DIRECTORS'
DISQUALIFICATION:
LAW AND PRACTICE

AUSTRALIA
LBC Information Services
Sydney

CANADA and USA
Carswell
Toronto

NEW ZEALAND
Brooker's
Auckland

SINGAPORE and MALAYSIA
Sweet & Maxwell Asia
Singapore and Kuala Lumpur

DIRECTORS' DISQUALIFICATION: LAW AND PRACTICE

ADRIAN WALTERS
AND
MALCOLM DAVIS-WHITE

London
Sweet & Maxwell
1999

Published by
Sweet & Maxwell Limited of
100 Avenue Road,
Swiss Cottage, London NW3 3PF
http://www.smlawpub.co.uk
Typeset by MFK Information Services Ltd, Hitchin, Herts.
Printed and bound in Great Britain by MPG Books Ltd, Bodmin, Cornwall

A C.I.P. catalogue record for this book
is available from the British Library

ISBN 0421 59940 5

No natural forests were destroyed to make this product,
only farmed timber was used and replanted.

©
Sweet & Maxwell Limited
1999

To the memory of Julie Süss-Francksen,
a wonderful student, colleague and friend

And to the Bear, the Bat and the Beaver

Preface

In some respects the Company Directors Disqualification Act 1986 and the practice and procedure applying to applications made under it resemble Dr Who's Tardis: small and compact on the outside, a labyrinth inside. The CDDA has emerged as the principal mechanism through which directors' obligations are enforced and developed. It is no longer possible to grasp the modern law of directors' duties without at least some passing acquaintance with the Act and the voluminous case law that has been generated under it. In writing this book, we have sought to provide practitioners, academics and students who are interested in the field of company and insolvency law with what we hope is a reasonably comprehensive and critical work of reference on the law and practice in relation to directors' disqualification. It almost goes without saying that the book is being published at a time of significant change. As well as developments in the area itself (see, in particular, the landmark decision in *Re Barings (No. 5)*, *Secretary of State for Trade and Industry v. Baker* [1999] 1 B.C.L.C. 433), we have been forced to contend both with the introduction of the new Civil Procedure Rules and the enactment of the Human Rights Act 1998. These developments are reflected in the text.

It is not possible in the space available to mention by name all those who have helped us during the course of the book's preparation but our debt to them is great. Special thanks go to the following who either read and commented on earlier drafts or provided us with information above and beyond the call of duty: Barry Rider, Andrew Hicks, John Armour, Michael Ashe, Jane Ridley, Frederique Dahan, Sandra Morton, Mark Mildred and Nicky Calthrop-Owen. We are grateful to Messrs Davies Arnold Cooper for details of their reform proposal which is briefly discussed in Chapter 9. We are also grateful to Patrick Chillery of the Insolvency Service who gave us permission to reproduce the Schedule setting out the information which, at present, is usually drawn to the attention of prospective applicants for permission to act notwithstanding disqualification. Mention must be made of the sterling work done by the library staff at Nottingham Trent University and, in particular, Terry Hanstock, Chris Garratt and Angela Donaldson. We also thank our publishers for their assistance and for preparing the tables and index. Adrian Walters would like to acknowledge colleagues both past and present (especially Michael Gunn, Peter Kunzlik, Liz Rodgers and Ian Williams who all provided a great deal of support and encouragement) and his wife, Rachel for her help generally and, in particular, at proof stage. Malcolm Davis-White would like to thank those at the Department of Trade and Industry, the Disqualification Unit within the Insolvency Service, the Treasury Solicitors' department and solicitors' firms who act as agents for the Treasury Solicitor in disqualification matters who have instructed him. Not only is he grateful to have been instructed by them on a number of interesting cases but he has valued their assistance in and knowledge of this area of law. To name names runs the risk of unintentional omission. Accordingly he does not do so. He hopes that those concerned know who they are. Finally, there are two people that he would like specifically to mention and thank. The first is his wife Sarah, who has had to put up with a lot. The second is Mr Justice Charles, who, whilst "Treasury Devil", taught him so much and with such good humour.

Finally, it should be noted that the views expressed in this book (and any mistakes) are those of the authors alone. We have sought to state the law as at June 1, 1999 but, where possible, have noted developments up to and including October 1, 1999.

AJW
MDW

October 1999

Contents

page

Preface   vii

Table of Cases   xvii

Table of Statutes   xxxv

Table of Statutory Instruments   xlvii

Table of Rules   li

para.

CHAPTER 1

Company Directors' Disqualification Act 1986: Introduction and Overview

Introduction   1.01
Company Directors' Disqualification Act 1986   1.02
    Outline of the CDDA   1.03
    Regulatory responsibility of the Department of Trade and
    Industry in relation to disqualifications under the CDDA   1.20
History and Evolution of the Disqualification Regime   1.21
    Phase one: bankruptcy   1.22
    Phase two: fraud during winding up and criminal offences in
    connection with the management of companies   1.23
    Phase three: persistent non-compliance with filing obligations
    under companies legislation   1.25
    Phase four: the development of the unfitness provisions   1.26
Summary and Conclusion   1.30

CHAPTER 2

The Nature and Purpose of Directors' Disqualification

Introduction   2.01
What was Parliament's Intention in Enacting the CDDA?   2.03
    Disqualification and abuse of the privilege of limited liability   2.03
    Protection of the public or punishment of the individual   2.07

	para.
What is the Nature of the Disqualification Process	2.21
Is disqualification a quasi-criminal process?	2.21
Re Cedac Ltd, Secretary of State for Trade and Industry v. Langridge	2.25
Other factors concerning the process which may influence the court's approach	
Summary and Conclusion	2.29

CHAPTER 3

Disqualification for Unfitness: Preliminary Matters

Introduction	3.01
The Inception of Section 6 Proceedings: Reporting by Office Holders	3.02
Statutory reporting obligations	3.02
Section7(4)	3.03
Insolvent Companies (Reports on Conduct of Directors) Rules 1996	3.05
Section 6(1): Substantive Preliminaries	3.09
"Director"	3.10
De facto directors	3.11
Shadow directors	3.25
Other categories of director	3.35
"Company"	3.38
Statutory extensions of "company"	3.39
Companies capable of being wound up under Part V of the Insolvency Act 1986	3.46
"Becomes Insolvent"	3.50
"Goes into liquidation"	3.51
Conduct in Relation to Lead and Collateral Companies	3.53
Can good conduct in collateral companies be taken into account?	3.54
Does there need to be some nexus or connection between the conduct in lead and collateral companies?	3.55
Can collateral allegations raised in one set of disqualification proceedings be raised against the same defendant in subsequent disqualification proceedings?	3.59
"Lead" and "collateral" allegations	3.60
Section 8(1): Preliminaries	3.61
Reports, information or documents	3.62

CHAPTER 4

Determining Unfitness (1): General Principles

Introduction	4.01
Section 6: Mandatory Disqualifications for Unfitness	4.02
Section 8: Discretionary Disqualification for Unfitness	4.04

	para.
Determining Unfitness	4.05
Statutory guidance	4.05
General judicial guidance	4.14
"Makes him unfit to be concerned in the management of a company": relevant conduct under section 6	4.21
Summary	4.26

CHAPTER 5

Determining Unfitness (2): Specific Instances of Unfitness and Period of Disqualification

Introduction	5.01
Specific Instances of Unfitness	5.02
Trading while insolvent	5.03
Failure to keep proper accounting records and the wider obligation to exercise financial responsibility	5.13
Deliberate failure to pay Crown or other non-pressing creditors and the concept of discrimination	5.20
Excessive remuneration	5.28
Misuse of bank account	5.30
Phoenix activity and serial failure	5.31
Lack of capitalisation	5.34
Failure in the preparation and filing of accounts/returns	5.35
Acceptance of customer pre-payments	5.37
Breach of transaction avoidance provisions	5.38
Non co-operation with insolvency practitioner	5.42
Breach of fiduciary duty	5.43
Fraud	5.45
Breach of miscellaneous statutory obligations	5.46
Specific instances of unfitness in section 8 cases	5.47
Unfitness and the General Law	5.49
Some problems of underlying rationale	5.50
What level of incompetence will justify an order under section 6?	5.51
Individual responsibility and collective failure	5.54
Standard of proof in unfitness proceedings	5.66
Period of Disqualification	5.67
Introduction	5.67
Court of Appeal "sentencing" guidelines	5.68
The Sevenoaks "brackets" in practice	5.71
Mitigating factors	5.75

CHAPTER 6

Procedure and Evidence in Civil Disqualification Proceedings

Introduction	6.01
The Relevant Courts	6.02
Jurisdiction to wind up companies	6.03
Time for determining jurisdiction	6.04
Jurisdiction under sections 7(2), 7(4) and 15	6.07
Transfer and proceedings commenced in the wrong court	6.08
Overseas directors: disputing the court's jurisdiction	6.13

                                                                    para.

     The Applicable Rules of Court   6.14
        Applicable rules: history   6.15
        Tasbian, Probe Data and the applicability of the Insolvency
           Rules   6.16
        Developments after *Tasbian* and *Probe Data*   6.19
        The current position   6.20
        The current position: sections 6 and 8   6.21
        The CPR and the Disqualification Practice Direction   6.22
     Conduct Before Proceedings are Commenced   6.25
        General points   6.25
        CDDA, s. 16(1): the "ten-day letter"   6.27
     Parties to Proceedings   6.31
        The general position   6.31
        The Secretary of State or official receiver as claimant 6.32
        The wrong claimant   6.33
        The number of defendants   6.34
        The number of lead companies   6.35
     Applications for the Making of a Disqualification Order   6.36
        Overview of procedure on an application for the making of a
           disqualification order   6.36
        Procedural timetable   6.38
        Other matters   6.47
        Parallel proceedings   6.49A
     Commencement of Proceedings   6.50
        Timing of proceedings: the two-year time period for com-
           mencement of proceedings under section 6   6.50
        Allegations of unfit conduct: sections 6 and 8   6.52
     Evidence   6.59
        Written evidence   6.59
        Hearsay evidence   6.64
        Expert evidence   6.75
        Character evidence   6.78
     Appeals   6.80
        Which provisions apply   6.80
        Appeal provisions applicable to civil proceedings generally 6.81
        Appeal provisions of the Insolvency Rules 1986   6.82
        Is permission to appeal needed in cases covered by Insolvency
           Rules 1986, rr. 7.47 and 7.49?   6.83
        Review powers   6.84
     Costs   6.85
     Miscellaneous   6.86
        Inspecting the court file   6.86
        Use of affidavits in other proceedings   6.87

CHAPTER 7

Permission to Commence Section 6 Proceedings Out of Time and the Impact of Delay in Civil Disqualification

     Introduction   7.01

para.

Permission to Commence Proceedings Out of Time under Section
7(2)   7.02
    General points   7.02
    Principles on which the discretion to grant permission is exer-
    cised   7.05
    Procedure on applications for permission under section 7(2) 7.29
Dismissal for Want of Prosecution   7.33
    Manlon Trading: Balancing the public interest against preju-
    dice suffered by the respondent   7.34
    Cases following the conventional approach   7.36
    Conclusion   7.38

CHAPTER 8

Civil Disqualification Proceedings: Termination Without a Full Trial

Introduction   8.01
Discontinuance of Proceedings   8.02
    Position under RSC/CCR   8.03
    Position under the CPR   8.04
    Costs   8.05
A Stay on the Business of Undertakings   8.06
    Cases where undertakings have been accepted   8.07
Summary Hearing: The *Carecraft* Procedure   8.08
    Carecraft statements   8.09
Uncontested Evidence   8.20
CPR Part 36, Offers "To Settle", *Calderbank* Offers   8.21

CHAPTER 9

Alternative Grounds for Disqualification

Introduction   9.01
    Scope of Chapter   9.01
    General introduction: sections 2 to 5 and 10   9.02
    Meaning of 'company' in sections 2 to 5 and 10   9.04
Section 2: Disqualification on Conviction of Indictable Offence   9.05
    Indictable offence   9.06
    Promotion, formation and management   9.07
    Offence in connection with promotion of a company   9.08
    Offence in connection with formation of a company   9.09
    Offence in connection with management of a company   9.10
    Specific management offences falling within section 2(1)   9.13
    Offence in connection with liquidation or striking off of a com-
    pany   9.29
    Offence in connection with receivership or management of a
    company's property   9.30
    Section 2: Procedure   9.31

para.

Section 3: Disqualification for Persistent Breach of Companies
Legislation   9.36
    Companies legislation   9.37
    Return, account, etc.   9.38
    Persistent default   9.40
    Section 3: procedure   9.41
Section 4: Disqualification for Fraud, etc. in Winding Up   9.42
    Section 4(1)(a): fraudulent trading   9.44
    Section 4(1)(b): fraud or breach of duty by an officer or liqui-
dator or receiver or manager of corporate property   9.45
    Section 4 procedure   9.47
Section 5: Disqualification on Summary Conviction   9.48
    Section 5: Procedure   9.50
Section 10: Disqualification Following Participation in Wrongful
Trading   9.51
    Insolvency Act 1986, s. 213   9.52
    Insolvency Act 1986, s. 214   9.53
    Section 10: Procedure   9.54
Factors Considered by the Court in Exercising its Discretion under
Sections 2 to 5 and 10   9.55
    The nature of the discretion   9.56
    Specific problems of discretion in the criminal courts   9.59
    Period of disqualification   9.66
Appeals Against Disqualification Orders Made Under Sections 2
and 5   9.71

CHAPTER 10

Individual Insolvency

Introduction   10.01
Automatic Disqualification of Undischarged Bankrupts   10.02
    History and rationale   10.03
    "Undischarged bankrupt"   10.06
    Overlap with other provisions in the CDDA 10.07
    Publicity   10.08
Disqualification Following Revocation of an Administration Order
Made Under Part VI of the County Courts Act 1984   10.09

CHAPTER 11

Disqualification Orders

Introduction   11.01
Disqualification Orders   11.02
    Picking and choosing   11.04

para.

Commencement and Coming into Effect of Disqualification Orders   11.18
   Civil proceedings under CDDA, ss. 7 to 8   11.19
   Civil proceedings under CDDA, ss. 2(2)(a), 3, 4, 10   11.21
   Criminal proceedings   11.22
   Is there a general power to stay or suspend a disqualification
   order under the inherent jurisdiction?   11.23
   Interim permission   11.25
Registration of Order   11.26

CHAPTER 12

The Legal Effect of Disqualification

Introduction   12.01
Scope of Disqualification   12.02
   The prohibitions   12.02
"Company"   12.05
   Extension to building societies and incorporated friendly
   societies   12.06
   Section 22 of the CDDA: general definitions   12.07
Director, Liquidator or Administrator, etc.   12.19
   Director   12.19
   Liquidator or administrator   12.20
   Receiver or manager   12.22
"Directly or Indirectly be Concerned or Take Part in the Promotion,
Formation or Management of a Company"   12.23
   Declaratory relief?   12.24
   "In any way, whether directly or indirectly, be concerned or
   take part in..."   12.25
   Promotion   12.26
   Formation   12.28
   Management   12.29
Knock-on Legal Effects of CDDA Disqualification   12.45
   Insolvency Act 1986   12.46
   Charities Act 1993   12.47
   Pensions Act 1995   12.48
   Police Act 1996   12.49
   Housing Act 1996   12.50
   Local Government Act 1972   12.51
   Does a CDDA disqualification result in formal removal from
   office?   12.52
   Regulatory and other consequences   12.53
Breach of the Prohibition   12.54
   Criminal liability and further disqualification   12.55
   Civil liability   12.56

CHAPTER 13

Permission to Act

Introduction   13.01

para.

The Approach of the Court in Exercising the Power to Grant Permission   13.03
    Scope of power   13.03
    Discretion   13.05
    The proper starting point   13.07
    The "need" requirement   13.09
    Protection of the public   13.26
    Conditional permission   13.32
    Types of condition   13.39
    Applications for permission to be involved in management   13.52
    Interim permission   13.54
    Applications for permission under sections 11 and 12   13.55
    Can an insolvency practitioner be granted permission to act as a liquidator, etc.?   13.56
    Future direction   13.57
Procedure on Applications for Permission   13.58
    Sections 17 and 12: Procedure on an application for permission to act notwithstanding a disqualification order   13.58
    Procedure on an application for permission to act notwithstanding automatic disqualification under section 11   13.69

page

APPENDIX 1

Company Directors Disqualification Act 1986   407

APPENDIX 2

Extracts From Previous Legislation   423

APPENDIX 3

Table of Former Provisions   445

APPENDIX 4

The Insolvent Companies (Disqualification of Unfit Directors) Proceedings Rules 1987   447

APPENDIX 5

Practice Direction: Directors Disqualification Proceedings   451

APPENDIX 6

Extracts from the Australian Corporations Law   461

APPENDIX 7

Guidelines for Applications for Permission under a Disqualification Order Issued by the Secretary of State   467

APPENDIX 8

Draft Carecraft Statement   469

Index   475

Table of Cases

A B Trucking and B A W Commercials, Re, unreported, June 3, 1987......... 4.02
A C Group Services, Re [1993] B.C.L.C. 1297............................. 5.57, 5.84
Adams v. Adams [1971] P. 188; [1970] 3 W.L.R. 934; 114 S.J. 605; [1970] 3
    All E.R. 572... 9.54, 13.63
Admiral Energy Group Ltd, Re; Official Receiver v. Jones, unreported, August
    19, 1996, Ch. C..................... 5.13, 5.23, 5.30, 5.31, 5.84
Agriplant Services Ltd, Re [1997] 2 B.C.L.C. 598, [1997] B.C.C. 842
    Ch. D.. 5.24
Agushi and Australian Securities Commission (1996) 19 A.C.S.R.
    322.. 4.02, 5.16, 5.42
Aldermanbury Trust plc, Re [1993] B.C.C. 598.................... 5.81, 5.84, 8.08
Altim Pty Ltd, Re [1968] 2 N.S.W.R. 762....................... 10.04, 13.08, 13.55
Amaron Ltd, Re; Secretary of State for Trade and Industry v. Lubrani [1998]
    B.C.C. 264.......... 2.20, 4.09, 4.10, 4.14, 4.18, 5.03, 5.05, 5.12, 5.29, 7.16,
              12.13, 13.01, 13.03, 13.05, 13.07, 13.08, 13.23, 13.24, 13.31,
                       13.36, 13.41, 13.42, 13.54, 13.56
Amberey Metal Form Components Ltd, Re; Secretary of State for Trade and
    Industry v. Jones [1999] B.C.C. 336.............. 3.11, 3.15, 3.17, 3.20, 3.22,
                                 3.23, 6.18, 6.27
American Cyanamid Co. v. Ethicon Ltd [1975] A.C. 396; [1975] 2 W.L.R. 316,
    119 S.J. 136; [1975] 1 All E.R. 504; [1975] F.S.R. 101; [1975] R.P.C.
    513, H.L.; reversing [1974] F.S.R. 312, C.A. 13.54
Amstrad Consumer Electronics plc v. British Phongraphic Industry Ltd [1986]
    F.S.R. 159, C.A.; affirming (1985) 135 New L.J. 1186; (1985) 82 L.S.
    Gaz. 3702; (1985) Comp. L.P. 38, C.A.; affirming [1986] F.S.R. 159;
    [1986] E.C.C. 531 12.24
Andrey Fashions Ltd, Re, unreported July 17, 1987........................... 4.02
Ansett, Re (1990) 3 A.C.S.R. 357... 10.05, 13.55
Arab Monetary Fund v. Hashim (No. 7) [1993] 1 W.L.R. 1014; [1992] 1
    W.L.R. 1176, [1992] 4 All E.R. 860, C.A. 6.63
Arbuthnot Latham Bank Ltd v. Trafalgar Holdings Ltd [1998] 1 W.L.R. 1426,
    [1998] 2 All E.R. 181, [1998] C.L.C. 615, *The Times*, December 29,
    1997 C.A.. 7.34, 7.38
Arctic Engineering Ltd, Re [1986] 2 All E.R. 346, [1986] B.C.L.C. 253, (1985)
    1 B.C.C. 563.. 9.37, 9.40, 9.46, 12.46
Armour v. Skeen [1976] I.R.L.R. 310, 1997 S.L.T. 71 .... 12.38
Armvent Ltd, Re [1975] 1 W.L.R. 1679, 119 S.J. 845, [1975] 3 All E.R.
    441 .... 6.67
Arrows Ltd (No. 4), Re [1995] 2 A.C. 75, [1994] 3 W.L.R. 656, [1994] 3 All
    E.R. 814, [1995] 1 Cr. App. R. 95, [1994] B.C.C. 641, H.L., [1994] 2
    B.C.L.C. 738, (1994) 144 N.L. J. Rep. 1203, *The Times*, July 26, 1994,
    The Independent, July 26, 1994, H.L. ; affirming [1993] Ch. 452, [1993]
    3 W.L.R. 513, [1993] 3 All E.R. 861, [1993] B.C.C. 473, [1993] B.C.L.C.
    1222, C.A... 3.68

ASFA Ltd v. RTZ Pension Property Trust Ltd, unreported, October 29,
    1998... 8.04
Ask International Ltd, Re; Secretary of State for Trade and Industry v. Keens,
    unreported, May 5, 1992, Ch. D.............................. 5.16, 5.71, 5.74
Astra Holdings plc, Re [1999] B.C.C. 121...................................... 3.63
Atlantic Computers plc, Re; Secretary of State for Trade and Industry v. Ash-
    man, unreported, June 15, 1998, Ch. D.... 2.16, 3.03, 3.62, 4.04, 5.19, 5.48
Atlantic Computers plc, Re; Secretary of State for Trade and Industry v.
    McCormick [1998] 1 B.C.L.C. 18, Ch. D.................................. 3.62
Attorney-General's Reference, unreported, April 28, 1999 .... 3.66
Attorney General's Reference Nos. 14, 15 and 16 of 1995, The Times, April 10,
    1997... 9.73, 11.04
Austinsuite Furniture Ltd, Re [1992] B.C.L.C. 1047......... 4.20, 5.19, 5.23, 5.29,
                                                5.37, 5.51, 5.64, 5.72, 5.78
Australian Securities Commission v. AS Nominees Ltd (1995) 18 A.C.S.R.
    459... 3.26, 3.27
Auto Electro and Powder Finishers, unreported, April 5, 1995................. 11.19
Automatic Self-Cleansing Syndicate Co. v. Cuninghame [1906] 2 Ch.
    34... 12.30

Bairstow v. Queens Moat Houses plc [1998] 1 All E.R. 343, The Times, Octo-
    ber 23, 1997, C.A. 6.70
Banque des Marchands de Moscou (Koupetschesky) v. Kindersley [1951] Ch.
    112, 66 T.L.R. (Pt. 2) 654, [1950] 2 All E.R. 549, 17 Sol. 258, 11 C.L.J.
    198, C.A. ; affirming (1950) 66 T.L.R. (Pt. 1) 1147...................... 3.48
Barings plc, Re; Secretary of State for Trade and Industry v. Baker [1998] Ch.
    356, [1998] 1 B.C.L.C. 16, [1998] B.C.C. 888......... 2.28, 3.07, 3.08, 4.24,
                                                5.53, 5.51, 5.76, 5.81
Barings plc, Re; Secretary of State for Trade and Industry v. Baker (No. 2)
    [1998] Ch. 356, [1998] 2 W.L.R. 667, [1998] 1 All E.R. 673, [1998] 1
    B.C.L.C. 590, [1999] B.C.C. 146, The Times, October 23, 1997, Inde-
    pendent, October 7, 1997, Ch. D....................... 3.02, 5.76, 9.35, 9.34
Barings plc (No. 3), Re; Secretary of State for Trade and Industry v. Baker
    [1999] 1 All E.R. 311, (sub nom. (No. 2); [1999] 1 B.C.L.C. 226,
    Ch. D.. 6.32, 6.49, 6.67, 6.68, 6.72
Barings plc (No.4), Re; Secretary of State for Trade and Industry v. Baker
    [1999] 1 All E.R. 1017, [1999] 1 BC.L.C. 262........... 13.08, 13.12, 13.13,
                                13.17, 13.23, 13.24, 13.25, 13.26, 13.29, 13.36, 13.49
Barings plc (No. 5), Re; Secretary of State for Trade and Industry v. Baker
    [1999] 1 B.C.L.C. 433, (1998) 95 (45) L.S.G. 38, (1998) 148 N.L.J.
    1474, The Times, October 10, 1998, Independent, October 9, 1998,
    Ch. D......... 2.16, 2.28, 4.03, 4.12, 4.24, 4.25, 5.50, 5.57, 6.24, 6.67, 6.75,
                                                6.76, 6.77, 6.79, 13.29
Barings plc, Re; Secretary of State for Trade and Industry v. Baker, unreported,
    February 24, 1998, Ch. D. 8.15
Barrandra Promotions Ltd, Re unreported July 4, 1996....................... 5.66
Bath Glass Ltd, Re [1988] B.C.L.C. 329, (1988) 4 B.C.C. 130........... 1.02, 3.54,
    3.55, 4.02, 4.08, 4.09, 4.15, 4.22, 5.03, 5.04, 5.12, 5.20, 5.26, 5.31, 5.35, 5.51,
                                                7.26, 9.53
Battery Specialists (Five Star) Ltd, unreported, February 23, 1998, Ch. D. 6.50
Baysington pty Ltd, Re (1988) 12 A.C.L.R. 412 .... 10.06

Birckett v. James [1978] A.C. 297, [1977] 3 W.L.R. 38, [1977] 2 All E.R.
    810 .... 7.34
Bishopgate Investment Management Ltd v. Maxwell (No. 2) [1994] 1 All E.R.
    261, [1993] B.C.L.C. 1282, *The Times*, February 16, 1993, C.A., affirm-
    ing [1993] B.C.L.C. 814, [1993] B.C.C. 120, *The Times*, January 12,
    1993 .... 4.11, 5.30, 5.55
Biss v. Lambeth, Southwark and Lewisham Health Authority [1978] 1 W.L.R.
    382, [1978] 2 All E.R. 125 .... 7.34
Blackheath Heating & Consulting Engineers Ltd, Re (1985) 1 B.C.C.
    99 .... 6.15
Blackspur Group plc, Re; Secretary of State for Trade and Industry v. Davies
    [1997] 1 W.L.R. 710, [1997] 2 B.C.L.C. 96, [1997] B.C.C. 488,
    Ch. D 6.58, 7.01, 7.03, 7.04, 7.05, 7.07, 7.08, 7.10, 7.12, 7.13, 7.17,
                                                                  8.02, 8.06, 8.07, 8.18
Blackspur Group plc, Re; Atlantic Computer Systems plc, Re [1998] 1 W.L.R.
    422, [1998] 1 B.LC.L.C. 676, [1998] B.C.C. 11, C.A 2.18, 3.09, 4.04,
                                                                  6.32, 8.02
Bloomgalley Ltd, Re; Secretary of State for Trade and Industry v. Neophytou
    unreported, October 15, 1993, Ch. D. 5.16
Blunt v. Corporate Affairs Commission (No.2) (1988) 14 A.C.L.R. 270,
    (1988) 6 A.C.L.R. 270, (1988) 6 A.C.L.C. 1077 .... 4.02, 4.15, 11.24
Bonus Breaks Ltd, Re [1991] B.C.C. 546 .... 13.28
Bourne v. Norwich Crematorium Ltd [1967] 1 W.L.R. 691, 111 S.J. 256,
    [1967] 2 All E.R. 576, 44 T.C .164, [1967] T.R. 49, 46 A.T.C.
    43 .... 12.39
Bown v. Gould & Swayne [1996] P.N.L.R. 130 .... 6.77
BPR Ltd, Re [1998] B.C.C. 259 Ch. D. 8.18
Bradford & Bingley Building Society v. Seddon [1999] 1 W.L.R. 1482, CA ... 6.49
Brazilian Rubber Plantations & Estates Ltd [1911] 1 Ch. 425 .... 2.03, 5.57
Brian D. Pierson (Contractors) Ltd, Re [1999] B.C.C. 26 .... 4.11, 5.55, 5.57,
                                                                  6.31, 9.53, 9.53, 9.54
Brian Sheridan Cars Ltd, Re [1996] 1 B.C.L.C. 327 .... 6.84, 11.08, 11.09,
                13.22, 13.32, 13.35, 13.37, 13.38, 13.40, 13.41, 13.50, 13.51, 13.57
Bristol & West Building Society v. Saunders [1997] Ch. 60, [1996] 3 W.L.R.
    473, [1997] 3 All E.R. 992, [1997] B.C.C. 83, [1996] B.P.I.R. 335
    Ch. D. 13.38
British & Commonwealth plc v. Spicer and Oppenheim [1993] A.C. 426,
    [1992] 3 W.L.R. 853, [1992] 4 All E.R. 876, [1993] B.C.L.C. 168, [1992]
    B.C.C. 977, (1992) 142 N.L.J. 1611, *The Times*, November 3, 1992,
    H.L., affirming [1992] Ch. 342, [1992] 2 W.L.R. 931, [1992] 2 All E.R.
    810, [1992] B.C.C. 165 and [1992] B.C.C. 172, [1992] B.C.L.C. 641,
    The Times, December 31, 1991, CA, reversing [1991] B.C.C 651 and
    [1991] B.C.C. 658, [1992] B.C.L.C. 306 and [1992] B.C.L.C. 314,
    Financial Times, November 6, 1991, *The Times*, November 8, 1991,
    Financial Times, August 6, 1991 .... 3.04
Brooks Transport (Purfleet) Ltd, Re [1993] B.C.C. 766 .... 5.31, 5.42, 5.72
Bulawayo Market Ltd, Re [1907] 2 Ch. 458 .... 3.36
Burnham Marketing Services Ltd, Re; Secretary of State for Trade and Industry
    v. Harper [1993] B.C.C. 518 .... 5.05, 5.18, 5.23, 5.35, 5.57, 5.77
Burrels Wharf Freeholds Ltd v. Galliard Homes Ltd, unreported, July 1,
    1998 .... 6.19, 6.24

Busytoday Ltd, Re [1992] 1 W.L.R. 683, [1992] 4 All E.R. 61, [1992] B.C.C. 480, [1993] B.C.L.C. 43 .... 6.83

C. & J. Hazell Holdings Pty Ltd, Re (1991) 9 A.C.L.C. 802, (1991) 4 A.C.S.R. 703 .... 13.57

Calderbank v. Calderbank [1976] Fam. 93, [1975] 3 W.L.R. 586, 119 S.J. 490, [1975] 3 All E.R. 333, 5 Fam. Law. 190, CA 8.09, 8.21

Cannonquest Ltd, Re; Official Receiver v. Hannan 11.08, 11.09, 11.10, 11.11, 11.12, 11.20, 11.24

Cardiff Savings Bank, Re [1892] 2 Ch. 100 .... 5.55

Carecraft Construction Co Ltd, Re [1994] 1 W.L.R. 172, [1993] 4 All E.R. 499, [1993] B.C.L.C. 1259, [1993] B.C.C. 336 .... 3.09, 5.67, 5.81, 6.46, 8.02, 8.06, 8.08, 8.09 8.09, 8.11, 8.12, 8.14, 8.15, 8.17, 8.18, 8.19, 8.20, 9.35, 13.13, 13.20, 13.29

Cargo Agency Ltd, Re [1992] B.C.L.C. 686, [1992] B.C.C. 388 .... 3.17, 5.29, 5.35, 5.77, 5.79, 8.02, 12.44, 13.06, 13.10, 13.13, 13.26

Carltona Ltd v. Commissioner of Works [1943] 2 All E.R. 560 .... 6.32

Cedac Ltd, Re; Secretary of State for Trade and Industry v. Langridge [1991] Ch. 402, [1991] 2 W.L.R. 1343, [1991] 3 All E.R. 591, [1991] B.C.C. 148, [1991] B.C.L.C. 543, The Times, March 4, 1991, CA, reversing [1990] B.C.C. 555 .... 2.17, 2.19, 2.24, 2.25, 6.27, 7.01, 7.19, 7.30, 9.33, 9.54, 9.59

Cedar Developments Ltd, Re [1994] 2 B.C.L.C. 714, [1995] B.C.C. 220   7.08, 7.09

Chartmore Ltd, Re [1990] B.C.L.C. 673 .... 2.24, 11.16, 12.25, 13.30, 13.31, 13.38, 13.48, 13.50

Chew v. N.C.S.C. (1985) 9 A.C.L.R. 527; [1985] W.A.R. 337 .... 13.48, 13.57

Choraria v. Sethia [1998] C.L.C. 625, (19988) 95 (7) L.S.G. 31, (1998) 142 S.J.L.B. 53, The Times, January 29, 1998, C.A. 7.38

Churchill Hotel (Plymouth) Ltd, Re [1988] B.C.L.C. 341, (1988) 4 B.C.C. 112 4.02

Circle Holidays International plc, Re; Secretary of State for Trade and Industry v. Smith [1994] B.C.C. 226 .... 6.19, 6.64, 6.69

City Equitable Fire Insurance Co Ltd, Re [1925] Ch. 407 .... 4.11, 4.25, 5.55

City Investment Centres Ltd, Re [1992] B.C.L.C. 956 .... 5.12, 5.37, 5.42, 5.51, 5.54, 5.57, 5.74, 5.79, 6.65

City Pram and Toy Co Ltd, Re [1998] B.C.C. 537 .... 5.05, 5.06, 5.08, 5.09, 5.10, 5.11, 5.12, 5.35, 5.37, 5.65, 5.84

Civica Investments Ltd, Re (1982) 126 S.J. 446, (1982) 79 L.S. Gaz. 919 .... 9.46, 9.57, 9.68, 9.69

Cladrose Ltd, Re [1990] B.C.L.C. 204, [1990] B.C.C. 11 .... 4.15, 5.18, 5.21, 5.23, 5.35, 5.51, 5.52, 5.58, 5.60, 9.36

Clasper Group Services Ltd, Re (1988) 4 B.C.C. 673, [1989] B.C.L.C. 143 .... 12.29

Cloghmor Ltd, Re unreported, November 17, 1994 .... 5.44

C M Van Stillevoldt v. El Carriers Inc. [1983] 1 W.L.R. 207, [1983] 1 All E.R. 699 .... 7.05

Commissioner for Corporate Affairs v. Bracht (1987) 7 A.C.L.C. 40, [1989] V.C. 821 ...... 12.19, 12.23, 12.25, 12.31, 12.32, 12.34, 12.35, 12.41, 12.42

—— v. Ekamper (1988) 12 A.C.L.R. 519, [1986] 1 W.L.R. 686, [1986] 2 All E.R. 346, [1986] B.C.L.C. 253, (1985) 1 B.C.C. 99 .... 9.46, 9.68

Compania Merabello San Nicholas SA, Re [1973] Ch. 75, [1972] 3 W.L.R. 471, 116 S.J. 631, [1972] 3 All E.R. 448 .... 3.48, 12.18

Company (No. 00996 of 1979), Re A [1980] 1 Ch. 138 .... 12.40
Company (No. 5009 of 1987) ex p. Copp, Re [1989] B.C.L.C. 13, (1988) 4
    B.C.C. 424.. 3.30, 3.31
Congratulations Franchising Ltd, Re; Secretary of State for Trade and Industry
    v. Davies, unreported, March 6, 1998............................ 13.11, 13.35
Continental Assurance Co of London Ltd, Re [1997] B.C.L.C. 48, [1996]
    B.C.C. 888, (1996) 93 (28) L.S.G. 29, (1996) 140 S.J.L.B. 156, *The*
    Times, July 2, 1996, Ch. D........... 2.16, 2.26, 5.44, 5.46, 5.53, 5.57, 5.59,
                   5.72, 5.74, 5.85, 6.53, 7.26, 8.17, 9.24, 11.23, 13.01, 13.54
Copecrest Ltd, Re; Secretary of State for Trade and Industry v. McTighe (No. 2)
    [1996] 2 B.C.L.C. 477, [1997] B.C.C. 224....... 4.14, 5.12, 5.23, 5.29, 5.31,
            5.42, 5.44, 5.72, 5.73, 5.74, 7.04, 7.06, 7.07, 7.11, 7.22, 8.17, 9.73
Country Farm Inns Ltd, Re; Secretary of State for Trade and Industry v. Ivens
    [1997] 2 B.C.L.C. 339, [1997] B.C.C. 801, *The Times*, September 24,
    1997, CA, affirming [1997] 2 B.C.L.C. 334, [1997] B.C.C. 396 3.53,
    3.55, 3.56, 3.57, 4.05
Craig Meats Ltd, Re, unreported April 25, 1996 .... 5.57
Credit Suiss v. Allendale Borough Council [1996] 3 W.L.R. 894, [1996] 4 All
    E.R. 129, [1996] 2 Lloyd's Rep. 241, [1996] 5 Bank. L.R. 249, *Times*,
    May 20, 1996, *Independent*, June 7, 1996, CA, affirming [1995] 1
    Lloyd's Rep. 315, (1994) 15 Bus. L.R. 220, (1995) 159 L.G. Rev. 549,
    Independent, June 17, 1994 QBD 11.90
Crestjoy Products Ltd, Re [1990] B.C.L.C. 677, [1990] B.C.C. 23............. 2.20,
                               2.23, 6.39, 7.03, 7.07, 7.23, 7.25, 7.30
CS Holidays Ltd, Re; Secretary of State for Trade and Industry v.
    Taylor.. 5.62
CSTC Ltd, Re; Secretary of State for Trade and Industry v. Van Hengel [1995] 1
    B.C.L.C. 545, [1995] B.C.C. 173.................. 4.05, 4.18, 5.29, 5.37, 5.59
C.U. Fittings, Re [1989] B.C.L.C. 556, (1989) 5 B.C.C. 210 4.02, 4.15, 4.25, 5.12,
                                                              5.26, 5.52
Cullen v. Corporate Affairs Commission (1988) 14 A.C.L.R. 789, (1989) 7
    A.C.L.C. 121.. 4.02, 12.34

Dawes & Henderson (Agencies) Ltd, Re; Secretary of State for Trade and In-
    dustry v. Dawes [1997] 1 B.C.L.C. 329, [1997] B.C.C. 121....... 4.22, 5.64,
                                                           5.75, 5.76, 6.78
Dawes & Henderson (Agencies) Ltd, Re; Secretary of State for Trade and In-
    dustry v. Coulthard, unreported, February 4, 1997, Ch. D. 8.17
Dawes & Henderson (Agencies) Ltd, Re; Secretary of State for Trade and In-
    dustry v. Shuttleworth, unreported, January 27, 1999........... 13.06, 13.13,
            13.14, 13.17, 13.18, 13.19, 13.23, 13.24, 13.25, 13.29, 13.36
Dawson Print Group Ltd, Re [1987] B.C.L.C. 601, (1987) 3 B.C.C.
    322.. 4.02, 4.15, 4.20, 5.20
Debtor (No 1 of 1987), Re [1989] 1 W.L.R. 271 .... 1.30
Debtor (No. 32–SD/1991), Re [1993] 1 W.L.R. 314 .... 6.84
Defence & Microwave Devices Ltd, Re, unreported, October 7, 1992,
    Ch. D... 5.42, 5.45, 5.73
Delonga and the Australian Securities Commission, Re (1994) 15 A.C.S.R.
    450, (1995) 13 A.C.L.C. 246... 4.02, 5.16
Department of Transport v. Chris Smaller (Transport) Ltd [1989] A.C. 1197,
    [1989] 2 W.L.R. 578, (1989) 133 S.J. 361, [1989] 1 All E.R. 897, (1989)
    139 N.L.J. 363, H.L.. 7.16, 7.34

Device & Microwave Devices Ltd, Re, unreported, October 7, 1992, Ch.D...   3.57
Dexmaster Ltd, Re [1995] B.C.C. 186, [1995] 2 B.C.L.C. 430............   6.49, 7.16
Diamond Computer Systems Ltd, Re; Official Receiver v. Brown [1997] 1
    B.C.L.C. 174 ....   3.57
Dicetrade Ltd, Re; Secretary of State for Trade and Industry v. Worth [1994] 2
    B.C.L.C. 113, [1994] B.C.C. 371...   6.85, 11.03, 11.15, 13.11, 13.59, 13.63,
                                                                    13.65, 13.66
DJ Matthews (Joinery Design) Ltd, Re (1988) 4 B.C.C. 518...   11.04, 13.15, 13.20
Dobson v. Hastings [1992] Ch. 394, [1992] 2 W.L.R. 414, [1992] 2 All E.R. 94
    [1992] Gazette, February 26, 1992, (1991) 141 N.L.J. 1625, The Inde-
    pendent, November 12, 1991, The Guardian, November 13, 1991, The
    Times, November 18, 1991......................................   6.18, 6.19, 6.86
Donoghue v. Stevenson [1932] A.C. 562, 20 M.L.R. 1, 86 L.Q.R. 454, 64 L.S.
    Gaz. 245, 103 S.J. 143...   5.55
Dorchester Finance Ltd v. Stebbing [1989] B.C.L.C. 498...........   5.30, 5.58, 5.65
Douglas Construction Services Ltd, Re [1988] B.C.L.C. 397, (1988) 4 B.C.C.
    553...   4.15, 4.16, 5.12, 5.52, 5.60
D' Jan of London Ltd, Re [1994] 1 B.C.L.C. 561, [1993] B.C.C. 646 ....   4.11,
                                                                    5.58, 5.65
D.J. Matthews (Joinery Design) Ltd, Re (1988) 4 B.C.C. 513............   4.02, 4.22,
                                                                    5.18, 5.31
DKG Contractors Ltd, Re [1990] B.C.C. 903 ....   9.53
Dominion International Group plc (No.2), Re [1996] 1 B.C.L.C. 572.........   3.53
Douglas Construction Services Ltd, Re [1988] B.C.L.C. 397, (1988) 4 B.C.C.
    553...   4.02, 5.31
Dovey v. Corey [1901] A.C. 477 ....   5.63
Drew v. H.M. Advocate 1996 S.L.T. 1062 ....   12.29
Drincqbir v. Wood..   5.57
Dwyer v. National Companies and Securities Commission (1989) 15 A.C.L.R.
    386, (1989) 7 A.C.L.C. 571.....................................   4.02, 4.15, 5.45
Dwyer v. N.C.S.C. (No.2) (1989) 14 A.C.L.R. 595............................   11.24

ECM (Europe) Electronics Ltd, Re [1991] B.C.C. 268, [1992] B.C.L.C.
    814...   4.03, 4.18, 5.29, 5.31, 5.35, 5.38
EDC v. United Kingdom [1998] B.C.C. 370......   2.28, 5.83, 5.84, 6.34, 7.01, 7.16
Elgindata (No.2), Re [1992] 1 W.L.R. 1207, [1993] 1 All E.R. 232, [1993]
    B.C.L.C. 119, (1992) 136 S.J.L.B. 190, [1992] Gazette, 15 July, 33, The
    Times, June 18, 1992, CA...   6.85
Eloc Electro–Optieck & Communicatie B.V. [1982] 2 All E.R. 1111...   3.48, 12.18
Erlanger v. New Sombrero Phosphate Company (1878) 3 Cr. App. Cas.
    1218...   12.26
Euromove Ltd, Re [1993] B.C.C. 549..   5.05
Eurostem Maritime Ltd, Re [1987] P.C.C. 190...........................   3.11, 3.48
Exchange Travel (Holdings) Ltd (No.3), Re [1996] 2 B.C.L.C. 524, [1996]
    B.C.C. 933..   5.39

Facia Footwear Ltd v. Hinchcliffe [1998] 1 B.C.L.C. 218....   4.09, 5.03, 5.28, 5.43
FAI General Insurance Co. Ltd v. Godfrey Merrett Robertson Ltd, unreported,
    December 21, 1998 ....   8.19
Ferrari Furniture Co. Pty Ltd, Re [1972] N.S.W.L.R. 790 ....   1.29
Firedart Ltd, Re; Official Receiver v. Fairhall [1994] 2 B.C.L.C. 340 ....   5.16,
                                                5.29, 5.52, 5.72, 5.74, 5.80, 5.81

First Energy (U.K.) Ltd v. Hungarian International Bank Ltd [1993] B.C.C.
  533, [1993] 2 lloyd's Rep. 194, [1993] B.C.L.C. 1409, [1993] N.P.C. 34,
  The Times, March 4, 1993, CA... 12.42
Fitch v. Officail Receiver [1996] 1 W.L.R. 242, [1996] B.C.C. 328, [1996]
  B.P.I.R. 152, (1996) 2 All E.R. 171, *The Times*, January 3, 1996, *Inde-
  pendent*, February 12, 1996... 6.84
Flatbolt Ltd, Re, unreported, February 21, 1986.................... 4.15, 5.21, 11.05
Focus, Re [1992] M.C.L.R. 515... 13.22, 13.29

G Barraclough (Soft Drinks) Ltd, Re; Secretary of State for Trade and Industry
  v. Cawthray, unreported, November 2, 1995.............................. 7.34
Gemini Display Ltd, Re, unreported, July 19, 1996, Ch. D. 6.50
General Mediterranean Holdings SA v. Patel, unreported, July 19, 1999...... 6.24
Gerald Cooper Chemicals, Re [1978] Ch. 262, [1978] 2 All E.R. 49.......... 9.53
Gibson Davies Ltd, Re [1993] B.C.C 11.......... 2.20, 12.35, 13.06, 13.11, 13.12,
                               13.13, 13.16 13.20, 13.24, 13.26, 13.29, 13.31, 13.33,
                               13.34, 13.35, 13.36, 13.37, 13.38, 13.46, 13.48, 13.49
Gluckstein v. Barnes [1900] A.C. 240... 12.26
Godwin Warren Control Systcms plc, Re [1993] B.C.L.C. 80, [1992] B.C.C.
  557......... 2.12, 3.55, 3.56, 3.57, 3.58, 4.08, 5.43, 5.49, 5.72, 9.23, 11.16,
                                                                          13.40
Golden Chemical Products Ltd, Re [1976] 1 Ch. 300, [1976] 3 W.L.R. 1, 120
  S.J. 401, [1976] 2 All E.R. 543... 6.32
Gower Enterprises Ltd, Re; Official Receiver v. Moore [1995] B.C.C. 293.... 3.52
Gower Enterprises Ltd (No.2), Re [1995] 2 B.C.L.C. 201, [1995] B.C.C.
  1081......................... 11.05, 11.06, 11.07, 11.08, 11.09, 11.13, 13.01
Gray v. Commissioner for Corporate Affairs (Vic) (1988) 13 A.C.L.R. 516 .. 11.24
Grayan Building Services Ltd, Re; Secretary of State for Trade and Industry v.
  Gray [1995] Ch. 241, [1995] 3 W.L.R. , [1995] 1 B.C.L.C. 276, [1995]
  B.C.C. 554......... 2.17, 2.23, 3.54, 4.02, 4.04, 4.10, 4.16, 4.18, 4.20, 4.22,
                     4.23, 4.24, 4.25, 5.13, 5.18, 5.26, 5.38, 5.52, 5.69, 5.71, 5.80,
                                                5.82, 5.84, 7.26, 7.34, 9.63, 13.07
Great Wheal Polgooth Company, Re (1883) 53 L.J. Ch. 42.............. 9.08, 12.26
Grovit v. Doctor [1997] 1 W.L.R. 640, [1997] 2 All E.R. 417, [1997] C.L.C.
  1038, 91997) 147 N.L.J. 633, (1997) 141 S.J.L.B. 107, (1997) 94(20)
  L.S.G. 37, *Times*, April 25, 1997, *Independent*, May 1, 1997, HL affirm-
  ing *Independent*, December 13, 1993................................ 7.34, 7.38
Gruppo Torras SA v. Al Sabah, unreported, July 5, 1999, Commercial
  Court... 6.85
GSAR Realisations Ltd, Re [1993] B.C.L.C. 409...... 4.09, 4.18, 5.10, 5.23, 5.26,
                                                    5.35, 5.42, 5.60, 5.71, 5.75
Guiness Peat Properties Ltd v. Fitzroy Robinson [1987] 1 W.L.R. 1027, (1987)
  131 S.J. 807, [1987] 2 All E.R. 716, (1987) 38 Build. L.R. 57, (1987) 137
  New L.J. 452, (1987) 84 L.S. Gaz. 1882 .... 3.07

Hamilton–Irvine, Re (1990) 8 A.C.L.C. 1057......................... 13.22, 13.57
Harrison, Re (1998) 153 A.L.R. 369.. 13.03, 13.07
H. Laing Demolition Building Contractors Ltd, Re; Secretary of State for Trade
  and Industry v. Laing [1998] B.C.C. 561.......................... 3.15, 3.34
Henderson v. Henderson (1843) 3 Hare 100........................ 3.59, 8.03, 8.12
Highfield Commodities Ltd, Re [1984] 3 All E.R. 884 .... 3.04

Highgrade Traders Ltd, Re [1985] 1 W.L.R. 149, (1984) 128 S.J. 870, [1984] 3
    All E.R. 884, [1985] P.C.C. 191, (1984) L.S. Gaz. 3589 .... 3.07
Hitco 2000 Ltd, Re; Official Receiver v. Cowan [1995] 2 B.C.L.C. 63, [1995]
    B.C.C. 161......... 4.18, 5.16, 5.17, 5.18, 5.30, 5.35, 5.52, 5.71, 5.77, 6.53,
                                                                        6.54, 6.55
Hoffmann-La Roche v. Secretary of State for Trade and Industry [1975] A.C.
    295, [1974] 3 W.L.R. 104, 118 S.J. 500, [1974] 2 All E.R. 1128, HL
    affirming [1973] 3 W.L.R. 805, 117 S.J. 713, sub nom. Secretary of State
    for Trade and Industry v. Hoffman–La Roche (F.) & Co. A.G. [1973] 3
    All E.R. 945, CA reversing [1973] 3 W.L.R. 805......................... 3.04
Hollington v. F. Hewthorn & Co. Ltd [1943] K.B. 587............. 6.66, 6.67, 6.68
Holpitt Pty Ltd v. Swaab (1992) 6 A.C.S.R. 488................................ 12.39
Home Treat Ltd, Re [1991] B.C.C. 165, [1991] B.C.L.C. 705.................. 9.45
Homes Assured Corporation plc, Re; Official Receiver v. Dobson [1994] 2
    B.C.L.C. 71, [1993] B.C.C. 573....................................... 6.32, 8.07
Howard v. Boddington (1877) 2 P.D. 203.. 6.28
Howard Davey & Co Ltd, Re, unreported, December 7, 1984, Ch. D......... 5.21
Howard Smith Ltd v. Ampol Petroleum Ltd [1974] A.C. 821, [1974] 2 W.L.R.
    689, [1974] 1 All E.R. 1126, P.C. 5.48
Hunter v. Corporate Affairs Commission (NSW) (1988) 13 A.C.L.R.
    250.. 11.24, 11.25
Hydrodam (Corby) Ltd, Re [1994] 2 B.C.L.C. 180, [1994] B.C.C. 161, The
    Times, February 19, 1994............ 3.12, 3.14, 3.23, 3.26, 3.27, 3.32, 3.33,
                                                                      3.34, 3.37

Ikarian Reefer, Re [1995] 1 Lloyd's Rep. 455, CA reversing [1993] 2 Lloyd's
    Rep. 68, [1993] F.S.R. 563, [1993] 37 E.G. 158, The Times, March 5,
    1993.. 6.77
International Tin Council, Re [1989] Ch. 309, (1988) 4 B.C.C. 653, 1989
    P.C.C. 90, CA 12.12
International Westminster Bank plc v. Okeanos Maritime, Re a Company (No.
    00359 of 1987) [1988] 1 Ch. 210, [1987] B.C.L.C. 450, (1987) 3 B.C.C.
    160... 3.48, 12.18
Ipcon Fashions Ltd, Re (1989) 5 B.C.C. 774.. 4.15, 5.31, 5.71, 5.77, 11.19, 13.54
IRC v. Robinson [1999] B.P.I.R 329.. 6.84
Issacs v. Robertson [1985] A.C. 97 .... 11.09

J & B Lynch (Builders) Ltd [1988] B.C.L.C. 376..................... 4.02, 5.21, 5.23
Jandra Ltd, Re, unreported, July 4, 1995... 6.50
Jaymar Management Ltd, Re [1990] B.C.L.C. 617, [1990] B.C.C. 303........ 2.25,
                                                                      6.27, 7.11
Jazzgold Ltd, Re [1992] B.C.C. 587 [1994] 1 B.C.L.C. 38................ 6.58, 7.03
Jefferson Ltd v. Bhetcha [1979] 2 All E.R. 1108, CA........................... 6.49B
Jeffrey S. Levitt, Re [1992] Ch. 457, [1992] 2 W.L.R. 975, [1992] 2 All E.R.
    509, [1992] B.C.L.C. 250, [1992] B.C.C. 137, The Times, November 6,
    1991... 1.30
John Shaw & Sons (Salford) Ltd v. Shaw [1935] 2 K.B. 113.................... 12.30
Joint Liquidators of Sasea Finance Ltd v. KPMG [1998] B.C.C. 216 .... 3.04

Kascot Interplanetary (U.K.) Ltd, Re [1972] 3 All E.R. 829............... 6.67, 6.72
Kaufman v. Belgium 50 D.R. 98.. 2.28

Kaytech International plc, Re; Secretary of State for Trade and Industry v.
    Potier [1999] B.C.C. 390............   3.17, 3.20, 3.22, 3.23, 3.34, 3.35, 5.23,
                                                          5.31, 5.45, 5.57, 5.79
Keypack Homecare Ltd, Re [1990] B.C.L.C. 440, [1990] B.C.C. 117.........   4.20,
                                                    5.21, 5.23, 5.28, 5.31, 5.39
Kleinwort Benson Ltd v. Barbak Ltd; The Myrto (No. 3) [1987] A.C. 597,
    [1987] 2 W.L.R. 1053, (1987) 131 S.J. 497, [1987] 2 All E.R. 289, [1987]
    1 F.T.L.R. 43, [1987] 2 Lloyd's Rep. 1, (1987) 84 L.S. Gaz. 1651, (1987)
    137 New L.J. 388, H.L. [1985] 2 Lloyd's Rep. 567.......................   7.07
Kreditbank Cassel GmbH v. Schenker Ltd [1927] 1 K.B. 826 ....   12.42
Kuwait Airways Corp. v. Iraqi Airways Co. (No. 2) [1994] 1 W.L.R. 985,
    [1995] 1 All E.R. 790, [1994] 1 Lloyd's Rep. 284, (1994) 138 S.J.L.B. 39,
    The Times, February 19, 1994....................................   11.08, 13.37
Kuwait Asia Bank EC v. National Mutual Life Nominees Ltd [1991] 1 A.C.
    187, [1990] 3 W.L.R. 297, [1990] 3 All E.R. 404, [1990] 2 Lloyd's Rep.
    95, [1990] B.C.C. 567, [1990] B.C.L.C. 868, [1990] B.C.C. 567, P.C...   3.26

Ladd v. Marshall [1954] 1 W.L.R. 1489, [1954] 3 All E.R. 745.................   7.31
Lagunas Nitrate Co. v. Lagunas Syndicate [1899] 2 Ch. 392 ....   12.26
Landhurst Leasing plc, Re; Secretary of State for Trad and Industry v. Ball
    [1999] 1 B.C.L.C. 286...   2.16, 5.57, 6.50
Land Travel Ltd, Re; Secretary of State for Trade and Industry v. Tjolle [1998]
    1 B.C.L.C. 333, [1998] B.C.C. 282........   2.19, 2.23, 2.28, 3.17, 3.19, 3.22,
                                  3.23, 3.24, 5.37, 5.45, 5.74, 6.34, 9.35, 9.56, 9.64
Langley Marketing Services, Re [1993] B.C.L.C. 1340, [1992] B.C.C.
    585...   6.19, 6.83
Lasercell Ltd, Re; Official Receiver v. Cummings, unreported, November 1,
    1991 Ch. D. 5.23
Launchexcept Ltd, Re; Secretary of State for Trade and Industry v. Tillman
    [1999] B.C.C. 703, CA...............   3.02, 3.03, 3.53, 3. 57, 3.59, 6.32, 6.49,
                                                          7.12, 8.03, 9.35
Linvale Ltd, Re [1993] B.C.L.C. 654....................   4.20, 5.23, 5.31, 5.52, 5.71
Litchfield Freight Terminal, Re; Secretary of State for Trade and Industry v.
    Rowe [1997] 1 B.C.L.C. 226, [1995] B.C.C. 197.................   6.05, 13.52
Lightning Electrical Contractors Ltd, Re [1996] 2 B.C.L.C. 302, [1996] B.C.C.
    950 ....   13.28
Living Images Ltd, Re [1996] B.C.L.C. 348, [1996] B.C.C. 112.........   2.20, 3.09,
                                              4.08, 4.18, 5.12, 5.39, 5.42, 5.66, 5.84
LM Fabrications Ltd, Re unreported, April 27, 1995.....................   5.42, 5.46
Lo-Line Electric Motors Ltd, Re [1988] Ch. 477, [1988] 3 W.L.R. 26, [1988] 2
    All E.R. 692, (1988) 132 S.J. 851, 1988 P.C.C. 236, [1988] 2 F.T.L.R.
    107, [1988] B.C.L.C. 698, (1988) 4 B.C.C. 415, (1988) 138 New L.J.
    119....   2.20, 3.11, 3.12, 3.17, 3.19, 4.02, 4.15, 4.19, 4.20, 5.21, 5.35, 5.51,
                    6.47, 6.52, 6.58, 7.26, 11.16, 12.19, 13.13, 13.41, 13.46, 13.57
Lombard Shipping and Forwarding Ltd, Re [1993] B.C.L.C. 238, [1992]
    B.C.C. 700...........................   3.03, 6.47, 13.24, 13.30, 13.31, 13.34
London & Clydeside Estates Ltd v. Aberdeen District Council [1980] 1 W.L.R.
    182, (1979) 124 S.J. 100, [1979] 3 All E.R. 876, (1979) 39 P. & C.R. 549,
    253 E.G. 1011..   6.28
London and General Bank, Re [1895] 2 Ch. 155 ....   9.45
Looe Fish Ltd, Re [1993] B.C.L.C. 1160, [1993] B.C.C. 348......   2.13, 3.66, 4.18,
                                                          5.47, 5.74, 6.52, 6.55

M. v. Home Office [1994] 1 A.C. 377, [1993] 3 W.L.R. 433, [1993] 3 All E.R.
537, [1995] 7 Admin. L.R. 113, (1993) 90(37) L.S. Gaz. 50, (1993) 143
N.L.J. Rep. 1099, (1993) 137 S.J.L.B. 199, *The Times*, July 28, 1993,
The Independent, July 28, 1993, H.L. ; affirming [1992] Q.B. 270,
[1992] 2 W.L.R. 73, [1992] 4 All E.R. 97, [1992] C.O.D. 97, (1991) 141
N.L.J. Rep. 1663, *The Times*, December 2, 1991, *The Independent*,
December 3, 1991, *The Guardian*, December 4, 1991, CA reversing
[1992] C.O.D. 11 .... 11.09
M C Bacon Ltd, Re [1991] Ch. 127, [1990] B.C.L. C. 324, [1990] B.C.C.
78... 1.30, 3.30, 5.39
McNulty's Interchange Ltd, Re [1989] B.C.L.C. 709, (1988) 4 B.C.C.
533... 4.02, 4.15, 5.03, 5.21, 5.52, 5.60
McQuillan, Re [1988] 7 N.I.J.B. 1, (1989) 5 B.C.C. 137...... 10.05, 13.08, 13.10,
13.55
Maelor Pty Jones Ltd, Re (1975) 1 A.C.L.R. 4 .... 13.17
Magna Alloys & Research Pty Ltd, Re (1975) 1 A.C.L.R. 203........... 1.29, 9.64,
12.34, 12.35, 13.03, 13.10, 13.29
Maidstone Building Provisions Ltd, Re [1971] 1 W.L.R. 1085, 115 S.J. 464,
[1971] 3 All E.R. 363 .... 9.52
Mainwaring v. Goldtech Investments Ltd [1999] 1 W.L.R. 745 .... 6.85
Majestic Recording Studios Ltd, Re [1989] B.C.L.C. 1, (1989) 4 B.C.C.
519............................... 4.02, 5.31, 5.57, 11.16, 12.35, 13.04, 13.29
Manlon Trading Ltd, Re; Official Receiver v. Aziz [1996] Ch. 136, [1995] 3
W.L.R. 839, [1995] 4 All E.R. 14, [1995] 1 B.C.L.C. 578, [1995] B.C.C.
579.............................. 2.20, 7.16, 7.31, 7.34, 7.35, 7.36, 7.38
Marsden, Re (1980) 5 A.C.L.R. 694.. 13.10, 13.29
Melcast (Wolverhampton) Ltd, Re [1991] B.C.L.C. 288........... 3.57, 4.20, 5.18,
5.23, 5.31, 5.53, 5.57, 5.72, 5.78
Meridian Global Funds Management Asia Ltd v. Securities Commission
[1995] 2 A.C. 500, [1995] 3 W.L.R. 413, [1995] 3 All E.R. 918, [1995] 2
B.C.L.C. 116, [1995] B.C.C. 942, (1995) 139 S.J.L.B. 152, (19995)
92(28) L.S. Gaz. 39, *The Times*, June 29, 1995, P.C............... 12.30, 12.42
Michael v. Gowland [1977] 2 All E.R. 328, [1977] 1 W.L.R. 296 .... 9.71
Midland Bank Trust Co. Ltd v. Hett, Stubbs & Kemp [1979] Ch. 384, [1978] 3
All E.R. 571 .... 6.77
Minimix Industries Ltd, Re (1982) 1 N.Z.C.L.C. 98, (1982) 1 A.C.L.C.
511 .... 13.22
Minotaur Data Systems Ltd, Re; Official Receiver v. Brunt [1999] 3 All E.R.
122, [1999] B.C.C. 57, [1999] B.P.I.R. 560 .... 6.31
Mirror Group Newspapers plc [1999] 2 All E.R. 641...................... 3.62, 3.63
Moonbeam Cards Ltd, Re [1993] B.C.L.C. 1099........................ 6.64, 6.65
Moonlight Foods (U.K.) Ltd; Secretary of State for Trade and Industry v. Hickling [1996] B.C.C. 678......... 3.08, 3.19, 3.21, 3.23, 3.24, 4.03, 4.18, 5.06,
5.12, 5.50, 5.60, 5.64, 5.11, 6.25
Montreal Street Railway Co. v. Normandin [1917] A.C. 170 .... 6.28
Moorgate Metals Ltd, Re; Official Receiver v. Huhtala [1995] 1 B.C.L.C. 503,
[1995] B.C.C. 143....... 2.11, 3.14, 3.17, 3.18, 4.08, 5.29, 5.44, 5.45, 5.51,
5.72, 5.78
Morris v. Stratford–on–Avon Rural District Council [1973] 1 W.L.R. 1059,
117 S.J. 601, [1973] 3 All E.R. 263.. 6.69
Murray v. Australian Securities Commission (1994) 12 A.C.L.C. 1... 13.22, 13.57

Mutual Reinsurance v. Peat Marwick Mitchell [1997] 1Lloyd's Rep. 253, [1997] 1 B.C.L.C. 1, [1997] P.N.L.R. 75, [1996] B.C.C. 1010, *Times*, October 15, 1996, CA 9.45

Nascimento v. Kerrigan, *The Times*, June 23, 1999 .... 6.82
New Generation Engineers Ltd, Re [1993] B.C.L.C. 435.... 2.11, 5.12, 5.16, 5.23, 5.40, 5.52, 6.55
New Technology Systems Ltd, Re [1996] B.C.C. 694............... 6.55, 6.56, 7.37
Noble Trees Ltd, Re [1993] B.C.L.C. 1185, [1993] B.C.C. 318........... 7.34, 7.36
Norman v. Theodore Goddard [1991] B.C.L.C. 1028, [1992] B.C.C. 14........ 4.11, 5.65
Normandy Marketing Limited, Re [1994] Ch. 198..................... 6.03, 12.12
NP Engineering and Security Products Ltd, Re; Official Receiver v. Pafundo [1998] 1 B.C.L.C. 208... 6.08, 6.09, 6.32
Nusca v. Da Ponte 1994 3 S.A. 251(B) 13.03

Oakfame Construction Ltd, Re [1996] B.C.C. 67.............................. 6.77
Official Receiver v. B. Ltd [1994] 2 B.C.L.C. 1................................... 7.36
—— v. Bond and Long, unreported, June 10, 1997 .... 8.12
—— v. Brady [1999] B.C.C. 258.. 2.01, 3.27
—— v. Cummings unreported, November 1, 1991, Ch. D............... 5.78, 5.81
—— v. Cooper [1999] B.C.C. 115 .... 8.09
Oldham Vehicle Contracts Ltd, Re; Official Receiver v. Vass [1999] B.C.C 516   5.57
Omaglass Ltd, Re unreported, April 6, 1995............................... 5.46, 5.49
Oriel Limited, Re [1986] 1 W.L.R. 180, (1985) 129 S.J. 669, [1985] 3 All E.R. 216, 1986 P.C.C. 11, (1985) 82 L.S. Gaz. 3446........................... 12.10

Packaging Direct Ltd, Re [1994] B.C.C. 213........................ 7.07, 7.13, 7.27
Pamstock Ltd, Re [1994] 1 B.C.L.C. 716, [1994] B.C.C. 264............ 3.54, 3.56, 3.57, 3.58, 4.20, 4.22, 4.25, 5.23, 5.30, 5.31, 5.35, 5.77, 6.85, 9.36
Parallel Computers Ltd, Re, unreported, October 29, 1996, Ch. D. 6.50
Park House Properties Ltd, Re [1997] 2 B.C.L.C. 530, [1998] B.C.C. 847..... 3.02, 3.08, 3.09, 4.19, 5.12, 5.21, 5.24, 5.31, 5.44, 5.56, 5.57, 5.61
Penrose v. Official Receiver [1996] 1 W.L.R. 482, [1996] 1 B.C.L.C. 389, [1996] B.C.C. 311, *Times*, December 19, 1995, Ch. D. 13.28
Peppermint Park Ltd, Re [1998] B.C.C. 23......................... 5.31, 5.57, 5.62
PFTZM Ltd, Re[1995] 2 B.C.L.C. 354, [1995] B.C.C. 280..................... 3.31
Philipp & Lion Ltd, Re [1994] 1 B.C.L.C. 739, [1994] B.C.C. 261 .... 6.50
Piercy v. S. Mills & Co. Ltd [1920] 1 Ch. D. 77 .... 5.48
Pinemoor Ltd, Re [1997] B.C.C. 708........................ 3.02, 3.08, 6.52, 6.75
Playcorp Pty Ltd v. Shaw (1993) 10 A.C.S.R. 212.............................. 3.35
Polly Peck International plc, ex p. Joint Administrators, Re [1994] B.C.C. 15.. 3.03, 3.04, 7.26
Polly Peck International plc (No.2), Re; Secretary of State for Trade and Industry v. Ellis [1994] 1 B.C.L.C. 661, [1993] B.C.C. 886, *The Times*, March 22, 1993, *The Independent*, March 31, 1993, C.A.......... 3.56, 4.18, 4.19, 4.22, 4.25, 5.63, 5.66, 7.13, 7.15, 7.16, 7.26, 7.31, 7.32, 11.06
Pritam Kaur v. S Russell 7 Sons Ltd [1973] Q.B. 336........................... 6.50
Probe Data Systems (No. 2), Re [1990] B.C.L.C. 574, [1990] B.C.C. 21 ...... 7.29
Probe Data Systems Ltd (No.3), Re; Secretary of State for Industry v. Desai [1992] B.C.C. 110, [1992] B.C.L.C. 405, C.A., affirming [1991] B.C.C. 428, [1991] B.C.L.C. 586...... 2.24, 6.17, 6.18, 6.21, 6.33, 7.05, 7.06, 7.13, 7.16, 7.20, 7.31, 12.13

Produce Marketing Consortium Ltd, Re [1989] 1 W.L.R. 745, [1989] 3 All
E.R. 1, [1989] B.C.L.C. 513, (1989) 5 B.C.C. 569 .... 5.13
Produce Marketing Consortium Ltd (No.2), Re [1989] B.C.L.C. 520, (1989) 5
B.C.C. 569 .... 9.53
P S Banarse & Co. (Products) Ltd, Re; Secretary of State for Trade and Industry
v. Banarse [1997] 1 B.C.L.C. 653, [1997] B.C.C. 425, Ch. D....... 8.13, 8.18
Puropint Ltd, Re [1991] B.C.L.C. 491, [1991] B.C.C. 121 .... 9.53

Quek Leng Chye v. A.G. [1985] 2 M.L.J. 279 P.C. 13.29

Rasool v. West Midlands Passenger Transport Executive [1974] 3 All E.R. 638   6.69
Ready Fish Ltd, Re; Secretary of State for Trade and Industry v. Arnold
unreported, February 23, 1995, Ch. D. 5.29
Record Leather Manufacturers (Aust.) Pty Ltd, RE (1980) 5 A.C.L.R. 19..... 13.29
Red Label Fashions Ltd; Secretary of State for Trade and Industry v. Kullar
[1999] B.C.C. 308. .... 3.11, 3.23
R. v. Appleyard (1985) 81 Cr. App. R. (S.) 319, [1985] Crim. L. R. 723,
C.A. 9.11, 9.21
——— v. Austen (1985) 7 Cr. App.. R. (S.) 214, (1985) 1 B.C.C. 88   9.05, 9.11, 9.20,
12.40
——— v. Bibi [1980] 1 W.L.R. 1193, 91981) 71 Cr. App. R. 360, (1980) 2 Cr.
App. Rep. (S.) 177, [1980] Crim. L.R. 732, C.A. 9.70
——— v. Boal [1992] 1 Q.B. 591, [1992] 2 W.L.R. 890, [1992] 3 All E.R. 177,
(1992) 136 S.J.L.B. 100, (1992) 156 J.P. 617, [1992] I.C.R. 495, [1992]
I.R.L.R. 420, (1992) 95 Cr. App. R. 272, [1992] B.C.L.C. 872, (1992)
156 L.G. Rev. 763, [1992] Gazette, 3 June, 26, The Times, March 16,
1992, C.A. 12.37, 12.39, 12.41
——— v. Bradley [1961] 1 W.L.R. 398, 125 J.P. 303, 105 S.J. 183, [1961] 1 All
E.R. 669, 45 Cr. App. R. 97, C.A. 11.18
——— v. Brockley (1994) 99 Cr. App. R. 385, [1994] B.C.C. 131, [1994] 1
B.C.L.C. 606, [1994] Crim. L.R. 671, (1994) 138 S.J.L.B. 5, The Times,
November 25, 1993. .... 12.55, 13.38
——— v. Campbell (1984) 78 Cr. App. R. 95, [1984] B.C.L.C. 83..... 12.23, 12.25,
12.31, 12.32, 12.33, 12.34, 12.35
——— v. Chance, ex p. Smith [1995] B.C.C. 1095. .... 6.49A
——— v. Cobbey (1993) 14 Cr. App. R. (S.) 82. .... 9.21, 9.66
——— v. Cole, Lees & Birch [1998] B.C.C. 87. .... 2.19, 9.64, 11.11
——— v. Corbin (1984) 6 Cr. App. R. (S.) 17, [1984] Crim. L.R. 303..... 9.05, 9.11,
9.20, 12.40
——— v. Director of the Serious Fraud Office, ex p Saunders [1988] Crim. L.R.
837 .... 3.68
——— v. Edwards [1998] 2 Cr. App. R. (S.) 213, [1998] Crim. L.R. 298 .... 9.66,
9.67, 9.70
——— v. Georgiou (1988) 87 Cr. App. R. 207, (1988) 4 B.C.C. 322, [1988] Crim
L.R. 472, (1988) 10 Cr. App. R. (S.) 137, [1988] Crim. L.r. 472, (1988) 4
B.C.C. 322. .... 9.11, 9.26, 12.40
——— v. Goodman [1993] 2 All E.R. 789, (1983) 97 Cr. App. R. 210, (1993) 14
Cr. App. R. (S.) 147, [1994] 1 B.L.C. 349, [1992] B.C.C. 625..... 9.05, 9.10,
9.11, 9.20, 9.21, 9.70, 9.73, 11.04, 12.40

R. v. Grantham [1984] Q.B. 675, [1984] 2 W.L.R. 815, [1984] 3 All E.R. 166,
　　(1984) 79 Cr. Ap.. R. 86, [1984] Crim. L.R. 492, (1984) 81 L.S. Gaz.
　　1437, C.A. 5.12
—— v. Green and Green (1981) 3 Cr. App. R. (S.) 22 .... 9.68
—— v. Hayden [1975] 1 W.L.R. 852, 119 S.J. 390, [1975] 2 All E.R. 558,
　　[1975] Crim. L.R. 350; sub nom R. v. Hayden (Joseph Anthony) 60 Cr.
　　App. R. 304, C.A. 9.71
—— v. Immigration Apeal Tribunal, ex p. Jeyeanthan [1999] 3 All E.R. 231 . 6.28
—— v. Institute of Chartered Accountants in England and Wales, ex p. Brindle
　　[1994] B.C.C. 297, CA; *The Times*, January 12, 1994, CA 6.49A
—— v. Kamzi (1985) 7 Cr. App. R. (S.) 115 .... 9.21
—— v. Medicines Control Agency ex p. Pharma Nord (U.K.) Ltd unreported,
　　May 22, 1998 .... 12.24
—— v. Menocal [1980] A.C. 598, [1979] 2 W.L.R. 876, [1976] 2 All E.R. 510;
　　sub nom. Customs and Excise Commissioners v. Menocal (1979) 123
　　S.J. 372, (1979) 69 Cr. App. R. 157, [1979] Crim. L.R. 651, H.L. ; revers-
　　ing [1979] Q.B. 46, [1978] 3 W.L.R. 602, (1978) 122 S.J. 661, [1978] 3
　　All E.R. 961, (1979) 69 Cr. App. R. 148, C.A. 11.12
—— v. Michael [1976] Q.B. 414, [1975] 3 W.L.R. 731, 119 S.J. 792, [1976] 1
　　All E.R. 629 .... 11.12
—— v. Miles [1992] Crim. L.R. 657, The Times, April 15, 1992, C.A. 9.44
—— v. Millard (1994) 15 Cr. App. R. (S.) 445, [1994] Crim. L.R. 146 .... 9.21,
　　　　　　　　　　　　　　　　　　　　　　　　　　　　　　　　　　9.66, 9.70
—— v. Newth [1974] N.Z.L.R. 760 .... 12.25, 12.34
—— v. Russen unreported, July 6, 1984 .... 9.25
—— v. Savage (1983) 5 Cr. App. R. (S.) 9.60
—— v. Saville [1981] 1 Q.B. 12 .... 11.12
—— v. Secretary of State for Trade and Industry, ex p. McCormick [1998]
　　B.C.C. 379, [1998] C.O.D. 160, (1998) 95(10) L.S.G. 27, *The Times*,
　　February 10, 1998, *Independent*, February 10, 1998, C.A. ; affirming
　　[1998] B.C.C. 381, *Independent*, January 15, 1998, Q.B.D.. 2.24, 3.63, 7.01
—— v. Secretary of State for Trade and Industry, ex p. Soden [1996] 1 W.L.R.
　　1512, [1996] 3 All E.R. 967, [1996] 2 B.C.L.C. 636, [1997] B.C.C.
　　308 .... 3.03
—— v. Shacter [1960] 2 Q.B. 252, [1960] 2 W.L.R. 258, 124 J.P. 108, 104
　　S.J.90, [1960] 1 All E.R. 61, 44 Cr. App. R. 42, 111 L.J. 6 .... 9.45
—— v. Shepherd (1983) 5 Cr. App. R. (S.) 124 .... 9.72
—— v. Smith (1996) 2 Cr. App. R. 1., [1996] 2 B.C.L.C. 109 .... 9.21
—— v. Teece (1994) 15 Cr. App. R. (S.) 302 .... 12.55
—— v. Theivendran (1992) 13 Cr. App. R. (S.) 601 .... 12.55
—— v. Thompson (1993) 14 Cr. App. R. (S.) 89 .... 12.55
—— v. Young (1990) 12 Cr. App. Rep. (S.) 262, [1990] Crim. L.R. 818, [1990]
　　B.C.C. 549 .... 2.19, 9.02, 9.34, 9.60, 9.61, 9.62, 9.63. 9.64, 9.66, 9.70
Registrar of Restrictive Trading Agreements v. W.H. Smith & Son Ltd [1969] 1
　　W.L.R. 1460, 113 S.J. 686, [1969] 3 All E.R. 1065, ; affirming [1968] 1
　　W.L.R. 1541, [1968] 3 All E.R. 721, sub nom. Registrar of Restrictive
　　Trading Agreements v. Smith (W.H.) (1968) 112 S.J. 782, [1968] C.L.Y.
　　389 .... 12.37, 12.38, 12.43
Restick v. Crickmore [1994] 1 W.L.R. 420, (1994) 138 S.J.L.B. 4, [1993]
　　N.P.C. 155, (1993) 143 N.L.J. 1712, *The Times*, December 3, 1993, C.A. 6.09

Rex Williams Leisure plc, Re; Secretary of State for Trade and Industry v. War-
    ren [1994] 3 W.L.R. 745, [1994] 4 All E.R. 27, [1994] B.C.C. 551,
    [1994] 2 B.C.L.C. 555, *The Times*, May 4, 1994, CA, affirming [1994]
    Ch. 1, [1993] 3 W.L.R. 685, [1993] 2 All E.R. 741, [1993] B.C.C. 79,
    [1993] B.C.L.C. 568, (1993) 143 N.L.J. Rep. 52...... 2.28, 3.62, 3.66, 6.15,
                                       6.36, 6.37, 6.49, 6.63, 6.67, 8.20
Richborough Furniture Ltd; Secretary of State for Trade and Industry v. Stokes
    [1996] 1 B.C.L.C. 507, [1996] B.C.C. 155....... 3.13, 3.16, 3.17, 3.18, 3.19,
                                  3.20, 3.21, 3.23, 3.24, 5.05, 5.16, 5.52, 5.72
Roebuck v. Mungovin [1994] 2 A.C. 224, [1994] 2 W.L.R. 290, [1994] 1 All
    E.R. 568, [1994] 1 Lloyd's Rep. 481, [1994] P.I.Q.R. 209, [1994] J.P.I.L.
    164, (1994) 144 N.L.J. Rep. 197, (1994) 138 S.J.L.B. 59, (1994) 91(13)
    L.S.G. 36, *Times*, February 4, 1994, *Independent*, February 8, 1994,
    H.L; reversing [1993] P.I.Q.R. 444... 7.37
Rolls Razor Ltd (No. 2), Re [1970] 1 Ch. 576, [1970] 2 W.L.R. 100, 113 S.J.
    938, [1969] 3 All E.R. 1386.. 6.81
Rolls Royce Ltd (No.2), Re [1970] Ch. 576, [1970] 2 W.L.R. 100, [1969] 3 All
    E.R. 1386... 6.18
Rolus Properties Ltd, Re (1988) 4 B.C.C. 446... 4.02, 4.15, 4.16, 5.12, 5.13, 5.14,
                                               5.34, 5.52, 5.79, 11.05
Ronald Mullen v. Birmingham City Council, May 27, 1999, QBD 6.63
Ronson v. Pounds 13 Cr. App. Rep. 153 .... 6.85
Routestone Ltd v. Minories Finance Ltd [1997] B.C.C. 180 .... 6.77

Salomon v. Salomon & Co. Ltd [1897] A.C. 22........................... 2.02, 2.16
Salter v. National Companies Securities Commission [1989] W.A.R. 296,
    (1988) 13 A.C.L.R. 253, (1986) 6 A.C.LC. 717......................... 10.06
Samuel Sherman plc, Re [1991] 1 W.L.R. 1070, [1991] B.C.C. 699 .... 3.66,
                                               4.09, 4.18, 5.47, 5.67
S & R Seafoods Ltd, Re, unreported, November 23, 1995...................... 5.57
Sasea Finance Ltd, Re [1998] 1 B.C.L.C. 559 .... 3.04
Saunders v. United Kingdom [1997] B.C.C. 872, (1997) 23 E.H.R.R. 313,
    (1997) 2 B.H.R.C. 358, *Times*, December 18, 1996, *Independent*, Janu-
    ary 14, 1997, ECHR, affirming *Independent*, September 30, 1994, Eur
    Comm HR 3.63
Savings & Investment Bank Ltd v. Gasco Investments (Netherlands) BV [1984]
    1 W.L.R. 271, [1984] 1 All E.R. 296...................................... 6.66
SBA Properties Ltd, Re [1967] 1 W.L.R. 799, [1967] 2 All E.R. 615 .... 6.67
Seagull Manufacturing Co Ltd (No. 2) [1994] Ch. 91, [1994] 2 W.L.R. 453,
    [1994] 2 All E.R. 767, [1994] 1 B.C.L.C. 273, [1993] B.C.C. 833....... 3.35,
                                                                   6.13
Seagull Manufacturing Co. Ltd (No.3), Re [1996] 1 B.C.L.C. 51, [1995] B.C.C.
    1088... 11.07, 11.09
Secretary of State for Trade and Industry v. Ashcroft [1998] Ch. 71, [1997] 3
    W.L.R. 319, [1997] 3 All E.R. 86, [1997] B.C.C. 634, (1997) 94(11)
    L.S.G. 35, (1997) 141 S.J.L.B. 57, Times, March 4, 1997 .... 6.67
—— v. Baker [1999] 1 B.C.L.C 433....................................... 2.16, 8.15
—— v. Bannister [1996] 1 W.L.R. 118, [1996] 1 All E.R. 993, [1996] 2
    B.C.L.C. 271, [1995] B.C.C. 1027, Times, July 26, 1995, Independent,
    August 11, 1995............ 11.19, 11.21, 11.223, 11.24, 11.25, 13.01, 13.54

Secretary of State for Trade and Industry v. Barnett [1998] 2 B.C.L.C. 64 .... 12.13
—— v. Brown (1995) S.L.T. 550................................. 13.24, 13.30, 13.31
—— v. Burrows, unreported, July 4, 1996............................. 11.23, 13.01
—— v. Carmichael [1995] B.C.C. 679... 7.07
—— v. Edwards [1997] B.C.C. 222........................... 11.08, 11.19, 11.24
—— v. Elms unreported, January 16, 1997, Ch. D. 3.23
—— v. Houston (No.2) 1995 S.L.T. 196................... 3.04, 6.50
—— v. Jabble [1998] 1 B.C.L.C. 598, [1998] B.C.C. 39, (1997) 94(35) L.S.G.
33, (1997) 141 S.J.L.B. 214, Times, August 5, 1997, C.A.......... 3.51, 3.52
—— v. Jebraille, unreported, December 20, 1997, Ch. D. 6.50
—— v. Lonrho plc [1992] B.C.C. 325, C.A. 6.32
—— v. McCormick [1998] 2 B.C.I..C. 18, Ch.D 2.23
—— v. Martin [1998] B.C.C. 184........................... 7.35, 7.36
—— v. Morrall [1996] B.C.C. 229... 7.07
—— v. Normand [1995] B.C.C. 158... 6.50
—— v. Palfreman 1995 S.L.T. 156, 1995 S.C.L.R. 172, [1995] 2 B.C.L.C. 301,
[1995] B.C.C. 193......................... 11.16, 13.04, 13.22, 13.30, 13.32
—— v. Palmer [1993] B.C.C. 650... 6.50
—— v. Phelps, unreported, April 11, 1996...................................... 11.08
—— v. Queen 1998 S.L.T. 735, [1998] B.C.C. 678, Times, August 27, 1997. 5.45
—— v. Renwick, unreported, July, 1997, Ch.D........ 13.11, 13.43, 13.54, 13.63
—— v. Rogers [1996] 1 W.L.R. 1569, [1996] 4 All E.R. 854, [1996] 2 B.C.L.C.
513, [1997] B.C.C. 155........ 8.06, 8.08, 8.09, 8.11, 8.12, 8.14, 8.17, 8.18
—— v. Rosenfield [1999] B.C.C. 413.................... 13.18, 13.22, 13.38, 13.40,
13.44, 13.48, 13.49
—— v. Sananes [1994] B.C.C. 375... 3.07
—— v. Shah, unreported, April 10, 1997.. 8.12
—— v. Shuttleworth, January, 27, 1999.. 11.04
—— v. Taylor [1997] 1 W.L.R. 407................................ 4.09, 5.04, 5.54
—— v. Worth [1994] 2 B.C.L.C. 113, [1994] B.C.C. 371 .... 13.11
Secretary of State for Trade and Industry, Petitioner [1998] B.C.C. 11 .... 6.05
Sevenoaks Stationers (Retail) Ltd, Re [1991] Ch. 164, [1990] 3 W.L.R. 1165,
[1991] 3 All E.R. 578, [1991] B.C.L.C. 325, [1990] B.C.C. 765, (1990)
134 S.J. 1367, C.A; reversing [1990] B.C.L.C. 668, Ch. D........ 4.16, 4.17,
4.18, 4.19, 4.20, 4.26, 5.05, 5.04, 5.21, 5.22, 5.23, 5.25,
5.51, 5.58, 5.67, 5.68, 5.70, 5.74, 5.75, 5.77, 5.85, 6.52,
6.55, 6.54, 6.58, 7.26, 8.09, 8.16, 8.17, 9.66, 9.69, 9.70, 13.29
Shocked v. Goldschmidt [1998] 1 All E.R. 372, Times, November 4, 1994,
Independent, December 5, 1994, CA... 6.84
Shou Yin Mar v. Royal Bank [1940] 3 D.L.R. 331 .... 12.43
Shneider, Re (1997) 22 A.C.S.R. 997....................... 9.24, 13.03
Smith v. Braintree District Council [1990] 2 A.C. 215 .... 1.30
Smith v. Director of the Serious Fraud Office [1993] A.C. 1, [1992] 3 W.L.R.
66, [1992] 3 All E.R. 456, (1992) 136 S.J.L.B. 182, [992] B.C.L.C. 879,
[1992] Crim. L.R. 504, [1992] C.O.D. 270, (1992) 142 n.l.j. 895, [1992]
Gazette, 15 July, 34, The Independent, June 12, 1992, The Times, June
16, 1992, Financial Times, June 17, 1992, The Guardian, July 1, 1992,
H.L., reversing [1992] 1 All E..R. 730, (1992) 135 S.J.L.B. 214, (1992)
95 Cr. App.R. 191, [1992] C.O.D. 188, [1992] Gazette, March 11 33,
The Independent, November 8, 1991, The Guardian, November 13,
1991, The Times, November 13, 1991, D.C. [1992] 3 All E.R. 546..... 3.68

S N Group plc, Re [1993] B.C.C. 808... 6.84
Southbourne Sheet Metal Co. Ltd, Re [1992] B.C.L.C. 361, [1991] B.C.C.
    732.. 2.24
Southbourne Sheet Metal Co. Ltd (No. 2) [1993] B.C.L.C. 135.......... 6.85, 8.04
Sparrow v. Sovereign Chicken Ltd unreported June 8 1994, C.A.............. 7.38
Stanford Services Ltd, Re [1987] B.C.L.C. 607, (1987) 3 B.C.C. 326...   4.02, 4.16,
                                                                       5.20, 5.29
Standard Chartered Bank of Australia Ltd v. Antico (1995) 131 A.L.R. 1.....   3.33
Stormont Ltd, Re; Secretary of State for Trade and Industry v. Cleland [1995]
    B.C.C. 203............................. 7.05, 7.06, 7.10, 7.13, 7.16, 7.23, 8.07
St James Club, Re (1852) 2 De. G. M. & G. 383, 42 E.R. 920 .... 12.12
St Piran, Re [1981] 1 W.L.R. 1300.. 6.67
Streamhaven Ltd, Re; Secretary of State for Trade and Industry v. Barnett
    [1998] 2 B.C.L.C. 64......................... 7.16, 13.13, 13.20, 13.23, 13.25
Surrey Leisure Ltd, Re; Official Receiver v. Keam [1999] 1 B.C.L.C.
    731... 6.30, 6.35
Sutton Glassworks Ltd, Re [1997] 1 B.C.L.C. 26, [1996] B.C.C. 174, Ch. D.   6.48
Swift 737 Ltd, Re; Secretary of State for Trade and Industry v. Ettinger [1993]
    B.C.L.C. 896, [1993] B.C.C. 312, The Times, February 18, 1993, C.A.,
    reversing in part [1992] B.C.C. 93, [1993] B.C.L.C. 1.......   2.08, 2.18, 4.18,
                                              4.20, 5.13, 5.84, 5.85, 9.36, 9.46, 10.07
Sykes (Butchers) Ltd; Secretary of State for Trade and Industry v. Richardson
    [1998] 1 B.C.L.C. 110, [1998] B.C.C. 484, (1987) 141 S.J.L.B. 111,
    (1997) 94(20) L.S.G. 37, Times, May 16, 1997, Ch. D............   3.12, 3.17,
                           3.19, 3.22, 4.09, 4.16, 5.35, 5.40, 5.41, 5.64, 5.83, 6.53, 6.55, 6.85
Synthetic Technology Ltd, Re; Secretary of State for Trade and Industry v.
    Joiner [1993] B.C.C. 549..............   5.05, 5.12, 5.23, 5.29, 5.72, 5.74, 9.36

T (A Minor), Re [1986] Fam. 160, [1986] 2 W.L.R. 538, (1986) 130 S.J. 88,
    [1986] 1 All E.R. 817, [1986] 1 F.L.R. 31, (1986) 16 Fam. Law. 184,
    (1986) 83 L.S. Gaz. 520, C.A. 6.28
T & D Services (Timber Preservation & Damp Proofing Contractors) Ltd, Re
    [1990] B.C.C. 592.............   3.53, 3.56, 5.18, 5.38, 5.42, 5.45, 5.74, 11.19
Tansoft Ltd, Re [1991] B.C.L.C. 339......   3.20, 3.56, 5.23, 5.42, 5.44, 5.72, 5.74,
                                                                                10.07
Tasbian Ltd (No. 1) [1991] B.C.L.C. 54, [1990] B.C.C. 318 .... 7.21
Tasbian Ltd (No. 2), Re; Offical Receiver v. Nixon [1991] B.C.L.C. 59, [1990]
    B.C.C. 322.. 6.16, 6.19, 6.21, 6.50
Tasbian Ltd (No.3), Re; Official Receiver v. Nixon [1993] B.C.L.C. 297,
    [1992] B.C.C. 358.. 3.24, 3.26, 3.28, 3.29, 3.31, 6.50, 7.06, 7.13, 7.21, 7.28
Tech Textiles Ltd, Re; Secretary of State for trade and Industry v. Vane [1998] 1
    B.C.L.C. 259...............   13.04, 13.07, 13.21, 13.22, 13.29, 13.32, 13.44,
                                                       13.46, 13.47, 13.48, 13.50
Tesco Supermarkets Ltd v. Nattrass [1972] A.C. 153, [1971] 2 W.L.R. 1166,
    115 S.J. 285, [1971] 2 All E.R. 127, 69 L.G.R. 403, 121 New L.J. 461, 39
    S.L.G. 221, Commercial Acct. 331, 5 N.Z.L.R. 357, H.L. reversing
    [1971] 1 Q.B. 133, [1970] 3 W.L.R. 572, 114 S.J. 664, [1970] 3 All E.R.
    357, 68 L.G.R. 722, D.C. 12.30
Thomas Christy Ltd, Re [1994] 2 B.C.L.C. 527 .... 6.49
Thorncliffe Finance Ltd, Re; Secretary of State for Trade and Industry v. Arif
    [1997] 1 B.C.L.C. 34, [1996] B.C.C. 586, Times, March 25, 1996,
    Ch. D..............   3.10, 4.04, 4.20, 5.14, 5.15, 5.42, 5.72, 5.61, 5.82, 5.83,
                                                                5.84, 13.01, 13.54

Thorne v. Silverleaf [1994] 1 B.C.L.C. 637, [1994] B.C.C. 109 .... 12.56
Thynne v. Thynne [1955] P. 272, [1955] 3 W.L.R. 465, 99 S.J. 580, [1955] 3
    All E.R. 129, 71 L.Q.R. 453, CA; reversing [1955] 3 W.L.R. 108, 99 S.J.
    437, [1955] 2 All E.R. 377 .... 11.08
Time Utilising Business Systems Ltd, Re [1990] B.C.L.C. 568, (1989) 5 B.C.C.
    851 .... 5.39, 6.10
TLL Realisations Ltd, Re, unreported, February 1, 1999 ...... 11.03, 11.15, 12.24,
        12.43, 13.03, 13.03, 13.17, 13.29, 13.32, 13.21, 13.28, 13.45, 13.53, 13.54
TMS (GB) Ltd, Re; Secretary of State for Trade and Industry v. White
    unreported, November 26, 1993, Ch. D 4.05
Tolj v. O'Connor (1983) 13 A.C.L.R. 653 .... 11.24
Topglass Windows Ltd, Re, unreported, September 26, 1995 .... 5.66
Travel and Holiday Clubs Ltd, Re [1967] 1 W.L.R. 711, 111 S.J. 272, [1967] 2
    All E.R. 606 .... 6.67
Travel Mondial (U.K.) Ltd, Re [1991] B.C.L.C. 120, [1991] B.C.C. 224   5.31, 1.19
Tucker v. D.P.P. [1992] 4 All E.R. 901 .... 9.72
Twycross v. Grant (1877) 2 C.P.D. 469 .... 12.27

Unisoft Group Ltd (No.3), Re [1994] 1 B.C.L.C. 609, [1994] B.C.C. 766 ..... 3.26
Universal Flooring and Driveways Ltd, Re; Secretary of State for Trade and
    Industry v. Woodward, unreported, May 15, 1997, Ch. D 7.16, 13.20

VAB Planting Ltd, Re unreported, April 11, 1986 .... 4.02
Van Reesma, Re (1975) 11 S.A.S.R. 322 .... 13.15
Verby Print for Advertising, Re; Secretary of State for Trade and Industry v.
    Fine [1998] 2 B.C.L.C. 23, [1998] B.C.C. 652 .... 3.08, 5.12, 5.23, 5.24,
                            5.25, 5.26, 5.27, 5.40, 5.66, 5.71
Victoria Society, Re; Knottingley [1913] 1 Ch. 167 .... 3.49

W & A Glaser Ltd, Re [1994] B.C.C. 199 .... 6.84
Walker v. Wilsher (1889) 23 Q.B. D. 335 .... 8.10
Wallace, Re (1983) 8 A.C.L.R. 311 .... 13.22
Walter L Jacob & Co. Ltd, Re; Official Receiver v. Jacob [1993] B.C.C.
    512 .... 3.51, 6.06, 6.50
W & M Roith Ltd, Re [1967] 1 W.L.R. 432110 S.J. 963, [1967] 1 All E.R. 427,
    [1966] C.L.Y. 1495, 30 M.L.R. 566 .... 5.29
Ward Sherrard Ltd, Re [1996] B.C.C. 418 .... 4.18, 5.06, 5.07, 5.08, 5.09,
                                5.12, 5.29, 5.31, 5.71
Wedgecraft Ltd, Re, unreported, March 7, 1986 ...... 4.02, 4.15, 5.21, 5.44, 13.54
Welfab Engineers Ltd, Re [1990] B.C.L.C. 833, [1990] B.C.C. 600 .... 5.06
Western Welsh International System Buildings Ltd, Re (1988) 4 B.C.C.
    449 .... 2.11, 4.02, 5.21, 5.37, 5.71
Westmercia Safetywear Ltd v. Dodd [1988] B.C.L.C. 250, (1988) 4 B.C.C. 30,
    CA 4.09, 5.03, 5.28, 5.43
Westmid Packing Services Ltd, Re; Secretary of State for Trade and Industry v.
    Griffiths [1998] 2 All E.R. 124, [1998] 2 B.C.L.C. 646, [1998] B.C.C.
    836.... 2.18, 2.23, 4.04, 4.22, 5.48, 5.57, 5.61, 5.67, 5.70, 5.74, 5.75, 5.76,
            5.81, 5.82, 5.83, 5.84, 6.21, 6.24, 6.76, 6.79, 6.85, 7.03, 7.05, 7.07,
            7.26, 7.30, 8.15, 8.17, 9.58, 9.66, 10.07, 13.01, 13.07, 13.26, 13.64
Westmid Packing Services Ltd (No.2), Re; Secretary of State for Trade and In-
    dustry v. Morrall [1996] B.C.C. 229 .... 3.24, 7.15, 7.16, 7.28

Whaley Bridge Printing Company v. Green (1880) 5 Q.B.D. 109 .... 12.26
White & Osmond (Parkstone) Ltd, Re... 5.12
Wills v. Corfe Joinery Ltd [1998] 2 B.C.L.C. 75, [1997] B.C.C. 511, [1997]
    B.P.I.R. 611, (1997) 94(7) L.S.G. 29, *Times*, January 21, 1997, Ch. D.. 5.39
Wimbledon Village Restaurant Ltd, Re; Secretary of State for Trade and indus-
    try v. Thompson [1994] B.C.C. 753........ 4.03, 5.06, 5.10, 5.11, 5.12, 5.23
Witney Town Football and Social Club, Re [1993] B.C.C. 874, [1994]
    B.C.L.C. 487 .... 12.12
Woodhouse v. Walsall Metropolitan Borough Council [1994] Env. L.R.
    30... 12.37, 12.38, 12.39, 12.43
Working Project Limited, Re [1995] 1 B.C.L.C. 226, [1995] B.C.C. 197,
    Times, October 27, 1994, *The Independent*, November 28, 1994,
    Ch. D.. 6.05, 6.06

Zim Metal Products Pty, Ltd, Re [1977] A.C.L.C. 29, (1977) 2 A.C.L.R.
    553... 13.10, 13.22, 13.29
Zucker v. Commissioner for Corporate Affairs [1980] A.C.L.C. 34.... 9.64, 13,29

Table of Statutes

1844 Joint Stock Companies
      Act (7 & 8 Vict.,
      c. 110).. 3.38, 9.04, 12.08,
                            12.12
1856 Joint Stock Companies
      Act (19 & 20 Vict.,
      c. 47)................. 12.08
      Joint Stock Banking
      Companies Act...... 12.08
1862 Companies Act (25 & 26
      Vict., c. 89).......... 12.08
1883 Bankruptcy Act (46 &
      47 Vict., c. 52) 10.09
1907 Limited Partnerships Act
      (7 Edw. 7, c. 24) 4.07
1908 Companies (Consoli-
      dation) Act (8 Edw.
      7, c. 69) (Ireland) ... 3.38,
                      9.04, 12.08
1914 Bankruptcy Act (4 & 5
      Geo. 5, c. 59)—
      s. 155.................. 10.04
1925 Law of Property Act (15
      & 16 Geo.5, c. 20).. 9.30,
                      9.45, 12.46
1928 Companies Act...... 1.21, 1.24,
                            10.03
      s. 75....... 1.23, 9.42, App. 2
         (1) 9.51
         (3) 9.50
         (4) 9.51
         (5) 9.50
      s. 84.............. 1.22, App. 2
1929 Companies Act (19 & 20
      Geo. 5, c. 23)........   1.26,
                 10.03, 11.13, 12.08
      s. 142.................. App. 2
      s. 217.................   1.24
      s. 275...... 1.23, 9.42, App. 2
         (1)............ 9.42, 9.51
1947 Companies Act (10 & 11
      Geo. 6, c. 47)—
      s. 33.................. App. 2

1947 Companies Act—cont.
      s. 33(1) 9.42
         (a) 9.05
         (b)............. 9.42
         (3) 6.28
1948 Companies Act (11 & 12
      Geo. 6, c. 38).... 1.23, 1.28
      s. 182................... 12.52
      s. 185 .... 12.52
      ss. 187–188............ App. 2
      s. 188........1.23, 1.25, 1.27,
                      11.18, 12.52
         (1)................ 9.42
         (a)............ 9.05
         (b) 9.42
         (3)................ 6.28
      s. 332............... 1.23, 9.51
      s. 441 .... 12.40
1956 Restrictive Trade Prac-
      tices Act (4 & 5 Eliz.
      2, c. 68)—
      s. 15 .... 12.37
1960 Administration of Justice
      Act (8 & 9 Eliz. 2, c.
      65)—
      s. 12 .... 8.17
1964 Police Act (c. 48)—
      Sched. 1B............... 12.49
1965 Industrial and Provident
      Societies Act (c.
      12)—
      s. 55 .... 3.49
1968 Criminal Appeal Act (c.
      19) 9.73
      s. 9(1).................. 9.73
      s. 11(1) 9.73
         (3)............9.73, 11.12
      s. 18(1) 9.73
         (2) 9.73
      s. 50 .... 9.73
      Trade Descriptions Act
      (c. 29)—
      s. 1(1)(a) 9.19

1968	Trade Descriptions Act —*cont.*	
	s. 14(1)(a)	9.19
	s. 20	9.19
	Civil Evidence Act (c. 64)........... 6.64, 6.69	
	s. 8	6.69
1971	Fire Precautions Act (c. 40)	12.37
1972	Local Government Act (c. 5)—	
	s. 80	10.06
	ss. 80–81	12.51
	Civil Evidence Act (c. 30)..... 6.63, 6.64, 6.69	
	s. 3	6.77
1973	Powers of Criminal Courts Act (c. 62)—	
	s. 7	9.60
1974	Health and Safety at Work Act (c. 37)....	9.18
	ss. 2–4	9.16
	s. 33	9.16
	s. 37........ 9.16, 9.17, 12.38	
	Control of Pollution Act (c. 40)................	12.38
	Friendly Societies Act (c. 46)....... 3.41, 3.49, 12.12	
	Rehabilitation of Offenders Act (c. 53)	5.45
1975	Criminal Procedure (Scotland) Act (c. 21)—	
	s. 289B	12.54
1976	Insolvency Act (c. 60) ...	1.27, 2.10
	s. 9.......... 1.27, 1.28, 4.02, 12.52, App. 2	
	(3)...................	6.28
	Companies Act (c. 69)—	
	s. 28................	1.25, 9.36
	ss. 28–29.............. App. 2	
	s. 29	11.26
1978	Interpretation Act (c. 30)—	
	s. 5	9.06
	Sch. 1............ 9.06, 9.48	
1980	Magistrates' Courts Act (c. 43)—	
	s. 32	12.54
	s. 108...................	9.71
1980	Magistrates' Courts Act —*cont.*	
	s. 108(3)...............	9.71
	s.111....................	9.72
	(2)................	9.71
	(4)................	9.72
	s. 142..................	11.12
	s. 144..................	9.06
1981	Supreme Court Act (c. 54)...... 6.47, 11.21, 11.22	
	s. 16	6.81
	s. 18(1)(h)..............	6.83
	ss. 33–34	3.04
	s. 47(1)....9.73, 11.22, 11.24	
	(2)	11.12
	s. 48	9.71
	(4)	9.71
	(6)	9.71
	s. 49(3)	11.23
	Companies Act (c. 62) ..	9.40, 10.03
	s. 93......... 1.25, 9.05, 9.36, 9.42, 12.52	
	ss. 93–94............... App. 2	
	(1)	1.23
	(1A)	9.50
	(1B)	11.13
	s. 94	1.27
	(1)	11.13
	s. 96	1.23
	Sched. 3................. App. 2	
	Para.9................	1.23
	Crown Court Act—	
	s. 46(1)	9.06
1982	Criminal Justice Act (c. 48)	9.73
	Insurance Companies Act (c. 50)	9.11
1983	Value Added Tax Act (c.55)—	
	s. 39	9.25
1984	County Courts Act (c. 28)........... 6.10, 6.47	
	s. 40(1)	6.08
	(2)............ 6.08, 6.10	
	(4)	6.08
	(8)	6.08
	s. 41(1)	6.08
	s. 42	6.09
	(1)	6.08
	(2)	6.08

1984 County Courts Act—
cont.
s. 42(7) 6.08
s. 77 .... 6.81
s. 112(6)................ 10.09
s. 114.................... 10.09
Part IV.................. 1.14
Part. VI...6.02, 10.01, 10.09,
12.03
1985 Companies Act (c. 6).... 3.10,
3.12, 3.47, 5.45, 6.66,
9.30, 11.04, 12.22,
13.18, 13.33
s. 1(2)(a) 2.03
(3A)................ 2.03
s. 14 .... 3.23
s. 49 .... 13.20
s. 51(2) 13.20
s. 117............. 9.09, 12.28
s. 151........ 5.46, 5.53, 9.24
s. 188(1)(b) 1.23
s. 221.......4.06, 4.10, 5.12,
5.13, 5.14, 5.15, 5.16,
5.17, 5.18, 5.35, 5.62,
5.63, 5.64, 13.20
(3)................ 5.16
(5)................ 5.13
s. 222.................... 4.06
s. 226.................... 4.06
s. 227.................... 4.06
s. 233.................... 4.06
s. 235.................... 5.19
s. 238.................... 5.41
s. 239.................... 5.41
s. 241.................... 9.39
s. 242........ 4.09, 4.10, 9.39
(4)................ 9.40
s. 242A 9.39
s. 244................... 9.39
s. 245B 9.40
s. 246–249 .... 2.03
s. 249A–249E.......... 2.03
s.282............... 3.10, 3.12
s. 285................... 3.12
s. 288................... 4.06
s. 295........... 11.03, 11.16
(6)................ 11.16
ss. 295–301 .... 11.16
ss. 295–302............ App. 2
s. 296............... 1.23, 9.05
s. 297............... 1.25, 9.36

1985 Companies Act—cont.
s. 298............... 1.23. 9.42
s. 300.......1.27, 2.20, 3.12,
4.02, 4.03, 4.04, 5.12,
5.26, 7.07, 12.19
s. 303.................... 2.03
ss. 306–307 .... 13.30
s. 309.. 2.04, 2.15, 5.26, 5.46
s. 317.................... 9.23
s. 320............... 5.19, 5.43
s. 342.................... 9.23
s. 346(4)................ 5.43
(5)................ 5.43
s. 349.................... 13.35
s. 352................... 4.06
s. 353................... 4.06
s. 363............... 4.06, 9.39
s. 379A................. 2.03
s. 381A–381C 2.03
s. 399................... 4.06
s. 411 .... 6.15
s. 415................... 4.06
s. 431................... 3.63
s. 431–432........ 3.63, 3.64,
3.66, 6.67
s. 432...............2.24, 3.03
(1)................ 3.63
(2)................ 3.63
s. 437................... 3.63
(3)................ 3.63
s. 441........ 3.63, 6.66, 6.67
s. 447.......3.66, 3.68, 3.69,
5.47, 6.67
(2)................ 3.66
(3)................ 3.66
(5)................ 3.66
(8)................ 3.66
s. 447–448 .... 3.66
s. 448.................... 3.66
s. 449........ 3.03, 3.63, 3.66
(1)(ba)....... 3.64, 3.66
(d)........ 3.64, 3.66
s. 451A............. 3.03, 3.63
(2)(a)........... 3.63
s. 455.................... 12.40
s. 458.......1.07, 1.23, 9.04,
9.21, 9.35, 9.42,
9.44, 9.50
s. 652.................... 9.39
s. 653.................... 9.39
s. 665.................... 12.14
ss. 675–676 .... 12.08

1985 Companies Act—*cont.*
 s. 689.................... 12.08
 s. 713.................... 9.40
 s. 718..... 3.47, 12.12, 12.17
 s. 721.................... 12.40
 s. 727.................... 9.45
 s. 735....... 3.38, 9.04, 12.08
  (1)(a).........3.38, 9.04
  (3)...........3.38, 9.04
 s. 740........... 3.37, 12.08
 s. 741(1)................ 3.11
  (2)................ 3.25
 s. 744..... 9.45, 12.08, 12.40
 s. 774A 12.17
 Sched. 1, Pt. I
  Para. 4(a) 4.10
   (f) 4.10
 Sched. 12, Pt. I
  Para. 1 .... 6.28
  Para. 4 .... 11.03
  Para. 5 .... 11.03
  Para. 6 .... 12.08
  Para. 7 .... 6.28
 Sched. 22............... 3.48
 Sched. 24.......... 9.23, 9.49
 Part. I............. 9.09, 12.28
 Part. VII.... 5.48, 9.39, 13.31
 Part XIV.... 2.13, 3.02, 3.03,
        3.66
 Company   Securities
  (Insider Dealing) Act
  (c. 8)............. 9.11, 9.21
 Insolvency Act (c. 65) ... 1.28,
   1.29, 1.30, 2.01, 2.04,
   2.07, 2.09, 4.09, 6.15,
   6.66, 9.04, 11.05
 ss. 12–16............... App. 2
 ss. 12–19 .... 3.26
 s. 13............... 3.61, 4.04
 s. 15............... 1.23, 9.51
 s. 16............... 1.23, 9.51
 s. 18 .... 12.56
 s. 22(8) 9.04
 s. 108.................. App. 2
  (2)............... 11.03
  (b)6.28
 s. 109.................. App. 2
 Sched. 2................ App. 2
 Sched. 6................ App. 2
  Para. 1(1)–(4) 11.03
  (14) 11.03
 Sched. 10, Pt. IV....... 12.14

1985 Civil Evidence Act... 6.64, 6.65
 Housing   Associations
  Act (c. 69) 12.50
1986 Company Directors' Disqualification Act (c.
  46)........ 1.01, 1.03, 1.21,
   1.24, 1.30, 2.01, 2.02,
   2.04, 2.05, 2.16, 2.17,
   2.18, 2.21, 2.22, 2.23,
   2.24, 2.28, 2.29, 3.01,
   3.13, 3.35, 3.38, 4.26,
   5.06, 5.65, 6.51, 6.75,
   6.85, 9.17, 11.01, 12.18,
   12.48, 12.49, 12.50,
   12.52, 12.53, 13.08,
   13.12, 13.19, 13.33,
   13.38, 13.42, 13.56,
   13.57, 13.61, 13.69,
        App. 1
 s. 1.... 1.04, 1.19, 3.24, 3.42,
   3.43, 3.45, 3.46, 3.48,
   6.84, 8.06, 9.04, 9.07,
   11.02, 11.03, 11.04,
   11.06, 11.13, 11.16,
   12.01, 12.02, 12.05,
   12.06, 12.08, 12.11,
   12.12, 12.13, 12.14,
   12.16, 12.17, 12.18,
   12.19, 12.20, 12.22,
   12.23, 12.24, 12.25,
   12.29, 12.46, 12.54,
      12.55, 13.51
  (1)...... 2.26, 3.38, 11.02,
   11.05, 11.06, 11.07,
   11.08, 11.10, 11.11,
   11.18, 11.23, 11.24,
   12.02, 13.01, 13.58,
        13.61
  (a)..... 3.10, 12.14, 13.10
  (a)–(c) 12.14
  (a)–(d) 11.13
  (b)... 11.13, 12.04, 12.14,
        12.46
  (b)–(c). 9.40, 12.46, 12.56
  (c)... 11.05, 11.13, 12.04,
    12.14, 12.22, 12.46
  (b)–(d)....... 11.11, 12.41
  (d).... 9.07, 11.11, 12.14,
        12.24
  (3)........ 9.27, 9.35, 9.54

1986   Company Directors' Disqualification Act—
cont.
s. 1(4)...............9.43, 9.47
s. 2.... 1.02, 1.05, 1.23, 2.01,
2.06, 2.19, 3.24, 3.45,
3.63, 3.64, 3.66, 3.69,
4.01, 5.45, 5.75, 6.01,
6.05, 6.18, 6.27, 6.38,
7.01, 7.33, 8.04, 9.02,
9.05, 9.07, 9.08, 9.11,
9.13, 9.14, 9.16, 9.17,
9.19, 9.20, 9.21, 9.24,
9.25, 9.26, 9.28, 9.29,
9.30, 9.32, 9.33, 9.34,
9.35, 9.36, 9.41, 9.43,
9.44, 9.46, 9.47, 9.50,
9.56, 9.57, 9.58, 9.60,
9.61, 9.62, 9.63, 9.64,
9.65, 9.65, 9.66, 9.69,
9.70, 9.71, 9.72, 9.73,
10.04, 11.11, 11.13,
11.17, 11.18, 11.22,
11.24, 12.17, 12.29,
12.33, 12.40, 12.41,
12.46, 12.52, 12.55,
13.60, 13.62
(1)....... 9.07, 9.08, 9.10,
9.11, 9.12, 9.13, 9.14,
9.16, 9.17, 9.29, 9.30,
9.31, 12.40
(2)...............9.06, 9.50
(a).... 6.02, 6.27, 6.60,
6.80, 11.21
(3)................... 9.31
ss. 2–4.......6.03, 6.31, 8.02,
9.54, 9.59
ss. 2–5....... 1.08, 1.09, 1.30,
2.01, 4.09, 9.01, 9.02,
9.03, 9.04, 9.50, 9.57,
9.58, 9.71, 11.02, 11.11,
11.18, 11.26, 13.62
ss. 2–6 .... 13.01
s. 3.... 1.06, 1.08, 1.25, 2.01,
2.19, 3.01, 3.48, 3.63,
3.63, 3.66, 3.69, 4.01,
6.01, 6.05, 6.27, 6.38,
6.60, 6.80, 7.33, 9.04,
9.36, 9.37, 9.40, 9.41,
9.48, 9.49, 9.50, 9.57,
9.64, 9.69, 11.21, 11.24,
12.46, 12.52

1986   Company Directors' Disqualification Act—
cont.
s. 3(1)....... 9.04, 9.36, 9.37,
9.40
(2)...............9.40, 9.49
(3)(b)........... 9.40, 9.49
(4)................... 6.02
(5)................... 9.41
s. 4.... 1.02, 1.07, 1.23, 2.09,
2.19, 3.01, 3.63, 3.64,
3.66, 3.69, 6.01, 6.05,
6.27, 6.38, 6.60, 6.80,
7.33, 9.04, 9.21, 9.42,
9.43, 9.44, 9.45, 9.46,
9.47, 9.57, 9.58, 9.64,
10.03, 11.21, 11.24,
12.46, 12.52
(1)................... 9.42
(a)... 9.04, 9.44, 11.13
(b).... 9.29, 9.30, 9.45,
9.46, 9.52, 11.13
(2)...............6.02, 9.45
(3)................... 9.46
ss. 4–11........... 3.45, 12.17
s. 5.... 1.02, 1.08, 1.25, 2.09,
2.19, 3.01, 3.48, 4.01,
6,27, 6.31, 7.01, 9.04,
9.36, 9.41, 9.48, 9.49,
9.50, 9.56, 9.57, 9.58,
9.64, 9.70, 9.71, 9.73,
11.11, 11.13, 11.17,
11.22, 12.52, 13.60
(1)........ 9.04, 9.48, 9.49
(2)...............9.48, 9.50
(3)...............9.48, 9.49
(4)(a) 9.48
s. 6.... 1.02, 1.09, 1.10, 1.20,
1.28, 2.01, 2.09, 2.10,
2.13, 2.14, 2.15, 2.18,
2.19, 2.20, 2.23, 2.24,
2.25, 2.27, 3.01, 3.02,
3.03, 3.06, 3.10, 3.12,
3.23, 3.25, 3.37, 3.38,
3.39, 3.40, 3.43, 3.45,
3.48, 3.50, 3.54, 3.55,
3.57, 3.59, 3.60, 3.63,
3.64, 3.66, 3.69, 4.01,
4.02, 4.04, 4.05, 4.08,
4.13, 4.15, 4.20, 5.01,
5.02, 5.03, 5.04, 5.35,
5.17, 5.45, 5.48, 5.49,

1986 Company Directors' Dis-
      qualification Act—
      cont.
  s. 6—cont... 5.55, 5.63, 5.67,
         5.68, 5.74, 6.02, 6.03,
         6.07, 6.13, 6.15, 6.16,
         6.19, 6.20, 6.21, 6.22,
         6.27, 6.28, 6.30, 6.31,
         6.32, 6.33, 6.35, 6.38,
         6.44, 6.47, 6.49, 6.50,
         6.51, 6.52, 6.60, 6.62,
         6.63, 6.67, 6.68, 6.80,
         6.84, 7.01, 7.07, 7.15,
         7.25, 7.27, 7.33, 7.34,
         7.36, 8.02, 8.03, 8.08,
         8.20, 9.03, 9.04, 9.05,
         9.18, 9.23, 9.35, 9.36,
         9.40, 9.46, 9.52, 9.53,
         9.54, 9.55, 9.57, 9.58,
         9.63, 9.65, 9.69, 9.70,
         9.71, 10.05, 10.07, 11.02,
         11.05, 11.06, 11.07,
         11.08, 11.09, 11.11,
         11.13, 11.18, 11.24,
         11.26, 12.05, 12.19,
         12.29, 12.52, 13.01,
         13.05, 13.27, 13.48,
         13.50, 13.57, 13.62
    (1)....... 3.02, 3.09, 3.60,
         3.61, 4.24, 6.13, 11.07
    (a).... 3.10, 3.15, 3.24,
         3.50, 3.51, 3.52,
         3.57, 4.05
    (b).... 3.02, 3.15, 3.23,
         3.51, 3.53, 3.54,
         3.57, 3.60, 4.04,
         4.08
    (c)................ 3.51
    (2)....... 2.50, 3.02, 3.50,
         4.04, 4.08, 4.21, 5.31,
         5.43, 6.35, 6.50, 7.03
    (a) 3.52
    (b) 6.50
    (3)....... 3.25, 6.02, 6.05,
         6.06, 6.07, 6.16, 6.21,
         7.29
    (a) 6.16
    (a)–(c)...... 6.02, 6.04,
         6.05, 6.16, 6.18,
         6.80
    (b)........... 6.06, 6.16

1986 Company Directors' Dis-
      qualification Act—
      cont.
  s. 6(3)(d).... 6.02, 6.08, 6.18,
         6.21, 6.27, 6.80
    (4)................... 5.67
  ss. 6–7....... 1.02, 1.12, 1.29,
         2.01, 6.32, 13.33,
         13.63
  ss. 6–8....... 1.30, 3.01, 3.43,
         3.48, 6.01, 9.02, 9.03,
         9.40
  ss. 6–9....... 1.02, 1.12, 1.26,
         2.01, 2.07, 2.09, 2.15,
         2.17, 3.09, 3.40, 3.43,
         3.12, 4.09
  ss. 6–10...... 3.43, 6.15, 6.18
  s. 7.... 1.10, 3.04, 3.25, 6.02,
         6.07, 6.20, 6.60, 10.07
    (1)....... 2.11, 3.02, 3.04,
         3.57, 6.31, 6.33, 6.65,
         8.02, 11.19
    (b) 6.65
    (2)....... 2.25, 2.28, 3.28,
         3.50, 3.53, 3.56, 3.57,
         5.63, 5.66, 5.83, 6.02,
         6.05, 6.07, 6.09, 6.13,
         6.16, 6.21, 6.27, 6.30,
         6.35, 6.50, 6.58, 6.60,
         6.62, 6.80, 7.01, 7.03,
         7.05, 7.06, 7.08, 7.09,
         7.13, 7.15, 7.16, 7.28,
         7.29, 7.32, 7.33, 8.07,
         11.06, 11.07
    (3)....... 1.24, 1.29, 3.02,
         3.04, 3.05, 3.52, 4.09,
         6.67
    (4)....... 1.24, 3.03, 3.04,
         6.02, 6.07, 6.13, 6.21,
         6.47, 6.62, 6.80, 7.12,
         7.26
  ss. 7–8.......... 11.21, 13.54
  s. 8.... 1.09, 1.11, 1.28, 2.01,
         2.13, 2.14, 2.15, 2.24,
         3.01, 3.03, 3.25, 3.38,
         3.61, 3.63, 3.64, 3.66,
         4.01, 4.04, 4.05, 4.20,
         5.01, 5.02, 5.47, 5.48,
         5.67, 5.74, 6.15, 6.18,
         6.20, 6.21, 6.22, 6.27,
         6.31, 6.32, 6.38,

1986 Company Directors' Disqualification Act—
   cont.
   s. 8—*cont...* 6.44, 6.52, 6.60,
    6.65, 6.66, 6.67, 6.68,
    6.80, 7.01, 7.33, 8.02,
    8.03, 8.08, 9.03, 9.05,
    9.18, 9.23, 9.55, 11.02,
    11.18, 11.19, 11.24,
    11.26, 12.29, 13.01,
    13.05, 13.33, 13.62,
    13.63
    (1)....... 1.24, **3.61**, 3.62,
     6.31, 8.02
    (2)................... 4.04
    (3)..............6.02, 6.27
   s. 9.... 1.12, 2.12, 2.14, 2.15,
    3.01, 3.25, 3.56, 3.57,
    4.05, 4.09, 4.13, 4.18,
    5.04, 9.23, 9.55
    (4)................... 5.21
    (4)–(5) 4.07
   s. 10.. 1.02, 1.09, 1.23, 1.30,
    2.90, 2.19, 4.01, 4.09,
    5.04, 6.01, 6.02, 6.10,
    6.20, 6.31, 6.52, 6.80,
    7.01, 9.01, 9.02, 9.03,
    9.04, 9.33, 9.42, 9.46,
    9.51, 9.52, 9.53, 9.54,
    9.55, 9.56, 9.58, 9.59,
    9.64, 9.70, 10.03, 11.02,
    11.18, 11.21, 11.26,
    13.62
    (1)....................9.51
    (2) 9.51
   s. 11.. 1.15, 1.16, 1.19, 1.22,
    2.01, 3.17, 3.22, 3.38,
    3.43, 3.46, 3.55, 5.12,
    5.84, 6.02, 6.62, 6.80,
    9.04, 9.27, 10.03, 10.04,
    10.05, 10.07, 11.26,
    12.01, 12.02, 12.06,
    12.08, 12.11, 12.13,
    12.17, 12.18, 12.19,
    12.22, 12.23, 12.25,
    12.29, 12.34, 12.46,
    12.54, 12.55, 12.56,
    13.01, 13.06, 13.10,
    13.51, 13.55, 13.56,
    13.64, 13.69

1986 Company Directors' Disqualification Act—
   cont.
   s. 11(1).. 10.02, 12.02, 13.01
    (2).......... 10.03, 13.69
    (3) 13.63
   s. 12.. 1.09, 1.14, 1.19, 3.38,
    3.43, 3.46, 3.48, 6.02,
    9.04, 10.09, 11.26,
    12.01, 12.02, 12.03,
    12.04, 12.06, 12.08,
    12.11, 12.12, 12.13,
    12.14, 12.16, 12.17,
    12.18, 12.19, 12.21,
    12.22, 12.23, 12.25,
    12.29, 12.46, 12.47,
    12.48, 12.52, 12.55,
    12.56, 13.01, 13.10,
    13.55, 13.56, 13.58,
    13.60, 13.61, 13.63
    (1) 13.01
    (2)...... 3.45, 9.04, 9.27,
     12.17, 12.56
   s. 13........1.16, 9.27, 11.08,
    11.09, 12.56, 13.38
   ss. 13–15........ 11.08, 12.54
   s. 14........ 1.16, 3.37, 12.55
    (2) 12.55
   s. 15.. 1.16, 1.17, 2.08, 2.09,
    2.11, 2.29, 3.42, 6.02,
    6.07, 6.10, 6.15, 6.18,
    6.20, 6.80, 9.04, 12.56,
    13.37, 13.38
    (1)(a) 12.56
    (b) 12.56
    (2) 12.56
    (3)
     (a) 12.56
     (b).............. 12.56
    (4) 12.56
    (5) 12.56
   ss. 15–17..........3.45, 12.17
   s. 16.. 6.26, 7.06, 7.07, 7.19,
    7.25, 7.27, 9.04, 9.54
    (1)......2.25, 2.26, 6.27,
     6.28, 6.29, 6.30,
     9.50, 9.54
    (2)...... 6.31, 8.02, 9.03,
     9.32, 9.50, 13.62
   s. 17.. 1.19, 6.02, 6.03, 6.65,
    9.04, 11.04, 11.13,

1986 Company Directors' Dis-
        qualification Act—
        cont.
    s. 17—*cont.*..... 11.14, 11.15,
            11.16, 11.17, 11.23,
            11.24, 11.26, 12.24,
            13.17, 13.36, 13.37,
            13.38, 13.51, 13.58,
            13.59, 13.60, 13.61,
            13.68, 13.69
        (1)......... 11.17, 13.58,
            13.59, 13.60
        (b).............. 13.59
        (2).. 13.62, 13.63, 13.66
    s. 18 ....   1.18
        (1) 11.26
        (2) 11.26
    s. 19(c)....... 3.43, 6.15, 6.18
    s. 20.. 3.43, 3.45, 6.15, 6.18,
            9.04, 12.17
    s. 21 ....   6.15
        (2)...... 3.43, 6.18, 6.19,
            6.21, 6.80, 12.14,
            13.68
    s. 22........3.45, 9.04, 12.07,
            12.17, 13.69
        (2) 12.12
        (a)...... 10.02, 12.15,
            12.17
        (b)...3.38, 3.46, 3.48,
            3.49, 3.60, 9.04,
            12.12, 12.14,
            12.16, 12.17,
            12.18
        (3)............. 3.51, 6.50
        (4)...... 3.11, 3.12, 3.25,
            12.19
        (5)............. 3.25, 12.19
        (6)............. 3.37, 9.45
        (7) 9.37
        (9).... 3.38, 9.04, 12.07,
            12.08, 12.17
    s. 22A....... 3.40, 3.44, 9.04,
            12.05
        (2) 12.06
    s. 22(3) 3.25
        (4) 3.40
    s. 22B...... 3.41, 3.44, 3.49,
            9.04, 12.06
        (3)........... 3.25, 3.38
        (4) 3.41
    s. 22C...... 3.44, 9.04, 12.06
    s. 24 ....   1.03

1986 Company Directors' Dis-
        qualification Act—
        cont.
    Sched. 1..... 1.12, 1.29, 2.01,
            3.40, 3.43, 3.45,
            3.57, 4.06, 4.07,
            4.09, 4.11, 4.12,
            4.13, 4.14, 5.03,
            5.04, 5.13, 5.21,
            5.35, 6.15, 6.18,
            9.04, 9.55, 12.17,
            13.05
        para 5A.............   3.42
    Sched. 2 .... 12.52
    Sched. 3 .... 12.52
        para.6...............   9.04
    Pt. I.......... 3.42, 4.05, 4.06
        Para. 1.... 2.15, 4.09, 5.03
        Paras 1–2........ 2.11, 9.23
        Para. 5 ....   4.10
    Pt II... 3.51, 4.05, 4.07, 4.08,
            5.37, 5.38, 5.42
        Para. 7 ....   2.15
        Para. 8(a) 4.10
    Insolvency Act (c. 45) ... 1.02,
            2.11, 2.22, 3.43, 5.62,
            6.53, 6.66, 6.82, 9.03,
            9.29, 9.30, 9.37, 12.46,
            12.55
        ss. 1–7 ....   9.45
        s. 7(5).................... 12.46
        s. 8................ 9.45, 13.07
            (3)(b) 3.02
        s. 9(4)....................   6.50
        s. 10 ....   1.13
        s. 13(2) 12.46
        s. 19(2)(a) 12.46
        s. 22 ....   4.07
        s. 29........ 9.30, 9.45, 12.22
        s. 40 ....   5.21
        s. 41 ....   9.40
        s. 45(2) 12.46
        s. 47 ....   4.07
        s. 53(6)(a) 6.50
        s. 66 ....   4.07
        ss. 84–90 ....   9.43
        s. 86 ....   6.06
        s. 92 .... 12.46
        s. 98 ....   4.07
        s. 99 ....   4.07
        s. 104.................. 12.46

1986 Insolvency Act—*cont.*	
s. 108 .... 12.46	
s. 117 ...... 6.03, 6.05, 12.18, 13.59	
(2) 11.17	
(4) 6.03	
(6) 6.03	
ss. 117–121 .... 9.54	
s. 120 .... 6.03, 13.59	
s. 123(1)(e) 5.03	
(2) 5.03	
s. 124A 3.02, 6.67	
s. 127 .... 4.07, 5.38, 5.39	
s. 129 .... 6.06	
s. 131 .... 4.07	
ss. 132–133 .... 1.24	
s. 170 .... 9.40	
s. 171(4) 12.46	
s. 172(5) 12.46	
s. 175 .... 5.21	
s. 206 .... 9.46	
s. 212(1)(c) 12.29	
s. 213 .... 1.23, 6.02, 6.20, 6.31, 9.03, 9.51, 9.52, 9.53, 9.54	
ss. 213–214 .... 1.13, 6.18	
s. 214 .... 1.02, 1.23, 2.09, 3.11, 3.26, 3.30, 4.11, 4.16, 5.03, 5.04, 5.05, 5.06, 5.12, 5.39, 5.50, 5.65, 6.02, 6.20, 6.31, 9.03, 9.04, 9.51, 9.53, 9.54	
(4) 4.11, 5.50	
s. 216 ...... 2.10, 5.34, 11.11, 13.20, 13.38	
s. 217 .... 12.56	
s. 218 .... 1.24, 3.06	
s. 220 .... 12.12	
(1) 3.49	
(3) 6.03	
s. 221 .... 3.48	
(2) 6.03, 12.12	
s. 225 .... 6.06	
s. 229 .... 9.04	
(1) 9.04	
(2) 12.12	
s. 230 .... 12.22	
(1) 12.20	
(2) 12.22	
(3) 12.20	
(4) 2.20	

1986 Insolvency Act—*cont.*	
s. 234 .... 4.07	
ss. 234–236 .... 3.04	
s. 235 .... 4.07, 7.26	
s. 236 .... 3.03, 3.04, 7.26	
s. 238 .... 4.07, 5.38, 5.39	
s. 239 .. 4.10, 5.38, 5.39, 5.40	
s. 240 .... 4.07, 5.38, 5.39	
s. 242 .... 4.07	
s. 243 .... 4.07	
s. 247 .... 6.50	
(2) 3.51	
s. 251 .... 3.11, 3.25	
ss. 264–277 .... 10.05	
ss. 279–280 .... 10.05	
s. 282 .... 10.05	
s. 350(2) 10.05	
s. 360 .... 1.22, 10.04	
s. 386 .... 5.21	
s. 388 .... 12.46	
(1) 12.02, 12.20, 12.22	
(a) 12.22	
(2A) 12.46	
s. 389 .... 12.20, 12.22, 12.46	
s. 390 .... 11.05, 12.03	
(4) 11.05, 11.13, 12.20, 12.22, 12.46, 12.47, 13.56	
(a) 12.02, 12.22, 13.56	
(b) 9.40, 10.06, 12.02, 12.04, 12.20, 12.21, 12.46, 13.56	
s. 391 .... 12.46	
(2) 12.46	
s. 392 .... 12.46	
s. 393(4) 12.46	
s. 411 .. 3.04, 6.17, 6.19, 6.80	
s. 420 .... 12.14	
(1) 3.43	
(2) 3.43	
s. 427 .... 10.07, 12.46	
s. 429 .... 10.09, 12.03, 12.2112.46, 13.56, 13.60	
(2) 1.14, 12.50	
(b) 6.02, 12.47, 12.48, 12.49	
s. 492(2) 10.09	
Sched. 6 .... 5.21	
Sched. 10 .... 9.49	

1986	Insolvency Act—*cont.*	
	Part. II	5.06
	Part. IV	9.54
	Part. V 3.38, 6.03, 6.06,	
	12.07, 12.12, 12.14,	
		12.18
	Part. XVI	4.06
	Part XIII.	2.10, 11.05
	Part. XXVI	12.07, 12.08
	Building Societies Act (c.	
	53) 3.40, 9.04, 12.06	
	s. 37	9.04
	ss. 88–90	9.04
	ss. 97–102	9.04
	s. 120	9.04
	Sched. 15	9.04
	Sched. 18, Para. 17(3).	9.04
	Financial Services Act (c.	
	60)	9.26
	s. 47	9.08, 9.22
	s. 94 ...... 3.64, 3.65, 3.67	
	(8)	3.64
	(9)	3.64
	s. 105 ...... 3.67, 3.68, 4.05	
	(3)	3.67
	(4)	3.67
	(5)	3.67
	s. 177	3.65, 3.67
	(5)	3.65
	s. 179–180 ...... 3.64, 3.67	
	s. 180(1)(c)	3.64
	s. 200	9.08
1987	Criminal Justice Act (c.	
	38)—	
	s. 1(3)	3.68
	ss. 1–2	3.68
	s. 2	3.68
	(2)	3.68
	(3)	3.66
	s. 3	3.68
	Criminal Justice (Scot-	
	land) Act (c. 41)	3.68
1988	Criminal Justice Act (c.	
	33)—	
	ss. 40–41	9.06
	s. 41	9.49, 9.50
	s. 172	9.73
	Pt. IV	9.34, 9.73
1989	Companies Act (c. 40)—	
	s. 1	9.39
	s. 11	9.39
	s. 23	4.06

1989	Companies Act—*cont.*	
	s. 82(1)	3.69
	s. 83	3.69
	s. 87(1)(b)	3.69
	s. 139(3)	4.06
	s. 211(3)	9.04
	s. 227	4.06
	s. 238	4.06
	Sched. 10	
	Para. 35(1)	4.06
	(3)	4.06
	Corporations Law	
	(Australia)—	
	s. 91A	App. 6
	s. 229(1)	10.04
	(3)....9.12, 9.24, 11.18	
	(a)	9.25
	ss. 229–230	App. 6
	s. 230	9.36
	s. 300	4.02
	s. 500	4.02
	s. 600	4.02, 4.14
	ss. 599–600 ..... 4.02, App. 6	
1990	Food Safety Act (c. 16)—	
	s. 36	9.19
	Courts and Legal Ser-	
	vices Act (c. 41)	10.09
	s. 13	10.09
	Environmental Protec-	
	tion Act (c. 43)—	
	s. 6	9.15
	s. 23(1)(a)	9.15
	s. 33(1)(a)	9.15
	s. 157	9.15
1991	Water Resources Act (c.	
	57)—	
	s. 85	9.15
	s. 217	9.15
1992	Offshore Safety Act (c.	
	15)	9.16
	Friendly Societies Act (c.	
	40) 3.41, 9.04, 12.06	
	s. 23	9.04
	s. 52	9.04
	s. 120(1)	3.41
	Sched. 10	9.04
	Sched. 21	
	Para. 8	3.41
	Charities Act (c. 41)—	
	ss. 45–46	12.48
1993	Charities Act (c. 10)—	
	s. 72	12.47

1993	Charities Act (c. 10)—	
	cont.	
	s. 72(1)(b)	10.06, 12.47
	(f)	12.47
	(3)(a)	12.47
	(4)	12.47
	ss. 72–72	12.48
	s. 73(1)	12.47
	(2)	12.47
	Criminal Justice Act (c. 36)—	
	s. 52	9.21
	s. 56	9.21
	s. 57	9.21
	s. 79(13)	9.73
	Sched. 5, Pt. I	
	Para.1	9.73
	Part V	3.65
1994	Value Added Tax Act (c. 23)—	
	s. 72	9.25
	Deregulating and Contracting Out Act (c. 40)—	
	s. 39	
	Sched. 11,	
	Para. 6	9.05
	Magistrates' Courts Act—	
	s. 3(2)	12.49
	Sched.2	12.49
1995	Environment Act (c. 25)—	
	Part I	9.15
	Pensions Act (c. 26)—	
	s. 3	12.48
	s. 4(1)(e)	12.48
	s. 6	12.48
	s. 29	12.48
	(1)(a)	10.06, 12.48
	(c)	12.48
	(f)	12.48
	s. 29(5)	12.48
	s. 30	12.48

	Civil Evidence Act (c. 38)	3.65, 6.64, 6.65, 6.67, 6.68, 6.69, 6.70, 12.50
	s.1	6.68
	(1)	6.69
	(3)	6.69
	(4)	6.69, 6.72
	s. 2	6.69, 6.72
	(1)	6.69
	(4)	6.69, 6.72
	s. 3	6.73
	s. 4	6.69
	(1)	6.69
	(2)	6.69
	(b)	6.73
	s. 5(2)	6.74
	s. 14(1)	6.69
	s. 16A	6.70
1996	Police Act (c. 16)—	
	Sched. 2,	
	Para, 11(1)(b)	10.06
	(c)	12.49
	Housing Act (c. 52)—	
	Sched. 1, Pt. II	
	Para. 4(2)(a)	10.06
	(b)	12.50
1997	Civil Procedure Act (c. 12)	6.23, 6.83
	s. 1	6.23
	s. 4(2)	6.70
	s. 5(1)	6.23
	Sched. 1	
	Para. 3	6.23
	Para. 6	6.23
1998	Human Rights Act (c. 42)	2.24, 3.24, 5.83, 6.45, 7.01, 7.38, 13.57
1999	Access to Justice Act (c. 22)—	
	s. 54	6.81B
	s. 56	6.80, 6.81A, 6.82, 6.83
	s. 57	6.81B

Table of Statutory Instruments

1949 Companies (Winding-
  Up) Rules (S.I. 1949
  No. 330) (L.4) 6.15
  r. 66 .... 6.36
  r. 68 .... 6.15
1981 Magistrates'   Courts
  Rules   1981   (S.I.
  1981 No. 552)—
  rr. 76–81 .... 9.71
  County Court Rules..... 6.18,
                          6.19
  Ord. 13
  r. 1(10) 6.81
      (11) 6.81
  Ord. 18................. 8.03
  Ord. 37................. 6.81
1982 Crown Court Rules (S.I.
  1982 No. 1109)—
  r. 7..................... 9.71
1985 Companies (Table A to
  F) Regulation 1985
  (S.I. 1985 No. 805). 12.30
1986 Insolvent   Companies
  (Disqualification of
  Unfit Directors) Pro-
  ceedings Rules (S.I.
  1986 No. 612)........ 6.15,
        6.18, 6.19, 6.60,
    6.80, 11.08, 11.25, 13.04
  r. 2(3).................. 6.39
  r. 3(3).................. 4.22
  r. 5.2................... 6.13
  r. 6.189................ 13.69
  r. 6.203................ 13.64
      (2) 13.69
      (d) 13.69
  rr. 6.203–6.205... 6.62, 6.80,
                        13.69
  r. 6.204(2) 13.69
  r. 6.205................ 13.69
  r. 6.223(A)............. 10.08
      (B) 10.08
  r. 7.47...... 6.16, 6.17, 6.21,
      6.82, 6.83, 6.84, 11.08

1986 Insolvent   Companies
  (Disqualification of
  Unfit Directors) Pro-
  ceedings Rules (S.I.
  1986 No. 612)—
  cont.
  r. 7.47(2).............. 6.16
  r. 7.48(2).............. 13.69
  r. 7.49............. 6.21, 6.82,
                    6.83, 6.84
  r. 7.51 .... 6.80
  r. 7.57(4).............. 6.62
  Ch. 22A 10.08
  (S.I. 1986 No. 1560)
    (C.56)............... 9.04
  Insolvency Practitioners
    (Recognised   Pro-
    fessional   Bodies)
    Order 1986 (S.I.
    1986 No. 1764)..... 12.42
  Companies (Disqualifi-
    cation   Orders)
    Regulation   (S.I.
    1986) No. 2067).... 11.26,
                        13.67
  Insolvent   Companies
    (Reports on Con-
    duct of Directors)
    No. 2 Rules (S.I.
    1986 No. 2134)..... 3.05
1987 Insolvent   Companies
    (Disqualification of
    Unfit Directors) Pro-
    ceedings Rules 1987
    (S.I.   1987   No.
    2023)........ 11.08, App. 4
  r. 2.......... 6.18, 6.19, 6.20,
                    6.60, 6.38
  r. 2.1(1) 6.21
      (4) 6.80
  r. 2.4................... 6.21
  r. 3.......... 6.65, 7.07, 7.10
      (1).................. 6.38

1987 Insolvent Companies
(Disqualification of
Unfit Directors) Pro-
ceedings Rules 1987
—cont.
r. 3(2)........ 6.64, 6.65, 6.73
(3)................... 6.52
r. 4....................... 6.39
r. 5..................... 6.38
(1)................... 6.40
(2)................... 6.40
(3)................... 6.41
r. 6..................... 6.38
(1)................... 6.41
(2)................... 6.42
r. 7.................. 6.44, 7.32
(1)..............6.39, 6.44
(3)................... 6.44
r. 8(2)................... 6.84
r. 9...... 11.19, 11.20, 11.21,
11.22, 11.24, 13.01,
13.54
1989 European Economic
Interest Grouping
Regulations (S.I.
1989 No. 638) 3.45,
12.17
Reg. 20..... 3.45, 9.04, 12.17
Sched. 4, Para. 20 ..... 12.17
Companies (Northern
Ireland) Order (S.I.
1989 No. 2404)
(N.I. 18) 1.03
Art. 5(1)................ 9.06
Art. 8(2)................ 9.46
1990 Companies Act 1989
(Commencement
No. 4 and Tran-
sitional and Saving
Provisions) Order
(S.I. 1990 No. 355)
(C. 13) 4.06
(S.I. 1990 No. 1392)
(C.41)................ 9.04
(S.I. 1990 No. 1707) (C.
46) 4.06
1991 High Court and County
Courts Jurisdiction
Order (S.I. 1991 No.
724)
Art. 7................... 6.10

1991 County Court Appeals
Order 1991 (S.I.
1999 No. 1877)..... 6.81
r. 4.................... 6.81
r. 19 .... 6.81
1994 General Product Safety
Regulations (S.I.
1994 No. 2328)..... 9.20
Insolvent Partnerships
Order (S.I. 1994 No.
2421)..... 2.24, 3.43, 3.50,
3.60, 4.06, 12.14
Art. 15.................. 12.42
Art. 16............ 3.50, 12.14
Sched. 8............ 3.50, 3.60
1995 Public Offers of Securities Regulations
1995 (S.I. 1995 No.
1537) 12.26
reg. 4(1) 9.07
reg. 16(2).............. 9.07
(S.I. 1995 No. 2945) 9.39
1996 Insolvent Partnerships
(Amendment) Order
(S.I. 1996 No.
1308)—
Art. 2(1)............... 3.43
Art. 3 .... 3.43
Art. 11................. 3.43
Art. 16..............3.43, 4.07
Sched. 8............ 3.43, 4.07
Insolvent Companies
(Reports on Con-
duct of Directors)
Rules (S.I. 1996 No.
1909)......3.05, 6.27, 6.80
r. 3..................... 3.05
r. 4..................... 3.05
r. 5(2)................... 3.35
r. 6..................... 3.04
r. 13.7 .... 6.18
Open-Ended Investment
Companies (Invest-
ment Companies
with Variable Capi-
tal) Regulations (S.I.
1996 No. 2827)...... 3.42,
4.06, 9.04, 12.16
reg. 6 .... 4.06

1998 The Rules of the Supreme Court (Amendment No. 2) (S.I. 1998 No. 3049) 6.83

1999 Insolvency (Amendment) Rules 1999 (S.I. 1999 No. 359).......... 11.25, 11.26
r. 6.233(B)(5) 10.08
High Court and County Courts Jurisdiction (Amendment) Order (S.I. 1999 No. 1014)—
Art. 7 .... 6.10

1999 Insolvency (Amendment) (No.2) Rules 1999 (S.I. No. 1022) 6.62
r. 7.57(6) 6.60
Insolvent Companies (Disqualification of Unfit Directors) Amendment Rules (S.I. 1999 No. 1023) 6.15, 6.16, 6.80
Civil Procedure (Modification of Enactments) Order 1999 (S.I. 1999 No. 1217) 6.71

Table of Rules

1965   Rules of the Supreme Court

Ord. 11................. 6.40

Ord. 15

     r. 6(2)................ 6.33

Ord. 20

     r. 3 .... 6.33

     r. 10................. 6.64

     r. 11................. 11.08

Ord. 21

     rr. 2–5 .... 8.03

     r. 2(3A).............. 8.03

        (3B) 8.03

        (4)............... 8.03

     r. 4 .... 8.03

Ord. 24,

     r. 13................. 3.07

        (1) 3.07

Ord. 28

     r. 1A(4).............. 8.03

Ord. 38

     r. 2A(4).............. 8.21

     r. 3............... 6.64, 6.69

     r. 21(3)(a) 6.72

     r. 25.............. 6.64, 6.69

     r. 26................. 6.69

     r. 29................. 6.69

     r. 36(2) 6.75

Ord. 40.7.............. 13.38

Ord. 41

     r. 5........6.64, 6.67, 6.72

Ord. 42

     r.3............. 11.08, 13.38

Ord. 58

     r. 3 .... 6.81

Ord. 59............6.80, 6.82

     r. 1A 6.83

     r. 1B.............6,81, 6.83

     r. 4............... 6.80, 6.81

Ord. 62

     r. 5(3)................ 8.03

     r. 10(1) 8.04

1998   Disqualification Practice Direction........6.22, 6.23, 6.32, 6.39, 6.63

Para. 4.1 .... 6.39

Para. 4.2 .... 6.38

Para. 4.3.......... 6.39, 6.44

Para. 5.1.......... 6.59, 6.63

Para. 6.1 .... 6.39

Para. 7.2 .... 6.40

Para. 7.3..... 6.10, 6.13, 6.40

Para. 8.3 .... 6.41

Para. 8.4 .... 6.41

Para. 9.1.......... 6.65, 6.60

Para. 9.2 .... 6.52

Para. 9.3 .... 6.38

        (2)........ 6.40, 6.63

Para. 9.4 .... 6.41

        (2) 6.63

Para. 9.5 .... 6.41

Para. 9.6 .... 6.42

        (2) 6.63

Para. 9.7 .... 6.43

Para. 9.8 .... 6.43

Para. 10.2............. 6.44

Para. 10.4............. 6.44

Para. 11 .... 6.43

Para. 12 .... 6.45

Para. 13 .... 6.46

Para. 13.4............. 6.23

Para. 16.1....... 11.21, 13.54

Para. 17.1.......... 6.63, 7.29

Para. 17.2............. 6.63

Para. 18 .... 3.04

Para. 18.1............. 6.07

Para. 19 .... 7.29

Para. 19.1............. 6.63

Para. 19.2(2).......... 6.13

Para. 20 .... 13.61

Para. 21 .... 13.61

Para. 21.1............. 6.63

Para. 22.1....... 13.64, 13.69

Para. 23 .... 13.63

Para. 25.1............. 6.63

Para. 26.2............. 6.13

1998	Civil Procedure Rules ... 6.01,
	6.18, 6.20, 6.21, 6.22,
	6.24, 6.25, 6.51, 7.01,
	7.32, 13.66, 13.68
r. 1.1	7.01
(2)(a)...........	6.26
(b)..............	6.26
(c)	6.26
r. 2.11	6.43
r. 3.1(2)(f)	8.07
r. 3.4	6.49
r. 5.4	6.86
(c)	6.86
r. 7.47........... 6.83, 6.84
r. 7.49........... 6.83, 6.84
r. 8.1(6)..............	6.23
r. 8.5(1)..............	6.48
r. 26.8	6.07
r. 29.5	6.43
r. 30.2(1)	6.08
(2)..............	6.08
(b).........	6.08
(3)	6.08
(4)	6.08
(7)	6.08
r. 30.3..... 6.07, 6.08, 6.10
(2)	6.08
r. 32.1	6.79
r. 32.5(5)	8.21
r. 32.6(2)	6.59
r. 32.12	6.87
r. 32.14	6.59
r. 32.15........... 6.60, 6.61
(1)...........	6.60
r. 33.2	6.72
r. 33.4	6.73
r. 33.5	6.74
r. 35.4	6.76
(4)	6.76
r. 35.7	6.76
r. 38.2	8.04
r. 38.2(a)(ii)	8.04

1998	Civil Procedure Rules—
	cont.
r. 38.3	8.04
r. 38.4	8.04
r. 38.5(3)	8.03
r. 38.6	8.04
r. 38.7	8.04
r. 39.2	8.17
r. 39.3	6.84
r. 40.7	13.54
r. 40.12	11.08
r. 44.3	8.03
(2)	6.85
r. 44.14	8.04
Practice Direction 7 ...	6.07
Para. 2.1.............	6.07
Practice Direction 29,
Para. 2.2......... 6.06, 6.10
Practice Direction 32
Para. 1.7.............	6.59
Part. 6	6.40
Part. 7	6.38
Part. 8............. 6.38, 6.40,
	9.32, 13.61
Part. 17.................	6.57
Part. 18.................	6.48
Part. 22.................	6.59
Part. 23.................	7.29
Part. 24.................	6.49
Part. 29.................	6.10
Part. 30.................	
Practice Direction	6.12,
	6.80
Part. 31.................	6.47
Part. 32.................	6.63
Part. 33.................	6.70
Part. 35.................	6.77
Part. 36.................	8.21
Part. 44.................	6.85
Part. 50.................	6.83
Sched. 1......6.81, 6.82, 6.83
Sched. 2	6.81

CHAPTER 1

Company Directors' Disqualification Act 1986: Introduction and Overview

INTRODUCTION

1.01 There is a strong case for saying that the the law relating to disqualification of directors has become one of the most significant parts of modern company law. Through the course of the 1990s, the number of disqualification orders made by the courts under the Company Directors' Disqualification Act 1986 ("CDDA") has increased dramatically and is now running at in excess of 1,000 per annum.[1] Moreover, in terms of the sheer volume of reported cases in the field of company law, disqualification cases are at the forefront. Indeed, it is strongly arguable that disqualification has become one of the principal means by which the general law of directors' obligations is enforced, with the consequence that the growing body of case law on the CDDA should now be regarded as a major driving force behind developments in company law. The aim of this chapter is to consider the history and evolution of disqualification legislation culminating in the enactment of the CDDA. Chapter 2 is also introductory in nature and seeks to analyse the rationale and purpose of disqualification as a form of regulatory sanction.

COMPANY DIRECTORS' DISQUALIFICATION ACT 1986

1.02 The CDDA is a single piece of consolidating legislation which governs the disqualification of directors and other persons who act improperly in the course of managing companies. The enactment of the CDDA brought down the curtain on a wider process of legislative reform which also led to the enactment of the Insolvency Act 1986.[2] Seen in that context, the CDDA was merely one part of a connected series of general reforms in the field of company and corporate insolvency law. Disqualification under the CDDA is essentially a method of enforcement. The CDDA sets out a number of grounds which, if established, trigger disqualification. These triggering events (which are discussed in outline further below) range widely and include, for example, criminal offences, defaults under companies legislation and breaches of the general law relating to the duties of company directors. The concept of unfitness which lies at the heart of the CDDA (see sections 6 to 9) and is its most significant aspect, rests

---

[1] See the Department of Trade and Industry, *Companies in 1990–1991* through to *Companies in 1997–1998* inclusive and the appendices to A. Hicks, *Disqualification of Directors: No Hiding Place for the Unfit?* (A.C.C.A. Research Report No. 59, 1998).
[2] The CDDA and Insolvency Act 1986 were enacted on the same day, July 25, 1986 as consolidation measures.

substantially on obligations imposed on directors by specific provisions of companies and insolvency legislation and by the general law.[3] As a regulatory technique, disqualification therefore provides an additional and ancillary response to these various forms of misconduct over and above the sanctions already provided by the ordinary criminal and civil law. As a process, disqualification is ancillary to *other forms of legal process*. In some cases, it is ancillary to criminal or civil proceedings in court.[4] In other cases, it is ancillary to formal corporate insolvency processes such as winding up or administration.[5] It should be noted that disqualification under the CDDA triggers provisions in other pieces of legislation (such as charities legislation) which have little or nothing to do with companies *per se*. As such, disqualification under the CDDA does more than simply prohibit the disqualified person from acting as a company director or from taking part in the management of companies. An outline of the scheme of the CDDA containing a synopsis of the main powers and provisions is set out below. The remainder of the chapter is devoted to a consideration of the history and legislative evolution of directors' disqualification provisions.

Outline of the CDDA

1.03   The main provisions of the CDDA can usefully be grouped under four broad headings namely, disqualification by the court, automatic disqualification, consequences of disqualification and permission to act notwithstanding disqualification. Not every provision of the CDDA is covered in this outline. There are a number of other miscellaneous provisions. These are tackled at appropriate points in the rest of the book. The CDDA applies to England, Wales and Scotland but not to Northern Ireland (section 24). However, the Companies (Northern Ireland) Order 1989 applies to Northern Ireland a disqualification regime which is the same in all material respects to that under the CDDA.

Disqualification by the court

1.04   Section 1 defines the scope of a disqualification order made by the court. A disqualification order imposes a wide prohibition. Broadly speaking, it prohibits the disqualified individual from being a company director or from engaging generally in the management of companies without the permission of the court. The making and commencement of disqualification orders is dealt with in Chapter 11 while the legal effect of a disqualification order is discussed more fully in Chapter 12.

1.05   Section 2 gives the court power to make a disqualification order against a person where he is convicted of an indictable offence in connection with the promotion, formation, management, liquidation or striking off of a company, or with the receivership or management of a company's property. The maximum period of disqualification is 15 years (except where the order is made by a court of summary jurisdiction in which case the maximum period is five years).

1.06   Section 3 gives the court power to make a disqualification order against a person where he has been persistently in default in relation to the provisions of compa-

---

[3] This is not exclusively so. See, *e.g. Re Bath Glass Ltd* [1988] B.C.L.C. 329, (1988) 4 B.C.C. 130 which establishes that insolvent trading can make a director unfit for the purposes of CDDA, s. 6 even in circumstances where his conduct would not attract liability for wrongful trading under section 214 of the Insolvency Act 1986: see discussion from para. 5.03 onwards.
[4] See, *e.g.* CDDA, ss 2 and 5 for two powers which are ancillary to criminal proceedings and CDDA, s. 10 for a power ancillary to civil proceedings.
[5] *ibid.*, ss 4, 6–7.

nies legislation requiring returns, accounts, documents or notices to be filed with the Registrar of Companies. The maximum period of disqualification is five years.

1.07 Section 4 gives the court power to make a disqualification order against a person if, during the course of the winding up of a company it appears either that he has been guilty (whether convicted or not) of an offence of fraudulent trading under the Companies Act 1985, s. 458, or he has otherwise been guilty while acting as an officer or as liquidator of the company or as a receiver or manager of its property, of any fraud in relation to the company or of any breach of duty in any of those capacities. The maximum period of disqualification is 15 years.

1.08 Section 5 gives the court power to make a disqualification order in cases where a person is convicted of a summary offence in consequence of a contravention of, or failure to comply with any provision of companies legislation requiring returns, accounts, documents or notices to be filed with the Registrar and in the previous five years he has received or been made the subject of not less than three convictions or default orders counting for the purposes of the section. The maximum period of disqualification is five years. Although the criteria are not identical, the power in section 5 is essentially directed at the same mischief as section 3, namely persistent default in the filing of accounts and returns. The main difference is that the power in section 3 is only exercisable by the civil courts whereas that in section 5 is exercisable by the criminal courts and, in particular, the magistrates' courts. Sections 2 to 5 inclusive are covered more fully in Chapter 9.

1.09 Section 6 *requires* the court to make a disqualification order against a person where satisfied that he is or was a director (or shadow director) of a company which has become insolvent and that his conduct as a director of that company (taken alone or taken together with his conduct as a director of any other company or companies) renders him unfit to be concerned in the management of a company. The court *must* disqualify an individual found to be unfit in accordance with section 6 for a minimum of two years. The maximum period of disqualification is 15 years. Section 6 differs from the various discretionary powers in sections 2 to 5 (see above) and sections 8, 10 and 12 (see below) in that it imposes a duty on the court to disqualify a person for at least two years where the requirements of the section are made out.

1.10 Section 7 sets out various procedural matters which relate to applications under section 6. Section 6 proceedings can only be brought by the Secretary of State for Trade and Industry (or the official receiver if the Secretary of State so directs in the case of a person who is or was a director of a company which is being wound up by the court). Section 7 imposes a two-year time limit for the commencement of proceedings, after which proceedings can only be commenced with the permission of the court. It also requires insolvency practitioners to provide reports on the conduct of directors of insolvent companies to the Secretary of State. In the early stages these reports are used to determine whether or not the Secretary of State should contemplate disqualification proceedings in a particular case. The various requirements in section 7 are discussed in Chapters 3, 6 and 7.

1.11 Section 8 gives the court power to make a disqualification order against a director (or shadow director) of a company on the application of the Secretary of State made following the receipt of information obtained as a result of certain specified types of statutory investigation or inspection. The court may exercise this power if it is satisfied that the director's conduct in relation to the company makes him unfit to be concerned in the management of a company. The maximum period of disqualification is 15 years.

1.12 Section 9 and Schedule 1 set out a number of non-exhaustive criteria to which the court must pay particular regard in determining, on an application under either section 6 or 8, whether an individual's conduct as a director (or shadow director) makes him unfit to be concerned in the management of a company. The maximum period of disqualification is 15 years. The unfitness provisions in sections 6 to 9 are the core provisions of the CDDA. Most of the disqualification orders made to date have been made on applications brought under these relatively new provisions (in particular, sections 6 to 7).[6] As a consequence, the vast majority of the reported cases are concerned with substantive and procedural aspects of unfitness proceedings. The central significance of these provisions within the overall scheme is reflected in the structure of this book of which Chapters 3 to 7 are devoted principally to an exposition of law and practice under sections 6 to 9. For all that, it is important that these provisions are not viewed in isolation from the other substantive provisions in the CDDA. One of the principal themes of this book is that the CDDA should properly be regarded as a legislative scheme with common features and objectives in which the concept of unfitness forms a central and unifying part.

1.13   Where a civil court orders a person to make a contribution to a company's assets under either the fraudulent or wrongful trading provisions in sections 213 to 214 of the Insolvency Act 1986, section 10 gives the court power, of its own motion, to disqualify that person. The maximum period of disqualification is 15 years. Further coverage of section 10 can be found in Chapter 9.

1.14   Where a person fails to make any payment which he is required to make by virtue of an administration order under Part VI of the County Courts Act 1984, the relevant county court may, if it thinks fit, by section 429(2) of the Insolvency Act 1986 revoke the administration order and direct that section 12 of the CDDA shall apply to that person for a specified period not exceeding two years. Section 12 simply records that where this power under the insolvency legislation is exercised, the person is disqualified from being a company director or from taking part generally in the management of companies without the permission of the court. This provision is discussed more fully in Chapters 10 and 12.

Automatic disqualification

1.15   Section 11 automatically disqualifies undischarged bankrupts from being company directors or from engaging generally in the management of companies without the permission of the court. This applies without the need for a court order under the CDDA and is the only provision of its type in the legislation. The position in relation to the automatic disqualification of undischarged bankrupts and the scope of the prohibition in section 11 are covered more fully in Chapters 10 and 12.

Consequences of disqualification

1.16   The CDDA imposes both criminal and civil penalties on those who act while disqualified. It is a criminal offence under section 11 for an undischarged bankrupt to act in breach of the automatic ban. Sections 13 and 14 also impose criminal penalties on those who act in breach of a disqualification order made by a court (or, in the case of section 14, those who are accessories to such a breach). Furthermore, section 15 provides that an individual is personally liable for certain debts of a company if he is at any time involved in the management of that company in breach of either a disqualification order or the automatic ban on undischarged bankrupts.

1.17   Section 15 also renders an individual personally liable for certain debts of a company if, while being involved in the management of that company, he acts or is

---

[6] See the Department of Trade and Industry, *Companies in 1990–1991* through to *Companies in 1997– 1998* inclusive and the appendices to A. Hicks, *Disqualification of Directors: No Hiding Place for the Unfit?* (A.C.C.A. Research Report No. 59, 1998).

willing to act on the instructions of another individual whom he knows either to be the subject of a disqualification order or an undischarged bankrupt. The penalties imposed by these provisions and other wider consequences of disqualification are discussed in Chapter 12.

1.18   Section 18 requires the Secretary of State to maintain a register of disqualification orders which is open to public inspection. The connected issues of registration and the publicising of disqualification orders are canvassed in Chapter 11.

Permission to act not withstanding disqualification

1.19   It is always open to a disqualified person to apply to the court for permission to act in certain prohibited capacities. This is inherent in the definition of a disqualification order in section 1 and in the terms of the prohibitions set out in sections 11 and 12. Section 17 is the main procedural provision of the CDDA governing applications for permission to act. The court's power to grant permission has considerable significance within the overall scheme, a point which is emphasised throughout this book and is developed, in particular, in Chapters 11 and 13.

Regulatory responsibility of the Department of Trade and Industry in relation to disqualifications proceedings under the CDDA

1.20   The Department of Trade and Industry is the regulator having principal responsibility for companies. The Secretary of State is not the only person who can commence disqualification proceedings under the CDDA.[7] However, in practice the majority of disqualification proceedings (including prosecutions of disqualified persons who act in breach of the prohibition) are initiated by the Secretary of State or his agents. For example, responsibility for the initiation of section 6 proceedings rests with the Disqualification Unit which forms part of the Insolvency Service, an executive agency of the Department of Trade and Industry.

HISTORY AND EVOLUTION OF THE DISQUALIFICATION REGIME

1.21   This section provides an outline of the origins and evolution of the various powers in the CDDA. Disqualification provisions relating to bankruptcy and fraudulent trading were first enacted in the Companies Act 1928 implementing reforms earlier proposed by the Greene Committee.[8] Since then there has been a sporadic process of consolidation and extension culminating in the reforms of the mid-1980s. In chronological terms, the various substantive provisions now contained in the CDDA evolved in roughly the four phases set out below.[9]

Phase one: bankruptcy

1.22   One concern of the Greene Committee, which reported in 1926, was the ease with which bankrupt individuals were able to continue trading through the medium of a limited company before obtaining their discharge. It has long been an offence for an undischarged bankrupt to attempt to obtain credit without disclosing his personal

---

[7] On the proper claimant in disqualification proceedings see generally Chaps 6 and 9.
[8] Report of the Company Law Amendment Committee (the Greene Committee), Cmd. 2657 (1926), especially paras 56–57 and 61–62.
[9] This account draws upon and seeks to refine the historical analysis offered in A. Hicks, "Disqualification of Directors—Forty Years On" [1988] J.B.L. 27, pp. 29–38. For another useful account see, L.H. Leigh, "Disqualification Orders in Company and Insolvency Law" (1986) 7 *The Company Lawyer* 179.

status.[10] Thus, it was considered unpalatable that an individual who had previously incurred liabilities in his own name which he had been unable to meet could, through incorporation, obtain further credit in the name of a company while enjoying the benefit of limited liability. The Greene Committee's recommendation that an undischarged bankrupt should automatically be prohibited from acting as a director or taking part in the management of a company without permission, first enacted as section 84 of the Companies Act 1928, reflected these concerns. The provision has since been extended so that an undischarged bankrupt is also now prevented from taking part in company promotion or formation.[11] That change apart, there is little to distinguish the original provision from its current incarnation which, after several consolidations and re-enactments, is now found in section 11 of the CDDA.

Phase two: fraud during winding up and criminal offences in connection with the management of companies

1.23   A comprehensive provision imposing civil and criminal liability for fraudulent trading was first introduced as section 75 of the Companies Act 1928 on the recommendation of the Greene Committee and then consolidated as section 275 of the Companies Act 1929. It created a range of sanctions, including a power to disqualify anyone held liable under its terms for a maximum period of five years. However, it only applied once the company was being wound up and so was limited in scope. As conceived, the main object of this provision (and thus, the power of disqualification) was to curb "security filling". This denotes the undesirable practice whereby a controller of a private company lends money to the company in return for security by way of floating charge and subsequently, knowing that the company is insolvent, "fills up" his security by obtaining goods on credit before putting the company into liquidation. Following the process of reform and consolidation which took place during 1947 and 1948,[12] the fraudulent trading provision emerged as section 332 of the Companies Act 1948. However, the court's power of disqualification was modified and separately re-enacted as part of the more extensive provision which emerged in section 188 of the 1948 Act. Section 188 created two powers:

(1)   Section 188(1)(a) gave the court power to disqualify a person convicted on indictment of any offence in connection with the promotion, formation or management of a company for a maximum period of five years. This is the earliest version of the modern power currently found in section 2 of the CDDA.[13]

(2)   Section 188(1)(b) gave the court power to disqualify a person who was found during the course of a winding up to have been guilty (whether convicted or not) of an offence of fraudulent trading under the Companies Act 1948, s. 332, or of any fraud in relation to the company or breach of duty perpetrated while acting as its officer for a maximum period of five years. The modern version of this power is now found in section 4 of the CDDA.[14]

---

[10] Report of the Review Committee, *Insolvency Law and Practice* (the Cork Committee), Cmnd. 8558 (1982), para. 132. See now, Insolvency Act 1986, s. 360.

[11] Companies Act 1981, Sched. 3, para. 9.

[12] For general background, see the Report of the Committee on Company Law Amendment (the Cohen Committee), Cmd. 6659 (1945), especially paras 150–151.

[13] Section 188(1)(a) was extended by Companies Act 1981, s. 93(1) to cover indictable offences in connection with the liquidation of a company or with the receivership or management of a company's property. The provision (as amended) was subsequently consolidated as Companies Act 1985, s. 296 before re-enactment as CDDA, s. 2. The maximum period of disqualification for a relevant conviction on indictment was increased from five years to 15 years by Companies Act 1981, s. 93(1).

[14] Section 188(1)(b) was extended to cover fraud or breach of duty committed by persons acting as liqui-

The final stage in this phase of development was the enactment of section 16 of the Insolvency Act 1985 which subsequently became section 10 of the CDDA. This empowers a civil court to disqualify an individual against whom it has made a fraudulent or wrongful trading declaration. This separate power was created broadly for three reasons. The first was the division of the composite fraudulent trading provision in section 332 of the 1948 Act into two self-contained provisions, one imposing criminal liability and the other imposing civil liability.[15] In the absence either of an amendment to what is now section 4 of the CDDA or the introduction of section 10, the courts would have had no power to disqualify an individual ancillary to a finding of civil liability for fraudulent trading.[16] The second reason behind the enactment of what is now section 10 was that it enabled the court to disqualify a person held liable under the wrongful trading provision which itself was only introduced for the first time in 1985.[17] The third reason was one of convenience. Section 10 enables the court making the fraudulent or wrongful trading declaration to make a disqualification order in the same proceedings without the need for a separate, free standing application.

1.24 By way of aside, it should be noted that a separate disqualification provision concerned with fraud was introduced in the Companies Act 1928 and consolidated as section 217 of the Companies Act 1929. As conceived, the power in section 217 was essentially ancillary to the investigative functions of the official receiver. In the case of any company which went into compulsory liquidation, the official receiver was at that time under a statutory obligation to provide a preliminary report to the court explaining the causes of the company's failure. It was also open to the official receiver, if he thought fit, to make a further report to the court stating that, in his opinion, fraud had been committed by any or all of the promoters, directors or other officers of the company in relation to its affairs. Faced with such a report, the court had power under the 1929 Act to summon the relevant individuals to be publicly examined by the official receiver or the company's liquidator and, in addition, it could disqualify them for up to five years under section 217.[18] The provision in section 217 was short-lived. It was repealed during the process of reform in 1947 to 1948. Nevertheless, in the light of the modern debate concerning the nature and purpose of disqualification legislation (which is examined in Chapter 2), it is interesting to reflect that section 217 is perhaps the earliest example of a disqualification provision based entirely on a public interest rationale, namely the public interest in exposing and explaining corporate failure and in calling delinquent directors to account.[19] On this point, it is also interesting to note that the structure of the modern unfitness provisions in the CDDA (discussed further below) is very similar to section 217 in that *locus standi* is conferred exclusively on agents of the state, and that the decision to proceed is usually based on a report on the

---

dators or as receivers or managers of a company's property by Companies Act 1981, s. 93(1). Criminal liability for fraudulent trading was also extended by Companies Act 1981, s. 96 to enable a person to be convicted whether or not the company has been or is in the course of being wound up (see now, the Companies Act 1985, s. 458). Section 188(1)(b) (as amended) was then consolidated as Companies Act 1985, s. 298 and finally re-enacted as CDDA, s. 4. The maximum period of disqualification was increased from five years to 15 years by Companies Act 1981, s. 93(1).

[15] See now, Companies Act 1985, s. 458 and Insolvency Act 1986, s. 213.

[16] It appears that the effect of section 75 of the 1928 Act (subsequently section 275 of the 1929 Act) which, as was seen above, did create a power to disqualify a person against whom a fraudulent trading declaration was made, was lost as part of the simplification of those provisions in the 1948 Act.

[17] Insolvency Act 1985, s. 15. See now, Insolvency Act 1986, s. 214.

[18] The concepts of public investigation and examination in compulsory liquidation survive: see now, Insolvency Act 1986, ss 132–133 and s. 218. For general background, see Report of the Cork Committee, *op. cit.*, paras 74–85, 653–657.

[19] See Report of the Cork Committee, *op. cit.*, especially paras 191–194, 1734–1736. Note also, the Cork Committee's attempt to restore the link between public examination and disqualification at para. 1819(b), a recommendation which was not taken up by Parliament.

company's affairs prepared and delivered to the Secretary of State in satisfaction of a statutory obligation.[20]

Phase three: persistent non-compliance with filing obligations under companies legislation

1.25   The court's power to disqualify for persistent breaches of companies legislation now contained in section 3 of the CDDA was first introduced in 1976[21] although it derives originally from a proposal of the Jenkins Committee made some 15 years earlier.[22] The related power in section 5 was originally introduced in 1981.[23] The aim was to make it easier to obtain a disqualification order for persistent default by enabling the convicting magistrates' court to make an order whereas an order under what is now section 3 can only be made by a court having winding up jurisdiction. These powers were introduced to widen the range of sanctions available to the Registrar of Companies for enforcing compliance with the disclosure and publicity requirements of companies legislation.

Phase four: the development of the unfitness provisions

1.26   The notion that the directors of an insolvent company should be called to account for the company's failure in the public interest is long-established in insolvency law. In this vein, the 1929 Act made provision for the court, on the application of the official receiver, to disqualify a company director or officer who had committed fraud.[24] However, it was only comparatively recently that provisions were enacted empowering the court to disqualify an individual, without proof of fraud, on the ground that his previous conduct as a director of a company which had become insolvent rendered him unfit to be concerned in the management of companies generally. The long and often controversial process which culminated in the enactment of the present unfitness provisions in sections 6 to 9 of the CDDA is outlined below.

Insolvency Act 1976

1.27   Reporting in 1962, the Jenkins Committee was critical of the narrow scope of the powers in section 188 of the 1948 Act described above. One of the Committee's recommendations was that the court should be given a broad power to disqualify any person who was shown, when acting as a director or when otherwise concerned in the management of a company, to have acted in an improper, reckless or incompetent manner in relation to the company's affairs. It is clear that this recommendation was driven, in part, by the feeling that something needed to be done about individuals who had presided over a number of corporate failures. As the Committee's report puts it:

"We recognise that it may be difficult to decide in any particular case whether a company director has acted so recklessly or incompetently that he should no longer be allowed to remain a director. But in serious cases, where, for example, a man

---

[20] See CDDA, ss 7(3), (4) and 8(1).
[21] Companies Act 1976, s. 28. The provision was subsequently carried back into Companies Act 1948, s. 188 by Companies Act 1981, s. 93 before further re-enactment, without material amendment, as Companies Act 1985, s. 297.
[22] Report of the Jenkins Committee, Cmnd. 1749 (1962), paras 80, 85. See further, the White Paper, *Company Law Reform*, Cmnd. 5391 (1973), paras 36–37.
[23] Companies Act 1981, s. 93.
[24] See para. 1.24.

has succeeded in steering a series of companies into insolvency, we think that the court should be able to put a stop to his activities."[25]

This concern was eventually given statutory expression in the form of section 9 of the Insolvency Act 1976.[26] Section 9 (later consolidated as section 300 of the Companies Act 1985) had three key elements:

(1) *Locus standi* to apply for a disqualification order was conferred exclusively on the Secretary of State and (in cases where a relevant company was in compulsory liquidation) the official receiver.

(2) The court's power to disqualify was only triggered where the respondent to the Secretary of State's or the official receiver's application had been a director (or shadow director) of *at least two companies* which had gone into insolvent liquidation within five years of each other.

(3) Subject to the requirement in (2), the court could, in its discretion, disqualify the respondent for up to five years[27] if satisfied that his conduct as a director of any of the relevant companies made him unfit to be concerned in the management of companies generally.

However, very few orders were made under this provision. There are no figures available before 1983 but between then and the repeal of the provision in 1985 a mere 23 orders were made.[28]

The Cork Committee

1.28 The Cork Committee reviewed the operation of the disqualification provisions in both the Companies Act 1948 and section 9 of the Insolvency Act 1976 as part of its exhaustive enquiry into the workings of English insolvency law which led ultimately to the enactment of the Insolvency Act 1985.[29] One of the reasons given by the Cork Committee to explain why there were so few applications under section 9 was that the Department of Trade and Industry had formed the narrow view that an application grounded on unfitness could only be made in a case where the director had been convicted of a criminal offence.[30] The Committee put forward a proposal for reform which, in keeping with its approach to the reform of insolvency law generally, was driven by the view that harmonisation of the law of personal and corporate insolvency was both necessary and desirable. It was felt that there should be at least some degree of automatic restriction on the future activities of directors of failed companies just as there was an automatic ban on undischarged bankrupts from acting as a director or taking part in corporate management.[31] Thus, the Committee recommended the strengthening of section 9 so that the court would be *obliged* to disqualify a person for at least two years (and up to a maximum of 15) where it appeared that his past conduct as a director of an insolvent company made him unfit.[32] This was roughly the formula

---

[25] *loc. cit.*
[26] Following on from the White Paper, *Company Law Reform*, Cmnd. 5391 (July 1973).
[27] Extended to 15 years by Companies Act 1981, s. 94.
[28] Three orders in 1983, eight orders in 1984 and 12 orders in 1985: see Department of Trade and Industry, *Companies in 1985.*
[29] Report of the Review Committee, *Insolvency Law and Practice* (the Cork Committee), Cmnd. 8558 (1982). For general background see, I.F. Fletcher, "The Genesis of Modern Insolvency Law—An Odyssey of Law Reform" [1987] J.B.L. 365.
[30] *ibid.*, para. 1763.
[31] *ibid.*, paras 1764–1766.
[32] *ibid.*, paras 1817–1818. Note also the Committee's recommendations at paras 1822–1823 (which led to the introduction of the personal liability provisions now found in section 15).

eventually adopted in what is now section 6 of the CDDA. There would no longer be a requirement for the director to have been involved in two corporate failures within five years. The insolvent liquidation of a single company would suffice. Furthermore, under this proposal, disqualification would become mandatory once unfitness was established to the satisfaction of the court. To that extent, disqualification on the ground of unfitness would no longer be a matter within the court's discretion. The Committee also recommended that the court should be empowered, but not required, to disqualify a person where it appeared to the Secretary of State, in consequence of a report received from inspectors appointed to conduct an investigation into the affairs of a company under companies legislation, that it was expedient in the public interest that the person concerned should be prohibited from being concerned (without the permission of the court) in the management of a company or a public company as the case may be.[33] This recommendation formed the basis of what is now the discretionary power of disqualification for unfitness in section 8 of the CDDA.

The White Paper: a revised framework for insolvency law

1.29 The Cork Committee's approach was eventually taken up in the Insolvency Act 1985, but only after a controversial attempt by the government of the day to push a more radical and draconian measure through parliament. In its White Paper, the government took up the Committee's recommendation but proposed additionally that the directors of any company which went into *compulsory liquidation* should be automatically disqualified from company management for three years unless they could satisfy the court that they should be exonerated.[34] This additional proposal, which shifted the onus onto the individual to demonstrate why he should not be disqualified, was embodied in the Insolvency Bill. However, the government was ultimately forced to abandon its original clause in the face of fierce parliamentary opposition.[35] A Cork-inspired mandatory disqualification provision was reintroduced and, after re-enactment, now appears as sections 6 to 7 of the CDDA. The onus remains firmly with the

---

[33] *ibid.*, para. 1819(c).

[34] *A Revised Framework for Insolvency Law*, Cmnd. 9175 (1984), paras 46–51.

[35] Several objections to automatic disqualification were raised during debate and the government was defeated on a division in the House of Lords: *Hansard,* H.L. Vol. 459, col. 628. The main objections to the proposal can be summarised as follows:

(1) unscrupulous directors could easily have evaded automatic disqualification by putting the company into *voluntary* liquidation: *Hansard,* H.L. Vol. 458, cols 909, 919; H.C. Vol. 78, cols 155, 210;

(2) automatic disqualification would be widely seen as a stigma: *Hansard,* H.C. Vol. 78, col. 190;

(3) automatic disqualification would deter skilled individuals from taking up non-executive directorships or consultancy positions in ailing companies where their expertise might most be needed: *Hansard,* H.L. Vol. 458, cols 884, 895, 898, 905–906, 918; H.C. Vol. 78, cols 185–186, 210;

(4) automatic disqualification would hamper the activities of the honest and stifle enterprise: *Hansard,* H.C. Vol. 78, col. 173;

(5) automatic disqualification would amount to a denial of natural justice by placing an unfair onus on the individual to establish his "innocence": *Hansard,* H.C. Vol. 78, col. 210 and the courts would become congested with rebuttal or leave applications as a result: *Hansard,* H.L. Vol. 458, col. 918; H.C. Vol. 78, col. 186.

On a comparative point, it is interesting to note that two automatic disqualification provisions enacted in Singapore during the 1980s were the subject of relentless criticism on similar grounds. For a general account of the Singapore experience see, A. Hicks, "Taking part in management—the disqualified director's dilemma" [1987] Mal. L.J. lxxiv and "Disqualification of Directors—Forty Years On" [1988] J.B.L. 27. Experience in Australia, where individuals convicted of a relevant criminal offence are automatically disqualified from taking part in the management of companies, suggests that there is some force in point (5) above. Many of the disqualification cases appearing in the Australian law reports have concerned applications by individuals who were automatically disqualified for leave to act: see, *e.g. Re Ferrari Furniture Co. Pty Ltd* [1972] N.S.W.L.R. 790; *Re Magna Alloys & Research Pty Ltd* (1975) 1 A.C.L.R. 203. For a theoretical critique of automatic disqualification provisions not confined to the specific case of company directors see, A. von Hirsch and M. Wasik, "Civil Disqualifications Attending Conviction: A Suggested Conceptual Framework" [1997] C.L.J. 599.

Secretary of State (or official receiver) to establish unfitness. A schedule of matters which the court must take into account when determining unfitness was introduced for the first time in the Insolvency Act 1985 and carried through into the CDDA. The prevailing view within both the executive and the legislature was that some form of "highway code" was needed to assist insolvency practitioners in complying with their reporting obligations[36] and the Secretary of State in deciding whether to apply for an order or not, as well as to assist the courts.[37] The contents of the Schedule reflect the experience of both the Insolvency Service and insolvency practitioners in their dealings with the directors of badly-run companies which end up in insolvency. They include breach of fiduciary duty, misapplication of company funds and default in filing accounts and returns. As such, the Schedule might be described as a statement of basic minimum standards.[38] The substantive power in section 6 captures the spirit of the Cork recommendations. A director involved in a single corporate insolvency is notionally at risk of disqualification and if the court makes a finding of unfitness under that provision it must disqualify the individual concerned for at least the minimum period of two years.[39]

SUMMARY AND CONCLUSION

1.30 The various substantive powers now to be found in the CDDA have evolved gradually and a number of distinct phases of historical development are discernible. This has not been an isolated process and it should be considered as one part of a wider process of legislative reform in the spheres of company and insolvency law culminating in the reforms of 1985 and 1986. It might be argued that the enactment of the CDDA served merely to bring a ramshackle collection of unconnected powers derived from companies and insolvency legislation together in one place. However, it is preferable to see the CDDA as a single legislative scheme in which the various disqualification provisions are harmonised. The Insolvency Act 1986 is generally treated as if it was a piece of codifying legislation. The prevailing judicial view of the insolvency legislation is that it should not be construed with reference to the law as it stood before its enactment.[40] Given that the CDDA was enacted broadly in the same period and that its core unfitness provisions were originally part of the Insolvency Act 1985, it is suggested that it should be treated more as a codifying than a consolidating statute. Further support for such a view derives from the structure of the CDDA itself. A striking feature of the CDDA is that matters which trigger jurisdiction under sections 2 to 5 and 10 can equally be treated as "unfitness" under sections 6 to 8. In a sense, the legislation is therefore bound together by the modern unfitness provisions which were originally enacted as part of the Insolvency Act 1985. Moreover, this view reflects the overall thrust of the historical process, in particular the shift of emphasis from provisions

---

[36] See now, CDDA, s. 7(3).

[37] See, *e.g. Hansard*, H.L. Vol. 461, cols 724, 732–733, Vol. 467, cols 1123–1124.

[38] *Hansard*, H.L. Vol. 467, col. 1124. For a full discussion of the contents of the Schedule, *cf.* Chap. 4. The idea that the disqualification legislation is concerned with setting and promoting standards of conduct for directors is canvassed further in Chap. 2.

[39] Section 6 is more unfavourable to the individual than comparable provisions in Australia: see, *e.g.* Corporations Law, ss 599–600. These are discretionary powers exercisable only where there have been at least two insolvencies: see further, J. Cassidy, "Disqualification of Directors Under the Corporations Law" (1995) 13 *Company and Securities Law Journal* 221, 235–238.

[40] See, *e.g. Re M C Bacon Ltd* [1990] B.C.L.C. 324, [1990] B.C.C. 78, *Re a Debtor (No. 1 of 1987)* [1989] 1 W.L.R. 271 (a case on statutory demands in personal insolvency), *Smith v. Braintree District Council* [1990] 2 A.C. 215, 237–238 (a case on section 285 of the Insolvency Act 1985) and *Re Jeffrey S Levitt* [1992] B.C.L.C. 250, [1992] B.C.C. 137.

based on fraud and bankruptcy in favour of the modern concept of unfitness, a concept which is not exclusively concerned with fraud or with behaviour that might be characterised as being criminally culpable.

CHAPTER 2

The Nature and Purpose of Directors' Disqualification

INTRODUCTION

2.01 Chapter 1 traced the historical evolution of disqualification legislation from its earliest origins in the 1920s to its final culmination in the CDDA. In broad terms, the enactment of the CDDA brought about two developments in the law concerning disqualification of directors. First, it served to pull together various long standing disqualification provisions scattered through companies and insolvency legislation into a single legislative scheme. Secondly, it marked the effective launch of a new regime, in the form of sections 6 to 9, which, among other things, made provision for the mandatory disqualification of directors on the ground of unfitness following corporate insolvency. While it is true to say that these new provisions in sections 6 to 9 had originally been enacted in the Insolvency Act 1985, they were barely in place a year before being re-enacted in the CDDA. With that in mind it makes more sense to regard the CDDA as their *de facto* point of commencement.[1]

Taking the provisions of the CDDA as a whole (with the exception of section 11 which bars undischarged bankrupts from taking part in the management of companies *automatically* without any need for a court order), the following common schematic features can be identified:

(1) The CDDA contains a number of separate jurisdictional "gateways" which potentially all lead to the same result, namely the possible imposition by the court of a disqualification order.

(2) A disqualification order amounts to a composite ban in the terms of section 1 which, for a specified period from the date of the order, precludes the disqualified person, amongst other things, from acting as a company director or from taking part in the promotion, formation or management of a company without the permission of the court.[2]

---

[1] The short title of the CDDA, "an Act to consolidate certain enactments relating to the disqualification of persons from being directors of companies, and from being otherwise concerned with the company's affairs" while strictly accurate, can be a little misleading. Before the CDDA came into force the two new powers in what are now sections 6 to 7 and 8 together with the criteria for determining unfitness in Schedule 1 were completely untested by the courts.

[2] On the scope of the ban, see generally Chap. 12. On the issue of permission to act notwithstanding disqualification, see generally Chap. 13. Where applicable the terms "claimant", "defendant" and "permission" are used to reflect the modern requirements of the CPR, the Disqualification Rules and the Disqualification Practice Direction. In disqualification proceedings, "defendant" is the modern equivalent of the pre-CPR term "respondent" and "permission" the term now used for "leave". On the issue of the applicable rules of procedure in proceedings under sections 6 and 8, see generally Chap. 6.

(3) All of the various jurisdictional "gateways" focus primarily on *individual* conduct within companies as opposed to the *collective* conduct of the board of directors. The courts only have jurisdiction to disqualify individuals on the basis of their personal conduct.[3] It is not open to the courts to impose a collective disqualification on a board of directors for what amounted to a collective failure. Each individual member of the board would have to be processed and his personal contribution to that collective failure assessed.[4]

(4) The court's power to disqualify under all of the various "gateways" is triggered by some *defined past misconduct* on the part of the individual (certain criminal offences in section 2, persistent filing defaults in section 3, unfit conduct in sections 6[4a] and 8 etc.) referable to a specified company or companies.

(5) Disqualification does not amount to an absolute ban. It is not possible under the CDDA for anyone to be disqualified by a court for a period in excess of 15 years. Moreover, the courts have statutory power to grant a disqualified person permission to act as a director or to take part in the management of a company during the currency of his disqualification.

(6) Breach of a disqualification order has the same legal consequences whether the order was made under CDDA, ss 2–5, 6, 8 or 10. This is true also in the case of a bankrupt who breaches the automatic ban in section 11.

Thus, in broad terms, the CDDA contains a range of powers which enable (and in the case of sections 6 to 7 oblige) the court to disqualify persons based on their previous misconduct, the logic being that this previous misconduct raises serious questions over their fitness or suitability to continue in the management of companies. While all the "gateways" are unlocked by their own particular "key", none of them are completely exclusive in scope. For example, a persistent failure to file accounts or annual returns can trigger disqualification under section 3 and could also be taken into account in determining whether a person is unfit within the meaning of section 6 or section 8. In the light of these common features the CDDA can justifiably be regarded as, in some sense, a coherent legislative scheme.

   2.02   The aim of this chapter is to explore two complex and related issues. First, the *rationale* of the CDDA is considered, in an attempt to determine the legislation's overall purpose and scope. Secondly, and in the light of that discussion, the *nature* of the jurisdiction established by the CDDA is explored: is disqualification simply an ancillary civil/administrative process or is it, as some have sought to argue, a *quasi-criminal* process even though it is administered, for the most part, by the civil courts? A number of important general points emerge from this discussion which provide a useful context for the detailed exposition of the CDDA's specific provisions contained in the rest of the book. First, at the rhetorical level there is a broad consensus that the main objective of the CDDA is not to punish miscreant directors but rather to protect the public from those who have abused the privilege of limited liability. However, there is far less consensus about how the nature of the jurisdiction should be characterised. As outlined in paragraph 2.01, above, it is clear that the legislation has some coherent features. At the same time, in terms of its overall structure and operation, the CDDA is by no means a straightforward legislative scheme. Indeed, as explained below, the jurisdiction has many difficult and ambiguous aspects. This makes the task of determining

---

[3] "Individuals" here includes individual companies which are also susceptible to disqualification under the CDDA: see *Official Receiver v. Brady* [1999] B.C.C. 258.
[4] On the approach of the court to issues of individual and co-responsibility see Chap. 5.
[4a] See, *e.g. Re Launchexcept Ltd, Secretary of State for Trade and Industry v. Tillman* [1999] B.C.C. 703 at 713.

the nature of the disqualification process a complex one. It is the contention of the present authors that uncertainties over how to characterise the nature of the jurisdiction will inevitably resurface in the courts. In other words, the way in which each judge perceives the broad nature of disqualification and its impact on the individual, may well affect that judge's approach to the task of applying and construing specific provisions of the CDDA. As such, there is scope for subtle differences in judicial approach and emphasis which may give rise to inconsistency and confusion. Judicial attitudes may also be shaped by concerns about the efficacy of disqualification as a regulatory technique.

WHAT WAS PARLIAMENT'S INTENTION IN ENACTING THE CDDA?

Disqualification and abuse of the privilege of limited liability

Origins of limited liability

2.03   In the light of the history and evolution of disqualification legislation, it is justifiable to take as a starting point the basic premise that disqualification is targeted at those who abuse the so-called privilege of limited liability. In a company limited by shares the liability of the shareholders who provide it with investment capital is limited to the amount, if any, unpaid on their shares.[5] This means that a shareholder cannot generally be required to contribute towards payment of the company's debts once he has paid for his shares in full. Thus, on the company's insolvency, each shareholder has no further liability for the company's debts and stands to lose only the amount of his initial investment. Statutory limited liability has been available in this form since the mid-nineteenth century.[6] Limited liability was originally intended to encourage widespread private investment in business and so enable entrepreneurs to raise the capital needed to fund their activities. The nascent limited company emerged primarily as a medium for raising capital from passive investors who had no active involvement in the running of the company's business. In its earliest form limited liability therefore went in tandem with what would now be recognised as the publicly-quoted limited company which continues to perform broadly that same economic function.[7] By the end of the nineteenth century, however, the limited company had emerged as a popular medium for small business. Erstwhile sole traders and partnerships were incorporating their businesses in increasing numbers so that they could trade with the benefit of limited liability. The limited company therefore became a *trading* mechanism for owner-managed businesses as well as performing its earlier function as a *financing*

---

[5] Companies Act 1985, s. 1(2)(a).

[6] For brief accounts of the history and origins of limited liability see, P.L. Davies, *Gower's Principles of Modern Company Law* (6th ed., 1997); B. Pettet, "Limited Liability—A Principle for the 21st Century?" (1995) 48 (II) *Current Legal Problems* 125; A. Hicks, "Corporate Form: Questioning the Unsung Hero" [1997] J.B.L. 306 and *Disqualification of Directors: No Hiding Place for the Unfit* (A.C.C.A Research Report No. 59, 1998).

[7] See Hicks, *op. cit.* This conception of the company as a mechanism for bringing together "passive" investors and "active" managers has exerted a powerful influence on company law which still treats those who manage the company's business as entirely separate from those who invest in and own the company (the shareholders). Thus, in law, the management and decision-making functions of a limited company are split between a board of directors (which in a private company may consist of a sole director) and the shareholders in general meeting. The influence on the development of directors' duties and, in particular, the common law duty of care and skill is also notable. The courts have shown a historical reluctance to employ the duty of care and skill as a means of imposing liability on directors for management failure: see, *e.g. Re Brazilian Rubber Plantations & Estates Ltd* [1911] 1 Ch. 425. Implicit in this approach is a refusal on the part of the courts to question management decision-making after the event especially given that the shareholders in general meeting have the power to select the board and deselect any directors who, in their collective view, are not up to scratch: see, *e.g.* the general power in Companies Act 1985, s. 303.

mechanism. The continuation of this shift in corporate culture was effectively sanctioned by the House of Lords decision in *Salomon v. Salomon & Co. Ltd* which left the way open for the mass incorporation of small, owner-managed businesses as private companies that has occurred in the twentieth century.[8] Official policy in the United Kingdom continues to rest firmly on the assumption that limited liability benefits the community at large by facilitating enterprise and, in particular, by encouraging entrepreneurs to start up in business without them being forced to put their entire personal wealth on the line.[9] Moreover, the limited company continues to be exalted as an appropriate vehicle for small, owner-managed businesses. This is borne out by the spate of deregulatory measures introduced in recent years to reduce the burden of regulatory compliance on small companies.[10]

Abuse of limited liability

2.04   Despite this prevailing emphasis on the facilitative aspect of company law, it has always been recognised that limited liability has disadvantages, the main one being that it transfers the risk of business failure to the company's creditors. The House of Lords in *Salomon* recognised that their refusal to impose personal liability on the principal shareholder for the insolvent company's debts had serious implications for unsecured creditors, although this did not sway them from their basic view that anyone complying with the registration formalities of the Companies Acts could lawfully trade with the benefit of limited liability. Nevertheless, this risk, which is inherent in the concept of limited liability, is regarded as acceptable given the concern of company law to encourage enterprise. At the same time, however, the recognition that limited liability confers benefits but also creates risks has given rise to the idea, commonly expressed in legal discourse, that limited liability is a *privilege* conferred by the state which should be used responsibly and not abused.[11] As such, there is a consensus that company law should have a regulatory function as well as a facilitative function. In particular, it is generally accepted that company law should provide some means of regulating companies in the interests of shareholders, investors, employees,[12] and, in

---

[8] [1897] A.C. 22, HL. The lower courts in *Salomon* imposed personal liability on the sole director and principal shareholder for the debts of an insolvent company. This decision was reversed in the House of Lords where it was held that a company lawfully incorporated by process of registration under the Companies Acts has a legal existence distinct from that of its members who are generally only liable to contribute personally to the company's assets to the extent provided by the legislation. When the case was decided, the idea of an owner-managed company in which investment and management functions could be combined was very new. It is perhaps not surprising that the lower courts resisted the notion that one man could invest in a company and manage its affairs at the same time while enjoying the benefits of limited liability. The "one man" company is now formally recognised by statute following implementation of the Twelfth Company Law Directive: see Companies Act 1985, s. 1(3A).

[9] See Hicks, *op. cit.* (Hicks supports open access to limited liability but questions the validity of this assumption in respect of owner-managers who may be best served by not incorporating or by the introduction of a registered incorporated partnership form); J. Freedman, "Small Business and Corporate Form: Burden or Privilege?" (1994) 57 M.L.R. 555 and S. Wheeler, "Directors' Disqualification: Insolvency Practitioners and the Decision-Making Process" (1995) 15 L.S. 283.

[10] See, *e.g.* Companies Act 1985, ss 379A, 381A–381C (simplified meeting procedures); ss 246–249 (simplified accounting procedures); ss 249A–249E (audit exemption).

[11] This highly influential notion is a variant of the concession theory of company law. Concession theory holds that a limited company can only be created by act of state so that when the state allows individuals to incorporate their business it confers a privilege which should be used in the public interest. The "privilege" idea has exerted a powerful influence in disqualification cases: see V. Finch, "Disqualifying Directors: Issues of Rights, Privileges and Employment" (1993) 22 I.L.J. 35. For a flavour of privilege rhetoric as used in the parliamentary debates accompanying the passage of what became the Insolvency Act 1985 to justify, *inter alia*, the introduction of more stringent disqualification powers see, *e.g. Hansard,* H.C. Vol. 78, cols. 145, 154 and the report of the proceedings of House of Commons Standing Committee E, Vol. 4 (Session 1984–85) commencing at col. 54 which is peppered with references to "the privilege of limited liability".

[12] See Companies Act 1985, s. 309.

the present context, creditors, one of the principal aims of regulation being to contain abuse of limited liability.[13] In broad terms, the enactment of the CDDA should be seen as part of this regulatory response.

2.05   A study of the available parliamentary materials suggests that the disqualification provisions now to be found in the CDDA were originally intended to address a number of quite specific concerns and abuses as set out below:

2.06   Security filling.   It is clear from the following statement found in the report of the Greene Committee[14] that the fraudulent trading provison introduced originally in 1928 was directed primarily at "security filling":

> "Our attention has been directed particularly to the case (met with principally in private companies) where the person in control of the company holds a floating charge and, while knowing that the company is on the verge of liquidation, 'fills up' his security by means of goods obtained on credit and then appoints a receiver."[15]

This practice is objectionable as, unless regulated, the director who knows that his company is insolvent is able to top up the value of any security referable to his loan account at the expense of trade creditors. The legislative response (in the form of the fraudulent trading provision) was to introduce a mixture of civil and criminal liability for trading of this character, while also making it a ground for disqualification.[16] It would seem that the more extensive power in section 2 of the CDDA to disqualify persons convicted of an indictable offence in connection with the promotion, formation or management of a company was introduced to deal with other comparable misuses of limited liability, such as the dishonest misappropriation of corporate assets.[17]

2.07   Under-capitalised companies.   Private companies are not subject to any minimum capital requirements and so it is perfectly lawful for anyone to incorporate a private company with an initial subscribed share capital of as little as £1 or £2.[18] The lack of a minimum capital requirement reflects the change of culture signalled by the *Salomon* decision (see para. 2.03, above) which saw a move away from the idea that the limited company performs primarily a capital-raising function. This means that limited liability can be purchased easily and cheaply.[19] Equally, however, it means that a person can incorporate a limited company without injecting any working capital and trade at the risk of the company's creditors. Concern over the enhanced risk which then under-capitalised companies pose for creditors and consumers is voiced

---

[13] Some have questioned the use of company law as a mechanism for protecting creditors. Many of the commentators who write from the standpoint of economic analysis argue that creditors will compensate themselves for the added risk of dealing with a limited company by increasing their prices or setting a higher rate of interest. Pettet, *op. cit.* provides a good account of this essentially deregulatory viewpoint. See also, B.R. Cheffins, *Company Law: Theory, Structure and Operation* (1997) especially Chap. 2 and T.G.W. Telfer, "Risk and Insolvent Trading" in *Corporate Personality in the 20th Century* (R. Grantham & C. Rickett (eds) 1998). For criticism of economic analysis see J. Dine, *Criminal Law in the Company Context* (1995), p. 32.
[14] Report of the Company Law Amendment Committee (the Greene Committee), Cmd. 2657 (1926).
[15] *ibid.*, para. 61
[16] *ibid.*, see para. 1.23. Trade creditors now commonly try to protect themselves against this abuse by including a term in their standard terms and conditions of sale providing that the seller retains title to the goods sold until such time as payment is received.
[17] See para. 1.23.
[18] Department of Trade and Industry statistics (see, in particular, the report produced annually which summarises the overall state of the register at Companies House) suggest that a very high proportion of companies have a share capital of £1,000 or less. See further discussion in A. Hicks, *op. cit.*
[19] See further, Hicks, *op. cit.*

frequently. The following extract from the report of the Jenkins Committee provides a good illustration:

> "The Board of Trade have referred in their evidence to the irresponsible multiplication of companies, particularly of 'one-man' companies; to the dangers of abuse through the incorporation with limited liability of very small, undercapitalised businesses... We are satisfied that this proliferation of small companies can and does lead to abuse..."[20]

Similar criticisms were put forward in the report of the Cork Committee[21] and during the parliamentary debate which preceded the enactment of the Insolvency Act 1985. The Cork Committee recommended that the disqualification regime should be strengthened as a means of "severely penalising those who abuse the privilege of limited liability by operating behind one-man, insufficiently capitalised companies...".[22] This recommendation led ultimately to the enactment of the unfitness provisions now found in CDDA, ss 6 to 9 and the introduction of the provision (now CDDA, s. 15) which renders a person who takes part in the management of a company while disqualified personally liable for that company's debts.

2.08 Failure to comply with disclosure obligations. In return for the benefit of limited liability, the limited company and its directors are required to comply with the extensive publicity requirements imposed by companies legislation. Of particular importance to creditors and shareholders alike are the recurring obligations requiring up-to-date accounts and annual returns to be filed with the Registrar of Companies. Any member of the public is entitled to carry out a search of the records at Companies House in order to access information filed by a limited company in accordance with these disclosure obligations. Disclosure is one of the main techniques offered by company law for safeguarding the interests of investors and creditors. A leading company law textbook has this to say about disclosure obligations:

> "In these ways ... members and the public (which, for practical purposes, means creditors and others who may subsequently have dealings with the company and become its members or creditors) are supposed to be able to obtain the information which they need to make an intelligent appraisal of their risks..."[23]

Perhaps not surprisingly, the CDDA reinforces the importance of these obligations by adding powers of disqualification to the range of criminal and other default sanctions made available in companies legislation.[24]

2.09 Insolvent/wrongful trading. Wrongful trading is the term coined by the Cork Committee to describe the abusive practice which occurs when the directors of a limited company allow it to continue trading and incurring fresh liabilities even

---

[20] Report of the Company Law Committee (the Jenkins Committee), Cmnd. 1749 (1962), para. 20 which echoes the view of those commentators opposed to the *Salomon* decision, a view most famously expressed by O. Kahn-Freund in "Some Reflections on Company Law Reform" (1944) 7 M.L.R. 54.
[21] Report of the Review Committee, *Insolvency Law and Practice* (the Cork Committee), Cmnd. 8558 (1982).
[22] *ibid.*, para. 1815.
[23] P.L. Davies, *Gower's Principles of Modern Company Law* (6th ed., 1997), p. 505.
[24] See CDDA, ss 3 and 5 (discussed more fully in Chap. 9). A court would also take into account non-compliance with these obligations in determining whether a person is unfit for the purposes of CDDA, ss 6 and 8: see, *e.g. Secretary of State for Trade and Industry v. Ettinger, Re Swift 736 Ltd* [1993] B.C.L.C. 896, [1993] B.C.C. 312, CA.

though they know or ought to know that the company has no reasonable prospect of survival. This practice is detrimental both to new creditors, who are persuaded to give credit to the company after the point of no return, and also to the company's existing creditors whose own prospects of recovering their money is diminished further given the overall increase in liabilities which the company cannot meet. The Cork Committee offered this summary:

> "The essence of wrongful trading is the incurring of liabilities with no reasonable prospect of meeting them; whether by incurring debts with no reasonable prospect of paying them, or by taking payment in advance for goods to be supplied with no reasonable prospect of being able to supply them or return the money in default."[25]

Cork also suggested that trading through an under-capitalised company could come within the concept of wrongful trading.[26] A combination of the wrongful trading provision now to be found in the Insolvency Act 1986, s. 214 (which empowers the court, on the application of a liquidator, to order the errant director to contribute personally to the company's assets) and the enactment of the CDDA (in particular, sections 6 to 9 and 15) were intended to address this problem.[27]

2.10   Phoenix companies and multiple insolvencies.   The "phoenix syndrome" is shorthand for a practice, much stigmatised in official reports, which takes the following form. The directors of a limited company trade the company into insolvency, place it into voluntary liquidation and then acquire its assets and business from a "friendly" liquidator at a knock-down price using a new, clean "phoenix" company as the vehicle for the purchase. The new company is said, like the phoenix, to rise from the ashes of the old. The directors and shareholders of both companies are the same and, in order to preserve any goodwill, the new company will adopt a name which is similar to that of the old company before trading is recommenced. By this process the directors succeed in recycling the assets of the business while shedding its liabilities.[28] It was stated in the report of the Jenkins Committee that the court should be given powers to curb the activities of individuals who succeed "in steering a series of companies into insolvency".[29] Parliament belatedly responded to this concern by introducing discretionary disqualification for unfitness in the Insolvency Act 1976.[30] This provision had little tangible impact and it was replaced, on the recommendation of the Cork Committee, by what is now section 6 of the CDDA. It is clear that this reform was inspired to a considerable extent by Cork's preoccupation with the phoenix syndrome. This is confirmed by the following extract taken from Chapter 45 of the Cork Committee's

---

[25] Report of the Review Committee, *op. cit.*, para. 1784.
[26] *ibid.*, para. 1785 and see para. 2.07. Wrongful trading also embraces the specific abuse of security filling described above at para. 2.06.
[27] Cork and the subsequent White Paper, *A Revised Framework for Insolvency Law*, Cmnd. 9175 (1984) both offered this mixed bag of civil liability combined with an extended disqualification regime, an approach ultimately taken up in the Insolvency Act 1985. Allegations of wrongful trading are routinely raised in unfitness proceedings: see generally Chap. 5. Civil liability for wrongful trading and disqualification are linked explicitly as a court imposing personal liability on a director under Insolvency Act 1986, s. 214 may disqualify him within the context of those proceedings under CDDA, s. 10. On the operation of section 214 generally see further, A. Walters, "Enforcing Wrongful Trading—Substantive Problems and Practical Disincentives" in *The Corporate Dimension* (Rider (ed.) 1998) and other works therein cited. Note that there was an earlier attempt by the Jenkins Committee, *op. cit.*, paras 499, 503 to introduce a "reckless trading" provision along similar lines.
[28] For a colourful description of the workings of this abusive practice see I.F. Fletcher, "The Genesis of Modern Insolvency Law—An Odyssey of Law Reform" [1987] J.B.L. 365.
[29] *op. cit.*, para. 80.
[30] See para. 1.27.

report, the main chapter setting out its proposals for strengthening the disqualification regime:

> "We have received many proposals for increasing the severity with which the directors of insolvent companies should be treated. It has been made evident to us that there is a widespread dissatisfaction at the ease with which a person trading through the medium of one or more companies with limited liability can allow such a company to become insolvent, form a new company, and then carry on trading much as before, leaving behind him a trail of unpaid creditors, and often repeating the process several times. The dissatisfaction is greatest where the director of an insolvent company has set up business again, using a similar name for the new company, and trades with assets purchased at a discount from the liquidator of the old company."[31]

Again, the CDDA should be seen as one aspect of the legislative response to the phoenix syndrome now operating in tandem with other reforms introduced in the mid-1980s such as the compulsory licensing of insolvency practitioners (under Part XIII of the Insolvency Act 1986) and the prohibition (in section 216 of the same Act) on the re-use of a company's name where that company has gone into insolvent liquidation.[32]

Enterprise, regulation and the wider objectives of the CDDA

2.11   As has been seen, much of the rhetoric in the official reports is directed at abuses of limited liability occurring within owner-managed private companies and so-called "one-man" companies. It can be concluded from this that one of the main objects of the CDDA (along with a series of other measures now to be found in the Insolvency Act 1986) was to offer creditors some form of protection against the abusive practices of owner-managers who choose to trade through the medium of a limited company. In a broader sense, the disqualification regime is therefore designed to address problems which have emerged within the context of the shift in corporate culture outlined in para. 2.03 above.[33] The CDDA's response to the trader who abuses the privilege of limited liability is to remove that trading privilege. The disqualified trader is prohibited from running a limited company and under CDDA, s. 15 he is personally liable for the debts of any company which he runs during the period of his

---

[31] *op. cit.*, para. 1813.
[32] On section 216 generally see G. Wilson, "Delinquent Directors and Company Names: The Role of Judicial Policy-Making in the Business Environment" (1996) 47 N.I.L.Q. 345; D. Milman, "Curbing the Phoenix Syndrome" [1997] J.B.L. 224. On insolvency practitioners see V. Finch, "Insolvency Practitioners: Regulation and Reform" [1998] J.B.L. 334.
[33] The impression that the CDDA is there primarily to regulate malpractice in small private companies is confirmed by the rhetoric of enforcement used by ministers within the Department of Trade and Industry who refer constantly to the need to curb the activities of "rogue traders" and "cowboy directors" in the interests of business and public confidence. See, *e.g.* "Dodgy Directors Top of Insolvency Service's Hitlist" (DTI Press Release P/95/543, August 15, 1995), "78% More 'Bad Bosses' Banned by Insolvency Service" (DTI Press Release P/96/126, February 20, 1996), "Unfit Directors of 'Phoenix' Companies Grounded as Disqualification Orders Soar" (DTI Press Release P/96/848, November 12, 1996), "Griffiths Goes Gunning Against Cowboy Directors" (DTI Press Release P/97/365, June 5, 1997), "Griffiths Double-Barrelled Attack on 'Phoenix' Directors" (DTI Press Release P/98/210, March 18, 1998), "Griffiths Promises No Let Up in Campaign to Ban Rogue Directors" (DTI Press Release P/98/338, April 30, 1998). These press releases suggest that the DTI sees disqualification as an exercise in maintaining public confidence which is mainly directed at tackling small traders who take advantage of limited liability to "rip off" creditors and consumers. One of our senior judges has expressed a similar view of the CDDA albeit extra-judicially: see Lord Hoffmann, "The Fourth Annual Leonard Sainer Lecture" (1997) 18 *The Company Lawyer* 194. DTI press releases can be accessed via the internet at http://www.dti.gov.uk/.

disqualification in breach of the prohibition. At the same time, however, it is notable that disqualification operates as an *ex post facto* measure. It is directed at those who have taken the opportunity to trade with the benefit of limited liability but who have then been found wanting in some respect. In seeking to strike a balance between the facilitative and regulatory aspects of company law, parliament has administered a dose of regulation while continuing to trumpet the virtue of the limited company as a vehicle for launching new businesses and the necessity of preserving relatively free access to limited liability as a means of encouraging enterprise. For all the complaints in official reports about the evils of under-capitalised companies,[34] proposals to curb abuse by increasing the price payable for the benefit of limited liability on incorporation or imposing some other form of entry requirement have been routinely rejected. One illustration of this is the short shrift consistently given to proposals to introduce a minimum share capital requirement for private companies.[35] Thus, the CDDA amounts to a legislative attempt to regulate abuse of limited liability within an overall legal framework which offers limited liability "on tap" and thereby continues to encourage the proliferation of private limited companies.[36] The underlying policy assumption is that limited companies are more of a "good thing" than a "bad thing" and that the purpose of regulation is to encourage the responsible use of limited liability without in any way discouraging enterprise.[37]

The impression that the legal framework is weighted in favour of "enterprise" over regulation is confirmed by the structure of the CDDA itself. There is nothing in the CDDA to say that business failure is wrong *per se*. The CDDA focuses on issues of individual misconduct within companies and business failure is merely one context in which that enquiry is carried out.[38] It also confers a statutory power on the courts to grant a disqualified person permission to act as a director of a specified company or companies. This gives the courts scope to assess whether there is any positive value in allowing the disqualified person to remain involved in the running of limited companies on the ground that beneficial economic activity might otherwise be stifled.[39] Another illustrative feature of the CDDA is the total absence of any *re-entry* requirement at the point when the period of disqualification expires. Once a disqualification order lapses, the person is immediately free to recommence trading with the benefit of limited liability without there being any procedure for assessing whether this is appropriate.[40]

---

[34] See para. 2.07 above.

[35] See, *e.g.* Report of the Committee on Company Law Amendment (the Cohen Committee), Cmd. 6659 (1945), para. 57.

[36] See Hicks, *op. cit.* Hicks is critical of this policy and argues persuasively for the introduction of an alternative unlimited corporate form for small business which would encourage less extensive use of limited companies and a resulting reduction in the abuse of limited liability. It is understood that the Law Commissions intend to propose legislation for a registered incorporated partnership form.

[37] There is considerable emphasis in the parliamentary debates on the need to encourage directors to monitor closely the financial circumstances of their businesses in the interests of creditors. See, *e.g. Hansard*, H.C. Vol. 78, cols 142, 145. Indeed, it is arguable that the CDDA was intended to reinforce various provisions of company law which already carry criminal sanctions, *e.g.* the requirement to keep proper books of account and financial records, a point taken up in Chap. 5.

[38] Automatic disqualification for directors involved with failed companies was categorically rejected by parliament, see para. 1.29. Furthermore, the Secretary of State must be satisfied that the public interest will be served before bringing disqualification proceedings against such a director for an order under section 6: see CDDA, s. 7(1).

[39] On permission to act generally, see Chap. 13.

[40] This is true even of a person who has been disqualified by the courts more than once. There is thus some emphasis in the law on encouraging entrepreneurs to try again in the hope that they have learned the lessons of previous business failures. Warner J. has frequently questioned the assumption that a director deemed unfit to act at the point of disqualification should automatically be deemed fit to act at the point when the period of disqualification expires: see *obiter* comments in *Re Western Welsh International System Buildings Ltd* (1988) 4 B.C.C. 449 at 451; *Re New Generation Engineers Ltd* [1993] B.C.L.C. 435 at 440–441; *Re Moorgate Metals Ltd, Official Receiver v. Huhtala* [1995] 1 B.C.L.C. 503 at 517, [1995] B.C.C. 143 at 154.

2.12   In summary, it is clear from its historical background and development that the CDDA was enacted to combat abuse of limited liability and create a culture of responsibility (which values limited liability as a privilege) primarily within private companies. As will become clear from the later chapters on the CDDA's unfitness provisions, judges often use opaque phrases such as "commercial morality" to denote the responsible use of limited liability. Moreover, it is clear that the disqualification regime was intended to perform this considerable regulatory function within an overall legal framework which seeks to preserve open and broadly unqualified access to limited liability. However, it is not suggested that the CDDA is concerned only with narrow issues of creditor protection in private limited companies. Read in the light of the general law of directors' obligations, it is apparent that the CDDA has a number of other objectives as set out below:

2.13   Shareholder/investor protection.   The unfitness provisions in sections 6 to 9 of the CDDA seek, in part, to protect shareholders. In determining whether a director is unfit for the purposes of sections 6 and 8, the court must have regard (among other things) to any misfeasance or breach of any fiduciary or other duty by the director in relation to the company and any misapplication or retention by the director of, or any conduct by the director giving rise to an obligation to account for, any money or other property of the company.[41] Such duties operate to protect shareholders as well as creditors. Furthermore, it is a prerequisite to proceedings under section 8 that information or documents have come into the possession of the Secretary of State following the exercise of one or more specified inquisitorial powers contained in companies and financial services legislation. These powers (which include the powers of company investigation contained in Part XIV of the Companies Act 1985) are broad in scope and their rationale embraces the protection of shareholders as well as creditors.[42]

2.14   Consumer protection.   The unfitness provisions in sections 6 to 9 have, to some extent, a consumer protection rationale. This is because, in determining whether a director is unfit for the purposes of section 6 (and section 8, if the relevant company is insolvent), the court must have regard to the extent of the defendant director's responsibility for any failure by the company to supply any goods or services which have been paid for (in whole or in part).[43] The wrongful acceptance or dissipation of customer deposits or pre-payments can therefore amount to unfit conduct under the CDDA.[44]

2.15   Employee protection.   The unfitness provisions in sections 6 to 9 are capable of being used for purposes of employee protection. Section 309 of the Companies Act 1985 confers a duty on the directors of a company to have regard in the performance of their functions to the interests of the company's employees in general, as well as the interests of its members. The duty is circumscribed in that it is owed to the company rather than to employees directly. However, a breach of the duty can be taken into account in disqualification proceedings under sections 6 and 8. This is because the court is required in such proceedings to have regard to "any … breach of any fiduciary or other duty by the director in relation to the company"[45] which clearly encompasses a breach of section 309.

---

[41] CDDA, s. 9, Sched. 1, Pt I, paras 1–2.
[42] For cases which illustrate the use of disqualification in connection with shareholder protection see *e.g. Re Godwin Warren Control Systems plc* [1993] B.C.L.C. 80, [1992] B.C.C. 557 and *Re Looe Fish Ltd* [1993] B.C.L.C. 1160, [1993] B.C.C. 348.
[43] CDDA, s. 9, Sched. 1, Pt II, para. 7.
[44] See para. 5.37.
[45] CDDA, s. 9, Sched. 1, Pt I, para. 1.

2.16 Wider public protection—raising standards. As discussed further below, the strong consensus which emerges from the case law is that the CDDA is concerned broadly with public protection and that protection is achieved (a) by prohibiting the defendant from taking part in the management of companies, (b) by deterring the defendant from future misconduct and (c) through general deterrence, *i.e.* by encouraging other directors to behave properly. Clearly, public protection, in this sense, is capable of extending beyond creditor protection to encompass the protection of the other constituencies mentioned above, namely, shareholders, consumers and employees. Moreover, it is clear from high profile cases such as *Re Atlantic Computers plc, Secretary of State for Trade and Industry v. Ashman*[46] and *Re Barings plc (No. 5), Secretary of State for Trade and Industry v. Baker*[47] that, while many disqualifications are of small traders who abuse limited liability, the concerns of the CDDA do extend beyond abuse of limited liability and creditor protection. *Atlantic* and *Barings* suggest that, in an appropriate case, the courts will disqualify a director who is incompetent in discharging his functions.[48] The upshot is that the application of the CDDA is not necessarily confined to cases involving "abuse of limited liability" in the sense that phrase is usually understood (*i.e.* misconduct by directors in small, owner-managed companies of the *Salomon* type which causes harm to creditors) nor to cases involving "commercial immorality" if that term is taken to encompass some want of probity or culpable misconduct but to exclude serious incompetence.[49] Again, there is some justification for such wider applications in the CDDA itself. The meaning of "company" in the CDDA is not confined to private limited companies but clearly encompasses public companies, companies limited by guarantee and unlimited companies. The effect is that a director of a company who does not enjoy the benefit of limited liability falls within the scope of the CDDA's powers of disqualification. Furthermore, a disqualified person cannot act in a prohibited capacity in relation to an unlimited company without the permission of the court.[50] Thus, it is suggested that the CDDA is directed not merely (as its history and evolution suggest) at those who abuse the privilege of limited liability but broadly at those who act improperly in the management of companies.

Protection of the public or punishment of the individual?

Protection of the public

2.17 The foregoing discussion has suggested that one main object of the CDDA (albeit not its exclusive object) is the regulation of abuse of limited liability. An enduring question is whether the primary purpose of disqualification is to protect the public from those who abuse limited liability or to punish directors for their past misconduct. A study of cases decided at appellate level under the core unfitness provisions (CDDA, ss 6 to 9) reveals a prevailing judicial consensus in favour of the view that the main purpose of the legislation is protection of the public. According to the cases, the CDDA seeks to protect the public in broadly two ways. First, by imposing a legal disability on

---

[46] June 15, 1998, Ch.D., unreported.
[47] [1999] 1 B.C.L.C. 433. See also *Re Continental Assurance Co of London plc* [1997] 1 B.C.L.C. 48, [1996] B.C.C. 888; *Re Landhurst Leasing plc, Secretary of State for Trade and Industry v. Ball* [1999] 1 B.C.L.C. 286.
[48] See discussion in Chap. 5.
[49] On "commercial morality" and the general approach of the courts to questions of unfitness, see discussion in Chap. 4.
[50] On the meaning of "company" in the CDDA, see chaps 3, 9 and 12.

the individual, disqualification puts that individual out of action. This is captured well in the extract below from Balcombe L.J.'s majority judgment in *Re Cedac Ltd, Secretary of State for Trade and Industy v. Langridge*[51]:

> "In my judgment the scope and purpose of the 1986 Act is clear. The ability to trade through a company with the protection of limited liability and with the use of capital subscribed by third partics, is of great economic advantage and confers considerable privileges upon persons so enabled. These privileges involve corresponding responsibilities and the public (in the form of creditors, shareholders and employees—the order in which I place them is of no significance) needs to be protected from persons whose conduct has shown that they have abused those privileges... Accordingly the purpose of the 1986 Act is to protect the public and its scope is the prevention of persons who have previously misconducted themselves in relation to companies, or have otherwise shown themselves as unfit to be concerned in the management of a company from being so concerned."

Secondly, it is said that disqualification aims to protect the public by deterring the disqualifed person from future misconduct and, through general deterrence, by encouraging other directors to behave properly thereby improving standards of corporate management. This emphasis on deterrence is evident in the following extract from Henry L.J.'s judgment in *Re Grayan Building Services Ltd, Secretary of State for Trade and Industry v. Gray*[52]:

> "The concept of limited liability and the sophistication of our corporate law offers great privileges and great opportunities for those who wish to trade under that regime. But the corporate environment carries with it the discipline that those who avail themselves of those privileges must accept the standards laid down and abide by the regulatory rules and disciplines in place to protect creditors and shareholders... The Parliamentary intention to improve managerial safeguards and standards ... is clear. The statutory corporate climate is stricter than it has ever been, and those enforcing it should reflect the fact that Parliament has seen the need for higher standards."

2.18   In the same case, Hoffmann L.J. advanced the view that disqualification for unfitness had been made mandatory under CDDA, s. 6 with the object of general deterrence in mind. In similar vein, in *Re Westmid Packing Services Ltd, Secretary of State for Trade and Industry v. Griffiths*, it was made clear by Woolf L.J. (again, in the context of section 6 proceedings) that the court can make a disqualification order solely for purposes of deterrence:

> "In *Re Lo-Line Electric Motors Ltd* [1988] Ch. 477, [1988] 3 W.L.R. 26, [1988] 2 All E.R. 692, [1988] B.C.L.C. 698, (1988) 4 B.C.C. 415 [see below at para. 2.20] Browne-Wilkinson V.-C. said that the primary purpose of section 300 of the Companies Act 1985 was to protect the public against the future conduct of companies by persons whose past records as directors of insolvent companies showed them to be a danger to creditors and others. That statement has often been approved by this court. But there is often a considerable time lag between the

---

[51] [1991] Ch. 402, [1991] B.C.L.C. 543, [1991] B.C.C. 148.
[52] [1995] Ch. 241, [1995] 3 W.L.R. 1, [1995] 1 B.C.L.C. 276, [1995] B.C.C. 554.

conduct complained of, its discovery and the disqualification proceedings actually coming to the court... One result of delay when it does occur is that there are occasions when disqualification must be ordered even though, by reason of the director's recognition of his previous failings and the way he has conducted himself since the conduct complained of, he is in fact no longer a danger to the public at all. In such cases it is no longer necessary for the director to be kept 'off the road' for the protection of the public, but other factors come into play in the wider interests of protecting the public, *i.e.* a deterrent element in relation to the director himself and a deterrent element as far as other directors are concerned."[53]

Deterrence was also strongly emphasised by the Court of Appeal in the earlier case of *Re Swift 736 Ltd, Secretary of State for Trade and Industry v. Ettinger*. Commenting on the defendant's repeated failure across several companies to comply with Companies Act requirements governing the keeping of proper accounting records and the filing of accounts and returns, Nicholls V.-C. had this to say:

"Those who make use of limited liability must do so with a proper sense of responsibility. The directors' disqualification procedure is an important sanction introduced by Parliament to raise standards in this regard. Those who take advantage of limited liability must conduct their companies with due regard to the ordinary standards of commercial morality. They must also be punctilious in observing the safeguards laid down by Parliament for the benefit of others who have dealings with their companies. They must maintain proper books of account and prepare annual accounts; they must file their accounts and returns promptly... Those who persistently fail to discharge their statutory obligations in this respect can expect to be disqualified, for an appropriate period of time, from using limited liability as one of the tools of their trade. The business community should be left in no doubt on this score."[54]

It is interesting to note that the Court of Appeal used this general approach as a basis for increasing the period of disqualification imposed by the trial judge from three years to five years. There are several other cases which support the view that the CDDA is intended primarily to offer dual protection to the public by taking disqualified directors out of circulation and by encouraging those who remain to act responsibly so improving the overall standard of management within companies.[55] A similar view was expressed by the National Audit Office in a report published in 1993 which reviewed the functions of the Insolvency Service's Disqualification Unit:

"The objectives under the Act are ... to protect the commercial world and the public at large by effective action against the abuse of limited liability through disqualification of individuals for periods determined by the courts ... further, by deterrence and by the promulgation of orders made by the courts, to contribute to fostering the integrity of markets generally and improving the standards of com-

---

[53] [1998] 2 All E.R. 124 at 131–132, [1998] 2 B.C.L.C. 646 at 654–655, [1998] B.C.C. 836 at 843.
[54] [1993] B.C.L.C. 896 at 899–900, [1993] B.C.C. 312 at 315.
[55] See, *e.g. Re Blackspur Group plc, Re Atlantic Computer Systems plc* [1998] 1 W.L.R. 422, [1998] 1 B.C.L.C. 676, [1998] B.C.C. 11, CA. The sabre-rattling tone of the DTI press releases cited earlier in the footnotes suggests that the politics of disqualification are dominated by the idea of deterrence and the need to promote public confidence.

pany stewardship in particular, but without inhibiting genuine enterprise and entrepreneurial management."[56]

This quote from an official source again shows that the main concern of policy makers has been to promote a climate of corporate responsibility without de-emphasising the role of the limited company as a vehicle for business.[57]

Is disqualification under CDDA, s. 2 a punishment?

2.19 It was stated by the Court of Appeal (Criminal Division) in the case of *R. v. Young* that a disqualification order made under CDDA, s. 2 is "unquestionably a punishment".[58] The court went on to state, *per* Brooke J., that a criminal court exercising jurisdiction under section 2 was in "a quite different situation" from a civil court exercising jurisdiction under section 6. Thus, the broad view in *Young* was that the purpose of disqualification under section 2 should be regarded as being totally different from the purpose of disqualification under the core unfitness provisions of the CDDA administered by the civil courts.[59] Although expressed at appellate level, this is an isolated view which can be criticised for the following reasons:

(1) When a criminal court considers disqualifying a person under section 2, it is first and foremost exercising jurisdiction *under the CDDA*. It just so happens that within the scheme of the legislation, this jurisdiction is ancillary to the court's primary criminal jurisdiction. Given the history and evolution of the CDDA and its overall concentration on regulating abuses of limited liability, there seems little justification for saying that disqualification under section 2 is somehow qualitatively different from disqualification under any other provision of the Act. A common approach to disqualification founded primarily on principles of public protection seems more appropriate. This criticism of *Young* can be supported with reference to the unitary features of the legislation identified above in para. 2.01.[60] Disqualification by the court under sec-

---

[56] National Audit Office, *The Insolvency Service Executive Agency: Company Director Disqualification* (1993), p. 4. This report cast grave doubt over whether the stated objectives of the CDDA were being met. Its main thrust was that insufficient numbers of unfit directors were being processed by the courts to achieve the twin aims of protection and deterrence, a criticism taken up in the 18th Report of the Committee of Public Accounts (1994 H.C. 167), *Insolvency Service Executive Agency: Company Director Disqualification*. For a more recent critical assessment of how the legislation is functioning when judged against its overall objectives see A. Hicks, *Disqualification of Directors: No Hiding Place for the Unfit?* (A.C.C.A, Research Report No. 59, 1998). Like the National Audit Office report, Hicks draws on empirical research to support his criticisms. His paper also stands as a set of proposals for reform. There is no systematic attempt in this book to study the operation of the CDDA using the methodology adopted by the NAO and Hicks. However, where possible, the book seeks to acquaint readers through footnotes with functional criticisms of the legislation and areas which are likely candidates for reform. It should be noted that the National Audit Office has now published a further report entitled *Company Director Disqualification—A Follow-up Report* (May 1999) which suggests that matters have improved since the publication of the earlier report.
[57] See para. 2.11 above. Hence perhaps the emphasis on general deterrence as a means of achieving at least some measure of *ex ante* regulation.
[58] (1990) 12 Cr.App.Rep.(S.) 262, [1990] Crim. L.R. 818, [1990] B.C.C. 549.
[59] This view is reflected in the reluctance sometimes shown by the criminal courts to use guidelines laid down by the civil courts in section 6 cases as a basis for determining the appropriate period of disqualification in section 2 cases: see paras 9.69–9.70.
[60] The criticism is echoed in more recent cases where it has been suggested that the criminal and civil courts should adopt a common approach to disqualification: see, *e.g. dicta* in *R. v. Cole, Lees & Birch* [1998] B.C.C. 87, CA; *Re Land Travel Ltd, Secretary of State for Trade and Industry v. Tjolle* [1998] 1 B.C.L.C. 333, [1998] B.C.C. 282. The need for a common approach is amply illustrated by the fact that the section 2 power is conferred on both the criminal and civil courts.

tion 2 (and, for that matter, sections 3, 4, 5 and 10) has exactly the same legal consequences as disqualification by the court under section 6. Both provisions should therefore be seen as operating for broadly similar ends.

(2) The view in *Young* contains the hint of a fallacy. It seems to assume that a disqualification imposed by a criminal court must necessarily be characterised as a punishment. This ignores the point that criminal sentencing may serve a variety of purposes such as general deterrence or rehabilitation as well as punishment. There is nothing wrong in principle with the idea of a criminal court exercising a jurisdiction which is concerned primarily with protection of the public. Much of the criminal law has a protective function anyway.

(3) Support for the view that the section 2 power should be regarded as protective rather than punitive can be derived from Commonwealth jurisdictions. Both Australia and Singapore, for example, have provisions under which directors are automatically disqualified on being convicted of certain criminal offences. These section 2 equivalents are regarded by the courts in those jurisdictions as being primarily concerned with protection of the public.[61]

R. v. Young is considered further in Chapter 9. For now it should be noted in passing that there is very little overt support for the idea that the principal purpose of disqualification is to punish directors despite the views expressed by Brooke J. in *Young*.

Re Lo-Line Electric Motors Ltd

2.20   It has been seen that, for the most part, the courts regard protection of the public as the main object of disqualification. At the same time, the courts generally concede that disqualification does have some negative or penal consequences for the disqualified person. The following oft-cited passage from *Re Lo-Line Electric Motors Ltd*[62] reflects this concession well:

"The primary purpose of [disqualification] is not to punish the individual but to protect the public against the future conduct of companies by persons whose past records as directors of insolvent companies have shown them to be a danger to creditors and others. Therefore the power is not fundamentally penal. But if the power to disqualify is exercised, disqualification does involve a substantial interference with the freedom of the individual. It follows that the rights of the individual must be fully protected."

Although *Lo-Line* was decided under the Companies Act 1985, s. 300, the statutory predecessor of CDDA, s. 6, it has been referred to with approval in several section 6 cases.[63] Thus, there is judicial recognition of the idea that disqualification impacts on the freedom of the disqualified person. This view that disqualification does have at least some impact on the disqualified person is difficult to contest. It imposes a legal disability on the disqualified and contravention of a CDDA disqualification carries

---

[61] See J. Cassidy, "Disqualification of Directors under the Corporations Law" (1995) 13 *Company and Securities Law Journal* 221 and A. Hicks, "Disqualification of Directors—Forty Years On" [1988] J.B.L. 27.
[62] [1988] Ch. 477, [1988] 3 W.L.R. 26, [1988] 2 All E.R. 692, [1988] B.C.L.C. 698, (1988) 4 B.C.C. 415.
[63] See, *e.g. Re Crestjoy Products Ltd* [1990] B.C.L.C. 677, [1990] B.C.C. 23; *Re Cedac Ltd, Secretary of State for Trade and Industry v. Langridge* [1991] Ch. 402, [1991] B.C.L.C. 543, [1991] B.C.C. 148, CA; *Re Gibson Davies Ltd* [1993] B.C.C. 11; *Re Living Images Ltd* [1996] 1 B.C.L.C. 348, [1996] B.C.C. 112; *Re Amaron Ltd* [1998] B.C.C. 264.

criminal penalties.[64] There is, however, considerable scope for disagreement about the *extent* to which disqualification interferes with individual freedom, a point taken up in the next section of this chapter.

What is the Nature of the Disqualification Process?

Is disqualification a quasi-criminal process?

2.21   According to the prevailing judicial consensus outlined above, the main purpose of disqualification under the CDDA is to protect the public although, at the same time, it is recognised that disqualification does have serious conseqences for the disqualified person. Any attempt to gauge the precise impact of disqualification on individual freedom is, however, fraught with difficulty and raises controversial questions about the proper scope of the CDDA and the nature of the disqualification process itself. There are broadly two competing views. At one extreme, disqualification might be seen as a civil/administrative regime which, much like a professional body exercising a disciplinary function over its members, operates to remove a trading privilege or licence in the public interest. This view sits comfortably with the rhetorical notion, expounded above, that the CDDA serves to protect the public from those who abuse the state-conferred privilege of limited liability rather than to punish the abuser. It follows, on this first analysis, that while disqualification clearly circumscribes the disqualified person's freedom to trade through the medium of a limited company, it does not restrict him altogether as he remains free to trade on his own account, albeit without limited liability. Alternatively, disqualification might be seen as a *quasi-criminal* process which interferes with an individual's *fundamental right* to trade, if he so chooses, with the benefit of limited liability. On this view, disqualification is regarded logically as penal because of its direct impact on the individual's rights and livelihood. Those who take this view would insist that disqualification is only a justifiable sanction where the defendant is "found guilty" of *culpable wrongdoing* (going beyond "mere incompetence") by a court applying the full protections and safeguards of criminal procedure in his favour. Clearly, this view has considerable ramifications for law and practice under the CDDA particularly in relation to legislative scope and issues of procedure.[65] It is now explored in greater detail.

2.22   The leading exponent of the view that disqualification is a quasi-criminal process is Professor Janet Dine.[66] Her work stems from a broad concern that many company law-related provisions administered for the most part by the civil courts, such as disqualification under the CDDA and wrongful trading under the Insolvency Act 1986, appear to be nothing more than criminal sanctions in disguise. Her argument proceeds from an analysis of the definition of crime which leads her to conclude that the most appropriate method of determining whether a particular legal rule is a rule of criminal or civil law is by reference to a series of indicators. She then analyses the

---

[64] See, *e.g. Re Manlon Trading Ltd, Official Receiver v. Aziz* [1996] Ch. 136, [1995] 3 W.L.R. 839, [1995] 4 All E.R. 14, [1995] 1 B.C.L.C. 578, [1995] B.C.C. 579, CA.

[65] This analysis of the nature of disqualification and its impact either in terms of a "privilege" view or a "rights" view was first put forward by V. Finch in "Disqualifying Directors: Issues of Rights, Privileges and Employment" (1993) 22 I.L.J. 35 as a basis for explaining inconsistencies in the approach taken by different judges in a number of section 6 cases.

[66] See variously, J. Dine, *Criminal Law in the Company Context* (1995), "Wrongful Trading—Quasi-Criminal Law" in *Insolvency Law and Practice* (H. Rajak ed. 1993), "Punishing Directors" [1994] J.B.L. 325 and "The Disqualification of Company Directors" (1988) 9 *The Company Lawyer* 213.

WHAT IS THE NATURE OF THE DISQUALIFICATION PROCESS?

CDDA regime in the context of these indicators[67] and concludes that, in many respects, disqualification strongly resembles a criminal sanction. In particular, she notes that disqualification is concerned, in a broad sense, with behaviour which harms the public and points to similarities between the disqualification process and criminal procedure. She also demonstrates the tendency of the courts in section 6 unfitness proceedings to determine unfitness by reference to a scale of culpability rather than by assessing the public's need for protection. Her overall conclusion is that the courts are administering a disqualification regime which has considerable penal elements without offering defendants anything like the safeguards provided for their counterparts in a criminal prosecution. Writing in 1988, Dine can be found lamenting the double failure of the civil courts to arrive at a proper legal classification of the CDDA regime and to acknowledge its uncanny resemblance to criminal process in these terms:

> "What is clear from the cases is that the courts regard disqualification as a serious matter. It is therefore disturbing that the classification of disqualification orders is unsettled. If they are akin to criminal sanctions as a number of indications ... appear to show then the director involved should be entitled to all the protections afforded to defendants in a criminal court, including the presumption of innocence, exact determination of the *mens rea* required, the criminal standard of proof, and the inability of the court to make 'assumptions' about behaviour in the absence of direct evidence. There is also a good case for better reporting of cases so that a proper 'law of sentencing' can be established."[68]

2.23 While it is now hardly possible to complain about a lack of reported disqualification cases, Dine's fundamental point concerning the ambivalence of disqualification still rings true today. It is possible to point to a number of features of law and practice under the CDDA which can be used to support her view:

(1) Disqualification involves the imposition of a legal disability which is wide in scope.[69] Thus, in administering a regime which operates to circumscribe individual freedom on the basis of a public interest justification, the courts are being asked to perform a function traditionally associated with the criminal law.

(2) The consensus view that disqualification is primarily concerned with public protection is easily reconcilable with Dine's view that it operates penally and is more akin to a criminal sanction. Most criminal sanctions have a protective as well as a punitive function.[70]

(3) The process of determining the appropriate period of disqualification is very similar to that of a criminal court sentencing a convicted offender. This has now been explicitly acknowledged by the Court of Appeal in *Re Westmid*

---

[67] The indicators used by Dine are:

    (1) Is the behaviour regarded as a moral wrong to be condemned?
    (2) Does the behaviour harm the public?
    (3) May the behaviour lead to the punishment of the defendant?
    (4) Are there similarities in procedure between this and core criminal cases?

[68] J. Dine, "The Disqualification of Company Directors", *op. cit.*, p. 218.
[69] On the consequences of disqualification and the extent of the prohibition, see generally, Chap. 12.
[70] The notion that a protective rule cannot operate punitively is the reverse of the *Young* fallacy alluded to in para. 2.19. It was seen in para. 2.20 that the courts have rightly not accepted this notion. As Dine herself puts it in "Wrongful Trading—Quasi-Criminal Law?", *op. cit.*, p. 175: "It is by no means clear why the punishment of the individual should necessarily be seen as an aim which excludes the protection of the public. The law against rape seeks to achieve both."

Packing Services Ltd, Secretary of State for Trade and Industry v. Griffiths.
Per Lord Woolf:

> "Despite the fact that the courts have said that disqualification is not a
> 'punishment', in truth the exercise that is being engaged in is little differ-
> ent from any sentencing exercise. The period of disqualification must
> reflect the gravity of the offence. It must contain deterrent elements. That
> is what sentencing is all about, and that is what fixing the appropriate
> period of disqualification is all about." [71]

It will be seen in Chapter 5 that the courts do take certain factors into account
by way of mitigation which strengthens the sentencing analogy.

(4) Mandatory disqualification under section 6 is capable of operating penally.
Once the court makes a finding on the evidence that the defendant's past conduct amounts to unfitness, it must disqualify him for at least the statutory
minimum of two years regardless of whether it is still necessary to protect the
public from that person by keeping him "off the road". In this way, a court
could well be forced to disqualify a defendant who has learned the lessons of a
previous business failure and built a new company which is being run properly
and successfully at the date of the hearing. This penal aspect of the legislation
is acknowledged by the courts and justified by reference to deterrence objectives. As Hoffmann L.J. put it in *Re Grayan Building Services Ltd*:

> "The purpose of making disqualification mandatory was to ensure that
> everyone whose conduct had fallen below the appropriate standard was
> disqualified for at least two years, whether in the individual case the court
> thought that this was necessary in the public interest or not. Parliament
> has decided that it is occasionally necessary to disqualify a company
> director to encourage the others." [72]

(5) It is currently not possible to compromise disqualification proceedings in the
same way that ordinary civil litigation can be compromised. While summary
procedures have been devised so that disqualification proceedings can be disposed of expeditiously without a full contested trial, these are subject to close
supervision by the court. The defendant cannot simply agree to accept a disqualification without the court making at least some assessment of the merits
and the appropriate period of disqualification. In this sense disqualification is
more like a criminal than a civil proceeding. [73]

Thus, there is something to be said for the view that disqualification is a quasi-criminal
process or, at very least, a hybrid process.

2.24   At the same time, there is also much to be said for the view that disqualification is a civil/administrative process. Many areas of business and professional life
are regulated by administrative or disciplinary tribunals which discharge public law
functions. The idea (stemming from the concession theory of companies) that limited

---

[71] [1998] 2 All E.R. 124 at 132, [1998] 2 B.C.L.C. 646 at 655, [1998] B.C.C. 836 at 843.
[72] [1995] Ch. 241 at 253, [1995] 3 W.L.R. 1 at 11, [1995] 1 B.C.L.C. 276 at 284, [1995] B.C.C. 554 at 574.
Similar views were expressed in *Re Crestjoy Products Ltd* [1990] B.C.L.C. 677, [1990] B.C.C. 23 and *Re
Land Travel Ltd, Secretary of State for Trade and Industry v. Tjolle* [1998] 1 B.C.L.C. 333, [1998] B.C.C.
282.
[73] On compromise generally and the *Carecraft* summary procedure in particular, see Chap. 8.

liability amounts to a state-conferred privilege or licence which the state can also revoke amounts to a plausible theory of disqualification. On this view, the removal of the privilege is justified in the wider state or public interest and so protection of the public rather than the impact on the individual is the dominant theme. Equally, on this view, the rules of natural justice operate to protect the individual and these should be respected.[74] A few points can be made in favour of the view that disqualification is more of a civil/administrative than a penal process:

(1) One assumption underlying the "quasi-criminal" view is that disqualification may have a very serious impact on the individual's livelihood.[75] This may be overstated. Disqualification does not prevent the disqualified person from carrying on a business either as a sole trader or in partnership, a point frequently emphasised by the courts.[76]

(2) Although at first sight, mandatory disqualification under section 6 appears to be penal (see para. 2.23 above), there is scope within the scheme of the legislation for the courts to ameliorate its impact. The disqualified person can always apply for permission to act as a director etc. of a specified company or companies. In a case where the court is obliged to disqualify even though it may no longer be in the public interest to do so, it is likely that an application for permission would be treated favourably.[77]

(3) The European Commission of Human Rights has expressed the view that disqualification proceedings constitute a dispute over "civil rights and obligations" within the meaning of Article 6(1) of the European Convention on Human Rights.[78] This means that the defendant is entitled to certain procedural rights such as a fair and expeditious trial. The English courts have also ruled that civil disqualification proceedings do not involve a "criminal charge" with the consequence that the defendant is not entitled to the additional safeguards in Article 6 which apply exclusively to criminal proceedings. In *R. v. Secretary of State for Trade and Industry ex. parte McCormick*,[79] a defendant in section 8 proceedings sought judicial review of the Secretary of State's decision to rely on compelled evidence obtained from him by company inspectors who had been appointed to investigate the affairs of the relevant company under section 432 of the Companies Act 1985. It was argued that the claim against him in the disqualification proceedings was a "criminal charge" within the meaning of Article 6(1) of the European Con-

---

[74] See further, Finch, *op. cit.* Finch draws a distinction between a "rights" view and a "privilege" view of disqualification. On the "rights" view, disqualification amounts to a serious interference with *substantive* rights whereas on the "privilege" view disqualification involves a public policy decision that pays due regard to the defendant's *procedural* rights. Procedural rights presumably include a right to have the issue of one's disqualification determined in accordance with Article 6 of the European Convention on Human Rights and/or the rules of natural justice.

[75] *ibid.*, p. 37.

[76] See, *e.g. Re Southbourne Sheet Metal Co. Ltd* [1992] B.C.L.C. 361, [1991] B.C.C. 732; *Re Chartmore Ltd* [1990] B.C.L.C. 673 and *Re Probe Data Systems Ltd (No. 3), Secretary of State for Industry v. Desai* [1991] B.C.L.C. 586, [1991] B.C.C. 428 all cited in Finch, *op. cit.* See also, *R. v. Secretary of State for Trade and Industry ex. parte McCormick* [1998] B.C.C. 381. Note that there is now some controversy as to whether a disqualified person is free to trade in partnership in the wake of the Insolvent Partnerships Order 1994 (S.I. 1994 No. 2421). The line taken in A. Mithani and S. Wheeler, *The Disqualification of Company Directors* (1st ed., 1996) is that the Insolvent Partnerships Order appears, rather oddly, to bring partnership within the scope of a disqualification order. On this point generally, see Chaps 3 and 12.

[77] See generally, Chap. 13.

[78] See *EDC v. United Kingdom* [1998] B.C.C. 370.

[79] [1998] B.C.C. 381, QBD and CA. See also *Secretary of State for Trade and Industry v. McCormick* [1998] 1 B.C.L.C. 18, Ch.D.

vention on Human Rights with the result that the use of the compelled evidence infringed his right, as a defendant in criminal proceedings, to be protected from self-incrimination. The Court of Appeal held that the Secretary of State was not bound to treat disqualification proceedings as if they involved a "criminal charge". It was reasonable for the Secretary of State to exercise the powers in the CDDA on the footing that disqualification involved nothing more than the withdrawal of a civil right. As the defendant's right to a fair trial under article 6 did not necessarily require him to be treated the same way in a civil case as in a criminal case, it was reasonable for the Secretary of State to rely on compelled evidence in civil disqualification proceedings. The decision in *McCormick* suggests that the disqualification process is seen from the human rights perspective as a civil/administrative law process rather than a criminal process. There can be little doubt that defendants will increasingly take points on the Convention following the enactment of the Human Rights Act 1998 and it remains to be seen whether the current view will hold.

Whatever the merits of these two broad views of the disqualification process, the analysis above illustrates that there are difficulties in drawing a clear line between civil and penal proceedings. This book cannot hope to resolve such problems of classification. However, it is important to note that the problem is likely to resurface in the courts and have an impact (whether explicit or implicit) on the way in which individual judges apply and construe specific provisions of the CDDA. This point is well illustrated by the differences of opinion which surfaced in the Court of Appeal in the case of *Re Cedac Ltd, Secretary of State for Trade and Industry v. Langridge*.[80]

Re Cedac Ltd, Secretary of State for Trade and Industry v. Langridge

2.25   This case concerned a short point arising from the Secretary of State's failure to comply with the procedural requirements of CDDA, s. 16(1). One effect of section 16(1) is that the Secretary of State is required to give the intended defendant to a proposed application for an order under section 6 at least ten days' notice of his intention to commence proceedings.[81] In *Cedac*, the defendant had received the ten-day notice on April 11, 1989 and the proceedings had then been issued on April 21, 1989. However, it was established in the earlier case of *Re Jaymar Management Ltd*[82] that the period of ten days must be calculated by excluding both the day on which the notice is given and the day on which proceedings are to be commenced. Accordingly, the notice should have been served no later than April 10, 1989. The short question was whether or not this failure to comply strictly with section 16(1) invalidated the proceedings or whether it was merely a procedural irregularity.[83] The question received two different answers. A majority of the Court of Appeal held that section 16(1) was directory rather than mandatory and that, as a consequence, the failure to comply did not render the proceedings a nullity. In a powerful dissenting judgment, Nourse L.J. took the opposite view. He thought that the ten-day notice requirement was mandatory and that the Secretary of State's non-compliance did therefore invalidate the entire proceedings. What is clear is that these two opposing conclusions stemmed from differing views about the nature of the disqualification pro-

---

[80] [1991] Ch. 402, [1991] B.C.L.C. 543, [1991] B.C.C. 148.
[81] On section 16(1) generally, see Chap. 6.
[82] [1990] B.C.L.C. 617, [1990] B.C.C. 303.
[83] In the overall context of the case this was an important question. If the proceedings were invalid, the Secretary of State could only have then commenced fresh proceedings with the permission of the court as the two-year time limit in section 7(2) for the commencement of section 6 proceedings had long since expired.

cess itself. The emphasis in the majority judgments is firmly on the idea that disqualification is a non-penal process primarily concerned with protecting the public and withdrawing the privilege of limited liability from those who abuse it.[84] Thus, while the majority accepted that the object of section 16(1) was to provide some form of protection to the individual, they gave much greater priority to the broader public interest than to the issue of individual rights in striking an overall balance. Taking this approach, Legatt L.J. felt content to characterise the ten-day notice as one which is "intended to inform of intentions rather than protect rights". By way of contrast, Nourse L.J. saw disqualification as being more of a penal process and so placed much more emphasis on safeguarding the individual. He characterised a disqualification order as "a substantial interference with the individual's freedom to do the job which he has chosen to do". It followed that he was unhappy to reach a conclusion which in any way diminished the protection potentially afforded to the individual by section 16(1).[85]

2.26 The Court of Appeal decision in *Cedac* shows how the debate about the nature of the disqualification process can influence the way in which cases under the CDDA are decided. In *Cedac*, the court's overall view of the status of the procedural provision in section 16(1) turned ultimately on Balcombe and Legatt L.JJ.'s impression that disqualification is essentially non-penal. There is then scope for subtle inconsistencies of judicial approach arising from differing conceptions of disqualification. Much may depend on where the judge chooses to place the emphasis in the process of striking a balance between protection of the public interest and the rights of the individual. Questions about the nature of the disqualification process may therefore have some considerable impact in shaping the substantive law under the CDDA and implications also for practice and procedure.[86]

Other factors concerning the process which may influence the court's approach

2.27 Lord Hoffmann took the opportunity to make a number of pertinent observations about the disqualification process when delivering the Fourth Annual Leonard Sainer Lecture in 1996. He gave four reasons why, in his view, the courts are uncomfortable over accepting the idea that disqualification is purely protective. These can be summarised as follows:[87]

(1) Disqualification is a very serious matter which may, in practice, make it difficult for the disqualified person to earn a living although, in theory, it does not prevent him from trading on his own account. Furthermore, a finding of unfitness under section 6 results in mandatory disqualification and this is so even

---

[84] For a flavour, see the extract from Balcombe L.J.'s judgment cited in para. 2.17.
[85] Nourse L.J. would have been prepared to give permission for fresh proceedings to be commenced out of time. Note that in deciding the case at first instance, Mummery J. had adopted a similar line to that taken by Nourse L.J.: see [1990] B.C.C. 555. For criticism of the majority view, see Dine, "Wrongful Trading—Quasi-Criminal Law?", *op. cit.*, pp. 175–176.
[86] Several areas of law and practice are affected. Different views about the nature of the disqualification process may, for example, lead to arguments about whether the prohibition in section 1(1) should be construed broadly or narrowly (see Chap. 12) and over the approach which should be adopted by the courts in determining unfitness (see Chap. 4). On this latter point see V. Finch, "Disqualification of Directors: A Plea for Competence" (1990) 53 M.L.R. 385 which illustrates the failure of the courts to establish a clear rationale for determining whether managerial incompetence amounts to unfitness. Procedural questions concerning, for example, amendment of proceedings, admissibility of evidence and standard of proof are similarly affected (see Chap. 6). The enactment of the Human Rights Act 1998 will probably only muddy the waters further.
[87] For the full text, see (1997) 18 *The Company Lawyer* 194. His Lordship's comments are mostly directed to section 6 proceedings.

where the misconduct happened several years ago and the director has since gone on to run a successful company while proceedings were pending. The difficulty with mandatory disqualification is that, if the court thinks the sentence is too harsh, it will be reluctant to make a finding of unfitness in the first place.

(2) The law does not impose any entry requirements on directors. No qualifications are required for becoming a director. It is not easy for the court to fix standards of conduct and competence *ex post facto* in the context of disqualification proceedings.

(3) There is an element of arbitrariness as to who ends up on the receiving end of disqualification proceedings. In the section 6 context, it depends first on the misconduct being followed by the company's insolvency. This is a matter of luck. In Lord Hoffmann's own words:

> "A rise in the market can compensate for the effect of some perfectly hair-raising piece of incompetence. One is very conscious of how thin is the line between success leading to wealth and a knighthood and failure leading to disqualification or even imprisonment."

(4) The operation of the process is necessarily weighted against those on the end of disqualification proceedings. This is particularly true of defendants in section 6 proceedings who, as former directors of insolvent companies, are likely to be impecunious and will not be able to afford to instruct lawyers to prepare their defence unless they are on legal aid.

2.28   For these reasons, Lord Hoffmann considers it unlikely that the courts will disqualify a director on the grounds of mere incompetence but will look for some breach of what he described as "accepted commercial morality".[88] These extra-judicial observations attributable to one of our most senior judges provide an interesting insight into judicial attitudes. It would appear that Lord Hoffmann instinctively regards disqualification as a quasi-penal process judging, in particular, from his opening comment on mandatory disqualification.[89] His comment concerning the *ex post facto* nature of disqualification also betrays a degree of discomfort about the operation of the CDDA within the overall structure of company law. It was seen in paras 2.03 to 2.16 how company law gives primacy to the objective of facilitating enterprise. Access to limited liability in the form of a private company is relatively cheap and beset by very few initial formalities. Directorship is not a true profession in any accepted sense of the term and, as Lord Hoffmann points out, individuals are not required to obtain any qualifications before assuming the office of director. It is perhaps not surprising to find some instinctive resistance to a process which sets standards of conduct "after the

---

[88] On the vexed issue of disqualification for incompetence see further Chap. 5 and *Re Barings plc (No. 5), Secretary of State for Trade and Industry v. Baker* [1999] 1 B.C.L.C. 433. It is suggested that directors can and should be disqualified on grounds of incompetence given the wider objectives of the CDDA described in paras 2.11–2.16. See also *Re Continental Assurance Co of London plc* [1997] 1 B.C.L.C. 48 at 57–58, [1996] B.C.C. 888 at 895–896 where, rejecting the defendant's submission that the CDDA was directed only to cases of abuse of limited liability by owner-managers, Chadwick J. stated that those dealing with the relevant company were entitled to expect that the defendant (a non-executive director and corporate financier) was sufficiently competent to be able to read and understand the company's statutory accounts and satisfy himself that transactions between the company and its subsidiaries were properly reflected in the accounts of the subsidiaries.

[89] See para. 2.23.

event" in circumstances where the law imposes no *ex ante* standard.[90] His lordship's final point, which is really a point about access to justice, is also significant. It suggests, whether rightly or wrongly, that the courts may be influenced in their approach to CDDA proceedings by the fact that the odds seem to be stacked in favour of the state over the individual. An important point flowing from this is that the courts may end up balancing the public interest in disqualifying miscreant directors against the broader public interest in the fair and expeditious administration of justice. Such a balancing act is perhaps inevitable given that disqualification is primarily a court-based process and that the need for improved efficiency in the administration of justice is currently high on the political agenda. It is important to appreciate therefore that *the impact which the litigation process itself* has on the individual may increasingly influence the approach of the courts under the CDDA.[91] Taken as a whole, Lord Hoffmann's observations suggest that the civil courts are generally pursuing a careful and judicious line in relation to disqualification.

SUMMARY AND CONCLUSION

2.29 The first two chapters have attempted to provide a background and context for the detailed exposition which follows in the remainder of the book. Two main points have emerged. First, while it is true to say that the evolution of directors' disqualification has been patchy, there now appears to be a relatively coherent legislative scheme. All the relevant powers are in one place and, as seen earlier in this chapter, the legislation has a number of unifying features. It is clear also that the legislation was conceived primarily as a creditor protection measure, the basic aim being to combat abuse of limited liability within private companies. This is reflected in the fact that if a disqualified person breaches the relevant prohibition he is exposed to personal liability for the relevant company's debts under CDDA, s. 15. At the same time, as was pointed

---

[90] Several commentators are critical of this apparent imbalance. Hicks, *Disqualification of Directors: No Hiding Place for the Unfit?* (A.C.C.A Research Report No. 59, 1998) at pp. 76–77 criticises the lack of any requirement to publicise directors' obligations under the law in a systematic way when a director takes up office and the lack of any positive standards of best practice. He recommends the enactment of a "Code for Creditors" which would bring together the principles that have been developed by the courts under the CDDA. Hicks argues that such a code could be used to inform directors (of private companies, in particular) of their obligations and serve as a set of *ex ante* standards against which directors could be judged in disqualification proceedings. Dine, *Criminal Law in the Company Context* (1995), p. 102 appears to favour the imposition of entrance qualifications. *In extremis*, Lightman J. has suggested extra-judicially that directors should be subject to some form of licensing requirement: see "The Challenges Ahead: Address to the Insolvency Lawyers' Association" [1996] J.B.L. 113. The Institute of Directors has introduced a form of voluntary "chartered" qualification: see CCH Company Law Newsletter, July 8, 1999.

[91] This kind of balancing exercise is carried out in determining applications for permission to commence section 6 proceedings out of time brought under section 7(2): see generally Chap. 7. For other judicial comments on the potentially oppressive impact of disqualification as a litigation process, see, *e.g. Re Rex Williams Leisure plc, Secretary of State for Trade and Industry v. Warren* [1994] Ch. 350, [1994] 2 B.C.L.C. 555, [1994] B.C.C. 551, CA; *Re Land Travel Ltd, Secretary of State for Trade and Industry v. Tjolle* [1998] 1 B.C.L.C. 333, [1998] B.C.C. 282. For an example of a decision at an interim stage which clearly reflects the view that the costs of disqualification proceedings are potentially punitive, see *Re Barings plc, Secretary of State for Trade and Industry v. Baker* [1998] Ch. 356, [1998] 1 B.C.L.C. 16, [1998] B.C.C. 888. The other important development in this context is the enactment of the Human Rights Act 1998 which incorporates the European Convention on Human Rights into English law. The jurisprudence on Article 6 of the Convention (right to a fair trial) is already beginning to have some impact in disqualification proceedings. In this respect, any lengthy delay on the part of the state in pursuing proceedings may give rise to a Convention remedy: see *EDC v. United Kingdom* [1998] B.C.C. 370 (though note that this was a first-stage decision by the European Commission of Human Rights rather than a decision of the full court). Also, on Lord Hoffmann's final point, it is an established principle of Convention jurisprudence that everyone who is a party to proceedings, whether criminal or civil, should have a reasonable opportunity of presenting his case to the court under conditions which do not place him at a substantial disadvantage as against his opponent (so-called "equality of arms": see, *e.g. Kaufman v. Belgium No. 10938/84, 50 D.R. 98, 115 (1986)*).

out in paras 2.13–2.15, the CDDA does encompass wider objectives of shareholder, employee and consumer protection. It is also suggested that the application of the CDDA is not restricted to cases involving abuse of limited liability but is directed, in a broad sense, at those who act improperly in the management of companies. Furthermore, the CDDA is not concerned merely with keeping wrongdoers "off the road", but also with the setting and raising of standards of conduct in the management of companies generally. Secondly, it appears that the unresolved debate about the nature of the disqualification process does have a considerable impact on law and practice under the CDDA. As a result, there is a likelihood that the kind of subtle differences of judicial approach that surfaced in the *Cedac* case will continue to arise from time to time. This makes the task of giving advice and predicting outcomes all the more difficult and has led some to question the efficacy and even the appropriateness of disqualification as a method of protecting the public.[92] The extra-judicial remarks of Lord Hoffmann referred to above suggest also that judicial perceptions of disqualification, placing it in the wider contexts of company law and the administration of justice, may also influence the way in which the courts apply the CDDA. The problem of whether disqualification should be classified as a penal or non-penal process, in particular, is one that is not easily resolved and is therefore likely to resurface on occasions in the courts.

---

[92] See, *e.g.* Finch, *op. cit.* and K.T.W. Ong, "Disqualification of directors: a faulty regime" (1998) 19 *The Company Lawyer* 7.

CHAPTER 3

Disqualification for Unfitness: Preliminary Matters

INTRODUCTION

3.01   The next three chapters examine the CDDA's core provisions on unfitness found in sections 6, 8 and 9. As the majority of disqualification orders are made under section 6 on the application of either the Secretary of State for Trade and Industry or the official receiver,[1] attention is focused principally on the elements which have to be made out before the court is obliged to make an order under that provision. Much of this chapter is concerned with the background to and inception of disqualification proceedings under section 6 and with a number of preliminary matters that must be established before the court goes on to consider the substantive issue of unfitness in such proceedings. The most significant element of section 6, which goes to the heart of the CDDA, is the concept of unfitness itself. Chapters 4 and 5 are devoted to a working exposition of this burgeoning area of the law. Section 8 is also covered in each of Chapters 3, 4 and 5. Although section 8 creates a distinct power which differs from section 6 in a number of respects, it too is concerned with unfitness. Chapters 6 to 8 then deal with various aspects of practice and procedure relating to civil disqualification proceedings generally (with particular reference to the unfitness provisions).

THE INCEPTION OF SECTION 6 PROCEEDINGS: REPORTING BY OFFICE HOLDERS

Statutory reporting obligations

3.02   As will be seen further below, jurisdiction under section 6 is only triggered where a relevant company or companies "becomes insolvent" (meaning, in general terms, the subject of a formal insolvency regime).[2] The effect of section 7(1) is that an application for a disqualification order under section 6 can only be made by the Secretary of State for Trade and Industry or, in the case of a company in compulsory liquidation, by the official receiver if the Secretary of State so directs. In practice, the Secretary of State's responsibilities in relation to the commencement and conduct of proceedings are discharged by the Insolvency Service's Disqualification Unit.[3] In gathering information about directors of insolvent companies who may arguably be unfit, the Disqualification Unit depends to a considerable extent on the co-operation of

---

[1] Any reference hereafter to the Secretary of State should be read as including a reference to the official receiver.
[2] See para. 3.50.
[3] An executive agency of the Department of Trade and Industry: see further, National Audit Office, *The Insolvency Executive Agency: Company Director Disqualification* (1993) and the 18th Report of the Committee of Public Accounts (1994 H.C. 167).

insolvency practitioners and the official receiver.[4] To reinforce co-operation, section 7(3) requires the relevant office holder of an insolvent company to report to the Secretary of State forthwith if it appears as respects a person who is or has been a director of that company that the conditions mentioned in section 6(1) are satisfied. In other words, the mandatory obligation to report a director arises if it appears to the office holder that *the court* would be likely to make a finding of unfitness against the director in the terms of section 6(1)(b). Thus, the office holder performs an extremely important screening function which underpins the entire disqualification process.[5] At the same time, the view of the insolvency practitioner is not decisive. It is for the Secretary of State to consider the available evidence and form a view as to whether proceedings should be commenced.[6] For the purposes of mandatory reporting the relevant office holder is:

(1) The official receiver in the case of a company or an insolvent partnership which is being wound up by the court in England and Wales.

(2) The liquidator in the case of a company which is being wound up voluntarily.

(3) The liquidator in the case of a company which is being wound up by the court in Scotland (where there is no equivalent of the official receiver).

(4) The administrator in the case of a company or an insolvent partnership in relation to which an administration order is in force.

(5) The administrative receiver in the case of a company which is in administrative receivership.

---

[4] The relevant insolvency practitioner will not necessarily be the only source of information. In the disqualification proceedings which followed the administration of Barings plc, the primary information came from the reports of inspectors appointed in Singapore and the report of the Board of Banking Supervision, H.C. 673 (1994–1995), July 1995: see generally, *Re Barings plc, Secretary of State for Trade and Industry v. Baker (No. 2)* [1998] 1 B.C.L.C. 590, [1999] B.C.C. 146. In other cases, the Secretary of State may also have the benefit of information and documents obtained pursuant to a power in Part XIV of the Companies Act 1985, especially in circumstances where the exercise of such a power is a precursor to the compulsory winding up of the relevant company on the Secretary of State's petition under section 124A of the Insolvency Act 1986.

[5] A survey of insolvency practitioners conducted by Andrew Hicks in 1997 revealed that office holders are not clear as to exactly when unfit conduct should be reported: see A. Hicks, *Disqualification of Directors: No Hiding Place for the Unfit?* (A.C.C.A. Research Report No. 59, 1998) especially Chaps 4 and 5. Over half of those who responded said that they report a director if they identify an *element* of unfit conduct. Others said that they report in cases where they think that the Disqualification Unit would want to investigate further. A handful said that they report in cases where they are of the personal view that the director should be disqualified. Strikingly, none of the survey participants said that they apply the statutory test in section 7(3) *i.e.* report a director in circumstances where it appears that *the court* would make a finding of unfitness. In the interests of consistency in reporting, Hicks argues that the law should be amended to require insolvency practitioners to report significant matters *indicative* of unfitness (in particular, any matters falling directly within Sched. 1) whether or not there is a *prima facie* case of unfitness viewing such matters cumulatively. This makes abundant sense given the difficulty of identifying the point at which the line between "mere misconduct" and unfit conduct is crossed and the refusal of the Court of Appeal in *Sevenoaks* to countenance a general test: see discussion on general judicial guidance in Chap. 4. Guidance notes issued by the Insolvency Service and Statement of Insolvency Practice 4: *Disqualification of Directors in England and Wales* issued by the Society of Practitioners of Insolvency in September 1998 refer practitioners to Sched. 1 and other matters not mentioned in the Schedule to which the Disqualification Unit attaches importance. In practice, this means that office holders are encouraged to report *indicative* conduct along the lines of the suggested reform. A further advantage of the indicative approach is that the Unit can build up a file and track the conduct of a director across a series of insolvent companies even though each insolvency involves a different office holder.

[6] See discussion in *Re Launchexcept Ltd, Secretary of State for Trade and Industry v. Tillman* [1999] B.C.C. 703; *Re Pinemoor Ltd* [1997] B.C.C. 708 and *Re Park House Properties Ltd* [1997] 2 B.C.L.C. 530, [1998] B.C.C. 847. In the *Barings* proceedings, at least one of the defendants was disqualified by the court even though the administrators were of the view that his conduct was not such as to make him unfit under section 6. Equally, an insolvency practitioner may form the view that a director's conduct is such as to make him unfit only for the Secretary of State to arrive at a different view.

The supervisor of a free standing corporate voluntary arrangement is not under a mandatory reporting obligation.[7]

Section 7(4)

3.03   A further power of information gathering is vested in the Secretary of State and official receiver by section 7(4). This enables the Secretary of State and official receiver to require the office holders listed above to provide further information and permit inspection of books and records relevant to the conduct of the director in question.[8] It appears from the decision of Vinelott J. in *Re Polly Peck International plc, ex. parte the joint administrators* that an office holder can disclose transcripts of private examinations conducted under section 236 of the Insolvency Act 1986 to the Secretary of State even if he has given an assurance that the transcripts would only be disclosed for the purposes of the relevant insolvency process. This is because the purposes of liquidation, adminstrative receivership and administration include the gathering of information as to the conduct of the company's directors and the obligation to report on such matters to the Secretary of State.[9] By the same reasoning, it appears that the Secretary of State or the official receiver could request production of the transcripts under section 7(4). In the light of *Soden v. Burns, R. v. Secretary of State for Trade and Industry, ex. parte Soden*[10] and *Re Atlantic Computers plc*,[11] a question arises as to whether notice should be given to a person who has been compelled to provide information or documents under section 236 of the Insolvency Act before the office holder passes any such information or documents to the Secretary of State under section 7(4). It is suggested that notice is not required. As explained above with reference to the *Polly Peck* decision, the subsequent use by the Secretary of State of such compelled material for the purposes of considering and/or bringing disqualification proceedings is inherent in the statutory purpose of section 236. The position is analogous to that where powers of investigation are exercised under Part XIV of the Companies Act 1985. In such cases, there is a statutory gateway in sections 451A and 449 of the Companies Act which permits the Secretary of State to make use of any information or documents obtained in the course of an investigation under Part XIV for the purposes of disqualification proceedings.[12] In relation to Part XIV, the Secretary of State's practice is not to give notice of the potential use of compelled information to the person

---

[7] This is consistent with the definition of "becomes insolvent" in section 6(2) the effect of which is that the court has no jurisdiction in relation to companies that have entered a free standing corporate voluntary arrangement. It is questionable why directors should be allowed to escape the clutches of section 6 simply because they manage to avoid a winding up. One justification for not requiring the supervisor of a corporate voluntary arrangement to report on the directors' conduct is that to do otherwise would undermine the relationship between the directors and the insolvency practitioner and thereby reduce its effectiveness as a medium for corporate rescue. However, the same might be said of administration and yet administrators do have a statutory obligation to report. As a result, where a corporate voluntary arrangement is coupled with an administration order (as contemplated by the Insolvency Act 1986, s. 8(3)(b)) then the insolvency practitioner is obliged to make a report in his capacity as the administrator if he determines that the conditions in section 6(1) are satisfied.

[8] For circumstances in which disqualification proceedings may be jeopardised if the Secretary of State does not avail himself of the power see *dictum* of Clarke L.J. in *Re Launchexcept Ltd, Secretary of State for Trade and Industry v. Tillman* [1999] B.C.C. 703. The existence of the power in section 7(4) does not necessarily mean that the Secretary of State can be compelled to disclose documents which are in the custody of an office holder to the defendant. In *Re Lombard Shipping and Forwarding Ltd* [1993] B.C.L.C. 238, [1992] B.C.C. 700 it was held that documents held by joint administrative receivers were not within the power of the Secretary of State for the purpose of ordering disclosure because the court has a discretion whether or not to order an office holder to comply with a request on an application under section 7(4) and so the Secretary of State has no absolute right to insist on production.

[9] [1994] B.C.C. 15.

[10] [1996] 1 W.L.R. 1512, [1996] 3 All E.R. 967, [1996] 2 B.C.L.C. 636, [1997] B.C.C. 308.

[11] [1998] B.C.C. 200.

[12] See further from para. 3.61.

who was compelled to provide it, in circumstances where its use is permitted by the statutory gateway. In *Soden v. Burns* and *Atlantic Computers*, the relevant information had been obtained under compulsion by inspectors appointed pursuant to section 432 of the Companies Act 1985. However, there was no statutory gateway permitting the information to be used either for the purposes of the insolvency of the relevant companies (section 236 of the Insolvency Act does not fall within the gateway in sections 451A and 449) or for private litigation. Hence, when the court was considering whether to compel further dissemination of the information (in *Soden v. Burns* by way of an order under section 236 and in *Atlantic Computers* by way of an order for disclosure), the persons who had been compelled to provide the information had to be notified first in order to give them an opportunity to object to its use for a purpose falling outside the scope of sections 451A and 449. As such, the cases of *Soden v. Burns* and *Atlantic Computers* can be distinguished from one where compelled information is used for a purpose expressly contemplated by statute, in which case notice is not required.

3.04   The Secretary of State may seek to remedy any non-compliance or inadequate compliance with a request under section 7(4) by applying to the court under rule 6 of the Insolvent Companies (Reports on Conduct of Directors) Rules 1996 (which are discussed generally below). On such an application, the court may make an order directing compliance within such period as may be specified. The court may provide in the order that all costs of and incidental to the application shall be borne by the relevant office holder. Paragraph 18 of the Disqualification Practice Direction provides that applications under section 7(4) may be made under CPR, Pt 8 or by application notice (under CPR, Pt 23) in existing disqualification proceedings. A number of issues arise. First, it is suggested that the power can be invoked either before or after proceedings are commenced. This would seem to follow from the wording of section 7(4) which states that the power can be invoked "for the purpose of determining whether to exercise, *or of exercising*, any function" under section 7 as a whole. The continuation of proceedings under section 6 (commenced in accordance with section 7(1)), is, it is suggested, an exercise of the function under section 7(1). That function does not cease once proceedings are issued, but continues until the proceedings are drawn to a close. Thus, if in the course of proceedings a defendant[13] raises a particular line of defence, the Secretary of State would be entitled to call for relevant ancillary papers or explanations from the office holder. This is a point of jurisdiction under the CDDA and so the Disqualification Practice Direction cannot itself confer a wider power than that conferred by section 7(4). Nevertheless, it is interesting to note that paragraph 18 of the Disqualification Practice Direction proceeds on the assumption that section 7(4) can be invoked even after substantive disqualification proceedings have been commenced. As a matter of discretion, it is suggested that the court would not refuse to make an order under section 7(4) on the basis that the Secretary of State could achieve the same or a similar result by issuing a witness summons under CPR, Pt 34. A second interesting question is whether or not the Secretary of State (on provision of relevant indemnities as to costs) could, by means of an application under section 7(4), require the office holder to invoke the powers under sections 234 to 236 of the

---

[13] Where applicable the terms "claimant", "defendant" and "permission" and "disclosure" are used to reflect the modern requirements of the CPR, the Disqualification Rules and the Disqualification Practice Direction. In disqualification proceedings, "defendant" is the modern equivalent of the pre-CPR term "respondent", "permission" the term now used for "leave" and "disclosure" the term now used for discovery. On the issue of the applicable rules of procedure in proceedings under section 6 and 8, see generally Chap. 6.

Insolvency Act. This difficult question raises two separate issues. The first issue is whether the relevant office holder would have grounds to resist such an order and the second issue is whether the person against whom the order is to be sought could raise objections. It is suggested that the first point raises both a question of jurisdiction and a question of discretion. As regards jurisdiction, the office holder can be required to furnish the Secretary of State with information and to produce documents under section 7(4). Although it might be said that the scope of section 7(4) is limited to information and documents in the office holder's possession, it is suggested that this is too narrow a reading. As an office holder has both a right and a duty to obtain the books and records of the relevant company, it should follow that he ought not to be able to resist an order to produce them under section 7(4) on the basis that he has not bothered to obtain them from the company's directors. If this is correct, there would seem to be no reason why, as a matter of jurisdiction, in a case where the office holder has neither obtained the company's books and records nor invoked the powers in sections 234 to 236 of the Insolvency Act, the court should not require the office holder to seek an order for production under those powers on an application under section 7(4) of the CDDA. The circumstances in which the court might exercise this jurisdiction is another matter. Clearly, if the application which the Secretary of State wishes the office holder to make is bound to fail, the court is hardly likely to order him to make such an application. A similar result is likely to follow if it is obvious that any order sought by the office holder will not be satisfied. The court might also wish to take into account the question of whether an indemnity has been offered to the office holder by the Secretary of State.[14] On the second issue, it appears that, as a general proposition, the person against whom an order was sought under section 236 of the Insolvency Act could object to the order if disqualification proceedings have already been commenced. The Secretary of State would normally be expected to use the powers available in the substantive proceedings under rules of court (whether by way of orders for disclosure, requests for further information or, in the case of third parties, by way of witness summonses) to obtain information rather than the power in section 236.[15] Before disqualification proceedings are commenced, the Secretary of State could have recourse to the wide powers in sections 33 to 34 of the Supreme Court Act 1981. However, it is suggested that, at that stage, the court would not necessarily refuse an order under section 7(4) on the ground that the information could be obtained under the Supreme Court Act. Quite simply, the power in section 236 of the Insolvency Act is much wider and is likely to be of much greater use. Furthermore, the position is analogous to that in the *Polly Peck* case discussed above. In other words, the Secretary of State would merely be seeking, through an application under section 7(4), to exploit the statutory purpose of section 236 and enable the relevant office holder to report fully on the conduct of any of the company's directors which falls below appropriate standards.

---

[14] In this context, it is a moot point whether the court might take into account the "law enforcement" nature of the powers being exercised by the Secretary of State together with the obligation of the office holder to report fully and fairly under sections 7(3) and 7(4) and not require the Secretary of State to provide indemnity. See, by analogy, the position with regard to cross-undertakings in damages where an interlocutory injunction is sought in a law enforcement context: see *Hoffmann-La Roche v. Secretary of State for Trade and Industry* [1974] 2 All E.R. 1128, HL; *Re Highfield Commodities Ltd* [1984] 3 All E.R. 884.

[15] See, by analogy, the ordinary position where office holders seek to invoke the power in section 236 after the commencement of litigation: see *British & Commonwealth plc v. Spicer and Oppenheim* [1993] A.C. 426, [1992] 3 W.L.R. 854, [1992] 4 All E.R. 876, [1993] B.C.L.C. 168, [1992] B.C.C. 977, HL; *Re Sasea Finance Ltd* [1998] 1 B.C.L.C. 559; *Re Atlantic Computers plc* [1998] B.C.C. 200; *Joint Liquidators of Sasea Finance Ltd v. KPMG* [1998] B.C.C. 216.

Insolvent Companies (Reports on Conduct of Directors) Rules 1996

3.05   The manner in which office holders are to make reports is governed by the Insolvent Companies (Reports on Conduct of Directors) Rules 1996.[16] The rules apply where the company has gone into voluntary liquidation, administration or administrative receivership but not compulsory liquidation.[17] There are a number of requirements under the rules:

(1) Any report made under section 7(3) of the CDDA should be made in prescribed Form D1 set out in the Schedule or in a form which is substantially similar (rule 3).

(2) If a section 7(3) report has not been submitted before the expiry of six months from the "relevant date", the office holder must submit a return in prescribed Form D2 set out in the Schedule or in a form which is substantially similar on every person who:

   (a) was, on the "relevant date", a director or shadow director of the company; or

   (b) had been a director or shadow director of the company at time in the three years immediately preceding the "relevant date" (rule 4).

(3) The "relevant date" for the purpose of (2) means:

   (a) the date on which the resolution for commencement is passed in the case of a creditors' voluntary winding up; or

   (b) the date on which the liquidator formed the opinion that the company's assets were insufficient to meet its debts, other liabilities and the expenses of winding up in the case of a company in members' voluntary liquidation; or

   (c) the date of the receiver's appointment in the case of an administrative receivership; or

   (d) the date of the administration order in the case of an administration.

(4) If the office holder vacates office earlier than one week before the expiry of six months from the "relevant date" as defined and he has not already submitted a D1 report or a D2 return, he must submit a D2 return as per (2) above within 14 days after vacating office.

3.06   The effect of these rules in practice is that the office holder must submit at least a D2 return in respect of every director and shadow director of company that goes into voluntary liquidation, administrative receivership or administration within the six months of taking office. The D2 return can be used either as an "interim return" or a "final return".[18] An interim return is submitted in circumstances where the office holder expects to be able to submit either a full D1 report or a final return at a later date. A final return is submitted where the office holder has not become aware of any

---

[16] S.I. 1996 No. 1909. These rules which were made pursuant to Insolvency Act 1986, s. 411, came into force on September 30, 1996 and replaced the earlier Insolvent Companies (Reports on Conduct of Directors) No. 2 Rules S.I. 1986 No. 2134. An equivalent set of rules applies in Scotland also with effect from September 30, 1996: see S.I. 1996 No. 1910.

[17] In the case of compulsory liquidation in England and Wales, the obligation to submit reports lies with the official receiver.

[18] See the Society of Practitioners of Insolvency, Statement of Insolvency Practice 4: *Disqualification of Directors in England and Wales* (September 1998), para. 5; "Dear IP" No. 36 (August 1996).

matters which would require him to submit a D1 report concerning a particular director. Office holders are encouraged by guidance notes and industry standards to submit
D1 reports and D2 final returns as quickly as they possibly can given that proceedings
for an order under section 6 must be commenced within two years of the company
becoming insolvent.[19] The overall position is that the office holder must submit either a
D1 report or a "nil" return on every director and shadow director of the insolvent
company. In a company where there is more than one office holder either consecutively
or concurrently (e.g. a liquidator following an administrator or an administrative
receiver appointed to a company already in liquidation) a D1 report or D2 return is
required from each office holder. However, in a case where joint office holders are
appointed (e.g. joint liquidators) the Unit only requires one report or return to be
submitted per director rather than one from each of the office holders.[20] Failure to
submit either a D1 report or return within the six month period is a criminal offence
punishable by fine under rule 4(7). Moreover, the Insolvency Service will report persistent non-compliance to the relevant office holder's authorising body.[21] The smooth
operation of the system thus depends heavily on the professional discipline of insolvency practitioners within the private sector. The office holder's costs in preparing
reports and returns forms part of his ordinary remuneration and is an expense of the
insolvency process. The costs are therefore borne by the insolvent estate (i.e. the company's creditors). The Unit will pay the office holder separately for work done by way
of further investigation or in agreeing and swearing affidavits and attending court
where the case is to proceed. However, the extent and likely cost of any additional
work should be discussed with the Unit before it is undertaken and separate payment
will only generally be made if the costs were authorised in advance.[22] It should be noted
that where the company is in liquidation, the liquidator is under a further obligation to
report a director to the appropriate authorities if it appears to him that the director has
been guilty of a criminal offence in relation to the company.[23]

Status of office holders reports in proceedings

3.07   One important question concerns whether the Secretary of State can be compelled to provide a copy of a D1 report to the defendant in the context of disclosure.
Orders for discovery and inspection were refused in two reported cases on the ground
that a D report amounted to a privileged communication.[24] However, an order for
inspection of an administrator's report was granted by Scott V.-C. in Re Barings plc,
Secretary of State for Trade and Industry v. Baker[25] and this should now be regarded as

---

[19] CDDA, s. 7(2): cf. Chaps 6 and 7. For examples of industry standards see, e.g. Statement of Insolvency
Practice 4 referred to above and the "Dear IP" letters issued by the Insolvency Service.
[20] Statement of Insolvency Practice 4, para. 6; "Dear IP" No. 36.
[21] "Dear IP" No. 32 (October 1994). It is also expected that insolvency practitioners will disclose copies of D
reports and returns when requested to do so by those carrying out monitoring visits on behalf of their
professional body: "Dear IP No. 35 (April 1996). For an insight into the possible impact of professional
monitoring on the office holder's decision whether to submit a report or a "nil" return see S. Wheeler,
"Directors' Disqualification: Insolvency Practitioners and the Decision-Making Process" (1995) 15 L.S.
283.
[22] Statement of Insolvency Practice 4; "Dear IP" No. 37 (January 1997).
[23] Insolvency Act 1986, s. 218.
[24] Secretary of State for Trade and Industry v. Sananes [1994] B.C.C. 375; Secretary of State for Trade and
Industry v. Houston (No. 2) 1995 S.L.T. 196. In Houston discovery was also refused on the ground of public
interest immunity. Under the former rules of court applicable prior to the CPR, it was important to distinguish "discovery" (disclosure of the existence of a document) and "inspection" (the process of making the
contents of the document available to the other side). Different rules governed these two separate processes
although unfortunately, as a matter of nomenclature, "discovery" was commonly used when it was "inspection" that was in issue. Disclosure and inspection of documents is now governed by CPR, Pt 31.
[25] [1998] Ch. 356, [1998] 1 B.C.L.C. 16, [1998] B.C.C. 888.

the definitive authority on the point. There were two separate questions facing the court. The first question was whether an order for inspection could be made in the instant case on the ground that inspection was "necessary either for disposing fairly of the cause or matter or for saving costs" under RSC Ord. 24, r. 13. The second question was whether, in any event, the D report was privileged in the hands of the Secretary of State. The Vice-Chancellor decided that inspection of the report was "necessary" under RSC Ord. 24, r. 13 and that it was not protected by legal professional privilege. Scott V.-C.'s reasoning and conclusions can be summarised as follows:

(1) While most of its factual contents could be extracted from other documents that were available to the defendant, the D report should be made available for inspection because its production would save the defendant the time and expense of trawling through the source material in order to produce his own organised analysis of the facts. In the judge's view, as the Secretary of State had enjoyed the benefit of the report, it was only fair that it should also be made available to the defendant. The threshold test that an order for inspection should only be made if the court is of the opinion that the order is necessary either for disposing fairly of the matter or for saving costs was therefore satisfied.[26]

(2) It was not remotely arguable that the D report was immune from disclosure in order to protect the inviolability of communications between the Secretary of State and the Secretary of State's legal advisers (*i.e.* to protect the confidentiality of legal advice). That was because the D report did not in any sense represent legal advice given to the Secretary of State. This ground of legal professional privilege was therefore not available.

(3) That part of legal professional privilege known as "litigation privilege", which confers immunity on documents brought into existence for the purposes of litigation should not be regarded as a species of privilege which is wholly distinct from legal professional privilege. Originally, litigation privilege only applied to documents which might cast light on the client's instructions to the lawyer or the lawyer's advice to the client regarding the conduct of the case or the client's prospects. More recent cases have dispensed with the connection orginally required between the claim to privilege and the principle that communications between a party and his lawyers should be immune from compulsory disclosure.[27] While he regarded the removal of such a connection as wrong in principle, Scott V.-C. was bound by these authorities to hold that privilege can be claimed in respect of a document provided that the document has been brought into existence for the dominant purpose of use in litigation.

(4) It was clearly arguable that the D report had been produced by the administrators for the dominant purpose of enabling the Secretary of State to decide whether or not to commence disqualification proceedings. However, it did not follow that the report was privileged. The usual rule in (3) above does not apply to reports which are required to be produced pursuant to a statutory

---

[26] RSC Ord. 24, r. 13(1). See now CPR, Pt 31.
[27] See, in particular, *Re Highgrade Traders Ltd* [1984] B.C.L.C. 151 and *Guinness Peat Properties Ltd v. Fitzroy Robinson* [1987] 1 W.L.R. 1027, [1987] 2 All E.R. 716.

duty. In such cases, it is not appropriate to examine the purpose of the office holder in making the report or the purpose of the statutory reporting obligations. Instead, the question is whether there is a public interest in the non-disclosure of the report's contents which is sufficient to override the administration of justice rationale reflected in the usual right of a litigant to inspect his opponent's documents. There being no claim of public interest immunity (nor any ground for such a claim) and there being no need to protect the D report as bearing on communications between the Secretary of State and the Secretary of State's legal advisers, there was no public interest weighing in the balance against inspection.

3.08   There are undoubtedly difficulties with the legal analysis of litigation privilege and the application of the relevant principles in *Barings*. A D report is not a "public" document in the sense of a document which is published and made available in the public domain. Moreover, the view (summarised in (3) above) that litigation privilege does not apply to statutory reports is problematic. Such documents are clearly produced (and required to be produced) for purposes of litigation. However, it must be assumed for now that D reports are not the subject of legal professional privilege.[28] This does not necessarily mean that the court will always make an order for inspection of a D report. The *Barings* case was exceptional in a number of respects. Whether the production of the D report will really save costs in the ordinary case is open to question. Furthermore, there is no obvious justification for the court to order inspection on grounds of fairness provided that any points made by the office holder in favour of the defendant are fairly set out in the office holder's affidavit.[29] It is suggested in the light of these matters that inspection of D reports will not be ordered with any great frequency. Such a view is likely to be consistent with the overriding objective of the CPR and also reflects the fact that the views of an office holder as to whether reported conduct constitutes unfitness, carry little or no weight in proceedings.[30] At the same time, to avoid creating the impression that he has something to hide, the Secretary of State may feel that voluntary disclosure of D reports is appropriate, even in a case where disclosure would not necessarily be ordered by the court. This is subject to two caveats. First, it may be doubted whether it would necessarily be right for D reports to be disclosed so readily in other civil proceedings (*i.e.* non-disqualification proceedings). This is particularly so if the Secretary of State decided not to commence disqualification proceedings. In such a case, it is suggested that the contents of the report should only be made available if the interests of the effective administration of justice demand it. Secondly, consideration has to be given to the position of other directors who may also be the subject of the D report in question.

It is clear from the tenor of the judge's concluding remarks in *Barings* that disqualification proceedings should be regarded as having more in common with criminal proceedings than ordinary civil proceedings concerning private rights. Indeed, he went so far as to make the point that in criminal proceedings the report would have had to be disclosed to the defence. This tension between the idea of civil "public interest" litigation (analogous to criminal proceedings) and "ordinary" civil litigation to which the "ordinary" rules of civil procedure governing disclosure, costs, evidence, etc. should apply is one that rears its head in other aspects of the law of directors' disqualification.

---

[28] Even if they were, the Secretary of State could waive such privilege. This was purportedly done in the *Barings* case prior to the delivery of the Vice-Chancellor's judgment.
[29] A requirement confirmed by *Re Moonlight Foods (U.K.) Ltd, Secretary of State for Trade and Industry v. Hickling* [1996] B.C.C. 678.
[30] See *Re Pinemoor Ltd* [1997] B.C.C. 708 and *Re Park House Properties Ltd* [1997] 2 B.C.L.C. 530, [1998] B.C.C. 847.

SECTION 6(1): SUBSTANTIVE PRELIMINARIES

3.09   Section 6(1), the CDDA's only mandatory disqualification provision, states:

"The court shall make a disqualification order against a person in any case where, on an application under this section, it is satisfied—

(a) that he is or has been a director of a company which has at any time become insolvent (whether while he was a director or subsequently), and

(b) that his conduct as a director of that company (either taken alone or taken together with his conduct as a director of any other company or companies) makes him unfit to be concerned in the management of a company."

The onus is on the claimant (who for these purposes is either the Secretary of State for Trade and Industry or the official receiver) to establish that the requirements of section 6(1) are made out.[31] It is for the court to decide whether the defendant is unfit, not the Secretary of State or any other party.[32] If the provision is broken down into its component parts, it is clear that the court must be satisfied on all of the following points before it is obliged to disqualify:

(1) that the defendant is or has been a director of a company;

(2) that that company has become insolvent; and

(3) that the defendant's conduct as a director of that company (either taken alone or taken together with his conduct as a director of any other company or companies) makes him unfit to be concerned in the management of a company.[33]

In most cases points (1) and (2) are not in dispute and the principal question before the court is whether the relevant conduct makes the defendant unfit. Nevertheless, there are cases in which a preliminary issue under (1), (2) or (3) is raised. These preliminary issues are dealt with in this chapter and the critical question as to what constitutes unfitness is addressed in the chapters which follow. A number of these preliminary matters involve the construction of particular terms (*e.g.* "director", "company") which are used throughout the CDDA. As a result, the material in this chapter does occasionally range beyond the particular context of sections 6 to 9 and is cross-referenced to other chapters which deal with core concepts.

"DIRECTOR"

3.10   "Director" is a core term of the CDDA and its importance is twofold. First, the court has no jurisdiction under section 6 in relation to conduct other than that of directors. Secondly and more generally, the term is relevant in determining the scope of

---

[31] *Re Verby Print for Advertising Ltd, Secretary of State for Trade and Industry v. Fine* [1998] 2 B.C.L.C. 23, [1998] B.C.C. 652. The burden of proof is the ordinary civil standard.
[32] *Re Carecraft Construction Co Ltd* [1994] 1 W.L.R. 172, [1993] 4 All E.R. 499, [1993] B.C.L.C. 1259, [1993] B.C.C. 336; *Re Park House Properties Ltd* [1997] 2 B.C.L.C. 530, [1998] B.C.C. 847; *Re Blackspur Group plc, Re Atlantic Computer Systems plc* [1998] 1 W.L.R. 422, [1998] 1 B.C.L.C. 676, [1998] B.C.C. 11, CA.
[33] Section 6(1) was broken down into these three requirements in *Re Living Images Ltd* [1996] 1 B.C.L.C. 348, [1996] B.C.C. 112.

any disqualification imposed under the CDDA, as a person disqualified by the court is prohibited (amongst other things) from being a director of a company without permission of the court.[34] There is no exhaustive definition of the term "director". The Companies Act 1985 simply requires all companies registered under it to appoint directors[35] and to provide the Registrar of Companies with basic details about them, including their signed written consent to act.[36] Furthermore, there is no statutory machinery governing the mode of appointment. This matter is left for the company to determine in its articles of association.[37] A director who has been formally appointed in accordance with the appropriate procedure set out in the relevant company's articles of association is known as a *de jure* director. There is no doubt that *de jure* directors fall within section 6(1)(a). However, the scope of "director" in the CDDA is not confined to *de jure* directors. The CDDA also applies to what have become known as *de facto* directors (that is, persons who are "in fact" directors) and, for section 6 purposes, it further embraces shadow directors. Thus, anyone falling within these wider legal categories is potentially vulnerable to disqualification under section 6. It is also clear on the wording of section 6(1)(a) that the provision catches former directors. A director (be that a *de jure*, *de facto* or shadow director) cannot automatically escape liability to disqualification simply by resigning or otherwise withdrawing from his position.[38]

De facto directors

3.11 The term "director", as defined in CDDA, s. 22(4), includes "any person occupying the position of director, by whatever name called".[39] This wording has received conflicting interpretations. In *Re Eurostem Maritime Ltd*,[40] it was held that a person who had been actively concerned in the administration of seven companies could be treated as "occupying the position of a director" even though he was not a *de jure* director. Browne-Wilkinson V.-C. took a narrower view in *Re Lo-Line Electric Motors Ltd*,[41] stating that the words "by whatever name called" are confined to matters of nomenclature only. On this view, section 22(4) obviously covers *de jure* directors who take the title "director". However, beyond that, it extends only to persons who are *de jure* (*i.e.* properly appointed) but who happen to go under a different title because, for example, the company's articles provide that the running of its business is committed to a board of "governors", "trustees" or "managers" rather than "directors". On this basis, the definition in section 22(4) would not extend to persons who act *as if* they are *de jure* directors even though they have not been formally appointed or in circumstances where their appointment is defective in some way.[42] It is this latter

---

[34] CDDA, s. 1(1)(a), see discussion in Chapter 12.
[35] Companies Act 1985, s. 282. A public company must have at least two directors unless it was incorporated before November 1, 1929 in which case one will do. A private company need only have one director.
[36] *ibid.*, ss 10 and 288.
[37] Ultimate control over the appointment of directors is commonly reserved to the members: see, *e.g.* Table A, arts 73–80.
[38] Resignation will not prevent a disqualification order being made on the basis of any conduct of the director up to the date of resignation which, either alone or taken together with other relevant conduct, is such as to make him unfit within the meaning of the CDDA. In some circumstances resignation may be the only option available. In such circumstances resignation itself will not amount to conduct which will found a disqualification order: see *Re Thorncliffe Finance Ltd, Secretary of State for Trade and Industry v. Arif* [1997] 1 B.C.L.C. 34 at 46, [1996] B.C.C. 586 at 596. However, it is quite possible that resignation in other circumstances (*e.g.* where a sole director and shareholder abandons the company) might itself amount to conduct making the former director unfit and that he would be treated as bearing responsibility (for the purposes of the CDDA) for further matters occurring after his resignation.
[39] Adopting wording also to be found in Companies Act 1985, s. 741(1) and Insolvency Act 1986, s. 251.
[40] [1987] P.C.C. 190.
[41] [1988] Ch. 477, [1988] 3 W.L.R. 26, [1988] 2 All E.R. 692, [1988] B.C.L.C. 698, (1988) 4 B.C.C. 415.
[42] *e.g.* because of some failure to follow correct procedures under the articles or companies legislation such as a rule concerning the convening of the relevant board or general meeting or a quorum requirement.

category, that is to say, "directors who assume to act as directors without having been appointed validly or at all"[43] that are properly regarded as *de facto* directors.

3.12   Although in *Lo-Line* the then Vice-Chancellor took the view that the statutory definition of director did not itself extend to *de facto* directors, he accepted that the court did have the power to disqualify a *de facto* director under the Companies Act 1985, s. 300, the statutory predecessor of section 6. He reached this conclusion on the basis that, as a matter of statutory construction of section 300, the word "director" included *de facto* directors. His reasoning, paraphrased below, can equally be applied to section 6:

(1)   The statutory definition of director is inclusive not exhaustive and so the meaning of the term must be determined by looking at the relevant legislation as a whole and at the immediate context in which the term appears. It is clear from the Companies Act 1985 that certain provisions applicable to directors can only be referring to *de jure* directors. One example is Companies Act 1985, s. 282 which requires every company to have a minimum number of directors. Equally, however, there are some sections where the term "director" must include a person who is not a *de jure* director. The best example is section 285 which validates the acts of a director whose appointment later turns out to have been defective in some way. Section 285 makes no sense unless it is read as referring to a *de facto* director. The upshot is that the word "director" in legislation may in some contexts include *de facto* directors but this will not always be so. Thus, the question of whether a given statutory provision applies to *de facto* directors or not will depend on the overall context of that provision.[44]

(2)   When considering disqualification for unfitness the court is required to examine the defendant's conduct "as a director". On the view that the paramount purpose of disqualification is public protection, it is difficult to see how Parliament could have intended that the issue of a person's vulnerability to disqualification should rest on the validity of his appointment. A *de facto* director whose past conduct raises questions about his suitability to be involved in the management of companies should not be able to escape disqualification just because he was never formally appointed or his appointment was defective.[45] The argument for construing "director" narrowly in favour of the individual based on the submission that disqualification is a process with penal elements was thus rejected in *Lo-Line*.

---

[43] *Re Hydrodam (Corby) Ltd* [1994] 2 B.C.L.C. 180, [1994] B.C.C. 161 *per* Millett J., a case concerning the applicability of Insolvency Act 1986, s. 214 to *de facto* and shadow directors rather than a disqualification case but one of general importance. The basic definition of a *de facto* director as a person who acts as a director without formal appointment is rarely contested in disqualification cases: see, *e.g. Re Red Label Fashions Ltd, Secretary of State for Trade and Industry v. Kullar* [1999] B.C.C. 308; *Re Ambery Metal Form Components Ltd, Secretary of State for Trade and Industry v. Jones* [1999] B.C.C. 336. Argument centres much more on what constitutes "acting as a director".

[44] It is important to note from this analysis that the *de facto* director is effectively a creature of statutory interpretation because the definition in CDDA, s. 22(4) is not exhaustive and, according to *Lo-Line* only ever includes persons who were acting *de jure*. There is a suggestion in *Re Sykes (Butchers) Ltd, Secretary of State for Trade and Industry v. Richardson* [1998] 1 B.C.L.C. 110 at 119, [1998] B.C.C. 484 at 490 to the effect that a *de facto* director finding brings the defendant within the statutory definition as a "person occupying the position of director, by whatever name called". This conflicts with the approach taken in *Lo-Line* and is best disregarded.

[45] It might be added that it would be odd for Parliament to make express provision bringing shadow directors within the scope of the CDDA, ss 6–9 while not intending the term "director" to cover persons who act as directors without formal or valid appointment.

3.13   The *Lo-Line* view is clearly a sensible one. It was seen in chapter 2 that the CDDA is directed broadly at those who abuse the privilege of limited liability or otherwise act improperly in managing companies. It would obviously defeat this broad purpose if a person could contrive to remove himself from the clutches of the legislation because the company conveniently failed to appoint him or his appointment was in some way defective. The point is particularly germane in relation to owner-managed private companies which are rarely run at the level of formality contemplated by companies legislation at least as concerns company decision-making. The basic view that the CDDA applies to *de facto* directors as well as *de jure* directors has been confirmed in several section 6 cases.[46] However, even though it is settled that the Act applies to *de facto* directors, this still leaves the difficulty of how they are to be identified. What acts or characteristics constitute a person a *de facto* director?

Legal ingredients of de facto directorship

3.14   It follows from what has been said so far that a person will only be treated as a *de facto* director if he has in some sense been acting as a director. A fuller description was put forward by Millett J. in *Re Hydrodam (Corby) Ltd*:

> "A *de facto* director is a person who assumes to act as a director. He is held out as a director by the company, and claims and purports to be a director, although never actually or validly appointed as such. To establish that a person was a *de facto* director of a company it is necessary to plead and prove that he undertook functions in relation to the company which could properly be discharged only by a director. It is not sufficient to show that he was concerned in the management of the company's affairs or undertook tasks in relation to its business which can properly be performed by a manager below board level."[47]

The *dictum* of Millett J. should not, of course, be read as if it were a statutory provision. Millett J.'s main purpose was to distinguish between *de facto* and shadow directors. On the facts of *Hydrodam*, Millett J. did not have to apply the test for *de facto* directors because the only arguable case against the defendants in that case was on the "shadow director" footing. In *Re Moorgate Metals Ltd, Official Receiver v. Huhtala*[48] Warner J. reviewed the *Hydrodam* case and qualified Millett J.'s *dictum* by finding that it is not a necessary condition of *de facto* directorship that the person concerned is held out as a director by having the label of "director" expressly attached to them. Indeed, on the facts of *Moorgate Metals*, the reason that the relevant defendant had not been appointed a *de jure* director (and the reason why he would not want to be held out as such) was fairly obvious: he was an undischarged bankrupt who did not have the court's permission to act as a director.

3.15   Millett J.'s *dictum* was adopted and applied in *Re H Laing Demolition Building Contractors Ltd, Secretary of State for Trade and Industry v. Laing*.[49] In that case the Secretary of State sought disqualification orders against a *de jure* director and two other individuals ("B" and "C") who were alleged to have been *de facto* directors of the same company. The principal ground of the application was that all three had caused the company to trade at the risk of creditors while knowing it to be insolvent. B and C were directors of another company, M Plc but were never formally appointed as

[46] See *Re Richborough Furniture Ltd, Secretary of State for Trade and Industry v. Stokes* [1996] 1 B.C.L.C. 507, [1996] B.C.C. 155 and other cases discussed in the main text below.
[47] [1994] 2 B.C.L.C. 180 at 183, [1994] B.C.C. 161 at 163.
[48] [1995] 1 B.C.L.C. 503, [1995] B.C.C. 143.
[49] [1996] 2 B.C.L.C. 324.

directors of the company itself. M Plc entered into a conditional contract to invest in and acquire the company which had been suffering cash-flow difficulties as a result of a significant expansion in its turnover. Before the contract was completed B and C had both become signatories on the company's bank account, the terms of the mandate describing B as a "director" and C as a "manager". Furthermore, there was evidence that B had signed a contract on behalf of the company under the standard rubric of "director", formally witnessing the affixing of the company's seal to a document. Evans-Lombe J. held that B and C's involvement in the company (the main aim of which was to oversee the completion of M plc's acquisition rather than to manage the company's business) was not sufficient to constitute them *de facto* directors. Even assuming that B had held himself out as a director by signing the contract, the evidence as a whole did not suggest unequivocally that he had assumed the role of director in the terms of Millett J.'s test. The judge made the further point that, even if it was accepted that B had constituted himself a *de facto* director through the act of signing the contract, it remained a question of fact as to how long such a directorship could be taken to have continued. By definition, *de facto* directorship must be capable of ending without formal resignation and, on the facts, the judge was satisfied that B had not continued to act for a sufficiently lengthy period after signing the contract to justify disturbing his overall conclusion.[50]

3.16   It would appear from Millett J.'s test and the manner of its application in *Laing* that the following two elements would have to be established for the court to make a finding of *de facto* directorship:

(1)   that both the company and the defendant had represented that he was a director of the company at the relevant time; and

(2)   that the defendant had undertaken functions which could only be performed by a director and not by a manager or some other senior employee below board level.[51]

However, this two-fold test has since been further developed and modified. In *Re Richborough Furniture Ltd; Secretary of State for Trade and Industry v. Stokes*,[52] Mr Timothy Lloyd Q.C. (sitting as a judge of the Chancery Division) doubted that the *Hydrodam* test amounted to an exhaustive test of *de facto* directorship applicable in every case. The main problem perceived by Mr Lloyd Q.C. was that under the first element anyone who, on the facts of a given case, could be shown to have run the company would only be exposed to disqualification if that person had been held out as

---

[50] *ibid.* at 346 This aspect of Evans-Lombe J.'s conclusion is susceptible to some mild technical criticism. It is arguable that if the judge was satisfied that the signing of the contract constituted C a *de facto* director at the time of signing, then it would have been correct to conclude that he was a director for the purposes of section 6(1)(a). This would not have altered the result as C's only identifiable "conduct as a director" under section 6(1)(b) would have been the signing of the contract and there was no allegation that this, on its own, made him unfit. Support for such an approach can be derived from the more recent case of *Re Ambery Metal Form Components Ltd, Secretary of State for Trade and Industry v. Jones* [1999] B.C.C. 336. In that case there was an allegation that the defendant had held himself out as joint-managing director of the relevant company in a letter addressed to a firm of accountants. It was held by a district judge that this "holding out" was an isolated incident relating only to a period of some four days. On appeal to the High Court, Jonathan Parker J. said that the correct approach was to look at the defendant's conduct in the round to see if he had in fact assumed the role of a director of the company and that, as such, it was significant that the defendant was prepared to sign a letter on the company's notepaper expressing himself to be joint-managing director. In other words, the judge in *Jones* was content to draw a wide inference as to the defendant's overall role within the company from the evidence of the letter.

[51] In *Laing*, the second "function" element was not proven. As such, it is suggested that the case would have been decided the same way had the judge applied the "equal footing" test discussed below in the main text.

[52] [1996] 1 B.C.L.C. 507, [1996] B.C.C. 155.

a director and claimed, and purported to be a director. This criticism has considerable force as it is by no means clear why a person's potential liability to disqualification should turn on what essentially is a required element in establishing agency. As Professor Morse has pointed out, the concept of holding out is concerned with the narrow issue of corporate contractual liability (*i.e.* whether a particular agent has the requisite authority to bind the company in contract) and the associated issue of security of transaction, whereas the CDDA is concerned with broader issues of public and creditor protection.[53] As such, it would be odd if the public lost protection simply because there was no holding out.[54] These criticisms directed at the first element in particular, prompted Mr Lloyd Q.C. to put forward his own description of a *de facto* director in *Richborough Furniture*:

"It seems to me that for someone to be made liable to disqualification under section 6 as a *de facto* director, the court would have to have clear evidence that he had been either the sole person directing the affairs of the company ... or, if there were others who were true directors, that he was acting on an equal footing with the others in directing the affairs of the company. It also seems to me that, if it is unclear whether the acts of the person in question are referable to an assumed directorship, or to some other capacity such as shareholder or ... consultant, the person in question must be entitled to the benefit of the doubt."[55]

3.17 This test abandons any formal "holding out" requirement and amounts to a reformulation of the second "function" element of Millett J.'s definition.[56] Its apparent virtue is that it can be used in a variety of circumstances. Where it is clear that the defendant was the only person running the company's business, there will be no difficulty in saying that he was a *de facto* director. Thus, cases like *Re Lo-Line Electric Motors Ltd*[57] are readily explicable. In *Lo-Line*, the defendant had been validly appointed as a director of a company. He then resigned, but subsequently resumed the sole running of the company without being formally reappointed after the only remaining *de jure* director had absconded to the United States. Browne-Wilkinson V.-C. had no difficulty in concluding that the defendant had constituted himself a *de facto* director by assuming sole control of the company's business. Equally, there is little difficulty if the evidence shows that the defendant was the *main* person actively managing the company's trading operations in circumstances where the *de jure* directors were involved to a lesser or a nominal degree.[58] The "equal footing" aspect of the *Richborough Furniture* test also appears to offer a means of resolving more complex

[53] G. Morse, "Shadow and *De Facto* Directors" in *The Corporate Dimension* (B. Rider (ed.), 1998) and *cf.* generally Chap. 2.
[54] See *Re Moorgate Metals Ltd, Official Receiver v. Huhtala* [1995] 1 B.C.L.C. 503, [1995] B.C.C. 143 considered above.
[55] [1996] 1 B.C.L.C. 507 at 524, [1996] B.C.C. 155 at 170.
[56] See Morse, *op. cit.* The decision in *Richborough Furniture* has led to the development of a much looser approach under which the court looks at all the relevant circumstances of the case: see *Re Land Travel Ltd, Secretary of State for Trade and Industry v. Tjolle* [1998] 1 B.C.L.C. 333, [1998] B.C.C. 282; *Re Kaytech International plc, Secretary of State for Trade and Industry v. Potier* [1999] B.C.C. 390, CA and further discussion below in the main text. The upshot is that evidence of holding out will often still be taken into account as a relevant factor: see, *e.g. Re Sykes (Butchers) Ltd, Secretary of State for Trade and Industry v. Richardson* [1998] 1 B.C.L.C. 110, [1998] B.C.C. 484; *Re Ambery Metal Form Components Ltd, Secretary of State for Trade and Industry v. Jones* [1999] B.C.C. 336 and the *Kaytech International* case itself.
[57] [1988] Ch. 477, [1988] 3 W.L.R. 26, [1988] 2 All E.R. 692, [1988] B.C.L.C. 698, (1988) 4 B.C.C. 415.
[58] See, *e.g. Re Moorgate Metals Ltd* [1995] 1 B.C.L.C. 503, [1995] B.C.C. 143 and see para. 3.18 below. A point of note arising from this case is that the *de facto* director had deliberately avoided formal appointment because he was an undischarged bankrupt and therefore automatically disqualified from directing or managing a company under CDDA, s. 11. *Re Cargo Agency Ltd* [1992] B.C.L.C. 686, [1992] B.C.C. 388 is another case in point although there it was conceded without argument that the relevant party had acted as a *de facto* director.

issues in cases where the alleged *de facto* director was acting alongside the appointed directors or was providing them with advice and assistance rather than taking the lion's share of responsibility for running the company's business. Thus, for example, it should assist the court in determining whether the activities of someone who claims to have acted as a "management consultant", "company doctor" or other service-provider amount to *de facto* directorship on the facts of a given case. The "equal footing" aspect is considered in more detail below.

De facto directors: the "equal footing" test

3.18 The "equal footing" approach has been considered or adopted in a number of cases with varying results. The question of whether the defendant was acting on an equal footing with the *de jure* directors in a given case is a question of fact. In *Re Moorgate Metals Ltd, Official Receiver v. Huhtala*,[59] a case decided a year before *Richborough Furniture*, there were two defendants, "R" and "H". The company, which traded as a metal merchant, was in substance a joint venture between the two. H was a *de jure* director and the company secretary but had no experience of the metal trade. He took responsibility for financial and administrative matters. R, in contrast, was an experienced metal trader. R had taken sole charge of the company's trading operation but was never formally appointed as a director (he was an undischarged bankrupt). Warner J. swiftly concluded that R was a *de facto* director and so liable to disqualification under section 6. All the evidence suggested that R and H were equal joint venturers. R was the driving force behind setting up the business. R and H shared the responsibility of managing the company and under this arrangement R was left in sole control of the company's trading without any formal limit being placed on the extent of the commitments that he could enter into on the company's behalf. R and H received equal remuneration. Finally, there was in evidence a promotional brochure published by the company that described R and H repeatedly as "partners". In the judge's words, they were "equals running the company between them".[60]

3.19   *Re Sykes (Butchers) Ltd, Secretary of State for Trade and Industry v. Richardson* is another case in which the defendant was held to be a *de facto* director.[61] The relevant company was the subsidiary of another company called Lemoncrest. The defendant, "R", was a director of Lemoncrest but he was never formally appointed as a director of the company, although there was some evidence that this was intended. The company's only *de jure* director was "O", who was also a director of Lemoncrest. The Secretary of State relied on several documents including the company's bank mandates and letters on company note paper that R had signed as "director" or "MD". The court also heard oral evidence from the company's bank manager, the company secretary and O to the effect that R had acted as if he was a director. Taking this evidence as a whole the registrar concluded that R was a *de facto* director, a finding upheld by Ferris J. on appeal. The decision seems to turn primarily on the fact that R had been held out as a director although Ferris J. did pay lip-service to the "equal footing" test from *Richborough Furniture*. The case suggests that strong evidence of holding out may well strengthen an inference of equality between the alleged *de facto* director and the appointed board, even though, as was seen above, there does not appear to be any formal threshold requirement of holding out.

---

[59] [1995] 1 B.C.L.C. 503, [1995] B.C.C. 143.
[60] It should be noted that the judge reached this conclusion without full argument as R did not appear and was not represented at trial.
[61] [1998] 1 B.C.L.C. 110, [1998] B.C.C. 484.

More often than not the "equal footing" test has tended to work in favour of defendants. By way of contrast with the decisions in *Lo-Line, Moorgate Metals* and *Sykes (Butchers)*, applications against alleged *de facto* directors in *Re Moonlight Foods (U.K.) Ltd, Secretary of State for Trade and Industry v. Hickling,*[62] *Re Land Travel Ltd, Secretary of State for Trade and Industry v. Tjolle*[63] and in *Richborough Furniture* itself were all dismissed because, on their facts, none of them was on an "equal footing". As will become clear, the decision in the *Land Travel* case also makes further modifications to the applicable test.

3.20 In *Richborough Furniture*, there were three defendants, two of whom, "S" and "Z", were *de jure* directors. It was alleged that the third defendant, "M", was a *de facto* director. The relevant company was part of a group which amounted in substance to a tripartite joint venture between S, an individual called Mr Bond (who was not the subject of proceedings) and various interests associated with Z. Z and M were married and, together with their son, ran an unincorporated business called the Jade Partnership which provided consultancy services to small businesses. Jade invested in the group and entered into a formal consultancy agreement with it. As a result, Jade, principally through M, provided financial management, accounting and administrative services to the company. Once the company started to struggle, M regularly negotiated with the Inland Revenue, Customs and Excise and pressing trade creditors. S's evidence was that he relied on M to perform the functions of a finance director and that M had some say in the decision to pay creditors. There was also evidence from the company's suppliers and creditors that S had introduced M to them as his "partner" and that M had referred to himself in telephone conversations as "the boss" or the "managing director". The key question was whether M had acted merely as a consultant or whether, in reality, he had assumed the role of a finance director. The position was complicated because, in effect, M was performing a dual role, acting as a consultant under the agreement while also representing Jade's interests as a shareholder in the group.[64] Sitting as a deputy High Court judge, Mr Timothy Lloyd Q.C. decided to give M the benefit of the doubt. While accepting that outsiders may have perceived that S and M were equals, he found that under the peculiar arrangement between Jade and the company, M had not been placed on an equal footing with the *de jure* directors. This was very much a border-line case. There is little doubt that within the company M was regarded as having primary responsibility for financial and accounting matters including keeping the company's books and the preparation of management accounts. He carried out tasks that were consistent with directorship. However, the judge considered that these tasks could equally have been carried out by a professional or an employee and that any say M had in the company derived from his

---

[62] [1996] B.C.C. 678.
[63] [1998] 1 B.C.L.C. 333, [1998] B.C.C. 282.
[64] The judge expressed the view that it was legitimate for M to represent Jade as against the other shareholders and, furthermore, that in a small quasi-partnership company, decisions which are ordinarily matters of day-to-day management for the board, including who to pay and when, could easily be regarded, especially at a time of crisis, as a question for the shareholders to decide. Given that the judge ruled in M's favour, this suggests that a shareholder who influences company decision-making *qua* shareholder might not be regarded as a *de facto* director. However, where the evidence shows that the defendant involved himself extensively in the company's affairs with the aim of protecting or enhancing his investment, it is doubtful that the court would rule that he had not constituted himself a *de facto* director simply on the ground that his actions were motivated *qua* shareholder: see *Re Kaytech International plc, Secretary of State for Trade and Industry v. Potier* [1999] B.C.C. 390 at 401, CA; *Re Ambery Metal Form Components Ltd, Secretary of State for Trade and Industry v. Jones* [1999] B.C.C. 336 at 349–350.

position as the representative of Jade's interests as a shareholder.[65] In other words, M had not unequivocally assumed the position of a director because it was possible to say that he was carrying out his functions in some other capacity, e.g. as consultant, employee or shareholder.

3.21   The facts of Re Moonlight Foods (U.K.) Ltd, Secretary of State for Trade and Industry v. Hickling are less complex but there are similarities in the outcome and underlying reasoning. There were three defendants, two de jure directors and an alleged de facto director, "C". C was a qualified accountant who served in the relevant company as company secretary. He was also an employee of the company's major shareholder. He acted as alternate director for one of the de jure directors and was a signatory on the bank mandate. Under the terms of a formal agreement between the company and its major shareholder, the shareholder provided the company with a financial management service in the person of C. C carried out functions that were consistent with those of a finance director including the preparation of cash flow forecasts and management accounts for the board. He attended board meetings but was always careful in the minutes, according to standard convention, to distinguish between the de jure directors who were present and himself as secretary, whom he recorded as being merely "in attendance". Applying the approach in Richborough Furniture to the letter, the judge dismissed the application against C. He was not satisfied that C was on an equal footing with the two de jure directors who were both active in the management of the company. Furthermore, C's acts were not necessarily referable to an assumed directorship. They were equally consistent with his role as either company secretary or as an employee of the major shareholder providing the company with services under the agreement.

3.22   The "equal footing" test was discussed and interpreted further in Re Land Travel Ltd, Secretary of State for Trade and Industry v. Tjolle. The alleged de facto director, "K", was one of three defendants. She had worked her way up in the relevant company from a part-time administrative assistant to the position of a senior employee, principally responsible for sales, marketing and customer care. The dominant force in the company was its founder, "T" who was described in evidence as "autocratic". K had become a de jure director of the company's parent, BNE, but not of the company itself. K had some limited power to commit the company to expenditure in relation to sales and marketing but most of the managerial decisions were made by T. There was evidence that K was called by various titles including "director" and "deputy managing director" to give her status in the eyes of customers and other employees. She signed company documents, including bank mandates, using these titles. However, she stopped using them and also resigned her directorship of BNE once she realised that the group was in default in relation to its filing obligations with the Registrar of Companies. Nevertheless, she continued to use the title "Chief Executive" and did attend regular meetings with T and the other de jure director. In her favour, all the evidence suggested that T was in absolute control of the company's affairs. The company's financial records were kept locked away so that K had no access to them. There was little to suggest that she played any real part in financial and strategic decision-making. Jacob J. held that K was a manager but not a de facto director and, in so doing, added the following gloss to the "equal footing" test:

---

[65] M maintained throughout that his role was one of offering advice and providing information to the company on behalf of Jade rather than of taking any formal decisions in relation to the running of the company. It is interesting to note that, at the relevant time, M was an undischarged bankrupt and the subject of a disqualification order made in the case of Re Tansoft Ltd [1991] B.C.L.C. 339. There may have been grounds for the court to draw some less favourable inferences from the evidence especially in relation to the role played by Jade. The judge did note in passing that M's involvement may have been sufficient to put him in breach of the disqualification order or the terms of CDDA, s. 11 as he had arguably taken part in management.

"For myself I think it may be difficult to postulate any one decisive test. I think what is involved is very much a question of degree. The court takes into account all the relevant factors. Those factors include at least whether or not there was a holding out by the company of the individual as a director, whether the individual used the title, whether the individual had proper information ... on which to base decisions, and whether the individual has to make major decisions and so on. Taking all these factors into account, one asks 'was this individual part of the corporate governing structure?', answering it as a kind of jury question. In deciding this, one bears very much in mind why one is asking the question... There would be no justification for the law making a person liable to misfeasance or disqualification proceedings unless they were truly in a position to exercise the powers and discharge the functions of a director. Otherwise they would be made liable for events over which they had no real control, either in fact or law."[66]

In the first part of the passage, the judge is not to be understood as enumerating tests which must all be satisfied if *de facto* directorship is to be established. On this approach, the court should consider all the relevant factors (including those matters mentioned), recognising that the crucial question is whether the defendant has assumed the status and functions of a director so as to make himself responsible under the CDDA as if he were a *de jure* director.[67] Although it was clear on the facts of *Land Travel* that K was called a "director" and held out as one, she did not form part of the real corporate governance of the company, not least because she never had access to detailed information concerning the company's financial position. The upshot is that while evidence of holding out can be taken into account, a person who takes the title "director" will not necessarily be regarded as a *de facto* director. It was seen above that it is not a necessary condition of *de facto* directorship that the alleged *de facto* director was held out as a director. Equally, it is clear from *Land Travel* that holding out is not necessarily of itself a sufficient condition to establish *de facto* directorship. It is merely one of a number of factors which can be taken into account. In the words of the judge:

"... [I]t is common experience that many business executives these days use (and are told to use) the title 'director' when they are no such thing... Titles such as 'marketing director', 'sales director' and so on are far from uncommon. It would potentially lead to injustice if all such individuals were to be treated in law as if they really were directors."[68]

However, the court may attach greater significance to evidence of holding out in other cases depending on all the relevant circumstances.[69] The central question remains whether the defendant is, in a real sense, on equal terms with the appointed directors and in *Land Travel* this was interpreted to mean, in effect, an equal ability to participate and share in decisions taken by those who form the company's governing structure.

---

[66] [1998] 1 B.C.L.C. 333 at 343–344, [1998] B.C.C. 282 at 290. This passage was cited with approval by the Court of Appeal in *Re Kaytech International plc, Secretary of State for Trade and Industry v. Potier* [1999] B.C.C. 390 at 402.
[67] *ibid.*
[68] [1998] 1 B.C.L.C. 333 at 345, [1998] B.C.C. 282 at 291. Jacob J. is right about the current usage of titles like "director". It is fashionable for businesses to use such job titles as status symbols with the object of motivating staff and for impressing outsiders.
[69] See, *e.g. Re Sykes (Butchers) Ltd, Secretary of State for Trade and Industry v. Richardson* [1998] 1 B.C.L.C. 110, [1998] B.C.C. 484; *Re Ambery Metal Form Components Ltd, Secretary of State for Trade and Industry v. Jones* [1999] B.C.C. 336; *Re Kaytech International plc, Secretary of State for Trade and Industry v. Potier* [1999] B.C.C. 390, CA.

Criticisms of the current law on de facto directors

3.23 The virtue of the "equal footing" test (as modified in *Land Travel*) is that it requires the court to look at the overall picture in each case to determine whether the alleged *de facto* director has assumed the position of a director. It is also capable of application in cases where the alleged *de facto* director is one of several people, including the *de jure* directors, who took some part in the company's affairs. There are, however, a number of problems with the current law on *de facto* directors:

(1) Despite the emergence of the "equal footing" test, the courts have still to arrive at a settled and consistent approach. In cases like *Sykes (Butchers)* there is considerable emphasis on the fact that the defendant was held out as a director. In other cases there is an emphasis on equality of function and latterly, in *Land Travel*, on equality of participation in the company's governing structure. In at least one case,[70] the judge simply ran the *dictum* from *Hydrodam (Corby)* and the "equal footing" test together to produce a composite test. This is all liable to give rise to confusion. The Court of Appeal's approval of the *Land Travel* approach in *Re Kaytech International plc, Secretary of State for Trade and Industry v. Potier* suggests that the correct test (as a matter of authority) is to ask whether in all the circumstances (no single factor necessarily being decisive) the defendant has assumed the status and functions of a director.[71]

(2) The "equal footing" aspect of the approach in *Richborough Furniture* and *Land Travel* is problematic. *Richborough Furniture* and *Moonlight Foods* suggest that even where the defendant has done *some acts* that are consistent with directorship, he will not be liable to disqualification if those acts are in part referable to some other position or capacity such as consultant, professional adviser, employee or shareholder. One possible justification for this narrow approach is that under section 6(1)(b) the court is required to consider his "conduct *as a director*" in determining whether the defendant is unfit. Therefore, it could be argued that it is unfair for anyone who has not unequivocally assumed the position of a director to be exposed to disqualification. However, if it is assumed (as the authorities suggest) that the primary purpose of disqualification is to protect the public then this argument becomes less compelling. The question in section 6 is whether the defendant's conduct makes him "unfit to be concerned *in the management of a company*". If the real purpose of the CDDA is to protect the public from those whose conduct makes them unfit to take part in company management there is a good argument for saying that the courts should take a broad approach and extend the scope of *de facto* directorship to include anyone who undertakes *some* acts or functions which are consistent with *de jure* directorship. The proper approach in *Richborough Furniture* and *Moonlight Foods* on this analysis, would have been for the court to conclude that M and C were *de facto* directors and then to have considered the question of unfitness.[72] This approach sits better with the

---

[70] *Secretary of State for Trade and Industry v. Elms,* January 16, 1997, Ch.D., unreported.
[71] [1999] B.C.C. 390 at 402. In *Kaytech International* the defendant, P, a chartered surveyor, was the moving spirit behind the incorporation of the relevant company. The trial judge found that P was extensively involved in the company over the eighteen months of its trading life. He was involved in the acquisition of leasehold premises for the company in different locations. He alone made arrangements for raising the company's initial capital (arrangements which turned out to be a fiction). There was evidence that P was held out or held himself out as being variously a "director", "joint founder" and "chief executive" of the company. It was held (both at trial and by the Court of Appeal) that P had constituted himself a *de facto* director.
[72] In *Land Travel,* Jacob J. covered himself by going onto decide that, even if K could be treated as a *de facto* director, her conduct in relation to the company did not make her unfit.

view that the main purpose of the CDDA is to protect the public and raise standards among those who run companies.[73]

(3) The suggestion in *Richborough Furniture* that there must be "clear evidence" and that defendants should be given "the benefit of the doubt" can be criticised on the basis that such formulations suggest that a criminal rather than civil standard of proof is being applied.[74]

(4) In *Richborough Furniture*, the judge's suggestion that where the acts in question could be referable to some other position or capacity, such as consultant, professional adviser, employee or shareholder, they would (or might) not be enough to establish *de facto* directorship is, to some extent (although not explicitly) reflected in *Re Red Label Fashions Ltd, Secretary of State for Trade and Industry v. Kullar*.[75] In that case, Lightman J. decided, on balance, that there was no unequivocal reference or indication that the relevant defendant "was or acted as a director rather than as a manager or dutiful wife". It seems clear from *Kaytech International* that such *dicta* should not be taken too far.[76] The proper test turns on the role in fact assumed and exercised, and not the reason or motive for taking up such role. A criticism which might be made of *Richborough Furniture* surrounds the application of the principle to the facts of the case. In most small private companies, as a practical matter, a shareholder will usually have a large say in the management of the company. It will frequently be the case that the distinction between director and shareholder will not be observed very carefully or formalistically.[77] As formulated and applied in *Richborough Furniture*, the test in cases where there are other *de jure* directors is, it is suggested, one that makes it too difficult to establish a *de facto* directorship given the overall purpose of the CDDA.

(5) Another problem with the "equal footing" test is that it seems to rest on the assumption that all appointed directors necessarily take an equal and active part in directing the company's affairs. The reality is that many *de jure* directors (admittedly, at their peril) take a nominal role and many others are in a

---

[73] The arguments in (2) draw on arguments put forward in Morse, *op. cit.* On the issue of public protection and the purpose of the CDDA generally see Chap. 2. A further oddity of the approach in *Richborough Furniture* and *Moonlight Foods* is that the emphasis on different capacities has echoes of the tiresome distinction often drawn in cases on section 14 of the Companies Act 1985 between those who the courts allow to enforce provisions in the articles of association because they are claiming *qua* member and those whose claim fails because it is brought in some other capacity, *e.g.* director. For an example of what can happen if too great an emphasis is placed on the "equal footing" aspect see *Re Red Label Fashions Ltd, Secretary of State for Trade and Industry v. Kullar* [1999] B.C.C. 308. In that case the claim against the defendant was dismissed on the basis that the evidence suggesting that she had jointly-run a small company with her co-defendant husband was consistent with her role as a manager, shareholder and wife and therefore not sufficient to constitute her a *de facto* director.

[74] On standard of proof see para. 5.66.

[75] [1999] B.C.C. 308. The judge states that he was referred to the relevant authorities but does not set them out in his judgment. In summary, he simply states that the authorities require him to consider whether or not the relevant defendant "assumed the role and exercised the role in management of a director".

[76] See [1999] B.C.C. 390 at 401 where Robert Walker L.J. suggested that Rimer J. (the trial judge in *Kaytech*) may have been straining his reasoning in discounting the interest of the relevant defendant as shareholder on the basis that the company's articles followed the almost universal practice of entrusting the management of its business to the board of directors. In Robert Walker L.J.'s view, this strained reasoning was "probably out of deference to Mr Lloyd Q.C.'s reference in *Richborough* to 'some other capacity such as shareholder'".

[77] In this respect the view of Jonathan Parker J. in *Re Ambery Metal Form Components Ltd, Secretary of State for Trade and Industry v. Jones* [1999] B.C.C. 336 is to be preferred. He states (at 349–350):
"If a substantial shareholder in a small company—a quasi-partnership company, for example—wishes, as well he may, to take an active part in running the affairs of the company in order to protect his investment, that raises the very question whether in so doing he may not be constituting himself a *de facto* director of the company."

minority or are forced to defer (for whatever reason) to the influence of a dominant personality or group on the board. Similarly, the *de jure* directors will often have different areas of responsiblity. The "equal footing" test should therefore be applied flexibly and not too literally.

(6) The approach in *Land Travel* (as approved in *Kaytech International*) is also not entirely satisfactory. The question of whether the defendant was part of the corporate governing structure is one that tends to concentrate attention narrowly on the formal decision-making organs of the company and, in particular, the board. This may be an appropriate approach in a large company or a company organised formally along the lines contemplated in companies legislation where the board functions in a formal sense and its area of activity is clearly demarcated. However, it does not accurately reflect the position in many small companies and owner-managed companies in which decision-making is often less formal. The impression from many of the section 6 cases discussed later in relation to unfitness is that in small private companies the board rarely meets. Each of the directors often takes responsibility for a particular area such as sales or financial matters and one of them may have a co-ordinating role. However, the idea deriving from legal theory that the board is the main organ of the company which operates formally and collectively to express the company's will does not always reflect commercial practice and reality. There is a danger that on a narrow reading of *Land Travel* a person who takes major decisions which have a significant impact on the company's affairs will not be regarded as a *de facto* director unless those decisions are taken in the context of a formal decision-making process. It is important therefore to stress the point (also made in *Land Travel* and *Kaytech International*) that the court should take into account all relevant factors. When considering the issue of *de facto* directors the court should consider, in particular, the specific corporate context in which the defendant was working, taking into account factors such as the size of the company and its organisational and decision-making structures.

3.24   As a whole these criticisms suggest that the courts would do well to adopt a looser test concentrating on whether the defendant has carried out at least some functions that one might usually expect a director of the company in question (or a company of its size and type) to carry out. This approach would better advance the protective cause of the CDDA while also reducing the scope for evasionary tactics. Admittedly, it may put a number of senior managers and consultants to the expense of defending unfitness proceedings. One commentator has gone further and suggested that section 6(1)(a) should be amended so that an application for disqualification could be made against any person who has taken part in the *management* of a company whether or not formally appointed as a director.[78] A final point of interest arising from the cases on *de facto* directors is that the debate concerning the nature of disqualification (considered in Chapter 2) is never far from the surface. The narrower view adopted in *Richborough Furniture* and *Moonlight Foods* is consistent with a view of the CDDA as quasi-penal legislation. Mr Lloyd Q.C. expressly stated that where it is unclear whether the defendant's acts are referable to an assumed directorship or to some other capacity then he is entitled to the benefit of the doubt. This approach

---

[78] A. Hicks, *Disqualification of Directors: No Hiding Place for the Unfit?* (A.C.C.A. Research Report No. 59, 1998). This amendment would remove the need for the claimant to establish that the defendant was a *de facto* director. The meaning of "take part in management", a lesser test, is covered in Chaps 9 and 12 with particular reference to CDDA, ss 1 and 2.

clearly operates in the defendant's favour.[79] Moreover, in *Land Travel*, it appears that the judge may have been influenced by the manner in which the proceedings had been conducted against K. In particular, he was unimpressed by the length of time it had taken to bring K's case to trial.[80] The important point to note is that a judge who places greater emphasis on the protective aspect of the legislation might well take a broader view as to what constitutes *de facto* directorship.[81]

Shadow directors

3.25   In contrast to *de facto* directors, shadow directors are entirely creatures of statute. Section 6(3) of the CDDA expressly provides that "director" includes a shadow director for the purposes of both sections 6 and 7 and section 22(5) states that:

> "'Shadow director', in relation to a company, means a person in accordance with whose directions or instructions the directors of the company are accustomed to act (but so that a person is not deemed a shadow director by reason only that the directors act on advice given by him in a professional capacity)."

The same exhaustive definition of "shadow director" is used throughout companies legislation as a whole.[82] Section 6 applies to shadow directors of building societies as well as of ordinary companies, although it does not encompass shadow directors of incorporated friendly societies.[83] The broad purpose behind this statutory extension of the term "director" is plain enough. It is designed to prevent persons who in substance dictate to the board and control the direction of a company's affairs from avoiding exposure to disqualification (or other forms of liability under companies legislation) by declining formal appointment. Whereas a *de facto* director is someone who usually acts as if he had been properly appointed (though see Moorgate Metals), a shadow director, as the term implies, lurks unseen in the shadows while the *de jure* directors, often his nominees or puppets, dance to his tune.

Judicial interpretation of "shadow director"

3.26   The issue of shadow directorship has not, to date, arisen frequently in reported disqualification cases.[84] However, the courts have been called upon to interpret and apply the statutory definition in a number of wrongful trading cases brought under section 214 of the Insolvency Act 1986. The guidance provided by these cases is clearly applicable in the context of disqualification for unfitness. The definition of "shadow director" in the CDDA and the Insolvency Act is the same. Furthermore,

---

[79] On the general question of standard of proof in unfitness proceedings see para. 5.66.

[80] A delay caused because the proceedings had been stayed pending the outcome of parallel criminal prosecutions brought against K's two co-defendants. Although no such point was taken directly in *Land Travel*, it is anticipated that defendants will increasingly be tempted to claim that the conduct of disqualification proceedings in some way infringes their rights under Article 6 of the European Convention on Human Rights now that the Human Rights Act 1998 has been enacted. It is clear from the Convention case of *EDC v. U.K.* [1998] B.C.C. 370 that a lengthy delay on the part of the claimant in bringing a case to trial will amount to a *prima facie* breach of the defendant's Article 6 rights.

[81] Contrast the broad view in *Re Tasbian Ltd (No. 3)* [1993] B.C.L.C. 297, [1992] B.C.C. 358, CA with the narrower view in *Re Westmid Packing Services Ltd (No. 2), Secretary of State for Trade and Industry v. Morrall* [1996] B.C.C. 229. In both cases the court was considering whether to allow the claimant to bring proceedings against an alleged *de facto* director out of time. On this issue generally, see Chap. 7.

[82] See Companies Act 1985, s. 741(2); Insolvency Act 1986, s. 251. It is clear to the point of overkill that sections 6 to 9 of the CDDA apply to shadow directors. There are express references in sections 8, 9 and 22(4) in addition to the reference in section 6(3) and the definition in section 22(5).

[83] CDDA, ss 22A(3), 22B(3).

[84] One of the few exceptions, *Re Tasbian Ltd (No. 3), Official Receiver v. Nixon* [1993] B.C.L.C. 297, [1992] B.C.C. 358, CA, is discussed in paras 3.28–3.29 below.

both the wrongful trading and unfitness provisions were enacted together as part of a series of measures targeted against those who act irresponsibly in the management of companies.[85] The starting point is again the case of *Re Hydrodam (Corby) Ltd*[86] which addressed the question of whether the directors of a parent company could be treated as shadow directors of an insolvent subsidiary for the purposes of a wrongful trading action. Having recited the statutory definition, Millett J. held that it is necessary for the claimant to allege and prove the following elements in order to establish that the defendant is a shadow director:

"(1) who are the directors of the company, whether *de facto* or *de jure*; (2), that the defendant directed those directors how to act in relation to the company or that he was one of the persons who did so; (3) that those directors acted in accordance with such directions; and (4) that they were accustomed so to act. What is needed is first, a board of directors claiming and purporting to act as such; and secondly, a pattern of behaviour in which the board did not exercise any discretion or judgment of its own, but acted in accordance with the directions of others."

Two important points emerge from this. First, it is clear there can only be a shadow director where the company has one or more *de jure* or *de facto* directors. A key element of the statutory definition is missing if there is no board of directors for the alleged shadow director to orchestrate and direct. Secondly, a pattern of consistent compliance by the board with the directions of the alleged shadow director needs to be established. The words "accustomed to act" suggest that occasional or "one-off" compliance will not suffice.[87] It also appears from the definition and its interpretation in *Hydrodam (Corby)* that the board as a whole must be acting on the alleged shadow director's instructions, rather than just an individual director or some of the directors.[88]

3.27   Millett J.'s four specific criteria set out above can properly be regarded as part of the *ratio* of *Hydrodam (Corby)*. However, the gloss added by the judge can be criticised. Any requirement that the board must be claiming and purporting to act as such is entirely superfluous. The definition simply requires the relevant company to have directors.[89] Furthermore, Millett J.'s judgment can be construed as suggesting that shadow directorship will not be established in cases where the board has, on occasions, exercised some independent discretion or judgment. The imposition of a requirement that the board must *never* have taken decisions on its own cannot be justified given the purpose and wording of the statutory provision. Customary compliance with the directions of the alleged shadow director is all that is required. Thus, there is no need to show that the board acted *on every occasion* at the direction of the alleged shadow

---

[85] This impression is confirmed by the structure of the Insolvency Act 1985 in which both provisions were first enacted. They appear alongside one another as part of a coherent block (see ss 12–19).

[86] [1994] 2 B.C.L.C. 180, [1994] B.C.C. 161.

[87] There must be more than one act and a course of conduct: *Re Unisoft Group Ltd (No. 3)* [1994] 1 B.C.L.C. 609, [1994] B.C.C. 766. Conversely, if there is a pattern of compliance, the fact that the board acted independently on a few occasions may not be sufficient for the alleged shadow director to escape liability. For an illustration from Australia see *Australian Securities Commission v. AS Nominees Ltd* (1995) 18 A.C.S.R. 459. Similar or identical definitions of "shadow director" are in force in other jurisdictions such as Australia, New Zealand and Hong Kong.

[88] *Kuwait Asia Bank EC v. National Mutual Life Nominees Ltd* [1991] 1 A.C. 187, [1990] B.C.L.C. 868, [1990] B.C.C. 567, P.C.; *Re Unisoft Group Ltd (No. 3)* [1994] 1 B.C.L.C. 609, [1994] B.C.C. 766. One interesting and open question is whether a person could constitute himself a *de facto* director in circumstances where he is not a shadow director as defined because only part of the board and not the board as a whole acts at his behest.

[89] Morse, *op. cit.*

director. As long as there is customary compliance, occasional acts of independent decision-making should not prevent a finding of shadow directorship.[90] A further point is that there are dangers in placing too much emphasis on questions of board discretion. Such an emphasis may allow an alleged shadow director to escape liability in a case where the board claims to have taken his "advice" and exercised its discretion to act on that "advice" even though, in substance, it always unquestioningly followed such advice or it would be unthinkable that it could or would in practice fail to follow it. The courts should therefore treat with some caution any suggestion that the board were freely taking and assimilating the alleged shadow director's "advice" but not acting on his directions or instructions.[91] In the United Kingdom, most of the reported cases on shadow directorship have been decided in favour of the alleged shadow director. From the cases it is possible to identify broadly three categories of potential shadow director: consultants and advisers to companies, financial institutions and parent companies (or their directors) in relation to their subsidiaries. These are considered in turn.

Consultants/advisers as shadow directors

3.28 There is a statutory defence for professional advisers such as solicitors or accountants in that a person is not deemed to be a shadow director by reason only that the directors act on advice given by him in a professional capacity. The issue of direct relevance for consultants and advisers is where precisely the line is drawn between the giving of advice and a higher order of involvement that goes beyond mere advice and might expose the adviser to liability as a shadow director. In this respect, the crucial distinction is between, on the one hand, the giving of advice and, on the other hand, the giving of "directions or instructions". A case providing some assistance is the Court of Appeal's decision in *Re Tasbian Ltd (No. 3), Official Receiver v. Nixon.*[92] The defendant in this case, "N", was a chartered accountant and an experienced "company doctor". The company, Tasbian, had never been profitable and N was enlisted to provide advice and assist in turning its fortunes around. N was formally appointed consultant to Tasbian and he was involved in the company for around a year. At no time was N a *de jure* director. He resigned from his consultancy position just before the company went into receivership. The claimant obtained permission under section 7(2) of the CDDA to bring unfitness proceedings against N out of time.[93] N applied to set aside the order giving permission principally on the ground that the evidence disclosed no arguable case that he was either a shadow or *de facto* director. The claimant relied on the following evidence to support a case of shadow or *de facto* directorship:

(1) N was appointed and paid by Tasbian.

(2) He negotiated an informal moratorium with creditors.

(3) He monitored trading and assisted the board.

(4) He negotiated with the DTI and the Inland Revenue and introduced Tasbian to a new factoring company.

---

[90] This criticism has considerable academic support: see variously Morse, *op. cit.*; N.R. Campbell, "Liability as a Shadow Director" [1994] J.B.L. 609 and P.M.C. Koh, "Shadow Director, Shadow Director, Who Art Thou?" (1996) 14 *Company and Securities Law Journal* 340.
[91] For an example of this approach see *Australian Securities Commission v. AS Nominees Ltd* (1995) 18 A.C.S.R. 459. Note, however, that the courts tend to be less suspicious where the alleged shadow director is a financial institution, see paras 3.30–3.31.
[92] [1993] B.C.L.C. 297, [1992] B.C.C. 358.
[93] On applications for permission under section 7(2) see generally Chap. 7.

(5) He was a signatory on, and at all times controlled the use of, Tasbian's bank account.

(6) He advised on the transfer of all of Tasbian's employees to a shell company which then acted as a "labour-only" sub-contractor to Tasbian.

(7) The *de jure* directors regarded N as a shadow director or even as managing director of Tasbian.

3.29   The Court of Appeal held that both the registrar and the judge had been right to allow the case against N to proceed as the evidence disclosed an arguable case. Balcombe L.J. laid particular emphasis on the fact that Tasbian's bank account could not be operated without N's consent. He was in a position to determine which of the company's creditors were paid and in what order. To this extent, it appeared that N was able to exercise control over Tasbian's affairs. *Tasbian (No. 3)* cannot be regarded as a definitive ruling because the Court of Appeal only had to decide whether there was a triable issue on the facts. Furthermore, while N's ability to dictate to the board over payment of creditors suggests shadow directorship, the facts as a whole suggest that the stronger case was one based on *de facto* directorship.

If the authorities discussed above on *de facto* directorship are anything to go by then, in the absence of compelling evidence, the English courts are likely to reject a case against a consultant or adviser based on alleged shadow directorship. There is a delicate balance to be struck. Clearly, those who control the direction of a company and demonstrate unfitness in the way that their control is exercised should be prime candidates for disqualification. Equally, however, the courts will be anxious not to expose consultants or advisers to disqualification too easily. To do so might stem the flow of advice to companies in financial difficulties. This would be unfortunate given the potential benefits of timely advice. A well-advised board may conclude that the company should immediately cease trading and go into liquidation which at least means that it is no longer incurring fresh debts which cannot be met. Alternatively, on proper advice, the board may be able to implement strategies which turn around the company's fortunes. Thus, where there is some doubt over whether an adviser has constituted himself a shadow director, the courts may well allow him some margin and construe the provision in his favour.[94] This will be doubly so if the court approaches the CDDA on the footing that it is quasi-criminal legislation and is therefore minded to apply its provisions restrictively.

Financial institutions as shadow directors

3.30   The position of banks and other financial institutions (such as venture capital providers) which take steps to protect their financial stake in a given company has been considered in a handful of cases. The difficulty for financial institutions in this context is that their incentive (and often their contractual entitlement) to assert some form of control steadily increases as the company gets more and more into financial difficulty. A particular concern for banks is that they are usually only prepared to extend the company's loan or overdraft facilities on conditions which may include the imposition of bank control over major managerial decisions.[95] Despite these concerns, general considerations of policy suggest that the courts will not readily make a finding of sha-

---

[94] An approach consistent with the overall "enterprise" bias of company law, see Chap. 2.
[95] Alarm over the possible impact of shadow directorship on financial institutions (especially in the context of bank rescues) caused the Financial Law Panel to produce a guidance paper, *Shadow Directorships* (1994). As well as containing a useful summary of the law, this provides practical guidance aimed at helping financiers reduce the risk of shadow director liability in a number of specific commercial situations.

dow directorship against a financier who is seeking to protect a legitimate financial interest. This general impression is confirmed by the cases.

The case of *Re a Company (No. 005009 of 1987) ex. parte Copp*[96] raised fears that banks could be made liable as shadow directors for wrongful trading in relation to their corporate customers. The company traded profitably but got into difficulties when it lost its main customer. Once the agreed unsecured overdraft limit was reached, the bank initiated an investigation and commissioned its own financial services section to prepare a report on the company containing detailed recommendations. The company went into liquidation and its liquidator brought wrongful trading proceedings against the bank under section 214 of the Insolvency Act 1986. The liquidator's case was that the implementation by the board of the recommendations contained in the report made the bank a shadow director, thus exposing it to liability for wrongful trading. The bank applied to strike out the proceedings on the ground that there was no sustainable cause of action. The application was refused by Knox J. on the basis that a claim against the bank as shadow director was not obviously hopeless on the facts. However, the allegation was later dropped at trial, seemingly with the approval of the trial judge.[97]

3.31 Since *Re a Company ex. parte Copp*, the courts have continued to take a cautious line. In *Re PFTZM Ltd*,[98] an allegation of shadow directorship was made against two representatives of the company's main financial backers. It had been agreed after the company got into financial difficulties that weekly management meetings would be held to discuss the company's business. These meetings, which took place for almost two years before the company went into liquidation, were attended by the financier's officers. The liquidator argued that there was a *prima facie* case of shadow directorship against the officers. The court rejected this argument. The thrust of Mr Paul Baker Q.C.'s judgment was that the officers were acting to protect the commercial interests of the financier as a secured creditor, and not acting as directors of the company. All the financier had done was to impose terms (through the medium of the meetings) on which it was prepared to continue the company's facility in the light of threatened default, a level of influence entirely consistent with the normal bank-customer relationship. The board retained the power to accept or reject these terms. Thus, in a situation like that in *Re PFTZM Ltd* where there may be little real choice but to accept the financier's terms, the courts are still likely to find that the board had enough of a free hand to defeat an allegation of shadow directorship.[99] This restrictive approach is likely to be followed under section 6 of the CDDA given the seriousness of the likely impact of disqualification on a financial institution and/or its officers.

---

[96] [1989] B.C.L.C. 13, (1988) 4 B.C.C. 424.
[97] *Re M C Bacon Ltd* [1990] B.C.L.C. 324 at 326, [1990] B.C.C. 78 at 79.
[98] [1995] 2 B.C.L.C. 354, [1995] B.C.C. 280.
[99] For criticism of this approach see Morse, *op. cit.* One might argue that a finding of shadow directorship is justifiable in a situation of "Hobson's choice" where the financial institution exercises control in a real sense over the company's direction. It is important to bear in mind that *liability* under the relevant provision will not automatically attach to a shadow director. There is a good case for saying that financial institutions which exercise substantial control over companies should act responsibly. A greater willingness on the part of the courts to uphold allegations of shadow directorship might serve to reinforce that obligation. The arguments against such an approach can be summarised as follows. First, shadow directorship was never really intended to catch company outsiders like banks. Furthermore, a narrow approach can be justified on the ground that financiers might otherwise refuse to become involved in attempts to keep companies afloat. English judges favour the latter view and are likely to place additional hurdles in the way of a claimant: see, *e.g.* P. Millett, "Shadow Directorship—A Real or Imagined Threat to Banks" (1991) 1 *Insolvency Practitioner* 14 expressing the view that a "conscious intention" to control the board is a necessary ingredient of shadow directorship. It is interesting to note that Balcombe L.J. in *Tasbian (No. 3)* (a case of a consultant acting in the interests of a major investor) considered that the motives behind the defendant's actions were irrelevant.

Parent companies and parent company directors as shadow directors

3.32 The concept of shadow directorship cannot easily be adapted to the situation of the modern corporate group. The reality in many groups of companies is that decisions affecting the group as a whole are usually taken by the board of the parent company. As such, the parent board will often exercise greater control over the direction of its subsidiaries than the *de jure* directors of each subsidiary. This raises the possibility that the parent company or its individual directors could be treated as shadow directors and expose themselves to disqualification under section 6 should any of the subsidiaries become insolvent.

Again, the leading case on the point is *Re Hydrodam (Corby) Ltd.*[1] Eagle Trust plc was the ultimate parent company of Hydrodam. Hydrodam went into liquidation and its liquidator commenced wrongful trading proceedings against two of the directors of Eagle Trust alleging that they were liable for wrongful trading as *de facto*[2] or shadow directors of Hydrodam. Millett J. struck out the application against the two directors and, in so doing, made the following points:

(1) Even assuming that the parent company has acted as a shadow director of the subsidiary, it does not automatically follow that an individual director of the parent is also a shadow director.

(2) While the individual director is someone who is collectively responsible for the conduct of the parent, it does not follow that he has ever given instructions to the directors of the subsidiary or that they were accustomed to act on his instructions. Even assuming that the directors of the parent, acting as a board, have collectively given instructions to the directors of the subsidiary, this would not turn the individuals on the parent board into shadow directors. This is because they would be acting collectively as agent for (or organ of) the parent with the result that the parent, not its individual directors, would be acting as a shadow director. Thus, the directors of the parent can only become shadow directors of the subsidiary if they issue instructions to the board of the subsidiary on an individual and personal basis.

3.33 It follows that it will be easier to make a case of shadow directorship against the parent company itself than against its individual directors.[3] The difficulty for the parent company, or indeed any controlling shareholder, is that in strict company law terms, the companies which it controls are separate legal entities. Each entity has directors who are under a fiduciary obligation to consider the interests of that entity which are not necessarily the same as the overall interests of the group. If the directors of a subsidiary simply accept and act on decisions handed down by the parent board without carefully considering whether those decisions are in the subsidiary's individual interest, the parent company is very likely to be acting as a shadow director.[4] Equally, however, where it appears in relation to a particular decision that the interests of the subsidiary dovetail with those of the group as a whole, it may be that the parent company will avoid a finding of shadow directorship. This is particularly so if it can be inferred that the subsidiary's directors exercised a meaningful judgment because, for

---

[1] [1994] 2 B.C.L.C. 180, [1994] B.C.C. 161. For the test of shadow directorship applied in this case *cf.* paras 3.26–3.27.
[2] See paras 3.14–3.17 and text which follows.
[3] There is comfort here too for the officers and employees of financial institutions. It appears from Millett J.'s *dictum* in *Hydrodam (Corby)* that if an agent is acting within the scope of the authority given him by his principal, the agent will not be exposed personally to a finding of shadow directorship.
[4] *Standard Chartered Bank of Australia Ltd v. Antico* (1995) 131 A.L.R. 1.

example, the matter was clearly considered at a board meeting. Again, much will depend on the court's attitude in relation to questions of policy. A court which takes a narrow view of the CDDA may be more prepared to find that the subsidiary's board was exercising a genuine discretion than one which takes a broad, protective approach. As we have seen, the courts in the United Kingdom are generally slow to uphold allegations of shadow directorship. This suggests that compelling evidence will be needed.

Pleading mixed allegations of shadow and de facto directorship

3.34 In *Hydrodam (Corby)*, Millett J. was critical of the liquidator's failure to distinguish sufficiently between his two allegations of shadow and *de facto* directorship. The judge asserted that the two are alternatives which do not overlap. This view has received subsequent support in *Re H Laing Demolition Building Contractors Ltd, Secretary of State for Trade and Industry v. Laing.*[5] However, the idea that shadow and *de facto* directorship are mutually exclusive and can never overlap is not sustainable on the authorities or in principle. The courts have accepted in interlocutory proceedings that it is possible for the claimant to advance a case both simultaneously and in the alternative that the defendant acted as a shadow and/or a *de facto* director on the same evidence.[6] Furthermore, one can envisage rare situations arising in which a person may simultaneously be acting as a shadow and *de facto* director. An obvious candidate is someone who, in the day to day management of the company, acts as a *de facto* managing director while also instructing the *de jure* directors how to act.[7] As Professor Prentice has pointed out, nothing of particular significance would flow from the person having a dual status.[8] The important point for the claimant is that the two concepts should not be confused. The case under each head should be pleaded separately and the evidence marshalled accordingly. It should be remembered that in respect of shadow directorship (but not *de facto* directorship) a defence covering mere professional advice is available. Claimants would be wise to heed Millett J.'s criticism. However, the point appears to go more to presentation of case than to substance.

Other categories of director

Foreign element

3.35 The CDDA contains no territorial restrictions. The court therefore has the power to disqualify a director who resides outside the normal jurisdiction of the United Kingdom courts. This applies whether the director is a U.K. or foreign subject. There is also no requirement that the conduct complained of must have occurred within the jurisdiction. However, the court may in its discretion refuse to allow proceedings to be served on a party outside the jurisdiction[9] where it is not satisfied that there is a good arguable case against that party under the CDDA.[10] One effect of all this is that a "sleeping" or nominee director who resides abroad and takes no active part in the company's affairs is exposed to an application for disqualification under section 6

---

[5] [1996] 2 B.C.L.C. 324, 329.
[6] Oddly enough at an earlier stage in the *Laing* proceedings: see *Re H Laing Demolition Building Contractors Ltd* [1998] B.C.C. 561. *Tasbian (No. 3)* discussed above in the main text provides further tacit support.
[7] See the *obiter* comments of Robert Walker L.J. in *Re Kaytech International plc, Secretary of State for Trade and Industry v. Potier* [1999] B.C.C. 390 at 402.
[8] D.D. Prentice, "Corporate Personality, Limited Liability and the Protection of Creditors" in *Corporate Personality in the Twentieth Century* (R. Grantham & C. Rickett (eds) 1998), p. 114.
[9] Disqualification Rules, r. 5(2).
[10] See generally *Re Seagull Manufacturing Co Ltd (No. 2)* [1994] 1 B.C.L.C. 273, [1993] B.C.C. 833. This practice is likely to be followed in Scotland and Northern Ireland.

if the company becomes insolvent. This point is of particular relevance to certain residents of offshore jurisdictions like the Channel Islands who routinely accept nominee directorships in return for a fee but play no part whatsoever in the running of the companies concerned.[11]

Alternate directors

3.36 A company's articles of association may permit a director to appoint an alternate director to act in his place and, in particular, to attend any board meetings that he is unable to attend in person. The model articles in Table A make such provision (articles 65–69). An alternate director can only be appointed if there is authority in the articles. The status of alternate directors is not entirely clear. However, it is suggested that alternate directors who have been properly appointed under the articles should be regarded as *de jure* directors bringing them squarely within the scope of the CDDA.[12]

Corporate directors

3.37 As considered above and as shown in, for example, *Hydrodam (Corby) Ltd*, it is conceptually possible for one company to constitute itself a shadow director of another company. Aside from this, it has long been recognised that a company can be a *de jure* director.[13] Furthermore, it is clear from section 14 of the CDDA that a body corporate[14] is capable of committing an offence of acting in breach of a disqualification order. It follows that a body corporate which holds directorships can be disqualified under the CDDA. The point was confirmed in *Official Receiver v. Brady*[15] where two nominee Jersey companies were disqualified from being directors under section 6.

"COMPANY"

3.38 "Company" is another core term of the CDDA. Like the term "director" its scope is important in two respects. First, it operates as an outer limit on the power of the courts to make disqualification orders under the CDDA. Thus, for example, under section 6 the court only has jurisdiction if the conduct complained of relates to a "company". Secondly, the term is acutely relevant to any person disqualified under the provisions of the CDDA. This is because a disqualified person is prohibited from engaging in various activities relating to the management of companies.[16] The discussion in this chapter is concerned only with the jurisdictional question.[17] The second aspect is considered fully in Chapter 12 on the legal effect of disqualification.

The effect of section 22(9) of the CDDA and section 735 of the Companies Act 1985 is that section 6 (and section 8) should be read as applying broadly to companies

---

[11] See, *e.g. Re Kaytech International plc, Secretary of State for Trade and Industry v. Potier* [1999] B.C.C. 390.
[12] Note however the Australian case of *Playcorp Pty Ltd v. Shaw* (1993) 10 A.C.S.R. 212 which, although not a disqualification case, suggests that an alternate director will only be caught if he has participated *qua* director in the running of the company. In other words, an alternate might not expose himself to an application for disqualification by reason of his appointment alone.
[13] *Re Bulawayo Market Ltd* [1907] 2 Ch. 458.
[14] Defined to include companies incorporated elsewhere in Great Britain (*i.e.* Scotland) but to exclude a corporation sole: CDDA, s. 22(6); Companies Act 1985, s. 740.
[15] [1999] B.C.C. 258.
[16] CDDA, ss 1(1), 11 and 12.
[17] Some separate consideration of the two questions is needed because there are entities which can be treated as "companies" for jurisdictional purposes but which are not "companies" for the purposes of the prohibition. For example, there has been some controversy over whether a person disqualified in the terms of CDDA, s. 1 is prohibited from trading in partnership but no doubt that a partnership firm is a "company" for the purposes of section 6 (see below main text). The question of whether "company" includes partnership for the purposes of section 1 as well is considered fully in Chap. 12.

formed and registered under the Companies Act 1985 or its precursors on or after July 14, 1856.[18] This encompasses guarantee companies and unlimited companies as well as companies limited by shares. There are two further points to be made about the definition of "company" for CDDA purposes. First, the definition has been expressly extended to bring a number of entities that are not directly regulated by companies legislation within the scope of the CDDA. Secondly, the term "company" (in so far as it appears in any provision of the CDDA apart from section 11) is expressly defined in section 22(2)(b) of the CDDA to include any company which is capable of being wound up under Part V of the Insolvency Act 1986. The scope of the term "company" is discussed accordingly under two sub-headings. Readers should be warned that much of the analysis is highly technical and arid. The issue is a complex one and any effort to arrive at clear interpretation is often hampered rather than helped by the way that the legislation has been drafted.

Statutory extensions of "company"

3.39 The CDDA has been expressly extended to bring those who manage the following types of organisation within the general scope of the Act and within section 6 in particular:

Building societies

3.40 Section 22A of the CDDA provides that the Act applies to conduct in relation to building societies regulated by the Building Societies Act 1986 as it applies to conduct in relation to ordinary registered companies. The two main effects of section 22A are that directors of building societies are liable to disqualification under section 6 and that a disqualified person cannot act as a director or officer of a building society without the permission of the court. The applicability of the unfitness provisions in sections 6 to 9 is expressly contemplated in section 22A(4) which provides that references to provisions of the Insolvency Act or the Companies Act in Schedule 1 of the CDDA include references to corresponding provisions of the Building Societies Act 1986.

Incorporated friendly societies

3.41 Section 22B of the CDDA provides that the Act applies to conduct in relation to incorporated friendly societies regulated by the Friendly Societies Act 1992 as it applies to conduct in relation to companies. The effects of section 22B are the same as those of section 22A in relation to building societies.[19] The applicability of the unfitness provisions to friendly societies is clearly contemplated by section 22B(4). The CDDA did not originally apply to friendly societies. Section 22B was inserted by the Friendly Societies Act 1992, s. 120(1) and Sched. 21, para. 8 with effect from February 1, 1993.[20] The 1992 Act makes provision for the conversion of incorporated friendly societies into companies in which case they fall squarely within the CDDA in any

---

[18] Companies formed and registered under the Joint Stock Companies Act 1844 or in Ireland under companies legislation up to and including the Companies (Consolidation) Act 1908 are excluded: Companies Act 1985, s. 735(1)(a), (3).
[19] The only difference is that in relation to incorporated friendly societies, the CDDA does not extend to shadow directors: section 22B(3).
[20] S.I. 1993 No. 16 (C. 1).

event. It should be noted that section 22B does not extend to unregistered friendly societies or friendly societies registered under the Friendly Societies Act 1974. These entities are considered below in para. 3.49.

Open-ended investment companies

3.42 The Open-Ended Investment Companies (Investment Companies with Variable Capital) Regulations 1996 inserted a new paragraph 5A in Schedule 1 of the CDDA.[21] In relation to Part I of the Schedule, this provides that references to provisions of the Companies Act shall be taken to be a reference to the corresponding provision of the 1996 Regulations. It is clear from this that directors of open-ended investment companies are exposed to disqualification under the unfitness provisions of the CDDA. It is not clear whether a person disqualified in the terms of section 1 from acting as a director, etc. of a company is prohibited from acting as director of an open-ended investment company. This is because the 1996 Regulations do not expressly amend or modify CDDA, s. 1 to include a reference to open-ended investment companies. This last point is considered further in Chapter 12 on the legal effect of disqualification.

Insolvent partnerships

3.43 Issues of partnership insolvency are governed by the Insolvent Partnerships Order 1994.[22] Article 16 of the Order provides that the CDDA, ss 6 to 10, 15, 19(c), 20 and Sched. 1 apply (with certain modifications) where an insolvent partnership is wound up as an unregistered company under Part V of the Insolvency Act.[23] Article 3 has the effect that references to companies in the provisions of the CDDA applied by the Order should be construed as references to insolvent partnerships. It is clear from these provisions and the modifications contained in Schedule 8 to the Order that an officer of an insolvent partnership is caught by CDDA, s. 6 and must be disqualified if the court is satisfied that his conduct as an officer of that partnership makes him unfit to be concerned in the management of a company. Indeed, conduct by a partner or former partner in relation to an insolvent partnership firm clearly triggers the possibility of disqualification under the unfitness provisions as a whole. For the purposes of CDDA, ss 6–9 a partnership "officer" means "a member or a person who has management or control of the partnership business".[24] It should be noted that CDDA, ss 6–8 have no application where the individual members of the firm present a joint bankruptcy petition under article 11 of the Insolvent Partnerships Order. In those circumstances, article 16 is not triggered because article 11 procedure does not involve the winding up of the firm as an unregistered company. Nevertheless, partners using article 11 are susceptible to automatic disqualification under section 11 of the CDDA as personal bankrupts. An issue of some controversy concerns whether a person disqualified in the terms of CDDA, ss 1, 11 or 12 is prohibited from trading in partnership as well as from running companies. The preferable view is that a disqualified person can trade in partnership because the Insolvent Partnerships Order is concerned only with insolvent partnerships (not partnerships generally) and it does not expressly amend or modify section 1 to include a reference to partnerships (whether solvent or

---

[21] S.I. 1996 No. 2827 with effect from January 6, 1997.
[22] S.I. 1994 No. 2421 as subsequently amended by the Insolvent Partnerships (Amendment) Order 1996 (S.I. 1996 No. 1308). For a general discussion, see G. Morse, *Partnership Law* (4th ed., 1998), Chap. 8.
[23] Article 16 mirrors the application of the rule-making powers in the Insolvency Act 1986 as provided for by section 21(2) of the CDDA. The Insolvent Partnerships Order was made under section 420(1), (2) of the Insolvency Act and section 21(2) of the CDDA.
[24] Insolvent Partnerships Order 1994, art. 2(1).

otherwise). Indeed, given the limits of the rule-making power in section 21(2) of the CDDA (which makes no reference to section 1) there is no power to make such amendment.[25] This difficult issue is considered fully in chapter 12 on the legal effect of disqualification.

Limited liability partnerships

3.44 Limited liability partnerships are a new form of body corporate which can be incorporated under the proposed new Limited Liability Partnerships Act. They are designed for use by groupings of professionals (e.g. solicitors or accountants) and combine certain features of ordinary partnerships with the main features of limited companies (i.e. corporate personality and limited liability). Draft regulations propose the insertion of a new section 22C in the CDDA which adopts the same approach as sections 22A and 22B. The position in relation to limited liability partnerships under the CDDA is therefore the same as that for building societies and incorporated friendly societies (subject to the Act being passed and coming into force).[25a]

European Economic Interest Groupings

3.45 The CDDA, ss 1, 2, 4–11, 12(2), 15–17, 20, 22 and Sched. 1 expressly apply where an EEIG is wound up as an unregistered company under Part V of the Insolvency Act. This is the effect of Regulation 20 of the European Economic Interest Grouping Regulations 1989.[26] For these purposes, the reference in CDDA, s. 6 to a director or past director of a company is taken to include a reference to a manager of an EEIG or anyone who has or has had control or management of an EEIG's business. Thus, there is little doubt that directors and managers of an insolvent EEIG could face disqualification under the provisions specified. As with partnership there is some doubt whether a disqualified person is prohibited generally from involvement in EEIGs. Although the 1989 Regulations make express reference to CDDA, s. 1 they do not expressly extend the wording of section 1 to include EEIGs. This point is discussed further in Chapter 12 on the legal effect of disqualification.

Companies capable of being wound up under Part V of the Insolvency Act 1986

3.46 Section 22(2)(b) of the CDDA provides that the term "company" includes "any company which may be wound up under Part V of the Insolvency Act 1986" in all provisions of the CDDA except for section 11. On a literal reading, this means that the various powers of disqualification in the Act extend to the directors, etc. of any *company* that can be wound up as an unregistered company under Part V. It also means that a person disqualified in the terms of either section 1 or section 12 of the CDDA is prohibited from being a director or from taking part in the management of such a company. The definition has the effect of bringing the following types of company within the CDDA's scope:

---

[25] For a contrary view, see A. Mithani & S. Wheeler, *The Disqualification of Company Directors* (1st ed., 1996), pp. 49, 198–200. The view expressed there was that a partnership is a "company which may be wound up under Part V of the Insolvency Act" within CDDA, s. 22(2)(b) because winding up of partnerships under Part V is expressly contemplated under the Insolvent Partnerships Order. The upshot is that "company" in CDDA, s. 1 includes "partnership". This view is subjected to detailed criticism in Chap. 12. The present authors' main contention is that a partnership is not a "*company* which may be wound up under Part V" (emphasis added) within section 22(2)(b). An opposite view is also now expressed in the later looseleaf edition of Mithani in Chap. 1 of Division 5.
[25a] At the time of going to press the relevant provisions had not been enacted.
[26] S.I. 1989 No. 638.

Unregistered companies as defined by the Companies Act

3.47   Certain provisions of the Companies Act 1985 are extended to apply to bodies corporate which are incorporated in Great Britain but are incorporated under a special Act of Parliament or by Royal Charter rather than under the Companies Act or any other public general Act.[27]

Foreign companies

3.48   A company incorporated outside Great Britain can be wound up by the court under Part V of the Insolvency Act (usually exercising jurisdiction under section 221). The court will only assume jurisdiction in relation to the winding up of an overseas company if there is some sufficient connection between the company and England and Wales. It will normally be a sufficient connection if the company has carried on business in England and Wales or if it holds assets here and there are people within the jurisdiction who have an interest in the distribution of those assets.[28] The result is that the provisions in sections 6 to 8 of the CDDA apply to overseas companies that are being wound up in England and Wales. Furthermore, where the lead company in section 6 proceedings is an English company, the defendant's conduct as a director of collateral overseas companies can also be taken into consideration.[29] An overseas company having a branch or an established place of business within the jurisdiction may also fall within sections 3 and 5 as certain provisions of companies legislation governing the filing of accounts and returns apply to these companies. The final consequence of note is that section 22(2)(b) has the effect of extending the meaning of "company" in sections 1 and 12. This means that a person disqualified by the court is technically prohibited from acting as a director or taking part in the management of an overseas company over which the English courts might usually be expected to assume winding up jurisdiction. The point is raised again in Chap. 12.

Unincorporated friendly societies

3.49   Section 22B of the CDDA (discussed in para. 3.41 above) does not extend to unregistered friendly societies or friendly societies registered under the Friendly Societies Act 1974. It might appear at first sight that these would be caught by the CDDA as they may be wound up as unregistered companies under Part V of the Insolvency Act.[30] However, section 22(2)(b) of the CDDA refers to any *company* which may be wound up under Part V. It does not expressly adopt the wider term "unregistered company" used in the Insolvency Act and defined to include "any association and any company"[31]. It is suggested that an unincorporated association capable of being wound up under Part V should not be treated as a "company" (*i.e.* an incorporated entity) falling within section 22(2)(b).[32]

The position in relation to industrial and provident societies needs to be mentioned briefly. Section 55 of the Industrial and Provident Societies Act 1965 provides that societies registered under that legislation should be treated as if they were ordinary

---

[27] Companies Act 1985, s. 718, Sched. 22.
[28] *Banque des Marchands de Moscou (Koupetschesky) v. Kindersley* [1951] Ch. 112, [1950] 2 All E.R. 549; *Re Compania Merabello San Nicholas SA* [1973] Ch. 75, [1972] 3 All E.R. 448; *Re Eloc Electro-Optieck & Communicatie BV* [1982] Ch. 43, [1981] 2 All E.R. 1111; *International Westminster Bank plc v. Okeanos Maritime, Re a Company No. 00359 of 1987* [1988] 1 Ch. 210, [1987] B.C.L.C. 450, (1987) 3 B.C.C. 160.
[29] *Re Eurostem Maritime Ltd* [1987] P.C.C. 190. See also *Re Dominion International Group plc (No. 2)* [1996] 1 B.C.L.C. 572 and para. 3.53.
[30] *Re Victoria Society, Knottingley* [1913] 1 Ch. 167.
[31] Insolvency Act 1986, s. 220(1).
[32] The same argument is developed in Chap. 12 in relation to partnerships.

registered companies for the purposes of winding up. This has the effect that industrial and provident societies will usually be wound up under the provisions of Part IV, not Part V of the Insolvency Act. It is strongly arguable that these societies fall outside the scope of the CDDA on the ground that they are not "companies" within section 22(2)(b). The argument is strengthened by the fact that Parliament has seen fit to extend the CDDA so that it specifically covers building societies and incorporated friendly societies (see paras 3.40–3.41) but has made no attempt to apply the Act's provisions expressly to industrial and provident societies.[33]

"BECOMES INSOLVENT"

3.50 For the purposes of section 6(1)(a) it must be established that the defendant is or has been a director of a company which has at any time "become insolvent". Section 6(2) states:

"For the purposes of ... section [6] and ... [7], a company becomes insolvent if—

(a) the company goes into liquidation at a time when its assets are insufficient for the payment of its debts and other liabilities and the expenses of the winding up,

(b) an administration order is made in relation to the company, or

(c) an administrative receiver of the company is appointed..."

This provision is important in two respects. First, the jurisdiction in section 6 is only triggered if the relevant company has "become insolvent". It can be seen from section 6(2) that the company needs to have entered into a relevant formal insolvency regime.[34] The company's "insolvency" in a commercial sense (*e.g.* where it is unable to pay its debts as they fall due) is not of itself sufficient to trigger the jurisdiction. A further implication is that a company which is dissolved and struck off the register without being the subject of a formal insolvency procedure has not "become insolvent" within section 6 and would first have to be restored to the register before proceedings could be commenced.[35] Secondly, the two-year time limit for commencing proceedings for an order under section 6 runs from the day on which the relevant company "became insolvent".[36] This second aspect is considered further in Chapter 6.

"Goes into liquidation"

3.51 Section 6(2)(b) and (c) are relatively straightforward. If the company has gone into administration, it is treated as insolvent for CDDA purposes from the date the administration order was made under Part II of the Insolvency Act 1986. If the

---

[33] For a contrary view, see C. Mills, "Does CDDA Apply to Industrial and Provident Societies?" (1997) 13 *Insolvency Law & Practice* 182. Mills argues that just because legislation makes provision for the winding up of a society as if it were an ordinary company under Part IV does not necessarily oust the court's jurisdiction under Part V (and with it, the application of the CDDA). Much seems to depend on the phrase "may be wound up under Part V". Mills contends that the court retains a residual jurisdiction under Part V and asserts that the question of whether the court is *likely* to exercise this jurisdiction is irrelevant. Even if an industrial and provident society could be wound up under Part V, the better view is that it is an "association" rather than a "*company* which may be wound up under Part V" and so does not fall within section 22(2)(b) of the CDDA.
[34] The position is similar in relation to insolvent partnerships: see Insolvent Partnerships Order 1994, art. 16 and Sched. 8. It is perhaps an anomaly that section 6(2) does not include a corporate voluntary arrangement.
[35] See further Chap. 6 on this point.
[36] CDDA, s. 7(2).

company has gone into administrative receivership, it is treated as insolvent for CDDA purposes from the date of the receiver's appointment.[37] At first sight, section 6(2)(a) is equally straightforward. The Insolvency Act definition of "goes into liquidation" is expressly adopted.[38] A company "goes into liquidation" if it passes a resolution for voluntary winding up or an order for its compulsory winding up is made by the court.[39] However, the court must also be satisfied that the company was insolvent on the balance sheet test (*i.e.* as having a deficiency of assets over liabilities) at the time it went into liquidation. This additional requirement to establish that the relevant company has gone into *insolvent* liquidation has the effect of excluding companies that are solvent when wound up from the ambit of section 6.

3.52   In determining whether the company was insolvent at the time it went into liquidation, one question that has arisen is how the court should go about computing the expenses of winding up. On a literal reading of section 6(2)(a), if the company's realisable assets were sufficient to meet its liabilities and projected winding up expenses at the time it went into liquidation, then it has not "become insolvent" for section 6 purposes. The problem with this is that the court is being asked to take expenses into account in determining whether the company had become insolvent, but viewed from a point when those expenses have not yet been incurred, namely the commencement of liquidation. In *Re Gower Enterprises Ltd, Official Receiver v. Moore*,[40] the company went into liquidation with a surplus of realisable assets over liabilities of around £100,000 according to its statement of affairs. In winding up the company's affairs, the liquidator incurred expenses (including his own remuneration) of around £180,000. If the expenses actually incurred were taken into account under section 6(1)(a) then the company could be treated as having become insolvent with an asset deficiency of £80,000. The court took a pragmatic view recognising that it is impossible to determine the amount of the winding up expenses at the date of winding up. Equally, however, it was considered inappropriate to use the figure for expenses actually incurred as to do so would mean that liability under the CDDA could turn on expenses that had been improperly or ill-advisedly incurred. To avoid this possible injustice, Evans-Lombe J. held that "expenses" in section 6(1)(a) should be construed as meaning "reasonable expenses". The unfortunate consequence is that in cases like *Gower Enterprises* the court will have to hear argument on whether the expenses were reasonably incurred and, if it decides that they were not, substitute its own "reasonable expenses" figure.[41] It is arguable that section 6(1)(a) should be amended so that the court's jurisdiction is triggered simply if the company goes into liquidation. So as not to deter directors from placing a company into liquidation where there is no question of insolvency, it could be made clear by further amendment (to section 7(3)) that there is no obligation on the liquidator in a members' voluntary liquidation to report on the question of fitness. This would eliminate any scope for defendants to raise time-

[37] The validity of an administration order or an administrative receiver's appointment cannot be challenged in disqualification proceedings: see *Secretary of State for Trade and Industry v. Jabble* [1998] 1 B.C.L.C. 598, [1998] B.C.C. 39, CA. The proper course is to stay the disqualification proceedings to allow the company to challenge the order or appointment in proceedings properly constituted for the purpose. The court is unlikely to stay disqualification proceedings if it considers that the challenge will fail *e.g.* in circumstances where the administration or receivership has long since been completed.
[38] Insolvency Act 1986, s. 247(2); CDDA, s. 22(3).
[39] In the case of compulsory liquidation, the company "goes into liquidation" under the CDDA on the date of the winding up order not the date of the petition: see *Re Walter L Jacob & Co. Ltd, Official Receiver v. Jacob* [1993] B.C.C. 512.
[40] [1995] B.C.C. 293.
[41] In *Gower Enterprises* the court, on inquiry, substituted a reduced figure but this still meant that there was an overall asset deficiency for the purposes of section 6(2)(a): see [1995] B.C.C. 293 at 297, [1995] 2 B.C.L.C. 107.

consuming side issues pertaining to the conduct of the liquidation.[42] In a sense, the requirement that a company be insolvent on a net asset basis when it is wound up is rather anomalous. There is no such requirement in the case of companies that go into administration or administrative receivership.

CONDUCT IN RELATION TO LEAD AND COLLATERAL COMPANIES

3.53   Under section 6(1)(b) the court must decide whether the defendant's conduct as a director of the relevant company (*i.e.* the one which has "become insolvent") "either taken alone or taken together with his conduct as a director of any other company or companies makes him unfit ...". The final preliminary issue concerns the extent to which the court can take into account the defendant's conduct in relation to other companies in proceedings under section 6. In what follows the terminology used in *Re Country Farm Inns Ltd, Secretary of State for Trade and Industry v. Ivens*[43] is adopted. The main company in the proceedings is referred to as the "lead company" and other companies in relation to which complaint is made are referred to as "collateral companies".

The basic point of section 6(1)(b) is that it allows the court to take into account evidence of the defendant's misconduct in the lead company either alone or "together with" evidence of his misconduct in relation to a collateral company or companies.[44] The court can rely on the "collateral company" evidence to tip the balance towards a finding of unfitness on the evidence as a whole. Alternatively, if the court is satisfied that the evidence in relation to the lead company is enough on its own to make the defendant unfit, it can take into account the "collateral company" evidence when determining the period of disqualification.[45] Thus, "collateral company" evidence may go either to the question of unfitness or to the question of length of disqualification. The effect is that the claimant can rely on evidence which tends to show a pattern of misconduct in relation to a series of failed companies over time. Three main questions have arisen for decision in this context. The first is whether the court can take account of good conduct on the defendant's part in collateral companies and weigh that against questionable conduct in the lead company to reach an overall conclusion concerning his fitness or unfitness. The second is whether there has to be some nexus or connection between the conduct complained of in the lead company and any collateral companies. The third is whether "collateral company" allegations raised in one set of disqualification proceedings can be raised in a later set of disqualification proceedings against the same defendant.

---

[42] The Court of Appeal has confirmed that a challenge on the ground that there was no deficiency of assets when the company went into liquidation can properly be made in disqualification proceedings as it goes directly to the issue of jurisdiction: see *dictum* of Millett L.J. in *Secretary of State for Trade and Industry v. Jabble* [1998] 1 B.C.L.C. 598, [1998] B.C.C. 39.

[43] [1997] 2 B.C.L.C. 334, [1997] B.C.C. 801, CA.

[44] There may be more than one lead company: see discussion in *Re Launchexcept Ltd, Secretary of State for Trade and Industry v. Tillman* [1999] B.C.C. 703. For that to be the case, the proceedings in respect of all the lead companies would need to be commenced within the two-year time period unless the permission of the court is obtained under section 7(2) to commence them late. It is conceivable that the Secretary of State might commence proceedings in relation to a number of lead companies where the prospective defendant is the director of several companies in an insolvent group. It should also be noted that conduct in relation to a subsidiary of the lead company can be taken into account if it involves a breach of duty which inflicts harm on both the subsidiary and the lead company even in circumstances where the court would not have had jurisdiction over the subsidiary in isolation (*i.e.* where the subsidiary was not capable of being a lead company): see *Re Dominion International Group plc (No. 2)* [1996] 1 B.C.L.C. 572.

[45] See *Re T & D Services (Timber Preservation & Damp Proofing Contractors) Ltd* [1990] B.C.C. 592 at 593.

Can good conduct in collateral companies be taken into account?

3.54   Counsel for the defendant in *Re Bath Glass Ltd*[46] submitted that it was open to the court to conclude that a disqualification order should not be made by taking into account a general record of good conduct in relation to collateral companies. This submission was based on an argument that the words "either taken alone or taken together with his conduct as a director of any other company ..." should be treated as general words enabling the court to reach the conclusion that a disqualification order is inappropriate (on the basis that the defendant is *fit*) by reference to the defendant's conduct as a director of other companies. Peter Gibson J. rejected the submission. He concluded that section 6(1)(b) obliges the court to judge whether the defendant was *unfit* by looking either at his conduct as a director of the lead company alone or at his conduct as a director both of the lead company and of any collateral companies. Once the court finds by either route that the defendant is unfit, it is bound to disqualify him. Counsel for the defendant's construction of section 6(1)(b) was rejected because it implied that the court has a discretion to refuse to order disqualification by allowing evidence of good conduct in collateral companies to cancel out evidence of unfit conduct in the lead company. The net result is that evidence of a general record of good conduct in relation to collateral companies is inadmissible in proceedings for an order under section 6 on the question of unfitness. Only additional evidence of misconduct can be allowed in. The broader (and related) issue of whether evidence of good conduct (in relation to any company, lead, collateral or otherwise) can be adduced on the question of unfitness is considered in Chapter 4.[47] It should be noted, however, that none of this necessarily stops the court from relying on evidence of good conduct in collateral companies to justify imposing a shorter period of disqualification than that which would otherwise have been appropriate.[48] The extent to which evidence of good conduct can be relied on to mitigate the period of disqualification is also discussed in Chapter 5.

Does there need to be some nexus or connection between the conduct in lead and collateral companies?

3.55   The "nexus" issue was first raised by Chadwick J. in *Re Godwin Warren Control Systems plc* where he made the following remarks:

> "There must, I think, be some nexus between the conduct in relation to other companies and the conduct in relation to the insolvent company. If this were not so, a director whose conduct in relation to the insolvent company was blameless would be at risk of disqualification because his conduct in relation to other companies (unconnected and not insolvent) was unsatisfactory. Where the position is that conduct in relation to other companies is quite independent of the conduct in relation to the insolvent company, it is not to be taken into account for the purposes of the decision which the court has to make under section 6(1)(b)."[49]

It appears that on this basis the judge refused to take into account evidence of the defendant's integrity in relation to companies which he had managed both before and after his involvement in the lead company in that case. Thus, all that *Godwin Warren*

---

[46] [1988] B.C.L.C. 329, (1988) 4 B.C.C. 130.
[47] See, in particular, *Re Grayan Building Services Ltd, Secretary of State for Trade and Industry v. Gray* [1995] Ch. 241, [1995] 3 W.L.R., [1995] 1 B.C.L.C. 276, [1995] B.C.C. 554, CA which adds further weight to the view put forward in *Bath Glass*.
[48] See *Re Pamstock Ltd* [1996] B.C.C. 341 at 349–350 *per* Morritt L.J.
[49] [1993] B.C.L.C. 80 at 92, [1992] B.C.C. 557 at 567.

really decided was that good conduct in collateral companies is irrelevant to the question of unfitness because there is no nexus between *good conduct* and the *misconduct* alleged in relation to the lead company. A similar conclusion could have been reached using the reasoning in *Bath Glass* (see para. 3.54 above) but this case was apparently not cited.[50] Chadwick J.'s *dictum* was subsequently interpreted in *Re Diamond Computer Systems Ltd, Official Receiver v. Brown* as meaning that there must be some link or connection between the alleged *misconduct* in relation to collateral companies and the alleged *misconduct* in relation to the lead company.[51]

3.56   The current leading authority on the nexus issue is the Court of Appeal's decision in *Re Country Farm Inns Ltd, Secretary of State for Trade and Industry v. Ivens*.[52] In that case, the two defendants were a husband and wife and the lead company in the proceedings was Country Farm Inns Ltd. It was alleged in relation to Country Farm that the husband was unfit solely on the basis that he had taken part in the company's management while an undischarged bankrupt (*i.e.* in breach of the automatic disqualification imposed by CDDA, s. 11). His wife was said to be unfit because she permitted him to act while disqualified. The Secretary of State asked the court to have regard to evidence of the defendants' conduct in relation to four other failed companies. The nature of the alleged misconduct in these collateral companies is not spelled out in detail in the reports of the case but it is clear that it differed from the alleged misconduct in the lead company as it was said to have occurred before the husband was made bankrupt. The preliminary issue before the court was whether the defendants' conduct as a director of the collateral companies was "conduct as a director of any other company or companies" which could legitimately be taken into account in determining the question of unfitness under section 6. It was common ground between the parties that there does have to be *some* nexus in the sense that the defendant must have been a director (whether *de jure*, *de facto* or shadow) of each of the lead and collateral companies and, further, that the alleged misconduct in the lead and collateral companies must be conduct *qua* director that tends to show unfitness. The defendants argued that misconduct as a director of collateral companies should only be taken into account where it is the same as or similar to the misconduct alleged in relation to the lead company or where it serves to throw light on, explain or remove doubt about the lead company allegations. In putting forward this argument, they relied on Chadwick J.'s *dictum* from *Godwin Warren*.[53] It was also pointed out that at the time when the application was commenced in relation to Country Farm, the Secretary of State could not have commenced proceedings based *solely* on the alleged misconduct in respect of the collateral companies (*i.e.* proceedings in which those companies would have been lead companies) without the permission of the court. This was because of the requirement in section 7(2) that proceedings for an order under section 6 should generally be commenced within two years of the day on which the relevant company became insolvent. In this case the four collateral companies had all become insolvent more than two years before the proceedings were commenced in relation to Country Farm. The implication of this argument was that unrelated conduct in collateral companies should only be taken into account if the proceedings were commenced

---

[50] See the comments of Judge Weeks Q.C. at first instance in *Re Country Farm Inns Ltd, Secretary of State for Trade and Industry v. Ivens* [1997] 2 B.C.L.C. 334 at 336–337, [1997] B.C.C. 396 at 397.
[51] [1997] 1 B.C.L.C. 174 at 179–180. The judge used the word "conduct" rather than "misconduct" but it is clear from the passage as a whole that he saw a need for a link to be established between the matters of complaint in the lead and collateral companies.
[52] [1997] 2 B.C.L.C. 334, [1997] B.C.C. 801.
[53] As later approved by the Court of Appeal in *Re Pamstock Ltd* [1996] B.C.C. 341, a case on costs. Lindsay J. also spoke approvingly of the *dictum* in *Re Polly Peck International plc (No. 2)* [1994] 1 B.C.L.C. 574 at 583, [1993] B.C.C. 890 at 898.

within two years of the *collateral companies* (as well as the lead company) becoming insolvent or if permission to proceed in relation to the collateral companies was first obtained under section 7(2).[54]

3.57   A unanimous Court of Appeal held that the defendants' conduct in relation to the four collateral companies could be taken into account in determining whether or not they were unfit. A number of important points concerning the construction of section 6(1)(b) emerge from Morritt L.J.'s leading judgment:

(1) The claimant is only required to establish a limited nexus between the allegations relating to the lead and collateral companies. The conduct complained of in respect of each company must be "conduct as a director" and conduct that tends to show unfitness. There is nothing in the CDDA to suggest that the conduct in collateral companies should be the same as or similar to the conduct relied on in relation to the lead company. The court is required by section 9 of the Act to have particular regard to matters mentioned in Schedule 1 when determining the question of unfitness. However, the only distinction drawn in section 9 is between solvent and insolvent companies. There is nothing in either section 9 or Schedule 1 requiring the court to draw some additional distinction between the types of conduct that can be taken into account in lead and collateral companies. As long as the conduct in the collateral companies tends to show unfitness it will generally be relevant and admissible.[55]

(2) Chadwick J.'s *dictum* in *Godwin Warren* rested on a false assumption. The judge assumed that a defendant would be at risk of disqualification based *solely* on his conduct as a director of a collateral company in the absence of some wider "nexus" requirement. Morritt L.J. accepted that the judge at first instance in *Country Farm* had been correct to hold that the court can only disqualify the defendant if it concludes that his conduct as a director of the lead company, "either taken alone or taken together with his conduct as director of any other company" makes him unfit. Thus, if the defendant's conduct as a director of the lead company is *in no way* unsatisfactory, it is not possible for the court to disqualify him on the basis of his conduct in relation to collateral companies. On the other hand, as long as the claimant can point to *some* relevant misconduct in the lead company, there is a clear implication that conduct in collateral companies can be used to tip the balance towards a finding of unfitness.[56]

(3) The two-year time limit in section 7(2) only applies to the lead company. It does not apply to collateral companies. This means that as long as the proceedings in relation to the lead company are brought in time, the claimant can also rely on allegations in relation to other companies that may have become

---

[54] On section 7(2) generally, see further Chaps. 6–7.
[55] To give an example, it is clearly contemplated in section 9 and Schedule 1 that the court should take into account the defendant's responsibility for the lead company giving a preference (Sched. 1 Pt II, para. 8) together with his responsibility for a failure by any collateral company to prepare annual accounts (Sched. 1 Pt I, para. 5). These can hardly be described as the same type of allegation but both go to the question of unfitness. On section 9 and Schedule 1 generally see Chap. 4.
[56] The claimant must be able to point to some element of relevant misconduct in the lead company but there is no requirement that that conduct, taken in isolation, must necessarily make the defendant unfit. The same finding was made by the Registrar of the Companies Court in the *Launchexcept* case: see *Re Launchexcept Ltd, Secretary of State for Trade and Industry v. Tillman* [1999] B.C.C. 703.

insolvent more than two years before the proceedings were commenced.[57] Although not canvassed in the Court of Appeal, this point does raise an issue of policy. It might be argued on a narrow view of the CDDA that it is unfair for the claimant to rely on matters of any great vintage. Otherwise, directors face the risk that a fresh corporate insolvency may trigger an inquiry into past failings in relation to which no proceedings were brought at the time. However, it must be remembered that the claimant is directed by section 7(1) to consider whether it is expedient in the public interest to bring proceedings for an order under section 6. Furthermore, on a wider view, it is clear that the CDDA is concerned with protecting the public from those who have traded a succession of companies into the ground at the expense of creditors. As such, it is legitimate (in a broad sense) for the court to take into account the full history of the defendant's involvement in companies where it illustrates an emerging pattern of misconduct over time and this is so even though "lead company" proceedings could no longer have been commenced against some of those companies without the court's permission under section 7(2). However, it will be interesting to see if, in an appropriate case, the court might strike out "lead company" proceedings as an abuse of process. It was suggested *obiter* by Mr Jules Sher Q.C. (sitting as a deputy High Court judge) in *Re Diamond Computer Systems Ltd, Official Receiver v. Brown* that it would be inappropriate "to disqualify a director of company 'x' for his misconduct as director of company 'y' in proceedings in respect of which the lead company is company 'x' where the essential burden of the complaint is his conduct as a director of company 'y' and not company 'x'"[58] The judge described this as allowing "the tail to wag the dog". It is suggested that if the claimant sought to rely on conduct in relation to the lead company solely as a means to avoid an application for permission to commence proceedings out of time under section 7(2) in circumstances where the "essential burden of complaint" was his conduct in relation to other companies, the court would resort to its power to strike out proceedings as an abuse of its process.[59]

(4) There is no requirement that a collateral company must necessarily have become insolvent. It is perfectly possible for the claimant to rely on the defendant's conduct in relation to *solvent* collateral companies as long as that conduct tends to show unfitness.[60] This point adds further force to the points in (2) and (3) above. The insolvency of the lead company is one of the crucial elements that triggers jurisdiction under section 6. As such, it must be correct to say that the claimant is required to point to some relevant misconduct in the lead company. Otherwise, it would follow logically that the defendant could be disqualified on the basis of conduct in *solvent* collateral companies alone, a result which sits uncomfortably alongside the triggering requirement that "he

---

[57] The claimant has been allowed to rely on such collateral allegations in several cases: see, *e.g. Re T & D Services (Timber Preservation & Damp Proofing Contractors) Ltd* [1990] B.C.C. 592 (in this case the three collateral companies all went into liquidation before either the Insolvency Act 1985 or the CDDA came into force); *Re Tansoft Ltd* [1991] B.C.L.C. 339; *Re Melcast (Wolverhampton) Ltd* [1991] B.C.L.C. 288; *Re Defence & Microwave Devices Ltd*, October 7, 1992, Ch.D., unreported; *Re Pamstock Ltd* [1994] 1 B.C.L.C. 716, [1994] B.C.C. 264.
[58] [1997] 1 B.C.L.C. 174 at 180.
[59] The dismissal of proceedings on grounds of abuse of process is discussed further in Chap. 6.
[60] It was indicated in *Country Farm* that, at least at that time, the Secretary of State was unlikely ever to rely on a defendant's conduct as a director of a solvent collateral company. However, the attitude of the Secretary of State in no way affects the construction of section 6 and may since have changed. There are positive reasons in the public interest (in particular, the notion that disqualification is concerned with raising standards of conduct) why such an approach should not be followed.

is or has been a director of a company which has at any time become insolvent" in section 6(1)(a). Equally, this point makes it difficult to see how section 7(2) has any relevance to collateral companies. The two-year time limit starts to run from the date when the lead company "became insolvent". Section 7(2) thus draws directly on the wording in section 6(1)(a). As there is no absolute requirement for collateral companies to have "become insolvent" it must follow that the two-year time limit does not apply to them (subject to the point concerning abuse of process in (3) above).

3.58   It is clear from the Court of Appeal's decision that the nexus "requirement" as conceived in *Godwin Warren* is now dead. However, the issue of collateral companies is not entirely free from difficulty. Morritt L.J.'s judgment does not deal with the suggestion made in *Diamond Computer* that the defendant should not be disqualified if the "essential burden of complaint" relates to his conduct in collateral companies. As indicated above, there may be circumstances in which the court would strike out disqualification proceedings based principally on allegations relating to the defendant's conduct in a collateral company as an abuse of process.[61] Having said that, the approach in *Country Farm* is consistent with the protective purpose of disqualification in that it allows both the claimant and the court, in an appropriate case, to reconstruct a pattern of misconduct across a number of companies over time.

Can collateral allegations raised in one set of disqualification proceedings be raised against the same defendant in subsequent disqualification proceedings?

3.59   In *Re Launchexcept Ltd, Secretary of State for Trade and Industry v. Tillman*,[62] "lead company" proceedings were commenced against the defendant, "T", claiming that his conduct in relation to Launchexcept Ltd made him unfit to be concerned in the management of a company. T had been a defendant in an earlier set of disqualification proceedings brought by the official receiver following the failure of a listed company called Honorbilt Group plc. In the Honorbilt proceedings, the official receiver had chosen to rely in part on T's conduct in relation to the filing of accounts and returns in respect of Launchexcept as one of a number of collateral companies. In the event, the Honorbilt proceedings were dismissed against T because he was not found to be responsible for any relevant misconduct in the lead companies. As a result, the court could not take into account the collateral allegations relating to Launchexcept (see discussion in para. 3.57). T sought to have the Launchexcept proceedings struck out as an abuse of process on the ground that the further charges in relation to Launchexcept could and should have been brought forward in the earlier Honorbilt proceedings. In so doing T relied on the principle in *Henderson v. Hen-*

---

[61] Note also the attitude of Vinelott J. in *Re Pamstock Ltd* [1994] 1 B.C.L.C. 716, [1994] B.C.C. 264 and see also the Court of Appeal's decision on costs in that case at [1996] B.C.C. 341. The claimant must strike a balance. It is right for the claimant to draw attention to all the companies in which the defendant has been involved that have gone into insolvent liquidation. Equally, he should draw attention to serious failures in the filing of returns and accounts in collateral companies even if these complaints, taken in isolation, do not justify a disqualification order, or an increased period of disqualification. However, the claimant should not put in evidence every matter that could possibly be the subject of complaint without discrimination. To do so may detain the court in dealing with matters of no substantial weight going back over a long period of time thus increasing costs. The defendant in *Pamstock* was disqualified for the minimum period of two years but he was only ordered to pay half of the official receiver's costs. This was because in the judge's view, the claimant's practice of raising every conceivable matter of complaint in relation to the collateral companies, however inconsequential, had unnecessarily increased costs. The courts are likely to adopt a more robust approach in this respect in the light of the CPR.
[62] [1999] B.C.C. 703.

derson[63] which requires a party to bring forward his whole case and prevents him raising in later proceedings any matter that could have been litigated in the original proceedings. On T's appeal against the refusal of the judge to strike out the Launchexcept proceedings, Chadwick L.J. said that the proper approach is to ask whether the course adopted by the Secretary of State in relation to the earlier proceedings was such that it would be manifestly unfair to the defendant to allow the later proceedings to continue against him or alternatively, whether a refusal to strike out or stay the later proceedings would bring the administration of justice into disrepute among right thinking people. On the facts of *Launchexcept* the Court of Appeal held that the later proceedings were not an abuse of process.[64] The effect is that it may be possible for collateral allegations from earlier proceedings to be raised against the same defendant in later "lead company" proceedings if, in all the circumstances, it is fair to the defendant to allow the later proceedings to go forward on that footing.

"Lead" and "collateral" allegations in the context of insolvent partnerships

3.60   It was seen above in the course of the discussion concerning the meaning of "company", that proceedings for an order under section 6 can be brought against the officers of an insolvent partnership. Schedule 8 of the Insolvent Partnerships Order makes a number of modifications to the CDDA to accommodate such proceedings. The important point for present purposes is that section 6(1) is modified in the context of insolvent partnerships to read as follows:

> "The court shall make a disqualification order against a person in any case where, on an application under this section, it is satisfied—
>
> (a)   that he is or has been an officer of a partnership which has at any time become insolvent (whether while he was an officer or subsequently), and
>
> (b)   that his conduct as an officer of that partnership (either taken alone or taken together with his conduct as an officer of any other partnership or partnerships, or as a director of any company or companies) makes him unfit to be concerned in the management of a company."

Section 6(1)(b) (as modified by the Insolvent Partnerships Order) thus treats the insolvent partnership as the equivalent of a lead company and entitles the court to take into account the defendant's conduct in both collateral partnerships and collateral companies. In all other respects the position is the same as outlined in paras 3.53–3.59. It is not clear whether evidence of misconduct in a "collateral partnership" can be taken into account in ordinary proceedings under section 6 (*i.e.* where the jurisdiction is triggered by a corporate as opposed to a partnership insolvency). To take an example, "M" is the director of a private company, "X Ltd" which has gone into liquidation. M has also been involved previously in a number of failed partnership businesses. The Secretary of State seeks a disqualification order under section 6 based on M's conduct as a director of X Ltd as lead company. The issue for the court would be whether it can also take into account M's conduct as an officer of the collateral partnerships to determine the question of unfitness. The better view is that the court could not look at M's conduct in relation to the failed partnerships. It is suggested that conduct relating to

---

[63] (1843) 3 Hare 100.
[64] The main points were (1) that the matters raised in the later proceedings were not the subject of any adjudication in the Honorbilt proceedings (2) the claimant was not seeking to re-litigate the question of whether or not T's conduct in relation to Launchexcept made him unfit (3) the claimant was not relying on the filing defaults which had been raised in the Honorbilt proceedings (4) the matters raised in *Launchexcept* had not come to light when the Honorbilt proceedings came on for trial.

collateral partnerships can only be taken into account in the circumstances expressly provided for in the Insolvent Partnerships Order (*i.e.* where jurisidiction is triggered by a partnership insolvency). However, this point is not without controversy.[65]

SECTION 8(1): PRELIMINARIES

3.61   Section 8(1) which is headed "disqualification after investigation of company" states:

> "If it appears to the Secretary of State from a report made by inspectors under section 437 of the Companies Act or section 94 or 177 of the Financial Services Act 1986, or from information or documents obtained under section 447 or 448 of the Companies Act or section 105 of the Financial Services Act 1986 or section 2 of the Criminal Justice Act 1987 or section 52 of the Criminal Justice (Scotland) Act 1987 or section 83 of the Companies Act 1989, that it is expedient in the public interest that a disqualification order should be made against any person who is or has been a director or shadow director of any company, he may apply to the court for such an order to be made against that person."

It follows that two preliminary requirements need to be satisfied before an order can be sought under section 8:

(1)   That the defendant is or has been a director or shadow director of a company. The terms "director", "shadow director" and "company" bear the same meaning in section 8(1) as they do in section 6(1) (see above).

(2)   That information relating to the defendant's conduct in relation to that company has come to light in the course of the exercise of one or more of the statutory powers of investigation specified in section 8(1). Section 8 proceedings must be based on information contained in a report made by company inspectors or on information or documents obtained under one or more of the provisions mentioned.

Subject to these requirements, the court may, at its discretion, make a disqualification order against the defendant where it is satisfied that his conduct in relation to the company makes him unfit to be concerned in the management of a company. The relevant company need not have become insolvent for the purposes of section 8.[66]

Reports, information or documents

3.62   Section 8(1) makes reference to two types of inquisitorial power, namely powers of investigation leading to the production of a report by company inspectors and powers to obtain information or documents. Each set of powers is considered in turn.[67]

---

[65] See the discussion in the notes to para. 3.43 and in Chap. 12. The difficult point concerns whether or not a partnership can properly be regarded as a "*company* which may be wound up under Part V of the Insolvency Act" (emphasis added) within CDDA, s. 22(2)(b). If it can then the phrase "any other company or companies" in section 6(1)(b) would include collateral partnerships.

[66] The concept of discretionary disqualification for unfitness following a company investigation etc. originates from the Cork Report (see para. 1819(c)) and the provision was first enacted as section 13 of the Insolvency Act 1985.

[67] For a review of the Department of Trade and Industry's investigatory powers giving a detailed insight into their scope and operation see Trade and Industry Committee, Third Report, *Company Investigations* (1990 H.C. 36). For certain criticisms of the practices which have evolved in relation to the exercise of such powers see *Re Mirror Group Newspapers plc* [1999] 2 All E.R. 641.

Powers of investigation leading to production of a report

3.63 *Section 437 of the Companies Act 1985.* Under sections 431–432 of the Companies Act, the Secretary of State for Trade and Industry has power to appoint inspectors to investigate the affairs of a company either of his own motion (in the circumstances specified in section 432(2)) or at the request of the company or its members (section 431). In addition, the Secretary of State is obliged to appoint inspectors where the court declares by order that the affairs of a company ought to be investigated (section 432(1)). Where an investigation is carried out under these powers, the inspectors are required by section 437 to make a final report to the Secretary of State on completion of the investigation. Information in such a report may form the basis of proceedings under section 8 of the CDDA. Section 441 of the Companies Act provides that a certified copy of any such report is admissible in any legal proceedings as evidence of the opinion of the inspectors in relation to any matter contained in it and, in proceedings under section 8 of the CDDA, as evidence of any fact stated in it. The report may therefore be relied upon as evidence in any subsequent section 8 proceedings.[68] Moreover, even if the report is not published (as it may be under section 437(3)), there is a statutory gateway in sections 451A and 449 which permits the Secretary of State to make use of any information or documents obtained in the course of the investigation for a variety of purposes including the institution of disqualification proceedings under the CDDA. In this respect, the Secretary of State is not restricted to using the information in section 8 proceedings. It is clear from sections 451A(2)(a) and 449(1)(ba), (d) that the information could be used in connection with disqualification proceedings initiated by the Secretary of State under sections 2, 3, 4 and 6 as well as section 8.

3.64 *Section 94 of the Financial Services Act 1986.* Under this provision, the Secretary of State has power to appoint inspectors to investigate the affairs of an authorised unit trust scheme or any other collective investment scheme and/or the affairs of the manager, trustee or operator of such a scheme. The power is similar to that found in sections 431 to 432 of the Companies Act. Where an investigation is carried out under section 94, the inspectors are required by section 94(8) to make a final report to the Secretary of State on completion of the investigation. The statutory gateway in sections 179 to 180 permits the Secretary of State to make use of any information obtained under section 94 (see, in particular, section 180(1)(c)) for a variety of purposes including, it appears, the institution of disqualification proceedings under the CDDA. This applies whether or not the Secretary of State exercises his power in section

---

[68] For an example of section 8 proceedings which followed an investigation under section 432(2) and the production of a report under section 437 see *Re Atlantic Computers plc, Secretary of State for Trade and Industry v. Ashman*, June 15, 1998, Ch.D., unreported. As well as the report itself, transcripts of interviews together with any material gathered in the course of the investigation are admissible as evidence in section 8 proceedings by way of an implied exception to the hearsay rule: see *Re Rex Williams Leisure plc, Secretary of State for Trade and Industry v. Warren* [1994] Ch. 350, [1994] 3 W.L.R. 745, [1994] 4 All E.R. 27, [1994] 2 B.C.L.C. 555, [1994] B.C.C. 551, CA or alternatively under the Civil Evidence Act 1995. However, inspectors' correspondence including internal memoranda, notes and other materials produced for internal use are inadmissible and do not have to be disclosed: see *Re Astra Holdings plc* [1999] B.C.C. 121. In *Saunders v. United Kingdom* (Case 43/1994/490/572) [1997] B.C.C. 872 the European Court of Human Rights held that the use in criminal proceedings of compelled evidence obtained from the defendant in the course of a company investigation was a violation of his right to a fair trial under Article 6 of the European Convention on Human Rights. It is not thought presently that this ruling has any impact on the use of compelled evidence in disqualification proceedings as these are regarded as civil rather than criminal proceedings and the right to protection from self-incrimination enshrined in Article 6 only applies in criminal proceedings: see *Re Atlantic Computers plc, Secretary of State for Trade and Industry v. McCormick* [1998] 1 B.C.L.C. 18, Ch.D.; *R. v. Secretary of State for Trade and Industry ex. parte McCormick* [1998] B.C.C. 381, QBD and CA. For further discussion see *Re Mirror Group Newspapers plc* [1999] 2 All E.R. 641.

94(9) to have the report published and, as in the case of Companies Act investigations, the effect of sections 179–180 is that information could be used in connection with disqualification proceedings under sections 2, 3, 4, and 6 as well as 8.

3.65 *Section 177 of the Financial Services Act 1986.* If it appears to the Secretary of State that there are circumstances suggesting that an insider dealing offence under Part V of the Criminal Justice Act 1993 may have been committed, he has power under section 177 to appoint inspectors to carry out such investigations as are requisite to establish whether or not any such offence has been committed. Where an investigation is carried out under section 177, the inspectors are required by section 177(5) to make a final report to the Secretary of State on completion of the investigation. The statutory gateway in sections 179–180 applies to any information obtained under section 177 in the same way as it does to information obtained under section 94 (see above).

Powers to obtain information or documents

3.66 *Sections 447 to 448 of the Companies Act 1985.* Under section 447(2) of the Companies Act, the Secretary of State may at any time, if he thinks there is good reason to do so, give directions to a company requiring it, at such time and place as may be specified in the directions, to produce specified documents. There is also power in section 447(3) for the Secretary of State to authorise a competent person to require a company to produce documents. Section 448 empowers a justice of the peace to issue a search warrant on the application of the Secretary of State or an inspector if satisfied that there are reasonable grounds for believing that there are on any premises documents whose production has been required (whether under section 447 or other provisions of Part XIV of the Companies Act) and which have not been produced in compliance with that requirement. The purpose of section 447 was originally to allow the Secretary of State to obtain information and documents from companies under suspicion with a view to deciding whether or not to appoint an inspector and launch a full company investigation under sections 431–432.[69] It is clear from section 449 that its further purpose is to enable the Secretary of State to form a view as to whether legal proceedings (including disqualification proceedings) should be commenced. The power in section 447 includes power to take copies of any documents produced and power to require the person who produced them, or any other person who is a present or past officer of, or is or was at any time employed by the company in question, to provide an explanation of any of them (section 447(5)). Any statement made by a person in compliance with a requirement to produce documents may be used in evidence against him (section 447(8)).[70] As in the case of full company investigations (discussed above) there is a statutory gateway in section 449 which permits the Secretary of State to make use of any information or documents obtained in the course of the investigation for a variety of purposes including the institution of disqualification

---

[69] See Report of the Company Law Committee (the Jenkins Committee), Cmnd. 1749 (1962), paras 214–215 and discussion in *A.G.'s Ref. (Section 447 of the Companies Act)* [1999] B.C.C. 590.

[70] In *A.G.'s Ref. (Section 447 of the Companies Act)* [1999] B.C.C. 590, it was held that the requirement in section 447(5) to provide an explanation is, as a matter of construction, not limited to a requirement to provide an exposition of the text of a document but is capable of including (a) a requirement to provide an explanation covering the contents of the document, its date of creation, authorship, provenance, accuracy, completeness, intended purpose, destination and significance of its contents, and of the use to which it was in fact put and (b) a requirement to provide an explanation of any discrepancy or apparent discrepancy between two or more documents produced or between any explanation provided and the contents of any document produced. The result is that a person can be called upon to give explanations which might incriminate himself as the effect of section 447(8) is to override the privilege against self-incrimination. It is suggested that the comparable provisions in section 105(4) of the Financial Services Act and section 2(3) of the Criminal Justice Act 1987 would be read in the same way.

proceedings under the CDDA. In this respect, the Secretary of State is not restricted to using the information in section 8 proceedings. It is clear from section 449(1)(ba), (d) that the information could be used in connection with disqualification proceedings initiated by the Secretary of State under sections 2, 3, 4 and 6 as well as section 8. Information obtained under these provisions has formed the basis of disqualification proceedings under both sections 8 and 6.[71]

3.67 *Section 105 of the Financial Services Act 1986.* This provision empowers the Secretary of State to investigate the affairs of any person who is or was carrying on investment business, or appears to the Secretary of State to be or have been carrying on investment business. By virtue of section 105(4), the Secretary of State can require the person under investigation or any other person to produce documents and provide explanations of any document produced. The person under investigation can also be required to attend before the Secretary of State and answer questions or furnish information with respect to any matter relevant to the investigation (section 105(3)). Any statement made by a person in compliance with a requirement imposed by virtue of section 105 may be used in evidence against him (section 105(5)). The statutory gateway in sections 179 to 180 applies to any information obtained under section 105 in the same way as it does to information obtained under sections 94 and 177 (see above).

3.68 *Section 2 of the Criminal Justice Act 1987.* Section 1(3) of the Criminal Justice Act empowers the Director of the Serious Fraud Office to investigate any suspected offence involving serious or complex fraud in England, Wales and Northern Ireland. By virtue of section 2(2), the Director may require a person under investigation or any other person whom it is believed has relevant information to answer questions or furnish information with respect to any matter relevant to the investigation. Such persons can also be required to produce documents and provide explanations of any document produced. However, the use to which statements made by a person in compliance with these requirements is more limited than that under sections 447 of the Companies Act and section 105 of the Financial Services Act (see section 2(8)).[72] There is a similar range of powers in the Criminal Justice (Scotland) Act 1987, the only difference being that these powers are exercisable at the behest of the Lord Advocate rather than the Serious Fraud Office which does not have jurisdiction in Scotland. The statutory gateway in section 3 of the Criminal Justice Act 1987 permits the Serious Fraud Office to disclose information obtained under sections 1 to 2 to other competent authorities. The provision appears to be wide enough to allow information to be disclosed to the Secretary of State or the official receiver for use under the CDDA.

3.69 *Section 83 of the Companies Act 1989.* This provision confers on the Secretary of State a similar range of powers to those contained in section 447 of the Companies Act 1985. The powers are exercisable by the Secretary of State for the purpose of assisting an overseas regulatory authority which has requested his assistance in connection with inquiries being carried out by it or on its behalf (see section 82(1)). A statement made by a person in compliance with a requirement imposed under section

---

[71] See *Re Samuel Sherman plc* [1991] 1 W.L.R. 1070, [1991] B.C.C. 699; *Re Looe Fish Ltd* [1993] B.C.L.C. 1160, [1993] B.C.C. 348 (both section 8) and *Re Rex Williams Leisure plc, Secretary of State for Trade and Industry v. Warren* [1993] B.C.C. 79, Ch.D., [1994] Ch. 350, [1994] 3 W.L.R. 745, [1994] 4 All E.R. 27, [1994] 2 B.C.L.C. 555, [1994] B.C.C. 551, CA (section 6—see [1993] B.C.C. 79 at 88—though, note the apparent confusion in the Court of Appeal).
[72] For discussion of the scope of these powers see *Smith v. Director of the Serious Fraud Office* [1992] 3 All E.R. 546, HL; *R. v. Director of the Serious Fraud Office ex. parte Saunders* [1988] Crim. L.R. 837; *Re Arrows Ltd (No. 4)* [1994] 3 All E.R. 814, [1994] 2 B.C.L.C. 738, [1994] B.C.C. 641, HL.

83 may be used in evidence against him. It appears from section 87(1)(b) that any information obtained could be used by the Secretary of State for the purpose of considering whether to commence disqualification proceedings under sections 2, 3, 4 and 6 as well as in relation to section 8 proceedings.

CHAPTER 4

Determining Unfitness (1): General Principles

INTRODUCTION

4.01   The central question arising in the law on directors' disqualification is: what constitutes "unfitness"? This question has been touched on in the course of the discussion in Chapter 3 concerning the preliminary conditions that must be met if the claimant is to succeed in obtaining a disqualification order under either section 6 or 8. Once the preliminaries are out of the way, the court must decide whether the defendant's[1] conduct as a director of the relevant company or companies "makes him unfit to be concerned in the management of a company". The concept of unfitness is at the heart of the CDDA. It appears to encompass many, if not all, of the specific wrongs targeted by the other substantive powers of disqualification contained in sections 2, 3, 4, 5 and 10. It is also central to the policy of the CDDA in that a significant part of company law's regulatory function (especially in relation to the protection of creditors) is exercised through the law on unfitness. Unfitness is the principal criterion chosen to distinguish legitimate enterprise from illegitimate failure to meet the standards required of directors which justifies disqualification. There is now a vast and expanding corpus of judicial pronouncements on the question of what conduct makes a person unfit. The sheer volume of the case law is a reflection of the ever-increasing numbers of directors being processed through the courts in unfitness proceedings.[2] The present chapter and Chapter 5 attempt to provide a synthesis of this important area of company law and some assessment of the contribution which the developing law on unfitness is making to the reshaping of directors' obligations generally.[3] Issues of general principle are dealt with in this chapter. A detailed exposition of specific instances of unfit conduct and important issues such as directorial incompetence and

---

[1] Where applicable the terms "claimant", "defendant" and "permission" are used to reflect the modern requirements of the CPR, the Disqualification Rules and the Disqualification Practice Direction. In disqualification proceedings, "defendant" is the modern equivalent of the pre-CPR term "respondent" and "permission" the term now used for "leave". On the issue of the applicable rules of procedure in proceedings under section 6 and 8, see generally Chap. 6.

[2] The number of directors disqualified in proceedings for an order under CDDA, s. 6 has increased considerably during the 1990s and especially following the National Audit Office's report of October 1993 which criticised the effectiveness of the Insolvency Service in implementing the legislation: see the statistical appendices in A. Hicks, *Disqualification of Directors: No Hiding Place for the Unfit?* (A.C.C.A Research Report No. 59, 1998) and discussion in Chap. 14 of the same work. See also National Audit Office, *Company Director Disqualification—A Follow-up Report* (May 1999).

[3] There is not the space to provide a full account of the general law of directors' obligations. Nevertheless, some attempt is made in the course of the next two chapters to explore how the law on unfitness interrelates with the general law of directors' duties and, in particular, the duty of directors to act in good faith and the duty of care and skill. Another prevailing theme (borne out by the detailed coverage of specific instances of unfitness in Chap. 5) is the tendency for disqualification to be used as a means to reinforce core obligations in companies legislation such as the requirements to keep proper accounting records and to prepare and file audited accounts.

co-responsibility is reserved to Chapter 5. Once the court has determined that a disqualification order should be made against the defendant on grounds of unfitness, it then has to determine the appropriate period of disqualification. The approach of the court in determining the length of disqualification and the factors that might be taken into account in mitigation are discussed towards the end of Chapter 5.

SECTION 6: MANDATORY DISQUALIFICATION FOR UNFITNESS

4.02   The final matter on which the court must be satisfied before a disqualification order can be imposed under section 6 is that the defendant's conduct as a director "makes him unfit to be concerned in the management of a company". This is a critical requirement because once the court has determined that the defendant is unfit, it *must* disqualify him for at least the statutory minimum period of two years. Section 6 is the only mandatory provision in the CDDA. It differs markedly from its statutory antecedents in section 9 of the Insolvency Act 1976 and section 300 of the Companies Act 1985. Under these earlier provisions, the court did not have jurisdiction at all unless the defendant had been a director of at least two companies which had gone into insolvent liquidation within five years of one another. Furthermore, the court was under no obligation to disqualify the defendant even if it was satisfied that his conduct in relation to those companies made him unfit. The question of whether or not to disqualify was a matter entirely within the discretion of the court. As such, it was open to the court to take a broad range of personal factors into account and weigh these in the balance before deciding that a disqualification order was appropriate.[4] Cases decided under these provisions should be approached with a degree of caution as they provide no sure guide as to what constitutes unfit conduct for the purposes of mandatory disqualification under section 6.[5] One major difficulty with some of the old cases is that the courts tended to be influenced in their deliberations as to what constituted unfitness by factors that ought properly to have been taken into account at a later stage when determining whether or not to disqualify an unfit director in the exercise of the

---

[4] See, *e.g. Re Churchill Hotel (Plymouth) Ltd* [1988] B.C.L.C. 341, (1988) 4 B.C.C. 112 (defendant's conduct in relation to four failed companies did make him unfit but not disqualified because his conduct had not been dishonest and there was evidence that he was running eight substantial companies in a responsible fashion, the businesses and employees of which would have been prejudiced by a disqualification order). The current position in Australia under sections 599–600 of the Corporations Law is, on its face, similar to that under section 300. These provisions confer discretionary powers on the court (section 599) and the Australian Securities Commission (section 600) to prohibit a person from managing a corporation for up to five years and are triggered broadly where the person has been a director of two companies which have gone into liquidation in the previous seven years. Although the term "unfitness" is not used, it is clear that sections 599–600 are targeted at unfit conduct in the CDDA sense and it is interesting to note that the Australian courts often rely on English authorities when applying the provisions: see *Blunt v. Corporate Affairs Commission (No. 2)* (1988) 14 A.C.L.R. 270, (1988) 6 A.C.L.C. 1,077; *Dwyer v. National Companies and Securities Commission* (1989) 15 A.C.L.R. 386, (1989) 7 A.C.L.C. 571; *Cullen v. Corporate Affairs Commission* (1988) 14 A.C.L.R. 789, (1989) 7 A.C.L.C. 121; *Re Delonga and the Australian Securities Commission* (1994) 15 A.C.S.R. 450, (1995) 13 A.C.L.C. 246; *Re Agushi and Australian Securities Commission* (1996) 19 A.C.S.R. 322 and discussion in J. Cassidy, "Disqualification of Directors Under the Corporations Law" (1995) 13 *Company and Securities Law Journal* 221 and A. Hicks, *Disqualification of Directors: No Hiding Place for the Unfit* (A.C.C.A Research Report No. 59, 1998), pp. 82–83.
[5] Old section 300 cases are still cited, the leading example being *Re Lo-Line Electric Motors Ltd* [1988] Ch. 477, [1988] 3 W.L.R. 26, [1988] 2 All E.R. 692, [1988] B.C.L.C. 698, (1988) 4 B.C.C. 415 which contains some authoritative *dicta* concerning the nature and purpose of disqualification: see para. 2.20.

discretion. There is a danger that a court considering these cases in section 6 proceedings may adopt too generous a standard of unfitness.[6]

Mandatory disqualification for unfitness was first conceived in the Cork Report as a means of providing stronger safeguards for the public against "those whose conduct has shown them to be unfitted to manage the affairs of a company with limited liability".[7] It was seen in Chapter 2 that mandatory disqualification is said to protect the public in two ways. It restrains the person who has abused limited liability and, through deterrence, it may encourage both the disqualified person himself and others to act responsibly.[8] Indeed, this second deterrent aspect is regarded as giving mandatory disqualification legitimacy in marginal cases. To take an illustration, let us say that "W" was a director of "X Ltd" which became insolvent. There is an allegation that W allowed X Ltd to trade while insolvent and disqualification proceedings are commenced. In the intervening period before trial W is involved in the management of two successful companies, "Y Ltd" and "Z Ltd". If the court finds that W's conduct in relation to X Ltd was such as to make him unfit, it is bound to disqualify him for at least two years even though he has proved himself to be capable of acting responsibly in relation to Y Ltd and Z Ltd. The Court of Appeal has said that the mandatory disqualification of someone in W's position can be justified on grounds of general deterrence.[9]

4.03   One danger with any provision of this nature is that in marginal cases like that of W there may be a tendency for the court to refuse to "convict" in the first place if it regards the mandatory "sentence" as being too harsh. Thus, although in strict theory the court has no discretion in the matter, there is room for different judges to reach different conclusions on the same or similar facts. The obligation to disqualify only arises if the court finds that the defendant's conduct "makes him unfit". As such, there is scope for the court to avoid disqualifying the defendant in a borderline case by finding that his conduct falls short of unfitness. Although nothing like as wide as the discretion under section 300 of the Companies Act 1985, this narrow "discretion" does have the potential to create a shifting boundary between "fitness" and "unfitness" leaving room for personal and policy factors to exert some influence.[10] Leaving aside this residual "discretion", there are some who are critical of mandatory disqualifi-

---

[6] For examples of such cases, see *Re Lo-Line Electric Motors, ibid.*; *Re Dawson Print Group Ltd* [1987] B.C.L.C. 601, (1987) 3 B.C.C. 322; *Re Douglas Construction Services Ltd* [1988] B.C.L.C. 397, (1988) 4 B.C.C. 553; *Re C.U. Fittings Ltd* [1989] B.C.L.C. 556, (1989) 5 B.C.C. 210 (all cases decided under Companies Act 1985, s. 300 in which no order was made principally on the ground that unfitness was not established). Equally, however, disqualification orders were made under the old provisions in a number of cases: see, *e.g. Re Stanford Services Ltd* [1987] B.C.L.C. 607, (1987) 3 B.C.C. 326 (two years); *Re Rolus Properties Ltd* (1988) 4 B.C.C. 446 (two years); *Re Western Welsh International System Buildings Ltd* (1988) 4 B.C.C. 449 (two defendants each disqualified for five years); *Re D.J. Matthews (Joinery Design) Ltd* (1988) 4 B.C.C. 513 (three years); *Re Majestic Recording Studios Ltd* [1989] B.C.L.C. 1, (1988) 4 B.C.C. 519 (two defendants disqualified for three and five years respectively); *Re McNulty's Interchange Ltd* [1989] B.C.L.C. 709, (1988) 4 B.C.C. 533 (eighteen months); *Re J & B Lynch (Builders) Ltd* [1988] B.C.L.C. 376 (three years); *Re Flatbolt Ltd*, February 21, 1986, unreported (five years); *Re Wedgecraft Ltd*, March 7, 1986, unreported (seven years); *Re VAB Plating Ltd*, April 11, 1986, unreported (eight years); *Re AB Trucking and BAW Commercials,* June 3, 1987, unreported (four years); *Re Andrey Fashions Ltd,* July 17, 1987, unreported (ten years).
[7] See Cork Report, para. 1808 and Chap. 45 generally. Further detail on the legislative history of section 6 is provided in Chap. 1.
[8] *cf.* para. 2.17.
[9] *Re Grayan Building Services Ltd, Secretary of State for Trade and Industry v. Gray* [1995] Ch. 241, [1995] 3 W.L.R. 1, [1995] 1 B.C.L.C. 276, [1995] B.C.C. 554. This issue is addressed further in the discussion of the phrase "makes him unfit" later in the main text.
[10] For classic examples of the operation of this hidden "discretion" under section 6 see *Re Bath Glass Ltd* [1988] B.C.L.C. 329, (1988) 4 B.C.C. 130; *Re ECM (Europe) Electronics Ltd* [1992] B.C.L.C. 814; *Re Wimbledon Village Restaurant Ltd, Secretary of State for Trade and Industry v. Thomson* [1994] B.C.C. 753; *Re Moonlight Foods (U.K.) Ltd, Secretary of State for Trade and Industry v. Hickling* [1996] B.C.C. 678. See further discussion in A. Hicks, *Disqualification of Directors: No Hiding Place for the Unfit?* (A.C.C.A Research Report No. 59, 1998), pp. 36–37.

cation on other grounds. The main criticism is directed at the narrowness of the parameters within which the court is obliged to operate. Returning to the example above, let us say that W's conduct in relation to X Ltd was a clear case of trading while insolvent, meriting a three-year disqualification. Some would argue that to disqualify W is punitive and unhelpful in the light of his subsequent conduct in relation to Y Ltd and Z Ltd. However, under the law as it stands, the court must confine its enquiry to W's misconduct in relation to X Ltd. It cannot say that his good conduct in the other companies outweighs his misconduct and makes him fit.[11] This has led some to argue that mandatory disqualification should be abandoned and a discretionary power reinstated.[12] There is a further anomaly, noted by Chadwick J. in *Re Thorncliffe Finance Ltd, Secretary of State for Trade and Industry v. Arif*, which is that mitigating factors cannot be taken into account to reduce the period of disqualification below the statutory minimum of two years.[13] Thus, a mitigating factor which can be used to reduce what, in the absence of mitigation, would be a three-year disqualification, cannot be used to reduce a two-year disqualification.

SECTION 8: DISCRETIONARY DISQUALIFICATION FOR UNFITNESS

4.04 In proceedings for an order under section 8 the final matter on which the court must be satisfied before a disqualification order can be imposed is that the defendant's conduct "in relation to the company makes him unfit to be concerned in the management of a company".[14] Thus, the court's power of disqualification under section 8 turns ultimately on a finding of unfitness although, in contrast to section 6, the decision of whether or not to disqualify is entirely at the court's discretion. The court must therefore engage in a two-stage process determining first whether the defendant's conduct shows him to be unfit and, if so, whether it is appropriate to disqualify him for some period.[15] The concept of discretionary disqualification for unfitness following a company investigation originated from the Cork Report[16] and the provision was first enacted as section 13 of the Insolvency Act 1985. As was seen in Chapter 3, proceedings for an order under section 8 must be based on information contained in a report made by inspectors or on information or documents obtained pursuant to various provisions of companies and financial services legislation. Only the Secretary of State has *locus standi* to apply and an application can only be made against a director or shadow director and, as with section 6, presumably a *de facto* director. One issue of considerable importance is the nature of the section 8 dis-

---

[11] See *Re Barings plc (No. 5), Secretary of State for Trade and Industry v. Baker* [1999] 1 B.C.L.C. 433 at 482–486.
[12] See generally A. Hicks, *Disqualification of Directors: No Hiding Place for the Unfit?* (A.C.C.A Research Report No. 59, 1998) and the thinly-veiled criticism of mandatory disqualification made by Vinelott J. in *Re Pamstock Ltd* [1994] 1 B.C.L.C. 716 at 737, [1994] B.C.C. 264 at 282. The stock response to this criticism is that, within the structure of the CDDA, it is always open to someone in W's position to apply for permission to act as a director of Y Ltd and Z Ltd while disqualified: see further discussion below of the phrase "makes him unfit".
[13] [1997] 1 B.C.L.C. 34 at 44–45, [1996] B.C.C. 586 at 595. On mitigation generally, see further Chap. 5.
[14] CDDA, s. 8(2). The court for these purposes is the High Court or, in Scotland, the Court of Session: CDDA, s. 8(3).
[15] *Re Atlantic Computers plc, Secretary of State for Trade and Industry v. Ashman*, June 15, 1998, Ch.D., unreported. One practical implication of this is that the defendant may seek to adduce separate evidence on the question of unfitness and in relation to the exercise of the discretion.
[16] See para. 1819(c).

cretion. At first sight, it might be thought that the court has the same sort of wide discretion under section 8 as it enjoyed under section 300 of the Companies Act 1985 (see above). However, it is suggested that the courts are likely to adopt a narrower approach to the section 8 discretion having regard to the way in which the law has developed under section 6. As was seen in Chapter 2, the idea that a disqualification order serves to protect the public not only by prohibiting the unfit director from taking part in the management of companies but also by deterring other directors and improving standards of conduct generally, is a consistent theme of cases decided under section 6.[17] One effect of this is that a disqualification order can be made for purposes of general deterrence even in circumstances where the director himself poses no particular risk to the public. It might be argued that this notion of deterrence has emerged as a means of justifying mandatory disqualification under section 6 in circumstances where the defendant's past conduct has been shown on the evidence to be manifestly unfit (with the result that the court must disqualify) even though by the date of trial he has mended his ways and is running other companies successfully and properly.[18] Nevertheless, it is submitted that the courts are likely to have regard to the section 6 cases and exercise their discretion under section 8 accordingly. Thus, if the court considers that it is appropriate to disqualify the defendant in order to protect the public either by "taking him off the road" or through general deterrence (or a combination of both), it will exercise its discretion to disqualify under section 8.[19] A further issue arising from the wording of section 8(2) is whether or not conduct which can be taken into account in determining unfitness is limited to "conduct as a director". It is clear that relevant conduct for section 6 purposes is limited to "conduct as a director of [a] company" (section 6(1)(b)). However, it appears that relevant conduct for section 8 purposes is wider as section 8(2) allows the court to determine whether or not the defendant is unfit with reference to his "conduct in relation to the company" not his "conduct as a director".

DETERMINING UNFITNESS

Statutory guidance

4.05 The starting point for the court faced with the task of determining whether the defendant is unfit to be concerned in the management of a company is the CDDA itself. Section 9 requires the court to have regard in particular to the matters mentioned in Part I of Schedule 1 and, where the relevant company has "become insolvent",[20] also to the matters mentioned in Part II of that Schedule. Thus, a distinction is drawn for these purposes between solvent and insolvent companies. The lead company in proceedings for an order under section 6 must have become insolvent because of the effect of section 6(1)(a). This means that in relation to a lead company in section 6 proceedings, the court must have regard to all the matters in Schedule 1. The position is the same in relation to any collateral company though if the collateral company has not

---

[17] See generally *Re Grayan Building Services Ltd* [1995] Ch. 241, [1995] 3 W.L.R. 1, [1995] 1 B.C.L.C. 276, [1995] B.C.C. 554, CA (discussed further in main text below); *Re Blackspur Group plc, Re Atlantic Computer Systems plc* [1998] 1 W.L.R. 422, [1998] 1 B.C.L.C. 676, [1998] B.C.C. 11, CA; *Re Westmid Packing Services Ltd, Secretary of State for Trade and Industry v. Griffiths* [1998] 2 All E.R. 124, [1998] 2 B.C.L.C. 646, [1998] B.C.C. 836, CA.
[18] The main thrust of *Re Grayan Building Services Ltd* [1995] Ch. 241, [1995] 3 W.L.R. 1, [1995] 1 B.C.L.C. 276, [1995] B.C.C. 554, CA (discussed further in main text below).
[19] The leading case under section 8 is *Re Atlantic Computers plc, Secretary of State for Trade and Industry v. Ashman*, June 15, 1998, Ch.D., unreported. Lloyd J.'s judgment and, in particular, his reliance on the general approach taken in section 6 cases like *Grayan*, lends support to the view expressed in the main text.
[20] Which phrase, according to section 9(2), bears the same meaning as that established in section 6(2).

become insolvent,[21] the court need only consider the matters in Part I of the Schedule in relation to that company.

The starting point in determining unfitness under section 8 is again section 9 which directs the court's attention to Schedule 1. The crucial difference between sections 6 and 8 is that under section 8 the relevant company need not have become insolvent. It is possible for the Secretary of State to commence section 8 proceedings in relation to a solvent company, in which case the court would only be required to pay particular regard to the matters mentioned in Part I of the Schedule. However, a company under investigation may often be or become insolvent in which case the Secretary of State has a choice of whether to apply for an order under either section 6 or 8. In these circumstances the Secretary of State may choose to proceed under section 6, given that a finding of unfitness would result in mandatory disqualification.[22] However, if the decision is taken to proceed under section 8, it is clear that the court may take into account the matters applicable where a company has become insolvent in Part II of the Schedule as well as the general matters in Part I.[23] The key question is the same as for section 6, *i.e.* does the defendant's previous conduct make him unfit? There is no doubt that in an appropriate case the court could take into account many of the specific instances of unfitness discussed later in Chapter 5 in the context of section 6. As such, section 8 arguably adds little to our understanding of unfitness save that the section 8 cases tend to be concerned more with issues of investor or shareholder protection than with creditor protection.[24] The contents of the Schedule are as follows.

Schedule 1, Part I—Matters Applicable in all Cases

4.06   In all cases where the court is asked to decide whether the defendant's conduct makes him unfit the court must have regard to the following matters in particular:

(1) Any misfeasance or breach of any fiduciary or other duty by the director in relation to the company.

(2) Any misapplication or retention by the director of, or any conduct by the director giving rise to an obligation to account for, any money or other property of the company.

(3) The extent of the director's responsibility for the company entering into any transaction liable to be set aside under Part XVI of the Insolvency Act (provisions against debt avoidance).

(4) The extent of the director's responsibility for any failure by the company to comply with any of the following provisions of the Companies Act, namely—

---

[21] It was indicated in *Re Country Farm Inns Ltd, Secretary of State for Trade and Industry v. Ivens* [1997] 2 B.C.L.C. 334 at 346, [1997] B.C.C. 801 at 808, CA that, at least at that time, the Secretary of State was unlikely ever to rely on a defendant's conduct as a director of a solvent collateral company. However, the attitude of the Secretary of State in no way affects the construction of section 6 as to jurisdiction and may since have changed in any event. There are positive reasons in the public interest (in particular, the notion that disqualification is concerned with raising standards of conduct) why such an approach should not be followed. On collateral companies generally, see Chap. 3.

[22] As was the case in *Re CSTC Ltd* [1995] 1 B.C.L.C. 545, [1995] B.C.C. 173 where relevant evidence had been obtained pursuant to section 105 of the Financial Services Act 1986 with the consequence that proceedings could presumably have been commenced under section 8.

[23] See *Re TMS (GB) Ltd, Secretary of State for Trade and Industry v. White*, November 26, 1993, Ch.D., unreported.

[24] See paras 5.47–5.48 below. This is not surprising given the link between section 8 and company investigations.

(a) section 221 (companies to keep accounting records);

(b) section 222 (where and for how long records to be kept);

(c) section 288 (register of directors and secretaries);

(d) section 352 (obligation to keep and enter up register of members);

(e) section 353 (location of register of members);

(f) section 363 (duty of company to make annual returns);[25] and

(g) sections 399 and 415 (company's duty to register charges it creates).

(5) The extent of the director's responsibility for any failure by the directors of the company to comply with—

(a) section 226 or 227 of the Companies Act (duty to prepare annual accounts); or

(b) section 233 of that Act (approval and signature of accounts).[26]

(5A) In relation to any person who is a director of an investment company with variable capital, any reference to a provision of the Companies Act shall be taken to be a reference to the corresponding provision of the Open-Ended Investment Companies (Investment Companies with Variable Capital) Regulations 1996 or of any regulations made under regulation 6 of those Regulations.[27]

Schedule 1, Part II—Matters Applicable Where Company Has Become Insolvent

4.07   In all cases where the court is asked to decide whether the defendant's conduct makes him unfit and the relevant company or companies have become insolvent, the court must have regard, in particular, to the following matters set out in Part II of the Schedule, in addition to those in Part I:

(6) The extent of the director's responsibility for the causes of the company becoming insolvent.

(7) The extent of the director's responsibility for any failure by the company to supply any goods or services which have been paid for (in whole or in part).

(8) The extent of the director's responsibility for the company entering into any transaction or giving any preference, being a transaction or preference—

---

[25] The reference in (f) to section 363 replaced an earlier reference to the former provisions in the Companies Act, ss 363–365 with effect from October 1, 1990: see Companies Act 1989, s. 139(4) and S.I. 1990 No. 1707 (C. 46).
[26] Para. (5) replaced an earlier para. which referred to the former sections 227 and 238 of the Companies Act with effect from April 1, 1990: see Companies Act 1989, s. 23 and Sched. 10, para. 35(1), (3); S.I. 1990 No. 355 (C. 13).
[27] Inserted by S.I. 1996 No. 2827 with effect from January 6, 1997. As a result, the matters in Pt I of the Schedule are equally applicable to conduct in relation to an open-ended investment company: see para. 3.42.

(a) liable to be set aside under section 127 or sections 238 to 240 of the Insolvency Act, or

(b) challengeable under section 242 or 243 of that Act or under any rule of law in Scotland.

(9) The extent of the director's responsibility for any failure by the directors of the company to comply with section 98 of the Insolvency Act (duty to call creditors' meeting in creditors' voluntary winding up).

(10) Any failure by the director to comply with any obligation imposed on him by or under any of the following provisions of the Insolvency Act—

(a) section 22 (company's statement of affairs in administration);

(b) section 47 (statement of affairs to administrative receiver);

(c) section 66 (statement of affairs in Scottish receivership);

(d) section 99 (directors' duty to attend meeting; statement of affairs in creditors' voluntary winding up);

(e) section 131 (statement of affairs in winding up by the court);

(f) section 234 (duty of any one with company property to deliver it up);

(g) section 235 (duty to co-operate with liquidator, etc.).

Power is delegated to the Secretary of State by CDDA, s. 9(4)-(5) to make orders modifying any of the provisons of Schedule 1. It should also be noted that section 9 and the Schedule have been modified to deal with cases involving insolvent partnerships by the Insolvent Partnerships Order 1994, art. 16 and Sched. 8.[28]

Section 6(2): Conduct Connected with the Company's Insolvency

4.08 Where a relevant company (including a collateral company) has become insolvent, the court can expressly take into account the defendant's conduct "in relation to any matter connected with or arising out of the insolvency of that company" in determining whether or not he is unfit for the purposes of section 6. This is the effect of the closing words of section 6(2). The wording was clearly intended to cover misconduct such as a failure on the part of a director to co-operate with an office holder.[29] As such, this part of section 6(2) clearly overlaps with some of the specific criteria mentioned in Schedule 1, Part II (which include failure to submit a statement of affairs, failure to deliver up company property and failure to co-operate with an office holder) and the wording is arguably superfluous. However, judicial treatment of the wording has not been so narrow. Peter Gibson J. has suggested that it is directed at the phoenix syndrome because it would allow the court to treat the defendant's conduct in causing a new company to arise phoenix-like from the ashes of an insolvent company as conduct "connected with or arising out of the insolvency" of the latter.[30] Furthermore, Chadwick J. expressed the view in *Re Godwin Warren plc* that disqualification proceedings are themselves "matters connected with or arising out of the insolvency of

---

[28] S.I. 1994 No. 2421. The Insolvent Partnerships Order does not amend the CDDA directly but provides that, in the case of an insolvent partnership, the Schedule is modified so as to apply in the form in which it appears in Sched. 8. The modified Schedule does not make pretty reading. A series of references to partnership and a specific paragraph relating to limited partnerships registered under the Limited Partnerships Act 1907 have been clumsily grafted onto the basic CDDA provisions dealing with companies.

[29] Parliamentary Debates, H.C. Standing Committee E, Session 1984–85, Vol. IV, col. 96.

[30] *Re Bath Glass Ltd* [1988] B.C.L.C. 329 at 331, (1988) 4 B.C.C. 130 at 132.

the company in respect of which they are brought" with the effect that where the defendant misleads the court during the course of proceedings, such conduct can be taken into account to determine whether he is unfit.[31] The point made by the judge was that the defendant's failure to tell the truth during the course of the *Godwin Warren* proceedings suggested that he did not appreciate the nature of a director's duties and so tended to indicate that he was unfit. There may be a problem with Chadwick J.'s view in that it is difficult to characterise such conduct as being conduct *qua* director within the meaning of section 6(1)(b) and section 6(2). In this respect, it is certainly arguable that the words "conduct in relation to any matter connected with or arising out of the insolvency" are governed by the general requirement that conduct must be "conduct as a director".

History and Legal Status of Schedule 1

4.09 The unfitness provisions now found in sections 6 to 9, together with the earliest version of Schedule 1, were originally enacted in the Insolvency Act 1985. The idea of a detailed schedule of indicative factors appears to have emerged first during the course of the Parliamentary debates on the Insolvency Bill.[32] There was a consensus in Parliament that the term "unfit" was too vague and that guidelines on the meaning of the term should be introduced into the legislation.[33] The theory was that guidelines were needed (a) to assist the courts, (b) to provide general guidance to directors on how they should act, (c) to assist insolvency practitioners in compiling "unfitness" reports on directors of insolvent companies[34] and (d) to assist the Secretary of State in deciding whether or not to commence proceedings in a particular case. The factors selected for inclusion in the Schedule reflected the experience of the Insolvency Service in dealing with the directors of failed companies and the comments of insolvency practitioners.[35] However, while there was general agreement that the Schedule ought to reinforce core statutory obligations (such as the duty of directors to keep accounting records which disclose with reasonable accuracy the company's financial position at any given moment), there was less consensus in the Parliamentary debate as to what other specific factors should be included.[36]

Looking at the factors as a whole, Schedule 1 reiterates a number of specific statutory obligations arising under the Companies Act and the Insolvency Act while also bringing directors' duties at common law within its scope. Schedule 1, Part I, paragraph 1 refers to breaches of "any fiduciary duty or other duty by the director in relation to the company". On this wording alone, it appears that the court can take into account any breach of a director's fiduciary obligations to act in good faith in the company's interests, to avoid conflicts of interest and duty and to avoid making secret

---

[31] [1993] B.C.L.C. 80 at 92, [1992] B.C.C. 557 at 567–568. The point was subsequently considered in *Re Moorgate Metals Ltd, Official Receiver v. Huhtala* [1995] 1 B.C.L.C. 503, [1995] B.C.C. 143 and applied in *Re Living Images Ltd* [1996] 1 B.C.L.C. 348, [1996] B.C.C. 112.

[32] The substantive powers in sections 6 and 8 are based on recommendations put forward in Chap. 45 of the Cork Report. Cork makes no mention of a schedule of indicative factors and neither does the White Paper, *A Revised Framework for Insolvency Law*, Cmnd. 9175 (1984).

[33] An amendment was introduced in the House of Lords and this eventually crystallised into the Schedule: see variously, Hansard, HL Vol. 461, cols 724–725, 727, 732–733, Vol. 467, cols 1123–1124.

[34] See now CDDA, s. 7(3) and generally, Chap. 3.

[35] Hansard, HL Vol. 467, col. 1124; Parliamentary Debates, H.C. Standing Committee E, Session 1984–85, Vol. IV, cols 125–126.

[36] Standing Committee E, Session 1984–85, Vol. IV, from col. 54. Note, in particular, the attempt by some members of the Standing Committee to add specific criteria requiring the court to have regard to the frequency of a defendant's involvement in corporate insolvencies and the adequacy of the relevant company's share capital.

profits from the use of the company's assets. Equally, the wording in paragraph 1 is sufficiently wide to encompass any breach of the director's common law duty of care and skill and of any statutory duties not expressly mentioned elsewhere in the Schedule (such as the duty to file audited accounts imposed by section 242 of the Companies Act 1985).[37] Moreover, the concept of unfitness clearly encompasses types of misconduct targeted specifically by other substantive provisions in the CDDA, *i.e.* sections 2 to 5 and 10. The Schedule amounts to nothing more than a summary restatement of existing obligations with a private company orientation laying particular emphasis (in Pt I) on proper record-keeping and financial reporting. There is nothing in section 9 or the Schedule that serves to augment the obligations imposed on directors by general company law.

4.10 It is clear that the criteria contained in the Schedule are not to be regarded as exhaustive. The court is required by section 9 to "have regard in particular" to matters mentioned in the Schedule. The effect of this is that the court is not limited to those matters in determining unfitness and may consider other matters falling outside the Schedule as well.[38] However, there are a number of points which are less clear. First, it is uncertain whether the factors mentioned in the Schedule should be given greater weight than factors not specifically mentioned. Neuberger J. expressed the view in *Re Amaron Ltd* that each allegation of unfitness should be dealt with on its merits irrespective of whether or not it falls in the Schedule.[39] It was pointed out in the earlier case of *Re Bath Glass Limited*[40] that while the Schedule makes express reference (see Part I, paragraph 5) to any failure by the defendant to comply with statutory duties to prepare and seek approval of annual accounts, no mention is made of failure to comply with the obligation to file accounts now found in section 242 of the Companies Act 1985. Even so, in the view of Peter Gibson J., a failure to comply with the filing obligation "is plainly a matter which can and should be taken into account". There is no other express guidance on the point save that it is clear from *Re Grayan Building Services Ltd, Secretary of State for Trade and Industry v. Gray* that section 6 should not be applied in a way that deprives the specific matters mentioned in the Schedule of any

---

[37] On directors' duties generally, see *Palmers Company Law*; P.L. Davies, *Gower's Principles of Modern Company Law* (6th ed., 1997), Chaps 22–23; J.H. Farrar & B.M. Hannigan, *Farrar's Company Law* (4th ed., 1998), Chaps. 26–28. For present purposes, it should be noted that the common law now accommodates the idea that in a company of doubtful solvency, the directors should give priority to the interests of the company's creditors rather than its members when discharging their fiduciary obligation to act in good faith in the company's interests: see *West Mercia Safetywear Ltd v. Dodd* [1988] B.C.L.C. 250, (1988) 4 B.C.C. 30, CA; *Facia Footwear Ltd v. Hinchcliffe* [1998] 1 B.C.L.C. 218. This means that any failure by the director of an insolvent company to take account of creditors' interests could amount to a breach of fiduciary duty falling within CDDA, Sched. 1, Pt I, para. 1. For general background, see D.D. Prentice, "Creditors' Interests and Directors' Duties" (1990) 10 O.J.L.S. 265, "Directors, Creditors and Shareholders" in E. McKendrick (ed.), *Commercial Aspects of Trusts and Fiduciary Obligations* (1992); R. Grantham, "The Judicial Extension of Directors' Duties to Creditors" [1991] J.B.L. 1 and N. Furey, "The Protection of Creditors' Interests in Company Law" in D. Feldman & F. Meisel (eds.) *Corporate and Commercial Law: Modern Developments* (1996).

[38] A point made during the parliamentary debate: Hansard, HL Vol. 461, cols 738, 740, Vol. 467, cols. 1123–1124; Standing Committee E, Session 1984–85, Vol. IV, col. 90 and made frequently by the courts: see, *e.g. Re Bath Glass Ltd* [1988] B.C.L.C. 329 at 332, (1988) 4 B.C.C. 130 at 132–133; *Re Samuel Sherman plc* [1991] 1 W.L.R. 1070 at 1073, [1991] B.C.C. 699 at 701; *Re GSAR Realisations Ltd* [1993] B.C.L.C. 409 at 421; *Secretary of State for Trade and Industry v. Taylor* [1997] 1 W.L.R. 407 at 412, *sub nom. Secretary of State for Trade and Industry v. Gash* [1997] 1 B.C.L.C. 341 at 346, *sub nom. Re CS Holidays Ltd* [1997] B.C.C. 172 at 176; *Re Amaron Ltd* [1998] B.C.C. 264 at 268; *Re Sykes (Butchers) Ltd, Secretary of State for Trade and Industry v. Richardson* [1998] 1 B.C.L.C. 110 at 125, [1998] B.C.C. 484 at 496. Arguably, most matters will fall within the Schedule given the apparent width of para. 1 which refers to "any misfeasance or breach of any fiduciary or other duty by the director in relation to the company".

[39] [1998] B.C.C. 264 at 268

[40] [1988] B.C.L.C. 329 at 332, (1988) 4 B.C.C. 130 at 132–133.

effect.[41] Secondly, there is no indication as to the relative weight to be given to each of the stated factors. It is apparent from the discussion in Chapter 5 on specific indicia of unfitness that a breach of section 221 of the Companies Act 1985 (Schedule 1, Part I, para. 4(a)) will generally be treated as more serious than, say, a failure to file annual returns (Schedule 1, Part I, para. 4(f)). This approach to relative weighting has been developed entirely by the courts. Thirdly, the CDDA gives no general guidance as to the *degree* of misconduct required to make a defendant unfit. It is fairly safe to say that a few isolated defaults in filing accounts and returns will probably not render a director unfit. However, it is notoriously difficult to draw the line between fitness and unfitness. The task of identifying individual matters which are relevant to the question of unfitness is a relatively easy one. It is much less easy to identify at what point a particular combination of factors will take the defendant across the line.[42] This leaves some margin for the exercise of what, for present purposes, can be described as judicial discretion.

"Extent of responsibility"

4.11 It has been seen that Schedule 1 does not have any immediate impact on the law of directors' obligations. It simply restates existing aspects of the law in varying degrees of detail. However, it is important to note that the majority of the criteria in the Schedule direct the court to evaluate "the extent of the director's responsibility" for the specified failure or default. The use of this wording serves to highlight a peculiar tension within company law. On the one hand, the board of directors tends to be treated in company law as the primary organ of the company, *i.e.* the principal means by which the company acts, especially in relation to those outside the company. In this sense, the directors are regarded as acting collectively rather than individually. On the other hand, the legal obligations of directors are owed by each director to the company on an individual basis and so, in law, the board is not an entity which owes a collective duty.[43] A difficult question falling between these two stools of collective and individual responsibility is whether the duties imposed on each individual director carry equal weight. To take an example, companies legislation draws no explicit distinction between executive and non-executive directors. As such, executive and non-executive directors have hitherto been treated broadly as equals for the purposes of their legal obligations. This is despite the fact that, in practice, executive and non-executive directors are clearly distinguishable in that executive directors are salaried senior employees as well as being directors. However, in recent times, the position in relation to the duty of care and skill at common law has become rather more nuanced. On this issue, the courts increasingly take an objective approach requiring each director to exercise the degree of care and skill that one may reasonably expect of a person carrying out that

---

[41] [1995] Ch. 241, [1995] 3 W.L.R. 1, [1995] 1 B.C.L.C. 276, [1995] B.C.C. 554, CA. See the comments of Hoffmann L.J. criticising the trial judge's ruling that conduct amounting to unlawful preference (specifically referred to Sched. 1, Pt II, para. 8(a)) should be disregarded because a remedy had been pursued against the defendants under section 239 of the Insolvency Act 1986 which would have brought the consequences of their actions home to them.
[42] See generally Hicks, *op. cit.* and see paras 4.02–4.03.
[43] See Davies, *loc. cit.*

director's particular function in the company.[44] This objective minimum standard based on the individual director's function in a given company gives the court scope to distinguish between directors according to their job descriptions, *e.g.* "finance director", "sales director", "non-executive" director and so on. However, it leaves a number of questions unanswered. For example, the extent to which the law imposes any common minimum standards which are applicable to *all* directors regardless of function is unclear. Is it true to say that each director must participate in the management of the company to at least some minimum degree? To what extent can a director escape liability by pointing to another director or employee of the company and saying that the particular default under scrutiny was within the scope of that person's function and responsibility, not his? Alternatively, does each director have to accept his share of collective responsibility? These issues have not as yet been fully worked through in the modern law of directors' obligations but, as will become clear, they often surface in disqualification proceedings.[45]

4.12   The effect of the "extent of responsibility" wording in Schedule 1 is that the court is required to focus primarily on the defendant's personal responsibility. At the same time, however, the use of the word "extent" suggests that the court must examine the defendant's conduct in the round, taking into account not only his own functions and responsibilities but also those of others in the company. The Schedule therefore clearly contemplates that the directors in a company may have *varying degrees* of responsibility although, like the common law, it sets no common minimum standards applicable to all directors. In disqualification cases, the broad tendency is for the courts to insist that each director is under at least a minimum obligation to make himself aware of the company's financial position even if he has no involvement in the day-to-day running of its business. The upshot is that the courts use the CDDA to fashion minimum standards but the precise nature of a director's responsibility in relation to a given company will ultimately depend on the facts of each case.[46] These important issues of minimum standards, directors' participation and co-responsibility are developed further in Chapter 5.[47]

---

[44] See *Norman v. Theodore Goddard* [1991] B.C.L.C. 1028, [1992] B.C.C. 14 and *Re D'Jan of London Ltd* [1994] 1 B.C.L.C. 561, [1993] B.C.C. 646 noted by A. Hicks (1994) 110 L.Q.R. 390. This minimum objective standard is drawn from the statutory test applicable in wrongful trading proceedings: see Insolvency Act 1986, s. 214(4). The standard can be adjusted upwards to reflect the general knowledge, skill and experience that the particular director possesses. The case of *Re Brian D Pierson (Contractors) Ltd* [1999] B.C.C. 26 provides a good example of how the test is applied in section 214 proceedings. A husband and wife were the only directors and shareholders of a company which went into creditors' voluntary liquidation in early 1996. The auditors' report on the accounts for the year to July 31, 1993 expressed doubt as to whether it was correct for those accounts to be prepared on a going concern basis. The evidence showed that the husband ran the company. The wife took no active part in management decisions but carried out clerical duties. Although her function was limited, she was held liable under section 214. The judge stated that the office of director has certain minimum responsibilities and functions which are not discharged by leaving the running of the company to another director without question. The function of "directing" requires some consideration of the company's affairs to be exercised. The test to be applied to the wife under section 214(4) was that of a reasonably diligent person who has taken on the office of director and this basic standard could not be reduced on the ground that the director in question exercised no particular function in the company's management.
[45] The position in relation to a director's participation still rests on the decision of Romer J. in *Re City Equitable Fire Insurance Co Ltd* [1925] Ch. 407 which suggests that a director is not bound to give continuous attention to the affairs of the company. It has been suggested subsequently by Hoffmann L.J. that the existence of a positive obligation to participate will depend on the particular context *i.e.* on factors such as how the particular company is organised.and the part which the director could reasonably have been expected to play: see *Bishopgate Investment Management Ltd v. Maxwell (No. 2)* [1994] 1 All E.R. 261 at 264, [1993] B.C.L.C. 1282 at 1285.
[46] See further the approach in *Re Barings plc (No. 5), Secretary of State for Trade and Industry v. Baker* [1999] 1 B.C.L.C. 433.
[47] See paras 5.54–5.65.

Criticisms of CDDA, s. 9 and Sched. 1

4.13 It has been mentioned already that the Schedule amounts to a mixed bag of broad and narrow criteria and that on certain points, such as the relative weight to be attached to each criterion, there is a lack of specific guidance. Another more general criticism of the CDDA is that it lacks any positive statement of basic standards. Given that one discernible purpose of disqualification is to protect the public by raising directors' standards of conduct through general deterrence, it is arguable that there should be a clear statutory statement of obligations and standards to which directors could refer. At the moment, directors are faced with the problem that the law concerning their obligations is somewhat inaccessible. They must refer to a plethora of statutory provisions and court decisions, including the vast number of cases decided under CDDA, s. 6 in order to arrive at a comprehensive understanding of directors' duties. This criticism has been taken up by the Law Commission.[48] As a consequence, it is possible that doubts concerning the moral legitimacy of disqualification may in certain circumstances surface within the adjudicative process.[49]

General judicial guidance

4.14 It has already been noted that the guidance in the statute is not exhaustive and that it is deficient in a number of respects. In particular, it is not clear what relative weight the court should attach to the various matters it takes into account and what *degree* of misconduct is required to take the defendant across the line from fitness into unfitness. As such, the courts have played a significant part in developing the law of unfitness. The court's basic task, having resolved any disputes of fact, is to decide whether the matters alleged by the claimant indicate that the defendant is unfit. In approaching this task, the court must look at each matter of misconduct and determine whether on its own, or taken cumulatively with other matters alleged and proven, that matter is sufficient to make the defendant unfit.[50] The court is entitled to conclude that the defendant is unfit on a single ground of complaint alone and this is so even if that ground is not one of the matters specifically mentioned in Schedule 1.[51] These mechanical statements provide only a bare framework. They tell us nothing about the *standard* which the court is supposed to apply to a set of proven allegations in determining whether the defendant's conduct falls on the acceptable or unacceptable side of the line. In the absence of any clear statement in the CDDA, it has been left to the courts to determine the appropriate standard for distinguishing between fit and unfit conduct.

Standard of unfitness: judicial paraphrasing

4.15 In several cases decided in the late-1980s, including some decided under the old provisions, there was an attempt by the judges to formulate something approach-

---

[48] Law Commission Paper No. 153, *Company Directors: Regulating Conflicts of Interests and Formulating a Statement of Duties* (1998), especially Section B, Part 14. It has also been suggested by Hicks, *op. cit.* that a code for creditors providing a concise statement of directors' obligations to creditors as found in Schedule 1 and distilled from disqualification cases should be established and distributed to new directors by Companies House as an *ex ante* measure. Hicks argues that this would assist the court and the law-abiding director while enhancing the moral justification for disqualification where the code is breached. One problem identified by the National Audit Office in its report of October 1993 and confirmed to an extent by Hicks' later work is that many directors are not even aware of the existence of the CDDA. This finding appears to undermine any notion that the CDDA is raising awareness of directors' legal obligations.
[49] Lord Hoffmann's extra-judicial comments made in the fourth annual Leonard Sainer Lecture (1997) 18 *The Company Lawyer* 194 (discussed earlier in Chap. 2) carry this implication.
[50] See *dictum* of Morritt L.J. in *Re Copecrest Ltd, Secretary of State for Trade and Industry v. McTighe (No. 2)* [1996] 2 B.C.L.C. 477 at 485, [1997] B.C.C. 224 at 230.
[51] *Re Amaron Ltd* [1998] B.C.C. 264.

ing a general threshold test. In *Re Dawson Print Group Ltd*, a section 300 case, Hoffmann J. stated:

> "There must, I think, be something about the case, some conduct which if not dishonest is at any rate in breach of standards of commercial morality, or some really gross incompetence which persuades the court that it would be a danger to the public if he were to be allowed to continue to be involved in the management of companies, before a disqualification order is made."[52]

Mere "mismanagement" on its own was not regarded by Hoffmann J. as being sufficient to satisfy this test. A similar refrain was taken up by Browne-Wilkinson V.-C. in *Re Lo-Line Electric Motors Ltd*:

> "Ordinary commercial misjudgment is in itself not sufficient to justify disqualification. In the normal case, the conduct complained of must display a lack of commercial probity although I have no doubt that in an extreme case of gross negligence or total incompetence disqualification could be appropriate."[53]

These *dicta* suggest that a line should be drawn with conduct amounting to either a breach of commerical morality or "gross" or "total" incompetence falling on the wrong side of the line, and mere "mismanagement" or "misjudgement" falling on the right side.[54] Furthermore, the use of phrases like "commercial morality" and "commercial probity" suggests that the courts are applying some sort of objective standard. A slightly different tack was taken by Peter Gibson J. in *Re Bath Glass Ltd*, an early section 6 case:

> "To reach a finding of unfitness the court must be satisfied that the director has been guilty of a serious failure or serious failures, whether deliberately or through incompetence, to perform those duties of directors which are attendant on the privilege of trading through companies with limited liability."[55]

4.16 It is clear from this *dictum* that conduct less culpable than dishonest or fraudulent conduct may be sufficient to support a finding of unfitness, a view which reflects

---

[52] [1987] B.C.L.C. 601 at 604, (1987) 3 B.C.C. 322 at 324–325. This test has been followed in Australia to determine when it will be appropriate for the Australian Securities Commission to exercise its discretion to disqualify a person under section 600 of the Corporations Law: see *Blunt v. Corporate Affairs Commission (No. 2)* (1988) 14 A.C.L.R. 270, (1988) 6 A.C.L.C. 1,077.
[53] [1988] Ch. 477 at 486, [1988] 3 W.L.R. 26 at 32, [1988] 2 All E.R. 692 at 696, [1988] B.C.L.C. 698 at 703, (1988) 4 B.C.C. 415 at 419. In the Australian case of *Dwyer v. National Companies and Securities Commission (No. 2)* (1989) 7 A.C.L.C. 733 at 746 Young J. suggested that it was necessary in disqualification proceedings under section 600 of the Australian Corporations Law to establish a high degree of incompetence because, at that time, there was no statutory requirement of competence imposed on company directors. Such an approach should be disregarded in the light of *Sevenoaks* (discussed below).
[54] For other early cases with a similar flavour see, *e.g. Re Flatbolt Ltd*, February 21, 1986, unreported; *Re Wedgecraft Ltd*, March 7, 1986, unreported (two decisions of Harman J. in which acts of "commercial immorality" were said to justify disqualification); *Re Rolus Properties Ltd* (1988) 4 B.C.C. 446 (gross incompetence without dishonesty capable of amounting to unfitness); *Re McNulty's Interchange Ltd* [1989] B.C.L.C. 709, (1988) 4 B.C.C. 533; *Re Douglas Construction Services Ltd* [1988] B.C.L.C. 397, (1988) 4 B.C.C. 553 (mere mismanagement not sufficient to justify disqualification); *Re C.U. Fittings Ltd* [1989] B.C.L.C. 556, (1989) 5 B.C.C. 210 (defendant's conduct not justifying disqualification as there was no lack of "commercial probity"); *Re Ipcon Fashions Ltd* (1989) 5 B.C.C. 774 (conduct contrary to "commercial morality" justifying disqualification); *Re Cladrose Ltd* [1990] B.C.L.C. 204, [1990] B.C.C. 11 (one of two defendants not disqualified because his conduct was insufficient to amount to "gross incompetence").
[55] [1988] B.C.L.C. 329 at 333, (1988) 4 B.C.C. 130 at 133.

the historical development of the unfitness provisions.[56] Again, it is implicit that there is some objective standard of competence to which the court must have regard. However, it is not clear from any of this coded language what terms such as "commercial morality", "mismanagement", "incompetence" and "serious failure" that have been frequently used, actually mean.[57] The court is therefore free to set its own standard according to the facts of the particular case and the attitude of the individual judge to disqualification as a matter of policy. This means that in marginal cases, there is scope for narrow approaches to disqualification, placing emphasis on enterprise and individual freedom, to compete with broader approaches, emphasising the need for creditor protection and the idea that limited liability is a freedom or privilege which should be used responsibly.[58] In simple terms, a narrow approach to disqualification is likely to produce a higher threshold test than a broad, protective approach. Any predisposition either way will therefore affect the standard applied.[59] Bearing in mind that disqualification for unfitness inevitably involves a trade-off between these competing policy objectives, it is impossible to eliminate the influence of policy on the question of where to draw the line. As such, any attempt to formulate a general, objective threshold test drawing a clear line between fitness and unfitness is beset by difficulties. Like the *dicta* quoted above, any broad test will tend to be so general as to be bereft of practical meaning and leave both claimant and defendant relying on some sort of judicial instinct or "sixth sense" for guidance. The main consequence of all this is that much greater guidance can be derived by identifying the various specific types of misconduct which lead, time and again, to the making of a disqualification order than from any general threshold test or broad statement of principle.

---

[56] In particular, the general shift away from the requirement to prove fraud in directors' liability provisions towards objective standards analogous to negligence, a shift exemplified by the wrongful trading provision in section 214 of the Insolvency Act 1986 which was introduced at the same time as section 6.

[57] For an amplification of this criticism, see J. Dine, *Criminal Law in the Company Context* (1995), Chap. 5. One problem with Peter Gibson J.'s "serious failure" test identified by Dine is that it is not clear whether it means that the conduct must have been seriously wrong (*i.e.* effectively contemplating a "gross negligence" standard) or simply that the conduct must have caused serious harm in the form of substantial loss to creditors (*i.e.* effectively contemplating an ordinary negligence standard). A similar problem besets the *dictum* of Vinelott J. in *Re Stanford Services Ltd* [1987] B.C.L.C. 607, (1987) 3 B.C.C. 326 to the effect that a disqualification order is justified in the public interest where the defendant has been guilty of a serious breach of his obligations causing loss to company creditors. It is suggested that the focus of the CDDA is on the defendant's conduct and the propensity of that conduct to cause loss, not on the question of whether loss was actually suffered on the facts of the case: see, *e.g. Re Sykes (Butchers) Ltd, Secretary of State for Trade and Industry v. Richardson* [1998] 1 B.C.L.C. 110 at 117–118, [1998] B.C.C. 484 at 489–490. In other words, the focus is different to that in ordinary civil litigation (*e.g.* a claim in contract or tort) where the claimant will usually have to establish loss in order to succeed.

[58] Indeed, there is scope for the court to vary its approach subtly to meet the requirements of a particular case. Compare, for example, the approaches taken by Harman J. in *Re Rolus Properties Ltd* (1988) 4 B.C.C. 446 (emphasis placed on the idea of limited liability as a privilege with the consequence that disqualification was justified where the defendant was "incompetent" in the sense of his inability to discharge the statutory responsibilities that go with limited liability) and *Re Douglas Construction Services Ltd* [1988] B.C.L.C. 397, (1988) 4 B.C.C. 553 (narrower approach construing "abuse of privilege" restrictively and emphasising the need for the court to avoid stultifying enterprise with the result that no order was made). The two cases are consistent but it is interesting to note how Harman J. strived to confine the categories of "abuse of privilege" in *Douglas Construction*.

[59] Commentators who, like Dine, see disqualification as essentially a form of criminal process, insist that the courts should explicitly follow a narrow approach and only disqualify persons whose behaviour involves a high degree of criminal culpability: see Dine, *op. cit.* and "Wrongful Trading—Quasi-Criminal Law" in *Insolvency Law and Practice* (H. Rajak (ed.) 1993), "Punishing Directors" [1994] J.B.L. 325 and "The Disqualification of Company Directors" (1988) 9 *The Company Lawyer* 213. Such an insistence appears to be at odds with the general shift away from directors' liability provisions based on fraud towards provisions like section 214 of the Insolvency Act based on a lesser threshold: see *dictum* of Hoffmann L.J. in *Re Grayan Building Services Ltd, Secretary of State for Trade and Industry v. Gray* [1995] Ch. 241 at 255, [1995] 3 W.L.R. 1 at 13, [1995] 1 B.C.L.C. 276 at 286, [1995] B.C.C. 554 at 575 suggesting that the court applies a standard not just of probity, but also of competence.

Re Sevenoaks Stationers (Retail) Ltd: *the apparent rejection of paraphrasing and the move towards a language of proper standards*

4.17 In *Re Sevenoaks Stationers (Retail) Ltd*, the Court of Appeal stated categorically that judicial statements, like those quoted above, should not be elevated to the status of legal principle at the expense of the plain words in the statute. Dillon L.J. made the following pertinent observations:

> "The test laid down in section 6 ... is whether the person's conduct as a director of the company or companies in question 'makes him unfit to be concerned in the management of a company'. These are ordinary words of the English language and they should be simple to apply in most cases. It is important to hold to those words in each case. The judges of the Chancery Division have, understandably, attempted in certain cases to give guidance as to what does or does not make a person unfit to be concerned in the management of a company... Such statements may be helpful in identifying particular circumstances in which a person would clearly be unfit. But there seems to have been a tendency, which I deplore, on the part of the Bar, and possibly also on the part of the official receiver's department, to treat the statements as judicial paraphrases of the words of the statute, which fall to be construed as a matter of law in lieu of the words of the statute. The result is to obscure that the true question to be tried is a question of fact—what used to be pejoratively described in the Chancery Division as 'a jury question'."[60]

4.18 The implication is clear. According to the Court of Appeal in *Sevenoaks Stationers*, unfitness is simply a question of fact. The courts are not to put any wider judicial gloss on the statutory language. In effect, this means that a court faced with the task of assessing whether or not the defendant is unfit has little guidance beyond the terms of section 9, the criteria in Schedule 1 and the facts of other cases. There is an obvious justification for Dillon L.J.'s position. Many of the so-called "judicial paraphrases" of unfitness, including those quoted above, derive from cases which were decided under the old provisions without the benefit of the detailed criteria now contained in Schedule 1. The treatment of broad judicial statements as if they were tests for unfitness having statutory force is arguably much less justifiable in the context of section 6 given that the court is now assisted by the specific guidelines in the Schedule. However, the approach in *Sevenoaks* can be criticised. It has been seen that Schedule 1 is not exhaustive. The court is entitled to look at conduct which does not necessarily fall within the Schedule to determine whether or not the defendant is unfit. Thus, it is arguable that the courts need to formulate some principles to enable consistency of judicial approach and to provide guidance to directors. Furthermore, it is difficult to see how the question of what conduct does or does not make a person unfit can be characterised purely as a question of fact. It is implicit in the concept of unfitness that the court is being asked to assess the defendant's behaviour against some objective benchmark. The difficult question of where one draws the line between conduct that is objectively fit and objectively unfit, albeit one primarily of degree, must be at least in some sense a question of law. It seems preferable therefore to characterise the question

---

[60] [1991] Ch. 164 at 176, [1991] 3 All E.R. 578 at 583, [1991] B.C.L.C. 325 at 330, [1990] B.C.C. 765 at 773.

as one of mixed law and fact.[61] These concerns may explain why some judges, while paying lip-service to Dillon L.J.'s *dictum*, have continued to provide generalised descriptions of the nature of the conduct which they have found amounts to unfitness.[62] At the same time, Dillon L.J.'s preference for a narrow focus on the facts and the plain words of the statute has been followed closely in several cases which is perhaps not surprising given that *Sevenoaks* is a Court of Appeal decision.[63] As the courts become increasingly costs conscious in the wake of the civil justice reforms recently introduced in England and Wales, a *Sevenoaks* approach giving emphasis to the autonomy of the statute and, by implication, devaluing the extensive citation of decided cases may well prove attractive.

4.19 A further important aspect of the decision in *Sevenoaks* is that the Court of Appeal set the standard of competence expected from directors at a higher level than that set in previous cases. In the words of Dillon L.J.:

"... I have no doubt at all that it is amply proved that [the defendant] is unfit to be concerned in the management of a company. His trouble is not dishonesty, but incompetence or negligence in a very marked degree and that is enough to render him unfit; I do not think it is necessary for incompetence to be 'total', as suggested by the Vice-Chancellor in *Re Lo-Line Electric Motors Ltd*, to render a director unfit to take part in the management of a company."[64]

The clear implication is that conduct falling short of total incompetence or total negligence may amount to unfit conduct attracting mandatory disqualification. As such, *Sevenoaks Stationers* suggests a shift towards a more exacting judicial standard of directorial competence and a lower threshold test for unfitness. In the light of Dillon L.J.'s general admonition it is difficult to know what to make of this. In particular, it is not clear where *Sevenoaks* leaves the distinction drawn in *Lo-Line* between "ordinary commercial misjudgment" and conduct lacking in "commercial probity".[65] The issue of disqualification on grounds of incompetence is considered further in Chapter 5.

---

[61] See *Re Grayan Building Services Ltd* [1995] Ch. 241 at 254, [1995] 3 W.L.R. 1 at 12, [1995] 1 B.C.L.C. 276 at 285, [1995] B.C.C. 554 at 575 and S. Wheeler, "*Re Sevenoaks*—Continuing the Search for Principle" (1990) 6 *Insolvency Law & Practice* 174. Wheeler argues that some form of explanatory test is needed in the interests of establishing uniformity of approach. In the absence of exhaustive statutory guidance, it is submitted that the court must at least have to direct itself on the question of what is and is not legally relevant. Lack of explanatory guidance may also impede the Disqualification Unit in deciding which cases to bring: see D. Henry, "Disqualification of Directors: A View from the Inside" in *Insolvency Law and Practice* (H. Rajak (ed.) 1993) pp. 182–183.
[62] See, *e.g Re CSTC Ltd, Secretary of Trade and Industry v. Van Hengel* [1995] 1 B.C.L.C. 545, [1995] B.C.C. 173 (phrases like "grossly negligent", "totally incompent" and "lack of moral probity" used as labels for unfit conduct although the court acknowledged that the words "unfit to be concerned in the management of a company" are ordinary English words that are simple to apply); *Re Polly Peck International plc (No. 2), Secretary of State for Trade and Industry v. Ellis* [1994] 1 B.C.L.C. 574, [1993] B.C.C. 890; *Re Living Images Ltd* [1996] 1 B.C.L.C. 348, [1996] B.C.C. 112 (reiterate Dillon L.J.'s *dictum* but proceed to suggest that an order for disqualification can only be made if the defendant has acted in a way which is "serious" or "blameworthy"). The older tests have still been used or echoed in the lower courts in several cases decided after *Sevenoaks Stationers*: see, *e.g. Re ECM (Europe) Electronics Ltd* [1992] B.C.L.C. 814; *Re Swift 736 Ltd, Secretary of State for Trade and Industry v. Ettinger* [1993] B.C.L.C. 896, [1993] B.C.C. 312; *Re Looe Fish Ltd* [1993] B.C.L.C. 1160, [1993] B.C.C. 348; *Re Moonlight Foods (U.K.) Ltd, Secretary of State for Trade and Industry v. Hickling* [1996] B.C.C. 678 at 693G.
[63] See, *e.g Re Samuel Sherman plc* [1991] 1 W.L.R. 1070, [1991] B.C.C. 699; *Re GSAR Realisations Ltd* [1993] B.C.L.C. 409; *Re Hitco 2000 Ltd, Official Receiver v. Cowan* [1995] 2 B.C.L.C. 63, [1995] B.C.C. 161; *Re Ward Sherrard Ltd* [1996] B.C.L.C. 418; *Re Amaron Ltd, Secretary of State for Trade and Industry v. Lubrani* [1997] 2 B.C.L.C. 115.
[64] [1991] Ch. 164 at 184, [1991] 3 All E.R. 578 at 590, [1991] B.C.L.C. 325 at 337, [1990] B.C.C. 765 at 780.
[65] An observation made by Lindsay J. in *Re Polly Peck International plc (No. 2), Secretary of State for Trade and Industry v. Ellis* [1994] 1 B.C.L.C. 574 at 579, [1993] B.C.C. 890 at 894–895. See also *Re Park House Properties Ltd* [1997] 2 B.C.L.C. 530 at 543–544, [1998] B.C.C. 847 at 858.

4.20   Since *Sevenoaks* the courts have relied less on general *dicta* from earlier authorities such as *Dawson Print* and *Lo-Line*. At the same time, there has been a shift towards a judicial language of "proper standards". In *Re Keypack Homecare Ltd*, a case decided shortly before the Court of Appeal ruled in *Sevenoaks*, Harman J. said that he preferred to use the phrase "lack of regard for proper standards" rather than "want of commercial morality" as the touchstone for unfitness.[66] A similar refrain has been taken up in subsequent cases. In *Re Pamstock Ltd*, Vinelott J. was obliged to disqualify the defendant for two years on finding that his conduct "fell short of the standard of conduct which is today expected of a director of a company which enjoys the privilege of limited liability".[67] In *Re Swift 736 Ltd, Secretary of State for Trade and Industry v. Ettinger* and *Re Grayan Building Services Ltd, Secretary of State for Trade and Industry v. Gray*, two cases which lay considerable stress on the value of disqualification as a general deterrent, the Court of Appeal spoke of "ordinary standards of commercial morality"[68] and posited the idea that conduct falling below the "appropriate standard" will attract disqualification.[69] In *Grayan*, it was made abundantly clear that a major concern of the CDDA was to raise standards of conduct. Thus, in determining unfitness, the court is required, in the words of Hoffmann L.J., to "... decide whether [the relevant] conduct, viewed cumulatively ... has fallen below the standards of probity and competence appropriate for persons to be fit to be directors of companies".[70] On the face of it, this all smacks of a semantic exercise. However, it does also amount to an explicit acknowlegement by the courts that an objective standard is being used to distinguish between unfitness and conduct falling short of unfitness. This increasing judicial emphasis on standards suggests that the courts take seriously the idea that disqualification has value as a deterrent and as a means of improving directors' awareness of their legal obligations. It may be that the change in emphasis amounts to a partial response by the courts to general criticisms, discussed above, concerning the inaccessibility of the law on directors' obligations. The recourse to objective standards again calls into question the notion from *Sevenoaks* that unfitness is purely a question of fact.[71] However, general judicial statements provide no guidance as to the precise content of "proper standards". Thus, there is just as much scope for the court to vary the standard according to the dictates of policy as there was with the older threshold tests. On a broad note, it can be said with confidence that the claimant is not required to establish that the defendant's conduct was criminally culpable. Unfitness can be proved without the need to establish dishonesty or fraud. Indeed, in several cases the courts have imposed disqualification orders of five years or more while acknowledging that the defendant had not been deliberately defrauding creditors or otherwise acting dishonestly.[72] This suggests that the courts are applying

---

[66] [1990] B.C.L.C. 440 at 444, [1990] B.C.C. 117 at 120.
[67] [1994] 1 B.C.L.C. 716 at 736, [1994] B.C.C. 264 at 281.
[68] [1993] B.C.L.C. 896 at 899, [1993] B.C.C. 312 at 315.
[69] [1995] Ch. 241 at 253, [1995] 3 W.L.R. 1 at 11, [1995] 1 B.C.L.C. 276 at 284, [1995] B.C.C. 554 at 574.
[70] *ibid.*
[71] Implicit in the conflict between the approaches in *Sevenoaks* (unfitness a question of fact) and *Grayan* (unfitness a question of mixed law and fact) are deeper questions about the autonomy of the trial judge in disqualification proceedings and the extent to which an appellate court will intervene with the trial judge's findings.
[72] See, *e.g. Sevenoaks* itself (defendant disqualified for seven years reduced to five on appeal where conduct not dishonest but markedly negligent/incompetent); *Re Melcast (Wolverhampton) Ltd* [1991] B.C.L.C. 288 (two defendants disqualified for seven and four years respectively despite the court finding that they had not acted dishonestly in the sense of lining their own pockets at the expense of creditors); *Re Austinsuite Furniture Ltd* [1992] B.C.L.C. 1047; *Re Thorncliffe Finance Ltd, Secretary of State for Trade and Industry v. Arif* [1997] 1 B.C.L.C. 34, [1996] B.C.C. 586 (in each case one defendant disqualified for seven years despite no finding of dishonesty); *Re Linvale Ltd* [1993] B.C.L.C. 654 (two defendants disqualified for five years despite no finding of dishonesty). The cases suggest that most disqualifications of less than five years are for misconduct that could not be characterised as criminally culpable.

something closer to a negligence standard. No further assistance can be derived from general judicial *dicta* concerning the question of where to draw the line between unfit and acceptable conduct. Chapter 5 seeks to demonstrate that the detail of individual cases decided under sections 6 and 8 provides a better source of practical guidance on the types of misconduct that are likely to attract disqualification than that provided by judicial generalisations.

"Makes him unfit to be concerned in the management of a company": relevant conduct under section 6

4.21   Before the court can make a disqualification order it must be satisfied under section 6(2) that the defendant's conduct as a director of the relevant company (either taken alone or taken together with his conduct as a director of any other company or companies) "makes him unfit" to be concerned in the management of a company. The extent to which the claimant can adduce evidence of misconduct from other, so-called collateral companies was considered in Chapter 3. A more general question concerning the nature and scope of the court's enquiry arises from the use of the present tense in the phrase "makes him unfit". Does this require the court to be satisfied that the defendant is, at the time of the hearing, *presently* unfit? If it does then the court would be entitled to assess at the date of trial whether the defendant still posed a genuine risk to the public for the future. In a broad enquiry of this nature, the court could take into account evidence of the defendant's general conduct (including responsible conduct) as a director of other companies during the period following the relevant company's insolvency up to the date of trial and/or other evidence that lessons from past failings have been learned making future repetition of the previous misconduct unlikely. Any improvement in the standard of the defendant's conduct during the intervening period might thus outweigh his past misconduct and indicate as at the date of trial his overall fitness to be concerned in the management of companies. This broad interpretation of the phrase "makes him unfit" does not, however, reflect the current state of the law.

"Tunnel vision": the narrow focus on past conduct

4.22   In *Grayan*,[73] the Court of Appeal held that the use of the present tense "makes" means only that the court has to make a decision on the evidence *presently before the court*. Following the line taken by Peter Gibson J. in *Re Bath Glass Ltd*,[74] Hoffmann L.J. stated:

> "The court is concerned solely with the conduct specified by the Secretary of State or official receiver under rule 3(3) of the Insolvent Companies (Disqualification of Unfit Directors) Proceedings Rules 1987. It must decide whether that conduct, viewed cumulatively and taking into account any extenuating circumstances, has fallen below the standards of probity and competence appropriate for persons fit to be directors of companies."[75]

The effect of this is that the court must determine the question of unfitness solely by reference to the evidence of *past conduct* adduced by the claimant in relation to the lead company and any collateral companies. The defendant may point to "extenuating circumstances" but evidence of extenuating circumstances is only admissible if it

---

[73] [1995] Ch. 241, [1995] 3 W.L.R. 1, [1995] 1 B.C.L.C. 276, [1995] B.C.C. 554.
[74] [1988] B.C.L.C. 329, (1988) 4 B.C.C. 130 see discussion in para. 3.54. See also Peter Gibson J.'s decision in *Re D.J. Matthews (Joinery Design) Ltd* (1988) 4 B.C.C. 513.
[75] [1995] Ch. 241 at 253, [1995] 3 W.L.R. 1 at 11, [1995] 1 B.C.L.C. 276 at 284, [1995] B.C.C. 554 at 573–574.

relates directly to the allegations of misconduct raised by the claimant.[76] Evidence of a
more general nature concerning the defendant's present suitability, the fact that he
may be running other companies successfully and responsibly at the date of trial and so
on, is not admissible as evidence of "fitness". The court makes no attempt to assess
whether the defendant is likely to behave wrongly again in the future. The question is a
narrow one: if accepted, does the present evidence of the defendant's past conduct
make him unfit? If it does then the court must disqualify him even if it is not necessarily
in the public interest to do so.[77] The court is required to have "tunnel vision":[78] it does
not enquire about the defendant's current fitness or competence but concentrates narrowly on evidence of past misconduct. Once a finding of unfitness has been made, the
court can, at that stage, consider wider evidence regarding his general conduct and
abilities as a director in determining the appropriate period of disqualification and/or
any application for permission to act. As Hoffmann L.J. put it in *Grayan*:

> "If this should be thought too harsh a view, it must be remembered that a disquali-
> fied director can always apply for [permission] under section 17 and the question
> of whether he has shown himself unlikely to offend again will obviously be highly
> material to whether he is granted [permission] or not. It may also be relevant by
> way of mitigation on the length of disqualification..."[79]

4.23   Let us consider by way of illustration, the impact of the *Grayan* approach on
the simple situation raised in paragraphs 4.02–4.03 above. W is a director of X Ltd. X
Ltd becomes insolvent and disqualification proceedings are commenced against W on
the ground that he caused X Ltd to continue trading while insolvent. Subsequently, W
becomes a director of two successful companies, Y Ltd and Z Ltd. There is clear evidence that W is running these companies in a responsible fashion without any repetition of the type of conduct that has attracted complaint in relation to X Ltd. On the
current approach, the court will only consider the alleged misconduct in X Ltd. If the
court is satisfied that such misconduct makes him unfit, it must disqualify W for at least
two years even though, in the light of his subsequent conduct, it does not appear to be
in the public interest to do so. The court can take into account W's responsible behaviour in relation to Y Ltd and Z Ltd if he makes an application for permission to act as a
director of those companies. Equally, this evidence and any other evidence suggesting
that W is unlikely to "reoffend" may be used in mitigation as a means of reducing the
length of disqualification.

4.24   A further point concerns the meaning of "*a* company" (emphasis added) in
the phrase "makes him unfit to be concerned in the management of a company". Some
have tried to argue that "a company" means "any company" with the effect that the

[76] [1995] Ch. 241 at 254, [1995] 3 W.L.R. at 11–12, [1995] 1 B.C.L.C. 276 at 285, [1995] B.C.C. 554 at
574. A possible example of admissible "extenuating circumstances" can be gleaned from the judgment of
Lindsay J. in *Re Polly Peck International plc (No. 2)* [1994] 1 B.C.L.C. 574 at 583, [1993] B.C.C. 890 at
898. The judge suggested that a defendant whose defaults, after an otherwise blameless career, consisted of
failing to ensure that proper accounting records were kept in accordance with section 221 of the Companies
Act 1985 would not be unfit if the defaults were wholly referable to a period of time during which his wife or
child were suffering from a terminal illness.
[77] Meaning the public interest in the defendant being "kept off the road". *Grayan* is authority for the view
that there may be a public interest in disqualifying such a defendant for purposes of encouraging others to
behave properly and of raising standards.
[78] A phrase commonly used by claimant's counsel: see, *e.g. Re Pamstock Ltd* [1994] 1 B.C.L.C. 716 at 737,
[1994] B.C.C. 264 at 282.
[79] [1995] Ch. 241 at 254, [1995] 3 W.L.R. 1 at 12, [1995] 1 B.C.L.C. 276 at 285, [1995] B.C.C. 554 at 574.
See further the Court of Appeal decision in *Re Westmid Packing Services Ltd, Secretary of State for Trade
and Industry v. Griffiths* [1998] 2 All E.R. 124, [1998] 2 B.C.L.C. 646, [1998] B.C.C. 836; *Re Dawes &
Henderson (Agencies) Ltd, Secretary of State for Trade and Industry v. Dawes* [1997] 1 B.C.L.C. 329,
[1997] B.C.C. 121 and para. 5.67 below.

claimant must establish on the evidence that the defendant is unfit to manage *any* company and the court cannot simply infer the defendant's general unfitness from evidence of his unfitness in relation to the company or companies which are the subject of the claim. The implication is that if the evidence of the defendant's misconduct in relation to the relevant company would not be sufficiently serious as to make him unfit in relation to some other hypothetical company or companies, he is not unfit within the meaning of section 6(1). In the above example, this might mean that the claim against W would be dismissed on the ground that his misconduct in relation to X Ltd was not sufficient to establish that he is unfit to manage any company (in particular, Y Ltd and Z Ltd). This argument was categorically rejected by Jonathan Parker J. in *Re Barings plc (No. 5), Secretary of State for Trade and Industry v. Baker*[80] in the following terms:

> "In my judgment it can be no defence to a charge of unfitness based on incompetence for a [defendant] to contend that even if he was grossly incompetent in discharging the management role in fact assigned to him, or which he in fact assumed, nevertheless he has not been shown to be unfit to be concerned in the management of *any* company, since it is possible to conceive of a management role (whether in the company or companies in question or in some other company altogether—real or imagined) which he could have performed competently— what I might call the 'lowest common denominator' approach. In the context of an issue as to unfitness it is neither here nor there whether a [defendant] could have performed some other management role competently. That is not the test of 'unfitness' for the purposes of section 6 (although of course it may be a relevant factor in the context of an application for [permission] under section 17 of the CDDA...). Under section 6 the court is concerned only with the conduct in respect of which complaint is made, set in the context of the [defendant's] actual management role in the company. If in his conduct in *that* role the [defendant] was guilty of incompetence to the requisite degree, then a finding of unfitness will be made and (under section 6) a disqualification order must follow."

Thus, the approach in *Barings* to the meaning of "a company" consolidates the view put forward in *Grayan* as to the meaning of "makes him unfit".[81]

Criticisms of Re Grayan Building Services Ltd

4.25 It may be thought that the disqualification of X in the earlier example is a harsh result. In *Grayan*, the claimant successfully appealed against the refusal of the trial judge to disqualify the two defendants, the Court of Appeal reaching the conclusion that they should each be disqualified for two years on the basis of the approach outlined above. One criticism of the *Grayan* approach is that it sits uncomfortably alongside the general view that the purpose of disqualification is not primarily to punish the defendant for his past misconduct.[82] The fact that the court may end up disqualifying the defendant even though by the date of trial he no longer poses any threat to the

[80] [1999] 1 B.C.L.C. 433 at 485.
[81] In *Barings* the defendants argued that evidence of their incompetence in relation to a large and complex plc did not show that they would be so incompetent as to make them unfit to be concerned in the management of a small company. The implication of such an argument is that there is a universal minimum standard of competence based on a "lowest common denominator", namely standards of conduct within small companies. It is suggested that the view put forward by the judge is correct because it recognises that the standard must be applied to the facts of each case. As Hoffmann L.J. put it in *Grayan* ([1995] Ch. 241 at 254, [1995] 3 W.L.R. 1 at 12, [1995] 1 B.C.L.C. 276 at 285, [1995] B.C.C. 554 at 574), the question of whether the relevant conduct falls below the appropriate standard must be adjudged "in its setting".
[82] See Chap. 2.

public seems punitive, a point made previously by Harman J. in *Re Crestjoy Products Ltd*, a case decided before *Grayan*.[83] This concern prompted Vinelott J. in *Re Pamstock Ltd* to question, *obiter*, the merits of mandatory as opposed to discretionary disqualification.[84] There are two partial responses to the criticism that the *Grayan* approach appears primarily punitive:

(1) Parliament has chosen to make disqualification for unfitness under section 6 mandatory not discretionary. Disqualification of a defendant like X may appear punitive but can also be justified on the ground that it may deter others from engaging in similar misconduct and lead to an improvement in standards of conduct generally. The point was made by Hoffmann L.J. in *Grayan* in the following terms:

> "If the court always had to be satisfied at the hearing that the protection of the public required a period of disqualification, there would be no need to make disqualification mandatory... The purpose of making disqualification mandatory was to ensure that everyone whose conduct had fallen below the appropriate standard was disqualified for at least two years, whether in the individual case the court thought that this was necessary in the public interest or not. Parliament has decided that it is occasionally necessary to disqualify a company director to encourage the others."[85]

Thus, in theory, mandatory disqualification serves the public interest not merely by taking persons who have shown themselves to be a danger to the public out of circulation but also through general deterrence. The implication is that any negative impact on the individual is a price worth paying in the pursuit of better standards.

(2) As Hoffmann L.J. points out, it is always open to a disqualified person to apply for permission to act as a director of a specified company or companies. On an application for permission, a defendant in X's position would be entitled to put a case as to why he should be allowed to continue as a director of Y Ltd and Z Ltd despite being disqualified. Thus, in theory, the power of the courts to grant permission operates as a check and balance within the structure of the Act that can be used to temper the impact of disqualification on the person.

---

[83] [1990] B.C.L.C. 677, [1990] B.C.C. 23.
[84] [1994] 1 B.C.L.C. 716 at 737, [1994] B.C.C. 264 at 282. *Grayan* and *Pamstock* are in stark contrast to the wide enquiry permitted under the discretionary provision formerly in section 300 of the Companies Act 1985: see, *e.g. Re Churchill Hotel (Plymouth) Ltd* [1988] B.C.L.C. 341, (1988) 4 B.C.C. 112. The approach taken by Lindsay J. in *Re Polly Peck International plc (No. 2)* [1994] 1 B.C.L.C. 574, [1993] B.C.C. 890 (a case concerning an application by the Secretary of State for permission to commence proceedings out of time under section 7(2)) provides another example of judicial discomfort with "tunnel vision". Laying particular emphasis on the use of the present tense and the indefinite article in the phrase "*makes* him unfit to be concerned in the management of *a* company" (emphasis added), Lindsay J. held that there was an onus on the claimant to establish that the defendant was *presently* unfit (*i.e.* at the date of trial) in relation to the management of companies generally. Thus, the judge adopted a higher threshold test and refused to accept that a finding of past unfitness should result *automatically* in a finding of present unfitness. At the same time, he recognised that the courts face a difficulty in dealing with uncorroborated evidence suggesting that the defendant is unlikely to "reoffend". To overcome this difficulty, Lindsay J. held that a finding of past unfitness should raise a presumption that the defendant is presently unfit. The onus would then be on the defendant to satisfy the court as to present fitness with reference to his general record in managing companies and any other positive performance indicators. It is clear that this complex approach does not survive the Court of Appeal's decision in *Grayan* as further glossed by Jonathan Parker J.'s judgment in *Re Barings plc (No. 5)*.
[85] [1995] Ch. 241 at 253, [1995] 3 W.L.R. 1 at 11, [1995] 1 B.C.L.C. 276 at 284, [1995] B.C.C. 554 at 574. It was suggested by Vinelott J. in *Re Pamstock Ltd* [1994] 1 B.C.L.C. 716 at 737, [1994] B.C.C. 264 at 282 that mandatory disqualification also serves a denunciatory function. The association of disqualification with notions of deterrence and denunciation only serves to strengthen the view, dismissed in Chap. 2, that disqualification is in some sense a criminal or hybrid proceeding.

Whatever the merits of the narrow approach taken by the Court of Appeal in *Grayan*, it currently represents the law.

Summary

4.26 The general guidance discussed so far on the meaning of unfitness can be summarised in the following propositions:

(1) The court is required first to consider the specific matters mentioned in Schedule 1 of the CDDA. The Schedule directs the court to assess the extent of the defendant's personal responsibility for each specified breach or default.

(2) Unfitness is a broad term that on the criteria in the Schedule appears to embrace any breach of directors' obligations under the general law. As the statutory guidance is not exhaustive, unfitness may also embrace types of misconduct that are not mentioned in the Schedule or are included within the scope of other substantive provisions in the CDDA.

(3) According to the Court of Appeal in *Sevenoaks*, the question of whether or not the defendant is unfit is a question of fact. In practice, the courts are applying some form of objective standard in determining unfitness and so the question is better characterised as one of mixed law and fact. The standard applied may vary according to the facts of the particular case and the subjective views of individual judges in relation to the competing policy issues. For this reason, it is not possible to draw a precise line between fitness and unfitness or determine with any certainty the degree of misconduct or the combination of factors that will take a defendant over onto the wrong side of the line.

(4) Although the threshold standard is variable, it appears more often than not to resemble a negligence standard. The court does not have to be satisfied that the defendant's behaviour was criminally culpable to make a finding of unfitness. In Chapter 5, it will be seen that the degree of culpability is of greater relevance at the stage when the court determines the appropriate period of disqualification.

(5) The court can take into account any proven allegations of misconduct in relation to lead and collateral companies. However, following *Grayan*, the court must have "tunnel vision" and concentrate only on the defendant's past conduct and whether or not it measures up to the standard fixed by the court. It is not concerned to assess whether or not the director is *now* fit. The director's general track record in relation to other companies that do not feature in the proceedings is irrelevant on the question of unfitness. If his track record in running companies is generally good then evidence of this may be admitted on an application for permission to act or by way of mitigation when the court comes to fix the period of disqualification.[86]

Armed with this account of the court's general approach to the question of unfitness, the next chapter considers the detail of individual cases decided under sections 6 and 8 and seeks to identify specific types of misconduct that are likely to result in disqualification.

---

[86] See *Re Westmid Packing Services Ltd* [1998] 2 All E.R. 124, [1998] 2 B.C.L.C. 646, [1998] B.C.C. 836, CA.

CHAPTER 5

Determining Unfitness (2): Specific Instances of Unfitness and Period of Disqualification

INTRODUCTION

5.01 This chapter follows on from the previous chapter and covers the following subject matter:

(1) Specific instances of unfitness as they have arisen in cases decided under sections 6 and 8 (principally, section 6).

(2) Concepts which are of increasing significance in the law of unfitness, such as incompetence and co-responsibility.

(3) Period of disqualification and mitigating factors.

SPECIFIC INSTANCES OF UNFITNESS

5.02 Numerous specific instances of unfit conduct can be derived from the plethora of reported cases decided under section 6 and 8. The examples that follow illustrate the wide scope of unfitness. In particular, it will be seen that there is considerable emphasis in section 6 cases on the need for directors to show responsibility by monitoring the company's financial position closely at all times and on the notion that, where the company is in financial difficulty, they should pay proper regard to the interests of creditors. Needless to say, unfitness embraces the more egregious forms of conduct such as fraud. At the same time, the courts routinely disqualify defendants whose conduct is less egregious but involves the failure to exercise financial responsibility and/or to pay due regard to the interests of company creditors. It is natural for section 6 cases to focus on the protection of creditors because of the requirement that the relevant company must have "become insolvent". However, it should be noted that section 6 (and section 8) are wide in scope and may be used to protect the "public" which, in appropriate circumstances, can include shareholders, investors, consumers and employees as well as creditors.[1]

Trading while insolvent

5.03 By far and away the most frequent allegation raised in proceedings for an order under section 6 is that the defendant caused the relevant company to continue

---

[1] See discussion in Chap. 2.

trading while insolvent to the detriment of its creditors.[2] Moreover, there are cases where the courts have found the defendant unfit on the basis of a single proven allegation of insolvent trading in relation to one company.[3] This is so despite the fact that trading while insolvent is not specifically mentioned in Schedule 1 (although it does arguably fall within the wide "any misfeasance or breach of any fiduciary or other duty..." wording in Schedule 1, Pt I, para. 1 as a failure on the part of a director to discharge his general duty to act in the interests of the company).[4]

Insolvent trading in the context of CDDA, s. 6 bears some relation to the concept of wrongful trading in section 214 of the Insolvency Act 1986. On the application of a liquidator under section 214, the court can declare that a director or shadow director of a company is liable to contribute personally to the company's assets provided that:

(1) the company has gone into insolvent liquidation; and

(2) at some time before the commencement of the winding up of the company, he knew or ought to have concluded that there was no reasonable prospect that the company would avoid going into insolvent liquidation; and

(3) the defendant fails to establish that, having reached the state of knowledge referred to in element (2), he took every step with a view to minimising the potential loss to the company's creditors as he ought to have taken.

If these elements are established, the court may make an order, but is not obliged to do so. The applicable standard (for the objective test of knowledge in element (2), and for determining whether the defendant took "every step") is that of a reasonably diligent person having both the general knowledge, skill and experience that may reasonably be expected of a person carrying out the same functions as are carried out by the defendant in relation to the company, and the general knowledge, skill and experience possessed by the defendant.

5.04 The essential mischief of insolvent and wrongful trading is similar. Both target the director who causes an insolvent company to continue incurring debts that the company is unlikely to be able to meet and that cannot generally be laid at the director's own door because he is protected by limited liability. However, it appears that the courts are entitled to find a defendant unfit under section 6 on the basis of insolvent trading without the claimant being required to make out a case that satisfies all the elements of section 214. In other words, the court can disqualify a director for conduct

---

[2] It should be noted for these purposes that there are two types of insolvency, namely "cash flow" insolvency (where the company cannot meet its debts as they fall due) and "balance sheet" insolvency (where liabilities exceed assets): see section 123(1)(e), (2) of the Insolvency Act 1986. A company which is "balance sheet" insolvent may be able to trade on despite its position and if it can meet its debts as they fall due and there is no immediate prospect of collapse, the directors will not necessarily be guilty of insolvent trading. As such, "insolvent trading" tends to denote the practice of trading on in circumstances where the company is "cash flow" or "balance sheet" insolvent and there is no reasonable ground for believing that it can survive.

[3] *Re McNulty's Interchange Ltd* [1989] B.C.L.C. 709, (1988) 4 B.C.C. 533; *Re Amaron Ltd, Secretary of State for Trade and Industry v. Lubrani* [1997] 2 B.C.L.C. 115 affd. [1998] B.C.C. 264.

[4] It arguably falls within Sched. 1, Pt I, para. 1 because, at common law, for the purposes of the general duty, the interests of the company are said to include its creditors where the company is of doubtful solvency: see, *e.g. West Mercia Safetywear Ltd v. Dodd* [1988] B.C.L.C. 250, (1988) 4 B.C.C. 30, CA; *Facia Footwear Ltd v. Hinchcliffe* [1998] 1 B.C.L.C. 218. However, it is clear from *Re Bath Glass Ltd* [1988] B.C.L.C. 329, (1988) 4 B.C.C. 130 that the court can make a finding of unfitness without the need to establish that the misconduct amounted to wrongful trading as defined in section 214 of the Insolvency Act 1986 (a point developed below in the main text). If "insolvent trading" at the lower *Bath Glass* standard gives rise to liability at common law then, ironically, section 214 might become redundant. On a separate point, it appears that the extent of a director's responsibility for the causes of the company becoming insolvent under Sched. 1, Pt II, para. 6 may involve a consideration of insolvent trading. Moreover, wrongful trading (as defined in section 214) is a ground of disqualification in its own right under CDDA, s. 10.

that *falls short* of wrongful trading, hence the use here of the distinct "insolvent trading" terminology. This point was first made by Peter Gibson J. in *Re Bath Glass Ltd* where he stated:

> "Take a case of wrongful trading. In proceedings brought by the liquidator under section 214 a director may be held liable under that section because for a short time before the commencement of the liquidation the director allowed the company so to trade and a small contribution might be ordered under that section... In contrast the test in section 6 is quite different: there is no single specified offence that is the condition to be satisfied for the court to make a disqualification order. What the court must have regard to is the director's conduct; that is a term of great generality and I do not doubt that it was deliberately so chosen... Any misconduct of the [defendant] *qua* director may be relevant, even if it does not fall within a specific section of the Companies Acts or the Insolvency Act... Even if... conduct *does not amount to wrongful trading within section 214, in my judgment it would still be conduct amounting to misconduct and so relevant to section 6.* Whether in any particular case that misconduct... proved to the satisfaction of the court, will justify a finding of unfitness will depend on all the circumstances of the case."[5]

The observation to the effect that misconduct falling short of wrongful trading can amount to unfit conduct is strictly *obiter* as, on the facts of *Bath Glass*, the judge held that the defendants' conduct, while "improper", was not sufficiently serious as to make them unfit. Nevertheless, the basic point that unfitness can be established without the *necessity* for the claimant to make a case under section 214 is an important one and Peter Gibson J.'s observations have been well-received in the Court of Appeal.[6] The justification for this position lies in the generality of the term "unfit" and the fact that there is no specific requirement in sections 6, 9 or the Schedule to establish that the defendant engaged in wrongful trading as defined in section 214. A further point is that the court can take into account evidence of insolvent trading in unfitness proceedings whether or not a liquidator has previously brought separate wrongful trading proceedings against the defendant.[7] Equally, there have been cases in which the courts have followed the wording in section 214 closely as a guide to determining whether a particular instance of insolvent trading amounts to unfit conduct exposing the perpetrator to disqualification.[8]

5.05   The current test favoured by the courts to determine if the defendant engaged in insolvent trading to a degree that makes him unfit is to ask whether he took "unwarranted risks with creditors' money". The test derives from the following statement of Evans-Lombe J. (as he now is) in *Re Synthetic Technology Ltd, Secretary of State for Trade and Industry v. Joiner*:

---

[5] [1988] B.C.L.C. 329 at 333, (1988) 4 B.C.C. 130 at 133–134 (emphasis added).
[6] *Re Sevenoaks Stationers (Retail) Ltd* [1991] Ch. 164 at 183, [1991] 3 All E.R. 578 at 590, [1991] B.C.L.C. 325 at 337, [1990] B.C.C. 765 at 779; *Re Copecrest Ltd, Secretary of State for Trade and Industry v. McTighe (No. 2)* [1996] 2 B.C.L.C. 477 at 486–487, [1997] B.C.C. 224 at 231.
[7] In a case where there are parallel wrongful trading proceedings, the defendant is doubly exposed to disqualification. If the action under section 214 succeeds the court dealing with those proceedings may, in its discretion, disqualify the defendant for up to 15 years under CDDA, s. 10: see further discussion in Chap. 9. If it fails, or no action is taken, the claimant may still be able to rely on allegations of insolvent trading in unfitness proceedings. Even if the court were to make a disqualification order under section 10, this does not appear to prevent the Secretary of State from seeking an additional period of disqualification under sections 6–7 on the basis of the defendant's conduct generally, including the conduct already scrutinised in the wrongful trading proceedings.
[8] See, *e.g. Secretary of State for Trade and Industry v. Taylor* [1997] 1 W.L.R. 407 at 412, *sub nom. Secretary of State for Trade and Industry v. Gash* [1997] 1 B.C.L.C. 341 at 346, *sub nom. Re CS Holidays Ltd* [1997] B.C.C. 172 at 176.

"From the combined judgments of Dillon L.J. in ... *Sevenoaks*[9] ... and Peter Gibson J. in ... *Bath Glass* ... it is apparent that a director can permit his company to continue to trade whilst insolvent, while not exposing himself to a charge of wrongful trading under section 214 ... but still be guilty of conduct amounting to misconduct under section 6. In the course of his submissions I was flattered by [counsel] commending to me words which I used in my judgment in the case of *Re Euromove Ltd*[10] where I sought to define such conduct as the taking of unwarranted risks with creditors' money by continuing to trade."[11]

This "unwarranted risks" test appears easier to satisfy than the statutory test for wrongful trading in section 214. Under section 214, the liquidator must establish that *at some given moment in time* the defendant knew or ought to have concluded that the company had no reasonable prospect of survival with the consequence that, as of that date, he should have caused the company to cease trading. Thus, there is an onus on the liquidator to plead and prove that there was an identifiable cut-off point that, at the very least, the defendant ought to have recognised. There is apparently no onus on the claimant in disqualification proceedings to establish a cut-off date beyond which the company should not have continued trading.[12] All that has to be shown is that the defendant allowed the company to continue trading at the expense or risk of its creditors rather than at the expense of the company and/or the defendant himself.[13] Although this amounts to a lesser overall burden, the claimant must still show that the defendant took "unwarranted risks", *i.e.* that his conduct was unreasonable in some way.

5.06   In a marginal case, the court must apply this objective test with care. In applying the test, the court is blessed with hindsight: it knows that the company has failed. A judge will be quite careful in reviewing, with hindsight, a decision to continue trading taken by a defendant in the heat of the moment. There is some justification for such a careful approach. First, the CDDA is not directed at business failure but rather at unfit conduct. In the interests of enterprise, it may be legitimate to allow a director to try and trade out of insolvency and turn the company around. If the company still fails then it is right that the courts should, with hindsight, be slow to characterise a legitimate

---

[9] [1991] Ch. 164, [1991] 3 All E.R. 578, [1991] B.C.L.C. 325, [1990] B.C.C. 765. *Per* Dillon L.J.:

"[The defendant] made a deliberate decision to pay only those creditors who pressed for payment. The obvious result was that the two companies traded, when in fact insolvent and known to be in difficulties at the expense of those creditors who ... happened not to be pressing for payment. Such conduct on the part of a director can well, in my judgment, be relied on as a ground for saying that he is unfit to be concerned in the management of a company."

There is further citation of this passage in para. 5.22 below.

[10] July 30, 1992, Ch.D., unreported.

[11] [1993] B.C.C. 549, 562.

[12] Indeed, it is dangerous to plead a case in disqualification proceedings along the lines of section 214. If the claimant couches an allegation in terms that the defendant knew or ought to have known at some specific date that the company was insolvent and could not survive, the case of *Re Burnham Marketing Services Ltd, Secretary of State for Trade and Industry v. Harper* [1993] B.C.C. 518 suggests that the court is likely to hold the claimant to the specific date pleaded (*i.e.* reliance on either an earlier or later date will not be permitted). This means that if the court refuses to accept or infer that the defendant knew, or should have known, that the position was hopeless on that date, the allegation is not proved.

[13] The reference to "creditors' money" is not technical and carries no implication of strict trust or proprietary right. Indeed, the test appears to track the view at common law that the directors of a struggling company should take account of creditors' interests when discharging their fiduciary obligation to the company to act in good faith. The test has been adopted in several cases since *Synthetic Technology*: see, *e.g. Re Living Images Ltd* [1996] 1 B.C.L.C. 348, [1996] B.C.C. 112; *Re Richborough Furniture Ltd, Secretary of State for Trade and Industry v. Stokes* [1996] 1 B.C.L.C. 507, [1996] B.C.C. 155; *Re Moonlight Foods (U.K.) Ltd, Secretary of State for Trade and Industry v. Hickling* [1996] B.C.C. 692; *Re City Pram and Toy Co. Ltd* [1998] B.C.C. 537; *Re Copecrest Ltd, Secretary of State for Trade and Industry v. McTighe (No. 2)* [1996] 2 B.C.L.C. 477, [1997] B.C.C. 224.

attempt at turning the business around as unfit conduct even though creditors may have suffered as a result. A related justification is that certain aspects of company law, for example the administration procedure in Part II of the Insolvency Act 1986, were enacted to promote corporate rescue. Some insolvent trading will be inevitable while the directors put together a rescue package or negotiate the sale of the company's business to a third party.[14] Secondly, there is the danger that if the courts take a hard line and disqualify directors who fail to put their companies into liquidation at the first sign of trouble, persons with appropriate expertise will be discouraged from taking up directorships. At the same time, a judge who regards limited liability as a state concession that must be used responsibly and the CDDA as a tool of creditor protection, may be more hawkish when determining whether or not the defendant took unwarranted risks and less inclined to take into account the fact that the court is blessed with hindsight. Thus, if the case against the defendant rests principally on an allegation of insolvent trading, the court is faced with an issue of some complexity.[15] As Neuberger J. put it in *Re Amaron Ltd*:

> "It is often a difficult matter to decide the point at which an unfortunate, and in retrospect, mistaken commercial assessment goes beyond the pale and becomes a decision which is such that it is either dishonest ... or culpable for some other reason ... so as to justify a disqualification order."[16]

The difficulties involved in reaching a judgment in an insolvent trading case can be illustrated by contrasting the final outcomes in *Re Ward Sherrard Ltd*[17] and *Re City Pram and Toy Co. Ltd*[18] with those in *Re Wimbledon Village Restaurant Ltd, Secretary of State for Trade and Industry v. Thomson*[19] and *Re Moonlight Foods (U.K.) Ltd, Secretary of State for Trade and Industry v. Hickling.*[20]

5.07   In *Ward Sherrard*, the defendants were directors of a company incorporated in 1987 to carry on the business of an advertising agency. In the first year of trading the company broke even but by the end of the second year (June 1989) the company was suffering from cashflow problems caused mainly by a rapid expansion of turnover. According to the audited accounts for the second year of trading, the company was balance sheet insolvent by June 1989. Moreover, the auditors qualified these accounts by saying, in effect, that the "going concern" basis on which they were prepared could prove over-optimistic unless the company was successfully refinanced. Subsequently, the defendants introduced close on £200,000 by way of directors' loans. However, in the final year and a half of trading, they withdrew some of this sum in lieu of salary with the effect that the overall net increase in the company's capital was quite small. Throughout the company's life, turnover consistently increased but increases in turnover were achieved at the expense of an increasing deficit on profit and loss account. A county court judge refused to disqualify the defendants, taking the view that their decision to continue trading was based on a genuine belief in the future viability of the company. His judgment laid emphasis on the injection of the loan monies and the continued rise in turnover following the auditors' qualification of the accounts. On the

---

[14] See, *e.g. Re Welfab Engineers Ltd* [1990] B.C.L.C. 833, [1990] B.C.C. 600.
[15] The application of the "no reasonable prospects" test in section 214 is attended by similar difficulties and competing policy considerations: see A. Walters, "Enforcing Wrongful Trading" in *The Corporate Dimension* (B. Rider (ed.) 1998).
[16] [1998] B.C.C. 264, 270.
[17] [1996] B.C.C. 418.
[18] [1998] B.C.C. 537.
[19] [1994] B.C.C. 753.
[20] [1996] B.C.C. 678. Compare also the different approaches at first instance and an appeal in *Re Grayan Building Services Ltd* [1995] Ch. 241, [1995] 3 W.L.R. 1, [1995] 1 B.C.L.C. 276, [1995] B.C.C. 554 and *Re Copecrest Ltd* [1996] 2 B.C.L.C. 477, [1997] B.C.C. 224.

claimant's appeal to the High Court, both defendants were disqualified for three years. It was held that they should have recognised that the company was in immediate need of a long term capital injection once the auditors had qualified the accounts. The funds injected by the directors had not stabilised the company's long term trading position because they had been repaid in the short term. Although turnover was increasing, there had been little prospect of financing the increase by outside borrowing on mortgage because of the general decline in property values occurring at the time. As such, the defendants' belief that the company's business was viable was unrealistic in all the circumstances and their conduct in continuing to trade after the date of the audit qualification in the absence of a long term refinancing of the company's business made them unfit.

5.08 Like *Ward Sherrard*, the case of *City Pram* also involved an appeal by the claimant to the High Court against an earlier refusal to disqualify the defendants. The company in this case was a family company, originally incorporated in 1947, which traded as a retailer of prams and children's toys from various shop premises. Having lost a lucrative concession with a leading department store in the late-1980s, the company's profitability declined drastically. During the early 1990s it suffered a series of misfortunes, through no fault of the two defendants, which were compounded by a general economic recession. The audited accounts for the year ended December 31, 1991 showed a substantial loss and were qualified by the auditors because of doubts over whether it was appropriate for them to be prepared on a "going concern" basis. The defendants, who were twin brothers, signed these accounts in October 1992 by which time the company's cashflow difficulties were acute. From that point, their strategy was to negotiate an increase in the company's overdraft facility to finance trading up to the end of 1992. The company normally did one third of its yearly turnover in the two months leading up to Christmas and the defendants believed that if borrowings were increased they would be able to trade out of difficulty by the beginning of 1993, a view shared by the company's auditors. The bank agreed to extend the overdraft limit in return for the provision of fresh personal security by the defendants and their father. However, trading over the Christmas period did not produce the anticipated increase in turnover and profitability. One of the defendants suffered a nervous breakdown further compounding the company's problems. By January 1993 the company could not hope to survive without the support of the bank and its major creditors. The bank took the view that it could justify supporting the company for a further three months. Some creditors agreed to repayment by instalments but others refused and so, on the advice of insolvency practitioners, the company was put into creditors' voluntary liquidation in April 1993. The Secretary of State's principal allegation was that the defendants had caused the company to trade while insolvent to the detriment of its creditors from October 1992 onwards. The registrar dismissed the application, holding that the defendants' decision to continue trading was based on reasonable grounds. While the company was undoubtedly insolvent in October 1992, he accepted that the defendants were justified in attempting to trade out of difficulty over the Christmas period especially as their decision was supported by the bank and the auditors. Moreover, the registrar concluded that the decision to trade on while trying to rally the support of creditors for the short period after Christmas was also reasonable in the circumstances. On appeal, the judge agreed with the registrar in relation to the period up to Christmas but disagreed in relation to the period of continued trading from January to April 1993:

"In my judgment, from January 1993, from the evidence the only conclusion which could properly be reached was that the conduct of ... the twins has to be

categorised as the taking of unwarranted risks with creditors' money by continuing to trade. If the company could not be restored to profit by the Christmas
trading there was no hope for it in the early months of 1993. Each twin clearly
permitted the company to continue to trade whilst insolvent . . . the law focuses on
the offence rather than the offender, albeit that the offender is honest and does not
lack commercial probity."[21]

The defendants were disqualified for two years.

5.09   In *Ward Sherrard* and *City Pram*, the courts were not prepared to allow the
defendants a great deal of margin for error. *Ward Sherrard* is the classic case of a
business which over-expands in its early years and fails to control overheads. It is
perhaps understandable that its directors saw fit to continue while turnover was
increasing. In theory at least, it is not true to say that the creditors in *Ward Sherrard*
were left wholly at the mercy of the defendants as they were in a position to make an
informed judgment over whether to advance further credit to the company once the
qualified accounts for June 1989 had been filed with the Registrar of Companies.
However, it is doubtful whether, in practice, many trade creditors monitor the company's position as disclosed to Companies House. The decision in *City Pram* looks even
harsher. The defendants were fighting to save an established family business against
the backdrop of an economic recession. The bank was consulted. The auditors were
consulted. The creditors themselves were consulted and when they refused to forebear,
the defendants put the company into liquidation. Creditors are always put at risk when
an insolvent company continues to trade. However, the question is whether it was
unreasonable for the defendants to take the decision to continue trading in the prevailing circumstances. It is arguable that the defendants in *City Pram* acted responsibly in
difficult circumstances.[22]

5.10   By way of contrast, the courts in *Re Wimbledon Village Restaurant Ltd* and
Re Moonlight Foods (U.K.) Ltd were prepared to allow the defendants a much greater
margin of error. In the first case, the Secretary of State sought disqualification orders
against three directors of "WVR Ltd", a company which traded in the restaurant business from March 1985 until it was put into creditors' voluntary liquidation in November 1989. The company was originally incorporated by the third defendant, "W" who
was an experienced restaurant proprietor. Financed by bank borrowings, it acquired
the lease of some licensed premises and began trading. W gave an unlimited personal
guarantee of the company's indebtedness to the bank. By the end of 1986, it was clear
that the restaurant was not a financial success and W's original co-venturers decided to
leave and withdrew their capital. At this point, W invited her two co-defendants, "IT"
and "GT" who were brothers, to join the company as directors. GT had an established
reputation as a successful manager of wine bars and so the new board decided to
reduce prices in the restaurant and open a wine bar in the basement of the premises. In
order to refinance WVR Ltd, IT and GT agreed to lend the company £50,000 in return
for a controlling interest. A further aspect of this agreement was that management of
the business was to be placed entirely in the hands of the two brothers. In return, they
agreed to indemnify W against any liability under her bank guarantee over and above
the level of her existing exposure at the date of the takeover. W remained a director so
as to monitor her personal exposure to the bank but played no further part in the
management of the business. It was accepted that the company was balance-sheet

---

[21] [1998] B.C.C. 537, 547.
[22] Equally, the decision can be justified because the defendants continued to accept customer deposits in the
period from January 1993 in circumstances where there must have been some doubt as to whether the items
ordered would ever be delivered: see para. 5.37.

insolvent at the time of the takeover but the view of the brothers, backed up by professional and family advice, was that its fortunes could be turned around. Initially, they managed to generate an increase in turnover. However, they never succeeded in making the business profitable. By the early months of 1989 the bank was questioning the company's continuing viability. A number of cheques had already been dishonoured by this stage. Basic accounting functions were not carried out properly and the company's books were not up to date. There was no immediate prospect of selling the business because the company's lease was up for renewal and the lessor had indicated that he was not prepared to grant a new lease on the grounds that he wished to occupy the premises for his own purposes. Further cheques were dishonoured, creditors who pressed for payment were strung along with excuses and in July 1989, by which time GT had left the business, the Inland Revenue took walking possession of the company's chattels. The company finally ceased trading in September 1989. The judge concluded that from the end of March 1989 onwards IT and GT should have realised that the company was only able to continue trading at the potential expense of its creditors:

> "In my judgment a dispassionate analysis at any point thereafter would have led to the conclusion that continued trading could only be justified if there was a real prospect of selling the business in the very near future. In the event no such sober analysis took place."[23]

There was never any genuine attempt either to value or market the business for sale and the company was faced with the added difficulty that the lessor was refusing to renew the lease. The Secretary of State alleged that the brothers were deliberately gambling at the expense of creditors in the period after March 1989 with the objective of driving down the bank overdraft so as to reduce or eliminate their personal exposure under the indemnity previously given to W. The judge refused to accept that there was any such conscious design but he did accept that the brothers' conduct had been unsatisfactory:

> "The picture I have is not one of a deliberate strategy to reduce the overdraft at expense of trade creditors and then to scuttle the ship, but rather one of allowing the ship to drift. Had the brothers been trading with personal liability, I doubt whether events would have taken quite the same course... In my judgment the way in which the business of the company was run from the end of March onwards was not the way in which such a business ought to have been run, given the possible consequences for trade creditors. I find that both [IT] and [GT] paid insufficient regard to the interests of creditors during this period. It was the responsibility of both of them to make an early and informed decision on what would be in the best interests of the company and its creditors. This did not happen ... and, while they may have genuinely believed that they would be able to sell the business and lease ... should the worst come to the worst, they did not have reasonable grounds on which to base such a belief. It was the product of wishful thinking."[24]

5.11 Despite this finding, the application against the brothers was dismissed. The judge emphasised that not every past impropriety necessarily leads to the conclusion that the person responsible is unfit and took into account what he described as "the peculiar combination of family and commercial circumstances in which they found

---

[23] [1994] B.C.C. 753 at 761.
[24] *ibid.* at 762.

themselves".[25] Left with a "significant measure of doubt", the judge decided to resolve it in the brothers' failure. W was also exonerated. Compared with *City Pram*, the approach in this case looks generous. The judge seems to have expected the claimant to establish a high degree of culpability (*i.e.* some conscious design) and was anxious, given the benefit of hindsight, not to apply too strict a standard.[26] Thus the approach in *Wimbledon Village Restaurant* more closely resembles the approach of a criminal court.

A similar approach was taken in *Re Moonlight Foods (U.K.) Ltd*. In this case the company, "M Ltd", ran a sandwich-making business, but traded for under two years before administrative receivers were appointed in February 1992. The company amounted in substance to a partnership between "D" and "T". D had previously been running a similar business but needed finance to expand. She was introduced to T who was the major shareholder and managing director of a building company. M Ltd was incorporated with a view to acquiring a sandwich-making business which was in the hands of receivers. T persuaded his company to invest in M Ltd (it acquired a controlling interest) and agreed to provide financial and accounting expertise. D agreed to provide her client list and experience of the business. "C", the finance director of T's company was appointed as M Ltd's secretary and it was agreed that he would attend to day to day accounting matters. The business was acquired from the receivers for around £60,000 of which £10,000 was paid by M Ltd with T's company meeting the balance. This sum of £50,000 was treated as an unsecured loan by T's company to M Ltd. A secured overdraft facility was negotiated with M Ltd's bankers. It is clear from these financing arrangements that the company had a high gearing from the start of its active trading life. With the loss of its major contract, M Ltd was already in financial difficulty before the end of 1990. The bank agreed to increase its overdraft limit in return for a guarantee from T's company. It is clear that creditors were pressing for payment throughout the company's life. Despite regular cash injections by T's company it was never profitable. Moreover, M Ltd's accounting records, the particular responsibility of C, were never in a satisfactory state. Several cheques were dishonoured. D and T appear to have been content to rely on profit and cashflow forecasts provided by C rather than any hard accounting information concerning the company's financial position. The auditors of T's company, mindful of the impact of the business on the group as a whole, were expressing grave reservations about M Ltd's viability and the lack of concrete accounting information from around September 1991 and onwards. By November 1991, they were describing the situation with regard to "problem creditors" as "dangerous". The company's salvation appears to have rested at this stage on a contract with British Homes Stores. However, British Home Stores reduced their order in December 1991 and discontinued orders altogether in January 1992. The bank appointed receivers a month later. The judge held that C was principally to blame for much of what went wrong but declined to disqualify him as he was never appointed a director and was not found to have acted as a *de facto* director. He then went on to deal with the question of whether D and T had taken "unwarranted risks":

"It is submitted that the directors should have realised that [C's] projections were

---

[25] *ibid.* at 764. Among the extenuating factors taken into account were general economic conditions (with particular reference to the rise in interest rates during 1989) and the breakdown of the brothers' personal relationship. Thus economic and personal factors were said to have contributed to the situation rather than any "innate or invincible incompetence" on the brothers' part.

[26] A judge following the sort of approach taken in *Synthetic Technology* and *City Pram* might well have taken a less generous view of the evidence (especially that concerning the pressing creditors and dishonoured cheques) and imposed a short period of disqualification. It is interesting to note that the judge in *Wimbledon Village Restaurant* (who became Hart J.) has subsequently cast doubt on his own decision: see *Re Landhurst Leasing plc* [1999] 1 B.C.L.C. 286 at 346–347.

unreliable because they had not been tested against management accounts... No lack of probity is suggested, and in my judgment the conduct of these directors in continuing to trade on what, with hindsight, may be seen to be inadequate information is not reprehensible enough to justify a finding that either of them is unfit... In this case I have found no dishonesty, no breach of common standards of commercial morality, no cynical disregard for others' interests and no gross incompetence on the part of either [D] or [T]. At worst they were guilty of naivety, over-optimism and misplaced trust."[27]

5.12 The approach taken in *Moonlight Foods* can best be described as circumspect. The judge accepted that it was appropriate to apply the test from *Synthetic Technology* rather than the wording of section 214. However, it appears from the passage quoted above, that the court required the claimant to establish a higher degree of culpability (*i.e.* dishonest or cynical conduct) than that suggested by the "unwarranted risks" test. At the same time, a likely explanation is that the judge was reluctant to disqualify D and T bearing in mind that he had refused to assume jurisdiction over C on the basis that he was not a "director". It appears that the judge was anxious to avoid a result that treated D and T more severely than the person he considered to be mainly responsible for the company's downfall.[28] He may also have been influenced in D's case by the fact that she was already disqualified under CDDA, s. 11 having been made bankrupt.

The four cases discussed illustrate the important, if trite point that the decision in a borderline case boils down ultimately to a matter of individual judgment. The courts in *Ward Sherrard* and *City Pram* applied a strict standard and allowed the defendants very little margin. The courts in *Wimbledon Village Restaurant* and *Moonlight Foods* applied a lesser test and were much more prepared to make allowance for the potentially distorting impact of judicial hindsight.[29] On this less strict approach, we see the courts paying greater deference to managerial decision-making and showing greater willingness to characterise the decision to continue trading as a commercial misjudgment. Thus, whereas the judge in *Ward Sherrard* dismissed as groundless a genuinely-held belief that the company could trade out of difficulty, the judge in *Moonlight Foods* was much more prepared to defer to the directors' subjective evaluation of the position. Scope therefore remains for the tacit operation of variants of the discredited "sunshine" or "blue skies" test applied previously in a number of fraudulent trading cases.[30] Even so, the counsel of perfection for the company director is to learn the lesson of the decisions in *Ward Sherrard* and *City Pram*. Where the company is insolvent, the decision to continue trading must be a well-informed one based on accurate,

---

[27] [1996] B.C.C. 678, 692–693.
[28] The decision not to assume jurisdiction over C is criticised in paras 3.21 to 3.24. A further explanation is that D and T were justified in delegating responsibility for the company's financial affairs to someone of C's experience and expertise. However, in several cases the courts have said, in effect, that all directors have an equal responsibility to monitor the company's financial position. Where, as here, there is a failure to keep adequate accounting records in accordance with section 221 of the Companies Act 1985, even directors who are not charged with the task of overseeing the book-keeping are routinely disqualified: see paras 5.13–5.19 and on the issue of apportionment of responsibility, paras 5.54–5.65.
[29] For further cases in which a less strict approach was adopted see, *e.g. Re Douglas Construction Services Ltd* [1988] B.C.L.C. 397, (1988) 4 B.C.C. 553; *Re C.U. Fittings Ltd* [1989] B.C.L.C. 556, (1989) 5 B.C.C. 210 (both decided under section 300 of the Companies Act 1985); *Re Bath Glass Ltd* [1988] B.C.L.C. 329, (1988) 4 B.C.C. 130. For other cases taking a strict approach see, *e.g. Re City Investment Centres Ltd* [1992] B.C.L.C. 956; *Re Amaron Ltd* [1998] B.C.C. 264.
[30] See, *e.g. Re White & Osmond (Parkstone) Ltd*, June 30, 1960 cited in *R. v. Grantham* [1984] Q.B. 675, [1984] 2 W.L.R. 815, [1984] 3 All E.R. 166, (1984) 79 Cr. App. Rep. 86, [1984] B.C.L.C. 270. So-called because the defendant who genuinely believed that the "sun would eventually shine" as far as the company's fortunes were concerned, was likely to escape liability even if the belief was groundless.

up to date financial information and a realistic, objectively justifiable evaluation of the company's prospects. Once taken, the decision must be regularly reviewed and the company's prospects reevaluated. Wise counsel from professional advisers should be heeded and unbridled optimism checked.[31] At the same time, *Wimbledon Village Restaurant* and *Moonlight Foods* show that the Secretary of State faces difficulties in making a case for disqualification based solely on an allegation of insolvent trading. It is always possible that the court may make subtle adjustments to the burden of proof to try and counter the effect of hindsight. It is perhaps a reflection of this that few applications for orders under section 6 are brought on the basis of insolvent trading alone. Indeed, the court is much more likely to make a finding of unfitness if there are other exacerbating factors present in the case that serve to strengthen the inference of insolvent trading and take the defendants decisively over the wrong side of the line. Several of the exacerbating factors commonly raised as subsidiary allegations in insolvent trading cases are discussed below. The range of factors provides a useful illustration of the combinations of (often-related) misconduct that can lead to a finding of unfitness and mandatory disqualification. While there is nothing to prevent the claimant raising these exacerbating factors in isolation, it is common for a number of them to be linked to an allegation of insolvent trading so as to illustrate a general failure on the defendant's part to exercise financial responsibility.[32] At the same time, some of the other specific factors discussed, such as breach of fiduciary duty or fraud, may well be sufficiently serious on their own to result in a finding of unfitness.

Failure to keep proper accounting records and the wider obligation to exercise financial responsibility

5.13   The cases suggest that a failure by the defendant to keep proper accounting records in accordance with section 221 of the Companies Act 1985 will increase the likelihood of disqualification whether it is linked to an allegation of insolvent trading or considered in isolation. Non-compliance with section 221 is a matter specifically mentioned in Schedule 1 of the CDDA. The section itself states:

> "(1) Every company shall keep accounting records which are sufficient to show and explain the company's transactions and are such as to—(a) disclose with reasonable accuracy, at any time, the financial position of the company at that time, and (b) enable the directors to ensure that any balance sheet and profit and loss account prepared ... complies with the requirements of this Act.
> (2) The accounting records shall in particular contain—(a) entries from day to day of all sums of money received and expended by the company, and the matters in respect of which the receipt and expenditure takes place, and (b) a record of the assets and liabilities of the company."

---

[31] On the dangers for directors who fail to follow good professional advice and plough on believing, without foundation, that the company's fortunes will turn around see *Re Synthetic Technology Ltd* [1993] B.C.C. 549; *Re Living Images Ltd* [1996] 1 B.C.L.C. 348, [1996] B.C.C. 112; *Re Park House Properties Ltd* [1997] 2 B.C.L.C. 530, [1998] B.C.C. 847.

[32] Even so the court will consider each distinct allegation separately: see *Re New Generation Engineers Ltd* [1993] B.C.L.C. 435, 438–439; *Re Copecrest Ltd, Secretary of State for Trade and Industry v. McTighe (No. 2)* [1996] 2 B.C.L.C. 477, [1997] B.C.C. 224, CA. Moreover, the courts have on occasions made disqualification orders based exclusively on what are described in the main text as "exacerbating factors". For an early case based exclusively on accounting defaults see *Re Rolus Properties Ltd* (1988) 4 B.C.C. 446. For a case in which the court made a disqualification order on the basis that the defendants had failed to pay Crown debts despite rejecting an allegation of insolvent trading see *Re Verby Print for Advertising Ltd, Secretary of State for Trade and Industry v. Fine* [1998] 2 B.C.L.C. 23, [1998] B.C.C. 652 discussed in paras 5.24–5.27 below.

Section 221(5) adds that where a company fails to comply with the provision every officer of the company in default is guilty of an offence (punishable by imprisonment or fine or both) unless he shows that he acted honestly and that in the circumstances the default was excusable. Breach of section 221 is regarded in the context of disqualification as a failure by the directors to keep themselves properly informed of the company's financial position. The upshot is that a decision to allow an insolvent company to continue trading will generally be treated as a failure of a higher order where the directors had no detailed grasp of the company's financial position and were, in effect, "trading blind". Thus, the courts are more likely to reach a finding of unfitness and less likely to make allowance for hindsight if the directors were taking decisions that were not well-informed.[33] The cases discussed below illustrate the use of disqualification proceedings as a forum to fashion a basic minimum standard of financial responsibility applicable to directors and as a principal means of enforcing section 221. This emphasis on the need for directors to exercise proper financial responsibility reflects concerns expressed both in the Cork Report and during the parliamentary debates that preceded the enactment of the current insolvency legislation.[34]

5.14   A total failure on the part of the defendant to maintain any proper accounting records at all is the sort of misconduct that is likely to tip the balance in an otherwise marginal case. Harman J. characterised this failure in the following terms in *Re Rolus Properties Ltd*:

> "The privilege of limited liability is a valuable incentive to encourage entrepreneurs to take on risky ventures without inevitable personal total financial disaster. It is, however, a privilege which must be accorded upon terms and some of the most important terms that Parliament has imposed are that accounts be kept and returns made so that the world can, by referring to those, see what is happening. Thus, a total failure to keep statutory books and to make statutory returns is significant for the public at large and is a matter which amounts to misconduct if not complied with and is a matter of which the court should take into account in considering whether a man can properly be allowed to continue to operate as a director of companies, or whether the public at large is to be protected against him on the grounds that he is unfit, not because he is fraudulent but because he is incompetent and unable to comply with the statutory obligations attached to limited liability."[35]

On this analysis, the obligation to comply with section 221 is part of the price exacted from those who choose to trade with the benefit of limited liability. If the company has no core accounting records the directors will be unable to ascertain the company's financial position with any certainty and will be faced with grave difficulties when the time comes to prepare and file audited accounts. This analysis was taken forward by Chadwick J. in *Re Thorncliffe Finance Ltd, Secretary of State for Trade and Industry v. Arif*[36] who attributed two distinct purposes to section 221. The first

---

[33] See *Re Grayan Building Services Ltd* [1995] Ch. 241 at 252, [1995] 3 W.L.R. 1 at 10, [1995] 1 B.C.L.C. 276 at 283, [1995] B.C.C. 554 at 573. This is true also of wrongful trading proceedings under section 214 of the Insolvency Act: see discussion of *Re Produce Marketing Consortium Ltd* [1989] 1 W.L.R. 745, [1989] 3 All E.R. 1, [1989] B.C.L.C. 513, (1989) 5 B.C.C. 569 in Walters, *op. cit.*
[34] See, *e.g.* Cork Report, Chap. 45; Hansard, HL Vol. 458, col. 885, Vol. 461 cols 712, 732–736, Vol. 467, cols 1130–1131, 1133, 1137. The importance of financial responsibility is further reflected by cases where the court has been prepared to make a finding of unfitness based exclusively on breaches of statutory accounting obligations: see, *e.g. Re Rolus Properties Ltd* (1988) 4 B.C.C. 446; *Re Swift 736 Ltd, Secretary of State for Trade and Industry v. Ettinger* [1993] B.C.L.C. 896, [1993] B.C.C. 312.
[35] (1988) 4 B.C.C. 446 at 447.
[36] [1997] 1 B.C.L.C. 34, [1996] B.C.C. 586.

purpose is to ensure that those who trade with the benefit of limited liability maintain sufficient accounting records to enable them to ascertain the company's financial position at a given moment. Chadwick J.'s view was that directors cannot act responsibly in deciding whether or not to continue trading in the absence of proper records. The second purpose is to ensure that the directors can prepare an accurate statement of affairs should the company fail so that an insolvency practitioner who takes office can readily identify the company's assets and take steps to recover or exploit those assets in the interests of creditors.[37]

5.15   In *Arif* the three defendants, "M", his son "S" and "D" were directors of a finance company called Thorncliffe Finance Ltd. Thorncliffe was acquired for the purpose of financing the businesses of four affiliated companies which were in the motor trade. M was a director of these affiliated companies. Thorncliffe was a source of hire purchase finance for customers who wished to purchase cars from the affiliated companies. It also provided the affiliated companies with the finance needed to purchase cars for resale from manufacturers or distributors. The affiliated companies ceased trading and Thorncliffe was placed in administrative receivership with an estimated deficiency as regards creditors in excess of £1.6 million. The thrust of the case against the defendants was that they had caused Thorncliffe to enter into transactions with the affiliated companies which led to the accrual of over £1 million worth of indebtedness without any proper financial controls and without security. This meant that Thorncliffe's fortunes had been inextricably tied to those of the affiliated companies. There had been some attempt by D to raise the issue of the inter-company indebtedness but no steps were ever taken to put security in place or to monitor asset levels within the affiliated companies. The inter-company indebtedness was allowed to grow unchecked with the effect that when the affiliated companies failed they brought Thorncliffe down with them. The evidence showed that the accounting records of Thorncliffe and the affiliated companies were insufficient to enable the various office holders to identify and recover any remaining assets. The defendants had been unable to prepare a statement of affairs for the purposes of the receivership. The judge held that the failure of the defendants to fulfil these statutory obligations made them unfit and all three were disqualified. In effect, the case can be interpreted as one where the defendants' general failure to act in the interests of Thorncliffe (manifested in their particular failure to protect its assets for creditors) was compounded by non-compliance with section 221. *Arif* confirms that there is a minimum obligation on directors to act with financial responsibility in the interests of creditors. If a decision is taken to continue trading in circumstances where the directors have no sure means of ascertaining whether the company is solvent or insolvent and trading at the risk of its creditors, the risk of disqualification on grounds of unfitness is substantially increased. The case also illustrates the "cascade" effect of failure to comply with section 221. If there are no proper accounting records, it is more than likely that the directors will also have failed in their obligation to prepare accounts and, where necessary, a statement of affairs. These additional matters of complaint will again increase the risk of disqualification.

5.16   The theme of proper financial responsibility has surfaced in several other cases. In *Re New Generation Engineers Ltd*[38] Warner J. characterised the defendant's failure to comply with section 221 as a failure to monitor the company's financial position that was itself indicative of unfitness. Part of the defendant's evidence was that he lacked accounting knowledge. The judge's response was to say that his lack of expertise made it necessary for him to have proper professional guidance in the matter

---

[37] [1997] 1 B.C.L.C. 34 at 42–43, [1996] B.C.C. 586 at 593–594.
[38] [1993] B.C.L.C. 435.

of the company's accounting records and financial position. This serves to reinforce the view that section 221 is being used by the courts to fashion a basic minimum standard that will not be relaxed simply because the defendant possesses no financial expertise.[39] In *Re Firedart Ltd, Official Receiver v. Fairall*[40] the defendant was found to be unfit on a number of grounds including trading while insolvent and failure to keep proper accounting records. Arden J. laid particular emphasis on the latter:

> "When directors do not maintain accounting records in accordance with the very specific requirements of section 221 of the Companies Act ... they cannot know their company's financial position with accuracy. There is therefore a risk that the situation is much worse than they know and that creditors will suffer in consequence. Directors who permit this situation to arise must expect the conclusion to be drawn in an appropriate case that they are in consequence not fit to be concerned in the management of a company."[41]

A notable feature of this case is that, for the purposes of the insolvent trading allegation, the judge rejected the defendant's view that the company had first become insolvent during 1988, finding that he ought to have concluded that it was insolvent before the end of 1986. This illustrates again how a breach of section 221 may persuade the court to treat other allegations with a greater degree of seriousness.[42] Thus, it is clear that the courts take the failure to maintain proper accounting records very seriously and will often infer from it a lack of regard for creditors' interests sufficient to constitute unfitness.[43]

5.17   It has been seen how the courts have used section 6 of the CDDA to fashion a minimum standard of financial responsibility applicable to directors based on the core accounting obligation in section 221 of the Companies Act. In several other cases, disqualification orders have been made on the basis of a more general failure to exercise financial responsibility not linked directly to a breach of section 221. In *Re Hitco 2000 Ltd, Official Receiver v. Cowan*[44] the relevant company traded for just under two years before going into compulsory liquidation. The defendant, who was the company's sole director, had expertise in buying and selling. He delegated the task of maintaining the company's accounting records to a series of unqualified book-keepers. His evidence was that he had no knowledge of the finer points of accounting and therefore relied on the book-keepers to compile the books and records. Payment of the company's debts was also delegated. The defendant's practice was to sign whole cheque books in blank leaving the book-keeper with instructions to pay as many of the company's outstanding debts as possible given available funds. The company encountered severe cash flow difficulties from the outset. No less than 84 cheques were dishonoured

---

[39] See further the treatment of the second defendant, Ms Zangus in *Re Richborough Furniture Ltd, Secretary of State for Trade and Industry v. Stokes* [1996] 1 B.C.L.C. 507, [1996] B.C.C. 155 and *Re Hitco 2000 Ltd* discussed below in main text.
[40] [1994] 2 B.C.L.C. 340.
[41] *ibid.* at 352.
[42] For further support see *Re Ask International Transport Ltd, Secretary of State for Trade and Industry v. Keens*, May 5, 1992, Ch.D. unreported and *Re Bloomgalley Ltd, Secretary of State for Trade and Industry v. Neophytou*, October 15, 1993, Ch.D. unreported. In *Ask International* the defendants allowed the company to continue to trade while insolvent despite a warning from the auditors concerning the inadequacy of its basic financial information. The judge found them to be unfit on the basis of "reckless or risky trading". In *Bloomgalley* the defendant's failure to keep proper stock records (a breach of Companies Act 1985, s. 221 (3)) influenced the court to conclude that he had caused the company to continue trading without justification.
[43] This also a theme of Australian jurisprudence under section 600 of the Corporations Law: see, *e.g. Re Delonga and the Australian Securities Commission* (1994) 15 A.C.S.R. 450, (1995) 13 A.C.L.C. 246; *Re Agushi and Australian Securities Commission* (1996) 19 A.C.S.R. 322.
[44] [1995] 2 B.C.L.C. 63, [1995] B.C.C. 161.

during its trading life and writs were issued by several creditors for undisputed sums. There was no allegation of non-compliance with section 221. Nevertheless, a full set of accounts was never produced and the fact that the defendant allowed the company to continue trading without making any realistic assessment of its prospects was sufficient to render him unfit. As the judge put it:

> "The company traded for a period of a year and ten months... In all that period of time the business ... was conducted without the [defendant] stopping once to make ... an appraisal and to ask himself the question: should I stop incurring credit and cease trading? I should say immediately that there is no ... question of want of probity on the [defendant's] part... But it does seem to me to be a case where trade was carried on by a sole director for the most part blind as to the true financial state of his company and thus quite unable to make an intelligent projection from time to time as to whether it was right to go on or not. In my judgment the [defendant's] greatest failing is that he did not ensure that he was provided with regular financial management information so as to enable him to answer that most difficult question which every director who trades with the privilege of limited liability is obliged to confront, especially in straitened financial circumstances, *i.e.* should I cease trading? ... How else could any reasonable decision be made as to whether continued trading from that point of time onwards would be at the risk and expense of creditors or not?"[45]

5.18   The defendant's disqualification in *Hitco 2000 Ltd* illustrates that, in the case of a sole director, the basic obligation to exercise financial responsibility extends beyond merely ensuring that core accounting records are compiled and kept up to date. A proper system of financial control must also be implemented to ensure that he receives current accounting information and can make well-informed decisions. *Hitco 2000* suggests that a sole director who abdicates control of the financial side of the business will equally be at risk of disqualification as one who fails to comply with section 221. The judge added that it was incumbent on a sole director who lacked financial expertise to ensure that he had constant professional guidance whatever the cost.[46] The upshot is that a director is vulnerable to disqualification if he has maintained no books and records as the court is likely to infer that any decision to continue trading was not made on a proper basis. Even where accounting records have been maintained, *Hitco 2000* suggests that a director will be exposed if he fails to monitor the company's financial position and allows the company to continue trading blindly against a background of persistent cash flow problems and creditor unrest. Further support for this view can be derived from *Re Grayan Building Services Ltd, Secretary of State for Trade and Industry v. Gray*.[47] In *Grayan*, the Secretary of State complained, in the context of a claim of insolvent trading, that the company's lack of management accounts was evidence of unfitness. This was disregarded by the trial judge on the basis that there is no statutory requirement for companies to produce management

---

[45] [1995] 2 B.C.L.C. 63 at 70, [1995] B.C.C. 161 at 167–168.
[46] [1995] 2 B.C.L.C. 63 at 74, [1995] B.C.C. 161 at 171. For further cases suggesting that a general abdication of financial control is likely to lead to a finding of unfitness especially in a small company see, *e.g. Re D.J. Matthews (Joinery Design) Ltd* (1988) 4 B.C.C. 513; *Re T & D Services (Timber Preservation & Damp Proofing Contractors) Ltd* [1990] B.C.C. 592; *Re Melcast (Wolverhampton) Ltd* [1991] B.C.L.C. 288; *Re Burnham Marketing Services Ltd, Secretary of State for Trade and Industry v. Harper* [1993] B.C.C. 518; *Re Pamstock Ltd* [1994] 1 B.C.L.C. 716, [1994] B.C.C. 264.
[47] [1995] Ch. 241, [1995] 3 W.L.R. 1, [1995] B.C.L.C. 276, [1995] B.C.C. 554, CA.

accounts. However, Hoffmann L.J. stated that the absence of up-to-date figures about the company's financial position is relevant to whether it is reasonable for directors to allow a company to continue trading at a time when it is unable to pay its debts as they fall due. Thus, it is suggested that a failure to produce regular financial information in the form of management accounts can amount to a failure to monitor the company's financial position in the *Hitco* sense. Furthermore, the court is unlikely to allow a director to rely on his lack of financial expertise as a defence to disqualification proceedings. This reinforces the point that directors are expected to attain a basic minimum standard of financial responsibility.[48]

5.19 A further general aspect of the duty to exercise financial responsibility is that accounting information must be presented in a way which gives a fair impression of the company's financial position. In *Re Austinsuite Furniture Ltd*[49] one of the defendants caused the lead company, "A Ltd" to acquire the business of "B Ltd", a company of which he was also a director. Both companies were on the verge of insolvency. A valuation of £2 million was placed on the business and goodwill of B Ltd despite the fact that it was insolvent and that A Ltd had been meeting its debts for the previous six months. It appears that the principal objective of the transaction was to put a rosier complexion on the respective balance sheets of A Ltd and B Ltd. Its effect was to enhance the assets of A Ltd by the value placed on the business acquired and the assets of B Ltd by the value of the consideration. In substance, no consideration was paid to B Ltd as A Ltd simply assumed responsibility for B Ltd's debts. The judge disqualified the defendant for seven years on a number of grounds but took a particularly dim view of this transaction:

"The position of [A Ltd] was in effect concealed by the extraordinary transaction purportedly entered into by [B Ltd] and [A Ltd]. If it had not been introduced into the accounts as filed at the Companies Registry, creditors ... would have been alerted to the true position of [A Ltd], with the almost certain consequence that [A Ltd] would have been compelled to cease trading at a time when its liabilities would have been less than they were in ... the following year."[50]

Not surprisingly, the auditors of A Ltd came in for considerable criticism for failing to satisfy themselves that some basis existed for the valuation placed on B Ltd's business and allowing what amounted to a fraud on creditors practised through the accounts to pass largely unchallenged.[51] A further example, and one on a much larger scale, is provided by the section 8 case, *Re Atlantic Computers plc, Secretary of State for Trade and Industry v. Ashman*.[52] In that case, several former group executives (though not all) were found to be unfit principally on the basis that Atlantic's accounts had failed to disclose the true extent of the company's contingent liabilities. The *Atlantic* case is considered in greater detail in para. 5.48 below.

---

[48] There are cases which suggest that a director may be less at risk where accounting functions have been delegated to someone holding appropriate professional qualifications: see, in particular, *Re Cladrose Ltd* [1990] B.C.L.C. 204, [1990] B.C.C. 11 and see paras 5.58–5.60.
[49] [1992] B.C.L.C. 1047.
[50] *ibid.* at 1060.
[51] The auditor's principal obligation under section 235 of the Companies Act 1985 is to certify that the annual accounts have been properly prepared and give a true and fair view of the state of affairs of the company. The audit report in A Ltd's case was qualified but the judge described the qualification as one lying "at the less serious end of the possible forms of qualification set out in the accounting standards". Given that A Ltd and B Ltd had common directors it also appears that the transaction may have required approval by both sets of shareholders under section 320 of the Companies Act.
[52] June 15, 1998, Ch.D., unreported.

Deliberate failure to pay Crown or other non-pressing creditors and the concept of discrimination

5.20   Another specific allegation frequently raised in disqualification proceedings is that the defendant caused the company to withold payment of sums owing to Crown creditors such as the Inland Revenue (in relation to PAYE and national insurance contributions) and Customs & Excise (in relation to VAT) with the effect that the company was only able to continue trading at the expense of such creditors. At first sight, the non-payment of Crown debts appears merely to be one aspect of the wider charge that the defendant allowed the company to continue trading while insolvent. This is much the way in which Ferris J. tackled it in Re GSAR Realisations Ltd:

> "... the non-payment of substantial Crown debts by a company which is in financial difficulties ... may support an inference that the directors have made a deliberate decision only to pay those creditors who pressed for payment, with the result that the company while insolvent has unfairly been using as working capital money which ought to have been paid to creditors... Looked at in this way, the non-payment of Crown debts is merely one aspect of the charge ... that he allowed the company to trade after he knew it had become unable to pay its debts. I shall deal with this complaint as part of the same general charge."[53]

It was also stated in Re Bath Glass Ltd that the non-payment of Crown debts is not to be regarded as significant unless the court can infer from it that the directors knew or ought to have have known that the company was trading while insolvent at the risk of creditors.[54] However, there are cases in which this ground appears to acquire an independent life of its own.

5.21   The debate concerning the precise status and treatment of Crown debts in the context of disqualification proceedings is one of long standing. The early cases decided before 1990 reveal a marked lack of judicial consensus. In a series of cases, Harman J. took the view that monies representing VAT paid by customers and deductions of tax and national insurance from employees' wages were held by the company on "quasi-trust". It followed that the company was obliged to account for these monies rather than "misapply" them for its own cash flow purposes. On this analysis the non-payment of Crown debts was regarded as more serious than the non-payment of ordinary trade debts in determining unfitness.[55] The justification for this approach appears to lie in the public nature of these liabilities and the Crown's status as an involuntary creditor. By contrast, in Re Dawson Print Group Ltd, Hoffmann J. refused to make any distinction between non-payment of Crown debts and ordinary trade debts in terms of relative seriousness.[56] Indeed, he voiced doubt over whether the failure to pay Crown debts would at that time have been regarded as sufficiently serious in the commercial world to justify a finding of unfitness in itself. Two points can be made in support of Hoffmann J.'s approach. First, non-payment of Crown debts is not one of the specific matters mentioned in Schedule 1 to which the court is directed to have particular regard. It might be inferred from this that Parliament and the Secretary of State (who has power to add further specific matters to the Schedule under section 9(4) of the

---

[53] [1993] B.C.L.C. 409, 412–413.
[54] [1988] B.C.L.C. 329 at 337, (1988) 4 B.C.C. 130 at 137.
[55] See, e.g. Re Howard Davey & Co Ltd, December 7, 1984, Ch.D. unreported; Re Flatbolt Ltd, February 21, 1986, Ch.D. unreported; Re Wedgecraft Ltd, March 7, 1986, Ch.D. unreported; Re Cladrose Ltd [1990] B.C.L.C. 204, [1990] B.C.C. 11.
[56] [1987] B.C.L.C. 601 at 604, (1987) 3 B.C.C. 322 at 325.

CDDA) do not currently regard such conduct as being particularly heinous.[57] Secondly, the Crown is protected to a certain extent by its preferential status in insolvency and this arguably compensates it for being in the position of an involuntary creditor.[58] Other judges steered a middle path between the two extremes of the "quasi-trust" and *Dawson Print* approaches. In *Re Stanford Services Ltd*, Vinelott J. seemed to indicate that failure to pay Crown debts was more serious than failure to pay trade debts because the Crown is an involuntary creditor. However, in reaching the conclusion that the defendant was unfit the judge laid no special emphasis on non-payment of Crown debts and simply inferred from the evidence that he had caused the company to trade while insolvent.[59] In *Re Lo-Line Electric Motors Ltd*, Browne-Wilkinson V.-C. expressed the view, without adopting Harman J.'s quasi-trust analysis, that the use of Crown monies to finance the continuation of an insolvent company's business was more culpable than the failure to pay trade debts. However, this conclusion appears to rest on the misapprehension that failure to account for PAYE and national insurance contributions deducted from wages was somehow prejudicial to employees.[60] The emphasis (apparent in cases like *Stanford Services* and *Lo-Line*) on the Crown's special status as an involuntary creditor led the courts to treat failure to pay Crown debts less seriously where the evidence showed that the Inland Revenue or Customs & Excise had agreed to accept payment by instalments.[61] Nevertheless, with the exception of *Dawson Print*, the view that failure to pay Crown debts should be treated more seriously than failure to pay trade debts appears to have been gaining in acceptance up to 1990.

5.22 The Court of Appeal decision in *Re Sevenoaks Stationers (Retail) Ltd*[62] brought a change in emphasis and laid the foundation for a broader approach. In this case there was evidence that substantial Crown debts had been allowed to accumulate at a time when the defendant knew that the relevant companies were in increasing financial difficulty. The Court of Appeal held that non-payment of Crown debts should not automatically be treated as evidence of unfitness and that the court should consider on the facts of the particular case whether to attribute any significance to the fact of such non-payment. Dillon L.J. adopted the following analysis:

"[The defendant] made a deliberate decision to pay only those creditors who pressed for payment. The obvious result was that the two companies traded, when in fact insolvent and known to be in difficulties, at the expense of those creditors who, *like the Crown*, happened not to be pressing for payment. Such conduct on the part of a director can well, in my judgment, be relied on as a ground for saying that he is unfit to be concerned in the management of a company. But what is relevant in the Crown's position is not that the debt was a debt

---

[57] Against this, there is nothing in the Act to suggest that misconduct falling within the Schedule should automatically be regarded as more serious than misconduct falling outside: see discussion in paras 4.09–4.10.

[58] Although note that this is not full protection as only limited amounts of Crown debt rank as preferential in receivership and liquidation: see Insolvency Act 1986, ss 40, 175, 386 and Sched. 6.

[59] [1987] B.C.L.C. 607 at 616–618, (1987) 3 B.C.C. 326 at 334–335.

[60] [1988] Ch. 477 at 488, [1988] 3 W.L.R. 26 at 34, [1988] 2 All E.R. 692 at 698, [1988] B.C.L.C. 698 at 705, (1988) 4 B.C.C. 415 at 421. The misapprehension was cleared up in *Re Sevenoaks Stationers Ltd* [1991] Ch. 164, [1991] 3 All E.R. 578, [1991] B.C.L.C. 325, [1990] B.C.C. 765. For other cases steering a middle course see *Re Western Welsh International System Buildings Ltd* (1988) 4 B.C.C. 449; *Re J & B Lynch (Builders) Ltd* [1988] B.C.L.C. 376.

[61] See, *e.g. Re McNulty's Interchange Ltd* [1989] B.C.L.C. 709 at 712, (1988) 4 B.C.C. 533 at 536; *Re Keypack Homecare Ltd* [1990] B.C.L.C. 440 at 445, [1990] B.C.C. 117 at 121. See, however, *Re Park House Properties Ltd* [1997] 2 B.C.L.C. 530, [1998] B.C.C. 847 which suggests that the Crown's failure to take action against the non-payer is no defence.

[62] [1991] Ch. 164, [1991] 3 All E.R. 578, [1991] B.C.L.C. 325, [1990] B.C.C. 765.

which arose from a compulsory deduction from employees' wages or a compulsory payment of VAT, but that the Crown was not pressing for payment, and the director was taking unfair advantage of that forbearance on the part of the Crown, and, instead of providing adequate working capital, was trading at the Crown's expense while the companies were in jeopardy. *It would be equally unfair to trade in that way and in such circumstances at the expense of creditors other than the Crown. The Crown is more exposed not from the nature of the debts but from the administrative problem it has in pressing for prompt payment as companies get into difficulties.*[63]

Thus, the Court of Appeal did not attach any special or added significance to the non-payment of Crown debts in determining whether the defendant was unfit and took a much broader approach. The implication of *Sevenoaks* is that where a company is insolvent, the deliberate practice of paying only those creditors who are pressing while withholding payment from creditors (which may include the Crown) who are not pressing is likely to result in a finding of unfitness. As such, the essence of the misconduct described by Dillon L.J. lies in the discriminatory impact of the practice on some of the creditors. In effect, if the directors adopt this type of practice, the company will continue to trade at the risk of its non-pressing creditors while other creditors receive preferential treatment.

5.23   Following on from *Sevenoaks* it appears increasingly that the courts will treat a director who discriminates between different creditors in this way more seriously than one who simply allows the company to trade while insolvent at the expense of all its creditors. In *Sevenoaks* itself, the Court of Appeal treated the discriminatory practice as a separate ground which added weight to other findings (including a general finding of trading while insolvent) and concluded that a five-year disqualification was appropriate. Even before *Sevenoaks* there are some indications that the lower courts were starting to move in this direction. In the earlier case of *Re Cladrose Ltd*, Harman J. indicated that a case where all the creditors suffer would be regarded as less serious than a case where trade creditors are paid but the Crown is deliberately left unpaid with the effect that the company is using Crown monies "as a sort of piggy-bank to pay others."[64] Similarly, in *Re Keypack Homecare Ltd*, the same judge distinguished the deliberate retention of Crown monies to subsidise continued trading from a case where the Crown is merely one unpaid creditor who has suffered along with all the other creditors as a result of a corporate insolvency.[65] These *dicta* and several cases decided after *Sevenoaks* follow a similar line and reinforce the view that while the failure to pay Crown creditors is not unfit conduct *per se*, the discriminatory practice of "robbing Peter to pay Paul" is more likely to lead to a finding of unfitness.[66] In the majority of these cases, the failure to pay non-pressing creditors is treated simply as a form of aggravated insolvent trading.

The cases suggest that the claimant is not required to prove that the defendant *intentionally* operated a policy of paying non-pressing creditors. If, for example, there is

---

[63] [1991] Ch. 164 at 183, [1991] 3 All E.R. 578 at 589–590, [1991] B.C.L.C. 325 at 337, [1990] B.C.C. 765 at 779. Emphasis added.
[64] [1990] B.C.L.C. 204 at 211, [1990] B.C.C. 11 at 16.
[65] [1990] B.C.L.C. 440 at 445, [1990] B.C.C. 117 at 121.
[66] See further *Re Tansoft Ltd* [1991] B.C.L.C. 339; *Re Burnham Marketing Services Ltd, Secretary of State for Trade and Industry v. Harper* [1993] B.C.C. 518; *Re GSAR Realisations* [1993] B.C.L.C. 409; *Re New Generation Engineers Ltd* [1993] B.C.L.C. 435; *Re Linvale Ltd* [1993] B.C.L.C. 654; *Re Pamstock Ltd* [1994] 1 B.C.L.C. 716, [1994] B.C.C. 264; *Re Synthetic Technology Ltd* [1993] B.C.C. 549; *Re Copecrest Ltd, Secretary of State for Trade and Industry v. McTighe (No. 2)* [1996] 2 B.C.L.C. 477, [1997] B.C.C. 224, CA; *Re Lasercell Ltd, Official Receiver v. Cummings*, November 1, 1991, Ch.D., unreported; *Re Admiral Energy Group Ltd, Official Receiver v. Jones*, August 19, 1996, Ch.D., unreported.

evidence that Crown monies were witheld over a sustained period, the court will usu-ally infer that the defendant was operating a deliberate policy of non-payment. In *Re Melcast (Wolverhampton) Ltd* where the evidence showed that Crown debts were rising consistently over a period of 18 months while amounts owing to trade creditors during the period were kept at the same level, the court readily inferred that the defend-ants had deliberately witheld payment from the Crown and used what money there was to keep an insolvent company temporarily afloat.[67] The case of *Re Austinsuite Furniture Ltd* suggests that the court will draw a similar inference where one company within a trading group is used as a vehicle to employ the group's workforce and during the whole of its existence it pays no PAYE or national insurance.[68] However, the court is likely to reach the opposite conclusion and attach less significance to the allegation if the evidence shows, for example, that Crown monies were witheld for only a short period just before the company ceased trading.[69] Equally, in a marginal case, the court may make adjustments to the overall burden of proof as seen above in *Re Wimbledon Village Restaurant Ltd.*

5.24   A special case requiring separate discussion is one where the defendants have benefited personally from the company's failure to pay non-pressing creditors. A clas-sic example of this is where the directors give personal guarantees to the company's bank and then operate a policy of paying off the bank at the expense of other creditors which has the effect of reducing their own exposure under the guarantees. This type of conduct raises a problem of classification. On the one hand, the payments could be classified as a deliberate policy of unfair discrimination in favour of the bank. On the other hand, it might be preferable to treat payments to the bank in these circumstances as a preference in favour of the guarantor.[70] The case of *Re Verby Print for Advertising Ltd, Secretary of State for Trade and Industry v. Fine*[71] illustrates some of the difficult-ies that can arise when this issue of classification is not resolved. The two defendants were the sole shareholders and directors of the company which traded in the printing business. Towards the end of 1992 the company suffered a downturn in its business and, anticipating serious financial difficulties, the defendants sought the advice of an insolvency practitioner. In March 1993, the company's creditors approved a corpor-ate voluntary arrangement but this collapsed before the end of April 1993, when the company lost the support of its debt factors. The defendants continued trading, but only with the aim of selling the company's business as a going concern. A buyer for most of its assets was found and the company ceased trading at the end of July 1993 before entering creditors' voluntary liquidation a month later. The company's state-ment of affairs revealed an estimated deficiency as regards Crown creditors of £38,000 and an overall deficiency in excess of £250,000. The Secretary of State sought disquali-fication orders on two grounds. The first ground was that the defendants allowed the company to trade while insolvent with no reasonable prospect of creditors being paid. The registrar rejected this ground and held that the defendants' conduct in consulting the insolvency practitioner and in continuing to trade with a view to a going concern sale constituted an adequate and timely response to the company's financial difficult-ies. The second ground was that the defendants discriminated against the Crown by using monies that could have been paid to the Crown to pay the bank and thereby reduced their own exposure under their personal guarantees. Thus it was alleged that

---

[67] [1991] B.C.L.C. 288.
[68] [1992] B.C.L.C. 1047.
[69] *Re J & B Lynch (Builders) Ltd* [1988] B.C.L.C. 376 at 379 (*dictum* of Mervyn Davies J.); *Re Keypack Homecare Ltd* [1990] B.C.L.C. 440 at 445, [1990] B.C.C. 117 at 121 (in relation to non-payment of VAT). See however, the *Verby Print* case discussed in main text below.
[70] By analogy with *Re Agriplant Services Ltd* [1997] 2 B.C.L.C. 598, [1997] B.C.C. 842.
[71] [1998] 2 B.C.L.C. 23, [1998] B.C.C. 652.

they took advantage of the Crown's forbearance for their own benefit. Up to late June 1993 the registrar found that there was real uncertainty as to what, if anything, was owed to the Crown. The position was investigated by an insolvency practitioner who advised that some £37,000 was owing in respect of PAYE and national insurance. The registrar concluded that the defendants' failure to take any steps towards paying off this liability once they became fully aware of it was sufficient misconduct to render them unfit.

5.25   The registrar's decision in *Verby Print* was upheld on appeal. Neuberger J. held that the registrar had been right to conclude that the defendants should have made some attempt to reduce the outstanding liability to the Crown, especially once they had completed the task of selling the company's assets at the end of July 1993. The judge's view of the evidence was that there was sufficient "slack" in the company's banking facilities for at least something to have been paid towards the Crown debt. In the circumstances, it could be inferred that the defendants' failure in this regard was a failure born of self-interest given their position as guarantors. It was argued for the defendants that before unfair discrimination against a creditor can justify a finding of unfitness, the claimant must show that there was an actual policy of discrimination and that the period under consideration in this case (one of two months) was too short to enable the court to infer that such a policy existed. Prompted by a concession from the Secretary of State, Neuberger J. held that a policy of unfair discrimination between creditors must be established, following the analysis put forward by Dillon L.J. in *Sevenoaks*. He characterised a "policy" as a decision which is conscious or unconscious taken for reasons which may be conscious or unconscious. On this analysis, the court can infer that there was a policy if, *in effect*, the company traded at the expense of a particular class of creditors whether or not that effect was consciously intended.[72] Moreover, the judge was not prepared to introduce any threshold requirement that has to be established before the "policy" can be said to be "unfair":

> "... to hold that the policy should have continued for a certain minimum period, or to impose any other fetter on what has to qualify before it can be a policy of unfair discrimination, appears to me to be wrong in principle and unhelpful in practice. Clearly, the shorter the period during which the policy exists, the less grave a view the court may take of the policy, all other things being equal. However, once the court finds, as it has done in the present case, that there has been what in normal language could be called a policy of unfair discrimination, it is not, in my judgment, possible to say that it is for some reason incapable of being a policy for the purposes of deciding whether a person is unfit ... because it continued for only a short time. In other words, once one finds a director permitting a company to engage in unfair discrimination between creditors, the only question for the court is whether, taking into account all the relevant factors relating to the policy (including the period for which the policy continued) that finding justifies the conclusion that the person concerned is unfit to be a director of a company."[73]

5.26   The striking aspect of the decision in *Verby Print* is that the defendants were disqualified on the ground that they unfairly discriminated against the Crown in circumstances where the court accepted that there was nothing illegitimate in their decision to allow the company to continue trading. Indeed, the court found that this decision was based on the reasonable view (supported by the insolvency practitioner)

---

[72] See further *Re Park House Properties Ltd* [1997] 2 B.C.L.C. 530, [1998] B.C.C. 847, a case decided by the same judge.
[73] [1998] 2 B.C.L.C. 23 at 39, [1998] B.C.C. 652 at 665.

that continued trading for the purposes of a sale was the best way of achieving a satis-factory realisation of the company's assets. Thus, *Verby Print* is not a case of the type envisaged by Ferris J. in *GSAR Realisations* where conduct amounting to unfair dis-crimination is treated as an aggravated form of insolvent trading. It is rather a case in which the related allegations of insolvent trading and unfair discrimination have become unhitched. There are dangers in treating unfair discrimination as an isolated ground for disqualification. If, as in *Verby Print*, the court accepts that the defendant was acting in the interests of creditors as a whole in continuing to trade while insol-vent,[74] it may seem odd that he should then be penalised for what amounts to a failure to pay non-pressing creditors. Even where continued trading is regarded as *legitimate*, it is likely that some creditors will lose out. Moreover, if the company is to survive, the directors will inevitably have to pay pressing creditors first especially if they include the bank and key suppliers. In this context, the emphasis on the concept of unfair discrimi-nation may produce a situation of "Hobson's choice": the directors face disqualifi-cation for deciding to pay Creditor X because it discriminates against Creditor Y whereas if they decide to pay Creditor Y they face disqualification for discriminating against Creditor X. The true basis of the decision in *Verby Print* appears to lie in prefer-ence rather than unfair discrimination. It was found on the evidence that the company had not been pressed into reducing the sum owed to the bank. Thus, it could readily be inferred that the defendants' primary motivation in paying the bank rather than the Crown was to prefer themselves.[75] As such, it is necessary to be careful over treating unfair discrimination as a separate ground for disqualification uncoupled from insol-vent trading. The mere fact that some creditors are, in the end, harmed more than others may be an inevitable result in a case of insolvent trading when the company eventually collapses. It is another matter if the directors deliberately decide to discrimi-nate and prefer some creditors over others in the absence of insolvent trading. In this respect, *Verby Print* can be contrasted sharply with the earlier case of *Re C.U. Fittings Ltd* decided under the former provision in section 300 of the Companies Act 1985. In *C.U. Fittings* the defendant had taken the decision to contine trading with the sole aim of realising some of the company's stock in the hope that a greater sum would be received for the stock in those circumstances than if the company was put straight into liquidation. The effect of this decision was that certain creditors such as the bank received payment while substantial VAT liabilities generated by the company's sales went unpaid. Hoffmann J. characterised the defendant's conduct as a mere misjudg-ment and declined to make a disqualification order:

> "The company here was not using the Crown's money as working capital for a trade that should not have been carried on. It was not at the relevant time doing anything more than winding down its business. It is true that in the event the effect of its choosing to realise some of its stock rather than going into liquidation has meant that [some creditors] have received payment, whereas the VAT liabilities ... remain unpaid. However, it seems to me that the choice as to whether to realise the stock without going into liquidation in the hope that substantially larger prices can be obtained, or to go into liquidation to preserve the preferential pos-ition of the commissioners cannot be a very easy one. Where a lack of commercial

---

[74] And, arguably, in the interests of the company's employees as well in accordance with the statutory duty in Companies Act 1985, s. 309.
[75] For the treatment of preferences in disqualification proceedings, see paras 5.38–5.41. It is interesting to note that a similar allegation was treated as a preference in *Re Grayan Building Services Ltd* [1995] Ch. 241, [1995] 3 W.L.R. 1, [1995] 1 B.C.L.C. 276, [1995] B.C.C. 554. *Grayan* and *Verby Print* stand in stark contrast to the altogether more generous approach adopted in a similar situation in *Re Bath Glass Ltd* [1988] B.C.L.C. 329, (1988) 4 B.C.C. 130.

probity is required, I think that a good deal more than a misjudgment on that question must be shown."[76]

5.27   At the same time, there is some attraction from the State's point of view in the concept of unfair discrimination, especially in relation to Crown debts. Indeed, despite the Court of Appeal's refusal in *Sevenoaks* to treat the Crown as a special case, it is hard to escape the conclusion that the courts are trying to get across the message that witholding payment from the Crown is not acceptable. If so (and the stiff approach taken in *Verby Print* suggests that it might be so) then disqualification is being used, in part, as a deterrence mechanism to support the enforcement effort of Crown agencies.

Excessive remuneration

5.28   An allegation sometimes raised is that the defendant remunerated himself at a level that was unsustainable given the company's financial circumstances. Again, this is not a matter which is spelled out in Schedule 1 but it amounts to a failure on the part of the defendant to pay due regard to the interests of the company (and, in particular, its creditors) and might best be categorised as a breach of fiduciary duty.[77] It is important to draw a distinction between "excessive remuneration" in the popular (and pejorative) sense (in which highly remunerated executive directors are commonly described as "fat cats") and excessive remuneration that is criticised on the ground that the company was not in financial position to afford it, even though, on an objective basis, it did not exceed the "going rate" for the services in question. Reported cases decided under section 6 have only been concerned to date with the question of remuneration in the latter sense. As such, it appears that the issue is more likely to arise in cases involving owner-managers who determine their own remuneration rather than in cases of executive directors who do not own the company and whose remuneration is determined by non-executive directors or some other independent means. Excessive remuneration is not usually relied on to establish unfitness in isolation. It is invariably treated as an exacerbating factor which taken in combination with related misconduct such as insolvent trading may result in a finding of unfitness. For instance, if X allows a company to trade while insolvent and is only able to maintain his own remuneration at the same levels as when the company was solvent by witholding payment from non-pressing creditors he is liable to disqualification on the combined grounds of insolvent trading, unfair discrimination and excessive remuneration. As with the other specific grounds discussed so far, it is a matter of fine judgment whether this ground will be established to the satisfaction of the court on the facts of a particular case. In *Re Keypack Homecare Ltd*, the company had been trading for over ten years and its annual turnover was in the region of £500,000. Aware that the company was in financial difficulties, the defendants agreed to take increased remuneration of some £25,400 between the two of them. In addition, they each enjoyed the use of a company car. Six months later the company went into liquidation. Although the defendants were disqualified on other grounds, Harman J. refused to accept that the decision with regard to remuneration amounted to unfit conduct:

"... the Secretary of State submits that it must be wrong for directors to increase their remuneration in the face of falling profits and a business that was not doing

[76] [1989] B.C.L.C. 556 at 560, (1989) 5 B.C.C. 210 at 214. Though query to what extent this can be regarded as authoritative in the light of the shift away from judicial paraphrases like "commercial probity" towards the language of "appropriate standards": see discussion in Chap. 4.
[77] See, *e.g. West Mercia Safetywear Ltd v. Dodd* [1988] B.C.L.C. 250, (1988) 4 B.C.C. 30, CA; *Facia Footwear Ltd v. Hinchcliffe* [1998] 1 B.C.L.C. 218.

very well. In my judgment, one cannot approach it as simply as that. I have to consider whether these [defendants] were, to use a colloquialism, 'living high on the hog' at the expense of the creditors of the company, and in my view their salaries ... are not such as in 1986 would of themselves cause any very serious eyebrow-raising for managerial people running a business with a turnover of approaching £0.5m even though the business was doing badly."[78]

5.29   In other cases the court has found that it was irresponsible for the defendants to take the "going rate" without giving any consideration to the company's financial position or its ability to pay.[79] In this regard, if the defendant is unaware of the true extent of the company's plight, a decision to maintain current levels of remuneration or increase them will compound his overall failure to exercise proper financial responsibility.[80] Similarly, the courts have said that there is no justification for a director to take increasing levels of remuneration from a company that has never made profits.[81] Perhaps not surprisingly, the courts have also castigated directors for allowing their company to pay salaries to family members or co-directors who perform little or no obvious function in return.[82] However, no director has yet been disqualified solely on the basis of these sorts of findings.

Misuse of bank account

5.30   This is a supplementary allegation sometimes raised to support a case based mainly on insolvent trading and/or failure to exercise proper financial responsibility. The phrase "misuse of bank account" is usually used to denote the practice whereby the defendant allows cheques to be drawn on the company's account without any regard for whether the bank will honour them or not. If there is evidence that the company "bounced" several cheques, this strengthens inferences of insolvent trading and lack of financial responsibility.[83] Moreover, in cases where the defendant delegated the task of paying creditors to an employee or book-keeper such evidence supports the contention that he abdicated responsibility for monitoring the company's financial position.[84] It was suggested *obiter* in *Re Hitco 2000 Ltd* that the practice of regularly drawing cheques in the hope that the bank account will remain within the overdraft limit when they are presented for payment is conduct capable of evidencing unfitness even where the cheques are ultimately met, although whether it does so in a particular case will depend on all the evidence.[85] In *Hitco*, it was also held that the

---

[78] [1990] B.C.L.C. 440 at 443–444, [1990] B.C.C. 117 at 120.
[79] See *Re Stanford Services Ltd* [1987] B.C.I..C. 607, (1987) 3 B.C.C. 326 (the question is not what the director needed to draw to cover living expenses but what the company can afford to pay); *Re Cargo Agency Ltd* [1992] B.C.L.C. 686, [1992] B.C.C. 388; *Re Synthetic Technology Ltd* [1993] B.C.C. 549; *Re Moorgate Metals Ltd, Official Receiver v. Huhtala* [1995] 1 B.C.L.C. 503, [1995] B.C.C. 143; *Re CSTC Ltd, Secretary of State for Trade and Industry v. Van Hengel* [1995] 1 B.C.L.C. 545, [1995] B.C.C. 173; *Re Amaron Ltd, Secretary of State for Trade and Industry v. Lubrani* [1997] 2 B.C.L.C. 115 affd. [1998] B.C.C. 264; *Re Readyfresh Ltd, Secretary of State for Trade and Industry v. Arnold*, February 23, 1995, Ch.D., unreported.
[80] *Re Firedart Ltd, Official Receiver v. Fairhall* [1994] 2 B.C.L.C. 340.
[81] *Re Austinsuite Furniture Ltd* [1992] B.C.I..C. 1047; *Re Ward Sherrard Ltd* [1996] B.C.C. 418; *Re Copecrest Ltd, Secretary of State for Trade and Industry v. McTighe (No. 2)* [1996] 2 B.C.L.C. 477, [1997] B.C.C. 224, CA. Contrast *Re ECM (Europe) Electronics Ltd* [1992] B.C.L.C. 814 where a defendant who drew a salary out of gross profits and reduced his level of remuneration once the company started to struggle was not disqualified.
[82] *Re Firedart Ltd, Official Receiver v. Fairhall* [1994] 2 B.C.L.C. 340; *Re CSTC Ltd, Secretary of State for Trade and Industry v. Van Hengel* [1995] 1 B.C.L.C. 545, [1995] B.C.C. 173. The directors must address their minds to whether a payment (especially a gratuitous one) serves the interests of the company by analogy with *Re W & M Roith Ltd* [1967] 1 W.L.R. 432, [1967] 1 All E.R. 427.
[83] See, *e.g. Re Admiral Energy Group Ltd, Official Receiver v. Jones*, August 19, 1996, Ch.D., unreported.
[84] *Re Pamstock Ltd* [1994] 1 B.C.L.C. 716, [1994] B.C.C. 264.
[85] [1995] 2 B.C.L.C. 63 at 68–69; [1995] B.C.C. 161 at 166.

practice of a director signing blank cheques and instructing employees to pay pressing creditors without exercising any proper control over their use of the cheque book can also amount to a misuse of the bank account. At trial, the only complaint made under this heading concerned the dishonoured cheques. The defendant argued, on appeal from a district judge, that the complaint about the use of the cheque book could not be relied on as it had not been put forward as a separate ground of unfitness at trial. Mr Jules Sher Q.C. (sitting as a deputy High Court judge) agreed with the defendant and held that the official receiver was not entitled in that case to rely upon the defendant's practice of leaving signed blank cheques with employees as conduct which of itself justified a finding of unfitness.[85a] However, such evidence was held to be relevant to the main allegation which had been properly raised against the defendant, namely his general abdication of responsibility in the realm of financial control.[86]

Phoenix activity and serial failure

5.31 One of Parliament's major priorities in enacting the CDDA was to address the so-called phoenix syndrome. There is no mention of this specific abuse in Schedule 1. Nevertheless, it has been suggested that the practice whereby directors use a phoenix company to acquire the assets of their insolvent company on the cheap with total disregard for its creditors is a matter connected with or arising out of the insolvency of the latter company for the purposes of CDDA, s. 6(2).[87] Whatever the technicalities, there is a strong likelihood that evidence of deliberate phoenix activity will result in a finding of unfitness given the amount of attention it attracted in the Cork Report and during parliamentary debate.[88] Again, however, it is the cases involving conduct falling short of deliberate phoenix activity which illustrate the complexity of the policy issues at stake.

The case of *Re Copecrest Ltd, Secretary of State for Trade and Industry v. McTighe (No. 2)*[89] is at the serious end of the scale although it did not amount to a classic phoenix case. One of the allegations in *McTighe* centred on a transfer of assets between two companies, "C Ltd" and "L Ltd", both of which were controlled by the defendants. The assets and goodwill of C Ltd, which had consistently made losses during its recent trading history, were sold to L Ltd in 1989 for the sum of £1.4 million payable by instalments over the next five years. L Ltd provided no security with regard to the deferred consideration. Only one instalment of £185,000 was ever paid and C Ltd was put into creditors' voluntary liquidation in 1990 with a deficiency in excess of £1 million, mostly made up of liabilities to the Crown. Its only asset was the unpaid debt of roughly £1.2 million owed by L Ltd. There is little doubt that the Court of Appeal regarded the transfer of C Ltd's assets to L Ltd as a device designed to put the assets out of the reach of C Ltd's creditors, enabling the business to continue free of its debts. The failure of the defendants as directors of C Ltd to obtain any security in respect of the deferred consideration payable by L Ltd was considered sufficiently serious on its own to justify a finding of unfitness.[90]

5.32 The pattern of conduct found in *Re Ipcon Fashions Ltd*[91] is a much more direct example of phoenix activity. The defendant carried on business in the clothing trade through a succession of small, owner-managed companies. The relevant com-

---

[85a] See further paras 6.52–6.58.
[86] See *Dorchester Finance Ltd v. Stebbing* [1989] B.C.L.C. 498 and, by analogy, *Bishopgate Investment Management Ltd v. Maxwell (No. 2)* [1994] 1 All E.R. 261, [1993] B.C.L.C. 1282, [1993] B.C.C. 120.
[87] *Re Bath Glass Ltd* [1988] B.C.L.C. 329 at 331, (1988) 4 B.C.C. 130 at 132. Although query in this context whether conduct must be "conduct as a director": see discussion in para. 4.08.
[88] See paras 2.05–2.10 and see I.F. Fletcher, "The Genesis of Modern Insolvency Law" [1987] J.B.L. 365.
[89] [1996] 2 B.C.L.C. 477, [1997] B.C.C. 224.
[90] [1996] 2 B.C.L.C. 477 at 487, [1997] B.C.C. 224 at 232.
[91] (1989) 5 B.C.C. 773.

pany, Ipcon Fashions Ltd was the successor to a business previously carried on at the same premises by a company called Lorenzo Fashions Ltd. Lorenzo Fashions was put into liquidation in 1985 with an estimated deficiency of over £100,000. Ipcon Fashions continued to use the trading name "Lorenzo". After a good start to its short trading life sales almost completely dried up and by mid-1986 the defendant decided, in his words, "to wind down the company's affairs with a view to paying all creditors". The business of Ipcon Fashions was transferred to a new company called Lorenzo London Ltd which carried on the same business. Although it now had no business to carry on, the defendant continued to incur liabilities through Ipcon Fashions and he and his wife each drew a salary without accounting for tax. A compulsory winding up order was made in respect of the company in October 1986. Hoffmann J. disqualified the defendant for five years. It is clear that the judge regarded this as a case in which the company and its creditors had been abandoned to their fate. The defendant's conduct in continuing to draw a tax-free salary and in maintaining the appearance that the company was still trading after the transfer of the business to Lorenzo London Ltd was considered "particularly reprehensible".

In *Re Keypack Homecare Ltd* the defendants were found to be unfit on the basis that they had arranged for stock to be transferred from an insolvent company to a successor company of which they were also directors. Harman J. described the successor as being "in the most obvious of senses a phoenix company, a complete reincarnation from the ashes of the old"[92] and disqualified both defendants for three years. *Ipcon Fashions* and *Keypack Homecare* suggest that the court will come down quite hard on any conduct that appears to involve a process of sheltering assets from creditors.[93] However, the fact that the directors use a fresh company to acquire the assets and business of their former insolvent company from its liquidator does not of itself render them unfit. It is not unlawful to set up a successor company and provided that the assets are acquired from the liquidator at a price ascertained by independent valuation, the directors will not be liable to disqualification on the ground of the acquisition alone.[94] This is consistent with the idea that company law is concerned with the facilitation of enterprise and not the punishment of business failure *per se*. However, it is incumbent on both the insolvency practitioner and the directors to ensure that the successor company acquires the former company's assets at market value and that the process is wholly transparent.[95]

5.33 The phoenix syndrome aside, there are cases where directors have been disqualified following their involvement in a number of failed companies. However, this is not to say that serial failure in the absence of phoenix activity automatically amounts

[92] [1990] B.C.L.C. 440 at 443, [1990] B.C.C. 117 at 119. The defendants asserted that the stock transfer had taken place on the advice of the first company's liquidator. This was found to be not proven but it is interesting to note that the liquidator had previously been removed from office on the application of a creditor: see the earlier application in *Re Keypack Homecare Ltd* [1987] B.C.L.C. 409, (1987) 3 B.C.C. 558.
[93] See also *Re Travel Mondial (U.K.) Ltd* [1991] B.C.L.C. 120, [1991] B.C.C. 224 (defendant who engineered phoenix succession disqualified for nine years); *Re Linvale Ltd* [1993] B.C.L.C. 654 (phoenix aspect—two defendants described as reckless but honest each disqualified for five years) and *Re Saver Ltd* [1999] B.C.C. 221.
[94] *Re Douglas Construction Services Ltd* [1988] B.C.L.C. 397 at 400, (1988) 4 B.C.C. 553 at 556; *Re Pamstock Ltd* [1994] 1 B.C.L.C. 716 at 720–721, [1994] B.C.C. 264 at 268. The directors must ensure that the successor company does not trade using a prohibited name in breach of section 216 of the Insolvency Act 1986. Misuse of a former company name by a successor company was raised but rejected in *Re ECM (Europe) Electronics Ltd* [1992] B.C.L.C. 814. However, such conduct has been taken into account for section 6 purposes whether or not the successor company becomes insolvent.
[95] An approach reflected in the guidance issued to its members by the Society of Practitioners of Insolvency: see Statement of Insolvency Practice 13, "Acquisition of Assets of Insolvent Companies by Directors" (November 1997). Nevertheless, the fact that the successor company goes into insolvent liquidation will not of itself make its directors automatically unfit. It is necessary to look at all the circumstances of the case.

to an independent ground for disqualification. It was seen in Chapter 3 that the court can take into account the defendant's conduct in relation to a series of companies under section 6(1)(b). As such, where the claimant can show that the defendant has repeated the same or a similar pattern of misconduct in several companies and thus failed to learn the lessons of previous business failures, there is an enhanced likelihood of disqualification.[96] It is the repetition of misconduct rather than serial business failure *per se* that will attract the attention of the court, an approach which reflects both the enterprise rationale of company law and the protective aspect of disqualification.

Lack of capitalisation

5.34   The failure of directors to ensure that their companies are properly financed is not in itself a separate ground of disqualification. This is hardly surprising given that the Companies Act imposes no minimum capital requirement on private companies making limited liability, on the face of it, a cheap commodity. Thus, the fact that a company with a paid up share capital of £2 becomes insolvent is not itself a justification for disqualifying its directors. This is consistent with the enterprise rationale of company law discussed at length in Chapter 2 and the *dictum* of Harman J. in *Re Rolus Properties Ltd* to the effect that the formation of a company with a small capital for the purposes of a speculative venture would not by itself warrant criticism.[97] Seen in this light, it is not surprising that Parliament refused to include a reference to inadequate capitalisation in Schedule 1 of the CDDA and make it a matter to which the court is required to pay particular regard.[98] At the same time, many corporate failures can be explained by lack of capitalisation and the official line is that companies trading on inadequate financial foundations pose an enhanced risk to creditors.[99] As a result, the court may be influenced in determining whether a director is unfit by the company's inadequate capitalisation especially where he causes the company to trade into an increasing deficiency without making any attempt to introduce fresh capital, whether by way of share capital or long term loan. Equally, the court will not be impressed in such circumstances if the director is drawing funds out of the company for his own personal remuneration or benefit. Thus, inadequate capitalisation may surface as a further aggravating factor in cases containing a mixture of allegations including some or all of insolvent trading, unfair discrimination, excessive remuneration and phoenix activity.[1] Moreover, the fact that a company is under-capitalised arguably enhances the obligation on its directors to exercise proper financial responsibility, especially in relation to the filing of accounts, so that potential creditors can make judgments on the basis of financial information that is reasonably current. Inadequate capitalisation is likely to be regarded more seriously in a public company than in a private company,

---

[96] See, *e.g. Re Majestic Recording Studios Ltd* [1989] B.C.L.C. 1, (1988) 4 B.C.C. 519; *Re Melcast (Wolverhampton) Ltd* [1991] B.C.L.C. 288; *Re Brooks Transport (Purfleet) Ltd* [1993] B.C.C. 766; *Re Admiral Energy Group Ltd, Official Receiver v. Jones*, August 19, 1996, Ch.D., unreported. A defendant who has persisted in the same pattern of misconduct across several companies will commonly be disqualified for five years or more see paras 5.67 *et seq*.
[97] (1988) 4 B.C.C. 446, 447.
[98] Parliamentary Debates, H.C. Standing Committee E, Session 1984–85, Vol. IV, in particular cols 100–101.
[99] See paras 2.05–2.10.
[1] See, *e.g. Re D.J. Matthews (Joinery Design) Ltd* (1988) 4 B.C.C. 513; *Re Ipcon Fashions Ltd* (1989) 5 B.C.C. 773; *Re Peppermint Park Ltd* [1998] B.C.C. 23. However, it is dangerous to assume that a so-called "aggravating factor" could never of itself lead to a finding of unfitness. Whether or not the defendant's conduct makes him unfit depends on all the facts of the case.

especially in circumstances where there has been a deliberate failure to comply with the minimum capital requirement.[2]

Failure in the preparation and filing of accounts/returns

5.35   Failure to prepare accounts is a matter specifically mentioned in Schedule 1 of the CDDA. The courts generally treat it as being less serious than a failure to maintain accounting records in breach of section 221 of the Companies Act. However, where the evidence shows that the company was in a poor state of financial health for an extended period of time, the failure to prepare full accounts may be indicative of a more general failure to monitor the company's financial position.[3] Failure to file accounts and/or returns (especially annual returns) is frequently raised as a supplementary allegation. Filing obligations are important in terms of underlying policy. For instance, if the directors have not filed accounts it is likely that none have been prepared and may suggest a wider failure on their part to exercise financial responsibility. Equally, filing defaults deprive creditors of information that might influence them in deciding whether or not to deal with a particular company.[4] The attitude of the courts appears to depend on the frequency of default. It is most unlikely that a director would ever be disqualified on the basis of a single default or a couple of isolated lapses.[5] This is particularly true if the company had already ceased trading at the time when the filing obligation arose as, in that case, the default could not possibly prejudice creditors.[6] However, where the evidence shows that the company was in a weak financial position throughout its trading history, the court may treat the matter more seriously.[7] Moreover, a director with professional expertise in the fields of accounting and finance stands a greater chance of being disqualified for defaults in the preparation and filing of accounts than a director who has no such expertise.[8] In a case where there is persistent default across several companies it is conceivable that the director responsible could be disqualified solely on the ground of failure to comply with statutory obligations. The case of *Re Swift 736 Ltd, Secretary of State for Trade and Industry v. Ettinger* provides a vivid illustration. This was an appeal in which the Secretary of State contended that the three year disqualification imposed by the judge was too short. The Secretary of State argued that the judge had not attached sufficient weight to the defendant's repeated failure as a director of some 11 companies to prepare and file accounts and

---

[2] See *Re Kaytech International plc, Secretary of State for Trade and Industry v. Potier* [1999] B.C.C. 390 where one defendant, a *de facto* director, was disqualified for the maximum period of fifteen years primarily on the basis of his false claim that the company had a paid up capital of £2.5 million.

[3] See, *e.g. Re Park House Properties Ltd* [1997] 2 B.C.L.C. 530, [1998] B.C.C. 847. In this sort of case, it is no defence for the defendant to rely on a dispute with the company's accountants or auditors as an explanation for the failure: see *Re Ward Sherrard Ltd* [1996] B.C.C. 418.

[4] Though by the same token, the failure to keep filed information up to date in accordance with Companies Act requirements may raise doubts about the company's management and creditworthiness. In this respect, it is interesting to note that the obligation to file annual returns is referred to in Schedule 1 but not the obligation to file annual accounts. Even so, Peter Gibson J. stated in *Re Bath Glass Ltd* [1988] B.C.L.C. 329 at 332, (1988) 4 B.C.C. 130 at 133 that failure to file accounts is "plainly a matter which can and should be taken into account".

[5] See, *e.g. Re Lo-Line Electric Motors Ltd* [1988] Ch. 477, [1988] 3 W.L.R. 26, [1988] 2 All E.R. 692, [1988] B.C.L.C. 698, (1988) 4 B.C.C. 415; *Re GSAR Realisations Ltd* [1993] B.C.L.C. 409; *Re Hitco 2000 Ltd* [1995] 2 B.C.L.C. 63; [1995] B.C.C. 161; *Re City Pram & Toy Co. Ltd* [1998] B.C.C. 537. Although not required to consider the terms of CDDA, s. 3 it is most unlikely in practice that the court would make a finding of unfitness based on conduct falling short of "persistent default" as therein defined: see *Re ECM (Europe) Electronics Ltd* [1992] B.C.L.C. 814 at 818. On section 3 generally see Chap. 9.

[6] See, *e.g. Re Bath Glass Ltd* [1988] B.C.L.C. 329, (1988) 4 B.C.C. 130; *Re Cargo Agency Ltd* [1992] B.C.L.C. 686, [1992] B.C.C. 388.

[7] See, *e.g. Re Burnham Marketing Services Ltd, Secretary of State for Trade and Industry v. Harper* [1993] B.C.C. 518 at 524; *Re Pamstock Ltd* [1994] 1 B.C.L.C. 716, [1994] B.C.C. 264.

[8] See, in particular, *Re Cladrose Ltd* [1990] B.C.L.C. 204; [1990] B.C.C. 11 (discussed further in para. 5.58 below).

annual returns. The Court of Appeal agreed and increased the period of disqualification to five years. This result and the tenor of the leading judgment leave little doubt that in an appropriate case the court will treat the failure to prepare and file accounts as unfit conduct. Nicholls V.-C. made the following robust assessment:

> "Limited liability is a valuable tool in the promotion of trade and business, but it must not be misused. Those who make use of limited liability must do so with a proper sense of responsibility. The ... disqualification procedure is an important sanction introduced by Parliament to raise standards in this regard. Those who take advantage of limited liability ... must ... be punctilious in observing the safeguards laid down by Parliament for the benefit of others who have dealings with their companies. They must maintain proper books of account and prepare annual accounts; they must file their accounts and returns promptly... Isolated lapses in filing documents are one thing and may be excusable. Not so persistent lapses which show overall a blatant disregard for this important aspect of accountability. Such lapses are serious and cannot be condoned even though ... they need not involve any dishonest intent... Those who persistently fail to discharge their statutory obligations ... can expect to be disqualified ... from using limited liability as one of the tools of their trade. The business community should be left in no doubt on this score. It may be that, despite the disqualification provisions having been in operation for some years, there is still a lingering feeling in some quarters that a failure to file annual accounts and so forth is a venial sin. If this is still so, the sooner the attitude is corrected the better it will be."[9]

5.36   It is clear from this that in cases of persistent default the courts will use disqualification in an attempt to deter others and so promote compliance with core statutory obligations. A further justification for this approach is that repeated failure to prepare and file accounts will often be symptomatic of a wider failure on the part of directors to keep a real grip on the financial position of their companies.[10] In the majority of cases, failure to prepare and file accounts etc. will not justify disqualification on its own. However, it may form part of a pattern of conduct or a combination of factors that lead to an overall finding of unfitness.

Acceptance of customer pre-payments

5.37   Disqualification was clearly intended to operate in some sense as a measure for consumer protection. In the case of a company which has become insolvent, the court is directed by CDDA, Sched. 1, Pt II to pay particular regard to the extent of the director's responsibility for any failure by the company to supply goods or services which have been paid for in advance. If a director allows the company to trade while insolvent and in so doing accepts customer deposits for goods or services that the company may not be in a position to deliver and dissipates those sums, the risk of disqualification is undoubtedly increased. Use of customer monies to prop up an ailing company will thus be treated as a significant aggravating factor in a case of insolvent trading.[11]

---

[9] [1993] B.C.L.C. 896 at 899–900; [1993] B.C.C. 312 at 315.
[10] See paras 5.13–5.19.
[11] See, e.g. Re Western Welsh International System Buildings Ltd (1988) 4 B.C.C. 449; Re Austinsuite Furniture Ltd [1992] B.C.L.C. 1047; Re City Pram & Toy Co. Ltd [1998] B.C.C. 537 (discussed fully in paras 5.06–5.12) and the Northern Ireland case of Re Omaglass Ltd, April 6, 1995, unreported (discussed in A. Hoey, "Disqualifying Delinquent Directors" (1997) 18 The Company Lawyer 130). In Re Land Travel Ltd, Secretary of State for Trade and Industry v. Tjolle [1998] 1 B.C.L.C. 333, [1998] B.C.C. 282 the principal defendant was convicted of fraudulent trading after customers of his travel company lost deposits worth £6.6 million on its collapse. He subsequently consented to a maximum 15 year disqualification under section 6 following the summary Carecraft procedure (on which see further Chap. 8).

This reflects the perception that the consumer is in a weaker bargaining position than the trade creditor and therefore in greater need of protection. Disqualification orders have been made against directors of financial services companies on related grounds. In *Re City Investment Centres Ltd*[12] three directors were disqualified for periods ranging from six to 10 years where the company had used client monies, which should have been used to execute dealings on behalf of clients, to make speculative loans and as working capital. Similarly, in *Re CSTC Ltd, Secretary of State for Trade and Industry v. Van Hengel*[13] the principal defendant was disqualified for six years, for failing among other things, to maintain separate client accounts and for using interest accrued on client monies as working capital.

Breach of transaction avoidance provisions

5.38   In contrast to wrongful trading which is not specifically referred to in the Schedule,[14] the court is directed by CDDA, Sched. 1, Pt II to pay particular regard to the extent of the director's responsibility for entering into transactions liable to be set aside under section 127 or sections 238 to 240 of the Insolvency Act 1986. These provisions confer various rights of action on a liquidator and also, in the case of sections 238–240, an administrator. Their overall purpose is to reverse transactions entered into by insolvent companies which benefit certain creditors at the expense of other creditors or which have the effect of unfairly reducing the assets available to meet creditors' claims. There is no doubt that misconduct capable of amounting to a breach of these provisions is relevant to the question of unfitness. Moreover, the fact that the liquidator has pursued the director in parallel civil proceedings for a remedy under these provisions does not mean that less weight should be attached to the same misconduct in any subsequent disqualification proceedings. In *Re Grayan Building Services Ltd* the judge found that conduct amounting to a preference did not make the defendants unfit because of the salutary effect on them of parallel proceedings under section 239. This finding was criticised by the Court of Appeal as depriving the reference to section 239 in Schedule 1 of any effect in the worst of cases.[15] Conversely, the pursuit of parallel civil proceedings is not a pre-condition for a finding of unfitness. If the liquidator (or, where relevant, the administrator) takes no action (because, for example, he lacks funds to cover the cost of litigation), it is still open to the court to disqualify a director for misconduct falling within the ambit of the provisions.[16]

5.39   It was seen above that in the case of an allegation of insolvent trading, the court can find unfitness without the claimant having to establish all the elements of wrongful trading under section 214 of the Insolvency Act.[17] At first sight, it is arguable that the position may differ with the provisions being considered here. By Schedule 1, Part II the court is expressly required to take into account a director's responsibility for the company entering into transactions "liable to be set aside" under section 127 or sections 238 to 240. This suggests that the claimant may need to adduce evidence showing that the transaction is one that satisfies all the elements of the relevant provision and could have been successfully challenged in parallel civil proceedings. The

---

[12] [1992] B.C.L.C. 956.
[13] [1995] 1 B.C.L.C. 545, [1995] B.C.C. 173.
[14] See paras 5.03 to 5.12.
[15] [1995] Ch. 241 at 256, [1995] 3 W.L.R. 1 at 14, [1995] 1 B.C.L.C. 276 at 287, [1995] B.C.C. 554 at 576. This formed part of the Court of Appeal's attack on the notion that the claimant must show that the defendant is *presently* unfit: see paras 4.21–4.25. For a case where conduct the subject of parallel civil proceedings under sections 238–239 was taken fully into account in subsequent disqualification proceedings see *Re T & D Services (Timber Preservation & Damp Proofing Contractors) Ltd* [1990] B.C.C. 592.
[16] Though note the cautious approach in *Re ECM (Europe) Electronics Ltd* [1992] B.C.L.C. 814.
[17] See paras 5.03 to 5.12.

case of *Re Living Images Ltd*[18] seems to reflect this view. One allegation in this case concerned the repayment of a loan made to the company by B, a close friend of the first defendant. The Official Receiver alleged that the repayment, which was made three months before the company went into liquidation, constituted an unlawful preference. To succeed under section 239, it must be shown that the company giving the preference was influenced by a desire to put a creditor or guarantor in a better position, in the event of the company's insolvency, than would otherwise have been the case. Laddie J. stuck closely to this requirement and held that a director must at least know of the desire to prefer and the fact that it has influenced the company to act for the benefit of a particular creditor before he can be disqualified on this ground. Following the guidance given by Millett J. in *Re M C Bacon Ltd*,[19] the leading case on section 239, the judge concluded that the company, through the defendants, had been influenced in repaying B by a desire to improve his position in the event of an insolvent liquidation. In disqualifying the first defendant for six years (on the basis of this and other proven allegations), Laddie J. noted that his willingness to prefer a friend at a time when the company was unable to pay its debts illustrated his indifference to the plight of the company's creditors as a whole. On this approach, a director who causes his company, in anticipation of its insolvent liquidation, to repay sums outstanding on his own loan account, could well be disqualified for preferring himself. Here it is much easier to satisfy the requirements of section 239 as, in the case of a preference given by a company to a connected person such as a director, there is a presumption that the company was influenced by the requisite desire to prefer.[20]

5.40   The approach in *Living Images* has not been adopted in every case. In *Re Sykes (Butchers) Ltd, Secretary of State for Trade and Industry v. Richardson*[21] the registrar disqualified the defendant for seven years having found him to be unfit on a number of grounds. One allegation found to be proved was that he caused the company to extinguish its bank overdraft to the detriment of other creditors and to his own benefit as guarantor of the company's indebtedness to the bank. The registrar found as a fact that the defendant was influenced at least in part by the desire to eliminate the exposure under his guarantee but rejected the Secretary of State's submission that repayment of the overdraft amounted to a statutory preference liable to be set aside under section 239. Nevertheless, the registrar allowed the Secretary to State to reformulate the case on the footing that the defendant had demonstrated a lack of probity in paying off the bank rather than trade creditors. On appeal, it was argued for the defendant that the registrar had been wrong to entertain a case based on this more general formulation especially as the Secretary of State had originally alleged that the conduct amounted to a statutory preference and nothing less. Ferris J. held that the Secretary of State had not put his case so narrowly:

"It would ... be surprising if the Secretary of State had been prepared to limit his case in the way suggested ... because it is apparent from the terms of section 6 ... that the court is to be concerned with conduct generally and not merely with contravention of specific provisions of the Companies Act ... or the Insolvency Act ...

---

[18] [1996] 1 B.C.L.C. 348, [1996] B.C.C. 112.
[19] [1990] B.C.L.C. 324, [1990] B.C.C. 78.
[20] See *Re Exchange Travel (Holdings) Ltd (No. 3)* [1996] 2 B.C.L.C. 524, [1996] B.C.C. 933; *Wills v. Corfe Joinery Ltd* [1998] 2 B.C.L.C. 75, [1997] B.C.C. 511. Even so, in disqualification proceedings the court will still need to consider the specific circumstances giving rise to the repayment of directors' loans: see *Re Keypack Homecare Ltd* [1990] B.C.L.C. 440 at 444–445, [1990] B.C.C. 117 at 120–121. For a similar approach to that in *Living Images* applying the statutory predecessor of section 239 (*i.e.* the old fraudulent preference provision) in unfitness proceedings see *Re Time Utilising Business Systems Ltd* [1990] B.C.L.C. 568, (1989) 5 B.C.C. 851.
[21] [1998] 1 B.C.L.C. 110, [1998] B.C.C. 484.

Moreover, although responsibility for a statutory preference liable to be set aside under ... the Insolvency Act ... is one of the matters to which the court, in determining unfitness, is to have particular regard ... it is clear that these matters are not the only ones to which the court may have regard. On examination I find that the Secretary of State has not in fact limited his case in this way. The reference to 'preference' has always been made in general terms, not in terms specific to any of the statutory provisions concerning preference which I have referred to."[22]

The implication is that the claimant can plead in the alternative that the alleged misconduct amounts either to a breach of the statutory provisions or conduct which falls short of a specific breach but is nevertheless indicative of unfitness. In a case like *Sykes (Butchers)* this means that if the claimant cannot establish a statutory preference, the court may still be persuaded to find unfitness on the alternative ground of unfair discrimination.[23] This was much the conclusion reached on similar facts in the *Verby Print* case discussed above in the context of Crown debts.

5.41 The wider approach to preference allegations taken in *Sykes (Butchers)* is problematic for directors. If a decision is made to continue trading despite insolvency on the basis that there is some prospect that the company may recover, it is inevitable in the interim that some creditors will not be paid. The directors may be forced to reduce the overdraft because of bank pressure and this will almost certainly have a discriminatory impact. In these kind of circumstances it is arguable, in the interests of fairness, that an allegation of unfair discrimination should be linked explicitly to a wider charge of insolvent trading or, failing that, treated more strictly as an allegation of statutory preference. The danger otherwise is that directors may find themselves disqualified on the ground of unfair discrimination without there being any enquiry as to whether the company, through them, was influenced by a desire to prefer the bank. For these reasons, a judge who tends to see disqualification as a quasi-penal measure would be likely to follow the stricter analysis adopted in *Living Images* than the approach in *Sykes (Butchers)* and *Verby Print* which appears to make the claimant's task of establishing unfitness somewhat easier.[24] Equally, it must be remembered that the focus of disqualification proceedings is on the director's conduct rather than on the cause of action under the Insolvency Act. It is therefore understandable that the courts do not regard it as essential to establishing unfitness, that the transaction under scrutiny should necessarily satisfy the statutory criteria (especially the prescribed periods).

Non-co-operation with insolvency practitioner

5.42 The combined effect of section 6(2) and Schedule 1, Part II of the CDDA is that the court must have particular regard to any failure by a director to co-operate with the relevant office holder. Non-co-operation covers a multitude of sins including failure to provide a statement of affairs, failure to deliver up company records or assets and, in the case of a compulsory liquidation, failure to attend appointments with an official receiver. The importance of full co-operation from the directors of a company that has entered a formal insolvency regime cannot be underestimated. Without

---

[22] [1998] 1 B.C.L.C. 110 at 125, [1998] B.C.C. 484 at 496.
[23] Similarly, in *Re New Generation Engineers Ltd* [1993] B.C.L.C. 435, Warner J. appears to have treated an allegation of preference as part of a wider complaint concerning the policy adopted for payment of creditors.
[24] These criticisms do not apply so readily to transactions at an undervalue. In that case, if the conduct complained of does not amount to a breach of section 238, the alienation of the company's property could arguably be treated as a general breach of fiduciary duty affecting *all* creditors. In other words, the difficulties raised by the concept of unfair discrimination would not usually be present. It is often argued that section 239 would serve creditors better if the mental "desire" element was to be removed. If so, it would be sufficient to show that the transaction has a preferential effect. Such a reform would probably have little impact in the disqualification context as scope would remain for competing approaches to develop along current lines.

co-operation, the office holder's attempts to identify the company's assets and quantify its liabilities may be hampered. Failure to co-operate may therefore result in further harm to creditors. In *Re Copecrest Ltd, Secretary of State for Trade and Industry v. McTighe (No. 2)*[25] the first defendant refused to explain the background to certain items in the statement of affairs of one company, a stance he maintained throughout the liquidation. In respect of two other companies, he failed to attend appointments with the Official Receiver. The Court of Appeal took the robust view that his persistent failure to co-operate was itself indicative of unfitness. In the majority of cases, non-co-operation is a supplementary allegation and is often an aggravating factor rather than a matter which, on the facts, leads automatically to a finding of unfitness.[26] Nevertheless, *McTighe* suggests that, in an appropriate case, persistent non-co-operation may of itself amount to unfit conduct.

Breach of fiduciary duty

5.43   Several of the areas already discussed such as insolvent trading and excessive remuneration could equally be characterised as breaches of fiduciary or statutory duty. It might be said, for instance, that a director who decides to continue trading in circumstances where the company has no recovery prospects is in breach of his fiduciary duty to act in the company's best interests. This is because the common law recognises that creditors' interests should be taken into account in ascertaining whether a director acted in the best interests of an insolvent company.[27] However, the point is rarely made explicit in disqualification jurisprudence. Where breach of fiduciary duty is specifically raised in unfitness proceedings, the allegation will usually centre on conflict of interest or misappropriation of company property.

In *Re Godwin Warren Control Systems plc*[28] the relevant company, Systems, acquired the business and assets of a company called Data Solutions Ltd. The first defendant, "O", failed to disclose to the board of Systems that he had a controlling interest in Data Solutions. Moreover, he took steps to reduce his registered shareholding in Data Solutions in order to circumvent the obligation to seek shareholder approval for the transaction under section 320 of the Companies Act.[29] Chadwick J. held that O's deliberate attempt to conceal his interest from both the board and shareholders of Systems made him unfit and disqualified him for six years. The case was seen as being particularly serious because O was a chartered accountant and Systems was a public company. It is interesting to note that O's disqualification was based on a rationale of investor rather than creditor protection. *Godwin Warren* once again illustrates the use of disqualification to reinforce basic rules concerning directors' self-dealing.

---

[25] [1996] 2 B.C.L.C. 477, [1997] B.C.C. 224.
[26] See *Re T & D Services (Timber Preservation & Damp Proofing Contractors) Ltd* [1990] B.C.C. 592; *Re Tansoft Ltd* [1991] B.C.L.C. 339; *Re Brooks Transport (Purfleet) Ltd* [1993] B.C.C. 766; *Re GSAR Realisations* [1993] B.C.L.C. 409; *Re City Investment Centres Ltd* [1992] B.C.L.C. 956; *Re Living Images Ltd* [1996] 1 B.C.L.C. 348, [1996] B.C.C. 112; *Re Thorncliffe Finance Ltd, Secretary of State for Trade and Industry v. Arif* [1997] 1 B.C.L.C. 34, [1996] B.C.C. 586; *Re Defence & Microwave Devices Ltd*, October 7, 1992, Ch.D., unreported; *Re L M Fabrications Ltd*, April 27, 1995, unreported (Northern Ireland). See also *Re Agushi and Australian Securities Commission* (1996) 19 A.C.S.R. 322 in which the defendant's failure to deliver up the company's books and records to the liquidator was regarded as being indicative of unfitness for the purposes of section 600 of the Australian Corporations Law.
[27] *West Mercia Safetywear Ltd v. Dodd* [1988] B.C.L.C. 250, (1988) 4 B.C.C. 30, CA; *Facia Footwear Ltd v. Hinchcliffe* [1998] 1 B.C.L.C. 218 and see J.H. Farrar & B.M. Hannigan, *Farrar's Company Law* (4th ed., 1998), pp. 382–385. It is arguable that this overriding fiduciary duty and the duty of care and skill are conflated in a situation of insolvency or near-insolvency, a point taken up below in para. 5.50.
[28] [1993] B.C.L.C. 80, [1992] B.C.C. 557.
[29] The transaction between Solutions and Systems would only have been caught by section 320 if O had retained either a controlling interest in Solutions or an interest in at least one-fifth of its share capital: Companies Act 1985, s. 346(4), (5).

5.44   There are several other cases in which the courts have had no trouble reaching a finding of unfitness based on serious breaches of fiduciary duty. The following have all been regarded in themselves as indicative of unfitness: diversion of assets or business away from the company whether the director benefited directly or not;[30] the siphoning off of company monies for personal use by directors[31] and illegal loans to directors.[32] A case where directors engage in misconduct of this nature at a time when the company's solvency is in doubt will undoubtedly be regarded as a serious one. On the other hand, it is important to recognise that a mere technical breach of duty is of itself unlikely to lead, in isolation, to a finding of unfitness.

Fraud

5.45   Many of the activities discussed in the previous paragraph might equally be categorised as fraud. This is especially true where the defendant has deliberately misappropriated assets belonging to the company. It is open to the court to disqualify a director on the basis of fraudulent conduct in respect of which he has already been convicted in a criminal court.[33] Equally, the court can take into account fraudulent conduct which has not previously been the subject of criminal proceedings. For instance, in *Re T & D Services (Timber Preservation & Damp Proofing Contractors) Ltd*[34] there was evidence that the defendant had obtained grants from a local authority by deception. Relying on this and other proven allegations, the judge disqualified him for ten years. Similarly, in *Re Defence & Microwave Devices Ltd*[35] allegations that the defendants defrauded the Inland Revenue and appended false audit certificates to annual accounts were found proven and take into account. In the context of a public company, a defendant who falsely claims that the company has an adequate paid up share capital when, in fact, it does not meet the minimum share capital requirements imposed on public companies by the Companies Act, is very likely to be found unfit.[36] Proven allegations of deception and/or dishonesty usually result in a lengthy period of disqualification.[37]

---

[30] *Re Living Images Ltd* [1996] 1 B.C.L.C. 348, [1996] B.C.C. 112 (diversion of contract); *Re Wedgecraft Ltd*, March 7, 1986, Ch.D., unreported (diversion of cashflow from one company to another controlled by the defendant, in the form of rent payments).
[31] *Re Tansoft Ltd* [1991] B.C.L.C. 339; *Re Continental Assurance Co. of London plc* [1997] 1 B.C.L.C. 48, [1996] B.C.C. 888; *Re Copecrest Ltd, Secretary of State for Trade and Industry v. McTighe (No. 2)* [1996] 2 B.C.L.C. 477, [1997] B.C.C. 224; *Re Park House Properties Ltd* [1997] 2 B.C.L.C. 530; *Re Cloghmor Ltd*, November 17, 1994, unreported (Northern Ireland).
[32] *Re Tansoft Ltd* [1991] B.C.L.C. 339; *Re Moorgate Metals Ltd, Official Receiver v. Huhtala* [1995] 1 B.C.L.C. 503, [1995] B.C.C. 143; *Re Copecrest Ltd, Secretary of State for Trade and Industry v. McTighe (No. 2)* [1996] 2 B.C.L.C. 477, [1997] B.C.C. 224. See also *Re Agushi and Australian Securities Commission* (1996) 19 A.C.S.R. 322, a case decided under section 600 of the Australian Corporations Law.
[33] Note that in *Re Land Travel Ltd, Secretary of State for Trade and Industry v. Tjolle* [1998] 1 B.C.L.C. 333, [1998] B.C.C. 282 the principal defendant had previously been convicted of fraudulent trading and disqualified for ten years under CDDA, s. 2. Nevertheless, the Secretary of State was able to bring proceedings seeking a longer period of disqualification under section 6. It appears also that the court can take into account conduct the subject of a previous conviction even if that conviction has become spent because of the operation of the Rehabilitation of Offenders Act 1974: *Secretary of State for Trade and Industry v. Queen* [1998] B.C.C. 678. However, this is subject to arguments of double jeopardy and abuse of process discussed further in Chaps 6 and 9.
[34] [1990] B.C.C. 592.
[35] October 7, 1992, Ch.D., unreported.
[36] *Re Kaytech International plc, Secretary of State for Trade and Industry v. Potier* [1999] B.C.C. 390.
[37] For a further example bearing this out see the case of the second defendant in *Re Moorgate Metals Ltd, Official Receiver v. Huhtala* [1995] 1 B.C.L.C. 503, [1995] B.C.C. 143. For an example from Australia see *Dwyer v. National Companies and Securities Commission* (1989) 15 A.C.L.R. 386; (1989) 7 A.C.L.C. 571 in which a person who allowed himself to be used as a nominee director in connection with a criminal conspiracy was disqualified under the Companies (New South Wales) Code.

Breach of miscellaneous statutory obligations

5.46   In *Re Continental Assurance Co. of London plc*[38] the first defendant allowed the funds of a subsidiary to be used in repaying sums borrowed by its parent company to finance the acquisition of the subsidiary. This amounted to financial assistance in breach of section 151 of the Companies Act. Chadwick J. took the breach of section 151 into account in finding the first defendant and a non-executive director of the company to be unfit. There is every reason to suppose that conduct in breach of analogous statutory provisions such as the rules prohibiting payment of dividends out of capital could also be taken into account.

On a different note, the courts of Northern Ireland have treated breaches of the directors' statutory obligation to have regard to the interests of employees[39] as a matter indicative of unfitness. In *Re L M Fabrications Ltd*[40] some importance was attached to the defendant's failure to maintain compulsory employers' liability insurance. In *Re Omaglass Ltd*[41] the company was under an obligation to maintain a bonus fund for its salesmen to meet commission payments. The defendant's failure to ensure that monies were transferred into the fund was taken into account as a failure to pay due regard to employees' interests. These cases suggest (in line with the present authors' suggestion in Chapter 2) that weight may be given to the interests of employees in disqualification proceedings.

Specific instances of unfitness in section 8 cases

5.47   At first glance the cases decided under section 8 tend to be concerned more with issues of investor protection than of creditor protection. This reflects the rationale of the various investigatory powers, the exercise of which is a precursor to section 8 proceedings. In *Re Samuel Sherman plc*,[42] the relevant company ceased trading and at the defendant's direction its assets were sold generating a surplus of some £300,000. Without consulting the company's shareholders, the defendant used the surplus to make speculative overseas investments in the oil and gas industries. These investments were *ultra vires* the company's memorandum of association. The company lost money on the investments and was eventually wound up with a surplus of only £26,000. The main criticism of the defendant (who was disqualified for five years) was not the speculative nature of the investments but the fact that he had caused the company to change its business without recourse to shareholders. In *Re Looe Fish Ltd*,[43] a set of disqualification proceedings which followed an investigation of the relevant company's affairs under section 447 of the Companies Act 1985, the defendants manipulated voting control of the company with a view to blocking a takeover bid from a rival faction. They hatched an elaborate scheme whereby the company issued sufficient extra shares to enable them to block action supported by the "true" majority. They then arranged for the company to repurchase these shares. Both defendants were disqualified for breach of duty despite their belief that they were acting in the company's best interests and not for financial gain or improper personal benefit.[44] Leaving preliminary matters aside, it is clear that the misconduct in both these cases could equally have led to a

---

[38] [1997] 1 B.C.L.C. 48, [1996] B.C.C. 888.
[39] The equivalent provision in England, Wales and Scotland is Companies Act 1985, s. 309.
[40] April 27, 1995, unreported.
[41] April 6, 1995, unreported. Both cases are discussed in A. Hoey, "Disqualifying Delinquent Directors" (1997) 18 *The Company Lawyer* 130.
[42] [1991] 1 W.L.R. 1070, [1991] B.C.C. 699.
[43] [1993] B.C.L.C. 1160, [1993] B.C.C. 348.
[44] There is an obvious analogy with common law authorities on improper share allotments such as *Piercy v. S. Mills & Co. Ltd* [1920] 1 Ch. 77 and *Howard Smith Ltd v. Ampol Petroleum Ltd* [1974] A.C. 821, [1974] 2 W.L.R. 689, [1974] 1 All E.R. 1126, P.C.

finding of unfitness under section 6. Moreover, in *Sherman* the defendant's persistent failure to comply with statutory obligations was taken into account much as it would have been under section 6.[45]

5.48 Investor protection was also the principal theme in the more recent case of *Re Atlantic Computers plc, Secretary of State for Trade and Industry v. Ashman*.[46] The case arose following a Companies Act investigation into the well-publicised collapse of Atlantic, a computer leasing company and its parent company, British & Commonwealth Holdings plc ("B&C"). Atlantic was successfully floated on the London Stock Exchange and later acquired by B&C. The collapse was linked to the mechanics of Atlantic's principal product, the "flexlease". Under the flexlease, Atlantic sold computer equipment to a financier at an initial profit which was then leased to the customer for a fixed term. Atlantic also entered into an agreement enabling the customer either to upgrade the equipment or to walk away from the lease before the term expired. In the event that the customer exercised the so-called "walk option", Atlantic was left with a liability to pay the outstanding rental for the unexpired term to the financier. The theory was that customers would favour an upgrade and therefore take fresh equipment under a new lease. Unfortunately, in practice, the "walk" liabilities were so large as to precipitate the collapse of the B&C group. Several former group executives (though not all) were found to be unfit. This finding was based principally on the failure of Atlantic to disclose the true extent of its contingent liabilities in its accounts both before the acquisition by B&C and later after the potential magnitude of the problem became apparent. A number of other substantive points emerge from Lloyd J.'s judgment:

(1) The court can take breaches of accepted standards of financial reporting into account in addition to breaches of statutory accounting obligations. The fact that Atlantic's accounting policies did not conform to fundamental accounting principles and to certain of the Statements of Standard Accounting Practice was taken into consideration as well as failure to comply in a number of respects with Part VII of the Companies Act 1985 (especially the requirement to maintain adequate and reasonably accurate accounting records).

(2) Where a director's conduct is honest and not lacking in commercial integrity, it does not necessarily follow that, if the conduct falls short of the standards of competence which might be expected by the City or others (whether or not by the law of directors' duties), of a director of a listed company, that director is thereby shown to be unfit to be concerned in the management of a company, however small, private and simple its affairs may be. Nevertheless, where obligations of disclosure and public announcement are concerned, in the case of a listed company, issues of commercial probity do arise, even in the absence of any issue of dishonesty or personal gain.

(3) Misleading statements attributable to a director in a prospectus or listing particulars can be taken into account. Here a statement in Atlantic's prospectus issued in the course of the company's flotation to the effect that only a small percentage of flexleases contained walk options was found to be misleading.

(4) The pursuit of a line of business (here the flexlease) which is inherently unviable does not necessarily make a director unfit. However, if a director allows the company to continue pursuing that line of business once he has

---

[45] His defaults included the failure to lay annual accounts before general meeting. The court regarded this failure to provide basic information to shareholders as particularly serious given their lack of any obvious practical remedy: see [1991] 1 W.L.R. 1070 at 1085–1086, [1991] B.C.C. 699 at 711–712.
[46] June 15, 1998, Ch.D., unreported.

been given cause to question its viability (as here once the size of the "walk" liabilities finally became apparent), this may be indicative of unfitness.

(5) The court must consider the extent of each defendant's personal responsibility for the relevant misconduct. However, as with section 6, a director cannot escape disqualification by taking no responsibility at all nor can he delegate the performance of his legal obligations entirely to someone else. In other words, the approach discussed below in paras 5.54 to 5.57 is equally applicable in section 8 proceedings.

(6) The court's approach to the standard of proof in section 8 cases is similar to that under section 6 (see para. 5.66 below).

(7) Once a finding of unfitness has been made, the court must then decide whether or not to disqualify. It appears that the matters regarded by the Court of Appeal in *Westmid Packing* as relevant to determining the period of disqualification in section 6 cases (discussed below in the section on period of disqualification) may be taken into account in determining whether or not to make a disqualification order under section 8 at all.[47]

UNFITNESS AND THE GENERAL LAW

5.49   As has been seen, unfitness is a broad concept and its categories are not closed. It is clear from cases like *Re Godwin Warren Control Systems plc* and *Re Omaglass Ltd* discussed above that disqualification orders under section 6 are used to protect the interests of shareholders and employees. This is true also of disqualification orders under section 8. Many of the reported cases involve directors of owner-managed private companies and so it is clear that one of the main (albeit not exclusive) objects of section 6 is the protection of creditors.[48] One difficulty that has already been encountered is the vexed question of how the courts draw the line between fitness and unfitness. Ultimately, this is a problem that cannot be resolved in terms of principles and legal tests alone. As has been seen above, the court reaches a finding of unfitness with reference to a specific factor or the cumulative effect of a combination of factors. The purpose of this section is to consider various other problems and concepts which arise in the substantive law of unfitness, especially those which raise issues relevant to the development of company law generally.

Some problems of underlying rationale

5.50   Implicit in the development of factors such as insolvent trading, excessive remuneration and financial responsibility is the recognition that directors have a duty to act in the interests of creditors as a whole where the company's solvency is in doubt. The precise implications of this central underlying principle in the law of unfitness have yet to be worked out fully either in disqualification cases or at common law. In particular, it is not clear how the general duty to act in creditors' interests differs in analytical terms from the duty of care and skill. For instance, trading while insolvent might be analysed as either a failure by the directors to consider the interests of creditors when taking the decision to continue trading or a failure to exercise reasonable care and skill in the light of the company's prospects. There is thus a tendency for the general duty and the duty of care and skill to become conflated. In the case of insolvent

---

[47] For instance, in *Atlantic* the judge considered and rejected a submission by two of the defendants that the court should refrain from disqualifying because of the length of time for which they had been in jeopardy: see paras 5.82–5.84. This factor and the earlier treatment of some of their co-directors were nevertheless taken into account in relation to the period of disqualification.
[48] See discussion in Chap. 7

trading, this may not matter. The precise relationship between the objective "unwarranted risks" test and the standard of diligence and skill in section 214(4) of the Insolvency Act may not be entirely clear. However, the underlying nature of the obligation is similar and there is equal scope for the court to defer to the directors by taking account of hindsight whether insolvent trading is treated as a breach of general duty or a breach of the duty of care and skill. Greater difficulty may be encountered where the relevant factor has no obvious foundation within the general law of directors' obligations outside the CDDA. The concept of unfair discrimination discussed above provides a good illustration of this problem. It is not clear whether its basis lies in a duty to act in the interests of all as opposed to some creditors or in the duty of care and skill or in the concept of preference or, indeed, in the obligation to account for certain monies to the Crown. What is clear is that unfair discrimination is now a common basis for disqualification even though there has been no real analysis of its rationale. While theoretical, the point is not without importance. Disqualification as a form of proceeding is ancillary to the general law of directors' obligations. Its purpose was probably not to create new obligations, although as has been seen with the concept of financial responsibility, it can be used to reinforce and develop the scope of existing obligations.[49] Given the recognition that disqualification does have some impact on individual freedom, it is arguable that the rationale underlying each specific instance of unfitness should be absolutely clear.

What level of incompetence will justify an order under section 6?

5.51   *Dicta* discussed in Chapter 4 from cases like *Lo-Line*, *Bath Glass* and *Sevenoaks* suggest that a director's incompetence may be sufficient to make him unfit although it is not clear what degree of incompetence is required. According to the judge in *Lo-Line* the incompetence would need to be "total" whereas in *Sevenoaks*, the Court of Appeal suggested that incompetence "in a very marked degree" would suffice. In the course of the disqualification proceedings brought against 10 former senior executives following the collapse of Barings Bank, the court has confirmed that "incompetence" is a basis for disqualification.[50] However, incompetence is not an easy thing to define and, as is suggested further below, it should not be regarded as having a broad meaning in the disqualification context. On the one hand, incompetence denotes a failure or inability to comply with basic obligations. On the other hand, it is often used, at least by the layman, as shorthand for bad commercial decision-making or risk-taking which causes the company loss, such as an unwise investment or a flawed decision to expand into an unfamiliar market. The courts are traditionally reluctant to intervene in cases involving commercial misjudgment or lack of business acumen. There are several reasons for this reluctance. First, the courts are not naturally equipped for dealing with questions of business judgment, especially when asked to substitute their own judgment after the event. Secondly, the whole purpose of limited liability is to encourage commercial risk-taking. This is because it protects the entrepreneur from the consequences of business failure. Creditors and shareholders inevitably suffer in the collapse of any company. However, the exposure of directors to liability and disqualification on the basis of commercial misjudgment would discourage legitimate risk-taking. Investors and creditors must therefore shoulder some of the

---

[49] Furthermore, the concept of insolvent trading (falling short of wrongful trading in section 214 of the Insolvency Act) and developments (in relation to the duty of care and skill) shown by cases like *Re Barings plc (No. 5)*, *Secretary of State for Trade and Industry v. Baker* [1999] 1 B.C.L.C. 433 suggest that the courts do rely on the width of the term "unfit" to make law because directors are now being disqualified for conduct which, in the past, might not have founded a cause of action in civil law.

[50] See, *e.g. Re Barings plc*, *Secretary of State for Trade and Industry v. Baker* [1998] B.C.C. 583 and the later decision of Jonathan Parker J. in *Re Barings plc (No. 5)* [1999] 1 B.C.L.C. 433.

risk of business failure if the rationale of limited liability is to be preserved and it is left to them to assess the management's capabilities before investing or extending credit. Thirdly, as Hicks has pointed out, it may be difficult to see any justification for disqualifying directors in these circumstances given that creditors are equally exposed to the consequences of commercial misjudgments in unincorporated businesses.[51] For these reasons, a director will not be found unfit solely on the basis of commercial misjudgment.[52]

5.52 It follows that when the courts equate "incompetence" with unfitness they are not referring primarily to matters of business judgment or commercial ability. At first sight, it is not immediately obvious where commercial misjudgment ends and incompetence justifying disqualification begins. For instance, in some early insolvent trading cases, directors escaped disqualification because the decision to allow their company to continue trading was treated as a commercial misjudgment or as mere mismanagement.[53] Nevertheless, on further analysis, it is apparent that the notion of incompetence is quite closely associated with the duty to exercise financial responsibility discussed earlier and also with the general concept of diligence. The impression from the cases is that incompetence may justify disqualification if it is more than mere misjudgment and amounts to culpable negligence. It is suggested that some or all of the following elements are common badges of such incompetence:

(1) failure to maintain proper accounting records and/or prepare accounts;

(2) lack of knowledge and/or appreciation of directors' obligations especially statutory accounting obligations;

(3) abdication of the responsibility to monitor the company's financial position and/or failure to maintain proper financial controls;

(4) failure to exercise diligent supervision over the company's activities.

For instance, in *Re Rolus Properties Ltd* the defendant's failure to maintain accounting records, prepare accounts and comply with filing obligations made him unfit "not because he is fraudulent but because he is incompetent and unable to comply with statutory obligations".[54] Similarly, in *Re Cladrose Ltd* the judge equated "total incompetence" with a "failure to understand the duty of directors, or to produce any sort of proper trading record",[55] in other words a combination of elements (1) and (2). The case against the second defendant in *Re Richborough Furniture Ltd, Secretary of State for Trade and Industry v. Stokes*[56] was also made up of elements (1) and (2). The principal allegations were that the directors allowed the company to take unwarranted risks

---

[51] A. Hicks, *Disqualification of Directors: No Hiding Place for the Unfit?* (A.C.C.A Research Report No. 59, 1998), p. 43. The argument is that questions of competence (meaning sound commercial judgment) and creditworthiness should therefore be regulated by the market.

[52] See, *e.g. Re Cladrose Ltd* [1990] B.C.L.C. 204; [1990] B.C.C. 11 in which the court did not question the decision of the defendants to acquire a motor dealership on the basis of an agency agreement terminable on one month's notice which provided no protection for the company against termination. See also *Re Moorgate Metals Ltd, Official Receiver v. Huhtala* [1995] 1 B.C.L.C. 503, [1995] B.C.C. 143 (directors' reliance on a single customer and a single supplier not regarded as unfit *per se*) and *Re McNulty's Interchange Ltd* [1989] B.C.L.C. 709, (1988) 4 B.C.C. 533 (attempt to acquire assets and business of company in receivership not evidence of unfitness). In contrast, a decision to acquire an insolvent subsidiary without carrying out any proper due diligence or valuation exercise is less likely to be treated as a mere misjudgment: see *Re Austinsuite Furniture Ltd* [1992] B.C.L.C. 1047; *Re City Investment Centres Ltd* [1992] B.C.L.C. 956.

[53] See, *e.g. Re Douglas Construction Services Ltd* [1988] B.C.L.C. 397, (1988) 4 B.C.C. 553; *Re C.U. Fittings Ltd* [1989] B.C.L.C. 556, (1989) 5 B.C.C. 210; *Re McNulty's Interchange Ltd* [1989] B.C.L.C. 709, (1988) 4 B.C.C. 533.

[54] (1988) 4 B.C.C. 446, 447.

[55] [1990] B.C.L.C. 204 at 213; [1990] B.C.C. 11 at 18.

[56] [1996] 1 B.C.L.C. 507, [1996] B.C.C. 155.

with creditors' monies and failed to maintain adequate accounting records. The second defendant had no previous experience in the management of companies and admitted in evidence to having no financial expertise. Nevertheless, she was found to be unfit, "largely through lack of experience and knowledge", and disqualified for three years. A third example is *Re Melcast (Wolverhampton) Ltd* in which a director who seems to have regarded himself as a mere employee and had, to paraphrase the judge, no concept of what being a director involved was disqualified for four years. These cases provide further support for the view pressed above that the courts are fashioning a minimum standard of financial competence and stewardship based on the statutory accounting obligations. Every director is expected to exercise financial responsibility. If the company has no accounting records or up to date financial information, the court is likely to conclude that the directors were not in a position to make sensible commercial judgments.[57] Lack of financial expertise or lack of awareness and understanding of basic obligations are no defence.[58]

5.53   A case involving element (3) in which the court made a finding of unfitness on the basis of incompetence is *Re Continental Assurance Co. of London plc*.[59] The company, "CAL", made various loans and cash transfers to its parent company, Yorkdale Holdings plc. Yorkdale used the monies to repay sums that it had borrowed from Scanbank to fund its original acquisition of CAL. The effect was that CAL had given financial assistance for the purchase of its shares in breach of section 151 of the Companies Act 1985. The third defendant, "B", was head of U.K. banking and, subsequently, head of U.K. corporate finance at Scanbank. He had responsibility for the bank's lending relationship with Yorkdale. In that capacity he was appointed as a non-executive director of Yorkdale and CAL. B's evidence was that he did not know about the inter-company transfers and he claimed that if he had known that CAL was lending money to Yorkdale to enable it to service the Scanbank loan, he would have recognised the implications and intervened. The conclusion of the court was that as a director of CAL, B should have made it his business to know about the inter-company loans and the reason behind them. CAL was Yorkdale's only source of income. It was clear from Yorkdale's accounts seen and approved by B that its income was insufficient to service the annual interest charges on the Scanbank loan. It was also clear that there was a rising trend of inter-company indebtedness. B's failure to appreciate what was going on amounted to an abdication of a director's basic responsibility to appraise himself of the company's financial position, a failure described by the judge as "serious incompetence or neglect". B was disqualified for three years.

A further example of disqualification based on a combination of elements (3) and (4) is provided by the various proceedings in *Re Barings plc* brought against senior executives following the collapse of Barings Bank.[60] The immediate cause of the bank's crash was the unauthorised trading activities of a group subsidiary, Baring Futures (Singapore) Pte Limited ("BFS") on the Singapore International Monetary Exchange. These activities were attributable to Nick Leeson, the senior floor trader and general man-

---

[57] See, *e.g. Re Firedart Ltd, Official Receiver v. Fairhall* [1994] 2 B.C.L.C. 340; *Re Grayan Building Services Ltd* [1995] Ch. 241, [1995] 3 W.L.R. 1, [1995] 1 B.C.L.C. 276, [1995] B.C.C. 554 and discussion in paras 5.13–5.19.
[58] *Re New Generation Engineers Ltd* [1993] B.C.L.C. 435; *Re Linvale Ltd* [1993] B.C.L.C. 654; *Re Hitco 2000 Ltd, Official Receiver v. Cowan* [1995] 2 B.C.L.C. 63, [1995] B.C.C. 161; *Re CSTC Ltd* [1995] 1 B.C.L.C. 545, [1995] B.C.C. 173 (in relation to the second defendant). These cases together with *Richborough Furniture* suggest *contra* V. Finch, "Disqualification of Directors: A Plea for Competence" (1990) 53 M.L.R. 385 that the courts will act in what Finch describes as "a purely protective manner" and disqualify as unfit, incompetent directors who fail to grasp the nature of their office and responsibilities.
[59] [1997] 1 B.C.L.C. 48, [1996] B.C.C. 888.
[60] [1998] B.C.C. 583 (Scott V.-C.) and [1999] 1 B.C.L.C. 433 (Jonathan Parker J.). For a full account of the collapse and analysis of its regulatory implications see the First Report of the Treasury Committee, *Barings Bank and International Regulation*, (1996 H.C. 65).

ager of BFS. The unauthorised trading produced losses amounting to some £827 million which were concealed by Leeson in an unnamed client account. One part of the proceedings concerned "M", the chairman of the bank's asset and liability committee. The case against M was that he had failed, despite his senior position, to monitor or control the trading activities of BFS. Over the final year of the bank's life, the level of funds transferred to BFS increased from £39 million to a high of £742 million on the eve of the crash. This huge outflow of funds which ultimately precipitated the collapse was allowed to go unquestioned. The judge found that M had failed to ensure that the funding to BFS was properly understood and controlled. His conduct was said to amount to incompetence and a failure to exercise diligent supervision. Applying the *dictum* in *Sevenoaks*, the judge held that M was incompetent in a sufficiently marked degree to make him unfit and disqualified him for four years. Subsequently, three other former executives, "B", "T" and "G" were disqualified by Jonathan Parker J. on the basis that each was guilty of serious failures of management in relation to Leeson's activities which demonstrated incompetence of such a degree as to justify a disqualification order. Again, the principal findings in the case of these executives were that they had failed to inform themselves properly as to the nature of BFS's business and to exercise anything approaching effective control over Leeson.

Individual responsibility and collective failure

5.54   In company law theory the board of directors is the primary agent or organ of the company. As such, the board acts collectively. However, in the realm of directors' obligations there is no settled or rigid concept of *collective responsibility*. Under section 6, the court is required to consider whether each individual director is unfit, and with regard to several of the matters listed in Schedule 1, to evaluate the extent of each director's personal responsibility. As Morritt J. put it in *Re City Investment Centres Ltd*, "the court is required to consider the extent of the responsibility of a particular director where the failure in question is of the directors as a whole".[61] Thus, it is acknowledged that the responsibilities of each director may differ in degree from those of his co-directors. A further implication is that the court does not take a blanket approach where disqualification proceedings are brought against more than one director of the same company. So, for instance, if proceedings are commenced against three directors of a company, the court will not necessarily say that all of them are unfit or that they should all be disqualified for an equal period simply because they are all on the board. The purpose in this section is to examine how the courts tackle a number of pressing questions which arise in the assessment of a director's individual responsibility especially (though not exclusively) in cases where there is more than one defendant.

Is every director on the board required to participate in management up to a basic minimum level?

5.55   In keeping with the spirit of the Cork Committee's recommendations, the courts have used section 6 to fashion a minimum standard of financial responsibility and competence. It has been seen that a director who fails to appraise himself of his company's financial position runs the risk of disqualification under section 6 if the company becomes insolvent. This is particularly so where accounting records have not been maintained. It follows that directors are expected to participate in the company's

---

61 [1992] B.C.L.C. 956, 960. See also *Secretary of State for Trade and Industry v. Taylor* [1997] 1 W.L.R. 407 *sub nom. Secretary of State for Trade and Industry v. Gash* [1997] 1 B.C.L.C. 341, *sub nom. Re CS Holidays Ltd* [1997] B.C.C. 172.

management to the minimum degree necessary for the exercise of proper financial responsibility. It is no longer safe for directors to assume that the court will adopt the more relaxed approach to participation evident at common law especially in the context of an insolvent or near-insolvent company.[62] The common law's "hands off" approach pays deference to the company's shareholders. It is left to the general meeting which, in theory, retains ultimate control over the selection and removal of board appointees, to remove incompetent directors and regulate the degree of participation required. This approach also reflects an outmoded view both of the way in which companies operate and of the law of negligence.[63] The stiffer approach under section 6 not only reflects the intrusion of creditors' interests once the company's solvency is in doubt, but also a modern view of the proper scope of directors' obligations.

5.56   Similarly, it would be unwise for a non-executive director who takes no part in the day to day management of the company to assume that his office is merely honorific. Indeed, as a consequence of developments such as the Combined Code on Corporate Governance, non-executive directors of public companies are expected to play a positive role in corporate governance and the courts are now unlikely to treat them merely as "gentleman amateurs" with few specific obligations as might have been the case in the past.[64] Moreover, the idea that a director can disassociate himself completely from the company's affairs has been challenged in several disqualification cases. In *Re Park House Properties Ltd* the principal defendant, "C", was disqualified for four years for a combination of insolvent trading, failure to exercise financial responsibility and breach of fiduciary duty. C had taken sole responsibility for the management of the company although his wife, son and daughter were also unpaid directors. Each of the three other directors were found to be unfit by virtue of sheer inactivity. In the words of the judge:

"... the best way in which the case against the three [defendants] can be summarised is by saying that they were three of the four directors of a company, they permitted the other director to run the company in a way which was inappropriate, they did nothing whatever to inform themselves of how the company was being managed, to what extent that management might be inappropriate, and therefore they did nothing to discourage or dissuade that director from running the company in this inappropriate way... Directors have duties, and if, having knowingly been appointed a director, a person does nothing, he is likely to be in breach of his duties, and if the company is involved in inappropriate activity, he

---

[62] The position at common law rests on the decision of Romer J. in *Re City Equitable Fire Insurance Co. Ltd* [1925] Ch. 407 which suggests that a director is not bound to give continuous attention to the affairs of his company. The case of *Re Cardiff Savings Bank* [1892] 2 Ch. 100 in which a director who attended only one board meeting during his whole life escaped liability is perhaps the most graphic illustration of the common law's latitude. Hoffmann L.J. has suggested more recently that the existence of a positive obligation to participate depends on the particular context, *i.e.* on factors such as how the particular company is organised and the part which the director could reasonably have been expected to play: see *Bishopgate Investment Management Ltd v. Maxwell (No. 2)* [1994] 1 All E.R. 261 at 264, [1993] B.C.L.C. 1282 at 1285. Even so, the thrust of the approach under the CDDA is that all directors are expected to exercise financial responsibility as a bare minimum. This is also now the position under the wrongful trading provision: see *Re Brian D Pierson (Contractors) Ltd* [1999] B.C.C. 26.

[63] The "traditional" view rests on cases like *City Equitable* which were decided before *Donoghue v. Stevenson* [1932] A.C. 562.

[64] For the "gentleman amateur" approach see, *e.g. Re Brazilian Rubber Plantations and Estates Ltd* [1911] 1 Ch. 425. For a case in which a non-executive director of a plc was disqualified on the ground that his failure to read and appreciate the company's statutory accounts fell short of the standards of competence that can reasonably be expected of external directors, see *Re Continental Assurance Co. of London plc* [1997] 1 B.C.L.C. 48, [1996] B.C.C. 888. It is suggested at para. 1.39 of the Law Commission Paper No. 153, *Company Directors: Regulating Conflicts of Interests and Formulating a Statement of Duties* (1998) that non-compliance with self-regulatory rules such as the Combined Code may come to be treated as evidence of unfitness.

risks associating himself with, and taking some responsibility for, that inappropriate activity... As a matter of principle, it appears to me that it cannot be right that a director ... can escape liability simply by saying that he knew nothing about what was going on."[65]

5.57 The upshot is that all directors, whatever their status, have a duty to make enquiries concerning the running of the company and must arrive at some appreciation of the results of those enquiries. A further implication is that it is not possible for a director, while he remains in office, to delegate away all of his functions and responsibilities. In *Re A & C Group Services Ltd*, "O" was a director and controlling shareholder of the company. For most of his period of office (some 10 years) the company made modest profits. O became ill and the company's profitability suffered as a result. O invited T to join the board and in the contemplation that T would eventually acquire the company, allowed him to take over responsibility for its management. Under T's management, the company engaged in a disastrous expansion resulting in trading losses of nearly £500,000. T was disqualified for six years on various grounds. Despite the fact that O's belief that T was about to buy him out was found to be genuine, he and his wife were each disqualified for two years. Citing the words of Byrne J. in *Drincqbier v. Wood*, the judge stated that a director who consents to be a director, has assumed a position involving duties which cannot be shirked by leaving everything to others.[66] The position taken in *Park House Properties* and *A & C Group Services* is reflected in a number of other cases.[67] The current state of the law in this area is perhaps best summarised with reference to the three propositions put forward by Jonathan Parker J. in *Re Barings plc (No. 5), Secretary of State for Trade and Industry v. Baker*[68]:

(1) Directors have, both collectively and individually, a continuing duty to acquire and maintain a sufficient knowledge and understanding of the company's business to enable them properly to discharge their duties as directors.

(2) While directors are entitled (subject to the company's articles of association) to delegate particular functions to those below them in the management chain and to trust their competence and integrity to a reasonable extent, the exercise of a power of delegation does not absolve a director from the duty to supervise the discharge of the delegated functions.

(3) No rule of universal application can be formulated as to the residual duty of monitoring and supervision referred to in (2) above. The extent of the duty,

---

[65] [1997] 2 B.C.L.C. 530 at 554, [1998] B.C.C. 847 at 866–867. The effect is that "nominee" directors who take no part at all in the affairs of the company are at grave risk: see further *Re Kaytech International plc, Secretary of State for Trade and Industry v. Potier* [1999] B.C.C. 390; *Re Oldham Vehicle Contracts Ltd, Official Receiver v. Vass* [1999] B.C.C. 516 and, in the wrongful trading context, *Re Brian D Pierson (Contractors) Ltd* [1999] B.C.C. 26.

[66] [1899] 1 Ch. 393, 406. If a "sleeping" director is in receipt of remuneration this may further enhance his minimum obligations. A further point which seems to be reflected in *A & C Group Services* is that an owner-manager like O may, in effect, be disqualified for failing to monitor his own investment. In other words, owner-managers may be expected to behave as responsible *owners* as well as responsible directors and should therefore be particularly careful when delegating management responsibility: see also *Re Burnham Marketing Services Ltd, Secretary of State for Trade and Industry v. Harper* [1993] B.C.C. 518 at 526–528.

[67] *Re Majestic Recording Studios Ltd* [1989] B.C.L.C. 1, (1988) 4 B.C.C. 519; *Re Melcast (Wolverhampton) Ltd* [1991] B.C.L.C. 288; *Re City Investment Centres Ltd* [1992] B.C.L.C. 956; *Re Peppermint Park Ltd* [1998] B.C.C. 23; *Re Westmid Packing Services Ltd, Secretary of State for Trade and Industry v. Griffiths* [1998] 2 All E.R. 124, [1998] 2 B.C.L.C. 646, [1998] B.C.C. 836, CA; *Re Barings plc (No. 5), Secretary of State for Trade and Industry v. Baker* [1999] 1 B.C.L.C. 433; *Re Landhurst Leasing plc, Secretary of State for Trade and Industry v. Ball* [1999] 1 B.C.L.C. 286. See also the Northern Ireland cases of *Re S & R Seafoods Ltd*, November 23, 1995, unreported and *Re Craig Meats Ltd*, April 25, 1996, unreported discussed in Hoey, *op. cit.*

[68] [1999] 1 B.C.L.C. 433 at 489.

and the question whether it has been discharged, must depend on the facts of each particular case, including the director's role in the management of the company.

Are higher standards of conduct expected from experienced directors and directors with special expertise?

5.58   It has been seen that directors cannot escape disqualification by reason of inexperience or lack of expertise where there has been a failure to exercise proper financial responsibility. This is because the courts treat the duty to monitor the company's financial position and associated obligations as a basic minimum standard applicable to all directors. At the same time, it appears that the courts do expect directors who possess particular expertise to achieve higher standards of conduct in relation to matters falling within the scope of that expertise. In *Re Cladrose Ltd*[69] the application concerned three insolvent companies of which the two defendants, "JP" and "DP" were owner-managers. There was a total failure in all three companies to produce audited accounts and file annual returns. However, this was not a case in which the directors failed to maintain accounting records. Indeed, the evidence was that all three companies had good core accounting records and that internal management accounts were regularly produced. JP claimed that he relied on DP, a qualified chartered accountant, to take responsibility for the production of full accounts and the filing of annual returns. It was accepted in evidence by DP that the default was largely his responsibility and that it was reasonable for JP to rely on him. The judge held that there was a collective failure but that the extent of JP's responsibility was insufficient to make him unfit. DP, however, was disqualified for two years for failing to perform duties falling squarely within the scope of his professional expertise. As a chartered accountant DP could "properly be expected, both by his fellow directors and by the court, to have a better knowledge and understanding of company law and of the formal duties to make returns ... than persons who do not hold that distinguished qualification."[70]

5.59   Similarly, in the case of *Continental Assurance* referred to above in para. 5.53, the court appeared to demand a higher standard of conduct from the defendant based on his experience as a banker and corporate financier. His failure as a non-executive director to appreciate that the subsidiary, CAL was giving unlawful financial assistance was described by Chadwick J. in these terms:

"Those in the position of [B], being senior employees of major banks, who accept appointment as directors of client companies of those banks, are lending their name and the status associated with their employer to the board of directors of that client company. Those dealing with the client company are entitled to expect that external directors appointed on the basis of their apparent expertise will exercise the competence required by the Companies Act 1985 in relation to the

---

[69] [1990] B.C.L.C. 204, [1990] B.C.C. 11.
[70] [1990] B.C.L.C. 204 at 208, [1990] B.C.C. 11 at 14. One distinguished commentator has argued that the decision was based more on punitive considerations than on a principle of public protection: see V. Finch, "Disqualification of Directors: A Plea for Competence" (1990) 53 M.L.R. 385. Finch contends that both directors would have been disqualified had a protective principle been in play as both were responsible by statute for preparing and filing accounts. For similar criticisms of the Court of Appeal decision in *Re Sevenoaks Stationers (Retail) Ltd* see S. Wheeler, "*Re Sevenoaks*—Continuing the Search for Principle" (1990) 6 *Insolvency Law & Practice* 174. Note however, that the CDDA's concern with individual responsibility is always likely to produce this kind of result and that the approach in *Cladrose* is consistent with recent developments at common law: see, *e.g. Dorchester Finance Co. Ltd v. Stebbing* [1989] B.C.L.C. 498; *Re D'Jan of London Ltd* [1994] 1 B.C.L.C. 561, [1993] B.C.C. 646. One doubts whether JP would have escaped disqualification in the event of a collective failure to maintain core accounting records.

affairs of the company of which they have accepted office as directors. The competence required by the 1985 Act extends, at the least, to a requirement that a director who is a corporate financier should be prepared to read and understand ... statutory accounts ... and satisfy himself that transactions between holding company and subsidiary are properly reflected in the statutory accounts of the subsidiary."[71]

This suggests that a non-executive appointed to represent the interests of a bank or venture capital financier is expected to bring at least some basic knowledge of accounts and financial reporting to the task. In relation to executive directors, the case of *Re Barings plc* suggests that the standard of conduct demanded may be greater for senior executives. The defendant's high status and the remuneration which accompanied it were said to carry with them, or at least to reflect, a high degree of responsibility including an obligation of diligent supervision. It was accepted that in a large organisation the senior management need to delegate functions to others. However, the judge stated that the responsibilities of high office require the incumbent to question from time to time whether the persons to whom duties have been delegated are discharging those duties efficiently.[72]

Is a director less exposed to disqualification if he relied on professional advice?

5.60   It has been seen in the case of *Re Cladrose Ltd* that a director may escape disqualification if it is reasonable for him to rely on the professional expertise of his co-director in relation to certain functions. Similarly, in the earlier case of *Re Douglas Construction Ltd* the court declined to disqualify the defendant who, in trying to refinance a struggling company, relied on professional advice.[73] In marginal cases such as these, a director's reliance on a professionally qualified co-director or on independent professional advice may tip the balance in his favour. However, it is not necessarily safe for a director to rely on a decision by the company's bank to extend its overdraft facility as a justification for continuing to trade.[74]

Should a director who proves unable to exert any influence over board policy despite best efforts consider resigning?

5.61   A difficult issue that is not easy to resolve concerns the position of a director who is incapable of excercising any influence over board decisions because he is in a minority or who is unwilling to exercise any technical influence he may have because of the presence in the company of a dominant personality. If, for instance, the company continues to trade while insolvent and the board makes no attempt to review its trading prospects, each individual director is at risk of disqualification even though for practical purposes he may have no real control over board decisions. We saw earlier that every director must make at least some attempt to acquaint himself with the com-

---

[71] [1997] 1 B.C.L.C. 48 at 57–58, [1996] B.C.C. 888 at 896.
[72] Note also *Re CSTC Ltd, Secretary of State for Trade and Industry v. Van Hengel* [1995] 1 B.C.L.C. 545, [1995] B.C.C. 173 which suggests that a finance director may have a particular responsibility to ensure that the company's financial controls are adequate and that levels of executive remuneration are reviewed regularly in the light of the overall financial position.
[73] [1988] B.C.L.C. 397, (1988) 4 B.C.C. 553. Even if the advice proves incorrect the director may still be exonerated provided that it is reasonable for the defendant to rely on the professional adviser: *Re McNulty's Interchange Ltd* [1989] B.C.L.C. 709, (1988) 4 B.C.C. 533. For a further case of successful reliance see *Re Moonlight Foods (U.K.) Ltd, Secretary of State for Trade and Industry v. Hickling* [1996] B.C.C. 678.
[74] See *Re GSAR Realisations Ltd* [1993] B.C.L.C. 409. The reason for this is that the bank is acting in its own interests as a lender rather than giving advice to the company or its directors. In any event, any claim to have relied on advice will be judged against the full background of the advice, *i.e.* what advice was sought and what information was provided to the adviser.

pany's affairs and, in particular, its financial position. Furthermore, the case of *Re Park House Properties Ltd* discussed above suggests that there is an obligation on every director to see that the board as a whole is acting responsibly.[75] For a director who for whatever reason has limited influence, this is a difficult proposition. What should a director do if he is unable to persuade his co-directors to act responsibly? Is resignation the best course? This question has received differing treatments.

In *Re Thorncliffe Finance Ltd, Secretary of State for Trade and Industry v. Arif*, a case discussed above in para. 5.15, it was suggested by Chadwick J. that a director should resign his office if he is unable to compel the board to act responsibly. Here, "D", the company's managing director, continued in office despite having identified the irregularity (namely the lack of security for inter-company indebtedness within a series of affiliated companies) which ultimately precipitated its downfall. He wrote expressing his concerns to the company's controller and made proposals for regularising the problem which were never implemented. He did resign later but the fact that he remained in office despite lacking the influence to address the problem was said to make him unfit and he was disqualified for three years. The judge's message was unequivocal:

> "In my view it should be made clear that those who assume the obligations of directors, which they know they cannot fulfil, are persons whose conduct makes them unfit to be concerned in the management of a company. It is no answer to that charge to say, 'I did what I could'. If a director finds that he is unable to do what he knows ought to be done then the only proper course is for him to resign."[76]

5.62   In the subsequent case of *Re CS Holidays Ltd, Secretary of State for Trade and Industry v. Taylor*, the same judge sought to confine the scope of this apparent obligation on a director to resign to circumstances where the defendant is unable to compel the board as a whole to comply with the statutory duty to maintain proper accounting records. The relevant defendant was one of the company's three directors. He also had a minor shareholding and was employed by the company on a small salary as a book-keeper. The company's bankers expressed concern that the company was trading while insolvent. The defendant reacted to this by producing a written report to the board recommending specific cost cutting measures. He discussed these recommendations with the company's auditor who said at trial that the company would have had a reasonable chance of trading out of its difficulties if they had been implemented. The company continued trading without following the recommendations. Later the auditor wrote to the company at the defendant's instigation making further recommendations that were again not acted on. The allegation against all three directors was that they allowed the company to continue trading while insolvent to the detriment of creditors. In relation to the defendant, it was argued that he ought to have resigned having failed to persuade the board to adopt his recommendations and that, by continuing in office, he benefited at the expense of the company's creditors because he continued to draw a salary. Significantly, the Secretary of State made no criticism of the way in which the defendant maintained the company's financial records and statutory books. The district judge's decision to dismiss the case against the defendant was upheld by Chadwick J. on appeal. The judge distinguished his previous decision in *Arif*

---

[75] See also *Re Westmid Packing Services Ltd, Secretary of State for Trade and Industry v. Griffiths* [1998] 2 All E.R. 124, [1998] 2 B.C.L.C. 646, [1998] B.C.C. 836 in which it was suggested that a board of directors should not allow one person to dominate them as to do so might amount to an abrogation of proper financial responsibility.

[76] [1997] 1 B.C.L.C. 34 at 46, [1996] B.C.C. 586 at 596.

by saying that his remarks there were made in the context of a failure by the directors to fulfil their statutory obligations and, in particular, the obligation imposed by section 221 of the Companies Act 1985. Thus, a failure to resign should not necessarily lead to the conclusion that a director is unfit. Directors have no *statutory* obligation to ensure that their company avoids trading while insolvent or at a loss. Their obligation under the Insolvency Act is to ensure that they do not cause the company, knowing it to be insolvent, to continue trading in circumstances where there is *no reasonable prospect* of avoiding insolvent liquidation. A director who, like the defendant, fails to resign having used such influence as he possesses to persuade the board to review its policy of continued trading is therefore in a different category from a director who remains in office in circumstances where he knows that the company is in breach of a statutory provision such as section 221. There is therefore a clear link between the "duty" to resign and the wider duty to exercise financial responsibility. Nevertheless, Chadwick J. left open the possibility that a director might be disqualified in appropriate circumstances for failing to resign in a case not involving breach of statutory accounting obligations:

> "I am not to be taken as expressing the view that there may not be circumstances in which a director who has ceased to exercise any influence in the deliberations of the board will be at risk of being held unfit if he fails to resign. The duties of a director include ... the duty to inform himself as to the company's affairs and the duty to make his views known to the other directors. If there comes a point at which his attendance at board meetings is purposeless because he must recognise that his co-directors take no account of his views ... it may well be appropriate to ask why he continues to remain as a director. If he continues to remain as a director in those circumstances for no purpose other than to draw his ... fees or to preserve his status, a court might well come to the conclusion that he was so lacking in appreciation of a director's duties that he was unfit...".[77]

Thus a powerless director who carries on in office despite having no practical influence on managerial policy is exposed to disqualification if it can be established that in continuing to draw his remuneration he acted without regard for creditors' interests. On the facts of *Taylor* the defendant was only paid a salary equivalent to that of a junior employee and Chadwick J. refused to interfere with the district judge's finding that he sought to gain no advantage at the expense of creditors in his capacity as a director.[78]

5.63   *Arif* and *Taylor* can be contrasted with the earlier case of *Re Polly Peck International plc, Secretary of State for Trade and Industry v. Ellis (No. 2)*.[79] The four defendants were at all times in a minority on the board and at the date on which the company went into administration they represented less than one-third of the serving directors. One of the defendants was the company's finance director while the others served as non-executive directors. The company's prime mover and chairman, Asil Nadir was not among the defendants. The case against the four was based on their failure to exercise adequate control over Nadir who had been able to move large amounts of funds out of the company into a series of foreign subsidiaries without any check. The need of the foreign subsidiaries for such substantial funding was never seriously questioned. The Secretary of State developed the case by arguing that the four defendants ought to have threatened their resignation in the face of the board's continuing failure to exercise any sort of control over Nadir's activities and that by

---

[77] [1997] 1 W.L.R. 407 at 414–415, [1997] 1 B.C.L.C. 341 at 349, [1997] B.C.C. 172 at 178–179.
[78] For a case arguably falling within the scope of Chadwick J.'s *dictum* see *Re Peppermint Park Ltd* [1998] B.C.C. 23 especially in relation to the third defendant, Mr Love.
[79] [1994] 1 B.C.L.C. 574, [1993] B.C.C. 890.

remaining in office they shared responsibility for the overall failure to institute proper controls. The question arising was whether the case was sufficiently strong for the court to grant the Secretary of State permission under section 7(2) to commence proceedings outside the two year time limit.[80] Lindsay J. refused to grant permission and in so doing expressed grave reservations over whether the failure of this small minority of directors to resign could be regarded as sufficiently serious to justify a finding of unfitness. It is perhaps significant that there was no suggestion that the directors were in breach of basic statutory obligations such as section 221 of the Companies Act. In other words, *Polly Peck* can arguably be distinguished from *Arif* on the same basis as *Taylor*.[81]

Can a director rely on an agreed division of labour?

5.64   In a case where the directors have failed collectively to comply with the minimum obligation of proper financial responsibility it is unlikely that any one of them would escape disqualification by trying to shift all of the blame onto the others. Although it is open to the court to find that one director is less responsible (and deserving of a lesser period of disqualification) than another, a defendant will rarely be able to shift all the responsibility for non-compliance with basic statutory obligations such as section 221 of the Companies Act onto a co-defendant. Moreover, if a defence along these lines is unsuccessful, the defendant running it risks being penalised in costs.[82] However, there are cases which suggest that the court will take account of the manner in which the company was run and, in particular, the functions and responsibilities undertaken by each individual member of the board. Thus, in circumstances where a particular task is habitually discharged by one director, the others may be able to shift responsibility onto him in the event that failure to discharge that task becomes an issue in disqualification proceedings. This is consistent with the approach of Schedule 1 which in relation to the majority of the matters listed requires the court to consider the extent of each defendant's personal responsibility. In *Re Cladrose Ltd*, as we have already seen, one defendant escaped disqualification where it was accepted that his co-defendant, a qualified chartered accountant, had assumed particular responsibility for the preparation and filing of accounts and returns. The decision turned on the court's view that it was reasonable in the circumstances for him to expect an accountant to discharge the board's statutory obligations.[83] Thus, if there is a habitual division of labour and it is reasonable for one director to rely on the expertise of another to

---

[80] On permission to commence proceedings for an order under section 6 out of time see generally Chap. 7.
[81] Moreover there is arguably an analogy between *Polly Peck* and the common law position as advanced in *Dovey v. Corey* [1901] A.C. 477. In that case the court held that the director of a bank was not liable to make good the bank's losses in circumstances where it had paid dividends out of capital and made advances on improper security. It was accepted that it was reasonable for the director in relation to these matters to rely on the bank's chairman and general manager whose skill and competence he had no cause to doubt. The suggestion that he should have taken steps to monitor the activities of lesser bank officials or check the audit files was rejected. The case of *Re Barings plc* discussed in the main text above suggests that the allegations raised in *Polly Peck* would now be couched in terms of directorial incompetence. In this respect it is noticeable that Lindsay J.'s approach demands a much higher threshold of culpability for a finding of unfitness than the approach in *Barings*. Indeed, as a matter of law (as opposed to policy) some aspects of the decision look distinctly shaky in the light of subsequent authority. This is particularly true of Lindsay J.'s "director-friendly" approach to the issue of present unfitness, on which see now *Grayan* discussed above in paras 4.21–4.25.
[82] See *Re Sykes (Butchers) Ltd, Secretary of State for Trade and Industry v. Richardson* [1998] 1 B.C.L.C. 110, [1998] B.C.C. 484 (one defendant, R, ordered to pay 25% of his co-defendant O's costs in circumstances where proceedings against O were dismissed and the trial had been substantially lengthened by reason of R's unsuccessful attempt to shift responsibility on to O).
[83] While there are dangers for a defendant who defends himself by saying that a particular default was someone else's responsibility, it is clear that his perceptions concerning the reliability of his co-defendants can be adduced in evidence: see also *Re Dawes & Henderson (Agencies) Ltd, Secretary of State for Trade and Industry v. Dawes* [1997] 1 B.C.L.C. 329, [1997] B.C.C. 121.

discharge his assigned function, the court may decide that the former was not sufficiently responsible to justify a finding of unfitness. This is particularly so in the context of a large company where division of function and the delegation of specific tasks
to individual directors and senior managers is a practical necessity. However, it will be
rare for a reliance-based defence to succeed in a case of a small company where there
has been a collective failure to discharge basic minimum obligations such as the duty to
maintain proper accounting records.[84] Furthermore, the defendant will need to show
that he was justified in relying on his co-defendant to discharge the relevant task or
function and that he did exercise at least some degree of supervision or monitoring of
its performance.

Summary

5.65   From the foregoing it appears that the CDDA, like section 214 of the Insolvency Act, is being used by the courts to fashion a minimum standard of skill and
competence. Every director has a basic obligation to exercise financial responsibility
and see that the board is in a position to make well-informed decisions. This obligation
appears to be non-delegable and an individual director will not be able to use ignor-
ance of basic responsibilities or lack of relevant experience as an excuse. At the same
time, it appears that a director who has special expertise or experience will be expected
to achieve standards of conduct at a level above the basic minimum required of directors who are not so qualified. This shift towards an objective minimum standard capable of being adjusted upwards to take into account the skill, knowledge and experience
of each director echoes judicial attempts to modernise the common law duty of care
and skill.[85] The focus of the CDDA on personal responsibility means that the court can
take into account the particular function and responsibilities of each director and any
agreed division or delegation of functions within the company in making its
assessment.

Standard of proof in unfitness proceedings

5.66   The basic standard of proof in proceedings for an order under section 6 is the
civil standard, i.e. the claimant must establish the defendant's unfitness on the balance
of probabilities. It has been argued by those who emphasise the quasi-penal nature of
disqualification that the stricter criminal standard of proof should apply.[86] However,
the application of a criminal standard of proof has been rejected. The courts have
recognised that some adjustment to the basic civil standard may be required where
certain facts are alleged in disqualification proceedings. In practice, the more serious

---

[84] Though see the generous approach in Re Austinsuite Furniture Ltd [1992] B.C.L.C. 1047 (director
responsible for production not disqualified despite failing to monitor the company's financial position, the
judge noting that he was a member of a large executive board which included a finance director and a
manager both with accounting qualifications) and Re Moonlight Foods (U.K.) Ltd, Secretary of State for
Trade and Industry v. Hickling [1996] B.C.C. 678 (two directors exonerated where responsibility for maintenance of accounting records said to rest with a chartered accountant).

[85] Norman v. Theodore Goddard [1991] B.C.L.C. 1028, [1992] B.C.C. 14 and Re D'Jan of London Ltd
[1994] 1 B.C.L.C. 561, [1993] B.C.C. 646 noted by A. Hicks (1994) 110 L.Q.R. 390. See also Dorchester
Finance Co. Ltd v. Stebbings [1989] B.C.L.C. 498 and the illuminating discussion in K. Wardman, "Directors, Their Duty of Care and Skill: Do the Provisions of the Company Directors Disqualification Act 1986
Provide a Basis for the Establishment of a More Objective Standard?" Business Law Review for March 1994
at p. 71. See also Re Barings plc (No. 5) [1999] 1 B.C.L.C. 433 where the judge considered the position at
common law as well as under section 6.

[86] Dine, op. cit. and see also Re Polly Peck International plc, Secretary of State for Trade and Industry v. Ellis
(No. 2) [1994] 1 B.C.L.C. 574 at 581, [1993] B.C.C. 890 at 896 where Lindsay J. (albeit faced with a
preliminary issue under section 7(2)) said that a director should be given the benefit of any reasonable doubt
because disqualification has penal consequences for the individual.

the allegation, the more cogent the evidence required to establish it. In *Re Living Images Ltd*, Laddie J. summarised the position thus:

> "These are civil proceedings. The appropriate standard of proof is therefore a balance of probabilities. However disqualification does involve a substantial interference with the freedom of the individual... Furthermore, some of the allegations ... may involve serious charges of moral turpitude... In such cases the court must bear in mind the inherent unlikeliness of such serious allegations being true. The more serious the allegation, the more the court will need the assistance of cogent evidence... But in the end these are civil, not criminal, proceedings. [Counsel] argued that the director must be given the benefit of any reasonable doubt... If that is the correct approach, then the standard of proof in these applications would be the same as that used in criminal proceedings."[87]

This approach to standard of proof and evidential burden is now fairly settled.[88]

Period of Disqualification

Introduction

5.67   If a director is found to be unfit the effect of section 6(4) is that the court must disqualify him for the minimum period of two years. The maximum period of disqualification which the court can impose is 15 years. Otherwise, the period of disqualification is a matter within the court's discretion. While it is possible for the parties, using the summary *Carecraft* procedure, to agree a statement of facts which indicate the defendant's unfitness and suggest what they consider to be an appropriate period of disqualification based on those facts, the court has the final say and it is not bound by any purported agreement between the parties as to period.[89] The Court of Appeal has provided some guidance concerning the exercise of the court's discretion in two cases, *Re Sevenoaks Stationers (Retail) Ltd*[90] and *Re Westmid Packing Services Ltd, Secretary of State for Trade and Industry v. Griffiths*.[91] The second of these decisions explicitly acknowledges that in fixing an appropriate period of disqualification the court is engaged in something akin to a sentencing exercise.

In contrast to section 6 there is no minimum period of disqualification under section 8. The maximum period is 15 years. It was said in *Re Samuel Sherman plc* that the lack of a minimum period did not mean that the court should treat directors more leniently under section 8 than under section 6.[92] In these three section 8 cases the court referred to the *Sevenoaks* brackets (discussed below) when assessing the appropriate period of disqualification although it was accepted in *Re Atlantic Computers plc*[93] that for misconduct falling within the lowest bracket the court can make an order of one year or less reflecting the fact that there is no statutory minimum period.

---

[87] [1996] 1 B.C.L.C. 348 at 355, [1996] B.C.C. 112 at 116.
[88] See also *Re Verby Print for Advertising Ltd* [1998] 2 B.C.L.C. 23, [1998] B.C.C. 652. A similar approach is taken in Northern Ireland: see *Re Topglass Windows Ltd*, September 26, 1995, unreported; *Re Barrandra Promotions Ltd*, July 4, 1996, unreported, discussed in Hoey, *op. cit.* This approach is consistent with ordinary principles: see *Bater v. Bater* [1951] p. 35 at 36–37; *Hornal v. Neuberger Products Ltd* [1957] 1 Q.B. 247 at 26; and *Khawaja v. Home Secretary* [1984] A.C. 74 at 113–114.
[89] On *Carecraft* and other forms of disposal or compromise see generally Chap. 8.
[90] [1991] Ch. 164, [1991] 3 All E.R. 578, [1991] B.C.L.C. 325, [1990] B.C.C. 765.
[91] [1998] 2 All E.R. 124, [1998] 2 B.C.L.C. 646, [1998] B.C.C. 836.
[92] [1991] 1 W.L.R. 1070 at 1085, [1991] B.C.C. 699 at 711.
[93] June 15, 1998, Ch.D., unreported.

Court of Appeal "sentencing" guidelines

The Sevenoaks "brackets"

5.68   In *Sevenoaks* Dillon L.J. endorsed a division of the potential 15-year disqualification period into three brackets as follows:

(1) A top bracket of over 10 years to be reserved for "particularly serious cases". These may include cases where a director who has already had one period of disqualification imposed on him falls to be disqualified again.

(2) A middle bracket of between six and 10 years for serious cases not meriting the top bracket.

(3) A minimum bracket of between two and five years to be applied where, though disqualification under section 6 is mandatory, the case is not, relatively speaking, very serious.

This guidance is rather vague. It appears that the court is required to determine the appropriate period of disqualification in each case according to a sliding scale of culpability. Perhaps suprisingly, there is no specific suggestion in *Sevenoaks* that the court should have regard to the overall purposes of the CDDA in exercising the discretion although Dillon L.J. did make the general statement that the undisputed purpose of section 6 is to protect the public, and in particular potential creditors of companies, from unfit directors. This leaves the impression that the public's need for protection is to be measured wholly by reference to the degree of the defendant's culpability. Care should be taken not to treat the *Sevenoaks* brackets as if they had the force of a statute. Each bracket encompasses a broad spectrum. It is difficult to be precise about whether conduct falling, for example, in the minimum bracket merits a two-year order or a three-year order and so on. What is important is that the broad spectrum of conduct should not vary within each bracket. A further point to note is that, on a literal reading, Dillon L.J.'s judgment leaves open the question of whether a disqualification of between five and six years falls within the middle or minimum bracket. The courts tend to make orders in round years, although they can (and occasionally do) make orders which involve fractions of years (provided, in the case of section 6, that the order is for not less than two years). It is suggested that the qualitative comparative difference between conduct that will justify a six-year order rather than a five-year order is no different in degree than that between conduct justifying a four-year order rather than a three-year order. The 15-year span is itself a spectrum and the *Sevenoaks* brackets should be treated as guidance and not as rigid categories.

Westmid Packing

5.69   In this case the Secretary of State failed to persuade the Court of Appeal to increase the period of disqualification imposed on two defendants by the trial judge. Lord Woolf M.R. took the opportunity to lay down some general guidance from which the following points emerge:

(1) Although disqualification is not strictly a punishment, the court is, in effect, engaged in a sentencing exercise. As such, the period of disqualification must reflect the gravity of the misconduct and (in keeping with the approach in *Grayan* discussed above) it must contain deterrent elements. The Court of Appeal thus acknowledges that disqualification is concerned with public protection in three senses: (a) keeping unfit directors "off the road", (b) deterring the unfit director from repeating the misconduct (*i.e.* individual deterrence)

and (c) deterring other directors (*i.e.* general deterrence). It is implicit in this acknowledgment that the court should, in some sense, be seeking to advance the overall purposes of the CDDA when fixing the period of disqualification.

(2) The court should start by arriving at the appropriate period to fit the gravity of the conduct. Allowance should then be made for any mitigating factors and the period reduced accordingly. The court should not be influenced in determining the period of disqualification by the existence of its power to grant a disqualified director permission to act. The power to grant permission is a separate question and if (as will often be the case) the defendant has cross-applied for permission anticipating that a disqualification order will be made, that question should only be considered after the period of disqualification has been fixed.

(3) On the question of unfitness, the court is required to have "tunnel vision" and concentrate only on the instances of past misconduct alleged by the claimant.[94] While the director's past misconduct is obviously relevant in determining the period of disqualification, the court is less restricted in the factors which can be taken into account. A wide variety of factors may be relevant including the director's general reputation, his age and state of health, the length of time taken to bring the matter to trial, whether he admitted any of the allegations, his general conduct before and after the unfit conduct and any periods of disqualification ordered by other courts on his co-directors. Some of these factors are considered further below in the discussion of mitigating factors.

(4) The citation of authorities as to the period of disqualification will, in the majority of cases, be unnecessary and inappropriate as, in relation to the period of disqualification in particular, the court should adopt a broad brush approach and exercise the jurisdiction in a summary manner.

5.70 It is possible at a theoretical level to criticise the Court of Appeal's guidelines. The emphasis in both *Sevenoaks* and *Westmid Packing* on the need to tailor the period of disqualification to the gravity of the offence seems to reflect a policy of tariff-based "punishment" rather than public protection. The court is not required to evaluate the extent of the risk posed to the public by the defendant for the future. Also, the point in (4) is something of a pious hope. In practice, there is a natural tendency for lawyers advising the parties to disqualification proceedings to try to match the given case to the facts of previous cases in much the same way as personal injury lawyers resort to previous fact patterns in order to advise on the likely quantum of a claim. Despite these criticisms, it is hard to see how the courts could do much better. The current approach is pragmatic and holds out at least some hope that directors will receive fair and consistent treatment. In what follows there is an attempt to flesh out these Court of Appeal guidelines and offer some practical insights as to how they are applied.

The Sevenoaks "brackets" in practice

Minimum bracket cases

5.71 The majority of cases fall within the miminum bracket of two to five years.[95]

---

[94] See para. 4.21 above.
[95] Between December 1986 and June 1997 of 4,269 disqualification orders made under section 6, 3,241 (*i.e.* over 75%) were for between two and five years (DTI Press Release P/97/365, June 5, 1997). In the two years ending on June 30, 1998 of 2,307 orders made under section 6, 1590 (*i.e* over 70%) were for between two and five years (DTI Press Release P/98/578, July 23, 1998).

In practice, the courts tend to make an order for a period within this bracket in cases of unfit conduct where there is no evidence that the director acted dishonestly or sought deliberately to milk the company at the expense of creditors. A straightforward case of insolvent trading even coupled with other allegations such as failure to monitor the company's financial position, filing defaults and excessive remuneration rarely results in more than a minimum bracket period of disqualification.[96] If there is an established pattern of this sort of conduct across two or three companies or a particular aggravating factor the court may be persuaded to make an order towards the top of the minimum bracket or into the middle bracket.[97] Although far from an exact science, it seems that in cases where there is no proven dishonesty or serious lack of probity the court is likely to assess the period at between two and five years depending on the degree of misconduct (*e.g.* factors such as how long the defendant allowed the company to continue trading while insolvent) and then, in accordance with the approach in *Westmid Packing*, apply a discount if there are any admissible mitigating factors.

Middle bracket cases

5.72   As a rule of thumb, if there is at least some evidence of deliberate, dishonest or self-serving conduct this may either of itself fall within the middle bracket or take what is otherwise a minimum bracket case up into the middle bracket. Thus, in *Re Godwin Warren Control Systems plc* where it was found that the first defendant had deliberately failed to disclose his personal interest in a corporate transaction to the company's directors and shareholders, he was disqualified for six years.[98] Evidence of deliberate breach of fiduciary duty involving the misappropriation of corporate assets may well result in a period of disqualification lying towards the top of the middle bracket especially when combined with other more mundane matters.[99] A similar fate may befall a director who deliberately and persistently disregards his statutory obligations or indulges in "repeat" misconduct in a number of companies without showing any

---

[96] See, *e.g. Re Hitco 2000 Ltd* [1995] 2 B.C.L.C. 63; [1995] B.C.C. 161 (short period of insolvent trading coupled with abdication of financial control, misuse of bank account, filing defaults: two years); *Re Grayan Building Services Ltd* [1995] Ch. 241, [1995] 3 W.L.R. 1, [1995] 1 B.C.L.C. 276, [1995] B.C.C. 554 (preference, insolvent trading, failure to keep proper accounting records, minor filing default: two years); *Re Verby Print for Advertising Ltd* [1998] 2 B.C.L.C. 23, [1998] B.C.C. 652 (policy of discrimination against Crown creditors: two years); *Re GSAR Realisations* [1993] B.C.L.C. 409 (insolvent trading, failure to co-operate with insolvency practitioner, late preparation and filing of accounts: three years); *Re Ward Sherrard Ltd* [1996] B.C.C. 418 (insolvent trading, excessive remuneration, late preparation and filing of accounts: three years); *Re Ask International Transport Ltd, Secretary of State for Trade and Industry v. Keens*, May 5, 1992, Ch.D. unreported (insolvent trading in face of warning from auditor as to inadequacy of financial information, failure to exercise proper financial responsibility: four years).

[97] See, *e.g. Re Linvale Ltd* [1993] B.C.L.C. 654 (insolvent trading in three successive companies with phoenix aspect albeit no dishonesty: five years) and *Re Ipcon Fashions Ltd* (1989) 5 B.C.C. 773, a similar case. Trading on customer deposits is likely to be an aggravating factor: see *Re Western Welsh International System Buildings Ltd* (1988) 4 B.C.C. 449 (five years) though note that when this case was decided the maximum period of disqualification was five years and it might now fall within the middle bracket.

[98] [1993] B.C.L.C. 80, [1992] B.C.C. 557. See also *Re Austinsuite Furniture Ltd* [1992] B.C.L.C. 1047 where the first defendant was disqualified for seven years. Here the court was strongly influenced by his conduct in procuring a company to enter into a worthless acquisition which was represented in the accounts in such a way that they gave a misleading impression of the company's true financial position.

[99] See, *e.g. Re Tansoft Ltd* [1991] B.C.L.C. 339 (repeated pattern of misconduct across three companies including misapplication of company monies: seven years); *Re Moorgate Metals Ltd, Official Receiver v. Huhtala* [1995] 1 B.C.L.C. 503, [1995] B.C.C. 143 (*de facto* director who caused company to trade while insolvent, took excessive remuneration, acted dishonestly and deceitfully and took part in the management of a company while bankrupt in breach of CDDA, s. 11 disqualified for 10 years) and *Re Continental Assurance Co. of London plc* [1997] 1 B.C.L.C. 48, [1996] B.C.C. 888 (executive director who instigated illegal financial assistance and used the assets of two companies as if they were his own disqualified for nine years).

sign that he has learned the lessons of previous insolvencies.[1] Middle bracket disqualifications have been imposed in cases where there was no allegation of dishonesty and the misconduct related to a single company or an insolvent group.[2] While rare, such cases illustrate the difficulty which practitioners face in trying to predict a possible outcome.

Top bracket cases

5.73 It is rare for a director to be disqualified for over 10 years.[3] To merit a disqualification in the top bracket it appears that the misconduct would need to be very severe. Criminally culpable conduct such as persistent fraudulent trading might fit the bill. Again, a pattern of serious "repeat" misconduct across a number of companies consisting primarily of dishonest misappropriation of corporate assets might well attract a period of disqualification within this bracket.[4]

Summary

5.74 Much seems to depend on the defendant's culpability and on whether the misconduct occurred in isolation or was repeated across several companies. In *Seven-oaks* the Court of Appeal endorsed the use of brackets in an attempt to introduce some consistency of approach. In particular, there was a perception that the High Court tended to impose lower periods of disqualification than county courts for conduct that was closely comparable. However, no rule of thumb will ever produce absolute consistency. For instance, it is difficult to determine what might tip the balance and turn minimum bracket conduct into middle bracket conduct or middle bracket conduct

---

[1] See, *e.g. Re Melcast (Wolverhampton) Ltd* [1991] B.C.L.C. 288 (first defendant guilty of "gross irresponsibility in his financial conduct" of two successive companies disqualified for seven years reduced from 10 years on grounds of his age); *Re Brooks Transport (Purfleet) Ltd* [1993] B.C.C. 766 (persistent conduct within two owner-managed companies described at best as "cavalier" and at worst as "a deliberate refusal to comply with legal requirements where [the defendant] considered them inconvenient or an obstacle to the conducting of the business...": seven years); *Re Copecrest Ltd, Secretary of State for Trade and Industry v. McTighe (No. 2)* [1996] 2 B.C.L.C. 477, [1997] B.C.C. 224, CA (second defendant's period of disqualification raised from 4 to 6 years on appeal where evidence of "repeat" failings in a number of companies including some responsibility for misappropriation of corporate assets) See also *Re Saver Ltd* [1999] B.C.C. 221.

[2] See, *e.g. Re Synthetic Technology Ltd, Secretary of State for Trade and Industry v. Joiner* [1993] B.C.C. 549 (sustained insolvent trading in loss-making company, excessive remuneration and filing defaults: seven years); *Re Firedart Ltd, Official Receiver v. Fairhall* [1994] 2 B.C.L.C. 340 (paradigm case of insolvent trading coupled with excessive remuneration and failure to maintain proper accounting records in relation to a single company: six years); *Re Richborough Furniture Ltd, Secretary of State for Trade and Industry v. Stokes* [1996] 1 B.C.L.C. 507, [1995] B.C.C. 155 (paradigm case of insolvent trading, misuse of bank account and failure to maintain proper accounting records in relation to a single company: first defendant disqualified for six years); *Re Thorncliffe Finance Ltd, Secretary of State for Trade and Industry v. Arif* [1997] 1 B.C.L.C. 34, [1996] B.C.C. 586 (first defendant disqualified for seven years primarily for failure to exercise proper financial responsibility within a group of companies despite no finding of dishonesty). It is perhaps significant that in *Synthetic Technology* the defendant appeared in person and that in *Firedart* the defendant made no appearance at all with the effect that the claimant's evidence was wholly unchallenged. Lesser periods might have resulted if there had been a more effective attempt to contest these proceedings or put forward mitigating factors. The use of the middle bracket in *Richborough Furniture* probably reflects the lenient treatment previously given to the same defendant in *Re Austinsuite Furniture Ltd* [1992] B.C.L.C. 1047.

[3] Between December 1986 and June 1997 of 4,269 disqualification orders made under section 6, only 82 (*i.e.* under 2%) were for between 11 years and the maximum 15 years (DTI Press Release P/97/365, June 5, 1997). In the two years ending on June 30, 1998 of 2,307 orders made under section 6, 41 (*i.e* again less than 2%) were for between 11 and 15 years (DTI Press Release P/98/578, July 23, 1998).

[4] See *Re Copecrest Ltd, Secretary of State for Trade and Industry v. McTighe (No. 2)* [1996] 2 B.C.L.C. 477, [1997] B.C.C. 224, CA in which the first defendant's period of disqualification was raised from eight to 12 years on appeal and *Re Defence & Microwave Devices Ltd*, October 7, 1992, Ch.D., unreported (principal defendant disqualified for 12 years in a case best characterised as a saga of dishonesty and irresponsibility).

into top bracket conduct. The "common sense" approach in *Westmid Packing* is perhaps a recognition of this difficulty. Some inconsistency is therefore inevitable and it creates problems for the practitioner faced with the task of advising on likely outcome, especially in circumstances where, as will often be the case, the ability to compromise the proceedings turns on a sensible and realistic appraisal of the appropriate period of disqualification. Moreover, as will be seen below, it is not always easy to gauge what impact mitigation will have on the determination of period.[5] It is also noticeable that defendants who are not represented or who litigate in person seem to attract what appear to be relatively higher periods of disqualification.[6] This is probably best explained by the failure of these defendants to mount an effective challenge to the claimant's evidence and/or a failure to put forward any compelling mitigation.

Mitigating factors

5.75   It was suggested in *Re Dawes & Henderson (Agencies) Ltd, Secretary of State for Trade and Industry v. Dawes* that the defendant can only rely in mitigation on matters which are relevant to the conduct established.[7] As has been demonstrated, this narrow approach was rejected in favour of a more flexible approach by the Court of Appeal in *Westmid Packing*. The specific factors discussed below suggest that the court may engage in a broad enquiry and take into account matters which are personal to the defendant including the impact of the disqualification process on him. A number of factors often taken into account at this stage are not strictly mitigating factors at all but rather points of emphasis. For instance, the court may lay emphasis on the fact that the defendant was not dishonest and/or did not benefit personally from his misconduct. Strictly speaking, this amounts to an assessment of the defendant's degree of culpability for the purposes of the *Sevenoaks* approach rather than genuine mitigation.[8] Needless to say, points like these bear repetition by defendant's counsel as they tend to indicate a period of disqualification within the minimum bracket. Thus, one aspect of "mitigation" is the attempt to draw out factors which point to a lesser degree of culpability and to emphasise what the defendant got right. It is difficult to know with any certainty the level of discount which the court might apply to reflect a

---

[5] Although the point is not made explicitly by Hoey, *op. cit.*, her discussion suggests that the court in Northern Ireland tends to impose higher periods of disqualification than the English High Court for comparable misconduct. It appears also that the criminal courts exercising their powers under CDDA, s. 2 do not always act in line with the approach of the civil courts under section 6 on the question of period: see discussion in Chap. 9.

[6] The cases suggest that an unrepresented defendant or a litigant in person are at a serious disadvantage: see, *e.g. Re T & D Services (Timber Preservation & Damp Proofing Contractors) Ltd* [1990] B.C.C. 592 (unrepresented defendant disqualified for 10 years); *Re Tansoft Ltd* [1991] B.C.L.C. 339 (litigant in person disqualified for seven years); *Re City Investment Centres Ltd* [1992] B.C.L.C. 956 (two unrepresented defendants disqualified for 10 and six years respectively, one litigant in person disqualified for six years); *Re Looe Fish Ltd* [1993] B.C.L.C. 1160, [1993] B.C.C. 348 (section 8 case in which an unrepresented defendant was disqualified for a period only six months less than his represented co-defendant despite the latter's more significant involvement in the relevant misconduct); *Re Synthetic Technology Ltd* [1993] B.C.C. 549 (litigant in person disqualified for seven years); *Re Firedart Ltd* [1994] 2 B.C.L.C. 340 (unrepresented defendant disqualified for 6 years in "standard" case of insolvent trading and failure to maintain accounting records); *Re Copecrest Ltd, Secretary of State for Trade and Industry v. McTighe (No. 2)* [1996] 2 B.C.L.C. 477, [1997] B.C.C. 224 (period of disqualification imposed on unrepresented defendant raised from eight to 12 years); *Re Continental Assurance Co. of London plc* [1997] 1 B.C.L.C. 48, [1996] B.C.C. 888 (unrepresented defendant disqualified for nine years); *Re Ask International Transport Ltd, Secretary of State for Trade and Industry v. Keens*, May 5, 1992, Ch.D (two unrepresented defendants disqualified for four years where insolvent trading had only occurred over a short period). For a more sympathetic approach see *Re Land Travel Ltd, Secretary of State for Trade and Industry v. Tjolle* [1998] 1 B.C.L.C. 333, [1998] B.C.C. 282.

[7] [1997] 1 B.C.L.C. 329 at 40, [1997] B.C.C. 121 at 130.

[8] See, *e.g. Re GSAR Realisations Ltd* [1993] B.C.L.C. 409.

particular mitigating factor. The cases suggest that the specific factors discussed below may be taken into account.[9] It appears that these various mitigating factors, which are admissible in proceedings for an order under section 6, are also relevant and admissible in section 8 proceedings.

General character and reputation

5.76 It appears that evidence relating to the defendant's general ability and conduct as a director can be adduced by way of mitigation. General evidence of good character is ordinarily inadmissible in civil proceedings because it is not probative of any issue. However, it was suggested in *Westmid Packing* that evidence relating to the defendant's conduct and track record in the discharge of the office of director may be admissible because it is relevant in determining the extent of the public's need for protection.[10] The evidence must be relevant. As Scott V.-C. put it in *Re Barings plc, Secretary of State for Trade and Industry v. Baker*, "it would not be relevant in the least whether the director was a good family man or whether he was kind to animals".[11]

Impact of corporate failure

5.77 It appears that if the defendant has suffered personal financial loss in the company's collapse that this can be taken into account in mitigation. At first sight, this seems somewhat incongruous in the light of the oft-stated view that disqualification is primarily concerned with the protection of the public. The rationale seems to be that the public needs less protection from a director who lost out along with creditors than from one who manipulated the company entirely for his own ends in circumstances where his personal fortune was not at stake. One difficulty is that in an owner-managed company, the controller's failure to monitor the running of the company and the value of his own investment may of itself indicate a lack of regard for creditors' interests.[12] Thus, in cases where an owner-manager is said to have abdicated responsibility, his personal financial loss may not be of much significance as a mitigating factor. Nevertheless, the impact of the company's failure on the defendant was taken into account in *Sevenoaks* and other cases.[13]

Age and/or state of health

5.78 In *Re Melcast (Wolverhampton) Ltd*, the court considered it appropriate to disqualify the first defendant for 10 years but reduced it to seven to take account of his

[9] Note that in the interests of economy of court time, the judge may frown upon the citation of numerous cases as to the appropriate period of disqualification: see *Westmid Packing* [1998] 2 All E.R. 124 at 134, [1998] 2 B.C.L.C. 646 at 658, [1998] B.C.C. 836 at 846.
[10] [1998] 2 All E.R. 124 at 133, [1998] 2 B.C.L.C. 646 at 657, [1998] B.C.C. 836 at 845 citing with approval *Re Barings plc* [1998] B.C.C. 583 at 590 *contra Re Dawes & Henderson (Agencies) Ltd* [1997] 1 B.C.L.C. 329, [1997] B.C.C. 121. General character evidence is admissible in criminal proceedings where there is a presumption that a person of good character would not commit a crime. The flexible approach taken in *Westmid Packing* appears to reflect the Court of Appeal's acceptance that the process of determining the appropriate period of disqualification is analogous to a criminal sentencing exercise.
[11] [1998] B.C.C. 583 at 590.
[12] See, *e.g. Re Burnham Marketing Services Ltd, Secretary of State for Trade and Industry v. Harper* [1993] B.C.C. 518.
[13] See also *Re Cargo Agency Ltd* [1992] B.C.L.C. 686, [1992] B.C.C. 388; *Re Pamstock Ltd* [1994] 1 B.C.L.C. 716, [1994] B.C.C. 264; *Re Hitco 2000 Ltd* [1995] 2 B.C.L.C. 63, [1995] B.C.C. 161 and contrast with *Re Ipcon Fashions Ltd* (1989) 5 B.C.C. 773 where a director who lost no personal capital in three successive failed companies having traded entirely at the risk of creditors was disqualified for five years. See also *Re Firedart Ltd* [1994] 2 B.C.L.C. 340 at 352 where Arden J. did not regard the defendant's guarantee of the bank overdraft and provision of personal security as a matter of mitigation. Given that the company was seriously undercapitalised from the start, the monies should, in the judge's view, have been injected in exchange for issues of share capital.

advancing age.[14] At the time of trial he was 68 and it was felt that a seven-year disqualification would adequately protect the public because there was little risk of him wanting to take an active part in the management of a company after the age of 75. Similarly in *Official Receiver v. Cummings*,[15] the defendant's age (53) was regarded as a mitigating factor. On the other hand, in *Re Moorgate Metals Ltd, Official Receiver v. Huhtala,* Warner J. did not consider that the second defendant's age (he would be 80 by the time the period of disqualification ended) was a reason for reducing the period.[16] At the opposite end of the spectrum, a young and inexperienced director might expect to receive some credit especially for a "first offence".[17] If the defendant is in ill health the court may be persuaded by analogy to apply a discount if the illness reduces the likelihood of him being able to take up directorships in the future. It is suggested that the restrictive approach in *Moorgate Metals* should apply where the defendant seeks to rely on age or ill health as a mitigating factor unless it can be shown that either factor bears directly on the unfit conduct.

Reliance on professional advice

5.79   It was seen in para. 5.60 above that in some cases the defendant may escape a finding of unfitness where he has relied on professional advice or on the special expertise of a co-director. Even if he is not able to persuade the court to dismiss the application altogether, it is likely that such reliance would be treated as a mitigating factor. Thus in *Re Rolus Properties Ltd*,[18] the court assessed the appropriate period of disqualification at between four and six years but reduced it to two years to take account of the fact that the defendant had procured the services of a chartered secretary to assist in the company's administration.[19]

Conduct after the unfit conduct

5.80   Instances of positive conduct after the unfit conduct have been taken into account in some cases. It will usually go to the defendant's credit if he co-operated fully with the insolvency practitioner appointed to take charge of the company's affairs following its collapse.[20] Moreover, it was suggested in *Re Firedart Ltd* that an attempt by the defendant to improve the position of creditors by making a payment to the liquidator might be a relevant mitigating factor.[21] This presumably reflects the idea that an act of contrition based on the defendant's recognition of the damage suffered by creditors is worthy of some discount. However, such an argument is unlikely to cut much ice if the payment was made in satisfaction of civil proceedings brought by the liquidator.[22]

---

[14] [1991] B.C.L.C. 288.

[15] November 1, 1991, Ch.D., unreported.

[16] [1995] 1 B.C.L.C. 503 at 520, [1995] B.C.C. 143 at 157.

[17] There is the hint of such an approach in the treatment of the defendant LS in *Re Austinsuite Furniture Ltd* [1992] B.C.L.C. 1047.

[18] (1988) 4 B.C.C. 446.

[19] See also *Re Keypack Homecare Ltd* [1990] B.C.L.C. 440, [1990] B.C.C. 117 where the defendants received some credit for having relied on bad professional advice.

[20] See, *e.g. Re Cargo Agency Ltd* [1992] B.C.L.C. 686, [1992] B.C.C. 388; *Re City Investment Centres Ltd* [1992] B.C.L.C. 956.

[21] [1994] 2 B.C.L.C. 340 at 352.

[22] See *Re Grayan Building Services Ltd* [1995] Ch. 241, [1995] 3 W.L.R. 1, [1995] 1 B.C.L.C. 276, [1995] B.C.C. 554 in which the Court of Appeal held that the trial judge had been wrong to take into account by way of mitigation the fact that the liquidator had previously achieved an advantageous settlement of proceedings brought against the defendants under section 239 of the Insolvency Act 1986.

Conduct during proceedings

5.81   Credit may be given if the defendant refrains from acting as a director while proceedings against him are pending.[23] To what extent the defendant will receive any credit for the way in which the proceedings are conducted on his behalf remains however something of a moot point. It was suggested in *Re Firedart Ltd* that a discount might be available if the defendant makes admissions during proceedings.[24] In *Re Barings plc*, Scott V.-C. stated categorically that there is no scope for plea bargaining in disqualification proceedings and that, as far as he was concerned, a director should not be given credit for assisting the court in its disposal of the case by not disputing the indisputable.[25] However, he does seem to have accepted that credit could be given to a director who realistically accepts that his conduct makes him unfit, as this indicates a state of mind which suggests that he may pose less of a danger to the public in the future than someone who adamantly insists that he was not responsible for any misconduct. The Court of Appeal in *Westmid Packing* disagreed with Scott V.-C. and the present state of the law is best reflected in the following passage from Lord Woolf M.R.'s judgment in that case:

> "In the criminal sentencing context ... there is no room for plea bargaining if by that it is meant some form of agreement as to the sentence if a plea is entered. But there can be negotiation as to the acceptability of an admission on a certain basis of fact, and that would seem to be as sensible in this context as in the criminal context. That is indeed already recognised in the *Carecraft* procedure.[26] Furthermore in the criminal context very little discount is given if there is an admission of what is 'indisputable', but an admission of what might otherwise have taken a great deal of time and expense to prove surely merits some recognition, provided of course that the starting point correctly reflects the gravity of the conduct."[27]

Thus, if the defendant admits an allegation before trial that would otherwise have occupied considerable court time, a discount may be appropriate. Once again, the idea that the exercise is closely analogous to criminal sentencing is to the fore.

Delay in bringing proceedings: de facto *disqualification*

5.82   In *Re Thorncliffe Finance Ltd, Secretary of State for Trade and Industry v. Arif*, the first defendant argued that, in fixing the appropriate period of disqualification, the court should have regard to the fact that since the institution of the proceedings he had been prevented from taking up appointments as a director because the sort of directorship which would be attractive to him (namely, one in a company engaged in the motor trade) would not be offered to a person against whom disqualification proceedings were pending. He therefore sought credit for what was described as the period of *de facto* disqualification between the commencement and conclusion of proceedings. Chadwick J. held that no credit could be given because of the structure of the CDDA. If the court makes a finding of unfitness, the court must disqualify the defendant for a minimum of two years even if he no longer poses any threat to the public

---

[23] *Official Receiver v. Cummings*, November 1, 1991, Ch.D., unreported.
[24] [1994] 2 B.C.L.C. 340 at 352.
[25] [1998] B.C.C. 583 at 590.
[26] On *Carecraft* generally see Chap. 8. This procedure allows cases to be disposed of summarily on the basis of an agreed statement of facts. It reduces court time that would otherwise be spent in contesting issues of fact. Strictly speaking, a *Carecraft* disposal is not a plea bargain because the parties cannot agree a period of disqualification (though see *Re Aldermanbury Trust plc* [1993] B.C.C. 598 at 602). It is left in the hands of the judge to determine the appropriate period based on an assessment of the agreed facts.
[27] [1998] 2 All E.R. 124 at 132, [1998] 2 B.C.L.C. 646 at 655, [1998] B.C.C. 836 at 844.

under the rule in *Re Grayan Building Services Ltd* discussed earlier. In circumstances like these where the minimum period of disqualification is appropriate it is not open to the court to give any credit for the period during which proceedings were pending. The judge concluded that, if a period of so-called *de facto* disqualification cannot be taken into account in a case of that nature, then it cannot be taken into account either in a case where the appropriate starting point, as in *Arif*, is a period of disqualification longer than the two-year minimum.[28] However, in *Westmid Packing*, the Court of Appeal disagreed expressly with Chadwick J.'s view and said that the length of time for which a director has been in jeopardy may be a relevant factor.

5.83   There are difficulties with both these conflicting views. Chadwick J.'s view suffers from a flaw in logic. It is clear that if the minimum period of disqualification is appropriate the court has *no scope whatsoever* for taking mitigating factors into account. The minimum period cannot be discounted. If *Arif* is correct in respect of *de facto* disqualification, it follows that mitigation of any sort can never be relevant because it is not possible for the court to rely on mitigating factors if to do so would reduce the period below two years. Equally, however, there is no clear guidance in *Westmid Packing* as to the circumstances in which a period of *de facto* disqualification might be taken into account. Strictly speaking, while proceedings are pending, the defendant is not *legally* restricted from taking up directorships. There is no obvious reason why the court should *automatically* conclude that the period between commencement of proceedings and trial operates as a *de facto* disqualification.[29] It might be different if there is cogent evidence establishing that the defendant was *de facto* disqualified or in cases where there has been an unreasonable delay on the part of the claimant in bringing the matter to trial. The task of determining the extent to which a defendant's right to due process can affect the substantive outcome of his case is a complex and controversial one. Once proceedings are commenced, it is clear that any unreasonable delay in bringing the case to trial will infringe the defendant's right to a fair trial under Article 6 of the European Convention on Human Rights.[30] At the same time, delay in the prosecution of disqualification proceedings arguably harms the public because the defendant is technically free to act as a director (and potentially free to indulge in "repeat" misconduct) until such time as a disqualification order is made. This tension between individual rights and the public interest may give rise to conflicting characterisations of the period between commencement of proceedings and trial. There is thus no guarantee that the court will always treat it as a period of *de facto* disqualification. The enactment of the Human Rights Act 1998 is likely to mean that the court's attention will increasingly be drawn to defendants' Article 6 rights. As such, it is not unreasonable to assume that any delay in proceedings which is not directly attributable to the defendant will be construed to his advantage. In other words, in attempting to strike a balance between the defendant's Article 6 rights and the public's need for protection, the courts are likely to err on the side of caution and give priority to the defendant's rights. This is especially so where the proceedings have been hanging over him for a considerable length of time (bearing in mind that the events which triggered the proceedings will be even further in the past). However, this is not to say that other factors such as the relative seriousness of the allegations (which, as has been seen, in effect determines the extent of the public's need for protection) will not be as relevant here as they are in deciding an application for permission to commence proceedings out of time under section 7(2).[31]

---

[28] [1997] 1 B.C.L.C. 34 at 44–45, [1996] B.C.C. 586 at 595.
[29] See *Re Sykes (Butchers) Ltd, Secretary of State for Trade and Industry v. Richardson* [1998] 1 B.C.L.C. 110, [1998] B.C.C. 484.
[30] See *EDC v. United Kingdom* [1998] B.C.C. 370.
[31] On which see generally Chap. 7.

5.84 As the conflicting views in *Arif* and *Westmid Packing* suggest, the courts are not as yet following any consistent approach. There has been a tendency in appeal cases for the appellate court to give the defendant some credit in respect of the length of time for which he was "in jeopardy".[32] Defendants have also received credit at first instance.[33] However, if the defendant's Article 6 rights are complied with and there is no specific evidence that the defendant's livelihood has been affected as a result of pending proceedings, there is no obvious reason why the courts should apply a discount as a matter of course. On a separate point, the general approach in *Westmid Packing* suggests that a court might be persuaded to give some form of discount if the defendant is already the subject of automatic disqualification on the ground of personal bankruptcy under section 11.[34]

Treatment of any co-director

5.85 Although not strictly a mitigating factor the courts do appear to be influenced by a desire to fix periods of disqualification which reflect a fair balance in cases involving a number of unfit co-directors.[35] Thus, the way in which one director is treated may well affect the court's treatment of his co-directors. Similarly, the outcome of proceedings against one director which have been compromised or discontinued may influence the court's attitude in determining for how long any co-director who has contested the proceedings to trial should be disqualified.[36]

---

[32] See *Re Grayan Building Services Ltd* [1995] Ch. 241, [1995] 3 W.L.R. 1, [1995] 1 B.C.L.C. 276, [1995] B.C.C. 554, CA and *Re City Pram & Toy Co. Ltd* [1998] B.C.C. 537. Both cases involved successful appeals by the Secretary of State against an earlier refusal to disqualify the defendants. In *City Pram* the court expressly adopted the practice followed by the Court of Appeal (Criminal Division) on successful appeals by the Crown against sentence in criminal cases and substituted a lesser period of disqualification than it felt the registrar should have ordered to reflect the additional strain placed on the defendants by the Secretary of State's appeal.

[33] See, *e.g. Re Aldermanbury Trust plc* [1993] B.C.C. 598; *Re A & C Group Services Ltd* [1993] B.C.L.C. 1297 (though here the credit given also reflected the fact that the defendant had spent some of the period between commencement of proceedings and trial under automatic disqualification as an undischarged bankrupt); *Re Admiral Energy Group Ltd, Official Receiver v. Jones*, August 19, 1996, Ch.D., unreported (eighteen month discount where proceedings had been pending for six and a half years). It is interesting to reflect that substantial delay often occurs because parallel criminal or regulatory proceedings are in train. In the light of *EDC v. United Kingdom* [1998] B.C.C. 370 it is likely that the courts will try to safeguard defendants against such delay (especially in cases where disqualification proceedings are stayed against the defendant pending the outcome of parallel proceedings against a co-defendant in which he is not involved). The fact that a defendant's conduct may expose him to parallel proceedings (and therefore additional "jeopardy") has not of itself attracted a discount: see, *e.g. Re Living Images Ltd* [1996] 1 B.C.L.C. 348, [1996] B.C.C. 112 (existence of parallel disciplinary proceedings brought by accountancy body not taken into account).

[34] See also *dictum* in *Re Swift 736 Ltd, Secretary of State for Trade and Industry v. Ettinger* [1993] B.C.L.C. 896, [1993] B.C.C. 312, CA suggesting that bankruptcy might be taken into account in an appropriate case.

[35] See, *e.g. Re Sevenoaks Stationers (Retail) Ltd* [1991] Ch. 164, [1991] 3 All E.R. 578, [1991] B.C.L.C. 325, [1990] B.C.C. 765 (where Dillon L.J. expressed doubt *obiter* as to whether it would have been right to disqualify the appellant for more than twice as long as his co-director who was not involved in the appeal) and *Re Swift 736 Ltd, Secretary of State for Trade and Industry v. Ettinger* [1993] B.C.C. 896, [1993] B.C.C. 312.

[36] See, *e.g. Re Continental Assurance Co. of London plc* [1997] 1 B.C.L.C. 48, [1996] B.C.C. 888 (where the court was influenced in its treatment of a non-executive director by the fact that one of his fellow directors had been disqualified for four years under the *Carecraft* procedure).

CHAPTER 6

Procedure and Evidence in Civil Disqualification Proceedings

INTRODUCTION

6.01 This chapter covers the following subject matter:

(1) Court procedure in civil disqualification proceedings. This encompasses procedure in relation to any application for a disqualification order in the civil courts and so includes material which is relevant not only to sections 6 to 8 of the CDDA but also disqualification proceedings under sections 2, 3, 4 and 10 (the substance of which is covered in Chapter 9). The impact of the new Civil Procedure Rules ("CPR") is reflected in this chapter. While, in a general sense the CPR represent a decisive shift towards a wholly new culture of civil litigation and a break with past practice, many of the cases decided under the old rules are good indicators of problems which are likely to arise and recur in disqualification proceedings under the new system. With that in mind, this chapter does trespass on the old law to a certain extent. Apart from the fact that the application of the CPR will only be worked out over time, the new rules are changing rapidly. It is therefore imperative that readers check the up-to-date position regarding the CPR.

(2) The application of the law of evidence in civil disqualification proceedings.

THE RELEVANT COURTS

6.02 In a number of cases the CDDA expressly identifies the civil courts in which proceedings must be commenced. They are as follows:

(1) Section 2(2)(a): any court having jurisdiction to wind up the company in relation to which the relevant offence was committed.

(2) Section 3(4): any court having jurisdiction to wind up any of the companies in relation to which the relevant offence or other default has been or is alleged to have been committed.

(3) Section 4(2): any court having jurisdiction to wind up any of the companies in relation to which the relevant offence or other default has been or is alleged to have been committed.

(4) Section 6(3) (which defines "the court" for the purposes of sections 6 and 7):

  (a) in the case of a person who is or has been a director of a company which is being wound up by the court, the court by which the company is being wound up;

(b) in the case of a person who is or has been a director of a company which is being wound up voluntarily, any court having jurisdiction to wind up the company;

(c) in the case of a person who is or has been a director of a company in relation to which an administration order is in force, the court by which that order was made;

(d) in any other case[1] (in England and Wales), the High Court or (in Scotland), the Court of Session.

(5) Section 8(3): (in England and Wales), the High Court or (in Scotland), the Court of Session.

(6) Section 10: the court making a declaration under section 213 or 214 of the Insolvency Act 1986.

(7) Section 11: the court by which the person was adjudged bankrupt.

(8) Section 12: the court making an order under section 429(2)(b) of the Insolvency Act 1986, revoking an administration order under Part VI of the County Courts Act 1984.

(9) Section 17:

(a) where permission is sought to promote or form a company: any court with jurisdiction to wind up companies;

(b) where permission is sought to be a liquidator, administrator or director of, or otherwise to take part in the management of a company, or to be a receiver or manager of a company's property, any court having jurisdiction to wind up that company.

It will be noted that there may be cases where the court hearing (for example) an application for the making of a disqualification order under section 6, does not have jurisdiction to grant permission to act notwithstanding a disqualification order under section 17. This may be a reason for seeking a transfer of the proceedings before trial.

No express provision is made as regards applications under sections 7(4) or 15 of the CDDA.

Jurisdiction to wind up companies

6.03 The jurisdiction of the courts to wind up companies is established by section 117 of the Insolvency Act 1986. The position is as follows:

(1) The High Court has jurisdiction to wind up any company registered in England and Wales.[1a]

(2) A county court has jurisdiction to wind up a company (concurrently with the High Court) where two conditions are satisfied:

---

[1] That is, one not covered by section 6(3)(a) to (c). The most common case will be where the company is in administrative receivership but section 6(3)(d) would apply equally where a company has been wound up and dissolved.
[1a] Winding up jurisdiction in Scotland is governed by section 120 of the Insolvency Act 1986 and is shared between the Court of Session and the sheriff courts.

(a) the company's paid-up share capital must not exceed £120,000;

(b) the registered office of the company must have been within the district of the relevant county court[2] for the longest period within the immediately preceding 6 months.[3]

As regards foreign companies and sections 2 to 4, 6 and 17 of the CDDA, the relevant deeming provisions for the purposes of establishing and allocating jurisdiction within the United Kingdom are set out in section 221(3) of the Insolvency Act. In summary, an unregistered company (as defined by Part V of the Insolvency Act 1986)[4] is deemed to be registered in England and Wales or Scotland according to which jurisdiction its principal place of business is situated. If it has a principal place of business situated in both countries, it will be deemed to be registered in both countries. The principal place of business situated in that part of Great Britain in which proceedings are being instituted is deemed to be its registered office. An unregistered company with a principal place of business situated in Northern Ireland cannot be wound up under Part V of the Insolvency Act unless it has a principal place of business situated in England and Wales and/or Scotland.[5] The circumstances in which the court will in fact exercise the jurisdiction to wind up in relation to foreign companies is considered in Chapter 12.

Time for determining jurisdiction

6.04 In this context it is section 6(3)(a)–(c) of the CDDA which has caused the most difficulty. Problems have arisen because of the use of the present tense in the identification of the court in question. Section 6(3)(a)–(c) read as follows:

"In this section and the next **"the court"** means—

(a) in the case of a person who is or has been a director of a company which *is being wound up* by the court, the court by which the company *is being wound up*;

(b) in the case of a person who is or has been a director of a company which *is being wound up* voluntarily, any court having jurisdiction to wind up the company;

(c) in the case of a person who is or has been a director of a company in relation to which an administration order *is in force*, the court by which that order was made..." (emphasis added).

Given that the qualifying factor is that a particular insolvency process (be it winding up or administration) "is" continuing, the two questions which have arisen are: (a) at what time is the test of the ongoing process to be satisfied and (b) at what point does the process end?

The time to apply the tests in section 6(3)(a)–(c)

6.05 So far as the time to apply the test is concerned, in two cases the High Court has decided that the time to test jurisdiction by asking whether the relevant process is

---

[2] For these purposes, the Lord Chancellor may by statutory instrument exclude specific county courts from having winding up jurisdiction and may attach their district (or part of their district) to another county court: Insolvency Act 1986, s. 117(4).

[3] *ibid.*, s. 117(6).

[4] See further Chap. 12 on the definitions of "company" and "unregistered company".

[5] Insolvency Act 1986, s. 221(2) and see *Re Normandy Marketing Limited* [1994] Ch. 198. Companies registered in Northern Ireland are wound up under the NI Order.

continuing is the date at which the disqualification proceedings are commenced.[6] On these authorities, section 6(3) is to be read as if the words "for the purposes of the commencement of the proceedings" were implicit.[7] Thus, where proceedings are validly commenced in a particular county court, in circumstances where jurisdiction arises because at that time the company is being wound up under a compulsory winding up order made by that court, jurisdiction will not cease half way through the disqualification proceedings when the winding up process is completed and at an end.[8] Similarly, where the registered office of a company is changed (by the voluntary liquidator) after commencement of a voluntary liquidation, disqualification proceedings will be properly commenced in the county court for the district of the new registered office (provided that for the purposes of section 117 of the Insolvency Act such registered office is the place which has longest been the company's registered office in the six months immediately prior to commencement of proceedings) and not the county court in whose district the registered office was situated before that time and up to the commencement of the voluntary liquidation.[9] The Inner House of the Court of Session has also ruled that the time at which jurisdiction is to be determined under section 6(3) is the date of the commencement of the disqualification proceedings and not the date of the relevant (earlier) insolvent event which triggers the two year period in section 7(2) for commencing proceedings.[10] It would appear that the time to apply the test of whether a court has jurisdiction to wind up a company (under sections 2, 3, 4 and 17) will be the same, that is, the time at which the proceedings are commenced.

At what point does a company cease to be in an insolvency process?

6.06 Whether or not an administration order "is in force" (under section 6(3)(b)) at any particular time is fairly easy to ascertain. However, the court has had to grapple with the issue of when a company "is being" wound up and when it ceases to be subject to this process. The commencement of the winding up is fairly easy to determine. In the case of a voluntary liquidation it is the date of the relevant resolution.[11] In the case of a compulsory liquidation, the liquidation is deemed to commence at the date of any earlier voluntary winding up or, if none, the date of presentation of the relevant petition although in practice it will not be known that the company is in the course of being compulsorily wound up unless and until a compulsory winding up order is made.[12] The High Court has decided that, for the purposes of section 6(3) of the CDDA, a company ceases to be in the course of being wound up only once it is finally dissolved and this is so even if its affairs have been fully wound up prior to that date.[13] In the case of a foreign company wound up as an unregistered company under Part V of the Insolvency Act 1986, the dissolution or ceasing in existence of the foreign company by virtue of the laws of its country of incorporation will not affect the ability of the courts within Great Britain to wind up or continue to wind up such a company.[14]

---

[6] *Re The Working Project Limited* [1995] 1 B.C.L.C. 226, [1995] B.C.C. 197 (in relation to section 6(3)(a)) and *Re Lichfield Freight Terminal* [1997] 2 B.C.L.C. 109, [1997] B.C.C. 11 (in relation to section 6(3)(b)). In the latter case the High Court was sitting as an appellate court.

[7] *Per* Carnwath J. in *Re The Working Project Limited* [1995] 1 B.C.L.C. 226 at 230, [1995] B.C.C. 197 at 201.

[8] *Re The Working Project Limited* [1995] 1 B.C.L.C. 226, [1995] B.C.C. 197 as decided in relation to the directors of Davies Flooring (Southern) Limited.

[9] *Re Lichfield Freight Terminal* [1997] 2 B.C.L.C. 109, [1997] B.C.C. 11.

[10] *Secretary of State for Trade and Industry, Petitioner* [1998] B.C.C. 437.

[11] Insolvency Act 1986, s. 86.

[12] *ibid.*, s. 129 and compare *Re Walter L. Jacob Co. Ltd, Official Receiver v. Jacob* [1993] B.C.C. 512.

[13] *Re The Working Project Limited* [1995] 1 B.C.L.C. 226, [1995] B.C.C. 197.

[14] Insolvency Act 1986, s. 225.

Jurisdiction under sections 7(2), 7(4) and 15

6.07   It is convenient to consider the position under these provisions separately.

(1) Applications for permission to commence proceedings under section 6 after the expiry of the two-year period from the onset of insolvency (section 7(2)) are dealt with in Chapter 7. The relevant court in which the application should be launched is the court having jurisdiction over the substantive disqualification proceedings that will be commenced if permission is granted (see section 6(3) as to the meaning of "the court" in sections 6 and 7). In the event that the court with jurisdiction alters between the issuing of the relevant application notice seeking permission and (if permission is given) the date of commencement of the substantive disqualification proceedings, the principle from the cases considered above will presumably apply: provided that the court to which the application for permission was made had jurisdiction at the time the application notice was issued, it will retain jurisdiction.

(2) Section 7(4) of the CDDA is dealt with in Chapter 3. If substantive disqualification proceedings are on foot, an application under section 7(4) can be brought within such proceedings.[15] It is also possible to bring an application by way of claim form under CPR, Pt 8 as provided for in the Disqualification Practice Direction. It is not clear to which court the application should be made and the safest course would be to make it in the High Court. However, it is possible that the court which would have jurisdiction with regard to the substantive proceedings (if brought) could entertain an application under section 7(4). A further possibility is that there may be power to apply under the Insolvency Rules to the court seised of the relevant insolvency proceedings.

(3) Proceedings seeking to impose civil liability on a disqualified person for acting in breach of a disqualification order can be brought either in the High Court or the relevant county court (subject to the relevant monetary limits).[16]

Transfer and proceedings commenced in the wrong court

Powers of transfer

6.08   There are wide powers of transfer. As explained below, the CPR (subject to modifications) apply to disqualification proceedings in civil courts. Transfer is regulated by CPR, Pt 30 and the relevant practice direction. In summary:

---

[15] Disqualification Practice Direction, para. 18.1.
[16] See the Practice Direction to Part 7 of the CPR. Where a county court has jurisdiction, proceedings may not be commenced in the High Court unless the value of the claim is more than £15,000 (Practice Direction 7, para. 2.1). However, there is jurisdiction to transfer proceedings between courts, which is considered in more detail below. In exercising the jurisdiction to transfer by reference to the financial value of claims, the starting point is that (in general) proceedings with a value of £50,000 or less should be heard in a county court (Practice Direction 29, para. 2.2). This starting point is subject to qualification. In deciding questions of transfer the court is also to have regard to the matters set out in CPR, r. 30.3 as discussed further below. Within a particular court there is then the further question of allocation to the relevant "track": the small claims track (broadly, claims having a financial value of not more then £5,000), the fast track (broadly, claims having a financial value of more than £5,000 but not more than £15,000) and the multi-track: see generally, CPR, Pt 26. However, in deciding track allocation, the court must also have regard to a number of other specific factors under CPR, r. 26.8 which share some similarities with those set out in CPR, r. 30.3.

(1) If proceedings are commenced in the wrong county court,[17] that county court can transfer them to the county court in which they should have been started or strike them out (CPR, r. 30.2(2)). A county court which does not have jurisdiction under the CDDA does not have the option of retaining CDDA proceedings which were wrongly commenced there (see CPR, r. 30.2(2)(b) and (7)). Application for transfer should be made to the county court in which the claim is proceeding (CPR, r. 30.2(3)).

(2) If proceedings are wrongly commenced in a county court when they should been commenced in the High Court,[18] there is power in that county court either to transfer the proceedings to the High Court or, if satisfied that the person bringing the proceedings knew, or ought to have known, that they should have been brought in the High Court, to strike them out (section 42(1), (7) of the County Courts Act 1984).

(3) If proceedings are wrongly commenced in the High Court when they should have been commenced in a county court, there is power in the High Court either to transfer the proceedings to a county court or, if satisfied that the person bringing the proceedings knew, or ought to have known, that they should have been brought in a county court, to strike them out (section 40(1), (8) of the County Courts Act 1984).

(4) If proceedings are correctly commenced in the High Court:

   (a) There is a general power in the High Court to transfer such proceedings between the Royal Courts of Justice and a district registry of the High Court (CPR, r. 30.2(4) and (5)). In deciding whether or not to transfer the court must have regard to the (presumably non-exhaustive) factors set out in CPR, r. 30.3(2)).

   (b) There is a power in the High Court under section 40 of the County Courts Act 1984 to transfer such proceedings to a relevant county court as long as that county court also has jurisdiction under the relevant provision of the CDDA. The exercise of the power is governed by section 40(2), (4) of the 1984 Act and CPR, r. 30.3.

(5) If proceedings are correctly commenced in a particular county court, there is no power to transfer them to another county court which does not have jurisdiction under the CDDA (CPR, r. 30.2(1) and (7)). However, *provided that the High Court does have jurisdiction*, there is power in the High Court (section 41(1) of the County Courts Act 1984) and a county court (section 42(2) of the County Courts Act 1984), to transfer the proceedings to the High Court. The exercise of these powers is governed by CPR, r. 30.3. Furthermore, provided that another county court also has jurisdiction, there is power for one county court to transfer the proceedings to that other county court if the court is satisfied that the criteria in CPR, r. 30.3 are satisfied (CPR, r. 30.2(1)).

---

[17] For example, in cases where the registered office has changed or where a winding up has been transferred from one county court to another.
[18] In these circumstances section 6(3)(d) applied. See, *e.g. Re NP Engineering and Security Products Ltd, Official Receiver v. Pafundo* [1998] 1 B.C.L.C. 208, CA, where the company had been wound up in a county court but was dissolved prior to issue of the disqualification proceedings.

Transfer from wrong court

6.09   In cases where proceedings are commenced in the wrong court, the court always has a discretion to transfer or strike out. The mere fact that the claimant ought to have known that the proceedings should have been commenced in a different court will not automatically result in the proceedings being struck out. In *Re NP Engineering and Security Products Ltd, Official Receiver v. Pafundo*[19] the court applied the principles set out in *Restick v. Crickmore*[20] (a case concerned with transfer of proceedings under section 42 of the County Courts Act 1984). In that case the established policy of the courts was described as being as follows:

> "... [P]rovided proceedings are commenced within the time permitted by the statute of limitations, are not frivolous, vexatious or an abuse of the process of the court and disclose a cause of action, they will not as a rule be struck out because of some mistake in procedure on the part of the [claimant] or his advisers. Save where there has been a contumelious disobedience of the court's order, the draconian sanction of striking out an otherwise properly constituted [claim/application], simply to punish the party who has failed to comply with the rules of court, is not part of the court's function. No injustice is involved to the defendant in transferring [a claim/application] which has been started in the wrong court to the correct court."[21]

In *NP Engineering*, the Court of Appeal, with regard to the question of the "wrong" court and in deciding to transfer rather than strike out, relied on the fact that (a) no-one had suggested that the proceedings were obviously frivolous or vexatious; (b) the proceedings (under section 6) were brought within the two-year period as required by section 7(2); (c) it made no practical difference to the defendants whether the proceedings were commenced in the county court or the High Court; (d) the proceedings were brought in the public interest; and (e) the function of the court on a transfer application was not to punish the incompetence of [the claimant]. Although the court may now be more willing to punish parties it is suggested that the basic approach should remain the same under the CPR.

Transfer from correct court

6.10   In cases where proceedings are commenced in the correct court, the court, in deciding whether or not to transfer the proceedings to another court (see powers in 6.08 above), is required to consider the factors set out in the relevant sections of the County Courts Act 1984 and CPR, r. 30.3:

(1)   In considering transfer from the High Court to a county court under section 40(2) of the County Courts Act 1984, the High Court must have regard to the convenience of the parties and of any other persons likely to be affected and

---

[19] [1998] 1 B.C.L.C. 208, CA. The first instance decision (see [1995] 2 B.C.L.C. 585, [1995] B.C.C. 1,052) is discussed in A. Mithani, "Disqualification Proceedings in the Wrong Court—A Dilemma for the Secretary of State?" (1996) 12 *Insolvency Law & Practice* 169.
[20] [1994] 1 W.L.R. 420.
[21] *ibid.* at 427.

the state of the business in the courts concerned.[22] The court must also now have regard to CPR, r. 30.3.

(2) Under CPR, r. 30.3 the court is obliged to consider:

    (a) the financial value of the claim and the amount in dispute, if different (this is not relevant in most proceedings brought under the CDDA though it will be relevant in cases under sections 10 and 15);

    (b) whether it would be more convenient or fair for hearings (including the trial) to be held in some other court;

    (c) the availability of a judge specialising in the type of claim in question;

    (d) whether the facts, legal issues, remedies or procedures involved are simple or complex[23];

    (e) the importance of the outcome of the claim to the public in general;

    (f) the facilities available at the court where the claim is being dealt with and whether they may be inadequate because of any disabilities of a party or potential witness.

(3) The factors enumerated in CPR, r. 30.3 largely mirror those previously set out in article 7 of the High Court and County Courts Jurisdiction Order 1991.[24] The one major change, which is not going to be relevant to most disqualification proceedings, is to the old rule of thumb that where the claim has a financial value of over £50,000, proceedings should be heard in the High Court and where the claim has a financial value of under £25,000, proceedings should be heard in a county court. The position now is that claims having a financial value of less than £50,000 will generally be heard in a county court (CPR, Pt 29; Practice Direction 29, para. 2.2). It is also to be noted that the previous restriction under article 7 of the 1991 Order preventing the court from making a transfer order solely on the ground that it would result in a more speedy trial of the proceedings no longer exists.

Transfer of applications for permission to act

6.11 In cases where legal proceedings seeking a disqualification order are started in a county court and (a) the person, if disqualified, would need to apply for permission to act in a relevant office or capacity otherwise prohibited by a disqualification order and (b) the relevant county court in question would not have jurisdiction to grant permission in relation to the particular company or companies for which permission is sought, consideration should be given to whether it is possible to transfer the proceedings to a court which would have jurisdiction both to make a disqualification order and to grant permission to act notwithstanding such order.

---

[22] For an example of this power being used in disqualification proceedings see *Re Time Utilising Business Systems Ltd* (1989) 5 B.C.C. 851 (the report in [1990] B.C.L.C. 568 does not cover this point). On the facts the case is actually wrongly decided in the light of subsequent decisions of the Court of Appeal (discussed below in main text) that in section 6 disqualification proceedings appeals from the district judge of a county court lie direct to the High Court judge and not to the county court judge.

[23] For an example of a pre-CPR case in which the High Court decided that this factor had been improperly invoked see *Re Time Utilising Business Systems Ltd* (1989) 5 B.C.C. 851.

[24] S.I. 1991 No. 724. This article was later omitted: see article 7 of the High Court and County Courts Jurisdiction (Amendment) Order 1999 S.I. 1999 No. 1014.

Appeals from transfer order

6.12   Once an order for transfer has been made there is some uncertainty as to whether or not the provisions on appeals set out in the Practice Direction to Part 30 of the CPR apply for the purposes of the appeal or whether the matter is regulated by the provisions on appeals set out in the Insolvency Rules. This matter is considered further below.

Overseas directors: disputing the court's jurisdiction

6.13   In cases under sections 6 and 8 where the court has granted permission to serve disqualification proceedings out of the jurisdiction under rule 5.2 of the Disqualification Rules and paragraph 7.3 of the Disqualification Practice Direction, the defendant served with the proceedings can apply to set aside service.[25] Indeed, the standard form of acknowledgment applicable to disqualification claims contains a relevant section on this topic. A question remains as to the practice in a case of a defendant served overseas by virtue of an order made under either paragraph 19.2(2)[26] or 26.2[27] of the Disqualification Practice Direction but it is presumed that the position is the same. The question of service outside the jurisdiction of disqualification proceedings under section 6 was considered in *Re Seagull Manufacturing Co. Ltd (No. 2)*.[28] In summary the conclusions from that case were as follows:

(1)   There is no jurisdictional limitation under section 6 of the CDDA. Section 6(1) can apply to any person, whether a British subject or a foreigner, irrespective of their presence here or at the time when the activities took place. The conduct need not have taken place within the jurisdiction.

(2)   Nevertheless, there remains a residual discretion in the court to refuse to order service out of the jurisdiction (or to set aside any such order for service and the service effected pursuant to such order) if the court is not satisfied that there is a "good arguable case".

THE APPLICABLE RULES OF COURT

6.14   To reach an understanding of the present position on applicable rules and the sort of points that remain unclear it is necessary to have some understanding of the history of the position.

Applicable rules: history

6.15   Immediately prior to the Insolvency Act 1985, civil disqualification proceedings were governed either by the Companies (Winding-Up) Rules 1949[29] (in particular, rule 68) or by the originating summons procedure in the High Court.[30] In 1986 new rules were introduced governing applications under sections 6 and 8 of the CDDA[31]

---

[25] This also applies in cases under other provisions of the CDDA where permission has been granted to serve proceedings outside the jurisdiction under paragraph 7.3 of the Disqualification Practice Direction.
[26] Governing applications under CDDA, ss 7(2) and 7(4).
[27] Governing applications in disqualification proceedings made by way of application notice.
[28] [1994] 1 B.C.L.C. 273, [1993] B.C.C. 833.
[29] S.I. 1949 No. 330 (L. 4). See, *e.g. Re Blackheath Heating & Consulting Engineers Ltd* (1985) 1 B.C.C. 99,383.
[30] See, *e.g.* discussion in *Re Rex Williams Leisure plc, Secretary of State for Trade and Industry v. Warren* [1994] Ch. 350, [1994] 3 W.L.R. 745, [1994] 4 All E.R. 27, [1994] 2 B.C.L.C. 555, [1994] B.C.C. 551, CA.
[31] The Insolvent Companies (Disqualification of Unfit Directors) Proceedings Rules 1986 S.I. 1986 No. 612.

and, in 1987 these were replaced by the Disqualification Rules. The latter rules have been amended, to take account of the adoption of the CPR in place of the Rules of the Supreme Court and the County Court Rules, by the Insolvent Companies (Disqualification of Unfit Directors) (Amendment Rules) 1999.[32] The current position is unfortunate in two main respects:

(1) The nomenclature of the Disqualification Rules is confusing: section 8 proceedings can be brought in relation to companies which have not become insolvent. The title to the Disqualification Rules is also something of a mouthful.[33]

(2) The jurisdiction to make rules by way of statutory instrument under section 21 of the CDDA is effected by incorporating rule-making powers in the Insolvency Act 1986[34] but is limited to sections 6 to 10, 15, 19(c) and 20 and Schedule 1 of the CDDA (which provisions are, for the relevant purpose, deemed incorporated into the Insolvency Act 1986). Accordingly, applications under other sections fall to be dealt with under the CPR and the jurisdiction to modify the CPR in such cases has to be found in the CPR themselves.

It would be sensible if the CDDA conferred a wide rule-making power to replace the present limited arrangements which have emerged piecemeal as a result of historical accident.

Tasbian, Probe Data and the applicability of the Insolvency Rules

6.16   Prior to the amendment of the Disqualification Rules in 1999,[35] there was considerable uncertainty on the question of applicable rules in disqualification proceedings. This uncertainty was caused primarily by the somewhat unsatisfactory decision of the Court of Appeal in *Re Tasbian Ltd (No. 2), Official Receiver v. Nixon.*[36] The point for the Court of Appeal in that case was whether or not, on an application for permission to commence proceedings under section 6 outside the two-year time limit laid down by section 7(2), an appeal from the registrar of the Companies Court lay to the Court of Appeal or a High Court judge. Clearly concerned that the Court of Appeal should not be overburdened with appeals from the Companies Court registrar, it was decided in *Tasbian* that an appeal lay to a High Court judge. The reasoning by which this result was reached was unfortunately somewhat compressed. The Disqualification Rules did not, at that point, contain any express provisions about appeals[37] and so the Court of Appeal turned to the wording of section 6(3) of the CDDA. The analysis proceeded thus. It was noted that the court with jurisdiction under section 6(3)(b) (company in voluntary winding up), is the court with "jurisdiction to wind up the company". In *Tasbian*, the relevant company was in compulsory winding up and so the relevant court having jurisdiction to disqualify was, under section 6(3)(a), the court by which the company was being wound up. Indeed, in all cases

---

[32] S.I. 1999 No. 1023.
[33] "Company Directors Disqualification Rules" would be simpler, as would the consolidation of all relevant statutory instruments within one single statutory instrument.
[34] See section 411.
[35] The Disqualification Rules were amended by the Insolvent Companies (Disqualification of Unfit Directors) Proceedings (Amendment) Rules 1999 S.I. 1999 No. 1023.
[36] [1991] B.C.L.C. 59, [1990] B.C.C. 322.
[37] In any event, although no reference was made to this, there was a question as to whether the Disqualification Rules applied to applications under section 7(2).

under section 6(3)(a)–(c), the court given jurisdiction under the CDDA is a court which has winding up jurisdiction over companies. The Insolvency Rules 1986 contain provisions about appeals in insolvency proceedings. Rule 7.47 of the Insolvency Rules governs appeals from "... a decision made in the exercise of ..." the jurisdiction to wind up companies. The jurisdiction to wind up companies was not to be narrowly construed as referring only to a court's power to make winding up orders. In the words of Dillon L.J.:

> "... [I]t is plain that [the jurisdiction to wind up companies] is not limited to the mere making of winding up orders. It is a conventional formula of long-standing under successive Companies Acts..."

Dillon L.J. concluded that in relation to rule 7.47(2) of the Insolvency Rules:

> "... any decision made by a registrar of the High Court, in the exercise of the jurisdiction of the Chancery Division as the court having jurisdiction to wind up companies, is subject to appeal to a single judge of the High Court and not to this court."

In other words, the fact that a disqualifying court was not making a winding up order or some other order in the course of a winding up did not prevent rule 7.47 of the Insolvency Rules applying in *Tasbian*.

6.17 The matter was considered further in *Re Probe Data Systems Ltd (No. 3), Secretary of State for Trade and Industry v. Desai.*[38] The Court of Appeal was asked to decide that *Tasbian* was wrongly decided and to overrule it, but refused to do so. In particular, the Court of Appeal was not prepared to apply the *per incuriam* rule to enable it to depart from the decision in *Tasbian*. The argument proceeded, in part, on the following footing:

> "[Counsel for the director] submitted that if the decision [in *Tasbian*] were allowed to stand, the ratio would require the review and appellate procedures of rule 7.47 to be applied not only to orders made under [the CDDA] but to all orders made under the Companies Act 1985. He pointed out that 'court', in the Companies Act 1985 is defined as 'the court having jurisdiction to wind up the company' (section 744), and submitted that Dillon L.J.'s reasoning would apply the Insolvency Rules to all orders made by 'the court' so defined."

The answer to this was given by counsel for the Secretary of State:

> "Mr Richards gave the answer to this hair-raising submission. Section 411 of the Insolvency Act 1986, under which the Insolvency Rules were made, gives the Secretary of State no power to make rules for the purposes of the Companies Act 1985. *Per contra*, section 21 of [the CDDA] does permit rules made under section 411 to apply to disqualification proceedings. The Insolvency Rules 1986 could not be given an ultra vires effect and could not possibly apply to proceedings under the Companies Act 1985. So there is nothing in the point."

6.18 These two decisions appear to have had the following consequences and to have raised the following points of difficulty:

---

[38] [1992] B.C.L.C. 405, [1992] B.C.C. 110.

(1) Appeals in cases brought under any section of the CDDA other than sections 6 to 10, 15, 19(c), 20 and Schedule 1 cannot be governed by the Insolvency Rules 1986. This is because it would be ultra vires for such rules to be construed as applying to any provision other than the provisions referred to in section 21(2) of the CDDA (which concerns rule-making). Accordingly, although the civil court with jurisdiction to make disqualification orders under, for example, section 2 is defined as the court "with jurisdiction to wind up companies", the relevant rules applying to such a court exercising its jurisdiction under section 2 and on any appeal, could not have been the Insolvency Rules. The relevant rules (pre-CPR) would have been the Rules of the Supreme Court or the County Court Rules.

(2) In certain cases under sections 6 to 10, 15 and 19(c), the civil court with jurisdiction is defined not by reference to a winding up jurisdiction but as "the High Court": see, for example, section 6(3)(d) and section 8. In such cases, it is suggested that the Insolvency Rules would have had no application. This is implicit in the reasoning of Dillon L.J. in *Tasbian* discussed above. It was obviously undesirable that the applicable rules on appeals in section 6 cases should vary depending on whether the proceedings were commenced under section 6(3)(a)–(c) or section 6(3)(d). However, any other conclusion would involve viewing "the High Court" as referred to in the CDDA, simply as a sub-category of the court "having jurisdiction to wind up".[38a] The 1999 amendments to the Disqualification Rules (discussed further below) now make it clear that appeals in proceedings under either section 6 or 8 are governed by the Insolvency Rules but that otherwise proceedings are governed by the Disqualification Rules and the CPR.

(3) No specific provision is made in the CDDA as to the court having jurisdiction under sections 10 and 15. It is suggested that the applicable rules were and are now to be determined (a) in section 10 cases, by reference to the rules governing substantive proceedings under sections 213–214 of the Insolvency Act 1986 and (b) in the case of applications under section 15, by reference to the ordinary rules of court (now the CPR).

(4) In cases where (following the decisions in *Tasbian* and *Probe Data*), the Insolvency Rules govern the question of appeals, it would seem to follow that the appeal itself will be an "insolvency proceeding" governed by the Insolvency Rules (see Insolvency Rules, r. 13.7). However, in another context (*i.e.* one not involving a question of appeals), it was decided that the applicable rules to proceedings under sections 6 and 8 were not the Insolvency Rules 1986 but rather the Rules of the Supreme Court (or the County Court Rules) by reason of rule 2 of the Disqualification Rules. This point (arising from *Dobson v. Hastings*) is considered in the next section below.

(5) In cases where appeals in disqualification proceedings were not governed by the Insolvency Rules, the position after *Tasbian* and *Probe Data* was thus:

    (a) Appeals from the registrar of the Companies Court sitting in the High Court lay to a High Court judge (rehearing only).[39]

[38a] This was the approach taken by the parties and acceded to by the judge in *Re Ambery Metal Form Components Ltd, Secretary of State for Trade and Industry v. Jones* [1999] B.C.C. 336. It is suggested that the decision on this point, while sensible, is wrong. The point is probably academic in the light of the 1999 amendment to the Disqualification Rules.

[39] See discussion in *Re Rolls Razor Ltd (No. 2)* [1970] Ch. 576, [1970] 2 W.L.R. 100, [1969] 3 All E.R. 1386.

(b) Appeals from a district judge in a county court lay to a county court judge under the County Court Rules.

(c) Appeals from a county court judge exercising original jurisdiction lay to the Court of Appeal and not to a High Court judge (as is the case under the Insolvency Rules).

Developments after *Tasbian* and *Probe Data*

6.19   In *Dobson v. Hastings*,[40] the question before the court concerned the right of the public to inspect the court file of a set of disqualification proceedings brought under section 6: was such a right governed by the ordinary rules of court or by the Insolvency Rules? Basing himself firmly on the wording of what was then rule 2 of the Disqualification Rules, Nicholls V.-C. rejected the notion that the proceedings were "insolvency proceedings" governed by the Insolvency Rules and held that (in the High Court) the Rules of the Supreme Court (which were in force at that time) applied. Rule 2 of the unamended Disqualification Rules formerly made provision for the form of application in proceedings under sections 6 and 8 and went onto provide that "the Rules of the Supreme Court 1965 or (as the case may be) the County Court Rules 1981 apply accordingly, except where these Rules make provision to inconsistent effect". Thus rule 2, in its previous incarnation, did not simply govern the form of application: it governed the proceedings as a whole.[41] Unfortunately, rule 2 was not discussed by the Court of Appeal in *Tasbian*. Further, rule 2 was not mentioned by Dillon L.J. when he came to set out the relevant provisions of the Disqualification Rules. It is suggested, in the light of *Dobson v. Hastings* and on the true construction of the Disqualification Rules, that *Tasbian* was in fact wrongly decided and that the Insolvency Rules (which were made exclusively under section 411 of the Insolvency Act)[42] should not have been held to apply to any proceedings under the CDDA.

The question of applicable rules in section 6 proceedings arose again in *Re Circle Holidays International plc, Secretary of State for Trade and Industry v. Smith*.[43] In that case, the proceedings were in a county court. The immediate question was whether or not the applicable rules concerning hearsay in affidavits were to be found in the County Court Rules or the Insolvency Rules. His Honour Judge Micklem decided that the County Court Rules applied. His reasoning is, it is suggested, compelling. Thus, it appears that the position reached prior to the adoption of the CPR and the 1999 amendments to the Disqualification Rules was that the ordinary rules of court were treated as applying to all matters other than appeals, which (at least in relation to proceedings under section 6) were governed by the Insolvency Rules.

The current position

6.20   The current position would appear to be as follows:

(1) Civil disqualification proceedings under any provision of the CDDA (including section 15) apart from sections 6, 7, 8 and 10 are governed by the CPR and the Practice Directions made thereunder.

---

[40] [1992] Ch. 394, [1992] 2 W.L.R. 414, [1992] 2 All E.R. 94.
[41] *Contra* Hoffmann J. in *Re Langley Marketing Services Ltd* [1993] B.C.L.C. 1340, [1992] B.C.C. 585.
[42] Contrast the Disqualification Rules which were also made pursuant to section 21(2) of the CDDA. It appears that this consideration may have less weight than previously thought: see by analogy discussion of the rules made under the Civil Procedure Act 1997 in relation to pre-action disclosure in *Burrels Wharf Freeholds Ltd v. Galliard Homes Ltd*, unreported, July 1, 1999.
[43] [1994] B.C.C. 226.

(2) Proceedings under sections 6 and 8 are governed by the Disqualification Rules. The provisions of the Disqualification Rules and applications under sections 7(2) and 7(4) are considered further below.

(3) Proceedings under section 10 are governed by the relevant rules governing the substantive proceedings in which the claim under section 213 or section 214 is brought.

The current position: sections 6 to 8

6.21   As regards proceedings under sections 6 to 8 of the CDDA:

(1) The Disqualification Rules apply to applications for the making of a disqualification order under section 6 (technically section 7(1)) and section 8 in the first instance rather than the CPR (see CPR, r. 2.1(2) and Disqualification Rules, r. 2). Rule 2.4 of the Disqualification Rules expressly provides that the appeal and review provisions of the Insolvency Rules (*i.e.* rr. 7.47 and 7.49) apply to proceedings under sections 6 and 8. The 1999 amendment to the Disqualification Rules expressly gives effect to the result in *Tasbian* and *Probe Data*. To the extent that the Disqualification Rules do not make "provision to inconsistent effect", and subject to the application of the Insolvency Rules, rr. 7.47 and 7.49, the CPR and the Practice Directions apply. In other words, the position appears to reflect that which was apparently reached prior to the adoption of the CPR, namely that the Insolvency Rules apply only in relation to questions of appeal and review.

(2) The only question which appears to remain is whether the appeal and review provisions of the Insolvency Rules apply to proceedings under section 7(2) for permission to commence proceedings out of time. It should be noted that "the court" in section 7(2) is the same as for substantive proceedings for an order under section 6 (section 6(3)). It is suggested that the appeal and review provisions of the Insolvency Rules do apply in section 7(2) cases given that applications for permission are very much allied to the substantive disqualification proceedings in relation to which permission is sought. Otherwise the CPR will apply.

(3) In relation to section 7(4) the position is more complex. To the extent that an application is made within existing disqualification proceedings, it is suggested that the procedural rules governing the substantive proceedings will apply. If an application is made within the relevant insolvency proceedings, it is suggested that the Insolvency Rules will apply. If a free standing application is made by way of claim form under CPR, Pt 8 (as contemplated by the Disqualification Practice Direction), the position is uncertain. The provisions governing court applications under section 7(4) are contained in the Insolvent Companies (Reports on Conduct of Directors) Rules 1996 (made pursuant to the rule–making power in CDDA, s. 21(2)).[44] This might indicate that the Insolvency Rules apply throughout. The better view, it is suggested, is that the CPR (including its relevant appeal provisions) will apply.

The CPR and the Disqualification Practice Direction

6.22   On April 26, 1999, the Disqualification Practice Direction (governing civil disqualification proceedings) was adopted. The broad effect of the Disqualification

---

[44] S.I. 1996 No. 1909. See discussion in Chap. 3.

Practice Direction is to apply the same sort of procedures envisaged in the Disqualification Rules to civil disqualification proceedings not expressly governed by the Disqualification Rules (which only apply to proceedings under sections 6 and 8). The CPR are not merely a new set of procedural rules. They represent (and seek to bring about) a revolution in civil procedure and the culture of civil litigation on a grand scale. As such, it is likely to be some time before the full ramifications of the CPR are clear and settled. However, it is worth making two points, one of a general nature and a second which relates more specifically to disqualification proceedings:

(1) Even prior to the adoption of the CPR, the judiciary were encouraged to apply the old rules in accordance with the new spirit. It is therefore wrong to assume that the adoption of the CPR represents a completely fresh start and clear break away from past practice, procedures and attitudes.

(2) Civil disqualification proceedings have always, to some extent, mirrored the approach to civil litigation now enshrined in the CPR. Cases have generally been brought before a judge fairly speedily and the technique of case management is not entirely novel as far as disqualification proceedings are concerned. Having said that, the way in which the court exercises its case management powers is likely to change. The exercise of case management techniques pre-CPR did not prevent a significant number of applications to strike out for delay, nor did it prevent the Court of Appeal expressing concerns about delay, cost and over-elaboration (see the discussion of *Westmid Packing* in para. 6.24 below).

The Disqualification Practice Direction

6.23   In considering the effect of the Disqualification Practice Direction, it is important to bear in mind that a practice direction may serve any one or more of three different functions:

(1) A practice direction may simply recite other provisions of law or practice as an *aide memoire* rather than create any new practice and procedure. To the extent that the Disqualification Practice Direction sets out provisions of the Disqualification Rules in relation to proceedings to which those rules apply, it is not a source of law with regard to practice and procedure. The power to make practice directions of this type derives from the court's inherent jurisdiction to regulate its own practice.

(2) As was the case before the Civil Procedure Act 1997 came into force, the court may, under its inherent jurisdiction, issue practice directions which regulate its own practice. An example of this sort of practice direction (which to an extent overlaps with (1) above) is the provision in paragraph 13.4 of the Disqualification Practice Direction that the court will normally sit in private when hearing a summary application under the *Carecraft* procedure.[45]

(3) Under the Civil Procedure Act 1997, practice directions may, in certain circumstances, modify, vary or disapply provisions of the CPR. This is a wholly new extension to the concept of practice directions which could not previously be used to change rules of procedure laid down by statutory instrument. Sec-

---

[45] On which, see generally Chap. 8.

tion 1 of the Civil Procedure Act 1997 sets out the relevant rule-making powers with regard to civil procedure generally. In so doing, section 1 expressly incorporates the provisions in Schedule 1 of the same Act. Paragraph 6 of Schedule 1 contains the most significant power. It states that the Civil Procedure Rules may, instead of providing for any matter, refer to provisions made or to be made about that matter by directions. It follows that rules of procedure, which formerly could only be made by statutory instrument, can now be made by practice direction as long as the relevant rules in the CPR, themselves made by statutory instrument, so provide. It also follows that both the jurisdiction to change rules of procedure and the distinction between court practice and court procedure are now blurred. In some cases, it is therefore necessary to consider whether or not a specific provision of the Disqualification Practice Direction contains a power for which there is authority under, for example CPR, r. 8.1(6). It should also be noted that there is a further provision relevant to practice directions in the Civil Procedure Act. In combination, paragraph 3 of Schedule 1 and section 5(1) provide that practice directions may be made governing the matters relating to transfer set out in paragraph 3 of Schedule 1.

The spirit of the CPR

6.24   As indicated above, the general concerns underlying the Woolf reforms and the encouragement to address public concern in relation to cost and delay in civil litigation, found judicial voice before the CPR came in. In *Re Westmid Packing Services Ltd, Secretary of State for Trade and Industry v. Griffiths*, the following observations were made by the Court of Appeal in relation to disqualification proceedings:

"... [W]e wish to discourage the belief that there is a complicated, arcane and inflexible code of evidential rules applicable in [disqualification] cases. In most cases the essential thing will be for the court, with the assistance of the parties, to use common sense and to adopt a practical and flexible approach to case management, so as to confine the evidence to that which is probative..."[46]

It was also said:

"We are concerned at the delay in the hearing of these cases... We feel that over-elaboration in the preparation and hearing of these cases and a technical approach as to what evidence is and is not admissible is contributing to delay. What is required and what the court should confine the parties to, is sufficient evidence to enable the court to adopt a broad brush approach."[47]

In *Re Barings plc (No. 5), Secretary of State for Trade and Industry v. Baker*, Jonathan Parker J. relied on these passages in connection with his refusal to admit certain alleged "expert" evidence.[48] The passages do have to be with treated with caution however. An overly "broad brush" approach may lead to the invocation of Article 6 of the European Convention on Human Rights. In addition, some provisions of the CPR have already been challenged as *ultra vires*.[48a]

[46] [1998] 2 All E.R. 124 at 132, [1998] 2 B.C.L.C. 646 at 656, [1998] B.C.C. 836 at 844.
[47] [1998] 2 All E.R. 124 at 134–135, [1998] 2 B.C.L.C. 646 at 658, [1998] B.C.C. 836 at 846.
[48] [1999] 1 B.C.L.C. 433 at 494.
[48a] See *e.g. Burrells Wharf Freeholds Ltd v. Galliard Homes Ltd*, unreported, July 1, 1999; *General Mediterranean Holdings SA v Patel*, unreported, July 19, 1999.

CONDUCT BEFORE PROCEEDINGS ARE COMMENCED

General points

6.25   Under the CPR, considerable emphasis is placed on the behaviour of the parties to litigation before proceedings are issued and the pre-action behaviour of the parties is something which the courts are required to consider and take into account. In particular, the intention is for "pre-action protocols" to be produced with a view to encouraging (a) more pre-action contact between the parties; (b) better and earlier exchange of information; (c) better pre-action investigation by both sides; (d) the parties to reach a position where they will be able to settle cases fairly and easily without recourse to litigation; (e) efficient and expeditious conduct of proceedings in the event that litigation does become necessary. Allowing for the fact that it is not, as yet, possible for the parties to "settle" proceedings by agreeing a disqualification by consent or for the Secretary of State to accept undertakings from the defendant not to be a director or take part in the management of a company etc., these aims are ones that the courts have been pursuing for some time. Moreover, the courts have expressed concern about the cost of disqualification proceedings and the way in which such proceedings can bear heavily upon defendants. Thus, for example, in *Re Moonlight Foods (U.K.) Ltd, Secretary of State for Trade and Industry v. Hickling*, His Honour Judge Weeks Q.C. had this to say:

> "At this stage I want to say a little about the [claimant's] duties. It is accepted that these are not ordinary adversarial proceedings but have an element of public interest and may entail penal consequences. It follows that there is a duty on the applicant to present the case against each [defendant] fairly. Many of these applications go by default or are defended by litigants in person, and the practice is for an official in the Department of Trade and Industry to swear a short affidavit referring to charges, specified in a detailed affidavit sworn by the receiver or liquidator. In my judgment that second affidavit should not omit significant available evidence in favour of any [defendant]. It should attempt to deal with any explanation already proffered by any of the [defendants]. It should endeavour to apportion responsibility as between the [defendants] and it should avoid sweeping statements for which there is no evidence. I do not know who drafted the receiver's affidavit in the present case, but it does seem to me to fall down on all four counts."[49]

6.26   In many cases, the Secretary of State depends heavily on the reporting insolvency practitioner to point up matters such as explanations of conduct which have already been offered and evidence which may favour a defendant. Nevertheless, if a pre-action protocol is formulated for disqualification proceedings, it would undoubtedly assist in minimising the problems which materialised in the *Moonlight Foods* case. Even in the absence of a specific pre-action protocol, the Practice Direction on protocols states (at paragraph 4) that:

> "In cases not covered by any approved protocol, the court will expect the parties, in accordance with the overriding objective and the matters referred to in CPR, r. 1.1(2)(a), (b) and (c), to act reasonably in exchanging information and documents relevant to the claim and generally in trying to avoid the necessity for the start of proceedings."

---

[49] [1996] B.C.C. 678 at 690.

The relevant sanctions are, in the context of disqualification proceedings, likely to be costs-based. Even in the absence of a specific pre-action protocol, it is suggested that there are likely to be changes in the way that disqualification proceedings are prepared and in the amount of contact between the parties before proceedings are commenced. As such, it is unlikely that the practice of sending out a "ten-day letter" under section 16 (see below) literally ten days before proceedings are to be commenced which contains very little information about the grounds of the claim and in circumstances where there has been no other contact between the parties, will remain the norm.

CDDA, s. 16(1): the "ten-day letter"

Mandatory or directory?

6.27   Section 16(1) of the CDDA starts with the words:

"A person intending to apply for the making of a disqualification order by the court having jurisdiction to wind up a company shall give not less than ten days' notice of his intention to the person against whom the order is sought..."

The effect of section 16(1) is that the claimant in civil disqualification proceedings brought under CDDA, ss 2(2)(a), 3, 4, 6 and 8[50] is required to give the intended defendant at least ten days' notice of his intention to commence the proceedings.[51] The first point which arises in relation to section 16(1) is whether the requirement for the defendant to be served with a "ten-day letter" is mandatory or directory. In *Re Cedac Ltd, Secretary of State for Trade and Industry v. Langridge*,[52] the defendant received the ten-day letter on April 11, 1989. Proceedings under section 6 were then issued on April 21, 1989. In the earlier case of *Re Jaymar Management Ltd*,[53] it was held that the period of 10 days must be calculated by excluding both the day on which the notice is given and the day on which proceedings are to be commenced. Accordingly, in *Cedac*, notice should have been given no later than April 10, 1989. The short question was whether or not this failure to comply strictly with section 16(1) rendered the proceedings a nullity or whether it was merely a procedural irregularity which the court, in its discretion, could excuse. On the facts, the point was extremely significant. If the failure to comply with the letter of section 16(1) rendered the proceedings a nullity, the Secretary of State could only have commenced fresh proceedings with the permission of the court as the two-year period for commencement in section 7(2) had long since expired.[54] In *Jaymar Management*, Harman J. held that non-compliance with section

---

[50] In relation to section 8 proceedings and section 6 proceedings in the High Court (see sections 6(3)(d) and 8(3)), this rests on the assumption that the High Court is treated as a "court having jurisdiction to wind up a company" under section 16(1). In any event, see the *dictum* of Balcombe L.J. in *Re Cedac Ltd, Secretary of State for Trade and Industry v. Langridge* [1991] Ch. 402, [1991] B.C.L.C. 543, [1991] B.C.C. 148 to the effect that a "ten-day letter" does not have to be served when the application for a disqualification order is made to a court other than the winding up court, "although doubtless the rules of natural justice will require that the person concerned should be given some notice that the court is contemplating making a disqualification order". In the context it appears that he was probably referring to *criminal* disqualification proceedings under sections 2 and 5 but his remark would apply more widely if section 8 cases and cases where section 6(3)(d) applied were held not to fall within section 16. On this point see also *Re Ambery Metal Form Components Ltd* [1999] B.C.C. 336.

[51] For the position in section 10 cases, which are not directly governed by section 16(1), see *dictum* of Balcombe L.J. in *Re Cedac Ltd, Secretary of State for Trade and Industry v. Langridge* [1991] Ch. 402, [1991] B.C.L.C. 543, [1991] B.C.C. 148 to the effect that the rules of natural justice require the defendant to be given some notice and see brief discussion in Chap. 9.

[52] [1991] Ch. 402, [1991] B.C.L.C. 543, [1991] B.C.C. 148, CA (reversing. *Re Cedac Ltd* [1990] B.C.C. 555).

[53] [1990] B.C.L.C. 617, [1990] B.C.C. 303.

[54] See Chap. 7.

16(1) went to jurisdiction and so rendered the proceedings a nullity. However, by a majority, the Court of Appeal in *Cedac* (effectively overruling *Jaymar Management*) held that section 16(1) was directory rather than mandatory and that, as a consequence, the failure to comply was a procedural irregularity that did not affect the validity of the proceedings.

6.28   The following points were made in support of this conclusion in the majority judgments:

(1) It was noted that the language in section 16(1) ("... shall not give less than ten days notice...") is mandatory but that there is no provision in the CDDA specifying what is to happen if notice is not given. It was also noted that section 16(1) could be traced back as far as section 33(3) of the Companies Act 1947[55] and that, while it appeared to be procedural rather than substantive in nature, it had always been in the primary legislation and not in rules made under the legislation.

(2) Although the language of section 16(1) is mandatory, the whole purpose of the CDDA must be considered and the importance of the provision that has been disregarded and the relation of that provision to the general object intended to be secured by the CDDA assessed in determining what are the legal consequences of breach. The correct approach is not to construe the provision in isolation to ascertain whether it is mandatory or directory. The court has to look at the purpose of the statute as a whole and should not decide the issue by simply stating that the provision is in mandatory or imperative form.[56]

(3) In Balcombe L.J.'s words, "... the purpose of the [CDDA] is to protect the public and its scope is the prevention of persons who have previously misconducted themselves in relation to companies, or have otherwise shown themselves as unfit to be concerned in the management of a company, from being so concerned". The object of the "ten-day letter" is the protection of the person against whom a disqualification application is to be made. It is necessary to conduct a balancing exercise between these two objects. In this respect, it is significant that the protection conferred by section 16(1) is limited for the following reasons: (a) notice is only required in relation to proceedings in a court having jurisdiction to wind up a company, *i.e.* it is not required in all proceedings brought under the CDDA; (b) the "ten-day letter" does not have to specify the grounds on which the application is to be made; (c) the period of the notice is too short for the intended defendant to be able to do much. On point (c), Legatt L.J. had this to say:

> "It does not enable [the intended defendant] to equip himself to answer the proceedings when served, nor give him much warning of them, nor enable him to do anything that without them he would be unable to do."

As such, in arriving at a proper balance, Legatt L.J. felt content to characterise the "ten-day letter" as one which is "intended to inform of intentions rather than protect rights".

---

[55] See subsequently, Companies Act 1948, s. 188(3); Insolvency Act 1976, s. 9(3); Companies Act 1985, Sched. 12, Pt. I, paras 1, 7; Insolvency Act 1985, s. 108(2)(b).
[56] See *Howard v. Boddington* (1877) 2 P.D. 203; *Montreal Street Railway Co. v. Normandin* [1917] A.C. 170; *London & Clydeside Estates Ltd v. Aberdeen District Council* [1980] 1 W.L.R. 182 and *Re T (A Minor)* [1986] Fam. 160. For a more recent discussion see *R. v. Immigration Appeal Tribunal ex. parte Jeyeanthan* [1999] 3 All E.R. 231.

(4) In all the cases to which section 16(1) applies (see above), except for applications under section 6, the CDDA imposes no time period in which proceedings are required to be commenced. Thus, if the requirement in section 16(1) were mandatory, and failure to comply rendered the subsequent proceedings a nullity, the Secretary of State (or whoever) could simply relaunch a fresh set of proceedings by serving the requisite "ten-day letter" correctly. In the words of Balcombe L.J., it is difficult to conceive that Parliament intended so pointless and wasteful a result.

6.29 It is fair to say that *Cedac* settles the point notwithstanding Nourse L.J.'s vigorous dissent.[57] However, it should be noted that Legatt L.J. accepted[58] that if the Secretary of State refrained altogether from complying with section 16(1), the failure to give due notice would enable the director to apply for, and if the court thought fit obtain, an order striking out the proceedings even though the provision was merely directory.

Contents of "ten-day letter"

6.30 In *Cedac*, both Balcombe and Legatt L.JJ. described the "ten-day letter" as "an unparticularised letter before action". It is clear in the light of *Cedac* and on the wording of section 16(1) that the letter need do no more than indicate that proceedings are to be commenced. The usual practice is for the letter simply to state that it is the claimant's intention to apply for a disqualification order under the relevant section of the CDDA, to name the relevant company or companies and to recite the terms of the order sought. There is no obligation on the claimant to specify the grounds or basis on which the order is to be sought. In *Re Surrey Leisure Ltd, Official Receiver v. Keam*,[59] the first defendant applied to strike out a set of section 6 proceedings on the ground that alleged non-compliance with section 16(1) vitiated the proceedings. The proceedings were brought in relation to the first defendant's conduct as a director of two lead companies within an insolvent group. However, the "ten-day letter", which was otherwise properly served, only made reference to one of these companies. Jonathan Parker J. dismissed the first defendant's application. He concluded that the "ten-day letter" complied with section 16(1):

"Section 16(1) contains no specific provisions as to what the required notice is to contain, save that it is to be not less than ten days of the would be [claimant's] intention to seek a disqualification order against the recipient 'by a court having jurisdiction to wind up a company'. The expression 'a company' in this context plainly refers to the lead company or companies. In my judgment, given the absence of any further specific statutory requirements as to the content of the notice, to hold that in order to comply with section 16(1) a notice must specify which is (or are) to be the lead company (or companies) in the intended proceedings would be to write into the sub-section a requirement which, for whatever reason, Parliament has not thought fit to include."[60]

It is likely that practice in relation to these so-called "unparticularised letters before action" will change and develop in the new legal culture. It is doubtful, given the

[57] On which see discussion in Chap. 2.
[58] Based on a concession by the Secretary of State. It was also common ground in *Surrey Leisure* (discussed below) that the court has such a discretion.
[59] [1999] 1 B.C.L.C. 731.
[60] *ibid.*, 737–738. The Court of Appeal subsequently upheld the judge's decision: see [1999] B.C.C. 847 from p. 854.

emphasis in the CPR on pre-action contact between potential litigants (discussed above) and the likely impact of the Human Rights Act 1998, that the practice described will remain unmodified.[61]

PARTIES TO PROCEEDINGS

The general position

6.31   As regards claimants for disqualification orders, the position in the civil courts is as follows:

(1) Applications for the making of a disqualification order under sections 2 to 4 (inclusive) can be brought by any of the Secretary of State for Trade and Industry, the official receiver,[62] or by the liquidator or any past or present member or creditor of a company in relation to which that person has committed or is alleged to have committed an offence or other default (CDDA, s. 16(2)). There must be a question as to the extent to which it could ever be proper for a liquidator to make such an application and, if it could be, in what circumstances it would be proper. In the case of corporate members or corporate creditors there may be question marks over the company's capacity to bring disqualification proceedings and, even assuming that the company has capacity, over whether the directors would be acting properly in causing the company to launch such proceedings.

(2) Although section 16(2) envisages that an application for the making of a disqualification order under section 5 of the CDDA can be made to the civil courts, this seems inconsistent with the express wording of section 5 itself (which confers jurisdiction only on criminal courts) and should probably be ignored.

(3) Applications for the making of a disqualification order under sections 6 and 8 can only be made by the Secretary of State or, under section 6, if the Secretary of State so directs in the case of a person who is or has been a director of a company which is being wound up by the court in England and Wales, by the official receiver (CDDA, ss 7(1), 8(1)).

(4) The civil court can act of its own motion under section 10 but equally the claimant in relevant proceedings under section 213 or 214 Insolvency Act 1986 could apply for an order. This again raises the question of whether it is ever proper for a liquidator to apply (and if so in what circumstances). In any event, it is suggested that the Secretary of State, as the person responsible for regulating companies, would have the ability to intervene[63] and that, when making (or being minded to make) a relevant declaration triggering jurisdiction under section 10, the court should always require notification to be given to the Secretary of State to give him a opportunity to apply and/or make representations (as happened in *Re Brian D Pierson (Contractors) Ltd*).[64]

---

[61] These factors are also likely to be relevant on applications for permission to commence section 6 proceedings out of time under section 7(2) on which see generally Chap. 7.
[62] For an analysis of the position of the official receiver as litigant see *Re Minotaur Data Systems Ltd, Official Receiver v. Brunt* [1999] 1 W.L.R. 1129, [1999] 3 All E.R. 122, [1999] B.C.C. 57, [1999] B.P.I.R. 560, CA.
[63] By analogy with *Adams v. Adams* [1971] P. 188 (especially at 197–198), [1970] 3 All E.R. 572.
[64] [1999] B.C.C. 26.

The Secretary of State or official receiver as claimant

6.32 When the Secretary of State is the claimant he or she will not usually take decisions personally but will act by a relevant officer under what is often referred to as the *Carltona* principle.[65] In practice, applications under sections 6–7 of the CDDA are dealt with by the Insolvency Service. In some cases, proceedings will be commenced in the name of the Secretary of State but an official receiver will have actual conduct of them. As a general rule, the official receiver may act by deputy official receivers (see the discussion of the relevant statutory provisions in *Re Homes Assured Corporation plc, Official Receiver v. Dobson*).[66]

Before proceedings can be commenced under section 6 or 8 of the CDDA, it must appear to the Secretary of State that it is expedient in the public interest that a disqualification order under the relevant section should be made. It is suggested that the same test would, in practice, apply to applications made by the Secretary of State under other sections of the CDDA and also to the question of the continuation of such proceedings once commenced. The latter question is considered further in Chapter 8. In principle, the question of whether or not it is expedient in the public interest to commence or continue proceedings will involve two issues: (a) the likelihood of the proceedings being successful and (b) the wider public interest (or public interests). However, even if the prospects of success are less than 50 per cent it might still be expedient in the public interest to commence proceedings and equally, if the prospects of success are more than 50 per cent it may not be expedient in the public interest to commence proceedings. If the proceedings are bound to fail or are for some other reason an abuse of the court's process, it would probably be inappropriate to commence or continue with them.

There is little doubt that in exercising his powers under the CDDA, the decisions of the Secretary of State are susceptible to judicial review. If the question is whether or not existing proceedings are bound to fail or are otherwise an abuse, the matter can be dealt with within the course of the proceedings rather than requiring a separate application for judicial review.[67] If the question is whether the Secretary of State has acted unreasonably in assessing the wider public interest (as referred to in (b) as contrasted with (a) above), and whether the result is that proceedings are commenced or are not commenced, the courts have shown a marked reluctance to interfere.[68]

The wrong claimant

6.33 On occasions, the Secretary of State directs the official receiver to commence proceedings under section 6 in circumstances where, the company not being in compulsory liquidation, such proceedings must be commenced and prosecuted in the name of the Secretary of State (section 7(1)). There have been cases where the official receiver

---

[65] See *Carltona Ltd v. Commissioner of Works* [1943] 2 All E.R. 560 and *Re Golden Chemical Products Ltd* [1976] 1 Ch. 300.
[66] [1994] 2 B.C.L.C. 71, [1993] B.C.C. 573.
[67] See in this respect the concession made in *Re Blackspur Group plc, Re Atlantic Computer Systems plc* [1998] 1 W.L.R. 422, [1998] 1 B.C.L.C. 676, [1998] B.C.C. 11, CA.
[68] See *R v. Secretary of State for Trade and Industry, ex. parte Lonrho plc* [1992] B.C.C. 325, CA (Secretary of State's refusal to apply under for orders under section 8 in the light of damning inspectors' report not perverse); *Re Atlantic Computer Systems plc* [1998] 1 W.L.R. 422, [1998] 1 B.C.L.C. 676, [1998] B.C.C. 11, CA (Secretary of State entitled to continue proceedings against defendant notwithstanding the offer of undertakings); *Re Barings plc (No. 3), Secretary of State for Trade and Industry v. Baker* [1999] 1 All E.R. 311 (*sub nom. (No. 2)*); [1999] 1 B.C.L.C. 226, ChD and CA (Secretary of State entitled to proceed against defendant even though he had already been dealt with by the relevant financial services regulator in relation to similar charges); *Re Launchexcept Ltd, Secretary of State for Trade and Industry v. Tillman* [1999] B.C.C. 703, CA (Secretary of State entitled to proceed against defendant in relation to a lead company which had given rise to different collateral allegations in earlier disqualification proceedings).

has mistakenly commenced the proceedings in his own name. On the problem coming to light, the Secretary of State's usual response has been to apply to amend the proceedings by substituting himself for the official receiver as claimant. The first such case to be reported was *Re Probe Data Systems Ltd.*[69] In *Probe Data*, Millett J. refused to grant the Secretary of State permission to amend the proceedings under RSC Ord. 20, r. 3 (by means of correcting the name of the claimant). However, in the later case of *Re NP Engineering and Security Products Ltd, Official Receiver v. Pafundo*[70] the Court of Appeal permitted substitution of the Secretary of State for the official receiver under RSC Ord. 15, r. 6(2), a rule not relied on in *Probe Data*. The same result as in *NP Engineering* would be likely to follow under what is now CPR, Pt 19.

The number of defendants

6.34   It is well established that there may be more than one defendant in a single set of disqualification proceedings. However, in appropriate circumstances, and as a matter of fairness in case management, the court may decide that the proceedings should continue against one defendant even if for some reason, such as illness or the existence of parallel criminal proceedings, the proceedings should not continue for the time being against another defendant. Thus, in *Re Land Travel Ltd, Secretary of State for Trade and Industry v. Tjolle,* Chadwick J. decided, in the circumstances, that it was appropriate to split the trial so that the proceedings continued against one defendant separately from those against the other two.[71] Moreover, in *EDC v. United Kingdom,*[72] the European Commission of Human Rights held that a defendant's right to a fair trial under Article 6 of the European Convention was infringed in circumstances where disqualification proceedings had been adjourned against him and his co-defendants pending the outcome of parallel criminal proceedings in which he was not a party. The upshot is that, in similar circumstances, the court may very well decide that there is little option but to split the trial.

The number of lead companies in section 6 cases

6.35   The concepts of "lead" and "collateral" companies are discussed at length in Chapter 3. In the case of *Re Surrey Leisure Ltd, Official Receiver v. Keam,*[73] a submission was made on behalf of the defendant to the effect that, on its proper construction, the CDDA does not allow a claimant to nominate more than one lead company in proceedings under section 6. The submission was roundly rejected by the judge:

> "I see no warrant for construing the [CDDA] in that restrictive manner. It has been said many times in the authorities that the purpose of the [CDDA] is to prevent persons acting as directors who are unfit to do so... That being so, I can see no reason in principle why [a claimant] for a disqualification order who seeks to establish unfitness in relation to more than one company should be obliged to limit himself to naming only one of those companies as the lead company, leaving the other or others to be treated as collateral companies, since by doing so he might be limiting his chances of obtaining an order. Nor can I find anything in the [CDDA], on its true construction, which justifies such an artificial, indeed arbitrary result."[74]

---

[69] [1989] B.C.L.C. 561, (1989) 5 B.C.C. 384.
[70] [1998] 1 B.C.L.C. 208.
[71] For the background see Jacob J.'s judgment in the case at [1998] 1 B.C.L.C. 333, [1998] B.C.C. 282.
[72] [1998] B.C.C. 370.
[73] [1999] 1 B.C.L.C. 731 (affirmed by the Court of Appeal: see [1999] B.C.C. 847 from p. 854.
[74] *ibid,* at 736–737. The Court of Appeal was struck by the fact that the official receiver could, in any event, issue separate proceedings for each lead company and then consolidate the proceedings.

The effect is that the claimant may name as many lead companies in section 6 proceedings as he wishes subject only to the requirement that (a) such companies have "become insolvent" within the meaning of section 6(2) and (b) the proceedings are brought within two-years or otherwise with the permission of the court under section 7(2).

Applications for the Making of a Disqualification Order

Overview of procedure on an application for the making of a disqualification order

6.36   The history of the matter is conveniently summarised by Hoffmann L.J. in *Re Rex Williams Leisure plc, Secretary of State for Trade and Industry v. Warren:*[75]

"... [W]hen a power to disqualify directors was first introduced in section 217 of the Companies Act 1929, the procedure was assimilated to that of the misfeasance summons, a summary procedure which went back to the Companies Act 1862: see rule 66 of the Companies (Winding up) Rules 1929. Misfeasance summonses had originally followed the traditional Chancery procedure of having all the evidence on affidavit, but in 1921 the Companies Court adopted a more common law approach. Astbury J. issued a Practice Note...:

'In a recent case tried in this court various defects in the present practice relating to the trial of misfeasance summonses ... were made apparent. The practice of allowing witnesses to give their evidence in chief by affidavits, prepared or settled for them by others, in cases where real disputes of fact exist and/or where various charges of misfeasance or breach of trust are involved, is open to grave objection, and when numerous or complicated issues of law or fact exist, the points relied upon are under the practice at present prevailing, as and when occasion demands, amended or raised for the first time and from time to time during the progress of the trial, which causes confusion, recalling of witnesses, possible injustice, waste of time and increased costs ... in future the practice in these cases shall be as follows: On the return of the summons the Registrar shall give directions as to whether points of claim and defence are to be delivered or not, as to the taking of evidence wholly or in part by affidavit or orally, as to cross-examination, and generally as to the procedure on the summons. No report or affidavit shall be made or filed until the Registrar shall so direct.'

Rule 66 of the Companies (Winding-up) Rules 1929 reflected this Practice Note, providing that no affidavit or report was to be filed in advance of the first appointment before the registrar and giving him a wide discretion as to the taking of evidence wholly or in part by affidavit or orally."

6.37   Hoffmann L.J. was referring here to the manner in which the relevant procedural rules have changed from time to time. His conclusion was that the Disqualification Rules are only part of a general trend towards a greater emphasis on written procedure in advance of the hearing. As he put it:

---

[75] [1994] Ch. 350, [1994] 3 W.L.R. 745, [1994] 4 All E.R. 27, [1994] 2 B.C.L.C. 555, [1994] B.C.C. 551, CA.

"The advantage of allowing both sides to discover each other's cases in detail before trial and cross-examination is perceived to outweigh the loss of spontaneity and the increase in costs in the pre-trial stage."

Since *Rex Williams* was decided the CPR have themselves further accentuated this trend.

Procedural timetable

6.38   The Disqualification Rules lay down a procedural timetable for applications for the making of disqualification orders under sections 6 and 8 of the CDDA. The Disqualification Practice Direction has largely replicated this regime for other civil applications under sections 2, 3 and 4. The procedure is broadly that under CPR, Pt 8 but with modifications.[76] There is no power to alter the procedure so that any proceedings become Part 7 proceedings.[77] The relevant timetable is as follows.

The Claim Form

6.39   A number of points arise regarding the Claim Form:

(1) The Claim Form is in a form prescribed by the Disqualification Practice Direction (see paragraph 4.2). The following matters are relevant:

(a) The heading will be entitled in the matter of the relevant company (which in cases brought under section 6 will be the name of the lead company or companies only) and in the matter of the CDDA (Disqualification Practice Direction, para. 5.1).

(b) The Claim Form is required to contain certain endorsements (Disqualification Rules, r. 4; Disqualification Practice Direction, para. 6.1). These endorsements are in the nature of notes for defendants setting out the applicable rules, the period of disqualification which can be imposed, the section of the CDDA pursuant to which the application is made and the time limits for filing evidence. Reference should also be made to rule 4 of the Disqualification Rules which provides that on the first hearing of the Claim Form in section 6 and 8 proceedings, the court can impose a period of disqualification of up to five years.

(c) The prescribed form of Claim Form sets out notes to assist the claimant in filling it in. These notes are not an integral part of the Claim Form and a defendant would have no grounds for complaint if they did not appear.

(2) In High Court cases, the Claim Form should be issued out of the office of the Companies Court registrar or a Chancery District Registry and, in the county court, out of the relevant county court office (Disqualification Practice Direction, para. 4.1).

---

[76] Disqualification Rules, rr. 2, 5 and 6; Disqualification Practice Direction, para. 4.2. See also CPR, r. 8.1(6).
[77] Disqualification Rules, r.2(3); Disqualification Practice Direction, para. 4.2.

(3) On issue of the Claim Form, the evidence relied upon in support of the claim must be filed with the court.[78] The evidence will be on affidavit or affirmation. Any exhibits to the evidence are lodged with the court but not formally "filed": they are returned at the conclusion of the case. In the case of proceedings brought in the name of the official receiver the evidence may take the form of a report by him. This form of evidence is considered further below.

(4) On issue of the Claim Form a hearing date is given for the first hearing of the application, before a district judge or the Companies Court registrar (as appropriate), which will be not less than eight weeks from the date of issue of the Claim Form (Disqualification Rules, r. 7(1); Disqualification Practice Direction, para. 4.3).

Service of Claim Form

6.40   A number of points also arise regarding service:

(1) The Claim Form, together with copies of the evidence in support and an acknowledgment of service must be served on the defendant (Disqualification Practice Direction, paras 9.3(3), 7.2, 7.4). The acknowledgment of service is again in a specially prescribed form (Disqualification Practice Direction, para. 8), reflecting the different procedural steps under the disqualification jurisdiction contrasted with an ordinary CPR, Pt 8 claim.

(2) Service of the Claim Form is the responsibility of the applicant. CPR, Pt 6 will apply in general except that the Claim Form may be served by first class post to the defendant's last known address and, if it is so served, the date of service is deemed to be the seventh day following the date on which the Claim Form was posted, unless the contrary is proved (Disqualification Rules, r. 5(1); Disqualification Practice Direction, para. 7.2).

(3) There is provision for the court to order service out of the jurisdiction which is a separate regime from that under RSC Ord. 11 (Disqualification Rules, r. 5(2); Disqualification Practice Direction, para. 7.3).

Acknowledgment and defendant's evidence

6.41   The position is as follows:

(1) Within 14 days of service of the Claim Form the defendant must file and serve on the other parties the acknowledgment of service (Disqualification Rules, r. 5(3); Disqualification Practice Direction, para. 8.3). If it is not filed within the prescribed period the defendant may attend the hearing of the application but may not take part in the hearing unless the court gives permission (Disqualification Practice Direction, para. 8.4).

(2) Within 28 days of service of the Claim Form the defendant must file in court any affidavit evidence in opposition to the application, lodge in court any exhibits and (at the same time) serve copies on the claimant (Disqualification Rules, r. 6(1); Disqualification Practice Direction, para. 9.4).

---

[78] CPR, r. 8.5(1); Disqualification Rules, r. 3(1) and Disqualification Practice Direction, para. 9.3. With the advent of the CPR, it is unlikely that the court will be sympathetic to "holding" evidence being filed on the basis that it will be supplemented later. For examples of judicial approach under the old rules see *Re Crestjoy Products Ltd* [1990] B.C.L.C. 677, [1990] B.C.C. 23 and *Re Jazzgold Ltd* [1994] 1 B.C.L.C. 38, [1992] B.C.C. 587.

(3) In cases where there is more than one defendant, each defendant is required to serve his evidence on the other defendants unless the court otherwise orders (Disqualification Practice Direction, para. 9.5). The court might otherwise order in cases where mutual exchange is more appropriate (for example, where there is a "cut throat" defence) or where one defendant is ready to serve but another is not. It is sensible practice for the defendants to agree a procedural course, or failing that, at least agree what should happen pending the first hearing with a view to saving the costs of an unnecessary application to the court. As the timetable envisages the service of evidence in reply by the claimant, it may be necessary to involve the claimant in any relevant discussion.

Further evidence of claimant

6.42 Within 14 days of receiving the defendant's evidence, the claimant should then serve any further evidence by way of evidence in reply (Disqualification Rules, r. 6(2); Disqualification Practice Direction, para. 9.6).

Extensions of time

6.43 So far as is possible, the timetable laid down by the Disqualification Rules or the Disqualification Practice Direction should be followed and all evidence filed before the first hearing (Disqualification Practice Direction, para. 9.8). It is to be hoped that the greater encouragement to consider matters before proceedings are launched will increase the possibility of achieving this. Nevertheless, there may be circumstances in which the timetable cannot be met. In those circumstances, there are two options:

(1) The parties themselves may be able to agree extensions of time. Prior to the first hearing, extensions may be made by written agreement. After the first hearing, extensions of time are governed by CPR, r. 2.11 and 29.5 (see Disqualification Practice Direction, para. 9.7).

(2) The court will regulate the procedural timetable as part of its case management function (Disqualification Practice Direction, para. 11).

The first hearing

6.44 The position is as follows:

(1) The date for the first hearing will have been fixed on the issue of the Claim Form for a date not less than eight weeks away (Disqualification Rules, r. 7(1); Disqualification Practice Direction, paras 4.3 and 10.2). The first hearing will be before a district judge or the Companies Court registrar in either case sitting in public (Disqualification Rules, r. 7(2); Disqualification Practice Direction, paras 4.3 and 10.2). The current practice in the Royal Courts of Justice is to list such applications for a Monday morning.

(2) On the first hearing date, the court will either determine the application or adjourn it. If the hearing is adjourned, the court will give directions and the parties should seek all interim directions that they need so far as possible with a view to avoiding the need for successive hearings (Disqualification Rules, r. 7; Disqualification Practice Direction, para. 10.4). The court's powers of case management are wide. In addition to the general powers in the CPR, the Disqualification Practice Direction highlights a number of matters which the

court and the parties should consider with regard to fixing the trial date and the like. One of the usual directions is that deponents to affidavits attend trial for cross-examination on so many days prior written notice and that, in default, their evidence is not to be read.

(3) In proceedings under sections 6 and 8, the judge is unable to disqualify for a period of more than five years on the first hearing. Accordingly, if on a provisional consideration, he takes the view that a period of more than five years is likely to be appropriate, he should adjourn the application giving reasons (Disqualification Rules, r. 7(4)(a)). The defendant, who may have decided not to defend on the basis that he is happy to accept a disqualification of five years or less, would then have an opportunity to take steps in the proceedings. If a defendant agrees or is present and is not prejudiced, there seems no reason why the hearing could not go ahead on the same day. It is suggested that failure to comply with the strict wording of the Disqualification Rules, r. 7(4) will not automatically prevent the hearing from going ahead if it is just for it to do so and that, in any event, the defendant can waive his rights under this rule.

The trial

6.45 Further procedural requirements are set out in paragraph 12 of the Disqualification Practice Direction dealing with such matters as trial bundles, skeleton arguments and other documents to be prepared by the claimant's advocate. The question of burden of proof is dealt with in Chapter 5. The court also has powers to limit evidence (see *e.g.* CPR, r. 32.1(2). Use of these powers is likely to raise questions of vires and compliance with the Human Rights Act 1998 especially in cases where the court declines to hear evidence on an issue that the parties wish to have decided. In the event that a party does not appear, the court has power to continue with the trial but there are provisions for the absent party to apply to set aside any order made in his absence (Disqualification Rules, r. 8; Disqualification Practice Direction, para. 14 and, by analogy, CPR, r. 39.3).

Summary procedure

6.46 If at any stage the parties wish to invite the court to deal with the matter on a *Carecraft* basis, they should inform the court immediately and obtain a date for the hearing (Disqualification Practice Direction, para. 13). The question of summary hearings under *Carecraft* is dealt with in greater detail in Chapter 8.

Other matters

Disclosure

6.47 Disclosure and inspection of documents is now governed by CPR, Pt 31. To the extent that the parties have documents physically within their possession, pre-trial disclosure may come more to the fore in the light of the pre-action protocols (see para. 6.25 above). Furthermore, the parties may have to give consideration to the powers of pre-action disclosure contained in the Supreme Court Act 1981 and the County Courts Act 1984 (see CPR, rr. 31.16 to 31.17). At present, it appears that the use of these powers to order pre-action disclosure (at least against non-parties) will be the exception rather than the rule except, perhaps, in cases where an administrator or administrative receiver has sold the company's business including its records. In that case, and if voluntary co-operation is not forthcoming, the claimant may need to persuade or require the office holder to exercise his powers under section 236 of the Insolvency Act 1986 and both parties may need to invoke the statutory powers for pre-action disclosure mentioned above. On the whole, in relation to section 6 proceedings where the official receiver is not the liquidator, it is rare for the claimant to hold many, if any documents which have not been exhibited in evidence. Such documents will usually be retained by the relevant office holder although the claimant may have received documents from other sources as a result of his own enquiries. In circumstances where the office holder physically retains documents, the question arises as to whether the Secretary of State is in "control" of those documents for the purposes of CPR, r. 31.8. In most cases the defendant will simply be unaware of the actual position. In the absence of special circumstances, it seems unlikely that the existence of the power in section 7(4) of the CDDA will be held to confer "control" on the claimant. In *Re Lombard Shipping and Forwarding Ltd,*[79] it was ruled that documents held by joint administrative receivers were not within the possession, custody of power of the Secretary of State for the purpose of ordering disclosure under the old rules. This was because the court has a discretion whether or not to order an office holder to comply with a request on an application under section 7(4) and so the Secretary of State has no absolute right to insist on production. However, it will be interesting to see whether a different result would follow if the defendant joined the relevant office holder so that the office holder and the claimant were both before the court. In those circumstances, the court might be prepared to consider whether, as between claimant and office holder, an order under section 7(4), is appropriate. In practice, the office holder will usually make documents available for inspection by the defendant on a voluntary basis but without giving disclosure by list. This can give rise to practical problems. First, the documents will often be in a chaotic state. Secondly, the office holder may seek to charge the defendant for making the documents available and/or for supervising the inspection. On the first point, as a general rule, the court is unlikely to require the preparation of a list as a means of saving time in that the defendant can usually be expected to have some acquaintance with his company's documents. It should be possible to deal with the issue of supervision by requiring the defendant's legal representative to attend and give any undertaking as to non-alteration and non-removal. The costs of getting the documents out of storage may be more problematic. If agreement cannot be reached, the defendant may have to consider issuing a witness summons to compel the office holder to produce the documents or an order under the CPR that the claimant should bear the relevant costs, such costs then being treated as costs in the proceedings. Where the official receiver is the liquidator he is technically in a position to make disclosure by way of list. However, unless the documents are extensive, it is likely that if he makes them available for inspection, the court would hold that any requirement of disclosure by list would be disproportionate given that the defendant ought to have at a least some passing acquaintance with the company's documents and should be able to identify those documents he wants to see.

Further information

6.48   The old difference between further and better particulars of pleading (now statements of case) and interrogatories has now gone (see now CPR, Pt 18). It should be noted that while, under the old rules, interrogatories were refused in *Re Sutton Glassworks Ltd,*[80] this did not mean that further information was not forthcoming in that case, as the Secretary of State had volunteered it. It is likely that if such infor-

---

[79] [1993] B.C.L.C. 238, [1992] B.C.C. 700.
[80] [1997] 1 B.C.L.C. 26.

mation was not produced voluntarily, the court would now be more willing to order its production in the spirit of the CPR. In making or responding to requests for information under CPR, Pt 18, it is essential to pay attention to the accompanying Practice Direction. One trap for the unwary is the power under paragraph 5 which enables the maker of a request, in certain circumstances, to apply for and obtain a court order without notice to the other side.

Summary judgment and/or strike out

6.49 Summary judgment was not available in originating summons procedure under the old law. However, the effect of Part 24 of the CPR is that the procedure for summary judgment is now applicable. It is not yet clear whether this will become a useful tool in disqualification proceedings.

There is power in CPR, r. 3.4 to strike out a statement of case and it is clear that this power can be used as a disciplinary measure, for example, in cases where there has been a failure to comply with rules of court, practice directions or court orders. Rule 3.4 refers expressly to statements of case but doubtless it will apply to affidavit evidence and claim forms. There are two other principal grounds on which the court can exercise the power to strike out: (a) where the statement of case discloses no reasonable grounds for bringing or defending the claim; and (b) where the statement of case is an abuse of the court's process or is otherwise likely to obstruct the just disposal of the proceedings. Going by the old law, the categories of abuse of process are not closed and it would appear that the court's jurisdiction to strike out disqualification proceedings will arise in the following (non-exhaustive) circumstances:

(1) On grounds of delay (see further discussion towards the end of Chapter 7).

(2) On grounds of double jeopardy. This point has been taken in recent cases. The case of *Re Barings plc (No. 2), Secretary of State for Trade and Industry v. Baker*[81] case involved an unsuccessful application by one of the *Barings* defendants for a stay of disqualification proceedings under section 6 of the CDDA on the ground that the issues arising had already been determined in regulatory proceedings brought against him by the Securities and Futures Authority. Moreover, on appeal those disciplinary proceedings were resolved in the defendant's favour. Although, in the event, the court refused to stay the disqualification proceedings, it is clear that, in an appropriate case, the court could strike proceedings out on this ground. Another closely connected scenario is where the issues raised in the disqualification proceedings have been aired in other civil proceedings. In *Re Thomas Christy Ltd*[81a] it was held to be an abuse of process for the claimant in proceedings against a liquidator to raise matters which had already been determined against him as the defendant in earlier disqualification proceedings. This suggests that there are circumstances where it may be an abuse of process for the claimant *or the defendant* to seek to contest points which have already been decided in other proceedings. However, since the decision in *Thomas Christy*, the courts have appeared reluctant to use this aspect of abuse of process as a means of preventing litigants from raising defences.[81b]

---

[81] [1999] 1 All E.R. 311, *sub nom. Re Barings plc (No. 3)* [1999] 1 B.C.L.C. 226, ChD and CA. See also *Re Launchexcept Ltd, Secretary of State for Trade and Industry v. Tillman* [1999] B.C.C. 703. Both cases contain a useful general test for what constitutes abuse of process.
[81a] [1994] 2 B.C.L.C. 527.
[81b] See *Bradford & Bingley Building Society v. Seddon* [1999] 1 W.L.R. 1482, CA indicating that an attempt to re-litigate an issue fully investigated and decided in earlier proceedings *may but will not necessarily* constitute an abuse of process.

(3) On grounds of loss of documents (*e.g.* by an insolvency practitioner). This category of potential abuse was raised in *Re Dexmaster Ltd*.[82] Again, while on the facts of the case the loss of documents was not regarded as being sufficiently prejudicial to justify striking out, it is clear that, in an appropriate case, there is jurisdiction.

(4) On grounds of ill health. It is possible that the court might stay or strike out proceedings against a defendant who is suffering from serious ill health. This point is discussed in the section on undertakings in Chapter 8.

Parallel proceedings

6.49A   In addition to the question of whether or not the existence of other (concluded) proceedings may make particular claims raised in disqualification proceedings susceptible to strike out on grounds of abuse, there is also the issue of the relationship between ongoing disqualification proceedings and other proceedings (civil or criminal) which, in factual terms, largely overlap. In such circumstances should the disqualification proceedings be stayed pending determination of the other proceedings? As a general rule, the position is that the court retains a discretion to stay disqualification proceedings where the continuation of those proceedings may prejudice the fairness of the other proceedings. However, the discretion should be exercised with great care and only where there is a real risk of serious prejudice leading to injustice.[82a] Although the discretion applies whether the parallel proceedings are civil, criminal or disciplinary, it is helpful to see the way in which it has been exercised in the disqualification sphere.

So far as parallel civil proceeding are concerned, the general rule is that the existence of other civil proceedings raising overlapping factual issues will not of itself be a good ground to stay disqualification proceedings. There is a public interest in disqualification proceedings being concluded speedily. In *Re Rex Williams Leisure plc*,[82b] an application to stay disqualification proceedings pending the determination of a set of civil proceedings brought by the company (acting by its administrators), and which had been dormant for almost two years, was rejected. The protection afforded to the public by the making of a disqualification order was not to wait on the determination of other claims against the director and the speed at which the parties chose to proceed with them. Having said that, there may be cases where the court would stay, or by use of its case management powers (for example, in fixing a trial date) would accommodate, another set of proceedings. One example might be where it would be unfair and unrealistic to expect the defendant to deal with both sets of proceedings at the same (or almost the same) time.

6.49B   The position regarding parallel criminal proceedings (actual or threatened) is more difficult and is likely to give rise to serious questions under Article 6 of the European Convention on Human Rights. The starting point is *Jefferson Ltd v. Bhetcha*.[82c] The mere fact that a defendant might give an indication of his likely defence to criminal charges by entering a defence in the civil proceedings was said in that case not to debar the claimant from pursuing the civil proceedings. However, the civil court has a discretion to stay the civil proceedings if justice requires. The exercise of this discretion has been considered in a number of disqualification cases. Two points commonly arise. The first is possible unfairness flowing from publicity which might be given to the disqualification proceedings (and the evidence and/or findings made in

---

[82] [1995] 2 B.C.L.C. 430.
[82a] See, albeit in a different context, *R. v. Institute of Chartered Accountants in England and Wales, ex. parte Brindle* [1994] B.C.C. 297, CA and compare *R. v. Chance ex. parte Smith* [1995] B.C.C. 1095.
[82b] [1994] Ch. 1 and 350.
[82c] [1979] 1 W.L.R. 898, [1979] 2 All E.R. 1108, CA.

such proceedings) prior to the criminal trial. The court can deal with this point by directing that the trial of the disqualification proceedings should take place after the criminal trial.[82d] It should be noted that, as the court is exercising a discretion, it will consider a number of factors including (a) the likely period of delay to the disqualification proceedings if stayed; (b) whether any undertakings have been given to protect the public in the meantime and (c) the possible impact of any delay on the trial of the disqualification proceedings (e.g. on the recollection of witnesses). The second (and, in practice, more difficult) issue, is to what extent the defendant should be obliged to file evidence in the disqualification proceedings. The question arising is whether the defendant's position in the criminal trial would be prejudiced by a requirement to file evidence in the disqualification proceedings on the ground that such evidence could (a) be put before the criminal court or (b) lead the prosecution to initiate further enquiries with a view to obtaining fresh evidence or (c) reveal the likely defence to the criminal charges and so enable the prosecution to tailor its case in the criminal proceedings accordingly. It is clear that each case will turn on its own particular facts.[82e] The one general principle that can be derived from the authorities is that the burden lies on the defendant to establish that a stay is appropriate and mere generalised allegations of possible prejudice are not likely to be persuasive.

COMMENCEMENT OF PROCEEDINGS

Timing of proceedings: the two-year time period for commencement of proceedings under section 6

6.50 Section 7(2) provides that an application for a section 6 disqualification order cannot be made later than the end of the period of two years beginning with the day on which the relevant company of which that person is or has been a director became insolvent, unless the permission of the court is first obtained. The two-year period starts to run on the day the relevant company "became insolvent" which means (a) the day the company went into liquidation (at a time when its assets were insufficient for the payment of its debts and other liabilities and the expenses of the winding up) or (b) the day an administration order was made in relation to the company or (c) the day an administrative receiver of the company was appointed (section 6(2)). The following points should be noted:

(1) Section 22(3) of the CDDA applies section 247 of the Insolvency Act 1986 "as regards references to a company's insolvency and to its going into liquidation". The effect is that in the case of compulsory winding up, a company "goes into liquidation" (and time starts to run under section 7(2)) on the date of the winding up order (unless it is already in voluntary winding up in which case time runs from the date of the earlier winding up resolution).[83]

(2) In *Re Tasbian Ltd, Official Receiver v. Nixon*, a problem arose in that two of the insolvency events in section 6(2) happened in quick succession. An administrative receiver was appointed on September 24, 1986. A compulsory wind-

---

[82d] See, e.g. *Re Landhurst Leasing plc*, July 4, 1995, Ch.D., unreported; *Re Battery Specialists (Five Star) Ltd*, February 23, 1998, Ch.D., unreported. Compare, however, *EDC v. United Kingdom* [1998] B.C.C. 370.

[82e] See, e.g. *Re Jandra Ltd*, June 19, 1995, Ch.D., unreported; . *Re Landhurst Leasing plc*, July 4, 1995, Ch.D., unreported; *Re Gemini Display Ltd*, July 19, 1996, Ch.D., unreported; *Re Parallel Computers Ltd*, October 29, 1996, Ch.D., unreported; *Secretary of State for Trade and Industry v. Jebraille*, December 20, 1997, Ch.D., unreported; *Re Battery Specialists (Five Star) Ltd*, February 23, 1998, Ch.D., unreported.

[83] *Re Walter L Jacob & Co. Ltd, Official Receiver v. Jacob* [1993] B.C.C. 512.

ing up order was made subsequently on November 10, 1986. The proceedings were commenced on November 8, 1988 within two years of the second event. The Court of Appeal held that time started to run from the happening of the first of the events mentioned in section 6(2) (here, the receivership) with the consequence that the proceedings were out of time.[84] However, both Dillon and Woolf L.JJ. suggested that where a company demonstrably returns to solvency after the first event (e.g. administration), it might fairly be said that the company only becomes insolvent for present purposes on the occurrence of the later event. On the facts of Tasbian it was not realistic to suppose that the company ever returned to solvency between September 24, 1986 and November 10, 1986. It is not entirely clear what Dillon and Woolf L.JJ. mean by a return to solvency in this context. It is suggested that a brief period of factual solvency would not be sufficient to disturb the basic rule. Thus, for example, in a situation where administrative receivers continue to trade and restore the company to factual solvency before selling off its business as a going concern, it is suggested that the administrative receivership rather than the subsequent liquidation would remain the triggering event. Indeed, apart from a situation where the first event is an administration, it is difficult to conceive of a situation where the company itself (as opposed to the company's assets and business) would be restored to financial health for these purposes. More often than not, the company will simply pass from one insolvency regime (e.g. administration or receivership) into another (usually liquidation) and any period of factual solvency in between should, it is suggested, generally be disregarded.

(3) An interim order under section 9(4) of the Insolvency Act 1986 is not an administration order within the meaning of section 6(2)(b) of the CDDA so, in a case where the Secretary of State applied for a disqualification order more than two years after the court made interim orders but within two years of the making of an administration order under section 8(3) of the Insolvency Act, the disqualification proceedings were commenced in time.[85]

(4) In the case of a company in administrative receivership, it appears that time only starts to run from the date on which the administrative receiver accepts appointment for the purposes of section 53(6)(a) of the Insolvency Act 1986.[86]

(5) If the two-year time period expires on a day when the court office is closed, the time is automatically extended to the next day on which it is open.[87]

6.51 Two other points should be mentioned. First, the two-year time period should not strictly be regarded as a limitation period. Its effect is that the application may only proceed if the court, in the exercise of what amounts to an unfettered discretion, considers that it should.[88] Secondly, section 6 proceedings are unique in this

---

[84] [1991] B.C.L.C. 54, [1990] B.C.C. 318, CA (affirming Peter Gibson J. at [1989] B.C.L.C. 720, (1989) 5 B.C.C. 729). After further litigation, the official receiver eventually obtained permission under section 7(2) to launch fresh proceedings out of time: see Re Tasbian Ltd (No. 3) [1993] B.C.L.C. 297, [1992] B.C.C. 358, CA and discussion in Chap. 7.

[85] Secretary of State for Trade and Industry v. Palmer [1993] B.C.C. 650 (Court of Session (Outer House)) affd. 1995 S.L.T. 188. For a further point arising from the particular requirements of procedure in the Scottish courts see Secretary of State for Trade and Industry v. Normand [1995] B.C.C. 158.

[86] For Scottish authority on the point see Secretary of State for Trade and Industry v. Houston 1994 S.L.T. 775 (Court of Session (Outer House)).

[87] Re Philipp & Lion Ltd [1994] 1 B.C.L.C. 739, [1994] B.C.C. 261 applying Pritam Kaur v. S Russell & Sons Ltd [1973] Q.B. 336.

[88] See further discussion in Chap. 7.

respect. In relation to all other forms of civil disqualification proceedings, the CDDA does not impose any time period for commencement. Once issued, however, proceedings will be subject to the court's powers of case management under the CPR and the Disqualification Practice Direction and Article 6 of the European Convention on Human Rights will also apply. In the light of these provisions, it is likely that a test will be developed under which it will not be permissible for stale proceedings to be commenced or continued.

Allegations of unfit conduct: sections 6 and 8

The requirement that allegations are clear

6.52   Rule 3(3) of the Disqualification Rules requires the evidence in support of an application for the making of a disqualification order under sections 6 or 8 of the CDDA to "include a statement of the matters by reference to which the defendant is alleged to be unfit to be concerned in the management of a company". A practice has developed whereby a summary of the main matters said to constitute unfitness is included at the end of one of the affidavits sworn on behalf of the claimant.[89] It has become common parlance to talk of this summary as constituting the "charges" though rule 3(3) refers neither to charges nor even to a summary of the allegations. The purpose of this requirement was adverted to in *Re Lo-Line Electric Motors Ltd*[90] and *Re Sevenoaks Stationers (Retail) Ltd.*[91] A number of points emerge from these two cases which are further illustrated by later reported cases.

The first point is that the basis of the requirement for allegations to be made clear is one of natural justice: the defendant should know the case that he has to meet. It follows that the spirit of rule 3(3) will apply in all civil disqualification proceedings and not be limited to those brought under sections 6 and 8, a point now reflected in paragraph 9.2 of the Disqualification Practice Direction (which covers all civil disqualification proceedings save for those under section 10). Moreover, in *Re Pinemoor Ltd,*[92] Chadwick J. said that those preparing and swearing affidavits in support of applications under the CDDA should be careful to distinguish between the facts which they were able to establish by direct evidence, the inferences which they invited the court to draw from those facts, and the matters which were said to amount to unfitness on the part of the defendant. These comments were directed more at practical issues. Chadwick J. went on to say that if these distinctions were observed, "... it might lead to [defendants] concentrating more closely on those factual matters to which they actually need to respond by affidavit evidence...".

6.53   The second point is that any summary of allegations is not to be read as if it were an indictment. The court will look at the substance of what is being alleged. The point is illustrated by the cases discussed below:

(1) In *Re Looe Fish Ltd,*[93] Jonathan Parker J. made clear that the summary of allegations should not be read as if it were an indictment. The director should know the substance of the allegations he has to meet but the requirement to summarise the allegations should not lead to "the technicalities associated with criminal charges". Once the director knows the case that he has to meet

---

[89] A practice alluded to in *Re Lo-Line Electric Motors Ltd* [1988] Ch. 477, [1988] 3 W.L.R. 26, [1988] 2 All E.R. 692, [1988] B.C.L.C. 698, (1988) 4 B.C.C. 415.
[90] [1988] Ch. 477 at 486–487.
[91] [1991] Ch. 164 at 176–177.
[92] [1997] B.C.C. 708.
[93] [1993] B.C.L.C. 1160 at 1171, [1993] B.C.C. 348 at 358.

the requirement is satisfied. Jonathan Parker J. might have gone even further. Although it was suggested by the Court of Appeal in *Sevenoaks* that a summary was necessary, this was probably not part of the *ratio* of the case. Indeed, as was suggested above, rule 3(3) does not necessarily require a summary of the allegations. It is suggested further that natural justice does not demand a summary. This may have been what Jonathan Parker J. was hinting at when he said that there was a requirement that the defendant should know the substance of the charge which he had to meet but, "... [o]nce that situation is reached, so that natural justice is satisfied, there is in my judgment no additional requirement to state, list or summarise the 'charges' against him...". In *Looe Fish*, the "charge" which was said not to have been spelled out was one of "breach of fiduciary duty" but it was admitted that the actual case was clear at all times. The express words of the relevant affidavit summarised the transactions of which complaint was made and referred to the fact that the transactions were illegal and that the end in question was achieved in an unscrupulous and illegal manner.

(2) In considering any "summary" of the allegations, it is necessary to consider the summary against the evidence it summarises. Thus in *Re Hitco 2000 Ltd*,[94] the substance of the allegation was that the defendant had allowed the company to "bounce" cheques. Further misconduct came to light, namely the defendant's practice of signing cheques in blank and leaving them for the book-keeper to use. Although the wording of the summary of the allegation looked at in isolation would have been wide enough to cover the conduct in relation to blank cheques it was not treated as such, because the summary of the allegation had to be looked at in the context of the matters it actually summarised. The applicant was not allowed to treat the wording of the summary as covering the separate allegation in relation to signing cheques in blank.[95]

(3) In *Re Continental Assurance Co. of London plc*, Chadwick J. had to deal with a submission that the summary of the allegations referred to the defendant having caused or allowed something to happen whereas the case as developed was one of "incompetence". Chadwick J. endorsed the view that it was essential that a director should know the criticism he was facing, but deplored "any tendency to introduce into this jurisdiction the inflexibility of a criminal indictment".[96] The defendant was said to have been well aware of what the criticisms of his conduct were. The judge continued:

> "It would defeat the purpose of the [CDDA] if, having held that [the defendant's] failure to do anything about the inter-company loans was due to gross incompetence rather than to deliberate abstention, I was precluded from holding that he was unfit to be concerned in the management of the company on the basis that the words 'cause and allow' in para. 53 of [the claimant's] affidavit were confined to deliberate wrongdoing."

---

[94] [1995] 2 B.C.L.C. 63 at 69, [1995] B.C.C. 161 at 166–167.
[95] The question was considered on appeal. By then it was too late to ask to "amend" the allegation and it was therefore an open question whether permission would have been granted (and on what terms) had permission been asked for at the trial.
[96] [1997] 1 B.C.L.C. 48 at 58–59, [1996] B.C.C. 888 at 896.

(4) In *Re Sykes (Butchers) Ltd, Secretary of State for Trade and Industry v. Richardson*,[97] Ferris J. found that it was clear on reading the summary of the allegation and the way in which the supporting facts had been set out in the main part of the affidavit, that an allegation of preferring creditors had not been limited to a narrow "charge" that the defendant had caused the company to give a preference in breach of the relevant statutory provisions in the Insolvency Act 1986.

6.54   A third point is that the claimant is limited to the allegations made in his evidence. The court can only consider those allegations in determining whether unfitness is established. Furthermore, the court cannot take other matters into account when it gets to the second stage of fixing the period of disqualification (or what is commonly referred to as "sentencing").[98] To a limited extent, this absolute rule requires some qualification. Although conduct which is not the subject of a clear allegation cannot be relied upon as a ground of unfitness or as a factor affecting the period of disqualification, it appears that such conduct may be taken into account, as a matter of evidence, to confirm the court's view of other evidence. It was seen above that in *Re Hitco 2000 Ltd*,[99] the judge found that a complaint based on the signing of blank cheques and leaving them for use by the book-keeper could not be relied upon by the claimant. The complaint did not form any part of the allegations of unfitness and there had been no application for permission to amend and so the basic rule applied. However, the court held that evidence of the defendant's conduct in relation to the blank cheques could be taken it into account in so far as it was relevant evidence confirming any other formal allegation. On the facts, the conduct was relevant to the general underlying complaint that the defendant had abdicated responsibility in the realm of financial control and failed to keep himself properly informed as to the state of the company's financial position.

Amending or adding to allegations

6.55   The court may, in appropriate cases, permit the claimant to alter or extend the allegations even after the trial has commenced. The key question is whether or not the defendant will suffer injustice as a result of the court allowing the claimant to rely on amended or additional allegations.[1] In this context, it is the potential injustice arising if a defendant does not have a fair and adequate opportunity to deal with any altered or additional allegation, which is of greatest relevance. In some cases the main issue will be whether the amendment or addition is necessary (see, *e.g. Hitco 2000* where the relevant allegation was raised for the first time on appeal).[2] In other cases the amended or additional allegation may simply be a different way of analysing existing matters which are already fairly and squarely in issue (see, *e.g. Looe Fish* and *Sykes (Butchers)* both discussed above). In the *Sevenoaks* case, the Court of Appeal adverted to the possibility that it might be necessary to add further allegations in circumstances where new matters arise from further evidence filed, or because further evidence comes to light or for some other reason. The requirements of justice would, in each case, depend upon the circumstances. In some cases, it will be necessary for the defendant to

---

[97] [1998] 1 B.C.L.C. 110, [1998] B.C.C. 484.
[98] See *Re Sevenoaks Stationers (Retail) Ltd* [1991] Ch. 164, [1990] 3 W.L.R. 1165; [1991] 3 All E.R. 578, [1991] B.C.L.C. 325, [1990] B.C.C. 765, CA. Other matters may be taken into account by way of mitigation: see Chap. 5.
[99] [1995] 2 B.C.L.C. 63, [1995] B.C.C. 161.
[1] See *Re New Generation Engineers Ltd* [1993] B.C.L.C. 435 at 438–439.
[2] [1995] 2 B.C.L.C. 63 at 69, [1995] B.C.C. 161 at 166–167.

be put on notice before the hearing, otherwise the raising of fresh matters during the hearing might come too late. In other cases an adjournment might be needed and it might be appropriate for one to be granted.[3] In other cases, if the defendant is represented by an experienced advocate, the advocate might be able to deal with the point without any adjournment "taking it in his stride".

Is permission needed to amend allegations?

6.56 In a sense this is a slightly academic issue. The practical question which it raises relates to the burden of proof (is it on the defendant to seek to "strike out" or have any proposed amendments disallowed or is it for the claimant to establish that it should be allowed?) However, few cases turn on burden of proof. The matter was considered by His Honour Judge Rich Q.C. (sitting as a High Court judge) in *Re New Technology Systems Ltd*.[4] In summary:

(1) If the allegation is filed in written evidence, the question will be whether such written evidence was permitted and, put more precisely, whether the new or amended allegation was also permitted under the relevant direction of the court.

(2) In many cases (including *New Technology Systems* itself), the further allegation will be contained in written evidence "in reply" to evidence of the defendant and the court will have made a direction permitting evidence in reply without specifically considering the question of amended allegations (because the point will not have been raised at the directions stage). The question then will be whether or not the amended allegation can properly be seen as being part of the evidence in reply. In some cases it will be allowed under the direction permitting the filing of evidence in reply. Three examples of such cases are: (a) where the allegation is a reformulation of an existing allegation (perhaps meeting a particular technical objection to the charge as laid); (b) where the evidence giving rise to the allegation is contained within the defendant's evidence in answer to the claimant's original evidence and (c) where the defendant's evidence seeks to refute one charge by alleging facts which give rise to another charge. In other cases, the amendment may not be treated as being allowed by the direction for evidence in reply.

(3) In practice, it may be unnecessary to consider the question of whether or not a particular allegation is or is not permitted by any existing direction of the court. It is open to the court to deal first with the next logical question, that is, assuming permission is needed, whether or not the court would be minded to give it.

6.57 It is suggested that it will not always be necessary for a new allegation to be included in written evidence and the parties can agree or the court can permit an alle-

---

[3] There may also be cases where an adjournment might be necessary to enable the defendant to deal with the point but such adjournment might not be fair to the defendant for other reasons, depending on (for example) at what stage of the proceedings the point was raised, how long the proceedings had been outstanding, how long ago the events in question arose and whether, if established, the new matters would be likely to seriously affect the end result one way or the other. The proportionality principle in Part I of the CPR (see rule 1.1(2)(c)) could be particularly important in this context. For an instructive pre-CPR case see *Re New Technology Systems Ltd* [1996] B.C.C. 694. In that case, the judge decided that there had been inordinate delay in the proceedings but found that the defendant's solicitor's conduct made such delay excusable. He did however strike out certain new allegations, even though the matter was not then ready for trial, but on terms that the claimant could refile the new evidence in a different form.
[4] [1996] B.C.C. 694.

gation to be made without the need for the claimant to waste time and costs filing further written evidence which is not really "evidence" but rather something that would normally be found in a statement of case. His Honour Judge Rich Q.C. recognised that the question of "amending" allegations is not the same as amending a pleading (or now " a statement of case") because the issue arises in the context of the wider question of whether further evidence should be admitted. It will be interesting to see to what extent the approach in this area will be coloured by experience under CPR, Pt 17.

The significance of the two-year period under section 7(2) on the question of amendment

6.58   The two-year period under section 7(2) is not strictly a limitation period.[5] As such, it is suggested that there is no presumption that because the period has expired either that (a) permission is automatically required to amend or add to allegations or that (b) any amended or further allegations should not be permitted. In this context, it has been said that it is unhelpful to treat the two-year period for commencing disqualification proceedings under section 6 as a limitation period.[6] It is suggested that in deciding whether to allow amended or additional allegations to be introduced, the court has an unfettered and general discretion and must consider all the circumstances. Usually the sort of circumstances that will be relevant are those referred to in the *Sevenoaks* and *Lo-Line* cases above, together with the issue of procedural fairness. The fact that the two-year period has expired before the time when the claimant is seeking to introduce amended or further allegations should not usually be treated as a decisive or significant factor weighing against him.[7] This is for the following reasons:

(1)   The two-year period in section 7(2) has two primary functions: (a) to aid good administration by encouraging the timeous obtaining of disqualification orders where the public needs to be protected against "unfit directors"[8] and (b) to protect potential defendants so that they know within a reasonable period whether they will have to face proceedings.

(2)   If proceedings are commenced within time, the two-year period will have served its purpose.

(3)   Good administration of the CDDA (referred to in (1) above), and the due administration of justice,[9] both factors underlying section 7(2), continue to be factors relevant to the exercise of the court's discretion in controlling proceedings generally. These factors are particularly relevant when the court is considering, for example, the exercise of the discretion to strike out for want of prosecution or whether to extend the time which a party has for the service of evidence.

(4)   Good administration of the CDDA and the due administration of justice may also weigh against the granting of permission to amend. However, in circumstances where the granting of permission (a) does not add to the overall timescale and/or (b) does not materially affect the defendant's ability to defend

---

[5] On section 7(2) generally, see Chap. 7.
[6] See *Re Blackspur Group plc, Secretary of State for Trade and Industry v. Davies (No. 2)* [1996] 4 All E.R. 289 at 298–299, [1997] 2 B.C.L.C. 317 at 327, [1997] B.C.C. 235 at 243–244, CA.
[7] See *Re Jazzgold Ltd* [1992] B.C.L.C. 587 at 594–5.
[8] *Re Blackspur Group plc, Secretary of State for Trade and Industry v. Davies (No. 2)* [1996] 4 All E.R. 289 at 298–299, [1997] 2 B.C.L.C. 317 at 327, [1997] B.C.C. 235 at 243–244, CA.
[9] Due administration of justice involves ensuring, for example, that a party is not permitted to draw out the proceedings with the result that the memories of witnesses fail and/or the proceedings become oppressive.

himself and/or (c) where the new or amended allegations are ones which the applicant considers it proper in the public interest to pursue, then it is suggested that any amendment should be readily allowed.

EVIDENCE

Written evidence

Form of written evidence: affidavits, witness statements, statements of truth

6.59   Evidence in connection with disqualification proceedings is by way of written evidence. In some cases affidavits are required. In what follows, references to affidavits should be taken as including a reference to affirmations.[10] In other circumstances, written evidence, verified by a statement of truth, can be used (in practice this would be by way of witness statement and/or an application notice; each of these must be verified by statement of truth).[11]

Affidavits

6.60   Affidavits are required in the following cases:[12]

(1) Substantive evidence (whether in support or in opposition) on an application for the making of a disqualification order. There is a specific exception in the case of the official receiver who may give evidence by way of report.[13]

(2) Substantive evidence (whether in support or in opposition) on an application for permission to act notwithstanding the making of a disqualification order.[14]

The requirement for affidavits in section 6 and 8 proceedings (as set out in the Disqualification Rules) has been extended to all civil disqualification proceedings governed by the Disqualification Practice Direction (namely, proceedings under sections 2(2)(a), 3, 4, 7 and 8 but not section 10). When the Disqualification Rules were amended to take account of the CPR, the opportunity was not taken to replace affidavits with written statements in proceedings under sections 6 and 8 of the CDDA. This contrasts with the position under the Insolvency Rules 1986.[15] The reason for this is likely to be that both the court and the Secretary of State may have to act on written evidence without it being tested. It would appear that affidavits are recognised by the CPR as being qualitatively different from witness statements, because, for example, affidavits are required in the case of applications for the making of search orders and freezing orders and in relation to contempt proceedings.[16] In practice, the main differ-

---

[10] See, *e.g.* paragraph 1.7 of PD 32 to the CPR (entitled "Written Evidence").
[11] See CPR, r. 32.6(2). Statements of truth are the subject of CPR, Pt 22. By CPR, r. 32.14, a person who makes or causes to be made a false statement in a document verified by a statement of truth without an honest belief in its truth is liable to proceedings for contempt of court brought by the Attorney General or with the permission of the court. In the case of affidavits there is, in such circumstances, the possibility of proceedings for perjury.
[12] CPR, r. 32.15: evidence must be given by affidavit if this required by the court, a provision contained in any other rule, a practice direction or any other enactment.
[13] In the case of proceedings under sections 7 and 8: rule 3(2) of the Disqualification Rules; in the case of other civil proceedings see paragraph 9.1 of the Disqualification Practice Direction. The power to impose such a requirement by practice direction would appear to follow from CPR, r. 32.15(1).
[14] Paragraph 22.1 of the Disqualification Practice Direction.
[15] As amended by the Insolvency (Amendment) (No. 2) Rules 1999 S.I. 1999 No. 1022 substituting new rule 7.57 (see especially rule 7.57(6)).
[16] CPR, Pt 25 and paragraph 3.1 of the relevant Practice Direction ("Interim Injunctions"). See also paragraph 1.4 of the Practice Direction to Part 32 ("Written Evidence").

ence appears to be that a false statement on oath will give rise to the possibility of proceedings for perjury whereas a false statement verified by statement of truth only opens up the possibility of proceedings for contempt of court. It should be noted that the old distinction between affidavits and witness statements (the latter could be used by other parties once filed, the latter could not) relied on unsuccessfully to challenge affidavit evidence in *Re Rex Williams Leisure*[16a] has now disappeared under the CPR (see CPR, r.32.5). Also, the old rule that a submission of "no case" could only be made if the party making it elected to call no evidence seems to have gone.[16b] It was recognised in *Rex Williams* that a witness could be asked questions designed to supplement his affidavit evidence before being cross-examined. However, the court would not normally permit a party to call brand new evidence which would take the other party by surprise. In cases where a party is unable to obtain affidavit evidence from a hostile witness, he may need to summons the witness to give oral evidence. In these circumstances, the party will have to apply to the court for permission to lead oral evidence. The likelihood is that the court will require the party to submit a "witness summary" (by analogy with CPR, r. 32.9).

6.61 In other types of civil disqualification proceeding, it is possible to rely on witness statements and indeed, there is an incentive to do so. This is because, although an affidavit may be used whenever written evidence is called for, there is the potential costs sanction of CPR, r. 32.15 if an affidavit is used when it is not required by the CPR or any other relevant provision.

Witness statements or application notices

6.62 In practice, written evidence by way of witness statement or application notice may be used in the following situations:

(1) Any interim application in the course of proceedings in which a disqualification order is sought or in the course of proceedings in which permission is sought to act notwithstanding the making of a disqualification order (such as an application to extend time, for disclosure, for further information, for summary judgment, to strike out and so forth).[17]

(2) An application for permission to act notwithstanding bankruptcy under section 11 and the Insolvency Rules, rr 6.203 *et seq*.[18]

(3) An application under section 7(2) for permission to commence section 6 proceedings after expiry of the two-year period.

(4) An application under section 7(4).

Affidavits and witness statements: formal requirements

6.63 The formal requirements are as follows:

(1) *Headings*: The headings to affidavits and witness statements must comply with the requirements of the Disqualification Practice Direction. This means that they must be entitled in the matter of the relevant company or companies

[16a] [1994] Ch. 1 and 350.
[16b] *Ronald Mullan v. Birmingham City Council*, May 27, 1999, QBD, unreported.
[17] Interim applications are governed primarily by CPR, Pt 23 and Practice Directions made in relation to it: see paragraph 24 of the Disqualification Practice Direction.
[18] See Insolvency Rules 1986, r. 7.57(5) as amended by the Insolvency (Amendment) (No. 2) Rules 1999 S.I. 1999 No. 1022.

and in the matter of the CDDA (Disqualification Practice Direction, paras 5.1, 19.1, 21.1, 25.1). In the case of section 6 proceedings, it is only necessary to set out the lead companies in the heading (Disqualification Practice Direction, para. 5.1). Affidavits must also comply with the relevant provisions of the CPR and the Practice Directions made thereunder. In relation to affidavits the following matters should clearly be written in the top right hand corner of the first page and on the back sheet:

(a) The party on whose behalf the affidavit is made.

(b) The initials and surname of the deponent.

(c) The number of the affidavit in relation to that deponent.

(d) The identifying initials and number of each exhibit referred to.

(e) The date sworn.[19]

The title of the proceedings should be set out save that it is not necessary to set out all the claimants (or all the defendants) if there are more than two.[20] In relation to witness statements, similar provisions apply (see paragraphs 17.1–17.2 of the Practice Direction to Part 32 of the CPR entitled "Written Evidence" ("PD 32").

(2) *Other matters*: The Practice Direction, "Written Evidence", which supplements Part 32 of the CPR, also contains similar provisions regarding affidavits and witness statements on the following matters (references to PD 32 unless otherwise stated):

(a) The body of the document (paragraph 4: affidavits; paragraph 16: affirmations; paragraph 18: witness statements).

(b) Exhibits (paragraphs 4.3, 11–15: affidavits; paragraphs 18.3–18.6: witness statements).

(c) Jurat (paragraph 5: affidavits)[21] and statement of truth (paragraph 20: witness statements).

(d) Format (paragraph 6: affidavits; paragraph 19: witness statements).

(e) Inability of person to read or sign affidavit (paragraph 7) or witness statement (paragraph 21).

(f) Alterations (paragraph 8: affidavits; paragraph 22: witness statements).

(g) Filing and written evidence in a foreign language (paragraph 10: affidavits; paragraph 23: witness statements). The Disqualification Practice Direction also contains provisions dealing with filing: broadly exhibits to affidavits are lodged with the court (rather than formally filed) and they are returned at the end of the relevant proceedings (Disqualification Practice Direction, paras 9.3(2), 9.4(2), 9.6(2)).

(h) Defects (paragraph 25).

---

[19] PD 32 to CPR, Pt 32 ("Written Evidence"), para. 3.2.
[20] *ibid.*, para. 3.1 and see also paragraph 4 of the Practice Direction to CPR, Pt 7 and paragraph 7 of the Practice Direction to CPR, Pt 20.
[21] See also paragraph 9 with regard to oaths and paragraph 16 on affirmations.

Hearsay evidence

6.64   The position with regard to hearsay evidence has changed substantially following the coming into force of the Civil Evidence Act 1995 ("CEA 1995"). Before the
commencement of the CEA 1995, the general position was that the Secretary of State
was entitled to adduce and rely on hearsay evidence by reason of implied statutory
exemptions arising from judicial construction of the CDDA. Furthermore, where section 6 proceedings were commenced by the official receiver and he filed a written
report (as he is entitled to do under the Disqualification Rules), such a report (and any
exhibits) could, by virtue of rule 3(2) of the Disqualification Rules, contain matters of
hearsay.[22] These exceptions, which were and remain extremely wide ranging, are considered in more detail below. The general position for defendants was less favourable.
A defendant was generally only able to rely on hearsay evidence if it came within an
established exception to the hearsay rule. The main established exception, deriving
from the Civil Evidence Acts 1968 and 1972 and complementary rules of court, was
fairly narrow. In the High Court, the notice procedure under RSC Ord. 38, r. 25 (and
following) expressly did not apply to affidavits. Moreover, affidavits (other than those
for use at interlocutory or interim hearings) could not contain hearsay by reason of
RSC Ord. 41, r. 5. However, there was power in the court to make an order permitting
hearsay evidence, but this power was rarely exercised.[23] A more relaxed approach was
taken to hearsay in affidavits in the county courts under CCR Ord. 20, r. 10: hearsay
evidence could be used provided that the affidavit stated which of the facts deposed to
were within the deponent's knowledge and which were based on information or belief
and, in the former case, the deponent's means of knowledge and, in the latter case, the
sources and grounds of the information and belief.[24] The CEA 1995 significantly
changes the position for defendants. Generally speaking, they are now entitled to rely
on hearsay evidence. While the CEA 1995 also applies in favour of the Secretary of
State, it appears that the Secretary of State can continue to rely on the exceptions which
were available to him before that Act came into force.

The express exception: section 6 proceedings where the official receiver is claimant

6.65   If the relevant company is being wound up by the court, the Secretary of State
may direct the official receiver to commence disqualification proceedings in the name
of the official receiver (CDDA, s. 7(1)(b)). In other cases, the official receiver may, in
practice, have conduct of the proceedings although the formal claimant is the Secretary
of State. In cases where the official receiver is the formal claimant, a special rule
applies. Under rule 3 of the Disqualification Rules, the official receiver may give evidence by written report rather than by affidavit. The effect of rule 3(2) is that such a
report will be treated as if it had been verified by the official receiver on affidavit and as
prima facie evidence of any matter contained in it. The courts have held that rule 3(2)
covers not only the body of the report itself, but also any exhibits to the report.[25] This
means that the official receiver's evidence may contain and exhibit matters of hearsay.
The admissibility of such evidence in no way depends on the Civil Evidence Acts. The

[22] See *Re Moonbeam Cards Ltd* [1993] B.C.L.C. 1099.
[23] RSC Ord. 38, r. 3. The exact scope of this power in relation to hearsay appears to have been uncertain
though see *Arab Monetary Fund v. Hashim (No. 7)* [1992] 1 W.L.R. 1176, [1992] 4 All E.R. 860, CA.
[24] See discussion in *Re Circle Holidays International plc* [1994] B.C.C. 226, Birmingham County Court.
[25] See *Re City Investment Centres Ltd* [1992] B.C.L.C. 956; *Re Moonbeam Cards Ltd* [1993] B.C.L.C.
1099.

same would appear to apply to any further report filed by the official receiver by way of reply to the defendant's filed evidence. If the official receiver files an affidavit rather than a report, the exception in rule 3(2) does not apply, but the implied statutory exception discussed below may apply. Under paragraph 9.1 of the Disqualification Practice Direction, the rule 3(2) provision might be said to have been purportedly extended to cover other CDDA proceedings (e.g. for permission to act under section 17) where the official receiver is a party. While the Disqualification Practice Direction is wider in scope than the Disqualification Rules (which only apply expressly to proceedings under sections 7(1) and 8), it is doubtful whether it can have created a wider express exception to the hearsay rule.[26] The paragraph is best understood as (a) setting out the position under rule 3(2) where such rule applies (i.e. in cases brought under section 7(1)(b)) and (b) otherwise confirming the position under CEA 1995 (see further below).

Express exceptions under the Companies Act 1985

6.66   The Companies Act 1985 creates specific exceptions to the hearsay rule. The most important exception in the present context is that in section 441 (as amended by the Insolvency Acts 1985 and 1986). This provides that a copy of the report of an inspector appointed under Part XIV of the Act which is certified by the Secretary of State, "... is admissible in any legal proceedings as evidence of the opinion of the inspectors in relation to any matter contained in the report and in proceedings under section 8 of the CDDA as evidence of any fact stated therein...". The first part of this passage deals solely with the mechanics by which an inspector's report may be proved but does not deal with the question of whether, *as a matter of the law of evidence*, such a report is admissible evidence.[27] However, the closing words, which refer to section 8, make plain that in proceedings under that section the report will be admissible evidence of any matter contained in it. This is likely to mean that, as well as hearsay evidence, material which contains evaluation of the recited facts will also be admissible: in other words, material commonly referred to as "opinion" evidence otherwise inadmissible under the line of authority starting, in modern times, with *Hollington v. F Hewthorn & Co. Ltd.*[28]

Proceedings under sections 6 and 8: the "implied statutory exception"

6.67   In cases decided under sections 6 and 8, the courts have construed the CDDA as containing an implied statutory exception to the hearsay rule which operates in favour of the claimant.[29] This implied statutory exception is now very wide. In *Re Barings plc (No. 2), Secretary of State for Trade and Industry v. Baker*, Evans-Lombe J. reached a conclusion in the context of a strike out application that meant, in his own words, that, "... the hearsay rule does not apply to evidence sought to be adduced by the Secretary of State in support of an application under [the CDDA]...".[30] It is

---

[26] There having been no relevant statutory instrument under either the CDDA or the Civil Procedure Act 1997: see discussion in para. 6.23.
[27] See *Savings & Investment Bank Ltd v. Gasco Investments (Netherlands) BV* [1984] 1 W.L.R. 271, [1984] 1 All E.R. 296.
[28] [1943] K.B. 587.
[29] These cases have concerned proceedings in which the claimant's evidence was required to be on affidavit rather than by way of written report. It is suggested that rule 3(2) (discussed above) does not extend the favourable hearsay regime applicable to official receiver's reports to affidavits. The point was argued but not decided in the *Ashcroft* case discussed further below.
[30] [1998] 1 B.C.L.C. 590 at 596, [1999] B.C.C. 146 at 151.

important to understand the incremental way in which the law has developed in this area because its historical development assists in explaining the limits now placed on the application of the hearsay rule. The "implied statutory exception" originates from a line of cases involving public interest winding up petitions. A summary explaining how the exception has developed is set out below:

(1) The relevant statutory scheme governing public interest winding up petitions formerly provided that the Secretary of State (originally the Board of Trade) could present a petition on the just and equitable ground if it appeared from a report of inspectors (appointed under what is now sections 431–432 of the Companies Act 1985), that it was expedient to do so. As Hoffmann L.J. explained in *Re Rex Williams Leisure plc, Secretary of State for Trade and Industry v. Warren*, it became established law that a report of inspectors could be adduced in evidence and relied upon as evidence in public interest winding up cases.[31]

(2) It was established in *Re Koscot Interplanetary (U.K.) Ltd*[32] that the relevant reports were evidence (as opposed to "material") and further established in *Re Armvent Ltd*[33] that a challenge to such evidence did not cause it to cease to be evidence and so require the Secretary of State to prove his case *de novo* "as though the inspectors had never come on the scene at all".

(3) The relevant statutory scheme was subsequently widened to allow the Secretary of State to take into account not only inspectors' reports produced under what is now sections 431–432 of the Companies Act 1985, but also material gathered under other Companies Act powers of investigation and inspection, including a "books and paper" appointment (see now section 447 of the 1985 Act).

(4) Under section 8 of the CDDA, the Secretary of State is entitled to apply for a disqualification order if it appears to him, from material gathered pursuant to various statutory powers,[34] expedient in the public interest that such an order should be made. In *Re Rex Williams Leisure plc, Secretary of State for Trade and Industry v. Warren*,[35] the Court of Appeal considered that the analogy between section 8 and the power to petition for winding up on public interest grounds (see now section 124A of the Insolvency Act 1986), was a powerful one and that hearsay evidence arising in the course of an appointment under section 447 of the Companies Act 1985 was admissible in disqualification proceedings on the basis of the implied statutory exception to the hearsay rule. If the evidence admitted under this exception was challenged, it was said that the Secretary of State might be well advised to supplement it by direct evidence because of its relative lack of weight. Nonetheless, hearsay evidence would remain evidence in the case. At first instance in *Rex Williams*,[36] Nicholls V.-C. put forward the cogent view that it would be absurd to expect the Secretary of State to construct a case based exclusively on evidence within his personal

[31] [1994] Ch. 350 (at 365–366), [1994] 3 W.L.R. 745, [1994] 4 All E.R. 27, [1994] 2 B.C.L.C. 555, [1994] B.C.C. 551. See also *Re Travel and Holiday Clubs Ltd* [1967] 1 W.L.R. 711, [1967] 2 All E.R. 606; *Re SBA Properties Ltd* [1967] 1 W.L.R. 799, [1967] 2 All E.R. 615; *Re Armvent Ltd* [1975] 1 W.L.R. 1679; *Re St Piran* [1981] 1 W.L.R. 1300.
[32] [1972] 3 All E.R. 829.
[33] [1975] 1 W.L.R. 1679.
[34] See Chap. 3.
[35] [1994] Ch. 350, [1994] 3 W.L.R. 745, [1994] 4 All E.R. 27, [1994] 2 B.C.L.C. 555, [1994] B.C.C. 551.
[36] [1994] Ch. 1, [1993] B.C.C. 79.

knowledge. Moreover there were sound reasons of procedure and economy which justified the Secretary of State's reliance on hearsay evidence:

"There is a measure of practical good sense in a procedure whereby the [claimant] has first to set out his case, with sufficient clarity and identification of the evidence being relied on for the defendant to know where he stands. Then the defendant puts in his evidence. The [claimant] can see what factual issues there are, and he can then take steps and incur expense in adducing where necessary first-hand evidence on these issues, before the hearing. In this way genuine issues can be resolved properly and fairly in the interests of the defendant and in the public interest."

(5) In *Secretary of State for Trade and Industry v. Ashcroft*,[37] the Court of Appeal applied the logic of *Rex Williams* to proceedings under section 6 of the CDDA in relation to hearsay evidence deriving from reports made to the Secretary of State by the relevant insolvency practitioner pursuant to section 7(3). Allowing the Secretary of State's appeal, Millett L.J. made the following points:

(a) The Court of Appeal in *Rex Williams* could have drawn a line between cases where the Secretary of State was applying for a winding up order and cases where he was applying for a disqualification order, but it had declined to do so.

(b) The Court of Appeal in *Rex Williams* could have drawn a line between evidence that was expressly admissible by statute under section 441 of the Companies Act 1985 (meaning inspectors' reports) and evidence that was not so admissible (for example, section 447 material), but it had declined to do so.

(c) There appeared to be no discernible distinction between material gathered by the Secretary of State's own officials and material deriving from information supplied to him by an office holder.

Having identified three safeguards—(a) that the information was obtained by a professional insolvency practitioner or department official who must have thought it worthy of credence; (b) that the Secretary of State must have thought it to have credence and (c) that the defendant would have an opportunity to challenge it—Millett L.J. ruled that the evidence was admissible. Hutchison and Hirst L.JJ. agreed, the latter approving the cogent considerations of policy identified in *Rex Williams* by Nicholls V.-C. and confirming that they applied with equal force in section 6 proceedings.

(6) In *Re Barings plc (No. 2), Secretary of State for Trade and Industry v. Baker*,[38] Evans-Lombe J. was faced with an application to strike out an affidavit filed on behalf of the Secretary of State on the ground that it contained inadmissible hearsay. The material in question comprised transcripts of interviews conducted by inspectors appointed in Singapore and by representatives of the Board of Banking Supervision enquiry with officers of the collapsed Barings group, as well as the final reports of those bodies. The judge held that all the relevant material was admissible evidence. The fact that the material in question was presented by an accountant rather than by an office holder and the fact that the material was not produced pursuant to the exercise of statutory powers did not affect its admissibility and did not amount to good grounds for dis-

---

[37] [1998] Ch. 97, [1997] 3 W.L.R. 319, [1997] 3 All E.R. 86, CA.
[38] [1998] 1 B.C.L.C. 590, [1999] B.C.C. 146.

tinguishing the case from *Ashcroft*. The key question was: "what was the information on which the Secretary of State took the decision to launch the proceedings?". He also held that, if necessary, the material was also admissible under the CEA 1995 on the ground that this had impliedly overruled RSC Ord. 41, r. 5.

(7) At the conclusion of section 6 proceedings against three of the former Barings executives, Jonathan Parker J. confirmed, in so far as he felt it was necessary in the light of Evans-Lombe J.'s earlier ruling, that the implied statutory exception went beyond "pure" hearsay to encompass the findings of fact made by relevant inspectors, *i.e.* evaluative judgments or "opinion" evidence of the sort normally inadmissible under the rule in *Hollington v. F Hewthorn & Co. Ltd.*[39]

Outstanding points on the implied statutory exception

6.68   Three main points are left outstanding following the discussion above:

(1) The status of hearsay evidence under the implied statutory exception, once such evidence is challenged.

(2) Whether the implied statutory exception is repealed by the CEA 1995.

(3) Whether there is an implied statutory exception to the hearsay rule in disqualification proceedings brought under other provisions of the CDDA (*i.e.* not restricted to proceedings under sections 6 and 8).

On the first point, it is clear from the cases in relation to both public interest winding up and disqualification, that if evidence is challenged, the Secretary of State may be well-advised, as a practical or tactical matter, to strengthen any hearsay evidence by first-hand evidence. However, he is not bound to do this and the hearsay material remains in evidence. On the second point, it is suggested that the wording of CEA 1995, s. 1 makes clear that other exceptions to the hearsay rule remain intact and that, technically speaking, the Act does not repeal the hearsay rule but simply provides a further exception (albeit one so wide that, in effect, it does abolish the rule). Given that the implied statutory exception to the hearsay rule also operates as an implied statutory exception to the rule in *Hollington v. Hewthorn*, it is, in any event, wider than the exception created by CEA 1995. On the third point, the language of Evans-Lombe J. in the *Barings (No. 2)* decision would suggest that the implied statutory exception is likely to apply in any civil disqualification proceedings where the application is made by the Secretary of State or at his direction.

The Civil Evidence Act 1995 ("CEA 1995")

6.69   The position, at least for defendants, has been changed greatly by the coming into force of the CEA 1995.[40] That Act does not abolish the hearsay rule in civil pro-

---

[39] [1943] K.B. 587. See *Re Barings plc (No. 5), Secretary of State for Trade and Industry v. Baker* [1999] 1 B.C.L.C. 433 at 495–496.

[40] See earlier discussion. In cases proceeding in a county court, either side could rely on hearsay evidence. In the High Court, the inability of a defendant to rely on hearsay as of right was, when contrasted with the position of the Secretary of State, manifestly unfair. In practice, the courts sometimes ameliorated the position by ordering under RSC Ord. 38 r. 3 that the defendant be permitted to prove a fact by adducing hearsay evidence on a particular point. This was invoked in at least one case where the combined effect of the notice procedure under RSC Ord. 38, r. 25 and following (which did not apply to affidavits) and the Civil Evidence Acts 1968 and 1972 would have enabled hearsay evidence to be admitted. See further discussion in *Re Circle Holidays International plc* [1994] B.C.C. 226, Birmingham County Court.

ceedings as such (see section 1(3), (4) which preserve existing exceptions to the rule), but does provide that evidence is not to be excluded on the ground that it is hearsay (section 1(1)).[41] As a general matter, the fact that evidence is hearsay goes to weight only and not to admissibility. In assessing weight, the court is required by section 4(1) to have regard to "... any circumstances from which any inference can reasonably be drawn as to the reliability or otherwise of the evidence...". A non-exhaustive list of circumstances is set out in section 4(2). These are largely a matter of common sense and, to a considerable extent, reflect the sort of factors that the court would have taken into account under the old legislation in deciding whether or not a party should be allowed to adduce hearsay evidence.[42] In considering the weight to be attached to hearsay evidence in disqualification proceedings, it is suggested that the principles set out in section 4 will, in practice, be applied, even if the evidence is admissible under some other exception outside the CEA 1995. Although section 2 of the CEA 1995 envisages a requirement on the party proposing to adduce hearsay evidence to give notice, this requirement is governed by rules of court which are considered below. The most important point to note is that the effect of failure to give notice differs fundamentally under the CEA 1995 compared with the position under the Civil Evidence Acts of 1968 and 1972. Under the old provisions, the giving of a notice was a pre-requisite to hearsay evidence being adduced. The court had power to dispense with the notice requirement but exercised this power sparingly.[43] In contrast, under the CEA 1995, a failure to give notice as required by section 2(1) and/or rules of court does not affect the admissibility of the evidence, but may be taken into account by the court when considering the exercise of its powers of case management and the issue of costs and as a matter adversely affecting the weight to be given to the evidence (section 2(4)). The other important difference is that under RSC Ord. 38, r. 26, the other party or parties were able to serve a counter-notice requiring the party giving the hearsay notice to call the maker of the relevant statements as a witness. Unless he could rely on a limited number of circumstances set out in section 8 of the Civil Evidence Act 1968,[44] the party who sought to adduce the hearsay evidence was forced to call the maker of the relevant statements as a witness and was otherwise not entitled to rely on that evidence. The CEA 1995 contains no provision for the service of counter-notices requiring the maker of any hearsay statements to be called as a witness. However, there is power in the other party or parties to ask that the maker be called for the purposes of cross-examination.

Transitional provisions under CEA 1995

6.70   Until recently, the position with regard to transitional provisions under the CEA 1995 was governed by the Court of Appeal decision in *Bairstow v. Queens Moat Houses plc*.[45] Despite confusion caused as a result of relevant changes to the RSC and CCR which were premised on a different basis, it was held in *Bairstow* that the CEA 1995 applied only to proceedings commenced on or after January 31, 1997 (being the date when that Act came into force). However, by a combination of a recent statutory instrument,[46] and the Practice Direction to Part 33 of the CPR, the result in *Bairstow*

---

[41] Note also the effect of section 14(1) which makes clear that the CEA 1995 is not to be taken as barring the exclusion of hearsay evidence on other grounds *e.g.* failure to comply with rules of court.

[42] See, *e.g. Rasool v. West Midlands Passenger Transport Executive* [1974] 3 All E.R. 638.

[43] See RSC Ord. 38, r. 29 and *e.g. Morris v. Stratford-on-Avon Rural District Council* [1973] 1 W.L.R. 1059, [1973] 3 All E.R. 263, CA.

[44] *e.g.* that the maker of the relevant statements was dead or overseas.

[45] [1998] 1 All E.R. 343.

[46] The Civil Procedure (Modification of Enactments) Order 1999 S.I. 1999 No. 1217 (made pursuant to section 4(2) of the Civil Procedure Act 1997) which, among other things, inserts a new section 16A into the CEA 1995.

has effectively been reversed. The position now is that the CEA 1995 applies to all claims commenced before January 31, 1997 unless (a) directions have been given or orders have been made as to the evidence to be given at the trial or hearing or (b) the trial or hearing began before April 26, 1999. It is unclear whether or not directions or orders will be treated as having been made for these purposes where evidence has been served as required by the Disqualification Rules and/or the Disqualification Practice Direction rather than by court order.

The provisions of the CPR on hearsay evidence

6.71   There is not scope in this book for a detailed consideration of either the CPR or the CEA 1995. The provisions of the CPR which are likely to be of most importance in disqualification proceedings are considered below.

6.72   The notice requirement.   As indicated above, section 2 of the CEA 1995 contemplates a notice requirement but provides that this requirement will be governed by rules of court. Under RSC Order 38, r. 21(3)(a) (as amended to take account of the CEA 1995), there was no requirement to serve hearsay notices in relation to material contained in affidavits. This probably applied as well to documents contained in exhibits to affidavits.[47] Although RSC Ord. 41, r. 5 did not permit affidavits (other than those prepared for use at interim or interlocutory hearings) to contain hearsay material, this rule was held to have been impliedly overruled (at least in disqualification proceedings) by the CEA 1995 in *Barings (No. 2)* (discussed above). The result was, to some extent, a victory for common sense. If the relevant material is set out in an affidavit, the other side has notice of what the material is and the fact that the party intends to rely on the material as hearsay evidence. Unfortunately, the provisions in Part 33 of the CPR do not fully reflect the position under the RSC. CPR, r. 33.3 currently provides that the requirement to serve a notice under section 2 of the CEA 1995 does not apply to affidavits or witness statements for use at trial "... which [do] not contain hearsay evidence". On the face of it, a party relying on an affidavit containing hearsay still needs to give notice under section 2. The service of a witness statement containing hearsay is deemed to comply with the section 2 notice requirement (see CPR, r. 33.2). However, the same is not true of affidavits even though, for all practical purposes, they fulfill the same function as witness statements. It seems anomalous that witness statements and affidavits are treated differently in this respect. In practice, the effect of a failure to serve a section 2 notice does not affect the admissibility of the evidence, but may be taken into account by the court when considering the exercise of its powers of case management and the issue of costs and as a matter adversely affecting the weight to be given to the evidence (section 2(4) of the CEA 1995). If the relevant information is set out in the affidavit, it is hard to see how the other party could be prejudiced by non-receipt of a section 2 notice and, it is suggested, that it would be unreal for the court to impose a costs sanction as punishment for a breach of the rules in circumstances where it appears that there is no requirement to serve a notice in the case of a witness statement. Furthermore, it is suggested that the weight of the evidence should not normally be affected if it is set out in proper detail in the affidavit. Section 2 only applies to hearsay evidence which is admissible exclusively under the exception in the CEA 1995. This means that it does not apply to evidence that would be admissible under an exception arising outside the CEA 1995 and under the CEA 1995 as well (section 1(4) of the CEA 1995).

---

[47] On the basis that the relevant rule of court was in a different form to that considered in *Re Koscot Interplanetary (U.K.) Ltd* [1972] 3 All E.R. 829 and/or on the basis that that case was wrongly decided.

6.73   Power of a party not relying on hearsay to ask the maker of hearsay statements to be called as a witness. Section 3 of the CEA 1995 stipulates that rules of court may provide that, where a party to civil proceedings adduces hearsay evidence of a statement made by some person and does not call that person as a witness, any other party to the proceedings may, with the court's permission, call that person as a witness and cross-examine him on the statement as if he had been called by the first party and as if the hearsay statement stood as evidence-in-chief. Although, section 3 does not apply to hearsay evidence which is admissible by reason of an exception arising outside the CEA 1995 (see section 1(4)), the relevant provisions of the CPR extend this power to all hearsay statements. This means that the provision applies to hearsay evidence which is relied on under either (a) rule 3(2) of the Disqualification Rules or (b) the implied statutory exception. CPR, r. 33.4 provides that the relevant application should be made not less than 14 days after the date on which notice of intention to rely on the hearsay statement was served. In the light of the discussion above, this will presumably be construed as meaning 14 days after service of any relevant affidavit. The 14-day period is likely to be extended to any later directions hearing if appropriate. The mere fact that a party can ask the court's permission to call the maker of the hearsay statement does not mean that the court will necessarily grant it. The court will probably want to be satisfied that the relevant statement is really significant and is materially challenged. Cases are likely to arise where it will be difficult to judge whether to ask permission to cross-examine or to submit that little weight should be given to the statement on the basis that the party seeking to rely on it could and should have been expected to have called the witness (see section 4(2)(a) of the CEA 1995). Before any application under CPR, r. 33.4 is made, it is important to discuss the position with the party relying on the hearsay statement. If that party knows that an application is to be made seeking permission to have the witness called, it is possible that the party will prefer to put in first-hand affidavit evidence from the maker of the statement and call that person to give evidence at trial.

6.74   Attacking the credibility of the maker of hearsay statements. If a party proposes to attack the credibility of the maker of a hearsay statement who is not to be called as a witness, he must give notice of his intention to do so not more than 14 days after service of the original notice of intention to rely on hearsay evidence (CPR, r. 33.5). This provision is further regulated by section 5(2) of the CEA 1995. As CPR, r. 33.5 is wider in scope than section 5(2), it is unclear to what extent section 5(2) will in fact apply. This may be a matter which requires clarification at a pre-trial or directions hearing. In any event, as evidence in disqualification proceedings is generally on affidavit, the point should become clear. In so far as a witness who is giving oral evidence, may find his credibility attacked, it appears that evidence may still be "sprung" on him, a point discussed further below in relation to cross-examination.

Expert evidence

**6.75   Before the CPR came into force, two particular problems were common in disqualification cases. First, because the evidence in support of disqualification proceedings contained a mixture of evidence, inference and submission confusion could arise as to whether the evidence purported to be expert evidence. The problem arose in particular with affidavits sworn by professional persons such as insolvency practitioners. As a result, on occasions, defendants would file what purported to be expert evidence to answer matters in the claimant's evidence which were perceived to be "expert" or "opinion" evidence. The case of *Re Pinemoor Ltd*[48] concerned an appli-

---

[48] [1997] B.C.C. 708.

cation by the Secretary of State to strike out purported expert evidence filed on behalf of the defendant director. The "evidence" in question was not, in truth, expert evidence. Chadwick J. struck the evidence out but subject to conditions. The main condition was that the Secretary of State serve notice on the defendant indicating any passages in the liquidator's affidavit which relied on expressions of expert opinion. If there were any, the defendant would have a further opportunity to file evidence in response. If there were none, it would be clear to the defendant that he was not facing a case based on the opinion of the Secretary of State's deponents. Chadwick J. also said that it was desirable for those who prepare and swear affidavits in support of applications under the CDDA to distinguish carefully between the facts which they were able to establish by direct evidence, the inferences which they invited the court to draw from those facts, and the matters which were said to amount to unfitness on the part of the defendant. If those distinctions were observed, the judge continued, it might lead defendants to concentrate more closely on those factual matters to which they actually needed to respond by affidavit evidence under rule 6 of the Disqualification Rules.

The second, connected problem, was that, in any event, there were occasions when defendants sought to rely on purported expert evidence when the evidence in question was not really expert evidence at all. Three choices were open to the claimant: (a) an application to strike out the evidence;[49] (b) to reserve the right to object to the evidence but to cross-examine the witness or (c) not to cross-examine and to await final submission.[50] These problems were probably exacerbated by the fact that permission was not required under the Rules of the Supreme Court to serve expert evidence contained in affidavits (see RSC Ord. 38, r. 36(2)). The position has now significantly changed and costs are likely to saved as there is now a requirement that the permission of the court be sought before expert evidence can be put in.

The position under the CPR

6.76 Part 35 of the CPR lays down a detailed code in relation to experts. No expert can be called nor expert evidence be put in without the permission of the court (CPR, r. 35.4). In seeking the permission of the court to adduce expert evidence, the relevant party is required to identify the expert's field of expertise and, where practicable, the identity of the party's preferred expert. The court has wide powers and can, for example, impose a ceiling on the costs recoverable from the other side in relation to the expert's fees and expenses (CPR, r. 35.4(4)) and, in cases where each side proposes to adduce expert evidence in a given field, impose a single joint expert on the parties (CPR, r. 35.7). The way in which these powers will be exercised is likely to develop over time. Although a number of difficult and interesting points arise in both theory and practice, these points are not peculiar to disqualification are accordingly beyond the scope of this book. The general point to make is that cases where expert evidence will be permitted in disqualification proceedings are likely to be quite rare.[51]

Expert evidence: general points

6.77 Although cases that have been reported in the field of disqualification are merely illustrations of the existing law of evidence, it is helpful to see how the relevant rules have been applied hitherto in the disqualification context:

---

[49] As happened in *Pinemoor* itself and in *Oakfame* (on which see further below).
[50] For a case in which the third course was adopted in relation to purported expert evidence from a merchant banker, see *Re Barings plc (No. 5), Secretary of State for Trade and Industry v. Baker* [1999] 1 B.C.L.C. 433.
[51] See *Re Barings plc (No. 5), Secretary of State for Trade and Industry v. Baker* [1999] 1 B.C.L.C. 433 at 494–495 on the need (following *Westmid Packing*) to admit evidence only where plainly relevant and helpful so as to avoid proceedings becoming "unwieldy, time-consuming and expensive".

(1) Any expert must be "independent".[52] Thus, it is not possible for the Secretary of State to put forward his or her principal deponent (who is setting out the case for disqualification) as an expert. That independence is now stressed an underpinned by Part 35 of the CPR. In September 1999, a draft code of guidance for experts under the CPR was produced. It is anticipated that, after consultation, this will become a practice direction.

(2) The expert must be properly qualified. In *Re Oakfame Construction Ltd*,[53] doubts were raised over the qualifications of the relevant deponents, but the court struck out the evidence in question without having to determine the point.

(3) The contents of the evidence must genuinely be "expert evidence":

(a) In *Re Oakfame Construction Ltd*,[54] the court struck out purported expert evidence which was in reality a combination of hearsay, advocacy and submissions rather than expert opinion. Although the "evidence" was useful to the defendants in "... priming themselves for making submissions and for cross-examining deponents...", it was not "material which can properly be placed before the court as expert testimony".

(b) In *Re Barings plc (No. 5)*,[55] evidence was adduced from Sir John Craven, a distinguished former merchant banker and businessman. His affidavit evidence was read as part of the evidence in the case but the question of its admissibility was left for closing speeches. Sir John Craven was not cross-examined so that his evidence (if admissible) remained unchallenged. The Secretary of State objected neither to Sir John's testimonial evidence nor to his factual account of the growth and development of merchant banking over time. Equally, there was no objection to evidence of Sir John's understanding of how the Barings group was organised in managerial terms and how it had developed. This evidence was simply a hearsay repetition of what had been communicated to him after the event and its purpose was to provide a factual basis for the statements of opinion which followed. The statements of opinion to which the Secretary of State took objection were those which amounted to comments and views as to the reasonableness or otherwise of one defendant's conduct in his role as chairman of the bank and of its principal management committee. The following useful points emerge from the decision:

(i) Section 3 of the Civil Evidence Act 1972 does not make admissible evidence which is otherwise irrelevant.[56] That section simply makes evidence "on a relevant matter" admissible.

(ii) As a general matter, expert evidence as to what is the legal test applicable in any proceedings is, by definition, inadmissible. Expert evidence on the question whether the legal test has been satisfied in a particular case *may* be relevant (for example, if it is evidence of "some practice in a particular profession, some accepted standard of

---

[52] See especially *The Ikarian Reefer* [1993] 2 Lloyd's Rep. 68.
[53] [1996] B.C.C. 67.
[54] *ibid.*
[55] [1999] 1 B.C.L.C. 433 at 489–495.
[56] See discussion in *Barings (No. 5)* of Jacob J.'s decision in *Routestone Ltd v. Minories Finance Ltd* [1997] B.C.C. 180.

conduct which is laid down by a professional institute or sanctioned by common usage...").[57] However, it will not be relevant if, on analysis, it amounts to no more than an expression of opinion as to what the expert would himself have done in similar circumstances.[58]

(iii) The issue in the case was one of whether or not the particular defendant was incompetent and, if so, incompetent in a sufficient degree to "make him unfit" within the meaning of section 6. On that issue, Sir John's evidence was of no assistance.

Character evidence

6.78 In *Re Dawes & Henderson (Agencies) Ltd, Secretary of State for Trade and Industry v. Dawes*,[59] Blackburne J. acceded to an application by the Secretary of State to strike out (among other things) two affidavits sworn on behalf of the defendants. The deponents were persons of responsibility within the commercial and legal world and their affidavits referred to the fitness, honesty and general good character of the defendants. The judge decided that, in so far as the affidavits expressed an opinion on each defendant's fitness to be a company director, they were inadmissible as the question of fitness or unfitness was for the trial judge to determine and that, in so far as they contained evidence of good character, they were equally inadmissible as the general character of the defendants was not in issue. The fact that the allegations involved imputations against the honesty of the defendants and that an adverse finding was likely to lead to a finding of unfitness and, in turn, to a disqualification order, did not justify a departure from the salutary rule which excludes evidence of general reputation. In civil proceedings, it is not possible to adduce evidence of general reputation with a view to proving that a person with an excellent reputation would not have done the things alleged against him. Blackburne J. also decided that any extenuating circumstances (of the type referred to in the *Grayan* case)[60] related to matters which might explain the conduct alleged by the Secretary of State, but did not extend to matters of the kind catalogued in the relevant affidavits which were entirely extraneous to the establishment or otherwise of the matters alleged. Moreover, the affidavits contained no material which might be relevant on the question of the appropriate period of disqualification as, again, the court was only concerned with the defendant's conduct in relation to the company named in the proceedings and any mitigation was also referable only to the conduct which had been established.

6.79 The question of character evidence was revisited by Scott V.-C. in one of the *Barings* hearings.[61] Although he accepted that general evidence of character and reputation was irrelevant to the question of whether or not specific past conduct as a director was such as to make the defendant unfit, he took a different view in relation to the period of disqualification which is a matter for the discretion of the court:

"I do not for my part see how it can be said that the evidence relating to the general ability and conduct as a director of the individual in question is necessarily irrelevant to the exercise of this discretion. I do not believe that discretion can be put into a closet from which general evidence of the sort I have described is excluded. Of course, not all evidence of character would be relevant. It would not be rel-

---

[57] *Midland Bank Trust Co. Ltd v. Hett, Stubbs & Kemp* [1979] Ch. 384 at 402, [1978] 3 All E.R. 571 at 582.
[58] *ibid.* and *Bown v. Gould & Swayne* [1996] P.N.L.R. 130.
[59] [1997] 1 B.C.L.C. 329, [1997] B.C.C. 121.
[60] On which see generally chaps. 2, 4 and 5.
[61] *Re Barings plc* [1998] B.C.C. 583.

evant in the least whether the director was a good family man or whether he was kind to animals. But evidence of his general conduct in the discharge of the office of director goes to the question of the extent to which the public needs protection against his acting in that office. It seems to me that evidence of that character is relevant to be taken into account by the court in exercising its discretion and cannot be excluded as being inadmissible."

The matter has now been settled by the Court of Appeal in *Re Westmid Packing Services Ltd, Secretary of State for Trade and Industry v. Griffiths* where the court agreed with the Vice-Chancellor's observations in the passage cited above.[62] General character and reputation evidence may be relevant to fixing the period of disqualification and on applications for permission to act notwithstanding disqualification, but it will not be relevant on the central issue of "unfitness".[63] Furthermore, the court should control evidence to minimise repetition which increases costs and wastes time (see now CPR, r. 32.1).

Appeals

Which provisions apply

6.80   The question of which procedural rules govern appeals is considered (in the context of applicable rules generally) in more detail above. In summary, it is suggested for the reasons discussed above that the position is as follows:

(1) Appeals in proceedings under sections 2(2)(a), 3 and 4 are governed by the provisions applicable to civil proceedings generally. The provisions in the Insolvency Rules 1986 regarding appeals have no application.[64]

(2) Appeals in connection with disqualification proceedings under sections 6 and 8 are governed by the relevant provisions of the Insolvency Rules 1986 (as amended).[65]

(3) Appeals in connection with applications under section 7(2) for permission to bring section 6 proceedings after the expiry of the relevant two-year period are probably governed by the relevant provisions of the Insolvency Rules 1986.[66]

(4) Appeals in connection with applications under section 7(4) will be governed by the procedural rules applicable to the original application.[67]

---

[62] [1998] 2 All E.R. 124, [1998] 2 B.C.L.C. 646, [1998] B.C.C. 836.
[63] Though note that testimonial evidence was not objected to and was accepted in evidence in *Barings (No. 5)* discussed above.
[64] The rule-making power in section 411 of the Insolvency Act 1986 is not extended to these provisions of the CDDA: see CDDA, s. 21(2) and discussion above in main text on the analogous position under the Companies Act 1985 in *Probe Data*.
[65] See Disqualification Rules, r. 2(4) following amendment by the Insolvent Companies (Disqualification of Unfit Directors) Proceedings (Amendment) Rules 1999 S.I. 1999 No. 1023. The question of whether the "High Court" for the purposes of section 6(3)(d) and section 8 was properly to be regarded as a court having jurisdiction to wind up companies has now become academic.
[66] This is certainly so as regards applications for permission to the court as provided by section 6(3)(a) to (c). The question with regard to applications to the court in section 6(3)(d) is whether as a matter of construction such applications are governed by the Disqualification Rules: is the application so closely connected to the substantive proceedings that it should be regarded as so covered and, if it is not, is it correct to say that the High Court can be treated as a court having winding up jurisdiction for the purposes of the Insolvency Rules (see discussion above under the heading "Applicable Rules").
[67] Which vary depending on whether the application is free standing or made in substantive disqualification proceedings: see para. 6.21 above.

(5) Appeals in connection with orders made under sections 10 and 15 are probably governed by the relevant provisions on appeals governing the substantive proceedings in which the order is made.

(6) Appeals in connection with applications for permission to act under section 11 are likely to be governed by the relevant provisions of the Insolvency Rules 1986 given that this sort of application is itself apparently governed by these rules. Having said that, there is an argument that the relevant rules (Insolvency Rules 1986, rr 6.203–6.205) are ultra vires because the rule-making power in section 411 of the Insolvency Act 1986 is not extended to proceedings of this nature by section 21(2) of the CDDA. If the rules are ultra vires, it would seem that the appeal provisions applicable to civil proceedings in general will apply.

(7) Appeals in the case of orders for transfer raise two questions: first, the court in which the appeal should be launched and second, the rules which should apply substantively to such appeals:

(a) As regards the court to which the appeal should be made, it is suggested that (i) if the applicable rules are the ordinary rules of civil procedure, then paragraph 5 of the Practice Direction to CPR, Pt 30 will apply to determine the court to which the appeal should be made and (ii) if the applicable rules would be the Insolvency Rules 1986, then the only possible conflict between those rules and the Practice Direction to Part 30 would be in cases where the order for transfer is between county courts or is an order made in county court proceedings by a judge of the county court. In the cases referred to in (ii) the question would be whether or not the provisions of the Practice Direction are inconsistent with the appeal provisions of the Insolvency Rules.[68] This would, in turn, depend on whether or not the order is regarded as one being made "in the exercise of" the winding up jurisdiction. It is suggested that, where the appeals provisions of the Insolvency Rules apply generally, then (i) they apply to orders for transfer as much as to any other interim order in the relevant proceedings and (ii) they will take effect in priority to the Practice Direction to CPR, Pt 30.

(b) As regards the nature of the appeal and the relevant procedure, it is suggested that if the reasoning in (a) above is correct, then the relevant provisions of the Insolvency Rules or of the CPR will apply accordingly.

In the cases of appeals to the Court of Appeal, it is essential not only to have regard to RSC Ord. 59, as appended at Schedule 1 of the CPR (at the time of writing), but also to the relevant practice directions of the Court of Appeal, especially the Consolidated Practice Direction. At the end of September 1999, a new draft CPR, Pt 59 (and accompanying draft practice directions) was issued for consultation purposes. The intention is to replace the current RSC provisions in Schedule 1 of the CPR and certain provisions of the CCR contained in Schedule 2 of the CPR. The position under these new drafts is touched on below, though not in detail. The purpose of the draft CPR, Pt 59 is to provide a common set of rules for all appeals to county courts, the High Court and the Civil Division of the Court of Appeal. Under the draft proposals there are two separate practice directions: one governing appeals to the Court of Appeal, the other

---

[68] See now Insolvency Rules 1986 (as amended), r. 7.51, which provides that the CPR and practice and procedure in the High Court or county courts applies "except so far as inconsistent" with the Insolvency Rules.

governing appeals to county courts and the High Court. These two draft procedural codes contain slight differences of detail (*e.g.* in relation to respondents' notices). It is unclear to what extent these provisions will impinge on the appeal and review provisions of the Insolvency Rules.

A further point is that section 56 of the Access to Justice Act 1999 allows for routes of appeal to be laid down by statutory instrument. At the time of writing, the matter was under review. It is likely that the approach taken will largely reflect that reached by the Court of Appeal Review Team and as set out in the Lord Chancellor's Department consultation paper of July 1998, *The Court of Appeal (Civil Division)—Proposals for Change to Constitution and Jurisdiction.*

Appeal provisions applicable to civil proceedings generally

6.81   As outlined above, in some cases the appeals provisions of the Insolvency Rules 1986 will apply. In other cases, the appeals provisions applicable to civil proceedings generally will apply. In summary these are as follows:

(1) Appeals from a High Court judge will be to the Court of Appeal. Permission to appeal (and cross-appeal) will be needed in all cases (except, for present purposes, in contempt proceedings).[69] The appeal will be a "true appeal". The time for appealing will be four weeks from the date the order was sealed or perfected.[70]

(2) Appeals from the registrar of the Companies Court will lie to a High Court judge. The position is not entirely clear but it is suggested that the appeal will be by way of rehearing,[71] that permission to appeal will not be needed and that the time for appealing is 28 days.

(3) Logically, appeals from a district judge sitting in the High Court should be governed in the same way as appeals from the Companies Court registrar. However, such appeals are probably governed by the amended provisions of RSC Ord. 58, r. 3, appended at Schedule 1 to the CPR. If this is correct, appeals on interim matters will be to the High Court judge (the time for appealing being seven days after the order was made or given) and appeals after trial will be to the Court of Appeal (the time for appealing being four weeks from the order being sealed or otherwise perfected).[72] The provisions regarding appeals from Masters are the same except that the time period is truncated to five days for permission to appeal to the judge.

(4) Appeals from a county court judge lie to the Court of Appeal.[73] Permission to appeal (or cross-appeal) will be needed in all cases (except contempt).[74] The appeal will be a "true appeal".[75] The time for appealing will be four weeks from pronouncement (not from the sealing or perfecting) of the relevant order.[76]

---

[69] See RSC Ord. 59, r. 1B as appended at Schedule 1 of the CPR
[70] See Supreme Court Act 1981, s. 16 and RSC Ord. 59 as appended at Schedule 1 of the CPR
[71] Following *Re Rolls Razor Ltd (No. 2)* [1970] Ch. 576, [1970] 2 W.L.R. 100, [1969] 3 All E.R. 1386.
[72] RSC Ord. 59, r. 4 as appended at Schedule 1 of the CPR.
[73] County Courts Act 1984, s. 77.
[74] See RSC Ord. 59, r. 1B as appended at Schedule 1 of the CPR. In effect, this replaces the previous provisions of the County Court Appeals Order 1991 S.I. 1991 No. 1877.
[75] *ibid.,* r. 19 as appended, etc.
[76] *ibid.,* rr. 4 and 19 as appended, etc.

(5) Appeals from a district judge sitting in a county court will be to the relevant county court judge under CCR Ord. 13, r. 1(10), (11) (in the case of interim matters) and CCR Ord. 37 (in the case of final matters and after trial). In each case, the relevant rules of the CCR are appended at Schedule 2 to the CPR. The time for appealing will be five and 14 days respectively. Permission is apparently not required.

6.81A It is likely that the powers under section 56 of the Access to Justice Act 1999 referred to above will be invoked to change the courts to which appeals should be directed. In broad summary, it is understood at the time of writing, that the position is likely to be as follows:

(1) Appeals in fast track cases heard at first instance by a district judge, whether or not the order is final, will be to a circuit judge.
(2) Appeals in fast track cases heard at first instance by a circuit judge, whether or not the order is final, will be to a circuit judge.
(3) Appeals in multi-track cases where the order is final will be to the Court of Appeal, regardless of the identity of the court which made the order.
(4) Appeals in multi-track cases where the order is not final will be to (a) a circuit judge in the case of orders made by a district judge; (b) a High Court judge in the case of orders made by a master, the registrar of the Companies Court or a circuit judge; and (c) the Court of Appeal in the case of orders made by a High Court judge.

6.81B Under draft CPR, Pt 59 (referred to above), two slightly different regimes will apply to appeals to the Court of Appeal and appeals to (or within) the High Court or a county court. This is reflected in the two draft practice directions that have been issued. In all cases permission to appeal will be required (except contempt proceedings; consideration is also being given as to whether or not permission should be required where the order is of a "quasi-criminal" nature: see Access to Justice Act 1999, s. 54 and draft CPR, r. 59.3). The time for lodging an appeal will be 28 days in the case of appeals from final orders and 14 days in all other cases (draft CPR, r. 59.4). For these purposes, time will run from the decision granting permission to appeal or the time when reasons are given for refusing permission. On a refusal of permission, it will usually be possible, as now, to seek permission from the appellate court. The appeal court will, in all cases, exercise a truly "appellate" role, *i.e.* the hearing will not be by way of re-hearing *de novo* as if the original order had not been made, but will focus on the reasoning of the judge whose decision is under appeal. A respondent's notice will be necessary in the case of all appeals to the Court of Appeal (draft CPR, r. 59.5; draft Practice Direction, "Appeals to the Court of Appeal", para. 6) and in some, but not all, cases in a county court or the High Court (draft CPR, r. 59.5; draft Practice Direction, "Appeals to the County Courts or High Court", para. 11.3). In some cases, the respondent will himself require permission. In suitable cases, it will be possible for an appeal to "leap-frog" directly to the Court of Appeal (Access to Justice Act 1999, s. 57; draft CPR, r. 59.16). It should be stressed that this is a tentative summary of what the authors understand to be the likely position as at September 1999. The position may well change.

Appeal provisions of the Insolvency Rules 1986

6.82 The combination of Insolvency Rules 1986, rr 7.47 and 7.49 and the relevant provisions applicable to the High Court would appear to be as follows:

(1) Appeals from the registrar of the Companies Court or a district judge (sitting in the High Court) will be to a High Court judge. The appeal is a "true appeal". The question of whether permission is needed is addressed below.

(2) Appeals from a county court (whether from a district judge or a judge) will be to a High Court judge. The appeal is a "true appeal". The question of whether permission is needed is addressed below.

(3) Appeals from a High Court judge exercising jurisdiction as an appeal court under (1) or (2) above, will be to the Court of Appeal under RSC Ord. 59 (as appended at Schedule 1 to the CPR). In considering the question of permission to appeal, the court will have regard to the fact that there has already been one appeal and accordingly will apply a more restrictive approach to the granting of permission that it would do in a case where there has been no earlier appeal.[77]

It is unclear whether or not any statutory instrument will be made under the Access to Justice Act 1999, s. 56, which will affect the above analysis. At the time of writing (September 1999), it is understood that the intention is not to alter the appeal routes as provided for by the Insolvency Act 1986 and the Insolvency Rules.

Is permission to appeal needed in cases covered by Insolvency Rules 1986, rr 7.47 and 7.49?

6.83   The following is subject to any changes that may flow from the new proposed CPR, Pt 59 and the Access to Justice Act 1999. It is suggested that permission to appeal to a High Court judge is not needed in such cases. This would appear to follow from the reasoning in *Re Busytoday Ltd*[78] and (to a limited extent) in *Re Langley Marketing Services Ltd*[79]:

(1) In *Langley Marketing*, Hoffmann J. confirmed that in the case of an appeal governed by the Insolvency Rules from the decision of a district judge sitting in the county court to a High Court judge, permission was not needed (whereas permission was needed for an appeal from such a district judge to a county court judge under the CCR). The decision suggests that the Insolvency Rules do not impose a condition that permission to appeal be obtained.

(2) In *Busytoday*, the question which arose was whether permission to appeal to a single High Court judge was needed under rule 7.47 in relation to interim (or interlocutory) orders made by the registrar of the Companies Court. At that time, permission to appeal was required for appeals to the Court of Appeal from interim (or interlocutory) decisions of a High Court judge. It was submitted that this requirement was part of the "procedure and practice" of the Supreme Court and that it was equally applicable to appeals under rule 7.47 by virtue of rule 7.49. Mummery J. rejected this submission on the basis that the requirement for permission was a matter of jurisdiction provided for by section 18(1)(h) of the Supreme Court Act 1981 (and reflected in RSC Ord. 59, r. 1A).

---

[77] See Court of Appeal Consolidated Practice Direction, para. 2.19.1 and, as regards its vires, see *Nascimento v. Kerrigan*, The Times, June 23, 1999, CA.

[78] [1992] 1 W.L.R. 683, [1992] B.C.C. 480.

[79] [1993] B.C.L.C. 1340, [1992] B.C.C. 585. Mr Registrar Rawson has decided that there is no requirement to obtain permission to appeal but had not given his reasons at the time of writing. That permission is not required has since been confirmed by a revision to paragraph 17.1 of the Practice Direction, "Insolvency Proceedings".

(3) The issue which arises is whether the changed requirements for permission to appeal in nearly all appeals to the Court of Appeal has, for the purposes of rules 7.47 and 7.49, now become part of the "procedure and practice" of the Supreme Court. It is suggested that the answer is the same as it was before. It is true that the original requirement for permission to appeal to the Court of Appeal was purportedly brought in by a Practice Direction of the Court of Appeal handed down on November 18, 1998 and said to come into effect from January 1, 1999. However, it is doubtful whether there was then any power to effect this change to statute by means of practice direction alone. Indeed, by S.I. 1998 No. 3049 (December 8, 1998), a new RSC Ord. 59, r. 1B was adopted which, in substance, repeated the relevant provisions of the Practice Direction. The Practice Direction has since been consolidated and what was formerly RSC Ord. 59, r. 1B remains, with the same numbering, as part of Schedule 1 to the CPR. The Court of Appeal Consolidated Practice Direction does not appear to have been made pursuant to any power conferred by the Civil Procedure Act 1997 and the CPR. Accordingly, the source and authority for the requirement for permission to appeal is to be found in RSC Ord. 59, r. 1B appended at Schedule 1 to the CPR. That Schedule (and CPR, Pt 50) is made by statutory instrument. Accordingly, whether it is regarded as (a) a provision originally enacted by statutory instrument under the Supreme Court Act 1981 and/or (b) as a provision enacted by or under the Civil Procedure Act 1997, the requirement for permission to appeal should be regarded as a jurisdictional requirement within the reasoning of Mummery J. in *Busytoday* and hence not part of the "procedure and practice" of the Supreme Court for the purposes of rule 7.49.

Review powers

6.84 In cases governed by the Insolvency Rules, r. 7.47 there is a general power of review in rule 7.49. This power is not to be exercised too freely or treated as an alternative to appeal.[80] In so far as a defendant does not attend at trial, there is specific provision in rule 8(2) of the Disqualification Rules and paragraph 14.2 of the Disqualification Practice Direction for judgment to be set aside. This power is likely to be exercised in the same way as the powers under CPR, r. 39.3[81] which also contains further ancillary powers to cover situations where neither party attends trial or the claimant fails to attend. The guiding principle is that the party applying for the judgment or order to be set aside must have (a) acted promptly once he ascertained the position, (b) a good reason for why he failed to attend the trial (c) a reasonable prospect of success at trial.

Costs

6.85 Particular points on costs relating to applications under the CDDA (*e.g.* for permission to act) which do not involve substantive proceedings for a disqualification order are dealt with elsewhere in this book. The general principle is that disqualification proceedings are no different to any other civil proceedings and the "public inter-

---

[80] See generally, and by way of analogy, *Re a Debtor (No. 32–SD/1991)* [1993] 1 W.L.R. 314; *Re S N Group plc* [1993] B.C.C. 808; *Re W & A Glaser Ltd* [1994] B.C.C. 199; *Fitch v. Official Receiver* [1996] 1 W.L.R. 242; *IRC v. Robinson* [1999] B.P.I.R. 329. The court was prepared to invoke the power, if necessary, to correct an incomplete order made under sections 6 and 1 in *Re Brian Sheridan Cars Ltd* [1996] 1 B.C.L.C. 327.
[81] See previously RSC Ord. 35, r. 2, CCR Ord. 37, r. 2 and *Shocked v. Goldschmidt* [1998] 1 All E.R. 372.

est" nature of the proceedings does not entitle the Secretary of State or official receiver to be treated differently on questions of costs to any other civil litigant. This is so, by way of example, whether the question concerns the basis on which costs are awarded[82] or costs payable on the withdrawal of proceedings.[83] The costs of disqualification proceedings can be high and, if a defendant is ultimately unsuccessful in resisting disqualification, he may find that the ultimate bill for costs is crippling. The judiciary often refer to the need for costs to be controlled and for disqualification proceedings to be dealt with in a summary fashion.[84] However, in many cases, at least where the case is fought, it is unlikely that costs will be significantly reduced. For this reason, the possibility of settlement through the mechanism of a summary hearing, may be a very attractive option (see Chapter 8). A number of general points can be made which arise from the CPR and the experience in disqualification proceedings to date:

(1) The question of what order as to costs should be made is a matter in the discretion of the court, taking into account all relevant factors (see generally CPR, Pt 44).

(2) As a general matter, costs will follow the event, that is the court will order the unsuccessful party to pay the successful party's costs (CPR, r. 44.3(2)). However, the court will perhaps be more ready than in the past to consider which party has won or lost on specific issues and to divide costs accordingly.[85] The court will also have regard (among other things) to the conduct of the parties during the course of the proceedings and costs can therefore become a disciplinary matter.[85a]

(3) In cases involving more than one defendant, a single costs order against all defendants will be treated as joint and several.[85b] Defendants may wish to give consideration to asking for costs to be apportioned. The court may, in appropriate circumstances, (a) make a single costs order but provide that, as between the defendants, the contribution of each defendant will be fixed in certain proportions or (b) apportion the costs separately so that the successful claimant receives an entitlement to costs in a fixed proportion as against each defendant. In carrying out an apportionment exercise, the court should probably consider the guidance given (albeit in criminal proceedings) in the course of the *Guinness* prosecutions.[86] The starting point would be to consider what a reasonable estimate of costs would be had each defendant been tried alone. There is something to be said for the view that, in an appropriate case, the total proportion of costs ordered against the defendants as a whole could be more than 100 per cent of the starting estimate provided that the claimant was not entitled to recover more than 100 per cent in total. Otherwise, the defendant might be relieved of costs that he would otherwise have had to pay had the proceedings been conducted separately against him and the claimant might receive much less than the costs otherwise attributable to that defendant

---

[82] *Re Dicetrade Ltd, Secretary of State for Trade and Industry v. Worth* [1994] B.C.C. 371, CA.

[83] *Re Southbourne Sheet Metal Co. Ltd (No. 2)* [1993] B.C.L.C. 135, CA.

[84] See, *e.g. Re Westmid Packing Services Ltd, Secretary of State for Trade and Industry v. Griffiths* [1998] 2 All E.R. 124, [1998] 2 B.C.L.C. 646, [1998] B.C.C. 836, CA.

[85] For a relevant case under the old law, see *Re Elgindata Ltd (No. 2)* [1992] 1 W.L.R. 1207 and, in the disqualification context, *Re Pamstock Ltd* [1994] 1 B.C.L.C. 716, [1994] B.C.C. 264, Ch.D. and, on the costs point [1996] B.C.C. 341, CA.

[85a] See, *e.g. Gruppo Torras SA v. Al Sabah*, July 5, 1999, Commercial Court, unreported, where successful defendants were deprived of up to two-thirds of their costs.

[85b] See *Mainwaring v. Goldtech Investments Ltd* [1999] 1 W.L.R. 745.

[86] *Ronson v. Pounds* 13 Cr. App. Rep. 153.

because of the financial position of other defendants. In such circumstances, there might be room for a complicated formula requiring the claimant to exhaust his remedies against one defendant first or go up to a specific amount on top of detailed provisions for contribution as between each defendant. The courts have, on occasions, apportioned costs as between defendants on the basis of the relative seriousness of the wrongdoing established against each defendant. However, it is suggested that the correct criterion is the length of time and costs involved in establishing a particular allegation rather than the degree of seriousness of the relevant conduct. The application of the latter as a criterion amounts to a punitive use of the costs rules. Even so, in practice, the more serious the allegation, the more time and cost is likely to be expended in establishing or defending an allegation. Finally, it should be noted that, in an appropriate case, there may be scope for an order that the claimant recover some (or all) of the costs he is ordered to pay to one defendant, from another defendant.[87]

MISCELLANEOUS

Inspecting the court file

6.86 The old law concerning inspection of the court's file in relation to disqualification proceedings can be found in *Dobson v. Hastings.*[88] The position is now governed by CPR, r. 5.4. This allows any party to proceedings to be supplied from the records of the court with a copy of any document relating to those proceedings provided he pays the prescribed fee and files a written request for the document. A non-party may search for, inspect and take a copy of the claim form and any judgment or order given or made in public on payment of the prescribed fee. Any other documents on the court file can only be inspected by a non-party with the court's permission (CPR, r. 5.4(c)).

Use of affidavits in other proceedings

6.87 There are restrictions on the use to which witness statements can be put. They cannot generally be used for other purposes (*e.g.* to stand as evidence in other non-disqualification proceedings) although there are narrow exceptions (see generally CPR, r. 32.12). There is no comparable rule restricting the use to which *affidavits* can be put. Equally, it is not clear whether a party would be the subject of an implied undertaking not to use them without say, the consent of the other party or parties and/or the permission of the court. The fact that affidavits and witness statements are for some purposes treated differently in the CPR appears somewhat anomalous.

---

[87] *Re Sykes (Butchers) Ltd, Secretary of State for Trade and Industry v. Richardson* [1998] 1 B.C.L.C. 110, [1998] B.C.C. 484.
[88] [1992] Ch. 394, [1992] 2 W.L.R. 414, [1992] 2 All E.R. 94.

CHAPTER 7

Permission to Commence Section 6 Proceedings Out of Time and the Impact of Delay in Civil Disqualification

INTRODUCTION

7.01   As has been seen, the effect of section 7(2) of the CDDA is that an application for a section 6 disqualification order cannot be made later than two years after the relevant company became insolvent unless the permission[1] of the court is first obtained.[2] Section 7(2) contains no formal guidance as to the approach which the court should adopt when faced with an application for permission to bring proceedings after the expiry of the two-year time limit. It has been left to the courts to develop their own approach. The factors which the courts take into account in determining whether or not to grant permission under section 7(2) form the main subject matter of this chapter.

On the question of whether the Secretary of State or official receiver[3] should be given permission to proceed against a director out of time, the court must perform a difficult balancing act. A number of competing aspects of the public interest are in play. First, at the heart of the CDDA, there is the broad interest in the protection of the public from directors whose past conduct makes them unfit to be concerned in the management of a company. Equally, the public's need for protection must be weighed against the rights of the individual director. It was seen in Chapter 2 that the impact of disqualification on the person can be characterised in broad terms as either the interference with a fundamental freedom or the removal of a special trading privilege. The tendency of the higher courts in England is to see disqualification more as a sanction for abuse of privilege than an interference with substantive human rights.[4] Even so, it is generally recognised that the individual has procedural rights which should be respected and accorded some weight. The time limit in section 7(2) is itself a form of procedural safeguard given that the Secretary of State has no automatic right to commence proceedings for a section 6 disqualification order after expiry of the two-year period. As

---

[1] The CDDA and cases decided before the reform of the civil justice system use the phrases "leave of the court" and "leave to act". In the light of the CPR, the Disqualification Rules and the Disqualification Practice Direction, the term "permission" is used throughout rather than the old term "leave" except in the case of direct quotes from the CDDA.
[2] There is no such time limit in the case of proceedings under the discretionary provisions in CDDA, ss 2–5, 10 (on which see Chap. 9) and s. 8.
[3] Reference hereafter to the Secretary of State should be read as including a reference to the official receiver.
[4] See, *e.g. Re Cedac Ltd, Secretary of State for Trade and Industry v. Langridge* [1991] Ch. 402, [1991] B.C.L.C. 543, [1991] B.C.C. 148, CA discussed in Chap. 2 and *R. v. Secretary of State for Trade and Industry ex. parte McCormick* [1998] B.C.C. 381, QBD and CA.

such, section 7(2) amounts to a possible indication from Parliament that directors are entitled to have disqualification proceedings commenced against them reasonably quickly and that, outside the two-year period, proceedings should only be started once the court has had an opportunity to balance the need for public protection against the director's rights.[5] A further related matter is the public interest in the fair and expeditious administration of justice coupled with the individual's right to a fair trial. The public interest in the fair and expeditious administration of justice is given expression in the overriding objective of the new Civil Procedure Rules.[6] The right to a fair trial is enshrined in Article 6 of the European Convention on Human Rights which now forms part of English law following the enactment of the Human Rights Act 1998. Under Article 6(1) everyone is entitled to a fair hearing within a reasonable time and this applies to proceedings which involve the determination of the individual's civil rights and obligations as well as to criminal proceedings.[7] The question of whether and if so, how, the English courts should give weight to a director's Article 6 rights on an application for permission under section 7(2) has yet to be considered directly. However, in the light of current public policy, the court is bound to scrutinise carefully the reasons why proceedings were not commenced promptly within the two-year time limit and construe any unjustifiable delay in the director's favour. As there are similarities in the way in which the courts approach an application for permission under section 7(2) and an application to dismiss for want of prosecution, applications of the latter type are also considered towards the end of this chapter.

PERMISSION TO COMMENCE PROCEEDINGS OUT OF TIME UNDER SECTION 7(2)

General points

7.02   The Secretary of State will need permission under section 7(2) in two circumstances:

(1) Where proceedings for a section 6 order are to be commenced more than two years after the relevant company became insolvent within the meaning of section 6(2).[8]

---

[5] It should be stressed that the courts do not regard section 7(2) as a limitation period in the classic sense of an absolute time-bar conferring a full immunity from suit: *Re Blackspur Group plc, Secretary of State for Trade and Industry v. Davies (No. 2)* [1996] 4 All E.R. 289 at 298–299, [1997] 2 B.C.L.C. 317 at 327, [1997] B.C.C. 235 at 243–244, CA. Indeed, the tendency is for applications under section 7(2) to be treated as glorified applications for an extension of time to comply with a procedural step. Factors similar to those relevant for section 7(2) purposes are often raised on applications to dismiss a claim for want of prosecution. For this reason, dismissal for want of prosecution in the context of disqualification proceedings is also considered later in this chapter.
[6] CPR, r. 1.1.
[7] It is fairly settled that disqualification proceedings constitute a dispute over "civil rights and obligations" within the meaning of Article 6(1) and that a director is therefore entitled to have the case against him determined within a reasonable time: see *EDC v. U.K.* [1998] B.C.C. 370. However, there is doubt over whether disqualification proceedings can be said to involve a "criminal charge" so as to afford a director the additional safeguards in Article 6(2) and (3): *R. v. Secretary of State for Trade and Industry ex. parte McCormick* [1998] B.C.C. 381, QBD and CA.
[8] A company "becomes insolvent" (and the two years starts to run) where (a) the company goes into liquidation at a time when its assets are insufficient for the payment of its debts and other liabilities and the expenses of winding up, (b) an administration order is made in relation to the company, or (c) an administrative receiver of the company is appointed. For a full discussion of section 6(2) and some of the problems which can arise see Chap. 6.

(2) Where the proceedings are issued within the two-year period against one or more defendants[9] but the Secretary of State later wishes to add a further defendant to proceedings after the two-year period has expired.[10]

One further situation that has arisen should not pass without comment. In *Re Blackspur Group plc, Secretary of State for Trade and Industry v. Davies (No. 2)*[11] proceedings under section 6 were commenced within the two-year time limit but the evidence in support of the proceedings was not ready to be filed and served with the originating process. The Secretary of State sought an extension of time to serve evidence until a date long after the expiry of the two-year period.[12] Although it was accepted by both parties that, in exercising his discretion, the judge should treat the application for an extension as if it had been an application for permission to issue the originating process out of time under section 7(2), Millet L.J. disagreed.[12a]

7.03   It was suggested by the Court of Appeal in *Re Blackspur Group plc, Secretary of State for Trade and Industry v. Davies (No. 2)* that section 7(2) serves two purposes. First, it reflects the public interest in the disqualification of unfit persons. The important point here is that a person who is unfit is free to act as a director until a disqualification order is made. As Hobhouse L.J. put it, "... the worse the case of unfitness, the greater need that a disqualification order be applied for and made at the earliest practicable date...".[13] Secondly, it gives the director a procedural right to object where proceedings are not commenced in time that he should not be subjected to a stale, oppressive or unmeritorious application. The crucial point here is that if the two-year period expires without the director hearing anything from the authorities, he should be entitled to assume that he is free to go about his business without the threat of proceedings. However, section 7(2) does not confer an immunity from suit. Its effect is that the application may only proceed if the court, in the exercise of what amounts to an unfettered discretion, considers that it should. Section 7(2) is thus more closely analogous to a procedural rule than to an absolute limitation and an application for permission resembles an application to extend the time available under rules of court for compliance with a procedural step. The same analysis led Millett L.J. to conclude in *Davies*

---

[9] Where applicable the terms "claimant" and "defendant" are used to reflect the modern requirements of the CPR, the Disqualification Rules and the Disqualification Practice Direction. In disqualification proceedings, "defendant" is the modern equivalent of the pre-CPR term "respondent" and so strictly the reference here should be to "defendants". However, confusion arises because on an application for permission under section 7(2) which is made by application notice under Pt 23 (see text below), the person against whom the order is sought is still referred to as the "respondent". Once permission is granted and the substantive disqualification proceedings are issued, the "respondent" becomes the "defendant"! For the avoidance of confusion, the term "respondent" is used in its Pt 23 sense in the discussion of section 7(2). We revert to the term "defendant" when discussing dismissal for want of prosecution as in those cases the defendant in the substantive disqualification proceedings is seeking to have them struck out.

[10] *Re Westmid Packaging Services Ltd, Secretary of State for Trade and Industry v. Griffiths* [1995] B.C.C. 203.

[11] [1996] 4 All E.R. 289, [1997] 2 B.C.L.C. 317, [1997] B.C.C. 235, CA (affirming Carnwath J. [1995] B.C.C. 835).

[12] In *Re Jazzgold Ltd* [1994] 1 B.C.L.C. 38, [1992] B.C.C. 587, it was suggested that the issue of the originating process within two years would be sufficient to comply with section 7(2) even if the evidence in support was filed and served outside the two years. However, it appears from certain observations made by Harman J. in *Re Crestjoy Products Ltd* [1990] B.C.L.C. 677 at 683, [1990] B.C.C. 23 at 28 that the view taken in the Disqualification Unit at the time of that decision was that all the supporting evidence had to be available at the time the originating process was issued.

[12a] Millett L.J. accepted that in such circumstances a similar approach would be adopted to that on an application to commence proceedings out of time and that similar factors would be taken into account. However, it would be easier to justify a failure to serve evidence than a failure to commence proceedings at all, especially where the proceedings have been served together with a statement of the grounds on which unfitness is alleged.

[13] [1996] 4 All E.R. 289 at 302, [1997] 2 B.C.L.C. 317 at 331, [1997] B.C.C. 235 at 246.

(No. 2) that the true function of the two-year period is not to provide the director with *absolute protection* but to ensure that he is aware in good time of the fact that proceedings are to be commenced and of the grounds for those proceedings:

> "One of the purposes which Parliament had in mind in enacting the two-year time limit must have been to allow directors of companies which have become insolvent a reasonable degree of security from disqualification with the passage of time. If they have been notified within the time limit, not only of the Secretary of State's decision to bring disqualification proceedings against them but also of the nature of the allegations upon which they are to be based, the statutory purpose has to this extent been fulfilled."[14]

7.04   The onus is on the Secretary of State to satisfy the court that permission to commence proceedings out of time should be granted. The Secretary of State must show that there is a good reason to justify an extension of the two-year period.[15] It appears that the court will only be prepared to grant prospective permission and not retrospective permission designed to enable existing proceedings already commenced (albeit out of time) to continue.[16]

Principles on which the discretion to grant permission is exercised

7.05   In *Re Probe Data Systems Ltd (No. 3), Secretary of State for Trade and Industry v. Desai*, Scott L.J. said:

> "In considering an application under section 7(2) for [permission] to commence disqualification proceedings out of time the court should, in my opinion, take into account the following matters: (1) the length of the delay, (2) the reasons for the delay, (3) the strength of the case against the director and (4) the degree of prejudice caused to the director by the delay."[17]

In the subsequent case of *Re Blackspur Group plc, Secretary of State for Trade and Industry v. Davies (No. 2)* Millett L.J. took the view that this was not an exhaustive statement and that all relevant circumstances should be taken into account including, but not limited to, the four particular matters mentioned by Scott L.J.[18] The main factors are considered in greater detail below. The general impression is that the pivotal factors to be balanced are the strength of the Secretary of State's case (meaning, in effect, the strength of the public interest in pursuing the respondent) and the countervailing effect of delay on the individual director. It cannot be emphasised enough that the court is exercising a discretion and that much may turn on the circumstances of the

---

[14] [1996] 4 All E.R. 289 at 299, [1997] 2 B.C.L.C. 317 at 328, [1997] B.C.C. 235 at 244.
[15] *Re Copecrest Ltd, Secretary of State for Trade and Industry v. McTighe* [1994] 2 B.C.L.C. 284 at 287, [1993] B.C.C. 844 at 852, CA; *Re Blackspur Group plc, Secretary of State for Trade and Industry v. Davies (No. 2)* [1996] 4 All E.R. 289 at 296, [1997] 2 B.C.L.C. 317 at 325, [1997] B.C.C. 235 at 241, CA.
[16] *Re Stormont Ltd, Secretary of State for Trade and Industry v. Cleland* [1997] 1 B.C.L.C. 437, [1997] B.C.C. 473; *Re Westmid Packaging Services Ltd, Secretary of State for Trade and Industry v. Griffiths* [1995] B.C.C. 203. However, the costs of such proceedings are not likely to be wholly wasted. The court is likely to order that the evidence in the proceedings commenced out of time should stand as evidence in any new proceedings for which permission is granted and may be prepared to adjourn issues of costs relating to the earlier proceedings to the final hearing of the new proceedings with "permission to apply" ("liberty to apply" in pre-CPR language) in the meantime.
[17] [1992] B.C.L.C. 405 at 416, [1992] B.C.C. 110 at 118. These factors derive from *C M Van Stillevoldt v. El Carriers Inc.* [1983] 1 W.L.R. 207, [1983] 1 All E.R. 699, CA which involved the exercise of a discretion to extend time for setting down a matter for hearing in the Court of Appeal.
[18] [1996] 4 All E.R. 289 at 296, [1997] 2 B.C.L.C. 317 at 325, [1997] B.C.C. 235 at 242.

particular case. Moreover, there is scope for differences in emphasis depending on the court's overall view of the disqualification process.[19]

Length of delay

7.06   It is clear that the court should take into account delay in bringing proceedings which occurs *before* the initial two years has expired. The court can and should consider why it was that the Secretary of State was unable to get his tackle in order within the two year period. To borrow some words of Harman J. at first instance in *Probe Data*, it is not correct to assume that the two years can be taken up by "any amount of indolence" just because Parliament has seen fit to allow the Secretary of State an initial period in which proceedings can be commenced as of right.[20]

The need for a section 7(2) application often arises in circumstances where proceedings were originally commenced in time but the validity of those original proceedings is contested by the defendant. A considerable period after expiry of the initial two years may well be used up in interlocutory proceedings to determine whether or not the original proceedings were incorrectly brought and should be struck out. Delays of this nature have not generally been taken into account by the court on an application by the Secretary of State to commence a fresh set of proceedings out of time.[21] This means that in many cases it is the nature of the delay *within* the two year period that will be critical.

7.07   In a case where the need for permission does not depend on the validity or otherwise of an earlier set of proceedings, the Secretary of State should make the application for permission without delay. If it is anticipated that the evidence in support of the substantive proceedings will not be ready in time, the application for permission should be made before the two-year period expires.[22] In *Re Crestjoy Products Ltd*[23] the respondents were sent ten-day letters in accordance with section 16 shortly before the expiry of the two-year period. However, the application for permission was not made until some ten weeks after the end of the two years. A further delay then occurred because the application for permission was drawn in the wrong form. Harman J. was not satisfied that a good reason for an extension of time had been shown and refused to give permission. Following the approach of Lord Brandon in *Kleinwort Benson Ltd v.*

---

[19] See general discussion in Chap. 2.

[20] [1991] B.C.L.C. 586 at 592, [1991] B.C.C. 428 at 433. See also *Re Copecrest Ltd, Secretary of State for Trade and Industry v. McTighe* [1994] 2 B.C.L.C. 284 at 287, [1993] B.C.C. 844 at 852, CA; *Re Stormont Ltd, Secretary of State for Trade and Industry v. Cleland* [1997] 1 B.C.L.C. 437, [1997] B.C.C. 473.

[21] See *Re Cedac Ltd* [1990] B.C.C. 555 (original proceedings held to be invalid by Mummery J. because the section 16 notice was one day short—period of delay arising while validity of original proceedings was contested not relevant—*n.b.* Mummery J. later reversed by CA on the section 16 point); *Re Probe Data Systems (No. 3), Secretary of State for Trade and Industry v. Desai* [1992] B.C.L.C. 405, [1992] B.C.C. 110, CA (original proceedings commenced incorrectly in the name of the official receiver rather than in the name of the Secretary of State—period of delay during which strike-out proceedings were on foot not taken into account); *Re Tasbian Ltd (No. 3), Official Receiver v. Nixon* [1993] B.C.L.C. 297, [1992] B.C.C. 358, CA (argument over whether original proceedings were commenced within time resolved in favour of respondent—court paying no attention to the period of delay occurring after the date of the original proceedings).

[22] It will assist the Secretary of State's prospects of success on an application for permission in these circumstances if the originating process is at least accompanied by a statement of the grounds on which it is alleged that the respondent is unfit: *Re Blackspur Group plc, Secretary of State for Trade and Industry v. Davies (No. 2)* [1996] 4 All E.R. 289 at 299, [1997] 2 B.C.L.C. 317 at 328, [1997] B.C.C. 235 at 244, CA (see paras 7.02–7.04). If this cannot be done in time, the director should know within the two years, at the very least, that the proceedings are to be brought and on what grounds in which case a very short delay *e.g.* of one day might not prove fatal: see *Secretary of State for Trade and Industry v. Carmichael* [1995] B.C.C. 679 (and note there that the court considered the scheduling and management of the case in the context of the Secretary of State's overall priorities and resources). The one situation in which failure to issue the originating summons or even to put the director on proper notice in time might be treated sympathetically is where the delay is wholly or partly attributable to the respondent's non co-operation with the insolvency practitioner: see *Re Copecrest Ltd* discussed below in para. 7.11.

[23] [1990] B.C.L.C. 677, [1990] B.C.C. 23.

Barbrak Ltd, The Myrto (No. 3)[24] (a case concerning an extension of time for service of a writ), the judge held that an extra hurdle must be overcome where permission is sought after expiry of the two-year period. The Secretary of State's failure to explain why an application for permission was not made before the expiry of the two-year period at the point when it must have been clear that the evidence required by rule 3 of the Disqualification Rules would not be ready in time proved fatal. It is striking that Harman J. had formed the view earlier in his judgment that mandatory disqualification under section 6 was "more nearly penal" when compared with disqualification under the former section 300 of the Companies Act 1985, "where a judge could, in the exercise of his discretion, say that although the conduct had been bad yet he was now convinced that a disqualification should not be made because, for example, the [defendant] had learnt his lesson".[25] Any delay by the Secretary of State in making the application for permission is likely to be compounded if the case against the respondent is not particularly strong.[26] However, even where the application for permission is made outside the two-year period, it should not be assumed that it will automatically fail. It is submitted that the court should consider all relevant factors and carry out a full balancing exercise while recognising that the Secretary of State's failure to apply for permission inside the two-year period will weigh in the respondent's favour.

Reasons for delay

7.08   One important question which has arisen is whether, on an application for permission under section 7(2), the Secretary of State must provide a good explanation for the failure to commence proceedings in time. In *Re Cedar Developments Ltd*,[27] the official receiver failed to commence proceedings in time as a result of an administrative muddle. The application for permission was made under a week after the two years had expired. Permission was refused. The judge took the view that disqualification proceedings are quasi-penal in nature with the effect that on an application for permission there is a real onus on the applicant to show a good reason why an extension of time should be granted. This onus had not been discharged. There was no sufficient explanation as to why it had taken the official receiver two years to get his tackle in order and why no margin had been allowed for unforeseen problems or mistakes of the type that had actually occurred. The court could not be expected to grant permission "semi-automatically" on the basis that the time limit had been missed by the small matter of a few days because of an administrative mistake. The judge added that in his view, "there can hardly be a good reason for permission without a good reason being shown why the time limit was missed".[28] In *Re Blackspur Group plc, Secretary of Trade and Industry v. Davies (No. 2)*, an attempt was made on behalf of the respondents to elevate this remark to the status of a threshold test. It was submitted that it is always necessary for the Secretary of State to provide a satisfactory explanation for the delay and, that if an adequate explanation is not forthcoming, the respondent is entitled to have the application for permission dismissed without consideration of any countervailing factors such as the strength of the case or lack of prejudice. The Court of Appeal categorically rejected the notion of a threshold test.

---

[24] [1987] A.C. 597, [1987] 2 All E.R. 289.
[25] [1990] B.C.L.C. 677 at 681, [1990] B.C.C. 23 at 26. For further discussion of *Crestjoy see* para. 7.25.
[26] See *Re Packaging Direct Ltd* [1994] B.C.C. 213; *Re Westmid Packing Services Ltd (No. 2), Secretary of State for Trade and Industry v. Morrall* [1996] B.C.C. 229. A notable feature of the *Packaging Direct* case was that the ten-day letters under section 16 were sent some nine months before the end of the two years indicating that the decision to proceed had actually been taken at that point. The application for permission was not made until nearly a year later, a delay described by Jacob J. as "very substantial and excessive".
[27] [1994] 2 B.C.L.C. 714, [1995] B.C.C. 220.
[28] [1994] 2 B.C.L.C. 714 at 719, [1995] B.C.C. 220 at 224.

7.09   The following salient points were made to support this conclusion:

(1) The Secretary of State is obliged to explain why he failed to issue the proceedings or serve the supporting evidence (as the case may be) in time. Once an explanation is given it becomes a matter to be considered along with all the other relevant circumstances. There is no justification for treating the adequacy of the explanation as a free standing or threshold test which must be satisfied before other considerations can be taken into account.

(2) The notion of a threshold test is incorrect in principle and unworkable in practice. In the absence of a deliberate decision to disregard the rules, there is no such thing as a "good" or "bad" reason for delay or a reason which is inherently acceptable or unacceptable. The correct test is whether the reason for delay may reasonably be accepted as sufficient to justify an extension of time in all the circumstances of the particular case. The court might be satisfied with an explanation such as forgetfulness for a minimal delay but not for a longer period of delay. Thus, while forgetfulness is not itself a satisfactory reason for delay, it might be accepted as sufficient to justify an extension of time where it was supported by other considerations including the fact that the delay was minimal.

(3) There is nothing in the test put forward by Scott L.J. in *Probe Data* to suggest that a "good" reason for the delay must be shown before any other factors are considered. The Secretary of State must show a good reason to justify being granted an extension of time but this is not the same as having to show a good reason for the delay as a pre-condition.[29]

(4) The notion of a threshold test runs contrary to the public interest in the disqualification of unfit directors. If there was such a test, directors responsible for serious misconduct would escape disqualification in cases where there is no "good"explanation for the delay without any consideration being given to the strength and serious nature of the charges against them. This result would also arguably elevate the status of the two-year period in section 7(2) closer to that of an immunity from suit.

7.10   On the facts of *Davies (No. 2)*, the Secretary of State issued the proceedings within the two-year period but was not able to file the evidence in support required by rule 3 of the Disqualification Rules in time. The problem had arisen because the directors of the relevant group of companies were also under investigation by the Serious Fraud Office which had taken possession of the group's books and records. The Secretary of State requested assistance from the Serious Fraud Office but this was not forthcoming until about six weeks before the two-year deadline was due to expire. Without access to the books and records it was not possible to prepare detailed evidence in support of the substantive proceedings. By the time the Serious Fraud Office agreed to make the relevant information available there was insufficient time to finalise the evidence before the end of the two-year period. It was accepted by the court that the reasons put forward by the Secretary of State were far from satisfactory. However, this was outweighed by a number of other countervailing considerations. The most important of these was the seriousness of the case against the respondents but also

---

[29] In *Re Cedar Developments Ltd* itself a submission to the effect that it is unnecessary to carry out a detailed balancing exercise unless a good reason can be shown as to why proceedings were not commenced in time was expressly rejected by the judge.

relevant was the absence of any prejudice to the respondents and the fact that the timetable for the disqualification proceedings had not been affected because the hearing could not take place realistically until after parallel criminal proceedings had been determined.[30]

7.11   If the delay or any part of it is attributable to the conduct of the respondent this will be a factor weighing in the Secretary of State's favour. In *Re Copecrest Ltd, Secretary of State for Trade and Industry v. McTighe*,[31] the Disqualification Unit did not receive the final D report from the liquidator of the relevant company until a date less than one month before the two-year period was due to expire. The application for permission was made one week after the end of the two years. Even so, the Court of Appeal allowed the Secretary of State's appeal against an earlier refusal by the judge to grant permission. The primary responsibility for the delay lay with the respondents. A statement of affairs had been sworn which suggested that the company, although unable to pay its debts as they fell due, was solvent on a balance sheet basis. The company had ceased trading and sold its assets and business to a second company controlled by the respondents for the sum of £1.4 million payable over five years. The company's only asset on liquidation was the unpaid balance of the purchase price, a sum of around £1.2 million which was said in the statement of affairs to be fully recoverable. The liquidator then spent some 18 months attempting to collect the debt on the basis that if payment was received the company would be solvent and its creditors would be paid in full. On this basis he also delayed in submitting a D report. Despite the liquidator's best efforts, the company received only a single payment of £5,000 and no concrete proposals for payment of the rest of the outstanding balance were ever forthcoming. The fact that the respondents had contributed to the delay by stringing the liquidator along with promises of payment taken together with the serious nature of the allegations made against them were critical factors weighing in the Secretary of State's favour. The Court of Appeal's overall conclusion is well-summarised in the following passage from Hoffmann L.J.'s judgment:

"[The Secretary of State] is not entitled to assume that any period of delay for which he is not responsible will automatically be added by the court on to the two-year period. He must take into account that such delays may curtail the period available to him. What, however, the learned judge does not appear to have taken into account is the directors' own responsibility for the delay on the part of the liquidator. The directors had sworn a statement of affairs showing the company to be solvent and thereafter tried ... to string the liquidator along with promises of payment. The respondents say that the liquidator should have realised much earlier that the debt would never be paid, but in my view it does not lie in the mouths of the directors to say that the liquidator should have realised that they were only prevaricating. I regard the directors' responsibility for the curtailment of the period available to the Secretary of State from 18 months to three weeks as a very significant feature in this case. ... If, therefore, one takes into account, as the judge did not, the directors' responsibility for the earlier delay and what the judge agreed to be the serious nature of the allegations being made

---

[30] Equally, if no satisfactory explanation is forthcoming, the court may refuse an application for permission where the case against a director is not particularly strong even though the Secretary of State erred in missing the two-year deadline by only a single day: *Re Stormont Ltd, Secretary of State for Trade and Industry v. Cleland* [1997] 1 B.C.L.C. 437, [1997] B.C.C. 473.
[31] [1994] 2 B.C.L.C. 284, [1993] B.C.C. 844.

against these directors, the balance, in my view, clearly comes down in favour of the grant of an extension."[32]

7.12 On a similar note, it is possible that the Secretary of State might receive a sympathetic hearing in circumstances where the insolvency practitioner delays in submitting a D report because his investigation into the company's affairs is hampered by a lack of proper books and records. It is logical that the Secretary of State should not be penalised for a delay which is directly attributable to the failure of directors to maintain proper books and records in breach of Companies Act requirements, not least because such a failure is itself indicative of their unfitness.[33] Against this, there is some onus on the Secretary of State to monitor the position closely and, where necessary, to use the threat of sanctions under the Insolvent Companies (Reports on Conduct of Directors) Rules 1996 and the powers in section 7(4) as a means to press the matter forwards.[34] A realistic timetable for each case needs to be set and periodically reviewed. The insolvency practitioner should be asked to estimate how long it might take him to submit a final report and assemble supporting evidence. If a case has been properly monitored in this way and the application for permission is made before the end of the two years, there is a fair chance that any delay which is not directly attributable to the Disqualification Unit will not weigh heavily against the Secretary of State.[35]

Strength of case

7.13 In *Re Blackspur Group plc, Secretary of State for Trade and Industry v. Davies (No. 2)*, the "strength of case" factor was expressed in terms of the public interest. Millett L.J. stated:

> "One factor which is always present but always relevant is the nature of the proceedings. The Secretary of State is not seeking to vindicate a private right, but to protect the public from the actions of a person alleged to be unfit to be a director of a company. Scott L.J.'s reference [in *Probe Data*] to 'the strength of the case against the director' must be read in this light."[36]

In similar vein, Hobhouse L.J. said:

> "If a 'good reason' has to be looked for, it is not a reason for the delay but a reason for giving [permission] . . . that reason will normally be found in the public interest that unfit directors be disqualified unless the proposed application under section 6 lacks substance or there is some sufficient countervailing factor."[37]

Seen in these terms, a strong case for disqualification will be a powerful factor weighing in the Secretary of State's favour on an application for permission. However,

---

[32] [1994] 2 B.C.L.C. 284 at 287–288, [1993] B.C.C. 844 at 852–853. Further support for the view that permission may be granted where the delay is occasioned by the conduct of the respondent can be derived from *dictum* of Harman J. in *Re Jaymar Management Ltd* [1990] B.C.L.C. 617 at 623–624, [1990] B.C.C. 303 at 308.

[33] See paras 5.13–5.19.

[34] See discussion in Chap. 3 and in *Re Launchexcept Ltd, Secretary of State for Trade and Industry v. Tillman* [1999] B.C.C. 703.

[35] See *dictum* of Millett L.J. in *Re Blackspur Group plc, Secretary of State for Trade and Industry v. Davies (No. 2)* [1996] 4 All E.R. 289 at 295, [1997] 2 B.C.L.C. 317 at 324, [1997] B.C.C. 235 at 240–241.

[36] [1996] 4 All E.R. 289 at 296–297, [1997] 2 B.C.L.C. 317 at 325, [1997] B.C.C. 235 at 242.

[37] [1996] 4 All E.R. 289 at 304, [1997] 2 B.C.L.C. 317 at 333, [1997] B.C.C. 235 at 248. Hobhouse L.J. drew an analogy with the approach taken on applications to dismiss disqualification proceedings for want of prosecution where the court rests its decision on an assessment of the public interest in allowing the proceedings to continue: see main text below.

it is not entirely clear what the Secretary of State is required to show in order to establish a "strong case". First, there is some debate as to whether the Secretary of State must establish a strong case by reference to *the allegations* or *the evidence*. Millett L.J. expressed the view in *Davies (No. 2)* that "the strength of the case" was a reference to the gravity of the charges made not to the strength or credibility of the supporting evidence.[38] However, in *Re Stormont Ltd, Secretary of State for Trade and Industry v. Cleland*, Lloyd J. concluded that, despite the observations of Millett L.J., the court should consider not just the nature and gravity of the charges made on their face but also whether and to what extent those charges are fairly raised by the evidence.[39] On this view, the court must form a provisional opinion of the Secretary of State's case having given some consideration to the supporting evidence and the respondent's evidence in reply. Lloyd J. was fortified in this conclusion by the approach in *Probe Data (No. 3)* where Scott L.J. considered affidavits sworn by the relevant office holder and the respondent before resolving the application in the Secretary of State's favour.[40] This appears to be the better view. However, as an application for permission is essentially interlocutory in nature and is designed to determine merely whether a case can go forward for trial, the court should be careful not to allow it to turn into a mini-trial.[41]

7.14   The second (and closely related) area of debate surrounds the applicable test for a "strong case". It was suggested by Balcombe L.J. in *Re Tasbian (No. 3), Official Receiver v. Nixon* that the case must be "fairly arguable":

> "On an application ... for [permission] to bring proceedings ... out of time what is the test to be applied? In my judgment, it is the same test as that which is used on any application to the court for [permission] to take some initiating procedure out of time, for example [permission] to appeal out of time. There can be no point in extending the time if the application is going to fail. If, however, the court is satisfied that the evidence shows a fairly arguable case on the applicant's part, then on this ground alone, that is leaving aside the reasons for the delay and any questions of prejudice to the other party, the court will not refuse [permission]."[42]

The implication is that the Secretary of State need only show that there is a reasonable prospect of success for this factor to count in his favour. However, in *Re Packaging*

---

[38] [1996] 4 All E.R. 289 at 297, [1997] 2 B.C.L.C. 317 at 325, [1997] B.C.C. 235 at 242. He expressed the same view (as Millett J.) in *Re Probe Data Systems (No. 2), Secretary of State for Trade and Industry v. Desai* [1990] B.C.L.C. 574, [1990] B.C.C. 21 although it should be noted that the overall view of the procedure to be adopted on an application for permission under section 7(2) put forward in that case was later superseded: see paras 7.29–7.30.

[39] [1997] 1 B.C.L.C. 437 at 447, [1997] B.C.C. 473 at 480.

[40] [1992] B.C.L.C. 405 at 416–417, [1992] B.C.C. 110 at 119–120. See also *Re Packaging Direct Ltd* [1994] B.C.C. 213 in which a "broad brush" assessment of the merits was favoured.

[41] *Re Packaging Direct Ltd* [1994] B.C.C. 213 at 215–216. There has been further debate over how the court should approach the available evidence. In *Re Polly Peck International plc (No. 2)* [1994] 1 B.C.L.C. 574 at 598, [1993] B.C.C. 890 at 910–911 Lindsay J. suggested that the court could treat any part of the respondent's evidence not expressly admitted in the Secretary of State's evidence or submissions as undisputed for the purposes of assessing the strength of the case. This approach (which reflects Lindsay J.'s view that the legislation is quasi-penal in effect) was not followed in *Re Stormont Ltd, Secretary of State for Trade and Industry v. Cleland* (see [1997] 1 B.C.L.C. 437 at 447, [1997] B.C.C. 473 at 480) because of the danger of the Secretary of State would feel bound to controvert everything that might be in issue in the respondent's case and the application for permission might thus become weighed down with a mound of evidence. The authors suggest that the seriousness of the *allegations* made is one factor to be taken into account and weighed in the balance and that the *evidential strength* of the case is another factor. However, given the nature of the hearing, the court should avoid spending a lot of time in weighing all the evidence to reach a view as to the evidential strength of the case. Only in the clearest of cases should the court decide that the evidence is too weak to sustain a case. It will be interesting to see if the CPR test for summary judgment has any impact.

[42] [1993] B.C.L.C. 297 at 301–302, [1992] B.C.C. 358 at 362.

Direct Ltd, Jacob J. indicated that an "arguable case" type of test was not appropriate and that what had to be established was a "strong case" taking into account all the available evidence while having regard in the overall balance to other factors such as the length of the delay and the explanation given for it.[43] In *Re Polly Peck International plc (No. 2)*,[44] Lindsay J. put forward a two-stage approach which amounts to a synthesis of these competing approaches. He suggested first that the court should apply an initial threshold test to determine whether the allegations made by the Secretary of State could result in disqualification assuming those allegations to be true. Only once this threshold is crossed should the court consider the strength of the case on the evidence and balance that along with the other relevant factors. If it is not crossed then, in Lindsay J.'s view, the application should fail without any consideration of other factors, "... as it would be pointless to allow to proceed a case which could not succeed".[45] Similarly, in *Re Stormont Ltd, Secretary of State for Trade and Industry v. Cleland*, Lloyd J. asked himself whether there was evidence on which the court might come to the conclusion that the conduct of the respondent as a director made him unfit to be concerned in the management of a company, describing this also as a "threshold test".[46] It is submitted that there is no necessity for this kind of threshold test. The true test is whether, on the available evidence and in the light of all the circumstances, the Secretary of State has shown a "good reason" why the court should grant permission. If the case is unlikely to succeed, the Secretary of State will find it very difficult to show a "good reason". Moreover, it is hard to imagine the Secretary of State going to the trouble of putting together a case unless it contains some allegations which are at least *indicative* of unfitness. It was seen in Chapter 4 that it is difficult in a marginal case to determine whether the respondent's conduct falls on the acceptable or unacceptable side of the line.[47] In the light of this difficulty the court will usually have to move to Lindsay J.'s second stage anyway with the result that the threshold test becomes superfluous. As such, a court faced with an application for permission is likely to adopt the safest course and carry out a full balancing exercise.

7.15   A further issue concerns the treatment of allegations relating to collateral companies. In *Re Westmid Packaging Services Ltd (No. 2), Secretary of State for Trade and Industry v. Morrall*,[48] the court did not give any weight to collateral allegations in assessing the seriousness of the case against the respondent. The judge made the point that the Secretary of State had chosen not to bring proceedings in relation to those allegations within two years of the collateral companies becoming insolvent. The inference drawn was that the Secretary of State did not regard the collateral allegations as having sufficient weight to justify full "lead company" proceedings. That being so, the court would not give them much weight either. It is suggested that this approach to collateral allegations in the context of an application under section 7(2) should be treated with caution. As a matter of principle, it is open to the Secretary of State to raise allegations concerning collateral companies more than two years after such companies became insolvent. The two-year rule applies to lead companies. The justification for this is that a pattern of repeated misconduct may only emerge after a series of insolvencies. Even if the judge in *Westmid Packing (No. 2)* was right on the facts to give little weight to the collateral allegations, it is suggested that it is wrong in principle to give no

---

[43] [1994] B.C.C. 213 at 218, 220.
[44] [1994] 1 B.C.L.C. 574, [1993] B.C.C. 890.
[45] [1994] 1 B.C.L.C. 574 at 591, [1993] B.C.C. 890 at 904.
[46] [1997] 1 B.C.L.C. 437 at 455, [1997] B.C.C. 473 at 487.
[47] See paras 4.14–4.20.
[48] [1996] B.C.C. 229.

weight to collateral allegations simply because the Secretary of State has not chosen to bring "lead company" proceedings on the back of those allegations.[49]

Degree of prejudice caused by delay

7.16   Prejudice to the respondent may arise in three possible forms. The first type of potential prejudice is the prolonged stress and worry that a director may suffer from having the threat of proceedings hang over him beyond the expiry of the two years. It was suggested in *Re Polly Peck International plc (No. 2)* that prolonged stress arising because the threat of proceedings remains a possibility for longer than it might otherwise have done may, on suitable facts, represent such serious prejudice that the court will refuse permission.[50] The second type of potential prejudice is that which the delay may have on the prospects for a fair trial. The strength of the director's evidence may weaken with the passage of time and the dimming of witnesses' memories. In *Polly Peck (No. 2)*, Lindsay J. calculated that the full trial in that case would have been delayed by at least a year as a result of the Secretary of State's failure to launch proceedings in time. One respondent was seeking to rely on evidence from three elderly co-directors, two of whom were suffering from failing health. The judge concluded that there was a real risk of prejudice to the respondent because, in the circumstances, the delay of a year was likely to result in a diminishing of the strength and availability of his evidence.[51] However, the delay in the overall timetable caused by the need for an application for permission should not be exaggerated as, in preparing evidence to be adduced on the "strength of case" factor, the parties may end up saving time later should the matter proceed.[52] The third type of potential prejudice is the impact which the threat of proceedings may have on a director's job prospects and livelihood. This has been taken into account in cases involving "professional" directors who earn their living from holding directorships. For instance in *Polly Peck (No. 2)*, the judge accepted the contention of one of the respondents that the continued risk of disqualification would reduce his prospects of obtaining employment at a level commensurate with his qualifications and experience. Moreover, as he had reached the age of 60, this amounted to real prejudice because he only had a few years left in which to earn a living and provide for his retirement.[53] However, it may be difficult for the owner-manager of

---

[49] For a full discussion of "lead" and "collateral" companies in proceedings under section 6 see Chap. 3.

[50] [1994] 1 B.C.L.C. 574 at 602, [1993] B.C.C. 890 at 914. One of the respondents was in his seventies and in poor health. In the light of the medical evidence, Lindsay J. thought that the mere prolongation of the proceedings would cause substantial prejudice to him. However, mere anxiety arising because of the prolongation of proceedings has not generally been treated as sufficient to justify the striking out of an action for want of prosecution: see, *e.g. Department of Transport v. Chris Smaller (Transport) Ltd* [1989] A.C. 1197, [1989] 2 W.L.R. 578, [1989] 1 All E.R. 897, HL and, in the disqualification context, *Re Manlon Trading Ltd, Official Receiver v. Aziz* [1996] Ch. 136, [1995] 3 W.L.R. 839, [1995] 4 All E.R. 14, [1995] 1 B.C.L.C. 578, [1995] B.C.C. 579, CA.

[51] [1994] 1 B.C.L.C. 574 at 603, [1993] B.C.C. 890 at 915. This can be contrasted with the decision in *Davies (No. 2)* discussed earlier where there was no prejudice because, in the light of the need to determine the parallel criminal proceedings first, the timetable for the disqualification proceedings was unaffected by the Secretary of State's failure to apply within two years. See also *Re Manlon Trading Ltd, Official Receiver v. Aziz* [1996] Ch. 136, [1995] 3 W.L.R. 839, [1995] 4 All E.R. 14, [1995] 1 B.C.L.C. 578, [1995] B.C.C. 579, CA. It remains to be seen whether the decision of the European Commission of Human Rights in *EDC v. United Kingdom* [1998] B.C.C. 370 will lead to a treatment of delay arising as a result of parallel proceedings which is more favourable to directors.

[52] See *Re Stormont Ltd, Secretary of State for Trade and Industry v. Cleland* [1997] 1 B.C.L.C. 437 at 455, [1997] B.C.C. 473 at 487. The loss by an office holder of company documents that could potentially assist the director might not be treated as being sufficiently prejudicial to justify the refusal of permission: see *Re Dexmaster Ltd, Secretary of State for Trade and Industry v. Joyce* [1995] 2 B.C.L.C. 430, [1995] B.C.C. 186 though note that this case involved an application to strike out proceedings which had been commenced in time rather than an application for permission under section 7(2).

[53] [1994] 1 B.C.L.C. 574 at 603, [1993] B.C.C. 890 at 915. See also *Re Westmid Packing Services Ltd (No. 2), Secretary of State for Trade and Industry v. Morrall* [1996] B.C.C. 229 at 244–245.

a small private company to establish that the continued threat of proceedings is prejudicial to his livelihood as it is open to him to carry on the same business without the benefit of limited liability.[54] This third type of prejudice is controversial because the impact which disqualification or the threat of disqualification may have in an individual case will often be a matter of pure speculation. Whether evidence of such prejudice is favourably or poorly received may depend in part on the court's overall view of the disqualification process and the legal nature of its impact on the person.[55] If this factor is to carry much weight it will need to be established at the very least that the prejudice arose as a result of the delay in the commencement of proceedings. It is technically possible for a respondent to resist an application for permission successfully without establishing that the delay has caused actual prejudice or given rise to a substantial risk that a fair trial will no longer be possible. The onus remains with the Secretary of State to show "good reason".[56] Equally, the Secretary of State will not necessarily fail simply because the court accepts that there is prejudice. It is a question of balancing all the factors.

The balancing exercise

7.17   It was seen above how the Court of Appeal carried out the balancing exercise in *Davies (No. 2)*, the unsatisfactory delay in that case being outweighed by the strength of the allegations, the lack of any prejudice to the respondents and the fact that the late-filing of the applicant's evidence had not delayed the hearing which would have to await the outcome of parallel criminal proceedings in any event. Further illustrations of how the court balances the various factors is provided in this section.

Successful applications

7.18   The following are examples of cases where the application for permission was successful:

7.19   *Re Cedac Ltd, Secretary of State for Trade and Industry v. Langridge*.[57]   In this case it was held at first instance that the original proceedings were invalid because the Secretary of State had failed to give at least ten days' notice of intention to proceed as required by section 16. However, the Secretary of State was given permission to

---

[54] See the observation of Harman J. at first instance in *Probe Data* [1991] B.C.L.C. 586 at 593, [1991] B.C.C. 428 at 434 to the effect that the director could have chosen to run his current business through the form of a partnership rather than a limited company. This finding was left untouched on the subsequent appeal. Several applications brought by owner-managers under section 17 for permission to act as directors while disqualifed have failed on similar reasoning: see *Re Streamhaven Ltd, Secretary of State for Trade and Industry v. Barnett* [1998] 2 B.C.L.C. 64; *Re Amaron Ltd* [1998] B.C.C. 264; *Re Universal Flooring and Driveways Ltd, Secretary of State for Trade and Industry v. Woodward*, May 15, 1997, Ch.D., unreported and further discussion in Chap. 13.

[55] See Chap. 2, the discussion of *de facto* disqualification in paras 5.82–5.84 and the further discussion below of "inherent" prejudice in the context of dismissal for want of prosecution. One possible solution to the problems of delay and potential prejudice which balances the protective aspect of the legislation and the rights of the individual director (giving priority to the former) is for the case to proceed and the defendant to be "compensated" for delay etc. by a reduction in any period of disqualification ordered. However, as was pointed out in *Re Manlon Trading Ltd, Official Receiver v. Aziz* [1996] Ch. 136, [1995] 3 W.L.R. 839, [1995] 1 B.C.L.C. 578, [1995] B.C.C. 579 and *Re Westmid Packing Services Ltd (No. 2), Secretary of State for Trade and Industry v. Morrall* [1996] B.C.C. 229 at 245, such a reduction could not be made where the defendant is liable to be disqualified on the facts for no more than the minimum period of two years.

[56] In contrast, on an application to dismiss a claim for want of prosecution, the onus is on the defendant (at least under pre-CPR law) who is generally required to establish that the delay has caused actual prejudice: see, *e.g. Birkett v. James* [1978] A.C. 297, [1977] 3 W.L.R. 38, [1977] 2 All E.R. 801 and see discussion below from para. 7.33.

[57] [1990] B.C.C. 555.

commence fresh proceedings out of time. The original proceedings had been issued in time. The allegations against the respondent (which included insolvent trading and causing the company to enter into a transaction at an undervalue) were described as "grave". There was no prejudice to the respondent as all the evidence filed in relation to the original proceedings was available for use in the fresh proceedings and so the timetable for the hearing had not been affected. These matters outweighed the Secretary of State's failure to provide an adequate explanation as to why the giving of notice and commencement of proceedings had been left until the end of the period.[58]

7.20 *Re Probe Data Systems Ltd (No. 3), Secretary of State for Trade and Industry v. Desai.*[59] The original proceedings were commenced in time in the name of the official receiver but were later struck out because the official receiver has no *locus standi* to commence proceedings in his own name where the relevant company went into creditors' voluntary liquidation.[60] The Court of Appeal (affirming Harman J.) gave the Secretary of State permission to commence fresh proceedings out of time. The original proceedings had been issued two weeks before the end of the two-year period. The evidence (supporting allegations of breach of fiduciary duty, undervalue transactions and insolvent trading) disclosed a "well arguable case" that the respondent was unfit. The delay attributable to the procedural error was reasonably explained. Any criticism which could be levelled at the authorities for failing to commence the original proceedings earlier than two weeks before expiry of the two years was outweighed by the strength of the case against the respondent.[61]

7.21 *Re Tasbian Ltd (No. 3), Official Receiver v. Nixon.*[62] The original proceedings were commenced less than two years after a compulsory winding up order had been made in relation to the relevant company. However, the company had gone into administrative receivership some two months before the date of the winding up order. The respondent successfully argued that the proceedings were out of time because the two year period ran from the date of the earlier receivership.[63] The Court of Appeal subsequently gave the official receiver permission to commence fresh proceedings out of time. The evidence disclosed an "arguable case" that the respondent, who was described as a consultant, had acted as a *de facto* director of the company. In particular, the evidence suggested that the respondent had exerted a considerable degree of control over the company's finances in that its bank account could not be operated without his consent. He also played an influential part in the decision to transfer all of the employees to a separate company set up for the purpose of supplying their services back to the company on a subcontracted basis. In addition to an "arguable case" for disqualification, the delay in the commencement of proceedings was, in the Court of

---

[58] The decision on the section 16 point was overturned on appeal and the original proceedings reinstated: see [1991] Ch. 402, [1991] B.C.L.C. 543, [1991] B.C.C. 148. The majority in the Court of Appeal expressed the view *obiter* that there would have been no ground for interfering with the judge's decision to grant permission had they upheld his conclusion on section 16.

[59] [1992] B.C.L.C. 405, [1992] B.C.C. 110.

[60] See *Re Probe Data Systems Ltd (No. 2)* [1990] B.C.L.C. 561, (1989) 5 B.C.C. 384. A different result was reached in *Re NP Engineering and Security Products Ltd* [1998] 1 B.C.L.C. 208, CA.

[61] The Court of Appeal was also unimpressed by the respondent's claim that the delay between 1988 (when the original proceedings were commenced) and the end of 1991 (when the decision under discussion was made) had led to the evidence of various witnesses being lost. These matters of potential prejudice were said to carry little weight given that the respondent had been aware since 1988 of the likelihood that he would be proceeded against. The implication is that he should have taken steps to obtain affidavits from relevant witnesses in 1988 on the basis that their evidence might still have been admissible if, as was claimed, they subsequently died or lost touch.

[62] [1993] B.C.L.C. 297, [1992] B.C.C. 358.

[63] See *Re Tasbian Ltd (No. 1)* [1991] B.C.L.C. 54, [1990] B.C.C. 318, CA.

Appeal's view, sufficiently explained by the official receiver's mistaken assumption that a fresh two years ran from the date of the winding up order.

7.22 *Re Copecrest Ltd, Secretary of State for Trade and Industry v. McTighe.*[64] The Secretary of State failed to commence proceedings in time because the final D report was only received by the Disqualification Unit just under a month before the end of the two year period. A further period of 11 weeks was allowed to pass before the Secretary of State issued the application for permission. This further period of delay attracted some criticism in the Court of Appeal. However, the overall balance favoured the Secretary of State given that much of the earlier delay was attributable to the uncooperative attitude displayed by the respondents towards the company's liquidator and that the allegations against them were serious in nature.[65]

7.23 *Re Stormont Ltd, Secretary of State for Trade and Industry v. Cleland.*[66] The original proceedings were issued one day late by mistake. Permission to commence fresh proceedings out of time was granted in respect of the first respondent. The Secretary of State and Treasury Solicitor were criticised for proceeding with "less urgency than they might have done" during the two-year period and, in allowing matters to run right up to the wire, they had risked the possibility of failing to commence proceedings in time. Against this, the judge was not satisfied that any real prejudice had been caused by the delay because much of the evidence had already been prepared and so the timetable for the proceedings would not be seriously affected. Moreover, the case against the first respondent (including allegations of excessive remuneration, misapplication of funds and misrepresentation of the company's financial position to creditors) was sufficiently strong to amount to a good reason why permission should be granted.[67]

Unsuccessful applications

7.24 By way of contrast, the following are examples of cases where the application for permission was dismissed:

7.25 *Re Crestjoy Products Ltd.*[68] The application for permission was not made until some ten weeks after the end of the two years even though notice under section 16 was given in time. The Secretary of State's explanation for the delay was that by the time investigations in relation to two of the four respondents were completed only three weeks of the two year period remained. Harman J. criticised the Secretary of State for failing to explain why it was not decided to proceed separately against the other two respondents (in relation to whom investigations were completed roughly two months before the end of the two years) and why the application for permission was not issued within the two years once it was realised that it would be impossible to prepare the evidence in support of substantive proceedings in time. The judge said that an extra hurdle must be overcome where the application to extend time is made after the relevant time limit has expired. Here there was no good reason to extend time principally because of the Secretary of State's failure to explain why it had taken ten

---

[64] [1994] 2 B.C.L.C. 284, [1993] B.C.C. 844.
[65] *cf.* discussion in paras 7.08–7.12 and on the nature of the allegations see *Re Copecrest Ltd, Secretary of State for Trade and Industry v. McTighe (No. 2)* [1996] 2 B.C.L.C. 477, [1997] B.C.C. 224, CA.
[66] [1997] 1 B.C.L.C. 437, [1997] B.C.C. 473.
[67] Permission was refused in relation to the second respondent as the case against him was regarded as "too weak". The only matter which the judge considered would go towards justifying a finding of unfitness in his case was an allegation that he had received excessive bonus payments.
[68] [1990] B.C.L.C. 677, [1990] B.C.C. 23.

weeks to issue the application for permission. The strength of the case against the respondents and the question of prejudice caused by the delay were not canvassed in the judgment. Moreover, Harman J. formed the view that mandatory disqualification under section 6 amounts to a serious matter involving a substantial interference with the freedom of the individual and this appears to have influenced his approach. One possible justification for the decision is that once a period well in excess of two years has passed by without proceedings being commenced the individual may fairly and reasonably assume that it is safe to take up directorships with the consequence that the late commencement of proceedings might give rise to actual prejudice. In other words, there may come a point (albeit one that is difficult to identify with any precision) where the prejudice becomes a very strong factor against the grant of permission to bring proceedings out of time because the delay is such that it gives the impression that no proceedings are contemplated. Thus, if the individual takes up new directorships on the reasonable assumption that he is immune from suit, it is arguably unfair for the Secretary of State to be given permission.[69]

7.26   *Re Polly Peck International plc (No. 2).*[70]   Application for permission to proceed out of time was made in relation to four respondents two of whom were non-executive directors. Disqualification proceedings were originally commenced within time, but these were later withdrawn by consent. The application for permission was eventually made just over three months after the expiry of the two-year period. The main difficulty facing the administrators and the Disqualification Unit in this case was the sheer size and complexity of the company's affairs. The company had subsidiaries in several countries including North Cyprus, Turkey, Hong Kong, the US, Switzerland, Liberia and the Cayman Islands and so the insolvency was on an international scale. The upshot was that the joint-administrators were late in submitting interim returns and by the time a final report on the company's directors was submitted, less than four months of the two years was left. Further delays occurred in the preparation of affidavit evidence first because of a failure on the part of the Treasury Solicitor to issue formal instructions to counsel and later because a question arose as to whether the joint-administrators could properly disclose information obtained by them through the use of powers in sections 235 and 236 of the Insolvency Act 1986 to the Secretary of State for the purposes of the disqualification proceedings.[71] Lindsay J. criticised the Secretary of State's lack of urgency and, in particular, the failure either to press the joint-administrators on their reporting obligations or to make use of the information gathering powers in section 7(4).[72] Moreover, the judge found that the

---

[69] However, if the respondents received notice of intention to proceed under section 16 within the two years this would arguably weaken this point. It is also to be noted that the exclusive concentration on the length of the delay in *Crestjoy* tends to elevate this factor to a threshold test of the kind discredited in *Davies (No. 2)*: cf. paras 7.08–7.10. Nevertheless, the Secretary of State can expect a rough ride in a case of this nature if he fails either (a) to issue the application for permission within the two years or (b) to issue the substantive disqualification proceedings within the two years coupled with an application for permission to file and serve the evidence in support out of time.

[70] [1994] 1 B.C.L.C. 574, [1993] B.C.C. 890.

[71] Directions from the court were sought on this point: see *Re Polly Peck International plc, ex. parte the joint administrators* [1994] B.C.C. 15.

[72] On which see discussion in Chap. 3. Lindsay J.'s view that there had been unreasonable delay is best summed up in the following passage from his judgment ([1994] 1 B.C.L.C. 574 at 590, [1993] B.C.C. 890 at 904):

"Even in this complicated matter, given the resources of the joint administrators, the powers available to the Secretary of State, the fact that almost from the outset it had been seen as a case in which disqualification proceedings might be appropriate and the other circumstances which I have described, the . . . proceedings could have been launched within the time prescribed by Parliament had only the matter been attended with a sense of purpose and, later, of urgency with which it should have been marked."

case against the respondents was not sufficiently serious to justify the giving of permission. The collapse of Polly Peck was caused by the movement of substantial funds
out of the company, ostensibly to support various of its subsidiaries. The person
directly behind this transfer of funds was the company's chairman, Asil Nadir. The
allegations against the respondents were essentially ones of incompetence. It was
claimed that they failed (a) to institute adequate financial controls over the expenditure and transfer of monies from the company; (b) to ensure that adequate financial
controls and reporting procedures were implemented and adhered to in respect of the
various subsidiaries; (c) to obtain appropriate responses to the question of the subsidiaries' need for substantial funding from the company; and (d) to monitor, or set up
proper procedures for monitoring the actual expenditure incurred by the subsidiaries,
the funds which had been provided to them and their ability to repay their indebtedness to the company as and when required or at all. It was further claimed that they
should have threatened to resign in the event that their attempts to rectify these matters
met with resistance from Nadir. There were no allegations of fraud or dishonesty and
the four respondents were at all times in a minority on the board. Lindsay J. held that
the case was so weak that it could not lead to disqualification and was prepared to
refuse permission on that basis alone without considering other factors.[73] On the sup-
position that this conclusion was wrong, the judge went on to carry out a full balancing
exercise and reached the same result. The case was simply not strong enough to justify
the granting of permission given the delay and (in relation to three of the respondents)
the risk of prejudice.[74]

7.27   Re Packaging Direct Ltd, Secretary of State v. Jones.[75]   The application for
permission was made some nine weeks after expiry of the two-year period. The judge
regarded the delay as culpable because notices of intention to proceed under section 16
had been sent to the respondents nine months before the end of the two years. This was
said to indicate that a firm decision to proceed had actually been made at that point.
The Secretary of State was criticised on two counts for lack of urgency. First, there was
a failure to ensure that the relevant office holder swore his affidavit in sufficient time to
enable the Secretary of State to commence proceedings within the two-year period.

---

[73] An initial threshold test was applied: see para. 7.14. According to the judge, the Secretary of State had not
crossed the initial threshold because the respondents' shortcomings did not amount to a serious and deliberate failure or a demonstrable lack of commercial probity (applying *Re Bath Glass Ltd* [1988] B.C.L.C. 329,
(1988) 4 B.C.C. 130 and *Re Lo-Line Electric Motors Ltd* [1988] Ch. 477, [1988] 3 W.L.R. 26, [1988] 2 All
E.R. 692, [1988] B.C.L.C. 698, (1988) 4 B.C.C. 415 on which see paras 4.14 *et seq*). Moreover, to the extent
that they were incompetent they had not been incompetent "in a very marked degree" (applying *Re Sevenoaks Stationers (Retail) Ltd* [1991] Ch. 164, [1991] 3 All E.R. 578, [1991] B.C.L.C. 325, [1990] B.C.C. 765,
CA *cf.* paras 4.17–4.20).
[74] There are a number of problems with Lindsay J.'s judgment. First, his views on the meaning of present
unfitness and the scope of the court's enquiry under section 6 probably do not survive the Court of Appeal
decision in *Re Grayan Building Services Ltd, Secretary of State for Trade and Industry v. Gray* [1995] Ch.
241, [1995] 3 W.L.R. 1, [1995] 1 B.C.L.C. 276, [1995] B.C.C. 554 see paras 4.21 *et seq*. Moreover, in the
light of the *Barings* disqualifications and cases like *Re Continental Assurance Co. of London plc* [1997] 1
B.C.L.C. 48, [1996] B.C.C. 888 and *Re Westmid Packing Services Ltd, Secretary of State for Trade and
Industry v. Griffiths* [1998] 2 All E.R. 124, [1998] 2 B.C.L.C. 646, [1998] B.C.C. 836, CA, the standards of
competence and financial vigilance now expected from directors are arguably much higher than they were
when *Polly Peck* was decided: see paras 5.51 *et seq*. Lindsay J.'s view that the director should be given the
benefit of any reasonable doubt because disqualification has penal consequences is also open to criticism: see
discussion in Chap. 5 on the applicable standard of proof. A further point (admittedly speculative) is that the
judge may have been influenced by the fact that, for practical reasons, no proceedings were contemplated
against Nadir. In other words, it might have seemed unfair that four directors comprising less than one-third
of the company's board were left exposed to disqualification when the man primarily responsible for the
company's collapse was not so exposed. For these reasons *Polly Peck* is perhaps best regarded as a unique
case.
[75] [1994] B.C.C. 213.

Secondly, the further nine-week delay between the end of the two years and the issue of the application for permission was indicative of what the judge described as a "relaxed approach". It was held that the case against the respondents was not, in the circumstances, strong enough to provide a good reason why permission should be granted.[76]

7.28   Re Westmid Packing Services Ltd (No. 2), Secretary of State for Trade and Industry v. Morrall.[77]   The application for permission concerned M, an alleged *de facto* director of the relevant company. Proceedings against the three *de jure* directors of the company were commenced in time. However, the Secretary of State did not become aware until about six months after the expiry of the two-year period that there might be a case against M. The Disqualification Unit was alerted to this possibility by the contents of an affidavit sworn by M which formed part of the evidence put forward by two of the *de jure* directors in the main proceedings. Some three months later, on counsel's advice, the Secretary of State made an ordinary application in the existing proceedings to join M as a respondent out of time. This application was struck out on the ground that the Secretary of State had adopted an incorrect procedure and should simply have applied for permission to commence proceedings out of time by fresh originating summons under section 7(2) of the CDDA.[78] By the time the application for permission was finally made nearly a full year had elapsed since the end of the two-year period. The Secretary of State came in for criticism on a number of counts. It was said that if proceedings against the *de jure* directors had been commenced more expeditiously it was possible that the evidence against M would have surfaced much earlier. The judge added that there was no satisfactory explanation as to why the Secretary of State had risked further delay by deciding to adopt what turned out to be an incorrect procedure for seeking permission. Moreover, a number of other factors weighed in M's favour. First, the judge formed the view that the case against M was a weak one. It was the Secretary of State's case that M had effectively acted as the financial director of the company. He was the *de jure* financial director of the company's parent and there was evidence that he was regarded as having direct responsibility for all financial matters within the group. He was a signatory to the company's bank account and was described as financial director in the mandate. Nevertheless, the judge appears to have taken the view that the evidence as a whole showed that the tasks carried out by M were consistent with those of a manager or a group accountant and did not fall within the exclusive province of a director.[79] Furthermore, the court gave little weight to collateral allegations relating to M's conduct as a *de jure* director of the parent company. The Disqualification Unit had known of M's involvement in the parent company within seven months of it going into administrative receivership but had not seen fit to launch proceedings against him in relation to that company as a lead company inside two years. The Secretary of State's decision not to bring substantive

---

[76] The case against the first respondent (who had been responsible for the day-to-day running of the company) was a fairly standard mixture of insolvent trading and related "low bracket" allegations (including failure to exercise financial responsibility, trading at the expense of Crown creditors and excessive remuneration). The evidence suggested that trading was only continued with a view to a going concern sale of the company's assets and that major creditors (including the Crown) were kept regularly informed of the position. This considerably weakened the case against him. The case against the second respondent (who was only involved with the company for around one day per week) was weakened by the fact that he had appointed, paid for and relied on a chartered accountant to oversee the company's finances and report to him.

[77] [1996] B.C.C. 229.

[78] See [1995] B.C.C. 203.

[79] This sort of approach to the meaning of *de facto* director is not without controversy: see discussion in paras 3.14–3.24 and note also the contrasting approach in *Re Tasbian Ltd (No. 3), Official Receiver v. Nixon* [1993] B.C.L.C. 297, [1992] B.C.C. 358, CA referred to above in the main text.

disqualification proceedings against M on the basis of the parent company allegations was treated as being indicative of the weakness of those allegations and of the public interest in pursuing them.[80] Thirdly, it was accepted that M would suffer prejudice if the Secretary of State was allowed to proceed given that he had taken up a number of directorships since the collapse of the company.[81]

Procedure on applications for permission under section 7(2)

Form of proceedings

7.29   An application for permission under section 7(2) should be made by application notice[82] to the court that would ordinarily have jurisdiction had the proceedings been issued in time.[83] Under the pre-CPR procedure there was some difference of judicial opinion over the procedure to be adopted. In *Re Probe Data Systems Ltd (No. 2)*,[84] Millett J. held that the proper procedure was for the Secretary of State (or, where appropriate the official receiver) to apply to the registrar without notice to the respondent, putting before the registrar the whole of his evidence both on the question of permission and on the merits. Following this procedure, if the registrar was satisfied that there was a *prima facie* case for granting permission he should then give directions for a full hearing. At that hearing (of which the respondent would be given notice), the respondent was entitled to oppose permission. However, according to Millett J., the respondent's evidence should do no more than challenge the reasons for granting permission and should not go to the merits, a point developed in the passage below:

> "Matters which will have to be considered by the registrar will include the gravity of the allegations made by the Secretary of State, the reasons for the delay and the extent, if any, to which the respondent may have contributed to the delay, and any reasons which the respondent may wish to put forward to show why he would be unfairly prejudiced as a result of the delay which has occurred. In dealing with the gravity of the allegations in my judgment the respondent ought not to controvert the soundness of the allegations or deal with their merit but ought to reserve his position. The question will be whether the allegations are sufficiently grave to require to be adjudicated on notwithstanding the expiry of the two-year period. The question will not be whether those allegations are well founded."

Millett J.'s view was that the "without notice" stage would provide a quick means of filtering out unjustified applications.

7.30   However, in *Re Crestjoy Products Ltd*,[85] it was suggested that only one hearing was appropriate and that the application should be made with the respondent being given notice of such hearing. Following this procedure, a separate originating process seeking a disqualification order would then be issued if permission was granted. Harman J. took the view in *Crestjoy* that the "without notice" stage proposed by Millett J. was unnecessary as it was unlikely that the Secretary of State would bring frivolous or baseless applications. The further difficulty with Millett J.'s approach is

---

[80] An approach criticised at para. 7.15 above.
[81] However, it is not clear from the facts whether M accepted these positions after expiry of the two years in the reasonable expectation that disqualification proceedings would not be commenced against him.
[82] CPR, Pt 23 and see Disqualification Practice Direction, paras 17.1 and 19.
[83] *i.e.* the High Court, the appropriate county court or (in Scotland) the Court of Session: see CDDA, s. 6(3).
[84] [1990] B.C.L.C. 574, [1990] B.C.C. 21.
[85] [1990] B.C.L.C. 677, [1990] B.C.C. 23.

that the courts do not simply consider the gravity of the unchallenged allegations against the respondent. As was indicated above,[86] the tendency is for the courts, in evaluating "strength of case", to form a provisional view on the merits in the light of the available evidence. The current practice of the Secretary of State and the courts is to follow the *Crestjoy* procedure, and for there to be one hearing of which the respondent is given notice.[87]

Interim nature of proceedings

7.31   Although an application for permission is made by originating summons the proceedings are generally regarded as interlocutory or interim in character.[88] This has the following consequences:

(1) The hearing will be based solely on written evidence[89] and (save in highly exceptional circumstances) without cross-examination of deponents.[90]

(2) It will not generally be appropriate for the court to order disclosure of any documents referred to in the Secretary of State's evidence in support of the application.[91]

(3) The rules in *Ladd v. Marshall*[92] governing the admissibility of fresh evidence on an appeal do not apply with full rigour to an appeal against a decision to grant permission.[93]

Costs

7.32   If the respondent successfully resists an application for permission he is generally entitled to an order for his costs to be paid by the Secretary of State. The successful respondents in *Re Polly Peck International plc (No. 2)* argued that they were entitled to costs on the indemnity basis of assessment on the ground of double default in that the Secretary of State had not only failed to commence proceedings within time but had also failed to persuade the court to grant permission under section 7(2). Lindsay J. decided that this alone was insufficient to displace the ordinary disposition of the court to order costs on the standard basis.[94] If the Secretary of State is successful then

---

[86] See paras 7.13–7.14.

[87] See also *Re Cedac Ltd* [1990] B.C.C. 555; *Re Westmid Packaging Services Ltd, Secretary of State for Trade and Industry v. Griffiths* [1995] B.C.C. 203. Other commentators have supported Millett J.'s two-stage approach. The authors are not persuaded that there is any great merit in it because it takes time and duplicates costs. For that reason, it is not likely to be favoured in the light of the overriding objective of the CPR.

[88] *Re Probe Data Systems Ltd (No. 3), Secretary of State for Trade and Industry v. Desai* [1992] B.C.L.C. 405 at 417, [1992] B.C.C. 110 at 120, CA.

[89] In contrast to substantive disqualification proceedings and applications for permission to act notwithstanding a disqualification order, such written evidence need not be by affidavit: contrast the Disqualification Rules with the Disqualification Practice Direction, paras 9.1, 22.1.

[90] In *Re Manlon Trading Ltd, Official Receiver v. Aziz* [1996] Ch. 136, [1995] 3 W.L.R. 839, [1995] 1 B.C.L.C. 578, [1995] B.C.C. 579 the registrar's decision to make an order for the cross-examination of deponents on an application for dismissal for want of prosecution was criticised by the Court of Appeal. Peter Gibson L.J. said that such an order would only be justified in "highly exceptional circumstances" adding that the utility of interlocutory proceedings as a method for bringing to an end or reducing the scope of a case would be destroyed if "they became occasions for lengthy trials within trials, extended by oral evidence".

[91] See *Re Polly Peck International plc, Secretary of State for Trade and Industry v. Ellis* [1993] B.C.C. 886. On disclosure (formerly discovery) generally see CPR Pt 31 and see Chap. 6.

[92] [1954] 1 W.L.R. 1489, [1954] 3 All E.R. 745, CA.

[93] *Re Probe Data Systems Ltd (No. 3), Secretary of State for Trade and Industry v. Desai* [1992] B.C.L.C. 405 at 417, [1992] B.C.C. 110 at 120, CA.

[94] [1993] B.C.C. 890, 917. The pre-CPR equivalent of assessment was taxation.

the usual order is for the costs to be costs in the disqualification proceedings. However, the matter is one for the discretion of the court and it is unclear whether, under the CPR, the practice is likely to change. It may well be that, in line with the general indication that costs will not necessarily follow "the event" and that the court may be more prepared to consider success or failure on particular issues and make "split" orders for costs, more complicated costs orders will be made in future. In any event, and even before the advent of the CPR, it was not unknown for the court to order the costs of a successful application for permission under section 7(2) to be paid by the applicant on the ground that the applicant was seeking an indulgence of the court.

DISMISSAL FOR WANT OF PROSECUTION

7.33   Many of the considerations taken into account on applications for permission under section 7(2) are also relevant in the context of an application by the defendant to strike out disqualification proceedings against him for want of prosecution. It is beyond doubt that proceedings for an order under section 6 are capable of being struck out for delay. The same is also true of other forms of civil disqualification proceedings (*i.e.* proceedings brought under any of sections 2, 3, 4 or 8) although, to date, the reported cases have generally been concerned with applications to strike out proceedings for an order under section 6. In these cases the courts have been content to apply the usual principles applicable in ordinary civil litigation albeit recognising that some adjustment of approach may be required to reflect the fact that disqualification is not an ordinary form of civil proceeding. The hope is that with more rigorous case management under the CPR there should be less scope for such applications. However, it has to be borne in mind that disqualification proceedings under sections 6 and 8 have hitherto been more rigorously controlled by the courts by reason of the requirement in the Disqualification Rules that they come before the court within a comparatively short period of issue.[95]

Manlon Trading: Balancing the public interest against prejudice suffered by the respondent

7.34   The leading authority in the disqualification context is the Court of Appeal decision in *Re Manlon Trading Ltd, Official Receiver v. Aziz*.[96] Here proceedings for an order under section 6 were issued in June 1990, on the last day of the two-year period. The defendant's evidence was filed in April 1991 at which point the official receiver was directed by the registrar to file and serve further evidence in reply by mid-May 1991. Between May and November 1991 the official receiver applied to the registar for five extensions of time all of which were granted. A period of a year elapsed without any further step being taken. In November 1992 the Treasury Solicitor gave notice of intention to proceed to the defendant's solicitors. However, it was not until late-January 1994 that the evidence in reply was finally filed and served. The Court of Appeal upheld Evans-Lombe J.'s decision[97] to strike out the proceedings. The following points emerge from the judgments:

---

[95] Disqualification Rules, r. 7. The extensions granted in *Manlon Trading* (main text below) illustrate the point.
[96] [1996] Ch. 136, [1995] 3 W.L.R. 839, [1995] 4 All E.R. 14, [1995] 1 B.C.L.C. 578, [1995] B.C.C. 579.
[97] Reported at [1995] 3 W.L.R. 271, [1995] 1 All E.R. 988, [1995] 1 B.C.L.C. 84, [1995] B.C.C. 579.

(1) The conventional approach to dismissal for want of prosecution in ordinary civil proceedings is applicable in disqualification proceedings. On the conventional approach the inherent jurisdiction to strike out on this ground should only be exercised where the court is satisfied:

> "... either (1) that the default has been intentional and contumelious, *e.g.* disobedience to a peremptory order of the court or conduct amounting to an abuse of process of the court; or (2) (a) that there has been inordinate and inexcusable delay on the part of the [claimant] or his lawyers, and (b) that such delay will give rise to a substantial risk that it is not possible to have a fair trial of the issues in the action or is such as is likely to cause or to have caused serious prejudice to the [defendants] ..."[98]

The conventional approach should be modified in disqualification cases to reflect the fact that disqualification proceedings are not brought to enforce private rights but are brought in the public interest and should not therefore be struck out lightly. The "public interest" nature of the proceedings must be balanced against any prejudice suffered by the defendant as a result of the inordinate and inexcusable delay.[99]

(2) As the defendant's present unfitness is determined by reference to his past conduct,[1] the public interest in obtaining the protection of a disqualification order does not diminish as time passes. However, a point may be reached where the prejudice to the defendant flowing from the passage of time deserves to be accorded greater weight than the public interest.

(3) It was largely conceded by the official receiver that the period of delay between May 1991 and January 1994 was inordinate and inexcusable.[2] The question for the court on the conventional approach was whether the defendant was seriously prejudiced as a result. In deciding the question of prejudice to the defendant, the court should take into account prejudice caused by delay both before and after commencement of the proceedings. Thus, where the Secretary

---

[98] *per* Lord Diplock in *Birkett v. James* [1978] A.C. 297, [1977] 3 W.L.R. 38, [1977] 2 All E.R. 801. A further effect of *Birkett v. James* is that the court would not strike out proceedings for an order under CDDA, s. 6 before the expiry of the two-year period on the basis that it would be open to the Secretary of State to commence a fresh set of proceedings without permission. At present the approach of the courts in civil proceedings follows *Birkett v. James*. However, in recent times, the courts have been more willing to treat a failure to meet court orders as an abuse of process: see *Grovit v. Doctor* [1997] 1 W.L.R. 640, [1997] 2 All E.R. 417, HL; *Arbuthnot Latham Bank Ltd v. Trafalgar Holdings Ltd* [1998] 1 W.L.R. 1426, [1998] 2 All E.R. 181, [1998] C.L.C. 615, CA. In this context it should be noted that the court will consider not only the effect of delay on the parties but also its effect on the reputation of civil justice and on parties to other sets of proceedings (see further main text below). See now also *Shikari v. Malik, The Times*, May 20, 1999, CA; *P. Key* (1999) 115 L.Q.R. 208 and para. 7.38 below.
[99] Though, in this respect, the views of Beldam L.J. should be contrasted with those expressed by Peter Gibson and Staughton L.JJ. The majority thought that the "public interest" nature of disqualification proceedings was a factor to be taken into account. Beldam L.J., however, seems to have treated the case entirely on the conventional basis and disregarded the special nature of disqualification proceedings.
[1] *Re Grayan Building Services Ltd, Secretary of State for Trade and Industry v. Gray* [1995] Ch. 241, [1995] 3 W.L.R. 1, [1995] 1 B.C.L.C. 276, [1995] B.C.C. 554, CA. See paras 4.21–4.25.
[2] On what constitutes "inordinate and inexcusable delay" see generally *Birkett v. James* [1978] A.C. 297, [1977] 3 W.L.R. 38, [1977] 2 All E.R. 801, HL; *Department of Transport v. Chris Smaller (Transport) Ltd* [1989] A.C. 1197, [1989] 2 W.L.R. 578, [1989] 1 All E.R. 897, HL. Under the old civil justice system a delay could only be treated as inordinate and inexcusable if it exceeded the period allowed by the RSC or CCR for taking a particular step. For this purpose the period allowed would include any court-sanctioned extension of time with the effect that proceedings delayed as a result of repeated extensions could not be struck out even if the delay was prejudicial to the defendant or harmful to the prospects of a fair trial: see *Re G Barraclough (Soft Drinks) Ltd, Secretary of State for Trade and Industry v. Cawthray*, November 2, 1995, Ch.D., unreported.

of State delays the institution of proceedings for an order under section 6 right until the end of the two-year period, he will be expected to show extra diligence in pressing the matter forward thereafter.[3]

(4) It was accepted that there was an *inherent* prejudice to a director in the pendency of disqualification proceedings. This inherent prejudice consists of (a) the practical disadvantage to the director of having his status and reputation called into question, (b) the loss of business opportunities arising should the allegations against the director become known to potential business partners and (c) the difficulty for the director in ordering his affairs with a view to the future while his status remains open to question. Such inherent prejudice can be inferred by the court without evidence of specific prejudice. However, it will rarely be sufficient on its own to justify striking out especially when taking into account the public interest in obtaining a disqualification order against the director and the fact that while proceedings are pending he remains free to act as a director.[4] Some additional prejudice must normally be shown. In *Manlon Trading* additional prejudice could be found in the effect of the delay on the memories of witnesses. The allegations against the defendant mostly concerned events that had taken place over six years before the official receiver's evidence in reply was finally served. Moreover, there was an allegation of fraudulent trading that related to events going back more than ten years. The Court of Appeal concluded that the inherent prejudice combined with the impact of the delay on the recollection of witnesses amounted to "serious prejudice" which outweighed the public interest in the continuation of the proceedings.[5]

7.35   The approach in *Manlon Trading* was subsequently applied in *Secretary of State for Trade and Industry v. Martin*.[6] In *Martin* the court found that the defendant had been seriously prejudiced by the delay in several respects. First, it emerged during the strike-out proceedings that the thrust of the Secretary of State's case against the defendant had changed from that advanced in the affidavit evidence supporting the originating summons. It was said that the delay in raising what the court regarded as new allegations would inevitably have led to the dimming of witnesses' memories in relation to the matters which were the subject of these allegations. Secondly, there was

---

[3] See generally *Department of Transport v. Chris Smaller (Transport) Ltd* [1989] A.C. 1197, [1989] 2 W.L.R. 578, [1989] 1 All E.R. 897, HL and, in the disqualification context, *Re Noble Trees Ltd* [1993] B.C.L.C. 1185, [1993] B.C.C. 318.
[4] Some judges would add that inherent prejudice is further reduced by the fact that the director is free to organise his business affairs in other ways without recourse to corporate form or limited liability: see para. 7.16. Note also that the anxiety suffered by the defendant as a result of having the proceedings hanging over him will, of itself, only be sufficient to justify striking out in an exceptional case: see *Department of Transport v. Chris Smaller (Transport) Ltd* [1989] A.C. 1197, [1989] 2 W.L.R. 578, [1989] 1 All E.R. 897, HL.
[5] This at least was the conclusion of Peter Gibson and Staughton L.JJ. (although the former was more critical of the judge's approach). Beldam L.J. referred in passing to the public interest in the disqualification of unfit directors but gave greater weight to a wider public interest in the efficient administration of justice and disposed of the appeal largely on the conventional approach. It is to be noted that the reliance on the dimming of witnesses' recollections does not fit very well with the finding of Evans-Lombe J. that it was possible to have a fair trial. Also, the express finding of Evans-Lombe J. that the ground of specific prejudice to job opportunities was not established makes the Court of Appeal's reliance on general or inherent prejudice look strained. It is suggested that the Court of Appeal judgments should be treated with caution with regard to the application of the law as stated to the facts of the case. This is because the Court of Appeal seems to have disagreed with the findings of fact made by the judge at first instance. However, he having heard oral evidence and the Court of Appeal not having done so, it was not possible for the latter (as it would usually be) to make its own findings on the basis of being in as good a position as the judge to evaluate the written evidence.
[6] [1998] B.C.C. 184.

specific prejudice in that the defendant had been suspended from one job on the commencement of the proceedings and rejected for others on the ground that the proceedings were pending. He had managed to obtain casual employment but the employer
concerned had refused to offer him a full contract of employment until the proceedings
were resolved. Thirdly, the defendant had the benefit of legal aid at the time when, in
the court's view, the trial should have taken place. As he had subsequently obtained
employment it was likely that he would no longer qualify for legal aid and it was felt
that as a result he would be prejudiced in financing his defence.[7] Fourthly, he had
suffered family problems which appear to have been attributable, at least in part, to the
continuing proceedings. The judge held that the prejudice to the defendant outweighed
the public interest in disqualifying the defendant. He agreed that the public interest is
not diminished by lapse of time but added that the quantum of the public interest may
be affected by factors such as the strength of the case, the seriousness of the allegations
and the fairness with which the proceedings have been conducted. As there were no
allegations of fraud or dishonesty the judge formed the view that, at best, the Secretary
of State would obtain a disqualification order falling within the minimum bracket
between two and five years. The public interest in a "minimum bracket" disqualification was not strong enough to justify the proceedings continuing. Furthermore, it
was found that the Secretary of State's case had not been presented in a proper, objective way as material favourable to the defendant had been omitted or down-played in
the office holder's affidavit evidence. Notably, a submission on behalf of the Secretary
of State that there was a heightened public interest in the defendant's disqualification
because members of the investing public had lost money in his venture and wished to
see justice done was categorically rejected. In the judge's words:

> "I do not accept that submission, and it seems to me that the purpose of disqualifi-
> cation is to protect the public for the future against directors whose past conduct
> shows them unfit to run a company. It is not to punish delinquent directors. . . Still
> less are disqualification proceedings designed to satisfy the understandable desire
> for revenge of creditors who blame directors for their losses. The creditors or their
> representatives can take other civil proceedings, if so advised, to recoup their
> losses."[8]

Cases following the conventional approach

7.36   In two cases decided before *Manlon Trading* the courts struck out disqualification proceedings by applying the conventional approach in ordinary civil litigation
without modification. In *Re Noble Trees Ltd*[9] proceedings for an order under section 6
were issued nine days before the expiry of the two-year period. Subsequently, the Secretary of State was late, in breach of a court order, filing evidence in reply and took only
limited steps for a period of almost 20 months after that evidence was eventually filed.
In reaching the conclusion that there had been an inordinate and inexcusable delay,
Vinelott J. said that greater diligence was expected of a litigant (including the Secretary
of State) who delays issuing proceedings right until the end of a limitation period.
Moreover, it was held that the defendant was prejudiced by the delay as he had

---

[7] Every party to litigation is entitled under Article 6 of the European Convention on Human Rights to be
given a reasonable opportunity of presenting his case to the court in conditions which do not place him at a
substantial disadvantage in relation to his opponent. Points like this one taken in *Martin* based on "equality
of arms" are likely to become an increasing feature of disqualification jurisprudence following the enactment of the Human Rights Act 1998.
[8] [1998] B.C.C. 184 at 190.
[9] [1993] B.C.L.C. 1185, [1993] B.C.C. 318.

invested time and expense pursuing business opportunities which would necessitate his appointment as a director. No other specific prejudice was identified. In *Official Receiver v. B Ltd*[10] proceedings for orders under section 6 were issued against two defendants three days before expiry of the two-year period. Again, the delay in this case arose initially because of the official receiver's failure to file evidence in reply on time. Subsequently, the official receiver did very little (apart from giving notice of intention to proceed) to move matters forward between September 1991 and January 1993. The official receiver conceded that the delay could not be excused and so the court was concerned solely with the question of whether the defendants had suffered serious prejudice as a result. The judge found that serious prejudice had arisen on the basis of evidence that the defendants were forced, owing to the existence of the proceedings, (a) to forego a number of specific opportunities to take up directorships and (b) to pursue their existing business interests through the medium of partnership rather than through a limited company. As in *Noble Trees*, no other specific prejudice was identified. It would appear that the decisions in both *Noble Trees* and *Official Receiver v. B Ltd* conflict to some extent with the Court of Appeal decision in *Manlon Trading*. In particular, it was concluded in both cases that prejudice to business interests was sufficient to justify striking out. The following points can be put forward by way of possible explanation for this discrepancy in treatment:

(1) The approach in *Noble Trees* and *Official Receiver v. B Ltd* is inherently more "director-friendly" for two reasons. First, it places no particular weight on the public interest in disqualifying directors. Secondly, it rests on the assumption that disqualification or the threat of disqualification amounts to a serious interference with individual freedom which has the effect of lowering the threshold required for the defendant to establish "serious prejudice". The passage below from the judgment in *Official Receiver v. B Ltd* betrays this kind of thinking:

> "Where a businessman has proceedings of this kind hanging over him, their mere existence is prejudicial in that he cannot order his affairs with any certainty. To some degree he has to accept that. If the application is prosecuted diligently ... he cannot complain of the effect upon the ordering of his affairs. Further, if he is found unfit, he cannot complain that he cannot continue to have the benefit of trading with the benefit of a limited liability for the period of disqualification, save with the permission of the court which may be withheld or granted subject to restrictive conditions. *Nevertheless, the right to be a director of a limited liability company is an important right.* It prejudices a businessman to leave him in a state of uncertainty for an inordinate period of time in relation to a specific business opportunity or interest which involves him becoming a director of a particular company. It is no answer ... that he can become involved in a manner short of becoming a director, *e.g.* by shareholder's agreement or a partnership..."[11]

(2) The Court of Appeal's view that inherent prejudice to business interests is insufficient to justify striking out is arguably confined to prejudice which is simply inferred from the nature of the proceedings. In *Noble Trees* and *Official Receiver v. B Ltd* the defendants gave specific evidence showing how

---

[10] [1994] 2 B.C.L.C. 1.
[11] *ibid.*, 15 (emphasis added) and see general discussion on the nature and impact of disqualification proceedings in Chap. 2.

their business interests had been affected and so the prejudice was not simply inferred. It will be recalled that in *Secretary of State for Trade and Industry v. Martin*, a case which follows the approach in *Manlon Trading*, the court also relied to an extent on specific evidence of prejudice to job prospects rather than inferred prejudice.

(3) *Noble Trees* is arguably a special case as confusion had arisen as to whether the proceedings had been struck out at an earlier stage because of the Secretary of State's failure to file evidence in reply in compliance with an "unless" order. It emerged some time later that the Secretary of State had not consented to an order in "unless" terms and the proceedings were restored before subsequently being dismissed for want of prosecution. The view of the judge was that the confusion would have come to light much earlier had the Secretary of State pursued the proceedings with proper diligence. The point for present purposes is that the defendant had for some time acted on the assumption that the proceedings were at an end and, in the circumstances, it is perhaps not surprising that the court concluded that the Secretary of State's delay in reviving the proceedings had caused prejudice to the defendant.

7.37 By way of contrast, in *Re New Technology Systems Ltd*,[12] aspects of the conventional approach were deployed to reject an application to strike out disqualification proceedings. Again, this was a case in which proceedings for an order under section 6 were issued just before the expiry of the two-year period. The defendant was nearly two years late in filing his evidence in an appropriate form. That step was finally taken in May 1994. A further year elapsed without any response from the official receiver. In a telephone conversation which took place in early-August 1995, the defendant's solicitors agreed to the official receiver being allowed an extension of time until September 1, 1995. This was despite the fact that the official receiver had not given notice of intention to proceed. Applying principles laid down in *Roebuck v. Mungovin*,[13] the court exercised its discretion in the official receiver's favour on the basis that the consent given by the solicitors was an indication of the defendant's willingness to excuse the delay. It must be open to doubt whether such an approach will find favour in the post-Woolf era.

Conclusion

7.38 The modified approach taken by the Court of Appeal in *Manlon Trading* and followed in *Martin* best reflects the current state of the law in this area as it takes some account of the public interest in the disqualification of directors. It remains to be seen how the jurisdiction will develop, both generally and in the disqualification context, in the post-Woolf era. However, the guess is that the culture-shift brought about by the introduction of the Civil Procedure Rules and the enactment of the Human Rights Act 1998 (meaning that Article 6 of the European Convention on Human Rights is now part of English law) may see it develop in a way which is increasingly favourable to directors. For instance, it may be that the onus on the director to establish "serious prejudice" will be considerably reduced. In any event, it is open to doubt whether cases decided before the introduction of the Civil Procedure Rules remain authoritative. Even before the advent of the new civil justice system, there were glimpses of what the future might hold. The conventional approach to dismissal for want of prosecution in

[12] [1996] B.C.C. 694.
[13] [1994] 2 A.C. 224.

ordinary civil litigation was itself already coming under strain in anticipation of the Woolf reforms. In *Grovit v. Doctor*, Lord Woolf hinted that in the future the court is likely to put less emphasis on the prejudice suffered by the litigants in an individual case and look more broadly at the adverse effect which delay can have on the reputation and efficiency of the civil justice system as a whole.[14] Similarly, in *Arbuthnot Latham Bank Ltd v. Trafalgar Holdings Ltd* it was held that proceedings could be struck out as an abuse of process on the ground of inordinate and inexcusable delay where that delay amounts to a wholesale disregard of prescribed time limits, the same judge observing that, "inordinate delay ... is going to be a consideration of increasing importance".[15] In an earlier case Sir Thomas Bingham expressed the hope that, "the time may come when the House of Lords will review the existing state of authority and give thought to the question whether on proof of inordinate and inexcusable delay the court should not have a more general discretion to dismiss an action for want of prosecution if, in all the circumstances, that seems the right course to take".[16] These developments point towards an approach in ordinary civil litigation in which there is a greater concentration on delay and a reduced emphasis on the present requirement to show "prejudice". It is not yet clear how the courts will accommodate the public interest in the disqualification of directors within the context of this shift in culture.

---

[14] [1997] 1 W.L.R. 640, [1997] 2 All E.R. 417, HL.

[15] [1998] 1 W.L.R. 1426, [1998] 2 All E.R. 181, [1998] C.L.C. 615, CA. A similar approach was taken in *Choraria v. Sethia* [1998] C.L.C. 625.

[16] *Sparrow v. Sovereign Chicken Ltd*, June 8, 1994, CA, unreported. In *Shakari v. Malik, The Times*, May 20, 1999, the Court of Appeal indicated that pre-CPR cases should not be taken as having a licence to go slower than cases commenced after April 26, 1999. Several cases decided after the CPR came into force have proceeded on the basis of the old authorities while leaving open the question of the precise scope of the principles to be applied in the light of the CPR: see, *e.g. Co-op v. Guardian*, July 28, 1999, CA, unreported; *Masterton v. Caird*, May 7, 1999, unreported; *Skellerton v. Granada*, June 28, 1999, unreported; *Goodfellow v. Woolwich*, April 28, 1999, unreported. However, in *Biguzzi v. Rank Leisure plc*, July 26, 1999 (decided just before *Co-op v. Guardian*), the Court of Appeal, headed by Lord Woolf M.R., indicated that the whole purpose of the CPR was that it should be a self-contained code, and that the authorities on strike out applications under the old rules were no longer relevant. It was said that under CPR, r. 34, the judge has an unqualified discretion to strike out proceedings where there has been a failure to comply with the rules.

CHAPTER 8

Civil Disqualification Proceedings: Termination Without a Full Trial

INTRODUCTION

8.01 This chapter examines some of the ways in which civil disqualification proceedings may be brought to an end without the matter proceeding to a full contested trial. Although the circumstances in which civil disqualification proceedings may be brought to a premature close are not fundamentally different to those in which other civil proceedings may be brought to an end, there are particular aspects of disqualification proceedings which involve modifications to the applicable rules. This chapter considers in particular:

(1) Discontinuance of the proceedings by the person bringing the proceedings.

(2) A stay of the proceedings on the basis of undertakings.

(3) A summary disposal of the proceedings, commonly referred to as a "*Carecraft*" hearing.

(4) A hearing at which the claimant's evidence is not contested.

(5) *Calderbank* offers.

DISCONTINUANCE OF PROCEEDINGS

8.02 The question of the proper claimant in disqualification proceedings is considered in Chapters 6 and 9. Proceedings seeking disqualification orders under sections 6 and 8 of the CDDA can only be brought by the Secretary of State or, in certain section 6 cases where he is so directed by the Secretary of State, by the official receiver. A pre-condition of such proceedings is that "... it appears to the Secretary of State ... expedient in the public interest that a disqualification order ... should be made" against the relevant person (sections 7(1) and 8(1)). The practice of the Secretary of State is to keep under review the question of whether it remains expedient in the public interest to continue with such proceedings. It is therefore possible that, because of new evidence relating to the conduct of the defendant or because of some other change in circumstances, it will cease to appear to the Secretary of State expedient in the public interest that a disqualification order should be made. In those circumstances the Secretary of State will withdraw the proceedings.[1] Civil proceedings brought against a person under sections 2 to 4 of the CDDA may be brought by the Secretary of State, the official receiver or by any liquidator or any past or present member or creditor of the company in relation to which the person has committed or is alleged to have committed an offence or other default.[2] Although the CDDA lays down no express limitations on the power of the Secretary of State or the official receiver to commence proceedings akin to those applicable to applications under sections 6 and 8 of the CDDA, it is suggested that in practice proceedings will only be commenced if it appears to such person expedient in the public interest that a disqualification order should be made. Equally, if it ceases to appear expedient in the public interest that such proceedings should be continued, they would doubtless be withdrawn. Subject to questions of abuse of the court's process, creditors and members can pursue what they perceive as their own interests. Liquidators, who will be under costs constraints and subject to a number of duties, not least as officers of the court in the case of companies in compulsory liquidation, will not have so much freedom of action.

Position under RSC/CCR

8.03   Prior to the application of the Civil Procedure Rules,[3] the mechanics of discontinuing (or, as it was then technically called, withdrawing) proceedings was governed in the High Court by RSC Ord. 21, rr 2–5 and, in the County Court, by CCR Ord. 18. In the High Court, the applicant could discontinue the proceedings commenced by originating summons without leave, by service of notice of discontinuance on the respondent within the time limit prescribed. In cases other than those under section 6 or 8, such notice could be served at any time not later than 14 days after service of the respondent's affidavit evidence filed pursuant to RSC Ord. 28, r. 1A(4) or, if there were two or more respondents, of such evidence last served (RSC Ord. 21, r. 2(3A)). If affidavit evidence was in fact served prior to expiry of the period laid down by RSC Ord. 28, r. 1A(4), the period for serving the notice of discontinuance was extended to the end of the period laid down for service of the affidavit evidence (RSC Ord. 21, r. 2(3B)). As the service of evidence in cases brought under section 6 and 8 is governed by the Disqualification Rules, this power to discontinue did not apply to such cases. However, in all cases, whether or not brought under section 6 or 8, the parties could expressly consent to a discontinuance at any time before trial by producing to the court a written consent as required by RSC Ord. 21, r. 2(4). In such circumstances, the respondent might well only have agreed to a discontinuance on terms preventing the bringing of new proceedings by the applicant (see RSC Ord. 21, r. 4). In the absence of written consent, it would have been necessary to seek leave of the court to a discontinuance. If an unusual costs order was sought the applicant might wish to seek leave to discontinue because a discontinuance without leave would otherwise result in the

---

[1] See *Re Carecraft Construction Co. Limited* [1994] 1 W.L.R. 172 (at 180H–181A), [1993] 4 All E.R. 499, [1993] B.C.L.C. 1259, [1993] B.C.C. 336:

> "... the Secretary of State can and should cause an application for a disqualification order under section 6 or section 8 to be abandoned if it ceases to appear to him that the making of a disqualification order against the [defendant] to that application is 'expedient in the public interest'. I was told that the Secretary of State does in fact act upon this principle and I have no doubt that this is so."

To similar effect see *Re Blackspur Group plc, Re Atlantic Computer Systems plc* [1998] 1 W.L.R. 422 at 426G–H, [1998] 1 B.C.L.C. 676 at 680, [1998] B.C.C. 11 at 15.

[2] Section 16(2) of the CDDA.

[3] As regards the applicable rules to civil disqualification proceedings see Chapter 6. In this chapter, the CPR terms "claimant" and "defendant" are used in preference to the former terms "applicant" and "respondent" in all respects, save for the present paragraph which is concerned exclusively with the position under the old rules.

applicant being obliged to pay the costs of the respondent (RSC Ord. 62, r. 5(3)). In the County Court it was possible to discontinue proceedings, by service of the appropriate notices, at any time before judgment or further order.

Position under the CPR

8.04   Under the CPR, discontinuance is dealt with in Part 38. Under CPR, r. 38.2 a claimant can discontinue a claim at any time and, in cases where there is more than one defendant, against all or any of the defendants. Court permission is required in the event that any party has given an undertaking to the court (CPR, r. 38.2(a)(ii)). The procedure for discontinuing is governed by CPR, r. 38.3. A notice of discontinuance must be filed and a copy served on every other party to the proceedings. The notice filed must state that copies have been served on every other party and, where there is more than one defendant, the notice must specify against which defendant the claim is discontinued. Discontinuance will take effect when the notice of discontinuance is served (CPR, r. 38.5). The defendant has the right to apply, within 28 days of service of the notice of discontinuance upon him, to have the notice set aside (CPR, r. 38.4). Subject to the notice not being set aside, the proceedings will come to an end on the date of service of the notice of discontinuance. This does not affect proceedings to deal with any question of costs.

Unless the court otherwise orders, a claimant who discontinues is liable for the costs incurred by a defendant prior to service of the notice of discontinuance against whom he discontinues (CPR, r. 38.6). If a claim is discontinued after the filing of a defence by the relevant defendant, permission of the court is required before another claim can be made arising out of facts which are the same or substantially the same as those relating to the discontinued claim (CPR, r. 38.7). In relation to disqualification proceedings under sections 6 or 8 of the CDDA, the procedure for the commencement of new proceedings following discontinuance is governed by the Disqualification Rules and Part 8 of the CPR, the matter proceeding by way of affidavit rather than by statements of case. By reason of the relevant Practice Direction, the CPR Part 8 procedure also applies in relation to civil proceedings commenced under sections 2, 3 or 4 of the CDDA. Accordingly, there would appear to be no automatic bar to the commencement of new proceedings following a discontinuance in such cases. However, in practice, a defendant would in most cases have the opportunity to raise a defence based upon the line of cases starting with *Henderson v. Henderson*,[4] and to apply to strike out the new proceedings as an abuse of process.

Costs

8.05   If proceedings are discontinued the most important question for a defendant may be the incidence of costs. If proceedings are discontinued without permission of the court and unless an order to contrary effect is made, the claimant will have to pay the defendant's costs (RSC Ord. 62, r. 5(3) and CCR, Ord. 18; CPR, r. 38.6). If permission to discontinue is obtained, costs are in the discretion of the court.[5] Equally, in cases where the court is asked to make a different costs order, it will retain the same discretion. However, the relevant discretion is to be exercised according to principle.

---

[4] (1843) 2 Hare 100. As regards the application of the principle in *Henderson v. Henderson* in the context of disqualification proceedings see *Re Launchexcept Limited, Secretary of State v. Tillman* [1999] B.C.C. 703.
[5] CPR, r. 38.6 provides that a claimant who discontinues is liable for the defendant's costs "unless the court otherwise orders". Although the proceedings are discontinued this does not affect proceedings to deal with any question of costs (CPR, r. 38.5(3)). In considering the allocation of costs the court will doubtless have regard to CPR, r. 44.3.

The fact that the claimant was the Secretary of State or the official receiver will not of itself justify the discretion being exercised any differently than if the claimant was a private individual. There are no special costs rules derived from the fact that the proceedings in question are public interest proceedings.[6] However, this does not mean that the claimant who discontinues will automatically have to pay the costs of the defendant. If a defendant has so conducted himself, for example by withholding his true defence when he has had an opportunity to disclose it, as to encourage the claimant to bring or continue the proceedings, he may be deprived of the whole or part of his costs.[7] The relevant principles have been considered by the Court of Appeal (albeit outside the disqualification context) in *ASFA Ltd v. RTZ Pension Property Trust Ltd.*[8] The guidance laid down there is broadly as follows. It will be necessary to consider why the proceedings have been discontinued. If they have been discontinued in circumstances tantamount to an admission of defeat then the normal rule as to costs will apply, unless good reason to the contrary can be shown. The normal rule is that the claimant should pay the defendant's costs. Normally, a "good reason" justifying an order that the defendant pay the claimant's costs will not be shown unless the claimant is able to demonstrate misconduct of the defence. Such misconduct will usually be some act, omission or course of conduct on the part of the defendant which is unreasonable or improper for the purposes of what was RSC Ord. 62, r. 10(1) (see now CPR, r. 44.14). To justify an order that there be "no order as to costs", thus depriving the defendant of his costs but without making him pay the claimant's costs, the test is less severe and is the wider one of "what is fair and just in all the circumstances". These principles would appear to apply equally in the context of civil disqualification proceedings. Furthermore, it is suggested that under the CPR the same sort of principles will apply.

It is conceivable that the discontinuing claimant in disqualification proceedings could be awarded costs. It is possible that a set of civil disqualification proceedings might become academic because, for example, a disqualification order which is perceived to be of no lesser period than that which would be achieved in the civil proceedings, is made against the defendant in parallel criminal proceedings (*e.g.* under CDDA, s.2). If the criminal proceedings are concerned with unrelated conduct and the claimant can show, on the basis of the filed evidence, that there is no defence to the civil proceedings, it is suggested that the court in the civil proceedings might well be prepared to order costs in favour of the discontinuing claimant, even in the absence of any misconduct on the defendant's part in the course of such proceedings.

A STAY ON THE BASIS OF UNDERTAKINGS

8.06   As presently worded, the CDDA does not permit a claimant and a defendant to obtain a disqualification order by consent. In all cases the court must itself be satisfied that there is jurisdiction to make a disqualification order and that a particular order is appropriate on the facts of the case.[9] The lack of any mechanism for the parties

---

[6] *Re Southborne Sheet Metal Co. Ltd (No. 2)* [1993] B.C.L.C. 135, [1992] B.C.C. 797, CA.
[7] The example given by Nourse L.J. in *Re Southborne Sheet Metal Co. Limited (No. 2)* [1993] B.C.L.C. 135 at 140, [1992] B.C.C. 797 at 801. For a non-disqualification case decided after the CPR came into force see *Gruppo Torras SA v. Al-Sabah*, July 5, 1999, Commercial Court, unreported.
[8] October 29, 1998, unreported.
[9] *Re Carecraft Construction Co. Limited* [1994] 1 W.L.R. 172 (at 181B–D), [1993] 4 All E.R. 499, [1993] B.C.L.C. 1259, [1993] B.C.C. 336; *Re Blackspur Group plc* [1998] 1 W.L.R. 422 (at 426H–427C), [1998] 1 B.C.L.C. 676, [1998] B.C.C. 11, CA; *Secretary of State for Trade and Industry v. Rogers* [1996] 1 W.L.R. 1569 (at 1574), [1996] 4 All E.R. 854, [1996] 2 B.C.L.C. 513, [1997] B.C.C. 155, CA.

to settle by consent has resulted in the development of a summary procedure whereby facts which are agreed or non-contested are put before the court, it is agreed that such facts warrant disqualification and the court is invited to make a disqualification order for a specific period (or a period within a bracket). This procedure, which has been developed in cases following *Re Carecraft Construction Co. Ltd*, is considered in detail below. The *Carecraft* procedure aside, there has been much judicial[10] (and other) enthusiasm for the idea that the Secretary of State should be able to "compromise" proceedings, achieving a disqualification order or the same effect as a disqualification order, without the court having to hear the matter and reach its own view on the merits. Nevertheless, unless and until there is amending legislation and subject to any effect of the CPR (on which see paragraph 8.07 below), it is clear from the Court of Appeal's decision in *Re Blackspur Group plc, Re Atlantic Computer Systems plc*[11] that the Secretary of State is entitled to insist that disqualification proceedings are carried through to trial (or a summary hearing under the *Carecraft* procedure) and is not obliged to accept a defendant's undertaking to refrain from acting in the relevant capacities set out in section 1 of the CDDA. In the *Atlantic* case, the Court of Appeal held that it is impossible to construct undertakings which have the identical effect to a disqualification order and that there will usually be reasonable grounds for the Secretary of State to adopt the position that adherence to the statutory scheme promotes good regulation. Furthermore, it will neither constitute an abuse of the court's process, nor provide grounds for judicial review, if the Secretary of State refuses to accept a defendant's offer of undertakings to refrain from acting in the prohibited capacities set out in section 1 of the CDDA. It is unclear what view the court would take in circumstances where the claimant was a private litigant. In theory, the view that the same principle should apply has much to commend it (unless perhaps the Secretary of State had refused to bring the proceedings and/or, for reasons unrelated to the merits of the case, considered that it was not expedient in the public interest for such proceedings to be brought or continued).

Cases where undertakings have been accepted

8.07   There have been exceptional cases where the Secretary of State has been prepared to accept undertakings and the proceedings have been stayed by the court on the basis of such undertakings. The sort of case where the Secretary of State has been prepared to accept undertakings are those where it would not have been possible to have a fair trial (for example, because of the ill health of the defendant).[12] In *Re Homes Assured Corporation plc*,[13] the court noted that it was common ground that the court had inherent power to stay proceedings on the ground of (among other things) oppression, although there was a "sharp dispute" as to whether it was appropriate to exercise such jurisdiction in that case. CPR, r. 3.1(2)(f) contains an express power to stay proceedings but, other than in relation to procedural matters which may arise, it is assumed that this power is likely to be applied in circumstances analogous to those in

---

[10] See the views of Sir Richard Scott V.-C. set out in *Practice Note (Chancery Division: Directors' disqualification applications)* [1996] 1 All E.R. 442, [1996] B.C.C. 11 and *Secretary of State for Trade and Industry v. Rogers* [1996] 1 W.L.R. 1569 (at 1574), [1996] 4 All E.R. 854, [1996] 2 B.C.L.C. 513, [1997] B.C.C. 155, CA. These sentiments were echoed by Rattee J. in *Re Blackspur Group plc* (as cited by Lord Woolf M.R. [1998] 1 W.L.R. 422 at 429D–H).
[11] [1998] 1 W.L.R. 422, [1998] 1 B.C.L.C. 676, [1998] B.C.C. 11.
[12] See *Re Homes Assured Corporation plc* [1996] B.C.C. 297 and *Re Company X*, February 1, 1996, Ch.D, unreported. In *Homes Assured*, there was medical evidence as to the health of the defendant, Sir Edward Du Cann, detailing both a heart condition and problems with short term memory and powers of concentration. This evidence satisfied the judge that it would be "hazardous and difficult" to embark on a trial of several weeks' duration where the defendant would be giving evidence and acting in person.
[13] [1996] B.C.C. 297.

which the power to stay was exercised prior to adoption of CPR and that, for present purposes, the *Atlantic* decision, considered above, remains good law.

In *Re Stormont Ltd, Secretary of State for Trade and Industry v. Cleland*,[14] the court refused the Secretary of State permission to commence proceedings pursuant to section 6 outside the two year period laid down by section 7(2). In the case of one of the defendants to the application the court would have been minded to grant permission but, in part in the light of undertakings offered by that defendant,[15] instead stayed the application on the basis of such undertakings. Some doubt has been cast on the reasoning in that case by the decision in *Re Blackspur Group plc, Re Atlantic Computer Systems plc*, although it is fair to point out that the Court of Appeal in the latter case did not expressly disapprove of the actual decision in *Cleland*. It is suggested that the decision in *Cleland* is exceptional and that a section 7(2) application will not ordinarily be defeated by the offer of undertakings.[16]

SUMMARY HEARING: THE *CARECRAFT* PROCEDURE

8.08   In *Re Carecraft Construction Co. Ltd*,[17] in the course of proceedings under section 6 of the CDDA, Ferris J. sanctioned a procedure whereby, without a full contested hearing, agreed or non-contested facts could be placed before the court and the court could be invited to make a disqualification order based on such facts. In the event that the court was not prepared to make a disqualification order as asked, the matter would go to a full trial. This procedure (subject to certain modifications) was approved by the Court of Appeal in *Secretary of State for Trade and Industry v. Rogers*.[18] *Re Carecraft Construction Co. Ltd* concerned proceedings pursuant to section 6 of the CDDA. The procedure has been adopted and utilised in proceedings under section 8 of the CDDA.[19] There would seem to be no reason in principle why the procedure should not be available in any civil disqualification proceedings.

Carecraft statements

8.09   The practice which has now developed is for an agreed document to be submitted to the court, sometimes called "a *Carecraft* statement".[20] A number of points arise in relation to the contents of such a document and the manner of negotiating it. The first general point is that the basis of the *Carecraft* procedure rests on agreement having been reached by the parties that the matter should be put before the court on a

---

[14] [1997] 1 B.C.L.C. 437, [1997] B.C.C. 473.
[15] The undertaking was apparently in the terms of section 1 of the Act with the important qualification that it was unlimited in time and precluded the possibility of permission being granted.
[16] In *Cleland* Lloyd J. accepted that there were differences between the undertakings offered and the effect of a disqualification order as discussed further by the Court of Appeal in the *Atlantic* case, but stated that the undertakings would achieve "the public protection aimed at by the 1986 Act". However the decision in the *Atlantic* case was grounded, in part, on the holding that undertakings did not achieve the public protection that an order would achieve.
[17] [1994] 1 W.L.R. 172, [1993] 4 All E.R. 499, [1993] B.C.L.C. 1259, [1993] B.C.C. 336.
[18] [1996] 1 W.L.R. 1569, [1996] 4 All E.R. 854, [1996] 2 B.C.L.C. 513, [1997] B.C.C. 155.
[19] *Re Aldermanbury Trust Ltd* [1993] B.C.C. 598.
[20] The Disqualification Practice Direction requires that, unless the court otherwise orders, a written statement should be provided containing any material facts which are agreed or not opposed and stating the period of disqualifiction which the parties accept is justified on the agreed facts or the band of years or bracket (meaning the three brackets put forward by the Court of Appeal in *Re Sevenoaks Stationers (Retail) Limited* [1991] Ch. 164, [1991] 3 All E.R. 578, [1991] B.C.L.C. 325, [1990] B.C.C. 765) into which they submit that the case falls. A draft form of *Carecraft* statement is included in the appendices.

certain basis.[21] If either party is not prepared to agree to the matter proceeding by way of the summary procedure, or to the form of the agreed document that is to be put before the court, there is little in practice that the other party can do to force the other party to accept his terms. One possibility for a defendant is to make a *Calderbank* offer (see para. 8.21 below) with a view to bringing pressure to bear. It is extremely unlikely that an application for judicial review of the Secretary of State's (or official receiver's) refusal to accept an offer to deal with the proceedings on a *Carecraft* basis (or to strike out proceedings as an abuse of process in such circumstances) would succeed. Unless the parties agree jointly to ask the court to give guidance as to the terms to be included in the *Carecraft* statement, as happened exceptionally in *Official Receiver v. Cooper*,[22] the court would not appear to have power at the behest of one party or of its own volition to impose "agreed" terms on the parties.

In practice, the Secretary of State and official receiver tend to use a fairly common format for the agreed document and a number of standard clauses are usually insisted upon. The format (and the content of the standard clauses) changes from time to time with experience. Although a particular clause may have been referred to without disapproval by the court, or even specifically approved, it does not follow that a party could be compelled to agree to such a term in a subsequent statement.

As a starting point to negotiation, it will usually be necessary for the defendant to put forward to the claimant the allegations that he is prepared not to dispute and the period of disqualification (or band of years) which he would be prepared to accept. A defendant can offer to dispose of proceedings on a *Carecraft* basis at any time.[23] However, it is obviously in the defendant's interests to dispose of proceedings as soon as possible. Unless the offer is to dispose of the proceedings on the basis that the claimant's evidence is not contested in its entirety,[24] the Secretary of State (or official receiver) may not be prepared to agree to a *Carecraft* disposal until the defendant has filed affidavit evidence in opposition. The defendant's evidence provides a basis for the claimant to judge whether it is appropriate for certain facts not to be placed before the court on the summary hearing. It also serves to focus the negotiations and reduce the risk that the parties conduct the case (by allegation and counter-allegation) in correspondence. The *Carecraft* procedure is also regulated by the Disqualification Practice Direction. In particular, the parties are required to inform the court immediately once they have decided to seek a summary disposal.

Basis of negotiations

8.10   Both parties will doubtless wish to conduct the relevant negotiations under the "without prejudice" banner. That relevant negotiations are "without prejudice"

---

[21] In *Official Receiver v. Cooper* [1999] B.C.C. 115 the court was invited to rule upon whether the *Carecraft* statement could be made expressly "without prejudice" (in other words, confidential save for the purposes of a summary disposal). However, in that case *both parties* invited the court to rule on the matter on the footing that if the qualifications proposed on behalf of the defendant were acceptable to the court, the official receiver would drop his objection to them. Conversely, if they were not acceptable to the court, it was agreed that the defendant would drop his insistence on the incorporation of a "without prejudice" term in the statement. If the parties cannot agree to submit the issue to the court in this way, it would seem that the court has no power to require the parties to include particular wording in any agreed statement, a point recognised by Jonathan Parker J. in the *Cooper* case.

[22] *ibid.*

[23] In *Secretary of State for Trade and Industry v. Rogers* [1996] 1 W.L.R. 1569 (at 1574B), the Vice-Chancellor could be taken to suggest that the Secretary of State's evidence would at the least have to be disputed before the Secretary of State could "exclude" certain allegations from a *Carecraft* statement. However, on a true reading of the judgment it is submitted that this is not in fact what was being said.

[24] In which case, it may be more appropriate to deal with the matter on an uncontested basis, as to which see para. 8.17 below.

will probably be implied,[25] but it will be safer to make that basis of proceeding express. In the event that the negotiations do not mature to fruition, the relevant course of negotiations can then be kept from the court on any full trial.[26] To avoid arguments about whether and when an agreement has been reached, it may also be sensible to conduct the negotiations on the basis that a clear step needs to be taken before final agreement is reached, for example, that the negotiations are "subject to agreement of a written statement to be placed before the court, such agreement to be signified by signature of such written statement by or on behalf of both parties".

What if the court will not make the order sought?

8.11   It is clear from the authorities discussed above that *the court*, rather than the parties, is the ultimate arbiter of whether or not the pre-conditions to the making of a disqualification order are satisfied, and as to the period of any disqualification order. It is therefore important that any agreed document is clear with regard to (a) the question of precisely what the court is being invited to do and, in particular, how far the court is entitled, on the basis of the agreed or non-disputed facts, to make a disqualification order for a period other than as invited by the parties and (b) what is to happen in the event that the court is not prepared to make the disqualification order as sought. As regards the first point, it is clear that the parties may invite the court to make a disqualification order for a specific period or for a period (to be determined by the court) within a specific band of years (see further below). The agreed statement should make clear whether, on the summary hearing, the court is restricted to making a disqualification order for the period (or within the band) as sought and, if it is not prepared to do so, the matter must go to a full trial or whether the court is entitled to reject the period of disqualification suggested by the parties and make an order for such period as it thinks fit, based on the facts as not disputed before it.[27] In the event that the court is constrained to refuse to make the order sought, with the result that the matter must go to a full trial, the parties will usually want the agreed statement to make provision for a different judge to hear the subsequent contested trial. In these circumstances, it will also be usual to provide that the statement remains confidential and that it (and its contents) cannot be used by either party at the subsequent trial or otherwise. Exceptionally, the parties might agree that, if the court is not prepared to dispose of the matter by way of a summary hearing, the same judge should go on to hear the full

---

[25] See *Phipson on Evidence*.

[26] The *existence* of such negotiations (as opposed to their content) might of course be a relevant factor for the court to know about *e.g.* on questions of delay in prosecuting the proceedings (see, *e.g. Walker v. Wilsher* (1889) 23 QBD 335).

[27] In *Carecraft*, Ferris J. said that the court should also consider the scope of the disputed evidence. He went on to suggest that if, in a section 6 case, the court was not satisfied of unfitness on the basis of the agreed or unchallenged evidence, and that it considered the remaining disputed evidence would not, even if accepted, tip the scales in favour of a finding of unfitness it would, no doubt, dismiss the application: see [1994] 1 W.L.R. 172 at 184A–C. It is submitted that the court would not have been able to act as suggested by Ferris J., unless the parties had *agreed* that it was open to the court on the summary hearing to act in that way. As is clear from *Secretary of State for Trade and Industry v. Rogers*, on a summary hearing the court should consider only the agreed or unchallenged evidence. Therefore, it seems unlikely that this point could now arise. If the defendant wished the court to determine the proceedings on the grounds that they could not succeed (even if the factual matters were established) his correct course would be to issue an application to strike out the proceedings on the ground that they were bound to fail. Although under the CPR the court has greater power to act of its own volition, it is suggested that a *Carecraft* hearing would normally be an inappropriate time to consider the question whether the proceedings should be struck out.

trial.[28] The statement might also usefully deal with what is to happen about the costs of the summary hearing (and of negotiating the *Carecraft* statement)[29] in the event that the court refuses to make the order as sought and the matter then proceeds to a full trial.

The relevant facts

8.12 In *Carecraft* itself, Ferris J. said that the court should consider not only the facts that were agreed but also the general scope of the disputed evidence.[30] The reason for this was said to be that such disputed evidence might substantially affect the seriousness of the unfitness if accepted. In such circumstances, Ferris J. envisaged that the court would refuse to deal with the matter as invited and would direct a full trial. However, this was inconsistent with the notion that the parties have complete freedom as to what facts they invite the court to act upon and that a claimant is free to conduct his case as he thinks fit and to withdraw any part of his case at any time. In *Secretary of State for Trade and Industry v. Rogers*, the Court of Appeal held that, on a *Carecraft* hearing, the court should not consider the scope of any disputed evidence or of any matters not put forward on the summary hearing but which formed allegations in the proceedings. It is for the Secretary of State to decide what matters to put forward or to persist in.[31] The court will not therefore be concerned with the nature and scope of any allegations or evidence not put before it as being agreed or not contested. However, it may be sensible for the *Carecraft* statement to make express provision with regard to the status of the disputed evidence in the event that a disqualification order is made (for example, should disputed matters be treated in an analogous way to criminal charges which have been left to "lie on the file" or be formally withdrawn?). If the status of the disputed facts is not expressly dealt with in the *Carecraft* statement, it is submitted that a defendant would have a strong argument that the claimant could not seek to establish such facts in other proceedings (whether proceedings seeking permission to act notwithstanding the making of the disqualification order or later disqualification proceedings) by reason of the principle in *Henderson v. Henderson*.[32] The facts in question

[28] For example, in circumstances where the *Carecraft* statement is agreed on the morning of a trial long fixed where there will, in any event, be a trial against one or more other defendants and there is no practical possibility of having the *Carecraft* hearing before a different judge and retaining the contested trial date. It may be unfair for non-Carecrafting defendants if the matter has to be adjourned to another date. Equally, it may be impracticable to "split" the trial so that there are two trials: one against the defendant who (unsuccessfully) sought a summary disposal and one against the other defendants. Although a non-Carecrafting defendant may object to the judge conducting the summary hearing first before going on to hear the full trial, in most cases it is difficult to see that the objection would have any legal merit. Any trial against more than one defendant carries with it the risk that one defendant will make admissions which are inconvenient to another defendant. It is difficult to see that it makes a difference whether the admissions in question are in the course of a full trial or at a stage immediately prior to the trial. They have even less weight if they do not bind the non-Carecrafting defendant. Further, the Carecrafting defendant may have agreed not to contest the facts which is different from making formal admissions. Moreover, if by the time of the trial an order has been made under the summary procedure against one or more defendants, that fact and the basis on which the order was made are likely to be made available to the trial judge (a) for the purposes of explaining why a defendant is not before him and (b) for the purposes of considering the appropriate period of disqualification if a further order is to be made as a result of the trial.
[29] The parties might, for example, agree that costs be reserved to the trial judge, or that they be costs in the disqualification proceedings.
[30] [1994] 1 W.L.R. 172 at 183G to 184A.
[31] [1996] 1 W.L.R. 1569 at 1574. It is submitted that the claimant is free to decide that certain allegations should not be put before the court on the summary hearing whether or not they are disputed and that the correct analysis is that "the Secretary of State is entitled to decide what allegations in support of the disqualification application he will put forward, or having put forward, will persist in" (at 1574D) and that he is not restricted to agreeing to a disposal only where his evidence "is disputed" (see at 1574B). If this view is wrong, it would seem difficult to justify the Secretary of State ever agreeing to a *Carecraft* disposal before the defendant has filed evidence.
[32] (1843) 2 Hare 100.

should be set out in the *Carecraft* statement and not incorporate evidence set out in affidavits by reference (for example, by reciting paragraph numbers in the affidavits as being not contested).[33] This minimises the risk that the judge will (incorrectly) go beyond the *Carecraft* statement[34] and also ensures that there is a single document clearly setting out the relevant facts, which the court can then append to any judgment resulting in a disqualification order (see further below) and which can be used (for example) on an application for permission to act.

8.13   It is important that the facts in question are not ambiguous. Any ambiguity will be resolved in favour of the defendant director. Thus in *Re P S Banarse & Co. (Products) Ltd, Secretary of State for Trade and Industry v. Banarse*, the judge was faced with a statement that the defendants "knew or ought to have known" that certain accounts, circulated to third parties, were false. He was not prepared to draw the inference of secondary fact that there was dishonesty (that is, that there was actual knowledge). The *Carecraft* statement:

> "... should not mince its words. Either the parties are in agreement as to the facts or they are not. If not, a trial will in the long run be the appropriate course. But if they are in agreement, the facts should be spelled out clearly and should leave no room for need for infilling or interpretation by way of inference of secondary fact."[35]

8.14   The defendant can either admit the recited facts or admit that there is evidence supporting those facts and not contest them. To minimise the risk of admissions being used against him in other proceedings, a defendant is best advised not to contest (rather than to admit) the relevant facts. If the *Carecraft* statement is put forward on the basis that certain facts are not contested then the statement should confirm that there is evidence which supports the relevant facts asserted (and, of course, this will need to be the case in fact). In the event that the parties are content to put forward further facts which are not the subject of filed affidavit evidence (for example, because further matters have come to light) then the choice is for further affidavit evidence to be filed or for express admissions to be made. If an express admission is made the defendant is best advised to make clear that the admission is for the purposes of the summary hearing only. Indeed, even where the defendant simply does not contest the allegations, he is best advised to require wording to be inserted into the *Carecraft* statement to the effect that that course is only being followed for the purposes of the summary hearing in question.[36] In the *Carecraft* case, Ferris J. expressly referred to the need for there to be evidence before the court which establishes unfitness: "a mere assertion of no evidential value, or a mere admission which is unsupported by evidence, would not by itself suffice".[37] In this context, a mere admission of unfitness is not enough but an admission of a primary or secondary fact or facts (such as that the company continued to trade at a time when the defendant knew that it would not avoid insolvent liquidation and that debts substantially increased during this period) would,

---

[33] A course approved by Ferris J. in *Secretary of State for Trade and Industry v. Shah*, April 10, 1997, Ch.D., unreported. It is also consistent with the Practice Direction of December 14, 1995 [1996] 1 All E.R. 442, [1996] B.C.C. 11.

[34] As seems to have happened at first instance in *Official Receiver v. Bond and Long*, June 10, 1997, unreported.

[35] [1997] 1 B.C.L.C. 653 at 658, [1997] B.C.C. 425 at 429.

[36] In *Secretary of State for Trade and Industry v. Rogers* [1996] 1 W.L.R. 1569 the agreement recited was that "the admissions and concessions expressly and impliedly made in this statement are made only for the purposes of facilitating a *Carecraft* disposal of the proceedings and are made entirely without prejudice to the defendant's rights in any other proceedings..." (see at 1575F–H).

[37] [1994] 1 W.L.R. 172 at 183F.

of course, itself be evidence. Ferris J. also said that the court is not bound to accept "unchallenged or admitted facts about which it is not, in all the circumstances, satisfied".[38] It is difficult to conceive of circumstances in which the court would not be prepared to accept unchallenged or admitted facts as to what actually happened at the relevant time (as compared with, for example, an admission of mixed fact and law that the relevant conduct was such as to render the defendant unfit).

Mitigation

8.15   It is usual for the claimant to insist that any mitigation is identified and set out in the *Carecraft* statement.[39] An important aspect of mitigation, best dealt with expressly, is that, if the facts were not "indisputable", the defendant should obtain credit for what is, in effect, a "guilty plea" and for the fact that he has recognised the error of his ways, thereby making him less of a risk to the public.[40] Thus, an agreement to the making of a disqualification order on a summary basis, may of itself be a mitigating factor on the grounds that the defendant has admitted (or not contested) that which might otherwise have taken a great deal of time and expense to prove, and that it indicates a state of mind which suggests that he may be less of a risk to the public than somebody who adamantly insists that any deficiencies were not his fault and that he is not to be blamed for anything that went wrong.

To the extent that the claimant agrees that certain specific matters of mitigation should be put before the court, the claimant will usually be unable to agree them as facts. The formula frequently adopted is that the claimant does not accept the truth of the matters but does not object to the court having regard to such matters in disposing of the summary hearing.

The suggested period

8.16   To minimise the need for oral submission (and, in practice, to reduce the burden of preparing the agreed statement) it is preferable if a single period can be suggested to the court. The alternative is for the parties to agree that an order should be made for a period falling within a certain bracket of years. The parties then make submissions to the court as to what specific period within the suggested bracket of years is appropriate. The Disqualification Practice Direction makes clear that a period of years can be suggested which need not coincide with or even fall exclusively within one of the three brackets referred to in *Re Sevenoaks Stationers (Retail) Ltd*, (that is two to five years, six to 10 years and above 10 years).[41]

The hearing

8.17   It is important for the judge to have an opportunity to read the papers in advance so that if he has any doubts about whether a disqualification order should be

---

[38] [1994] 1 W.L.R. 172 at 183G.

[39] Thus avoiding (or minimising) disputes as to whether certain "mitigation" raised at the summary hearing is in fact inconsistent with the agreed or non-contested facts set out in the *Carecraft* statement. An analogous situation arose in a summary hearing in the Barings proceedings (*Re Barings plc, Secretary of State for Trade and Industry v. Baker*, February 24, 1998, Ch.D, unreported). The summary hearing was conducted on the basis that the claimant's evidence was not contested rather than technically under the *Carecraft* procedure. The director (Mr Broadhurst) produced a mitigation statement, passages of which were objected to on the grounds that they did not amount to mitigation but contradicted the non-disputed evidence of the claimant. The defendant eventually agreed that such passages should be redacted. This issue prolonged the hearing.

[40] See *Re Westmid Packing Services Ltd, Secretary of State for Trade and Industry v. Griffiths* [1998] 2 All E.R. 124 at 132, CA to some extent qualifying what was said by Sir Richard Scott V.-C. in *Re Barings plc, Secretary of State for Trade and Industry v. Baker* [1998] B.C.C. 583 at 590.

[41] [1991] Ch. 164, [1991] 3 All E.R. 578, [1991] B.C.L.C. 325, [1990] B.C.C. 765. As regards periods of disqualification and the *Sevenoaks* brackets see further Chapter 5.

made or whether a disqualification order for the period suggested by the parties is appropriate, those doubts can be expressed as soon as possible.[42] In an extreme case he may allow the parties a brief adjournment to re-consider their positions. In the event that there remains a fundamental difference between the judge's evaluation of the statement and that of the parties, he may be obliged to adjourn the matter for a full trial. The Disqualification Practice Direction provides that, unless the court otherwise orders, a summary hearing will be held in private, although if the court is minded to make a disqualification order it will usually give judgment and make the order in public. The status and remaining practical significance of section 12 of the Administration of Justice Act 1960 in the light of the CPR remains unclear. However, CPR, r. 39.2 and the accompanying Practice Direction make clear that a private hearing is one to which the public will not be admitted without permission of the court and that the transcript of a judgment or order made in private will not be available to the public (*i.e.* non-parties) without permission of the court. The "without prejudice" nature of the *Carecraft* process, and the fact that it is aimed at encouraging settlement by permitting "admissions" to be withdrawn if the court refuses to make the order sought by the parties, suggest strongly that summary hearings should be fully private unless and until judgment is given making the order sought by the parties. The judge cannot be bound by any agreement of the parties as to the appropriateness of disqualification or of any suggested period and may come to the view that the relevant facts do not merit a finding of unfitness or that the conduct in question merits a different period of disqualification to that suggested by the parties.[43] However, if the parties are agreed that the facts in question justify a disqualification order, it will be unusual for the court to disagree.[44] This is no doubt in part because the Secretary of State has experience in the area.[45] Equally, it will be unusual for the court to disagree with a period of disqualification agreed by the parties.[46] In considering the period of disqualification, it is suggested that the court should apply a similar practice to that of an appellate court.[47] The court should be prepared to make the order for the period sought, even if the judge would himself have imposed a slightly different period, provided that the period suggested by the parties is within the reasonable range of what a reasonable court could impose on the basis of the agreed facts. Given that the fixing of the period of disqualification is discretionary and different persons might quite legitimately consider that different periods of disqualification were appropriate on the same facts, it would be undesirable (and would act as a disincentive to agree to a disposal of disqualification proceedings under the *Carecraft* procedure),[48] if the court was to refuse to make an order for the period sought by the parties on the basis that the judge considered that a period of say one year's difference should be imposed. The suggested approach may in fact be applied without being articulated. However, some support for it can be found,

---

[42] *Secretary of State for Trade and Industry v. Rogers* [1996] 1 W.L.R. 1569 at 1575A–B.
[43] *ibid.* at 1574H–1575A: "In summary, the *Carecraft* procedure can effectively and without the judges's consent, limit the facts on which the judge can base his judgment as to the order that should be made; but the *Carecraft* procedure cannot oblige the judge to make a disqualification order and cannot bind him as to the period of disqualification to be imposed." See also at p. 1574E–G.
[44] *ibid.* at 1574E–F.
[45] For a (fully-contested) case where the court would have imposed a longer period of disqualification had it not been for the (lower) period suggested by the Secretary of State (and in which some emphasis was placed on the Secretary of State's status as the regulator responsible for companies): see *Re Continental Assurance Co. of London plc* [1997] 1 B.C.L.C. 48, [1996] B.C.C. 888.
[46] *Secretary of State for Trade and Industry v. Rogers* [1996] 1 W.L.R. 1569 at 1574F–G.
[47] See *Re Copecrest Ltd, Secretary of State v. McTighe (No. 2)* [1996] 2 B.C.L.C. 477 at 485, [1997] B.C.C. 224 at 230 and *Re Westmid Packing Services Ltd, Secretary of State v. Griffiths* [1998] 2 All ER 124 at 130.
[48] Or, at the least, to a disposal on the basis of putting to the court a fixed period of disqualification as opposed to a bracket of years thereby protracting the summary hearing by making it (to some degree) contentious as between the parties.

by way of analogy, in the judgment of Ferris J. in the *Carecraft* case itself. In *Carecraft*, Ferris J. suggested that the court should consider the scope of the disputed evidence to see whether or not the resolution of the dispute might substantially affect the period of disqualification. As discussed above, that approach was held to be wrong in the *Rogers* case but it is interesting to note how it was applied in *Carecraft*. On the facts in the *Carecraft* case, Ferris J. considered that a resolution of the disputed evidence might affect the period of disqualification otherwise to be imposed by a year or so.[49] Nevertheless, he did not think that this was sufficient to require him to refuse to make the order sought and to direct that the matter come on for a full trial. In effect, his view was that it was not necessary for him to refuse to make an order for the period sought where the period that might have been imposed in other circumstances would have been slightly different. The suggested approach is arguably inconsistent with that adopted by Sir Richard Scott V.-C. in *Re Dawes and Henderson (Agencies) Ltd, Secretary of State for Trade and Industry v. Coulthard*[50] where, on a *Carecraft* hearing, he refused to make a disqualification order for a period of five years, as sought, but was prepared to make an order of four years (which course the parties eventually agreed to). Apart from the actual language of the judgment in the *Rogers* case, the facts in that case also support the suggested approach. In *Rogers*, the trial judge was found wrongly to have made a finding of dishonesty. This finding was overturned by the Court of Appeal. Nevertheless, the Court of Appeal imposed the same period of disqualification as the trial judge (and as that sought by the parties at first instance).

8.18   In reaching his decision the judge cannot travel outside the terms of the *Carecraft* statement. The court cannot make findings based on affidavit evidence not contained within the *Carecraft* statement or findings which go beyond those expressed in the statement. Thus, in the *Rogers* case, there was nothing in the *Carecraft* statement to say that the director in question had acted dishonestly. However, the judge conducting the summary hearing made a finding of dishonesty. The Court of Appeal found that he had not been entitled to make such a finding as dishonesty formed no part of the agreed (or non-disputed) facts.[51] In *Re P S Banarse & Co. (Products) Ltd, Secretary of State for Trade and Industry v. Banarse,*[52] the court reaffirmed the proposition that the court could not be asked to draw inferences of secondary fact from the primary facts agreed.

It is convenient if the judge annexes the *Carecraft* statement to his judgment, or incorporates it within his judgment.[53] This saves judicial time otherwise spent in paraphrasing the statement and avoids the risk of inaccuracies in such a precis. The Disqualification Practice Direction requires the written statement to be annexed to the disqualification order, unless the court otherwise orders. It is suggested that it will be a rare case in which an order to the contrary will be made. The general public interest in the proper administration of justice as well as the public interest flowing from disqualification orders being made on the basis of publicly-found facts, both point strongly to the *Carecraft* statement being publicly available once it forms the basis of a judgment disqualifying a person.[54] In addition, if permission to act is granted subsequently on terms that the original order is publicised by service, then annexing the *Carecraft* statement to the order provides a convenient mechanism for publicising both the order and

[49] [1994] 1 W.L.R. 172 at 185B–E.
[50] February 4, 1997, Ch.D., unreported.
[51] [1996] 1 W.L.R. 1569 at 1578E–1579A.
[52] [1997] 1 B.C.L.C. 653, [1997] B.C.C. 425.
[53] A course suggested in *Re BPR Ltd* [1998] B.C.C. 259.
[54] See the following passage in *Re Blackspur Group plc* [1998] 1 W.L.R. 422 at 433H, CA: "The factual basis for making orders ... ensures that disqualification orders ... have a real deterrent effect and, in that way, afford public protection against the menace of persons unfit to enjoy the privileges of limited liability".

the reasons for the disqualification. If the *Carecraft* statement is incorporated in or annexed to the judgment and such statement is very substantial this might provide a reason to make an order to the contrary.

Status of the Carecraft statement after the making of an order

8.19   To the extent that the relevant judgment annexes or recites the *Carecraft* statement or the statement is annexed to the disqualification order, it will obviously be in the public domain. However, in some cases only a very short judgment is given and the statement is not incorporated or annexed. Some formulations have been adopted in *Carecraft* statements which suggest that the statement can or should remain confidential and unavailable to the public, even where a disqualification order is made on the basis of the agreed (or non-disputed) facts contained in it. Where the court finds expressly that certain facts are not made out or that the conduct which they disclose is beyond criticism or falls outside the factual matrix of conduct which, taken cumulatively, justified the making of a disqualification order, there may be an argument for keeping those facts confidential. However, it seems extremely unlikely that access to the statement would not be given by the court were a third party to seek it. The court is usually obliged to give reasons for its judgment. The statement contains the relevant facts on the basis of which the court makes the disqualification order. As such, it is suggested that when a disqualification order is made following the *Carecraft* procedure, the public are entitled to be given access to the *Carecraft* statement and that the parties do not have the ability to prevent such access.[55] Accordingly, it will be rare for the court to direct that the *Carecraft* statement should not be annexed to the disqualification order.

UNCONTESTED EVIDENCE

8.20   It is always open to a defendant not to contest the evidence which is put before the court. There is no obligation on a defendant to file evidence. In those circumstances, it would remain open to the defendant to dispute jurisdiction (for example, on the basis that the evidence did not disclose conduct such as to make the defendant unfit within the meaning of section 6). Alternatively, the defendant could accept that jurisdiction to make a disqualification order was established, but dispute the relevant period for which the order should be made.

Even after evidence is filed by a defendant it is open to him to seek to withdraw it so that the case proceeds on the basis of the claimant's evidence alone. However, once filed, evidence cannot simply be withdrawn without agreement. A claimant might wish to rely upon evidence filed by a defendant as furthering the claimant's case. The filing of an affidavit by one party may entitle the other party to rely on such evidence and to cross-examine the deponent.[56] If the claimant's evidence is not contested in its entirety it may be appropriate to deal with the matter by way of a summary hearing or it may be more appropriate simply to deal with the matter at trial.

There is no reason why the parties cannot agree a modification of the *Carecraft* procedure in circumstances where the defendant is not contesting the claimant's evi-

---

[55] See, by analogy, *FAI General Insurance Co. Ltd v. Godfrey Merrett Robertson Ltd*, December 21, 1998, unreported.

[56] See discussion in *Re Rex Williams Leisure plc* [1994] Ch. 1 at 6G to 10E (especially at 9D) and 350 (Court of Appeal) at 360E to 364B. It is to be noted that the procedural difference between affidavits (which could not be "withdrawn" once filed), and witness statements in the High Court (which had to be served but could not be relied on by any other party until the witness was called) that existed prior to the CPR (see RSC Ord. 38, r. 2A(4)) has now disappeared (see CPR, r. 32.5(5)).

dence. A statement could be agreed and the court invited to deal with the matter by way of a summary hearing. The statement could record that the claimant's evidence was not disputed for the purposes only of a summary disposal of the case (reserving the defendant's rights in other proceedings), and also set out agreement as to one or more matters normally covered by a *Carecraft* statement (*e.g.* that the case be put to the court on the agreed basis that the court has jurisdiction to make and should make a disqualification order and that the court be invited to make an order of a specific period or within a specific bracket having regard to the facts and any stated matters of mitigation).

CPR PART 36, OFFERS "TO SETTLE", *Calderbank* Offers

8.21 If the defendant wishes to dispose of the proceedings on a certain basis but the claimant will not agree, what can he do? One possibility is to make what, to date, has commonly been referred to as a *Calderbank* offer[57]: *i.e.* an offer "without prejudice save as to costs". The terms of such offer cannot be referred to at trial, other than with regard to the question of costs. If, after trial, the claimant achieves less than what has been offered then, although he may have succeeded at trial, he may be deprived of all or part of the costs which would otherwise have been ordered in his favour. The ability to make such an offer would appear to survive CPR, Part 36. Given the peculiar nature of disqualification proceedings, it is suggested that the detailed provisions of CPR, Part 36 are unlikely to have much practical application to such proceedings.[58] The practical difficulty which faces a defendant seeking to make a *Calderbank* offer is that the parties cannot simply compromise the proceedings by agreeing a period of disqualification. As discussed above, it is *the court* which must be satisfied that it has jurisdiction to make a disqualification order, that such order should be made and as to what is an appropriate period of disqualification. An offer merely to submit to a disqualification order for a period of years is therefore of no utility. It is difficult to see why a claimant should be penalised for refusing to "accept" such an offer when, even if such offer was accepted, the court would not act on it without making determinations of fact. There needs at least to be an offer to agree or not contest particular evidence. Even then, the defendant faces difficulties. In making such an offer, it is not clear how much detail the defendant would need to go into in identifying the facts he was prepared to admit or not contest. Would it be reasonable for the Secretary of State to refuse any such offer until he had seen affidavit evidence from the defendant? Similarly, if the defendant was only prepared to submit to an order of a fixed period, would it be reasonable for the claimant to refuse to agree to put the matter before the court on that basis on the ground that the court has a discretion as to period and the specific period "offered" by the defendant was more narrow than the reasonable range within which the court could reasonably have made an order? The difficulties facing a defendant in formulating a *Calderbank* offer probably explain, at least in part, why there are no reported cases of a claimant in civil disqualification proceedings being deprived of costs on the basis that he failed to "beat" a *Calderbank* offer.

---

[57] *Calderbank v. Calderbank* [1976] Fam. 93.
[58] Although, for present purposes, the possibility of a claimant making a *Calderbank* offer is perhaps highlighted by CPR, Pt 36.

CHAPTER 9

Alternative Grounds for Disqualification

INTRODUCTION

Scope of chapter

9.01 The following substantive powers of disqualification are considered in this chapter:

(1) The range of powers in CDDA, ss 2 to 5 grouped under the heading "disqualification for general misconduct in connection with companies".

(2) The power in CDDA, s. 10 headed "participation in wrongful trading".

General introduction: sections 2 to 5 and 10

9.02 Most of the chapter is devoted to an examination of the scope and operation of sections 2 to 5. The powers of disqualification created by those provisions are directed for the most part at persons who have committed certain substantive criminal offences or other types of criminal default. As such, it is arguably appropriate to characterise these powers as powers of *criminal* disqualification. However, it will be seen that these powers are not the exclusive preserve of the criminal courts. For instance, the power of disqualification in section 2 is exercisable by either the criminal or civil courts. Confusion has arisen as to whether the rationale of disqualification in a criminal court is or should be different from the rationale of disqualification in the civil courts.[1] The view maintained in this chapter can be summarised as follows:

(1) When the court (be that a criminal or a civil court) exercises a power of disqualification under sections 2 to 5, it is first and foremost exercising jurisdiction under the CDDA.

(2) The CDDA as a whole is best seen as a coherent legislative scheme with common features and a common purpose. Jurisdiction under the CDDA is generally triggered by some past misconduct of the individual (whether "general misconduct" under sections 2 to 5, or unfitness under sections 6 to 8, etc.) which raises doubts over his suitability to direct or manage companies. The effect of disqualification and the sanctions for breach of a disqualification order are the same whether the individual is disqualified under sections 2 to 5, 6 to 8 or section 10. This suggests that the various powers in the CDDA share a common rationale and, as such, the criminal and civil courts should, in general terms, adopt a common approach when exercising jurisdiction under it.[2]

---

[1] *R. v. Young* (1990) 12 Cr.App.Rep. (S.) 262, [1990] Crim L.R. 818, [1990] B.C.C. 549, CA suggests that the approach of the criminal and civil courts should be distinct. See further discussion at paras 2.19 and below at paras 9.59–9.65.

[2] See para. 2.01.

9.03 Three further points can be made by way of general introduction and by way of comparison between sections 2 to 5 and the unfitness provisions in sections 6 to 8 discussed in Chapters 3, 4 and 5. First, in contrast with section 6 but in common with section 8, the three provisions in sections 2 to 5 confer on the relevant court a *discretionary* power of disqualification. Thus, even if the court has jurisdiction to disqualify under sections 2 to 5, it is not bound to make a disqualification order. Secondly, in contrast with the unfitness provisions, sections 2 to 5 do not apply exclusively to company directors. The provisions in sections 2 to 5 are thus broader in scope and illustrate the important point that the CDDA is not concerned exclusively with the disqualification of directors and can extend to other persons within the corporate context. Thirdly, and again by way of contrast with the unfitness provisions, *locus standi* to apply for a disqualification order under sections 2 to 5 is not confined to the Secretary of State and the official receiver alone.[3] The power of disqualification exercisable by a civil court under section 10 is triggered by a declaration of personal liability under either section 213 or 214 of the Insolvency Act 1986. The power in section 10 is also discretionary.

Meaning of "company" in sections 2 to 5 and 10

9.04 The width of the term "company" is considered in Chapter 3 (where the court's jurisdiction under section 6 is explored) and in Chapter 12 (which considers the extent of the prohibitions in sections 1, 11 and 12). The main points of that discussion are restated briefly below but with particular reference to sections 2 to 5 and 10:

(1) It appears that the powers of disqualification in sections 2 to 5 and 10 apply to conduct in relation to building societies and incorporated friendly societies because of the effect of sections 22A and 22B of the CDDA. However, it is not entirely clear whether sections 3, 4(1)(a) and 5 are applicable to building societies and incorporated friendly societies because those sections make reference to specific provisions of companies legislation which are not expressly applied by the CDDA to these entities. The point is that under sections 3, 4(1)(a) and 5, a person is only liable to disqualification if he has committed a triggering breach of a type specified in each section. Sections 22A and 22B do make some modifications to other sections of the CDDA (*e.g.* they expressly provide that Schedule 1 of the CDDA, which is relevant to the question of unfitness, should be read as referring to the corresponding provisions of the Building Societies Act 1986 and the Friendly Societies Act 1992). However, they do not modify sections 3, 4(1)(a) and 5.[4] It appears that section 10 may be capable of applying to building societies and incorporated friendly societies

---

[3] CDDA, s. 16(2).
[4] The point is that a person is only liable to disqualification if he has committed a triggering breach of a type specified in the relevant CDDA provision. Thus, for example, under section 3 the triggering event is persistent default in relation to certain specified provisions of the Companies Act 1985 and the Insolvency Act 1986. As a building society regulated by the Building Societies Act 1986 is not, by definition, a "company" for all the purposes of companies legislation, its directors cannot commit a triggering breach. Obviously, if a building society converts into a company under sections 97–102 of the Building Societies Act then the point falls away. The position in relation to limited liability partnerships looks set to be much clearer. The draft Limited Liability Partnerships Regulations will insert a new section 22C in the CDDA. It is clear from the draft that the meaning of "companies legislation" in sections 3(1) and 5(1) of the CDDA will be extended to cover both the new Limited Liability Partnerships Act and the Regulations. The effect is that sections 3 and 5 will have clear application to limited liability partnerships. Furthermore, it is clear from the draft Regulations that (a) section 458 of the Companies Act will apply (bringing LLPs within the scope of section 4(1)(a) of the CDDA) and that (b) the Insolvency Act will have extensive application with the consequence that wrongful or fraudulent trading proceedings will clearly lie (bringing section 10 of the CDDA into play). The fact that these regulations are so explicit strengthens the arguments in the main text in relation to building societies and incorporated friendly societies.

because these entities are capable of being wound up under the Insolvency Act which suggests that wrongful or fraudulent trading proceedings might lie.[5] In relation to building societies, this view is confirmed by the legislative history of section 22A. Originally, the provisions of what are now sections 6 and 10[6] were extended to building societies by an amendment made to their immediate statutory predecessors in the Insolvency Act 1985.[7] The amendment was not expressly carried across on consolidation into the CDDA although it continued in force by virtue of the saving provision in Schedule 3, para. 6. Section 22A was inserted by the Companies Act 1989, s. 211(3) and the former amendment repealed with effect from July 31, 1990.[8] Nevertheless, it is suggested that section 22A should be read in the light of the original amendment to bring building societies expressly within the scope of the CDDA's unfitness provisions and section 10.

(2) The effect of section 22(9) of the CDDA and section 735 of the Companies Act 1985 is that sections 2 to 5 and 10 should be read as applying broadly to companies formed and registered under the Companies Act 1985 or its precursors on or after July 14, 1856.[9] This encompasses guarantee companies and unlimited companies as well as companies limited by shares. The references to provisions of companies legislation in sections 3, 4(1)(a) and 5 can be read as including references to corresponding provisions of the former Companies Acts and the Insolvency Act 1985 (section 22(8) of the CDDA).

(3) By virtue of section 22(2)(b) of the CDDA, sections 2 to 5 and 10 should be read as applying to a company which may be wound up under Part V of the Insolvency Act 1986. The view expressed elsewhere (see, in particular, Chapter 12) is that the CDDA only extends to *companies* which are capable of being wound up under Part V and does not encompass other associations or bodies which fall within the meaning of the broader term "unregistered companies" used in Part V. The effect of this analysis is that sections 2 to 5 appear capable of applying to foreign companies, open-ended investment companies[10] and EEIGs registered in Great Britain (which appear to be treated as bodies corporate having legal personality)[11] but are not applicable to partnerships, unin-

---

[5] See, *e.g.* the effect of the Building Societies Act 1986, ss 37, 88–90, Sched. 15 and, more generally, section 229 of the Insolvency Act 1986. See also the Friendly Societies Act 1992, ss 23, 52 and Sched. 10.

[6] Together with what is now section 214 of the Insolvency Act 1986.

[7] With effect from January 1, 1987: see Building Societies Act 1986, s. 120 and Sched. 18, para. 17(3) and S.I. 1986 No. 1560 (C. 56).

[8] S.I. 1990 No. 1392 (C. 41).

[9] Companies formed and registered under the Joint Stock Companies Act 1844 or in Ireland under companies legislation up to and including the Companies (Consolidation) Act 1908 are excluded: Companies Act 1985, s. 735(1)(a), (3).

[10] The Open-Ended Investment Companies (Investment Companies with Variable Capital) Regulations 1996 S.I. 1996 No. 2827 which came into force on January 6, 1997 expressly contemplate that an open-ended investment company can be wound up under Part V of the Insolvency Act suggesting that companies of this type are caught by sections 2, 4 and 10.

[11] Though again it is not clear whether the provisions of companies legislation referred to expressly in sections 3, 4(1)(a) and 5 and which trigger jurisdiction are applicable to open-ended investment companies and EEIGs. The effect of regulation 20 of the European Economic Interest Grouping Regulations 1989 S.I. 1989 No. 638 should be noted. This states that where an EEIG is wound up as an unregistered company under Part V, the provisions of sections 1, 2, 4 to 11, 12(2), 15 to 17, 20 and 22 of, and Schedule 1 to, the CDDA shall apply in relation to an EEIG as if any reference to a director or past director of a company included a reference to a manager of the EEIG and any other person who has or has had control or management of the EEIG's business and the EEIG were a company as defined by section 22(2)(b) of the CDDA. This seems to contemplate the express application of sections 2, 4 and 10 (but not 5) to EEIGs. However, their application is only triggered *where an EEIG is wound up as an unregistered company*. This suggests (bizarre though it may seem) that an application under those sections could only be made following the winding up of an EEIG.

corporated friendly societies and industrial and provident societies none of which are strictly *companies* within the meaning of section 22(2)(b) of the CDDA. Similarly, it appears that section 10 will apply to *companies* falling within Part V as, by virtue of section 229(1) of the Insolvency Act, the provisions of Part IV of that Act (including the wrongful and fraudulent trading provisions) are applicable to such entities.

SECTION 2: DISQUALIFICATION ON CONVICTION OF INDICTABLE OFFENCE

9.05   Under section 2, the court may make a disqualification order against a person where he is convicted of an indictable offence (whether on indictment or summarily) in connection with the promotion, formation, management, liquidation or striking off of a company or with the receivership or management of a company's property. Section 2 is broader than sections 6 and 8 as it is not limited in application to directors (whether *de jure, de facto* or shadow)[12] but applies equally to employees, managers, company secretaries, or insolvency practitioners convicted of an offence falling within its scope. It is clear that the court's discretion to disqualify a person under section 2 only arises if that person has been convicted of a relevant indictable offence. In the absence of such a conviction, the court's power simply does not arise.[13] However, it is not necessary to establish that the company is or became insolvent, which contrasts with the substantive requirement in section 6.

The provision was first enacted in section 33(1)(a) of the Companies Act 1947 (subsequently re-enacted as section 188(1)(a) of the Companies Act 1948).[14] In its original form, the provision enabled the court to disqualify a person "convicted on indictment of any offence in connection with the promotion, formation or management of a company" for up to five years. The current wording (which extended the scope of the original provision to encompass persons summarily convicted of an indictable offence and "offences in connection with the receivership or management of a company's property") was substituted by the Companies Act 1981, s. 93 and later consolidated as section 296 of the Companies Act 1985, the immediate predecessor of the present section 2.[15] While some of the cases cited in this chapter were decided under the Companies Act 1948, they are still relevant given this process of consolidation and the similarity of the statutory wording.[16]

Indictable Offence

9.06   In England and Wales, an indictable offence is an offence which, if committed by an adult, is triable on indictment, whether it is exclusively so triable or triable either way.[17] The position is the same in Scotland (by virtue of section 2(2) of the Act)

---

[12] See para. 3.10 where these terms are defined and discussed in the context of section 6.
[13] The position differs in other jurisdictions, *e.g.* Australia, New Zealand, Ireland, South Africa and Singapore where the offender is *automatically* disqualified on conviction for a relevant offence without the need for a court order. For an example see Australia's Corporations Law, s. 229(3).
[14] On the recommendation of the Cohen Committee: see Report of the Committee on Company Law Amendment, Cmnd. 6659 (1945), para. 150.
[15] The "liquidation or striking off" wording was substituted for the former wording "or liquidation" in section 2(1) by the Deregulation and Contracting Out Act 1994, s. 39 and Sched. 11, para. 6 with effect from July 1, 1995 (S.I. 1995 No. 1433).
[16] See, *e.g.* the treatment of *R. v. Corbin* (1984) 6 Cr.App.R. (S.) 17, [1984] Crim. L.R. 303 and *R. v. Austen* (1985) 7 Cr.App.R. (S.) 214, (1985) 1 B.C.C. 99,528 (both decided under the 1948 Act) in *R. v. Goodman* [1993] 2 All E.R. 789, (1993) 97 Cr.App.R. 210, (1993) 14 Cr.App.R. (S.) 147, [1994] 1 B.C.L.C. 349, [1992] B.C.C. 625.
[17] Interpretation Act 1978, s. 5, Sched. 1.

and in Northern Ireland (by virtue of article 5(1) of the NI Order). It is thus clear that the offence need only be *capable* of prosecution on indictment and that there will be jurisdiction to disqualify on conviction following either a summary trial or trial on indictment.[18]

Promotion, formation and management

9.07 The terms "promotion", "formation" and "management" appear in both section 2(1) and section 1(1)(d) of the CDDA. In section 2 their function is *jurisdictional*: if an offender commits an offence falling within their scope he is liable to disqualification. In section 1 they serve to delineate the boundaries of a disqualification order: a disqualified person cannot without the permission of the court be concerned or take part in company promotion, formation or management. For convenience, a full discussion of the terms is reserved to Chapter 12 in which section 1 is considered.[19] The analysis found there (which addresses fundamental questions like "what is a promoter?", "what is 'management'?", etc.) should be treated as applying equally to the terms as they appear in section 2(1). At the same time, it is important to bear in mind that for section 2 purposes there is jurisdiction to disqualify if the offender is convicted of an offence "in connection with" promotion, formation or management etc. It is not clear whether there is any difference in practical effect between this wording and the "in any way, whether directly or indirectly, be concerned or take part in" promotion, formation or management wording used in section 1(1)(d). It is suggested that the "in connection wording" is capable of being construed just as widely.

Offence in connection with promotion of a company

9.08 The common law on promoters was devised principally as a means of protecting investors in the context of a public offer. As such, it is arguable that the offence of making false or misleading statements where the company's securities are offered to the public is one in connection with the promotion of a company for the purposes of section 2(1).[20] The same may also be true of the offence of offering securities to the public without publication of a prospectus.[21] The fact that "any person" convicted of an offence "in connection with the promotion of a company" is liable to disqualification begs the question whether professional advisers, such as lawyers, accountants or merchant bankers specialising in corporate finance could be treated as "promoters" for section 2 purposes. At common law, a person who simply discharges his professional duties, *e.g.* by drafting a prospectus or preparing a profit forecast on the basis of information supplied by the client, is not regarded as a promoter.[22] However, the

---

[18] In England and Wales a prosecution on indictment must be brought before the Crown Court: Supreme Court Act 1981, s.46(1), while summary offences are usually tried by a magistrates court. Summary jurisdiction and procedure are governed principally by the Magistrates' Courts Act 1980 and by rules promulgated under section 144 of that Act although it is possible for a Crown Court to deal with a summary offence included as part of an indictment: Criminal Justice Act 1988, ss 40–41. The position in Northern Ireland in relation to the issues of procedure discussed in this chapter is similar to that in England and Wales: see generally the Judicature (Northern Ireland) Act 1978. In Scotland offences which are capable of being prosecuted on indictment are tried in either the High Court of Justiciary (which is Scotland's supreme criminal court) or in a sheriff court while summary jurisdiction is exercised by both the sheriff and district courts.
[19] See para. 12.23.
[20] See, *e.g.* Financial Services Act 1986, ss 47 and 200. This presupposes that any public offering amounts to "promotion", a view which does not sit entirely comfortably with the common law on promoters: *cf.* paras 12.26–12.27.
[21] Public Offers of Securities Regulations 1995 (S.I. 1995 No. 1537), regs. 4(1) and 16(2). One example of a case in which directors were disqualified following conviction for an equivalent offence in Singapore is the *City Country Club* saga chronicled in A. Hicks, "Commercial Candour and Integrity in Singapore" (1986) 28 Mal. L.R. 288.
[22] *Re Great Wheal Polgooth Company* (1883) 53 L.J. Ch. 42.

corporate financier or accountant who actively solicits potential investors for a corporate venture or in the course of a public offer could well be treated as one. In any event, the width of the "in connection with" prefix probably renders the point academic.

Offence in connection with formation of a company

9.09 "Formation" is arguably narrower than "promotion" and appears to refer only to the process of incorporation encompassing the preparation and filing of the documents required by Part I of the Companies Act 1985 and the issue of a certificate of incorporation by the Registrar of Companies. It might be argued that "formation" should bear an extended meaning and also encompass other legal requirements with which a company must comply before it can commence trading. It could then be said in the case of a public company that the offence of trading or exercising borrowing powers without a certificate under the Companies Act 1985, s. 117 is an offence "in connection with the formation of a company". Again, the point is academic as such an offence almost certainly amounts to one "in connection with" the management of a company in any event.

Offence in connection with management of a company

9.10 It appears from this wording that the court's jurisdiction to disqualify only arises if there is a demonstrable link between (a) the *offender* and a company's management and (b) the *offence* itself and a company's management. Thus, generally, it will only be possible to show that the offence is one "in connection with ... the management of a company" if it can be established first, that the offender is someone who identifiably occupies a management position or discharges or assists in the discharge of a managerial function[23] and second, that there is a nexus between the particular offence and the activity of management. Perhaps wisely, Parliament chose not to define "management" even though it is a term of central importance within the scheme of the CDDA. It is therefore left to the courts to determine as a matter of law and on the facts of each case whether an offender has committed an offence in connection with management for the purposes of section 2(1). The leading case is *R. v. Goodman*.[24]

R. v. Goodman

9.11 The question for the Court of Appeal (Criminal Division) in *R. v. Goodman* was whether the Crown Court had acted within its jurisdiction when disqualifying the appellant, the former chairman of a public company, following his conviction for an offence of insider dealing under the Company Securities (Insider Dealing) Act 1985. The principal ground of appeal was that there was no jurisdiction to make an order under section 2(1) because the offence for which the appellant had been convicted was not one "in connection with the management of a company". Staughton L.J. said that there were three possible ways of looking at the test to be applied:

(1) It could be said that the "indictable offence" referred to in section 2(1) is limited to offences which involve breach of some rule of law as to what must or must not be done in the management of a company. Examples might include

---

[23] On which see further paras 12.29–12.44.
[24] [1993] 2 All E.R. 789, (1993) 97 Cr.App.R. 210, (1993) 14 Cr.App.R. (S.) 147, [1994] 1 B.C.L.C. 349, [1992] B.C.C. 625.

failure to keep proper accounts or file returns, *i.e.* offences involving non-compliance with companies legislation. In the light of the authorities cited in support of the test in (2) below, the court rejected this test as too narrow.

(2) A second, wider approach is to say that any indictable offence committed by a person *in the course of managing a company* should fall within section 2(1). In support of this wider test, Staughton L.J. cited three previous Court of Appeal decisions, *R. v. Corbin*,[25] *R. v. Austen*[26] and *R. v. Georgiou*.[27] The appellant in *Corbin* had pleaded guilty to several counts of obtaining property by deception. The facts were that he ran a business selling yachts through the medium of three companies. To support the business, he fraudulently obtained money from a number of finance companies. He also defrauded customers, obtained yachts and other items of property from suppliers by deception and committed mortgage fraud. Corbin appealed against a five-year disqualification order on the ground that the court had lacked jurisdiction to make it. It was argued on his behalf that "the management of a company" must mean the *internal* management of a company's affairs and that Corbin's offences were not within the subsection because they related to third parties (*i.e.* the finance companies) who were *outside* the company. The court rejected this argument emphasising that Parliament had chosen to enact the words, "in connection with the management of a company" rather than "in respect of the management of a company". The court in *Austen* followed *Corbin* to uphold a disqualification order which had been imposed by the trial judge following the appellant's conviction for similar offences. In the process, the court refused to differentiate between management of a company's internal and external affairs.[28] The court went a stage further in *Georgiou*. The appellant carried on an insurance business through the medium of a company without proper authorisation under the Insurance Companies Act 1982. Again, the short question was whether that offence was one "in connection with the management of a company". The court rejected the appellant's submission that section 2(1) should be construed as applying only if the company has been used as a vehicle for the commission of indictable offences and upheld a five-year disqualification order:

> "The combined effect of [the decisions in *Corbin* and *Austen*] is not to confine the phrase 'in connection with management' to offences involving any actual misconduct of the company's affairs, whether internal or external. In our judgment carrying on an insurance business through a limited company is a function of management and if that function is performed unlawfully in any way which makes a person guilty of an indictable offence it can properly be said that that is in connection with the management of the company."

The overall effect of *Corbin*, *Austen* and *Georgiou* is that an offender is liable to disqualification under section 2 if convicted of either (a) an indictable offence committed in the course of running a company's business and (b) an indictable offence which involves the running of a company's business with-

[25] (1984) 6 Cr.App.R. (S.) 17, [1984] Crim. L.R. 303.
[26] (1985) 7 Cr.App.R. (S.) 214, (1985) 1 B.C.C. 99,528.
[27] (1988) 87 Cr.App.R. 207, (1988) 10 Cr.App.R. (S.) 137, [1988] Crim. L.R. 472, (1988) 4 B.C.C. 322.
[28] See also *R. v. Appleyard* (1985) 81 Cr.App.R. 319 (offender disqualified following conviction for offences of conspiracy to obtain property by deception from an insurance company).

out statutory authority where such authority is required because of the special nature of the business.[29]

(3) A third possibility is to say that any indictable offence which has *some relevant factual connection* with the management of a company should fall within section 2(1). It was the third test which was preferred by the court in *Goodman*, although the reasons supporting this conclusion are only briefly stated. As Nolan has pointed out, it is difficult to ascertain what is meant by a "factual connection", let alone a *"relevant* factual connection".[30] Staughton L.J. regarded the test as being wider than that in (2) above and, yet at the same time, he seems to have accepted that Goodman's offence of insider dealing satisfied a stricter test "because as chairman it was unquestionably his duty not to use confidential information for his own private benefit". However, there is a difference between a director who misuses confidential information in breach of duty and a director who (as in *Corbin, Austen* and *Georgiou*) conducts the company's business in a manner which is unlawful. Thus, sense can only be made of *Goodman* by accepting that it does go further than the three authorities discussed above. Indeed, it appears in the light of *Goodman* that section 2(1) extends to (a) self-dealing offences of a type predicated on the equitable fiduciary obligations owed generally by directors to their companies[31] and (b) any other offence which, in some sense, touches upon the management of the company.

9.12   While it is difficult to ascertain the ambit of the "relevant factual connection" test, the approach in *Goodman* suggests that the courts will not be unduly restrictive in construing section 2(1). Nevertheless, it is clear from the "in connection" wording that if a director or manager of a company is convicted of offences which do not relate to the company he is not liable to disqualification under section 2(1). Thus, for example, if a director is convicted of an isolated offence of shoplifting the court cannot disqualify him even though his offence may raise serious questions about his honesty and overall fitness to occupy a fiduciary position. His "fitness and properness" can only be judged by reference to his activities in relation to a specified company or companies. This contrasts with the position in other jurisdictions where a person convicted of certain types of offence faces disqualification regardless of whether that offence has any connection with a company or not. In Australia, a conviction for an offence of serious fraud results in automatic disqualification for five years. The position in the Republic of Ireland is similar.[32] The formal position in these jurisdictions reflects a more general-

---

[29] It might be argued that (a) and (b) are too wide because it is possible for sole traders or members of partnerships to commit these types of offence without risk of disqualification, *i.e.* there is nothing specifically *corporate* about the offences in *Corbin, Austin* and *Georgiou*. This argument can be raised in relation to many regulatory offences such as health and safety etc. which apply to business managers regardless of whether the business is incorporated. However, the justification for a wide approach rests on the CDDA's protective rationale including its concern with raising standards of conduct. In other jurisdictions, certain offences (generally offences of dishonesty or fraud as opposed to regulatory offences) committed *outside* the corporate context lead to automatic disqualification: see, *e.g.* Australian Corporations Law, s. 229(3)(b).
[30] R. Nolan, "Disqualifying directors" (1994) 15 *The Company Lawyer* 278.
[31] See further para. 9.23 for a discussion of self-dealing offences which appear to fall within section 2(1).
[32] The relevant provision in Australia is the Corporations Law, s. 229(3) which is discussed in J. Cassidy, "Disqualification of Directors under the Corporations Law" (1995) 13 *Company and Securities Law Journal* 221. The predecessor to section 229(3) was even wider in scope, extending to "any offence involving fraud or dishonesty punishable on conviction by imprisonment for a period of not less than three months": see Cassidy, *op. cit.* and J.F. Corkery, "Convicted Offenders and Section 227 of the National Companies Code: Restrictions on Certain Persons Managing Companies" (1983) 1 *Company and Securities Law Journal* 153. For Ireland, see G. McCormack, *The New Companies Legislation* (1991), Chap. 8. The position in New Zealand, South Africa and Singapore is similar to that in Australia and Ireland.

ised attempt to prevent those whose integrity and probity have been called into question from running companies and controlling corporate assets.

Specific "management" offences falling within section 2(1)

9.13   It has been suggested that the courts are unlikely to construe section 2(1) restrictively. A liberal approach to construction is certainly consistent with the view that the CDDA as a whole is a coherent legislative scheme concerned with protecting the public from those whose misconduct has cast doubt on their ability or suitability to run companies.[33] The aim under this sub-heading is to identify a range of possible offences of which a conviction might trigger the jurisdiction in section 2. The range of offences discussed below illustrates the potential width and practical relevance of section 2. However, it is not claimed that what follows provides an exhaustive account of every indictable offence which could conceivably fall within section 2(1). The discussion is intended to be illustrative rather than exhaustive.

Corporate offences committed with the consent or connivance of, or attributable to the neglect of a director or manager

9.14   Companies are liable to prosecution for a variety of regulatory offences in the fields of environmental protection, health and safety and consumer protection. In several instances, a director or manager of a company can also be prosecuted personally if it can be proved that the offence for which the company is liable was committed with the consent or connivance of, or was attributable to any neglect on the part of that director or manager. If a director or manager is convicted of an offence of this type the court's power to disqualify him under section 2 is very likely to arise as it will usually be easy to show the required connection between the offence and the management of a company in the light of the authorities discussed above. The trend in recent years has been to criminalise the conduct of directors and senior managers as well as that of the company and so the opportunities for the courts to consider section 2 are likely to increase rather than diminish in the future. Having said that, it must be appreciated that while conviction for an indictable offence is a *necessary* condition for the operation of section 2, it is not of itself a *sufficient* condition and there has, as yet, been very little debate as to whether disqualification is an appropriate response to offences of this nature.[34] Nevertheless, the relevant agencies which are responsible for enforcement should be aware that the court's discretion under section 2(1) is likely to arise where a director or manager is convicted of a corporate regulatory offence.

9.15   Environmental offences.   A wide range of indictable offences can be committed under environmental legislation. These offences are directed at mischiefs ranging from pollution of the environment to unauthorised disposal of waste. So, for example, it is an offence to carry on a prescribed process without authorisation[35] or to deposit controlled waste in or on land unless a waste management licence authorising

---

[33] See general discussion in Chap. 2.
[34] Such offences can also be committed by sole traders or members of partnership firms without risk of disqualification under section 2 (although the effect of the Insolvent Partnerships Order 1994 is that members of partnership firms are exposed to possible disqualification under section 6 on grounds of unfitness). Moreover, the use of disqualification in such contexts as environmental and consumer protection amounts to a tacit recognition that wider constituencies or "stakeholders" are deserving of some accommodation within the framework of company law. The question of whether company law can or should encompass such interests is hotly contested: see Chap. 5 of *Modern Company Law: The Strategic Framework* (February 1999), a consultation document issued by the Company Law Review Steering Group as part of the Department of Trade and Industry's review of core company law.
[35] Environmental Protection Act 1990, ss 6, 23(1)(a).

the deposit is in force[36] or to cause pollution of controlled waters.[37] All of these offences can be committed by "a person" (which, of course, includes a company, a director or senior manager) and are triable either way. If any of these offences are committed by a company and it is proved that the offence was committed with the consent or conniv-ance of, or is attributable to any neglect on the part of any director, manager, secretary or other similar officer or any person who was purporting to act in any such capacity, then he, as well as the company, is guilty of an offence and liable to prosecution.[38] Until recently, much of the responsibility for the enforcement of environmental legislation lay at the door of local authorities. Following the establishment of the Environment Agency for England and Wales and the Scottish Environment Protection Agency under Part I of the Environment Act 1995, enforcement is now largely concentrated in these bodies. As such, a considerable increase in prosecutions of directors and managers for environmental crime can be expected, with the added possibility that, on conviction, section 2 will come into play.

9.16 Health and safety offences. The Health and Safety at Work Act 1974 imposes duties on employers (including corporate employers) to take steps both to secure the health, safety and welfare of employees and to protect the public generally against risks to health and safety arising in the workplace.[39] Under section 33 of the 1974 Act, a person who fails to discharge any of these duties commits an offence which is triable either way. Section 37 contains precisely the same "consent, connivance or neglect" wording already observed in the context of environmental legislation with the consequence that individual directors or managers of a corporate offender can be pros-ecuted alongside the company. Responsibility for enforcement lies with the Health and Safety Executive which was established under the 1974 Act.

It was acknowledged during parliamentary debate on the Offshore Safety Bill[40] in 1991 that section 2 is capable of applying to offences under health and safety legis-lation. In the course of debate, an attempt was made in the House of Lords to amend section 2(1) to make express reference to offences under Part 1 of the 1974 Act and related legislation. Viscount Ullswater expressed the government's opposition to the amendment in the following terms:

> "To return to the particular amendment, the main reason why the government oppose the amendment is that they believe it is unnecessary or perhaps even coun-ter-productive. It is unnecessary because in our view section 2 of the Company Directors Disqualification Act 1986 is capable of applying to health and safety matters... We believe that the scope of section 2(1) ... is very broad and that 'management' includes the management of health and safety... Finally, I men-tioned our view that the amendment could be counter-productive. By that I meant that the proposed text could have the effect of narrowing the scope of section 2(1) ... which currently we construe very broadly. There is a danger that in seeking to define the circumstances in which section 2(1) applies, the courts will interpret the section as applying only to those specified circumstances and none other."[41]

9.17 Technical considerations aside, Viscount Ullswater also doubted whether, in practice, the court's power to disqualify directors and managers under section 2 would

---

[36] *ibid.*, section 33(1)(a).
[37] Water Resources Act 1991, s. 85.
[38] Environmental Protection Act 1990, s. 157; Water Resources Act 1991, s. 217.
[39] See, in particular, Health and Safety at Work Act 1974, ss 2–4.
[40] Subsequently enacted as the Offshore Safety Act 1992.
[41] *Hansard*, HL Vol. 532, cols 1431–1432, (1991).

have much effect in improving standards of health and safety. He reasoned that it will always be easier to prove a case against an employer generally than against individual directors and pointed out that even if a director is successfully prosecuted, the court may decide that disqualification would serve no useful purpose. This view seems to reflect both the general philosphy underpinning the 1974 Act with its primary emphasis on the use of administrative sanctions (such as improvement and prohibition notices) as a means to encourage employers to take constructive remedial action and doubts as to whether it is either appropriate or practical to apportion blame for collective management failure between individual directors.[42] Nevertheless, the section 2(1) power has been exercised to disqualify offenders following conviction under section 37 of the 1974 Act.[43]

Another interesting reform initiative was launched in 1991 by the City solicitors' firm, Davies Arnold Cooper. The principal aim of the Davies Arnold Cooper proposals was to insert a new mandatory provision in the Company Directors Disqualification Act 1986 *obliging* the court to disqualify a director or officer of a company or a person concerned in the management of any undertaking (whether a company or not) if satisfied on the balance of probabilities:

(a) that the company or undertaking in question is being or has been carried on in a manner which poses or has posed a serious risk to the health, safety or welfare of any person or class of persons, and

(b) that his conduct as a director or officer or person concerned in the management of the undertaking (and having regard also to his conduct in the same capacity in relation to other companies or undertakings) shows such disregard for the health, safety or welfare of any person or class of persons as to make him unsuited to be concerned in the management of a company or other undertaking without the permission of the court.

9.18 It was proposed that *locus standi* to apply for an order on such grounds would be conferred on the Secretary of State (presumably meaning the Secretary of State for Trade and Industry), inspectors appointed under the 1974 Act, chairmen of relevant public enquiries and coroners. The proposal goes much further than the rejected amendment to the Offshore Safety Bill discussed above. First, as under section 6, the court would be *obliged* to make an order if the terms of the provision were satisfied. Second, the proposal targets those who run unincorporated businesses as well as the directors, officers and managers of companies. Finally, and perhaps of most significance, an individual could be disqualified under this provision without first being convicted of an indictable offence. It is understood that Davies Arnold Cooper's proposals met with a negative response from the Government of the day and the firm has, as yet, been unable to find an MP prepared to champion their cause in the form of a private member's bill. Viscount Ullswater's observations cited above suggest that any attempt to persuade Parliament to enact disqualification provisions covering specific

---

[42] For background to the 1974 Act see Report of the Committee on Safety and Health at Work (the Robens Committee), Cmnd. 5034 (1972). Albeit in a different context, the collapse of the prosecution brought against P. & O. following the capsize of the *Herald of Free Enterprise* illustrates how difficult it can be in practice to apportion individual responsibility for collective or systemic failure: see the discussion in C.M.V. Clarkson, "Kicking Corporate Bodies and Damning Their Souls" (1996) 59 M.L.R. 557.

[43] See, *e.g.* the cases of Rodney James Chapman and William Eid. Chapman was disqualified in 1992 following his conviction for an offence under the 1974 Act at Lewes Crown Court. Chapman's case is discussed in G. Slapper, "A safe place to work" *Law Society's Gazette*, No. 38, October 22, 1992. Eid was disqualified for three years on December 1, 1995 by Leicester Crown Court after pleading guilty to various charges brought under section 37 relating to breaches of health and safety regulations (including regulations concerning the employment of child labour): see *Health and Safety Bulletin* for February 1996.

areas of concern, such as health and safety, is likely to run into difficulty. Moreover, it may be that the breaches of health and safety legislation could be taken into account as grounds of unfitness in proceedings under sections 6 or 8 of the CDDA.

9.19   Consumer protection.   The Trade Descriptions Act 1968 is a good example of legislation which aims to protect the consumer. This Act makes it an offence, in the course of a trade or business, to apply a false trade description to goods[44] or to make false statements concerning the provision of services.[45] The provisions of the 1968 Act encompass any person involved in a trade or business including companies and their directors or senior managers. The offences referred to above are triable either way and, as such, are capable of falling within section 2. As is the case with environmental and health and safety offences, section 20 of the 1968 Act contains "consent, connivance and neglect" wording which exposes, among others, the directors and managers of a corporate offender to criminal liability. Responsibility for the enforcement of this legislation lies with the Trading Standards Departments of local authorities.

The General Product Safety Regulations 1994,[46] and the Consumer Protection Act 1987 impose criminal liability on, among others, producers and suppliers of unsafe consumer goods and products. However, it appears that these product safety offences are only triable summarily and thus, do not fall within the scope of section 2. In contrast, under the Food Safety Act 1990 there are several indictable offences affecting food suppliers and retailers which could potentially come within section 2. Again, the directors and managers of a corporate offender are exposed to personal liability and, arguably, the possibility of disqualification, by virtue of "consent, connivance and neglect" wording in section 36 of the 1990 Act.

Financial crime

9.20   It is often argued that the public perceive crimes such as fraud or insider dealing as being less serious than "traditional" crimes such as murder or rape where there is an obvious victim.[47] Nevertheless, cases like *Corbin, Austen* and *Goodman* (discussed above) show that the courts have been willing to disqualify directors who perpetrate offences of theft, obtaining property by deception, fraud or insider dealing in the course of running a company. Furthermore, the use of section 2 in the field of financial crime has become increasingly visible in recent years following the establishment of the Department of Trade and Industry's Investigations Division in 1988 to coordinate the Department's main investigation and enforcement activities. The Investigations Division[48] is responsible for the prosecution of insider dealing and a range of other offences under the companies, financial services and insolvency legislation and, on the evidence of its quarterly press-releases, has made a considerable effort to promote the use of section 2 in these areas. Some specific examples of indictable offences in the field of financial crime which could prompt a response under section 2 are given below.

9.21   Fraudulent trading.   If a company's business is carried on with intent to defraud creditors or for any fraudulent purpose, then every person who was knowingly a party to the carrying on of the business in that manner commits an indictable

---

[44] Trades Descriptions Act 1968, s. 1(1)(a).
[45] *ibid.,* s. 14(1)(a).
[46] S.I. 1994 No. 2328.
[47] For a general introduction to these issues see M. Levi, *Regulating Fraud* (1987).
[48] On the role and responsibilities of DTI Investigations Division see generally, Trade and Industry Select Committee, Third Report, *Company Investigations* (1989–90 H.C. 36).

offence under section 458 of the Companies Act 1985. Section 458 applies regardless of whether the company has been, or is in the course of being wound up. Several directors convicted of this offence or related offences have been disqualified under section 2 and often for periods in excess of five years.[49] The court's power to disqualify a person convicted of this offence under section 2 overlaps to a certain extent with the power to disqualify a person guilty of fraud during the course of a winding up contained in section 4. The section 4 power and the overlap between sections 2 and 4 are explored further below.

9.22 Insider dealing. The regulation of insider dealing in listed securities remains controversial. The academic debate over whether there is any proper justification for regulation continues to rage.[50] Even those who favour prohibition increasingly take the view that the civil law may provide a more appropriate regulatory weapon than the criminal law.[51] Nevertheless, there is a gathering consensus that insider dealing in securities on the basis of unpublished, price-sensitive information amounts to a fraud on other market participants and that, as such, it should be prohibited in order to preserve public confidence in the fair operation of securities' markets.[52] Whatever the state of the debate, an individual currently commits an indictable offence under the Criminal Justice Act 1993, s. 52 if, having information as an insider,[53] he deals in securities that are price-affected in relation to that information, or encourages others to deal, or discloses the information to others. In *R. v. Goodman* discussed above, the appellant had been convicted of an offence under the Company Securities (Insider Dealing) Act 1985, now repealed. To prove an offence under that Act, the prosecution had to establish that there was a connection between the insider and the relevant corporate issuer. This is no longer a requirement as a person will now be treated as an insider simply by virtue of his *knowlege* that the relevant information is unpublished and derives from an inside source.[54] This recasting of the offence has led some to speculate that a court might not now be as willing as it was in *Goodman* to contemplate the use of section 2 in a case of insider dealing.[55] It remains strongly arguable, however, that a director of a company convicted of the current insider dealing offence in relation to the shares of that company is just as likely to be disqualified under section 2 as a director convicted under the previous legislation. Although decided under the previous legislation, *Goodman* suggests that an offence of insider dealing should be treated as a breach of directors' duties. An application of the "relevant factual connection" test would surely lead to the conclusion that a breach of directors' duties involving dealings in the company's shares which results in a conviction is an "offence in connection with ... management". The insider dealing offence can thus be converted into a straightforward issue of corporate governance bringing it within the scope of

---

[49] See, *e.g. R. v. Kazmi* (1985) 7 Cr.App.R. (S.) 115 (disqualified for five years); *R. v. Cobbey* (1993) 14 Cr.App.R. (S.) 82 (disqualified for six years); *R. v. Millard* (1994) 15 Cr.App.R. (S.) 445, [1994] Crim. L.R. 146 (disqualified for 15 years, reduced to eight years on appeal) and *R. v. Smith* (1996) 2 Cr.App.R. 1, [1996] 2 B.C.L.C. 109 (disqualified for 12 years). Directors have also been disqualified following conviction for insurance fraud: see, *e.g. R. v. Appleyard* (1985) 81 Cr.App.R. 319.

[50] See, *e.g.* H. McVea, "What's wrong with insider dealing?" (1995) 15 L.S. 390 ; D. Campbell, "Note: what *is* wrong with insider dealing?" (1996) 16 L.S. 185.

[51] See B. Rider, "Civilising the Law—The Use of Civil and Administrative Proceedings to Enforce Financial Services Law" (1995) 3 *Journal of Financial Crime* 11. At the time of going to press a new Financial Services and Markets Bill was going through Parliament which, if enacted, will expand the range of available sanctions beyond the purely criminal.

[52] B. Rider and M. Ashe, *Insider Crime—The New Law* (1993).

[53] On which, see further Criminal Justice Act 1993, ss 56, 57.

[54] *ibid.*

[55] See "Disconnecting insiders" (1994) 15 *The Company Lawyer* 130; R. Nolan, "Disqualifying directors" (1994) 15 *The Company Lawyer* 278.

section 2. On the same analysis, the director of a corporate broking business who engages in insider dealing on behalf of himself and his clients commits offences in the course of managing the company and could face disqualification. Individuals have been disqualified following conviction for other abuses in relation to securities' markets. For example, in 1990 an individual was disqualified for five years after he was found guilty of making a bogus takeover announcement.[56]

9.23   Self-dealing offences.   If a director dishonestly misappropriates the assets of his company then he commits both an offence of theft and breaches his fiduciary duties. There seems little doubt that the court can disqualify a director who has been convicted of an indictable offence *against* his company. Such an offence will invariably amount to a breach of fiduciary duty and, as in the case of insider dealing above, it can be readily characterised as an offence "in connection with the management of a company" because the fiduciary duties form part of the legal environment in which directors and senior managers are obliged to operate when running companies. On this analysis, it would be open to the court to disqualify a director who has been convicted of the self-dealing offences contained in sections 317 and 342 of the Companies Act 1985.[57]

9.24   Financial assistance.   Subject to various exceptions, a company and its subsidiaries are generally prohibited by the Companies Act 1985, s. 151 from providing financial assistance to anyone who is acquiring, proposing to acquire or has acquired shares in the company. If section 151 is breached, the company and every officer of it who is in default commits an indictable offence.[58] In *Re Continental Assurance Co. of London plc,* a disqualification order was made under section 6, in part based on breaches of this provision.[59] If the director in that case had been convicted of the offence it appears that an order could equally have been made under section 2.[60]

9.25   Tax evasion.   A director who uses the corporate form to perpetrate VAT or excise fraud runs the risk of disqualification if convicted. Customs and Excise are well aware of the section 2 power and directors convicted of offences under the VAT Act have suffered disqualification following conviction.[61]

---

[56] "Trade and Industry minister toughens stance on dishonest directors", *The Guardian,* September 4, 1990. For related abuses which could attract disqualification see Financial Services Act 1986, s. 47.

[57] These offences (section 317: failing to disclose interest in contract; section 342: authorising or permitting company to enter into prohibited loan transaction with director) are both indictable: Companies Act 1985, Sched. 24. Prosecutions for this type of offence are rare. However, given the overlapping nature of the CDDA's provisions, a director who commits such offences may well be judged unfit on an application to disqualify him under either section 6 or 8: see section 9, Sched. 1, Pt I, paras 1–2 and, *e.g. Re Godwin Warren Control Systems plc* [1993] B.C.L.C. 80, [1992] B.C.C. 557.

[58] Companies Act 1985, s. 151(3), Sched. 24.

[59] [1997] 1 B.C.L.C. 48, [1996] B.C.C. 888.

[60] The Australian case of *Re Shneider* (1997) 22 A.C.S.R. 997 which concerned an application to relax the automatic ban imposed on those convicted of certain offences by section 229(3) of the Corporations Law provides some limited support for this view. Shneider had been convicted of charges relating to a company which was found to have provided financial assistance for the purchase of its own shares. The court does not appear to have doubted the necessity of the application which suggests that the offence is one "in connection with the management of a corporation" within section 229(3)(a) of the Corporations Law.

[61] See, *e.g. R. v. Dealy, The Times,* December 13, 1994 where the defendant was disqualified following conviction under VAT Act 1983, s. 39 (see now VAT Act 1994, s. 72). In *R v. Russen,* July 6, 1984, unreported, the Court of Appeal lifted disqualification orders imposed by the Crown Court on the two appellants following their conviction on several counts of conspiracy to defraud the Inland Revenue. The court did not deny that a conviction for these types of offence could trigger jurisdiction under section 2(1). In the circumstances of the case, it was simply felt that the trial judge had been wrong to exercise the discretion to disqualify.

Carrying on an unauthorised investment business through the medium of a company

9.26 There are various types of specialised business, especially in the area of financial services, which cannot be conducted without formal authorisation from an external regulator. Thus, for example, a person who carries on unauthorised investment business is guilty of an offence under financial services legislation. Anyone wishing to carry on investment business must, generally speaking, seek authorisation from the Financial Services Authority ("the regulator").[62] It is clear by analogy with *R. v. Georgiou* (discussed above) that anyone convicted of conducting unauthorised investment business through the medium of a company is liable to disqualification under section 2. This appears to be the case even if the business has otherwise been carried on properly. Disqualification under the CDDA is just one of a range of possible sanctions available to deal with those who commit an offence by carrying on unauthorised investment business. The leading principle of financial services regulation is that only those who are considered "fit and proper" should be permitted to carry on investment business. Thus, even outside the CDDA context, anyone convicted of an offence involving dishonesty or incompetence is likely to face difficulties obtaining or retaining authorisation to engage in investment business. Moreover, the regulator may well conclude that a person with convictions for the offence of carrying on unauthorised investment business is not fit and proper.[63] Equally, it is important to note that proceedings under the CDDA are not precluded simply on the ground that a regulator has taken disciplinary action against the director in respect of the same or related matters. This is because disqualification under the CDDA differs in object and effect from regulatory proceedings and the tests applied in each case are different.[64]

Acting in contravention of a CDDA disqualification

9.27 Anyone who acts in contravention of (a) a disqualification order, (b) the automatic ban on undischarged bankrupts in CDDA, s. 11 or (c) the ban in CDDA, s. 12(2) commits an indictable offence under section 13 of the CDDA. If convicted, it is open to the court to impose a further period of disqualification as contravention of section 13 can be regarded as an offence "in connection with the management of a company".[65] Section 1(3) of the CDDA provides that where a disqualification order is

---

[62] Which for all intents and purposes has now taken over the functions previously discharged under the Financial Services Act 1986 by the Securities and Investments Board, the self-regulating organisations (principally the Securities and Futures Authority, the Investment Management Regulatory Organisation and the Personal Investment Authority) and the recognised professional bodies (such as the Law Society and the Institute of Chartered Accountants).

[63] For an insight into how the regulator might apply this test of fitness and propriety see the decision of the Financial Services Tribunal in the matter of Noble Warren noted at (1989) 4 *Butterworths Journal of International Banking and Financial Law* 334. The regulator also has devolved power under Financial Services Act 1986, s. 59 to direct that an individual shall not be employed in connection with investment business if it appears that he is not a fit and proper person to be so employed. To do so, a so-called "disqualification direction" must be entered on the register which the regulator is required to maintain under section 102. A disqualification direction can remain in force for an indefinite period and would further widen the scope of any CDDA disqualification. However, as of March 1996, there were only 15 persons on the register for whom such a direction was in force: Press Release No. PN/SIB/014/96, March 29, 1996.

[64] *Re Barings plc (No. 2)* [1999] 1 All E.R. 311, *sub nom. Re Barings plc (No. 3)* [1999] 1 B.C.L.C. 226, *sub nom. Re Barings plc (No. 4)* [1999] B.C.C. 639, Ch.D. and CA. This aspect of the *Barings* proceedings involved an unsuccessful attempt by one of the defendants, B, to have disqualification proceedings against him under section 6 stayed on the ground that he had already successfully resisted disciplinary proceedings brought by the Securities and Futures Authorities in which substantially the same charges were made. B was eventually disqualified under section 6 for six years.

[65] See, *e.g. R. v. Thompson* (1993) 14 Cr.App.R. (S.) 89.

made against a person who is already subject to such an order, the periods specified in the orders are to run concurrently not consecutively. So, for example, if X is disqualified for six years and then disqualified a second time for 10 years, four years into the first ban, the second ban starts to run from year four, not year six. A director or manager convicted of an offence under section 14 is similarly liable to disqualification. Section 14 imposes criminal liability on a body corporate which acts in contravention of a disqualification order and contains the "consent, connivance and neglect" form of words encountered earlier in the discussion of corporate regulatory offences.

Summary

9.28   The examples given above illustrate the width of the "relevant factual connection" test in *Goodman*. The fact that some of the offences discussed could equally be committed outside the corporate context (*e.g.* those relating to health and safety, the environment and the carrying on of an unauthorised business) does not take them outside the jurisdiction of section 2. If the offence is committed in the course of the management of a company's business (*Corbin, Austen* and *Georgiou*) or the offence, in some sense, touches upon management (*Goodman*), the offender is liable to disqualification under the section. Thus, the courts have quite considerable scope for using section 2 to further the protective policy of the CDDA as a whole. That being said, the question of whether the court should exercise this wide jurisdiction remains a matter of discretion in each case.[66]

Offence in connection with liquidation or striking off of a company

9.29   This wording encompasses certain provisions of the Insolvency Act 1986 which impose a duty on various people, including the officers of an insolvent company, to co-operate with the liquidator.[67] It would also expose an insolvency practitioner convicted of theft or fraud in relation to a company of which he was liquidator to possible disqualification under section 2.[68] In this respect, the powers to disqualify under section 2(1) and section 4(1)(b) overlap. The extent of this overlap is considered below. "Striking off" refers to the process by which a company is dissolved and removed from the register of companies.[69]

---

[66] In *R v. Russen*, July 6, 1984, unreported, the Court of Appeal lifted disqualification orders imposed by the Crown Court on the two appellants following their conviction on several counts of conspiracy to defraud the Inland Revenue. It was accepted that the offences fell within the scope of section 2. However, it was concluded that the trial judge had been wrong to exercise his discretion as, the offences aside, the companies were being conducted in an otherwise respectable fashion and the expertise of the appellants was essential to their continued successful (and presumably "respectable") operation (this despite the fact that the appellants were serving prison sentences). Dine suggests in "The Disqualification of Company Directors" (1988) 9 *The Company Lawyer* 213 that the court in *Russen* must have formed the view that the appellants were unlikely to repeat their fraud and that it was therefore unnecessary to disqualify them in order to protect the public. For similar reasoning in the context of section 3 see *Re Arctic Engineering Ltd* discussed in main text below.
[67] See, *e.g.* Insolvency Act 1986, ss 235, 430 and Sched. 10. Failure to co-operate with an office holder can also be taken into account in determining whether a respondent is unfit for the purposes of sections 6–8: CDDA, s. 9 and Sched. 1.
[68] Furthermore, an order in the form of CDDA, s. 1 apart from disqualifying him from acting as a liquidator or administrator (s. 1(1)(b)) or a receiver or manager of a company's property (s. 1(1)(c)) would automatically bar him from acting as an insolvency practitioner within the meaning of section 388 of the Insolvency Act 1986: *ibid.*, s. 390(4) and see discussion in Chap. 12. The same point applies to an insolvency practitioner convicted of an offence in connection with receivership or management of a company's property (see text below).
[69] The reference to "striking off" was added by an amendment introduced by the Deregulation and Contracting Out Act 1994, s. 39 and Sched. 11, para. 6 with effect from July 1, 1995 (S.I. 1995 No. 1433).

Offence in connection with receivership or management of a company's property

9.30   The phrase, "receiver or manager of the property of a company" is defined in section 29 of the Insolvency Act 1986 in such a way as to include administrative receivers, receivers of part only of a company's property and receivers appointed subject to the Law of Property Act 1925. Strictly, this definition only applies where the phrase is used in the Companies Act 1985 and the Insolvency Act 1986. Nevertheless, it is suggested that "receivership or management..." in section 2(1) should be read in the same way. As in the case of liquidation above, this wording encompasses certain provisions of the Insolvency Act which impose a duty on various people, including a company's officers, to co-operate with a receiver.[70] Moreover, an insolvency practitioner convicted of theft or fraud in relation to corporate assets of which he was receiver or manager may face disqualification under section 2. Again, in this respect, there is an overlap between section 2(1) and section 4(1)(b) which is considered further below.

Section 2: Procedure

9.31   Any of the following courts have power to make a disqualification order under section 2:

(1) A civil court having jurisdiction to wind up the company in relation to which the offence was committed.

(2) The convicting court.

(3) In the case of a summary conviction in England and Wales, any other magistrates' court acting for the same petty sessions area.[71]

If a court of summary jurisdiction makes a disqualification order under section 2, the maximum period of disqualification it can impose is five years. Otherwise, the maximum period of disqualification is 15 years (section 2(3)).

Court having winding up jurisdiction (civil cases)

9.32   The High Court has jurisdiction to wind up any company in England and Wales. In respect of a company which has a paid up share capital of £120,000 or less, the county court for the district in which the company's registered office is situated has concurrent winding up jurisdiction with the High Court.[72] The position in relation to civil disqualification proceedings in a court of winding up jurisdiction is considered in more detail in Chapter 6 and so what follows is a brief summary only.

Locus standi to apply is conferred on the following by section 16(2):

(1) The Secretary of State.

(2) An official receiver.

---

[70] See, *e.g.* s. 47 and Sched. 10.

[71] The position in Northern Ireland is very similar: see NI Order, article 5(2).

[72] Insolvency Act 1986, s. 117. In Scotland, the Court of Session and the sheriff courts have a similar concurrent jurisdiction: *ibid.*, section 120. The position in Northern Ireland is the same as for England and Wales.

(3) The liquidator or any past or present member or creditor of any company in relation to which the offence was committed.[73]

This procedure makes it possible for the Secretary of State, for example, to apply for a disqualification order against a person who has been convicted of a relevant offence but was not disqualified by the convicting court. Anyone intending to apply to a court with winding up jurisdiction for a section 2 order is required by section 16(1) to give at least ten days' notice to the intended respondent before issuing the application.[74] The application is by way of Claim Form under Part 8 of the CPR. Civil proceedings for an order under section 2 are not subject to any express limitation period. Once issued, however, they will be subject to the court's powers of case management under the CPR, the Disqualification Practice Direction and Article 6 of the European Convention on Human Rights. Any delay in the bringing of proceedings might therefore be taken into account by the court as a possible justification for refusing to exercise its discretion to make a disqualification order.

Convicting court

9.33   This will be the Crown Court (or, in Scotland, the High Court of Justiciary) if the trial is on indictment and a magistrates' court (or, in Scotland, a sheriff court) in the case of a summary trial. The convicting court can make a disqualification order of its own motion as an adjunct to the sentencing process. In *Re Cedac Ltd, Secretary of State for Trade and Industry v. Langridge*, Balcombe L.J. observed that the 10-day notice rule in section 16(1) does not apply to proceedings where the court is empowered to make a disqualification order of its own motion, although he went on to suggest *obiter* that "doubtless the rules of natural justice will require that the person concerned should be given some notice that the court is contemplating making a disqualification order".[75] It is difficult to know what to make of this *dictum* as the reference to a "court empowered to make a disqualification order of its own motion" could refer equally to civil disqualification following participation in wrongful trading under section 10 or criminal disqualification under section 2. In any event, there is no particularly compelling justification for a special requirement that an offender be given advance notice of his exposure to disqualification under section 2. The role of the prosecution in criminal sentencing is simply to remind the court of its powers for dealing with the offender. The prosecution does not *apply* for a disqualification order in the same way that the Secretary of State might in civil proceedings. It is submitted that in criminal proceedings the offender is deemed to be aware of all the possible sentencing consequences (including disqualification) which might be visited on him following conviction. If so, it is questionable whether any particular significance attaches to Balcombe L.J.'s observation in the context of criminal disqualification.

---

[73] Section 16(2) reads: "... or by the liquidator or any past or present member or creditor of any company in relation to which that person has committed *or is alleged to have committed an offence or other default*" (our emphasis). Section 16(2) also applies to applications for disqualification orders under sections 3 and 4 which do not require a conviction: see sections 3(4) and 4(2). The wording emphasised above should therefore be read as referring to those sections and not section 2. In the event of an application by the liquidator etc., the Secretary of State would presumably be entitled to intervene in the proceedings.

[74] For further discussion of the notice requirement in section 16(1) and the implications of non-compliance, see Chap. 6. A full account of procedure in civil disqualification proceedings (which does encompass CDDA, ss 2, 3, 4 and 10 as well as ss 6–8) is reserved to that chapter.

[75] [1991] Ch. 402 (at 414F), [1991] B.C.L.C. 543, [1991] B.C.C. 148.

Double exposure under section 2

9.34   A question of some difficulty which arises in relation to section 2 is whether the Secretary of State could apply to a court with winding up jurisdiction for an order in circumstances where the convicting court declined to make an order, or where it did make an order but for a period considered by the Secretary of State to be too short. At first sight, it appears that there is nothing in the wording of section 2 to prevent the court making an order in such circumstances. Indeed, it appears from the scheme of the CDDA that it is possible for the Secretary of State to apply to a civil court under section 2 either (a) where the criminal court has declined to exercise its power under section 2 at all or (b) where the criminal court has previously disqualified the individual. Clearly, if such circumstances arose, it would remain within the discretion of the civil court whether or not to make an order. One peculiarity of this double exposure is that a civil application for an order would amount, in effect, to an appeal against sentence. This appears somewhat anomalous in that the prosecution generally has no right of appeal against sentence in criminal proceedings.[76] However, if it is right to regard the criminal courts as performing a different function (namely, a punitive function) to that performed by their civil counterparts when exercising powers under the CDDA,[77] that would be a reason for allowing the later proceedings to go ahead.[78] On the other hand, if as is argued throughout this book, it is correct to say that the CDDA contains a set of powers which share common features, a common purpose and common consequences, it is arguable that a civil court should not exercise its discretion to "correct" any error by the convicting court.

9.35   It is not clear to what extent, if any, the common law presumption against "double jeopardy" has any application in these circumstances. The difficulty is that it would appear that the *same consequences* (*i.e.* disqualification) can be visited on the offender twice in separate proceedings arising out of the same or related matters. At the same time, section 2 specifically envisages that a civil court has power to disqualify a person following a criminal conviction and the CDDA therefore appears to sanction "double jeopardy". Faced with an application to stay the later civil proceedings on grounds of double jeopardy, it is suggested that the civil courts are likely to apply the approach taken by the Court of Appeal in *Re Barings plc (No. 2), Secretary of State for Trade and Industry v. Baker*.[79] That case involved an unsuccessful application by one of the *Barings* defendants for a stay of disqualification proceedings under section 6 of the CDDA on the ground that the issues arising had already been determined in regulatory proceedings brought against him by the Securities and Futures Authority. The test applied by the Court of Appeal was to ask whether the later civil proceedings amounted to an abuse of process. On this question, the view expressed was that the court should intervene and stay the proceedings where to allow them to continue would bring the administration of justice into disrepute among right-thinking people. It is suggested, following this approach, that the later civil proceedings would not amount to an abuse of process if additional matters are relied on which were not before the criminal court.[80] However, it would arguably be different if the claimant in the civil proceedings relies solely on the matters which grounded the criminal conviction or any guilty plea. In those circumstances, the civil claim might be treated as an abuse of process because it amounts to an attempt by the claimant to get around the problem that the prosecution generally has no right of appeal in criminal cases. In the event that a second order was made by a civil court, the periods specified in the two orders would run concurrently by virtue of section 1(3) of the CDDA.

Section 3: Disqualification for Persistent Breach of Companies Legislation

9.36   Section 3(1) provides that the court may make a disqualification order against a person where it appears that he has been persistently in default in relation to provisions of the companies legislation requiring any return, account or other document to be filed with, delivered or sent, or notice of any matter given, to the Registrar of Companies. Section 3 is perhaps best seen as a "last resort" option among the range of sanctions available to deal with companies (and relevant officers) that fail to comply with the disclosure and publicity requirements of companies legislation. Technically, an individual can be disqualified under section 3 regardless of whether the company to which the default relates is insolvent or not. In the case of a director of an insolvent company, complaints of this nature are much more likely to be brought against him as evidence of unfitness in proceedings for an order under section 6.[81] Like section 2, section 3 does not apply exclusively to directors and may be of concern to other officers including company secretaries. Section 3 also overlaps substantially with section 5 which is discussed further below. The power to disqualify for persistent breaches of companies legislation is a relative newcomer which was first introduced by the Companies Act 1976, s. 28. It was subsequently re-enacted first as the Companies Act 1981, s. 93 and later as the Companies Act 1985, s. 297 which was the immediate predecessor of the current provision.[82]

---

[80] For some assistance, see *Re Land Travel Ltd, Secretary of State for Trade and Industry v. Tjolle* [1998] 1 B.C.L.C. 333, [1998] B.C.C. 282. In this case, the first defendant, "T", pleaded guilty to an offence of fraudulent trading under section 458 of the Companies Act 1985 and was disqualified for ten years under section 2 as well as receiving a prison sentence. T's guilty plea (and consequent disqualification) related only to his conduct over a three month period. The Secretary of State was of the opinion that T's conduct overall (including matters to which he had not pleaded guilty in the criminal proceedings) merited a maximum period of disqualification of 15 years. Separate civil proceedings were brought under section 6 and T consented to a 15–year disqualification under the *Carecraft* procedure. For *Carecraft* purposes, T made admissions covering a two-year period. Jacob J. was clearly of the view that it was open to the Secretary of State to seek a further order against T in civil proceedings. However, the court did not consider (and, as T had agreed to submit to a *Carecraft* disposal, it was presumably not argued) whether the section 6 proceedings amounted to an abuse of process on grounds of double jeopardy. Although *Land Travel* is a section 6 case, it is suggested that the same principles should apply to any later civil disqualification proceedings, whichever section of the CDDA is relied on.
[81] Sections 6, 9, Sched. 1 and see Chap. 4. For examples of cases in which failure to file accounts and/or returns was taken into account in disqualification proceedings under section 6 see *Re Cladrose Ltd* [1990] B.C.L.C. 204, [1990] B.C.C. 11; *Re Synthetic Technology Ltd, Secretary of State for Trade and Industry v. Joiner* [1993] B.C.C. 549; *Re Swift 736 Ltd, Secretary of State v. Ettinger* [1993] B.C.L.C. 896, [1993] B.C.C. 312 and *Re Pamstock Ltd* [1994] 1 B.C.L.C. 716, [1994] B.C.C. 264. Defaults of this nature could also be taken into account in disqualification proceedings under section 8.
[82] Comparable provisions are in force in other jurisdictions such as Australia and Ireland: see, *e.g.* Australian Corporations Law, s. 230.

Companies legislation

9.37   For the purposes of section 3, companies legislation includes the Companies Acts and the Insolvency Act 1986 (insofar as it relates to companies).[83] Thus, an insolvency practitioner who persistently fails to file returns and documents with the Registrar of Companies as required under insolvency legislation is liable to disqualification under section 3. This is borne out by the proceedings brought against an insolvency practitioner in *Re Arctic Engineering Ltd*[84] discussed further below.

Return, account, etc.

9.38   Section 3(1) covers any return, form, document or notification which is required to be filed at Companies House. In particular, a company is mandatorily obliged from time to time to file an annual return and a set of accounts. Given the importance and recurring nature of these particular obligations, it is no surprise that the Department of Trade and Industry and Companies House treats them as key indicators of regulatory compliance.[85] As such, one might expect to see some use being made of section 3 to enforce compliance with these important filing obligations.

Annual return and accounts

9.39   The Companies Act 1985, s. 363 requires every company to file an annual return before the end of the period of 28 days after the company's return date.[86] The company commits a summary offence if it fails to comply which is punishable by fine. Where a company is guilty of this offence, every director or secretary of the company is similarly liable unless he shows that he took all reasonable steps to avoid the commission or continuance of the offence. The core accounts and audit provisions are contained in Part VII of the Companies Act 1985. Generally, the directors are obliged to lay copies of audited accounts and a directors' report on those accounts before a general meeting of the company in every financial year. The accounts and report must then be filed at Companies House within a prescribed period of time.[87] A variety of penalties can be imposed on a company and its directors for non-compliance with the obligation to file accounts including fines and civil penalties.[88] A further means by which Companies House promotes compliance with these obligations is by invoking the procedure in the Companies Act 1985, s. 652. This provision allows the Registrar to commence striking off proceedings against a company if he has reasonable cause to believe that the company is not carrying on business or is not in operation. The view taken at Companies House is that a company's repeated failure to file annual returns and accounts amounts to "reasonable cause". The problem for the company if it fails to respond once the Registrar has invoked this procedure is that it will be struck off the register. Although it would still then be possible to apply to court for an order restoring the company to the register,[89] the Registrar's current practice is to refuse consent to such an application until all outstanding documents have been filed. Thus, it is important to bear in mind that disqualification for "persistent default" is merely one of a

---

[83] Section 22(7).
[84] [1986] 1 W.L.R. 686, [1986] 2 All E.R. 346, [1986] B.C.L.C. 253, (1985) 1 B.C.C. 99, 563.
[85] See, *e.g.* Department of Trade and Industry, *Companies in 1995–96* (HMSO, 1996), para. 13 and Table F3 which set out the compliance rates for annual returns and accounts in the period 1991–1996.
[86] The return date is the date to which the annual return is made up and is fixed initially as the anniversary of the date of incorporation.
[87] Companies Act 1985, ss 241, 242 and 244.
[88] For civil penalties see, s. 242A, *ibid.*, inserted by Companies Act 1989, ss 1 and 11 with effect from July 1, 1992 (S.I. 1995 No. 2945).
[89] Companies Act 1985, s. 653.

range of regulatory sanctions and techniques which are available and that the main priority of Companies House where possible is to get companies to comply with the law by submitting returns without recourse to court proceedings.[90]

Persistent default

9.40 Under section 3(2), the fact that an individual has been persistently in default may be conclusively proved by showing that in the five years ending with the date of the application for a disqualification order, he has been adjudged guilty (whether or not on the same occasion) of three or more defaults in relation to the provisions of companies legislation described in section 3(1). For the purposes of this conclusive presumption, an individual is treated as having been "adjudged guilty" if he has either been convicted of a non-filing offence or a court order has been made against him under any of the five provisions mentioned in section 3(3)(b) all of which require him to remedy some specific default.[91] Even if persistent default can be conclusively proved in this way, the court is not *obliged* to disqualify the defendant. The question of whether or not to do so remains a matter of discretion and the onus does not shift to the defendant to show why he should not be disqualified.[92] If the individual has not been adjudged guilty of three defaults then the conclusive presumption does not apply and the onus would be on the claimant to prove persistent default in some other way. In *Re Arctic Engineering Ltd*,[93] (a case decided under the old provision in its Companies Act 1981 form), the Secretary of State applied for a disqualification order against an insolvency practitioner but did not seek to rely on the conclusive presumption. The defendant, an accountant of considerable experience, had been in default in relation to 35 returns concerning the liquidation or receivership of 34 companies over a five-year period. However, he had not been convicted of an offence and a default order had never been made against him although in several instances he had only complied after summonses had been issued and served. The court had to determine whether these defaults amounted to "persistent default" in circumstances where the conclusive presumption was not available. Hoffmann J. held that the term "persistently" connotes some degree of continuance or repetition and that a person may persist in the same default or persistently commit a series of defaults. Taking the conclusive presumption

---

[90] See, *e.g.* 36th Report of the Committee of Public Accounts (1984 H.C. 511), *Reliability of Companies Register*. Section 3 does not appear to have played a significant role in improving compliance during the nineties. Working from figures in the Department of Trade and Industry's annual report, *Companies in 1995–96* (HMSO, 1996) it appears that the compliance rate in England and Wales for filing annual returns improved from 85.8% for the year ended June, 30 1991 to roughly 92% by March 1996 and for filing accounts from 86.1% to roughly 95% over the same period. Yet prosecutions by the department for failure to file annual returns steadily declined in numbers from 3,780 in 1991–92 to 884 in 1995–96 and for failure to file accounts from 7,534 in 1991–92 to 2,297 in 1995–96. It is not possible to ascertain precisely how many people were disqualified under section 3 as the report gives an aggregate figure for disqualifications under sections 2–5 without further breakdown. However, there were less than 200 disqualifications per year under sections 2–5 as a whole from 1991 to 1996. It appears that the marked improvement in relation to accounts is attributable to a combination of factors, the main ones being the introduction of civil penalties in 1992 and the sustained compliance campaign which Companies House has continued to wage following criticism of its enforcement record by the Public Accounts Committee. During the eighties in Singapore, an amendment providing for *automatic* disqualification of those in "persistent default" was enacted in direct response to the problem of poor compliance: see A. Hicks, "Disqualification of Directors for Persistent Default in Filing Documents: Section 155, Companies Act" (1985) 27 Mal. L.R. 329, "Disqualification of Directors—Forty Years On" [1988] J.B.L. 27. It is understood that it was not a success.
[91] The five provisions specifically mentioned in section 3(3)(b) are Companies Act 1985, ss 242(4), 245B and 713 and the Insolvency Act 1986, ss 41 and 170.
[92] Support for this proposition can be found in *Re Arctic Engineering Ltd* (discussed in main text) and an Australian case, *Commissioner for Corporate Affairs v. Ekamper* (1988) 12 A.C.L.R. 519, 522.
[93] [1986] 1 W.L.R. 686, [1986] 2 All E.R. 346, [1986] B.C.L.C. 253, (1985) 1 B.C.C. 99,563.

provision as a guide, the judge regarded the defendant's 35 defaults as "amply sufficient to be called persistent". In reaching this conclusion, Hoffmann J. rejected counsel for the defendant's submission that the term "persistently" connoted a *culpable
disregard* of filing obligations. Thus, it is clear from *Arctic Engineering* that the court
should not take the defendant's culpability into account when determining whether
there has been "persistent default". The question is broadly one of fact and degree.
However, once the discretion to disqualify has arisen, the defendant's culpability can
be taken into account in deciding whether to disqualify and, if so, for how long. In
Arctic Engineering Hoffmann J. declined to disqualify the defendant. The consequences would have been serious for both his employees and clients.[94] Moreover, the
judge took the view that it was unnecessary to disqualify the defendant with a view to
preventing similar defaults in the future and seems to have felt that the very fact that
the Secretary of State had brought the disqualification proceedings would itself have a
corrective effect. He also took into account the fact that *Arctic Engineering* was the
first case in which the Secretary of State had brought proceedings without relying on
the conclusive presumption. It is unlikely that a court would be so lenient now given
the strong line that has been taken in relation to filing defaults in more recent section 6
cases.[95] On a slightly different note, it is clear from *Arctic Engineering* that in circumstances where a company eventually complies with its filing obligations but only in
response to the commencement of criminal or default proceedings, the withdrawal of
those proceedings is not a representation that the default in question will be disregarded for the future so as to estop the Secretary of State from relying on it in disqualification proceedings (whether under section 3 or sections 6 to 8).

Section 3: Procedure

9.41   An application under section 3 can only be made to a court having jurisdiction to wind up any of the companies in relation to which the offence or other default
has been or is alleged to have been committed. The criminal courts have no jurisdiction
under section 3 to disqualify an individual following his conviction for a filing offence
(although they would appear to have jurisdiction under section 2 if such offence is
indictable).[96] This is in contrast to the related power in section 5 (discussed below)
which is exercisable by criminal courts of summary jurisdiction. The procedure under
section 3 and the range of potential claimants is the same as for an application to a
court having winding up jurisdiction under section 2.[97] The maximum period of disqualification which can be imposed is five years (section 3(5)).

---

[94] The position would be even more serious now as a defendant in similar circumstances would be exposed to
disqualification from acting as an insolvency practitioner under section 390(4)(b) of the Insolvency Act
1986 as well as disqualification from the capacities mentioned in CDDA, s. 1(1)(b)–(c).
[95] See, *e.g. Re Swift 736 Ltd, Secretary of State v. Ettinger* [1993] B.C.L.C. 896, [1993] B.C.C. 312, CA
which suggests that the courts will use their powers of disqualification for purposes of deterrence, *i.e.* in an
attempt to improve the general standard of compliance with basic disclosure requirements in companies
legislation. It appears that before *Arctic Engineering*, the Secretary of State would only proceed where there
had been previous convictions for non-filing offences followed by continuing default: see *Re Civica Investments Ltd* [1983] B.C.L.C. 456 and two unreported cases noted by B. Rider at (1981) 2 *The Company
Lawyer* 129 and 174. It is unlikely that the Secretary of State would proceed in relation to three or less
defaults where the conclusive presumption is unavailable. However, in the light of the *Swift* case, it is suggested that a pattern of non-compliance could be sufficiently serious on its facts to amount to "persistent
default" even where the conclusive presumption is not available because there are no specific convictions or
default orders.
[96] The point is somewhat academic but one might expect a court considering such offences in the context of
section 2 to regard its discretion as being subject to the parameters set out in sections 3 and 5. In other words,
it is highly unlikely that a court would disqualify an offender convicted of an indictable filing offence in the
absence of persistent default.
[97] See para. 9.32 and Chap. 6 on civil procedure generally.

SECTION 4: DISQUALIFICATION FOR FRAUD ETC. IN WINDING UP

9.42   Section 4(1) states:

"The court may make a disqualification order against a person, if in the course of a winding up, it appears that he—

(a) has been guilty of an offence for which he is liable (whether he has been convicted or not) under section 458 of the Companies Act (fraudulent trading), or

(b) has otherwise been guilty, while an officer or liquidator of the company or receiver or manager of its property, of any fraud in relation to the company or of any breach of his duty as such officer, liquidator, receiver or manager."

The provision first appeared in something like its present form as section 33(1)(b) of the Companies Act 1947 (shortly after re-enacted as section 188(1)(b) of the Companies Act 1948)[98] though the scope of (b) above was restricted to officers. The extended wording covering liquidators and receivers or managers was substituted by section 93 of the Companies Act 1981 and the provision was later consolidated as section 298 of the Companies Act 1985, the immediate predecessor of section 4.

9.43   The governing precondition for the operation of section 4 is that the fraud must be discovered during the course of a winding up. This means that the court's discretion to disqualify a person can only arise if the conduct relates to a company which is being or has been wound up.[99] Although the company itself must have ended up as the subject of some form of liquidation procedure, it appears that the section applies to fraud whether it occurred before or during the winding up (*i.e.* at any stage of the company's life). Like section 2, section 4 is not confined in application to directors. In contrast to section 2, the court has jurisdiction to make an order under section 4 if the person is "guilty" of the conduct described in the section; a conviction is not required. Moreover, it appears from section 1(4) of the CDDA that disqualification proceedings could be commenced even if a criminal prosecution based on the same subject matter is pending.[1]

Section 4(1)(a): fraudulent trading

9.44   The Companies Act 1985, s. 458 provides that if any business of a company is carried on with intent to defraud creditors of the company or of any other person, every person who was knowingly a party to the carrying on of the business in that manner is liable to imprisonment or a fine, or both. Section 458 applies whether or not the company has been, or is in the course of being wound up. The upshot is that *anyone*

---

[98] The powers now contained in sections 2 and 4 originally appeared together in section 33(1) of the Companies Act 1947 and later section 188(1) of the Companies Act 1948: see para. 9.05. Under section 275 of the Companies Act 1929 (first enacted as section 75 of the Companies Act 1928) a criminal court had power of its own motion to disqualify an offender convicted of fraudulent trading though note that (a) a conviction was necessary and (b) it appears from the wording of section 275(1) that the company needed to go into liquidation before the offence could be charged. Section 10 of the CDDA can also be traced back to this provision in the Companies Acts 1928–1929 (see main text below).

[99] As long as there is or has been a winding up, it does not appear to matter whether it is an insolvent winding up or not. Thus, it suffices if the company is in members' voluntary winding up following a declaration of solvency by its directors: see Insolvency Act, ss 84–90.

[1] Section 1(4) states that: "A disqualification order may be made on grounds which are or include matters other than criminal convictions, notwithstanding that the person in respect of whom it is to be made may be criminally liable in respect of those matters". But see paras 6.49A to 6.49B above on parallel proceedings.

knowingly a party to fraudulent trading as defined, appears liable to disqualification under section 4 regardless of whether they have been convicted or not, provided that (for section 4 purposes) the company has been wound up. However, in *R. v. Miles*,[2] the Court of Appeal held that section 458 can only apply to those who exercise a controlling or managerial function and so section 4(1)(a) of the CDDA may not be as wide in scope as it first appears. If the fraudulent conduct came to light in the course of a winding up *and* the perpetrator was subsequently convicted of the offence, he is liable to disqualification under *either* section 4 or section 2. If a person is convicted of the offence *before* the company enters winding up, then at that point he could only be disqualified under section 2.

Section 4(1)(b): fraud or breach of duty by an officer or liquidator or receiver or manager of corporate property

9.45   Section 4(1)(b) applies to a prescribed class of persons. The term "officer" is not defined exhaustively but includes a director, manager or company secretary[3] and a shadow director.[4] The phrase, "receiver or manager of the property of a company" is defined in section 29 of the Insolvency Act 1986 in such a way as to include administrative receivers, receivers of part only of a company's property and receivers appointed subject to the Law of Property Act 1925. Although this definition does not expressly extend to the CDDA, it is submitted that "receiver or manager ..." in section 4(1)(b) should be read in the same way.

There are doubts as to whether an auditor, a supervisor of a corporate voluntary arrangement (made under the Insolvency Act 1986, ss 1–7) or an administrator (appointed by the court under the Insolvency Act 1986, s. 8) fall within the scope of section 4(1)(b). An auditor and an administrator have both been held to be an "officer" for the purposes of other statutory provisions.[5] A case could also be made for saying that a supervisor of a corporate voluntary arrangement and an administrator are managers bringing them within the scope of the term "officer" which includes a "manager". Equally, however, it is arguable that all three fall outside the scope of section 4 as while section 4(2) expressly provides that "officer" includes a shadow director, there is no express reference to an auditor, a supervisor of a corporate voluntary arrangement or an administrator.

9.46   Section 4(1)(b) applies to fraud and breach of duty. It is thus not confined to fraudulent trading and may encompass fraudulent activities of a type proscribed by section 206 of the Insolvency Act 1986 (which include concealment, destruction or falsification of company books and records) and general misfeasance. An insolvency practitioner convicted of a fraud offence is liable to disqualification under either section 4 or 2. If he has not yet been convicted, section 2 would not be available.

Where a director has acted fraudulently or in breach of duty and this comes to light during an insolvent winding up, it may give rise to proceedings for an order under section 6 which are discussed extensively in earlier chapters. There is also an overlap between section 4 and section 10 which is considered further below.

---

[2] [1992] Crim. L.R. 657.
[3] CDDA, s. 22(6) which applies Companies Act 1985, s. 744. The difficult question as to the scope of the terms "manager" and "management" is discussed principally in Chap. 12 though see also text from para. 9.10.
[4] Section 4(2). For a full discussion of the terms "director" and "shadow director" see Chap 3.
[5] See, *e.g. Re London & General Bank* [1895] 2 Ch. 155 (though in that case "officer" was defined expressly in the company's articles of association to include an auditor); *R. v. Shacter* [1960] 2 Q.B. 252; *Re Home Treat Ltd* [1991] B.C.C. 165 (relieving provision in Companies Act 1985, s. 727 held to apply to an administrator). For a more recent case concerning whether auditors should be regarded as officers, see *Mutual Reinsurance v. Peat Marwick Mitchell* [1997] 1 B.C.L.C. 1, CA.

Section 4: Procedure

9.47 An application under section 4 can only be made to a court having jurisdiction to wind up any of the companies in relation to which the offence or other default has been or is alleged to have been committed. The procedure under section 4 is the same as for an application to a court having winding up jurisdiction under section 2 (see above). The maximum period of disqualification which can be imposed under section 4 is the overall statutory maximum of 15 years (section 4(3)). The fact that a criminal prosecution may be pending in relation to the matters complained of is not a bar to separate disqualification proceedings based on the same matters under section 4 (section 1(4)).

Section 5: Disqualification on Summary Conviction

9.48 Section 5 covers much the same substantive ground as section 3. The main difference is that the power in section 5 is excercisable by the criminal courts whereas section 3 is the exclusive preserve of the civil courts. Section 5(2) provides that where a person is convicted of a summary offence counting for the purposes of the section, the court by which he is convicted (or, in England and Wales, any other magistrates' court acting in the same petty sessions area) may make a disqualification order against him for a period up to a maximum of five years if the circumstances specified in section 5(3) are present.

The first point to note is that the court's discretion to disqualify can only be triggered by a conviction for a "summary offence" which, for the purposes of section 5, means an offence which is triable only summarily (*i.e.* by a magistrates' court or the Scottish equivalent).[6] According to section 5(1), an offence counting for the purposes of the section is one of which a person is convicted (either on indictment or summarily) in consequence of a contravention of, or failure to comply with, any provision of the companies legislation requiring a return, account or other document to be filed with, delivered or sent, or notice of any matter to be given, to the Registrar of Companies (whether the contravention or failure is on the person's own part or on the part of any company). Thus, like section 3, section 5 is directed at non-compliance with statutory filing obligations but, unlike section 3, it enables the convicting magistrates court to disqualify the offender subject to what follows.

9.49 The circumstances specified in section 5(3) are that, during the five years ending with the date of conviction, the person has had made against him, or has been convicted of, in total, not less than three default orders[7] and offences counting for section 5 purposes (including the current conviction and any other offence of which he is convicted on the same occasion). Thus, the court's jurisdiction under section 5 arises on a "totting up" basis. There will, of course, need to be at least one conviction because the jurisdiction can only arise where a person is convicted of a relevant summary offence. Otherwise, any combination of default orders and convictions will suffice, provided that there is an aggregate of at least three in the previous five years. Furthermore, while the triggering conviction must be one for a *summary* offence, it appears from the wording of section 5(1) that previous convictions for summary *or* indictable

---

[6] Interpretation Act 1978, Sched. 1. This definition applies for Scotland as well as England and Wales: CDDA, s. 5(4)(a). For Northern Ireland, the relevant wording is, "... convicted by a court of summary jurisdiction" which has the same effect: NI Order, article 8(2).

[7] Which bear the same meaning as in section 3(3)(b), see para. 9.40.

offences can be counted.[8] There is a close analogy between section 5(3) and the conclusive presumption of "persistent default" in section 3(2) which triggers the court's discretion to disqualify under that section. At the same time, there is a substantive difference between sections 5 and 3. Jurisdiction under section 5 cannot arise without a conviction which itself must be combined with at least two previous convictions and/or default orders. Anything less will not trigger the jurisdiction. Under section 3, an aggregate of three or more convictions or default orders is clearly *sufficient* for the court's jurisdiction to arise because of the conclusive presumption of "persistent default". However, the applicant is not compelled to rely on the conclusive presumption and so three or more convictions or default orders are technically not a *necessary* pre-condition for the operation of section 3.[9]

Section 5: Procedure

9.50   The principal procedural difference between section 5 and section 3 is that a convicting court can exercise the power to disqualify under section 5 but not under section 3. The section 5 power was originally introduced by section 93(1A) of the Companies Act 1981. The aim was to make it easier to obtain a disqualification order for persistent default than it had previously been. Thus, the 1981 Act conferred a power on the convicting court to disqualify individuals in relation to filing offences where it had only been possible before that to apply to a court having winding up jurisdiction for an order under what is now section 3. The convicting court for section 5 purposes will almost invariably be a magistrates' court (or Scottish equivalent) although it could now technically be the Crown Court.[10] The convicting court can make a disqualification order of its own motion, in effect as part of the sentencing process. The 10-day notice rule in section 16(1) does not apply to criminal proceedings.[11]

It appears that section 16(2), which governs any application for a disqualification order made to a court with jurisdiction to wind up companies, proceeds on the basis that there is *locus standi* in a variety of parties to apply for an order under section 5. It starts by stating that, "[a]n application to a court with jurisdiction to wind up companies for the making against any person of a disqualification order under *any of sections 2 to 5* may be made by...". This suggests that an application for an order under section

---

[8] Section 5(1) starts:

"An offence counting for the purposes of this section is one of which a person is convicted (*either on indictment or summarily*)..." (our emphasis).

It is not clear whether "offence" in section 5(1) should be read as being subject to "summary offence" in section 5(2). As section 5(1) reads, "[a]n offence..." not "[a] *summary* offence" it is arguable that convictions for indictable offences can be counted for purpose of totting up. It is now possible for a person to be convicted of a summary offence *on indictment* because of the effect of the Criminal Justice Act 1988, s. 41. This allows a magistrates' court which commits a person to the Crown Court for trial of an "either way" offence to commit him for trial of a summary offence as well provided that the summary offence arises out of circumstances which appear to be the same as or connected to those giving rise to the "either way" offence. However, this development post-dates the enactment of section 5 and so it must be doubted whether Parliament intended the "offence" in section 5(1) to refer exclusively to *summary* offences whether tried summarily or on indictment under the 1988 Act procedure. If this is correct, then for absolute clarity, it might be preferable if section 5(1) read, "[a]n offence counting for the purposes of this section is an offence (whether indictable or summary)..." though, it has to be said, that there is not exactly an abundance of indictable filing offences (10 only in the Companies Act 1985: see Sched. 24; none at all in the Insolvency Act 1986: see Sched. 10). The principal offences discussed in the main text (failure to file accounts and annual return) are summary offences.

[9] Something of an academic point: see discussion of the *Arctic Engineering* case at para. 9.40.

[10] It is possible in defined circumstances under the Criminal Justice Act 1988, s. 41 for a summary offence to be tried on indictment.

[11] See discussion at para. 9.33.

5 would lie to a court with winding up jurisdiction. However, this is inconsistent with the wording of section 5(2) which confers the power of disqualification only on the convicting court (or, in England and Wales, any other magistrates' court acting for the same petty sessions area as the convicting court). While it is possible for either the convicting court or a court having winding up jurisdiction to exercise the power in section 2, both are specifically referred to in section 2(2). There is no reference in section 5 to a court with winding up jurisdiction and, accordingly, the section 5 power is exercisable only by a criminal court.

SECTION 10: DISQUALIFICATION FOLLOWING PARTICIPATION IN WRONGFUL TRADING

9.51   Section 10(1) states:

"Where the court makes a declaration under section 213 or 214 of the Insolvency Act that a person is liable to make a contribution to a company's assets, then, whether or not an application for such an order is made by any person, the court may, if it thinks fit, also make a disqualification order against the person to whom the declaration relates."

The statutory title, "participation in wrongful trading", is somewhat misleading as section 10 is triggered by the imposition of civil liability for fraudulent trading (section 213 of the Insolvency Act) as well as wrongful trading (section 214 of the Insolvency Act). The court imposing civil liability for fraudulent or wrongful trading can make a disqualification order under section 10 of its own motion. A declaration of personal liability under either provision is a prerequisite. Jurisdiction under section 10 does not arise if the fraudulent or wrongful trading proceedings are dismissed.

Section 10 can be traced all the way back to the Companies Acts 1928 and 1929. Section 75(1) of the Companies Act 1928 (consolidated as section 275(1) of the 1929 Act) is the earliest version of the civil fraudulent trading provision now found in section 213 of the Insolvency Act 1986. Section 75(4) contained an equivalent power in relation to fraudulent trading to that now found in section 10 of the CDDA though at that time the maximum period of disqualification was five years.[12] The power was not carried over into the Companies Act 1948 (see section 332) but was later revived in section 16 of the Insolvency Act 1985 (the immediate predecessor of the present provision) and extended to encompass wrongful trading which was itself introduced for the first time by section 15 of the same Act. The maximum period of disqualification under section 10 is currently 15 years (section 10(2)).

Insolvency Act 1986, s. 213

9.52   If in the course of the winding up of a company it appears that any business of the company has been carried on with intent to defraud creditors of the company or creditors of any other person, or for any fraudulent purpose, any persons knowingly party to such activities may be liable to contribute personally to the company's assets under section 213. An application can only be made by a liquidator. "Any persons who were knowingly parties to the carrying on of the business. . ." are exposed to liability under section 213 and therefore also exposed to disqualification under section 10 of

---

[12] Section 75(3) of the 1928 Act also created an offence of fraudulent trading (the earliest version of what is now section 458 of the Companies Act 1985). An offender convicted of the offence was also liable to disqualification by the convicting court under section 75(4).

the CDDA. In *Re Maidstone Building Provisions Ltd*[13] it was held that to be "knowingly party to the carrying on of the business" a person would need to have taken some active steps in the management of the business. At the same time, it appears that the provision would catch a creditor who accepts money knowing it was obtained by fraudulent means.[14] As such, the potential applicability of the provision is not confined to company directors. The power of disqualification for fraudulent trading in section 10 overlaps with the power in section 4(1)(b) discussed earlier. Allegations of fraudulent trading could also be raised against a director as a means of indicating his unfitness in proceedings for an order under section 6.

Insolvency Act 1986, s. 214

9.53   On the application of a liquidator under section 214, the court can declare that a director or shadow director of a company is liable to contribute personally to the company's assets provided that:

(1) the company has gone into insolvent liquidation; and

(2) at some time before the commencement of the winding up of the company, he knew or ought to have concluded that there was no reasonable prospect that the company would avoid going into insolvent liquidation.

If these elements are established, the court may make an order, but is not obliged to do so.[15] A defence is available if the respondent in section 214 proceedings establishes that having reached the state of knowledge referred to in (2), he took every step with a view to minimising the potential loss to the company's creditors as he ought to have taken. The applicable standard (for the objective test of knowledge in (2), and for determining whether the respondent took "every step") is that of a reasonably diligent person having both the general knowledge, skill and experience that may reasonably be expected of a person carrying out the same functions as are carried out by the respondent in relation to the company, and the general knowledge, skill and experience possessed by the respondent.[16] Section 214 applies only to directors, former directors and shadow directors and so is more limited in scope than section 213 which applies to "any persons who were knowingly parties to the carrying on of the business...". However, a director who exercises no particular function or takes no active part in the carrying on or management of the company's business will not necessarily be absolved of liability under section 214.[17] Allegations of wrongful or insolvent trading are frequently raised in proceedings for an order under section 6 of the CDDA. The advantage of section 6 is that a disqualification order can be obtained in section 6 proceedings without the need for any previous wrongful trading proceedings. Moreover, if the court is satisfied that the wrongful or insolvent trading makes the respondent unfit it must disqualify him for at least two years.[18] There is therefore a greater likelihood that a director will be disqualified under section 6 than under section 10.

---

[13] [1971] 1 W.L.R. 1085, [1971] 3 All E.R. 363.
[14] *Re Gerald Cooper Chemicals Ltd* [1978] Ch. 262, [1978] 2 All E.R. 49.
[15] For discussion of the requirements see *Re Produce Marketing Consortium Ltd (No. 2)* [1989] B.C.L.C. 520, (1989) 5 B.C.C. 569; *Re DKG Contractors Ltd* [1990] B.C.C. 903; *Re Purpoint Ltd* [1991] B.C.L.C. 491, [1991] B.C.C. 121; *Re Sherborne Associates Ltd* [1995] B.C.C. 40 and A. Walters, "Enforcing Wrongful Trading" in *The Corporate Dimension* (B. Rider (ed.), 1998).
[16] This is an objective minimum standard: see *Re Brian D Pierson (Contractors) Ltd* [1999] B.C.C. 26.
[17] *ibid.*
[18] On the treatment of wrongful and insolvent trading allegations in unfitness proceedings see Chap. 5. A further advantage of proceeding under section 6 is that trading while insolvent falling short of wrongful trading in section 214 may be sufficient to justify a finding of unfitness: see *Re Bath Glass Ltd* [1988] B.C.L.C. 329, (1988) 4 B.C.C. 130.

Nevertheless, the power in section 10 has been exercised. In *Re Brian D Pierson (Contractors) Ltd*[19] the two directors of a failed company were disqualified for five and two years respectively under section 10 following the making of contribution orders against them under section 214 of the Insolvency Act. The report of this case simply records that the judge made disqualification orders after discussion with counsel for the liquidator and the respondents, and in the light of written comments received from the Department of Trade and Industry's solicitors.[20]

Section 10: Procedure

9.54   The relevant court for section 10 purposes is, of course, the court seised of the main civil proceedings under either section 213 or 214 of the Insolvency Act. This will be a court having winding up jurisdiction over the company in relation to which complaint is made.[21] The court may make a disqualification order "whether or not an application for such an order is made by any person". This clearly means that the court can make a disqualification order of its own motion but also seems to imply that an application could be made by someone other than the liquidator who is bringing the main civil proceedings. However, section 16 of the CDDA (which governs applications to a court of winding up jurisdiction for orders under sections 2 to 4) makes no specific provision for *locus standi* in relation to section 10 and so it is difficult to know what to make of this wording. It does appear that any "application" would have to be made in the main action. It would be odd, as well as inconsistent with section 16, if the word "application" in section 10 were to be read as including "originating application". It is settled that the 10-day notice provision in section 16(1) does not apply in cases where the court is empowered to make a disqualification order of its own motion. However, in *Re Cedac Ltd, Secretary of State for Trade and Industry v. Langridge*, it was suggested *obiter* by Balcombe L.J. that "doubtless the rules of natural justice will require that the person concerned should be given some notice that the court is contemplating making a disqualification order".[22] As a matter of practice, the court should refer the matter to the Secretary of State and invite written representations on the question of disqualification.[23] Indeed, it is suggested that the Secretary of State would have *locus* to intervene in the proceedings and apply for a disqualification order as the person have regulatory responsibility under the CDDA.[24] One final point of some significance is that the director of an insolvent company against whom wrongful trading proceedings are commenced faces a double exposure to disqualification under section 10 and (assuming proceedings are commenced) under section 6. For instance, a director first disqualified under section 10 may subsequently be disqualified in proceedings for an order under section 6 in which the court could take account of wider matters indicative of unfitness rather than just wrongful trading. In those circumstances, the periods of disqualification specified in the two orders would run concurrently (section 1(3)).

FACTORS CONSIDERED BY THE COURT IN EXERCISING ITS DISCRETION UNDER SECTIONS 2 TO 5 AND 10

9.55   If the preconditions of any of sections 2 to 5 or 10 are satisfied, the relevant court has *jurisdiction* to make a disqualification order. However, it remains at the

---

[19] [1999] B.C.C. 26.
[20] A disqualification order was also made in *Re Purpoint Ltd* [1991] B.C.L.C. 491, [1991] B.C.C. 121.
[21] See sections 117–121 in Pt IV of the Insolvency Act 1986.
[22] [1991] Ch. 402 (at 414F), [1991] B.C.L.C. 543, [1991] B.C.C. 148.
[23] See *Re Brian D Pierson (Contractors) Ltd* [1999] B.C.C. 26 at 58.
[24] By analogy with *Adams v. Adams* [1971] P. 188, [1970] 3 All E.R. 572.

court's *discretion* whether or not to make an order. The CDDA provides considerable guidance on the factors which the court should take into account when determining the question of unfitness under sections 6 and 8.[25] However, it contains no express guidance as to how the court should go about exercising its discretion under sections 2 to 5 or 10.

The nature of the discretion

9.56 In deciding whether to exercise its discretion the court is faced with two questions:

(1) Is it appropriate to disqualify the individual?

(2) If so, what is the appropriate period of disqualification?

A number of basic points can be made about the discretion in (1). First, while Parliament has decided that a power of disqualification should be *available* in the circumstances defined in sections 2 to 5 and 10, it has been left to the court to decide whether it is *appropriate* to impose an order in an individual case. Thus, for example, in the cases of sections 2 and 5, a conviction for an offence which triggers the court's discretion is not itself regarded as a sufficient justification for the conclusion that the convicted individual should not be involved in the management of a company. This contrasts with the position in other jurisdictions such as Australia where an individual convicted of a relevant offence is *automatically* disqualified without the need for any further order of the court.[26] Equally, once it has decided to impose an order, it is also left to the court to determine the period of disqualification. The only guidance provided by the CDDA on this second question comes in the form of the statutory maxima of five or 15 years. Parliament has thus left it almost entirely to the courts to establish the principles on which the discretion should be exercised.

9.57 It is not easy to determine how the discretion will be exercised in a given case or to point with any certainty to a set of factors and say that those factors will (or should be) taken into account. This raises the fundamental questions canvassed in the second chapter about the nature of the court's power to disqualify an individual, the general purpose (or purposes) of the CDDA and the proper functions of the criminal and civil courts in the context of disqualification. It has been seen that sections 2 to 5 are concerned primarily with conduct which is defined by reference to criminal offences or defaults. However, only section 5 is the exclusive preserve of the criminal courts. Indeed, the powers in sections 3 and 4 are only exercisable by a civil court. This begs the question of whether the nature and purpose of disqualification as administered by the civil courts is somehow different from that in the criminal courts. The argument of this book is that the various powers in the CDDA share common features and a common purpose. It follows that the criminal and civil courts should adopt a common approach when exercising jurisdiction under it. It has been seen, for instance, that an order under section 2 can be made *either* by the convicting criminal court of its own motion *or* on a later application to a civil court. In the absence of any specific guidance in the CDDA, it is difficult to argue that Parliament intended the criminal and civil courts to adopt different approaches when exercising the *same*

---

[25] Section 9, Sched. 1: see discussion in Chap. 4.
[26] Australian Corporations Law, s. 229(3).

power.[27] A further question arises as to what form a common approach should take. In *Re Civica Investments Ltd,*[28] a High Court case decided under a statutory predecessor of section 3, Nourse J. (as he then was) made the following observations about the nature of the discretion which support an analogy with the process of sentencing in a criminal court:

"... [T]he function of the court has been to consider what, if any, is the appropriate period of disqualification to impose. It might be thought that that is something which, like the passing of sentence in a criminal case, ought to be dealt with comparatively briefly and without elaborate reasoning. In general I think that that must be the correct approach."

9.58 He added that in exercising its discretion, the court should disregard its power to give permission to act in the future notwithstanding the disqualification.[29] The Court of Appeal has subsequently likened the process of determining the appropriate period of disqualification on a finding of unfitness under section 6 to a criminal sentencing exercise.[30] In keeping with these authorities, it is suggested that the discretion in sections 2 to 5 and 10 should be regarded in a general sense as a sentencing discretion but that the court should take account of the protective aims of the CDDA (including deterrence) developed more fully by the Court of Appeal in the context of section 6 proceedings.[31]

Specific problems of discretion in the criminal courts

9.59 For the purposes of the present discussion, criminal courts do differ from civil courts in one obvious respect. A civil court exercising the powers in sections 2 to 4 and 10 of the CDDA is concerned only with the question of disqualification. Its sole function is to consider whether or not to make a disqualification order and, if so, for how long. A convicting criminal court has a wider remit. As Nourse L.J. pointed out in his

---

[27] A view which receives some support in *Re Land Travel Ltd, Secretary of State for Trade and Industry v. Tjolle* [1998] 1 B.C.L.C. 333, [1998] B.C.C. 282. In that case, the first defendant in section 6 proceedings had been previously disqualified for ten years by a criminal court under section 2 following his conviction for an offence of fraudulent trading. The Secretary of State persisted with the section 6 proceedings (which arose out of similar circumstances) because it was felt that a maximum 15–year disqualification should be sought in the public interest. In the course of criticising the criminal court for "under-disqualifying" the defendant, Jacob J. stated that: "... it is self-evident that civil and criminal courts should be applying the same standards: the purpose of disqualification—to protect the public from the activities of persons unfit to be concerned in the management of a company—is the same in both kinds of court". On the facts of *Land Travel*, this criticism appears somewhat harsh. The defendant had pleaded guilty in the criminal proceedings to fraudulent trading over a period of some three months whereas for the purposes of a *Carecraft* disposal of the section 6 proceedings, he agreed to a 15–year disqualification based on admitted misconduct of a much greater magnitude.

[28] [1983] B.C.L.C. 456.

[29] The implication being that the court should make a sentencing decision based on the facts and taking account of any mitigation. It should not impose the maximum period of disqualification and treat an application for permission to act as the forum for mitigation.

[30] *Re Westmid Packing Services Ltd, Secretary of State for Trade and Industry v. Griffiths* [1998] 2 All E.R. 124, [1998] 2 B.C.L.C. 646, [1998] B.C.C. 836. The question of whether it is appropriate to disqualify does not, of course, arise on a finding of unfitness under section 6: see Chaps 4 and 5 on section 6 proceedings.

[31] It has been argued that CDDA powers are quasi-criminal in nature and that civil courts exercising those powers should *in all respects* (*i.e.* as to questions of procedure and evidence as well as "sentencing") behave like criminal courts: see J. Dine, "Wrongful Trading—Quasi-Criminal Law" in *Insolvency Law and Practice* (H. Rajak (ed.) 1993) and "Punishing Directors" [1994] J.B.L. 325. Dine's view is discussed more fully in Chap. 2. There can be little doubt that this view has had an influence in some cases. However, it does not receive wide support in the authorities. The view of the present authors is that the "sentencing" analogy is appropriate for reasons of pragmatism. As there is no guidance in the CDDA with regard to discretion or period of disqualification it is not surprising that the courts have drawn such an analogy. It does not mean that a civil court should behave like a criminal court on questions of procedure and evidence.

dissenting judgment in *Re Cedac Ltd, Secretary of State for Trade and Industry v. Langridge*,[32] a disqualification order is only one of a *range* of orders which a criminal court can make in dealing with a convicted offender. Disqualification will therefore not necessarily be considered in isolation. This has had some impact on the use of the discretion in the criminal courts as the decisions of the Court of Appeal (Criminal Division) in *R. v. Young*[33] and *R. v. Holmes*[34] illustrate. These cases explore the extent to which a sentencer is able to *combine* a disqualification order under section 2 with other types of order from the range of possible sentences available to a criminal court.

R. v. Young

9.60   The appellant pleaded guilty to an offence of managing a company without the permission of the court while he was an undischarged bankrupt. The offence had been committed during 1984 and 1985 before the appellant's discharge from bankruptcy in 1986. The trial judge conditionally discharged him for three years and disqualified him for two years under section 2. He appealed against the making of the disqualification order. The Court of Appeal held that a conditional discharge and a disqualification order are incompatible and, with some reluctance, quashed the disqualification order. The following extract from Brooke J.'s *ex tempore* judgment forms the narrow *ratio* of *Young*:

> "It appears to the court that as the order for disqualification under section 2 of the Act is unquestionably a punishment, it would be quite inappropriate for a punishment of this kind to be linked with a conditional discharge in a case ... in which the sentencing court thought that a punishment was inexpedient."

Although not immediately apparent from this passage, it is clear from the grounds of appeal that the court based its decision on what was then section 7 of the Powers of Criminal Courts Act 1973 which provided that a court may not grant a conditional discharge unless it is satisfied that it is inexpedient to inflict punishment. In *R. v. Savage*,[35] this was construed to mean that a conditional discharge cannot be combined with a punitive order and although *Savage* was not considered in *Young*, the court applied the same logic. Thus, the effect of *Young* is that the exercise of the discretion under section 2 may be constrained by other aspects of the sentencing process. Having determined that disqualification is a "punishment", the sentencer must be careful to ensure that a disqualification order is compatible with other aspects of the overall sentence.

R. v. Holmes

9.61   The appellant pleaded guilty to an offence of fraudulent trading. He received a suspended prison sentence and was disqualified for 12 months under section 2. He was also ordered to pay compensation of £25,000 to the National Westminster Bank plc, the victim of his fraudulent activities. This case differed from *Young* in that the appeal was against the criminal compensation order and not the disqualification order. However, the main question again concerned the compatibility of a disqualification order with other types of order available to the sentencer. The Court of Appeal held that a criminal compensation order was inconsistent with an order disqualifying

---

[32] [1991] Ch. 402 at 423F.
[33] (1990) 12 Cr.App.Rep. (S.) 262, [1990] Crim L.R. 818, [1990] B.C.C. 549.
[34] (1992) 13 Cr.App.Rep (S.) 29, [1991] Crim L.R. 790, [1991] B.C.C. 394.
[35] (1983) 5 Cr.App.R. (S.) 216.

the appellant from acting as a director. In the court's view, it was wrong in principle to disqualify an individual at the same time as imposing a compensation order on him if disqualification might prejudice his ability to earn the means to pay the compensation order. This suggests that the Court of Appeal would have quashed the disqualification order if that, rather than the compensation order, had been the subject of the appeal.

The position in the civil courts

9.62   The view of the Court of Appeal (Criminal Division) at least in relation to section 2 is that the courts have a "completely general and unfettered power" (*per* Brooke J. in *Young*) but one which they should exercise in accordance with established sentencing practice paying particular regard to the overall balance of the sentence. The discretion of the civil courts in relation to section 2 does not appear to be so fettered. There is nothing to suggest that a civil court could not have imposed disqualification orders had free standing applications been made in *Young* and *Holmes*. However, while civil courts are not subject to the constraints of the overall sentencing process, it seems unlikely that the court would exercise its discretion in subsequent civil proceedings for an order under section 2 without paying any regard to the approach taken on the question of disqualification in the earlier criminal proceedings.

Should a power of disqualification exercised by a criminal court under the CDDA be regarded as a punishment?

9.63   A further implication of *Young* is that a criminal court may use its powers of disqualification to punish an offender even if it has ceased to be necessary to disqualify him in order to protect the public (whether by keeping him "off the road" and/or by deterring him and others from "re-offending"). Having concluded that disqualification was a "punishment", the Court of Appeal was constrained by statute to quash the disqualification order because of its incompatibility with a (non-punitive) conditional discharge. This constraint apart, it is clear that Brooke J. would otherwise have regarded a disqualification order as appropriate despite the fact that the appellant had been trading successfully for three-and-a-half years since obtaining his discharge from bankruptcy and could hardly have been regarded as a present danger to the public. It is clear that a disqualification order can be imposed under section 6 in circumstances where the defendant no longer poses any risk to the public. However, this is explained by the fact that disqualification under section 6 is mandatory.[36] Brooke J.'s view of disqualification as punishment rests on the proposition that a criminal court exercising jurisdiction under section 2 is in a "quite different situation" from a civil court exercising jurisdiction under section 6.

9.64   The related assumptions that (a) criminal courts exercising jurisdiction under the CDDA are doing something fundamentally different from their civil counterparts and that (b) criminal disqualification is concerned exclusively with punishment are suspect for the following reasons:[37]

> (1) When a criminal court considers disqualifying a person under sections 2 or 5, it is first and foremost exercising jurisdiction *under the CDDA*. It just so happens that within the scheme of the legislation, this jurisdiction is ancillary to the court's primary criminal jurisdiction. Given the history and evolution of the CDDA and its overall concentration on regulating abuses of limited liabil-

---

[36] See discussion in *Re Grayan Building Services Ltd, Secretary of State for Trade and Industry v. Gray* [1995] Ch. 241, [1995] 3 W.L.R. 1, [1995] 1 B.C.L.C. 276, [1995] B.C.C. 554, CA.
[37] Restating criticisms first voiced in Chap. 2.

ity, there seems little justification for saying that disqualification by a criminal court is somehow qualitatively different from disqualification by a civil court. A common approach to disqualification founded primarily on principles of public protection seems more appropriate. This criticism of *Young* can be supported with reference to the unitary features of the CDDA identified at the beginning of Chapter 2. Disqualification by the court under section 2 (and, for that matter, sections 3, 4, 5 and 10) has exactly the same legal consequences as disqualification by the court under section 6. Both provisions should therefore be seen as operating for broadly similar ends. Moreover, the fact that the criminal courts have been given jurisdiction in section 2 (and also section 5) can be seen simply as a device designed to save the necessity of further civil proceedings.

(2) If the decision in *Young* is correct then it follows that a criminal court using the power in section 2 is engaged in a quite different exercise from a civil court using the same power. This would be an odd result.[38]

(3) The view in *Young* appears to contain a fallacy. It seems to rest on the assumption that a disqualification imposed by a criminal court must necessarily be characterised as a punishment. This ignores the point that criminal sentencing may serve a variety of purposes such as general deterrence or rehabilitation as well as punishment. There is nothing wrong in principle with the idea of a criminal court exercising a jurisdiction which is concerned primarily with protection of the public. Much of the criminal law has a protective function anyway.[39]

(4) Support for the view that the section 2 power should be regarded as protective rather than punitive can be derived from Commonwealth jurisdictions. Both Australia and Singapore, for example, have provisions under which directors are automatically disqualified on being convicted of certain criminal offences. These section 2 equivalents are regarded by the courts in those jurisdictions as being primarily concerned with protection of the public.[40]

9.65   It is not absolutely clear whether Brooke J. (who did not enjoy the luxury of being able to reserve judgment) meant that disqualification under section 2 can *only* be seen as a punishment and nothing else. If the argument of the authors is correct, it would be preferable for the criminal courts to adopt broadly the same view of the CDDA that has been adopted by the civil courts in relation to section 6 (*i.e.* that disqualification is concerned primarily with protection of the public).[41]

---

[38] This criticism is echoed in more recent cases where it has been suggested that the criminal and civil courts should adopt a common approach to disqualification: see, *e.g.* dicta in *R. v. Cole, Lees & Birch* [1998] B.C.C. 87, CA; *Re Land Travel Ltd, Secretary of State for Trade and Industry v. Tjolle* [1998] 1 B.C.L.C. 333, [1998] B.C.C. 282. The need for a common approach is amply illustrated by the fact that the section 2 power is conferred on both the criminal and civil courts.

[39] On this point see generally, D.A. Thomas, *Principles of Sentencing* (2nd ed., 1979); A. Ashworth, *Principles of Criminal Law* (2nd ed., 1995); N. Walker and N. Padfield, *Sentencing: Theory, Law and Practice* (2nd ed., 1996).

[40] See J. Cassidy, "Disqualification of Directors under the Corporations Law" (1995) 13 *Company and Securities Law Journal* 221; A. Hicks, "Disqualification of Directors—Forty Years On" [1988] J.B.L. 27 and, *e.g. Re Magna Alloys & Research Pty Ltd* (1975) 1 A.C.L.R. 203 at 205; *Zuker v. Commissioner for Corporate Affairs* [1980] A.C.L.C. 34,334 at 34,338. As the offender is automatically disqualified without further order on conviction of a relevant offence, this view has been articulated by Australia's civil courts on applications for permission to act rather than by the criminal courts.

[41] A further point is that it is not clear from the report whether the Crown made submissions on the appeal. Equally, it appears that the Secretary of State was not invited to make representations. Doubts have also been expressed in subsequent cases as to the reasoning in *Young*: see *R. v. Cole, Lees & Birch* [1998] B.C.C. 87 at 91, CA.

Period of disqualification

Section 2 cases

9.66   There are signs (*Young* notwithstanding) that the criminal courts do follow broadly the same sort of approach as their civil counterparts on the question of the appropriate period of disqualification.[42] The cases on section 2 in the criminal courts suggest that the two main factors taken into consideration are the culpability of the offender and the public's need for protection. In *R. v. Cobbey*,[43] the Court of Appeal upheld a six-year disqualification order made against the appellant who had pleaded guilty to a count of fraudulent trading. The facts were that over a period of 10 months the appellant caused a company to obtain goods, services and credit with no prospect of paying for them and accepted deposits from customers in respect of contracts which he then failed to perform. In all, the company incurred liabilities of around £68,000 during this period which could not be met. The Court of Appeal held that a six-year disqualification order was an appropriate reflection of the appellant's culpability, the harm which he had caused to creditors and customers and the need to protect the public from him in the future. As Auld J. put it:

> "It is a case of dishonesty—dishonesty extending over several months, causing loss to many... The fact that he may have derived little or no personal benefit from his dishonesty has little relevance to the losses he caused and might cause again to others until he has learnt the importance of straight and careful business dealings."

In *R. v. Millard*,[44] the Court of Appeal held that an order of eight years' duration was appropriate to deal with an individual described as "devious ... manipulative, and thoroughly dishonest in the conduct of the affairs of [his] companies". In this case, the fraudulent conduct had lasted for a period of four years and resulted in a deficiency of approximately £728,000. The Court of Appeal thought that it was appropriate to disqualify Millard for two years longer than Cobbey because he had caused a greater degree of harm over a longer period.[45]

9.67   In the important case of *R. v. Edwards*,[46] the Court of Appeal reduced the period of disqualification imposed at trial on the appellant from ten to three years. The appellant was a minor participant in a fraudulent scheme involving the use of companies to acquire large quantities of goods on credit which were subsequently re-sold for cash at a discount. Each company would operate for only a short period of time before it ceased trading. As the following extract from Potter L.J.'s judgment illustrates, the Court of Appeal favoured a broad protective approach which is arguably of general application:

> "The rationale behind the power to disqualify is the protection of the public from the activities of persons who, whether for reasons of dishonesty, or of naivety or

---

[42] For the approach of the civil courts under section 6 see *Re Sevenoaks Stationers (Retail) Ltd* [1991] Ch. 164, [1990] 3 W.L.R. 1165; [1991] 3 All E.R. 578, [1991] B.C.L.C. 325, [1990] B.C.C. 765, CA; *Re West-mid Packing Services Ltd, Secretary of State for Trade and Industry v. Griffiths* [1998] 2 All E.R. 124, [1998] 2 B.C.L.C. 646, [1998] B.C.C. 836, CA and general discussion in Chap. 5.
[43] (1993) 14 Cr.App.R. (S.) 82.
[44] (1994) 15 Cr.App.R. (S.) 445, [1994] Crim. L.R. 146.
[45] Nevertheless, Millard could count himself lucky. The Court of Appeal substituted an eight-year order for the maximum 15–year order originally imposed by the trial judge. A differently-constituted Court of Appeal in *R. v. Edwards* (see main text below) clearly felt that Millard had received light treatment.
[46] (1998) 2 Cr.App.R. (S.) 213, [1998] Crim L.R. 298.

incompetence in conjunction with the dishonesty of others, may use or abuse their role and status as a director of a limited company to the detriment of the public. Frauds of the kind in this case archetypally give rise to a situation in which the exercise of the court's power is appropriate. In the case of this appellant, it appears that, in a period of unemployment, he was persuaded to participate in a fraudulent enterprise as a director, for which role, by reason of his inexperience, he was quite unsuited. While it is said that he did not appreciate the fraud until late on ... it is clear that he pleaded guilty on the basis that he had at some stage towards the end of the enterprise participated knowingly in it. It seems to us that such a position might well in principle arise again, whatever his present intentions may be."

However, in comparison with his co-defendants and Millard (see above), Edwards had played only a minor role in the scheme. In all the circumstances, it was felt that a three-year disqualification was appropriate.

9.68 It is possible that the court might decline to exercise its discretion at all in a case of less culpable wrongdoing or where it is not obvious that the public are in need of protection. Thus, in *R. v. Green and Green*,[47] the Court of Appeal quashed two-year disqualification orders made against the appellants on two grounds. First, it was held that they had not set out to use the corporate form for fraudulent purposes but had over-expanded in an unfavourable economic climate and then continued to trade at the expense of creditors while taking an over-optimistic view of the company's survival prospects. Secondly, the court also took account of the fact that in the five years which had elapsed between the winding up of the company and the trial, the appellants had been running another company successfully and so the disqualification orders would effectively remove their livelihood.[48]

Should the criminal courts apply the Court of Appeal's guidelines from Re Sevenoaks Stationers (Retail) Ltd in determining the period of disqualification?

9.69 In *Re Sevenoaks Stationers (Retail) Ltd*[49] the Court of Appeal (Civil Division) was given its first chance to consider whether the period of disqualification imposed on an individual by the High Court following a finding of unfitness under section 6 of the 1986 Act had been appropriate. The Court of Appeal took the opportunity to lay down guidelines with a view to the establishment of consistent practice. It was held that the 15–year period of disqualification available should be divided into three brackets: a top bracket of over ten years which should be reserved for particularly serious cases, a middle bracket of six to ten years for serious cases which do not merit the top bracket and a minimum bracket of two to five years for less serious cases. One question which has arisen is whether these guidelines should be applied by the criminal courts in determining periods of disqualification. The first obvious point to make is that the guidelines provide no direct assistance to magistrates' courts in determining how they should exercise their powers under sections 2 and 5 as the maximum period of disqualification which a court of summary jurisdiction can impose is limited to five

[47] (1981) 3 Cr.App.R. (S.) 22.
[48] The degree of the offender's culpability is also regarded by the civil courts as being relevant in determining the appropriate period of disqualification: see *Re Civica Investments Ltd* [1983] B.C.L.C. 456, 458 and the Australian case, *Commissioner for Corporate Affairs v. Ekamper* (1988) 12 A.C.L.R. 519. Although there are no reported cases, it is assumed that the approach under sections 4 and 5 would be similar.
[49] [1991] Ch. 164, [1990] 3 W.L.R. 1165, [1991] 3 All E.R. 578, [1991] B.C.L.C. 325, [1990] B.C.C. 765. The case is discussed more fully in Chaps 4 and 5.

years.[50] The question is therefore only of direct relevance to the Crown Court exercising its powers under section 2.

9.70   In both *R. v. Millard* and *R. v. Edwards*, the Court of Appeal (Criminal Division) expressly applied the *Sevenoaks* guidelines. In *Millard* the view was that the case fell into the middle bracket; in *Edwards*, the minimum bracket.[51] It has been suggested with reference to *R. v. Young* that guidance given in relation to section 6 is not necessarily applicable to cases before the criminal courts despite the practice adopted in *Millard* (and later followed in *Edwards*).[52] However, this view rests on Brooke J.'s conclusion (criticised above) that the criminal courts under section 2 and the civil courts under section 6 are engaged in different exercises. In any event, *Young* is distinguishable on this point as the question of what is an appropriate period of disqualification was not addressed. There is no reason in principle why the criminal courts should not use the guidelines in *Sevenoaks Stationers*. Indeed, these guidelines are closely analogous to the sentencing guidelines which the Court of Appeal (Criminal Division) regularly provides to the criminal courts in relation to various types of offence and so they are likely to feel quite at home in applying them.[53] The only slight caveat is that there is no minimum period of disqualification under sections 2 and 5 with the result that the minimum bracket of two to five years for section 6 cases needs some adjustment to take account of the fact that a criminal court can impose a disqualification order of less than two years' duration. In relation to section 10, it is safe to assume that the court would adopt a similar approach on the question of period to that taken by the civil courts under section 6.

APPEALS AGAINST DISQUALIFICATION ORDERS MADE UNDER SECTIONS 2 AND 5[54]

9.71   Appeals against disqualification orders made under sections 2 to 5 of the CDDA by a civil court having winding up jurisdiction fall to be dealt with in the same way as other civil appeals against a section 6 order and, from a High Court or County Court judge, lie generally to the Court of Appeal, or, in Scotland, to the Court of Session. Either party can appeal.[55]

---

[50] This is equally true of a civil court exercising its powers under section 3. Nevertheless, one would expect these courts to adopt a similar approach with regard to periods of disqualification towards the top end of the five-year maximum. See, *e.g. Re Civica Investments Ltd* [1983] B.C.L.C. 456, 458 where Nourse J. said that "the longer periods of disqualification are to be reserved for cases where the defaults and conduct of the person in question have been of a serious nature, for example, where defaults have been made for some dishonest purpose, or wilfully and deliberately, or where they have been many in number and have not been substantially alleviated by remedial action…".
[51] The Court of Appeal in *Edwards* felt that *Millard* was a "top bracket" case, a disagreement which reflects the universal difficulties experienced by courts in applying any type of general sentencing guidance.
[52] See, *e.g.* [1994] Crim L.R. 146, 147.
[53] *R. v. Bibi* (1980) 2 Cr.App.Rep. (S.) is an example of a case which sets out sentencing guidelines. For a general discussion of such guidelines see Walker and Padfield, *op. cit.* Staughton L.J. cast doubt in *R. v. Goodman* on whether it is appropriate to apply the *Sevenoaks* guidelines in criminal proceedings. Again, this misses the point that when a criminal court is considering disqualification it is first and foremost exercising jurisdiction *under the CDDA*. It just so happens that within the scheme of the Act, the jurisdiction is ancillary to the court's primary criminal jurisdiction.
[54] The main concern here is procedure relevant to appeals from the criminal courts. The position in civil disqualification proceedings is considered more fully in Chap. 6. The coverage here is limited and for a fuller understanding of criminal procedure readers should refer to standard practitioner works such as *Archbold* and *Stone's Justices' Manual*.
[55] For a fuller account, see Chap. 6 which also covers appeals from a district judge (county court) and the registrar of the Companies Court.

Appeals from a magistrates' court against sentence lie generally to the Crown Court.[56] It appears that an appeal either against the making of a disqualification order under sections 2 or 5 (magistrates' courts have no power to disqualify under sections 3 to 4) or against the length of disqualification imposed by the magistrates will lie as an offender has a right of appeal against "any order" made by a magistrates' court when dealing with him,[57] although this right does not extend to appeals against either an order for the prosecution's costs[58] or an order requiring a legally-aided person to contribute towards defence costs.[59] Notice of appeal must be given to the clerk to the justices not later than 21 days after the day on which the decision or sentence appealed against was given.[60] There is a risk, on appeal, that the Crown Court might increase the length of disqualification rather than reduce it or quash the order.[61] However, the Crown Court cannot increase the length of disqualification beyond the statutory maximum period of five years which the magistrates can impose. The prosecution has no right of appeal to the Crown Court. Scottish appeals from inferior courts of summary jurisdiction lie ultimately to the High Court of Justiciary, Scotland's supreme criminal court.

9.72   Under the Magistrates' Courts Act 1980, s. 111, "any person who was party to proceedings before a magistrates' court, or was aggrieved by the conviction, order, determination or other proceeding of the court", may appeal by way of case stated to the Divisional Court of Queen's Bench Division on the ground either that the magistrates' decision was wrong in law or in excess of jurisdiction. The significant point is that it is theoretically open to the prosecution as well as the defence to challenge an exercise of the magistrates' discretion under sections 2 or 5 using the "case stated" procedure whereas the prosecution has no right of appeal to the Crown Court. The application must be made within 21 days after the day on which the magistrates made their decision.[62] A defendant using this procedure will lose his right of appeal to the Crown Court.[63] Also, the risk for a defendant is that the Divisional Court will decline to review a sentence (including, it is submitted, a criminal disqualification order), if the right of appeal to the Crown Court has not been exercised or exhausted.[64] Presumably, a similar fate would befall an application for judicial review.

9.73   Appeals against sentences imposed by the Crown Court are governed generally by the Criminal Appeal Act 1968 and lie to the Court of Appeal (Criminal Division). Again, it appears that the term "sentence" is sufficiently wide to include a disqualification order made under section 2.[65] Indeed, a number of appeals against section 2 orders have been heard, many of which are discussed elsewhere in this chapter. Unless the trial judge certifies that the case is fit for appeal, leave to appeal must be

---

[56] Supreme Court Act 1981, s. 48; Magistrates' Courts Act 1980, s. 108. Note that in relation to procedure on appeal in the criminal courts we deal exclusively with appeals against sentence which is taken to include a disqualification order under the CDDA. We do not deal with the procedure relating to appeals against *conviction* or a combined appeal against conviction and sentence.
[57] Supreme Court Act 1981, s. 48(6); Magistrates' Courts Act 1980, s. 108(3).
[58] Magistrates' Courts Act 1980, s. 108(3).
[59] *R. v. Hayden* [1975] 1 W.L.R. 852, [1975] 2 All E.R. 558.
[60] Crown Court Rules 1982 (S.I. 1982 No. 1109), r. 7. Under the rules, the Crown Court may extend time for giving notice of appeal either before or after expiry of the 21–day period.
[61] Supreme Court Act 1981, s. 48(4).
[62] Magistrates' Courts Act 1980, s. 111(2). The High Court cannot generally extend the 21–day period: *Michael v. Gowland* [1977] 2 All E.R. 328, [1977] 1 W.L.R. 296. Procedure is governed by the Magistrates' Courts Rules 1981 (S.I. 1981 No. 552, as subsequently amended), rr. 76–81. The application should be made to the Justices' clerk.
[63] Magistrates' Courts Act 1980, s. 111(4).
[64] *R. v. Shepherd* (1983) 5 Cr.App.R. (S.) 124; *Tucker v. Director of Public Prosecutions* [1992] 4 All E.R. 901.
[65] Criminal Appeal Act 1968, s. 50 as substituted by Criminal Justice Act 1993, s. 79(13), Sched. 5, Pt I, para. 1 with effect from August 14, 1995 (S.I. 1995 No. 1958).

obtained from the Court of Appeal[66] The appellant must either serve the trial judge's certificate on the appropriate Crown Court officer together with a notice of appeal or apply to the Court of Appeal for leave to appeal within 28 days from the date of the original order.[67] On an appeal against sentence, the Court of Appeal cannot increase the sentence and thus cannot generally increase the period of disqualification.[68] The prosecution has no direct right of appeal. However, under the procedure introduced by Part IV of the Criminal Justice Act 1988, the Attorney General may refer certain sentences to the Court of Appeal if it appears to him that the sentencing of a person in the Crown Court has been unduly lenient. This procedure is available exclusively in respect of offences triable only on indictment and in a limited range of other instances specified by statutory instrument. On an Attorney General's reference, the Court of Appeal can impose a heavier sentence than that previously imposed (provided it does not exceed the sentencing powers of the court below) In *Attorney General's Reference Nos 14, 15 and 16 of 1995*, the Court of Appeal used this power to impose lengthy disqualification orders on two of three defendants who had been convicted of offences of market-rigging in relation to the shares of public companies.[69] An appeal does not generally lie from a section 2 order made in Scotland's High Court of Justiciary as this is the supreme court of jurisdiction in respect of criminal matters north of the border.

A final question which is of some importance in practice is whether the court has power to suspend or stay a disqualification order pending hearing of an appeal against it. The CDDA itself contains no such express power. It has been pointed out by Professor Sealy that a *magistrates' court* appears to have no power to suspend or stay a disqualification order.[70] If so, then as Sealy points out, the best that can be done for the defendant is to seek an expedited hearing of his appeal. In contrast, it appears from the wording of the Supreme Court Act 1981, s. 47(1) that the Crown Court does possess this power.[71] The power of the courts to suspend or stay the effect of disqualification orders is discussed further in Chapter 11.

---

[66] Criminal Appeal Act 1968, ss 9(1) and 11(1), as amended by the Criminal Justice Act 1982. Procedure is governed by the Criminal Appeal Rules 1968 (S.I. 1968 No. 1262 as subsequently amended). See also *Guide to Proceedings in the Court of Appeal Criminal Division* [1983] Crim. L.R. 415.

[67] Criminal Appeal Act 1968, s. 18(1); Criminal Appeal Rules, r. 2. The Court of Appeal can extend the 28–day period: Criminal Appeal Act 1968, s. 18(2).

[68] *ibid.*, s. 11(3). This contrasts with the position under section 6 of the Act where the Court of Appeal (Civil Division) can and has increased the period of disqualification on appeal by the Secretary of State: see, *e.g. Re Copecrest Ltd, Secretary of State for Trade and Industry v. McTighe (No. 2)* [1996] 2 B.C.L.C. 477, [1997] B.C.C. 224 discussed in Chap. 5 above.

[69] *The Times*, April 10, 1997. It appears that the trial judge had not disqualified the defendants. The court decided not to disqualify the third defendant, Hendry who was in poor health and received, *per* McCowan L.J., "very great credit for having established, despite his ill health, a small business on which he and his family are dependent". The disqualification orders which the court did make are not beyond criticism. The two other defendants, Ward and Howarth, were disqualified from holding any directorship of a *public company* for periods of seven and five years respectively. The CDDA does not confer jurisdiction on the court to make an order which differentiates between public and private companies: see Chap. 11 and *R. v. Goodman* [1993] 2 All E.R. 789, (1993) 97 Cr.App.R. 210, (1993) 14 Cr.App.R. (S.) 147, [1994] 1 B.C.L.C. 349, [1992] B.C.C. 625, nor do the criminal courts have the power to achieve a similar effect through a grant of permission to act in certain capacities notwithstanding disqualification. The Attorney General's reference procedure is available in respect of criminal sentencing in England, Wales and Northern Ireland but does not extend to Scotland: see Criminal Justice Act 1988, s. 172.

[70] L.S. Sealy, "Company directors' disqualification—suspension of disqualification pending appeal" (1989) 5 *Insolvency Law & Practice* 102. A perusal of the Magistrates' Courts Rules 1981 and *Stone's Justices' Manual* confirms the view that there is no express power of stay pending appeal although magistrates' courts can defer sentence or pass a suspended sentence. There appears to be no reason in principle why magistrates' courts should not be able to stay a disqualification order albeit that they are creatures of statute and there is no express power comparable to that available in the Crown Court under the Supreme Court Act 1981.

[71] Section 47(1) states that: "A sentence imposed or other order made by the Crown Court when dealing with an offender shall take effect from the beginning of the day on which it is imposed, *unless the court otherwise directs*" (our emphasis).

CHAPTER 10

Individual Insolvency

INTRODUCTION

10.01   This brief chapter is concerned with the substantive provisions of the CDDA which apply in the context of personal as opposed to corporate insolvency. They are:

(1) Automatic disqualification of undischarged bankrupts.

(2) Disqualification following revocation of an administration order made under Part VI of the County Courts Act 1984.

In the immediate context the first is by far and away the most important of the two. Moreover, as it affects all bankrupts automatically without the need for any special court order it is arguably one of the most important provisions in the whole of the CDDA.[1] Only the broad scope of the two provisions is considered here. The consequences of disqualification and applications for permission to act while disqualified are considered in Chapters 12 and 13 for the CDDA as a whole.

AUTOMATIC DISQUALIFICATION OF UNDISCHARGED BANKRUPTS

10.02   Section 11(1) of the CDDA states:

"It is an offence for a person who is an undischarged bankrupt to act as a director of, or directly or indirectly to take part in or be concerned in the promotion, formation or management of, a company, except with the leave of the court."

Thus, once a person is made an undischarged bankrupt and for as long as he so remains, he is automatically prohibited from acting as a company director, etc. without the permission of the court. "Company" for these purposes includes an unregistered company and a company incorporated outside Great Britain which has an established place of business in Great Britain.[2] The provision only applies to individ-

---

[1] As insolvent partnerships are treated as companies for CDDA purposes the applicability of the CDDA to them is considered elsewhere: see, in particular, Chaps 3 and 12. It suffices to say that where an insolvent partnership is being wound up as an unregistered company under the terms of the Insolvent Partnerships Order 1994 and there are concurrent bankruptcy petitions against the individual partners then those partners will be susceptible to automatic disqualification.
[2] CDDA, s. 22(2)(a).

uals made bankrupt in the courts of England, Wales and Scotland. It does not extend to an individual adjudicated bankrupt by a foreign court.

History and rationale

10.03   The automatic prohibition of undischarged bankrupts from acting as a director of, or directly or indirectly taking part in the management of a company was first enacted in the Companies Acts of 1928 and 1929. It was therefore one of the earliest directors' disqualification provisions to be introduced. Only the fraudulent trading aspects of the provisions in CDDA, ss 4 and 10 have origins going back as far. The provision was extended by an amendment introduced in the Companies Act 1981 to prevent undischarged bankrupts from taking part in company promotion or formation. Apart from that change, there is little substantive difference between the present section 11 and the original provision.

The provision was originally introduced on the recommendation of the Greene Committee.[3] The problem identified by the Greene Committee was the ease with which undischarged bankrupts were able to continue trading and to obtain credit through the medium of a limited company:

> "The evidence upon this subject discloses a state of affairs which is difficult to deal with but in our opinion demands a remedy. Many cases have been brought to our notice where bankrupts who have not obtained their discharge have been able, by using the machinery of the Companies Acts, to continue trading under the disguise of a limited company, with results often disastrous to those who have given credit to the company. In many cases, traders have been far too ready to give credit to private companies of which they know nothing, without making any or sufficient inquiries as to the financial standing of the company or the persons who control it, and to this extent it may fairly be said that the trouble lies at their own door. This is particularly the case where manufacturers in periods of trade depression have been eager at any risk to find a sale for their goods. But in spite of these considerations, we are of opinion that an amendment of the law so as to prohibit an undischarged bankrupt from taking part in the management of a company without the leave of the Bankruptcy Court concerned is desirable."[4]

10.04   The obvious anomaly was that it has long been an offence for an undischarged bankrupt to obtain credit without disclosing relevant information about his personal status.[5] In the absence of what is now the section 11 offence, a bankrupt was free to obtain credit through the medium of a separate corporate entity and enjoy the benefit of limited liability. Thus, the requirement on the bankrupt to disclose his personal status when seeking credit could effectively be side-stepped. A similar automatic

---

[3] Report of the Company Law Amendment Committee (the Greene Committee), Cmd. 2657 (1926).
[4] *ibid.*, para. 56. It remains the position that an undischarged bankrupt seeking permission to act in any of the prohibited capacities must apply to the court by which he was adjudged bankrupt or, in Scotland, by which sequestration of his estates was awarded: CDDA, s. 11(2) and see generally Chap. 13.
[5] See now the Insolvency Act 1986, s. 360. For the former provision see the Bankruptcy Act 1914, s. 155. The present provision also makes it an offence for a bankrupt to engage (whether directly or indirectly) in any business under a name other than that in which he was adjudged bankrupt without disclosing to all persons with whom he enters into any business transaction the name in which he was so adjudged.

prohibition has been adopted in several other jurisdictions including Australia, New Zealand, Ireland, South Africa, Hong Kong and Singapore.[6]

The quote from the Greene Committee suggests that the rationale of section 11 is quite narrow. However, it is arguable that the provision does not serve merely to buttress the offence of obtaining credit without disclosure of bankrupty but has a wider purpose. In keeping with the rationale of the CDDA as a whole, it is suggested that a wider aim of section 11 is to protect the public by prohibiting individuals whose bankruptcy suggests that they may be deficient in running their own affairs from being involved in the management of companies. Support for this view can be derived from the decision of the Supreme Court of New South Wales in *Re Altim Pty Ltd*, a case which concerned an application by an undischarged bankrupt for permission to act in prohibited capacities notwithstanding disqualification. In that case, Street J. described the purpose of an equivalent provision in the following terms:

> "The section under which this application is made proceeds upon the basis that a person who is an undischarged bankrupt is *prima facie* not to be permitted to act as a director or to take part in the management of a company. . . It should be borne in mind that the section is not in any sense a punishment of the bankrupt. . . The prohibition is entirely protective, and the power of the court to grant [permission] is to be exercised with this consideration in the forefront."[7]

10.05   It is striking that the applicant was refused permission in *Altim Pty* because, according to the judge, his history of failed financial ventures was ". . . such as to raise real doubts as to whether he should, whilst an undischarged bankrupt, be let loose again to take part in the commercial life of this community, in a managerial capacity in connection with a company".[8] The case suggests, by analogy, that section 11 amounts to a presumption that an individual who becomes bankrupt is unfit to be involved in the management of companies.[9]

"Undischarged bankrupt"

10.06   The bankruptcy of an individual commences with the day on which a bankruptcy order is made against him.[10] The automatic prohibition takes effect and continues from that point until such time as the individual is discharged from bankruptcy or the order is otherwise annulled. Discharge from bankruptcy will normally occur automatically on the expiry of two years from the date of the order in the case of a

---

[6] See, *e.g.* Australia's Corporations Law, s. 229(1) and discussion in *Re Altim Pty Ltd* [1968] 2 N.S.W.R. 762. Several of these jurisdictions, notably Australia, have introduced automatic disqualification provisions that are much wider in scope than section 11. For instance, under the Corporations Law a person convicted of an offence in connection with the promotion, formation or management of a corporation is automatically prohibited from managing any other corporation without the permission of the court for a period of five years. This is in contrast to the discretionary power of the courts to make a disqualification order in similar circumstances under CDDA, s. 2. One consequence is that Australian jurisprudence on disqualification is dominated by cases concerned with applications for permission. The potential increase in court time that might need to be devoted to the hearing of applications for permission was one of the objections used to defeat the U.K. Government's attempt in the mid-1980s to extend automatic disqualification to the directors of any company going into compulsory liquidation: see Chap. 1.
[7] [1968] 2 N.S.W.R. 762 at 764.
[8] *ibid.*
[9] *Altim Pty* has been expressly followed in a number of cases: see, *e.g. Re Ansett* (1990) 3 A.C.S.R. 357, Supreme Court of Victoria; *Re McQuillan* (1989) 5 B.C.C. 137, Northern Ireland High Court. A further point which strengthens this view is that the approach in cases like *McQuillan*, which involve an application by a bankrupt for permission to act, is similar to that taken on an application for permission to act by a person disqualified under CDDA, s. 6. See further Chap. 13.
[10] For the circumstances in which and by whom a bankruptcy petition may be presented see Insolvency Act 1986, ss 264–277.

summary administration and three years in any other case.[11] The prohibition ceases on discharge. The prohibition is confined in application to undischarged bankrupts. It does not apply to an insolvent individual who enters into an individual voluntary arrangement under Part VIII of the Insolvency Act 1986 unless such individual is and remains an undischarged bankrupt while subject to the arrangement.[12] An undischarged bankrupt is also disqualified from acting in various other capacities.[13]

Overlap with other provisions in the CDDA

10.07 In practice, it is not uncommon for a disqualification under CDDA, s. 6 to overlap with the automatic prohibition in section 11. The failure of a company may well lead to the bankruptcy of its directors, more often than not because they have personally guaranteed the company's indebtedness to certain creditors (in particular, the bank). The automatic disqualification of a director in this situation is no bar to proceedings being brought against him under sections 6–7. Clearly, the Disqualification Unit may decide that it would be expedient to proceed against the director with a view to securing a disqualification order for a longer period than the two or three years during which he might normally expect to remain an undischarged bankrupt. Thus, to an extent, the individual cannot really complain if, having suffered automatic disqualification, he is later re-disqualified by an order under section 6. However, it does appear that in determining the appropriate period of disqualification in any subsequent section 6 proceedings, the court will give the defendant a discount to reflect his automatic disqualification under section 11.[14] In this context, it might be questioned whether there would be any point in pursuing, in the public interest, a "minimum bracket" case against a director who is already or has already been disqualified automatically under section 11.[15]

---

[11] On discharge from bankruptcy (including provision for special cases) see sections 279 280, *ibid*. On the court's power to annul a bankruptcy order see section 282, *ibid*. Even if a person's bankruptcy is annulled there is Australian authority to suggest that the prohibition still applies for the period when he was considered a bankrupt: see *Re Baysington Pty Ltd* (1988) 12 A.C.L.R. 412 at 418; *Salter v. National Companies Securities Commission* [1989] W.A.R. 296, (1988) 13 A.C.L.R. 253 at 256, (1988) 6 A.C.L.C. 717. Although the offence under CDDA, s. 11 is not a "bankruptcy offence" for the purposes of the Insolvency Act 1986, s. 350(2), it must be doubtful whether a prosecution under section 11 would be instituted after an annulment.

[12] In this respect the CDDA is considerably narrower than the Australian Corporations Law which automatically disqualifies any "insolvent under administration". As well as undischarged bankrupts, this term embraces persons who have not been declared bankrupt but have executed a deed of arrangement or entered a composition which has not yet been fully administered.

[13] Including charity trustee (Charities Act 1993, s. 72(1)(b)), pension fund trustee (Pensions Act 1995, s. 29(1)(b)), member of a police authority (Police Act 1996, Sched. 2, para. 11(1)(b)), insolvency practitioner (Insolvency Act 1986, s. 390(4)(a)), member of Parliament (Insolvency Act 1986, s. 427), member of a local authority (Local Government Act 1972, s. 80). An undischarged bankrupt who serves as a director, trustee or committee member of a housing association is also susceptible to removal by the Housing Corporation (Housing Act 1996, Sched. 1, Pt II, para. 4(2)(a)).

[14] In *Re Tansoft Ltd* [1991] B.C.L.C. 339 the defendant was bankrupt at the date of trial and the earliest date on which he would be likely to obtain his discharge from bankruptcy was still some two years off. As a result, any period of disqualification imposed under section 6 would overlap with that resulting from the defendant's bankruptcy. Warner J. regarded this as a neutral factor that carried no weight for the purposes of determining the appropriate period of disqualification. However, *dicta* in *Re Swift 736 Ltd, Secretary of State for Trade and Industry v. Ettinger* [1993] B.C.L.C. 896, [1993] B.C.C. 312, CA and *Re Westmid Packing Services Ltd, Secretary of State for Trade and Industry v. Griffiths* [1998] 2 All E.R. 124, [1998] 2 B.C.L.C. 646, [1998] B.C.C. 836, CA suggest that a previous or current disqualification under section 11 would now be taken into account.

[15] See further, A. Hicks, *Disqualification of Directors: No Hiding Place for the Unfit?* (A.C.C.A. Research Report No. 59, 1998), p. 36. Note that the position could be affected by a DTI proposal to differentiate between bankrupts who, as responsible risk-takers, have simply been unfortunate and so-called "rogue" bankrupts who are guilty of culpable behaviour: see DTI Press Release P/99/575, July 2, 1999. Under this proposal, responsible risk–takers could be discharged from bankruptcy earlier but "rogues" could face disqualification for up to 15 years.

Publicity

10.08   The Secretary of State is required to maintain a register of bankruptcy orders under Chapter 22A of the Insolvency Rules 1986 which is open to public inspection.[16] Rules 6.223(A) and (B) require the official receiver to enter on the register specified bankruptcy information received by him in relation to any bankruptcy order.[17] The Secretary of State is also obliged to enter such specified bankruptcy information (subject to exceptions) relating to any bankruptcy order made in the five years prior to March 22, 1999 as was in his possession on that date. Provision is also made for the deletion of information from the register following discharge or annulment. The register of bankruptcy orders should therefore serve a similar purpose to the register of disqualification orders maintained under section 18 of the CDDA which has no application to section 11 disqualifications.[18]

DISQUALIFICATION FOLLOWING REVOCATION OF AN ADMINISTRATION ORDER MADE UNDER PART VI OF THE COUNTY COURTS ACT 1984

10.09   Under Part VI of the County Courts Act 1984 (as amended by the Courts and Legal Services Act 1990, s. 13), a county court has power in prescribed circumstances to make an administration order against a judgment debtor who is unable to satisfy the amount of a judgment against him.[19] The effect of such an administration order is that no creditor of the individual who has received notice that the order is to be made may proceed unilaterally against the individual or his property without the court's permission.[20] The order may provide for the payment of the individual's debts by instalments and either in full or in part.[21] Section 429 of the Insolvency Act 1986 provides that, where an individual fails to make any payment which he is required to make by virtue of the administration order, the relevant county court may, in its discretion, revoke the order and impose restrictions on the individual, including a direction that section 12 of the CDDA shall apply to him for a period of up to two years. Section 12 of the CDDA simply provides that, where the court has exercised its discretion to revoke the administration order and make such a direction, the individual affected shall not, without the permission of the relevant county court, act as a company director or liquidator or directly or indirectly take part or be

---

[16] This amendment to the Insolvency Rules was introduced by the Insolvency (Amendment) Rules 1999 S.I. 1999 No. 359 with effect from March 22, 1999.

[17] "Specified bankruptcy information" is defined in r. 6.233(B)(5). The definition is wide ranging and includes, among other things, the date of the bankruptcy order, the bankrupt's name, gender, date of birth and last known address and, significantly, full details concerning the bankrupt's discharge.

[18] See para. 11.26.

[19] An order can only be made where the debtor's whole indebtedness does not exceed the County Court limit. The procedure, originally introduced in the Bankruptcy Act 1883, was designed with the small debtor in mind. For history and background see Report of the Review Committee, *Insolvency Law and Practice* (the Cork Committee), Cmnd. 8558 (1982) at paras 68–73, 151–165. For criticisms of the procedure (some of which were addressed in the Courts and Legal Services Act 1990) see paras 272–280, *ibid*.

[20] County Courts Act 1984, s. 114. The effect is similar albeit not as wide as that of an interim order under Pt VIII of the Insolvency Act 1986 (which a debtor applies for in contemplation of an individual voluntary arrangement) or a company administration order under Pt II of the same Act.

[21] County Courts Act 1984, s. 112(6).

concerned in the promotion, formation or management of a company. The effect of section 429 of the Insolvency Act 1986 is that a disqualification under section 12 cannot exceed two years.[22]

---

[22] Under section 429(2) of the Insolvency Act, the court clearly has a discretion over whether to revoke the administration order. However, there is some argument as to whether, having decided to revoke the order, the court is bound to impose a disqualification in the terms of section 12 of the CDDA. It is suggested that the word "and" between "revoke the administration order" and "make an order directing that this section and section 12 of the CDDA shall apply" in section 429(2) should be treated as conjunctive. In other words, it appears that when the court revokes an administration order, it must disqualify as well.

CHAPTER 11

Disqualification Orders

INTRODUCTION

11.01 The following matters are considered in this chapter:

(1) The form of a disqualification order.

(2) The commencement of a disqualification order.

(3) Registration of a disqualification order.

These matters are relevant in all cases of disqualification by the court under the CDDA.

DISQUALIFICATION ORDERS

11.02 Where a person is disqualified under any of CDDA, ss 2 to 5, 6, 8 or 10, the terms of the disqualification order are prescribed by section 1. A disqualification order is defined by section 1(1) as:

"... an order that [the disqualified person] shall not, without the leave of the court:

(a) be a director of a company, or

(b) be a liquidator or administrator of a company, or

(c) be a receiver or manager of a company's property, or

(d) in any way, whether directly or indirectly, be concerned or take part in the promotion, formation or management of a company

for a specified period beginning with the date of the order."

11.03 It is clear from the terms of section 1 that a disqualified person may make a separate application for permission to act in specific respects (see Chapter 13). The Court of Appeal has encouraged such applications to be heard immediately after a disqualification order has been made if at all possible.[1] This step serves to protect the defendant's[2] position especially where he holds directorships or managerial positions

---

[1] *Re Dicetrade Ltd, Secretary of State for Trade and Industry v. Worth* [1994] 2 B.C.L.C. 113 at 116, [1994] B.C.C. 371 at 373G. See also Park J.'s comments in *Re TLL Realisations Ltd*, February 1, 1999, Ch.D., unreported. It is clear that there is power in the terms of section 1 to grant permission. Procedure is governed by section 17. The position was no different under former provisions namely the Companies Act 1985, ss 295, Sched. 12, paras 4, 5; Insolvency Act 1985, s. 108(2), Sched. 6, para. 1(1)–(4), (14).

[2] Where applicable the terms "claimant" and "defendant" are used to reflect the modern requirements of the CPR, the Disqualification Rules and the Disqualification Practice Direction. In disqualification proceedings, "defendant" is the modern equivalent of the pre-CPR term "respondent". Similarly, the term "permission" is used instead of "leave".

in companies other than those which are the subject of the proceedings. A question which has frequently taxed the courts is whether the court is bound by section 1 to impose an absolute ban prohibiting the disqualified person from engaging in *all* of the activities mentioned in section 1(1)(a) to (d) (set out above) or whether, alternatively, the court can pick and choose from section 1 as if it were a menu and, *in the absence of a formal application for permission to act in a particular capacity,* make a selective disqualification order or a disqualification order which permits the disqualified person to participate in the management of a specified company or companies. A closely-related procedural question is whether the form or minute of order should recite the words of section 1 in full. Both questions are considered below.[3]

Picking and choosing

11.04 It is clear from section 1 that the court cannot make an order differentiating between the various types of company that can be incorporated under the Companies Act 1985. Strictly, the ban applies in relation to all companies whether limited by shares, limited by guarantee or unlimited or whether public or private.[4] Thus, for example, the court has no jurisdiction to disqualify a person in relation only to public companies and leave him free to act as a director or manager of any private company.[5] Such effect could, in theory, be achieved if the court which made the disqualification order, assuming it had jurisdiction to do so under section 17 of the CDDA, immediately granted the disqualified person general permission to act in the prohibited capacities in relation to all private companies. It is important to note in this context that such result could not be achieved by a criminal court (which has no power to grant permission under the CDDA) nor by a county court (which can only grant permission in relation to those companies over which it can exercise winding up jurisdiction). It is also difficult to conceive of circumstances in which the court would be prepared to grant such general permission. Historically, there have been several cases in which the court has been prepared to qualify a disqualification order in some way without the defendant having made a formal application for permission to act. So far as these cases proceed on the assumption that the court is making a *qualified* order rather than a disqualification order coupled with the grant of permission to act, they can no longer be regarded as good law. They fall into two broad categories as follows.

Selective orders

11.05 Before the decision in *Re Gower Enterprises Ltd (No. 2)*[6] it was an established practice of the Companies Court in section 6 cases to draw up disqualification orders which only made express reference to paragraphs (a) and (d) of section 1(1).[7] No mention was made in these orders of paragraphs (b) and (c). The consequence of such an order (on its face, at least) was that the defendant was not formally disqualified from acting as a liquidator or administrator of a company or as a receiver or

---

[3] Note that this discussion has no application to the automatic disqualification of undischarged bankrupts under section 11 or a disqualification in the terms of section 12. It applies only to court-imposed disqualifications under sections 2–5, 6, 8 and 10.

[4] Though the court is likely to look favourably on an application by a disqualified person for permission to act in relation to an unlimited company: see *Re DJ Matthews (Joinery Design) Ltd* (1988) 4 B.C.C. 518, *Secretary of State for Trade and Industry v. Shuttleworth*, January 27, 1999, Ch.D., unreported.

[5] *R. v. Goodman* [1993] 2 All E.R. 789, (1993) 97 Cr.App.R. 210, (1993) 14 Cr.App.R. (S.) 147, [1994] 1 B.C.L.C. 349, [1992] B.C.C. 625, CA. *Attorney General's References Nos 14, 15 and 16 of 1995, The Times,* April 10, 1997 must be regarded as wrong on this point.

[6] [1995] 2 B.C.L.C. 201, [1995] B.C.C. 1081.

[7] Thus following the form of originating summons (or, in the county courts, originating application) issued by the Secretary of State or official receiver which usually sought a disqualification order under section 6 but then went on to describe such order by setting out the prohibitions in section 1(1)(a) and (d) only.

manager of a company's property. The practice first surfaced in two cases decided by Harman J.[8] There was some logic underlying this approach. Since the enactment of the Insolvency Act 1985, a person can only generally carry out the activities in paragraphs (b) and (c) if he holds a professional qualification enabling him to act as an insolvency practitioner. A person made the subject of a disqualification order under the CDDA is automatically disqualified from acting as an insolvency practitioner by section 390(4) of the Insolvency Act 1986. In the *Rolus* case, Harman J.'s view was that there was little to be gained from formally disqualifying a person under paragraphs (b) and (c) where that person was not qualified to act as an insolvency practitioner under what is now Part XIII of the Insolvency Act 1986.[9] In other cases, the view was taken that an order in the terms of paragraphs (a) and (d) would adequately protect the public and section 390 of the Insolvency Act does not seem to have been in mind. The practice of omitting paragraphs (b) and (c) from the court's order was rejected in *Re Gower Enterprises (No. 2)*, a case which was to have considerable repercussions.

11.06 In *Gower Enterprises (No. 2)*, the point arose in relation to the form of the originating summons which, in line with the established practice, sought an order under section 6 of the CDDA but then went on to press specifically for an order in the terms of paragraphs (a) and (d) only. Counsel for the official receiver advanced the view that the word "or" between each of paragraphs (a), (b), (c) and (d) in section 1(1) should be read as "and/or" thus enabling the court to pick and choose. Mr Robert Reid Q.C., sitting as a deputy High Court judge, rejected this construction, preferring instead the view expressed by Lindsay J. in *Re Polly Peck International plc (No. 2)*[10] that the provisions of section 1(1)(a) to (d) are cumulative in effect on the basis that the word "or" was intended to be conjunctive. As a result, the deputy judge concluded that an order which did not formally prohibit the disqualified person from engaging in *all* the activities described in section 1(1) was not a disqualification order for the purposes of the CDDA. Conversely, the court had no jurisdiction to limit the scope of a disqualification order to some but not all of the four paragraphs in the subsection. On the facts, it was held that the originating summons was not defective and that a full section 1 order could be granted either under the standard claim in the originating process for "further or other relief" or, if necessary, as a result of an amendment to the summons.[11]

11.07 The decision in *Gower Enterprises (No. 2)* raised two immediate problems. First, it was unclear what impact it would have on all the other current section 6 proceedings which had been brought in line with the established practice. An obvious solution was for the court to allow the amendment of any originating summons so affected. However, if following *Gower Enterprises (No. 2)*, a selective order was not a disqualification order, it was arguable that a selective originating summons was liable to be struck out as disclosing no cause of action. If this was right, then the Secretary of State or official receiver would be forced to commence fresh proceedings. As in the majority of these cases the two-year time limit for commencing proceedings would already have expired, it would then have been necessary for the Secretary of State to apply for permssion under section 7(2) to re-commence proceedings out of time.[12] This

---

[8] *Re Flatbolt Ltd,* unreported, February 21, 1986; *Re Rolus Properties Ltd* (1988) 4 B.C.C. 446. These cases were both decided prior to the enactment of the CDDA although nothing turns on this.

[9] This did not deal with the point that the prohibition on acting as a receiver and manager under CDDA, s. 1(1)(c) is in fact wider than the prohibition (on acting as an *administrative receiver*) flowing from section 390 of the Insolvency Act.

[10] [1994] 1 B.C.L.C. 574, 581–582, [1993] B.C.C. 890, 897A.

[11] Which amendment the judge would have been minded to permit notwithstanding that the two-year time limit under section 7(2) had expired.

[12] On applications for permission under section 7(2) generally, see Chap. 7.

point was taken by counsel for the defendant in another first instance case, *Re Seagull Manufacturing Co. Ltd (No. 3)*[13] decided a fortnight after *Gower Enterprises (No. 2)*. No doubt fully appreciating the ramifications, Blackburne J. skilfully turned the argument on its head and refused to dismiss the official receiver's originating summons. On the assumption (following *Gower Enterprises (No. 2)*) that there was no jurisdiction to make a selective order, he reasoned that the court would be bound, as a matter of course, to make a blanket order in the terms of section 1(1) once the official receiver had established the conditions for disqualification set out in section 6(1). The fact that the order sought in the originating summons omitted any reference to paragraphs (b) and (c) was of no consequence as the court would be obliged to make a blanket order if the case against the defendant was made out. Blackburne J. went further, suggesting that it would be sufficient for the originating summons simply to ask for "an order under section 6 of the CDDA, full stop, without condescending to set out ... what that order should contain". If the summons, having asked for such an order, then went on to describe such order inaccurately, this would not affect the relief that was in fact being sought. The ruling in *Seagull Manufacturing* quickly cleared away any of the difficulties which *Gower Enterprises (No. 2)* appeared to raise in relation to the form and contents of originating summonses and applications in pending section 6 proceedings.[14] Nevertheless, the practice currently adopted in the civil courts is to seek an order under the relevant section (usually section 6 or 8) and then to set out the full terms of section 1(1).

11.08 The second and more pressing problem concerned all the existing disqualification orders, still in force when *Gower Enterprises (No. 2)* was decided, which had been drawn up according to the old practice. The apparent effect of the decision was that these orders were not disqualification orders at all! This presented the DTI with a difficulty where they were seeking to prosecute a person for breach of the order under section 13 of the CDDA. Could breach of a selective order found criminal and/or civil proceedings under sections 13 to 15 of the CDDA? The Secretary of State's response was to apply in several of these cases for the original order to be corrected using the so-called "slip rule" so as to include reference to all four paragraphs of section 1(1). Once an order has been drawn up and entered, the High Court has power both under its inherent jurisdiction and pursuant to CPR, r. 40.12 (formerly RSC Ord. 20, r. 11) to correct accidental errors in its order and/or to ensure that its order carries out the meaning and intention of the court.[15] This power is discretionary and will not be exercised if injustice would be caused as a result. The first reported case in which the court used the slip rule to correct a selective disqualification order was *Re Brian Sheridan Cars Ltd*.[16] In this case, the deputy judge held that it was appropriate to use the slip rule in RSC Ord. 20, r. 11 to correct a disqualification order previously made under section 6. The defendant was not prejudiced by the correction because he had clearly assumed that the original order was valid (he had made an application for permission to act as a director of certain specified companies) and the addition of a reference to

---

[13] [1996] 1 B.C.L.C. 51, [1995] B.C.C. 1088.

[14] The solution adopted by Mr Robert Reid Q.C. in *Gower Enterprises (No. 2)* was to accept that the standard claim in the originating summons for "further or other relief" was sufficient to encompass a full disqualification order. That point aside, he would have been prepared to give the official receiver permission to amend even though the two-year period for commencement of fresh proceedings had by then elapsed. This aspect of the judgment is reported at [1995] B.C.C. 1081, 1085 *et seq.* and referred to by Blackburne J. in *Seagull Manufacturing (No. 3)*.

[15] For the position pre-CPR see, *e.g. Thynne v. Thynne* [1955] P. 272, [1955] 3 W.L.R. 465, [1955] 3 All E.R. 129. County courts have the same power under the CPR (formerly under CCR Ord. 15, r. 5).

[16] [1996] 1 B.C.L.C. 327, [1995] B.C.C. 1035. See also *Secretary of State for Trade and Industry v. Edwards* [1997] B.C.C. 222; *Secretary of State for Trade and Industry v. Phelps,* April 11, 1996, Tunbridge Wells County Court, unreported.

paragraphs (b) and (c) made no odds because he had not acted as a liquidator, administrator or receiver etc. since the date of the original order.[17] In granting the application, the court backdated the correction to the date of the original order.[18] A question having been raised as to whether rule 7.47 of the Insolvency Rules applied, the deputy judge added that he would have been prepared to correct the order also under rule 7.47 and the court's inherent jurisdiction.[19]

11.09   In upholding Harman J.'s decision at first instance in *Re Cannonquest Ltd, Official Receiver v. Hannan*,[20] the Court of Appeal appears to have resolved most of the remaining problems which arose in the wake of *Gower Enterprises (No. 2)*. Again, the case involved an application to correct a selective order using the slip rule. The defendant, "H", had been disqualified under section 6 for a period of six years in 1991. It was subsequently alleged that he had acted in breach of the order and a criminal prosecution had been commenced against him under section 13. The immediate result was the same as that in *Re Brian Sheridan Cars Ltd*. Harman J. corrected the order and ruled that it should be treated as having effect from its pronouncement (*i.e.* from 1991) in its corrected form. In the judge's view, this in no way prejudiced the defendant. It was not a case of the court retrospectively rendering him criminally liable by correcting the original order. It was simply that the order failed to express the court's true intention which was to make a disqualification order pursuant to the CDDA. Developing the point taken by Blackburne J. in *Seagull Manufacturing (No. 3)*, Harman J. added that the court could make an order expressed simply to be a disqualification order without the need to recite in full the words in section 1(1)(a)—(d). This is because the scope of the ban is defined by the *statute* rather than by the order.

The Court of Appeal decided that while the order in *Cannonquest* was imperfect and incomplete, it was nonetheless a disqualification order which was effective to disqualify H from doing what was set out in the imperfect order. This conclusion was based on two foundations. The first was that both the judge's power to disqualify H and the extent of the prohibition rested on the statute. The judge had intended to and had pronounced a period of disqualification. The second was the well-established principle that orders of a court of unlimited jurisdiction should be obeyed unless and until they are set aside. The same principle applied to require obedience to an order which said that it was a disqualification order, even if on paper, the full terms of the order were not fully and accurately set out.[21] As such, it was inconceivable that an

---

[17] Correcting the order would be prejudicial if since the date of the original order the person has engaged in activities covered by section 1(1) but not by the order itself. Even then, it is arguable that the prejudice could be avoided by the grant of retrospective and prospective permission to engage in those activities at the time of the correction.

[18] While the deputy judge took the view that a correction under the slip rule must logically be backdated to the date of the original order, he added *obiter* that he would otherwise have been prepared to backdate the alteration using the power in RSC Ord. 42, r. 3, on which see, *Kuwait Airways Corp. v. Iraqi Airways Co. (No. 2)* [1994] 1 W.L.R. 985, [1995] 1 All E.R. 790. If corrected disqualification orders had been made to run from a later date (*e.g.* the actual date on which the court sanctioned the alteration), this would have given rise to the problem of prior breach (*i.e.* a breach of the corrected order falling within the terms added by the court under the slip rule but which occurred before the date of alteration). Furthermore, without some downward variation of the period of disqualification, the court would inadvertently have been increasing the length of the ban. Fortunately, the Court of Appeal decision in *Re Cannonquest Ltd, Official Receiver v. Hannan* (see text) has now arguably removed the need for the court to vary selective orders using the slip rule.

[19] The precise applicability and interrelationship of the rules of court, the Insolvency Rules and the Disqualification Rules in disqualification proceedings has been something of a vexed question: see Chap. 6 for a full discussion.

[20] [1997] 2 B.C.L.C. 473, [1997] B.C.C. 644.

[21] See *Isaacs v. Robertson* [1985] A.C. 97 at 101E–103F; *M v. Home Office* [1994] 1 A.C. 377 at 423G–424D; *Credit Suisse v. Allendale Borough Council* [1996] 3 W.L.R. 894 at 919B–926H, 932E–939B. The High Court (which made the order in *Cannonquest*) and the Crown Court are both part of the Supreme Court and are generally regarded as courts of unlimited jurisdiction for this purpose.

application to set aside a selective order on a technicality could ever succeed if the defendant would be left undisqualified as a result. Morritt L.J. added that, even if he was wrong on the first point, namely that the order as orally pronounced was a disqualification order, there would still be power to correct the order under the slip rule. Waller L.J. did not deal with this further point and Simon Brown L.J. expressly reserved his position.

11.10 In *Cannonquest,* the Court of Appeal were not technically dealing with the position in respect of conduct which contravened *part* of the prohibition in section 1(1) but where the relevant part (typically paragraphs (b)–(c)) was not included in the terms of the imperfect order. Thus, the case is only direct authority for the proposition that an imperfect disqualification order is effective to prohibit the person from engaging in activities *described in the terms of the order* (typically section 1(1)(a) and (d) activities). However, the reasoning of the decision goes further and supports the proposition that a selective order is an effective, albeit imperfect, disqualification order that disqualifies the relevant person from acting in all the ways described in section 1(1). The logic of the decision is that if an order is expressed to be made under any of the various powers in the CDDA, then it will be treated as a blanket order in the terms of section 1(1) whether it expressly recites the contents of paragraphs (a) to (d) in full or not. In the light of this, there is no necessity for the court to correct any remaining selective orders under the slip rule.[22] After *Cannonquest,* it certainly makes little sense for the persons concerned to incur the cost of contesting any further slip rule motions pursued by the Secretary of State. Although the position is now fairly settled it is still advisable in drawing up a disqualification order to take a "belt and braces" approach and recite paragraphs (a) to (d) in full.

11.11 The cases discussed so far in connection with the slip rule were section 6 cases brought in the High Court. An important question is whether or not the criminal courts have a similar power to correct selective disqualification orders previously made under either section 2 or 5. In *R. v. Cole, Lees and Birch,*[23] the defendants were convicted in the Liverpool Crown Court of acting as directors of a company which was known by a prohibited name contrary to section 216 of the Insolvency Act 1986. Exercising the court's power under section 2, the trial judge made disqualification orders against all three defendants. However, the orders as orally pronounced were selective. Two of the defendants were only disqualified from acting as directors. In other words, the orders pronounced in their cases made no express reference to any of the activities described in section 1(1)(b)–(d). The third defendant was disqualified from being a director, liquidator or administrator or a receiver or manager of a company's property but there was no reference in the order pronounced to the prohibition from being concerned or taking part in promotion, formation or management set out in section 1(1)(d). On their appeal against conviction and disqualification, the Criminal Division of the Court of Appeal decided that the orders could be made valid by each appellant being generally disqualified in the full terms of section 1(1) from the date of sentence and for the periods stated by the judge. Thus, the actual result was the same as that in *Cannonquest.* What the Court of Appeal appears to have done was to accept that the sentence as passed was a disqualification order (albeit one imperfectly pronounced) and, as in *Cannonquest,* to regularise the position by making it absolutely clear that the order was what it always had been. However, it is not entirely clear from the judgments on what basis the Court of Appeal achieved this result particularly when one bears in mind that, unlike Harman J. in *Cannonquest,* it was not exercising an original jurisdiction. The following explanation is suggested.

---

[22] This was certainly the view of Simon Brown L.J. in *Cannonquest.*
[23] [1998] B.C.C. 87.

11.12   The Court of Appeal (Criminal Division) unquestionably has power under the Criminal Appeal Act 1968, s. 11(3) to quash an imperfect disqualification order and replace it with any order that the Crown Court could have made when it originally dealt with the matter. The Crown Court has an inherent power analogous to the slip rule which enables it to cure irregularities in its own orders.[24] As such, it was open to the Court of Appeal to make the order which the Crown Court could have made. The argument that section 11(3) of the Criminal Appeals Act 1968 does not permit the Court of Appeal (Criminal Division) to make an order if its effect would be to increase the appellant's original sentence was considered and rejected by the Court of Appeal. It is suggested that the answer to that argument is the same answer as the one given in the civil context by the Court of Appeal (Civil Division) in *Cannonquest*. The original order having been, and having always been a disqualification order, the use of the slip rule to "perfect" the imperfections in the order as pronounced (and/or, in the civil courts, as drawn up on paper) does not retrospectively increase the sentence or impose a new penalty or disqualification.

11.13   Although the decision in *Gower Enterprises (No. 2)* potentially created a number of problems, these have now been resolved. Even so, its basic premise that the court lacks jurisdiction to "pick and choose" and should therefore pronounce a disqualification order in the comprehensive terms of section 1(1)(a)–(d) is now the law. Indeed, despite the problems raised by the decision, the DTI decided not to appeal it and a number of compelling reasons can be found within the overall scheme of the CDDA to support the basic premise:

(1)   The focus in section 6 is on the previous conduct of the defendant *as a director*. If the court finds that the defendant's past conduct as a director is such as to make him unfit to be concerned in the management of a company it is obliged to make a disqualification order even if, for example, it considers that the defendant has since learned his lesson and is not now unfit. It is difficult to see how the court could have been left with no discretion as to the making of a disqualification order under section 6 and yet, at the same time, a discretion as to which activities could be prohibited within the terms of the order.

(2)   As the focus in section 6 is on the defendant's conduct as a director, it is difficult to imagine circumstances in which the conduct of, for example, a liquidator acting as such could ever be taken into account as a ground of unfitness on an application under that section. If conduct in other capacities is likely to be irrelevant, it is difficult to see when in a section 6 case the court would ever be able to disqualify a defendant from engaging in the activities described in section 1(1)(b) and (c). Furthermore, if there were a discretion as to the scope of the order then the court would first have to be satisfied that there was evidence of unfitness in relation to *each* of the four capacities set out in section 1(1) before making an order in relation to that capacity. The notion of a discretion sits uncomfortably alongside section 6 where only conduct *qua* director is relevant. The same considerations apply *mutatis mutandis* to sections 2 to 5 of the CDDA but on the assumption that the focus in cases under those

---

[24] *R. v. Michael* [1976] Q.B. 414; *R v. Saville* [1981] 1 Q.B. 12. It is only possible for a magistrates' court to correct orders made in criminal proceedings under the Magistrates' Courts Act 1980, s. 142. This power is analogous to the Crown Court's power of review under the Supreme Court Act 1981, s. 47(2) in that it can only be employed during the 28–day period beginning on the date of sentence (see, *e.g. R. v. Menocal* [1980] A.C. 598). This contrasts with the wider inherent powers available in the High Court and the Crown Court which are not time-constrained.

provisions will be on a particular offence or default committed by a person acting in a particular capacity (*e.g.* as a director or manager).

(3) In conferring various powers (and in section 6, a duty) to make a disqualification order, the CDDA focuses exclusively on particular types of conduct, for example, conduct *qua* director (section 6), an offence (sections 2, 4(1)(a) and 5), persistent default (section 3) and other specified conduct (section 4(1)(b)). However, it draws no express connection between the conduct triggering the power or duty to make a disqualification order and specific paragraphs of section 1(1). Thus, for example, in a case where the conduct triggering the making of an order is conduct as a liquidator (*e.g.* under section 4(1)(b)), the CDDA does not expressly limit the form of order to a prohibition under section 1(1)(b) alone. On the contrary, once the relevant power or duty is triggered, the CDDA provides that the court may, or shall, make a disqualification order as defined. These wider schematic factors tend to support the reasoning in *Gower Enterprises (No. 2)*.

(4) The construction of section 1(1) favoured in *Gower Enterprises (No. 2)* sits more naturally alongside the court's power to grant permission to act conferred by section 1 and regulated by section 17. Section 6 of the CDDA which obliges the court to make a disqualification order allows no scope for the consideration of the defendant's *present* activities. The legislative scheme is such that evidence of that nature can only be put before the court on an application for permission to act. The overall rationale of the regulatory regime established by the CDDA is that the court is empowered or obliged to make a full disqualification order based on the defendant's *past* conduct and the width of that overall prohibition is tempered by the court's ability to grant permission. The idea of a blanket prohibition is also consistent with the historical evolution of section 1(1).[25]

(5) The making of a disqualification order has "knock-on effects" under other legislation.[26] For example, a disqualified person is barred from acting as an insolvency practitioner (and therefore as a liquidator) by section 390(4) of the Insolvency Act 1986. The existence of these "knock-on" provisions gives some credence to the theory that parliament intended the prohibition to be comprehensive and wide-ranging.

11.14   The comprehensive nature of the prohibition coupled with the lack of jurisdiction to make selective orders has serious consequences for a person who holds directorships in several companies and is found to be unfit in relation to just one or two of them. He will find himself unable to continue as a director or manager of companies in relation to which there has been no complaint about his conduct. The only course of action available to a person faced with this situation is to make an application for permission to act under section 17.

"Specific excepted company" orders

11.15   The effect of section 1 is that the disqualified person can no longer act as a director or participate in the management of *any* company whatsoever. This does not

---

[25] Note, in particular, the amendments to the former disqualification provisions introduced by the Companies Act 1981, s. 93(1B) and s.94(1) the purpose of which was to extend the scope of the prohibition to include reference to liquidators and receivers. The incremental way in which the prohibition has developed tends to support the view that it is a blanket ban which has gradually expanded in scope from the time when the Companies Act 1929 was enacted down to the present.

[26] See further Chap. 12.

just apply to the person's position in the company or companies with which the proceedings were directly concerned. It means that he will be forced to resign any other directorships or managerial positions which he holds. This is so even where there is no complaint about his conduct in relation to those other companies. The blanket nature of the ban can be justified with reference to the areas of policy discussed in Chapter 2 and the schematic factors discussed above in para. 11.13. Even so, certain courts have the power to waive the full effect of an order by granting the disqualified person permission to take part in the management of a specified company or companies. The availability of this power means that the court can take into account whether the activities contemplated by the disqualified person pose any risk to the public. The law and practice relating to applications for permission to act is considered generally in Chapter 13. Suffice it to say for now that the procedure on applications for permission is governed by section 17 of the CDDA. If the disqualified person wishes to participate in the management of a specified company, the basic position is that he should make a formal application for permission to any court having jurisdiction to wind up that company. It is common practice in section 6 proceedings for the defendant to make an application to be heard immediately after the making of a disqualification order.[27] There are, however, a number of cases in which the court has been prepared to exclude specified companies from the scope of the order even in the absence of a formal application for permission. These cases suggest that the court may be able to make what can be described as a "specific excepted company" order under section 1 without the need for a formal application for permission.

11.16　Such an approach was first taken by Mervyn Davies J. in *Re Majestic Recording Studios Ltd*,[28] a case decided under the former provisions in sections 295 to 301 of the Companies Act 1985. The judge disqualified the second defendant, "C", for a five-year period on the ground that his conduct in relation to five specified companies made him unfit. However, he included a proviso in the order to the effect that C would be allowed to act as a director of a sixth company, Morton Music Ltd (which had not featured in the proceedings) during the five-year period provided that (a) an independent accountant approved by the court acted as his co-director throughout and that (b) three years' worth of outstanding accounts were filed by a specified date. It is perhaps significant that it was indicated through counsel that C would not oppose disqualification as long as he was allowed to continue as a director of Morton Music Ltd. Affidavit evidence concerning Morton Music Ltd had been put in at a late stage by C and its auditors. It appears that the judge was content to dispense with the requirement for a formal application for permission although he did express some doubt as to whether there was jurisdiction to make a "specific excepted company" order under sections 295 to 301 of the Companies Act 1985.[29] Shortly afterwards, the then Vice-Chancellor, Sir Nicolas Browne-Wilkinson, arrived independently at a similar conclusion in *Re Lo-Line Electric Motors Ltd*.[30] In that case, the court disqualified the defendant for three years but allowed him to remain as a director of two family companies subject to a number of conditions. Browne-Wilkinson V.-C. appears to have assumed that the Companies Act 1985, s. 295 gave him the power to make a "specific excepted com-

---

[27] A practice welcomed by the Court of Appeal in *Re Dicetrade Ltd, Secretary of State for Trade and Industry v. Worth* [1994] 2 B.C.L.C. 113 at 116, [1994] B.C.C. 371 at 373G. See also Park J.'s comments in *Re TLL Realisations Ltd*, February 1, 1999, Ch.D., unreported.

[28] [1989] B.C.L.C. 1, (1988) 4 B.C.C. 519.

[29] The applicable provisions regarding the scope of disqualification orders and applications for permission in *Majestic Recording* were Companies Act 1985, s. 295 and Sch. 12, Pt I, para. 4. The current provisions in CDDA, ss 1 and 17 are identical in all material respects.

[30] [1988] Ch. 477, [1988] 3 W.L.R. 26, [1988] 2 All E.R. 692, [1988] B.C.L.C. 698, (1988) 4 B.C.C. 415. This case was also decided under the old Companies Act provisions.

pany" order without the need for a formal application under section 295(6), the then equivalent of CDDA, s. 17. Again, affidavit evidence from the defendant and the auditors concerning the two family companies was before the court. This approach appears to have been followed in a number of section 6 cases although it is not clear from the reports of any of them whether the court was simply dispensing with the requirement for a formal application under section 17.[31] The entire phenomenon can probably be attributed to the pragmatism of both the judiciary and the DTI. It should not be seen as the court assuming a general jurisdiction to grant a partial disqualification order. The cases referred to were decided almost exclusively in the Chancery Division of the High Court. This court has the power to wind up any company in England and Wales and can therefore assume jurisdiction under section 17(1) to hear applications for permission brought in any disqualification case proceeding before it. If affidavit evidence concerning the companies in respect of which permission is sought is before the court (as, *e.g.* in *Majestic Recording*) and the Secretary of State adopts a neutral position, it makes sense for the disqualifying court to assume jurisdiction under section 17(1) and dispense with the need for a formal notice of application so that costs can be saved.[32] The "specific excepted company" order is thus in reality a full disqualification order coupled with a further order for permission notwithstanding the disqualification order.[33]

11.17 Unfortunately, it is not open to the criminal courts to adopt this convenient practice when exercising their powers to disqualify under sections 2 and 5. This is because section 17 does not confer jurisdiction on the criminal courts to hear applications for permission. The only course for a person disqualified in a criminal court is to make a free standing application for permission to a civil court having jurisdiction under section 17. A similar problem arises in the county courts where the defendant, having been disqualified, is seeking permission to act as a director or manager of a company the registered office of which is situated outside the district of the particular county court dealing with the disqualification proceedings.[34] An additional problem is that the disqualification order is likely to have taken effect before the free standing application is listed for hearing in these cases. This is distinctly unfortunate in a case in which permission is highly likely to be granted. The ability of these courts to suspend the effect of an order so as to give a disqualified person time to apply elsewhere for permission is discussed further below.

COMMENCEMENT AND COMING INTO EFFECT OF DISQUALIFICATION ORDERS

11.18 Section 1 provides that the period of disqualification runs from the date on which the court makes the order. In other words, if X is disqualified by the court for three years on April 1, 1999 the three-year period runs from that date and will expire on March 31, 2002. This applies to all disqualification orders made by a court pursuant to a substantive power contained in the CDDA (*i.e.* CDDA, ss 2 to 5, 6, 8 and 10). To modify the above example, this means that if X is disqualified by a criminal court

[31] See, *e.g. Re Chartmore Ltd* [1990] B.C.L.C. 673; *Re Godwin Warren Control Systems plc* [1993] B.C.L.C. 80, [1992] B.C.C. 557 and *Secretary of State for Trade and Industry v. Palfreman* [1995] B.C.C. 193. See also D. Milman, "Partial Disqualification Orders" (1991) 12 *The Company Lawyer* 224.
[32] This is the basis on which the Court of Session proceeded in *Secretary of State for Trade and Industry v. Palfreman* [1995] B.C.C. 193, 194D.
[33] Any other explanation falls foul of *Gower Enterprises (No. 2)* (see above at paras 11.06 *et seq.*).
[34] See CDDA, s. 17(1)(b) and the Insolvency Act 1986, s. 117(2).

under section 2 following his conviction of a relevant offence and he also receives a custodial sentence, the disqualification runs from the date of pronouncement of sentence not the date of X's release from prison.[35] One question of considerable practical importance which is discussed further below is to what extent the court has any power to direct that a disqualification order will not come into effect until some time after it is pronounced (*e.g.* pending either the hearing of an appeal against the order or the determination of an application for permission to act).

Civil proceedings under CDDA, ss 7 to 8

11.19   Proceedings under section 7(1) (in the High Court or the county courts) and section 8 (in the High Court) are governed by the Disqualification Rules. Rule 9 provides that a disqualification order in section 7(1) or section 8 proceedings takes effect at the beginning of the 21st day after the day on which the order is made unless the court orders otherwise. The apparent implication is that the period of disqualification ordered in these proceedings should generally run from the 21st day after the date of order and not from the date of order itself. Thus, at first sight, rule 9 appears to conflict with the mandatory terms of section 1 defining a disqualification order as an order that the defendant shall not, without permission of the court, be a director etc. for a specified period beginning with the date of the order.[36] This apparent conflict between rule 9 and section 1 was considered and resolved by Evans-Lombe J. in *Secretary of State for Trade and Industry v. Edwards*.[37] He held that the two provisions do not conflict and that the effect of rule 9 is merely to *suspend* the operation of the order for 21 days. The period of disqualification still runs from the date on which the court made the order even though, in relation to the first 21 days of the period, the order is unenforceable. Thus, a suspension of the order's effect under rule 9 is akin to a temporary stay. The relevant person is still treated as being disqualified while the stay remains in operation but the prohibition has no bite during that period. The court can abridge or extend the 21–day period.[38] Rule 9 serves a useful purpose. The 21–day stay gives the disqualified person a short period of breathing space during which he can re-arrange his affairs without being in breach of the disqualification order while he does so. In the absence of rule 9, a person who loses contested disqualification proceedings would be faced with considerable practical difficulties in respect of any current directorships etc. By suspending the full operation of the order using rule 9, the court can at least give him time to resign those positions and, where necessary, to take steps in conjunction with the relevant company or companies to appoint a replacement.

---

[35] *R. v. Bradley* [1961] 1 W.L.R. 398, [1961] 1 All E.R. 669, CA. The provision considered in this case was the Companies Act 1948, s. 188. The point has even greater force now given the mandatory nature of CDDA, s. 1(1). Even so, the fact that the period of disqualification runs concurrently with any period of imprisonment imposed on the disqualified person has been the subject of criticism in the past: see the Report of the Jenkins Committee, Cmnd. 1749 (1962) at para. 81. The position under the CDDA can be contrasted with that under section 229(3) of the Australian Corporations Law where, if the person is sentenced to imprisonment, the period of disqualification only starts to run on his release.
[36] A view expressed by Chadwick J. in *Re Auto Electro and Powder Finishers*, April 5, 1995, Ch.D., unreported and echoed by Morritt L.J. in *Secretary of State for Trade and Industry v. Bannister* [1996] 1 W.L.R. 118, [1996] 2 B.C.L.C. 271, [1995] B.C.C. 1,027.
[37] [1997] B.C.C. 222.
[38] In *Re Travel Mondial (U.K.) Ltd* [1991] B.C.L.C. 120, [1991] B.C.C. 224 Browne-Wilkinson V.-C. extended the rule 9 period so that the order took effect from 21 days after personal service of the order on the director. In *Re T & D Services (Timber Preservation & Damp Proofing Contractors) Ltd* [1990] B.C.C. 592 Vinelott J. disqualified the defendant for ten years but deferred the operation of the order for two weeks to give him time to sort out the affairs of a company which had not featured in the proceedings. In *Re Ipcon Fashions Ltd* (1989) 5 B.C.C. 573, Hoffmann J. gave permission to a disqualified person to continue to act as a director for eight weeks to enable him to make alternative arrangements for the management of a company of which he remained director and manager at the date of trial.

11.20   Evans-Lombe J.'s view receives support from the judgment of Harman J in *Re Cannonquest Ltd, Official Receiver v. Hannan* in which the following explanation of rule 9 was given:

> "The rule provides a perfectly sensible and practical provision that the man is to have a few days to put his house in order and be in a position to comply with the disqualification order pronounced against him, but that disqualification order shall run from the date of its pronouncement."[39]

It is important to realise that the suspended effect of the order under rule 9 does not affect the time at which the order will expire. Thus, shortening the 21–day period will not bring forward the date on which the order will expire.

Civil proceedings under CDDA, ss 2(2)(a), 3, 4, 10

11.21   In cases brought in the civil courts seeking a disqualification order under any of sections 2(2)(a), 3 or 4 of the CDDA, paragraph 16.1 of the Disqualification Practice Direction in effect brings the position into line with that under sections 7 to 8 by applying the same wording as set out in rule 9 to such proceedings. So far as orders under section 10 are concerned, the High Court would have power to stay or suspend such an order under the Supreme Court Act 1981.[40] The position in the county courts in relation to section 10 is more problematic. The county courts are entirely creatures of statute and have no inherent jurisdiction as such. It is open to doubt whether a county court has any jurisdiction to stay an order other than that conferred by rule 9 and the Disqualification Practice Direction. The availability of a power to stay in section 10 cases would alleviate the problem which can arise because a given county court has no jurisdiction to grant the defendant permission to act as a director or manager of a company the registered office of which is situated outside its district.

Criminal proceedings

11.22   The Disqualification Rules do not apply to cases involving disqualification in the criminal courts. Even so, it appears that the Supreme Court Act 1981, s. 47(1) confers a power on the Crown Court to suspend the operation of a disqualification order similar to the power contained in rule 9. Section 47(1) provides that a sentence imposed or other order made by the Crown Court when dealing with an offender shall take effect from the beginning of the day on which it was imposed *unless the court otherwise directs*. The similarity between this and the wording in rule 9 is striking and it appears that it would allow the Crown Court, in much the same way, to suspend the operation of an order for a short period to enable the disqualified person to re-arrange his affairs. It is conceivable that the Crown Court could also exercise the power of suspension in section 47(1) to enable a disqualified person to bring an application for permission to act before a civil court. This is a point of considerable importance bearing in mind that the criminal courts have no jurisdiction to hear applications for

---

[39] [1997] 2 B.C.L.C. 473, [1997] B.C.C. 644. Morritt L.J. indicated in *Secretary of State for Trade and Industry v. Bannister* [1996] 1 W.L.R. 118, [1996] 2 B.C.L.C. 271, [1995] B.C.C. 1027 while reaching no decision on the point, that the rule making authorities should direct attention to the question of whether or not rule 9 is *ultra vires* the CDDA. The solution adopted by Evans-Lombe and Harman JJ. should remove any fears on this for the time being.
[40] See *Secretary of State for Trade and Industry v. Bannister* [1996] 1 W.L.R. 118, [1996] 2 B.C.L.C. 271, [1995] B.C.C. 1027.

permission and are therefore unable to deal with the question of permission in the course of the main proceedings. In relation to sections 2 and 5 of the CDDA, the magistrates' courts appear to have no power which would enable them to postpone the full effect of a disqualification order until some time after the date of sentence.[41]

Is there a general power to stay or suspend a disqualification order under the inherent jurisdiction?

11.23   It should be apparent from the foregoing discussion that there is jurisdiction in the High Court, the county courts and the Crown Court to stay or suspend the operation of a disqualification order. In *Secretary of State for Trade and Industry v. Bannister*[42] it was held that both the High Court and the Court of Appeal have power under their inherent jurisdiction to stay or suspend an order made in unfitness proceedings pending an appeal by the defendant.[43] However, in refusing the defendant's application for a stay, the Court of Appeal made it very clear that this inherent power should only be exercised in exceptional circumstances. The following reasons were advanced in support of this conclusion:

(1) The whole purpose of the CDDA is to protect the public from those who by reason of their past conduct have shown themselves to be unfit to act as a director or in the management of a company. A relevant factor weighing against the exercise of the inherent power was that it would leave the public effectively unprotected. The Court of Appeal's approach in *Bannister* suggests that the paramount need to protect the public should generally outweigh any personal hardship which might be suffered by the defendant if a stay is refused.[44]

(2) It is open to the civil courts having jurisdiction under section 17 to grant the defendant permission to act as a director etc. On an application for permission, the practice is to require the applicant to provide evidence in relation to his current activities and, in particular, the financial standing and management structure of any company with which he wishes to become or remain involved. The court can also grant permission subject to conditions. As such, an application for permission provides the court with a more appropriate means of balancing the personal interests of the disqualified person over against the overriding need to protect the public than an application for a stay. Thus, the discretion to stay or suspend a disqualification order pursuant to the

---

[41] L.S. Sealy, "Company directors' disqualification—suspension of disqualification pending appeal" (1989) 5 *Insolvency Law & Practice* 102. A perusal of the Magistrates' Courts Rules 1981 and *Stone's Justices' Manual* confirms the view that there is no express power to stay the effect of an order although magistrates' courts can defer sentence or pass a suspended sentence. There appears to be no reason in principle why magistrates' courts should not be able to stay a disqualification order albeit that they are creatures of statute and there is no express power comparable to that available in the Crown Court under the Supreme Court Act 1981.
[42] [1996] 1 W.L.R. 118, [1996] 2 B.C.L.C. 271, [1995] B.C.C. 1,027.
[43] There being nothing in the CDDA to exclude the jurisdiction as statutorily recognised and preserved by the Supreme Court Act 1981, s. 49(3).
[44] Those who regard the legislation as having primarily a penal objective would no doubt wish to give greater weight to the evidence of financial and personal hardship put forward by the defendant in this case. While the decision in *Bannister* can be criticised because it proceeds on the false assumption that there is a conflict between rule 9 and section 1(1), the Court of Appeal's general approach, which places emphasis on the overall scheme and structure of the CDDA, is more workable than one which takes the personal consequences of disqualification as its starting point.

inherent power should, in practice, only be exercised in exceptional circumstances where the alternative remedy provided by section 17 is inadequate.[45]

11.24   It is important to add that in *Bannister* the Court of Appeal assumed that there was a conflict between the requirement in section 1(1) that an order commences on the date it is pronounced and the operation of rule 9. Ultimately the point was left open by Morritt L.J. in the leading judgments in both *Bannister* and *Cannonquest*. However, the approach of Harman (at first instance in *Cannonquest*) and Evans-Lombe JJ. (in *Secretary of State for Trade and Industry v. Edwards*) suggests that it is open to the High Court (and a county court), *as a matter of jurisdiction,* to stay the effect of a disqualification order made under CDDA, ss 6 or 8 by virtue of rule 9. The same power is conferred in civil proceedings under sections 2, 3 and 4 by reason of paragraph 16.1 of the Disqualification Practice Direction. The same can be said of the Crown Court's power to stay orders under section 47(1) of the Supreme Court Act 1981. It is suggested that the approach in *Bannister* should still be used as a guide to how these various powers should be exercised. Thus, it is generally more appropriate for the court to grant interim permission to act rather than stay the order. The advantage of using section 17 from a schematic perspective is that the disqualification can take full effect on the date of the order which gives priority to the protective aspect of the CDDA.[46] If a director needs permission to act only for specific companies a general suspension of the disqualification order seems to go too far. This approach also fits better with the obligation to file particulars of the disqualification order for registration, a requirement (discussed below) which is not affected by the suspension of the order's effect. At the same time, it is arguable that the Crown Court, in particular, should be prepared to exercise its power to stay more liberally than the civil courts given that the criminal courts generally have no power to grant permission to act.

Interim permission

11.25   The upshot of *Secretary of State for Trade and Industry v. Bannister* is that while the High Court and Court of Appeal retain a residual power to stay the full effect of a disqualification order, the courts should generally fall back on the scheme of the CDDA and, where appropriate, grant interim permission rather than a stay. As a means of dealing with the situation pending (a) an appeal against the disqualification order or (b) the full hearing of an application for permission to act, this approach has much to commend it. The question of interim permission is considered further in Chapter 13.

REGISTRATION OF ORDER

11.26   Section 18(1) of the CDDA empowers the Secretary of State to make regulations requiring officers of courts to furnish him with particulars of (a) all disqualifi-

---

[45] Morritt L.J. described as exceptional circumstances, "... the extreme case in which the court below went badly wrong and the very existence of the disqualification order causes irreparable harm to the person apparently disqualified.": [1996] 2 B.C.L.C. 271, 275D–E. This means that in practical terms the question of a stay under the inherent jurisdiction will invariably have to be taken to the Court of Appeal, a point well-illustrated by *Re Continental Assurance Co. of London plc.* [1997] 1 B.C.L.C. 48, [1996] B.C.C. 888 affd. *sub nom. Secretary of State for Trade and Industry v. Burrows,* July 4, 1996, CA, unreported.
[46] The approach taken on this question in Australian disqualification cases has been similar to that in *Bannister*: see, *e.g. Tolj v. O'Connor* (1988) 13 A.C.L.R. 653; *Hunter v. Corporate Affairs Commission (NSW)* (1988) 13 A.C.L.R. 250; *Gray v. Commissioner for Corporate Affairs (Vic)* (1988) 13 A.C.L.R. 516; *Dwyer v. NCSC (No. 2)* (1989) 14 A.C.L.R. 595 although some doubts were expressed by Young J. about the appropriateness of granting interim permission as opposed to a stay in *Blunt v. Corporate Affairs Commission (NSW)* (1988) 13 A.C.L.R. 648, 652.

cation orders made, (b) any action taken by a court in consequence of which such an order is varied or ceases to be in force, or (c) any permission granted by a court for a disqualified person to act in a prohibited way notwithstanding the order. The current regulations are the Companies (Disqualification Orders) Regulations 1986.[47] The effect of these regulations is that particulars of any disqualification order made under CDDA, ss 2 to 5, 6, 8 or 10 and of any grant of permission to act under section 17 notwithstanding such order must be notified to Companies House on the appropriate prescribed form. This must be done within 14 days of the order being made or permission being granted.[48] The Secretary of State (acting by the Registrar of Companies) is required by section 18(2) to maintain a register of disqualification orders and of cases in which permission to act has been granted. The register, which was first established under section 29 of the Companies Act 1976, is open to public inspection.[49] There is no provision for registration of a disqualification order made in the terms of section 12.

In relation to undischarged bankrupts, there is no disqualification order to register as disqualification flows automatically from the making of the bankruptcy order under section 11. However, as a result of an amendment introduced by the Insolvency (Amendment) Rules 1999,[50] the Secretary of State is now required to maintain a register of bankruptcy orders and this requirement goes some way towards assisting Companies House to identify whether persons seeking to incorporate companies are disqualified by reason of bankruptcy.[51]

---

[47] S.I. 1986 No. 2067 (as amended by S.I. 1995 No. 1509).

[48] It is not clear whether the court can direct that a disqualification order need not be registered within the 14–day period if the operation of the order is stayed or suspended using the powers discussed in the text from para. 11.18. It has been held that the courts of New South Wales do have power to make such a direction and override a similar requirement in the Companies (NSW) Code: see *Hunter v. Corporate Affairs Commission* (1988) 13 A.C.L.R. 250.

[49] A simple name search of the register can now be carried out by accessing the Companies House website on http://www.companieshouse.gov.uk. It is clear that the maintenance of a complete and accurate register is essential to the publicising and enforcement of disqualification. However, levels of notification have not always been as they might: see National Audit Office, *The Insolvency Service Executive Agency: Company Director Disqualification* (1993) and A. Hicks, *Disqualification of Directors: No Hiding Place for the Unfit?* (A.C.C.A Research Report No. 59, 1998), Chap. 11.

[50] S.I. 1999 No. 359 (amending the Insolvency Rules 1986).

[51] On the problems of cross-checking and enforcement which arose before the introduction of the central register see Hicks, *loc. cit.*

CHAPTER 12

The Legal Effect of Disqualification

INTRODUCTION

12.01 Like disqualification from driving a motor car, disqualification under the CDDA is, in the broadest sense, a form of legal incapacitation. However, the respective scope of the prohibitions under sections 1, 11 and 12 of the CDDA is much less clear than the scope of a driving ban. This chapter explores the legal scope of the prohibitions and their "knock-on" consequences for the disqualified person. It also considers the consequences of a person acting in breach of the prohibitions.

SCOPE OF DISQUALIFICATION

The prohibitions

12.02 The relevant provisions of the CDDA are sections 1, 11 and 12. Section 1(1) estalishes the parameters of a disqualification order imposed by the court under the CDDA. A disqualification order is described in section 1(1) as:

"... an order that [the disqualified person] shall not, without the leave of the court:

(a) be a director of a company, or

(b) be a liquidator or administrator of a company, or

(c) be a receiver or manager of a company's property, or

(d) in any way, whether directly or indirectly, be concerned or take part in the promotion, formation or management of a company

for a specified period beginning with the date of the order."

Section 11(1), which imposes a ban which is closely analogous to that set out in section 1, prohibits an undischarged bankrupt from acting as a director of, or directly or indirectly taking part in or being concerned in the promotion, formation or management of a company, except with the permission of the court.[1] The ban under section 11

---

[1] The CDDA and cases decided before the reform of the civil justice system use the phrases "leave of the court" and "leave to act". In the light of the CPR, the Disqualification Rules and the Disqualification Practice Direction, the term "permission" is used throughout rather than the old term "leave" except in the case of direct quotes from the CDDA.

is automatic and takes effect without the need for a court order.[2] Although, unlike an order under section 1, section 11 itself contains no express ban on occupying various other offices, such as liquidator, section 390(4)(a) of the Insolvency Act 1986 extends the disqualification to acting as an insolvency practitioner with the same practical effect.

12.03   Section 12 of the CDDA lays down a prohibition, without permission of the court, from acting as a director or liquidator of, or directly or indirectly taking part or being concerned in the promotion, formation or management of, a company. That prohibition will come into effect as a result of a court order made under section 429 of the Insolvency Act 1986. If a person fails to make a payment to which he is required to make under an administration order under Part VI of the County Courts Act 1984, the court may revoke the administration order, apply the disqualification in section 12 of the CDDA and apply various other disabilities set out in section 429 of the Insolvency Act 1986 (*e.g.* a restriction on obtaining credit without disclosing the fact that the section applies to him). Although the consequence of the application of section 12 of the CDDA is that the person cannot act as a liquidator, there is no general automatic disqualification from acting as an insolvency practitioner under section 390 of the Insolvency Act 1986, as there is in cases where a disqualification order is made or the person is an undischarged bankrupt.

It is unfortunate that the relevant prohibitions are similar and yet differently worded and defined. The interaction between the relevant bans under the CDDA and that on acting as an insolvency practitioner under section 390 of the Insolvency Act 1986 also differ in a most unfortunate manner. As a matter of general policy it is extremely difficult to see why different prohibitions should apply in each of the three cases in question. This lack of consistency reflects the way in which various provisions, which have come into being at different times and for different reasons, have been pulled together into a single Act of Parliament without a proper consideration of the same as part of one effective code.

12.04   On a first reading of the CDDA, it appears that the bans contemplated by the Act are extremely comprehensive in scope, the aim being to prohibit the disqualified person from having any involvement in the direction and running of companies without the express permission of the court.[3] The immediate consequence for anyone who holds directorships or managerial positions in any company is that he will have to resign from them or obtain permission of the court to remain in such positions. The consequences for insolvency practitioners who hold offices will extend beyond the prohibitions set out in sections 1(b), (c) and 12 of the CDDA by virtue of the disqualifi-

---

[2] A further difference between sections 1(1) and 11(1) is that the latter does not expressly prohibit an undischarged bankrupt from acting as a liquidator, administrator or receiver or manager. Note, however, that an undischarged bankrupt is automatically disqualified from acting as an insolvency practitioner under Insolvency Act 1986, s. 390(4)(a) which means that he cannot act as a liquidator, provisional liquidator, administrator, administrative receiver or supervisor of a corporate voluntary arrangement: section 388(1), *ibid*. It appears that an individual can act as a receiver or manager or a receiver in Scotland without being formally authorised to act as an insolvency practitioner. Again, however, an undischarged bankrupt is prohibited from taking up these positions: sections 31, 51(3), *ibid*. There is no provision for a bankrupt to obtain permission from the court to act as an insolvency practitioner notwithstanding his bankruptcy. On the question of the interaction between section 1 of the CDDA, which envisages that the court can grant permission to act in certain capacities notwithstanding a disqualification order and section 390(4)(b), which might suggest that the effect of a disqualification order is to create an absolute ban upon acting as an insolvency practitioner: see Chap. 13 regarding applications for permission to act notwithstanding disqualification.
[3] The question of whether the court can make partial or selective orders under section 1, *e.g.* an order disqualifying a person from acting as a company director but allowing him to take part in the management of companies is discussed in Chap. 11. Applications for permission to act are considered generally in Chap. 13.

cation on acting as an insolvency practitioner imposed by section 390(4)(b) of the Insolvency Act 1986.

"Company"

12.05 The prohibitions restrict the disqualified person from acting in various capacities in relation to *companies*. The meaning of "company" was considered earlier in Chapter 3. However, the discussion there was confined to the question of jurisdiction to disqualify. In some cases the meaning of "company" is the same whether one is considering the scope of a power to disqualify or the extent of the prohibitions. For example, by virtue of section 22A of the CDDA it is clear that the court's power of disqualification in section 6 could be used in relation to building societies and that the prohibition in section 1 also extends to building societies. However, the position is not always simple and needs to be checked in each case. It is not safe to assume that a disqualified person must be prevented from acting as a director, etc. of a particular type of body simply because the court is able in certain situations to exercise powers of disqualification in relation to that type of body.[4]

Extension to building societies and incorporated friendly societies

12.06 Section 22A(2) of the CDDA provides that the Act applies to building societies as it applies to companies. Thus references in the CDDA to "company" are taken as references to a "building society". Similarly section 22B of the CDDA provides that the Act applies to incorporated friendly societies as it applies to companies and references to "company" shall include references to an incorporated friendly society. As a result of these sections the prohibitions flowing from an order under section 1 of the CDDA or under sections 11 and 12 of the CDDA will apply to such bodies with the result that a disqualified person (or an undischarged bankrupt or a person subject to section 12) cannot, without permission of the court, be a director or officer of a building society (within the meaning of the Building Societies Act 1986), or a member of the committee of management or officer of an incorporated friendly society (within the meaning of the Friendly Societies Act 1992) nor in any way, whether directly or indirectly, be concerned or take part in the promotion, formation or management of such bodies. The position in relation to limited liability partnerships will be the same as for building societies and incorporated friendly societies once the proposed Limited Liability Partnerships Act is enacted.[5]

Section 22 of the CDDA: general definitions

12.07 Section 22 sets out the general definition of "company" in the CDDA. In section 11 the expression "includes an unregistered company and a company incorporated outside Great Britain which has an established place of business in Great Britain". "Elsewhere" it "includes any company which may be wound up under Part V of the Insolvency Act 1986". In addition, section 22(9) provides that "any expression for whose interpretation provision is made by Part XXVI of the Companies Act ... is to be construed in accordance with that provision." The effect of these definitions is considered in more detail below.

[4] The point is particularly pertinent in the context of insolvent partnerships.
[5] It is proposed by regulation to insert a new section 22C into the CDDA having the same effect as sections 22A and B.

Part XXVI of the Companies Act 1985: Companies formed and/or registered under the companies legislation

12.08 By virtue of section 22(9) of the CDDA and section 735 of the Companies Act 1985, the prohibitions in sections 1, 11 and 12 should be read as including relevant prohibitions in relation to companies formed and registered under the Companies Act 1985 or its precursors (other than under the Joint Stock Companies Act 1844 and any companies registered in Ireland under companies legislation up to and including the Companies (Consolidation) Act 1908).[6] Accordingly, the prohibitions are not restricted by reference to companies limited by shares but include guarantee companies and unlimited companies.[7] A number of companies have been registered under the Companies Act 1985 or its precursors (other than the Joint Stock Companies Act 1844) but which were not formed under the Companies Act 1985 or such precursors. However such companies are treated, for the purposes of the Companies Act 1985, as if they were also formed under the Companies Act 1985[8]. The broad effect is that the prohibitions in the CDDA apply in relation to companies registered under the Companies Act 1985 or its precursors on or after July 14, 1856.

Section 11: unregistered companies—British corporations and persons enjoying chartered rights

12.09 By virtue of section 22(2) of the CDDA, the prohibition imposed by section 11 applies in relation to "unregistered companies". By virtue of sections 22(9) of the CDDA and sections 744A and 718 of the Companies Act 1985, unregistered companies include bodies corporate[9] incorporated in and having a principal place of business in Great Britain other than (a) any body incorporated by or registered under any public act of Parliament, (b) any body not formed for the purpose of carrying on a business which has for its object the acquisition of gain by the body or its individual members, (c) any body for the time being exempted by direction of the Secretary of State (or Board of Trade) and (d) any investment company with variable capital within the meaning of the Open-Ended Investment Companies (Investment Companies with Variable Capital) Regulations 1996. Also included within the definition of unregistered companies are any unincorporated body of persons entitled by virtue of letters patent to any of the privileges conferred by the Chartered Companies Act 1837 and not falling within any of the exceptions set out in (a) to (c) above.

Section 11: Non-British corporations with an established place of business in Great Britain

12.10 The prohibition on bankrupts having a relevant involvement in companies is extended by section 22(2)(a) to what are, in effect, overseas companies as defined by

---

[6] The Joint Stock Companies Act 1856; the Joint Stock Companies Acts 1856, 1857; the Joint Stock Banking Companies Act 1857 and the Act to enable Joint Stock Banking Companies to be formed on the principle of limited liability; the Companies Act 1862; the Companies (Consolidation) Act 1908; the Companies Act 1929 and the Companies Acts 1928 to 1983. Companies registered under any of that legislation in what is now Ireland are excluded as are companies formed under the Joint Stock Companies Act 1844.

[7] However, the court may be more minded to grant permission to a person to act in relation to an unlimited company than a limited company: see Chap. 13.

[8] See Part XXII of the Companies Act 1985 especially ss 675–676, 689 and Sched. 21, para. 6.

[9] As defined by section 740 of the Companies Act 1985, a body corporate includes neither a corporation sole nor a Scottish firm.

section 744 of the Companies Act 1985. The question of what constitutes an "established place of business" in this context was considered by Hirst J. in *Cleveland Museum v. Capricorn Art*[10] who drew upon *Palmer's Company Law* (24th ed., 1987) and the earlier decision in *Re Oriel Limited*.[11] In summary, it appears that a company will have an established place of business within Great Britain if it has a specified or identifiable place at which it carries on business. It is not essential that there be some visible sign or physical indication of a connection with particular premises (though the absence of such factors may point against there being an established place of business). It is not necessary that the main activities of the company be carried out at the locality in question and it is sufficient if the activities carried on at the relevant place within Great Britain are restricted to matters incidental to its main business. The term "established" connotes more than the mere setting up of a place of business at a specific location but also a degree of permanence, something intended to have more than a fleeting character. In the words of Oliver L.J. in *Re Oriel Limited*:

> "... If for instance, agents of an overseas company conduct business from time to time by meeting clients or potential clients in the public rooms of an hotel in London, they have, no doubt, "carried on business" in England, but I would for my part find it very difficult to persuade myself that the hotel lounge was "an established place of business". The concept, as it seems to me, is of some more or less permanent location, not necessarily owned or even leased by the company, but at least associated with the company and from which habitually or with some degree of regularity business is conducted."[12]

12.11 It appears from this that a place of business is capable of being sufficiently "permanent" at the moment that it is set up, so that it is not automatically the case that it will only become "established" after a passage of time. Two general points should be made. First, it is unfortunate that the definition of what is a "company" for the purposes of the relevant prohibition in section 11 should differ from that in sections 1 and 12. There seems no real policy reason why this should be so. Secondly, it is unfortunate that the relevant definition raises the possibility that an involvement with a company which has a place of business within the jurisdiction would not be prohibited in cases where the place of business had not become (or was not "intended" to be) sufficiently "permanent" or, put another way, was so "fleeting" as to prevent it becoming "established". In such cases, damage could still be inflicted on the British public by, for example, the conduct of a bankrupt director.

Section 1: a company which may be wound up under Part V of the Insolvency Act 1986

12.12 By virtue of section 22(2)(b) of the Act, a "company" within sections 1 and 12 of the Act includes a company which may be wound up under Part V of the Insolvency Act 1986. The power to wind up companies under Part V of the Insolvency Act 1986 identifies such companies by the expression "unregistered company". This may cause confusion with the term "unregistered company" as defined by section 744 and 718 of the Companies Act 1985. Accordingly, and for present purposes, a company liable to be wound up under Part V of the Insolvency Act 1986 is referred to as a "Part V company". Part V companies are defined by exclusion, rather than inclusion. Thus, the effect of section 220 of the Insolvency Act 1986 is that "any association and

[10] [1990] B.C.L.C. 546.
[11] [1986] 1 W.L.R. 180, CA.
[12] [1986] 1 W.L.R. 180 at 184.

company" may be wound up under Part V with limited exceptions. Those exceptions are (a) a company registered in any part of the United Kingdom under legislation relating to companies in Great Britain[13] and (b) an association or company with a principal place of business situated in Northern Ireland (unless it also has a principal place of business situated in England and Wales and/or Scotland).[14] The main examples of Part V companies are companies formed under private Act of Parliament, foreign companies (considered further below), companies incorporated by private (or "special") Act of Parliament, companies incorporated by royal charter and companies incorporated by order in council. Although the words "any association" are very wide the courts have not so construed them.[15] Moreover, it is suggested that although Part V of the Insolvency Act 1986 is headed "winding up of unregistered companies", the use in section 22(2) of the CDDA of the expression "*a company* which may be wound up" is significant. Section 22(2) of the CDDA neither uses the expression "*any association or* company which may be wound up under Part V..." nor "any *unregistered* company which may be wound up under Part V..." nor "*any body* which may be wound up under Part V...". On this basis it is submitted that the prohibitions in section 1 relate to *companies* which may be wound up under Part V of the Insolvency Act 1986 and not associations or other bodies liable to be wound up under that Part (such as certain types of unincorporated associations which are not partnerships).[16] There is further support for this view in section 229(2) of the Insolvency Act which provides that an "unregistered company" is not, except in the event of its being wound up, deemed to be a company under the Companies Act.

Partnerships

12.13   It seems that the prohibitions in sections 1 and 11 of the CDDA do not extend to partnerships. This was certainly the assumption of Harman J. in *Re Probe Data Systems (No. 3) Limited*[17] and it is an assumption that is widely made on applications for permission to act notwithstanding the making of a disqualification order[18]. The position is considered first in relation to sections 1 and 12 and then in relation to section 11.

**12.14   *Sections 1 and 12 of the CDDA.*   The question is whether or not partnerships are "companies liable to be wound up under Part V of the Insolvency Act 1986"

---

[13] Section 220(1)(b) Insolvency Act 1986. Theoretically this exception would probably include a company registered under the Joint Stock Companies Act 1844 although it is to be doubted whether there are many (if any) such companies left in existence.

[14] Section 221(2) Insolvency Act 1986. See also *Re Normandy Marketing Limited* [1994] Ch. 198, holding that a company incorporated in Northern Ireland can be wound up as un unregistered company under section 220 of the Insolvency Act 1986, provided that it has a principal place of business in England and Wales. The point is of limited importance as the NI Order effectively extends the provisions of the CDDA to Northern Ireland.

[15] See, *e.g. Re St James Club* (1852) 2 De G.M. & G. 383, 42 ER 920; *Re International Tin Council* [1989] Ch. 309 and *Re Witney Town Football and Social Club* [1993] B.C.C. 874.

[16] For example, unincorporated friendly societies registered under the Friendly Societies Act 1974. The same is arguably true of industrial and provident societies which are treated as if they were ordinary registered companies for the purposes of winding up (*i.e.* they are wound up under Pt IV not Pt V of the Insolvency Act). The point is that they are simply not "companies" within the meaning of section 22(2) of the CDDA and so fall outside its scope. The view is strengthened by the fact that Parliament has seen fit to extend the CDDA so that it specifically covers non-corporate entities such as building societies, incorporated friendly societies and limited liability partnerships (see main text above) but not unincorporated friendly societies or industrial and provident societies. For a contrary view in relation to the latter see C. Mills, "Does CDDA Apply to Industrial and Provident Societies?" (1997) 13 *Insolvency Law & Practice* 182.

[17] [1991] B.C.L.C. 586 at 593, [1991] B.C.C. 428 at 434.

[18] See, *e.g. Re Streamhaven Ltd, Secretary of State for Trade and Industry v. Barnett* [1998] 2 B.C.L.C. 64; *Re Amaron Ltd* [1998] B.C.C. 264.

within section 22(2)(b) of the CDDA. Although, under article 7 of the Insolvent Partnerships Order 1994 ("the 1994 Order"), the provisions of Part V of the Insolvency Act 1986 (as modified by the 1994 Order) are applied to insolvent partnerships and the court is thereby enabled to wind up insolvent partnerships, it is submitted that partnerships do not thereby become "companies" liable to be wound up under Part V of the Insolvency Act 1986 on the following reasoning:

(a) Partnerships are not wound up under Part V but under the 1994 Order.

(b) A partnership is not a "company" and section 22(2)((b) refers to "companies" liable to be wound up not "bodies" liable to be wound up (see para. 12.12 above).

(c) The CDDA was enacted on July 25,1986. At that stage partnerships were not capable of being wound up under Part V of the Insolvency Act 1986. (The reference to "any partnership", formerly contained in section 665 of the Companies Act 1985, was removed by Part IV of Schedule 10 to the Insolvency Act 1985). The power to wind up partnerships as if under Part V of the Insolvency Act 1986 was conferred by the predecessor of the 1994 Order, the Insolvent Partnerships Order 1986. That Order was made on 8 December 1986. It was made under powers conferred by sections 420 of the Insolvency Act 1986 and section 21(2) of the CDDA. Neither conferred authority to alter the meaning or width of the prohibitions contained in section 1 of the CDDA. They are also expressly limited to conferring power to extend the provision of the relevant statutes to *insolvent* partnerships.

(d) Article 16 of the 1994 Order extends sections 6 to 10 of the CDDA (amongst other sections) to insolvent partnerships with modifications (in particular to deal with the fact that partnerships do not have "directors"). Its predecessor was to similar effect. The fact that such modification was necessary (not least to deal with the fact that there are no "directors" of a partnership) suggests that "company" in sections 6 to 10 does not itself include a partnership. It would be strange if "company" had a different meaning in section 1 of the CDDA.

(e) Furthermore, sections 1(1)(a), (b) and (c) of the CDDA clearly do not apply to partnerships. A modification akin to that effected by the 1994 Order in relation to sections 6 to 10 would be necessary. It would be anomalous if "company" meant one thing in sections 1(a) to (c) and another thing in section 1(1)(d).

(f) It is arguable on policy grounds that the prohibition should not extend to partnerships. There is a strong indication that the CDDA is directed primarily at those who abuse the privilege of limited liability.[19] Given the difficulty of formulating a consistent policy other than in general terms such as "protection of the public", this argument that the policy of the CDDA is not to disqualify persons from acting in partnership without permission is not especially compelling. On the plain words of the statute, it is clear that a disqualified person cannot be a director or take part in the management of an unlimited company.

The cumulative effect of these arguments is that a person disqualified in the terms of sections 1 and 12 can act in relation to a partnership without permission of the court.

[19] See generally Chap. 2.

12.15 *Section 11 of the CDDA.* There seems to be no reason why the prohibitions lying on undischarged bankrupts should be taken as relating to partnerships. Partnerships are not companies within the meaning of the terms set out in section 22(2)(a) of the CDDA.

Open-ended investment companies

12.16 The Open-Ended Investment Companies (Investment Companies with Variable Capital) Regulations 1996[20] expressly assume that an open-ended investment company would be wound up under Part V of the Insolvency Act. These regulations do not expressly modify sections 1 and 12 of the CDDA to include reference to an open-ended investment company. Nevertheless, it is submitted that a person disqualified under the terms of either section 1 or 12 is disqualified from acting in the prohibited capacities in relation to such an entity. This is because an open-ended investment company appears to be a *"company* which may be wound up under Part V..." for the purposes of section 22(2)(b) of the CDDA.

European Economic Interest Groupings

12.17 The European Economic Interest Grouping Regulations 1989[21] expressly assume that an EEIG can be wound up as an unregistered company under Part V of the Insolvency Act. On such winding up, the effect of regulation 20 is that CDDA, ss 1, 2, 4–11, 12(2), 15–17, 20, 22 and Sched. 1 expressly apply to an EEIG. However, the effect of regulation 20 appears to be circumscribed by the fact that the provisions of the CDDA mentioned only apply *where an EEIG is wound up as an unregistered company under Part V.* In other words, it does not expressly extend sections 1 and 12 *for all purposes.* As such, it is far from clear that a person disqualified either on the basis of his conduct in relation to an ordinary registered company or under section 12 would be disqualified from acting in relation to an EEIG. Having said that, the regulations clearly contemplate that an EEIG registered in Great Britain is a body corporate with its own legal personality.[22] On this basis, it is arguable that an EEIG is a *"company* which may be wound up under Part V..." for the purposes of section 22(2)(b) of the CDDA. As a result, it is suggested that a person disqualified under the terms of section 1 or 12 is disqualified from acting in the prohibited capacities in relation to an EEIG.

The position in relation to section 11 is even more complex. Regulation 20 refers expressly to section 11 and might be read as suggesting that an undischarged bankrupt cannot act in the management of an EEIG. However, the regulation appears only to apply to an *EEIG which is wound up.* The only literal sense that can be made of this is that an undischarged bankrupt is prohibited from acting in relation to an EEIG which is wound up. The question then arises as to whether an EEIG could amount to either an "unregistered company" or "a company incorporated outside Great Britain which has an established place of business in Great Britain" within section 22(2)(a) of the CDDA (see generally paras 12.09–12.11 above). It appears that an EEIG is not an "unregistered company" for the purposes of section 22(9) of the CDDA and sections 774A and 718 of the Companies Act 1985 because EEIGs are brought within the scope of the exceptions in section 718 by virtue of Schedule 4, paragraph 20 of the 1989 Regulations. Moreover, an EEIG registered in Great Britain under the 1989 Regulations is clearly not "a company incorporated outside Great Britain...". However, it does appear that an undischarged bankrupt is prohibited from acting in the management of

---

[20] S.I. 1996 No. 2827.
[21] S.I. 1989 No. 638.
[22] *ibid.*, reg. 3.

an EEIG registered in other member states of the European Union to the extent that local law requires an EEIG to be registered as a body corporate.[23]

Sections 1 and 12: Foreign companies

12.18   Although the position may be regarded as not entirely certain, it is suggested that companies which are incorporated overseas but which provide particulars under Part XXIII of the Companies Act still fall to be wound up under Part V of the Insolvency Act 1986 and that they are not "registered" companies for the purposes of section 117 in Part IV of the Insolvency Act 1986. So far as unregistered overseas or foreign companies are concerned, the court has a fairly wide power to wind up such companies. Foreign companies will be liable to be wound up wherever there is a "sufficiently close connection" with the jurisdiction.[24] Such closeness is capable of being established, for example, where there are assets within the jurisdiction or where the company has carried on business within the jurisdiction.[25]

The test for whether a foreign company "may be wound up under Part V" within the meaning of section 22(2)(b) of the CDDA is thought to require consideration of whether, at the relevant time, there is a sufficient connection between the company and England and Wales such as to justify the court exercising its winding up jurisdiction under Part V. The effect otherwise would be that the prohibitions in sections 1 and 12 would relate to any foreign company, even if it did not in fact have any connection with the jurisdiction, on the ground that at some time in the future such connection might be established. Even so, the prohibitions under section 1 still appear to apply very widely to overseas companies. This is clearly necessary as otherwise disqualification could be avoided by the device of using a foreign company.[26] It may be questioned whether the ability to wind up companies as unregistered companies is a sufficiently certain or satisfactory test for determining the prohibitions in section 1 of the CDDA. As noted above, it is also questionable whether it is sensible for there to be different definitions of "company" applying to sections 1 and 12 as contrasted with section 11 of the CDDA.

DIRECTOR, LIQUIDATOR OR ADMINISTRATOR ETC.

Director

12.19   The prohibitions in sections 1, 11 and 12 of the CDDA each encompass acting as a "director".[27] There is no doubt that the prohibitions encompass acting as a properly and legally appointed director. The need for a separate prohibition distinct from the prohibition on being involved or taking part in management is to protect the public as much from the supine director who fails to involve himself in management

---

[23] Regulation 2137/85 on the EEIG leaves it to member states to determine whether or not groupings registered at their registries have legal personality (see Article 1(3)).

[24] *International Westminster Bank plc v. Okeanos Maritime, Re a Company No. 003.59 of 1987* [1988] 1 Ch. 210, [1987] B.C.L.C. 450, (1987) 3 B.C.C. 160.

[25] *Re Compania Merobello San Nicholas SA* [1973] Ch. 75, [1972] 3 All E.R. 448; *Re Eloc Elektro-Optieck and Comunicatie BV* [1982] Ch. 43, [1981] 2 All E.R. 1111.

[26] In the House of Lords debate which preceded the enactment of what is now section 6 of the CDDA, concern was expressed that: "... Rogues may well use Jersey or other overseas companies to avoid risk of disqualification" and that the sanction of disqualification ought to extend to all companies which trade in the United Kingdom and are therefore likely to be compulsorily wound up there. (See Lord Bruce of Donington, *Hansard*, HL Vol 459, cols 571–572).

[27] In section 1, the disqualified person is banned from *being* a director. In sections 11–12, the ban is on *acting* as a director. It might be argued that there is nothing to stop a person disqualified under sections 11 or 12 being *appointed* as a director provided that he does not *act* as such. The point has very little to commend it in practical terms.

when he ought to have done so as from the active director. A shadow director, namely a person in accordance with whose directions or instructions the directors of a company are accustomed to act,[28] is not encompassed within the term "director" in sections 1, 11 or 12 of the CDDA but a ban on acting in such a capacity is, in practice, applied by the prohibition on being involved or taking part in management. A *de facto* director, that is a person who acts as a director although not duly appointed as such, is also caught by the relevant bans. The concepts of shadow and *de facto* directors are considered in more detail in Chapter 3. For present purposes it suffices to say that under sections 1, 11 and 12 of the CDDA, the prohibition on being a *de facto* director results from one or more of the following matters: section 22(4) of the CDDA; the true construction of "director" (in sections 1, 11 and 12) in the light of the policy of the CDDA[29]; and the prohibition on being concerned or taking part in management.[30]

Liquidator or administrator

12.20 An undischarged bankrupt is absolutely prohibited from acting as a provisional liquidator, liquidator or administrator by virtue of section 390(4)(a) of the Insolvency Act 1986. The relevant prohibition flows from the disqualification of the undischarged bankrupt as an insolvency practitioner and not from the terms of the CDDA. Accordingly, there is no power in the court to grant dispensation from this prohibition in the form of permission to act. Only insolvency practitioners are able to hold the offices of provisional liquidator, liquidator or administrator (sections 230(1), (3) and (4), 388(1) and 389 of the Insolvency Act 1986). The requirement that a liquidator is a qualified insolvency practitioner applies equally whether the company is in insolvent or solvent liquidation.[31]

The position with regard to persons the subject of a disqualification order under section 1 of the CDDA is less clear. This is because section 1 imposes a prohibition which, in effect, overlaps with section 390(4)(b) of the Insolvency Act 1986. The former prohibition expressly restricts the disqualified person from holding the offices of liquidator or administrator but, in terms, says that the court can grant permission to hold such offices. However, section 390(4)(b) disqualifies a person "subject to a disqualification order" from being an insolvency practitioner. Only qualified insolvency practitioners can act as liquidators or administrators (sections 230(1), (3) and (4), 388(1) and 389 of the Insolvency Act 1986). Section 390(4) of the Insolvency Act does not make clear whether the incapacity to act as an insolvency practitioner which flows from the making of a disqualification order under the CDDA is capable of being lifted if the court is otherwise minded to grant the disqualified person permission to act as a liquidator or administrator under section 1 of the CDDA.

12.21 Persons subject to section 12 are expressly prohibited from being liquidators. In the context this would appear to include provisional liquidators. However, such persons are not automatically disqualified from acting as administrators as the

[28] CDDA, s. 22(5).
[29] See the approach of Browne-Wilkinson V.-C. in relation to section 300 of the Companies Act 1985 (the predecessor of CDDA, s. 6) and *de facto* directors in *Re Lo-Line Electric Motors Ltd* [1988] Ch. 477 (at 488D–490F), [1988] 3 W.L.R. 26, [1988] 2 All E.R. 692, [1988] B.C.L.C. 698, (1988) 4 B.C.C. 415.
[30] In Australia the courts consider that the policy of their disqualification legislation does not require the prohibition on being a "director" to be limited to actual or purported appointments: *Commissioner for Corporate Affairs v. Bracht* (1989) 7 A.C.L.C. 40 (at 46), [1989] V.R. 821.
[31] An insolvent liquidation will be either a compulsory or creditors' voluntary liquidation. A solvent liquidation will be a members' voluntary liquidation. See generally, Insolvency Act 1986, Pt IV.

Insolvency Act does not extend the disqualification from acting as an insolvency practitioner to such cases.[32]

Receiver or manager

12.22   Section 11 contains no express prohibition against acting as a receiver or manager. However, by virtue of sections 230(2), 388(1)(a), 389 and 390(4)(a) of the Insolvency Act 1986, an undischarged bankrupt is disqualified automatically from acting as an administrative receiver of a company. There is no power in the court to relax such ban. The prohibition would apparently not prevent a bankrupt acting as a receiver who was not an administrative receiver but a receiver of part only of a company's property or of the company's income from property (*i.e.* a Law of Property Act receiver). However, this point is dealt with by section 31 of the Insolvency Act.

A disqualification order under section 1 expressly places a prohibition on the disqualified person acting as a receiver or manager of a company's property. The phrase, "receiver or manager of the property of a company" is defined in section 29 of the Insolvency Act 1986 in such a way as to include administrative receivers, receivers of part only of a company's property and receivers of income arising from that property. Strictly, this definition only applies to the phrase as it appears in the Companies Act 1985 and the Insolvency Act 1986. Nevertheless, it is suggested that section 1(1)(c) should be read in the same way. It is apparently possible for a person to act as a receiver or manager (as long as he is not an administrative receiver) without being qualified to act as an insolvency practitioner. The combined effect of sections 230, 388 and 389 of the Insolvency Act 1986 is to require a person appointed as a company's *administrative receiver* to be qualified to act as an insolvency practitioner. However, this requirement is not extended to other types of receiver. Thus, a person who is the subject of a disqualification order under the CDDA is doubly-disqualified from acting as an administrative receiver because of the effect of section 390(4) of the Insolvency Act 1986. His disqualification from acting as either a receiver of part or an income receiver takes effect only under the CDDA. As in the case of a liquidator or an administrator (see above), there are doubts about the ability of the court to grant permission to act as an administrative receiver, notwithstanding the making of a disqualification order. Section 12 contains no prohibition on acting as a receiver or manager and does not result in an automatic ban under section 390(4) of the Insolvency Act 1986. There is no express reference in sections 1, 11 or 12 to a supervisor of a corporate voluntary arrangement. Again, however, a person can only act in that capacity if he is qualified to act as an insolvency practitioner. The effect is that undischarged bankrupts and persons the subject of a disqualification order under section 1 are automatically banned while persons disqualified in the terms of section 12 fall outside the scope of the ban in section 390(4).

"DIRECTLY OR INDIRECTLY BE CONCERNED OR TAKE PART IN THE PROMOTION, FORMATION OR MANAGEMENT OF A COMPANY"

12.23   This prohibition applies under each of sections 1, 11 and 12 of the CDDA. In terms of the scope of disqualification, this is the most difficult aspect of the prohibition to pin down. The use of the phrase "directly or indirectly" makes clear that a

---

[32] Section 390(4)(b) applies to a disqualification order made under the CDDA. Strictly the disqualification in section 12 is not a disqualification order under the CDDA but a disqualification under section 429 of the Insolvency Act the scope of which is defined in the CDDA.

disqualified person would be in breach of the prohibition if he appoints a nominee to act in the promotion, formation or management of a company on his behalf. However, "indirect" involvement is not limited to such cases and is potentially quite wide. None of the terms "promotion", "formation" or "management" are statutorily defined and so the scope of the prohibition has a fluid quality. Given the wide variation in possible forms of involvement and the wide range of potential companies and corporate structures that arise, such fluidity is probably inevitable. In the words of Ormiston J. in *Commissioner for Corporate Affairs v. Bracht*, "... [c]ircumstances and procedures may vary widely from company to company".[33] This makes it difficult to do other than give a broad description of the prohibitions and suggests that it would be unwise for Parliament to attempt any more precise definitions. It will depend on all the facts of the case whether a disqualified person has acted in breach of the prohibition. Faced with the question, "do these activities amount to management?", the court will need to take a contextual approach and construe the term "management" in the light of both the overall scheme and purpose of the CDDA and the specific corporate context in which the person was operating.

Hicks has criticised this indeterminacy. He has stressed that disqualification is penal in character and has argued with particular reference to "management", that the terms "promotion", "formation" and "management" should be construed restrictively so that the disqualified person can be in no doubt about what he can and cannot do.[34] The argument that disqualification has at least some penal element cannot seriously be contested.[35] Nevertheless, it can be argued against Hicks that the terms "promotion", "formation" and "management" should be construed broadly to reflect the width of the statutory language, the protective purposes of the CDDA and the fact that it is open to the disqualified person to apply to the court for permission to act if he is any doubt as to whether he would breach the prohibition by engaging in a particular activity.[36] The prevailing judicial view is that the primary purpose of the legislation is protective rather than penal and, as such, the courts have tended to take a broad view when construing the terms of the prohibition. This view is considered elsewhere.[37] Ultimately, the question of whether a person is acting in a prohibited way is an issue of mixed law and fact. Where a person is prosecuted for acting in breach of the prohibition, it will be for the trial judge to direct the jury as to the scope of the prohibition and for the jury then to decide on the evidence whether the person has, in fact, breached the prohibition

Declaratory relief?

12.24   In at least one case following the making of a disqualification order, a party wishing to take up employment with a company has sought permission to act notwithstanding the disqualification under sections 1 and 17 and, in the alternative, a declara-

---

[33] (1989) 7 A.C.L.C. 40 (at 50), [1989] V.R. 821.
[34] A. Hicks, "Taking part in management—the disqualified director's dilemma" [1987] 1 Mal. L.J. lxxiv.
[35] See discussion of the nature and purpose of disqualification (including the "quasi-criminal" view) in Chap. 2.
[36] *Per* Beldam J. dealing with a similar criticism made by counsel in *R. v. Campbell* (1984) 78 Cr.App.R. 95, [1984] B.C.L.C. 83 (at 88E):

> "In the opinion of the court that criticism is amply met ... by the fact that there is provision ... for such a person, in the case of doubt, to apply to the court for [permission] to do that which he seeks to do. If he applies to the court then any question of ambiguity would be resolved because the court would either say that he could or could not do that which he proposed to do."

Note, however, that Beldam J.'s view has received judicial criticism: see *Commissioner for Corporate Affairs v. Bracht* (1989) 7 A.C.L.C. 40 (at 49), [1989] V.R. 821.
[37] See Chap. 2 for a general discussion concerning the scheme and purpose of the CDDA

tion that the activities that he wished to pursue would not involve a breach of the prohibition in section 1(1)(d).[38] The declaratory relief was not pursued but there are serious obstacles in the way of seeking such relief in this context. First, the question of whether certain activities fall within the wide wording of section 1(1)(d) will depend upon all the circumstances of the case and detailed evidence as to those circumstances. It is meaningless to list a number of activities in the abstract. In most cases, to provide an answer by way of declaration, the court would have to investigate in detail the entire factual context and circumstances which would probably necessitate disclosure. Secondly, and as a matter of discretion, it is doubtful that the court should grant declaratory relief. This is because the court could only deal with the facts as found by it at the time it made its investigation. Those facts might change in the future, making the declaration not only academic but misleading.[39]

"In any way, whether directly or indirectly, be concerned or take part in ..."

12.25   The degree of involvement in prohibited activities is very widely expressed in each of sections 1, 11 and 12. There are slight differences in wording in each case. Again, it is difficult as a matter of policy to see why there should be variations in terminology which only result in uncertainty and invite litigation over nuances of language. In contrast to similar legislation applying in the Australian state of Victoria,[40] it is clear, in each case, that the words "directly or indirectly" govern both "take part in" and "be concerned in".

In *Commissioner for Corporate Affairs v. Bracht*,[41] the Supreme Court of Victoria had to consider whether a disqualified person had acted in breach of an equivalent prohibition on being involved in management. Ormiston J. considered that the simple words "take part in" connoted and proscribed the active participation of a disqualified person in the prohibited activity. Such participation would have to be "real". Having referred to English and New Zealand authority,[42] the judge turned to a consideration of the concept of "being concerned in" a particular activity and decided that it connoted participation at a variety of levels and at differing intensities with the effect that it is much wider in scope than the concept of "taking part in". The level of participation could be relatively modest and would not require the participant to have a financial interest in or to derive any material benefit from the relevant activity. In practice, these descriptions of participation have to be construed together with and as part of the prohibited activity to which they relate.

Promotion

12.26   The terms "promotion" and "promoter" have no statutory definition. For guidance as to the meaning of the phrase "promotion of a company" it is necessary to look to the common law, that being the background against which the prohibition is to be construed.[43] A considerable body of case law was generated in the nineteenth and early-twentieth centuries concerning so-called company promoters. The courts developed the law of promoters to tackle a form of fraud on investors which was very popular in that age. Unscrupulous individuals would form companies and sell personal

---

[38] *Re TLL Realisations Ltd*, February 1, 1999, Ch.D., unreported.
[39] See, *e.g. Amstrad Consumer Electronics plc v. British Phonographic Industry Ltd* [1986] F.S.R. 159 and *R. v. Medicines Control Agency ex. parte Pharma Nord (U.K.) Ltd* (1998) 44 B.M.I.R. 41.
[40] Section 227 of the Companies (Victoria) Code, considered in *Commissioner for Corporate Affairs v. Bracht* (1989) 7 A.C.L.C. 40 (at 48–49), [1989] V.R. 821.
[41] *ibid.*
[42] *R. v. Campbell* (1984) 78 Cr.App.R. 95, [1984] B.C.L.C. 83; *R. v. Newth* [1974] N.Z.L.R. 760.
[43] *Palmer's Company Law*, Pt V.

assets, such as land or an existing business, to the companies at a price often well in excess of their market value. The public would then be invited by advertisement or prospectus to invest in shares in these companies and lost money instantly because the value of the shares which they had purchased reflected the real value of the company's assets. Public offers in those days were nothing like as heavily regulated as they are now[44] and so it was left to the judges to devise methods of protecting investors. One method which the courts adopted was to impose fiduciary obligations on company promoters.[45]

12.27 In *Twycross v. Grant*,[46] Cockburn C.J. defined a company promoter as a person "who undertakes to form a company with reference to a given project and to set it going, and who takes the necessary steps to accomplish that purpose".[47] This would encompass any person who incorporates a company (or acquires one "off the shelf" from a company formation agent), raises its initial finance, acquires its initial assets and engages on its behalf in other related activities generally associated with a business "start-up". It is important to note that "promotion" is a very wide concept and can include activities carried out by a person somewhat removed from the group of persons primarily motivated in forming and promoting the company. Thus, an individual who arranges for a person to become a director or who places shares or negotiates arrangements on behalf of the company or even who puts a supplier in touch with persons who may form a company to exploit, purchase or distribute his goods may be a promoter. Cockburn C.J.'s definition suggests that promotion can only encompass activities which are carried out during a company's formation and the early stages of its life. However, it is clear that the term "promoter" extends beyond this and will cover a person who subsequent to the formation of a company, agrees to float off its capital in accordance with the intention of those who came together to form the company.[48] It is tempting to read "promotion" as being even wider still so as to extend to activities which involve the use of a company to raise finance from the investing public *at any stage* of its life. Such a reading is consistent with modern usage of the term "promotion" to denote a marketing or publicity campaign designed to generate sales of a particular product or service. Furthermore, the abuse with which the judges were grappling in the old cases on company promoters was not the formation of the com-

---

[44] Pending the enactment of a new Financial Services and Markets Act, public offers of listed securities are governed by Pt IV of the Financial Services Act 1986 (with much of the responsibility for regulation delegated to the Stock Exchange) and public offers of unlisted securities are governed by the Public Offers of Securities Regulations 1995 (S.I. 1995 No. 1537). The latter regulations came into force on June 19, 1995 coinciding with the launch of the Alternative Investment Market. It is now virtually impossible to incorporate a trading company from scratch and immediately offer shares in the venture to the public. A market listing of the shares will not be granted under the rules of the London Stock Exchange unless the company can demonstrate at least a three-year trading history. This requirement does not apply to the Alternative Investment Market. Nevertheless, directors of companies coming to AIM are required to provide comfort as to the adequacy of the company's working capital and, if the company has been trading for less than two years, an undertaking that they will not dispose of any interests in the company's listed securities for a period of one year from the date of admission to trading. On securities regulation generally see B. Rider, C. Abrams and M. Ashe, *CCH Guide to Financial Services Regulation* (3rd ed., 1997).
[45] See, *e.g. Erlanger v. New Sombrero Phosphate Company* (1878) 3 App. Cas. 1218; *Gluckstein v. Barnes* [1900] A.C. 240.
[46] (1877) 2 C.P.D. 469.
[47] See also *Whaley Bridge Printing Company v. Green* (1880) 5 Q.B.D. 109 at 111:

> "The term promoter is a term not of law, but of business operations familiar to the commercial world by which a company is generally brought into existence. In every case the relief granted must depend on the establishment of such relations between the promoter and the birth, promotion and floating of the company, as render it contrary to good faith that the promoter should derive a secret profit from the promotion. A man who carries about an advertising board in one sense promotes a company, but in order to see whether relief is obtainable by the company what is to be looked at is not a word or name, but the acts and relations of the parties."

[48] *Lagunas Nitrate Co. v. Lagunas Syndicate* [1899] 2 Ch. 392 at 428.

pany *per se,* but the use of the company, through the mechanism of a public offer, as a vehicle for defrauding investors. Such a wider construction would thus reflect the true spirit of the old case law. However, this does not seem consistent with the authorities against the background of which the CDDA was enacted. Moreover, such an interpretation is probably not necessary as most of the acts that might be capable of falling within the prohibition on involvement in promotion would be likely to be caught by the prohibition on being involved in management. A person subject to the relevant prohibitions under the CDDA puts himself at risk if he takes up employment with, for instance, a firm of stockbrokers which regularly sponsors public offers or a merchant bank in which he is expected to arrange underwriting or provide advice to corporate clients who are seeking to launch a public offer. The same may be true of a disqualified person who acts as a financial adviser and prepares business plans for new companies which he then "touts" to lenders or other financiers with a view to raising capital for his clients.[49] At common law a person who simply discharges professional duties in connection with a public offer, for example, by drafting a prospectus or preparing a profit forecast on the basis of information supplied by the client, is not regarded as a promoter.[50] However, there is a real risk that such a person might be treated as "directly or indirectly" being concerned or taking part in the promotion of a company. It is important to keep in mind that the prohibition in the CDDA is not a prohibition on being a promoter but a prohibition on being involved or taking part in promotion.

Formation

12.28   "Formation" is arguably narrower than "promotion" and appears to refer only to the process of incorporation encompassing the preparation and filing of the documents required by Part I of the Companies Act 1985 and the issue of a certificate of incorporation by the Registrar of Companies. It is arguable that "formation" should bear an extended meaning and also encompass other legal requirements with which a company must comply before it can commence trading (*e.g.* the requirement to obtain a certificate under section 117 of the Companies Act 1985 before a newly-incorporated public company can commence trading). It is clear that a disqualified person is not allowed to carry on in business as a company formation agent without the court's permission.

Management

12.29   "Management" of companies is a key concept within the CDDA generally. It is an activity involvement in which is prohibited by each of sections 1, 11 and 12 of the CDDA. In addition, under section 2 of the CDDA, a person may be disqualified following his conviction for an indictable offence in connection with, among other things, the "management ... of a company". Moreover, under sections 6 and 8, the court is required to consider whether or not specific defined misconduct is such as to make the person "unfit to be concerned in ... management...".

As suggested earlier, the fluidity of the concept of "management" is such that the court will have to take a contextual approach and construe it in the light of both the

---

[49] Some, if not all of the activities mentioned may amount to "investment business" and be caught by financial services legislation in which case the person would, in any event, need to obtain authorisation from the Financial Services Authority: see Rider et al, *op. cit.* A person who is disqualified under the CDDA would not automatically have any existing authorisation revoked but it may be withdrawn or suspended if the relevant regulator considers that he is no longer a fit and proper person to carry on investment business. Equally, if a disqualified person applies for an authorisation it is open to the relevant regulator to refuse the application if it does not consider the applicant to be fit and proper.
[50] *Re Great Wheal Polgooth Company* (1883) 53 L.J. Ch. 42.

overall purpose of the CDDA and the specific corporate context in which the disqualified person was operating. The court must therefore form a view of the purpose or
purposes of the legislation. This will determine whether it adopts a broad or restrictive
approach when construing the term "management".[51] At the same time, the court will
need to take into account factors such as the size of the company and its organisational
and decision-making structure in determining whether or not the disqualified person
has directly or indirectly been concerned or taken part in the management of *that particular company*. If the disqualified person takes on sole responsibility for the running
of a small private family company, it should not be difficult to prove that he has
breached the prohibition. Indeed, it may be possible to argue that he was acting as a *de
facto* director as well as being concerned in the management of such a company.[52] In
other cases, it may be difficult to distinguish between those who are merely subordinates or employees within a particular company and those who are concerned or taking part in management.[53] The larger and more complex the organisation in question,
the more difficult it becomes to determine whether or not a given person is discharging
a "management" function.

   12.30   As yet, only limited assistance can be derived from ordinary principles of
company law on this issue. The main tendency in general company law and company
law theory has been towards a crude, hierarchical view of the company in which the
board of directors is portrayed as the principal *locus* of managerial power. This reflects
a basic concern within company law to offer an account of the internal constitution of
a limited company and of the roles played by its principal participants, namely the
directors and shareholders, and some explanation of how those participants interre-
late.[54] The doctrine of identification (also known as *alter ego* theory), which has been
used as a means of determining whether a company can be criminally liable for
offences with a *mens rea* element, has tended to reinforce the view of the company as a
narrow hierarchy. To determine whether a company can be directly criminally liable
for a *mens rea* offence under this doctrine, a two-stage approach is followed. First,
there must be an individual within the company who has committed the *actus reus*
while possessing the requisite *mens rea*. Secondly, according to the cases, this individual must be sufficiently high up within the corporate structure so as to form part of the
company's "directing mind and will". Only then does it become possible for the company to be identified with the individual so that his actions and state of mind can be

---

[51] See general discussion in Chap. 2.
[52] See discussion on *de facto* directors in Chap. 3 and para. 12.19 above. For an example of a case which
illustrates the point that it is relatively easy to prove breach of the prohibition in the context of a small private
company see *Drew v. HM Advocate* 1996 S.L.T. 1062. In that case, an undischarged bankrupt bought a
company off the shelf and used it to obtain goods and services on credit without any intention of paying for
them. His appeal against conviction on the ground that he was merely an employee of the company was flatly
rejected by the Scottish High Court of Justiciary.
[53] See, *e.g. Re Clasper Group Services Ltd* (1988) 4 B.C.C. 673, a decision on the scope of the similar wording in Insolvency Act 1986, s. 212(1)(c). As noted earlier, Hicks, *op. cit.* is critical of this indeterminacy.
While Parliament did not attempt a comprehensive definition, it was suggested in the Cork Report (Report
of the Review Committee, *Insolvency Law and Practice*, Cmnd. 8558 (1982), para. 1811) that the phrase
"being concerned in management" would only embrace "... those responsible for the general management
and policy of the company...".
[54] See, *e.g.* division of powers cases like *Automatic Self-Cleansing Syndicate Co. v. Cuninghame* [1906] 2
Ch. 34, CA and *John Shaw & Sons (Salford) Ltd v. Shaw* [1935] 2 K.B. 113, CA and also Table A, article 70:
Companies (Tables A to F) Regulations 1985 (S.I. 1985 No. 805). A particular concern of theorists, which
has arguably helped to foster this view of the company, is the separation of ownership and control observ-
able in public companies on which see, A.A. Berle and G.C. Means, *The Modern Corporation and Private
Property* (1932). A key aspect of the "corporate governance" project which continues to generate a vast
literature is the attempt , on one hand, to explain the development of corporate managerial power in public
companies and, on the other, to suggest means by which this power can be constrained or legitimised: see,
e.g. M. Stokes, "Company Law and Legal Theory" in *Legal Theory and Common Law* (W. Twining ed.
1986).

said to be those of the company. While the doctrine of identification is now the subject of considerable criticism from a number of quarters, its influence has been pervasive and the concept of the "directing mind" has tended to encourage a view which equates "the management" with the board of directors.[55] This one-dimensional view fails to reflect the organisational and structural diversity of modern companies and of large companies in particular. To develop the same point, it also fails to reflect the fact that in a complex, multi-layered corporate organisation, true managerial power may be wielded as much by senior employees as by the board of directors.[56] However, this tension between the prevailing judicial view of corporate structures and commercial reality has only surfaced rarely in the context of disqualification. This may be because the courts are encouraged by the protective rationale of the CDDA to take a "broad brush" approach and are not subject to the usual strictures which apply when questions of criminal culpability fall to be determined.

Disqualification cases on the meaning of "management"?

12.31 The two leading disqualification cases which explore the boundaries of the prohibition are *R. v. Campbell*[57] and the important Australian case, *Commissioner for Corporate Affairs v. Bracht*.[58] The main issue before the appellate court in both cases was whether a person had breached the prohibition on being concerned or taking part in the management of a company while disqualified and thereby committed an offence.

---

[55] The leading case which supports the doctrine is *Tesco Supermarkets Ltd v. Nattrass* [1972] A.C. 153. For recent academic criticism of the doctrine see C. Wells, *Corporations and Criminal Responsibility* (1993); C.M.V. Clarkson, "Kicking Corporate Bodies and Damning Their Souls" (1996) 59 M.L.R. 557 and G.R. Sullivan, "The Attribution of Culpability to Limited Companies" [1996] C.L.J. 515. The thrust of much of this criticism is that the scope of corporate criminal liability under the doctrine is very limited because of the requirement to find a culpable individual within the company's high-ranking officials. For recent judicial criticism see *Meridian Global Funds Management Asia Ltd v. Securities Commission* [1995] 2 A.C. 500, [1995] 2 B.C.L.C. 116, P.C. and see also the views of the Law Commission expressed in its report *Involuntary Manslaughter*, Law Com. No. 237 (1996). The critics (like the doctrine they criticise) are concerned primarily with questions of *corporate* as opposed to individual responsibility. By contrast, the disqualification legislation is concerned more with questions of *individual* responsibility for corporate failure or for wrongdoing in a corporate context. Nevertheless, the discussion is instructive because it illustrates the narrow way in which the courts have tended to view corporate structures.

[56] From the evidence it received, the Bullock Committee identified "at least nine different company structures: from the small company with a board of executive managers closely involved in every aspect of a company's affairs, to the decentralised group with a holding company board appointing senior managers and allocating resources, but leaving operating policy to its subsidiary boards.": Report of the Committee of Enquiry on Industrial Democracy, Cmnd. 6706 (1977), para. 20, p. 65. Another objection advanced by commentators who argue that corporate culpability should be free standing and not predicated on the culpability of individuals within a company is that, in reality, decision-making in large companies is often the product of *corporate* policies and procedures not of individual decisions: see Clarkson, *op. cit.* p. 561 referring to the collapse of the P & O trial which followed the capsize of the *Herald of Free Enterprise*. Wells, *op. cit.*, Chap. 7, develops this point with reference to organisation theory. She identifies two basic organisational models which she labels "organisational process" and "bureaucratic politics". Both models differ radically from the legal view of the company as a narrow hierarchy and both cast doubt on the view that corporate decisions can necessarily be seen as deriving from a specific, fully responsible individual within the company. These ideas have implications not only in relation to corporate criminality. They provide a fresh perspective from which to analyse whether or not an individual can be said to have been involved in "management" and illustrate the contextual nature of that enquiry. They also illustrate how difficult it can be to identify a single individual within a large company who is possessed in full of the relevant culpability. Conversely, this has implications for any attempt, in the context of disqualification, to apportion responsibility for corporate failure among individual members of the board. The disqualification legislation is concerned primarily with issues of individual responsibility. The CDDA has no concept of *collective* unfitness, only *individual* unfitness. Thus, in a large company, it may be difficult to pinpoint a specific culprit for what is, in form, a *collective* failure. This is precisely the difficulty which led to the collapse of the P & O trial referred to above. However, as the judgments in the *Barings* disqualifications illustrate, the courts do not appear to be having too many difficulties in apportioning collective responsibility under the CDDA: see discussion in Chaps 4 and 5.

[57] (1984) 78 Cr.App.R. 95, [1984] B.C.L.C. 83.

[58] (1989) 7 A.C.L.C. 40, [1989] V.R. 821.

The appellant in *Campbell* was the subject of a five-year disqualification order. The Crown's case was that he had acted in breach of the prohibition over a five-month period by giving advice and practical support to a company which was in financial difficulties. It emerged from the evidence that he had taken part in a number of activities. His brief had been to make proposals with a view to turning the company's fortunes around and in so doing he had engaged in the following activities:

(1) Advising the chairman extensively with regard to the overall structure and financing of the company.

(2) Taking part in negotiations leading to the resignation of one of the directors.

(3) Placing advertisements for the sale of part of the company's business and dealing with all responses to the advertisements.

(4) Negotiating directly with the company's bankers, the Inland Revenue and other unpaid creditors.

(5) Conducting meetings with the company's employees.

(6) Taking steps to raise additional finance for the company.

12.32   The appellant's case was that he had acted as an independent management consultant and could not be said to have been concerned or have taken part in management because he had never controlled the company's decision-making process. The Court of Appeal upheld his conviction and in so doing endorsed a crude distinction drawn by the trial judge between the management of certain *specific aspects* of a company's activities (such as production, sales and trading) and the *central management* of a company, said to comprise the matters normally undertaken by its directors or officers. The trial judge had then directed the jury to look at the overall picture and say in the light of that whether the appellant had taken part in management and not simply to consider the isolated tasks which he had undertaken. What is not absolutely clear from the report of the Court of Appeal's decision is how the distinction between "specific aspects of a company's activities" and "central management" is to be applied to answer the basic question, "is this 'management' or not?". One view of *Campbell* might be that the distinction simply illustrates the variety of activities which are capable of being classified as "management" in which case the Court of Appeal was not confining the scope of "management" to the central direction of a company's affairs.[59] An alternative view might be that in endorsing the distinction drawn by the trial judge, the Court of Appeal was saying that the management of isolated aspects of a company's business is *not* of itself "management" for the purposes of the CDDA and thus the scope of the term *is* confined to the central management and direction of the company, a view consistent with the narrow hierarchical model of the company discussed above.[60] *Campbell* is usually regarded as authority for a wide, flexible construction of the term "management". Much, in particular, is made of the following passage from Beldam J.'s judgment:

"... [T]he wording is so widely cast that it is the opinion of this court that it is intended to insulate persons, against whom an order of disqualification has been made, from taking part in the management of company affairs generally. It is cast in the widest of terms... It would be difficult to imagine a more comprehensive phraseology designed to make it impossible for persons to be part of the management and central direction of company affairs."[61]

---

[59] Hicks, *op. cit.*
[60] The view of *Campbell* expressed by Ormiston J. in *Commissioner for Corporate Affairs v. Bracht*.
[61] [1984] B.C.L.C. 83 at 88.

12.33   However, this is merely a comment on the width of the prefix "whether directly or indirectly be concerned or take part in..." and there is nothing in it to suggest that the term "management" embraces activities undertaken by individuals who are neither directors nor officers.[62] In any event, a case can be made on the evidence for saying that Campbell had been "directly or indirectly" involved in *central management* and at a stretch, it is even arguable that he may have acted either as a *de facto* or shadow director.[63] Not only had he advised the chairman closely on the steps that the company needed to take to escape its financial difficulties, he also appears to have played some significant part in implementing his own recommendations. The appellant's contention that he had merely acted as a consultant was always under strain. However, it is misleadingly simplistic to regard *Campbell* as strong authority for a wide, flexible construction of "management" because the Court of Appeal did not conclusively determine whether the term can ever encompass activities which fall outside the scope of "central management".

12.34   In *Bracht*,[64] the Commissioner of Corporate Affairs laid an information against the defendant alleging that over a two-year period he had been concerned in or had taken part in the management of a company while bankrupt in contravention of the State of Victoria's equivalent of CDDA, s. 11. The information was dismissed by a magistrate and the matter came before the Supreme Court of Victoria on the Commissioner's application for review of the magistrate's decision. The company concerned was a small family company of which the defendant's parents-in-law were the only directors. It appears from the evidence that Bracht had negotiated credit facilities backed by bank guarantees on the company's behalf and had handled a rent review relating to the company's leasehold factory premises. The magistrate found that the final say in all financial decisions rested with one of the directors who had retained effective control of the company's affairs throughout. Based on this finding, she was not satisfied beyond reasonable doubt that Bracht had undertaken a managerial function or held a managerial position within the company. The principal ground of review put forward by the Commissioner was that the magistrate had been wrong to hold that the final say of the director in relation to all decisions affecting the company precluded her from finding that Bracht had been concerned in management. The Supreme Court of Victoria ruled that the magistrate had misdirected herself as to the meaning of the provision, set aside the order dismissing the information and remitted the case to the magistrates for rehearing. In a lucid reserved judgment, Ormiston J. held that the term "management" embraces activities which involve policy and decision-making relating to a company's business affairs and which affect the whole or a substantial part of the company to the extent that the consequences of the formation of those policies or the making of those decisions may have some significant bearing on the financial standing of the company or the conduct of its affairs. On this view, if a person is in a position of authority which enables him to influence the affairs of a company and to implement policies or decisions which have a wide-ranging effect on the company, then he occupies a position of management whatever his official job title and whether or not he

---

[62] It is interesting to reflect on the fact that section 2 of the CDDA contemplates the possibility that individuals below board level might be involved in management. It empowers the court to disqualify *any person* convicted of an indictable offence in connection with the management of a company. This suggests that "management" is not an activity which is reserved to directors and officers alone. On section 2 generally, see Chap. 9.

[63] See Chap. 3 for a full discussion of these terms. The decision in *Campbell* can certainly be justified if it is accepted that the primary purpose of the legislation is to protect the public, especially given that the appellant was extensively involved in negotiating on the company's behalf with existing and potential creditors. It is the case's value as a workable precedent which is questioned.

[64] (1989) 7 A.C.L.C. 40, [1989] V.R. 821.

serves on the board of directors.[65] There must be an element of decision-making which affects the company as a whole, but those responsible need not form part of the board. Thus, in a closely controlled company, it is possible that a disqualified person who owns a majority of the shares could use his voting power in such a way as to breach the management prohibition even where he has not taken up a position on the board.[66] Equally, a person may be engaged in "management" where powers and functions are delegated to him which are likely, if exercised, to have a significant effect on the business and financial standing of the company. The *Bracht* test is wider and more commercially realistic than that in *Campbell* and should arguably be adopted by the courts in this jurisdiction. The width of the test reflects both Ormiston J.'s view that disqualification legislation is primarily protective and the fact that significant responsibilities can be delegated widely within large companies with the result that managerial power in those companies is often diffuse.[67] As to the *degree* of participation prohibited by the provision, Ormiston J. construed the phrase "being concerned in" as meaning that the involvement must be more than passing and must involve some measure of responsibility.[68] Overall, the judge was satisfied that a disqualified person may breach the prohibition even though ultimate responsibility for his decisions lies elsewhere.[69] This may be so in a small company or a large company, though Ormiston J. was careful to emphasise that circumstances and procedures from company to company may vary widely.

12.35   The main significance of *Bracht* when compared with *Campbell* lies in the court's decisive conclusion that "management" extends beyond "central management" and its implicit rejection of the entrenched hierarchical view of corporate

---

[65] As Ormiston J. put it at (1989) 7 A.C.L.C. 40, 46–47, [1989] V.R. 821, 828–829:

"There seems little doubt that the concern of the legislatures has been with the exercise of managerial control, not confined to the level of the board of directors but extending to all who perform management functions... Whilst it is easy to exclude from the concept of management those activities of a corporation which consist in the carrying out of day to day routine functions in accordance with predetermined policies, whether they be clerical or involve the ordering or supplying of goods or services on its behalf, it is harder to fix on those elements which are critical to management. It cannot be confined to those matters performed by the board of directors or a managing director, for those are already the subject of the prohibition against acting as a director."

[66] *Re Magna Alloys & Research Pty Ltd* (1975) 1 A.C.L.R. 203, 207.
[67] *Per* Ormiston J. at (1989) 7 A.C.L.C. 40, 48, [1989] V.R. 821, 830–831.

"... [T]here are those involved in large, discrete parts of a corporation's business, who, although not participating in the central administration of that corporation, nevertheless are involved in its management to the extent that their policies and decisions have a significant bearing on its business and its overall financial health. One has only to look at the published annual reports of public companies to realise that the results of one or more 'divisions' of a company can affect in large measure its general performance...".

Ormiston J. thus implicitly rejects a crude hierarchical view of corporate structure. The judge did betray some signs of discomfort over the notion that the purpose of the legislation is primarily protective. Note his criticism of the Court of Appeal's observation in *Campbell* to the effect that it is always open to a disqualified person to apply for permission: (1989) 7 A.C.L.C. 40, 49, [1989] V.R. 821, 832.
[68] See para. 12.25.
[69] Endorsing a similar view expressed *ex tempore* by Quilliam J. in *R. v. Newth* [1974] 2 N.Z.L.R. 760, a New Zealand authority. *Newth* was also a case in which a bankrupt was prosecuted on the ground that he had taken part or been concerned in management. Quilliam J. held that it is sufficient to show that the disqualifed person took a hand in the real business of the company and it is irrelevant whether any action he took was given the approval of someone else or not. There is scope here for circular arguments based on policy. As the decisions in *Bracht* and *Newth* bear out, the view that disqualification legislation is primarily protective may lead to the conclusion that a disqualified person should not be in a position to take decisions which could significantly influence the overall standing of the company. However, if the disqualified person is genuinely subject to close supervision by some other person and cannot be said to have a high degree of decision-making independence, it is arguable that the public are sufficiently protected. Both *Bracht* and *Newth* receive further support from *Cullen v. Corporate Affairs Commission* (1989) 7 A.C.L.C. 121, (1989) 14 A.C.L.R. 789, a decision of the Supreme Court of New South Wales.

structures. Ormiston J.'s open-ended formulation, which emphasises the protective aspect of the prohibition, has the potential to produce some interesting and perhaps ironic results. If the argument that the purpose of disqualification is primarily protective is accepted, then there should be no objection to a disqualified person holding a position in management where his activities are subject to close supervision by some other person or persons (such as the board of directors or a director nominated specifically for the task or an individual who reports regularly to the board).[70] This kind of purposive flexibility would go some way towards meeting the arguments of critics, like Hicks, who prefer an approach which is more restrictive than that in *Bracht*. Even so, the best advice for a disqualified person in a comparable position remains for him to apply for permission so that the court can formally approve any supervisory arrangements.

Non-disqualification cases on the meaning of "management"

12.36 It is not only in the context of disqualification legislation that the courts have been slow to put forward comprehensive definitions of the terms "manager" and "management". While there is some guidance (especially as to the scope of "manager") to be found in non-disqualification cases, these authorities should be handled cautiously. Relevant terms have to be construed against their statutory background. In relation to disqualification itself, it can be argued with reference to the general objectives and scheme of the CDDA that a wide reading of these terms is justifiable because the disqualified person is afforded the opportunity to apply for permission to act. The views advanced in the cases discussed below turn ultimately on the nature and purpose of the legislative provisions under immediate consideration and it is important to keep in mind that the overall context may differ considerably from disqualification.

12.37 On balance, the courts have tended to adopt a restrictive view in non-disqualification cases. In *Registrar of Restrictive Trading Agreements v. W H Smith & Son Ltd*[71] the Court of Appeal held that the local branch managers of two large companies which both operated a nationwide business were not managers of the companies for the purposes of section 15 of the (now repealed) Restrictive Trade Practices Act 1956. Consequently, the court had no jurisdiction to summon them for formal examination by the Registrar who was seeking to ascertain whether they had entered into an illegal price-fixing arrangement. Lord Denning M.R. followed *Gibson v. Barton*,[72] a case decided under nineteenth century companies' legislation, and defined "manager" as a person, "who is managing in a governing role the affairs of the company itself".[73] A similar conclusion was reached in two criminal appeal cases, *R. v. Boal*[74] and *Woodhouse v. Walsall Metropolitan Borough Council.*[75] In both cases the main issue was the extent to which a director, manager, secretary or other company officer can be held

---

[70] See Hicks, *op. cit.*, referring to Woon, "Disqualification for Unfitness under Section 149 of the Companies Act" (1985) 27 Mal. L.R. 149, 156. Reflecting this view, the courts in the United Kingdom have been prepared to give disqualified persons permission to act subject to the implementation of some form of supervisory regime by the companies concerned: see, *e.g. Re Majestic Recording Studios Ltd*, [1989] B.C.L.C. 1, (1988) 4 B.C.C. 519 (permission granted subject to the appointment of an independent chartered accountant approved by the court to act as co-director alongside the disqualified person); *Re Chartmore Ltd* [1990] B.C.L.C. 673 (permission granted subject to a requirement that the company convene a monthly board meeting with a representative from its auditors in attendance); *Re Gibson Davies & Co. Ltd* [1995] B.C.C. 11 (permission granted subject to implementation of a detailed regime of specific safeguards). For a relevant case on this point from Australia see *Re Magna Alloys & Research Pty Ltd* (1975) 1 A.C.L.R. 203. On permission to act generally, see further discussion in Chap. 13.
[71] [1969] 1 W.L.R. 1460, [1969] 3 All E.R. 1065.
[72] (1875) L.R. 10 Q.B. 329.
[73] [1969] 1 W.L.R. 1460, 1468A.
[74] [1992] 1 Q.B. 591.
[75] [1994] Env. L.R. 30.

co-extensively liable for corporate regulatory offences. In *Boal,* the appellant was employed by a company as assistant general manager of its bookshop. On a day when he had been left in charge of the shop to cover the general manager's absence on holiday, local fire inspectors carried out an inspection of the company's premises and found a number of serious breaches of the fire certificate. Both the appellant and the company were indicted on charges under the Fire Precautions Act 1971. At trial, the appellant pleaded guilty having been advised that he was clearly a manager within the meaning of the relevant provision. He received a suspended prison sentence but his conviction was quashed on appeal. The Court of Appeal applied *Gibson v. Barton* and *Registrar of Restrictive Trading Agreements v. W H Smith & Son Ltd* to reach the conclusion that the appellant had not been engaged in managing the whole affairs of the company. As Simon Brown J. put it in his leading judgment:

> "The intended scope of [the provision] is, we accept, to fix with criminal liability only those who are in a position of real authority, the decision-makers within the company who have both the power and responsibility to decide corporate policy and strategy."[76]

12.38 An identical approach was taken by the Divisional Court in *Woodhouse v. Walsall Metropolitan Borough Council* in quashing the appellant's conviction for an offence under the Control of Pollution Act 1974. The appellant was described as the general manager of a company's waste disposal site. He reported to the director with responsibility for special waste who, in turn, made a monthly report concerning the site to the company's board. On the evidence, the appellant was in a position to issue instructions concerning the running of the site to a site manager and two supervisors. He also had the authority to expend company money subject to clearance from the director with responsibility for special waste. However, he had no authority to hire employees and the site manager apparently had a right to query the appellant's decisions on commercial or legal matters arising from the running of the site. Applying Simon Brown J.'s test from *Boal,* the Divisional Court concluded that the appellant was not in a "position of real authority" in the sense of being a decision-maker within the company possessing the power and responsibility to decide corporate policy and strategy.[77] The restrictive approach in these cases can be explained by the fact that they were either criminal cases or cases from which criminal proceedings could have flowed. It is clear from the extract from Lord Denning's judgment in *Registrar of Restrictive Trading Agreements v. W H Smith & Son Ltd* which follows that his objection to a broad construction of the term "manager" stemmed from the criminal law implications of the provision under consideration:

> "It is not right in this section to give the word 'manager' . . . an extended meaning. It is contrary to the spirit of our law. The law of England abhors inquisitorial powers. It does not like to compel a man to testify against himself. It never wants him to incriminate himself or to be faced with interrogation against his will. It prefers the case to be proved against him rather than that he should be condemned out of his own mouth. When Parliament thinks it right to give the power to administer questions, it should do so in clear terms, specifying who is the person to be made guilty of a criminal offence."[78]

---

[76] [1992] 1 Q.B. 591, 597H–598A.
[77] In the Scottish case of *Armour v. Skeen* [1976] I.R.L.R. 310, 1997 S.L.T. 71, the appellant's conviction under Health and Safety Act 1974, s. 37, a similar provision to those under consideration in *Boal* and *Woodhouse,* was upheld. The difference there was that the court found as a fact that the appellant was the person within the organisation responsible for actually formulating its health and safety policy.
[78] [1969] 1 W.L.R. 1460, 1467E.

12.39   The Federal Court of Australia took a similarly narrow view when construing the insolvent trading provisions of the New South Wales Companies Code in *Holpitt Pty Ltd v. Swaab*.[79] The relevant provision imposed both criminal and civil liability for a company's insolvent trading on, "any person who was a director of the company, or took part in the management of the company...". The court held that it would be inappropriate to give the phrase "took part in ... management" a loose meaning and thus create a vague, pervasive criminal liability. Applying the *noscitur a sociis* rule of construction,[80] the judge ruled that the use of the word "director" suggested that those embraced by the provision were restricted to people whose management role could be likened to that of a director. On this view, if the board delegates some part of its functions and gives the delegate full discretion to act independently of its instructions, then he can be said to be taking part in management. However, the same conclusion will not necessarily follow just because a subordinate is given *some measure* of discretion in carrying out a delegated task (as was the case in *Boal* and *Woodhouse*).[81]

12.40   *Re A Company (No. 00996 of 1979)*[82] is a non-disqualification case in which the court favoured a broader view. The case concerned an application by the Director of Public Prosecutions for an order under section 441 of the Companies Act 1948 (subsequently re-enacted as section 721 of the Companies Act 1985) authorising an inspection of a company's books and records. The court was empowered by that section to order an inspection if the DPP demonstrated that there was reasonable cause to believe that a person had, "while an officer of a company, committed an offence in connection with the management of the company's affairs" and that evidence of its commission was to be found in the company's books and records. The application came about because there was reason to believe that a departmental manager had been issuing fraudulent statements to customers demanding greater sums from them than the company was actually owed. Reversing the decision at first instance and ordering the inspection, the Court of Appeal held that the phrase "officer of a company" (which by section 455 included "a director, manager or secretary")[83] should not be narrowly construed and included anyone who exercises some form of supervisory control which reflects the company's general policies or is related to its general adminstration.[84] This was in keeping with the overall object of the provision which was to enable the state to investigate criminal activities that might otherwise remain hidden behind the corporate veil. The Court of Appeal also rejected Vinelott J.'s view at first instance that "an offence in connection with the management of the company's affairs" was limited to offences within the framework of companies legislation which involve some internal misconduct by an officer of which the company itself is a victim.[85]

---

[79] (1992) 6 A.C.S.R. 488.
[80] A rule of language which holds that words "derive colour from those which surround them" (as Stamp J. put it in *Bourne v. Norwich Crematorium Ltd* [1967] 1 W.L.R. 691).
[81] A view deriving from *dicta* of Lord Reid in *Tesco Supermarkets Ltd v. Nattrass* [1972] A.C. 153, 171.
[82] [1980] 1 Ch. 138.
[83] "Officer" is defined identically in Companies Act 1985, s. 744. For a discussion of the term stressing, as we do here, a contextual approach to its construction see A. Hofler, "Elephants and Officers: Problems of Definition" (1996) 17 *The Company Lawyer* 258.
[84] See, in particular, the judgment of Shaw L.J. at [1980] 1 Ch. 138, 144.
[85] The Court of Appeal's approach here is echoed in disqualification cases decided under section 2 of the CDDA which favour a broad view of the words, "an ... offence ... in connection with the ... management ... of a company..." in section 2(1): see *R. v. Corbin* (1984) 6 Cr.App.R. (S.) 17, [1984] Crim. L.R. 303, CA; *R. v. Austen* (1985) 7 Cr.App.R. (S.) 214, (1985) 1 B.C.C. 99,528, CA; *R. v. Georgiou* (1988) 87 Cr.App.R. 207, (1988) 10 Cr.App.R. (S.) 137, [1988] Crim. L.R. 472, (1988) 4 B.C.C. 322, CA and *R. v. Goodman* [1993] 2 All E.R. 789, (1993) 97 Cr.App.R. 210, (1993) 14 Cr.App.R. (S.) 147, [1994] 1 B.C.L.C. 349, [1992] B.C.C. 625, CA all of which are discussed in Chap. 9.

Summary

12.41   The case of *Commissioner for Corporate Affairs v. Bracht* suggests that a broader view than that put forward in cases such as *Boal* is likely to be favoured in the disqualification context. A broad approach to construction is justifiable for the following reasons:

(1)   If the paramount consideration under the CDDA is protection of the public, a narrow view in which those said to be engaged in management are closely identified with the board of directors is inappropriate. Furthermore, such a narrow view fails to reflect the fact that in many companies true control may vest in the senior management rather than the board of directors.

(2)   Taken as a whole, the CDDA reflects a general concern that the public should be protected from those whose past conduct raises doubts about whether they should be allowed to act in the *management* of companies. If the only concern of the CDDA was to prevent undesirable individuals from serving as company directors then there would be no need for the further prohibitions in section 1(1)(b)–(d). To put it another way, the fact that Parliament has seen fit to add a prohibition preventing disqualified persons from being concerned in the management of companies generally, reflects a wider attempt to exclude those people from being involved in running companies whether as directors or otherwise. Furthermore, in exercising a number of the CDDA powers, the court is not required to focus exclusively on the defendant's conduct *as a director*. This is particularly true of section 2 and, again, reflects the wider concerns of the legislation.

(3)   Disqualification is not an absolute prohibition in two senses. First, it is open to the disqualified person to apply for permission to act. Secondly, the person is disqualified from acting in various capacities *in relation to companies*. He is not strictly prevented from earning a living. These factors tend to support the broad view.

(4)   Finally, the prohibition is not simply against being a "manager". The disqualified person is prohibited "in any way, whether directly or indirectly..." from being concerned or taking part in the management of a company. It is important to keep in mind that the prohibition in the CDDA is not a prohibition on being a manager but a wide ban on being involved or taking part in management.

Do common law rules of agency provide any guidance as to the scope of "management"?

12.42   It is a central tenet of company law that the company is a fictional legal entity which can only act and transact through human agents. To determine whether the act of an individual human being can be attributed to a company, what Lord Hoffmann has described as "the rules of attribution" must be applied.[86] The law of agency is a major source of such rules. Agency rules enable us to determine, in a transactional context, whether the acts of a particular individual, the agent, can bind his principal, the company, in contract.[87] The basic rule is that the company, as principal, is bound

---

[86] *Meridian Global Funds Management Asia Ltd v. Securities Commission* [1995] 2 B.C.L.C. 116, 121.
[87] For a general introduction concerning the application of agency rules to companies see, P.L. Davies, *Gower's Principles of Modern Company Law*, (6th ed., 1997), Chaps 9 and 10. The law on the criminal liability of corporations discussed above in para. 12.30 is a source of another set of attribution rules this time in a non-transactional context.

by transactions entered into by any of its agents, provided that they were acting within the scope of their authority which can be actual, usual or ostensible authority. In keeping with the hierarchical view of corporate structures explained above, the board of directors has been regarded in law as the primary agent or organ of the company. However, it can be difficult to determine whether the company, as principal, is bound in circumstances where the third party has dealt not with the board or an individual director, but with an employee or manager who is not a director. In the absence of formal authorisation (actual authority), the answer will depend on whether that individual acted with usual authority (the authority which a person in his position and in the type of business concerned can reasonably be expected to have) or with ostensible authority (the authority which he has been held out by the company as having and which the company is therefore estopped from denying). Older cases suggest that the ostensible authority of an individual who manages a branch or area of a company's business is limited in scope.[88] However, it appears now that a manager will generally have ostensible authority to undertake everyday transactions relating to the area of business for which he is responsible.[89] In *First Energy (U.K.) Ltd v. Hungarian International Bank Ltd*[90] it was held that a senior manager in charge of a branch office had ostensible authority to make offers of loan facilities in the bank's name which, if accepted by customers would bind the bank in contract, even though he lacked actual authority in this respect.

12.43   The question which the agency rules raise for present purposes is whether an agent who has actual, usual, or ostensible authority to bind the company can be equated with a "manager" or with a person who is concerned or taking part in its management. A similar question arose in a Canadian case, *Shou Yin Mar v. Royal Bank*.[91] This case has parallels with *Registrar of Restrictive Trading Agreements v. W H Smith & Son Ltd* discussed above, in that it concerned an application for an order that an individual be summoned to court for formal examination. The individual concerned was a former employee whose job description had been the "Chinese Manager" of a branch of the bank because of his responsibility for the branch's Chinese business. Under the applicable rule, the court only had jurisdiction to order his examination if he could be shown to have been a former "officer" of the bank. Dismissing the former employee's appeal against an order for examination, the British Columbian Court of Appeal held that the description "Chinese Manager" implied that the individual had some control and authority in relation to Chinese business sufficient to constitute him an "officer" even though he had no subordinates and had himself been subordinate to the branch manager and branch accountant. O'Halloran J.A. referred to his "apparent authority" (deriving, it seems, from his job title) and held that this should be regarded as his real authority, at least for the purpose of determining whether he could be examined as a former officer. The possible use of agency rules as a means of mapping the scope of disqualification is problematic however. It is clear from cases like *Woodhouse v. Walsall Metropolitan Council* discussed above that the board may confer *actual* authority on an agent in relation to defined tasks without necessarily constituting that agent a manager in law. Thus, much depends on the *width* of the agent's authority. The agent's actual, usual or ostensible authority may be quite limited in scope. Even the lowliest employee may have ostensible authority to bind the company for certain narrow purposes. Thus, agency rules can only serve as a useful guide if it can be said that the disqualified person has usual or ostensible authority to

---

[88] *e.g. Kreditbank Cassel GmbH v. Schenkers Ltd* [1927] 1 K.B. 826, CA.
[89] P.L. Davies, *op. cit.*, p. 226.
[90] [1993] B.C.L.C. 1409, CA.
[91] [1940] 3 D.L.R. 331.

bind the company in relation to major transactions which affect the whole or a substantial part of the company.[92] This is not suprising given that agency rules serve transactional purposes, their main objective being to ensure that those who deal with companies enjoy security of transaction.[93] Cases may arise in which agency rules are applied liberally to promote this objective. Even if strong emphasis is placed on the protective aspect of disqualification, it would be going too far to say that every individual who has ostensible authority to bind the company should necessarily be treated as a "manager".

Do "permission to act" cases provide any guidance as to the scope of "management"?

12.44 It has already been mentioned that a significant schematic feature of the CDDA is that a disqualified person may apply to the court for permission to engage in activities which fall within the scope of the prohibitions. The law and practice relating to applications for permission is considered fully in Chapter 13. One might expect the authorities which deal with the question of whether a disqualified person should be given permission to act during the currency of a ban to shed some light on the scope of the prohibition itself.

In *Re Cargo Agency Ltd,*[94] Harman J., having disqualified the defendant for two years under section 6, gave permission for him to be "engaged as a general manager" of a subsidiary of his then current employer. Unfortunately, the report is silent as to what precisely his activities as a general manager entailed. It is possible to discern from Harman J.'s simultaneous refusal to allow the defendant in *Cargo Agency* to become a *director* of the subsidiary that a person can be a manager without necessarily being a director. This is not particularly helpful.[95] Similarly, in *Re TLL Realisations Ltd,*[96] Park J. was faced with an application by a disqualified person for permission to act as a manager. In the end, he gave the applicant permission to act as a manager with joint responsibility for the internal accounting and financial function of a group of private companies but recorded his view as to the correctness of a concession by the applicant's counsel to the effect that the activities in question would, without permission, have involved a breach of the prohibition in section 1.[97] In general, permission to act cases provide little firm guidance. The current practice of the court is either to grant or refuse the application without really analysing whether what is proposed amounts to management or not. There has not been a reported case where the court refused to make an order on an application for permission on the ground that the disqualified person did not require permission to engage in the activities forming the subject matter of the application. If there is any doubt as to the necessity of the application, the applicant is entitled to the benefit of it and to the certainty of the protection which is enshrined in an order granting permission to act.[98]

---

[92] Applying *Commissioner for Corporate Affairs v. Bracht* discussed at para. 12.34 above.
[93] P.L. Davies, *loc. cit.*
[94] [1992] B.C.L.C. 686, [1992] B.C.C. 388.
[95] The same conclusion can be drawn from the fact that Parliament saw fit to add the separate "management" prohibition in section 1(1)(d) to the "director" prohibition in section 1(1)(a).
[96] February 1, 1999, Ch.D., unreported.
[97] It is clear that Park J. regarded the applicant, whose activities were said to be more significant than mere book-keeping while falling short of the role of a full finance director, as being at the very least "concerned" in management.
[98] A point first made by Hicks in 1987, *op. cit.*, p. lxxviii which has so far stood the test of time.

KNOCK-ON LEGAL EFFECTS OF CDDA DISQUALIFICATION

12.45 There are "knock-on" consequences for the disqualified person under the following statutes.

Insolvency Act 1986

12.46 It has been seen that an undischarged bankrupt and a person who is made the subject of a disqualification order under the CDDA is automatically disqualified from acting as an insolvency practitioner by section 390(4) of the Insolvency Act 1986. To the average disqualified director this is no hardship. However, the consequences for a licensed insolvency practitioner disqualified under the CDDA are obviously very serious.[99] The effect of section 390(4) is that he *automatically* ceases to be qualified to act as an insolvency practitioner. In other words, his disqualification under the Insolvency Act does *not* depend on the formal withdrawal of his authorisation by the relevant licensing authority.[1] In relation to a company, the effect is that he could no longer accept an appointment to act as liquidator, provisional liquidator, administrator or administrative receiver or as supervisor of a corporate voluntary arrangement and, in relation to an individual he could no longer accept an appointment to act as trustee in bankruptcy or supervisor of an individual voluntary arrangement.[2] Any current appointments to these offices or positions would have to be relinquished immediately.[3] It appears from section 388 that a disqualified person can act as a receiver or manager of *part* of a company's property or as an income receiver (*e.g.* as a receiver under the Law of Property Act 1925) without being formally authorised to act as an insolvency practitioner. However, a disqualification order under section 1 (though not a section 11 or 12 disqualification) prohibits the disqualified person from acting as a receiver or manager by virtue of section 1(1)(c) of the CDDA in any event. Section 389 of the Insolvency Act 1986 makes it an offence for a person to act as an insolvency practitioner in relation to a company or an individual without being qualified. So, for example, an insolvency practitioner who, while the subject of the prohibition in section 1, continues to act as liquidator or administrator of a company commits an offence under both the Insolvency Act 1986 and the CDDA. As was noted above, persons subject to section 12 of the CDDA are expressly prohibited from acting as liquidators but not as administrators or receivers. It appears that strictly an order in the

---

[99] It is conceivable that a licensed insolvency practitioner could be the subject of disqualification proceedings arising directly from his conduct *as* an insolvency practitioner under section 2, section 3 (see, *e.g. Re Arctic Engineering* [1986] 1 W.L.R. 686, [1986] 2 All E.R. 346, [1986] B.C.L.C. 253, (1985) 1 B.C.C. 99,563) or section 4.

[1] Insolvency practitioners can be licensed to act either by a professional body recognised under Insolvency Act, s. 391 or by a competent authority as defined in section 392, *ibid*. Recognised professional bodies include the Institute of Chartered Accountants in England and Wales and the Insolvency Practitioners Association. For a full list see the Insolvency Practitioners (Recognised Professional Bodies) Order 1986 (S.I. 1986 No. 1764). The recognised professional bodies are required by Insolvency Act 1986, s. 391(2) to maintain and enforce rules for securing that their members are fit and proper persons to act as insolvency practitioners. An insolvency practitioner who is authorised to act directly by the Secretary of State (at present the only "competent authority") is liable to have his authorisation withdrawn if he ceases to be "a fit and proper person" under s. 393(4), *ibid*.

[2] Insolvency Act 1986, s. 388. The same applies in the case of appointments to act as liquidator, provisional liquidator, administrator or trustee of an insolvent partnership or supervisor of a partnership voluntary arrangement: *ibid*. s. 388(2A) and see Insolvent Partnerships Order 1994 (S.I. 1994 No. 2421), art. 15.

[3] This would give rise to an office holder's vacancy within all the companies in relation to which the individual had been acting as liquidator, administrator etc.: Insolvency Act 1986, s. 171(4) (voluntary liquidation), s. 172(5) (compulsory liquidation), s. 19(2)(a) (administration), s. 45(2) (administrative receivership) Where such a vacancy occurs it may be filled by the company's creditors or the court: for specific provisions, see Insolvency Act 1986, ss 92, 104 and 108 (liquidation), s. 13(2) (administration), s. 7(5) (corporate voluntary arrangement).

terms of section 12 does not trigger the automatic disqualification in section 390(4) of the Insolvency Act as the order is made under section 429 of the Insolvency Act and is not "a disqualification order made under the CDDA..." within the meaning of section 390(4)(b). The effect is that a person disqualified in the terms of section 12 is not prohibited from acting as an administrator or a receiver. A further point of some difficulty is the question of permission to act. The ban in section 390(4) is absolute and there is no power of dispensation in the Insolvency Act. However, the CDDA clearly contemplates that a disqualified person could be given permission to act in some or all of the capacities of liquidator (sections 1(1)(b) and 12), administrator, receiver or manager (section 1(1)(b)–(c)). It is not clear whether the grant of permission to act in any of these capacities under the CDDA can take effect as a dispensation of the ban imposed by section 390(4). On a final note, a person who is adjudged bankrupt in any part of the United Kingdom is disqualified from sitting or voting in the Houses of Parliament by virtue of section 427 of the Insolvency Act.

Charities Act 1993

12.47   A person who is made the subject of a disqualification order under the CDDA is automatically disqualified by section 72(1)(f) of the Charities Act 1993 from acting as a charity trustee. The Charity Commissioners have the power to waive this automatic disqualification in individual cases but cannot exercise this power to allow the disqualified person to remain as the trustee of a charity which is an incorporated body.[4] Equally, it is clear that section 72(1)(f) does not apply where the court has granted the disqualified person permission to act under the CDDA in relation to a corporate charity.[5] Section 73(1) of the Charities Act 1993 makes it an offence for a person to act as a charity trustee while disqualified under section 72. However, the effect of section 73(2) is that a person who continues to act as a director of a corporate charity in breach of the section 1 prohibition only commits an offence under the CDDA.[6] An undischarged bankrupt is also disqualified from acting as a charity trustee by section 72(1)(b) of the Charities Act. In contrast to the position under section 390 (4) of the Insolvency Act 1986 discussed in the previous paragraph, a person the subject of an order under section 429(2)(b) of the Insolvency Act 1986 (which would encompass a person disqualified in the terms of CDDA, s. 12) is also disqualified by section 73(1)(f).

Pensions Act 1995

12.48   This legislation was introduced in the wake of the Maxwell scandal to tighten regulation of occupational pension schemes. A person who is made the subject of a disqualification order under the CDDA is automatically disqualified by section 29(1)(f) of the Pensions Act 1995 from acting as a trustee of an occupational pension scheme established under a trust. A corporate trustee is similarly disqualified by section 29(1)(c) from so acting where any of its directors is the subject of a disqualification falling within section 29. The Occupational Pensions Regulatory Authority established by the Act has the power to waive this automatic disqualification.[7] Section 30 of the Pensions Act 1995 makes it an offence for a person to act as a trustee while disqualified. The Authority also has the power to suspend a trustee where CDDA proceedings

---

[4] Charities Act 1993, s. 72(4).
[5] *ibid.*, s. 72(3)(a).
[6] Note that ss 72–73, *ibid.*, are re-enactments of the Charities Act 1992, ss 45–46 which originally came into force on January 1, 1993.
[7] Pensions Act 1995, s. 29(5). This power is identical to that of the Charity Commissioners under the Charities Act 1993.

against him are pending.[8] An undischarged bankrupt is also disqualified from acting as a pension trustee by section 29(1)(b) of the Pensions Act. A person the subject of an order under section 429(2)(b) of the Insolvency Act 1986 (which would encompass a person disqualified in the terms of CDDA, s. 12) is also disqualified by section 29(1)(f).

Police Act 1996

12.49 By Schedule 2, paragraph 11(1)(c) of this Act, a person who is made the subject of a disqualification order under the CDDA is automatically disqualified from being a member or from being appointed as a member of a police authority. The same provision formerly appeared in the Police Act 1964, Sched. 1B (as inserted by the Police and Magistrates' Courts Act 1994, s. 3(2), Sched. 2). The position is the same in respect of undischarged bankrupts and persons the subject of an order under section 429(2)(b) of the Insolvency Act 1986.

Housing Act 1996

12.50 By Schedule 1, Part II, paragraph 4(2)(b) of this Act, the Housing Corporation, which is responsible for the regulation of housing associations, may make an order removing a director, trustee or committee member of a housing association (now termed a registered social landlord) where he is the subject of a disqualification order under the CDDA.[9] A person disqualified under CDDA who is a director of a housing association constituted as a company limited by guarantee would have to resign anyway unless the court gives him permission to act. This is also true of a trustee of a housing association constituted as a registered charitable trust by virtue of the automatic disqualification provisions in the Charities Act 1993 (see above). Otherwise, a disqualification order under the CDDA does not automatically trigger disqualification under the Housing Act 1996. The onus is on the Housing Corporation to take steps to remove the person. The position is the same in relation to undischarged bankrupts and persons the subject of an order under section 429(2) of the Insolvency Act 1986.

Local Government Act 1972

12.51 The effect of sections 80–81 of this Act is that a person adjudged bankrupt is disqualified from being a member of a local authority until such time as he is discharged from bankruptcy or the bankruptcy order is annulled.

Does a CDDA disqualification result in formal removal from office?

12.52 The question of whether a person the subject of a CDDA disqualification is required to vacate office as a director depends on the relevant company's articles of association. Under article 81 of the present Table A, a person must vacate the office of director if, among other things, he (a) becomes prohibited by law from being a director, or (b) becomes bankrupt or makes any arrangement or composition with his creditors. Similar provision is made in article 88 of the former Table A in the Companies Act

---

[8] Pensions Act 1995, s. 4(1)(e). The Authority is also empowered to issue an order prohibiting a person from continuing as trustee of a scheme in prescribed circumstances: *ibid.*, s. 3. Penalties for breach of either a prohibition or suspension order are set out in s. 6, *ibid.*
[9] This provision came into force on October 1, 1996. The Housing Corporation previously had power under the Housing Associations Act 1985 to remove a housing association committee member in certain circumstances (*e.g.* bankruptcy or mental disorder). The 1996 Act extended these powers to encompass persons disqualified under CDDA.

1948.[10] While a disqualified person who continues in office would obviously be in breach of the prohibition, the point is not entirely academic. If no provision is made in the articles, it is arguable that the disqualified person would still retain authority to act on the company's behalf at least within the terms of the company's constitution.

Regulatory and other consequences

12.53 CDDA disqualification may have regulatory consequences for a disqualified person who is a member of a professional body. Similarly, if the disqualified person is someone who is carrying on authorised business under financial services or related legislation, the disqualification could prompt the Financial Services Authority to withdraw his authorisation on the ground that he is no longer a fit and proper person. These are both matters of discretion for the appropriate professional body or regulator. In the context of securities regulation, it is a requirement of the Listing Rules of the London Stock Exchange that the directors of an issuer disclose details of any bankruptcies or disqualification orders in the prospectus or listing particulars. On a different note, it is quite conceivable that a CDDA disqualification could have an adverse effect on the disqualified person's individual credit rating.

BREACH OF THE PROHIBITION

12.54 If a disqualified person acts in breach of the prohibitions in section 1, 11 or 12 he is liable to criminal prosecution and possible civil sanctions under sections 13 to 15 of the CDDA.[11]

Criminal liability and further disqualification

12.55 A person who acts in breach of the prohibitions in sections 1, 11 or 12 commits an "either way" offence. If convicted on indictment, he is liable to imprisonment for not more than two years or a fine or both. If convicted summarily, he is liable to imprisonment for not more than six months or a fine not exceeding the statutory maximum,[12] or both. A body corporate the subject of a disqualification order which acts in breach of the prohibition in section 1 is also guilty of an offence. By virtue of section 14, where a body corporate is guilty of the offence and it is proved that the

[10] One difference of note is that a director is required to vacate office under article 88 where, among other things, he ceases to be a director by virtue of sections 182 or 185 of the 1948 Act or he becomes prohibited from being a director by reason of any order made under section 188 of the 1948 Act (being the statutory predecessor of CDDA, ss 2 and 4). This is narrower than the present Table A and has the effect that a person disqualified under post-1948 Act provisions such as CDDA, ss 6 or 8 would not automatically be required to vacate office as a director under the constitution of a company having articles in the form of 1948 Act Table A. A reference to section 9 of the Insolvency Act 1976 (the earliest unfitness provision) was read into article 88: *ibid*, section 9(8). Section 93 of the Companies Act 1981 also had the effect of consolidating what are now sections 3 and 5 of the CDDA as part of section 188 of the 1948 Act. However, the CDDA makes no express adjustment to the wording of article 88 and the effect of the 1976 Act and 1981 Act provisions is not preserved by the savings in CDDA, Scheds. 2 and 3. By contrast, where a person is a director at the time of his disqualification under the Australian Corporations Law, his office is automatically terminated *by operation of the statute* and so the issue does not turn on whether there is provision in the relevant company's articles of association.

[11] The Department of Trade and Industry launched a hotline in January 1998 which aims to encourage members of the public to report anyone suspected of acting as a director, etc. while bankrupt or subject to a disqualification order. The 24–hour telephone number is 0845–6013546. For a critical view of the enforcement process generally see A. Hicks, *Disqualification of Directors: No Hiding Place for the Unfit?* (A.C.C.A Research Report No. 59, 1998), pp. 51–57.

[12] The statutory maximum in England and Wales means the prescribed sum under section 32 of the Magistrates' Courts Act 1980; in Scotland, the prescribed sum under section 289B of the Criminal Procedure (Scotland) Act 1975.

offence occurred with the consent or connivance of, or was attributable to any neglect on the part of any director, manager, secretary or other similar officer[13] of the body corporate, or any person who was purporting to act in any such capacity then that person also commits an offence. The basic offence is one of strict liability. Where the disqualified person breaches the prohibition as a matter of fact, the offence is committed even if he genuinely believes that his actions do not amount to a breach. In *R. v. Brockley*[14] a person who had carried on the business of a hotel company was convicted of the section 11 offence. His defence rested on the belief, based on legal advice, that he had been automatically discharged from bankruptcy under the provisions of the Insolvency Act 1986 before starting up the company's business. An appeal against conviction was unsuccessful. The Court of Appeal held that as the offence was one of strict liability, it was incumbent on the bankrupt to ensure that his bankruptcy had in fact been discharged before engaging in a prohibited activity. A person convicted of any of these offences is liable to further disqualification under section 2 of the CDDA as each offence is an "indictable offence ... in connection with the ... management ... of a company" within that section.[15]

Civil liability

12.56 By virtue of section 15(1)(a) of the CDDA, a person is personally responsible for all the relevant debts of a company if at any time he is involved in the management of the company in contravention of a disqualification order or of section 11. "Relevant debts" for this purpose are such debts and other liabilities of the company as are incurred at a time when that person was involved in the management of the company (section 15(3)(a)). Liability is joint and several with the company and any other person who may be personally liable for the debts whether under section 15 or otherwise (section 15(2)). The upshot is that a creditor owed a relevant debt could proceed against either the company or the disqualified person for the whole amount. A person is "involved in management" if he is a director of the company or if he is concerned, whether directly or indirectly, or takes part, in the management of the company (section 15(4)). Strictly, this means that a disqualified person who acts in breach of the prohibitions on being a liquidator, administrator or receiver or manager in section 1(1)(b)–(c) would not be personally liable under section 15 for any relevant debts. Civil liability under section 15(1)(a) is free standing. In other words, a disqualified person risks personal liability whether or not he is prosecuted for the criminal offence (see above). One oddity of section 15(1)(a) is that it does not appear to impose personal liability on a person who acts in breach of the terms of section 12.[16]

It is not only a disqualified person who can incur civil liability. By virtue of section 15(1)(b), a person is also personally responsible for all the relevant debts of a company if at any time as a person who is involved in the management of the company, he acts or is willing to act on instructions given without the permission of the court by a person whom he knows at that time to be the subject of a disqualification order or to be an undischarged bankrupt. This provision is directed primarily at those who might be prepared to act as nominees or "front men" in a company run by a disqualified person. "Relevant debts" for this purpose are such debts and other liabilities of the company as are incurred at a time when that person was acting or willing to act on the instructions

---

[13] Including members where the affairs of the body corporate are managed by its members: CDDA, s. 14(2).
[14] [1994] B.C.C. 131, [1994] Crim L.R. 671.
[15] See, *e.g. R. v. Theivendran* (1992) 13 Cr.App.R. (S.) 601; *R. v. Thompson* (1993) 14 Cr.App.R. (S.) 89; *R. v. Teece* (1994) 15 Cr.App.R. (S.) 302.
[16] No reference is made to section 12 in contrast to the criminal provision in section 13 which specifically refers to contravention of section 12(2).

of the disqualified person (section 15(3)(b)). Liability is again joint and several while "involved in management" bears the same meaning as it does in section 15(1)(a). A person who as at any time acted on the instructions of a disqualified person is rebuttably presumed to have been willing at any time thereafter to act on any instructions given by that person (section 15(5)).[17] It does not appear that a person who acts on the instructions of someone disqualified in the terms of section 12 is covered by section 15(1)(b).

---

[17] Civil liability along these lines was first introduced in section 18 of the Insolvency Act 1985. There is an analogous provision imposing similar liabilities where there is contravention of the restriction on re-use of company names in section 217 of the Insolvency Act 1986 which also derives from section 18. For a case where a creditor successfully sued a director under the latter provision see *Thorne v. Silverleaf* [1994] 1 B.C.L.C. 637, [1994] B.C.C. 109, CA.

CHAPTER 13

Permission to Act

INTRODUCTION

13.01 The power of the courts to grant a disqualified person permission to act[1] as a director or take part in the management of specified companies is an important schematic feature of the CDDA. It has been emphasised throughout this book that it is not possible to arrive at a complete understanding of the purpose and operation of the legislation unless the court's power to grant permission is taken fully into account. It has been seen that sections 2 to 6, 8 and 10 of the CDDA confer various powers on the courts (and in the case of section 6, a duty) to make a disqualification order, each of which focuses on particular types of past misconduct. A disqualification order made pursuant to these various powers is a *blanket* prohibition. As was seen earlier in Chapter 11, the court is bound to impose a complete ban prohibiting the disqualified person from engaging in any of the activities covered by section 1(1).[2] Thus, a person who is the subject of a disqualification order is prohibited from being a director of a company, and from in any way, whether directly or indirectly, being concerned in or taking part in the promotion, formation or management of a company and from acting as a liquidator, administrator, receiver or manager of a company or its property. An undischarged bankrupt is automatically prohibited by section 11 from acting as a director of, or directly or indirectly taking part in or being concerned in the promotion, formation or management of a company. A person disqualified in the terms of section 12 is prohibited from acting as a director or liquidator of, or directly or indirectly taking part or being concerned in the promotion, formation or management of, a company. As was seen in Chapter 12, the scope of these various prohibitions is extensive. However, none of the prohibitions is absolute because sections 1(1), 11(1) and 12(1) all provide that the disqualified person is disqualified from engaging in a prohibited activity or acting in a prohibited capacity *without the permission of the court*. Thus, a central unifying feature of the CDDA is that a person disqualified in the terms of any of sections 1, 11 and 12 may apply for permission to act notwithstanding disqualification. It has been seen that the power of the court to grant permission has significant implications for law and practice in relation to the CDDA generally. The following points can be made:

---

[1] The CDDA and cases decided before the reform of the civil justice system use the phrases "leave of the court" and "leave to act". In the light of the CPR, the Disqualification Rules and the Disqualification Practice Direction, the term "permission" is used throughout rather than the old term "leave" except in the case of direct quotes from the CDDA. In similar vein, where appropriate the modern terms "claimant" and "defendant" are used. Under the CPR, the parties on an application for permission to act brought on application notice within substantive disqualification proceedings would still be referred to as "applicant" and "respondent": see further below on procedure generally.

[2] *Re Gower Enterprises Ltd (No. 2)* [1995] 2 B.C.L.C. 201, [1995] B.C.C. 1,081: see paras 11.04 *et seq.*

(1) The rationale of the CDDA is that the court is empowered or obliged to make a full disqualification order based on the defendant's *previous* conduct and the width of the overall prohibition is tempered by the court's power to grant permission. The same point can be made in relation to sections 11 and 12 (although in the former case disqualification is automatic and an order of the court is not required). This suggests that, in exercising their substantive powers to disqualify, the courts should be concerned first and foremost to protect the public and promote high standards of conduct and that, generally, any other factors (such as the defendant's *present* conduct or circumstances) should be taken into account either by way of mitigation or (possibly) in the context of an application for permission.[3]

(2) The courts should take a wide, flexible view when construing the terms of the prohibition in section 1(1) (or section 11(1)), taking into account the fact that there is power under the CDDA to grant permission.[4]

(3) The courts should be careful in exercising any power, either inherent or conferred by rule 9 of the Disqualification Rules, to "stay" the effect of a disqualification order. It is generally more appropriate, having regard to the overall scheme of the Act, to consider the grant of *interim permission* under the disqualification order in relation to specific companies rather than to direct that the order is not to come into full effect until some time after it is pronounced.[5]

13.02   This chapter examines the principles on which the court exercises the power to grant permission to act, the factors which are taken into account and the relevant procedural issues.

The Approach of the Court in Exercising the Power to Grant Permission

Scope of power

13.03   The courts in England and Wales will generally only grant an application by a disqualified person for permission where it relates to a specific company or companies, a point borne out by the authorities which are discussed in greater detail below. This practice suggests that the courts are of the view that an application for a general relaxation of the prohibition (*e.g.* permission to act generally as a director of any company) should not be countenanced during the currency of a disqualification order. Support for this view can be derived from the result in *Re Shneider*[6] in which it was held that an equivalent provision of the Australian Corporations Law did not empower the court to go beyond a limited relaxation of the ban in respect of a specific company and lift the ban to permit a disqualified person to participate in the management of companies generally. However, in *Re Harrison*[7] the Federal Court of

---

[3] *Re Westmid Packing Services Ltd, Secretary of State for Trade and Industry v. Griffiths* [1998] 2 All E.R. 124, [1998] 2 B.C.L.C. 646, [1998] B.C.C. 836, CA.
[4] See Chap. 12. The ability to grant permission has been relied on as mitigating the fact that the prohibition is wide and, to some extent, uncertain.
[5] *Secretary of State for Trade and Industry v. Bannister* [1996] 1 W.L.R. 118, [1996] 2 B.C.L.C. 271, [1995] B.C.C. 1,027; *Re Continental Assurance Co. of London plc* [1997] 1 B.C.L.C. 48, [1996] B.C.C. 888 affd. *sub nom. Secretary of State for Trade and Industry v. Burrows*, July 4, 1996, CA, unreported; *Re Thorncliffe Finance Ltd, Secretary of State for Trade and Industry v. Arif* [1997] 1 B.C.L.C. 34, [1996] B.C.C. 586; *Re Amaron Ltd* [1998] B.C.C. 264 and see para. 13.54 below.
[6] (1997) 22 A.C.S.R. 497.
[7] (1998) 153 A.L.R. 369.

Australia considered the matter further. The question there arose in connection with what is now section 229(3) of the Corporations Law which automatically prohibits a person from acting in certain capacities for five years following a relevant conviction. The court considered the purpose of such a prohibition and interestingly confirmed the view (often expressed in the English courts) that the purpose of such prohibition was not punitive but rather, was designed "to protect the public and to prevent the corporate structure from being used to the financial detriment of investors, shareholders, creditors and persons dealing with the company" and was "calculated to act as a safeguard against the corporate structure being used by individuals in a manner which is contrary to proper commercial standards".[8] In reasoning that is extremely persuasive, Van Doussa J. rejected the view that, *as a matter of jurisdiction*, the court could not grant a general permission or a permission covering a series of companies which are not described individually but share certain defined characteristics (*e.g.* private companies). However, he accepted that the circumstances in which the court would think it appropriate to grant such a permission would be very rare for the reasons set out in *Re Shneider* and having regard to the policy considerations underlying the provision:

> "This is particularly so in the case of trading companies. Without knowing the particulars of the type of companies, the nature of their business, the nature of their management structure, and the intended involvement of the applicant in their management, it would be impossible to know whether it was appropriate to make an order in general terms that did not specify particular corporations by name".[9]

On the facts of that case and subject to certain conditions, the court was prepared to give a general permission to act in relation to one defined category of companies, identified by their characteristics rather than by specific company names, but not in relation to a second category.[10]

13.04 Applications tend to be granted more readily in relation to companies with which the disqualified person was involved at the time of his disqualification and which had not featured in the main disqualification proceedings.[11] A second common feature of English practice is that permission to act, when given, is invariably only given subject to detailed conditions and safeguards. Doubt has been expressed in some

---

[8] Citing Bowen L.J. in *Magna Alloys & Research Pty Ltd* (1975) 1 A.C.L.R. 203 at 205 in relation to the statutory predecessor of section 229.
[9] This echoes *dictum* of Neuberger J. in *Re Amaron Ltd* [1998] B.C.C. 264 at 278 on the need for the court to be given up to date information about the company or companies in relation to which permission is sought.
[10] Permission was granted to be a director of "not for profit" organisations of a community service kind on condition that the relevant board retained four or more members in addition to the applicant. The court was not prepared to make a blanket order in relation to companies that consulted the applicant for sales and marketing advice. A similar "general" permission was granted in relation to one of the disqualified Barings' directors, Mr Tuckey. In his capacity as a corporate banker, there was a concern that he might be involved, in a degree otherwise prohibited, in the promotion or formation of companies that would be undertaken by clients in the course of (for example) a restructuring. Permission to be so involved was granted. See also *Re TLL Realisations Ltd*, February 1, 1999, Ch.D., unreported. In this case, the court gave a disqualified person permission to carry out specific functions within a specified company and its existing subsidiaries. An extension of the permission was requested to cover subsidiaries that might be acquired in the future in the course of the group's expansion. The jurisdiction of the court to make such an order was not disputed but Park J., in his discretion, reluctantly refused to accede to this request. In South Africa it appears that the courts are prepared to relax the ban generally without reference to specific companies although the applicant is required to make a stronger case for general permission than for permission to act as a director of a specified company: see, *ex parte K* 1971 4 S.A. 289 (D); *Nusca v. da Ponte* 1994 3 S.A. 251(B).
[11] See *Re TLL Realisations Ltd*, February 1, 1999, Ch.D., unreported where Park J. suggested that the case for permission is stronger if the disqualified person is already involved in the company and had discharged his duties without complaint than a case in which the disqualified person wants to take on a new employment which he did not have before.

quarters as to whether the courts have the power to impose conditions on the grant of permission. Nevertheless, the practice is now well-established and unlikely to be challenged.[12] The sorts of conditions and safeguards which are commonly imposed are discussed further below.

Discretion

13.05   While the CDDA contains detailed guidance in Schedule 1 on the factors to be taken into account in determining whether a person's conduct makes him unfit for the purposes of sections 6 and 8, there is, by contrast, no express statutory guidance as to how the courts should go about exercising their discretion when faced with an application for permission.[13] The factors which the courts should (or might) take into account are left to be judicially determined in the light of the overall objectives of the legislative scheme. The courts in England and Wales have generally taken the view that the CDDA is concerned primarily with protecting the public from those whose past conduct makes them unfit to act as directors or managers of companies.[14] However, the application of that rationale in the context of applications for permission has not been consistent and a settled approach to the discretion is still emerging. The three points which can be made with confidence judging from the case law in this jurisdiction are, first, that the onus lies firmly with the applicant seeking permission to establish that it should be granted (the standard of proof being the balance of probabilities)[15]; secondly, that the application will usually only be considered if it relates to a specified company or companies; and thirdly, that in cases where permission is granted, it is frequently granted only subject to conditions and safeguards. In determining whether or not to grant permission, one approach favoured until recently by the courts has been to apply a two-stage test. On this approach the applicant is required to show:

(1) that there is a *need* for the applicant to act as a director or take part in the management of the company or companies specified in the application; and

(2) that, if an order giving permission is made, the public will be adequately protected.

13.06   This test originates from some words of Harman J. in *Re Cargo Agency Ltd*[16] which were later adopted by Sir Mervyn Davies in *Re Gibson Davies Ltd*.[17] For the purposes of a complete exposition, the two limbs of this test are analysed in detail below. However, as will become clear, the courts do not apply the so-called "need" requirement rigorously in every case and there is now doubt as to whether the two-stage test (incorporating the "need" requirement) truly represents (or should rep-

---

[12] For hesitancy on whether the phrase "permission of the court" can properly be construed as meaning "on such terms and conditions as the court thinks fit" see *Re Majestic Recording Studios Ltd* [1989] B.C.L.C. 1, (1988) 4 B.C.C. 519 and the Scottish case of *Secretary of State for Trade and Industry v. Palfreman* [1995] 2 B.C.L.C. 301, [1995] B.C.C. 193 though see the practice of the courts discussed in main text below and *dictum* of Arden J. in *Re Tech Textiles Ltd, Secretary of State for Trade and Industry v. Vane* [1998] 1 B.C.L.C. 259 at 267. The question does not arise in other jurisdictions, notably Australia, where the Corporations Law confers express power on the courts to impose such conditions or restrictions as they think fit when granting permission.
[13] Contrast also the precise substantive and procedural guidelines in the Insolvency Rules 1986 which pertain to an application for permission by an undischarged bankrupt: see further below, para. 13.69.
[14] See Chap. 2.
[15] On standard of proof see *Re Amaron Ltd* [1998] B.C.C. 264.
[16] [1992] B.C.L.C. 686, [1992] B.C.C. 388: "It seems to me that Mr Newey must be right that applications for [permission] pursuant to section 1 should only be granted where there is a need for them to be granted, and should only be granted upon evidence of adequate protection from danger."
[17] [1995] B.C.C. 11.

resent) the present state of the law. It is suggested that the test is better seen as one of whether or not, in all the circumstances, permission should be granted. The "circumstances" that will be relevant are those traditionally considered under the headings of "need" and "protection of the public" but under the suggested test no single factor would necessarily be decisive and, for example, the question of "need" would be regarded as a flexible matter encompassing a spectrum of possibilities. This approach is supported by the view expressed by Scott V.-C. in *Re Dawes & Henderson Ltd, Secretary of State for Trade and Industry v. Shuttleworth*[18]:

> "The discretion given to the court under the 1986 Act to grant [permission] to an individual against whom a disqualification order has been made, enabling him during the currency of the disqualification order to act as a director of a particular company, is a discretion unfettered by any statutory condition or criterion. It would in my view be wrong for the court to create any such fetters or conditions. The reason why it would be wrong is that no-one, when sitting in any particular case to give judgment, can foresee the infinite variety of circumstances that might apply in future cases before the court. When Parliament has given the courts an unfettered discretion I do not think it is for the courts to reduce the ambit of that discretion. But in exercising the statutory discretion courts must, of course, not take into account any irrelevant factors. The emphasis given in a judgment on a particular case on particular circumstances in that case is not necessarily a guide to the weight to be attributed to similar circumstances in a different case."

It is likely that these observations will be treated as extending to applications for permission to act in other prohibited capacities (*i.e.* not just as director) and applications by persons disqualified under section 11.

The proper starting point

13.07   It is suggested that the starting point should be that a person who has been disqualified is, on the face of it, unfit to act as a director or otherwise take part in the management of companies. As such, there should be a firm onus on the applicant to demonstrate why it is appropriate to grant him permission. As Van Doussa J. put it in *Re Harrison*[19]:

> "It must be a clear and appropriate case before the court gives [permission] so as to remove what Parliament prima facie thought was a necessary restriction."

The standard of proof is the civil standard on the balance of probabilities.[20] Nevertheless, for reasons considered further below, it is suggested that the courts need to apply a critical approach when considering an applicant's evidence and that they should not be overly-impressed by the mere fact that evidence may not have been challenged.[21] As discussed below, the Secretary of State will often have no basis on which to challenge the applicant's evidence. Moreover, the courts should be careful to avoid granting permission too readily as to do so might undermine the purposes for which the person was disqualified in the first place. It will be recalled that the purposes of disqualifi-

---

[18] January 27, 1999, Ch.D., unreported.
[19] (1998) 153 A.L.R. 369.
[20] See *Re Amaron Ltd* [1998] B.C.C. 264.
[21] In this sense, it is suggested that the court should approach the matter as it would an application for the making of an administration order under section 8 of the Insolvency Act 1986 or an application for relief under section 127 of the same Act: mere assertions without supporting evidence should not be enough.

cation include deterrence and the raising of standards of conduct among directors generally.[22] The value of disqualification as a form of protection (especially as a deterrent) would be undermined if a disqualified person is promptly given permission to act in a prohibited capacity or capacities. This general point was well made by Arden J. in *Re Tech Textiles Ltd, Secretary of State for Trade and Industry v. Vane*:

> "As respects the exercise of the discretion to grant leave there is no express guidance in the statute. It is clearly relevant to the exercise of this discretion to consider the end which disqualification seeks to achieve and the reasons why that end is thought desirable. It is clear ... that the purpose ... of the 1986 Act is protective rather than penal, and this is the starting point. In practice ... [it] ... also has a deterrent function since honest directors will not wish their conduct to result in disqualification proceedings. Advisers can perform the valuable function of drawing client directors' attention to these provisions and no doubt should often do so in the best interests of their clients. [Permission] ... is not to be too freely given. Legislative policy requires the disqualification of unfit directors to minimise the risk of harm to the public, and the court must not by granting [permission] prevent the achievement of this policy objective. Nor would the court wish anyone dealing with the director to be misled as to the gravity with which it views the order that has been made."[23]

13.08 In *Re TLL Realisations Ltd*[24] the court considered the question of whether too ready a grant of permission might not bring the CDDA into disrepute. The main problem with too generous an approach is that it tends to undermine the deterrent function of disqualification but the concern may go wider than that. In *Re Barings plc (No. 4), Secretary of State for Trade and Industry* Scott V.-C. accepted the general proposition that the question of permission involves a consideration of the purposes for which the original disqualification, against which partial relief is sought, was imposed:

> "The reasons for granting [permission], if [permission] is granted, must be consistent with the reasons why the disqualification was imposed in the first place."[25]

In that case, however, the Vice-Chancellor tended to dwell on protection of the public in the sense that the disqualified person is kept "off the road", rather than the deterrent function of a disqualification order. It is suggested, in the light of these general points, that the court should only exercise the discretion to grant permission if satisfied on cogent evidence that it is appropriate to do so bearing in mind all the purposes of disqualification (including deterrence).[26]

The "need" requirement

13.09 As indicated above, it has become commonplace for the courts to talk in terms of a two-stage requirement for the applicant to establish (a) that there is the

---

[22] See Chap. 2 and *Re Grayan Building Services Ltd, Secretary of State for Trade and Industry v. Gray* [1995] Ch. 241, [1995] 3 W.L.R. 1, [1995] 3 W.L.R. 1, [1995] 1 B.C.L.C. 276, [1995] B.C.C. 554, CA; *Re Westmid Packing Services Ltd, Secretary of State for Trade and Industry v. Griffiths* [1998] 2 All E.R. 124, [1998] 2 B.C.L.C. 646, [1998] B.C.C. 836, CA.
[23] [1998] 1 B.C.L.C. 259 at 267.
[24] February 1, 1999, Ch.D., unreported.
[25] [1999] 1 All E.R. 1017 at 1023, [1999] 1 B.C.L.C. 262 at 268.
[26] See also *Re McQuillan* (1989) 5 B.C.C. 137 at 140 (citing *Re Altim Pty Ltd* [1968] 2 N.S.W.R. 762) and *Re Amaron Ltd* [1998] B.C.C. 264 at 277.

relevant "need" to be a director and (b) that if permission is given, the public will continue to be adequately protected. It is suggested that the use of this language of "need" is unfortunate in that it has tended to obscure the basis for and circumstances in which permission will be granted. Thus, as has become clear in more recent cases, "need" is better seen as a flexible concept having a spectrum of meanings. Furthermore, "need" is not a gateway or threshold condition which must be satisfied before the court will consider other factors (as some of the earlier authorities imply), but is simply one among a number of factors that the court will consider in deciding whether permission will be given. Before summarising the current position further it is necessary to consider the authorities to see how the "need" requirement has developed.

The court will not act in vain

13.10   The concept of "need" first arose in *Re Cargo Agency Ltd*.[27] Having disqualified a Mr Keeling for the minimum period of two years, Harman J. was faced with an application by Mr Keeling for permission to be engaged as a general manager and/or as a director or otherwise to be involved in the management of a named company, a wholly-owned subsidiary of Rolls Royce plc. Mr Keeling had been carrying out this role for 18 months or so and the Secretary of State offered no opposition to his continuing in that occupation. Harman J. was prepared to give him permission to be engaged as a general manager but not permission to act as a director or otherwise to be involved in management. At that time, his being a director was not "an immediate issue" and so there was no "need" for a wider permission. This was because there were other directors in place who were capable of ensuring that the company continued to trade and flourish. In this context, the requirement to show "need" was little more than a requirement to show that there was some purpose to the court giving permission. As at the time there was no issue or question of the applicant being a director, it was inappropriate for the court to give permission. Narrow permission, analogous to the permission granted in *Cargo Agency* has also been granted in a number of Australian cases.[28]

The concept of "need" in the *Cargo Agency* sense arose again in *Re McQuillan*,[29] a case in which the Northern Ireland High Court was faced with an application by a bankrupt for permission to act as a director. The bankrupt did not wish to resume acting as a working director but wished to return to the board of a company of which he was a director and shareholder prior to his bankruptcy with a view to causing the company to bring proceedings against certain persons (including a receiver and manager appointed by a secured creditor). The court refused permission on two connected grounds. The first was that there was no "need" for the bankrupt to become a director. He could achieve his objective by a derivative action if the shares formerly owned by him were re-assigned by his trustee. The second ground was akin to that in *Cargo Agency*. In order to become a director the bankrupt would need not only the permission of the court, but would also need to be re-appointed by the company in general meeting. This was not a practical possibility because the company's sole shareholder

---

[27] [1992] B.C.L.C. 686, [1992] B.C.C. 388.
[28] *Re Magna Alloys & Research Pty Ltd* (1975) 1 A.C.L.R. 203; *Re Zim Metal Products Pty Ltd* [1977] A.C.L.C. 29,556, (1977) 2 A.C.L.R. 553 although note that the decision in the former case, in particular, did not turn on the question of need. This approach is not beyond criticism. An order granting the applicant a narrow permission to take part in management will need to be tightly drawn so that it is quite clear what the applicant can and cannot do. Otherwise, there is a risk that his activities may amount to *de facto* or shadow directorship which would put him in breach of the prohibitions in sections 1(1)(a), 11 and 12 of the CDDA: see further para. 13.52 below. For judicial criticism of the approach in *Magna Alloys* and *Zim Metal*, see *Re Marsden* (1980) 5 A.C.L.R. 694, 702 *per* Legoe J.
[29] (1989) 5 B.C.C. 137.

was not prepared to co-operate in the calling of a general meeting and in voting for the bankrupt's re-appointment. The court would not give permission where in so doing it would be giving permission in vain because of the opposition of the shareholder. It is suggested that this sense of "need" as a requirement to show that the court will not be acting in vain if an order is made is one which remains. In other words, there must be a good reason why permission should be given.

Desire or need of the applicant and of the company

13.11   In considering "need", the courts have gone further than a requirement to show that the court is not acting in vain. In *Re Gibson Davies Ltd*[30] Sir Mervyn Davies (sitting as a judge of the Chancery Division on an appeal from a district judge) approached the matter by considering whether there was a "need" and then whether or not, if an order was made, the public would be adequately protected. The circumstances were that the applicant had been disqualified for five years and he was seeking permission to be a director of a company called Congratulations Franchising Ltd. Interim permission was apparently in place between September 1993 and the date of the judgment on appeal in July 1994.[31] Sir Mervyn Davies discounted the desire of the applicant to be a director. However, he gave greater weight to evidence of the applicant and two others suggesting that the company was "much in need" of the applicant's services as the guiding light of the company. The district judge had considered evidence to the effect that if the applicant could not act as a director, the company would fail and jobs would be lost. Although such a consequence would be unfortunate, he considered that this danger was overstated and that the company could prosper equally well if the applicant was employed as chief salesman. Sir Mervyn Davies disagreed with this conclusion. He referred on a number of occasions to the "uncontradicted" evidence put forward by the applicant. In relation to this aspect of the judgment, it is suggested that the court should not rely so readily on the mere fact that evidence put forward is "uncontradicted". Unless the Secretary of State has relevant information to the contrary or is to be expected to seek and obtain disclosure and to cross-examine,[32] the court should be slow to take the fact that evidence is uncontradicted as a positive factor adding weight to the applicant's evidence. Secondly, the judge held that the district judge had reached a conclusion which was not "justified" on the evidence. Finally, he made the point that if, as suggested by the district judge, the applicant was employed as a chief salesman he would inevitably be concerned in management (and therefore in breach of the disqualification order). It is suggested that this last point gives rise to the question of whether in *Gibson Davies* the proper course would have been to give the applicant permission to act in a reduced capacity. However, this question was not explored further. The apparent elevation of the "need" requirement to the status of a pre-condition or threshold test in some of the later authorities stems essentially from *Gibson Davies*.

13.12   As a general matter, it is suggested that the authorities as a whole can be relied upon to support the following propositions which mark a shift away from the apparent rigidity of the two-stage approach in *Gibson Davies*:

---

[30] [1995] B.C.C. 11. For substantive disqualification proceedings arising out of the subsequent collapse of the company in relation to which permission was given see *Re Congratulations Franchising Ltd, Secretary of State for Trade and Industry v. Davies*, March 6, 1998, Ch.D., unreported and discussion below.

[31] A protracted period likely now to attract criticism: see, *e.g.* comments of Chadwick J. in *Secretary of State for Trade and Industry v. Renwick*, July 1997, Ch.D., unreported criticising the effective grant of interim permission for nine months and discussion further below in main text.

[32] Which would greatly lengthen hearings for permission apparently against the general guidance given by the Court of Appeal in *Re Dicetrade Ltd, Secretary of State for Trade and Industry v. Worth* [1994] 2 B.C.L.C. 113, [1994] B.C.C. 371.

(1) The word "need" is misleading and too narrow. Even given the width of the prohibitions under the CDDA, cases where "necessity" can be established in the sense that the applicant will not be able to earn a livelihood or the company will collapse unless he is granted permission to be (say) a director are probably going to be rare. The function of the court is, it is suggested, to weigh such "need", "desire" or "legitimate interest"[33] as is established with other factors pointing in favour or against the grant of permission.

(2) Any "desire" of the applicant to act in a prohibited capacity will carry much less weight than a "desire" or "need" of the company concerned ("desire" also carrying less weight than "need"). The "desire" or "need" of the relevant company may itself range in degree from a straightforward "desire" to have the applicant "on board",[34] to a "need" to have a person with the skills and experience of the applicant or to a "need" to have the applicant fulfilling a specific role or capacity for which permission is sought.

(3) In considering the "need" or "legitimate interests" of the company (to use parlance from more recent cases), there will be cases where the interests of the company cannot or should not be distinguished from those of the applicant.

These propositions and the shift away from a two-stage test towards a more nuanced "in all the circumstances" test are discussed further below.

The retreat from Gibson Davies

13.13 Although there are cases which suggest that the "desire" of the applicant for permission is irrelevant, such cases probably go to far. In *Re Gibson Davies Ltd* Sir Mervyn Davies discounted the desire of the applicant to be a director on the basis that "... such desire is, to my mind, not a need for present purposes".[35] However, in *Re Lo-Line Electric Motors Ltd*,[36] the court made reference to the "need" of the applicant to be a director, although it is not clear from the judgment what this "need" was based on. Similarly, in *Re Cargo Agency Ltd*,[37] Harman J. gave permission for a person to act as a general manager but it was not suggested in the judgment that the applicant had established, for example, that he could not have obtained employment elsewhere without breaching the terms of the disqualification order. Subsequent cases have confirmed that "need" is not a threshold requirement and that the "desire" or "need" of the applicant to obtain permission can be taken into account. In *Re Barings plc (No. 4), Secretary of State for Trade and Industry v. Baker*,[38] Scott V.-C. considered an application for permission made by Mr Norris, the former Chief Executive Officer of Barings who was disqualified for four years on grounds of unfitness under the summary *Carecraft* procedure.[39] In anticipation that a disqualification order would be made against him, Mr Norris made an application for permission to remain as a non-

---

[33] All terms which have been used by the courts in this context.
[34] See *Re Barings plc (No. 4), Secretary of State for Trade and Industry v. Baker* [1999] 1 All E.R. 1017, [1999] 1 B.C.L.C. 262.
[35] [1995] B.C.C. 11 at 15. In *Re Dawes & Henderson Ltd, Secretary of State for Trade and Industry v. Shuttleworth*, January 27, 1999, Ch.D., unreported Scott V.-C. suggested that the relevant passage from the judgment of Sir Mervyn Davies appeared to elevate the requirement of need into something like a *sine qua non* for the making of an order, an approach which he criticised.
[36] [1988] Ch. 477, [1988] 3 W.L.R. 26, [1988] 2 All E.R. 692, [1988] B.C.L.C. 698, (1988) 4 B.C.C. 415.
[37] [1992] B.C.L.C. 686, [1992] B.C.C. 388.
[38] [1999] 1 All E.R. 1017, [1999] 1 B.C.L.C. 262.
[39] On *Carecraft* see generally Chap. 8.

executive director of three named private companies. In each case, he did not "need" to act as a director because he was able to provide the same services and be remunerated accordingly as a consultant. Equally, the three companies did not "need" him to act as a director for the same reason. Nevertheless, on the facts of the case, permission to act as a director was given on terms.[40] Having decided that no relevant "need" (of company or applicant) had been established, Scott V.-C. said that the court should keep in balance the importance of protecting the public from the conduct which led to the disqualification order and the need for the applicant to act as a director.[41] On its face this raises a conundrum: if no "need" was established, what was there to balance? There are two possible answers which may overlap. The first is to say that "need" does not have to be established. The reference to a requirement to keep "need" and "protection of the public" in balance could simply be read as a suggestion that, in a case where the grant of permission poses no great danger to the public, it would be "out of balance" to require the applicant to establish "need". The second (and arguably more satisfactory) answer is to say that "need" does not have to be established as a precondition, but that the "needs" or "interests" of the relevant company and the applicant (which may vary in degree from "desire" to absolute "need") are relevant factors to be taken into account in determining whether, in all the circumstances, permission should be granted. On this view, it may be that in some cases, these factors will not be strong enough to outweigh other factors (principally, the public's need for protection) which weigh against the grant of permission.[42] Scott V.-C. returned to this question in *Re Dawes & Henderson Ltd, Secretary of State for Trade and Industry v. Shuttleworth*.[43] In that case, he referred, with approval, to the following words of Rattee J. in *Re Streamhaven Ltd, Secretary of State for Trade and Industry v. Barnett*:

> "In my judgment, the question I should ask myself is whether it is necessary for [the applicant] to be a director of a company in order to protect some legitimate interest of [the applicant] himself, or of any third party, which it is in all the circumstances of the case reasonable that the court should seek to protect... The extent to which it may be reasonable for the court to seek to protect the interests of the applicant himself in such a case must depend on all the circumstances giving rise to his disqualification."[44]

13.14   This move from "need" to "legitimate interest" and from a two-stage test to an "in all the circumstances" test, suggests further that "need" (beyond a narrow requirement to show that the court would not be acting in vain) is not a pre-condition of permission. In *Dawes & Henderson*, Scott V.-C. stressed that the court should only take into account relevant factors but firmly rejected any notion that the court should fetter its discretion in deciding whether or not to grant permission by any pre-conditions or criteria.[45] Thus, he held that it would not be right to ignore any "personal, non-commercial purposes" of the applicant. On the facts of the case, the relevant "interest" lay in the ability of the applicant's business to defer tax which was

---

[40] To ensure that Norris would not assume any executive responsibilities in relation to the three companies, permission was granted in each case on condition that he remain an unpaid non-executive and that he be barred from entering into a director's service contract.

[41] [1999] 1 All E.R. 1017 at 1024, [1999] 1 B.C.L.C. 262 at 269.

[42] In *Barings* itself, the court perceived that there was little risk that Norris's failings as a senior executive of a multi-national bank would recur by allowing him to take up a non-executive position in the three private companies which formed the subject matter of his application.

[43] January 27, 1999, Ch.D., unreported.

[44] [1998] 2 B.C.L.C. 64 at 72.

[45] See passage cited in 13.06 above.

apparently only possible by running the business through the medium of a company. However, it is important to recognise that Scott V.-C. did not say in *Dawes & Henderson* that "need" was an irrelevant factor. The mere fact that "need" is not a condition of obtaining permission did not mean that it would cease to be relevant factor in most cases. In many cases its absence would be fatal:

> "In a case where no need has been demonstrated on the company's part to have the applicant as director or, from a business point of view, on the applicant's part to be a director, there would need, I think, to be only a very small risk to the public which the granting of [permission] might produce to justify the refusal of the application. *Per contra*, if a substantial and pressing need on the part of the company, or on the part of the individual in order to be able to earn his living, could be shown in favour of the grant of [permission] then it might be right to accept some slight risk to the public if the [permission] sought were granted."

13.15 On the facts of the case, permission was granted to the applicant to act as a director of an *unlimited* company.[46] However, the Vice-Chancellor expressed the view that had the application been one to act as a director of a *limited* company, it would have been "a very difficult one indeed" to advance even bearing in mind the other positive factors which were relied upon as justifying the grant of permission. The mere fact that the company in question is *unlimited* and that there may be little practical difference between the applicant carrying on business as a sole trader or through an unlimited company[47] may not be decisive in all cases. In some cases, the previous misconduct (for example, misconduct involving dishonesty or want of probity) might not justify the court in allowing the person to act in a prohibited capacity, even in relation to an unlimited company. In summary, it is suggested that the position on "need" is currently as follows:

(1) There is no threshold requirement but the court must take into account and consider the "need" or "legitimate interests" of the applicant and the relevant company as part of all the circumstances of the case.

(2) The "legitimate interests" of the applicant and the company may go beyond mere commercial interests.

(3) Such "legitimate interests" as are established have to be weighed with the other factors (particularly, the question of public protection) pointing for and against the grant of permission.

(4) The strength of the "legitimate interests" which are required in any one case to tip the scales in favour of the grant of permission will depend on all the circumstances: there is no one standard or strength of "interest" or "need" the presence of which will automatically justify the grant (or the absence of which will automatically justify the refusal) of permission.

(5) In many cases, the absence of a strong "need" for permission will result in permission being refused. As a general rule, it will be a rare case where permission will be given in the absence of some need of the company for the services of the applicant in a prohibited capacity.

---

[46] See also further discussion of *Streamhaven* in main text below and the case of *Re DJ Matthews (Joinery Design) Ltd* (1988) 4 B.C.C. 513.
[47] The identifiable difference is that creditors need to wind up an unlimited company first before they can "get into [the applicant's] wallet".

Legitimate interest of the applicant of less weight than the legitimate interest of the company

13.16 The general proposition that the "interests" of the applicant weigh less heavily than the "interests" of an outside third party is borne out by authority. *Re Gibson Davies Ltd* itself is best seen as a case where the "interest" of the applicant in obtaining permission was not strong enough on its own to overcome the factors pointing against the grant of permission, but the weight given to the "interests" of the company and its employees was enough to tip the balance. The Australian courts have likewise accorded lesser weight to the applicant's personal needs as the following *dictum* of Zelling J. in *Re Maelor Pty Jones Ltd* illustrates:

> "Every disqualification under any Act involves in some way a hardship to an applicant and in some cases it may even threaten his livelihood and, it may be, his only source of livelihood, but when Parliament enacts disqualification sections such as these, it must be taken to know that that is their effect. Clearly in the opinion of Parliament the protection of the public outweighs the punitive effect the section may have on a person to whom it applies."[48]

13.17 This approach was also followed in *Re TLL Realisations Ltd*[49] where Park J. considered that the need for the disqualified person to earn a living, while relevant, would be less influential than the need of the company to have the work done by that person for the purposes of its business. This general point is considered further below in connection with other cases. In *Barings*[50] and *Dawes & Henderson*,[51] permission was given although no "need", either of the company or of the applicant was made out. While the approach in these cases to the question of need should now be followed (see discussion above), they are best regarded as exceptional. Thus, in *Barings* Scott V.-C. went so far as to say:

> "In *Re Amaron Ltd* [1998] B.C.C. 264 ... the judge addressed the question whether the applicant had established 'need' and held that he had not. But this was a case in which the applicant had allowed the company to trade while insolvent and to retain money owed to creditors in order to fund continued trading. The need to ensure protection of the public from management techniques of that character would, in my view, have made it virtually impossible for a section 17 application to have succeeded."[52]

13.18 He returned to this theme in *Dawes & Henderson* where he laid stress on the fact that the grounds on which the applicant had been disqualified did not involve any dishonesty, want of probity, deliberate breaches of the Companies Act 1985 or circumstances where any preferences or imprudent loans had been granted out of a desire for personal gain: "... in short, the improprieties alleged were of inadequate management and not of any dishonesty or want of probity". However, it is suggested that it would be wrong to assume that the fact that a director was disqualified for incompetence is going to be enough, in itself, to satisfy the court that permission is appropriate where there is only a weak "legitimate interest" in the application being granted. The relative weight to be given to the interests of the applicant and the interest

---

[48] (1975) 1 A.C.L.R. 4, 13–14. Also reported as *Re Van Reesma* (1975) 11 S.A.S.R. 322.
[49] Feburary 1, 1999, Ch.D., unreported.
[50] [1999] 1 All E.R. 1017, [1999] 1 B.C.L.C. 262.
[51] January 27, 1999, Ch.D., unreported.
[52] [1999] 1 All E.R. 1017 at 1023, [1999] 1 B.C.L.C. 262 at 269.

of the company is perhaps best reflected in the following extract from the judgment of His Honour Judge Cooke in *Secretary of State for Trade and Industry v. Rosenfield*:

> "I think that the question of need is best approached by saying simply does this order need to be made, and in whose interests does it need to be made? Now, so far as the director himself is concerned, I would take a good deal of persuasion that there were many, if any, cases where one can say properly the order needs to be made because the director would like it for his own purposes. The answer to that may very well be that if the director had landed himself in this position he must suffer a certain amount of inconvenience, but it does not follow that 'need' is to be construed restrictively so far as the needs of others are concerned."[53]

13.19   In *Dawes & Henderson*, Scott V.-C. observed that the policy behind the CDDA is that "... individuals against whom disqualification orders are made should nonetheless be able to earn their living in whatever business they may choose to turn their hand to". At first sight, this appears to imply that the "needs" of an applicant should be given considerable weight (*contra* the *dictum* of Judge Cooke). However, it is suggested that the Vice-Chancellor's observation should be read as a reference to carrying on a business as a sole trader or in partnership. This is because in the passage of the judgment which follows, the Vice-Chancellor referred to the applicant having "identified a business that he wants to carry on" and stated that it was consistent with the policy of the CDDA that he should carry it on *in his own name and at his own risk*, he being personally liable for its debts in the event of failure. It is suggested that this interpretation is consistent with the fact that the CDDA does not prohibit disqualified persons from carrying on in business as such. It only prohibits them from acting in certain capacities or carrying on certain functions in connection with companies. Thus, it is not the policy of the CDDA that disqualified persons should be able to carry on in business through the medium of a company. The policy is that they should only be able to do so with the permission of the court. As is stressed throughout this chapter, such permission should only be granted if it is consistent with the purposes for which the original disqualification was imposed and the CDDA generally.

Separate third party legitimate interests

13.20   In considering the "legitimate interests" of the company (or another third party), it is important to identify those cases where the company has no separate interest from that of the applicant and, where it does have a separate interest, what that interest is and how heavily it weighs in the balance. It is clear that there may be cases where the "interests" of the applicant and the company are indistinguishable. In *Re Streamhaven Ltd, Secretary of State for Trade and Industry v. Barnett*,[54] Rattee J. considered whether or not it was necessary for the applicant to be a director of the relevant company in order to protect some legitimate interest of the applicant or of a third party, which it was, in all the circumstances of the case, reasonable that the court should protect. In some cases it may be legitimate for the company to be regarded as having an interest separate from that of the applicant. For example, the relevant company may be long established and have outside investors and several employees. In such a case, it will be possible to say that the interests of the company are separate from those of the applicant as a matter of substance as well as form. In other cases, especially

---

[53] [1999] B.C.C. 413 at 416.
[54] [1998] 2 B.C.L.C. 64.

where the applicant is, in effect, seeking permission to act as an owner-manager, it may be artificial to distinguish the "interests" of the company from those of the applicant. *Streamhaven* was a case which fell into the latter category. The applicant and his wife were disqualified for four and two years respectively under the *Carecraft* procedure on the grounds that their conduct in relation to the relevant company, Streamhaven Ltd, which had traded in the restaurant business, made them unfit. Both parties accepted in the *Carecraft* statement that they had permitted the company to trade while insolvent, had failed to keep proper accounting records under section 221 of the Companies Act 1985 and had acted in breach of section 216 of the Insolvency Act 1986 by permitting the company to carry on its restaurant business under the same trade name that had been used when it was being run by a previous company which itself had gone into insolvent liquidation. The application for permission concerned a phoenix company controlled by the applicant and his wife which had acquired the restaurant business from Streamhaven acting by its liquidator. The applicant's evidence was that the restaurant business was identified with the applicant himself. He had devised the style of food for which the restaurant was known. He alone had dealt with the restaurant's suppliers. He claimed that, if he was not granted permission to act as a director, there would be no one who could run the company's business with the result that it would have to cease to trade. This would mean that bank loans would be called in and that 14 employees would lose their jobs. On the basis of this evidence, it was argued that the company needed the applicant as a director. Rattee J. refused to grant permission. His first point, as intimated above, was that it was unreal to distinguish the company's needs from the needs of the applicant where the relevant company was owned and run entirely by the applicant and his wife. The question of whether the court should protect the interests of the applicant in such a case must, according to Rattee J., depend on all the circumstances giving rise to his disqualification. On the facts, the judge was not satisfied that it was appropriate for the court "to protect [the applicant's] ability to run the business under the existing name, with the advantages to him of limited liability..." in circumstances where the relevant company was the third incorporated incarnation of the same business in the same hands and its previous incarnations had collapsed at the expense of creditors. It follows that Rattee J. was not satisfied that the "interest" of the applicant in being a director was strong enough in all the circumstances as to require or justify the grant of permission. In this respect, the judge accepted the suggestion made on behalf of the Secretary of State that if the company could not continue in business without the applicant as a director, steps should be taken to enable the applicant to continue as a sole trader or in partnership with his wife without the benefit of limited liability.[55] This suggests that an applicant who was disqualified on the ground of abuse of limited liability will find it difficult to satisfy the court that it is appropriate for him to be given permission to act, in effect, as an owner-manager of a limited company in the absence of any other compelling third party interest. The court might be prepared to grant permission in such a case if the applicant is seeking to trade through the medium of an unlimited company.[56] However, it is

---

[55] A similar conclusion was reached in *Re Universal Flooring and Driveways Ltd, Secretary of State for Trade and Industry v. Woodward*, May 15, 1997, Ch.D., unreported.
[56] See, *e.g. Re DJ Matthews (Joinery Design) Ltd* (1988) 4 B.C.C. 513, 518. In that case which was decided under the old Companies Act provisions, the judge suggested that the defendant's application for permission might be looked upon favourably if he re-registered the relevant company as an unlimited company. For the appropriate re-registration procedure see Companies Act 1985, s. 49. There appears to be a flaw in the approach suggested in *DJ Matthews* in that an applicant required to re-register his company as an unlimited company for the purposes of obtaining permission will be unable to convert it back into a limited company once his period of disqualification has expired: *ibid.*, s. 51(2). Note also, however, that a limited company can have directors with unlimited liability if its memorandum so provides: *ibid.*, ss. 306–307.

suggested in the light of *Dawes & Henderson* (discussed above) that there could still be difficulties in obtaining permission in such circumstances. *Streamhaven* appears to confirm the point that the applicant will have a stronger case for permission if the legitimate interest of the company or some other third party can be identified as being separate from the interests of the applicant.

13.21 The existence of a separate legitimate interest has been recognised in a number of cases. In *Re Tech Textiles Ltd, Secretary of State for Trade and Industry v. Vane*, Arden J. made the point that there will be companies where the involvement of the applicant in the capacity sought is vital to customer or investor confidence.[57] In that case, the applicant was given permission to act as a director of a single company as the evidence showed that, in practice, it was important to the company and others that the applicant remained as a director. The applicant was said to be particularly important to the company because of his expertise and contacts in the specialist industry in which the company was engaged. The court accepted that in the circumstances it was important to customers and suppliers that he remained on the board.

Similarly, in *Re TLL Realisations*,[58] some weight was given to the company's need for the applicant's specialist expertise. In that case, Park J. said that the court could take into account two distinct "needs" or "interests": (a) the need of the disqualified person to earn a living, and (b) the need of the company to have work done by the applicant for the purpose of its business. The judge stated that each factor carries some weight, although he would expect (b) to be more influential. Within (b) he identified two different "needs": (i) a need for the company to have some person filling the particular office or capacity in question and (ii) a need for the services of the particular applicant. Park J. went on to say that while there may be gradations between these types of case, the argument for permission will generally be more cogent in case (ii). It is suggested that this helpful characterisation should not be applied too rigidly. In practice, the two "needs" identified in (b) are but two particular points on a wide spectrum of "legitimate interest" or "need". It is possible to conceive of circumstances where it is highly desirable that a particular person carry out a particular function within a company (which would be a stronger legitimate interest than simply a requirement that somebody fill the position in question) but where it cannot be said that the applicant is the only possible person who could fill the role in question.

13.22 An earlier case which arguably reflects a similar approach is the decision of the Court of Session in *Secretary of State for Trade and Industry v. Palfreman*. In that case, permission was granted in the light of evidence tending to show that "... the [applicant] held a position of considerable responsibility in the companies which relied upon his goodwill for their successful trading and to remove him from management of the companies could have serious effects for a number of people, not least the employees...".[59] The company's dependence (and, by extension, that of innocent parties such as employees) on the applicant has also been treated as an important factor in several cases decided by the Australian and New Zealand courts.[60] Equally, however, there are cases where the court has not been persuaded that there is a sufficiently strong

---

[57] [1998] 1 B.C.L.C. 259 at 269. The existence of a separate legitimate interest may provide a possible rationale for the decisions in *Gibson Davies* (discussed above) and *Palfreman* (discussed below).
[58] February 1, 1999, Ch.D., unreported.
[59] [1995] B.C.C. 193, 195D. The employees in this case numbered some 350.
[60] See, *e.g. Re Zim Metal Products Pty Ltd* [1977] A.C.L.C. 29,556, (1977) 2 A.C.L.R. 553; *Re Hamilton-Irvine* (1990) 8 A.C.L.C. 1,057, *Murray v. Australian Securities Commission* (1994) 12 A.C.L.C. 1; *Re Wallace* (1983) 8 A.C.L.R. 311; *Re Minimix Industries Ltd* (1982) 1 N.Z.C.L.C. 98,381, (1982) 1 A.C.L.C. 511; *Re Focas* [1992] M.C.L.R. 515. In England and Wales see also *Secretary of State for Trade and Industry v. Rosenfield* [1999] B.C.C. 413.

"legitimate interest" to justify the grant of permission for a disqualified person to act as a director of a dormant or semi-dormant company.[61]

13.23 Even if some separate interest can be identified, the court may still take the view that it is not sufficiently worthy of protection to justify any relaxation of the prohibition. In *Re Amaron Ltd*[62] an outsider (*i.e.* a non-disqualified person) owned 25 per cent of the share capital and was a director of the company in relation to which permission was sought. The evidence showed that the applicant was the "guiding force" behind the company and that the outsider did not take any direct responsibility for running the company. It was held that any alleged detrimental effects on the company (which can be taken to include any prejudice to the outsider) could be met by the applicant and the outsider continuing to trade through the medium of a partnership: a similar solution to that adopted in *Streamhaven*.[63] The facts of the case are of interest because the general approach of the judge to the question of "need" (even taking into account that he was applying the law as it stood before *Barings* and *Dawes & Henderson*), demonstrates the level of detailed evidence that an applicant is required to produce. As indicated above, the judge took the view that much of the impact on the company's business, which it was alleged would follow if permission was not granted, could be alleviated if the applicant and the outsider set up in partnership and continued to trade from the same premises. Any unfortunate tax consequences which might arise if the premises were transferred from the company to the partners could be avoided by the company retaining ownership of them. Any disadvantage flowing from the applicant not having the status of director would be avoided given that, if the business was run as a partnership, there would be no directors and no expectation that the applicant should be a director. The suggestion that the outsider might be prejudiced was not made out on the evidence and, having heard from the gentleman in question, it appeared to the judge that "... he had not considered the matter and was in any event far from suggesting that he would not be prepared to carry on the business in partnership ... [t]he possibility certainly did not seem to worry him when it was raised with him.".[64] A question also arose in *Amaron* concerning a non-transferable waste transfer station licence which was vested in the company. The licence was not produced in court and, on the evidence, it appeared likely that if the premises remained vested in the company, the licence would not have to be transferred or renewed because ownership of the premises to which it attached was not changing. However, the judge did give interim permission for a transitional period of six weeks to enable matters to be sorted out, but subject to specific measures designed to protect the public.

13.24 In arriving at an overall assessment of the company's needs or legitimate interests the court may find it useful if evidence is adduced from an independent third

---

[61] See, *e.g. Re Brian Sheridan Cars Ltd* [1996] 1 B.C.L.C. 327 at 342 (permission refused in relation to a company which was not trading) and *Re Tech Textiles Ltd, Secretary of State for Trade and Industry v. Vane* [1998] 1 B.C.L.C. 259 at 271. In *Tech Textiles* permission was refused in relation to an investment holding company which did nothing more than hold shares in the main trading company but which was said (by the applicant) to need his services as a director (and, in particular, his knowledge and experience of the relevant industry) in relation to pursuing investment opportunities. It was said also that his position in negotiations would lack status and credibility if he was not a director. It was held that no strong interest had been shown as the evidence did not explain how the company could pursue any acquisitions or investment opportunities in the light of its stated financial position.

[62] [1998] B.C.C. 264.

[63] It is striking that in *Re Amaron Ltd* there was no offer from the applicant to ensure, by way of safeguard, that a professionally-qualified director (such as an accountant) was appointed to the board. As a consequence, Neuberger J. was not satisfied that the public would be adequately protected in any event.

[64] [1998] B.C.C. 264 at 279–280.

party such as a firm of chartered accountants.[65] However, the evidence will need to be up to date and reflect the current position of the company.[66] It is clear from authorities which follow the old two-stage approach that *some* evidence as to the company's needs should be put before the court. It is suggested that this remains the position even if (as is indicated above) the court's function on an application for permission cannot properly be understood without reference to *Barings* and *Dawes & Henderson*. In *Re Lombard Shipping & Forwarding Ltd*,[67] an application for permission to continue as director of a corporate residents association was refused even though it was not a normal trading company and, it appeared that there was no great risk to the public in allowing the applicant (who had been disqualified for the minimum period of two years under section 6) to remain on the board. The deputy judge summed up the position as follows:

> "The difficulty here is that I have got no evidence at all about the operation of that company apart from the fact that [the applicant] has been a director for 12 years. I have no evidence as to whether any other director is available to do the work or whether it is essential for [the applicant] to carry on because there is no other available person."

This point is arguably of general relevance. Thus, it will always be sensible for the applicant to adduce up to date evidence to assist the court on both the question of "legitimate interest" and the question of public protection. Only this will satisfy the broad requirement for cogent evidence discussed right at the outset with reference to *Tech Textiles*. As Neuberger J. put it in *Re Amaron Ltd*:

> "At least in the absence of special factors, the court must have an up to date (and substantial) account of the position of a company in respect of which a section 17 application is made. Otherwise, it is difficult for an applicant to establish that the public can be protected if he is permitted to act as a director (or indeed that there is a need that he be a director)" [68]

Summary

13.25   In the light of *Barings* and *Dawes & Henderson* it is doubtful whether the old two-stage test should now be followed. The critical question is whether, if permission is granted, the public will be adequately protected from the risk that the conduct which led to the applicant's disqualification might recur. The notion that the "need" requirement amounts to a threshold test applicable in every case is now under considerable strain. However, this is not to say that "need" (understood as a range or spectrum of factors) cannot be taken into account in an appropriate case. For example, in the context of owner-managed companies, it may well be that variants of the approach in *Streamhaven* will continue to be used as a means of balancing the primary interest in the protection of the public against other interests such as the interests of investors and employees. As such, there is clearly room for the court to weigh the "needs" of such constituencies in the exercise of the discretion. However, in a case like *Streamhaven* where the only identifiable "need" is that of the applicant, the likelihood

---

[65] See, *e.g. Secretary of State for Trade and Industry v. Brown* (1995) S.L.T. 550, 552 I–J, 553C–D; *Re Gibson Davies Ltd* [1995] B.C.C. 11, 14B. This evidence will also be useful in relation to the issue of public protection particularly, where relevant, on such matters as the state of the company's internal financial controls.
[66] *Re Amaron Ltd* [1998] B.C.C. 264 at 278.
[67] March 22, 1993, Ch.D, unreported.
[68] [1998] B.C.C. 264 at 278.

is that primacy will be given to the protection of the public. A further point flowing from this is that cases like *Streamhaven* would probably have been decided in the same way in any event. Thus, on the *Barings* approach, the court might well have concluded that the risk of further abuses of limited liability were too great to justify the granting of permission, a point reflected in the extract from Scott V.-C.'s judgment cited in 13.17 above.[69]

Protection of the public

13.26   It is suggested that in the light of *Barings* and the discussion of the "need" requirement above, that the rigid two-stage test posited in *Cargo Agency* and *Gibson Davies* should not be followed. The better view is that the court should simply ask whether, in all the circumstances of the case, permission should be granted. In considering whether permission should be granted, the court should bear in mind the reasons for the original disqualification and the purposes which the disqualification is to serve. Key among these is the protection of the public achieved through (a) keeping the disqualifed person "off the road", (b) deterring the disqualifed person and (c) deterring others from failing to meet the proper standards required of company directors by the courts.[70] For these purposes (as was argued in Chapter 2), the "public" should be given the widest possible meaning and taken to include investors, creditors, employees, customers and so on. In this respect, while each case will turn on its own particular facts, it is suggested that the applicant will have to give satisfaction on some or all of the points touched on below if he is to convince the court that the public will be adequately protected if permission is granted. Typically, the court will only be satisfied on the question of adequate public protection subject to the inclusion of detailed conditions and safeguards in the order. The courts' main concern on the authorities, has been to ensure, as far as possible, that there is no repetition of the types of conduct which led to the applicant's disqualification in the first place. In considering this question, it is suggested that the court should not be concerned solely to prevent a repetition of the precise conduct or failings which led to the disqualification but to protect the public against the fault which underlies the relevant conduct in question, be that dishonesty, want of probity or even incompetence. An incompetent director is as capable of causing loss and damage to the public as is a dishonest director.[71]

Factors taken into account

13.27   Most of the authorities to date have concerned applications for permission made by persons who were disqualified on grounds of unfitness under section 6. Applications have been successful in those cases where the applicant has convinced the courts that, on balance, there is unlikely to be any repetition of his previous unfit conduct. The court will pay close attention to the specific findings of unfitness which were made against the applicant (or, in a case not directly involving the unfitness provisions, the specific conduct which triggered the disqualification) and also to conditions within the company the subject of the application so as to be satisfied that the company is not a breeding ground for further misconduct.

13.28   It is suggested that the court is not restricted, and should not restrict itself, to a consideration of whether or not the specific past failings of the applicant which led to his disqualification are likely to be repeated. Thus, in a case such as *Re TLL Realis-*

---

[69] The decision in *Re Amaron Ltd* [1998] B.C.C. 264 is open to a similar re-interpretation.
[70] See *Re Westmid Packing Services Ltd, Secretary of State for Trade and Industry v. Griffiths* [1998] 2 All E.R. 124, [1998] 2 B.C.L.C. 646, [1998] B.C.C. 836, CA.
[71] On the range of meanings embraced by the term "incompetence" see Chap. 5.

ations Ltd[72] where the applicant was disqualified for his failings as a finance director but sought permission to act as a manager and not as a director, the mere fact that the applicant might be supervised in his new position as manager is not, it is suggested, a reason for the court to refuse to consider matters such as the financial position of the relevant company, its current standard of book-keeping and the like. There are a number of reasons why this should be so. The first arises from the general point that, once disqualified, a person has to ask the permission of the court to act in a certain capacity. The indulgence sought is an indulgence both to him and the company in question. The court should be satisfied that it is right to grant such an indulgence. It would seem strange to a member of the public if the court was aware that the company was, for example, teetering on the edge of insolvency, failing to file accounts and returns and the like and yet gave permission for the applicant to take part in such a company on the ground that he would not be directly involved in the "problem" matters. Equally, it would be odd if the court did not enquire or require evidence about such matters. In this respect, it is suggested that the position is different to that under section 216 of the Insolvency Act 1986, where the courts have said that permission to use a prohibited name will be given if the vice targeted by the provision (broadly arising in connection with phoenix operations) is not present, irrespective of whether the director in question might otherwise be unfit or the new company might otherwise be in financial difficulties.[73] Other powers are available to the Secretary of State (such as powers to initiate company investigations, winding up proceedings or further disqualification proceedings) to deal with any future problems which may arise in the company in relation to which permission is sought. However, the mere existence of such powers and mere absence of the particular vice which led to the original disqualification should not, it is suggested, prevent the court from refusing permission if there is concern that the company may be about to collapse or that it is not being run according to proper standards. A second reason is that if the company in relation to which permission is sought is itself not being properly run, this must raise doubts about the extent to which the applicant can or will be properly supervised and prevented from repeating the failings which led to his disqualification. A third reason is that if a person is required to exercise some management function, the likelihood is that he will have some autonomy. Otherwise there would be no point in appointing him. As such, he represents a potential weak link in the management structure. The weakness of that link can only be considered in the context of the overall management structure and health (financial or otherwise) of the company. The cases suggest that the following (non-exclusive) factors are likely to be taken into account in considering the question of "public protection":

13.29 *Seriousness and type of conduct.* Most of the applicants granted some form of permission by the courts in England and Wales have been persons disqualified for periods of five years or less and whose conduct was therefore considered by the disqualifying court to fall within the lowest bracket of seriousness on the *Sevenoaks Stationers* guidelines.[74] The fact that even in these cases the court considered it necess-

---

[72] February 1, 1999, Ch.D., unreported.

[73] Contrast the approach in *Re Bonus Breaks Ltd* [1991] B.C.C. 546 with that in *Penrose v. Official Receiver* [1996] 1 W.L.R. 482, [1996] 1 B.C.L.C. 389, [1996] B.C.C. 311 and *Re Lightning Electrical Contractors Ltd* [1996] 2 B.C.L.C. 302, [1996] B.C.C. 950. See also discussion in G. Wilson, "Delinquent Directors and Company Names" (1996) 47 N.I.L.Q. 345.

[74] *Re Sevenoaks Stationers (Retail) Ltd* [1991] Ch. 164, [1990] 3 W.L.R. 1165, [1991] 3 All E.R. 578, [1991] 1 B.C.L.C. 325, [1990] B.C.C. 765 and see Chap. 5. Of the successful applicants in reported cases, the ones disqualified for the longest periods were those in *Re Majestic Recording Studios Ltd* [1989] B.C.L.C. 1, (1988) 4 B.C.C. 519 and *Re Gibson Davies Ltd* [1995] B.C.C. 11 (both five years). In *Re TLL Realisations Ltd*, February 1, 1999, Ch.D., unreported, the successful applicant was (unusually) the subject of an eight-year disqualification order.

ary to impose conditions (see further below) suggests that a disqualified person whose previous conduct was held to fall within the middle or highest brackets of seriousness will find it correspondingly more difficult to persuade the court to grant his application. The nature and seriousness of the applicant's previous conduct is a factor which is also weighed in the balance in Commonwealth jurisdictions.[75] In the light of *Barings, Tech Textiles* and *Dawes & Henderson* (discussed above), it is clear that the court will also look carefully at the type of conduct which led to the applicant's disqualification and the nature of the company in relation to which permission is sought. *Re Barings plc (No. 4), Secretary of State for Trade and Industry v. Baker*[76] concerned Mr Norris, the former Chief Executive Officer of Barings. Mr Norris was disqualified for four years on grounds of unfitness under the summary *Carecraft* procedure. The case against him did not involve any imputation of dishonesty nor was it alleged that he had abused the privilege of limited liability. It was based exclusively on Mr Norris's incompetence. Particular emphasis was placed on Mr Norris's failure, despite his senior position, to monitor the activities of the rogue trader, Nick Leeson and the demand for funds which those activities had generated. Thus, Mr Norris had to accept his share of the responsibility for the board allowing to go unquestioned the huge outflow of funds from Barings plc into its Singaporean subsidiary which ultimately precipitated the collapse.[77] In anticipation that a disqualification order would be made against him, Mr Norris made an application for permission to remain as a non-executive director of three specified private companies. He had been invited to join the boards of these companies having previously advised them in a consultancy capacity. The companies were involved in various businesses ranging from publishing to film and video production. Despite Mr Norris's failure to demonstrate any strong need for permission, his application was granted. The Vice-Chancellor approached the application by asking whether, on the facts, the public interest required that permission be refused and dispensed with the question of need. He stated:

"The court in considering whether or not to grant [permission] should, in particular, pay attention to the nature of the defects in company management that led to the disqualification order and ask itself whether, if [permission] were granted, a situation might arise in which there would be a risk of recurrence of those defects. In a case like the present there seems to me to be virtually no risk at all of such a recurrence. [N will not be placed] ... in a position in which an inadequate discharge of executive responsibilities of the sort that justified the disqualification

---

[75] See, *e.g. Re Magna Alloys & Research Pty Ltd* (1975) 1 A.C.L.R. 203; *Re Zim Metal Products Pty Ltd* [1977] A.C.L.C. 29,556, (1977) 2 A.C.L.R. 553; *Zuker v. Commissioner for Corporate Affairs* [1981] V.R. 72, [1980] A.C.L.C. 34, 334 also reported as *Re Record Leather Manufacturers (Aust.) Pty Ltd* (1980) 5 A.C.L.R. 19; *Re Marsden* (1980) 5 A.C.L.R. 694, 702 (Australia). Note that the overall approach taken in Australia on the issue of permission is followed in both New Zealand and Singapore: see, *e.g. Re Focas* [1992] M.C.L.R. 515 (New Zealand); *AG v. Derrick Chong Soon Choy, Quek Leng Chye v. AG* [1985] 1 M.L.J. 97, *Quek Leng Chye v. AG* [1985] 2 M.L.J. 270, P.C. (Singapore). The Singapore cases cited arose in the wake of the City Country Club scandal which is chronicled and widely discussed in A. Hicks, "Commercial Candour and Integrity in Singapore" (1986) 28 Mal. L.R. 288. Note further that the applicants in these Commonwealth cases had all suffered *automatic* disqualification without further court order under a series of closely-comparable statutory provisions following their conviction for various *criminal offences*. There is no direct equivalent in England and Wales. Nevertheless, useful guidance can still be derived from these cases because the courts in all of these jurisdictions share the broad view of our courts that the primary purpose of disqualification legislation is the protection of the public.
[76] [1999] 1 All E.R. 1017, [1999] 1 B.C.L.C. 262.
[77] The former chairman of the bank's asset and liability committee consented to a disqualification order on similar grounds: see *Re Barings plc* [1998] B.C.C. 583. For the fate of three other senior executives see *Re Barings plc (No. 5), Secretary of State for Trade and Industry v. Baker* [1999] 1 B.C.L.C. 433 and see generally discussion in Chap. 5.

order ... will have any possibility of occurring. In [no] case does his directorship carry with it any executive responsibilities at all. Accordingly, the fact that a need for [N] to be given the ... [permission] that he seeks and that companies want him to be given has not been established is not, in my judgment, a sufficient reason for withholding [permission]."

To ensure that Mr Norris would not assume any executive responsibilities in relation to the three companies, permission was granted in each case on condition that he remain an unpaid non-executive and that he be barred from entering into a director's service contract.[78] It is clear from *Barings* that the court is required to consider the question of recurrence with reference to the applicant's previous conduct and the nature of the company in relation to which permission is sought.

13.30   *Trading prospects of company.* The fact that the company the subject of the application is trading successfully has tended to weigh in the applicant's favour. The applicant will need to show that trading conditions in the company are such that any specific misconduct highlighted by the original disqualification proceedings is unlikely to be repeated. For example, a person disqualified for allowing an insolvent company to continue trading at the expense of its creditors will need to demonstrate that the company is solvent and paying its debts as they fall due. In *Secretary of State for Trade and Industry v. Palfreman,*[79] the principal reason for the applicant's disqualification was that a company of which he was a non-executive director had traded while insolvent mainly at the expense of preferential creditors. A factor which contributed to the success of his application for permission to continue as a director of two other companies was evidence from the Inland Revenue and Customs & Excise indicating that those companies were currently honouring their obligations to the tax authorities. It was also noted that the turnover of both companies was substantial. By way of contrast, in *Re Lombard Shipping & Forwarding Ltd*[80] the application failed because, among other reasons, one of the companies was encountering difficulty in paying its rates, a recurrence of a specific problem which had come to light in the original disqualification proceedings. Equally, where lack of working capital is identified as a problem during the course of the disqualification proceedings, it is likely, on a permission application, that the court will want to see some evidence to suggest that the company is adequately capitalised.[81] The court will also want to be satisfied that directors' remuneration is paid at a level which the company can properly sustain.[82]

13.31   *Financial controls.* The applicant will need to adduce some evidence showing that the company the subject of the application has adequate financial controls and is complying with the statutory obligations in Part VII of the Companies Act 1985 as to the keeping of proper books of account and the filing of accounts and returns with the Registrar of Companies. Again, this will be especially important where complaints over lack of financial controls and/or filing defaults were upheld in

---

[78] It may be questioned whether such conditions in fact provide any protection, a point taken up below in the main text.
[79] [1995] 2 B.C.L.C. 301, [1995] B.C.C. 193.
[80] March 22, 1993, Ch.D., unreported.
[81] *Re Chartmore Ltd* [1990] B.C.L.C. 673 although in that case Harman J. decided that his concerns about the company's lack of capitalisation could be assuaged by granting the applicant permission to act as its director for one year only with liberty to apply under the order for permission to be extended, "... it being understood that, if it turns out that the responsible and careful manner heretofore adopted has not been continued, there may well be no extension of that permission..." (676G–H).
[82] *Secretary of State for Trade and Industry v. Brown* (1995) S.L.T. 550, 552L; *Re Amaron Ltd* [1998] B.C.C. 264.

the original disqualification proceedings.[83] A lack of up to date, reliable financial information about the company may well prove fatal to the application. If the evidence is inadequate or incomplete the court will usually dismiss the application rather than give the applicant time to adduce further evidence although this would not preclude a fresh application at a later date.[84] Even if the evidence produced is satisfactory, the court will usually require safeguards (*e.g.* the appointment of independent directors or regular attendance by the auditors at board meetings) with the aim of ensuring that the company's internal controls are the subject of continuous review.

Conditional permission

13.32   Even if the court is minded to grant the application, it is unlikely to give unconditional permission. The prevailing view is that the court may grant permission "on such terms and conditions as it thinks fit" despite the lack of express words in the statute to that effect.[85] The current practice of the courts in England and Wales, where permission is granted, is to insist either that the applicant offers certain safeguards which are then built into the order or to make an order which is limited in time and does not cover the full period of the disqualification (or some combination of the two approaches). This suggests that the court will not derogate lightly from the terms of the disqualification order and reflects the view expressed in *Re Brian Sheridan Cars Ltd*[86] that a person granted permission to act as a director of a specified company is being accorded a privilege or indulgence.[87] In this respect it is interesting to note that most of the reported cases where the court has granted conditional permission concerned persons who had been disqualified for five years or less and typically no more than three years.[88] A secondary issue concerning the technical difference between a fully conditional order and an order for permission granted on undertakings is considered below.

Permission: a derogation from protection of the public

13.33   It is important to recognise that any grant of permission is an erosion of the protection of the public otherwise afforded by a CDDA disqualification. In *Re Gibson Davies Ltd*,[89] the applicant had been disqualified for five years. The findings of unfitness related to a small company of which the applicant had been a director. It was established that the applicant had caused that company to trade while insolvent and enter into a transaction which amounted to a preference. It was also established that misleading invoices had been raised, excessive remuneration had been paid to the directors and accounts had not been filed. The case was somewhat unusual in that the applicant made no attempt to defend the disqualification proceedings but did apply

---

[83] See, *e.g. Re Chartmore* [1990] B.C.L.C. 673 at 676A; *Re Gibson Davies Ltd* [1995] B.C.C. 11 at 14B; *Secretary of State for Trade and Industry v. Brown* (1995) S.L.T. 550.

[84] *Re Lombard Shipping & Forwarding Ltd*, March 22, 1993, Ch.D., unreported. *Per* the deputy judge:

"I find that on the evidence put before me I am unable to give [permission] for Mr Woollen to continue. [Counsel] said there may be an inadequacy in the evidence but it could be put right. It is not for the court to negotiate in that sort of way and say what will be satisfactory and what not."

See also *Re Amaron Ltd* [1998] B.C.C. 264 on the importance of current evidence of the relevant company's financial position.

[85] See, *e.g. Re Tech Textiles Ltd, Secretary of State for Trade and Industry v. Vane* [1998] 1 B.C.L.C. 259 at 267. The Scottish courts have followed the English lead on grounds of comity while expressing doubt as to whether there is power to impose conditions: see *Secretary of State for Trade and Industry v. Palfreman* [1995] 2 B.C.L.C. 301, [1995] B.C.C. 193.

[86] [1996] 1 B.C.L.C. 327.

[87] See also the view in *Tech Textiles* cited above in para. 13.07 above.

[88] For an exception see *Re TLL Realisations Ltd*, February 1, 1999, Ch.D., unreported (eight years).

[89] [1995] B.C.C. 11.

later to set aside the disqualification order[90] or, failing that, for permission to act as a director of the English subsidiary of an Irish company. The application for permission was initially refused but granted by the Companies Court on appeal. The applicant originally offered the following specific safeguards:

(1) No cheque or financial agreement be signed or executed on the company's behalf by the applicant alone.

(2) Any director's loans owed by the company to the applicant shall not be repaid unless all creditors of the company are paid first.

(3) The applicant shall not be granted or accept any security over the company's assets.

(4) The applicant's total emoluments shall not exceed £380 per week or such greater sum as shall hereafter be agreed in writing by the Secretary of State, such consent not to be unreasonably withheld.

(5) The applicant shall procure the company to file annual returns and accounts at Companies House within the time limits set out in the Companies Act 1985.

(6) The applicant will procure the company to complete the implementation of accounting controls as set out by Mr Hear of Robson Rhodes in his affidavit sworn on February 3, 1994.

(7) The applicant will procure the company to prepare monthly management accounts and submit the same to Robson Rhodes or to the company's auditors for the time being.

(8) Robson Rhodes or the company's auditors for the time being shall be instructed to report to the board of directors in writing any matters of concern related to the management or financial control of the company and in default of prompt and appropriate action by the directors of the company will bring these matters to the attention of the Secretary of State's solicitors.

(9) In the event that the company seeks to change the identity of its auditors, the applicant will procure the company only to instruct auditors who are willing to accept and act on the obligations set out above.

(10) The applicant will take no step as a shareholder or director of Congratulations Ltd, that is the Irish company,[91] which would in any way impede, direct or control the activities of the company.

13.34   The accounting items referred to in (6) above were:

(a) All cheques over £2,500 to be signed by more than one director.

(b) All cheques below £2,500 to be signed both by the applicant and the company's financial controller, Mrs Richards.

(c) Monthly management accounts to be reviewed by Robson Rhodes.

(d) The company to complete the implementation of the internal accounting controls recommended by Robson Rhodes.

(e) Robson Rhodes to accept the obligation in (8) above.

---

[90] Rule 8(2) of the Disqualification Rules enables the court to set aside or vary any disqualification order made in the defendant's absence under either sections 6–7 or section 8.
[91] The applicant owned 50% of the issued shares in the Irish company and was a director. The company's two other directors held the balance of the shares.

After the hearing some alterations were made to these conditions by consent. Those alterations were all in the applicant's favour. First, the requirement in (4) for increases in emoluments to be approved by the Secretary of State in writing was replaced by a provision under which variations would be allowed subject only to the unanimous consent of the board of directors. Secondly, the various accounting controls were set out individually as a separate condition in the order. The two main purposes of all these conditions was to ensure that control of the company (and, indirectly, the Irish parent) remained vested at all times in the board as a whole (as opposed to the applicant alone who was merely one of three directors)[92] and that its business would be the subject of close and continuous scrutiny by the auditors. The conditions were also designed to meet any fears which the court might have as to the possible future repetition of the applicant's previous conduct.[93] In terms of safeguards, the conditional order made in *Gibson Davies* is the most detailed example to date.

13.35   The subsequent events which followed the granting of permission in *Gibson Davies* are instructive.[94] The original disqualification order was made in February 1993. The order granting permission for the applicant, Mr Davies to act as a director of Congratulations Franchising Ltd ("Congratulations") was made in July 1994. In January 1995, Congratulations went into creditors' voluntary liquidation with a deficit of over £400,000. Disqualification proceedings were subsequently commenced in relation to the conduct of a number of the directors of Congratulations including Mr Davies. One main ground of complaint in these proceedings was that there had been non-compliance with the conditions in the order granting Mr Davies permission to act. Two aspects of this complaint amounted to a re-run of the position that was reached in *Re Brian Sheridan Cars Ltd*.[95] First, the applicant for permission had failed to abide by the conditions which he had offered. Secondly, the other members of the board, on whom the court was relying to protect the public, had also failed to ensure that the conditions were met.[96] Breaches of conditions (1), (4), (5) and (6) of the conditions in the order were found to have occurred. The following further allegations of misconduct were raised against Mr Davies:

(1)   That he hampered the realisation by the liquidator of an asset of the company by asserting that it belonged to the Irish company. This allegation was found to be made out.

(2)   That he accepted payments from intending advertisers for a directory which was not published in circumstances where the money was mixed with the general funds of the company, that the company was under-capitalised and that these monies were used to finance the company. These allegations were found to be made out.

---

[92] See further, *Re Lombard Shipping & Forwarding Ltd*, March 22, 1993, Ch.D., unreported, where the court was even more explicit in expressing the view that an applicant should not be allowed to occupy a position of unbridled control.

[93] The conditions concerned with financial controls were clearly designed with the previous insolvent trading complaint in mind. Conditions (2) and (3) appear to have been offered to allay fears over possible preferences while conditions (4) and (5) also addressed issues which had come to light in the original disqualification proceedings.

[94] See the judgment of His Honour Judge Boggis Q.C. (sitting as a judge of the Chancery Division) in *Re Congratulations Franchising Ltd, Secretary of State for Trade and Industry v. Davies*, March 6, 1998, Ch.D., unreported.

[95] [1996] 1 B.C.L.C. 327.

[96] On this point, the position in *Brian Sheridan* was arguably worse as two professional individuals, one of whom was a solicitor, had been appointed to the relevant boards.

(3) That he deliberately prevented access to the company's records by interfering with the relevant computer programme. This allegation was found not proven.

(4) That there had been a technical breach of section 349 of the Companies Act by reason of the company using a shortened version of its name in gift albums. This allegation was admitted.

(5) That he caused the company to withhold payment of Crown monies (approximately £64,000) and used them to finance the company's business. This allegation was admitted.

(6) That he failed to ensure that the company's accounts were audited and filed by the due date. This allegation was found to be made out.

13.36 In the result, Mr Davies was found to be unfit and disqualified for 12 years. What this case shows, if there were any doubt about the matter, is that however widely conditions are framed, the protection of the public is inevitably eroded by the grant of permission. Indeed, it may be that if the approach put forward by Scott V.-C. in the *Barings* and *Dawes & Henderson* cases, was to be followed, the court would be much more wary of granting permission in a similar case to this in the future. In the original case, Mr Davies was disqualified for five years apparently[97] for (a) causing the company to enter into a transaction affording a preference to himself and another director; (b) allowing the company to continue trading thereby allowing the position of creditors to be eroded after distraint had been levied by the Inland Revenue; (c) raising misleading invoices; (d) paying undue remuneration when trading losses were increasing and (e) failing to file audited accounts. The following extract from the Vice-Chancellor's judgment in *Barings* bears repetition here:

> "In *Re Amaron Ltd* [1998] B.C.C. 264 ... the judge addressed the question whether the applicant had established 'need' and held that he had not. But this was a case in which the applicant had allowed the company to trade while insolvent and to retain money owed to creditors in order to fund continued trading. The need to ensure protection of the public from management techniques of that character would, in my view, have made it virtually impossible for a section 17 application to have succeeded."[98]

It is suggested that this approach ought to be followed in cases like *Gibson Davies*. Ironically, the greater the number of conditions that are placed on the grant of permission, the greater the indication that there is a potential risk to the public in granting it. It is suggested that the court in *Gibson Davies* was attempting to regulate the management of the company in a way which itself demonstrated that permission should not have been given. It is also suggested that the decision to grant permission in *Gibson Davies* was made without sufficient emphasis being given to the deterrence aspect of disqualification.

Conditions or undertakings?

13.37 In *Gibson Davies* the applicant was granted permission to be and remain a director of the English subsidiary "upon condition that [he] do abide by the conditions set out in the schedule hereto".[99] The safeguards referred to above were then incorpor-

---

[97] A note of the district judge's judgment was not available to Sir Mervyn Davies: see [1995] B.C.C. 11 at 12.
[98] [1999] 1 All E.R. 1017 at 1023, [1999] 1 B.C.L.C. 262 at 269.
[99] [1995] B.C.C. 11, 17C.

ated in the schedule. Similarly, the disqualified person in *Re Brian Sheridan Cars Ltd* was originally given permission "... subject to and so long as ..." he complied with various conditions set out in the order.[1] The effect of drawing the order in these terms is that if the applicant fails to comply with any of the safeguards, he puts himself automatically in breach of the prohibitions contained in the original disqualification order. This is because the continuance of permission is expressed to depend on full and continuing compliance with the safeguards. A conditional order of this nature must therefore be honoured to the letter failing which the applicant exposes himself (and, given the scope of the civil sanction in section 15, possibly others) to the full range of criminal and civil sanctions for which provision is made in the CDDA.[2] *Re Brian Sheridan Cars Ltd* is a case which illustrates the point well. There, the defendant, who was the subject of a three-year disqualification order, had originally been granted permission to act as a director of three companies, subject to a number of conditions, for one year only with effect from July 4, 1994. He failed to comply with all of the conditions, in particular, those requiring the relevant companies to appoint a specified firm of auditors and an independent director. The court acceded to his later application for renewal of the order, giving him permission for a second year. There was a further application before the court to vary the order of July 4, 1994 with retrospective effect. The deputy judge explained the thinking behind this further application:

> "The reason why the [defendant] is anxious that I should not merely amend the section 17 order, but also backdate it, is that it would thereby validate the defendant's directorship of the companies, whereas, if I did not backdate any amending order, the defendant would have been acting as a director of the companies contrary to the provisions of the Act, because he would not have complied with the terms on which the court had given him permission to act as director of the companies."[3]

13.38 The defendant's advisers appreciated that if the amendments were not backdated he would be exposed to criminal and civil liability under the CDDA because of his failure to comply with the conditions as originally drawn and this would still be the case even if the order for permission was renewed for a further year on fresh conditions. While acknowledging that the court has power to backdate its orders,[4] the deputy judge refused to backdate the order in this case and thus left the defendant exposed, at least in theory, to the possibility of enforcement proceedings under the CDDA. To grant the application, he observed, would be to send out the message, "... that the court does not really expect directors granted the indulgence contemplated by a section 17 order to take their responsibilities seriously [and] [n]othing would be more regrettable or inappropriate, or, indeed, inconsistent with the clear purpose of the Act".[5] As such, the Secretary of State will usually favour a conditional order in the form adopted in *Gibson Davies* and *Brian Sheridan* so that the applicant is exposed to prosecution under section 13 the moment he breaks any of the conditions. However, the applicant will prefer the order to state that he is given permission *absolutely* with any safeguards expressed as undertakings offered by the applicant to the court.[6] The advantage for the applicant is that while breach of undertaking would put him in contempt of court, this form of order is worded in such a way that breach does not result in

---

[1] [1996] 1 B.C.L.C. 327, 337A.
[2] See sections 13–15 and Chap. 12.
[3] [1996] 1 B.C.L.C. 327, 344A–B.
[4] See *Kuwait Airways Corp. v. Iraqi Airways Co. (No. 2)* [1994] 1 W.L.R. 985, [1995] 1 All E.R. 790 and see the discussion in Chap. 11.
[5] [1996] 1 B.C.L.C. 327, 344G.
[6] The order appears to have been drawn in this form in *Re Chartmore Ltd* [1990] B.C.L.C. 673.

the automatic cessation of permission and, thus, does not trigger the criminal and civil sanctions in the CDDA. Those who favour this alternative approach would argue that the public is protected as any breach of undertaking can be enforced in contempt proceedings which may themselves lead to criminal penalties. Moreover, some have argued that it is inappropriate for the applicant to be exposed to criminal prosecution and civil liability under the CDDA for failure to comply with conditions of an ongoing nature especially where there are doubts as to how those conditions should be construed.[7] The problem with undertakings from the point of view of the Secretary of State is that in contempt proceedings there is a higher burden of proof than in criminal proceedings for breach of the prohibition (the offence in section 13 is a strict liability offence).[8] As a matter of theory, as well as in practice for the reasons considered above, it would seem right that any terms on which permission is granted should be drafted as conditions. If the applicant fails to comply with the terms on which permission is granted, why should he not be treated as being without permission and disqualified? If the purpose of the conditions is to protect the public, it would be strange if the direct civil protection afforded by section 15 of the CDDA was not available to those directly affected by a breach of such conditions. The matter was considered by His Honour Judge Cooke (sitting as a High Court judge) in *Secretary of State for Trade and Industry v. Rosenfield*.[9] The judge came to the view that it was better that the relevant terms be framed as conditions to the order rather than as undertakings, for the sort of reasons considered above. He felt that any difficulties arising because of delays in compliance or mischance could be dealt with by drafting. It is worth noting in this respect that particular conditions can cause problems. One example is a condition as to joint signatures on cheques. If it is not obeyed on one occasion, will permission cease for ever after or just in respect of that individual cheque? Each case will turn on its own facts and careful consideration will have to be given to the terms of any draft order granting permission on, and subject to, the continued observance of conditions. There is always the possibility that permission could be given retrospectively in an appropriate case where, for example, there was a minor infraction of a condition on one occasion only or for a short period by mistake.[10]

Types of condition

13.39   In considering what conditions are appropriate in a particular case, it is important that conditions previously imposed in a different case are not unthinkingly

---

[7] See, A. Mithani & S. Wheeler, *The Disqualification of Company Directors* (1st ed., 1996), p. 230. Arguably, the applicant should at least be given a short period of time to comply with any conditions requiring, for example, the appointment of new directors or auditors. Otherwise, he would be in breach immediately the order is pronounced unless the new appointments have already been made. It was suggested, *obiter*, in *Brian Sheridan* [1996] 1 B.C.L.C. 327, 346G that if the court, adopting such an approach, makes an order on terms which have to be complied with by a certain time, it would be a desirable practice for the court to require the applicant to file an affidavit (with a copy to be served on the Secretary of State or the Official Receiver) within a specified time confirming compliance.

[8] *R. v. Brockley* [1994] Crim. L.R. 671; [1994] 1 B.C.L.C. 606; [1994] B.C.C. 131: see Chap. 12. Furthermore, the Secretary of State would have to police the undertakings: see generally on this point discussion in *Secretary of State for Trade and Industry v. Rosenfield* [1999] B.C.C. 413 at 419.

[9] [1999] B.C.C. 413 at 419.

[10] A possibility recognised (but not adopted on the facts) in *Re Brian Sheridan Cars Ltd* [1996] 1 B.C.L.C. 327 at 344–345. The relevant jurisdiction considered in that case was RSC Ord. 42, r. 3. That rule gave specific power to backdate orders. The only equivalent power would now appear to be contained in CPR, r. 40.7 but that rule provides that an order takes effect from its pronouncement or later: it does not deal with the question of whether the order can have retrospective effect. It is suggested that the question of backdating an order is one of mechanism. The real issue is whether or not permission can be granted retrospectively (whether or not the order in question is backdated or not). Common sense would suggest that, as a matter of jurisdiction, the court should be able to grant permission retrospectively. The question is ultimately one of statutory construction (see, by analogy, *Bristol & West Building Society v. Saunders* [1997] B.C.C. 83).

adopted. Such conditions may not be appropriate in that they might not go far enough in meeting the particular respects in which the public require protection.[11] It is also important to consider whether a particular condition is required and/or designed to fulfil the role of making the order easier to police, whether as its sole or as an ancillary object. What follows is an account drawn from the authorities of the types of conditions that have been imposed.

Publicity

13.40 It is frequently the case that the court requires publicity to be given to the order (and its conditions) so that (a) people can be warned that they are dealing with a disqualified person and/or (b) any persons entrusted with the task of monitoring and controlling the applicant and/or ensuring that he abides by any conditions are aware of the terms on which permission is granted. Although the terms of a disqualification order (and the grant of any permission) must be entered on the register of disqualification orders (see Chapter 11), the courts do not seem to have taken the drastic step of requiring publicity to be given to the world of the fact of disqualification (for example, by requiring the person to describe himself as "... disqualified, but acting with the permission of the court...").[12] A requirement for publicity will usually comprise of two further elements: (a) notification of the fact that the person is disqualified and has been given permission and (b) the reasons for the original disqualification.

(1) In *Re Brian Sheridan Cars Ltd*,[13] notification had to be given to:

    (a) General Accident Fire & Life Assurance Company (in effect, the financier of the schemes which the relevant company was seeking to implement).

    (b) The proposed independent directors to be appointed to the board (being a solicitor and an accountant)[14]

    (c) The proposed nominated auditors.

Notification was to be achieved by service of copies of the judgments and orders relating to the disqualification and the grant of permission on the above. As on the facts of the case, this condition had been breached, it was suggested that an affidavit of service should also have been required as a policing mechanism.

(2) In *Re Godwin Warren Control Systems plc*,[15] permission was granted to one of the disqualified persons to remain in a management role as chief executive provided that the order made and a note of the reasons set out in the judgment were brought to the attention of the boards of directors of the two relevant companies. Permission to act as a director in relation to two other companies was envisaged in the event that further directors (other than the disqualified person's wife) were appointed to the board provided that, in considering any application in relation to these companies, the judge was satisfied that their other shareholders were aware that the court had made a disqualification order and the reasons for it.

---

[11] See, *e.g. Secretary of State for Trade and Industry v. Rosenfield* [1999] B.C.C. 413 at 417 where the conditions initially offered by the applicant were said not to address the concerns at "the heart of the case".
[12] Along the lines of the old practice which required companies to add to their names "(and reduced)" following a reduction of capital under the Companies Acts.
[13] [1996] 1 B.C.L.C. 327.
[14] As noted earlier, this did not apparently guarantee the applicant's compliance with the conditions for permission.
[15] [1993] B.C.L.C. 80, [1992] B.C.C. 557.

Independent controls at board or other level

13.41   As a condition of permission, the court frequently requires that an independent person is appointed to the board and/or that such a person has primary day to day responsibility for any area in which the applicant's previous conduct suggests particular failings, thereby insulating the applicant, to some extent, from those areas. In such cases, the court needs to be satisfied that the person so appointed is fully aware of all the facts relating to the original disqualification and the grant of permission (see publicity above). There will also need to be a mechanism governing what is to happen in the event that the person appointed ceases to hold the relevant position (for example, by making provision for a short period of interim permission to allow time for a further application to the court). The company will need to demonstrate that it can afford the services of such a person.[16]

In *Re Lo-Line Electric Motors Ltd*,[17] the then Vice-Chancellor made it a condition of granting permission that a named individual remained a director of the relevant companies. The individual was described as being "primarily responsible for the financial management of the business and [having] shown himself to be capable and responsible".

In *Re Brian Sheridan Cars Ltd*,[18] a solicitor and an accountant were required to be appointed to each of the relevant boards to ensure that legal, accounting and financial standards were properly observed. The latter was expressly required to be the finance director.

13.42   In *Re Amaron Ltd*,[19] Neuberger J. said that the normal course followed by the courts is:

"... [T]o ensure that one or more professional persons, such as an accountant, is appointed to the board. This enables the order to have effective teeth: (a) if the company becomes insolvent then the accountant director may be liable himself to be disqualified under the 1986 Act[20]; (b) the accountant director has the powers of a director..."[21]

In that case, the condition offered was that a chartered accountant would monitor the activities of the company and report back to the court in the event of any dissatisfaction. It was not proposed that the accountant would join the board. Neuberger J. took the view that there was no good reason why the more usual proposal of an accountant-director could not have been made. He explained himself thus:

"... [A]lthough [the accountant] is prepared to have a monitoring obligation, it is something of an imposition on him to require him to give undertakings to come back to the court in certain circumstances. If he gives no such undertakings then the situation is of doubtful value. Thus, if he performs his tasks unsatisfactorily it is pretty unclear whether anyone who suffers has a cause of action against him or whether the court has any sanction against him."[22]

---

[16] See *Re Amaron Ltd* [1998] B.C.C. 264.
[17] [1988] Ch. 477, [1988] 3 W.L.R. 26, [1988] 2 All E.R. 692, [1988] B.C.L.C. 698, (1988) 4 B.C.C. 415.
[18] [1996] 1 B.C.L.C. 327.
[19] [1998] B.C.C. 264.
[20] He will also, of course, owe directors' duties both at common law and under statute which might involve civil and/or criminal liability if not observed.
[21] [1998] B.C.C. 264 at 278.
[22] *ibid.* at 278–279. Furthermore, it is difficult to see how such a monitoring obligation could be drafted as a condition other than on the basis that the accountant is employed by the company on such and such (non-revocable) terms.

13.43   In *Secretary of State for Trade and Industry v. Renwick*,[23] Chadwick J. said:

"It must be only in exceptional circumstances that a court—which has been satis-fied of unfitness and has made an order disqualifying the director for four years—can take the view that, nevertheless, the person disqualified should continue to have what was, in effect, uncontrolled direction and management of another company."

13.44   In *Re Tech Textiles Ltd, Secretary of State for Trade and Industry v. Vane*,[24] there was a requirement (in relation to one company) that another person hold the position of finance director and a requirement (in relation to a second company) that another person hold the position of managing director or finance director.

In *Secretary of State for Trade and Industry v. Rosenfield*, His Honour Judge Cooke referred to:

"... [S]omething which I indicated would concern me in my main judgment, is the need to have on the board somebody of financial expertise. The companies in the past had nobody of any financial expertise on the board. They had expert traders, but they had people who had no real idea of how the figures were going. It seems to me to be absolutely essential that there is somebody with the appropriate degree of expertise on the board."[25]

In that case, the condition was expressed in terms that if the nominated person ceased to be a director, the permission would continue for two months after his departure so that a replacement could be found and a further application made to the court to vary the order.

13.45   In *Re TLL Realisations Ltd*,[26] permission was granted allowing the appli-cant to be engaged in management. Although, the applicant had been disqualified for his failings as a finance director, the only relevant condition imposed was that the applicant be supervised by a named individual who acted as company secretary to a number of the companies in question and who was "knowledgeable and experienced in the internal financial administration" of companies.

Control of the company in general meeting

13.46   In *Re Lo-Line Electric Motors Ltd*,[27] the order was conditional on a named individual and his family retaining voting control of one company and that company retaining voting control of a second company.

In *Gibson Davies* (see above), one of the conditions was that the applicant took no steps in his capacity as 50 per cent shareholder and director of the company's parent, to impede, direct or control the activities of the company's directors.

In *Tech Textiles*, a condition was imposed to the effect that the relevant company remained a subsidiary of another named company.

Other outside assistance

13.47   In *Tech Textiles* the order was made subject to conditions that a consultant was appointed to ensure that accounts were properly filed, monies owed to the govern-

[23] July 1997, Ch.D., unreported.
[24] [1998] 1 B.C.L.C. 259.
[25] [1999] B.C.C. 413 at 418.
[26] February 1, 1999, Ch.D., unreported.
[27] [1988] Ch. 477, [1988] 3 W.L.R. 26, [1988] 2 All E.R. 692, [1988] B.C.L.C. 698, (1988) 4 B.C.C. 415.

ment paid and that no risks were taken with creditors' funds. Further conditions were that a named firm (or some other comparable firm of chartered accountants) be appointed to act as auditors and provide company secretarial services. A condition regulating the identity of the auditors was also imposed in *Brian Sheridan*.

Financial controls

13.48   In the nature of things, it is frequently the inadequacy or absence of financial management which is at the heart of many disqualification cases, especially those brought under section 6.[28] If permission is granted in such cases, financial controls of two particular types will usually be required: (a) general financial management controls and (b) specific controls designed to prevent the recurrence of previous malpractice on the applicant's part.

In addition to the appointment of named directors and auditors, further conditions are frequently imposed in relation to such persons. For example, in *Gibson Davies*, the controls recommended by the accountants were required to be implemented and the auditors were required to report on any matters of concern to the board. In both *Tech Textiles* and *Re Chartmore Ltd*,[29] there was a requirement for monthly board meetings (in the latter case to be attended by the auditors).

In *Tech Textiles, Gibson Davies* and *Rosenfield*, conditions were imposed requiring the provision of regular (monthly or quarterly) management accounts. In *Gibson Davies* these were to be submitted to the auditors. Controls over the signing of cheques were imposed in *Tech Textiles* and *Gibson Davies*.

13.49   Limits have also been placed on the amount of remuneration that the applicant can receive and conditions imposed requiring the applicant (in certain circumstances) to subordinate any investment or loan and to take no security (see *Gibson Davies* and *Rosenfield*). In *Barings (No. 4)*, the conditions imposed were that the applicant was to remain an unpaid non-executive director of the relevant companies and was not to enter into a service contract with any of them. The purpose of these conditions is not entirely clear. Mr Norris's remuneration from the company as a consultant was unregulated and the absence of paid terms of employment as a director would not necessarily restrict the role and duties that he might undertake. In *Rosenfield*, inter-company loans were regulated by condition as this was an area that had caused particular problems in the past.

Permission for a limited period

13.50   The question of interim permission is considered further below. On occasions, the court has granted permission limited to a year or so with the idea that the matter should then come back before the court. In cases of doubt or where, say, the company is new and its financial position is uncertain, there are strong grounds for granting such a limited permission. The further advantage of limited permission is that it enables the court to check that any conditions are being complied with and evaluate whether it is appropriate for permission to continue. In cases where conditions are imposed to minimise risks to the public, there is something to be said for the view that the court should keep the position under review.

In *Re Chartmore Ltd*,[30] Harman J. disqualified the defendant for two years under section 6. The judge found that the defendant's company had been inadequately capitalised and had lacked proper financial controls. Consequently, the company had

---

[28] See discussion of the concept of financial responsibility in Chap. 5.
[29] [1990] B.C.L.C. 673.
[30] [1990] B.C.L.C. 673.

continued to trade at the expense of its creditors despite being insolvent. The defendant's application for permission to act as a director of another company was granted on his undertaking that the existing system of monitoring the business by a full monthly board meeting attended by the auditors would continue. The official receiver expressed some concern over how the undertaking would be policed and the judge was hesitant because the company was uncomfortably similar to the one which had featured in the main proceedings in that it too appeared to be inadequately capitalised. The solution arrived at by the court was to give permission *for one year of the two year period only* with the defendant to have liberty to apply to the registrar for further permission at his own cost before the expiry of the order. It was made clear that on any application for renewed permission the defendant would need to adduce evidence showing that the company continued to be properly run along the lines of the undertaking. Permission for a limited period was similarly granted at an earlier stage in the proceedings which ultimately came before the court in *Re Brian Sheridan Cars Ltd*.[31]

Conditions: the role of the court and the Secretary of State

13.51　　Under sections 1 and 17 and section 11 of the CDDA, it is for the court (not the Secretary of State, official receiver or some other person) to be satisfied that permission should be granted. For the same reason, it will not usually be appropriate for a condition to be imposed that something should be done to the satisfaction of, say, the Secretary of State or for the Secretary of State to be required generally to "police" the management of a company in relation to which permission has been granted.[32]

Applications for permission to be involved in management

13.52　　Applications for permission to be involved in management (rather than to act as a director) cause difficulties. The danger is that if the permission is too widely couched, the court will, in effect, be granting the applicant permission to act as a *de facto* or shadow director without the sorts of safeguards that might be imposed were he to have asked for permission to act as a director. In two cases, the court has dealt with this difficulty by describing very precisely what the permission has been given for in the order. In *Re Lichfield Freight Terminal Ltd, Secretary of State for Trade and Industry v. Rowe*,[33] Her Honour Judge Alton refused the applicant permission to act as a director but did give him permission to do the following:

(1) Make arrangements on behalf of the company for the collection and delivery of goods.

(2) Give quotations for pricing for deliveries in accordance with a preset formula determined by the board.

(3) Negotiate the pricing and storage by the company of goods for third parties in accordance with a preset formula determined by the board.

(4) Price opportunities for the company's business for the consideration of the board.

(5) Interview drivers with a view to recommending their engagement to the board.

---

[31] [1996] 1 B.C.L.C. 327, 336H–I. See also *Re Tech Textiles Ltd, Secretary of State for Trade and Industry v. Vane* [1998] 1 B.C.L.C. 259.
[32] See further *Re Brian Sheridan Cars Ltd* [1996] 1 B.C.L.C. 327 at 346.
[33] November 19, 1997, Birmingham County Court, unreported.

(6) Act as a transport manager with responsibility for purchases of day to day consumables, making arrangements for maintenance of vehicles and tachographs (any purchase in excess of £250 to be approved by the board) and negotiating for the consideration of the board terms for the purchase and sale of vehicles and equipment.

(7) Check proof of delivery forms and invoices.

13.53   In *Re TLL Realisations Ltd*,[34] there was a similar attempt to specify in detail the activities that the applicant was permitted to engage in. The order expressly permitted him to do the following:

(1) Review a business and assemble reports for the company into the past, present and future operation of such business.

(2) Assist in the acquisition of a business by the company to the extent of carrying out research into its accounting position and liaising with the company's solicitors in the preparation of draft contracts for the purchase and establishment of a business.

(3) Act as a joint cheque signatory or counter signatory in every case signing with one other.

(4) Recommend and set up accounting books, systems and procedures appropriate to the trading activities of the company and maintain, expand and amend such systems as necessary to meet statutory requirements.

(5) Produce on request financial forecasts, including profit and loss and cash flow figures.

(6) Produce management accounts as required, including explanations of all items which vary from forecast.

(7) Produce annual accounts and submit them for approval by the board of directors and/or audit.

(8) Produce draft agreements, reports and documentation in respect of the trading activities of group companies and provide advice and accounting matters as and when requested.

(9) Subject to and in accordance with express prior instructions from the directors of any group company (a) without power to bind any such company, carry out negotiations with any customer; (b) place orders with any supplier of any such company, provided that each such order is specifically authorised by the company's board of directors; (c) dispose of property of any such company, provided that each such disposal is specifically and separately authorised by the said board of directors.

(10) Monitor and report on the accounts of any group company.

(11) Report to the board of directors of any group company in relation to financial and commercial issues.

[34] February 1, 1999, Ch.D., unreported.

Interim permission

13.54   It is conceivable that a disqualified person might wish to seek a stay of a disqualification order for a short period either (a) to allow him to prepare evidence in support of an application for permission or (b) pending appeal or (c) to enable him to make arrangements for the running of companies of which he is, for example, a director at the time of his disqualification. It was seen in Chapter 11 that there is jurisdiction in the civil courts to stay or suspend the operation of a disqualification order either under rule 9 of the Disqualification Rules (for orders made in proceedings commenced under sections 7 to 8) or under CPR, r. 40.7 and paragraph 16.1 of the Disqualification Practice Direction and/or (in the case of the High Court and the Court of Appeal) under the inherent jurisdiction. There is similar jurisdiction in the Crown Court. However, in the light of *Secretary of State for Trade and Industry v. Bannister*, the preferred approach is for the disqualified person to seek interim permission to act rather than a stay of the disqualification order.[35] The practice of granting interim permission has been followed by the courts in a number of cases since *Bannister*.[36] It is clear from these cases that interim permission should be granted for a short time only.[37] Moreover, it appears from *Re Amaron Ltd*[38] that in a case where interim permission is sought pending the hearing of an appeal or an application for full permission, the court will apply the guidelines laid down in *American Cyanamid Co. v Ethicon Ltd*.[39] A further point which emerges from Park J.'s judgment in *Re TLL Realisations*[40] is that the court is unlikely to tolerate a situation in which the applicant repeatedly seeks to extend an interim permission or the making of an application for interim permission without notice to the Secretary of State.

Applications for permission under sections 11 and 12

13.55   It was seen in Chapter 10 that the original purpose of automatic disqualification under section 11 was to prevent undischarged bankrupts from using the medium of a company to obtain credit and so circumvent the restriction on bankrupts obtaining credit without disclosing their personal status. Equally, there is support for

---

[35] [1996] 1 W.L.R. 118, [1996] 2 B.C.L.C. 271, [1995] B.C.C. 1,027, CA see paras 11.18–11.25. Even before the decision in *Bannister* there are cases where interim permission was granted rather than a stay: see *Re Wedgecraft Ltd*, March 7, 1986, Ch.D., unreported and *Re Ipcon Fashions Ltd* (1989) 5 B.C.C. 773.
[36] See *Re Thorncliffe Finance Ltd, Secretary of State for Trade and Industry v. Arif* [1997] 1 B.C.L.C. 34, [1996] B.C.C. 586; *Re Continental Assurance Co. of London plc, Secretary of State for Trade and Industry v. Burrows* [1997] 1 B.C.L.C. 48, [1996] B.C.C. 888; *Re Amaron Ltd* [1998] B.C.C. 264.
[37] In *Secretary of State for Trade and Industry v. Renwick*, July 1997, Ch.D., unreported Chadwick J. criticised a district judge who had purportedly relied on his earlier decision in *Re Thorncliffe Finance Ltd, Secretary of State for Trade and Industry v. Arif* [1997] 1 B.C.L.C. 34, [1996] B.C.C. 586. In *Renwick*, the district judge had adjourned the question of permission to a High Court judge. However, the adjournment was on terms that the matter did not come on before the judge for around nine months with interim permission in the meantime and six months to file further evidence in support of the application. The main reason for such a lengthy adjournment seems to have been the prospect that recoveries might be made in a claim being pursued against pension advisers, thereby improving the financial position of the relevant company. This was an entirely different situation from *Arif* in which a two month adjournment was allowed to enable the latest year end accounts to be made up (and to cover the Christmas holiday) in circumstances where there were interests other than the applicant at stake, evidence from professional advisers that both companies were properly managed and run and further evidence that the applicant would be deprived of any source of income unless interim permission was granted. There was no such evidence in *Renwick* and, on the facts of that case, Chadwick J. doubted whether it was appropriate to grant interim permission at all, let alone the nine months in fact allowed.
[38] [1998] B.C.C. 264 at 275.
[39] [1975] A.C. 396.
[40] February 1, 1999, Ch.D., unreported.

the view that section 11 serves the wider aim of protecting the public by prohibiting individuals who have gone bankrupt from being involved in the management of companies. The prevalence of such a view suggests that the courts will adopt much the same approach on an application for permission by an undischarged bankrupt as is adopted on an application for permission to act notwithstanding a disqualification order.[41] For similar reasons, it is unlikely that the courts would adopt a radically different approach to an application for permission made by a person disqualified in the terms of section 12.

Can an insolvency practitioner be granted permission to act as a liquidator etc.?

13.56   A person disqualified under an order in the terms of section 1 is prohibited from acting as a liquidator, an administrator or a receiver or manager of a company's property without the permission of the court. A person disqualified in the terms of section 12 is prohibited from acting as a liquidator without the permission of the court. One point of some difficulty (canvassed earlier in Chapter 12) is whether an insolvency practitioner disqualified in the terms of these provisions could seek permission to act as a liquidator etc. under the CDDA. Section 390(4) of the Insolvency Act 1986 provides that a person is not qualified to act as an insolvency practitioner (and therefore as a provisional liquidator, liquidator, administrator, administrative receiver or supervisor of a corporate voluntary arrangement) if he has been adjudged bankrupt or is subject to a disqualification order made under the CDDA. Moreover, there is no power in the court to grant dispensation from this prohibition in the form of permission to act under the Insolvency Act. It is suggested that the position is as follows:

(1) In the case of an insolvency practitioner the subject of a disqualification order in the terms of section 1, the court strictly has jurisdiction to grant him permission to act as a liquidator, administrator or administrative receiver *under the CDDA*. However, in such a case the absolute prohibition in section 390(4)(b) bites and the court cannot use its jurisdiction under the CDDA to override it. However, it is apparently possible for a person to act as a receiver or manager (not being an administrative receiver) without being a qualified insolvency practitioner. As such, the court would be in a position to exercise its jurisdiction to grant an insolvency practitioner permission to act as a receiver and manager as section 390(4)(b) does not bite in that case.

(2) In the case of an insolvency practitioner the subject of a disqualification order in the terms of section 12, the court strictly has jurisdiction to grant him permission to act as a liquidator. It appears (somewhat anomalously) in this case that the absolute prohibition in section 390(4)(b) does not bite as it applies only to a person who is "subject to a disqualification order made under the CDDA". Strictly, a disqualification order in the terms of section 12 is not a disqualification order "made under the CDDA" but one made under section 429 of the Insolvency Act the scope of which is defined in the CDDA. As such, the court could exercise its jurisdiction under the CDDA to grant an insolvency practitioner permission to act as a liquidator notwithstanding the prohibition in section 12. It is suggested that the court is, however, likely to lean against this construction.

[41] See *Re Altim Pty Ltd* [1968] 2 N.S.W.R. 762, Supreme Court of New South Wales; *Re Ansett* (1990) 3 A.C.S.R. 357, Supreme Court of Victoria; *Re McQuillan* (1989) 5 B.C.C. 137, Northern Ireland High Court.

(3) In the case of an insolvency practitioner who is an undischarged bankrupt the position is more straightforward. The relevant prohibition flows from section 390(4)(a) of the Insolvency Act (which is absolute) and not from the wording of section 11 of the CDDA with the effect that the court has no jurisdiction to grant an undischarged bankrupt to act in any capacity which requires him to be qualified as an insolvency practitioner.

Future direction

13.57   The main concern articulated in the cases on permission to date has been to ensure that the public are adequately protected in a narrow sense from a recurrence of the conduct which caused the applicant to be disqualified in the first place. The future direction of this particular aspect of disqualification jurisprudence is likely to be affected by many of the issues discussed in Chapter 2 concerning the broad rationale of the CDDA and the difficult balance to be struck between the public interest and the rights of the disqualified person. There is a strong argument for saying that even greater primacy should be given to the protection of the public than is currently the case.[42] As was pointed out in *Brian Sheridan*, the disqualified person is seeking a dispensation or indulgence in circumstances where his previous misconduct has resulted in disqualification. This suggests that the courts should exercise their power to grant permission sparingly. A further point that has not yet been taken on board by the courts is that too great a willingness to grant permission may undermine the wider purposes of the CDDA such as deterrence and the raising of standards among directors generally. If a person is found to be unfit and disqualified, in part, to deter others, it would be incongruous were the court simply to rubber stamp an application for permission. On the other hand, the influence of the quasi-criminal view of disqualification (see Chapter 2) is quite likely to spread in the light of the shift (with the enactment of the Human Rights Act) towards a more rights-based legal culture. One possible consequence of this is that the courts may seek to use the power to grant permission as a means of tailoring a proportionate response to individual cases. Thus, for example, a court which is obliged to disqualify under section 6 in a case where the defendant poses no obvious risk to the public at the date of trial, may consider it appropriate to temper the width of the prohibition by granting him permission to act. Such an approach may be attractive to a judge who doubts whether the curtailment of individual freedom flowing from a mandatory disqualification under section 6 is justified in moral terms or who regards the disqualification process as essentially arbitrary.[43]

---

[42] Indeed, the *dicta* cited earlier from *Barings* and *Dawes & Henderson*, might suggest that the rigorous approach taken to substantive disqualification (see, *e.g.* the *Grayan* case discussed in Chaps 2 and 4) is beginning to seep through into the area of permission to act.

[43] See the extra-judicial views of Lord Hoffmann discussed in Chapter 2. For the faint outlines of a proportionate approach see *Re Lo-Line Electric Motors Ltd* [1988] Ch. 477, [1988] 3 W.L.R. 26, [1988] 2 All E.R. 692, [1988] B.C.L.C. 698, (1988) 4 B.C.C. 415 and the Australian case of *Chew v. N.C.S.C.* (1985) 9 A.C.L.R. 527; [1985] W.A.R. 337. On proportionality generally, see A. von Hirsch and M. Wasik, "Civil Disqualifications Attending Conviction: A Suggested Conceptual Framework" [1997] C.L.J. 599. These writers argue that disqualifications should ordinarily be seen as civil risk-prevention measures and that, as such, the imposition of a wide constraint (like the one imposed in the terms of CDDA, s. 1) is only legitimate if it amounts to an appropriate and proportionate response reflecting the magnitude of any future risk. Furthermore, if this approach is followed, there is no reason why the court should not take personal factors (such as the impact of the prohibition on the disqualified person) into account when considering applications for permission. The applicant's personal hardship has, on occasions, been taken into account in Australia: see, *e.g. Re Zim Metal Products Pty Ltd* [1977] A.C.L.C. 29,556, (1977) 2 A.C.L.R. 553; *Re Hamilton-Irvine* (1990) 8 A.C.L.C. 1,057; *Re C. & J. Hazell Holdings Pty Ltd* (1991) 9 A.C.L.C. 802, (1991) 4 A.C.S.R. 703; *Murray v. Australian Securities Commission* (1994) 12 A.C.L.C. 1, a practice consistent with the rhetorical notion that disqualification is not intended to operate primarily as a punishment.

PROCEDURE ON APPLICATIONS FOR PERMISSION

Sections 17 and 12: Procedure on an application for permission to act notwithstanding a disqualification order

Which court?

13.58   The substantive power to grant permission to act notwithstanding a disqualification order is conferred by section 1(1) and section 12. However, it is not open to every court to exercise this power. The basic procedure governing applications for permission in such cases is contained in section 17(1). This identifies the courts to which an application for permission can be brought. In summary, section 17(1) provides as follows:

(1) An application for permission to promote or form a company must be made to any court having jurisdiction to wind up companies.

(2) An application for permission to be a director of a company, or otherwise to take part in the management of a company must be made to any court having jurisdiction to wind up that company.

(3) An application for permission to be a liquidator or administrator of a company or to be receiver or manager of a company's property must, as in (2) above, be made to any court having jurisdiction to wind up that company.

13.59   The jurisdiction of the courts to wind up companies is established by section 117 of the Insolvency Act 1986 and is discussed fully in Chapter 6. In practice, the combined effect of section 117 of the Insolvency Act and section 17(1) of the CDDA is as follows:

(1) It is always open to a disqualified person to bring his application for permission in the High Court.[44]

(2) In respect of a company which has a paid up share capital of £120,000 or less, the county court for the district in which the company's registered office is situated has concurrent winding up jurisdiction with the High Court.[45] Thus, if A wishes to apply for permission to act as a director of B Ltd where B Ltd has a paid up capital which does not exceed £120,000, A could apply in either the High Court or the county court for the district of B Ltd's registered office.

(3) If, however, A wishes to apply for permission to act as a director of several companies all having their registered offices in different county court districts, it will be sensible for A to make a single application in the High Court. This avoids the necessity of a series of separate applications in all of the relevant county courts as envisaged by section 17(1)(b). In cases where a county court seised of the substantive disqualification proceedings would not have jurisdiction under section 17 to grant permission to act (*e.g.* because the registered office of the company in relation to which permission might need to be sought is in a different county court district), this may be a reason for applying

---

[44] *i.e.* the Companies Court in the Royal Courts of Justice, London or a Chancery District Registry having winding up jurisdiction.

[45] Insolvency Act 1986, s. 117. The position in Scotland (*ibid.*, section 120) and Northern Ireland is similar.

for the proceedings to be transferred to the High Court under Part 30 of the CPR.

(4) It is not possible for a criminal court to exercise the power to grant permission.

13.60   Where disqualification proceedings are brought in the High Court, it is possible for the defendant to make the application for permission in the original proceedings. The application for permission will only then be determined if the court makes a disqualification order. By making such an application the defendant can avoid having to expend the further time and cost of bringing a free standing application for permission after the court has disposed of the original proceedings. It comes then as no surprise that the practice of dealing with both the disqualification and the question of permission at the same hearing is one that the civil courts have encouraged.[46] One difficulty with the legislation is that this sensible practice cannot be adopted in the criminal courts in section 2 or section 5 cases.[47] This is because the power to grant permission is restricted by section 17(1) to civil courts having winding up jurisdiction. Thus, if A is disqualified by the Crown Court under section 2, he will have to make a free standing application for permission to the High Court (or relevant county court) under section 17. As such, the legislation envisages that cases will arise in which the person is disqualified by a criminal court and yet granted permission by a civil court.[48] A variation of this difficulty arises where A is disqualified in a county court and is seeking permission to act as a director etc. of a company the registered office of which is situated outside that county court's jurisdiction. The general position there is that he will have to make a free standing application to either the High Court or the county court for the relevant district.

Applications for permission to act notwithstanding disqualification in the terms of section 12 should be made to the relevant county court which made the order pursuant to section 429 of the Insolvency Act. Section 17 has no application in such a case.

Form of application and applicable rules of court

13.61   Applications for permission made under either sections 1(1) and 17 or under section 12 of the CDDA are now governed by paragraph 20 of the Disqualification Practice Direction. This provides that the application should be made either by claim form under Part 8 of the CPR or by application notice in an existing disqualification application. Paragraph 21 of the Disqualification Practice Direction provides that every claim form or application notice by which an application for permission to act is begun, and all affidavits, notices and other documents in the application must be entitled in the matter of the company or companies in question and in the matter of the Company Directors Disqualification Act 1986. Applications for permission made under a disqualification order which was made under any statutory predecessor of the CDDA are also governed by paragraph 20 of the Disqualification Practice Direction.

---

[46] *Re Dicetrade Ltd, Secretary of State for Trade and Industry v. Worth* [1994] 2 B.C.L.C. 113 at 116, [1994] B.C.C. 371, 373F–G, CA. The court cannot make a partial or qualified disqualification order. It is obliged to make an order in the full terms of section 1. As such, it may be sensible for a defendant who holds directorships and/or managerial positions within other companies not directly in issue in the disqualification proceedings to consider making an application within the main proceedings: see Chap. 11.

[47] Though in any event it is questionable whether or not the criminal courts (let alone all prosecutors) have the expertise to consider the question of permission.

[48] The existence of this anomaly provides further support for the view expressed elsewhere by the authors that the civil and criminal courts should adopt a single, composite approach to the application of the CDDA. It makes no sense whatsoever for the criminal courts to work with one set of assumptions concerning the *raison d'etre* of disqualification if the civil courts administering the provision for permission are working with a different set of assumptions.

Section 17(2): Defendant to application for permission

13.62   It appears from section 17(2) that the defendant to the application for permission should ordinarily be the party who applied originally for the disqualification order—in other words, the roles of the original parties are reversed. Section 17(2) provides as follows:

> "On the hearing of an application for permission made by a person against whom a disqualification order has been made on the application of the Secretary of State, the official receiver or the liquidator, the Secretary of State, official receiver or liquidator shall appear and call the attention of the court to any matters which seem to him to be relevant, and may himself give evidence or call witnesses."

Common sense dictates that the subsection should be construed in such a way that *only* the original applicant in the main disqualification can be made defendant in the proceedings on the application for permission. It is submitted that the following summary reflects both the true intention of parliament and current practice:[49]

(1) Where the applicant for a disqualification order under any of sections 2 to 5, section 6 or section 8 is the Secretary of State then the Secretary of State should be made the defendant in any subsequent application for permission.[50]

(2) Where the applicant for a disqualification order under any of sections 2 to 5 or section 6 is the official receiver then the official receiver should be made the defendant in any subsequent application for permission.

(3) Where the applicant for a disqualification order under any of sections 2 to 5 is the liquidator of any company in which the conduct giving rise to disqualification took place[51] then, prima facie, that liquidator should be made the defendant to any subsequent application for permission. The Secretary of State should also be made a defendant as the person having responsibility for the regulation of companies.

(4) Where the court makes an order of its own motion under either section 2 or section 10 it would presumably make sense, there having been no formal applicant for the original order, for the Secretary of State to be made defendant to any subsequent application for permission.

(5) The members or creditors (past or present) of any company in which the conduct giving rise to disqualification took place have *locus standi* to bring an application for a disqualification order under sections 2 to 5 inclusive (section 16(2)). However, section 17(2) gives no indication as to the position on an application for permission where the applicant for the original order under those substantive provisions is a member or creditor. It is not clear whether there is any significance in this omission. It has been argued that the most appropriate course of action here would be for the court to direct that the Secretary of State, as the appointed guardian of the public interest, should be made a party to the application or, at the very least receive notice so that he

---

[49] Any possible doubt could be avoided if the subsection were to read, "... on the hearing of an application for permission made by a person against whom a disqualification order has been made on the application of the Secretary of State, the official receiver or the liquidator then the *same party shall correspondingly appear* and call the attention of the court etc..."
[50] The right to bring section 8 proceedings vests exclusively in the Secretary of State, a point which reinforces the need for a common sense approach to the construction of section 17(2).
[51] See section 16(2).

could, if he wished, file evidence and appear at the hearing of the application.[52] In that case, (as in the case of a liquidator in (3) above), it would be sensible for the applicant to contact the Treasury Solicitor and ask whether he would be prepared to accept service on the Secretary of State's behalf.

13.63 Certain difficulties caused by the wording of section 17(2) are now resolved by paragraph 23 of the Disqualification Practice Direction which provides that, in all cases (including applications under section 12), the claim form or application notice (as appropriate), together with the supporting evidence, must be served on the Secretary of State. In any event, in cases where the Secretary of State was not originally party to the disqualification proceedings or in cases where the disqualification order was made in criminal proceedings in which the Secretary of State was not the prosecutor, it is suggested that he would have standing to appear and make representations as the person with regulatory responsibility for companies by application of the principle in *Adams v. Adams*.[53]

In practice, the defendant will usually be either the Secretary of State or the official receiver given that the majority of disqualification orders are made under sections 6 to 7 and section 8. The use of the words "shall appear" in section 17(2) indicate that the defendant (whether the Secretary of State or otherwise) is under a mandatory obligation to attend the hearing and draw the court's attention to any matters which might assist the court in determining the application.[54] The court is not, of course, limited to a consideration of matters raised by any defendant, whether or not the Secretary of State.[55] Where the Secretary of State does not oppose the application it appears that he can discharge this obligation by writing a letter to the court drawing any particular points to its attention and indicating his intention not to attend the hearing.[56] In relation to an application for permission by an undischarged bankrupt, section 11(3) provides that the official receiver is under a duty to oppose the application if he is of the opinion that it is contrary to the public interest that the application should be granted. This wording differs from the more neutral wording in section 17(2) which provides only that the Secretary of State etc. "shall appear and call the attention of the court to any matters which seem to him to be relevant, and may himself give evidence or call witnesses". Despite the more neutral wording in section 17(2), it is suggested that the Secretary of State should, in an appropriate case, oppose the application and, in the event that the application is successful in such a case, it would be open to the Secretary of State to appeal.

Evidence

13.64 Paragraph 22.1 of the Disqualification Practice Direction provides that evidence in support of an application for permission to act shall be by affidavit. The ques-

---

[52] A. Mithani and S. Wheeler, *op. cit.*, p. 222.

[53] [1971] P. 188 especially at 197–198.

[54] *Re Dicetrade Ltd* [1994] 2 B.C.L.C. 113 at 116–117, [1994] B.C.C. 371 at 373–374, CA. As the current tests applied by the court are predicated heavily on the notion of public protection, there is much force in the view that it is preferable for the Secretary of State to be made defendant to all applications for permission however one reads the statute.

[55] See the following comment of Chadwick J. in *Secretary of State for Trade and Industry v. Renwick*, July 1997, unreported:

> "... I do not myself take the view that [on an application for permission] the court is circumscribed by those matters to which the Secretary of State draws attention. The purpose of section 17(2) ... is to provide assistance to the court by giving it the benefit of the Secretary of State's observations. It is not the purpose of section 17(2) to limit the court's own discretion whether or not to grant [permission] in respect of a person..."

[56] *Re Dicetrade Ltd* [1994] 2 B.C.L.C. 113 at 117, [1994] B.C.C. 371 at 374. Indeed, it appears from this passage that a letter in such terms to the applicant or the solicitors on record for the applicant will suffice.

tion of what matters should be covered by such evidence follows from the discussion above. Current practice is for the Secretary of State or official receiver to request that evidence deals with the points set out in an annexed schedule (a copy of the current version is in the appendices). It is obviously sensible that the evidence should include the matters that a bankrupt is required to put in evidence when seeking permission to act notwithstanding his automatic disqualification under section 11.[57] In addition, the question of relevant evidence on such hearings was considered by the Court of Appeal in *Re Westmid Packing Services Ltd, Secretary of State for Trade and Industry v. Griffiths*.[58] Although the applicant's general reputation may be relevant, "detailed or repetitive evidence" should not be allowed. On this authority, it also appears that evidence of the applicant's "age and state of health, the length of time he has been in jeopardy, whether he has admitted the offence, his conduct before and after the offence" are also relevant.[59]

Costs

13.65 In *Re Dicetrade Ltd, Secretary of State for Trade and Industry v. Worth*[60] the Court of Appeal made the following points:

(1) If the application for permission can be dealt with within the original disqualification proceedings and the Secretary of State merely puts forward matters which the court ought to consider but does not oppose the application, the question of permission is unlikely to take up much time in the context of the overall hearing. In such circumstances, the appropriate order may well be "no order for costs". (This point is questionable. The costs of the application may well encompass the additional cost of preparing for the hearing as well as costs of attendance. The Secretary of State may have carried out investigations and entered into correspondence clarifying matters and/or pointing out gaps in the applicant's evidence).

(2) On a free standing application for permission, there is no general principle which entitles the Secretary of State to be paid his costs of attending on the application automatically even if the Secretary of State, on consideration, does not oppose the application. (It is not clear how far this goes. Certainly, if the Secretary of State needlessly appears, he could not expect to obtain an order for costs. Similarly, if the Secretary of State needlessly prolongs any application, he might expect to have an order for costs made against him. What happens if (a) the application is dismissed or (b) the application is granted but the Secretary of State has played a useful role in bringing relevant matters to the court's attention is unclear).

13.66 If *Dicetrade* is applied, it appears that the starting assumption is that the Secretary of State is merely there to assist the court and that both sides should generally bear their own costs. However, it is suggested that such a starting assumption does not adequately reflect the position. The significant point is that the applicant is asking the court for an indulgence and the need for the application has been brought on the applicant by his own misconduct. The crux of the application is that the applicant is seeking to rid himself of a legal disability. Moreover, the Secretary of State, etc. is required to appear by section 17(2) which means that costs will have to be incurred by him in

---

[57] See Insolvency Rules, r. 6.203 and below.
[58] [1998] 2 All E.R. 124, [1998] 2 B.C.L.C. 646, [1998] B.C.C. 836.
[59] See discussion of mitigating factors in Chap. 5.
[60] [1994] B.C.C. 371.

deciding whether or not to oppose the application even if ultimately the decision is taken not to oppose. As such, it is suggested that the Secretary of State should generally be entitled to an order for costs whatever the outcome unless his opposition to an application is found to be unreasonable (in which case the applicant might arguably be entitled to at least some of his costs). Costs in disqualification proceedings are discussed more fully in Chapter 6. It remains to be seen how the courts will approach such issues in the light of the CPR. Although the matter remains in the discretion of the court and, to some extent, each case will turn on its own facts, it is suggested that the correct approach is as follows:

(1) If the application is dismissed, it will be usual for the applicant to be ordered to pay the Secretary of State's costs on the standard basis. Although the Court of Appeal in *Dicetrade* cited the comment of Chadwick J. that there was no "lis" between the parties, it is hard to see how this fits in with other remarks of the Court of Appeal to the effect that such proceedings are "no different to other civil proceedings" and that "the Secretary of State must take his chance in such litigation, just like any other litigant...".

(2) If the application is granted, an order that the applicant pay the Secretary of State's costs will generally be made if the Secretary of State has been of assistance to the court and has not acted improperly or wasted time arguing issues which were ultimately decided in the applicant's favour, or turned up unnecessarily when a letter drawing relevant points to the court's attention would have sufficed. To some extent this approach follows from the actual result in *Dicetrade*. The application for permission was granted. At first instance, there was no order for costs at all. On appeal, the Court of Appeal made an order that the applicant for permission pay the costs of the Secretary of State. This was on the basis that a separate hearing had been necessary because the applicant had not been ready to proceed at an earlier stage. Had the applicant been ready earlier, the hearing might not have led to further costs being incurred over and above the costs in the original disqualification proceedings (though see comment above). This result (which reflects current practice) can be further justified on the following ground. The applicant for permission is under a disability and has been disqualified for his own misconduct. As a price of obtaining permission and relief from such disability, he should expect to have to pay the reasonable costs of the regulator who is required to consider his application and bring relevant matters to the court's attention. The position is analogous to that of a tenant seeking relief from forfeiture.

Registration of order granting permission

13.67 Where permission is granted by a court for a person the subject of a disqualification order to do any thing which he is otherwise prohibited from doing, details of the order granting permission must be notified to the Secretary of State for entry on the registration of disqualification orders (see generally the Companies (Disqualification Orders) Regulations 1986).[61]

Appeals

13.68 Appeals from orders granting permission granting permission to act notwithstanding a disqualification order in the terms of section 1 would appear to be

[61] S.I. 1986 No. 2067 (as amended by S.I. 1995 No. 1509) and see para. 11.26 above.

governed by the ordinary rules applicable under the CPR rather than by the Insolvency Rules. This conclusion flows from the discussion in Chapter 6 and the fact that section 21(2) of the CDDA does not apply the rule-making power under the Insolvency Act to any of sections 1, 12 or 17. At present this would appear to mean that appeals from a district judge in the county court lie to a county court judge. Appeals from a county court judge would lie (with permission) to the Court of Appeal. Appeals in the High Court would lie from the registrar to a judge (but by way of rehearing only) and appeals from a High Court judge would lie (with permission) to the Court of Appeal. The subject of appeals is considered in more detail in Chapter 6. As explained there, the position in relation to appeals is currently under review and likely to change.

Procedure on an application for permission to act notwithstanding automatic disqualification under section 11

13.69 Applications by undischarged bankrupts for permission under section 11 of the CDDA are apparently governed by rules 6.203—6.205 of the Insolvency Rules. The reason for doubt is that section 22 of the CDDA does not expressly apply the relevant rule-making power under the Insolvency Act to section 11. In what follows, it is assumed that the relevant provisions of the Insolvency Rules do apply. The present rules provide that evidence may be given by way of affidavit which is in keeping with the position under sections 1, 17 and 12 (see paragraph 22.1 of the Disqualification Practice Direction). The application will be made to the court which made the bankruptcy order (section 11(2) of the CDDA). If the bankruptcy proceedings have been transferred to another court, there is a practical argument for saying that the application should be made to the court in which the bankruptcy proceedings are continuing but the CDDA does not seem to allow for this possibility. The evidence in support should contain (at the very least) the specific matters set out in rule 6.203(2). These matters include details of the business of the company, where such business is to be carried on, the persons primarily responsible for running the company (and presumably their positions), the manner in which the applicant proposes to take part or be concerned in the promotion, formation or management of the company, any emoluments and benefits to be obtained from the position[62] if permission is granted, the date of incorporation and the amount of the company's authorised share capital. These matters are modified to some extent in the event that the company does not exist at the time of the application. As the test of whether permission should be granted is an "in all the circumstances" test, the sort of matters considered in relation to permission to act notwithstanding a disqualification order will also be relevant. The official receiver and the bankrupt's trustee must be notified of the venue and served with copies of the application and supporting affidavit or written statement (rule 6.204(1)). The official receiver then has the right to file a report of any matters which he considers ought to be drawn to the court's attention. Any report so filed must be copied forthwith to the bankrupt and his trustee (rule 6.204(2)). Rule 6.204(4) provides that the official receiver and the bankrupt's trustee may appear on the hearing of the application, and may make representations and put to the bankrupt such questions as the court may allow. Section 11(2) of the CDDA requires the official receiver to be served with the claim form and further provides that it is his duty, if he is of the opinion that it is contrary to the public interest that the application should be granted, to attend on the hearing of the application and oppose it. It is not clear quite how section 11(2) and rule 6.204(4) interact. One difficulty which a bankrupt faces given the requirement under

---

[62] Rule 6.203(2)(d) refers to emoluments and benefits from the directorship but this is presumably too narrow.

the Insolvency Rules to notify his trustee is that a successful application for permission to act may well trigger an application for an income payments order under rule 6.189 of the Insolvency Rules. Indeed, the making of an income payments order when permission is granted is specifically contemplated by rule 6.205. It is suggested that the position on costs should be the same as that outlined above in relation to permission to act under a disqualification order. Appeals are presumably governed by rule 7.48(2) of the Insolvency Rules which governs appeals in bankruptcy.

APPENDIX 1

COMPANY DIRECTORS DISQUALIFICATION ACT 1986

(1986 Chapter 46)

ARRANGEMENT OF SECTIONS

SECTION   *Preliminary*

1. Disqualification orders: general

*Disqualification for general misconduct
in connection with companies*

2. Disqualification on conviction of indictable offence
3. Disqualification for persistent breaches of companies legislation
4. Disqualification for fraud, etc., in winding-up
5. Disqualification on summary conviction

Disqualification for unfitness

6. Duty of court to disqualify unfit directors of insolvent companies
7. Application to court under sec. 6; reporting provisions
8. Disqualification after investigation of company
9. Matters for determining unfitness of directors

Other cases of disqualification

10. Participation in wrongful trading
11. Undischarged bankrupts
12. Failure to pay under county court administration order

Consequences of contravention

13. Criminal penalties
14. Offences by body corporate
15. Personal liability for company's debts where person acts while disqualified

Supplementary provisions

16. Application for disqualification order
17. Application for leave under an order

18. Register of disqualification orders
19. Special savings from repealed enactments

Miscellaneous and general

20. Admissibility in evidence of statements
21. Interaction with Insolvency Act
22. Interpretation
22A. Application of Act to building societies
22B. Application of Act to incorporated friendly societies
23. Transitional provisions, savings, repeals
24. Extent
25. Commencement
26. Citation
SCHEDULES

SCHEDULE
1. Matters for determining unfitness of directors
2. Savings from Companies Act 1981 ss. 93, 94 and Insolvency Act 1985 Schedule 9
3. Transitional provisions and savings
4. Repeals

Company Directors Disqualification Act 1986

(1986 CHAPTER 46)

An Act to consolidate certain enactments relating to the disqualification of persons from being directors of companies, and from being otherwise concerned with a company's affairs.

[25TH JULY 1986]

Preliminary

Disqualification orders: general

1.—(1) In the circumstances specified below in this Act a court may, and under section 6 shall, make against a person a disqualification order, that is to say an order that he shall not, without leave of the court—

(a) be a director of a company, or

(b) be a liquidator or administrator of a company, or

(c) be a receiver or a manager of a company's property, or

(d) in any way, whether directly or indirectly, be concerned or take part in the promotion, formation or management of a company,

for a specified period beginning with the date of the order.

(2) In each section of this Act which gives to a court power or, as the case may be, imposes on it the duty to make a disqualification order there is specified the maximum (and, in section 6, the minimum) period of disqualification which may or (as the case may be) must be imposed by means of the order.

(3) Where a disqualification order is made against a person who is already subject to such an order, the periods specified in those orders shall run concurrently.

(4) A disqualification order may be made on grounds which are or include matters other than criminal convictions, notwithstanding that the person in respect of whom it is to be made may be criminally liable in respect of those matters.

Disqualification for General Misconduct in Connection with Companies

Disqualification on conviction of indictable offence

2.—(1) The court may make a disqualification order against a person where he is convicted of an indictable offence (whether on indictment or summarily) in connection with the promotion, formation, management, liquidation or striking off of a company, or with the receivership or management of a company's property.

(2) "The court" for this purpose means—

(a) any court having jurisdiction to wind up the compnay in relation to which the offence was committed, or

(b) the court by or before which the person is convicted of the offence, or

(c) in the case of a summary conviction in England and Wales, any other magistrates' court acting for the same petty sessions area;

and for the purposes of this section the definition of **"indictable offence"** in Schedule 1 to the Interpretation Act 1978 applies for Scotland as it does for England and Wales.

(3) The maximum period of disqualification under this section is—

(a) where the disqualification order is made by a court of summary jurisdiction, 5 years, and

(b) in any other case, 15 years.

Disqualification for persistent breaches of companies legislation

3.—(1) The court may make a disqualification order against a person where it appears to it that he has been persistently in default in relation to provisions of the companies legislation requiring any return, account or other document to be filed with, delivered or sent, or notice of any matter to be given, to the registrar of companies.

(2) On an application to the court for an order to be made under this section, the fact that a person has been persistently in default in relation to such provisions as are mentioned above may (without prejudice to its proof in any other manner) be conclusively proved by showing that in the 5 years ending with the date of the application he has been adjudged guilty (whether or not on the same occasion) of three or more defaults in relation to those provisions.

(3) A person is to be treated under subsection (2) as being adjudged guilty of a default in relation to any provision of that legislation if—

(a) he is convicted (whether on indictment or summarily) of an offence consisting in a contravention of or failure to comply with that provision (whether on his own part or on the part of any company), or

(b) a default order is made against him, that is to say an order under any of the following provisions—

    (i) section 242(4) of the Companies Act (order requiring delivery of company accounts),

  (ia) section 245B of that Act (order requiring preparation of revised accounts),

  (ii) section 713 of that Act (enforcement of company's duty to make returns),

  (iii) section 41 of the Insolvency Act (enforcement of receiver's or manager's duty to make returns), or

  (iv) section 170 of that Act (corresponding provision for liquidator in winding up),

in respect of any such contravention of or failure to comply with that provision (whether on his own part or on the part of any company).

(4) In this section **"the court"** means any court having jurisdiction to wind up any of the companies in relation to which the offence or other default has been or is alleged to have been committed.

(5) The maximum period of disqualification under this section is 5 years.

Disqualification for fraud, etc., in winding up

4.—(1) The court may make a disqualification order against a person if, in the course of the winding up of a company, it appears that he—

  (a) has been guilty of an offence for which he is liable (whether he has been convicted or not) under section 458 of the Companies Act (fraudulent trading), or

  (b) has otherwise been guilty, while an officer or liquidator of the company or receiver or manager of its property, of any fraud in relation to the company or of any breach of his duty as such officer, liquidator, receiver or manager.

(2) In this section **"the court"** means any court having jurisdiction to wind up any of the companies in relation to which the offence or other default has been or is alleged to have been committed; and **"officer"** includes a shadow director.

(3) The maximum period of disqualification under this section is 15 years.

Disqualification on summary conviction

5.—(1) An offence counting for the purposes of this section is one of which a person is convicted (either on indictment or summarily) in consequence of a contravention of, or failure to comply with, any provision of the companies legislation requiring a return, account or other document to be filed with, delivered or sent, or notice of any matter to be given, to the registrar of companies (whether the contravention or failure is on the person's own part or on the part of any company).

(2) Where a person is convicted of a summary offence counting for those purposes, the court by which he is convicted (or, in England and Wales, any other magistrates' court acting for the same petty sessions area) may make a disqualification order against him if the circumstances specified in the next subsection are present.

(3) Those circumstances are that, during the 5 years ending with the date of the conviction, the person has had made against him, or has been convicted of, in total not less than 3 default orders and offences counting for the purposes of this section; and those offences may include that of which he is convicted as mentioned in subsection (2) and any other offence of which he is convicted on the same occasion.

(4) For the purposes of this section—

  (a) the definition of "summary offence" in Schedule 1 to the Interpretation Act 1978 applies for Scotland as for England and Wales, and

  (b) **"default order"** means the same as in section 3(3)(b).

(5) The maximum period of disqualification under this section is 5 years.

Disqualification for Unfitness

Duty of court to disqualify unfit directors of insolvent companies

6.—(1) The court shall make a disqualification order against a person in any case where, on an application under this section, it is satisfied—

(a) that he is or has been a director of a company which has at any time become insolvent (whether while he was a director or subsequently), and

(b) that his conduct as a director of that company (either taken alone or taken together with this conduct as a director of any company or companies) makes him unfit to be concerned in the management of a company.

(2) For the purposes of this section and the next, a company becomes insolvent if—

(a) the company goes into liquidation at a time when its assets are insufficient for the payment of its debts and other liabilities and the expenses of the winding up,

(b) an administration order is made in relation to the company, or

(c) an administrative receiver of the company is appointed;

and references to a person's conduct as a director of any company or companies include, where that company or any of those companies has become insolvent, that person's conduct in relation to any matter connected with or arising out of the insolvency of that company.

(3) In this section and the next **"the court"** means—

(a) in the case of a person who is or has been a director of a company which is being wound up by the court, the court by which the company is being wound up,

(b) in the case of a person who is or has been a director of a company which is being wound up voluntarily, any court having jurisdiction to wind up the company,

(c) in the case of a person who is or has been a director of a company in relation to which an administration order is in force, the court by which that order was made, and

(d) in any other case, the High Court or, in Scotland, the Court of Session;

and in both sections **"director"** includes a shadow director.

(4) Under this section the minimum period of disqualification is 2 years, the maximum period is 15 years.

Applications to court under s. 6; reporting provisions

7.—(1) If it appears to the Secretary of State that it is expedient in the public interest that a disqualification order under section 6 should be made against any person, an application for the making of such an order against that person may be made—

(a) by the Secretary of State, or

(b) if the Secretary of State so directs in the case of a person who is or has been a director of a company which is being wound up by the court in England and Wales, by the official receiver.

(2) Except with the leave of the court, an application for the making under that section of a disqualification order against any person shall not be made after the end of the period of 2 years beginning with the day on which the company of which that person is or has been a director became insolvent.

the office-holder responsible under this section, that is to say—

company which is being wound up by the court in England and Wales,
iver,

of a company which is being wound up otherwise, the liquidator,

(c) in the case of a company in relation to which an administration order is in force, the administrator, or

(d) in the case of a company of which there is an administrative receiver, that receiver,

that the conditions mentioned in section 6(1) are satisfied as respects a person who is or has been a director of that company, the office-holder shall forthwith report the matter to the Secretary of State.

(4) The Secretary of State or the official receiver may require the liquidator, administrator or administrative receiver of a company, or the former liquidator, administrator or administrative receiver of a company—

(a) to furnish him with such information with respect to any person's conduct as a director of the company, and

(b) to produce and permit inspection of such books, papers and other records relevant to that person's conduct as such a director,

as the Secretary of State or the official receiver may reasonably require for the purpose of determining whether to exercise, or of exercising, any function of his under this section.

Disqualification after investigation of company

8.—(1) If it appears to the Secretary of State from a report made by inspectors under section 437 of the Companies Act or section 94 or 177 of the Financial Services Act 1986, or from information or documents obtained under section 447 or 448 of the Companies Act or section 105 of the Financial Services Act 1986 or section 2 of the Criminal Justice Act 1987 or section 28 of the Criminal Law (Consolidation) (Scotland) Act 1995 or section 83 of the Companies Act 1989, that it is expedient in the public interest that a disqualification order should be made against any person who is or has been a director or shadow director of any company, he may apply to the court for such an order to be made against that person.

(2) The court may make a disqualification order against a person where, on an application under this section, it is satisfied that his conduct in relation to the company makes him unfit to be concerned in the management of a company.

(3) In this section "the court" means the High Court or, in Scotland, the Court of Session.

(4) The maximum period of disqualification under this section is 15 years.

Matters for determining unfitness of directors

9.—(1) Where it falls to a court to determine whether a person's conduct as a director or shadow director of any particular company or companies makes him unfit to be concerned in the management of a company, the court shall, as respects his conduct as a director of that company or, as the case may be, each of those companies, have regard in particular—

(a) to the matters mentioned in Part I of Schedule 1 to this Act, and

(b) where the company has become insolvent, to the matters mentioned in Part II of that Schedule;

and references in that Schedule to the director and the company are to be read accordingly.

(2) Section 6(2) applies for the purposes of this section and Schedule 1 as it applies for the purposes of sections 6 and 7.

(3) Subject to the next subsection, any reference in Schedule 1 to an enactment contained in the Companies Act or the Insolvency Act includes, in relation to any time before the coming into force of that enactment, the corresponding enactment in force at that time.

(4) The Secretary of State may be order modify any of the provisions of Schedule 1; and such

an order may contain such transitional provisions as may appear to the Secretary of State necessary or expedient.

(5) The power to make orders under this section is exercisable by statutory instrument subject to annulment in pursuance of a resolution of either House of Parliament.

Other Cases of Disqualification

Participation in wrongful trading

10.—(1) Where the court makes a declaration under section 213 or 214 of the Insolvency Act that a person is liable to make a contribution to a company's assets, then, whether or not an application for such an order is made by any person, the court may, if it thinks fit, also make a disqualification order against the person to whom the declaration relates.

(2) The maximum period of disqualification under this section is 15 years.

Undischarged bankrupts

11.—(1) It is an offence for a person who is an undischarged bankrupt to act as director of, or directly or indirectly to take part in or be concerned in the promotion, formation or management of, a company, except with the leave of the court.

(2) "The court" for this purpose is the court by which the person was adjudged bankrupt or, in Scotland, sequestration of his estates was awarded.

(3) In England and Wales, the leave of the court shall not be given unless notice of intention to apply for it has been served on the official receiver; and it is the latter's duty, if he is of opinion that it is contrary to the public interest that the application should be granted, to attend on the hearing of the application and oppose it.

Failure to pay under county court administration order

12.—(1) The following has effect where a court under section 429 of the Insolvency Act revokes an administration order under Part VI of the County Courts Act 1984.

(2) A person to whom that section applies by virtue of the order under section 429(2)(b) shall not, except with the leave of the court which made the order, act as director or liquidator of, or directly or indirectly take part or be concerned in the promotion, formation or management of, a company.

Consequences of Contravention

Criminal penalties

13. If a person acts in contravention of a disqualification order or of section 12(2), or is guilty of an offence under section 11, he is liable—

(a) on conviction on indictment, to imprisonment for not more than 2 years or a fine or both; and

(b) on summary conviction, to imprisonment for not more than 6 months or a fine not exceeding the statutory maximum, or both.

Offences by body corporate

14.—(1) Where a body corporate is guilty of an offence of acting in contravention of a disqualification order, and it is proved that the offence occurred with the consent or connivance of, or was attributable to any neglect on the part of any director, manager, secretary or other similar officer of the body corporate, or any person who was purporting to act in any such capacity he, as well as the body corporate, is guilty of the offence and liable to be proceeded against and punished accordingly.

(2) Where the affairs of a body corporate are managed by its members, subsection (1) applies in relation to the acts and defaults of a member in connection with his functions of management as if he were a director of the body corporate.

Personal liability for company's debts where person acts while disqualified

15.—(1) A person is personally responsible for all the relevant debts of a company if at any time—

(a) in contravention of a disqualification order or of section 11 of this Act he is involved in the management of the company, or

(b) as a person who is involved in the management of the company, he acts or is willing to act on instructions given without the leave of the court by a person whom he knows at that time to be the subject of a disqualification order ot to be an undischarged bankrupt.

(2) Where a person is personally responsible under this section for the relevant debts of a company, he is jointly and severally liable in respect of those debts with the company and any other person who, whether under this section or otherwise, is so liable.

(3) For the purposes of this section the relevant debts of a company are—

(a) in relation to a person who is personally responsible under paragraph (a) of subsection (1), such debts and other liabilities of the company as are incurred at a time when that person was involved in the management of the company, and

(b) in relation to a person who is personally responsible under paragraph (b) of that subsection, such debts and other liabilities of the company as are incurred at a time when that person was acting or was willing to act on instructions given as mentioned in that paragraph.

(4) For the purposes of this section, a person is involved in the management of a company if he is a director of the company or if he is concerned, whether directly or indirectly, or takes part, in the management of the company.

(5) For the purposes of this section a person who, as a person involved in the management of a company, has at any time acted on instructions given without the leave of the court by a person whom he knew at that time to be the subject of a disqualification order or to be an undischarged bankrupt is presumed, unless the contrary is shown, to have been willing at any time thereafter to act on any instructions given by that person.

Supplementary Provisions

Application for disqualification order

16.—(1) A person intending to apply for the making of a disqualification order by the court having jurisdiction to wind up a company shall give not less than 10 days' notice of his intention to the person against whom the order is sought; and on the hearing of the application the last-mentioned person may appear and himself give evidence or call witnesses.

(2) An application to a court with jurisdiction to wind up companies for the making against any person of a disqualification order under any of sections 2 to 5 may be made by the Secretary of State or the official receiver, or by the liquidator or any past or present member or creditor of any company in relation to which that person has committed or is alleged to have committed an offence or other default.

(3) On the hearing of any application under this Act made by the Secretary of State or the official receiver or the liquidator the applicant shall appear and call the attention of the court to any matters which seem to him to be relevant, and may himself give evidence or call witnesses.

Application for leave under an order

17.—(1) As regards the court to which application must be made for leave under a disqualification order, the following applies—

(a) where the application is for leave to promote or form a company, it is any court with jurisdiction to wind up companies, and

(b) where the application is for leave to be a liquidator, administrator or director of, or otherwise to take part in the management of a company, or to be a receiver or manager of a company's property, it is any court having jurisdiction to wind up that company.

(2) On the hearing of an application for leave made by a person against whom a disqualification order has been made on the application of the Secretary of State, the official receiver or the

liquidator, the Secretary of State, official receiver or liquidator shall appear and call the attention of the court to any matters which seem to him to be relevant, and may himself give evidence or call witnesses.

Register of disqualification orders

18.—(1) The Secretary of State may make regulations requiring officers of courts to furnish him with such particulars as the regulations may specify of cases in which—

(a) a disqualification order is made, or

(b) any action is taken by a court in consequence of which such an order is varied or ceases to be in force, or

(c) leave is granted by a court for a person subject to such an order to do anything which otherwise the order prohibits him from doing;

and the regulations may specify the time within which, and the form and manner in which, such particulars are to be furnished.

(2) The Secretary of State shall, from the particulars so furnished, continue to maintain the register of orders, and of cases in which leave has been granted as mentioned in subsection (1)(c), which was set up by him under section 29 of the Companies Act 1976 and continued under section 301 of the Companies Act 1985.

(3) When an order of which entry is made in the register ceases to be in force, the Secretary of State shall delete the entry from the register and all particulars relating to it which have been furnished to him under this section or any previous corresponding provision.

(4) The register shall be open to inspection on payment of such fee as may be specified by the Secretary of State in regulations.

(5) Regulations under this section shall be made by statutory instrument subject to annulment in pursuance of a resolution of either House of Parliament.

Special savings from repealed enactments

19. Schedule 2 to this Act has effect—

(a) in connection with certain transitional cases arising under sections 93 and 94 of the Companies Act 1981, so as to limit the power to make a disqualification order, or to restrict the duration of an order, by reference to events occurring or things done before those sections came into force,

(b) to preserve orders made under section 28 of the Companies Act 1976 (repealed by the Act of 1981), and

(c) to preclude any applications for a disqualification order under section 6 or 8, where the relevant company went into liquidation before 28th April 1986.

Miscellaneous and General

Admissibility in evidence of statements

20. In any proceedings (whether or not under this Act), any statement made in pursuance of a requirement imposed by or under sections 6 to 10, 15 or 19(c) of, or Schedule 1 to, this Act, or by or under rules made for the purposes of this Act under the Insolvency Act, may be used in evidence against any person making or concurring in making the statement.

Interaction with Insolvency Act

21.—(1) References in this Act to the official receiver, in relation to the winding up of a company or the bankruptcy of an individual, are to any person who, by virtue of section 399 of the Insolvency Act, is authorised to act as the official receiver in relation to that winding up or bankruptcy; and, in accordance with section 401(2) of that Act, references in this Act to an official receiver includes a person appointed as his deputy.

(2) Sections 6 to 10, 15, 19(c) and 20 of, and Schedule 1 to, this Act are deemed included in

Application of Act to incorporated friendly societies

22B.—(1) This Act applies to incorporated friendly societies as it applies to companies.

(2) References in this Act to a company, or to a director or an officer of a company include, respectively, references to an incorporated friendly society within the meaning of the Friendly Societies Act 1992 or to a member of the committee of management or officer, within the meaning of that Act, of an incorporated friendly society.

(3) In relation to an incorporated friendly society every reference to a shadow director shall be omitted.

(4) In the application of Schedule 1 to the members of the committee of management of an incorporated friendly society, references to provisions of the Insolvency Act or the Companies Act include references to the corresponding provisions of the Friendly Societies Act 1992.

Transitional provisions, savings, repeals

23.—(1) The transitional provisions and savings in Schedule 3 to this Act have effect, and are without prejudice to anything in the Interpretation Act 1978 with regard to the effect of repeals.

(2) The enactments specified in the second column of Schedule 4 to this Act are repealed to the extent specified in the third column of that Schedule.

Extent

24.—(1) This Act extends to England and Wales and to Scotland.

(2) Nothing in this Act extends to Northern Ireland.

Commencement

25. This Act comes into force simultaneously with the Insolvency Act 1986.

Citation

26. This Act may be cited as the Company Directors Disqualification Act 1986.

SCHEDULES

Section 9   SCHEDULE 1

MATTERS FOR DETERMINING UNFITNESS OF DIRECTORS

PART I

MATTERS APPLICABLE IN ALL CASES

1.   Any misfeasance or breach of any fiduciary or other duty by the director in relation to the company.

2.   Any misapplication or retention by the director of, or any conduct by the director giving rise to an obligation to account for, any money or other property of the company.

3.   The extent of the director's responsibility for the company entering into any transaction liable to be set aside under Part XVI of the Insolvency Act (provisions against debt avoidance).

4.   The extent of the director's responsibility for any failure by the company to comply with any of the following provisions of the Companies Act, namely—

(a) section 221 (companies to keep accounting records);

(b) section 222 (where and for how long records to be kept);

(c) section 288 (register of directors and secretaries);

(d) section 352 (obligation to keep and enter up register of members);

(e) section 353 (location of register of members);

(f) section 363 (duty of company to make annual returns); and

(h) sections 399 and 415 (company's duty to register charges it creates).

5.   The extent of the director's responsibility for any failure by the directors of the company to comply with—

(a) section 226 or 227 of the Companies Act (duty to prepare annual accounts), or

(b) section 233 of that Act (approval and signature of accounts).

5A.   In the application of this Part of this Schedule in relation to any person who is a director of an investment company with variable capital, any reference to a provision of the Companies Act shall be taken to be a reference to the corresponding provision of the Open-Ended Investment Companies (Investment Companies with Variable Capital) Regulations 1996 or of any regulations made under regulation 6 of those Regulations (SIB regulations).

PART II

MATTERS APPLICABLE WHERE COMPANY HAS BECOME INSOLVENT

6.   The extent of the director's responsibility for the causes of the company becoming insolvent.
7.   The extent of the director's responsibility for any failure by the company to supply any goods or services which have been paid for (in whole or in part).
8.   The extent of the director's responsibility for the company entering into any transaction or giving any preference, being a transaction or preference—

(a) liable to be set aside under section 127 or sections 238 to 240 of the Insolvency Act, or

(b) challengeable under section 242 or 243 of that Act or under any rule of law in Scotland.

9.   The extent of the director's responsibility for any failure by the directors of the company to comply with section 98 of the Insolvency Act (duty to call creditors' meeting in creditors' voluntary winding up).
10.   Any failure by the director to comply with any obligation imposed on him by or under any of the following provisions of the Insolvency Act—

(a) section 22 (company's statement of affairs in administration);

(b) section 47 (statement of affairs to administrative receiver);

(c) section 66 (statement of affairs in Scottish receivership);

(d) section 99 (director's duty to attend meeting; statement of affairs in creditors' voluntary winding up);

(e) section 131 (statement of affairs in winding up by the court);

(f) section 234 (duty of any one with company property to deliver it up);

(g) section 235 (duty to co-operate with liquidator, etc.).

Section 19   SCHEDULE 2

SAVINGS FROM COMPANIES ACT 1981 ss. 93, 94, AND INSOLVENCY ACT 1985 SCHEDULE 9

1.   Sections 2 and 4(1)(b) do not apply in relation to anything done before 15th June 1982 by a person in his capacity as liquidator of a company or as receiver or manager of a company's property.
2.   Subject to paragraph 1—

(a) section 2 applies in a case where a person is convicted on indictment of an offence which he committed (and, in the case of a continuing offence, has ceased to commit) before

15th June 1982; but in such a case a disqualification order under that section shall not be made for a period in excess of 5 years;

(b) that section does not apply in a case where a person is convicted summarily—

(i) in England and Wales, if he had consented so to be tried before that date, or

(ii) in Scotland, if the summary proceedings commenced before that date.

3. Subject to paragraph 1, section 4 applies in relation to an offence committed or other thing done before 15th June 1982; but a disqualification order made on the grounds of such an offence or other thing done shall not be made for a period in excess of 5 years.

4. The powers of a court under section 5 are not exercisable in a case where a person is convicted of an offence which he committed (and, in the case of a continuing offence, had ceased to commit) before 15th June 1982.

5. For purposes of section 3(1) and section 5, no account is to be taken of any offence which was committed, or any default order which was made, before 1st June 1977.

6. An order made under section 28 of the Companies Act 1976 has effect as if made under section 3 of this Act; and an application made before 15th June 1982 for such an order is to be treated as an application for an order under the section last mentioned.

7. Where—

(a) an application is made for a disqualification order under section 6 of this Act by virtue of paragraph (a) of subsection (2) of that section, and

(b) the company in question went into liquidation before 28th April 1986 (the coming into force of the provision replaced by section 6),

the court shall not make an order under that section unless it could have made a disqualification order under section 300 of the Companies Act as it had effect immediately before the date specified in sub-paragraph (b) above.

8. An application shall not be made under section 8 of this Act in relation to a report made or information or documents obtained before 28th April 1986.

Section 23(1)   SCHEDULE 3

Transitional Provisions and Savings

1. In this Schedule, **"the former enactments"** means so much of the Companies Act, and so much of the Insolvency Act, as is repealed and replaced by this Act; and **"the appointed day"** means the day on which this Act comes into force.

2. So far as anything done or treated as done under or for the purposes of any provision of the former enactments could have been done under or for the purposes of the corresponding provision of this Act, it is not invalidated by the repeal of that provision but has effect as if done under or for the purposes of the corresponding provision; and any order, regulation, rule or other instrument made or having effect under any provision of the former enactments shall, insofar as its effect is preserved by this paragraph, be treated for all purposes as made and having effect under the corresponding provision.

3. Where any period of time specified in a provision of the former enactments is current immediately before the appointed day, this Act has effect as if the corresponding provision had been in force when the period began to run; and (without prejudice to the foregoing) any period of time so specified and current is deemed for the purposes of this Act—

(a) to run from the date or event from which it was running immediately before the appointed day, and

(b) to expire (subject to any provision of this Act for its extension) whenever it would have expired if this Act had not been passed;

and any rights, priorities, liabilities, reliefs, obligations, requirements, powers, duties or exemptions dependent on the beginning, duration or end of such a period as above mentioned shall be under this Act as they were or would have been under the former enactments.

4.   Where in any provision of this Act there is a reference to another such provision, and the first-mentioned provision operates, or is capable of operating, in relation to things done or omitted, or events occurring or not occurring, in the past (including in particular past acts of compliance with any enactment, failures of compliance, contraventions, offences and convictions of offences) the reference to the other provision is to be read as including a reference to the corresponding provision of the former enactments.

5.   Offences committed before the appointed day under any provision of the former enactments may, notwithstanding any repeal by this Act, be prosecuted and punished after that day as if this Act had not passed.

6.   A reference in any enactment, instrument or document (whether express or implied, and in whatever phraseology) to a provision of the former enactments (including the corresponding provision of any yet earlier enactment) is to be read, where necessary to retain for the enactment, instrument or document the same force and effect as it would have had but for the passing of this Act, as, or as including, a reference to the corresponding provision by which it is replaced in this Act.

Section 23(2)   SCHEDULE 4

                                         REPEALS

Chapter	Short title or title	Extent of repeal
1985 c. 6.	The Companies Act 1985.	Sections 295 to 299. Section 301. Section 302. Schedule 12. In Schedule 24, the entries relating to sections 295(7) and 302(1).
1985 c. 65.	The Insolvency Act 1985.	Sections 12 to 14. Section 16. Section 18. Section 108(2). Schedule 2. In Schedule 6, paragraphs 1, 2, 7 and 14. In Schedule 9, paragraphs 2 and 3.

TABLE OF DERIVATIONS

Note: The following abbreviations are used in this Table:
"CA" = The Companies Act 1985 (c. 6).
"IA" = The Insolvency Act 1985 (c. 65).

Provision	Derivation
1	CA sec. 295(1), (2), (4); IA Sch. 6 para. 1(1)–(3).
2	CA ss. 295(2), 296.
3	CA ss. 295(2), 297.
4	CA ss. 295(2), 298.
5	CA ss. 295(2), 299.
6	CA sec. 295(2); IA ss. 12(1), (2), (7)–(9), 108(2).
7	IA sec. 12(3)–(6).
8	CA sec. 295(2); IA ss. 12(9), 13, 108(2).
9	IA ss. 12(9), 14.
10	CA sec. 295(2); IA ss. 16, 108(2).
11	CA sec. 302.
12	IA sec. 221(2).
13	CA ss. 295(7), 302(1), Sch. 24.
14	CA sec. 733(1)–(3); IA Sch. 6 para. 7.
15	IA sec. 18(1) (part), (2)–(6).
16	CA sec. 295(6) (part), Sch. 12 paras. 1–3; IA sec. 108(2), Sch. 6 para. 1(4).
17	CA sec. 295(6) (part), Sch. 12 paras. 4, 5; IA sec. 108(2), Sch. 6 paras. 1(4), 14.
18	CA sec. 301: IA sec. 108(2), Sch. 6 para. 2.
19	CA sec. 295(6); and see Sch. 2.
20	IA sec. 231 (part).
21	IA ss. 106, 107, 108(1), (2), 222(1), 224(2), 227, 229, 234.
22	IA sec. 108(1)–(4).
23	—
24	IA sec. 236(4)(*a*).
25	—
26	—
Sch. 1	IA Sch. 2.
Sch. 2	CA Sch. 12 Pt. III; IA Sch. 9 paras. 2, 3.
Sch. 3	—
Sch. 4	—

APPENDIX 2

EXTRACTS FROM PREVIOUS LEGISLATION

- Insolvency Act 1985, ss. 12-16, 108, 109; Scheds 2, 6
- Companies Act 1985, ss. 295-302, Sched. 12
- Companies Act 1981, ss. 93-94; Sched. 3
- Companies Act 1976, ss. 28-29
- Insolvency Act 1976, s. 9
- Companies Act 1948, ss. 187-188
- Companies Act 1947, s. 33
- Companies Act 1929, ss. 142, 275
- Companies Act 1928, ss. 84, 75

INSOLVENCY ACT 1985, ss. 12–16

PART II

COMPANY INSOLVENCY ETC.

CHAPTER I

DISQUALIFICATION AND PERSONAL LIABILITY OF DIRECTORS AND OTHERS

Duty of court to disqualify unfit directors of insolvent companies

12.—(1) The court shall make a disqualification order against a person in any case where, on an application under this section, the court is satisfied—

(a) that he is or has been a director of a company which has at any time become insolvent (whether while he was a director or subsequently); and

(b) that his conduct as a director of that company (either taken alone or taken together with his conduct as a director of any other company or companies) makes him unfit to be concerned in the management of a company.

(2) The period specified as the period of the disqualification in a disqualification order made under this section shall not be less than two years.

(3) If it appears to the Secretary of State that it is expedient in the public interest that a disqualification order under this section should be made against any person, an application for the making of such an order against that person may be made—

(a) by the Secretary of State; or

(b) if the Secretary of State so directs in the case of a person who is or has been a director of a company which is being wound up by the court in England and Wales, by the official receiver.

(4) Except with the leave of the court, an application for the making under this section of a disqualification order against any person shall not be made after the end of the period of two years beginning with the day on which the company of which that person is or has been a director became insolvent.

(5) If—

(a) in the case of a person who is or has been a director of a company which is being wound up by the court in England or Wales, it appears to the official receiver;

(b) in the case of a person who is or has been a director of a company which is being wound up otherwise than as mentioned in paragraph (a) above, it appears to the liquidator;

(c) in the case of a person who is or has been a director of a company in relation to which an administration order is in force, it appears to the administrator; or

(d) in the case of a person who is or has been a director of a company of which there is an administrative receiver, it appears to that receiver,

that the conditions mentioned in subsection (1) above are satisfied as respects that person, the official receiver, the liquidator, the administrator or, as the case may be, the administrative receiver, shall forthwith report the matter to the Secretary of State.

(6) The Secretary of State or the official receiver may require the liquidator, administrator or administrative receiver of a company or the former liquidator, administrator or administrative receiver of a company—

(a) to furnish him with such information with respect to any person's conduct as a director of the company; and

(b) to produce and permit inspection of such books, papers and other records relevant to that person's conduct as such a director,

as the Secretary of State or the official receiver may reasonably require for the purpose of determining whether to exercise, or of exercising, any function of his under this section.

(7) For the purposes of this section a company becomes insolvent if—

(a) the company goes into liquidation at a time when its assets are insufficient for the payment of its debts and other liabilities and the expenses of the winding up;

(b) an administration order is made in relation to the company; or

(c) an administrative receiver of the company is appointed,

and references in this section to a person's conduct as a director of any company or companies include, where that company or any of those companies has become insolvent, references to that person's conduct in relation to any matter connected with or arising out of the insolvency of that company.

(8) In this section "the court" means—

(a) in the case of a person who is or has been a director of a company which is being wound up by the court, the court by which the company is being wound up;

(b) in the case of a person who is or has been a director of a company which is being wound up voluntarily, any court having jurisdiction to wind up the company;

(c) in the case of a person who is or has been a director of a company in relation to which an administration order is in force, the court by which that order was made; and

(d) in any other case, the High Court or, in Scotland, the Court of Session.

(9) In this section and sections 13 to 15 below "director" includes a shadow director within the meaning given by section 741(2) of the 1985 Act.

Disqualification after investigation of company

13.—(1) If it appears to the Secretary of State from a report made by inspectors under section 437 of the 1985 Act, or from information or documents obtained under section 447 or 448 of that Act, that it is expedient in the public interest that a disqualification order should be made against any person who is or has been a director of any company, he may apply to the court for such an order to be made against that person.

(2) The court may make a disqualification order against a person where, on an application under this section, the court is satisfied that his conduct in relation to the company makes him unfit to be concerned in the management of a company.

(3) In this section "the court" means the High Court or, in Scotland, the Court of Session.

Matters for determining unfitness of directors

14.—(1) Where it falls to a court to determine whether a person's conduct as a director of any particular company or companies makes him unfit as mentioned in section 12(1) or 13(2) above, the court shall, as respects his conduct as a director of that company or, as the case may be, each of those companies, have regard in particular—

(a) to the matters mentioned in Part I of Schedule 2 to this Act; and

(b) where the company has become insolvent, to the matters mentioned in Part II of that Schedule;

and references in that Schedule to the director and to the company shall be construed accordingly.

(2) Subsection (7) of section 12 above applies for the purposes of this section and Schedule 2 to this Act as it applies for the purposes of that section.

(3) Subject to subsection (4) below, any reference in Schedule 2 to this Act to any enactment contained in the 1985 Act or this Act shall include, in relation to any time before the coming into force of that enactment, a reference to the corresponding enactment in force at that time.

(4) The Secretary of State may by order modify any of the provisions of Schedule 2 to this Act; and such an order may contain such transitional provisions as may appear to the Secretary of State necessary or expedient.

(5) The power to make orders unders this section shall be exercisable by statutory instrument which shall be subject to annulment in pursuance of a resolution of either House of Parliament.

Responsibility for company's wrongful trading

15.—(1) Subject to subsection (3) below, if in the course of the winding up of a company it appears that subsection (2) below applies in relation to a person who is or has been a director of the company, the court, on the application of the liquidator, may declare that that person is to be liable to make such contribution (if any) to the company's assets as the court thinks proper.

(2) This subsection applies in relation to a person if—

(a) the company has gone into insolvent liquidation;

(b) at some time before the commencement of the winding up of the company, that person knew or ought to have concluded that there was no reasonable prospect that the company would avoid going into insolvent liquidation; and

(c) that person was a director of the company at that time.

(3) The court shall not make a declaration under subsection (1) above with respect to any person if it is satisfied that after the condition specified in subsection (2)(b) above was first satisfied in relation to him that person took every step with a view to minimising the potential loss to the company's creditors as (assuming him to have known that there was no reasonable prospect that the company would avoid going into insolvent liquidation) he ought to have taken.

(4) For the purposes of subsections (2) and (3) above the facts which a director of a company ought to know or ascertain, the conclusions which he ought to reach and the steps which he ought to take are those which would be known or ascertained, or reached or taken, by a reasonably diligent person having both—

(a) the general knowledge, skill and experience that may reasonably be expected of a person carrying out the same functions as are carried out by that director in relation to the company; and

(b) the general knowledge, skill and experience that that director has.

(5) The reference in subsection (4) above to the functions carried out in relation to a company by a director of the company includes a reference to any functions which he does not carry out but which have been entrusted to him.

(6) Subsections (3) to (6) of section 630 of the 1985 Act (responsibility for company's fraudulent trading) shall have effect in relation to a declaration under subsection (1) above as they have effect in relation to a declaration under subsection (2) of that section, and this section is without prejudice to that section.

(7) For the purposes of this section a company goes into insolvent liquidation if it goes into liquidation at a time when its assets are insufficient for the payment of its debts and other liabilities and the expenses of the winding up.

Disqualification of persons held to be liable to contribute to company's assets

16. Where a court makes a declaration under section 15 above or section 630 of the 1985 Act that any person is to be liable to make a contribution to a company's assets, then, whether or not an application for such an order is made by any person, the court may, if it thinks fit, also make a disqualification order against the person to whom the declaration relates.

INSOLVENCY ACT 1985, ss. 108(1), (2), 109

Construction of Part II

108.—(1) The provisions of this Part shall be construed as one with the 1985 Act and—

(a) so far as relating to the disqualification of directors and others involved in the management of companies, with Part IX of that Act; and

(b) so far as relating to receivers or managers, with Part XIX of that Act; and

(c) so far as relating to the winding up of companies, with Part XX of that Act,

and references in that Act to itself and to any of those Parts of that Act shall be construed accordingly.

(2) The following provisions, namely—

(a) sections 295 and 301 of the 1985 Act (disqualification orders and register of such orders); and

(b) paragraphs 1 and 3 to 5 of Part I of Schedule 12 to that Act (procedure for applying for and obtaining disqualification orders and applications for leave under such orders),

shall apply for the purposes of sections 12, 13 and 16 above; and references in those provisions to sections 296 to 299 of that Act shall be construed accordingly.

Minor and consequential amendments of 1985 Act

109.—(1) The 1985 Act shall have effect with the amendments specified in Schedule 6 to this Act (being minor and consequential amendments relating to the disqualification of directors and others involved in the management of companies and the insolvency and winding up of companies).

(2) In the 1985 Act refernces to general rules under section 663(1) or (2) of that Act shall have effect as references to rules under section 106 above.

(3) In the 1985 Act "administrative receiver" has the same meaning as in this Part.

INSOLVENCY ACT 1985, Scheds 2 and 6

Section 14   SCHEDULE 2

Matters for Determining Unfitness of Directors

PART I

MATTERS APPLICABLE IN ALL CASES

1. Any misfeasance or breach of any fiduciary or other duty by the director in relation to the company.

2. Any misapplication or retention by the director of, or any conduct by the director giving rise to an obligation to account for, any money or other property of the company.

3. The extent of the director's responsibility for the company entering into any transaction liable to be set aside under section 212 of this Act.

4. The extent of the director's responsibility for any failure by the company to comply with any of the following provisions of the 1985 Act, namely—

(a) section 221 (companies to keep accounting records);

(b) section 222 (where and for how long records to be kept);

(c) section 288 (register of directors and secretaries);

(d) section 352 (obligation to keep and enter up register of members);

(e) section 353 (location of register of members);

(f) sections 363 and 364 (company's duty to make annual return);

(g) section 365 (time for completion of annual return) and

(h) sections 399 and 415 (company's duty to register charges it creates).

5. The extent of the director's responsibility for any failure by the directors of the company to comply with section 227 (directors' duty to prepare annual accounts) or section 238 (signing of balance sheet and documents to be annexed) of the 1985 Act.

PART II

MATTERS APPLICABLE WHERE COMPANY HAS BECOME INSOLVENT

6. The extent of the director's responsibility for the causes of the company becoming insolvent.

7. The extent of the director's responsibility for any failure by the company to supply any goods or services which have been paid for (in whole or in part).

8. The extent of the director's responsibility for the company entering into any transaction of giving any preference, being a transaction or preference liable to be set aside under section 101 of this Act or section 522 of the 1985 Act or challengable under section 615A of 615B of that Act or under any rule of law in Scotland.

9. The extent of the director's responsibility for any failure by the directors or the company to comply with section 85 of this Act.

10. Any failure by the director to comply with any obligation imposed on him by or under section 482 of the 1985 Act (Company's statement of affairs) or section 39, 53, 66, 85, 98 or 99 of this Act.

Section 109   SCHEDULE 6

AMENDMENTS OF 1985 ACT

Disqualification etc.

1.—(1) Section 295 (disqualification orders: introductory) shall be amended as follows.

(2) In subsection (1) after the word "liquidator" there shall be inserted the words "or administrator" and in that subsection and subsection (3) for the words "sections 296 to 300" there shall be substituted the words "sections 296 to 299".

(3) In subsection (2), at the end there shall be inserted the words—

"; and where a disqualification order is made against a person who is already subject to such an order the periods specified in those orders shall run concurrently."

(4) In subsection (6), for the "Parts I and II of Schedule 12 have" there shall be substituted the words "Part I of Schedule 12 has".

2. In section 301(1) (register of disqualification orders), for the words "sections 296 to 300" there shall be substituted the words "sections 296 to 299".

. . .

7.—(1) Section 733 (liability of directors for offences by company under certain provisions) shall be amended as follows.

(2) In subsection (1), after "216(3)" there shall be inserted "295(7)".

(3) In subsection (3), for the words "210 or 216(3)" there shall be substituted the words "210, 216(3) or 295(7)".

. . .

14. In paragraph 4(3) of Part I of Schedule 12 (orders under sections 296 to 299), for the words "liquidator or director" there shall be substituted the words "liquidator, administrator or director".

COMPANIES ACT 1985, ss. 295–302

Disqualification

Disqualification orders: introductory

295.—(1) In the circumstances specified in sections 296 to 300, a court may make against a person a disqualification order, that is to say an order that he shall not, without level of the court—

(a) be a director of a company, or

(b) be a liquidator of a company, or

(c) be a receiver or manager of a company's property, or

(d) in any way, whether directly or indirectly, be concerned or take part in the promotion, formation or management of a company,

for a specified period beginning with the date of the order.

(2) The maximum period to be specified is—

(a) in the case of an order made under section 297 or made by a court of summary jurisdiction, 5 years, and

(b) in any other case, 15 years.

(3) In this section and sections 296 to 300, "company" includes any company which may be wound up under Part XXI.

(4) A disqualification order may be made on grounds which are or include matters other than criminal convictions, notwithstanding that the person in respect of whom it is to be made may be criminally liable in respect of those matters.

(5) In sections 296 to 299, any reference to provisions, or to a particular provision, of this Act or the Consequential Provisions Act includes the corresponding provision or provisions of the former Companies Acts.

(6) Parts I and II of Schedule 12 have effect with regard to the procedure for obtaining a disqualification order, and to applications for leave under such an order; and Part III of that Schedule has effect—

(a) in connection with certain transitional cases arising under sections 93 and 94 of the Companies Act 1981, so as to limit the power to make a disqualification order, or to restrict the duration of an order, by reference to events occurring or things done before those sections came into force, and

(b) to preserve orders made under section 28 of the Companies Act 1976 (repealed by the Act of 1981).

(7) If a person acts in contravention of a disqualification order, he is in respect of each offence liable to imprisonment or a fine, or both.

Disqualification on conviction of indictable offence

296.—(1) The court may make a disqualification order against a person where he is convicted of an indictable offence (whether on indictment or summarily) in connection with the promotion, formation, management or liquidation of a company, or with the receivership or management of a company's property.

(2) "The court" for this purpose means—

(a) any court having jurisdiction to wind up the company in relation to which the offence was committed, or

(b) the court by or before which the person is convicted of the offence, or

(c) in the case of a summary conviction in England and Wales, any other magistrates' court acting for the same petty sessions area;

and for purposes of this section the definition of "indictable offence" in Schedule 1 to the Interpretation Act 1978 applies in relation to Scotland as it does in relation to England and Wales.

Disqualification for persistent default under Companies Act

297.—(1) The court may make a disqualification order against a person where it appears to it that he has been persistently in default in relation to provisions of this Act or the Consequential Provisions Act requiring any return, account or other document to be filed with, delivered or sent, or notice of any matter to be given, to the registrar of companies.

(2) On an application to the court for an order to be made under this section, the fact that a person has been persistently in default in relation to such provisions as are mentioned above may (without prejudice to its proof in any manner) be conclusively proved by showing that in the 5 years ending with the date of the application he has been adjudged guilty (whether or not on the same occasion) of three or more defaults in relation to those provisions.

(3) A person is treated under subsection (2) as being adjudged guilty of a default in relation to any such provision if—

    (a) he is convicted (whether on indictment or summarily) of an offence consisting in a contravention of or failure to comply with that provision (whether on his own part or on the part of any company), or

    (b) a default order is made against him, that is to say an order under—

        (i) section 244 (order requiring delivery of company accounts), or
       (ii) section 499 (enforcement of receiver's or manager's duty to make returns), or
      (iii) section 636 (corresponding provision for liquidator in winding-up), or
      (iv) section 713 (enforcement of company's duty to make returns),

in respect of any such contravention of or failure to comply with that provision (whether on his own part or on the part of any company).

(4) In this section "the court" means any court having jurisdiction to wind up any of the companies in relation to which the offence or other default has been or is alleged to have been committed.

Disqualification for fraud, etc. in winding up

298.—(1) The court may make a disqualification order against a person if, in the course of the winding up of a company, it appears that he—

    (a) has been guilty of an offence for which he is liable (whether he has been convicted or not) under section 458 (fraudulent trading), or

    (b) has otherwise been guilty, while an officer or liquidator of the company or receiver or manager of its property, of any fraud in relation to the company or of any breach of his duty as such officer, liquidator, receiver or manager.

(2) In this section "the court" means the same as in section 297; and "officer" includes a shadow director.

Disqualification on summary conviction

299.—(1) An offence counting for the purposes of this section is one of which a person is convicted (either on indictment or summarily) in consequence of a contravention of, or failure to comply with, any provision of this Act or the Consequential Provisions Act requiring a return, account or other doucment to be filed with, delivered or sent, or notice of any matter to be given, to the registrar of companies (whether the contravention or failure is on the person's own part or on the part of any company).

(2) Where a person is convicted of a summary offence counting for those purposes, the court by which he is convicted (or, in England and Wales, any other magistrates' court acting for the same petty sessions area) may make a disqualification order against him if the circumstances specified in the next subsection are present.

(3) Those circumstances are that, during the 5 years ending with the date of the conviction, the person has had made against him, or has been convicted of, in total not less than 3 default orders and offences counting for the purposes of this section; and those offences may include that of which he is convicted as mentioned in subsection (2) and any other offence of which he is convicted on the same occasion.

(4) For the purposes of this section—

    (a) the definition of "summary offence" in Schedule 1 to the Interpretation Act 1978 applies for Scotland as for England and Wales, and

    (b) "default order" means the same as in section 297(3)(b).

Disqualification by reference to association with insolvent companies

300.—(1) The court may make a disqualification order against a person where, on an application under this section, it appears to it that he—

    (a) is or has been a director of a company which has at any time gone into liquidation (whether while he was a director or subsequently) and was insolvent at that time, and

(b) is or has been a director of another such company which has gone into liquidation within 5 years of the date on which the first-mentioned company went into liquidation,

and that his conduct as director of any of those companies makes him unfit to be concerned in the management of a company.

(2) In the case of a person who is or has been a director of a company which has gone into liquidation as above-mentioned and is being wound up by the court, "the court" in subsection (1) means the court by which the company is being wound up; and in any other case it means the High Court or, in Scotland, the Court of Session.

(3) The Secretary of State may require the liquidator or former liquidator of a company—

(a) to furnish him with such information with respect to the company's affairs, and

(b) to produce and permit inspection of such books or documents of or relevant to the company,

as the Secretary of State may reasonably require for the purpose of determining whether to make an application under this section in respect of a person who is or has been a director of that company; and if a person makes default in complying with such a requirement, the court may, on the Secretary of State's application, make an order requiring that person to make good the default within such time as may be specified.

(4) For purposes of this section, a shadow director of a company is deemed a director of it; and a company goes into liquidation—

(a) if it is wound up by the court, on the date of the winding-up order, and

(b) in any other case, on the date of the passing of the resolution for voluntary winding up.

Register of disqualification orders

301.—(1) The Secretary of State may make regulations requiring officers of courts to furnish him with such particulars as the regulations may specify of cases in which—

(a) a disqualification order is made under any of sections 296 to 300, or

(b) any action is taken by a court in consequence of which such an order is varied or ceased to be in force, or

(c) leave is granted by a court for a person subject to such an order to do any thing which otherwise the order prohibits him from doing;

and the regulations may specify the time within which, and the form and manner in which, such particulars are to be furnished.

(2) The Secretary of State shall, from the particulars so furnished, continue to maintain the register of orders, and of cases in which leave has been granted as mentioned in subsection (1)(c), which was set up by him under section 29 of the Companies Act 1976.

(3) When an order of which entry is made in the register ceases to be in force, the Secretary of State shall delete the entry from the register and all particulars relating to it which have been furnished to him under this section.

(4) The register shall be open to inspection on payment of such fee as may be specified by the Secretary of State in regulations.

(5) Regulations under this section shall be made by statutory instrument subject to annulment in pursuance of a resolution of either House of Parliament.

Provision against undischarged bankrupt acting as director, etc.

302.—(1) If any person being an undischarged bankrupt acts as director or liquidator of, or directly or indirectly takes part in or is concerned in the promotion, formation or management of, a company except with the leave of the court, he is liable to imprisonment or a fine, or both.

(2) "The court" for this purpose is the court by which the person was adjudged bankrupt or, in Scotland, sequestration of his estates was awarded.

(3) In England and Wales, the leave of the court shall not be given unless notice of intention to apply for it has been served on the official receiver in bankruptcy; and it is the latter's duty, if he is

of opinion that it is contrary to the public interest that the application should be granted, to attend on the hearing of the application and oppose it.

(4) In this section "company" includes an unregistered company and a company incorporated outside Great Britain which has an established place of business in Great Britain.

COMPANIES ACT 1985, Sched. 12

Section 295   SCHEDULE 12

SUPPLEMENTARY PROVISIONS IN CONNECTION WITH DISQUALIFICATION ORDERS

PART I

ORDERS UNDER SECTIONS 296 TO 299

Application for order

1. A person intending to apply for the making of an order under any of sections 296 to 299 by the court having jurisdiction to wind up a company shall give not less than 10 days' notice of his intention to the person against whom the order is sought; and on the hearing of the application the last-mentioned person may appear and himself give evidence or call witnesses.

2. An application to a court with jurisdiction to wind up companies for the making of such an order against any person may be made the Secretary of State or the official receiver, or by the liquidator or any past or present member or creditor of any company in relation to which that person has committed or is alleged to have committed an offence or other default.

Hearing of application

3. On the hearing of an application made by the Secretary of State or the official receiver or the liquidator the applicant shall appear and call the attention of the court to any matters which seem to him to be relevant, and may himself give evidence or call witnesses.

Application for leave under an order

4.—(1) As regards the court to which application must be made for leave under a disqualification order made under any of sections 296 to 299, the following applies.

(2) Where the application is for leave to promote or form a company, it is any court with jurisdiction to wind up companies.

(3) Where the application is for leave to be a liquidator or director of, or otherwise to take part in the management of a company, or to be a receiver or manager of a company's property, it is any court having jurisdiction to wind up that company.

5. On the hearing of an application for leave made by a person against whom a disqualification order has been made on the application of the Secretary of State, the official receiver or the liquidator, the Secretary of State, official receiver or liquidator shall appear and call the attention of the court to any matters which seem to him to be relevant, and may himself give evidence or call witnesses.

PART II

ORDERS UNDER SECTION 300

Application for order

6.—(1) In the case of a person who is or has been a director of a company which has gone into liquidation as mentioned in section 300(1) and is being wound up by the court, any application under that section shall be made by the official receiver or, in Scotland, the Secretary of State.

(2) In any other case an application shall be made by the Secretary of State.

7. Where the official receiver or the Secretary of State intends to make an application under the section in respect of any person, he shall give not less than 10 days' notice of his intention to that person.

Hearing of application

8. On the hearing of an application under section 300 by the official receiver or the Secretary of State, or of an application for leave by a person against whom an order has been made on the application of the official receiver or Secretary of State—

(a) the official receiver of Secretary of State shall appear and call the attention of the court to any matters which seem to him to be relevant, and may himself give evidence or call witnesses, and

(b) the person against whom the order is sought may appear and himself give evidence or call witnesses.

COMPANIES ACT 1981, ss. 93–94

Restrictions on participation in management of companies and disclosure of directorships

Disqualification of directors and others from managing companies, etc.

93.—(1) In section 188 of the 1948 Act (orders of court restraining persons from managing companies) the following subsections shall be substituted for subsections (1) and (2)—

"(1) Where—

(a) a person is convicted of a indictable offence (whether on indictment or summarily) in connection with the promotion, formation, management or liquidation of a company or with the receivership or management of the property of a company; or

(b) it appears to the court that a person has been persistently in default in relation to the relevant requirements; or

(c) in the course of the winding up of a company it appears that a person—

(i) has been guilty of an offence for which he is liable (whether he has been convicted or not) under section 332 of this Act; or

(ii) has otherwise been guilty, while an officer or liquidator of the company or receiver or manager of the property of the company, of any fraud in relation to the company or of any breach of his duty as such officer, liquidator, receiver or manager;

the court may make a disqualification order against that person.

(1A) Where a person is convicted of a summary offence which is a relevant offence and, during the five years ending with the date of that conviction, he has had made against him or has been convicted of, in total, not less than three default orders and relevant offences (including that and any other offence of which he is convicted on the same occasion), the court by which he is convicted of that offence or, in England and Wales, any other magistrates' court acting for the same petty sessions area may make a disqualification order against that person.

(1B) For the purposes of this section, a "disqualification order" is an order that the person against whom the order is made shall not without leave of the court be a liquidator or a director or a receiver without leave of the court be a liquidator or a director or a receiver or manager of the property of a company or in any way, whether directly or indirectly, be concerned or take part in the promotion, formation or management of a company for such period, not exceeding the relevant period, as may be specified in the order.

(1C) Subsection (1)(a) and (c)(ii) of this section shall not apply in relation to anything done before the date on which section 93 of the Companies Act 1981 came into force by a person in his capacity as liquidator of a company or as receiver or manager of the property of a company.

(2) Subject to subsection (1C) of this section, subsection (1)(a) of this section—

(a) shall apply in any case where a person is convicted on indictment of an offence which he committed (and, in the case of a continuing offence, had ceased to commit) before the date on which section 93 of the Companies Act 1981 came into force but in such a case a disqualification order shall not be made for any period in excess of five years;

(b) shall not apply in any case where a person is convicted summarily—

(i) in England and Wales, if he had consented so to be tried before that date; or
(ii) in Scotland, if the summary proceedings commenced before that date.

(2A) Subject to subsection (1C) of this section, subsection (1)(c) of this section shall apply in relation to any offence committed or other thing done before the date on which section 93 of the Companies Act 1981 came into force but a disqualification order made on the grounds of such offence or other thing done shall not be made for any period in excess of five years.

(2B) The powers conferred on any court by subsection (1A) of this section shall not be exercisable in any case where a person is convicted of an offence which he committed (and, in the case of a continuing offence, had ceased to commit) before the date referred to in subsection (2)(a) of this section; and for the purposes of sub-sections (1)(b) and (1A) no account shall be taken of any offence which was committed or any default order made before 1st June 1977.

(2C) For the purposes of an application made under subsection (1)(b) of this section, the fact that a person has been persistently in default in relation to the relevant requirements may (without prejudice to its proof in any other manner) be conclusively proved by showing that in the five years ending with the date of the application he has been adjudged guilty (whether or not on the same occasion) of three or more defaults in relation to those requirements.

A person shall be treated as being adjudged guilty of a default in relation to a relevant requirement for the purposes of this sub-section if he is convicted of any relevant offence or a default order is made against him.

(2D) In this section, except where the context otherwise requires—
"company" includes any company which may be wound up under Part IX of this Act;
"the court"—

(a) in relation to the making of a disqualification order under subsection (1) of this section means any court having jurisdiction to wind up any of the companies in relation to which the offence or other default has been or is alleged to have been committed;

(b) in relation to the making of a disqualification order against any person by virtue of subsection (1)(a) of this section, includes the court by or before which he is convicted of the offence there mentioned and, in the case of a summary conviction in England and Wales, any other magistrates' court acting for the same petty sessions area;

(c) in relation to the granting of leave to promote or form a company, means any court with any jurisdiction to wind up companies; and

(d) in relation to the granting of leave to be a liquidator or a director of or otherwise take part of the management of a company or to be a receiver or manager of the property of a company, means any court having jurisdiction to wind up that company;

"default order" means an order made against any person under sections 337, 375 or 428 of this Act (enforcement of duties of liquidators, receivers and managers and companies to make returns, etc.) or under section 5(1) of the Companies Act 1976 (order requiring failure to deliver accounts within required time to be made good) by virtue of any contravention of or failure to comply with any relevant requirement (whether on his own part or on the part of any company);

"officer", in relation to any company, includes any person in accordance with whose directions or instructions the directors of the company have been accustomed to act;

"petty sessions area" has the meaning given by section 150 of the Magistrates' Courts Act 1980;

"relevant offence" means an offence of which a person is convicted (whether on indictment or summarily) by virtue of any contravention of or failure to comply with any relevant requirement (whether on his own part or on the part of any company);

"the relevant period" means—

(a) in relation to an order made by a court of summary jurisdiction or an order made in pursuance of subsection (1)(b) above, five years; and

(b) in relation to any other order, fifteen years; and

"relevant requirement" means any provision of the Companies Acts 1948 to 1981 which requires any return, account or other document to be filed with, delivered or sent, or notice of any matter to be given, to the registrar.

(2E) For the purposes of this section, the definitions of "indictable offence" and "summary offence" contained in Schedule 1 to the Interpretation Act 1978 shall apply in relation to Scotland as they apply in relation to England and Wales.

(2F) A disqualification order may be made on grounds which are or include matters other than criminal convictions notwithstanding that the person in respect of whom the order is to be made may be criminally liable in respect of those matters.".

(2) The following subsection shall be substituted for subsection (4) of section 188—

"(4) An application to a court with jurisdiction to wind up companies for the making of a disqualification order against any person may be made by the Secretary of State or the official receiver or by the liquidator or any past or present member or creditor of any company in relation to which that person has committed or is alleged to have committed an offence or other default; and on the hearing of any such application made by the Secretary of State or the official receiver or the liquidator or of any application for leave made by a person against whom a disqualification order has been made on the application of the Secretary of State, official receiver or liquidator, the Secretary of State, official receiver or liquidator shall appear and call the attention of the court to any matters which seem to him to be relevant, and may himself give evidence or call witnesses."

(3) Subsection (5) of section 188 shall cease to have effect.

(4) After subsection (6) of section 188 there shall be inserted the following subsection—

"(7) The Power under section 193(2) of the Criminal Procedure (Scotland) Act 1975 to substitute a fine for a period of imprisonment shall in relation to a conviction on indictment under subsection (6) of this section be construed as including a power to impose such fine in addition to that period of imprisonment.".

(5) Section 28 of the 1976 Act (power of High Court and Court of Session to make disqualification orders for persistent failure to comply with the relevant requirements) shall cease to have effect; but any order made under section 28 shall have effect as if made under section 188 of the

1948 Act and any application made before the appointed day for such an order shall be treated as an application for an order under section 188.

Prohibition on directors of insolvent companies from acting as liquidators, etc.

94.—(1) In subsection (1) of section 9 of the Insolvency Act 1976 (power of court to disqualify persons from acting as directors, etc.) for the words from "the court may" to the end there shall be substituted the words—
	"the court may make an order that that person shall not, without the leave of the court—

    (a) be a director of or in any way, whether directly or indirectly, be concerned or take part in the promotion, formation or management of a company; or

    (b) be a liquidator of a company; or

    (c) be a receiver or manager of the property of a company;

for such period as may, subject to subsection (1A) below, be specified in the order.
	(1A) The period which may be specified in any order under subsection (1) above shall begin with the date of the order and may not exceed five years if none of the conduct to which the court has regard under subsection (1)(b) occurred after the day appointed for the coming into force of section 94 of the Companies Act 1981, or fifteen years in any other case.".
	(2) In subsection (7) of that section, for the definition of "company" there shall be substituted the following definition—
	" "company" includes any company which may be wound up under Part IX of the Companies Act 1948;".
	(3) The following subsection shall be inserted in that section after subsection (7)—
	"(7A) An order under subsection (1) may be made on grounds which are or include matters other than criminal convictions notwithstanding that the person in respect of whom the order is to be made may be criminally liable in respect of those matters."

COMPANIES ACT 1981, Sched. 3—paras 9, 36

9. In section 187 (restrictions on undischarged bankrupts acting as directors, etc.) after the words "acts as director" there shall be inserted the words "or liquidator" and after the words "is concerned in the" there shall be inserted the words "promotion, formation or".

Companies Act 1976 (c. 69)

36. In section 29(1) of the 1976 Act (register of disqualification orders)—

    (a) for the words from "that a person" to "in the order" there shall be substituted the words "under section 188 of the Act of 1948 or section 9 of the Insolvency Act 1976;"; and

    (b) the words from "This subsection" to the end shall cease to have effect.

COMPANIES ACT 1976, ss. 28–29

Disqualification orders

Disqualification for persistent default in relation to delivery of documents to registrar

28.—(1) Where, on the application of the Secretary of State, it appears to the High Court that a person has been persistently in default in relation to relevant requirements of the Companies Acts, the court may make an order that that person shall not, without the leave of the court, be a director of or in any, whether directly or indirectly, be concerned or take part in the management of a company for such period beginning with the date of the order and not exceeding five years as may be specified in the order.

In the preceding provisions of this subsection "the court", in relation to the granting of leave, means any court have jurisdiction to wind up the company as respects which leave is sought, and in the application of this section to Scotland the references in this subsection to the High Court shall be construed as references to the Court of Session.

(2) Any provision of the Companies Acts which requires any return, account or other document to be filed with, delivered or sent, or notice of any matter to be given, to the registrar of companies is a relevant requirement of the Companies Acts for the purposes of this section.

(3) For the purposes of this section, the fact that a person has been persistently in default in relation to relevant requirements of the Companies Acts may, subject to subsection (4) below (and without prejudice to its proof in any other manner), be conclusively proved by showing that in the five years ending with the date of the application he has been adjudged guilty (whether or not on the same occasion) of three or more defaults in relation to any such requirements.

A person shall be treated as being adjudged guilty of a default in relation to a relevant requirement of the Companies Acts for the purposes of this subsection if—

(a) he is convicted of any offence by virtue of any contravention of or failure to comply with any such requirement (whether on his own part or on the part of any company); or

(b) an order is made against him under section 428 of the Act of 1948 (enforcement of duty of company to make returns to the registrar) or under section 5(1) above.

(4) No account shall be taken for the purposes of this section of any offence which was committed or, in the case of a continuing offence, began before the date on which this section comes into operation.

(5) The Secretary of State shall give not less than ten days' notice of his intention to apply for an order under this section to the person against whom the order is sought, and on the hearing of the application that person may appear and himself give evidence or call witnesses.

(6) On the hearing of any application for an order under this section, or of any application for leave under this section by a person against whom an order under this section has been made, the Secretary of State shall appear and call the attention of the court to any matters which seem to him to be relevant and may himself give evidence or call witnesses.

(7) If any person acts in contravention of an order under this section he shall in respect of each offence be liable—

(a) on conviction on indictment, to imprisonment for a term not exceeding two years or to a fine or to both; or

(b) on summary conviction, to imprisonment for a term not exceeding six months or to a fine not exceeding £400 or to both.

(8) In this section "company" includes an unregistered company (wherever incorporated) within the meaning of Part IX of the Act of 1948.

Registrar of disqualification orders

29.—(1) The prescribed officer of any court which—

(a) makes an order, after the coming into operation of this section, that a person shall not, without the leave of the court, be a director of or in any way, whether directly or indirectly, be concerned or take part in the management of a company for such period as may be specified in the order, or

(b) grants leave in relation to any such order which is so made,

shall, at such time and in such manner and form as may be prescribed, furnish the Secretary of State with the prescribed particulars of the order or the grant of leave.

This subsection applies whether the order is made under section 188 of the Act of 1948, section 9 of the Insolvency Act 1976, or section 28 above.

(2) The Secretary of State shall, from the particulars with which he is furnished under subsection (1) above, maintain a register of such orders and of cases in which the court has granted leave.

(3) On the expiration of an order of which particulars are entered on the register, the Secretary of State shall delete from the register—

(a) those particulars, and

(b) any particulars of cases in which the court has granted leave in relation to that order.

(4) The register shall be open to inspection on payment of such fee as may be specified by the Secretary of State in regulations made by statutory instrument.

(5) A statutory instrument containing regulations made under subsection (4) above shall be subject to annulment in pursuance of a resolution of either House of Parliament.

INSOLVENCY ACT 1976, s. 9

Disqualification of directors of insolvent companies

9.—(1) Where on an application under this section it appears to the court—

(a) that a person—
  (i) is or has been a director of a company which has at any time gone into liquidation (whether while he was a director or subsequently) and was insolvent at that time; and
  (ii) is or has been a director of another such company which has gone into liquidation within five years of the date on which the first-mentioned company went into liquidation; and

(b) that his conduct as director of any of those companies makes him unfit to be concerned in the management of a company,

the court may make an order that that person shall not, without the leave of the court, be a director of or in any way, whether directly or indirectly, be concerned or take part in the management of a company for such period beginning with the date of the order and not exceeding five years as may be specified in the order.

(2) In the case of a person who is or has been a director of a company which has gone into liquidation as aforesaid and is being wound up by the court—

(a) any application under this section shall be made by the official receiver or, in Scotland, the Secretary of State; and

(b) the power to make an order on the application shall be exercisable by the court by which the company is being wound up;

and in any other case any application under this section shall be made by the Secretary of State and the power to make an order thereon shall be exercisable by the High Court or, in Scotland, the Court of Session.

(3) Where the official receiver or Secretary of State intends to make an application under this section in respect of any person, he shall give not less than ten days' notice of his intention to that person, and on the hearing of the application that person may appear and himself give evidence or call witnessses.

(4) On the hearing of an application under this section by the official receiver or Secretary of State, or of an application for leave under this section by a person in respect of whom an order has been made on the application of the official receiver or Secretary of State, the official receiver or Secretary of State shall appear and call the attention of the court to any matters which seem to him to be relevant and may himself give evidence or call witnesses.

(5) If any person acts in contravention of an order made under subsection (1) above he shall in respect of each offence be liable—

(a) on conviction on indictment, to imprisonment for a term not exceeding two years or to a fine or to both; or

(b) on summary conviction, to imprisonment for a term not exceeding six months or to a fine not exceeding £400 or to both.

(6) The Secretary of State may require the liquidator or former liquidator of any company—

(a) to furnish him with such information with respect to the company's affairs; and

(b) to produce and permit inspection of such books or documents of or relevant to the company,

as the Secretary of State may reasonably require for the purpose of determining whether to make an application under this section in respect of any person who is or has been a director of that company; and if a person makes default in complying with any such requirement the court may, on the application of the Secretary of State, make an order requiring that person to make good the default within such time as may be specified.

(7) In this section—
"company" includes an unregistered company (wherever incorporated) within the meaning of Part IX of the Companies Act 1948;
"director", in relation to a company, includes any person in accordance with whose directions or instructions the directors of the company have been accustomed to act;
and for the purposes of this section a company goes into liquidation if it is wound up by the court, on the date of the winding up order and, in any other case, on the date of the passing of the resolution for voluntary winding up.

(8) In Schedule 1 to the said Act of 1948, in regulation 88 of Part I of Table A and article 38 of Table C the references to an order under section 188 of that Act (disqualification of directors) shall include a reference to an order under this section.

(9) Subsection (1) above does not apply unless at least one of the companies there mentioned has gone into liquidation after the date of the coming into force of this section; and the conduct to which regard may be had under paragraph (b) of that subsection does not include conduct as director of a company that has gone into liquidation before that date.

COMPANIES ACT 1948, ss. 187–188

Provisions as to undischarged bankrupts acting as directors

187.—(1) If any person being an undischarged bankrupt acts as director of, or directly or indirectly takes part in or is concerned in the management of, any company except with the leave of the court by which he was adjudged bankrupt, he shall be liable on conviction on indictment to imprisonment for a term not exceeding two years, or on summary conviction to imprisonment for a term not exceeding six months or to a fine not exceeding five hundred pounds or to both such imprisonment and fine:

Provided that a person shall not be guilty of an offence under this section by reason that he, being an undischarged bankrupt, has acted as director of, or taken part or been concerned in the management of, a company, if he was on the third day of August, nineteen hundred and twenty-eight, acting as director of, or taking part or being concerned in the management of, that company and has continuously so acted, taken part or been concerned since that date and the bankruptcy was prior to that date.

(2) In England the leave of the court for the purposes of this section shall not be given unless notice of intention to apply therefore has been served on the official receiver, and it shall be the duty of the official receiver, if he is of opinion that it is contrary to the public interest that any such application should be granted, to attend on the hearing of and oppose the granting of the application.

(3) In this section the expression "company" includes an unregistered company and a company incorporated outside Great Britain which has an established place of business within Great Britain, and the expression "official receiver" means the official receiver in bankruptcy.

(4) Subsection (1) of this section in its application to Scotland shall have effect as if the words "sequestration of his estates was awarded" were substituted for the words "he was adjudged bankrupt".

Power to restrain fraudulent persons from managing companies

188.—(1) Where—

(a) a person is convicted on indictment of any offence in connection with the promotion, formation or management of a company; or

(b) in the course of winding up a company it appears that a person—

(i) has been guilty of any offence for which he is liable (whether he has been convicted or not) under section three hundred and thirty-two of this Act; or

(ii) has otherwise been guilty, while an officer of the company, of any fraud in relation to the company or of any breach of his duty to the company;

the court may make an order that that person shall not, without the leave of the court, be a director of or in any way, whether directly or indirectly, be concerned or take part in the management of a company for such period not exceeding five years as may be specified in the order.

(2) In the foregoing subsection the expression "the court", in relation to the making of an order against any person by virtue of paragraph (a) thereof, includes the court before which he is convicted, as well as any court having jurisdiction to wind up the company, and in relation to the granting of leave means any court having jurisdiction to wind up the company as respects which leave is sought.

(3) A person intending to apply for the making of an order under this section by the court having jurisdiction to wind up a company shall give not less than ten days' notice of his intention to the person against whom the order is sought, and on the hearing of the application the last-mentioned person may appear and himself give evidence or call witnesses.

(4) An application for the making of an order under this section by the court having jurisdiction to wind up a company may be made by the official receiver, or by the liquidator of the company or by any person who is or has been a member or creditor of the company; and on the hearing of any application for an order under this section by the official receiver or the liquidator, or of any application for leave under this section by a person against whom an order has been made on the application of the official receiver or the liquidator, the official receiver or liquidator shall appear and call the attention of the court to any matters which seem to him to be relevant, and may himself give evidence or call witnesses.

(5) An order may be made by virtue of sub-paragraph (ii) of paragraph (b) of subsection (1) of this section notwithstanding that the person concerned may be criminally liable in respect of the matters on the ground of which the order is to be made, and for the purposes of the said sub-paragraph (ii) the expression "officer" shall include any person in accordance with whose directions or instructions the directors of the company have been accustomed to act.

(6) If any persons acts in contravention of an order made under this section, he shall, in respect of each offence, be liable on conviction on indictment to imprisonment for a term not exceeding two years, or on summary conviction to imprisonment for a term not exceeding six months or to a fine not exceeding five hundred pounds or to both.

COMPANIES ACT 1947, s. 33

Power to restrain fraudulent persons from managing companies

33.—(1) Where—

(a) a person is convicted on indictment of any offence in connection with the promotion, formation or managment of a company; or

(b) in the course of winding up a company it appears that a person—

    (i) has been guilty of any offence for which he is liable (whether he has been convicted or not) under section two hundred and seventy-five of the principal Act (which relates to the responsibility of directors for fraudulent trading); or

    (ii) has otherwise been guilty, while an officer of the company, of any fraud in relation to the company or of any breach of his duty to the company;

the court may make an order that that person shall not, without the leave of the court, be a director of or in any way, whether directly or indirectly, be concerned or take part in the management of a company for such period, not exceeding five years, as may be specified in the order.

(2) In the foregoing subsection the expression "the court", in relation to the making of an order against any person by virtue of paragraph (a) thereof, includes the court before which he is convicted, as well as any court having jurisdiction to wind up the company, and in relation to the granting of leave means any court having jurisdiction to wind up the company as respects which leave is sought.

(3) A person intending to apply for the making of an order under this section by the court having jurisdiction to wind up a company shall give not less than ten days' notice of his intention to the person against whom the order is sought, and on the hearing of the application the last mentioned person may appear and himself give evidence or call witnesses.

(4) An application for the making of an order under this section by the court having jurisdiction to wind up a company may be made by the official receiver, or by the liquidator of the company, or by any person who is or has been a member or creditor of the company; and on the hearing of any application for an order under this section by the official receiver or the liqui-

dator, or of any application for leave under this section by a person against whom an order has been made on the application of the official receiver or the liquidator, the official receiver or liquidator shall appear and call the attention of the court to any matters which seem to him to be relevant, and may himself give evidence or call witnesses.

(5) An order may be made by virtue of sub-paragraph (ii) of paragraph (b) of subsection (1) of this section notwithstanding that the person concerned may be criminally liable in respect of the matters on the ground of which the order is to be made, and the purposes of the said sub-paragraph (ii) the expression "officer" shall include any person in accordance with whose directions or instructions the directors of the company have been accustomed to act.

(6) If any person acts in contravention of an order made under this section, he shall, in respect of each offence, be liable on conviction on indictment to imprisonment for a term not exceeding two years, or on summary conviction to imprisonment for a term not exceeding six months or to a fine not exceeding five hundred pounds or to both.

COMPANIES ACT 1929, ss. 142, 275

Provisions as to undischarged bankrupts acting as directors

142.—(1) If any person being an undischarged bankrupt acts as director of, or directly or indirectly takes part in or is concerned in the management of, any company except with the leave of the court by which he was adjudged bankrupt, he shall be liable on conviction on indictment to imprisonment for a term not exceeding two years, or on summary conviction to imprisonment for a term not exceeding six months or to a fine not exceeding five hundred pounds, or to both such imprisonment and fine:

Provided that a person shall not be guilty of an offence under this section by reason that he, being an undischarged bankrupt, has acted as director of, or taken part or been concerned in the management of, a company, if he was on the third day of August, nineteen hundred and twenty-eight, acting as director of, or taking part or being concerned in the management of, that company and has continuously so acted, taken part, or been concerned since that date and the bankruptcy was prior to that date.

(2) In England the leave of the court for the purposes of this section shall not be given unless notice of intention to apply therefore has been served on the official receiver and it shall be the duty of the official receiver, if he is of opinion that it is contrary to the public interest that any such application should be granted, to attend on the hearing of and oppose the granting of the application.

(3) In this section the expression "company" includes an unregistered company and a company incorporated outside Great Britain which has an established place of business within Great Britain, and the expression "official receiver" means the official receiver in bankruptcy.

(4) Subsection (1) of this section in its application to Scotland shall have effect as if the words "sequestration of his estates was awarded" were substitued for the words "he was adjudged bankrupt."

Responsibility of directors for fraudulent trading

275.—(1) If in the course of the winding up of a company it appears that any business of the company has been carried on with intent to defraud creditors of the company or creditors of any other person or for any fradulent purpose, the court, on the application of the official receiver, or the liquidator or any creditor or contributory of the company, may, if it thinks proper so to do, declare that any of the directors, whether past or present, of the company who were knowingly parties to the carrying on of the business in manner aforesaid shall be personally responsible, without any limitation of liability, for all or any of the debts or other liabilities of the company as the court may direct.

(2) Where the court makes any such declaration, it may give such further directions as it thinks proper for the purpose of giving effect to that declaration, and in particular may make provision for making the liability of any such director under the declaration a charge on any debt or obli-

gation due from the company to him, or on any mortgage or charge or any interest in any mortgage or charge on any assets of the company held by or vested in him, or any company or person on his behalf, or any person claiming as assignee from or through the director, company or person, and may from time to time make such further order as may be necessary for the purpose of enforcing any charge imposed under this subsection.

For the purpose of this subsection, the expression "assignee" includes any person to whom or in whose favour, by the directions of the director, the debt, obligation, mortgage or charge was created, issued or transferred or the interest created, but does not include an assignee for valuable consideration (not including consideration by way of marriage) given in good faith and without notice of any of the matters on the ground of which the declaration is made.

(3) Where any business of a company is carried on with such intent or for such purpose as is mentioned in subsection (1) of this section, every director of the company who was knowingly a party to the carrying on of the business in manner aforesaid, shall be liable on conviction on indictment to imprisonment for a term not exceeding one year.

(4) The court may, in the case of any person in respect of whom a declaration has been made under subsection (1) of this section, or who has been convicted of an offence under subsection (3) of this section, order that that person shall not, without the leave of the court, be a director of or in any way, whether directly or indirectly, be concerned in or take part in the management of a company for such period, not exceeding five years, from the date of the declaration or of the conviction, as the case may be, as may be specified in the order, and if any person acts in contravention of an order made under this subsection he shall, in respect of each offence, be liable on conviction on indictment to imprisonment for a term not exceeding two years, or on summary conviction to imprisonment for a term not exceeding six months or to a fine not exceeding five hundred pounds, or to both such imprisonment and fine.

In this subsection the expression "the court" in relation to the making of an order, means the court by which the declaration was made or the court before which the person was convicted, as the case may be and in relation to the granting of leave means any court having jurisdiction to wind up the company.

(5) For the purposes of this section, the expression "director" shall include any person in accordance with whose directions or instructions the directors of a company have been accustomed to act.

(6) The provisions of this section shall have effect notwithstanding that the person concerned may be criminally liable in respect of the matters on the ground of which the declaration is to be made and where the declaration under subsection (1) of this section is made in the case of a winding up in England, the declaration shall be deemed to be a final judgment within the meaning of paragraph (g) of subsection (1) of section one of the Bankruptcy Act, 1914.

(7) It shall be the duty of the official receiver or of the liquidator to appear on the hearing of an application for leave under subsection (4) of this section, and on the hearing of an application under that subsection or under subsection (1) of this section the official receiver or the liquidator, as the case may be, may himself give evidence or call witnesses.

COMPANIES ACT 1928, ss. 75, 84

Provisions with respect to fraudulent trading

75.—(1) If in the course of a winding-up it appears that any business of the company has been carried on with intent to defraud creditors of the company or creditors of any other person or for any fraudulent purpose, the court, on the application of the official receiver or the liquidator, or any creditor or contributory of the company, may, if it thinks proper so to do, declare that any of the directors, whether past or present, of the company who were knowingly parties to the carrying on of the business in manner aforesaid shall be personally responsible, without any limitation of liability, for all or any of the debts or other liabilities of the company as the court may direct.

(2) Where the court makes any such declaration, it may give such further directions as it thinks

proper for the purpose of giving effect to that declaration, and in particular may make provision for making the liability of any such director under the declaration a charge on any debt or obligation due from the company to him, or on any mortgage or charge or any interest in any mortgage or charge on any assets of the company held by or vested in him, or any company or person on his behalf, or any person claiming as assignee from or through the director, company or person, other than an assignee for valuable consideration (not including consideration by way of marriage) given in good faith and without notice of any of the matters on the ground of which the declaration is made, and may from time to time make such further order as may be necessary for the purpose of enforcing any charge imposed under this subsection.

For the purpose of the foregoing provision the expression "assignee" includes any person to whom or in whose favour by the directions of the director the debt, obligation, mortgage or charge was created issued or transferred or the interest created.

(3) Where any business of a company is carried on with such intent or for such purpose as is mentioned in subsection (1) of this section, every director of the company who was knowingly a party to the carrying on of the business in manner aforesaid, shall be liable on conviction on indictment to imprisonment for a term not exceeding one year.

(4) The court may, in the case of any person in respect of whom a declaration has been made under the foregoing provisions of this section or who has been convicted of an offence under the foregoing provisions of this section, order that that person shall not, without the leave of the court, be a director of or in any way whether directly or indirectly, be concerned in or take part in the management of a company for such period, not exceeding five years, from the date of the declaration or of the conviction, as the case may be, as may be specified in the order, and if any person acts in contravention of an order made under this subsection he shall, in respect of each offence, be liable on conviction on indictment to imprisonment for a term not exceeding two years, or on summary conviction to imprisonment for a term not exceeding six months or to a fine not exceeding five hundred pounds, or to both such imprisonment and fine.

In this subsection the expression "the court" in relation to the making of an order, means the court by which the declaration was made or the court before which the person was convicted, as the case may be, and in relation to the granting of leave means any court having jurisdiction to wind up the company.

(5) For the purposes of this section, the expression "director" shall include any person who occupies the position of a director or in accordance with whose directions or instructions the directors of a company have been accustomed to act.

(6) The provisions of this section shall have effect notwithstanding that the person concerned may be criminally liable in respect of the matters on the ground of which the declaration is to be made, and where the declaration under subsection (1) of this section is made in the case of a winding-up in England, the declaration shall be deemed to be a final judgment within the meaning of paragraph (g) of subsection (1) of section one of the Bankruptcy Act, 1914.

(7) It shall be the duty of the official receiver or of the liquidator to appear on the hearing of an application for leave under subsection (4) of this section, and on the hearing of an application under that subsection or under subsection (1) of this section the official receiver or the liquidator, as the case may be, may himself give evidence or call witnesses.

Provisions as to undischarged bankrupts acting as directors

84.—(1) If any person being an undischarged bankrupt acts as director of, or directly or indirectly takes part in or is concerned in the management of, any company including an unregistered company and a company incorporated outside Great Britain which has an established place of business within Great Britain except with the leave of the court by which he was adjudged bankrupt, he shall be liable on conviction on indictment to imprisonment for a term not exceeding two years or on summary conviction to imprisonment for a term not exceeding six months or to a fine not exceeding five hundred pounds or to both such imprisonment and fine:

Provided that a person shall not be guilty of an offence under this section by reason that he, being an undischarged bankrupt, has acted as director of, or taken part or been concerned in the management of, a company, if he was at the passing of this Act acting as director of, or taking part, or being concerned in the management of that company and has continuously so acted, taken part, or been concerned since the passing of this Act and the bankruptcy was prior to the passing of this Act.

(2) The leave of the court for the purposes of this section shall not be given unless notice of intention to apply therefor has been served on the official receiver and it shall be the duty of the official receiver, if he is of opinion that it is contrary to the public interest that any such application should be granted, to attend on the hearing of and oppose the granting of the application.

(3) In this section the expression "official receiver" means the official receiver in bankruptcy.

APPENDIX 3

TABLE OF FORMER PROVISIONS

This table traces the derivation and/or origin of the substantive provisions of the CDDA prior to their enactment.

CDDA	Insolvency Act 1985	Companies Act 1985	Companies Act 1981*	Companies Act 1976	Insolvency Act 1976	Companies Act 1948	Companies Act 1947	Companies Act 1929	Companies Act 1928
s.1(1)	ss.108(2), 109(1), Sched. 6, para. 1(1)	s.295(1)	s.93 (CA 1948, s.188(1B)) s.94 (IA 1976, s.9(1), (1A))	—	s.9(1)	s.188(1)	s.33(1)	s.275(4)	s.75(4)
s.1(2)	s.108(2)	s.295(2), Sched. 12, para. 10	s.93 (CA 1948, s.188(1C), (2), (2A)), s.94 (IA 1976, s.9(1), (1A))	—	s.9(1)	s.188(1)	s.33(1)	s.275(4)	s.75(4)
s.1(3)	ss.108(2), 109(1), Sched. 6, para. 1(3)	—	—	—	—	—	—	—	—
s.1(4)	s.108(2)	s.295(4)	s.93 (CA 1948, s.188(2F)) s.94(IA 1976, s.9(7A))	—	—	s.188(5)	s.33(5)	—	—
s.2	—	ss.295(2), 296	s.93 (CA 1948, s.188(1) (a), (1C), (2), (2A)–(2B), (2D)–(2E))	—	—	s.188(1)(a), (2)	s.33(1)(a), (2)	—	—
s.3	—	ss.295(2), 297	s.93 (CA 1948, s.188(1) (b), (2B), (2C), (2D))	s.28	—	—	—	—	—
s.4	—	ss.295(2), 298	s.93 (CA 1948, s.188(1) (c), (1C), (2A), (2D))	—	—	s.188(1)(b)	s.33(1)(b)	s.275(3), (4)	s.275(3), (4)
s.5	—	ss.295(2), 299	s.93 (CA 1948, s.188(1A), (2B), (2D), (2E))	—	—	—	—	—	—
s.6(1)	s.12(1)	s.300(1)	—	—	s.9(1)	—	—	—	—
s.6(2)	s.12(7)	—	—	—	s.9(1), (9)	—	—	—	—
s.6(3)	s.12(8), (9)	s.300(2), (4)	—	—	s.9(2), (7)	—	—	—	—
s.6(4)	s.12(2), s.108(2)	s.295(2)	s.94(IA 1976, s.9(1A))	—	s.9(1)	—	—	—	—
s.7(1)	s.12(3)	Sched. 12, para. 6	—	—	s.9(2)	—	—	—	—
s.7(2)	s.12(4)	—	—	—	—	—	—	—	—
s.7(3)	s.12(5)	—	—	—	—	—	—	—	—
s.7(4)	s.12(6)	s.300(3)	—	—	s.9(6)	—	—	—	—

CDDA	Insolvency Act 1985	Companies Act 1985	Companies Act 1981*	Companies Act 1976	Insolvency Act 1976	Companies Act 1948	Companies Act 1947	Companies Act 1929	Companies Act 1928
s.8	ss.12(9), 13, 108(2)	s.295(2)	—	—	—	—	—	—	—
s.9	ss.12(9), 14	—	—	—	—	—	—	—	—
s.10	s.16, 108(2)	s.295(2)	—	—	—	s.188(1)(b)	s.33(1)(b)	s.275(1), (4)	s.75(1), (4)
s.11	—	s.302	Sched. 3, para. 9 (CA 1948, s.187)	—	—	s.187	—	s.142	s.84
s.12	s.221(2)	—	—	—	—	—	—	—	—
s.13	s.221(5)	ss.295(7), 302(1), Sched. 24	—	s.28(7)	s.9(5)	ss.187(1), 188(6)	s.33(6)	ss.142(1), 275(4)	ss.84(1), 75(4)
s.14	Sched. 6, para. 7	s.733(1)–(3)	—	—	—	—	s.33(3)	—	—
s.15	s.18	—	—	—	—	—	—	—	—
s.16(1)	ss.108(2), 109(1), Sched. 6, para. 1(4)	s.295(6), Sched. 12, paras. 1, 7	—	s.28(5)	s.9(3)	s.188(3)	s.33(3)	—	—
s.16(2)	ss.108(2), 109(1), Sched. 6, para. 1(4)	s.295(6), Sched. 12, para. 2	s.93(2) (CA 1948, s.188(4))	s.28(1)	s.9(2)	s.188(4)	s.33(4)	—	—
s.16(3)	ss.108(2), 109(1), Sched. 6, para. 1(4)	s.295(6), Sched. 12, paras. 3, 8	s.93(2) (CA 1948, s.188(4))	s.28(6)	s.9(4)	s.188(4)	s.33(4)	—	—
s.17(1)	ss.108(2), 109(1), Sched. 6, paras. 1(4), 14	s.295(6), Sched. 12, para. 4	—	—	—	—	—	—	—
s.17(2)	ss.108(2), 109(1), Sched. 6, para. 1(4)	ss.295(6), 302(3), Sched. 12, paras. 5, 8	s.93(2) (CA 1948, s.188(4))	s.28(6)	s.9(4)	ss.187(2), 188(4)	s.33(4)	ss.142(2), 275(7)	ss.84(2), 75(7)
s.18	ss.108(2), 109(1), Sched. 6, para. 2	s.301	Sched. 3, para. 36 (CA 1976, s.29(1))	s.29	—	—	—	—	—
s.19	—	s.295(6)	—	—	—	—	—	—	—
s.20	s.231**	—	s.636(3)	—	—	s.365***	—	—	—
s.21	ss.106, 107, 108(1)–(2), 222(1), 224(2), 227, 229, 234	—	—	—	—	—	—	—	—
s.22	s.108(1)–(4)	ss.295(3), 302(4)	s.94(IA 1976, s.9(7))	s.28(8)	s.9(7)	s.187(3)	—	s.142(3)	s.84(3)
ss.23–26	—	—	—	—	—	—	—	—	—
Sched. 1	Sched. 2	—	—	—	—	—	—	—	—

* The Companies Act 1981 was an amending statute. The relevant provisions amended by the 1981 Act are referred to in parenthesis. "CA 1948" means the Companies Act, 1948; "IA 1976" means the Insolvency Act 1976; "CA 1976" means the Companies Act 1976.

** See now section 433 of the Insolvency Act 1986.

*** Section 20 has its origins in earlier provisions which dealt with the use of statements made by persons in the context of (a) winding up or (b) the exercise of the powers of investigation now contained in Part XIV of the Companies Act 1985. See also section 50 of the Companies Act 1967.

APPENDIX 4

THE INSOLVENT COMPANIES (DISQUALIFICATION OF UNFIT DIRECTORS) PROCEEDINGS RULES 1987

S.I. 1987 No. 2023 (AS AMENDED BY THE INSOLVENT COMPANIES (DISQUALIFICATION OF UNFIT DIRECTORS) PROCEEDINGS (AMENDMENT) RULES 1999 S.I. 1999 No. 1023

Made on 25 November 1987 by the Lord Chancellor, under s. 411 and 413 of the Insolvency Act 1986 and s.21 of the Company Directors Disqualification Act 1986. Operative from 11 January 1988.

CITATION, COMMENCEMENT AND INTERPRETATION

1.—(1) These Rules may be cited as the Insolvent Companies (Disqualification of Unfit Directors) Proceedings Rules 1987 and shall come into force on 11th January 1988.
(2) In these Rules—

(a) "the Companies Act" means the Companies Act 1985,

(b) "The Company Directors Disqualification Act" means the Company Directors Disqualification Act 1986,

(c) "CPR" followed by a Part or rule by number means that Part or rule with that number in the Civil Procedure Rules 1998,

(d) "practice direction" means a direction as to the practice and procedure of any court within the scope of the Civil Procedure Rules,

(e) "registrar" has the same meaning as in paragraphs (4) and (5) of Rule 13.2 of the Insolvency Rules 1986, and

(f) "file in court" means deliver to the court for filing.

(3) These Rules apply with respect to an application for a disqualification order against any person ("the defendant"), where made—

(a) by the Secretary of State or the official receiver under section 7(1) of the Company Directors Disqualification Act (on the grounds of the person's unfitness to be concerned in the management of a company), or

(b) by the Secretary of State under section 8 of that Act (alleged expedient in the public interest, following report of inspectors under section 437 of the Companies Act, or information or documents obtained under section 447 or 448 of the Act),

on or after the date on which these Rules come into force.

Form and Conduct of Application

2.—(1) The Civil Procedure Rules 1998, and any relevant practice direction, apply in respect of any application to which these Rules apply, except where these Rules make provision to inconsistent effect.

(2) An application shall be made by claim form as provided by the relevant practice direction and the claimant must use the CPR Part 8 (alternative procedure for claims) procedure.

(3) CPR rule 8.1(3) (power of the court to order the claim to continue as if the claimant had not used the Part 8 procedure), CPR rule 8.2 (contents of the claim form) and CPR rule 8.7 (Part 20 claims) do not apply.

(4) Rule 7.47 (appeals and reviews of court orders) and rule 7.49 (procedure on appeal) of the Insolvency Rules 1986 apply.

The Case Against the Defendant

3.—(1) There shall, at the time when the claim form is issued, be filed in court evidence in support of the application for a disqualification order; and copies of the evidence shall be served with the claim form on the defendant.

(2) The evidence shall be by one or more affidavits, except where the claimant is the official receiver, in which case it may be in the form of a written report (with or without affidavits by other persons) which shall be treated as if it had been verified by affidavit by him and shall be prima facie evidence of any matter contained in it.

(3) There shall in the affidavit or affidavits or (as the case may be) the official receiver's report be included a statement of the matters by reference to which the defendant is alleged to be unfit to be concerned in the management of a company.

Endorsement of Claim Form

4. There shall on the claim form be endorsed information to the defendant as follows—

(a) that the application is made in accordance with the Rules;

(b) that, in accordance with the relevant enactments, the court has power to impose disqualifications as follows—

 (i) where the application is under section 7 of the Company Directors Disqualification Act, for a period of not less than 2, and up to 15, years; and

 (ii) where the application is under section 8 of that Act, for a period of up to 15 years;

(c) that the application for a disqualification order may, in accordance with these Rules, be heard and determined summarily, without further or other notice to the defendant, and that, if it is so heard and determined, the court may impose disqualification for a period of up to 5 years;

(d) that if at the hearing of the application the court, on the evidence then before it, is minded to impose, in the defendant's case, disqualification for any period longer than 5 years, it will not make a disqualification order on that occasion but will adjourn the application to be heard (with further evidence, if any) at a later date to be notified; and

(e) that any evidence which the defendant wishes to be taken into consideration by the court must be filed in court in accordance with the time limits imposed under Rule 6 (the provisions of which shall be set out on the claim form).

SERVICE AND ACKNOWLEDGEMENT

5.—(1) The claim form shall be served on the defendant by sending it by first class post to his last known address; and the date of service shall, unless the contrary is shown, be deemed to be the 7th day next following that on which the claim form was posted.

(2) Where any process or order of the court or other document is required under proceedings subject to these Rules to be served on any person who is not in England and Wales, the court may order service on him of that process or order or other document to be effected within such time and in such manner as it thinks fit, and may also require such proof of service as it thinks fit.

(3) The claim form served on the defendant shall be accompanied by an acknowledgment of service as provided for by practice direction and CPR rule 8.3(2) (dealing with the contents of an acknowledgement of service) does not apply.

(4) The acknowledgement of service shall state that the defendant should indicate—

(a) whether he contests the application on the grounds that, in the case of any particular company—

   (i) he was not a director or shadow director of the company at a time when conduct of his, or of other persons, in relation to that company is in question, or
   (ii) his conduct as director or shadow director of that company was not as alleged in support of the application for a disqualification order.

(b) whether, in the case of any conduct of his, he disputes the allegation that such conduct makes him unfit to be concerned in the management of a company, and

(c) whether he, while not resisting the application for a disqualification order, intends to adduce mitigating factors with a view to justifying only a short period of disqualification.

EVIDENCE

6.—(1) The defendant shall, within 28 days from the date of service of the claim form, file in court any affidavit evidence in opposition to the application he wishes the court to take into consideration and shall forthwith serve upon the claimant a copy of such evidence.

(2) The claimant shall, within 14 days from receiving the copy of the defendant's evidence, file in court any further evidence in reply he wishes the court to take into consideration and shall forthwith serve a copy of that evidence upon the defendant.

(3) CPR rules 8.5 (filing and serving written evidence) and 8.6(1) (requirements where written evidence is to be relied on) do not apply.

THE HEARING OF THE APPLICATION

7.—(1) When the claim form is issued, the court will fix a date for the first hearing of the claim which shall not be less than 8 weeks from the date of issue of the claim form.

(2) The hearing shall in the first instance be before the registrar in open court.

(3) The registrar shall either determine the case on the date fixed or adjourn it.

(4) The registrar shall adjourn the case for further consideration if—

(a) he forms the provisional opinion that a disqualification order ought to be made, and that a period of disqualification longer than 5 years is appropriate, or

(b) he is of opinion that questions of law or fact arise which are not suitable for summary determination.

(5) If the registrar adjourns the case for further consideration he shall—

(a) direct whether the case is to be heard by a registrar or, if he thinks it appropriate by the judge, for determination by him;

(b) state the reasons for the adjournment; and

(c) give directions as to the following matters—

  (i) the manner in which and the time within which notice of the adjournment and the reasons for it are to be given to the defendant,
  (ii) the filing in court and the service of further evidence (if any) by the parties,
  (iii) such other matters as the registrar thinks necessary or expedient with a view to an expeditious disposal of the application, and
  (iv) the time and place of the adjourned hearing.

(6) Where a case is adjourned other than to the judge, it may be heard by the registrar who originally dealt with the case or by another registrar.

MAKING AND SETTING ASIDE OF DISQUALIFICATION ORDER

8.—(1) The court may make a disqualification order against the defendant, whether or not the latter appears, and whether or not he has completed and returned the acknowledgement of service of the claim form, or filed evidence in accordance with Rule 6.

(2) Any disqualification order made in the absence of the defendant may be set aside or varied by the court on such terms as it thinks just.

COMMENCEMENT OF DISQUALIFICATION ORDER

9. Unless the court otherwise orders, a disqualification order takes effect at the beginning of the 21st day after the day on which the order is made.

RIGHT OF AUDIENCE

10. Official receivers and deputy official receivers have right of audience in any proceedings to which these rules apply, whether the application is made by the Secretary of State or by the official receiver at his direction, and whether made in the High Court or a county court.

REVOCATION AND SAVING

11.—(1) The Insolvent Companies (Disqualification of Unfit Directors) Proceedings Rules 1986 ("the former Rules") are hereby revoked.

(2) Notwithstanding paragraph (1) the former Rules shall continue to apply and have effect in relation to any application described in paragraph 3(a) or (b) of Rule 1 of these Rules made before the date on which these Rules come into force.

Appendix 5

Practice Direction: Directors Disqualification Proceedings

Part One

1. Application and interpretation

1.1 In this practice direction:

    (1) "the Act" means the Company Directors Disqualification Act 1986;

    (2) "the Disqualification Rules" means the rules for the time being in force made under section 411 of the Insolvency Act 1986 in relation to disqualification proceedings[1];

    (3) "the Insolvency Rules" means the rules for the time being in force made under sections 411 and 412 of the Insolvency Act 1986 in relation to insolvency proceedings;

    (4) "CPR" means the Civil Procedure Rules 1998 and "CPR" followed by "Part" or "Rule" and a number means the part or Rule with that number in those Rules;

    (5) "disqualification proceedings" has the meaning set out in paragraph 1.3 below.

    (6) "a disqualification application" is an application under the Act for the making of a disqualification order;

    (7) "registrar" means any judge of the High Court or the county court who is a registrar within the meaning of the Insolvency Rules;

    (8) "companies court registrar" means any judge of the High Court sitting in the Royal Courts of Justice in London who is a registrar within the meaning of the Insolvency Rules.

1.2 This practice direction shall come into effect on 26 April 1999 and shall replace all previous practice directions relating to disqualification proceedings.

1.3 This practice direction applies to the following proceedings ("disqualification proceedings"):

    (1) disqualification applications made:

        (a) under section 2(2)(a) of the Act (after the person's conviction of an indictable offence in connection with the affairs of the company);

        (b) under section 3 of the Act (on the ground of persistent breaches of provisions of companies legislation);

        (c) under section 4 of the Act (on the ground of fraud etc);

        (d) by the Secretary of State or the official receiver under section 7(1) of the Act (on the ground of the person's unfitness to be concerned in the management of a company); or

        (e) by the Secretary of State under section 8 of the Act (following a report made by inspectors or in consequence of information or documents obtained);

    (2) any application made under section 7(2) or 7(4) of the Act; and

    (3) any application made under sections 12(2) or 17 of the Act and any application for permission to act notwithstanding a disqualification order which was made under any statutory predecessor of the Act;

    (4) any application for a court order made under CPR Part 23 in the course of any of the proceedings set out in sub-paragraphs (1) to (3) above.

---

[1] The current rules are the Insolvent Companies (Disqualification of Unfit Directors) Proceedings Rules 1987.

2. Multi-track

2.1 All disqualification proceedings are allocated to the multi-track. The CPR relating to allocation questionnaires and track allocation shall not apply.

3. Rights of audience

3.1 Official receivers and deputy official receivers have right of audience in any proceedings to which this Practice Direction applies, including cases where a disqualification application is made by the Secretary of State or by the official receiver at his direction, and whether made in the High Court or a county court.[2]

Part Two

Disqualification applications

4. Commencement

4.1 A disqualification application must be commenced by a claim form issued:
   (1) in the High Court out of the office of the companies court registrar or a chancery district registry; and
   (2) in the county court, out of a county court office.
   Sections 2(2)(a), 3(4), 4(2), 6(3) and 8(3) of the Act identify the courts which have jurisdiction to deal with disqualification applications.
4.2 Disqualification applications shall be made by the issue of a claim form in the form annexed hereto and the use of the procedure set out in CPR Part 8,[3] subject to any modification of that procedure under this practice direction and (where the application is made under sections 7 or 8 of the Act) the Disqualification Rules.[4] CPR rule 8.1(3) (power of the Court to order the application to continue as if the claimant had not used the Part 8 Procedure) shall not apply.
4.3 When the claim form is issued, the claimant will be given a date for the first hearing of the disqualification application. This date is to be not less than eight weeks from the date of issue of the claim form.[5] The first hearing will be before a registrar.

5. Headings

5.1 Every claim form by which an application under the Act is begun and all affidavits, notices and other documents in the proceedings must be entitled in the matter of the company or companies in question and in the matter of the Act. In the case of any disqualification application under section 7 of the Act it is not necessary to mention in the heading any company other than that referred to in section 6(1)(a).

6. The claim form

6.1 CPR Rule 8.2 does not apply. The claim form must state:
   (1) that CPR Part 8 (as modified by this practice direction) applies, and (if the application is made under sections 7 or 8 of the Act) that the application is made in accordance with the Disqualification Rules[6];
   (2) that the claimant seeks a disqualification order, and the section of the Act pursuant to which the disqualification application is made;
   (3) the period for which, in accordance with the Act, the court has power to impose a disqualification period.
   The periods are as follows:-

   (a) where the application is under section 2 of the Act, for a period of up to 15 years;

---

[2] Rule 10 of the Insolvent Companies (Disqualification of Unfit Directors) Proceedings Rules 1987.
[3] Rule 2(2) of the Insolvent Companies (Disqualification of Unfit Directors) Proceedings Rules 1987 as amended.
[4] For convenience, relevant references to the Insolvency Companies (Disqualification of Unfit Directors) Proceedings Rules 1987, which apply to disqualification applications under sections 7 and 8 of the Act (see rule 1(3)(a) and (b)) are set out in footnotes to this Practice Direction.
[5] Rule 7(1) of the Insolvent Companies (Disqualification of Unfit Directors) Proceedings Rules 1987.
[6] Rule 4(a) of the Insolvent Companies (Disqualification of Unfit Directors) Proceedings Rules 1987.

(b) where the application is under section 3 of the Act, for a period of up to 5 years;

(c) where the application is under section 4 of the Act, for a period of up to 15 years;

(d) where the application is under section 5 of the Act, for a period of up to 5 years;

(e) where the application is under section 7 of the Act, for a period of not less than 2, and up to 15 years[7];

(f) where the application is under section 8 of the Act, for a period of up to 15 years.[8]

(4) in cases where the application is made under sections 7 or 8 of the Act, that on the first hearing of the application, the court may hear and determine it summarily, without further or other notice to the defendant, and that, if the application is so determined, the court may impose a period of disqualification of up to 5 years but that if at the hearing of the application the court, on the evidence then before it, is minded to impose, in the case of any defendant, disqualification for any period longer than 5 years, it will not make a disqualification order on that occasion but will adjourn the application to be heard (with further evidence, if any) at a later date that will be notified to the defendant[9];

(5) that any evidence which the defendant wishes the court to take into consideration must be filed in court in accordance with the time limits set out in paragraph 9 below (which time limits shall be set out in the notes to the Claim Form).[10]

7. Service of the claim form

7.1 Service of the claim forms in disqualification proceedings will be the responsibility of the parties and will not be undertaken by the court.

7.2 The claim form shall be served by the claimant on the defendant. It may be served by sending it by first class post to his last known address; and the date of service shall, unless the contrary is shown, be deemed to be the 7th day following that on which the claim form was posted.[11] CPR r.6.7(1) shall be modified accordingly. Otherwise CPR Part 6 applies.

7.3 Where any claim form or order of the court or other document is required under any disqualification proceedings to be served on any person who is not in England and Wales, the court may order service on him to be effected within such time and in such manner as it thinks fit, may require such proof of service as it thinks fit,[12] and may give such directions as to acknowledgement of service as it thinks fit.

7.4 The claim form served on the defendant shall be accompanied by an acknowledgement of service.

8. Acknowledgement of service

8.1 The form of acknowledgement of service is annexed to this practice direction. CPR rr. 8.3(2) and 8.3(3)(a) do not apply to disqualification applications.

8.2 The form of acknowledgement of service shall state that the defendant should indicate[13];

(1) whether he contests the application on the grounds that, in the case of any particular company:—

(a) he was not a director or shadow director of that company at a time when conduct of his, or of other persons, in relation to that company is in question; or

(b) his conduct as director or shadow director of that company was not as alleged in support of the application for a disqualification order;

(2) whether, in the case of any conduct of his, he disputes the allegation that such conduct makes him unfit to be concerned in the management of a company; and

[7] Rule 4(b)(i) of the Insolvent Companies (Disqualification of Unfit Directors) Proceedings Rules 1987.
[8] Rule 4(b)(ii) of the Insolvent Companies (Disqualification of Unfit Directors) Proceedings Rules 1987.
[9] Rule 4(c) and (d) of the Insolvent Companies (Disqualification of Unfit Directors) Proceedings Rules 1987.
[10] Rule 4(e) of the Insolvent Companies (Disqualification of Unfit Directors) Proceedings Rules 1987.
[11] Rule 5(1) of the Insolvent Companies (Disqualification of Unfit Directors) Proceedings Rules 1987.
[12] Rule 5(2) of the Insolvent Companies (Disqualification of Unfit Directors) Proceedings Rules 1987.
[13] Rule 5(4) of the Insolvent Companies (Disqualification of Unfit Directors) Proceedings Rules 1987.

(3) whether he, while not resisting the application for a disqualification order, intends to adduce mitigating factors with a view to reducing the period of disqualification.

8.3 The defendant shall:
   (1) (subject to paragraph 7.2 above) file an acknowledgement of service in the prescribed form not more than 14 days after service of the claim form; and
   (2) serve the acknowledgement of service on the claimant and any other party.

8.4 Where the defendant has failed to file an acknowledgement of service and the time period for doing so has expired, the defendant may attend the hearing of the application but may not take part in the hearing unless the court gives permission.

9. Evidence

9.1 Evidence in disqualification applications shall be by affidavit, except where the official receiver is a party, in which case his evidence may be in the form of a written report (with or without affidavits by other persons) which shall be treated as if it had been verified by affidavit by him and shall be prima facie evidence of any matter contained in it.[14]

9.2 In the affidavits or (as the case may be) the official receiver's report in support of the application, there shall be included a statement of the matters by reference to which it is alleged that a disqualification order should be made against the defendant.[15]

9.3 When the claim form is issued:
   (1) the affidavit or report in support of the disqualification application must be filed in court;
   (2) exhibits must be lodged with the court where they shall be retained until the conclusion of the proceedings; and
   (3) copies of the affidavit/report and exhibits shall be served with the claim form on the defendant.[16]

9.4 The defendant shall, within 28 days from the date of service of the claim form[17]:
   (1) file in court any affidavit evidence in opposition to the disqualification application that he or she wishes the court to take into consideration; and
   (2) lodge the exhibits with the court where whey shall be retained until the conclusion of the proceedings; and
   (3) at the same time, serve upon the claimant a copy of the affidavits and exhibits.

9.5 In cases where there is more than one defendant, each defendant is required to serve his evidence on the other defendants unless the court otherwise orders.

9.6 The claimant shall, within 14 days from receiving the copy of the defendant's evidence[18]:
   (1) file in court any further affidavit or report in reply he wishes the court to take into consideration; and
   (2) lodge the exhibits with the court where they shall be retained until the conclusion of the proceedings; and
   (3) at the same time serve a copy of the affidavits/reports and exhibits upon the defendant.

9.7 Prior to the first hearing of the disqualification application, the time for serving evidence may be extended by written agreement between the parties. After the first hearing, the extension of time for serving evidence is governed by CPR rr. 2.11 and 29.5.

9.8 So far as is possible all evidence should be filed before the first hearing of the disqualification application.

10. The first hearing of the disqualification application

10.1 The date fixed for the hearing of the disqualification application shall be not less than 8 weeks from the date of issue of the claim form.[19]

10.2 The hearing shall in the first instance be before the registrar.[20]

---

[14] Rule 3(2) of the Insolvent Companies (Disqualification of Unfit Directors) Proceedings Rules 1987. Section 441 of the Companies Act 1985 makes provision for the admissibility in legal proceedings of a certified copy of a report of inspectors appointed under Part XIV of the Companies Act 1985.

[15] Rule 3(3) of the Insolvent Companies (Disqualification of Unfit Directors) Proceedings Rules 1987.

[16] Rule 3(1) of the Insolvent Companies (Disqualification of Unfit Directors) Proceedings Rules 1987.

[17] Rule 6(1) of the Insolvent Companies (Disqualification of Unfit Directors) Proceedings Rules 1987.

[18] Rule 6(2) of the Insolvent Companies (Disqualification of Unfit Directors) Proceedings Rules 1987.

[19] Rule 7(1) of the Insolvent Companies (Disqualification of Unfit Directors) Proceedings Rules 1987.

[20] Rule 7(2) of the Insolvent Companies (Disqualification of Unfit Directors) Proceedings Rules 1987.

10.3 The registrar shall either determine the case on the date fixed or give directions and adjourn it.[21]

10.4 All interim directions should insofar as possible be sought at the first hearing of the disqualification application so that the disqualification application can be determined at the earliest possible date. The parties should take all such steps as they respectively can to avoid successive directions hearings.

10.5 In the case of disqualification applications made under sections 7 or 8 of the Act, the registrar shall adjourn the case for further consideration if:—

  (1) he forms the provisional opinion that a disqualification order ought to be made, and that a period of disqualification longer than 5 years is appropriate,[22] or

  (2) he is of opinion that questions of law or fact arise which are not suitable for summary determination.[23]

10.6 If the registrar adjourns the application for further consideration he shall:—

  (1) direct whether the application is to be heard by a registrar or by a judge.[24] This direction may at any time be varied by the court either on application or of its own initiative. If the court varies the direction in the absence of any of the parties, notice will be given to the parties;

  (2) consider whether or not to adjourn the application to a judge so that the judge can give further directions;

  (3) consider whether or not to make any direction with regard to fixing the trial date or a trial window;

  (4) state the reasons for the adjournment.[25]

11. Case management

11.1 On the first or any subsequent hearing of the disqualification application, the registrar may also give directions as to the following matters:

  (1) the filing in court and the service of further evidence (if any) by the parties[26];

  (2) the time-table for the steps to be taken between the giving of directions and the hearing of the application;

  (3) such other matters as the registrar thinks necessary or expedient with a view to an expeditious disposal of the application or the management of it generally[27];

  (4) the time and place of the adjourned hearing[28]; and

  (5) the manner in which and the time within which notice of the adjournment and the reasons for it are to be given the the parties.[29]

11.2 Where a case is adjourned other than to a judge, it may be heard by the registrar who originally dealt with the case or by another registrar.[30]

11.3 If the companies court registrar adjourns the application to a judge to give further directions, the application will usually be listed before the companies court judge in a Monday morning list.

11.4 If the companies court registrar adjourns the application to a judge, all directions having been complied with and the evidence being complete, the application will be referred to the Listing Office and any practice direction relating to listing shall apply accordingly.

11.5 In all disqualification applications, the Court may direct a pre-trial review ("PTR"), a case management conference or listing questionnaires (in the form annexed to this practice direction) and will fix a trial date or trial period in accordance with the provisions of CPR Part 29 ("The Multi-Track") as modified by any relevant practice direction made thereunder.

11.6 In contested disqualification applications, the registrar may, at a hearing of the claim, direct:

  (1) that a PTR be fixed for a date approximately six weeks after the close of evidence;

---

[21] Rule 7(3) of the Insolvent Companies (Disqualification of Unfit Directors) Proceedings Rules 1987.
[22] Rule 7(4)(a) of the Insolvent Companies (Disqualification of Unfit Directors) Proceedings Rules 1987.
[23] Rule 7(4)(b) of the Insolvent Companies (Disqualification of Unfit Directors) Proceedings Rules 1987.
[24] Rule 7(5)(a) of the Insolvent Companies (Disqualification of Unfit Directors) Proceedings Rules 1987.
[25] Rule 7(5)(b) of the Insolvent Companies (Disqualification of Unfit Directors) Proceedings Rules 1987.
[26] Rule 7(5)(c)(ii) of the Insolvent Companies (Disqualification of Unfit Directors) Proceedings Rules 1987.
[27] Rule 7(5)(c)(iii) of the Insolvent Companies (Disqualification of Unfit Directors) Proceedings Rules 1987.
[28] Rule 7(5)(c)(iv) of the Insolvent Companies (Disqualification of Unfit Directors) Proceedings Rules 1987.
[29] Rule 7(5)(c)(i) of the Insolvent Companies (Disqualification of Unfit Directors) Proceedings Rules 1987.
[30] Rule 7(6) of the Insolvent Companies (Disqualification of Unfit Directors) Proceedings Rules 1987.

(2) that each party complete a listing questionnaire and return it to the court not later than two clear working days before the hearing of the PTR.

11.7 At the hearing of the PRT, the registrar may give any further directions as appropriate and, where the application is to be heard in the Royal Courts of Justice in London, unless the trial date has already been fixed, will direct Counsel's clerks to attend Room TM 4.09 to obtain an appointment to fix a trial date within 5 days from the hearing of the PTR. The parties may not by agreement extend the period for attendance to fix a trial date. In the event of non-compliance, the court will fix a date for trial and give notice of the date to the parties.

11.8 In all cases, the parties must inform the court immediately of any material change to the information provided in a listing questionnaire.

12.   The trial

12.1 Trial bundles containing copies of:—
  (1) the claim form;
  (2) the acknowledgement of service;
  (3) all evidence filed by or on behalf of each of the parties to the proceedings, together with the exhibits thereto;
  (4) all relevant correspondence; and
  (5) such other documents as the parties consider necessary;
     shall be lodged with the court.

12.2 Skeleton agruments should be prepared by all the parties in all but the simplest cases whether the case is to be heard by a registrar or a judge. They should comply with all relevant guidelines.

12.3 The advocate for the claimant should also in all but the simplest cases provide: (a) a chronology, (b) a dramatis personae, (c) in respect of each defendant, a list of references to the relevant evidence.

12.4 The documents mentioned in paragraph 12.1–12.3 above must be delivered to the court in accordance with any order of the court and/or any relevant practice direction.
  (1) If the case is to be heard by a judge sitting in the Royal Courts of Justice, London, but the name of the judge is not known, or the judge is a deputy judge, these documents must be delivered to the Clerk of the Lists. If the name of the judge (other than a deputy judge) is known, these documents must be delivered to the judge's clerk;
  (2) If the case is to be heard by a companies court registrar, these documents must be delivered to Room 409, Thomas More Building, Royal Courts of Justice. Copies must be provided to the other party so far as possible when they are delivered to the court.
  (3) If the case is to be heard in the Chancery district registries in Birmingham, Bristol, Cardiff, Leeds, Liverpool, Manchester or Newcastle, the addresses for delivery are set out in Annex 1;
  (4) If the case is to be heard in a county court, the documents should be delivered to the relevant county court office.

12.5 Copies of documents delivered to the court must, so far as possible, be provided to each of the other parties to the claim.

12.6 The provisions in paragraphs 12.1 to 12.5 above are subject to any order of the court making different provision.

13.   Summary Procedure

13.1 If the parties decide to invite the court to deal with the application uder the procedure adopted in *Re Carecraft Construction Co. Ltd* [1994] 1 W.L.R. 172, they should inform the court immediately and obtain a date for the hearing of the application.

13.2 Whenever the *Carecraft* procedure is adopted, the claimant must:
  (1) except where the court otherwise directs, submit a written statement containing in respect of each defendant any material facts which (for the purposes of the application) are either agreed or not opposed (by either party); and
  (2) specify in writing the period of disqualification which the parties accept that the agreed unopposed facts justify or the band of years (*e.g.* 4 to 6 years) or bracket (*i.e.* 2 to 5 years; 6 to 10 years; 11 to 15 years) into which they will submit the case falls.

13.3 Paragraph 12.4 of the above applies to the documents mentioned in paragraph 13.2 above unless the court otherwise directs.

13.4 Unless the Court otherwise orders, a hearing under the Carecraft procedure will be held in private.

13.5 If the Court is minded to make a disqualification order having heard the parties' representations, it will usually give judgment and make the disqualification order in public. Unless the court otherwise orders, the written statement referred to in paragraph 13.2 shall be annexed to the disqualification order.

13.6 If the Court refuses to make the disqualification order under the Carecraft procedure, the Court shall give further directions for the hearing of the application.

14. Making and setting aside of disqualification order

14.1 The court may make a disqualification order against the defendant, whether or not the latter appears, and whether or not he has completed and returned the acknowledgement of service of the claim form, or filed evidence.[31]

14.2 Any disqualification order made in the absence of the defendant may be set aside or varied by the court on such terms as it thinks just.[32]

15. Service of disqualification orders

15.1 Service of disqualification orders will be the responsibility of the claimant.

16. Commencement of disqualification order

16.1 Unless the court otherwise orders, a disqualification order takes effect at the beginning of the 21st day after the day on which the order is made.[33]

Part Three

Applications under sections 7(2) and 7(4) of the Act

17. Applications for permission to make a disqualification application after the end of the period of 2 years specified in section 7(2) of the Act

17.1 Such applications shall be made by Application Notice under CPR Part 23, and Part 23 and the Part 23 Practice Direction shall apply save as modified below.

18. Applications for extra information made under section 7(4) of the Act

18.1 Such applications may be made:
(1) by Practice Form N.208 under CPR Part 8; or
(2) by Application Notice in existing disqualification claim proceedings.

19. Provisions applicable to applications under sections 7(2) and 7(4) of the Act

19.1 **Headings:** Every claim form and notice by which such an application is begun and all affidavits, notices and other documents in relation thereto must be entitled in the matter of the company or companies in question and in the matter of the Act.

19.2 **Service:**
(1) Service of application notices seeking orders under section 7(2) or 7(4) of the Act will be the responsibility of the applicant and will not be undertaken by the court.
(2) Where any application notice or order of the court or other document is required in any application under section 7(2) or section 7(4) of the Act to be served on any person who is not in England and Wales, the court may order service on him to be effected within such time and in such manner as it thinks fit, may require such proof of service as it thinks fit, and may make such directions as to acknowledgement of service as it thinks fit.

Part Four

Applications for permission to act

20. Commencing an application for permission to act

20.1 This practice direction governs applications for permission made under:

---

[31] Rule 8(1) of the Insolvent Companies (Disqualification of Unfit Directors) Proceedings Rules 1987.
[32] Rule 8(2) of the Insolvent Companies (Disqualification of Unfit Directors) Proceedings Rules 1987.
[33] Rule 9 of the Insolvent Companies (Disqualification of Unfit Directors) Proceedings Rules 1987.

(1) section 1(1) and section 17 of the Act;

(2) section 12 of the Act; and

(3) any application for permission made under any disqualification order which was made under any statutory predecessor of the Act.

20.2 Sections 12 and 17(2) of the Act identify the courts which have jurisdiction to deal with applications for permission to act. Subject to these sections, such applications may be made:

(1) by Practice Form N.208 under CPR Part 8; or

(2) by application notice in an existing disqualification application.

21. Headings

21.1 Every claim form or application notice by which an application for permission to act is begun, and all affidavits, notices and other documents in the application must be entitled in the matter of the company or companies in question and in the matter of the Act.

22. Evidence

22.1 Evidence in support of an application for permission to act shall be by affidavit.

23. Service

23.1 In all cases, the claim form or application notice (as appropriate), together with the evidence in support thereof, must be served on the Secretary of State.

Part Five

Applications

24. Form of application

24.1 CPR Part 23 and the Part 23 practice direction (General Rules about Applications for Court Orders) shall apply in relation to applications governed by this practice direction (see paragraph 1.3(4) above) save as modified below.

25. Headings

25.1 Every notice and all affidavits in relation thereto must be entitled in the same manner as the Claim Form in the proceedings in which the application is made.

26. Service

26.1 Service of application notices in disqualification proceedings will be the responsibility of the parties and will not be undertaken by the court.

26.2 Where any application notice or order of the court or other document is required in any application to be served on any person who is not in England and Wales, the court may order service on him to be effected within such time and in such manner as it thinks fit, and may also require such proof of service as it thinks fit.

Part Six

Disqualification proceedings other than in the royal courts of justice

27.1 Where a disqualification application is made by a claim form issued other than in the Royal Courts of Justice this practice direction shall apply with the following modifications:

(1) Upon the issue of the claim form the court shall endorse it with the date and time for the first hearing before a district judge. The powers exercisable by a registrar under this practice direction shall be exercised by a district judge.

(2) If the district judge (either at the first hearing or at any adjourned hearing before him) directs that the disqualification claim is to be heard by a High Court judge or by an authorised circuit judge he will direct that the case be entered forthwith in the list for hearing by that judge and the court will allocate (i) a date for the hearing of

the trial by that judge and (ii) unless the district judge directs otherwise a date for the hearing of a PTR by the trial judge.

Annex 1

Birmingham: The Chancery Listing Officer, The District Registry of the Chancery Division of the High Court, 33, Bull Street, Birmingham B4 6DS.

Bristol: The Chancery Listing Officer, The District Registry of the Chancery Division of the High Court, 3rd Floor, Greyfriars, Lewins Mead, Bristol BS1 2NR.

Cardiff: The Chancery Listing Officer, The District Registry of the Chancery Division of the High Court, 1st Floor, 2, Park Street, Cardiff CF1 1NR.

Leeds: The Chancery Listing Officer, The District Registry of the Chancery Division of the High Court, Leeds Combined Court Centre, The Court House, 1, Oxford Row, Leeds LS1 3BG.

Liverpool and Manchester: The Chancery Listing Officer, The District Registry of the Chancery Division of the High Court, Manchester Courts of Justice, Crown Square, Manchester M60 9DJ.

Newcastle: The Chancery Listing Officer, The District Registry of the Chancery Division of the High Court, The Law Courts, Quayside, Newcastle upon Tyne NE1 3LA.

APPENDIX 6

EXTRACTS FROM THE AUSTRALIAN CORPORATIONS LAW

- Corporations Law, s. 91A
- Corporations Law, ss. 229–230
- Corporations Law, ss. 599–600

CORPORATIONS LAW, s. 91A

Effect of such a prohibition, notice or disqualification

91A.—(1) This section has effect for the purposes of sections 229, 230, 588Z, 599, 600, 1317EA and 1317EF.

(2) A person manages a local corporation if the person, in this jurisdiction or elsewhere, is a director or promoter of, or is in any way (whether directly or indirectly) concerned in or takes part in the management of, the corporation.

(3) A person manages a corporation (other than a local corporation) if the person:

(a) in this jurisdiction, does an act as a director or promotor of or is in any way (whether directly or indirectly) concerned in or takes part in the management of, the corporation; or

(b) in this jurisdiction or elsewhere, does an act as a director or promoter of, or is in any way (whether directly or indirectly) concerned in or takes part in the management of, the corporation in connection with:

(i) the corporation carrying on business in this jurisdiction; or

(ii) an act that the corporation does, or proposes to do, in this jurisdiction; or

(iii) a decision by the corporation whether or not to do, or to refrain from doing, an act in this jurisdiction.

(4) Except as provided in this section, a person is not taken to manage a corporation.

CORPORATIONS LAW, ss. 229–230

Certain persons not to manage corporations

229.—(1) An insolvent under administration must not, without the leave of the Court, manage a corporation ...

(3) A person who has, whether before or after the commencement of this part, been convicted:

(a) on indictment of an offence against an Australian law, or any other law, in connection with the promotion, formation or management of a body corporate or corporation; or

(b) of serious fraud; or

(c) of any offence for a contravention of section 232, 590, 591, 592, 595, 996 or 1307, of Part 6.6, of Division 2 of Part 7.11, or of a previous law corresponding to any of those provisions, or

(d) of an offence of which the person is guilty because of subsection 1317FA(1);

shall not, within 5 years after the conviction or, if the person was sentenced to imprisonment, after release from prison, without the leave of the Court, manage a corporation.

(3A) Section 91A defines what, for the purposes of this section, constitutes managing a corporation.

(4) In any proceeding for a contravention of subsection (3), a certificate by a prescribed authority stating that a person was released from prison on a specified date is *prima facie* evidence that that person was released from prison on that date.

(5) When granting leave under this section, the Court may impose such conditions or restrictions as it thinks fit and a person shall not contravene any such condition or restriction.

(6) A person intending to apply for leave of the Court under this section shall give to the Commission not less than 21 days notice of the person's intention so to apply.

(7) The Court may at any time, on the application of the Commission, revoke leave granted by the court under this section.

(8) Any leave granted by a court under a corresponding previous law of this jurisdiction before the commencement of this Part has effect for the purposes of this section as if it had been granted by the Court under this section.

Court may order person not to manage corporation

230.—(1) Where, on application by the Commission or a person who is a prescribed person in relation to the body corporate concerned, or any of the bodies corporate concerned, the Court is satisfied:

(a) that:

(i) a body corporate has, during a period in which a person (in this subsection called the "relevant person") was a relevant officer of the body corporate repeatedly breached relevant legislation; and

(ii) the relevant person failed to take reasonable steps to prevent the body corporate so breaching relevant legislation; or

(b) that:

(i) each of 2 or more bodies corporate has, at a time when a person (in this subsection also called "the relevant person") was a relevant officer of the body corporate, breached relevant legislation; and

(ii) in each case the relevant person failed to take relevant steps to prevent the body corporate from breaching relevant legislation; or

(c) that:

(i) a person (in this subsection also called the "relevant person") has repeatedly breached relevant legislation; and

(ii) on 2 or more of the occasions when the relevant person breached relevant legislation, the relevant person was a relevant officer of a body corporate (whether or not the relevant person was a relevant officer of the same body corporate on each of those occasions); or

(d) that, at any time during a period in which a person (in this subsection also called the "relevant person") has been or was a relevant officer of a body corporate (other than a corporation), the relevant person did an act, or made an omission, that would have constituted a contravention of subsection 232(2) or (4) in relation to the body if the body had been a corporation at that time;

the Court may by order prohibit the relevant person, for such period as is specified in the order, from managing a corporation.

(2) Where an order has been made under subsection (1) on the application of a person other than the Commission, the person shall, within 7 days after the making of the order, lodge an office copy of the order.

(3) A person who is subject to a section 230 order (whether made before or after the commencement of this section) must not manage a corporation.

(3A) Section 91A defines what, for the purposes of this section, constitutes managing a corporation.

(4) In this section, a reference to a period in which a person has been or was a relevant officer of a body corporate includes a reference to such a period that elapsed, or part of which elapsed, before the commencement of this Part.

(5) For the purposes of this section:

(a) a body corporate or other person shall be taken to have breached relevant legislation if the body corporate or other person has contravened a provision of a relevant enactment; and

(b) a body corporate or another person may be taken to have repeatedly breached relevant legislation if the body corporate or other person has:

(i) on 2 or more occasions, contravened a particular provision of a relevant enactment;

(ii) contravened 2 or more provisions of a relevant enactment; or

(iii) contravened provisions of 2 or more relevant enactments.

(6) In this section:
"body corporate" includes an unincorporated registrable body;
"prescribed person", in relation to a body corporate, means:

(a) a liquidator or provisional liquidator of the body corporate;

(ba) an administrator of the body corporate;

(bb) an administrator of a deed of company arrangement executed by the body corporate;

(b) a member of the body corporate;

(c) a creditor of the body corporate; or

(d) a person who is authorised by the Commission to make applications under this section, or to make an application under this section in relation to the body corporate;

"relevant enactment" means this Law or a previous law corresponding to provisons of this Law;
"relevant officer", in relation to a body corporate, means a director, secretary or executive officer of the body corporate.

CORPORATIONS LAW, ss. 599–600

Court may order persons not to manage certain corporations

599.—(1) This section applies to a relevant body:

(a) that has been wound up, or is in the course of being wound up, because of inability to pay its debts as and when they became due;

(b) that has been in the course of being wound up because of inability to pay its debts as and when they became due, where the winding up has been stayed or terminated by an order under section 482;

(c) that has been or is under administration;

(ca) that has executed a deed of company arrangement, even if the deed has terminated;

(d) that has ceased to carry on business because it was unable to pay its debts as and when they became due;

(e) in respect of which a levy of execution was not satisfied;

(f) in respect of property of which a receiver, or a receiver and manager, has been appointed, whether by a court or pursuant to the powers contained in an instrument, whether or not the appointment has been terminated; or

(g) that has entered into a compromise or arrangement with its creditors.

(2) Unless cause to the contrary is shown the Court may, on an application by the Commission and on being satisfied as the the the matters referred to in subsection (3), make an order prohibiting a person specified in the order from managing a corporation during such period not exceeding 5 years after the date of the order as is specified in the order.

(3) The Court shall not make an order under subsection (2) unless it is satisfied:

(a) that the person to whom the application for an order relates was given notice of the application;

(b) that, within the period of 7 years before notice of the application was given to the person referred to in paragraph (a), whether that period commenced before or after the commencement of this section, that person was a director of, or was concerned or took part in the management of, 2 or more relevant bodies to which this section applies; and

(c) that:

    (i) in the case of each of those 2 relevant bodies; or

    (ii) where the person was a director of, or was concerned or took part in the management of, more than 2 relevant bodies to which this section applies—in the case of each of 2 or more of those bodies;

    the manner in which affairs of the body had been managed was wholly or partly responsible for the body being wound up, being under administration, having executed a deed of company arrangement, ceasing to carry on business, being unable to satisfy a levy of execution, being subject to the appointment of receiver, or a receiver and manager, or entering into a compromise or arrangement with its creditors.

(4) A person who is subject to a section 599 order (whether made before or after the commencement of this section) must not manage a corporation.

(5) Section 91A defines what, for the purposes of this section, constitutes managing a corporation.

Commission may order persons not to manage corporations

600.—(1) For the purposes of this section:

(b) a relevant body is a section 600 body at a particular time if, and only if, within the period of 7 years ending at that time, a liquidator of the body has, under:

    (i) subsection 533(1); or

    (ii) a previous law corresponding to subsection 533(1);

    reported, or lodged a report with respect to, a matter relating to the ability of the body to pay its unsecured creditors; and

(c) a person shall be taken to be a relevant person in relation to a relevant body that is or was a section 600 body if, and only if, the person was a director of the body at any time during the period of 12 months ending on the day of the beginning of the winding up of the body.

(2) The Commission may give to a person who is a relevant person in relation to 2 or more

relevant bodies that are, at the time of service, section 600 bodies a notice in writing requiring the person to show cause why the Commission should not serve on the person a notice under subsection (3).

(3) Where the Commission:

(a) has served on a person a notice under subsection (2); and

(b) has given the person an opportunity of being heard in relation to the matter;

the Commission shall, unless it is satisfied that it is not appropriate to do so, serve on the person a notice in writing prohibiting the person, for such period not exceeding 5 years as is specified in the notice, from managing a corporation.

(4) Where:

(a) the Commission has served a notice under subsection (2) on a person who is a relevant person in relation to 2 or more relevant bodies that were, at the time of service, section 600 bodies; and

(b) those 2 bodies have at any time been related to each other, or any of those bodies has at any time been related to any other of those bodies, as the case may be;

the Commission shall have regard to that fact in considering whether or not it is appropriate to serve on the person a notice under subsection (3).

(5) A person who is subject to a section 600 notice (whether served before or after the commencement of this section) must not, without the leave of the Court, manage a corporation.

(6) Section 91A defines what, for the purposes of this section, constitutes managing a corporation.

APPENDIX 7

GUIDELINES FOR APPLICATIONS FOR PERMISSION UNDER A DISQUALIFICATION ORDER ISSUED BY THE SECRETARY OF STATE

The Secretary of State has a duty to appear on a number of such applications and to call the attention of the Court to any matters which seem to him to be relevant, and may himself give evidence or call witnesses.

The Secretary of State considers that the applicant for leave under a disqualification order should:

(i) support his application to the Court with full and particularised affidavit evidence which is supported by appropriate exhibits, and

(ii) serve such evidence on the Secretary of State to as to give him a proper opportunity to consider it fully before the hearing of the application.

The stance taken by the Secretary of State on each application, and thus for example whether he should give evidence and oppose the application or indicate that he does not oppose it, can only be decided having regard to the circumstances thereof.

However, if in the view of the Secretary of State the evidence that is served by the applicant omits relevant information, or lacks particularity or appropriate supporting material the Secretary of State would generally draw such matters to the attention of the Court and invite it to take them into account as a factor against granting leave.

The Secretary of State considers that the information set out below should normally be included in the applicant's evidence. This list of information is not intended to be comprehensive, it is only a guideline. In some cases further information will be necessary and in others some of the matters listed may not be relevant.

1. Details of the disqualification order made by the Court against the Applicant, including the length of the order made, details of the company of which your client was a director and details of his directorship of that company.

2. In a case where the disqualification order has been made following criminal charges, details of the charges of which the Applicant was convicted, details of the sentence imposed and details of the disqualification order made.

3. Details of the company in respect of which the Applicant seeks leave to act. Such details should include

    (a) the company's name, date of incorporation, registered office, paid up share capital, directors and auditors;

    (b) a detailed description of the Applicant's role and involvement with that company to date;

    (c) the Applicant's interests in that company, including share ownership;

    (d) a copy of the Memorandum and Articles of Association of the company; an up to date company search conducted in respect of it giving full details of all the information filed in respect of the company with the Registrar of Companies;

(e) a description of the company's performance together with copies of the audited accounts for the company for the past two years if the company has been trading for that length of time and in any event up to date management accounts;

(f) details of the management of the company; details of board members; board meetings and an overall description of the management structure of the company, describing those who are principally responsible for the conduct of the company's affairs, an account of their roles and responsibilities including the Applicant's role;

(g) details of the principal activities undertaken by the company during the past two years including its investments;

(h) details of any overdraft facilities of the company and of all securities over assets of the company and by way of guarantee for the indebtedness of the company to its bank and others;

(i) details of all steps taken to avoid a repetition of the acts and omissions which founded the making of the disqualification order.

4. A description of the Applicant's proposed involvement as a director of the company and why it is necessary that he should be so involved, including all the circumstances relied on by the Applicant in support of his assertion that his involvement as a director and/or manager of the affairs of the company is important to it. This should be supported by an auditors report or some other appropriate independent evidence on the effect of the Applicant not being involved as director or manager.

5. Details of the Applicant's remuneration, emoluments and other benefits from the company, including a copy of any service agreement.

APPENDIX 8

DRAFT CARECRAFT STATEMENT

IN THE HIGH COURT OF JUSTICE   NO. [   ]

CHANCERY DIVISION

COMPANIES COURT

IN THE MATTER OF [COMPANY NAME] LIMITED/PLC

AND IN THE MATTER OF THE COMPANY DIRECTORS DISQUALIFICATION ACT 1986

BETWEEN:

THE SECRETARY OF STATE FOR TRADE AND INDUSTRY

Claimant

-and-

(1) [NAME]
(2) [NAME]
(3) [NAME]

Defendants

STATEMENT OF FACTS NOT IN DISPUTE FOR THE PURPOSES OF A "CARECRAFT" SETTLEMENT AS BETWEEN THE SECRETARY OF STATE AND THE FIRST AND SECOND DEFENDANTS

1. **Introduction**

1.1 On the [date] the Secretary of State issued proceedings under Section 6 of the Company Directors Disqualification Act 1986 ("the 1986 Act") for Disqualification Orders against the Defendants in the terms of Section 1(1) of the 1986 Act.

1.2 Subject to the Court, the Secretary of State and the First and Second Defendants ("Mr. [name]" and "Mr. [name]" are willing to dispose of the proceedings by way of the shortened form of procedure sanctioned in *Re Carecraft Construction Co. Limited* [1994] 1 W.L.R. 172 as clarified by the decision of the Court of Appeal in *Secretary of State for Trade and Industry v. Rogers* [1996] 4 All E.R. 854. The proceedings as against the Third Defendant ("Mr. [name]") are continuing to trial, the [hearing of which is due to start on [date]].

1.3 The purpose of this Statement is to identify, in relation to the allegations of unfitness relied on by the Secretary of State, the core material facts which (for the purposes of a "Carecraft" disposal of these proceedings), are not disputed by Mr. [name] and Mr. [name]. None of the facts set out below are disputed and it is acknowledged that there is affidavit evidence verifying each of the same.

1.4 The Secretary of State submits that by reference to the undisputed facts the conduct of Mr. [name] and Mr. [name] as directors of [company name Limited/PLC] ("the Company") has been such as to make each of them unfit to be concerned in the management of a company and that, accordingly, the Court is bound (by Section 6(1) of the 1986 Act) to make a Disqualification Order against him. It is further submitted by the Secretary of State that the conduct of Mr. [name] and Mr. [name] is such that Disqualification Orders [for a period of / within the range of [   ] to [   ]] years (which, subject to the Court, have been agreed by the parties) are appropriate.

1.5 Mr. [name] and Mr. [name] accept that, by reference to the facts which are not in dispute, the Court can be satisfied as to their unfitness to be concerned in the management of a company, and that it would be appropriate to make Orders against them [for a period of / within the range of [   ] to [   ] years. They also agree that if, pursuant to this Statement, there is a "Carecraft" disposal of these proceedings, then there should additionally, be Orders that they should pay the Secretary of State's costs of these proceedings [in the sum of £   ]. As Mr. [name] is Legally Aided, it should be directed that the determination of the amount of costs to be paid by him be postponed (in accordance with Regulation 127 of the Civil Legal Aid (General Regulations) 1989 for such time as the Court thinks fit.

1.6 The Secretary of State, Mr. [name] and Mr. [name] all agree that, if the Court is unwilling to approve a "Carecraft" disposal of these proceedings, then no further reference may be made by any party to this Statement, or to the fact of any proposed "Carecraft" settlement or to any admissions made herein, during the course of these proceedings. The parties agree that, in any event, they will jointly apply to the Court for direction that a different Judge should hear the contested trial.

1.7 In the event of Disqualification Orders being made by reference to this Statement, the Secretary of State and Mr. [name] and Mr. [name] agree that they will jointly apply for a direction that this Statement be annexed to the Court's judgment.

1.8 The structure of the remainder of this Statement is as follows:

1.8.1 Section 2 contains the general background information relevant to the allegations of unfitness made against Mr. [name] and Mr. [name].

1.8.2 Sections 3, 4, 5 and 6 deal, respectively with each of the four allegations of unfitness that are made in subparagraphs [   ] of the affidavit sworn herein by Mr. [name of Applicant's deponent] on the [date].

1.8.3 Section 7 deals with an allegation of unfitness which is not contained in affidavit evidence but which has recently come to the attention of the Secretary of State. The Secretary of State and the First Defendant invite the Court to take these facts and matters into account when considering whether to approve the Carecraft disposal of these proceedings.

1.8.4 Section 8 sets out certain additional facts which the Court may wish to take into account by way of mitigation. The Secretary of State and Mr. [name] have agreed that no further facts (other than those set out in Section 8) may be adduced at the Carecraft hearing by way of mitigation.

2. General Background

2.1 The Company was incorporated and started trading in [date]. Its business was [details].

2.2 Mr. [name] and Mr. [name] founded the Company and remained its principal directors throughout. The only other director was Mr. [name] who was on the board from [date] until [date].

2.3 Mr. [name] and Mr. [name] each owned 300 of the 650 issued £1 ordinary shares in the Company.

2.4 Though Mr. [name] and Mr. [name] shared responsibility for the overall management of the Company, Mr. [name] was additionally in charge of accounting records whilst Mr. [name] had particular responsibility for arranging contracts and preparing estimates.

2.5 On the [date] Joint Administrative Receivers were appointed pursuant to the terms of a debenture dated the [date] in favour of [name].

2.6 A Statement of Affairs for the Company as at [date] sworn by Mr. [name] shows an estimated deficiency as regards creditors of [   ] this figure includes trade creditors amounting to [   ] and sums due to the Crown totalling [   ].

2.7 In the balance sheet included in the last set of audited accounts for the Company (being those for the year ending [date] the Company's excess of assets over liabilities amounted to [ ]. Accordingly, the deterioration in the net asset position on the Company going into receivership was [ ] according to the Statement of Affairs. The Statement of Affairs, however, does not make allowance for work in progress, or bad debt relief for VAT purposes.

3. Trading at the Risk of the Creditors

3.1 The allegation, contained in paragraph [ ] of Mr. [name of the Applicant's deponent]'s affidavit, is that Mr. [name] and Mr. [name]:
"... caused the Company to continue to trade after [date] when they should have known that the Company had no prospect of paying creditors."

3.2 In relation to the period from [date] to [date] and to the extent disclosed by the undisputed facts set out in paragraph 3.3 below, Mr [name] and Mr [name] admit this allegation.

3.3 The core facts material to this Allegation are the following:

3.3.1 The audited accounts for each of the years ending [date], [date] and [date] and the draft balance sheet for the year ending [date] showed that the Company had Net Current Liabilities as follows:

Year ending 31 August	Net Current Liabilities (£s)
[year]	[ ]
[year]	[ ]
[year]	[ ]
[year]	[ ]

3.3.2 As shown in paragaph 2.7 above, in the final period of trading (from the [date] being the date of the last audited accounts, to the appointment of the Joint Administrative Receivers on the [date] the Company's net asset position on going into receivership showed a deterioration of [ ] from a net asset position of [ ] to a deficit of [ ].

3.3.3 Betwen [date] and [date], [number] creditors took proceedings against the Company to enforce payment of debts amounting to [ ]. Of these, some were paid, leaving a net balance as at the date of the Statement of Affairs of [ ].

3.3.4 As from [date] the Company was subject to constant pressure from its bank to reduce the borrowing on its overdraft. This pressure was exacerbated by delays in payment by its own trade debtors from [date] onwards.

3.3.5 Between [date] and [date] the Company drew some [no] cheques (to the total value of approximately [ ] which were dishonoured. (Further details are to be found at paragraph 6.3.1 below).

3.3.6 By the date of the appointment of the Joint Administrative Receivers, amounts totalling [ ] for VAT and [ ] for PAYE and NIC were stated in the Statement of Affairs to be due to the relevant Crown departments. These sums included liabilities which dated back to [date].

3.3.7 In late [date] Mr [name] and Mr [name] consulted [name] about the continued viability of the Company following the voluntary liquidation of a major creditor. It was on [name] contacting the bank that the Receivers were appointed.

4. Crown Debts

4.1 The allegation, contained in paragraph [ ] of Mr [name]'s affidavit, is that Mr [name]:
"... caused the Company to retain monies due to the Crown which at the date of the receivership was approximately [ ], thereby providing them with involuntary finance for the Company's continued trading".

4.2 To the extent disclosed by the undisputed facts set out in paragraph 4.3 below (and save that the amount shown in the Statement of Affairs as being due to the Crown was [ ] rather than [ ] as alleged) Mr [name]and Mr [name] admit this Allegation.

4.3 The core facts material to this Allegation are the following:

4.3.1 The Statement of Affairs shows the sum of [ ] as being then due to HM Customs & Excise in respect of unpaid VAT.

4.3.2 Subsequent to the swearing of the Statement of Affairs, HM Customs & Excise produced a claim to the effect:

(1) that the total debt due from the Company was [   ] which sum included [   ] by way of interest, penalties and surcharges;

(2) that the VAT of [   ] due for the quarter ended [date] and payable on [date] had not been paid, and that no VAT had been paid for the quarters ended [date] and [date].

4.3.3 The Statement of Affairs shows an overall total of [   ] as being then due to the Inland Revenue in respect of unpaid PAYE and NIC.

4.3.4 As at the date of the receivership some of the total due to the Inland Revenue dated back to [date]. (Payments had been made for PAYE and NIC for [date].

4.3.5 The Crown was treated less favourably than the Company's trade creditors as is evidenced by the fact that between the [date] and the [date] the liabilities to trade creditors rose from [   ] to [   ] whilst in the same period the amounts due to the Crown increased from [   ] to [   ]. The increase in Crown debts was very largely due to non-payment of VAT, NIC and PAYE from [date] onwards.

5. Excessive Remuneration Contributing to the Company's Insolvency

5.1 The allegation, contained in paragraph [   ] of Mr [name]'s affidavit, is that Mr [name] and Mr [name]

". . . were responsible for the Company becoming insolvent by affording themselves a high level of remuneration".

5.2 To the extent disclosed by the undisputed facts set out in paragraph 5.3 below Mr [name] and Mr [name] admit this allegation.

5.3 The core facts material to this Allegation are the following:

5.3.1 The table set out below shows the total remuneration and benefits recorded in the audited accounts as having been received by Mr [name] and Mr [name] for each of the years ending 31st August 1988, 1989 and 1990. Also shown are the Company's turnover and net profit (loss) for the years in question.

	Turnover £	Net Profit/Loss £	Remuneration £ (inc pension contribution)
[year]	[ ]	[ ]	[ ]
[year]	[ ]	[ ]	[ ]
[year]	[ ]	[ ]	[ ]
Totals:	[ ]	[ ]	[ ]

5.3.2 If Mr [name] and Mr [name] had taken more modest remuneration they would have provided the Company with a "buffer" of accumulated profits for the future. In the event, when the Company began to make losses, there was very little by way of funds available to absorb these losses; as a result the Company rapidly became insolvent on a balance sheet basis.

5.3.3 When the Company started to become less successful, Mr [name] and Mr [name] took substantial reductions in their salaries. For the 12 months ended [date], their respective salaries were reduced to [   ] each; from the 3rd April 1991 to the 27th July 1991 Mr [name]'s drawings were [   ] and Mr [name] were [   ]. Thereafter no further drawings from the Company were taken by either of them.

5.3.4 Mr [name] and Mr [name] also provided to [   ] a joint and several personal guarantee in the sum of [   ]. They also paid [   ] from a pension fund for their benefit to the Company's bank account in 1991. Further Mr [name] also paid much of the bill for the Company's last accountants Messrs [name] in late 1991.

6. Misuse of Bank Account

6.1 The allegation, contained in paragraph [   ] of Mr [name]'s affidavit, is that Mr [name] and Mr [name]:

"...were responsible for the misuse of the Company bank account."

6.2 To the extent disclosed by the undisputed facts set out in paragraph 6.3 below, Mr [name] and Mr [name] admit this allegation.

6.3 The core facts material to this allegation are the following:

6.3.1 As already stated in paragraph 3.3.5 above, between [date] and [date] the Company drew some [no] cheques, to a total value of approximately [   ], which were dishonoured. Some [no] of these, to a value of [   ], were honoured on re-presentation. This left a total of [   ] cheques, to a value of approximately [   ] which were "referred to drawer" on at least one occassion; the majority of these cheques (save for those drawn in [date] and [date] were honoured on re-presentation.

6.3.2 Mr [name]and Mr [name] accept that they failed adequately to monitor the fluctuations in the Company's bank account.

7. Failure to file accounts

7.1 [Because the facts and matters set out below only came to the attention of the Applicant recently they have not been verified by affidavit in these proceedings. Nevertheless these facts and matters [have been agreed/are not disputed as] between the Applicant and the First Defendant, and the Applicant is satisfied as to their veracity. Accordingly the Applicant and the First Defendant jointly invite the Court to take these facts and matters in to account when considering whether to approve the *Carecraft* disposal of these proceedings. [In the event that these proceedings are disposed of on a *Carecraft* basis The Secretary of State expressly reserves the right to issue or cause to be issued further proceedings under the Company Directors Disqualification Act 1986 in relation to any further matters of misconduct which may come to his attention in relation to A Limited after the date of this statement].

7.2 The First Defendant accepts that he failed to ensure that A Limited prepared or filed audited accounts with the Registrar of Companies contrary to the provisions of the Companies Act 1985 (as amended) to the extent disclosed by the accepted facts set out in paragraph 7.3 to 7.5 below.

7.3 A Limited ("A") was incorporated on [date]. From [date], when it was acquired from company formation agents, the First Defendant was its sole director and sole beneficial shareholder, one share being registered in his name and one share being registered in the name of [name] who held it on trust for the First Defendant.

7.4 A commenced trading on [   ]. It went into creditors' voluntary liquidation on [   ].

7.5 A failed to prepare or file audited accounts for the years ended (date), (date) (date) or (date). These accounts were due for filing on (date) and (date) respectively. The First Defendant accepts that as sole director he was responsible for ensuring that audited accounts were prepared and filed, and he accepts that he did not do so.

8. Mitigation

8.1 The First and Second Defendants wish the Court to have regard to the matters set out in paragraphs 8.2 to 8.3 below. No further evidence or allegations will be relied upon in mitigation other than those set out in this statement. The Applicant, whilst not accepting the truth of these matters, does not object to the Court taking them into account for the purpose of disposing of this matter summarily.

8.2 The First Defendant invested £... into the Company as an unsecured creditor and appears as a creditor in that sum in the Statement of Affairs. He raised this money by way of a loan from his bank secured by means of a charge on his home. He is presently repaying this loan at the rate of £... per month.

8.3 Second Defendant was ill between [date] and [date] and was not able to attend the company's premises during that period.

Signed:
For the Secretary of State
For the Respondent, AB
DATE:

Index

Accounting. *See also* **Bank accounts, Filing requirements**
  assuming responsibility for, 5.64
  criminal offences, 5.13, 9.39
  failure to keep proper records, 5.13–5.19
  financial control, 5.18
  incompetence, 5.52
  information, 5.18–5.19
  limited liability, 5.14
  permission to act, 13.31, 13.48
  persistent breach of companies legislation, 9.38–9.39
  preparation, failure of, 5.35–5.36
  professional advisers, 5.16–5.17
  standards, 5.48
  statement of affairs, 5.15
  trading while insolvent, 5.07, 5.11, 5.13
  unfitness, 5.35–5.36, 5.64
  valuation, 5.19
Acknowledgement of service, 6.41
Administration orders,
  bankruptcy, 10.01, 10.09
  commencement of proceedings, 6.50
  disqualification orders, 1.14
  fraud, 9.45
  interim orders, as, 6.50
  judgments orders, 10.09
  jurisdiction, 6.04
  legal effects of disqualification, 12.03, 12.20–12.21
Administrative receivership,
  commencement of proceedings, 6.50
  criminal offences, 9.30
  legal effects of disqualification, 12.22
Advisers, 3.28–3.29, 5.60. *See also* **Professional advisers**
Affidavits,
  affirmations, 6.59
  character, 6.78
  Civil Procedure Rules 1998, 6.60, 6.63

Affidavits—*cont.*
  Disqualification Practice Direction, 6.60, 6.63
  experts, 6.75
  false statements, 6.60
  filing, 6.63
  hearsay, 6.64, 6.72–6.73
  unfitness, 6.52–6.53
  use of, in other proceedings, 6.87
Agency, 12.42–12.43
Alter ego companies, 12.30
Alternate directors, 3.36
Ancillary process, disqualification as, 1.02, 2.02
Appeals, 6.80–6.84
  case stated, 9.72
  costs, 9.71
  Court of Appeal, 9.73
  court rules, 6.16, 6.18, 6.21
  Crown Court, 9.72–9.73
  delay in bringing proceedings, 5.84
  discretion, 9.72
  disqualification orders, 9.71–9.73
    suspending or staying, 9.73
  duration of disqualification, 9.71
  Insolvency Rules, 6.21, 6.80–6.83
  magistrates' courts, 9.71–9.72
  permission to, 6.83, 13.68–13.69
  review powers, 6.84
  Scotland, 9.71
  sentencing, 9.71–9.73
  time limits, 6.81
  transfer of proceedings, 6.12, 6.80
  winding up, 9.71
Applications for disqualifications, 6.36–6.49
  acknowledgment of service, 6.41
  adjournment, 6.44
  Carecraft, 6.46
  case management, 6.44
  claim forms, 6.38–6.40
    endorsements, 6.39
    issue of, 6.39
    service of, 6.40

Applications for disqualifications—
cont.
delay, 6.49
directions, 6.44
disclosure, 6.47
Disqualification Practice Direction,
6.38–6.40, 6.43–6.44
Disqualification Rules, 6.37–6.39,
6.43–6.44
documents, loss of, 6.49
double jeopardy, 6.49
evidence, 6.39–6.41
further, 6.42
hearings,
dates, 6.39
first, 6.44
historical background, 6.36
information, further, 6.48
judgments,
summary, 6.49
misfeasance summons, 6.36
service, 6.40–6.41
statements of case, 6.49
summary judgments, 6.49
summary procedure, 6.46
timetable, 6.38–6.46
time limits, 6.38–6.46
Appointment of directors,
articles of association, 3.10
de facto directors, 3.12–3.13, 3.19
shadow directors, 325
Articles of association, 3.10
Assets,
contribution to company's, 1.13
disqualification orders, 1.13
phoenix companies, 5.32
Auditors,
fraud, 9.45
permission to act, 13.34
supervision, 13.34
Australia,
discretion, 9.56
legal effects of disqualification,
12.25
management, 12.33–12.34, 12.39
permission to act, 13.03, 13.16,
13.22
Automatic disqualification,
bankrupts, 1.15–1.18, 10.01–10.08
Company Directors'
Disqualification Act 1986,
1.15–1.18, 2.01
permission to act, 13.69

Bank accounts,
financial responsibility, 5.30
misuse of, 5.30
trading while insolvent, 5.30
unfitness, 5.30
Bankruptcy, 10.01–10.09
acting for undischarged person, 1.17
administration orders, 10.01, 10.09
automatic disqualification, 1.15,
10.01–10.08
companies, acting through, 1.22
Company Directors Disqualification
Act, overlap between, 10.07
credit, obtaining, 10.04
criminal offences, 1.16, 10.02,
10.04, 12.55
duration of, 10.06
formation, 10.03
fraudulent trading, 10.03
Greene Committee, 1.22, 10.03–
10.04
history, 10.03–10.05
individual voluntary arrangements,
10.06
insolvency practitioners, 13.56
insolvent partnerships, 3.43
judgment debtors, 10.09
legal effect of, 12.02
management, 10.05, 12.34
partnerships, 12.15
permission to act, 13.10, 13.55,
13.64, 13.69
prohibitions, 13.01
promotion, 10.03
public protection. 10.04
publicity, 10.08
rationale, 10.03–10.05
registration of orders, 10.08, 11.26
undischarged, 1.15, 10.01–10.08
Banks,
shadow directors, 3.30–3.31
wrongful trading, 3.30
Board of directors,
collective responsibility, 5.54
Cork Committee, 5.55
delegation, 5.57
disqualification orders, 2.01
failure to exert influence over policy
of, 5.61–5.63

Board of directors—*cont.*
  financial responsibility, 5.55
  independent controls, 13.41–13.45
  knowledge, 5.57
  management, participation in, 5.55
  monitoring financial position, 5.57
  negligence, 5.55
  non-executive directors, 5.55
  permission to act, 13.41–13.45
  personal responsibility, 5.54
  resignation, 5.61–5.63
  shadow directors, 3.27
  supervision, 5.57
  trading while insolvent, 5.61
  unfitness, 4.11, 5.54, 5.60–5.63
Breach. *See also* **Persistent breach of companies legislation**
  Company Directors'
    Disqualification Act 1986, 2.01
  disqualification orders, 1.16–1.17
  duty, of, 9.45–9.46
  fiduciary duties, 5.43, 5.72, 9.23
  filing requirements, 1.25
  fraud, 9.45–9.46
  incompetence, 2.28
  personal liability, 1.16–1.17, 2.30
  statutory obligations, 5.46–5.47,
    5.63
  trading while insolvent, 5.43
  transactions avoidance, 5.38–5.41
  unfitness, 5.46, 5.57
Building societies,
  companies, as, 3.40, 9.04
  disqualification, 3.40
  legal effects of disqualification,
    12.05–12.06

Calderbank letters, 8.09, 8.21
Capital. *See* **Capitalisation,** Under-
  capitalised companies
Capitalisation, 5.34
Care and skill,
  incompetence, 5.50
  unfitness, 4.09, 5.50, 5.65
Carecraft procedure, 6.46
  admissions, 8.14, 8.17
  Calderbank offers, 8.09
  conduct, 8.19
  discontinuance of proceedings, 8.06,
    8.08–8.19
  dishonesty, 8.18
  disqualification orders, 8.08, 8.11–
    8.12, 8.19

Carecraft procedure—*cont.*
  Disqualification Practice Direction,
    8.09, 8.16–8.18
  duration of disqualification, 8.16–
    8.17
  evidence, 8.09, 8.12–8.13, 8.17–
    8.18
  hearings, 8.17
  judgments, statements annexed to,
    8.18
  judicial review, 8.09
  mitigation, 8.15
  modification of, 8.20
  negotiations, 8.09, 8.10
  permission to act, 13.20
  public interest, 8.18
  refusal to make order, 8.11, 8.17
  relevant facts, 8.12–8.14
  settlement, 8.17
  standard clauses, 8.09
  statements, 8.09–8.19
  status after making an order, 8.19
  suggested period, 8.16
  without prejudice, 8.10, 8.17
Case management,
  applications for disqualification
    orders, 6.44
  Civil Procedure Rules 1998, 6.23
  criminal offences, 9.32
  parties, 6.34
  want of prosecution, 7.33
Case stated, 9.72
Character, 5.76, 6.78–6.79
Charities, 12.47
Chartered rights, 12.10–12.11
Civil liability,
  fraudulent trading, 1.23
  legal effects of disqualification,
    12.56
  permission to act, 13.38
Civil Procedure Rules 1998,
  Calderbank letters, 8.21
  case management, 6.22
  costs, 6.25–6.26
  criminal offences, 9.32
  discontinuance of proceedings, 8.04
  European Convention on Human
    Rights, 6.24
  experts, 6.24, 6.76
  hearsay, 6.71, 6.73
  impact of, 6.22

Civil Procedure Rules 1998—*cont.*
  inspection, 3.08, 6.68
  jurisdiction, 6.15
  overriding objectives, 3.08
  part 36 offers, 8.21
  permission to act, 13.68
  Practice Directions, 6.20
  pre-action protocols, 6.25–6.26
  settlement, 6.25
  spirit of the, 6.24
  ten-day letters, 6.27–6.30
  time limits, 7.01, 7.38
Civil proceedings. *See also* **Civil Procedure Rules 1998, Transfer of proceedings**
  affidavits, 6.87
  appeals, 5.83, 6.80–6.84
  applicable rules, 6.14–6.24
  commencement of proceedings, 6.50–6.58
  conduct,
    commencement of proceedings, before, 6.25–6.30
    courts, 6.02
      inspecting the file of, 6.86
      rules of, 6.014–6.024
  delay in bringing, 5.82–5.84
  discretion, 9.57, 9.59, 9.62–9.63
  disqualification orders, 6.02, 6.36–6.49, 11.19–11.21
  duration of disqualification, 5.82–5.84
  evidence, 6.59–6.79
  inspecting the court's file, 6.86
  jurisdiction, 6.02–6.12
    disputing, 6.13
    overseas, 6.13
  parties, 6.31–6.35
  winding up, 6.02
Client money, 5.37
Codification, 1.30
Co-directors, 5.60, 5.85
Collateral companies,
  conduct, 3.53–3.60
    connection or nexus, 3.55–3.58
  disqualification orders, 3.54
    subsequent proceedings, 3.59
  insolvent partnerships, 3.60
  parties, 6.35
  striking out, 3.58–3.59
  unfitness, 3.53–3.54, 4.05, 4.21, 4.26

Collective disqualification, 2.01
Collective investment schemes, 3.64
Combined Code of Corporate Governance, 5.56
Commencement of disqualification orders, 11.18–11.25
Commencement of proceedings, 6.50–6.58
  administration orders, 6.50
  administrative receivership, 6.50
  liquidation, 6.50
  notice, 2.25
  public interest, 6.32
  quasi-criminal process, 2.25
  time limits, 6.50–6.58
  unfitness allegations, 6.52–6.58
  winding up, 6.50
  wrong court, proceedings commenced in, 6–08–6.12
Coming into force of disqualification orders, 11.18–11.25
Companies. *See also* **Types of companies (eg Private companies, Small companies)**
  assets of, contribution to, 1.13
  bankrupts acting through, 1.22
  criminal offences, 9.27
  definition, 3.38–3.45, 9.04
  legal effects of disqualification, 12.05–12.18
  names, 2.10
  permanent establishment, 12.10–12.11
  restoration to register, 3.50
  unfitness, 3.38–3.39
  winding up, 3.46–3.50, 9.04
Compensation orders, 9.61
Competence. *See* **Incompetence**
Complex fraud. *See* **Serious fraud**
Compliance,
  filing requirements, 1.25
  reporting, 3.04
Compromise. *See* **Settlement**
Compulsory liquidation, 1.29
Concealment, 5.43
Conditional discharge, 9.60, 9.63
Conduct,
  board of directors, 2.01
  Carecraft procedure, 8.18
  character, 6.78
  collateral companies, 3.53–3.60
    connection or nexus between, 3.55–3.58

Conduct—*cont.*
conduct following unfit, 5.80
de facto directors, 3.12, 3.23
defined past misconduct, 2.01
delay, 7.11
discontinuance of proceedings, 8.05
discretion, 9.57
disqualification orders, 1.10–1.12,
11.10, 11.13, 11.15
duration of disqualification, 5.68–
5.69, 5.71–5.75, 5.80
evidence, 3.54
extenuating circumstances, 4.22
health and safety offences, 9.17
improvement in, 4.21
information, 3.61
insolvency practitioners, 3.06
investigations, 3.61
jurisdiction, 2.01
lead companies, 3.53–3.60
connection or nexus between,
3.55–3.58
management, 12.29, 12.40–12.41
past, 2.01, 4.22–4.25, 11.13, 12.41,
13.29, 13.57
pattern of, 3.53, 3.57
permission to act, 13.05, 13.07,
13.29, 13.35, 13.57
professional, 3.06
public interest, 3.57
relevant, 4.21–4.25
serial failure, 5.33
seriousness, 13.29
similar, 3.56
specific excepted company orders,
11.15
standards, 2.28
time limits, 7.11
types, 13.29
unfitness, 4.04, 4.06–4.08, 4.21–
4.25, 5.80
wrongful trading, conduct falling
short of, 5.04
Conflicts of interest, 5.43–5.44
Connected persons, 5.39
Consequences of disqualification,
1.16–1.18
Consolidation, 1.30

Consultants,
de facto directors, 3.20, 3.24
management, 12.31–12.33
shadow directors, 3.28–3.29
Consumer protection,
criminal offences, 9.19
false statements, 9.19
food safety, 9.19
limited liability, 2.14
permission to act, 13.21
pre-payments, 5.37
product safety, 9.19
unfitness, 2.14
Contempt of court, 13.38
Cork Committee,
limited liability, 2.07
phoenix companies, 5.31
unfitness, 1.28–1.29, 4.02, 4.04
wrongful trading, 2.09
Corporate directors,
disqualification orders, 3.37
shadow directors, as, 3.27
unfitness, 3.27
Corporate governance, 3.22, 5.56
Costs,
appeals, 9.71
apportionment, 6.85
Calderbank letters, 8.21
Civil Procedure Rules 1998, 6.25–
6.26
discontinuance of proceedings, 8.03,
8.04
estimates, 6.85
follow the event, 6.85
insolvency practitioners, 3.06
permission to act, 13.65–13.66
settlement, 6.85
split orders, 7.32
time limits, 7.32
unfitness, 5.64
County courts,
jurisdiction, 6.03, 6.05
transfer of proceedings, 6.08, 6.10
Courts. *See also* **County courts, Court
rules, High Court, Jurisdiction,
Transfer of proceedings**
Company Directors'
Disqualification Act 1986,
1.03–1.20
appeals, 9.71–9.73
contempt, 13.38
criminal offences, 9.31–9.35, 9.48,
9.50

Courts—*cont.*
  discretion, 1.28, 9.55–9.70
  disqualification, by, 1.03–1.20
  factors which may influence the
    approach of, 2.27–2.28
  permission to act, 13.01–13.69
  unfitness, 1.28
  wrong courts, proceedings
    commenced in, 6.08–6.12
Court rules, 6.14–6.24. *See* **Civil
  Procedure Rules 1998**
  appeals, 6.16, 6.18, 6.21
  Disqualification Rules, 6.15–6.21
  history, 6.15
  Insolvency Rules, 6.16–6.19, 6.21
  permission to act, 13.61
  Probe Data, 6.16–6.18, 6.21
  Tasbian, 6.16–6.18, 6.21
  winding up, 6.18
Creditor protection. *See also* **Non-
  pressing creditors**
  capitalisation, 5.34
  de facto directors, 3.16
  discrimination, 5.22–5.27
  duration of disqualification, 5.77
  fiduciary duty, breach of, 5.43
  financial responsibility, 5.15
  incompetence, 5.51
  insolvency practitioners, failure to
    co-operate with, 5.42
  trading while insolvent, 5.08–5.10
  transaction avoidance, 5.38
  unfitness, 5.02
Criminal offences. *See also* **Indictable
  offences, Quasi-criminal process,
  Sentencing, Summary offences**
  accounts, 5.13, 9.39
  acting in contravention of
    disqualification, 9.27
  administrative receivership, 9.30
  adjournments, 6.34
  bankrupts, 1.16, 10.02, 10.04,
    12.55
  case management, 9.32
  charges, 2.25
  Civil Procedure Rules 1998, 9.32
  companies, 9.27
  compensation orders, 9.61
  conditional discharge, 9.60, 9.63
  connivance, 9.14–9.19
  consent, 9.14–9.19
  consumer protection, 9.19

Criminal offences—*cont.*
  convictions, 9.05–9.35
    aggregate, 9.49
  courts, 9.31–9.35, 9.48, 9.50
    convicting, 9.33
  criminal charges, 2.24
  default orders, 9.49
  discretion, 9.57, 9.59–9.65
  disqualification,
    grounds for, 9.01
    orders, 1.08, 9.32–9.33, 9.48,
      9.50, 11.09, 11.11, 11.22
  Disqualification Practice Direction,
    9.32
  double jeopardy, 9.34–9.35
  duration of disqualification, 9.69–
    9.70
  environmental, 9.15
  European Convention on Human
    Rights, 9.32
  false statements, 9.08
  filing requirements, 9.41, 9.48
  financial assistance with purchase of
    own shares, 9.24
  financial crime, 9.20–9.26
  formation, 9.07, 9.09
  fraudulent trading, 1.23, 9.21, 9.44
  health and safety, 9.16–9.18
  indictable, 9.05–9.35
  insider dealing, 9.11, 9.20, 9.22
  insolvency practitioners, 9.29, 12.46
  Investigations Division, 9.20
  jurisdiction, 2.19, 9.07, 9.10–9.11,
    9.28, 9.31–9.32, 9.34
  legal effects of disqualification,
    12.55
  limited liability, 2.08
  liquidation, 9.29
  locus standi, 9.32, 9.50
  management, 9.07, 9.10–9.28, 9.30,
    12.31, 12.39
    mens rea, 12.30
    relevant factual connection, 9.11–
      9.12, 9.28
  misleading statements, 9.08
  natural justice, 9.33
  negligence, 9.14–9.19
  parallel proceedings, 6.34
  permission to act, 11.17, 13.38
  persistent default of companies
    legislation, 9.49–9.50
  procedure, 9.31–9.35, 9.50

Criminal offences—*cont.*
  promotion, 9.07, 9.08
  prospectuses, 9.08
  public protection, 9.13
  punishment, 2.19
  quasi-criminal process, 2.25
  receivership, 9.
  reporting, 3.06, 3.08
  returns, 3.06
  self-dealing offences, 9.23
  sentencing, 9.33
  striking off of companies, 9.29
  summary offences, 1.08, 9.48–9.50
  tax evasion, 9.25
  time limits, 3.06
  totting up, 9.49
  unauthorised investment business,
    carrying on, 9.26
  unfitness, 1.28
  waste disposal, 9.15
  winding up, 9.32, 9.34
Crown debts,
  deliberate failure to pay, 5.20–5.27
    seriousness of, 5.21, 5.23
  deterrence, 5.27
  discrimination, 5.22–5.27
  quasi-trusts, 5.21
  trading while insolvent, 5.20–5.26
  unfitness, 5.20–5.27
Customs and Excise, 5.20, 9.25

De facto **directors,**
  appointment, 3.12–3.13, 3.19
  conduct, 3.12, 3.23
  consultants, 3.20, 3.24
  corporate governance, 3.22
  creditor protection, 3.16
  criticism of law on, 3.23–3.24
  de jure directors, 3.11–3.15, 3.18,
    3.21
  definition of directors, 3.12
  disqualification, 3.12, 3.15–3.18,
    3.23–3.24
  equal footing test, 3.17–3.23
  finance directors, 3.20
  holding out as, 3.17, 3.19, 3.22
  legal effects of disqualification,
    12.19
  legal ingredients of, 3.14–3.17
  management, 3.24, 12.30, 12.33
  number of, 3.12
  permission to act, 13.52

De facto **directors**—*cont.*
  representations, 3.16
  sole control, 3.17–3.18
  shadow directors, 3.14, 3.26, 3.28–
    3.29
    mixed allegations, 3.34
  shareholders, 3.23
  senior managers, 3.24
  small companies, 3.23
  standard of proof, 3.23
  termination, 3.15
  unfitness, 3.11–3.24
De facto **disqualification,** 5.82–5.84
De jure **directors,**
  alternate directors, 3.36
appointment, 3.10
  de facto directors, 3.11–3.15, 3.18,
    3.21
  shadow directors, 3,26
Debts. *See* **Creditor protection, Crown
  debts**
Declarations,
  fraudulent trading, 1.23
  legal effects of disqualification,
    12.24
  permission to act, 12.24
  wrongful trading, 1.23
Definition of directors, 3.10
  de facto directors, 3.11–3.12
  legal effects of disqualification,
    12.19
  shadow directors, 3.25
Delay,
  appeals, 5.83
  applications for disqualification
    orders, 6.49
  conduct, 7.11
  duration of disqualification, 5.82–
    5.84
  European Convention on Human
    Rights, 5.83
  fair trials, 5.83
  inordinate and inexcusable, 7.34,
    7.36, 7.38
  length of, 7.06–7.07
  prejudice, 7.16, 7.23, 7.25, 7.38
  proceedings, in bringing, 5.82–5.84
  reasons for, time limits, 7.08–7.12
  time limits, 7.05–7.12, 7.16, 7.23,
    7.25, 7.38
  want of prosecution, 7.33–7.36

Delegation,
board of directors, 5.57
management, 12.34, 12.39
unfitness, 5.59, 5.64
Department of Trade and Industry.
See also **Secretary of State for
Trade and Industry**
Investigations Division, 9.20
regulation, 1.20
Deterrence,
Crown debts, 5.27
duration of disqualification, 5.69
permission to act, 13.08, 13.26,
13.57
unfitness, 4.02, 4.04, 4.13, 4.25
Disciplinary procedure, 2.21
Disclosure. *See also* **Filing
requirements**
applications for disqualification
orders, 6.47
duration of disqualification, 5.72
insolvency practitioners, 6.47
limited liability, 2.08
Official Receiver, 6.47
Secretary of State, 6.47
unfitness, 5.48
Discontinuance of proceedings, 8.01–
8.21
Calderbank offers, 8.21
Carecraft, 8.06, 8.08–8.20
Civil Procedure Rules 1998, 8.04
conduct, 8.05
costs, 8.03, 8.04
Disqualification Rules, 8.03
evidence, 8.20
notice, 8.04
procedure, 8.03, 8.04
public interest, 8.01
settlement, 8.06, 8.21
time limits, 8.03, 8.04
Secretary of State, 8.01
stay of proceedings, 8.06–8.07
undertakings, 8.06–8.07
Discovery, 3.07–3.08
Discretion,
appeals, 9.72
Australia, 9.56
civil proceedings, 9.57, 9.59, 9.62–
9.63
compensation orders, 9.61
conditional discharge, 9.60, 9.63
conduct, 9.57

Discretion—*cont.*
courts, 1.28, 9.55–9.70
criminal offences, 9.57, 9.59–9.65
disqualification orders, 9.03, 9.55–
9.70
suspension or staying, 11.23
duration of disqualification, 9.58,
9.66–9.70
guidance, 9.56
jurisdiction, 9.63
management, 12.39
nature, 9.56–9.58
permission to act, 13.05–13.07,
13.14
reporting, 3.04
sentencing, 9.59–9.60, 9.62
shadow directors, 3.27
time limits, 7.05–7.28
unfitness, 1.28, 4.02–4.04, 4.25
Discrimination,
creditor protection, 5.22–5.27
Crown debts, 5.22–5.27
excessive remuneration, 5.28
incompetence, 5.550
transaction avoidance, 5.41
unfitness, 5.20–5.27, 5.50
Dishonesty,
Carecraft procedure, 8.18
duration of disqualification, 5.71,
9.66
unfitness, 4.20
Disqualification orders, 11.01–11.26.
See also **Applications for
disqualification orders, Legal
effect of disqualification**
acting for person subject to, 1.17,
9.27
administration orders, 1.14
appeals, 9.71–9.73
assets, contribution to, 1.13
blanket orders, 11.07
breach of, 1.16
personal liability for, 1.16–1.17
Carecraft procedure, 8.08, 8.11–
8.12, 8.19
civil proceedings, 11.19–11.21,
11.23–11.24
collateral companies, 3.54
coming into force, 11.18–11.25
commencement of, 11.18–11.25
Companies Directors
Disqualification Act 1986, 2.01

Disqualification orders—*cont.*
conduct, 1.10–1.12, 11.10, 11.13, 11.15
consent, 8.06
corporate directors, 3.37
correcting, 11.08–11.12
courts, issued by, 1.04–1.14, 11.18–11.25
criminal offences, 9.32, 9.33, 9.48, 9.50, 11.09, 11.11, 11.22
definition, 11.01
discretion, 9.03, 9.55–9.70, 11.23
Disqualification Practice Direction, 11.21, 11.24
Disqualification Rules, 11.19, 11.22
duration of, 1.05–1.14, 11.19
filing requirements, 1.06, 1.08, 1.25
fraud, 9.42
fraudulent trading, 1.07, 1.13
hearsay, 6.67
indictable offences, convicted of, 1.05
insolvency, 1.09–1.10
insolvency practitioners, 11.05, 11.13, 12.46, 13.56
insolvent partnerships, 3.60
interim permission, 11.25
investigations, 3.61
jurisdiction, 2.19, 6.02
  gateways, 2.01
knock on effects, 11.13
limiting the scope of, 11.06
locus standi, 1.27, 9.03
management, 11.13, 11.15
mistakes, 11.08–11.12
originating summons, 11.06–11.07
parties, 6.31
permission to act, 6.11, 11.03–11.04, 11.13, 11.15, 11.17, 11.25
persistent breach of companies legislation, 9.36, 9.40
picking and choosing, 11.04–11.17
procedure, 1.10
prohibitions, 12.02–12.04, 12.08, 13.01
public protection, 11.23
punishment, 2.19
registration, 11.26
scope, 1.04
Secretary of State for Trade and Industry, 1.010–1.11, 1.20

Disqualification orders—*cont.*
selective orders, 11.05–11.14
sentencing, 9.33, 11.18, 11.22
slip rule, 11.08–11.12
specific excepted company orders, 11.15–11.17, 11.24
staying, 9.73, 11.21, 11.23–11.24, 13.01, 13.54
summary offences, convicted of, 1.08
suspending, 9.73, 11.19–11.24, 13.54
time limits, 1.10, 7.01, 11.07
unfitness, 1.09, 1.12, 4.04, 11.13
wrongful trading, 1.13, 9.54
Disqualification Practice Direction, 6.22–6.24
affidavits, 6.63
applications for disqualification orders, 6.38–6.40, 6.45
Carecraft procedure, 8.09, 8.17, 8.18
criminal offences, 9.32
disqualification orders, 11.21, 11.24
hearsay, 6.65
permission to act, 13.54, 13.61, 13.63–13.64
review powers, 6.84
unfitness, 6.52
witness statements, 6.63
Disqualification Rules,
applications for disqualification orders, 6.37, 6.39, 6.43–6.44
court rules, 6.15–6.21
discontinuance of proceedings, 8.03
disqualification orders, 11.19, 11.22
hearsay, 6.64, 6.65, 6.70
permission to act, 13.01, 13.54
review powers, 6.84
want of prosecution, 7.33
Disqualification Unit, 1.20, 3.02
Division of labour, 5.64
Documents, 3.62–3.69
applications for disqualification orders, 6.49
copies, 3.66
disqualification, 3.66, 3.69
evidence, 3.66–3.67, 3.69
inspection, 3.07–3.08
investigations, 3.66–3.68
investment business, 3.67
loss of, 6.49

Documents—*cont.*
  overseas authorities, assisting, 3.69
  power to obtain, 3.66–3.69
  privilege, 3.07–3.08
  production, 3.04, 3.66–3.68
  reporting, 3.04
  Scotland, 3.68
  search warrants, 3.66
  serious fraud, 3.68
  unfitness, 4.04
Double jeopardy, 6.49, 9.34–9.35
Duration of disqualification orders,
    1.04–1.14, 5.67–5.85
  age, 5.78
  appeals, 9.71
  Carecraft procedure, 8.16–8.17
  character, 5.76
  co-directors, treatment of, 5.85
  conduct, 5.68–5.69, 5.71–5.75
    conduct following unfit, 5.80
    proceedings during, 5.81
  corporate failure, 5.77
  Court of Appeal guidelines, 9.69–
    9.70
  creditor protection, 5.77
  criminal courts, 9.69–9.70
  de facto disqualification, 5.82–5.84
  delay in bringing proceedings, 5.82–
    5.84
  deterrence, 5.69
  disclosure, 5.72
  discounts, 5.81, 5.84
  discretion, 9.58, 9.66–9.70
  dishonesty, 5.71, 9.66
  excessive remuneration, 5.71
  fiduciary duty, 5.72
  filing requirements, 5.71
  fraudulent trading, 5.73
  guidance, 5.68–5.71
  increase in, 9.71
  maximum period, 2.01, 5.67
  misappropriation, 5.73
  mitigation, 5.69, 5.71, 5.74–5.85
  monitoring financial position, 5.71
  plea bargaining, 5.81
  professional advice, 5.79
  public protection, 5.77, 5.78, 5.83,
    9.66–9.68
  reputation, 5.76
  sentencing, 5.69, 5.81

Duration of disqualification orders—
  cont.
  Sevenoaks brackets, 5.67–5.77,
    9.69–9.70
    middle, 5.72, 5.74, 9.69–9.70
    minimum, 5.71, 5.74, 9.69
    top, 5.73, 5.74, 9.69
  state of health, 5.78
  suspension, 11.19
  trading while insolvent, 5.71
  unfitness, 1.27, 1.29, 4.01, 4.03,
    5.67, 5.69
  Westmid Packing, 5.69–5.70, 5.74,
    5.84

EEIGs. *See* European Economic
    Interest Groupings
Effect of disqualification. *See* Legal
    effect of disqualification
Employees. *See also* Senior employees
  health and safety, 9.16–9.18
  Northern Ireland, 5.46
  protection of, 2.15, 5.46, 9.16–9.18
  unfitness, 2.15, 5.46
Enterprise, 2.11–2.12
Entry requirements, 2.27, 2.28
Environmental offences, 9.15
European Convention on Human
    Rights,
  Civil Procedure Rules 1998, 6.24
  criminal offences, 9.32
  delay, 5.83
  fair trials, 2.24, 5.83, 6.34
  quasi-criminal process, 2.24
  parallel proceedings, 6.34
  time limits, 7.01, 7.38
European Economic Interest
    Groupings,
  companies, as, 3.45
  disqualification, 3.45
  legal effects of disqualification,
    12.17
  managers, 3.45
  unregistered companies, 12.17
  winding up, 12.17
Evidence, 6.59–6.79. *See also* Experts,
    Hearsay, Witnesses
  applications for disqualification
    orders, 6.39–6.40, 6.42
  Carecraft procedure, 8.09, 8.12–
    8.13, 8.17–8.18
  character evidence, 6.78–6.79
  conduct, 3.54
  documents, 3.66–3.67, 3.69

Evidence—*cont.*
  further, 6.42
  overseas regulatory authorities, 3.69
  permission to act, 13.07, 13.11,
      13.24, 13.28, 13.64
  reports, 3.63
  statements of truth, 6.59
  unfitness, 6.56–6.57
  written, 6.59–6.63
Evolution of disqualification regime,
    1.21–1.30
Examinations, 3.03
Excessive remuneration,
  discrimination, 5.28h
  duration of disqualification, 5.71
  executive directors, 5.28
  fiduciary duties, breach of, 5.28
  financial responsibility, 5.29
  permission to act, 13.30–13.31,
      13.49
  trading while insolvent, 5.28
  unfitness, 5.28–5.29
Executive directors, 4.11, 5.28
Expenses, 3.52
Experienced directors, 5.58–5.61, 5.65
Expertise of directors,
  permission to act, 13.21, 13.44
  unfitness, 5.58–5.61
Experts, 6.75–6.77
  affidavits, 6.75
  Civil Procedure Rules 1998, 6.24,
      6.76
  opinions, 6.75, 6.77
  striking out, 6.75, 6.77
Extraterritoriality, 3.35

Failure. *See* Serial failure
Fair trials,
  European Convention on Human
      Rights, 2.24, 5.83, 6.34
  delay, 5.83
  quasi-criminal process, 2.24
  time limits, 7.01, 7.16
  want of prosecution, 7.34
False statements, 6.60, 9.08, 9.19
Fiduciary duties,
  breach of, 5.43, 5.72, 9.23
  concealment, 5.43
  conflicts of interest, 5.43–5.44
  creditor protection, 5.43
  duration of disqualification, 5.72
  excessive remuneration, 5.28
  promotion, 12.26

Fiduciary duties—*cont.*
  self-dealing, 5.43, 9.23
  trading while insolvent, 5.43
  unfitness, 4.09, 5.43
Filing requirements,
  Company Directors'
      Disqualification Act 1986, 1.25
  breach, 1.25
  criminal offences, 9.41, 9.48
  disqualification orders, 1.06, 1.08,
      1.25
  duration of disqualification, 5.71
  failure to keep proper records, 5.13–
      5.19
  financial responsibility, 5.36
  incompetence, 5.52
  Jenkins Committee, 1.25
  limited liability, 2.08, 5.15
  monitoring financial position, 5.35–
      5.36
  permission to act, 13.31
  persistent breach of companies
      legislation, 9.48–9.41
  persistent non-compliance with,
      1.25
  preparation, failure to, 5.35–5.36
  public protection, 2.18
  striking off, 9.39
  unfitness, 4.06, 4.10, 5.13–5.19,
      5.35–5.36, 5.48, 5.58
Finance directors, 3.20, 4.12
Financial assistance for purchase of
    own shares,
  criminal offences, 9.24
  incompetence, 5.53
  unfitness, 5.46
Financial crime, 9.20–9.26. *See also*
    **Financial assistance for purchase
    of own shares, Fraud, Fraudulent
    trading, Insider dealing, Self-
    dealing**
Financial institutions, 3.30–3.31. *See
    also* **Banks**
Financial responsibility,
  bank accounts, 5.30
  board of directors, 5.55
  capitalisation, 5.34
  creditor protection, 5.15
  excessive remuneration, 5.29
  filing requirements, 5.35
  financial control, 5.18
  incompetence, 5.52

Financial responsibility—*cont.*
  independent control, 13.41–13.45
  obligation to exercise, 5.13–5.19,
    5.64
  permission to act, 13.31, 13.48–
    13.49
  resignation, 5.72
  standards, 5.13, 5.17
  unfitness, 5.13–5.19, 5.64–5.65
Financial services, 12.53
Fitness. *See* **Unfitness**
Food safety, 9.19
Foreign companies,
  jurisdiction, 3.48, 6.03
  legal effects of disqualification,
    12.18
  sufficient connection, 12.18
  winding up, 3.48, 6.06, 12.18
Foreign element. *See also* **Overseas**
  regulatory authorities
  nominee directors, 3.35
  jurisdiction, service outside the, 3.35
  unfitness, 3.35
Formation,
  bankruptcy, 10.03
  criminal offences, 9.07, 9.09
  definition, 9.09, 12.28
  indirectly or indirectly concerned,
    12,23–12.44
  legal effects of disqualification,
    12.23, 12.28
Fraud, 9.42–9.47. *See also* **Fraudulent**
  trading, Serious fraud
  administrators, 9.45
  auditors, 9.45
  breach of duty, 9.45–9.46
  disqualification orders, 9.42
  insolvency practitioners, 9.46
  liquidators, 9.45
  managers, 9.45
  office holders, 9.45
  perception of, 9.20
  procedure, 9.47
  promotion, 12.26
  receivers, 9.45
  shadow director, 9.45
  statements, 12.40
  unfitness, 1.26, 4.20, 5.45
  winding up, 9.43, 9.47
Fraudulent trading,
  bankruptcy, 10.03
  civil liability, 1.23

Fraudulent trading—*cont.*
  criminal offences, 1.23, 9.21, 9.44
  declarations, 1.23
  disqualification orders, 1.07
  duration of disqualification, 5.73
  Greene Committee, 1.23
  history of regime, 1.24
  limited liability, 2.05
  official receiver, 1.24
  security filling, 2.05
  sentencing, 1.23
  winding up, 1.23, 9.44
Friendly societies,
  companies, as, 3.41, 9.04
  incorporated, 3.41, 9.04
  unfitness, 3.41
  unincorporated, 3.49
  winding up, 3.49

General meetings, 13.46
Greene Committee, 1.21–1.23, 2.05,
  10.03–10.04
Groups of companies, 3.32
Guarantee companies, 12.08

Hearings,
  applications for disqualification
    orders, 6.39, 6.44–6.45
  date, 6.39
  time limits, 7.29–7.31
Hearsay, 6.64–6.74
  affidavits, 6.64, 6.72, 6.73
  Civil Procedure Rules 1998, 6.71,
    6.73
  credibility, 6.73
  disqualification orders, 6.67
  Disqualification Practice Direction,
    6.65
  Disqualification Rules, 6.64–6.65,
    6.70
  exceptions, 6.64–6.67
    implied statutory, 6.67–6.68
  notice, 6.64, 6.69, 6.72
  official receiver, 6.65
  public interest, 6.67–6.68
  reports, 6.66–6.67
  Secretary of State, 6.65, 6.67
  time limits, 6.73
  winding up, 6.67, 6.68
  witnesses, calling makers of hearsay
    statements as, 6.73

Health and safety,
conduct, 9.18
criminal offences, 9.16–9.18
employee protection, 9.16–9.18
enforcement, 9.16
locus standi, 9.18
High Court,
jurisdiction, 6.03, 6.05
transfer of proceedings, 6.08, 6.10
History of disqualification regime,
1.21–1.30
Holding out, 3.17, 3.19, 3.22
Housing associations, 12.50
Human rights. *See* **European**
Convention on Human Rights

Income payments orders, 13.69
Incompetence,
accounting, 5.52
care and skill, 5.50
commercial judgments, 5.51–5.52
creditor protection, 5.51
definition, 5.51
discrimination, 5.50
filing requirements, 5.52
financial assistance for purchase of
own shares, 5.53
financial responsibility, 5.52
investor protection, 5.51
limited liability, 5.51
negligence, 5.52
permission to act, 13.18, 13.27,
13.29
risks, 5.51–5.52
section 6 orders, 5.51–5.53
standards, 5.50
time limits, 7.26
trading while insolvent, 5.50, 5.52
unfitness, 4.16, 4.19, 4.22, 5.65
level of, 5.50–5.53
unwarranted risks test, 5.50
Incorporated friendly societies, 3.41,
9.04
Indictable offences, 9.05–9.35
disqualification orders, 1.05
limited liability, 2.06
Individual insolvency. *See* **Bankruptcy**
Individual voluntary arrangements,
10.06
Industrial and friendly societies, 3.49

Information, 3.62–3.69. *See also*
Documents
accounting, 5.18–5.19
applications for disqualification
orders, 6.48
conduct, 3.61
further, 6.48
investigations, 3.03, 3.61
power to obtain, 3.66–3.69
reporting, 3.03–3.04
Secretary of State, 3.03
transcripts of private examinations,
3.03
unfitness, 4.04
Inland Revenue,
failure to pay, 5.20, 5.21, 5.24, 5.26
unfitness, 5.20, 5.21, 5.24, 5.26
Insider dealing,
criminal offences, 9.22
investigations, 3.65
knowledge, 9.22
management, 9.11
Insolvency. *See also* **Insolvency**
practitioners, Insolvency Service,
Trading without insolvency
"becomes insolvent", 3.50–3.52,
4.05
Cork Committee, 1.28–1.29
disqualification orders, 1.10
limited liability, 2.09–2.10
liquidation, 3.51–3.52
multiple insolvencies, 2.10
partnerships, 3.43
restoration to register, 3.50
unfitness, 1.28–1.29
Insolvency practitioners,
authorisation, 12.46
bankrupts, 13.56
costs, 3.06
creditor protection, 5.42
criminal offences, 9.29, 12.46
disclosure, 6.47
disqualification orders, 11.05,
11.13, 12.46, 13.56
fraud, 9.46
legal effects of disqualification,
12.03–12.04
licensing, 12.46
liquidation, 9.29, 12.20, 13.56
non-co-operation with, 5.42
aggravating factor, as, 5.42
permission to act, 12.46, 13.56
professional conduct, 3.06
reporting, 3.02, 3.06

Insolvency practitioners—*cont.*
statement of affairs, 5.42
time limits, 7.12
unfitness, 5.42
Insolvency Rules,
appeals, 6.21, 6.80–6.83
court rules, 6.17–6.19, 6.21
Insolvency Service, 1.20
Insolvent partnerships,
bankruptcy, 3.43
collateral companies, 3.60
companies, as, 3.43
disqualification, 3.43
orders, 3.60
lead companies, 3.60
legal effects of disqualification,
12.14
unfitness, 3.43, 4.07
Inspection,
Civil Procedure Rules 1998, 3.08,
6.86
court's file, 6.86
documents, 3.07–3.08
inspectors,
appointment of, 3.63
reporting, 3.07–3.08
Investigations,
conduct, 3.61
criminal offences, 9.20
disqualification orders, 3.61
documents, 3.66–3.68
DTI Investigations Division, 9.20
information, 3.03, 3.61
insider dealings, 3.65
reports, leading to, 3.63
serious fraud, 3.68
time limits, 7.12
Investment business,
authorisation, 9.26
criminal offences, 9.26
documents, 3.67
'fit and proper', 9.26
unauthorised, carrying on, 9.26
Investor protection,
limited liability, 2.13
permission to act, 13.21
unfitness, 5.47–5.48

Jenkins Committee, 1.25, 1.27, 2.07,
2.10
Joint and several liability, 12.56

Judgments,
administration orders, 10.09
applications for disqualification
orders, 6.49
bankruptcy, 10.09
Carecraft procedure, 8.18
debtors, 10.09
summary, 6.49
Judicial review, 6.32, 8.09
Jurisdiction,
administration orders, 6.04
ambiguity, 2.02
Civil Procedure Rules 1998, 6.15
Company Directors'
Disqualification Act 1986, 2.02
conduct, 2.01
county courts, 6.03, 6.05
criminal offences, 2.19, 9.07, 9.10–
9.11, 9.28, 9.31–9.32, 9.34
discretion, 9.63
disputing the court's, 6.13
disqualification orders, 2.01, 2.19,
6.02
foreign companies, 3.48, 6.03, 6.06
High Court, 6.03, 6.05
liquidation, 6.06
overseas directors, 6.13
reporting, 3.04
service, outside the, 3.35, 6.13
good arguable case, 3.35
time for determining, 6.04–6.12
transfer of proceedings, 6.08–6.12
winding up, 6.02–6.12, 9.32, 9.34
wrong court, proceedings
commenced in wrong, 6.07–
6.12
wrongful trading, 9.54

Knowledge,
board of directors, 5.57
insider dealing, 9.22
trading while insolvent, 5.03
wrongful trading, 9.53

Lead companies,
conduct, 3.53–3.60
connection or nexus, 3.55–3.58
insolvent partnerships, 3.60
parties, 6.34
striking out, 3.57
time limits, 3.57, 7.15
unfitness, 3.54, 4.26

Legal effects of disqualification,
    12.01–12.56
  administration orders, 12.03
  administrative receivers, 12.22
  administrators, 12.20–12.21
  Australia, 12.25
  breach of prohibitions, 12.54–12.56
  building societies, 12.05–12.06
  charities, 12.47
  chartered rights, 12.10–12.11
  civil liability, 12.56
  companies, 12.05–12.18
    definition, 12.05, 12.07, 12.11
    permanent establishments, 12.10–
      12.11
  criminal offences, 12.55
  de facto directors, 12.19
  declaratory relief, 12.24
  directors, 12.19
  European Economic Interest
      Groupings, 12.17
  financial services, 12.53
  foreign companies, 12.18
  formal removal from office, 12.52
  formation, 12.23, 12.28
  friendly societies, 12.06
  guarantee companies, 12.08
  housing associations, 12.50
  imprisonment, 12.55
  insolvency practitioners, 12.03–
      12.04, 12.46
  joint and several liability, 12.56
  knock-on effects, 12.45–12.53
  limited liability partnerships, 12.06
  liquidators, 12.03, 12.20–12.21
  local authorities, 12.51
  managers, 12.22, 12.29–12.44,
      12.56
  New Zealand, 12.25
  nominees, 12.56
  open-ended investment companies,
      12.16
  partnerships, 12.13–12.15
  pensions, 12.48
  personal liability, 12.56
  police, 12.49
  prohibitions, 12.02–12.04, 12.08,
      12.23–12.44
    breach of, 12.54–12.56
  promotion, 12.23, 12.26–12.27
  receivers, 12.22

Legal effects of disqualification—*cont.*
  regulation, 12.53
  scope of, 12.02–12.04
  shadow directors, 12.19
  unlimited companies, 12.08, 12.10–
      12.11
  unregistered companies, 12.12
  vacating office, 12.52
  winding up, 12.12
Legal professional privilege. *See*
    Privilege
Legislation. *See* **Persistent breach of
    companies legislation**
Liability. *See* **Civil Liability, Limited
    liability, Personal liability**
Limitation periods. *See* **Time limits**
Limited liability, 2.28. *See also*
    Limited liability partnerships
  abuse of privilege of, 2.03–2.17,
      2.30, 13.20, 13.25
  accounting, 5.14
  Company Directors'
      Disqualification Act 1986,
      2.04–2.05, 2.11–2.12, 2.16
  consumer protection, 2.14
  Cork Committee, 2.07, 2.09
  criminal offences, 2.08
  disadvantages, 2.04
  disclosure, 2.08
  employee protection, 2.15
  enterprise, 2.11–2.12
  filing requirements, 2.08, 5.36
  fraudulent trading, 2.06
  Greene Committee, 2.06
  incompetence, 5.51
  indictable offences, 2.06
  insolvency, 2.09
    multiple, 2.10
  investor protection, 2.213
  Jenkins Committee, 2.07, 2.10
  one man companies, 2.11
  origins, 2.03
  permission to act, 13.20, 13,26
  personal liability, 2.04, 2.11
  Phoenix companies, 2.10
  private companies, 2.03, 2.16
  public protection, 2.16, 2.17–2.18
  publicity, 2.08
  purpose of, 2.03
  quasi-criminal process, 2.21, 2.24
  regulation, 2.05, 2.11–2.12
  risks, 2.05, 2.07, 5.51

Limited liability—*cont.*
security filling, 2.06
shareholders, 2.13
small companies, 2.03, 2.16
standards, 2.16
under-capitalised companies, 2.07,
2.09, 2.11
unfitness, 2.10
wrongful trading, 2.09
Limited liability partnerships,
companies, as, 3.44
legal effects of disqualification,
12.06
Liquidation. *See* **also Compulsory**
liquidation
commencement of proceedings, 6.50
criminal offences, 9.29
fraud, 9.45
'goes into', 3.51–3.52
insolvency, 3.51–3.52
practitioners, 12.20, 13.56
legal effects of disqualification,
12.03, 12.20–12.21
shadow directors, 3.30–3.31
winding up, 3.51–3.52
Local authorities, 12.51
Locus standi,
criminal offences, 9.32, 9.50
disqualification orders, 1.27, 9.03
health and safety offences, 9.18
Secretary of State, 1.27
wrongful trading, 9.54

Management,
agency principles, 12.42–12.43
alter ego companies, 12.30
apparent authority, 12.43
Australia, 12.33–12.34, 12.39
bankruptcy, 10.05, 12.34
board of directors, 5.55–5.57
central, 12.32–12.33, 12.35
conduct, 12.29, 12.40–12.41
consultants, 12.31–12.33
criminal offences, 9.07, 9.10–9.28,
9.30, 11.13, 12.31, 12.39
consent to connivance, 9.14–9.19
mens rea, 12.30
de facto directors, 3.24, 12.29, 12.3
definition, 12.29, 12.31–12.41
delegation, 12.34, 12.39
directing mind and will, 12.30
discretion, 12.44

Management—*cont.*
disqualification, 3.38
orders, 11.15
European Economic Interest
Groupings, 3.45
fraud, 9.45
fraudulent statements, 12.40
guidance, 12.42–12.43
indirectly or directly concerned,
12.23–12.44
insider dealing, 9.11
legal effects of disqualification,
12.22, 12.29–12.44, 12.56
mismanagement, 4.15–4.16
ostensible authority, 12.42–12.43
permission to act, 12.41, 12.44,
13.10, 13.28–13.29, 13.36
applications for, 13.52–13.53
position of real authority, 12.38
promotion, 12.27
property, 9.20, 9.45
public protection, 9.13
senior employees, 12.41
shadow directors, 3.26, 12.33
small companies, 12.34
unfitness, 4.11, 4.21–4.25
Misappropriation, 5.73
Misconduct. *See* **Conduct**
Misleading statements, 5.48, 9.09
Mismanagement, 4.15–4.16
Mitigation,
Carecraft procedure, 8.15
duration of disqualification, 5.69,
5.71, 5.74–5.85
Monitoring financial position,
board of directors, 5.57
filing requirements, 5.35–5.36
permission to act, 13.40, 13.42
unfitness, 5.02, 5.16, 5.18, 5.58,
5.64

Natural justice,
criminal offences, 9.33
unfitness, 6.52–6.53
Nature of disqualification, 2.01–2.29
Negligence,
board of directors, 5.55
incompetence, 5.52
unfitness, 4.19–4.20, 4.26
New Zealand, 12.25, 13.22

Nominee directors,
foreign element, 3.35
legal effects of disqualification, 12.56
offshore companies, 3.35
Non-executive directors,
board of directors, 5.56
Combined Code of Corporate Governance, 5.56
permission to act, 13.29–13.30
unfitness, 4.11, 5.58
Non-pressing creditors,
Crown, 5.20–5.27
deliberate failure to pay, 5.20–5.27
discrimination, 5.22–5.27
unfitness, 5.20–5.27
Non-resident directors, 3.35
Northern Ireland, 1.03, 5.46
Notice,
commencement of proceedings, 2.25
hearsay, 6.64, 6.69, 6.72
permission to act, 13.40
quasi-criminal process, 2.25
ten-day letters, 6.27–6.30
Number of disqualifications, 1.01

Occupational pensions, 12.48
Office holders,
definition, 9.45
fraud, 9.45
joint, 3.06
relevant, 3.02
reporting by, 3.02–3.08
section 6 proceedings, 3.02–3.08
status of, 3.07–3.08
unfitness, 3.02–3.08
Official receiver,
deputy, 6.32
disclosure, 6.47
fraudulent trading, 1.24
hearsay, 6.65
parties, 6.32–6.33
time limits, 7.01
Offshore companies, 3.35
One-man companies, 2.11
Open-ended investment companies, 3.42, 12.16
Overdrafts, 5.08
Overseas regulatory authorities, 3.69

Parallel proceedings,
adjournment, 6.34

Parallel proceedings—cont.
criminal offences, 6.34
European Convention on Human Rights, 6.34
preferences, 5.38–5.39
transaction avoidance, 5.38–5.39
Parent companies,
shadow directors, 3.32–3.33
time limits, 7.28
Part 36 offers, 8.21
Parties to proceedings, 6.31–6.35
collateral companies, 6.35
defendants, number of, 6.34
disqualification orders, 6.31–6.32
lead companies, 6.35
Official Receivers, 6.32–6.33
Secretary of State, 6.32–6.33
wrong claimants, 6.33
Partnerships. *See also* **Insolvent partnerships, Limited liability partnerships**
bankrupts, 12.15
legal effects of disqualification, 12.13–12.15
permission to act, 12.13, 13.19
prohibitions, 12.13–12.15
winding up, 12.14
Payments. *See* **Pre-payments**
Pensions, 12.48
Period of disqualification. *See* **Duration of disqualification**
Permanent establishments, 12.10–12.11
Permission to act, 13.01–13.69
accounts, 13.48
appeals, 13.68, 13.69
applications, 11.15, 13.55, 13.58–13.69
defending, 13.62–13.63
form of, 13.61
auditors, 13.34
Australia, 13.03, 13.16, 13.22
bankrupts, 13.10, 13.55, 13.64, 13.69
board of directors, 13.41–13.45
burden of proof, 13.07
Carecraft procedure, 13.20
civil liability, 13.38
Civil Procedure Rules 1998, 13.68
conditions, 13.04, 13.11, 13.26, 13.29, 13.32–13.51
court's role, 13.51

Permission to act—*cont.*
  conditions—*cont.*
    Secretary of State, 13.51
    types of, 13.39–13.51
  conduct, 13.05, 13.07, 13.35, 13.57
    seriousness and type of, 13.29
  costs, 13.65–13.66
  courts,
    applicable rules, 13.61
    powers of, 13.01–13.57
    scope of, 13.03–13.06
    vain, not acting in, 13.10
    which, 13.58–13.60
  criminal offences, 11.17, 13.38
  customer confidence, 13.21
  de facto directors, 13.52
  declaratory relief, 12.24
  dependence of company on director,
    13.22–13.23
  deterrence, 13.08, 13.26, 13.57
  discretion, 13.05–13.07, 13.14
  dishonesty, 13.18
  disqualification orders,
    automatic, 13.69
    notwithstanding, 1.19, 11.03–
      11.04, 11.13, 11.15, 11.17,
      11.25
    stay of, 13.01
  Disqualification Practice Direction,
    13.54, 13.61, 13.63–13.64
  Disqualification Rules, 13.01, 13.54
  evidence, 13.07, 13.11, 13.24,
    13.28, 13.31, 13.54, 13.64
  excessive remuneration, 13.30,
    13.49
  expertise, 13.21, 13.44
  factors to be taken into account,
    13.27–13.28
  filing requirements, 13.20, 13.31
  financial control, 13.31, 13.48–
    13.49
  future direction, 13.57
  general meetings, control of
    company in, 13.46
  guidance, 13.05
  income payments orders, 13.69
  incompetence, 13.18, 13.26, 13.29
  independent control, 13.41–13.45
  insolvency practitioners, 12.46,
    13.56
  interim, 11.25, 13.01, 13.11–13.12,
    13.54
  investor confidence, 13.21

Permission to act—*cont.*
  legitimate interest, 13.14–13.25
    applicant's interest of less weight
      than company, 13.16–13.19
    third party, 13.20–13.25
  limited liability, 13.20, 13.25
  limited period, for, 13.50–13.51
  liquidation, 13.56
  management, 12.41, 12.44, 13.10,
    13.28–13.29, 13.36, 13.52–
    13.53
  monitoring financial position, 13.42
  need requirement, 13.05–13.06,
    13.09–13.26
    desire or need of applicant or
      company, 13.11–13.15
  New Zealand, 13.22
  non-executive directors, 13.29–
    13.30
  notice, 13.40
  outside assistance, 13.47
  partnerships, 12.13, 13.19
  personal liability, 13.19
  phoenix companies, 13.20
  preferences, 13.36
  procedure, 13.58–13.69
  public interest, 13.29, 13.57, 13.69
  public protection, 13.03, 13.05–
    13.06, 13.08, 13.13, 13.25–
    13.31, 13.57
    derogation from, 13.33–13.36
    undertakings, 13.38
  publicity, 13.40
  registration, 13.67
  relevant factors, 13.14–13.15
  safeguards, 13.04, 13.26, 13.37,
    13.52
  Secretary of State, 13.51, 13.63
  shadow directors, 13.52
  sole traders, 13.19
  specified companies, 13.05
  standard of proof, 13.07
  supervision, 13.28, 13.34, 13.40
  threshold test, 13.11, 13.15
  transfer of proceedings, 6.11
  undertakings, 13.37–13.38
  unfitness, 13.07, 13.27, 13.29,
    13.33, 13.36, 13.43
  unlimited companies, 13.15, 13.20
  witness statements, 6.62

Persistent breach of companies legislation, 9.36–9.41
accounting, 9.38–9.39
annual returns, 9.38–9.39
'companies legislation', meaning of, 9.37
criminal offences, 9.41, 9.49–9.50
disqualification orders, 9.36, 9.40
filing requirements, 9.38–9.41
persistent default, 9.40
procedure, 9.41
winding up, 9.41
Personal liability,
bankrupt, acting for, 1.17
breach, 1.16–1.17, 2.30
disqualification orders,
acting for person under, 1.17
breach of, 1.17
legal effects of disqualification, 12.56
limited liability, 2.04, 2.11
permission to act, 13.19
shadow directors, 3.27
trading while insolvent, 5.03
wrongful trading, 9.52–9.53
Phoenix companies,
assets, acquisition of, 5.32
Cork Report, 5.31
limited liability, 2.10
permission to act, 13.20
unfitness, 4.08, 5.31–5.32
Police authorities, 12.49
Pre-action protocols, 6.25–6.26
Preferences,
parallel proceedings, 5.38–5.39
permission to act, 13.36
transaction avoidance, 5.38–5.41
Pre-payments,
acceptance of, 5.37
client money, use of, 5.37
consumer protection 5.37
trading while insolvent, 5.37
unfitness, 5.37
Private companies, 2.3, 2.11
Privilege, 3.07–3.08
Probe Data, 6.18–6.18, 6.21
Product safety, 9.19
Professional advisers,
accounts, 5.16–5.17
co-directors, as, 5.60
duration of disqualification, 5.79
shadow directors, 3.28–3.29
unfitness, 5.60

Professional conduct, 3.06
Promotion,
bankruptcy, 10.03
criminal offences, 9.07, 9.08
definition, 12.26–12.27
directly or indirectly concerned, 12.23, 12.26–12.27
fiduciary duties, 12.26
fraud, 12.26
legal effects of disqualification, 12.23, 12.26–12.27
management, 12.27
Public companies, 2.16
Public interest,
Carecraft procedure, 8.18
commencement of proceedings, 6.32
conduct, 3.57
discontinuance of proceedings, 8.02
hearsay, 6.67–6.68
permission to act, 13.29, 13.57, 13.69
time limits, 7.01, 7.09
unfitness, 1.26, 1.28
want of prosecution, 7.34–7.35
Public protection,
bankruptcy, 10.04
Company Directors' Disqualification Act 1986, 2.17–2.19
criminal offences, 9.13
derogation from, 13.33–13.36
deterrence, 2.17–2.18
discretion, 9.68–9.70
disqualification orders, 11.23
duration of disqualification, 5.77, 5.78, 5.83
filing requirements, 2.18
limited liability, 2.16, 2.17–2.18
management, 9.13
permission to act, 13.03, 13.05–13.06, 13.08, 13.13, 13.25–13.31, 13.57
derogation from, 13.33–13.36
undertakings, 13.38
quasi-criminal process, 2.21, 2.22
standards, 2.18
ten-day letters, 6.29
unfitness, 2.17–2.18, 2.27, 4.02, 4.04, 4.13, 5.02
Publicity,
limited liability, 2.08

Publicity—*cont.*
  permission to act, 13.40
Purpose of disqualification, 2.01–2.29

Qualifications, 2.27, 2.28
Quasi-criminal process,
  Company Directors'
    Disqualification Act 1986,
    2.21–2.26, 2.28
  criminal charges, 2.24
  disciplinary procedure, 2.21
  disqualification of directors, as,
    2.21–2.26
  European Convention on Human
    Rights, 2.24
  fair trials, 2.24
  judiciary, 2.26
  limited liability, 2.21, 2.24
  livelihood, impact on individual's,
    2.24
  notice of intention to commence
    proceedings, 2.25
  public protection, 2.21, 2.22
  sentencing, 2.22
  shadow directors, 3.29
  unfitness, 2.22
  wrongful trading, 2.22

Records. *See* Filing requirements
Receivership,
  criminal offences, 9.30
  fraud, 9.45
  legal effects of disqualification,
    12.22
Registration,
  bankruptcy orders, 10.08, 11.26
  disqualification orders, 1.18, 11.26
  permission to act, 13.67
  restoration of companies, 3.50
Regulation. *See also* Overseas
    regulatory authorities
  Department of Trade and Industry,
    1.20
  legal effects of disqualification,
    12.53
  limited liability, 2.04, 2.11–2.12
Removal from office, 12.52
Remuneration. *See* Excessive
    remuneration
Reporting,
  compliance, 3.04
  co-operation 3.02

Reporting—*cont.*
  costs, 3.06
  criminal offences, 3.06, 3.08
  discovery, 3.07–3.08
  discretion, 3.04
  Disqualification Unit, 3.02
  documents, production of, 3.03–
    3.04
  dominant purpose, 3.08
  information, 3.03–3.04
  insolvency practitioners, 3.02, 3.06
  inspection, 3.07–3.08
  investigations, 3.03
  jurisdiction, 3.04
  office holders, 3.02–3.08
    status of, 3.07–3.08
  official receiver, 3.02–3.03
  privilege, 3.07–3.08
  returns, 3.05–3.06
  rules on, 3.05–3.06
  Secretary of State, 3.02–3.04, 3.07–
    3.08
  section 6 proceedings, 3.02–3.08
  statutory requirements, 3.02–3.06
  time limits, 3.05–3.06, 7.26
  transcripts of private examinations,
    3.03
  unfitness, 3.02–3.08
Reports, 3.62–3.69 . *See also*
    Reporting
  certified copies, 3.63
  collective investment schemes, 3.64
  evidence, 3.63
  hearsay, 6.66–6.67
  investigations, leading to, 3.63
  unfitness, 4.09
  unit trust schemes, 3.64
Representations, 3.16
Reputation, 5.76
Rescues, 5.06
Resignation,
  accounting, 5.62
  board of directors,
    failure to exercise influence over,
      5.61–5.63
  breach of statutory obligations, 5.63
  failure to resign, 5.62
  financial responsibility, 5.62
  trading while insolvent, 5.62
  unfitness, 5.61–5.63
Restoration to register, 3.50

Returns,
   criminal offences, 3.06
   interim, 3.06
   persistent breach of companies
      legislation, 9.39
   reporting, 3.3.05–3.06
   time limits, 3.06
Review powers, 6.84
Risks. *See also* **Unwarranted risks test**
   incompetence, 2.05, 2.07, 5.51–5.52
   limited liability, 5.51

Sales directors, 4.11
Scotland,
   appeals, 9.71
   documents, 3.69
   serious fraud, 3.69
Search warrants, 3.66
Secret profits, 4.09
**Secretary of State for Trade and
   Industry,**
   disclosure, 6.47
   discontinuance of proceedings, 8.02
   disqualification orders, 1.10–1.11,
      1.20
   hearsay, 6.65, 6.67
   information, 3.03
   judicial review, 6.32
   locus standi, 1.27
   parties, 6.32–6.33
   permission to act, 13.51, 13.63
   reporting, 3.02–3.04, 3.07–3.08
   time limits, 7.01, 7.04, 7.06–7.07,
      7.12–7.16, 7.20, 7.28
   unfitness, 1.29
Security, 2.05
Selective orders, 11.05–11.14
Self-dealing,
   criminal offences, 9.23
   fiduciary duty, breach of, 5.43, 9.23
Senior employees,
   management, 12.41
   unfitness, 4.11, 5.58
Sentencing,
   appeals, 9.71–9.73
   criminal offences, 9.33
   discretion, 9.59–9.60, 9.62
   disqualification orders, 9.33, 11.18,
      11.22
   punishment, 2.19
   quasi-criminal process, 2.22

Serial failure,
   conduct, 5.33
   unfitness, 5.31–5.33
Serious fraud,
   documents, 3.68
   investigations, 3.68
   Scotland, 3.68
   time limits, 7.10
Service,
   acknowledgment of service, 6.41
   applications for disqualification
      orders, 6.40–6.41
   claim forms, 6.40
   jurisdiction, outside the, 3.35, 6.13
      good arguable case, 3.35
   setting aside, 6.13
Setting aside transactions, 5.38–5.39
Settlement,
   Carecraft procedure, 8.17
   Civil Procedure Rules 1998, 6.25
   costs, 6.85
   discontinuance of proceedings, 8.06
   offers, 8.21
Sevenoaks **brackets,** 5.68–5.77, 9.69–
   9.70
Shadow directors,
   advisers, 3.28–3.29
   appointment, 3.25
   banks, 3.30–3.31
   board of directors, 3.27
   consultants, 3.28–3.29
   control, 3.28–3.29
   corporate directors, 3.37
   de facto directors, 3.14, 3.23, 3.26,
      3.28–3.29
      mixed allegations, 3.34
   de jure directors, 3.25, 3.26
   definition, 3.25
   discretion, 3.27
   disqualification, 3.25–3.26
   financial institutions, 3.30–3.31
   fraud, 9.4545
   groups of companies, 3.32
   guidance, 3.26
   interpretation, 3.26–3.29
   legal effects of disqualification,
      12.19
   liability, 3.27
   liquidation, 3.30–3.31
   managers, 3.26, 3.34, 12.33
   mixed allegations, 3.34
   parent companies, 3.32–3.33

Shadow directors—*cont.*
permission to act, 13.52
professional advisers, 3.28
quasi-criminal process, 3.29
subsidiary companies, 3.32–3.33
unfitness, 3.25–3.34
wrongful trading, 3.26, 3.30, 3.32
Shareholders, 2.13
Shares. *See* **Financial assistance for purchase of own shares**
Skill and care. *See* **Care and skill**
Slip rules, 11.8–11.12
Small businesses,
de facto directors, 3.23
limited liability, 2.3, 2.16
management, 12.34
Sole traders, 13.19
Specific excepted companies, 11.15–11.17, 11.24
Standards,
accounting, 5.48
conduct, 2.28, 5.58–5.59
experience directors, 5.58–5.59
financial responsibility, 5.13, 5.17
judicial paraphrasing, 4.15–4.20
language of proper, 4.17–4.20
limited liability, 2.16
permission to act, 13.07
public protection, 2.18
special expertise, directors with, 5.58–5.59
trading while insolvent, 5.03
unfitness, 1.29, 4.11–4.21, 4.25–4.26, 5.48, 5.58–5.59
Standing. *See* **Locus standi**
Statement of affairs, 5.15, 5.42
Statements of case, 6.49
Statements of truth, 6.59
Statutory obligations,
breach of, 5.46–5.47, 5.63
resignation, 5.63
Stay of proceedings,
discontinuance of proceedings, 8.06–8.07
undertakings, 8.06–8.07
Striking off companies,
criminal offences, 9.29
filing requirements, 9.39
insolvency practitioners, 9.29
Striking out,
applications for disqualification orders, 6.49

Striking out—*cont.*
collateral companies, 3.58–3.59
experts, 6.77
lead companies, 3.57
statements of case, 6.49
transfer of proceedings, 6.09
want of prosecution, 7.33–7.34, 7.36–7.37
Subsidiaries, 3.32–3.33
Summary judgments, 6.49
Summary offences, 1.08, 9.48, 9.50
Summary procedure. *See Carecraft* procedure
Supervision,
auditors, 13.34
board of directors, 5.58
permission to act, 13.28, 13.34

Tasbian, 6.16–6.18, 6.21
Tax evasion, 9.25
Ten-day letters,
Civil Procedure Rules 1998, 6.27–6.30
contents of, 6.30
notice, 6.27–6.30
public protection, 6.29
Threshold test,
permission to act, 13.11, 13.15
time limits, 7.08–7.09, 7.14
unfitness, 4.15–4.16, 4.19–4.20, 4.26
Time limits. *See also* **Want of prosecution**
applications for disqualification orders, 6.38–6.46
balancing exercise, 7.17, 7.26
Civil Procedure Rules, 7.01, 7.38
commencement of proceedings, 6.50–6.51
conduct, 7.11
costs, 7.32
criminal offences, 3.06
delay, 7.05–7.12
length of, 7.06–7.12
prejudice caused by, 7.16, 7.23, 7.25, 7.38
reasons for, 7.08–7.12
discontinuance of proceedings, 8.03, 8.04
discretion, 7.05–7.28
disqualification orders, 1.10, 7.01, 11.07

Time limits—*cont.*
European Convention on Human
Rights, 7.01, 7.38
extensions of, 6.43, 7.04, 7.08–7.09
procedure, 7.29–7.32
successful applications, 7.18–7.22
unsuccessful applications, 7.24–
7.28
fair trials, 7.01, 7.16b
freedom of individual, 7.25
hearings, 7.29–7.31
hearsay, 6.73
incompetence, 7.26
insolvency practitioners, 7.12
interim nature of proceedings, 7.31
investigations, 7.12
lead companies, 3.57, 7.15
Official Receiver, 7.01
parent companies, 7.28
permission to start proceedings out
of time, 7.01–7.38
public interest, 7.01, 7.09
public protection, 7.01
reporting, 3.05, 7.26
returns, 3.06
Secretary of State, 7.01, 7.04, 7.06–
7.07, 7.12–7.16, 7.20, 7.28
serious fraud, 7.10
seriousness of case, 7.10, 7.22
strength of case, 7.13–7.16, 7.21
threshold test, 7.08–7.09, 7.14
unfitness, 6.58
Trading while insolvent,
accounts, 5.07, 5.11, 5.13
bank accounts, 5.30
board of directors, 5.61
burden of proof, 5.12
commercial misjudgement, 5.52
creditor protection, 5.08–5.10
Crown debts, 5.20–5.26
duration of disqualification, 5.71
exacerbating factors, 5.18
excessive remuneration, 5.28
fiduciary duty, breach of, 5.43
incompetence, 5.50, 5.52
knowledge, 5.03
margin of error, 5.09–5.10, 5.12
overdrafts, 5.08
personal liability, 5.03
pre-payments, 5.37
reasonableness, 5.08–5.09
rescue, 5.06

Trading while insolvent—*cont.*
resignation, 5.62
standards, 5.03
transaction avoidance, 5.41
unfitness, 5.03–5.12, 5.50
unwarranted risks test, 5.05–5.06,
5.11–5.12
wrongful trading, 5.03, 5.04–5.05
Transfer of proceedings,
appeals, 6.12, 6.80
correct court, from, 6.10
county courts, 6.08, 6.10
High Court, 6.08, 6.10
jurisdiction, 6.08–6.12
permission to act, applications for,
6.11
powers of, 6.08
striking out, 6.09
value of claims, 6.10
wrong court, from, 6.09
Transaction avoidance,
breach of provisions, 5.38–5.41
connected persons, 5.39
creditor protection, 5.38
discrimination, 5.41
parallel proceedings, 5.38–5.39
preferences, 5.38–5.40
setting aside transactions, 5.38–5.39
trading while insolvent, 5.41
unfitness, 5.38–5.41
wrongful trading, 5.39
Transcripts, 3.03
Triggering events, 1.02, 1.27, 1.30,
2.01
Trusts,
charitable, 12.47
Crown debts, 5.21
pensions, 12.48
quasi-trusts, 5.21

Under-capitalised companies, 2.07,
2.09, 2.11
Undertakings,
acceptance of, 8.07
contempt, 13.38
discontinuance of proceedings,
8.06–8.07
permission to act, 13.37–13.38
stay of proceedings, 8.06–8.07
Unfitness, 3.01–3.69
advisers, 5.60
affidavits, 6.52–6.53

Unfitness—*cont.*
  allegations, 6.52–6.57
    amending or adding to, 6.55–6.58
    clarity of, 6.52
    permission needed to amend,
      6.56–6.57
  bank accounts, muse of, 5.30
  board of directors, 4.11, 5.54–5.57
    failure to exert influence over,
      5.61–5.63
  breach of statutory obligations,
    5.46, 5.57
  burden of proof, 3.09
  capitalisation, lack of, 5.34
  care and skill, 4.09, 5.50, 5.65
  case law, volume of, 4.01
  character, 6.78
  collateral companies, 3.53–3.54,
    4.05, 4.21, 4.26
  commencement of proceedings,
    6.52–6.58
  companies, 3.38–3.49, 3.53–3.60
  Company Directors Disqualification
    Act 1986, 1.02, 1.26–1.30,
    2.01, 2.19, 3.01–3.69
  compulsory liquidation, 1.29
  conduct, 4.04, 4.06–4.08, 4.21
    conduct following unfit, 5.80
    experienced directors, 5.58–5.61
    past, 4.22–4.25
    relevant, 4.21–4.25
    special expertise, directors with,
      5.58–5.61
  consumer protection, 2.15
  Cork Committee, 1.28–1.29, 4.02,
    4.04
  costs, 5.64
  courts, discretion, 1.28
  creditor protection, 5.02
  criminal offences, 1.28
  Crown, deliberate failure to pay,
    5.20–5.27
  Customs and Excise, 5.20
  determining, 4.01–4.26, 5.01–5.66
  degree of, 4.10
  delegation, 5.59, 5.64–5.65
  deterrence, 4.02, 4.04, 4.13, 4.25
  directors, 3.10–3.11
    alternate, 3.36
    corporate, 3.37
    de facto, 3.11–3.24
    experienced directors, 5.58–5.61

Unfitness—*cont.*
  directors—*cont.*
    foreign element, 3.35
    shadow, 3.25–3.34
    special expertise, directors with,
      5.58–5.61
  disclosure requirements, 5.48
  discretion, 4.02–4.04, 4.25
  discrimination, 5.20–5.27, 5.50
  dishonesty, 4.20
  disqualification orders, 1.09, 1.12,
    4.04 , 11.13
  Disqualification Practice Direction,
    6.52
  dividends, non-payment of, 5.46
  division of labour, directors relying
    on, 5.64
  documents, 4.04
  duration of disqualification, 1.27,
    1.29, 4.01, 4.03, 5.67, 5.69,
    6.54
  employee protection, 2.15, 5.46
  evidence, 6.56–6.57
  evolution of regime, 1.26–1.29
  excessive remuneration, 5.28–5.30
  executive, 4.11
  experienced directors, 5.58–5.61
  extenuating circumstances, 4.22
  fiduciary duties, 4.09, 5.43
  filing requirements, 4.06, 4.10,
    5.13–5.19, 5.35–5.36, 5.48
    responsibility for, 5.58, 5.64
  finance directors, 4.12
  financial assistance for purchase of
    own shares, 5.46
  financial reporting, 5.48
  financial responsibility, obligation to
    exercise, 5.13–5.19, 5.64–5.65
  fraud, 1.26, 4.20, 5.45
  friendly societies, 3.41
  guidance, 4.05–4.20, 4.26
  history and legal status of provisions
    relating to, 4.09–4.10
  incompetence, 4.15–4.16, 4.19,
    4.22, 5.48, 5.51–5.53
  information, 4.04
  Inland Revenue, 5.20, 5.21, 5.24,
    5.26
  insolvency, 1.28–1.29, 3.50–3.52
    becoming insolvent, 4.05
  insolvency practitioners, non-
    cooperation with, 5.42
  insolvent partnerships, 3.43, 4.07

Unfitness—*cont.*
  investor protection, 5.47–5.48
  Jenkins Committee, 1.27
  judicial guidance, 4.14–4.20
  language, 4.17–4.20
  lead companies, 4.26
  limited liability, 2.10
  managers, 4.12, 4.21–4.25, 5.55–
    5.57
  mandatory disqualification, 4.02–
    4.03
  misleading statements, 5.48
  mismanagement, 4.15–4.16
  monitoring financial position of
    companies, 5.02, 5.16, 5.18,
    5.58, 5.64
  natural justice, 6.52–6.53
  negligence, 4.20
  non-executive directors, 4.11, 5.58
  non-pressing creditors, 5.20–5.27
  open-ended investment companies,
    3.42
  permission to act, 13.07, 13.27,
    13.29, 13.33, 13.36, 13.43
  phoenix companies, 4.08, 5.31–5.33
  policy, 4.16
  pre-payments, acceptance of, 5.37
  professional advisers, 5.60
  public interest, 1.26, 1.28
  public protection, 2.17–2.18, 2.27,
    4.02, 4.04, 4.13, 5.02
  quasi-criminal process, 2.22
  reporting by office-holders, 3.02–
    3.08
  reports, 4.09
  resignation, 5.61–5.63
  responsibility,
    accounts, 5.58
    collective, 4.11, 5.54–5.67
    extent of, 4.07, 4.11–4.12, 4.14
    individual, 4.11–4.12, 4.26, 5.48,
      5.54–5.67
  sales director, 4.13
  Secretary of State, 1.29
  secret profits, 4.09
  section 6 proceedings, 3.02–3.08
  section 6(1) provisions, 3.09–3.10
  section 8(1) preliminaries, 3.61–
    3.69
  senior employees, 4.11, 5.59
  serial failure, 5.31–5.33
  special expertise, directors with,
    5.58–5.61

Unfitness—*cont.*
  specific instances, 5.01–5.66
  standard of proof, 5.66
  standards, 1.29, 4.11–4.21, 4.25–
    4.26, 5.58–5.61, 5.65
  threshold test, 4.15–4.16, 4.19–
    4.20, 4.26
  time limits, 6.58
  trading while insolvent, 5.93–5.12,
    5.50
  transaction avoidance provisions,
    breach of, 5.38–5.41
  triggering events, 1.27, 1.30
  want of prosecution, 7.34
  White Paper, 1.29
Unincorporated friendly societies, 3.49
Unit trusts schemes, 3.64
Unless orders, 7.36
Unlimited companies, 12.08, 13.15,
  13.20
Unregistered companies,
  European Economic Interest
    Grouping, 12.17
  legal effects of disqualification,
    12.10–12.11, 12.12
  winding up, 3.47
Unwarranted risks test,
  incompetence, 5.50
  trading while insolvent, 5.05–5.06,
    5.11–5.12

Vacating office, 12.52
Valuation, 5.19

Want of prosecution, 7.33–7.37
  case management, 7.33
  delay, 7.33–7.35
    inordinate and inexcusable, 7.34,
      7.36
  Disqualification Rules, 7.33
  fair trials, 7.34
  Manion Trading, 7.34
  prejudice, 7.34–7.36
  public interest, 7.34–7.35
  striking out, 7.33–7.34, 7.36–7.37
  unfitness, 7.34
  unless orders, 7.36
Waste disposal, 9.15, 12.38
Winding up,
  appeals, 9.71
  commencement of, 6.06
    proceedings, 6.50

Winding up—*cont.*
  companies capable of being, 3.46–
      3.50, 9.04
  court rules, 6.18
  criminal offences, 9.32, 9.34
  disqualification, 3.46
  European Economic Interest
      Grouping, 12.17
  expenses, 3.52
  foreign companies, 3.48, 6.06,
      12.18
  fraud, 9.43, .45
  fraudulent trading, 1.23, 9.45
  hearsay, 6.67
  industrial and provident societies,
      3.49
  jurisdiction, 6.02–6.12, 9.32, 9.34
  legal effects of disqualification,
      12.12, 12.14
  liquidation, 3.51–3.52
  persistent breach of companies
      legislation, 9.41
  unincorporated friendly societies,
      3.49
  unregistered companies, 3.47
Without prejudice, 8.10, 8.17

Witnesses,
  hearsay statements makers, called
      as, 6.73
  statements,
      Disqualification Practice
          Direction, 6.63
      formal requirements, 6.62
      permission to act, 6.62
Wrongful trading, 9.51–9.54
  banks, 3.30
  conduct falling short of, 5.04
  Cork Committee, 2.09
  declarations, 1.23
  defence, 9.53
  disqualification orders, 9.54
  jurisdiction, 9.54
  knowledge, 9.53
  limited liability, 2.09
  locus standi, 9.54
  personal liability, 9.51–9.53
  procedure, 9.54
  quasi-criminal process, 2.22
  shadow directors, 3.26, 3.30, 3.32
  trading while insolvent, 5.03, 5.04–
      5.05
  transaction avoidance, 5.39